Get a camera

Get some stock

Go shoot a MOVIE...

The Guerilla Film Makers Handbook

To Chris and Jo

For Mum and Dad

To Zee...
We couldn't have done it without you

To Jon...
Thank you for your friendship and wisdom

Continuum
80 Maiden Lane
Suite 704
New York NY 10038

Continuum
The Tower Building
11 York Road
London SE1 7NX

First published in 2004
Reprinted 2011

Library of Congress Control Number: 2004100536

ISBN 9780826414649

Layout and design by Chris Jones
Printed and bound in the United States of America

The Guerilla Film Makers Handbook

By
Genevieve Jolliffe
and Chris Jones

US Editorial
Andrew Zinnes

Production
Cara Williams and
Claire Trevor-Roper

Acknowledgements

We would like to thank all the contributors in this book for sharing with us their experience and expertise, helping to shed light on how parts of the US film industry work. We would also like to thank everyone who has helped Living Spirit produce its first three feature films; *The Runner, White Angel* and *Urban Ghost Story,* especially those who have supported us, both financially and emotionally, while navigating the shark infested, ship wrecked waters of low-budget film making. You were our life jackets.

To all those people who said it could be done, our sincere thanks for your encouragement.

Special thanks in particular for words of advice received on a running track all those years ago.

Thanks also for the phrase 'the surest way to succeed is to be determined not to fail'.

We would also like to express our gratitude to the following for their help in producing this book -

David Barker, you are sooooo cooool! Thanks for your unending patience and encouragement.

Jim, thanks for your illustrations.

Special thanks to Lynn & Stan Morris, Tom Hunter, Tariq Jalil, Dave Lasdon, Louise Runge, Kevin Foxe, Betsey Dennis, Steven Fishman and Simon Broad.

Thanks also to all the people who helped hone down the mountain of interviews...Rachel Gibbs, Lucia Landino, Adam Morris, Dominic Beeton, Ben Lock, Robyn Morrison, Pearl Howie, Kim Lomax, Julie Thomlinson, Vanita Eden, Andrew Adamides, Charly Gamble, Steve Wilson, Steve Munro, Brendan Deere, Carol Ann Walters, Halima Sufi and Linda Haysman.

Thanks also to Mums, Dads and families.

The Guerilla Film Makers Handbook

Introduction

Long ago in a country far, far away, two crazy and desperate British filmmakers had a dream. They wanted to make movies. And great movies at that. Lofty aspirations for a couple of kids with nothing more than determination and a very large amount of naivete. Yet they managed to make a movie while still in their teens. Certainly not a great movie. Actually, a terrible movie. It was called *The Runner*. Undeterred, they made another, this one called *White Angel*. Not too bad this time, they obviously learned something on the first. But sadly, this one landed them in prison! You'd think they would have reconsidered film as a career by now, but no, determination and naivete can be put to very good use. And so they made a third feature film, *Urban Ghost Story*. And it's even better than the first two, and about to be released in the USA on DVD! (2004)… *'We may enjoy some measure of success yet',* they said with naivete and determination!

Zap back in time, and it was while languishing in the cells after our second film, the serial killer thriller White Angel, that the idea for *The Guerilla Film Makers Handbook* came to us. *'You'd never believe what happened to us when we made our movie…'* And so the book was birthed. At first a cathartic volume, which quickly expanded into the stories of other film makers, pitfalls to avoid, tips and tricks, and interviews with experts who we hoped would *'tell the truth'* about how it all works.

It is the fusion of these elements - expert advice combined with film makers war stories - that is the essence of the book. We hope it is aspirational, inspirational and educational in equal measure. And so we present to you The Guerilla Film Makers Handbook - USA. *'Hollywood here we come!'* But, wait, you say. Hollywood and independent film? Isn't that an oxymoron? Anyone who takes a look at the films at Sundance or watches the Oscars will understand that the line between these two formerly disparate worlds is blurring. Art house movies can have big stars working for scale and Hollywood blockbusters rely on indie filmmakers to bring fresh voices to stale genres.

The interviewees in this book were chosen for their experience rather than their supposed affiliation with a style of filmmaking. The knowledge they convey can be applied to either school of thought - indie or establishment, you just have to scale back, rework or expand on their nuggets of wisdom to fit it to what you want to do. It should be noted that the various informational boxes peppered throughout the book come from the authors, not the interviewees. You will also see a few anonymous interviews. We wanted those interviewees to be free to answer honestly and not politically.

The road to fame and fortune, okay, the road to actually getting a movie made, is long and hard. We hope that this book will be a welcome partner on that journey. And when you get your movie made, drop us an email! We love to share success stories, and just getting your film made is a success story worth shouting about! So the best of luck, never give up, and we hope to see you at the Oscars in, let's see, 2009?

Genevieve Jolliffe & Chris Jones
Living Spirit Pictures
February 29, 2004
www.livingspirit.com
mail@livingspirit.com

Experts Contents

TRAINING

DEVELOPMENT

ORGANIZATIONS

FINANCE

TALENT

PRODUCTION

POST PRODUCTION

SALES

AFTERMATH

CASE STUDIES

GLOSSARY

INDEX

Tips Contents

POST PRODUCTION

SALES

AFTERMATH

Quick Guide To Low Budget Movie Making

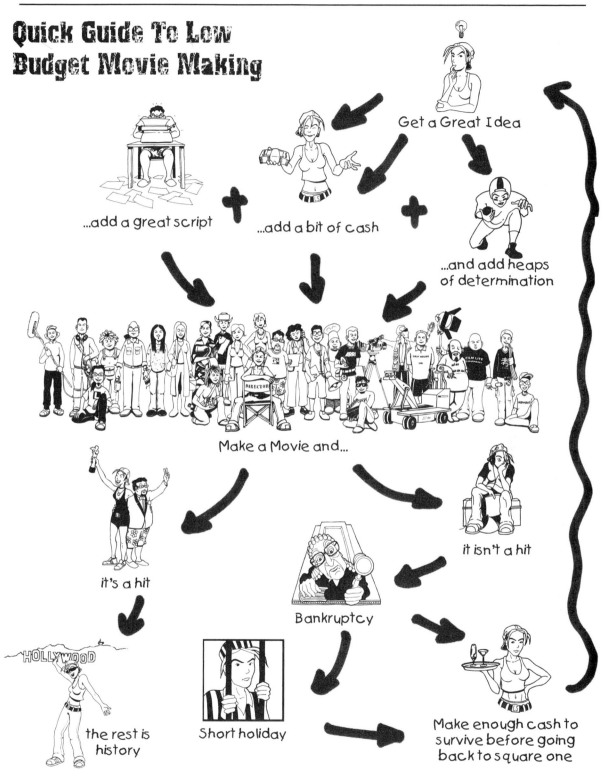

Get a Great Idea

...add a great script + ...add a bit of cash + ...and add heaps of determination

Make a Movie and...

it's a hit

it isn't a hit

Bankruptcy

HOLLYWOOD

the rest is history

Short holiday

Make enough cash to survive before going back to square one

Training

This section deals with how to start a potential career. Go to film school or not? Who else is out there that can help you?

Development

This section is all about taking that idea through to a project. What should you develop? Who for? How long will it take? What pitfalls should be avoided?

Organizations

This section is all about the groups that are out there, organizations that you can join, what they offer and how they might help you realize that dream. Other organizations are professional bodies whom you will deal with when you make you film.

Finance

This section is all about money, the risks, the benefits, how much you might need, where to spend it. It does not detail where the pot of gold is at the end of the rainbow however.

Talent

This section is all about the major talent, mainly the director, cast and working with kids.

Production

This section is all about the shooting of the movie. Who will do what, when and where.

Post Production

This section is all about how to technically and artistically complete your movie after having shot it. It also begins to detail the implications of international sales.

Distribution

This section is all about preparing and selling your movie, and film festivals. It also covers supporting your movie once it is 'out there'.

Aftermath

This section deals with what happens when the dust settles, for better or for worse.

Case Studies

This section is about other filmmakers, the authors included, and the films they have made, the successes they have enjoyed and the failures they have endured and learned from.

Film School Graduates
Amy Collins and Becky Rolnick

FILM SCHOOL?

Q - Why film school?

Becky - As an undergraduate I majored in political science and journalism after which I developed an interest in filmmaking and did a 6 week intensive film course at NYU that I absolutely loved. It gave me enough exposure to filmmaking that I knew that I wanted to pursue it as a career. From there I started pouring through the trades and working any job I could get "hired" to do on low budget films that were being scraped together on credit cards. I spent time interning in London and then I worked for a year as an executive assistant at a film company. Through all of this, I came to understand that film school would give me the space to immerse myself in film theory, history and creativity while connecting me to an invaluable community of artists and giving me hands on experience with sophisticated equipment that I wouldn't otherwise get. Of course, the big film school irony is that at the end of the day, you still come out and work for free.

Amy - I always loved movies. During my undergraduate degree at Berkeley, I took an acting class and became fascinated with the whole craft. I realized very quickly, though, that I was a terrible actor but I knew I wanted to be involved in film, but behind the camera. So I interned at a news station and on a documentary that later became Oscar nominated. After graduation I moved to LA, and took an internship at a producer's office, and that's when I knew I wanted to go to film school. You get to a point where you look at the people you work for, who are in powerful positions, and you say either *'I want to do that'* or *'that's not for me'*.

Q - Did you need to have made a short film to get into USC?

Becky - No. I was asked to send in a required personal statement (a few pages saying who you are, why film school is the right place for you, etc.) and an artistic resume, where I could send pictures or copies of anything artistic I'd done, from films and photographs, to poetry and woodwork. I was also asked to write an essay on an emotionally intense moment in my life. I guess they were trying to see how well I could tell a story.

Q - Was film school a better route for you two than working your way up in the industry?

Becky - Ironically, when you come out of film school, you most likely end up being a PA again! It's a hard pill to swallow as you feel much more capable. Often, there's a stigma in the industry that film school grads have a sense of entitlement and that they need to start at the beginning and pay their dues. Some do, some don't, but hopefully going to film school gives you the skills to help you advance quickly, even if you start at an entry level.

Amy - You reach a level of maturity where you can say *'I am a production assistant. It is my job to get coffee for this person. It doesn't reflect on me as a person, but that is my job description.'* The people who move up quickly are the people who realize this, and do their job with a smile on their face. This industry is based on relationships. People want to work with people they like and people who make their job easier. It's also important to remember that landing a feature right out of film school as a director is very much an anomaly. Most people have many years of work experience behind them before they are coined *'overnight'* successes. Having said that, the idea of working your way up in the industry really depends on what it is you want to do. There is no set path to becoming a director, whether you go to film school or not.

Q - How long was the program at USC?

Amy - It's supposed to be three years. In your first year, everyone takes the same classes, then you begin to specialize. Making a thesis film is what can really set people back time-wise. Most people who make these films are at USC for longer than three years.

Q - Did everyone have to produce or direct for their thesis film?

Becky - No, there are different ways to fulfill graduation requirements. You could write a script as your thesis, or work in some capacity on an advanced project. You have to fulfill a thesis requirement in some way, otherwise you won't graduate. Although having a diploma from film school doesn't mean that much. It would mean I could get a teaching job somewhere, but it doesn't really translate into work in the industry.

Q - Why USC?

Amy - Actually, I had a bias against USC, as the reputation of it was very Hollywood and I thought it would be a *"boys club"*. My dream was to go to NYU. The Coen Brothers and Martin Scorcese went there and I admire them. I sent in a non-sync, 16mm short film with my application that I'd made through a UCLA Extension course. It was called *The Magical Blue Box* and it was terrible! Hence I didn't get in, but I did get a thick envelope from USC. When you get one of those, you think, *'Oh my God, I got in, I'm so excited'*. My heart was racing, I opened it up and it said, *'Dear Berne, Congratulations on being accepted to USC'* and I said, *'Who the hell is Berne?'* I called the admissions woman who discovered that there was a mix up. Berne was a Swedish girl who had been accepted. She then went to find out about my case while I was left hanging on to the phone wondering if Berne had received my rejection letter. She then came back and told me that I was in too!

Becky - USC wasn't my first choice. It wasn't just about the school for me, but the location. I was from the East Coast and I wanted to stay on the East Coast, but I was rejected by every other school. It's ironic because USC is actually rated first or second in the country. It was a great feeling to be accepted because I felt like someone out there felt I was capable of going somewhere in the industry. Even if it's baby steps to start with, someone is saying, *'yep, she can do it'.*

Q - Would you recommend Film School?

Becky - Yes. Film school is so exciting because you dive into this world and you don't come up for air for 3 years. It's a real community where everyone is as passionate as you are and you find yourself constantly crewing up on everyone else's projects, *'I'll help you shoot if you help me edit'.* You are engulfed in this world. If you choose not to go to film school but work in the film world, it's not the same because you're not helming the process and you can't get such hands-on experience. You get a total sense of discovery and community at film school, where you all have the same energy and goals. It's fantastic.

Q - Did you feel the Hollywood vibe at USC?

Amy - Yes. Because of USC's ties and connections to alumni like George Lucas, Robert Zemeckis etc. and also because it happens to be based in LA which meant that people would come to the school for events, Q & A sessions, and to give lectures. It's beneficial to hear about first hand experiences from people working in the industry and I'm not sure that if you went to film school in another state where there isn't a large entertainment industry, that you would have such resources.

Becky - You can also get an internship locally. A friend of mine got to shadow Ron Howard on *The Grinch* for example.

Q - Did you work with 35mm at film school?

Amy - You can work with 35mm if you take advanced cinematography or chose to shoot your advanced thesis project on 35mm. But in intermediate cinematography classes as well as intermediate projects financed by the school, students work with 16mm.

Q - How many films are financed by the school?

Amy - The school finances 4 intermediate 16mm narrative projects a semester. These projects are made in a workshop that centers more on the learning

Amy Collins directs her first short film.

experience than the ultimate quality of the films. Students have to pay for advanced projects out of their own pocket, but there are 15 projects selected a semester for which students can use the school's equipment, insurance and SAG agreements. Roughly 30-40 of these projects are pitched a semester. My project wasn't picked so I had to do another type of thesis film in which I would receive the university credit for the film, but I had to pay for everything. I couldn't use the school's equipment, insurance, or SAG agreement.

Becky - The only upshot to doing the film on your own is that at the end of the day, you own it, whereas for me, USC owns my film. I had a time limit (my film was 14 1/2 minutes) and I had to battle for that as it wasn't supposed to be over twelve. Amy's was 27 minutes and nobody had any say over that.

Virgin Directors

Different directors have different styles and methods of working with their actors and the crew. Some will scream and shout, others prefer a relaxed working environment, there are 'actor directors', there are 'camera directors'... And, then there are 'virgin directors', first timers who are trying to figure out which one of the above they are (if any!).

1. Be prepared. Know what you want for each scene and know what camera set-ups are needed.

2. The most overlooked area of directing is casting. Get the cast right (and script) and you'll find the journey much easier.

3. Have a read-through with the actors at least once. Reading out loud and performing the script is very different to reading it alone - this reading will illuminate the interplay among the characters and any problems can be modified in a script rewrite.

4. Rehearse. With the physical acting out of the scenes, you will get a feel for anything that isn't working. It's better for problems to arise in rehearsals than on set. Don't over rehearse so that your cast can still recreate the magic when in front of the camera. The rehearsal will help give your actors a sense of the whole story rather than just their own character journey.

5. Have good communication with your actors and crew so that they know exactly what you want. Use storyboards, shot lists or floor plans.

6. Know your script intimately. Actors may ask you for the background to scenes for their motivation is in this scene.

7. As a low budget filmmaker you are often the producer too. Make sure that when directing you let go of as much producer's work as possible. Delegate!

8. Creative ideas can come from anywhere - listen to your crew and cast. The director will ALWAYS get the credit.

9. Cover the scene! Make sure you have enough shots to make it work in the edit. Don't believe that your screenplay, actors and direction is so good that you won't need to cut it - you will.

10. Substance over style. Get the story right and get great performances before you worry about flashy shots.

11. Rest when you can. Politely request others to get you tea, coffee and food and avoid decisions you don't have to make.

12. Steal your brothers iPod so you can listen to music. It will take you away from the set and help clear your mind.

13. Learn everybody's name! If you're interested enough to learn their name, they feel respected and appreciated.

14. Stay on schedule and budget. Your resources are VERY limited and indulgence in one area will mean drastic cut backs in another. You only have a film is you shoot the whole script!

15. Study acting, indeed act yourself, you will learn so much about the job. Avoid giving actors blank direction such as 'you're angry now'.

16. Keep working. Don't think that when you wrap that is the end of the shoot. Keep shooting new scenes and cutaways as you need them.

17. Have production meetings with your crew. Explain what has been done, what is left to be done. Everyone will feel more like a team and a team will make for a happy relaxed crew who will deliver their best.

18. Learn how to edit. Editing is directing after the fact.

19. Recognize that your first film will mostly be about learning how to make a film!

TRAINING

Is Film School For You?

Quentin Tarantino once famously said something to the effect of 'take the money you plan on using to pay for film school and use it to make your first film.' Not all agree, but it is fair to say that not all film schools are the same. You may not be right for one of the top film schools, but may shine and better exploit a lesser school. Then again, you may find yourself frustrated and bogged down in theory when you thought you were taking on a practical course!. Speak to the tutors, students, ex students, and watch their films before you decide. Be clear abnout YOUR expectations.

For Film School

1. The film industry is about networking. Film school provides you with a whole class of contacts.

2. You are more likely to receive grants as a student.

3. Professors are there to give advice about how the system and equipment works.

4. You can screen your work at the school film festivals.

5. As a student, you usually receive discounts on things like processing, rentals, and licensing fees.

6. Cheap to free equipment rental.

7. Some schools, such as USC, have mentoring programs with alumni who are professionals.

8. You will not have a diploma, which is not that important, but graduates can often get a foot hold through the 'old school' contacts.

9. You will make friends with a group of like minded people, often remaining friends for life.

Against Film School

1. No expensive tuition, so you can put all your funds into making your film.

2. Some competitive film schools only make a few of their students films a year. Your idea may have to wait or never see the light of day. No film school, and you can make your film whenever you are ready.

3. No competition for equipment with other students.

4. You have to learn everything yourself, which costs time and money.

5. Hiring professionals is expensive and you will not have a free and somewhat experienced labor pool.

6. You have to make your own contacts.

7. You may not get on with the system or professors. Film makers are often rebels, and schools don't like rebels.

8. Comedy and commercial work is sometimes looked down upon in film schools.

9. Expensive (upwards of $25K a year, pro / adult courses can be $1000 per class).

Q - How many people ended up making their own film with their own money?

Amy - Out of the 50 people in our class, I think about 5 ended up making films with their own cash. Even though USC has a reputation for being a mainstream school, the students are encouraged to tell dramatic, personal stories that are not mainstream. If the vision of the film you want to make doesn't fit with your teachers' sensibilities, your film can fall by the wayside. That was my experience. By going out and making my film on my own, I didn't have to shape it to anyone else's vision. If you are someone who's lucky enough to go into the film world professionally, there's going to be very few times during your career when you're going to be able to have that experience. That's the silver lining to not making a University mentored project.

Becky - Faculty mentors pick projects based on a set of criteria personal to them, in conjunction with guidelines set down by the university. A lot of the films that get made on the independent basis that Amy chose often end up being stronger films.

Q - If someone wanted to include your short with others on DVD for distribution, who would get the income for it if the film school owns your film?

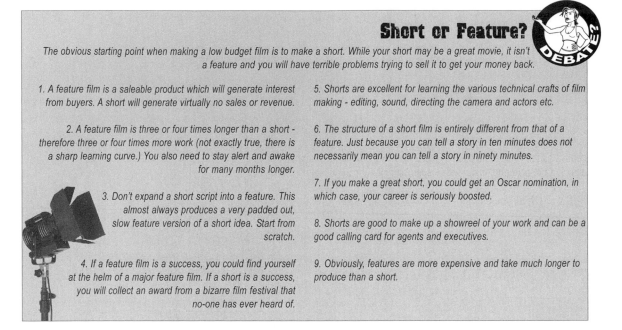

Short or Feature?

The obvious starting point when making a low budget film is to make a short. While your short may be a great movie, it isn't a feature and you will have terrible problems trying to sell it to get your money back.

1. A feature film is a saleable product which will generate interest from buyers. A short will generate virtually no sales or revenue.

2. A feature film is three or four times longer than a short - therefore three or four times more work (not exactly true, there is a sharp learning curve.) You also need to stay alert and awake for many months longer.

3. Don't expand a short script into a feature. This almost always produces a very padded out, slow feature version of a short idea. Start from scratch.

4. If a feature film is a success, you could find yourself at the helm of a major feature film. If a short is a success, you will collect an award from a bizarre film festival that no-one has ever heard of.

5. Shorts are excellent for learning the various technical crafts of film making - editing, sound, directing the camera and actors etc.

6. The structure of a short film is entirely different from that of a feature. Just because you can tell a story in ten minutes does not necessarily mean you can tell a story in ninety minutes.

7. If you make a great short, you could get an Oscar nomination, in which case, your career is seriously boosted.

8. Shorts are good to make up a showreel of your work and can be a good calling card for agents and executives.

9. Obviously, features are more expensive and take much longer to produce than a short.

Becky - If your film is made through the film school, as I made my film, you don't own your film. The school does. If you've made your film like Amy and not received any access to the school's resources, then the school doesn't own it, Amy owns it. Technically she would be the one to make any money if a deal ever came her way.

Q - Would you say it's a good idea to get an industry mentor?

Amy - Yes, if you can. Robert Zemeckis, for example, is someone who has gotten involved in some of the thesis projects that the school endorsed. In my case, I was at a function where I approached a Hollywood director to mentor my project. It turned out the timing was right. He responded to the material and agreed to be involved in a limited capacity. In Hollywood, people like to put a label on something, and if your film has a seal of approval from someone who's well known, in some way that raises your stock. So having him as a mentor has benefited me on some level, I think, as it's peaked people's interest, and made them think that this director has endorsed my project. I was lucky because he also happened to be a really nice man and gave a lot of great notes.

Becky - I wanted a professional Foley artist for my film, and I anguished over how I was going to do this. I ended up cold calling a major post production studio and asked them outright. Not only did they give me a professional foley and mix for free, but they donated a final mix too.

Q - Do you think you learned something different from Becky in having to make your own film?

Amy - I came out feeling like I was ready to make a feature, because I'd gone through every step of the process on my own. I had to do things the way they are done in the real world, as opposed to how they are done within the University, which I think was ultimately the best learning experience I could have had.

Becky - In the real world, post film school, my film was well received critically, but not commercially. I had a few meetings after the 'First Look' screening, which is the School's screening for the industry. But soon it became a matter of how am I going to pay my bills? The first year out of film school was the toughest as I didn't have many real world connections, and I was suddenly faced with the real world. My back up skill was editing, and that's been keeping me alive since. A faculty member once advised me *'If they're looking for a director, they're not going to come ask Becky the editor'*. He felt that if I wanted to direct, I should focus on that alone. Write scripts, push my way through doors, but even those things are an uphill battle. You still have to worry about things like paying the rent, buying food, paying student loans. I realize that nothing is going to happen over night. Everything in this industry is future oriented and it's hard to stay motivated. More than talent, it takes stamina and sheer will. I have ended up working a lot in television which suits my personality as it's a more stable environment.

Amy - I made a 27 minute comedic film and I got rejected from practically every film festival I applied to. I felt like a failure. I set up my own screening, and an agent from a respected company approached me there. I signed with them and was so excited, thinking that this was the beginning. However, months went by and nothing was happening. I realized that having a successful short film alone had no real status in Hollywood. You need a great idea and a great script. At that point, I had neither. After USC's "First Look" screening, I was approached by a manager who I decided to sign with, hoping that two people looking after me rather than one would help get me and my film out there. Since then, I've been going on a lot of general meetings. It's been great, because I'm making contacts with people in the industry and I'm finding out what projects are out there. It's also forced me to become more creative as I'm writing and pitching ideas constantly. Taking the next step will ultimately be up to me, whether that means nailing a take on a project or going out with a spec script that I can get set up.

Q - Do you think you should make a commercial film as your calling card short film?

Becky - It's hard to tell. I had a friend who made a dramatic, character driven film and she got into lots of festivals and did well. But, there's been no attention from agents. Make a film that you're passionate about, whether it's commercial or not. If you do that, you'll get the best film you are capable of making, regardless of its commercial value, and that's the most important thing. There is no right answer though. If you're in the industry long enough, the one thing everyone has in common - possibly the only thing everyone has in common, in fact - is that absolutely everyone has a different story about how they got where they wanted to be.

Amy - Agents and managers look at people and films in terms of what they can "sell". If you have a project that they don't know how to "sell", it isn't any less valid, but it puts you at a disadvantage. Filmmakers who make genre pieces, like comedies, musicals, or horror films, generally get more mileage from their shorts. Certain genres are going to be more accessible in a short space of time. With comedy for instance, you can make someone laugh in 5 seconds, but with drama you have to involve someone in the story and characters, so it takes longer to get drawn in. You ultimately have to make the film you want to make, though. You can never be sure what will lead to what, so enjoy the process.

Q - Was film school a good experience?

Becky - Film school is great. It gave me hands on experience, taught me a ton that I wouldn't have otherwise had exposure to, allowed me to participate in an amazing and passionate community, and exposed me to great mentors and professionals. In the industry, most of the jobs I have gotten have been through people I went to school with. Often, I'll get a random e-mail asking if I can do work. Ultimately, it's an industry of whom you know, the more people you know that are working, the more work you will get as they pull you in.

Amy - I encountered a lot more conflict from the University throughout my film school experience, so I was ultimately left disenchanted. To be a filmmaker requires ambition though, and when it comes down to it, I probably would not have had the motivation to go out, track down the resources and make twelve short films on my own without the structure provided by the school. I saw myself grow so much over the time I was there. There is an enormous learning curve in that environment and it's great to be able to shut out the outside world for a brief time and get to only focus on creative things. That being said, it is by no means the only way to do it. You come out of film school with some idea of what your own personal strengths are. I would never trade what I got from that experience.

Film Help Websites

www.mandy.com
www.assistantdirectors.com
www.shadesofday.com
www.film-makers.com
www.tdfilm.com
www.filmmaking.net
www.indiefilms.com

Internet Shorts Websites

Atom Films: www.atomfilms.com
Ifilm: www.ifilm.com
Hypnotic: www.hypnotic.com
BMW Films: www.bmwfilms.com
Cyber Film School:
www.cyberfilmschool.com
Catatonic: http://
www.catatonicfilms.com/films9/
Zap2It: http://alliance.zap2it.com
Nibblebox (animated):
www.nibblebox.com
Urban Entertainment:
www.urbanentertainment.com
Bijou Café: www.bijoucafe.com

David Von Ancken
Bullet in the Brain

NO FILM SCHOOL?

Q - What is your film background?

David - I never went to film school. Filmmaking wasn't something I wanted to do until I was at college. I was too much of a coward to jump into it straight away. I studied economics and history and started writing short stories. After university, I worked in NYC in corporate real estate for ten years and slowly carved out free time to work on my own films when I realized my future wasn't going to be in corporate America. It still took me several years to edge out.

Q - How did your first short film come about?

David - A friend of mine, Ken McIntyre, who was well known in the jazz world, challenged me years ago to make a film using his saxophone as dialogue. So, I wrote a film called *Box Suite*, a black and white avant-garde jazz piece. I put up the entire budget of $10k and shot it. Once we had a rough cut, we took it up to Ken's studio and he composed an original score, which served the dialogue, and it worked really well.

Q - How did 'Bullet in the Brain' come about?

David - I read the short story by Tobias Wolff in *The New Yorker*. It was four pages long and it really knocked me on my ass. The story is about what happens to a professor who antagonizes a bank robber to the point where he shoots him in the head, and what happens when the bullet hits the front of his brain. The brain operates so much faster than the bullet, that even though he's dead within a thousandth of a second, his brain accelerates around the bullet and the professor has an eternity to live in his head for that moment. So, I rang ICM who represented Tobias Wolff, to see if I could get an option and explained why I wanted to do it. They forwarded him a copy of my first short, he liked it, and had them cut me a good deal. In fact, the price went down by eight fold for the option. It was about a thousand bucks, maybe a little less. I decided this would be an exercise in NOT spending my own money, which of course in the end, didn't work out. I applied for a grant from the New York State Council of the Arts (NYSCA), which provides filmmaking grants for people that live in New York City. Their maximum was $20k and we got around $16k. They provided me with a tax free status (501c3) through the NYFA (New York Foundation for the Arts) that they would administer. That enabled me to go out and get investors who could legitimately give us money as a tax write off. We managed to get four investors - one of them came to me, as she had seen my other short, and she donated money but wanted to remain anonymous. Then there were two others that the producer, C.J Follini, found.

Q - What was the budget of your film?

David - We shot 35mm and got the film in the can for $43k. We got some great deals which kept costs down, a $3k telecine for $500 for instance, unlimited Avid time for two months, and when they kicked us out, we found another. I was carrying around my Avid drives for three months! Panavision knew one of our DPs, James Fidiler, so we were given two free 35mm Panavision rigs. Kodak would only give us 20% off, and then Fuji stepped up and gave us a great deal which resulted in 75% off market price.

Q - On that budget, could you hire a professional crew and pay them?

David - Yes. We only shot for six days, so everybody got paid. We had 30 people on the crew. I had two DP's, my primary DP, Pete Konzal who had shot my previous short and a couple of commercials that I had done, and my second DP, James who I had done a PSA with. Pete shot the larger set pieces, and James shot some of the action pieces and beauty shots.

Q - Why two DPs?

David - I could have given it to one, but I'm friends with both, and both expressed a desire to work on it. It can be a problem when you have two DP's on set as they are territorial. But Pete was the primary DP, and James was cool with that. They didn't get in each other's way, and they worked well together.

Q - How did you mange to get the actor Tom Noonan on board?

David - I loved Tom in *Manhunter* and *What Happened Was,* a two person play that Tom put on film. We got Tom the script and he said yes. Then, through connections, Dean Winters (who played O'Riley in *Oz*) approached me and said he was interested in playing the bank robber. It was a small part where he shoots Tom in the head. Those guys Tom and Dean rocked it. When I said, 'cut', no one moved in that bank.

Q - Was money ever an issue with these actors, did you have any actor problems?

David - We paid them all SAG minimums, which they were OK with. We had kids in one scene, which caused a problem. SAG kids are tough as you only get them for 8 hours from the time they leave their house until they return. So, if I did it again, I would just use locals.

Q - Did you need a permit to shoot on the streets in New York?

David - Although permits are free in NY, you have to have $3m in insurance before you can even rent anything. If you don't have the permits the cops will shut you down. Otherwise, they're usually co-operative. You don't need a permit for hand held, but as soon as you put sticks down, it's required. There was a lot of time spent finding the right bank for free. You can get a bank in NY, but it's going to cost you $10k a day, and there won't be any props in it. We went to Brunswick, NJ, and found a bank that was beautiful, it had just been vacated.

Q - The film has a voice over, what happened about that?

David - George Plimpton was one of my first choices, so we sent him a rough cut of the film, which was already looking good, and he knew Toby Wolff and so he said 'yes' and did it for almost nothing. He read the script once and nailed it.

Q - How long was the shooting and the post?

David - Shooting was 6 days, pre production was about a month. This is all while I was doing other things, like working on a real job. Post was three months, but it was all part time. I would grab an editor at 12 o'clock at night after he'd been working for twelve hours and we'd edit until 6 in the morning, and I worked them to the bone. I used two editors too. They were both working full time, and I burnt my first one out. The film initially was 24 minutes long and then we just kept chopping it

Chrysler Million Dollar Film Festival

Chyrsler? Sponsoring a film festival? Yes, indeed. It has been a mission of the automotive manufacturer to support the arts and The Chrysler Million Dollar Film Festival is their project aimed at assisting emerging filmmakers to reach their dreams. Supported by Hypnotic (an online acquisitions / production / distribution company) and Universal Pictures, the Chrysler Million Dollar Film Festival collects shorts from filmmakers and chooses 25 to go to Park City, UT, to showcase their films at the Sundance Film Festival and work on a 5 minute Chrysler branded short film script. The 10 best travel to New York City where they have 10 days to cast, shoot edit and show their short. 5 are chosen to move to the final stage where they develop a $1,000,000 feature film package (an actual scene, poster, publicity materials). The five finalists pitch their projects at the same time at the Toronto Film Festival and one lucky winner wins a million-dollar feature film production and distribution deal.

For more details go to www.hypnotic.com

up on the Avid until it was 13 minutes. Your short can never be short enough. I hate watching long shorts. Filmmakers want to put everything that they've ever done in their life, emotionally, into their short. So they want to make a 25 minute short and after 6 minutes, they've told everything they have to tell. Tell the story and then cut it down by a third.

Q - How did the Hypnotic Chrysler award come about?

David - I submitted my film and treatment for a feature. The award for the winner was that they would give you a million dollars to make a feature. However, the treatment never worked out with Hypnotic. Thankfully, my lawyer made sure I had an out, and I actually regained control of the screenplay. Three days later it was sold to Jason Kliot and Joanna Vicente at Open City films.

Q - Did you get an agent after Bullet?

David - Yes. The film played in more than 30 film festivals from Rotterdam, San Francisco, St Louis to NY. It was great, and we got some amazing publicity. The press seemed to love it. People started seeing the movie, and several agents were interested. They'd heard a lot about the movie through word of mouth. I was lucky as I ended up getting a manager AND an agent. I didn't even know if I needed a manager or agent. I just thought, '*Okay, why not?*'. They're very different people who hit different parts of the market. Living in New York, it helps having two sets of people in LA. I keep a lawyer in New York though. I chose my agent as he is a straightforward guy. He may not be with one of the big firms, but he gives me his full attention. My manager promotes my name, gives me scripts to read, and is constantly looking out for stuff for me. I've now got twice the resources to draw on for meetings and contacts. I've been doing a lot of writing, and I've not had to work in corporate America for 2 years because of the film, and having an agent and manager. It's easier to get writing jobs, although if you can write and direct, people seem to pay more attention. I love directing more than writing as I love the team that you build around you when you make a movie, where writing can be isolating.

Q - What was the time period between finishing the film and getting an agent?

Directing Books

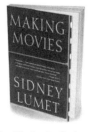

Film Directing Shot By Shot: Visualizing From Concept To Screen by Steven Katz
This book focuses on the 'storytelling' of filmmaking by showing how a script can be turned into storyboards and provides a rich selection of techniques for filmmakers.

Directing Actors: Creating Memorable Performances for Film & Television by Judith Weston
Weston provides a great insight into filmmaking - that it is collaborative. From this stand point, she explains how to make a movie using an exchange of ideas from everyone involved in the process, especially the actors.

The Film Director by Richard Bare
A veteran director gives a solid nuts-and-bolts handbook for the beginning director, especially those working with low budgets. Extremely practical and pragmatic, it covers, among other topics, shooting, staging, camera style, rehearsing, and editing - even how to get a job directing for a studio!

Making Movies by Sidney Lumet
The director of such classics as Dog Day Afternoon and Serpico takes us on a filmmaking journey, through the process of American filmmaking. Written with passion for the craft and a genuine love of life. An invaluable insight.

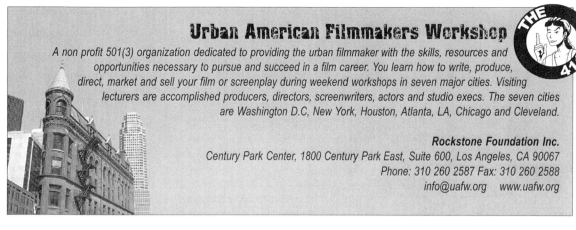

David - Dean Winters showed it to his producers. They then offered me a chance to direct an episode. It was a great experience. That's when I got my agent. When you're directing a high caliber show as *Oz*, you can't say enough good things about it. Yes, I enjoyed it, I friggin' loved it! I wished that there had been another episode! For me, I worked 20 hour days, but I found myself on 3 hours sleep being more awake than usual!

Q - You're based in New York, have you thought about going out to LA?

David - I'm not going to go to LA unless work brings me there. I don't need to have it rain all the time.

Q - What has happened to the film now?

David - We sold it to Hypnotic. You have to remember that you'll never make your money back on a short, I don't care if you spent 50 bucks. We spent $43k, were lucky enough to get a grant, lucky enough to get some great actors and lucky that it came out alright... but we're still not going to come close to ever making $43k back.

Q - Is a short a calling card that will lead to other things?

David - Could be! While making my first short, which I don't show anybody, I met my DP, Pete. I then managed to shoot a couple of commercials, and from making my second short, where I had hired a great actor in a TV show, I ended up directing TV! I've been writing spec scripts and doing rewrites for studios and am now pitching TV shows and features! Without *Bullet* I wouldn't have an agent or a manager and I wouldn't get into any of these meetings.

Q - What advice would you give new filmmakers?

David - Get a group of people you like working with and go shoot. Give responsibility, delegate and trust. A lot of people micro manage everything, wanting to do it all. For me, the beauty of it is creating a team and having fun with those people. Yes you're going to work really hard sometimes, in really uncomfortable situations. Yes, you're gonna get up early, go to bed late, it's gonna be taxing, but at the end of the day you'll have something to show. There are a lot of people who go out, spend a lot of money on CGI and expensive DP's for their calling cards, but whether it looks hot or not is less important. I was at the One Reel film festival in Seattle where the film that won was a little super 8mm movie, black and white, and mute. It told a simple story, and it was by far the best film. It was up against all these expensive 35mm movies. Short is certainly better. Film festivals love them short too. Make sure you have a good bunch of friends who will be very honest with you and will keep on telling you to make it SHORT!

Susan O'Leary
Fox Searchlab

STUDIO TALENT SEARCH

Q - What is Fox Searchlab?

Susan - Fox Searchlab is a Fox Searchlight Pictures sponsored talent incubator launched in January 2001. Fox Searchlab was created to encourage new cinematic voices and provide opportunity to aspiring filmmakers. To that end, the Lab identifies, supports and showcases emerging filmmakers. The Lab provides a small production budget, and equipment to create a short film that serves as an audition piece. The Lab and the Lecture Series are located on the 20th Century Fox studio lot. Fox Searchlight Pictures signs the helmers to first look deals and hopes to build relationships with tomorrow's top directors. Fox Searchlight Pictures is proud of its heritage of working with first-time directors like Jonathan Glazer (*Sexy Beast*), Mark Romanek (*One Hour Photo*), Peter Cattaneo (*The Full Monty*), Bob Dolman (*Banger Sisters*), and Kimberly Peirce (*Boys Don't Cry*). Fox Searchlab is an extension of this heritage. The mentoring aspect of Searchlab is embodied in the Lecture Series. The Series runs year round and to date has included (among others), Bryan Singer, John Toll, Leonardo DiCaprio, Tobey Maguire, John Frankenheimer, Kimberly Peirce, Peter Bart, Frank Darabont, Michael Khan, Baz Luhrmann, Robert Towne, Ridley Scott, Billy Bob Thornton, David Fincher, Mike White and Jay Roach. Searchlab shares the Lecture Series and the digital short films via www.foxsearchlight.com to extend the geographic reach of the program.

Q - Who decides which films go on from the lab and have a deal with Fox Searchlight?

Susan - The Lab screens the short films for Fox Searchlight executives who then decide which filmmakers they are interested in pursuing.

Q - What are you looking for in applicants?

Susan - An original voice, an emerging filmmaker ready to make a film for Fox Searchlight pictures within one or two years. The Lab monitors national and international film schools and 55 film festivals worldwide, in addition to receiving approximately 3000 annual submissions from the public, and industry professionals.

Q - Is there a fee to apply?

Susan - There is no application fee. The Lab employs a rolling submission process, and while we have limitations on the number of filmmakers we can take in any given fiscal year, we are always searching for new talent.

Q - What's the time scales and can they use their own crews?

Susan - The cast and crew work for free. The $2.5k production budget generally covers food, gas, props and maybe a location. The faster the filmmakers gets the short delivered (and screened by searchlight executives), the sooner the relationship between the filmmaker and searchlight can begin. Ddelivery times vary greatly and are agreed to on an individual basis.

Q - While they are making the film, what additional resources can the lab offer?

Susan - Executive oversight for development of the short film script and physical production, production insurance, camera, post facilities, wardrobe department, grip and electric.

Q - How does the first look deal work with Searchlight?

Susan - The Lab contract is a non-exclusive first look directing deal with Fox Searchlight Pictures.

Q - What success stories has the Lab had?

Susan - To date, the Lab has sponsored 38 lectures with high profile industry talent. Searchlab currently has 80 filmmakers in the program from all over the world. In 2003, three lab shorts have screened at the Sundance Film Festival and one lab short garnered consideration for an Academy Award nomination. In 2004, three more Lab shorts will screen at Sundance and again, a lab short has been short listed for an Academy award nomination. Fox Searchlight Pictures is developing a Lab-generated feature film by new director Kiran Ramchandran (expanding his short film, *Kid Bang*, into a screenplay that he is attached to direct). After creating a short film for the Lab, Jessy Tererro directed his first feature film for MGM entitled *Soul Plane*. Lab director Kevin Connelly is up for his first feature film with Nick Cassavetttes penning the screenplay. Searchlight is interacting with other lab directors on various levels too and lab directors often attain representation after participating.

Q - What is it that really stands out from people in their submission?

Susan - Does the story work? Does the ending work? Is it well cast? Production values are nice but do not carry the day at the submission level.

Q - When they make these shorts, can they take them out on the film festival circuit?

Working From Home

1. Working from home can reduce your overheads and maximize your time. You won't have to rent offices and you can start work the moment you get out of bed, then work late into the night.

2. Working from home can decrease your work time – it's all too easy to sleep in or get distracted into fixing the kitchen sink, etc. It's difficult to separate business from pleasure. Have one or two people around to keep yourself from getting bored or lonely. It happens and it sucks.

3. Try to keep a normal work schedule during the day. Elmore Leonard stated once, that he goes to his downstairs office and writes from 9AM to noon or so, takes an hour lunch break and then goes back to the office and writes until 5-6PM. How many novels has he written?

4. If you intend to shoot a movie from home, rent a very big place and we mean BIG! Preferably in the country where you can't disturb neighbors. A call to the police from an angry neighbor could shut down production and force you to relocate.

5. If you mess around too much, be prepared to be evicted – landlords DON'T like the self-employed. Keep it quiet.

6. Inviting a client or investor into your living room can have two effects. It can either make you look very amateur, or it can make you look grass roots and honest. People do like home grown talent and this is an angle which could be very effective. Just look as professional as possible and stress that working from home is a way of minimizing overhead.

7. Mom and Dad may say it is OK to make your film at home – just remember, they don't expect 50 friends to move in with you.

8. Get DSL or a cable modem. It makes research and file sharing more efficient. You can sometimes get cheaper rates through package deals with your phone, cable or satellite TV provider.

9. This may seem very LA, but exercise can wake you up when you feel burnt out.

Film Schools

NYU
Department of Film & TV
70 Washington Square South
New York, NY 10012
Tel: 212-998-1918
http://www.nyu.edu/tisch/
Equipment Available: 35mm,16mm, DV,
Avid, Linear Editing Machines.

UCLA
School of Theater, Film and Television
405 Hilgard Avenue
Box 951361
Los Angeles, CA 90095-1361
Tel: 310-825 5761
Fax: 310-825 3383
webmaster@emelnitz.ucla.edu
Equipment available: 35mm, Super 8, Hi8,
SVHS, VHS, Media 100, Final Cut Pro,
Linear Editing Machines.

USC
School of Cinema-Television
University Park Campus
Los Angeles, CA 90089
Tel. 213-740-8358
admissions@cinema.usc.edu
Equipment Available: 35mm, 16mm, DV,
DAT, Avid, Linear Editing Machines.

AFI
2021 North Western Avenue
Los Angeles, CA 90027
Tel: 323-856 7600
Fax: 323-467 4578
shardman@AFIonline.org
Equipment Available: 35mm, 16mm, Avid,
Adobe Premiere, Linear Editing Machines.

Columbia University
School of The Arts
305 Dodge Hall
Mail Code 1808
2960 Broadway
New York, NY 10027
Tel. 212-854-2815
film@columbia.edu
Equipment available: 16mm, DV, Media
100, Adobe Premiere, Final Cut Pro, Linear
Editing Machines.

Boston University
Department of Film & Television
121 Bay State Road
Boston, MA 02215
1-800-992-6514 or 617-353-3471
Equipment Available:16mm, DV, Avid,
Media 100, Linear Editing Machines.

University of Texas – Austin
Department of Radio-Television-Film
CMA 6.118
Austin, TX 78712-1091
Tel. (512) 471-4071
Fax: (512) 471-4077
Equipment Available:16mm, Super 8,
DV, SVHS, VHS, Linear Editing
Machines.

Florida State University
School of Motion Picture, Television
&Recording Arts
University Center 3100A
Tallahassee, FL 32306-2350
850.644.7728
FAX 850.644.2626
information@filmschool.fsu.edu
Equipment Available: 35mm,16mm,
DV, Linear Editing Machines.

Northwestern University
Department of Radio Television Film
Northwestern University
1905 Sheridan Road
Evanston, IL 60208
Phone: 847-491-7315
Fax: 847-467-2389
rtvfinfo@northwestern.edu
Equipment Available: 16mm, DV,
Betacam SP, DV, Hi8, DAT, Nagra,
Avid, Linear Editing Machines.

Los Angeles Film School (LAFS)
6363 Sunset Boulevard
Hollywood, CA 90028
Tel: 323-860 0789
info@lafilm.com
Equipment Available: 35mm, 16mm,
DV, VHS, SVHS, 3/4 Umatic, Avid,
Adobe Premiere, Linear Editing
Machines.

University of North Carolina at Greensboro
Department of Broadcasting &Cinema
205 Brown Building
P.O. Box 26170
Greensboro, NC 27402-6170
Tel: 336-334-5360
Fax: 336-334-5039
jbcullen@dewey.uncg.edu
Equipment Available: 16mm, Super 8, DV,
SVHS, VHS, Adobe Premiere, Final Cut
Pro, Linear Editing Machines.

Wesleyan University
Wesleyan Station
Middletown, Connecticut, 06459
Tel: 860-685-2000
wesleyan.edu/course/filmc.htm
Equipment Available: 16mm, DV, SVHS,
VHS, Avid, Linear Editing Machines.

Chapman University
School of Film & Television
Cecil B. DeMille Hall
333 North Glassell Street
Orange, CA 92866
Tel: 714-991.6765
ftvinfo@chapman.edu
Equipment Available: 35mm, 16mm, DV,
Hi8, D-Vision, Linear Editing Machines.

Howard University
Film
2400 Sixth Street, NW
Washington, DC 20059
Tel: 202-806-6100
Equipment Available: 35mm, 16mm, Super
8, VHS, SVHS, DV, SVHS, VHS, Avid,
Linear Editing Machines.

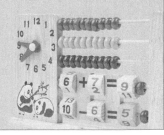

Susan - Yes, while Fox owns the short film, the Lab encourages festival exposure. The shorts serve as talent show pieces and can contribute to building a directorial career.

Q - What about filmmakers not in LA?

Susan - The Lab searches for talent without regard for nationality. That said, LA based filmmakers receive more help given their proximity to the studio as the Fox Searchlab is located on the Fox studio lot.

Q - What kind of film do you think new filmmakers should make?

Susan - They should direct the material they feel most passionately about - and in the tone and genre they want to pursue in their debut film. The Lab approves the short film script or concept before it goes into production, and the rough cut before it locks. Within this mini-green lighting structure, the only other requirement is that the short film be a narrative. It helps if the filmmakers have a screenplay that can be pitched to the studio if the short film finds an enthusiastic Searchlight executive audience.

Q - Then you'll have the studio's attention?

Susan - The proposed material that follows is as important as the success of the short film. Demonstrating visual story telling talent is imperative, but the studio must also be interested in the film material.

Q - What mistakes do you encounter with new filmmakers?

Susan - Do you have a good story and is it worth telling? Who is your audience? Are you passionate about the material? Casting often represents 60% of a director's creative influence on a film, so cast wisely.

Q - What advice would you offer a new filmmaker who's out there embarking on shorts or features?

Susan - As a newcomer creating a directorial calling card (short film), it doesn't matter what you shoot on - so consider going digital and saving yourself time and money. If the story works, format is often irrelevant. That said, shooting an exterior sweeping epic on digital is not yet a great idea given the limitations of the current technology. If you've got talent, 35mm will follow. The important thing is to create a piece of work you are proud of that, something that you can shop.

Q - Would you say the same for features?

Susan - If you want to be a director, direct. the smaller the budget, (generally) the greater the creative freedom. try to get your finished work into festivals to obtain representation, notice as a filmmaker and 'buzz'.

Global Film School

Want to go to film school but can't get in because it is too competitive? Or, perhaps you want to go, but don't want to quit your job to move to Los Angeles or New York. Well, maybe the Global Film School is your answer. Created by the UCLA School of Theater, Film & Television, the Australian Film Television & Radio School and the National Film & Television School of Great Britain and London as a way to "democratize film making" the school provides online classes in film making with courses presided over by some of the top professionals in the field. More importantly, the school's website acts as a distribution site for the students whose work will be viewed online by film studios, television network and representation companies.

Global Film School, 8800 West Sunset Blvd, West Hollywood, CA 90069
Tel: 310-360-2406 www.globalfilmschool.com

Eli Holzman
Project Greenlight

PROJECT GREENLIGHT

Q - What is Project Greenlight?

Eli - Project Greenlight is a documentary television program contest for first time writers and directors that results in the production of a feature film. We wanted it to be an meritocracy in the film landscape, and an opportunity for people who never get heard, or who don't have an opportunity, to get a foot in the door. Stacey Sher said '*filmmakers are the rock stars of the new millennium*' - kids can pick up a camera and make a movie in the same way that people used to pick up a guitar and start a band. With that in mind, we try to give hopeful writers and directors a chance, as well as doing something that would be beneficial to more than just the winner of the contest.

Q - What do you look for in the projects you make?

Eli - The same things that we look for at a studio or as a producer - a great script. Something that succeeds in what it is trying to do. If it's a comedy, you should be laughing. It has to be a movie that can be made within constraints too, *Blair Witch* and *Reservoir Dogs* being good examples. Genre-wise, the movie needs to consider its audience, and we try to find movies that will find an audience. Ideally, it's an audience like the audience for the TV show as those are the people who are most invested. Three or four million people a week are seeing *Project Green Light* and that's a great audience for a movie. That's a $30m audience for a budget of our size (around $1m). We're trying to tap into that audience and deliver them a script that appeals to them.

Q - What do you require from the prospective writers and directors?

Eli - Writers send in the whole script, directors send in a three minute clip of their work. Everyone then has to read a few screenplays and watch some clips. This process allows us to narrow down the field, at which point my colleagues read the scripts, watch the directing samples and begin to narrow it down even further. For a kid who lives in the middle of nowhere, they could enter this contest, and even if they came away with nothing else, they'll have four or five reviews from like minded people who've read their script.

Additional assignments are also required throughout the process - for instance for one assignment we gave them a video camera, editing software and a month to shoot a script we wrote, which was three pages of nonsensical dialogue. It was written to be ambiguous in terms of tone, character, gender, setting, so as to invite the broadest possible spectrum of directorial interpretation. What we got back was amazing.

Last year 10,000 people entered the contest, about 7500 were screenwriters and 2500 were directors. The writers upload their screenplays (in industry format and as a PDF) along with information about themselves. The computer then sorts the submissions and re-distributes them to be read in electronic format by other entrants. Each screenplay is read within a month of the deadline, and is read on average by nine other entrants. They then submit reviews and answer about 50 questions - they have to rate the female characters dialogue, the male characters dialogue etc., as well as answer a number of questions designed to identify scripts that may be too expensive, because ultimately, we will want an opportunity to make a film with a restricted budget of ideally around

$1m. We then take the top 50 scripts, selected by the other entrants and calculated by our computer, and we invite the writers to send us a videotape of themselves appearing on camera and pitching their script - so it's more than just a piece of paper and so we can see who they are. The reason for doing it this way is that any person that talks to the studio about 'their' movie can later claim the studio ripped off their idea and start a law suit. So we limit the amount of creative work we are exposed to.

With those videos and scripts in hand, we get together and pick ten scripts to come to Sundance to meet us. There is a big difference between the few very good, commercial, producible scripts and the others, so they stand apart. We interview the writers for half an hour each, about their script and how they saw it. Usually we have creative issues with notes in the script, to see how they were going to react - would they be flexible, stubborn or resolute to the point of stifling the project? Are they intelligent and well spoken? Then we interview the directors who would talk about the scripts. Then we make our decision and choose the winners. From that moment, they enter into 10 weeks of pre-production - cast and crewing, getting ready, budgeting, schedule, location etc. There's a shoot period, then post immediately, then the movie comes out in mid-August.

Q - Stepping back, how does the selection of the directors work?

Eli - It's pretty much on the same timeline as the writers. The directors submit three minute clips of short films that they have produced and directed, either original work or work specifically made for this contest. You can enter as many times as you like. The directors are obliged to review other directors submissions and rate them based on a form that we have created for them, and also read the scripts. We have a computer system set up so that if you give shitty scores to everyone, we'll kick you out. The computer determines the top 250 directors and we ask them to send in tapes pitching themselves as directors. The vast majority are a white guy on a couch staring into the camera saying *'I'm a story teller'* and boring you to tears for the next 3 minutes. We watch these tapes, argue, and pick the final 10 from the last 50. We then announce the top ten writers and directors at the same time. The ten directors are sent computer editing software and a high end DV camera and have 25 days to shoot something based on the script we send them. They also have to write reviews of all 10 scripts and talk about which ones they want to direct and why.

Q - Do they have to use that DV camera?

Eli - No. Some shot on film. One took all the stuff, sold it on E-bay and used the money for locations and costumes, as she had access to a camera and editing facilities. Any way you get it done is fine by us. The more inventive the better. It's how they use the format. You can make video look terrific. We took everything into account. How it looks counts. Absolutely. If you don't have a film camera and you're in the Green Light contest and you are a director, then don't pick a story that needs beautiful film shots and a stunning filmic look to be successful. Look at *Time Code* or *Breaking The Waves*, they're great movies shot on video and pick something that suits the medium. We're looking for technical ability first. People who can deliver films that are beautifully lit and shot, who understand composition and get great performances, telling dynamic stories. Then beyond technical ability, we're also looking for sensibility and whether it compliments the material.

Q - So the filmmakers get a chance to network during their time at Sundance?

Eli - We have a big party filled with agents and everyone we can get to come. We also send their scripts to agents and make them aware. We champion the scripts that we personally love and try to get them out there to people. It's a huge publicity and promotional platform for the contest and as a business, Green Light only makes sense for Miramax or anyone involved if we can recoup our investment. We believe we're going to make a big hit film one of these days. We believe that that's possible and the investment is a less risky one based on all the attention by the television show contest. If you look at the free publicity in terms of one would normally spend millions on marketing a movie, Project Green Light comes with $10m worth of free marketing and then the studio goes, *'I'll gamble $1m based on this other bit of it.'* It's a great opportunity to bring our contestants into the fold and expose them to the industry. Also its the home of independent film, or if not the home, the hall of fame, so it's appropriate.

Q - Will your film get screened at the next Sundance if you win the contest?

Eli - Not necessarily. The movie still has to be selected by the Sundance judges.

Q - In the editing, it must be difficult when something is moved and taken out of context?

Eli - That's what making a documentary is. You try to stay as true to events as you can with the understanding that you're telling a story. You're not going to change anything drastically for the benefit of the story, but if we all know that someone said, *'no'* and then exited the room in a huff, but the camera wasn't there for it, but you need that beat because it's vital for people to understand what took place, and there's a shot of that person slamming a door that happened the day before, you could edit that shot in there to help the story. We try to stay away from that because we try to be as accurate as possible, but sometimes you have to make a tough choice in the service of a compelling narrative. We film so much material that you can't possibly put it all in. The vast majority of what you shoot ends up on the floor, so the few things you select will be the best moments to illustrate what's going on. It's never a complete picture of what's going on, but we do the best we can with the cut.

Q - And the critics are looking for something to criticize...

Eli - Definitely, especially as the show made it seem like the movie wasn't going to be great. But in the case of *Stolen Summer*, I don't think it really hurt us as the movie ultimately just didn't have an audience, and we can only blame ourselves. That's not based on the talent of anyone involved. For me, it was instructive to see an intelligent person, surrounded by a team of very skilled

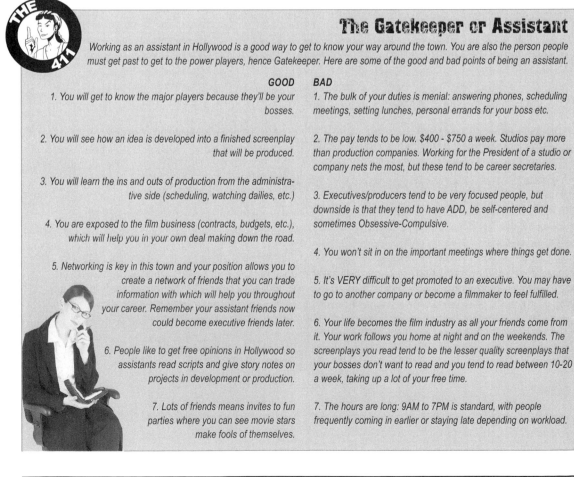

The Gatekeeper or Assistant

Working as an assistant in Hollywood is a good way to get to know your way around the town. You are also the person people must get past to get to the power players, hence Gatekeeper. Here are some of the good and bad points of being an assistant.

GOOD	BAD
1. You will get to know the major players because they'll be your bosses.	1. The bulk of your duties is menial: answering phones, scheduling meetings, setting lunches, personal errands for your boss etc.
2. You will see how an idea is developed into a finished screenplay that will be produced.	2. The pay tends to be low. $400 - $750 a week. Studios pay more than production companies. Working for the President of a studio or company nets the most, but these tend to be career secretaries.
3. You will learn the ins and outs of production from the administrative side (scheduling, watching dailies, etc.)	3. Executives/producers tend to be very focused people, but downside is that they tend to have ADD, be self-centered and sometimes Obsessive-Compulsive.
4. You are exposed to the film business (contracts, budgets, etc.), which will help you in your own deal making down the road.	4. You won't sit in on the important meetings where things get done.
5. Networking is key in this town and your position allows you to create a network of friends that you can trade information with which will help you throughout your career. Remember your assistant friends now could become executive friends later.	5. It's VERY difficult to get promoted to an executive. You may have to go to another company or become a filmmaker to feel fulfilled.
6. People like to get free opinions in Hollywood so assistants read scripts and give story notes on projects in development or production.	6. Your life becomes the film industry as all your friends come from it. Your work follows you home at night and on the weekends. The screenplays you read tend to be the lesser quality screenplays that your bosses don't want to read and you tend to read between 10-20 a week, taking up a lot of your free time.
7. Lots of friends means invites to fun parties where you can see movie stars make fools of themselves.	7. The hours are long: 9AM to 7PM is standard, with people frequently coming in earlier or staying late depending on workload.

professionals and to realize that they couldn't really fuck up too badly. First time directors tend to be too acquiescent or deferential. In a way, that's good, they shouldn't stifle talented people and tell them when they don't have the experience to match. By the same token, you need to have a vision that you are working towards. It should be a malleable one, and informed by the council of your seasoned peers. If there is not a vision there, you're in trouble. Not being prepared enough is the thing that shocks me. If I were making a first time film, I'd have the thing storyboarded and every single thing would be thought through, so the conversation with the DP would be a case of *'this is exactly how I want this shot to look.'*

Q - What common mistakes do you see from new filmmakers?

Eli - On the screenwriting side, first time efforts tend to be overwritten, too much detail and repetition. Like here… *Interior, office….* *Eli sits at a chair in an office.* It's like yeah, when you said interior office, we knew there was a chair and desk. That's a basic writing mistake. Others include poor structure, generic characters, dialogue that isn't differentiated very well… You can get a copy of the coverage form we give to people when they submit screenplays, it's pretty instructive. Every question it asks you deals with character, story, structure… All little things to be looked for in the script and people tend to ignore or lose them. The worst amateur scripts are the ones that are just sprawling, with notes scrawled, and scenes that don't advance the story in any way, characters that you don't care for… In terms of direction, anything that doesn't look professional tends to look bad, and things look professional when they are well made. If your cuts are sloppy, if your choice of camera angles are bad, if the quality of your audio is bad, your work isn't going to look or sound good. I'm a believer in production design. It makes a tremendous difference. People that know how to light, dress and give a good, solid professional look to their work make an impression. A person on the first Project Greenlight series had a cool trick. She'd been a TV editor for years and when she wants to check a cut after having seen thousands of them on her Avid, she brings the tape home and watches it on her own TV because she's used to sitting at home and watching network television or movies and subconsciously, she holds her work to that standard, the standard that we're all accustomed to. Everyone knows when they like or don't like something. That's easy. Articulating *why* is more difficult. What might not appeal to me might appeal to someone else.

Q - What is your advice for new filmmakers?

Eli - For writers, the most important trait to learn is work ethic, and sitting down and writing at their computer every day for a certain amount of time. Read a great deal. If you are going to be a screenwriter, you should read 1000 scripts! You'll learn as much from the good as the bad. It's invaluable training. Read scripts from movies that have been made, scripts that haven't and are published shooting drafts, but read! Study your craft. Also learn about the business. You're developing a product to sell to a manufacturer, so get a sense of what those manufacturers are looking for and keep an open mind. If your hope is to sell a script, have an idea who your buyers are. Directors should get their foot in the door by writing. If you write a good script, hopefully you'll have enough leverage to get your foot in the door and get an opportunity to direct. If you have the bug and you just want to go out and shoot stuff, I'd say be realistic. A lot of people have grandiose ideas as to what will work and I think they do themselves a disservice, by not trying to do their best. I'm always surprised by the ideas people have here in LA. They say, *'oh, I'm shooting this pilot'* and yet, those pilots don't sell! They aren't usually good enough to get someone a job and I think, *'unless you are doing it to entertain yourself, what's the point?'* Unless you are using it as a calling card or want to get noticed, in which case it needs to be pretty spectacular. It needs to be a case of when you watch it, there's no question, you can trust them to direct something amazing.

Michelle Satter
Sundance Labs

Q - What are the various 'labs' that you offer?

Michelle - We offer three Labs each year: a 5-day Screenwriters Lab in January, which are the 5 days immediately preceding the Film Festival, the June Filmmakers Lab, which is 3 1/2 weeks in June (usually beginning the day after Memorial Day), and another 5-day Screenwriters Lab which takes place immediately following the Filmmakers Lab in June.

Q - What is the application process?

Michelle - Each spring we have an open application period during which anyone can apply for all of the following year's programs. The deadline varies from year to year, but it is usually somewhere between April 15 and May 5. Open applicants are considered for all three of the following year's Labs, so if someone applied in April 2003 they'll be considered for the 2004 January Screenwiters lab and the 2004 June Filmmakers/Screenwriters Labs. In order to apply through open application, applicants must have a complete draft of a narrative feature-length screenplay (can be a rough draft). For the first stage of application, we ask for a cover letter introducing the applicant and letting us know the status of the project, a resume/bio on the applicant and any key crew he/she may be collaborating with (i.e. a co-writer or producer - but if no one but the applicant is involved, that's fine), a two-page synopsis of the script, the first 5 pages of the script, and a $30.00 processing fee. Those applicants selected to move on to the second round of consideration will be asked to send in their complete screenplay. Applications are available on our website at www.sundance.org, typically around February 15 (this application process is open to US based filmmakers only - international applicants should visit our website for information on whom to contact about applying.) In addition to our open application process, our staff also does year-round outreach, utilizing a national network of alumni, creative advisors, filmmakers, producers, agents, film festival and film school staff and other industry professionals to garner recommendations, and we also solicit scripts from filmmakers whose work we have seen and appreciated.

Q - What are you looking for when selecting?

Michelle - We consider both the filmmaker and the screenplay when making selections for the Lab. We're looking for unique voices telling compelling stories we haven't seen before on screen. We're also interested in supporting projects which are exploring new methods of storytelling or are pushing the envelope in terms of narrative. Finally, we're looking to support filmmakers who are committed to making their films independently and on low budgets. Typically, filmmakers selected for the June Filmmakers Lab have been through a previous Screenwriters Lab, whether it's the January Lab immediately previous or a Screenwriters Lab from an earlier year. We have, on occasion, selected projects for the Filmmakers Lab that have not been through a writers lab, but that's the exception rather than the rule.

Q - How much does it cost and do you provide accommodation?

Michelle - There is no cost to attend a Lab - we cover the costs of airfare, lodging and meals.

Q - How many people are in each lab?

Michelle - We typically select 12 people for the January Screenwriters Lab and 8 people for the June Filmmakers Lab. The 8 Filmmakers Lab fellows stay on for the June Screenwriters Lab, and we also select 5 new projects to join them at the June Screenwriters Lab.

Q - How long do the labs last?

Michelle - The Screenwriters Labs are 5 days long, and the Filmmakers Lab is usually just under 4 weeks.

Q - Do all the labs occur at the same time and in the same location? And are there networking parties within and across labs?

Michelle - All the Labs take place at the Sundance Village in Utah and happen at different times. There are other Labs besides the Feature Film Program Labs (Theater Lab, Composers Lab) that take place later on in the summer, but none of these labs overlap and there are no networking parties across all the Labs.

Q - Do you have guest speakers who attend?

Michelle - We don't have guest speakers per se - we have Creative Advisors who meet one-on-one with the Fellows during the Screenwriters Lab and who follow the Fellows through the rehearsal, shooting, and editing process during the Filmmakers Lab. We also have evening screenings of advisors' work, after which they lead an informal Q & A. At the Screenwriters Lab, the Creative Advisors are all screenwriters (past advisors have included Frank Pierson, Joan Tewkesbury, Scott Frank, Walter Bernstein, Callie Khouri, Chris McQuarrie, and Alice Arlen) and at the Filmmakers Lab, there are Creative Advisors who are directors, DP's, editors, and actors (past advisors have included David Cronenberg, Sydney Pollack, Terry Gilliam, Sally Field, Alexander Payne, Kathy Bates, Denzel Washington, Agnieszka Holland, Alfonso Cuaron, and Jocelyn Moorhouse.)

Q - What are the major benefits to the participants?

Michelle - At the Screenwriters Lab, the aim is to help each Fellow get to the most compelling version of his/her next draft, while staying true to their unique voice and perspective. At the Filmmakers Lab, each filmmaker is allowed to take risks and work collaboratively, exploring their material away from the pressures of production and financial responsibility.

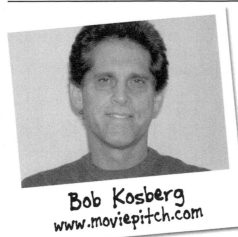

Bob Kosberg
www.moviepitch.com

Q - You are renowned for being the Hollywood pitch king. How did that come about?

Bob - Well I didn't set out with that in mind, I just wanted to work in the movie business. I was lucky and went to film school (UCLA) and when I graduated I did lots of odd jobs in the movie business to make a living, which is when I began collecting ideas that I might want to write someday. Five years later I teamed up with another young writer named David Simon, who I had met during one of my odd jobs. We had one thing in common, we had a lot of ideas! I'd been collecting them, he'd been collecting them, and we decided to go to the studios with the one agent that I had a relationship with, and pitch some.

We were lucky enough to sell a few ideas over a short period of time and I started to notice that I was a little better at finding ideas and pitching them than I was as a writer. That was where my talent seemed to be. But I didn't really know how you made a living as a pitcher. That's not really a job description. So we pursued the writing careers and we got a job at Disney as office bound writers for the next two years. While we were there, this natural urge in me was to play hooky and run around town to the studios and pitch the latest idea that popped into my head. My partner was more of a dedicated writer and he would sit in the office and write while I would tackle the ideas that the two of us had, and be the designated pitcher. When the Disney contract ran out I had built up a reputation of having sold a bunch of pitches, just good ideas being told well, and gradually became known as someone who was good at telling stories. In that first couple of years after Disney I sold ten projects. Most successful people sell two or three things in a lifetime, so I was doing well! Although it's not easy because most people don't really value ideas. One would think they would, because good ideas can be worth $millions. Nobody wants to put a $value on something that can be said in three sentences, and yet oftentimes, great movies can be summarized in three sentences.

Another reason ideas are so devalued is that people are looking for screenplays, because a script is so much closer to the final product. But how often do you find a great screenplay? The reason I sell so many projects as pitches is because there aren't enough great screenplays. If this town were full of great screenplays, I'd be out of business.

Q - It's incredible considering the whole movie comes from that idea...

Bob - The theory is that if it's just an idea, it still has to be written to become a fantastic screenplay and it then may not work. But that's not true. There are many examples of great ideas that are not written well that still turn into successful films because the idea in of itself is so compelling. Of course, if you get a screenwriter and you execute a good idea in a brilliant way, it's all the better. I'm not arguing against the fact that you need a good writer to develop the good idea, but on the other hand, what's a good writer going to do with a lousy idea? So I'd rather start with a good idea and know that I can always hold on to that as the core concept, through the various drafts and working with writers. In America, they have that cliché, *'ideas are a dime a dozen'.* I think it's the exact opposite. I think bad ideas are a dime a dozen, but good ideas are one in a million. On the other hand, there's the human nature factor. Everyone wants to hear the next good idea. You just never know. When someone walks in your door they could pitch the next *Star Wars* or *ET*. It's like when you are in a theatre and the movie starts, you always have faith that you are going to see a great movie. When someone opens their mouth to pitch, there's always this moment too.

All the major stars have production companies, as do the producers and directors, and then there are the studios - and they are all looking for great scripts first and foremost, but when they reach the conclusion that they all have reached, that there aren't enough screenplays to satisfy everyone, in comes someone like me with a bag of good ideas. That gives me numerous doors to walk into with nothing more than an idea. If one person doesn't like it, there's ten more people down the street who might. That's the most interesting thing. You'll pitch an idea fifty times and forty-nine people will tell you you're an idiot, and the fiftieth person will tell you you're a genius. Once in a while, you'll hear a studio head acknowledge that all he wants to hear is one simple, good idea. There are people who have made great livings in the movie business, who have said in public interviews that they recognise the value of a good idea. The joy for me is that not many people seem to be prospecting out in the ideas world, so I find a lot of them, and people also bring them to me because I've gotten a reputation, for better or worse, as being someone who's open to good ideas.

Q - Are you inundated with ideas?

Bob - Yes, because people don't know where else to go with them. I have a website now (www.moviepitch.com) and hundreds come in every week. I recently ran a pitch seminar where 500 people pitched to me, 30 seconds at a time. At the end, I had a migraine, but out of those 500, I heard 2 great ideas that I will now try to sell into the Hollywood system.

Q - How does the system work when you pitch an idea?

Bob - I present the idea, which is owned by the person who brought it to me, so in legal terms, we're talking about the 'underlying rights'. If the studio is interested, they must immediately have a lawyer or business affairs person contact the original writer or creator and negotiate a payment. That payment can be a three month option for $1k, or it can be a six month or year's option to buy an outline or treatment that's been written (that might be anywhere between $10-$20k, and the option keeps being renewed. So you might make $20 - $40k over a course of two or three years. If the writers have a good project, not only should they get paid up front, but when the movie is produced, they should have negotiated a 'balloon payment', a much larger sum of money that could be anywhere between $25-$100k, payable when the movie is made. From a studio point of view, they're making a $70m movie, so it's nothing for them to reward the person who had the original idea.

You could also tell the studio that you don't want to sell the idea unless you can write the screenplay, which some people do. Sometimes, the pitch gives you the leverage to do that. They like the idea, fine. Now pay me to write the script. Now you're into $75-$150k for a first draft, all because they like your pitch.

A real pitch, a pure pitch, means you've written nothing. Everything depends on your ability to walk into a room and entertain someone with nothing more than the ability to tell them your story. We're now going back to cave man days when people sat around camp fires and told each other stories and some of them were interesting and fun and some of them were boring. So what makes a good pitch is no different than someone telling you a story as a friend might over drinks tonight. They'll either interest you with their story or they won't.

A good pitch will simply make the person who's listening, hear it in such a way that they want to see the movie. The best pitches tend to be the ones that are strongest on plot. It's hard to tell a pitch that's all about character because there's really no plot movement from A to B to C. The best pitches tend to be what Hollywood terms 'high concept', very high in plot, that sound unusual, different, strange, weird, off-beat, because they immediately capture your attention. They may be silly like *The Man Who Meets The Mermaid*, but the minute you hear it, you're a bit intrigued.

Bob Kosberg's website at www.moviepitch.com is the perfect place for new film makers just bustin' with ideas to go pitch a movie... And Bob's reputation means that if it's any good, it may get sold, and YOU may make some money and get some attention.

The next part about pitching is simply telling the story in classic terms, which hasn't changed for millions of years - a beginning, a middle and anend. Hopefully you have an ability in a good pitch to summarize. So you're telling the beginning, the middle and the end in less than five minutes, maybe ten minutes, and by telling a short story, you've done your pitch. You leave the room hoping that the person you've pitched to understands the movie and can re-pitch it to their bosses with the same beginning, middle and end, and everybody then is on the same page and understands the story. Do they like it or don't they?

Q - How do people get to an agent with a good idea?

Bob - The problem in Hollywood has always been a Catch 22 - you can't succeed unless you have an agent, and you can't get an agent unless you're already selling. So how do you do it? Usually, you need to write a lot of material for free. Eventually, that gets seen by someone, then an agent shows up wanting to represent you, but of course, they're only there when they can make 10%.

I'm one of the few people who can help those who don't want to write a screenplay for free. They just want to sell an idea. There aren't agents or lawyers who are going to represent those kind of people. They only want to represent screenwriters, not idea

Tips on Negotiating Yourself or Your Movie

For the most part, your agent, manager or lawyer will do this for you as that is their job. Further, if you are a member of a guild, the parameters of how much you get paid for some jobs exist and are immutable. However, if you don't have representation or if the job is non-union... read on...

1. Be reasonable. If you ask for ridiculous amounts of money, if you yell and scream at business affairs people, studio executives or producers without provocation, if you play the part of the prima donna just because you feel entitled, you will get little or nothing. And, if you do get something, you better be the best, most creative, most box office generating film maker ever because in this town, people talk...

2. That said, if you create a property, and someone wants to buy it, you have power.

3. One way to get more money and autonomy is to get hired for multiple things. A writer/director gets more cash than someone who does only one job. If you have enough power, perhaps you can get a producing credit, which carries more weight.

4. Be knowledgeable about the companies that you are dealing with. This will help you plan your negotiations.

5. Try to get as much money up front as possible. Back end deals are reliant on success and honesty, neither of which you can control.

6. Try to retain as many rights as possible. George Lucas kept the merchandising rights to Star Wars and he never had to eat out of can again.

7. Deals are typically structured in steps, such as writing a treatment, then a first draft, a second draft and a polish. The studio pays you some money upon commencement and completion of each step. This gives the studio the option to kill a project if they wish, without paying all that is due, although they would generally give you some compensation. Get as much money in the early parts to minimize your risk.

8. If you are negotiating the sale of a finished film, remember that there are many ways to distribute your work, and more countries in the world than the just the US. Ask yourself if you can get more money by selling all windows (theatrical, TV/ cable, Home DVD, etc.) at once or in separate pieces. Each country is a separate territory and that, for instance, selling the rights to all of Asia might not be as lucrative as going country by country.

9. Read your contracts. Look out for loopholes where power is given to you in one clause, and then taken away in another. Make sure all parameters are clearly defined. If you are confused - HIRE A LAWYER!

10. Know when to walk away. Some things sound good, but after examination, they can be a nightmare. Never be afraid to walk away from a deal.

Pitching Tips

You either love it or hate it, but pitching to high powered executives is a fact of life for the aspiring filmmaker in Hollywood.

1. Have the great hook, and if they bite, you'd better have it thought through!

2. Rehearse your pitch and try it out on friends. Everyone is a consumer when it comes to finding out just how hot that idea is.

3. Have more than one great pitch, if they don't like the first, move onto the second, and even third.

4. Get to the point. There may be a little small talk, but dive straight in. Both your time and their time is precious.

5. Have energy, both in the pitch itself, and in your desire to pitch to anyone who could get your movie made.

6. Look professional. You don't need a thousand dollar suit, but don't go in looking like a penniless student.

7. No matter how the pitch goes, ask questions, chat and form allegiances. This is a business of connections and personalities.

---

people. There was a little old lady from Arkansas who heard about me and she e-mailed me saying *'Dear Bob, I understand you sell ideas. What would you think of a true story about a man living in the Statue of Liberty?'* and I was immediately fascinated. There was no great originality on her part, but she was smart enough to recognize something. I sold it to Universal studios and she made about $50k for doing nothing more than having a nose for a good idea and Xeroxing a magazine article. And then Michelle Pfeiffer was offered $10m to star in it, although it has yet to be made (like so many other projects, it's stuck in development hell).

Q - If a new filmmaker goes into a studio with ten ideas and has five minutes to pitch the whole lot, what should they do?

Bob - You don't want to walk into a room with ten ideas and try to pitch all of them as it cheapens the ideas. You may have passion for all ten, but unfortunately the system is set up in such a way so that it sounds like you don't. Pick one or two, make the first one three minutes long and the second one two minutes long. Remember, there are no rules. This way you've given your two best pitches and they've gotten a sense of what each one is about, and they can judge if they like you or your ideas. Even if they don't buy them, you can come back two weeks later and try two more. Within a month, you will have pitched all of your ideas! Of course you can go to other studios and companies too. Eventually, you're on a merry go round in Hollywood where you're meeting lots of people and you're exposing all your ideas. So the trick is to be concise and to learn the ability to summarize. The best pitches are short, an entire two hour movie boiled down to it's essence. It's not that Hollywood has such a short attention span that they will never want to discuss the story with you, it's just that in the beginning, you have to wow them with the high concept hook and a little bit of the story. If people like the two or three minute pitch, they'll spend hours with you discussing it in greater depth.

Don't try to cram it all in at first. Some people go way off on tangents and start talking about how their characters have blue eyes and what cereal they eat in the morning. And nobody cares at that point. They just want to know the beats of the main story.

Q - What is the biggest challenge for a filmmaker when pitching?

Bob - Number one is to have something that will excite people in the room, something that is truly different, special or unusual. The challenge is always figuring out whether or not you truly do have something that is different. People also go in with something that they're passionate about, but they have no idea about it on a critical level, or whether it is original or not. The chances are it is derivative, and if you take in something derivative, the studio executives are going to know it in thirty seconds because that's what they do all day long. I don't mind walking in and telling an executive that I have a pitch that's like ET, but in my very next sentence, I'll say, *'but this is where it's different...'* I want to be able to tell them the spin, the hook, the difference, the poster. Something about the idea that I think will wow them! If you walk in and say, *'I have a story about two people who fall in love'* that might be a great movie some day but it wont sell in a room as a pitch, because you are offering nothing new.

Q - You have to be passionate as well?

Bob - The cosmetic part of pitching, passion, will only take you so far. When you have a good idea, it's important to express it well and passion is part of that. But let's say it's a bad idea and you express it with tremendous passion. It's still a bad idea, just pitched passionately. People tell me '*Bob, you're very articulate, we think you sell a lot of pitches because you pitch very well. You're passionate, you're enthusiastic*'. I think that I am good at pitching, but that's not why the pitches sell. They sell because the ideas are strong, the story is strong, the concept is unusual. Passion is icing on the cake, but you've still got to have the cake.

Oftentimes I pitch to a VP of development and then I leave. And by the time I've gotten home I hear that the pitch has been bought. But it wasn't bought by the person that I pitched it to, it was bought by the person who the person I talked to pitched it to later. So how good was my verbal pitch? It wasn't my pitch that sealed the deal, it was that the idea travelled well down the hall.

When you walk into the room to pitch, the people that aren't in the room, but they're there almost as ghosts, are the marketing people, who's job it is to sell your project to the world after you leave. So they're telling the studio executives, '*wait a minute, you just told us you heard a really good pitch, but we don't know how to market that...*' I try to do the work for the advertising people by letting them know that after I've done the whole pitch, this is how it ends up on a poster. I give them the one line that belongs along with the title. We pitched a romantic comedy called, Stepping Out, a love story between a man who's afraid of everything and a woman who's afraid of nothing. A glib little line, nothing special about it, but if they liked the story, and then they hear a poster line, they can start to envision how they can take what I've just pitched all over the world and draw people in.

That's a hard concept to get your head around as all you're thinking about is that you have a wonderful story that you want to tell, and you get frustrated when someone tells you to put it in one sentence, because how can one sentence convey something that is so important to you!? You have to separate your project from your ego. *Shakespeare In Love* won a lot of Academy Awards and I can still tell you that film in one sentence - 'Shakespeare has writer's block and he meets the woman who inspires Romeo and

Pitching Competitions and Festivals

International Screenwriters Conference - American Screenwriters Association

The American Screenwriters Association (ASA) exists to serve the largest most under represented writers' population today – the emerging screenwriter. In an effort to help and educate new screenwriters, the ASA puts on a 4 day event in LA offering workshops dedicated to screenwriters. These range from analyzing scripts, mastering the 2 minute pitch, one-on-one consultations to hands-on pitching. Speakers have included experts such as Michael Hauge (author of "Writing Screenplays That Sell") and Linda Seger (author of 'Making a Good Script Great"). Registration is open to all and ranges from $425 for ASA members to $600 to the general public.

For information contact - American Screenwriters Association - 269 South Beverly Drive, Suite 2600, Beverly Hills, CA 90212-3807 Phone/Fax: 866-265-9091   asa@goasa.com   www.asascreenwriters.com.

The Hollywood Pitch Festival - Conference and Pitchfest and the From Concept to Sale Conference.
***** Screenwriter magazine recommendation.*
For 2 intense days over a weekend, over 50 of the film and television industry's top professionals (studio and production company executives, agents, managers, producers, and managers) are under one roof to pitch to and meet with. This includes one-on-one pitch meetings, agency submissions, networking, and intensive, hands-on training for writers (featuring Hollywood's A-List filmmakers as your instructors). Sponsored by Fade In magazine, Waterman Pens and Borders Books. Festival limited to 175 attendees.

For information call 1-800-646-3896 or visit www.hollywoodawards.com.
Hollywood Film Festival, 289 S. Robertson, #469, Beverly Hills, CA 90211

Juliet.' There's no such thing as a movie that can't be boiled down to one sentence, it's just that people don't want to do it. When you ask them to tell you their idea in one sentence, either they can't because they're too attached, or they can't because their movies aren't pitchable.

Q - So is every good movie a good pitch?

Bob - A lot of good movies were never pitched, they were based on novels, or were already written, so did not need to be pitched in the same way. Pitches tend to sell because they fall into a category - high concept plot driven movies. So when I have projects that people bring me that I think are good movies, but I can't pitch them, I tell them '*I really like that, but I can't pitch it. When it's a finished script, I would love to read it.*' I have two lists. On my A list are my high concept, plot driven pitches and on my B list are all the projects I really love and believe in, but I'll never be able to pitch them. People have to define up front, *is it pitchable?*

None of this is meant to sound like I'm some kind of pompous guru trying to make pitching and screenwriting some kind of science. It's mostly fun and games and it's actually pretty easy once you learn the rules - what they like to hear as a pitch, what they like to read as a screenplay, what subject matter is hot, and what's not. Those kind of things are basic, and you get them from reading the trade papers of Hollywood.

It's a small town and once you know a few key people, you're in, and then you find out very quickly, there are about fifteen people that are important for you to know, who can say '*yes*' to you, and about five million people that aren't important to you. The trick is to get to the fifteen people that can say '*yes.*'

Q - Is it a good idea when you're pitching to describe your movie, for instance, as a cross between Fatal Attraction meets Wizard Of Oz?

Bob - When you're pitching, inevitably, someone will say, '*oh, it's a lot like Fatal Attraction*', and someone else will say, '*crossed with ET*' and all of a sudden, as it travels down the hall and everyone is saying, '*it's Fatal Attraction' meets 'ET*'. But you've got to have a story. There's nothing wrong with saying, '*It's a little bit like ET, but in this sense, it's a little bit like Star Wars*', and then let them use the short hand '*ET meets...*' Most executives don't want to hear a writer walk in and throw that around as if that's some kind of magical way to sell a project because it sounds too glib. Nor do they want to hear the other cliché, '*imagine Bruce Willis and Julia Roberts...*' It's like people who walk in and say '*there's tremendous ancillary value to this. You can build a ride at Disneyland*'. They don't want to hear about the ride until they've heard your pitch. It's way too presumptuous. First tell me you've got a good idea, then we'll talk about the roller coaster.

Q - What mistakes have you come across from new filmmakers who have done their pitch and are writing their screenplay?

Bob - The first mistake is writing something that they shouldn't have written in the first place because the idea is never going to get made, it's way too esoteric or complicated. I think you have to find things that have these strong, high concept hooks to them that are you able to explain. I wouldn't set out to write something that's too complicated. Don't become paralyzed by trying to make every scene perfect. You should force yourself to write everyday and plow through to the end so you have a first draft, rather than make every scene perfect. Most people say that good writing is rewriting. As long as you are writing, you can always go back and rewrite. The people I know who get most paralyzed are those young writers who are trying to be too perfect too soon.

Q - When you read a script, what are you looking for?

Bob - For me, the set up for the plot must be interesting and different, and I like to feel like I must keep turning the pages. If after the first act, they either haven't given me a story at all, or they haven't given me anything even slightly new that I find intriguing, then it's not going to matter how good the writing is. I'm looking for someone to be able to set up a story quickly. Not to be vague or confusing. It's the same test that I would give a movie that's already been made. I start to get restless after twenty minutes and want to yell at the screen '*what is this movie about?*' That's what I'm saying to the script as I read it, '*what is this story about?*' Help me understand it as quickly as you can.

Beyond the story I'm looking for what most people are looking for, dialogue that's stimulating, interesting or entertaining. Characters that engage me because they are very relatable, and I root for them because I want to see what's going to happen to them next, or it holds me in the grip of suspense. There was a famous executive in Hollywood who said to people who came in to pitch, '*either make me laugh, or make me cry, or get out!*'

It's blunt, but when you're reading a script, you're hopefully going to start smiling if its a comedy or getting emotional if it's a drama. And if a writer hasn't been able to communicate those feelings to you, then it's going to be bland, and most scripts are bland, boring and do not contain an idea in terms of a story that is very different. The combination of all those things is deadly and you end up not wanting to finish the script. On the other hand, you may read a script that has some brilliant dialogue. It doesn't have a great story, but I might say to them '*I didn't find your story interesting but you're clearly a writer with talent and I want to work with you on something else*'. Writers who don't have a high concept pitch or plot shouldn't be afraid of writing a script that demonstrates their writing ability, but they should be aware that their script probably won't sell. What they're doing is furthering their career by demonstrating their writing ability. Then they might be hired by somebody who does have a really great story to bring to them. The irony is that most great writers don't necessarily have great ideas.

Q - How do you protect or copyright ideas?

Bob - There is no one answer. If you have a good idea, try not to pitch it to everyone. The more people you talk to, the more hear it, and inevitably someone could steal your idea or something from your idea. So there's a danger there but there is nothing you can do to prevent it, other than deal with reputable people. There are little things you can do but they're not 100% protection. The Writers Guild of America allows you to register a one page idea for $20 (and you don't need to be a member). If you pitch that idea later on down the line and someone tries to steal it, you have some legal evidence. Whether you can win in court and prove they stole your idea, maybe yes, maybe no, but it's better than not having it. If you write a finished script, there is even more evidence.

I don't know anyone who regularly copyrights or protects every idea they have. I think you have to accept the cruel facts of life that if you're out there pitching all the time and running ideas by people, yes, it could happen, but it's the way the system's built. But, 99% of the way the system works on a daily basis is legitimate. People selling ideas, studios entering into contracts, people getting paid for what they do etc. The truth is, if you have a good idea and you go to a studio, there's no logical reason for anyone to steal it from you because they're going to buy it instead.

Q - Any advice for new filmmakers?

Bob - If you want to go into the Hollywood system and feel this is the only thing that you want to do, you will ultimately succeed (to varying degrees) because you won't give up. Is this the business that you live and die for? That you're obsessed with? Persistence. Or do you want to be a filmmaker just because you think it might be fun or you could make some money, or even just because you think you have something to say. All of these are reasons but they're not enough. Most of the people I know that have those reasons eventually give up because its too hard.

Every day you have to push that rock up the hill, and even when you're being reasonably successful, you're constantly being crushed by the rock falling back on you. You have to be a little crazy to want to play in this game, but once you decide you love it, then it's the only game in town. Be on the look out for good ideas - they are the one constant. Good ideas will take you anywhere you want to go, in any part of Hollywood. There was never a meeting or a place that I couldn't get into as long as I had that one thing, *a good idea.*

The Writers Bookshelf

'Story' by Robert McKee
Already legendary. It's a huge tome that is crammed with detail, both practical and esoteric. It's not for the faint hearted as it reads like a cross between a psychology manual and / or rocket scientists notebook. Still, it's the ESSENTIAL book. Another one to leave in the bathroom and read in bite sized chunks. More than a few pages at a time will make your head hurt, it's so dense and challenging. Buy it now!

'Writing Screenplays That Sell'
by Michael Hague
A great starter book that really gets the juices flowing. Light-weight in comparison to Vogler and McKee but probably the best place to start if you are working on your first screenplay. Also includes details on getting agents and selling your screenplay. Practical and pragmatic.

'The Writer Got Screwed (but didn't have to)'
by Brooke A. Wharton
Written by an entertainment lawyer, it could be argued that this should be the first book on screenwriting that you read. It's a modest investment for the disasters it could help you avoid. Among other topics, it covers areas such as how to protect your work, contracts, release forms, managers, agents and lawyers etc.

'The Screenwriter's Workbook'
by Syd Field
Along with several other books written by Syd Field, TSWW has proved invaluable to authors at all levels, although those starting out will probably benefit from his clear, concise and structured concepts more. 'Four Screenplays', *another book by Syd Field is particularly fun for the dissection of four Hollywood movies. Very practical and easy to get your head around.*

'Adventures In The Screentrade' *and* **'Which Lie Did I Tell?'** by William Goldman
Both are about as compulsive a read as you can get on the film making business. Told from the perspective of the writer, the books are humorous, insightful and truthful accounts of Goldman's various misadventures in the writing and making, and failing to make, various projects. Wanna know what it is really like inside the monster that is the studio system? Then read these books.

'Bird by Bird: Some Instructions On Writing and Life' by Anne Lamott
Not so much a book on writing, more a book about what it is to be a writer. This book will have you laughing out loud as you recognise yourself in the text. It may not directly make your screenplay much better, but it will encourage you to keep going and keep aiming high.

'Making a Good Script Great'
by Linda Segar
A great book to read even before you start writing. While ideal for beginners, seasoned writers will find themselves coming back to this book. More advanced than Syd Field, but not so baffling as McKee, this is the ideal antidote to days of writers block.

'Teach yourself Screenwriting'
by Raymond G Frensham
This tiny tome is ideal for short journeys or the bathroom. It's easy to read, filled with diagrams and covers everything in such a direct and concise way, it makes you wonder why the other books are so much longer. Considering how small it is, the detail contained is staggering. Overall, the best value for money book on the subject.

Keya Khayatian
UTA

THE LITERARAY AGENT

Q - What is your job?

Keya - I'm a motion picture literary agent. I represent writers and director's, and have a background in books.

Q - As an unknown writer, how can you get your work to an agent?

Keya - For a first time writer, it's just about getting as many people as you can in the film industry to read it. I receive a lot of query letters, and also hear about scripts through my assistant and through other agents. If you don't know anyone at an agency, not even an assistant, then you would send a query letter to an agent who you've heard might be looking for projects. All agents are looking for good projects. If you know someone, even an assistant or a reader, and you can just get your script read it will help.

Q - What do you look for in a screenplay?

Keya - It's hard to put your finger on any one thing. For me, it's an original voice. I'm looking for really strong characters, material that has ideas in it, and I don't mean high concept, but gets at something deeper through the story, whether it be human emotion or phenomenon.

Q - How do you find the right agent?

Keya - It has to do with a personal connection, someone who understands and is passionate about your work, who will be the right advocate for you. You may meet someone at a film festival, you may get a call from someone who heard about your script. An agent can find you in any number of ways.

Q - How does the spec script market work?

Keya - The spec script market is exactly that, *it's speculative*. An agent will find a script that they believe in, come up with a strategy, then *'go out with it'*. Most spec scripts go out *'wide'*, which means they are sent out to a number of producers. Once a producer is interested, it's then submitted to studios and the studio will decide whether they should buy it or not. Another route for spec scripts is if there is an attachment, like an actor or director who is interested, who can then help sell the studio on that script. Sometimes scripts don't need a producer. If you really believe in something and it's really strong, you may go directly to studios and try to sell it that way. Having a script that can go out and people can read is the first step in any writer or writer / director's career.

Q - What are the advantages and disadvantages of pitching an idea?

Keya - Having a pitch or an outline, may be the first step in writing a screenplay, but in terms of a pitch being a sales tool, it's really not helpful unless you're someone who has delivered in the past. If you're a screenwriter who has had some movies made, or has sold work in the past, who is a known quantity, then it's a lot easier. It's still difficult to sell, but it's easier. If you're a new writer, in my opinion, it is too hard to sell something based on a pitch, because you don't have a script that someone can read to then take a chance on your writing the pitch into a movie.

Q - How do you determine your writer fee or payment?

Keya - The Writers Guild determines minimums, but it's about what leverage you have, and in every case it's different. If a writer who's never sold a project before is being hired to write a project, the studio will usually adhere pretty strongly to 'scale, plus ten' - that means the agent will try to negotiate an additional 10% above the scale salary, so the writer gets the full Writers Guild minimum. The Writers Guild sets the bar for what a new screenwriter will get paid for their first job. If you have a spec script that you're going out with, it depends on how badly people want it, how many people want it and how you can take advantage of the need for the material. As with any business, you can set your own price and negotiate the price from there. If a screenwriter has been hired to write a script and they've had a movie that has a buzz, then you've got an opportunity to increase their quote because they've gotten a movie made. There are all sorts of milestones when you're negotiating. If a writer has written a project that an incredible director has attached themselves to, and it looks like it's going to be that directors' next movie, you've got an advantage. If you've done good work and people have recognized that, you're likely to get a raise from one job to the next. Many studios are now going for one step deals, a defensive move when they don't want to risk too much money up front on a project. A one step deal entails writing a draft, and if it's coming along well, the studio then will have the option to move forward the project. If they don't want to continue, they can bail out without paying more.

Q - What does the two step deal involve?

Keya - Writing a draft and then doing a rewrite.

Q - How many drafts would there be?

Keya - Every project is different. Sometimes a project comes in and it's terrific, and with the first draft they get a director and actors, but that's rare. Some scripts go through a number of writers, where one writer will do a draft and a rewrite and then the studio will look for another writer because they don't feel the script got to where they wanted it to creatively. A studio may also bring in another writer if they don't get the caliber of actors they are aiming for, with the hope being that they'll have better luck with another writer.

Q - What's the difference between a page one rewrite and a polish?

Keya - A page one rewrite is when a project is really in dire-straights and needs to be reconceived. Maybe there's an idea in there that works but the entire script doesn't work and it needs to be overhauled. In this case you may be able to get more pay than if you're doing a rewrite. A polish is maybe four weeks of work when the studio thinks the script is pretty close to where they want it to be, but they feel it needs some work.

Q - If a script is bought outright by a studio, how much can a writer expect to be paid?

Keya - Scripts are sold for $millions if every studio wants it. However, a script may go out and if only one person wants it, you may only get Guild minimum, or slightly more. It depends on the appetite of the studio for the material.

Q - What is a sample?

Keya - The best way to get everybody to read your script all at once is to send it out as a spec script, as everyone is always looking for new material. That way a lot of people get to know your

Hundreds of thousands of screenplays will circulate around Hollywood every year. The overwhelming majority will be very poor. But if your work sparkles, an agent may pick you up, get a producer onboard, get the producer to get the studios excited then a deal can be cut. And all your hard work may result in some cash, another job, a movie... All you have to do is write the GREAT MOVIE!

work. If it doesn't sell, it becomes a sample that may be given to producers looking for a writer. Getting your script read is always the most important thing. You target your material to the right producers and executives. But, for instance, while a producer might be known for comedy, they may now want to do something more dramatic. My responsibility is to have ongoing conversations with producers and studios and to be in touch with what people are looking for. There is never an exact fit, but there are certain producers that are known for certain material. As much as we all struggle not to be pigeon-holed by what we do, inevitably producers will get scripts based on what they've become known for. The goal is to balance the experience and track record someone has with the aspiration for what they want to do next.

Q - How many 'samples' do you like to give out to producers?

Keya - It depends. If there is a sample that is perfect, a producer may read it and be happy enough to go to the writer with a project. Sometimes, if a producer reads a sample and says, '*it doesn't have the comedy I'm looking for*', you might send another sample. It depends on the project and producer. Some producers are very thorough and they will read everything a writer has written before they hire them, others won't. When a writer goes into that creative meeting to get the job, the more prepared they are and able to talk about a project, the more it gives the producer confidence that the writer will be able to execute what they are looking for, so being prepared is really important for getting a job. A good meeting can sometimes help push it over the edge.

Q - How likely is it that an available sample will be bought?

Keya - Usually it's because someone falls in love with the script, an actor for example, then it can come together.

Q - What's the difference between buying a script outright, and buying an option?

Keya - Paying for an option gives a studio or producers a period of time in which they can elect to buy the script. For example, if a studio or producer options a script for twelve months, they can use that time to either do rewrites, or attach elements such as actors or a director, to figure out if they'll be able to put the movie together and then decide to buy the script or not. Usually the studio will option the script and have a second option which they can then pick up if say, the first option expires and they are moving forward on it but not as fast as they'd like, and want some more time. They will then exercise their right to pick it up for an additional amount of time. The standard has become 18 months for a certain amount of money, with another option to renew for an

A question of Genre...?

Should your first film (or any) be a genre film? Here are some pros and cons to help you decide. You could also add, to pitch or not to pitch as genre films tend to be 'high concept' and plot driven, where non genre films tend to be more esoteric and character driven.

Pros

Genre films are easier to write because the genre (action, horror, comedy, romantic comedy, sci-fi etc.) has certain rules and conventions on how characters act and what they do. Beware of breaking these rules.

Genre films can get funding more easily because they sell more consistently in the US and abroad.

If you are clever in the way you construct your story, a strong genre film can be produced on low budgets and in a small number of locations.

Cons

It's difficult to come up with a unique genre story because most ideas have been done.

Familiarity can be off-putting to the film business, but not necessarily to private investors.

It's tough to attract big stars, or even high caliber actors to these lower budget films.

If no big stars are attached, then distributors may pass, as it doesn't compete with the big movies out there.

They are not accepted into film festivals as readily as the more "dramatic" or "indie" films.

Options

What is an Option?

It is the exclusive right to purchase a property (script, play or book) at a later date by paying a percentage of the eventual purchase price. This enables the producer to set up/develop the project with less risk than buying the property outright. During the term of the option, no one else is permitted to acquire rights to the property in question and the buyer has the length of the option period to purchase the property in full. At the end of the option period, the buyer (producer) can either abandon the project (and lose the option price already paid), negotiate an option renewal, or purchase the property in full.

How much will it cost and how long will it last?

The standard option fee is usually 10% of the purchase price but is always negotiable. However the option fee could be waived in lieu of the producer's efforts to set up the project. If this is the case, it's recommended to pay at least $1 so that money has changed hands in order to enforce the contract. This option price is 'applied' against the eventual total purchase of the property (i.e you deduct the deposit from the total purchase price of the property).

The option period is generally 18 months. The option renewal period is generally 12-18 months, with extra monies agreed.

Points to be aware of...

1. WGA minimums don't cover authors of books, articles or plays.

2. There are other factors that the writers can negotiate. i.e an author could ask for bestseller bonuses where additional sums can be paid if the book is placed on certain best seller lists. A stage play writer could ask for bonuses if their play wins a 'Tony'. There might also be negotiations for profit participation in net receipts.

3. Producers must ensure that if they sign a book purchase that they receive a publishers release. Here the publisher acknowledges that they don't own the film or any ancillary rights in the book and ensures that the buyer can exploit such rights.

4. Writers may want to reserve certain rights, such as radio and television rights, stage play rights and print publication.

5. Producers (buyers) will want to make sure they can make changes to the work when adapting it. This is the bugbear of screenwriters who have no control over their moral rights.

6. Producers will want to protect themselves by obtaining warranties from the writers, ensuring that the work doesn't infringe another's copyright, defame or invade anyone's privacy. They'll also want the writer to indemnify the producer, agreeing to reimburse the buyer (producer) for any breach of warranty by the writer.

7. Credits. If the writer is covered by WGA, credits are straightforward and determined by the WGA. However, if non-union, the writer must make sure they receive the proper credit and billing.

8. As a Producer, make sure that you're under no obligation to actually produce a film.

9. Make sure that in the event that the producer doesn't produce your property as a movie within a negotiated timescale (usually 3-7 years from when the rights were acquired) that the property reverts back to you.

10. Remember, when buying an option, you must at the same time, work out the terms of the purchase agreement. Without negotiating the underlying literary purchase agreement your option will mean nothing. The seller is under no obligation to sell to you on the terms you propose.

Book Recommendations to buy...The Screenwriter's Legal Guide (2nd Ed) by Stephen F. Breimer. Also The Writer Got Screwed (but didn't have to) by Brooke A. Wharton.

extra 12 or 18 months. An outright purchase is different in that the studio or producer then owns the script. Only in the most competitive situation will one be able to command an outrageous fee for an option. When the numbers go higher, it's usually a purchase.

Q - Once a producer has acquired a project, what happens next?

Keya - They will go to the studio and convince them to buy it. It's important to have a producer as your ally, who's going to fight for you, who will help the studio visualize the movie and see why it's a great project to pick up.

Q - If a producer has a personal relationship with a writer, is it okay for them to discuss projects without consulting the agent?

Keya - Some agents have a policy whereby everything has to go through them and they keep their writers isolated. Others think it is important for writers to have relationships. If you write a movie for a producer and you have a great relationship with that producer, and then that producer has a great idea and they call and discuss it with the writer, that's okay with me. It would be courteous for the producer to call the agent and fill them in because the best client / agent relationships have an open line of communication.

Q - What are the advantages and disadvantages of a bigger agency over a smaller agency?

Dogme Films

In '95, Danish filmmakers Lars Von Trier and Thomas Vinterberg grew weary of how technology had overtaken the filmmaking process and wanted to get back to a purer form. They created Dogme Films, which followed a strict set of rules that stripped away the gloss of the modern movie and forced a director to work with the basics: story, actors and the camera. The rules (which consist of things like the camera must be handheld and no props may be used) were open to interpretation by the filmmaker and brought an extra layer of creativity to the process as the director sought ways of dealing with each challenge. While no longer in existence, the spirit of 'Dogme' prevails and filmmakers are encouraged to try and tell their tales using the rules listed below. So grab your miniDV camera NOW!

THE VOW OF CHASTITY

1. Shooting must be done on location. Props and sets must not be brought in (if a particular prop is necessary for the story, a location must be chosen where this prop is to be found).

2. The sound must never be produced apart from the images or vice versa. (Music must not be used unless it occurs where the scene is being shot).

3. The camera must be hand-held. Any movement or immobility attainable in the hand is permitted. (The film must not take place where the camera is standing; shooting must take place where the film takes place).

4. The film must be in color. Special lighting is not acceptable. (If there is too little light for exposure the scene must be cut or a single lamp be attached to the camera).

5. Optical work and filters are forbidden.

6. The film must not contain superficial action. (murders, weapons, etc. must not occur.)

7. Temporal and geographical alienation are forbidden. (That is to say that the film takes place here and now.)

8. Genre movies are not acceptable.

9. The film format must be Academy 35 mm.

10. The director must not be credited.

Furthermore I swear as a director to refrain from personal taste! I am no longer an artist. I swear to refrain from creating a "work", as I regard the instant as more important than the whole. My supreme goal is to force the truth out of my characters and settings. I swear to do so by all the means available and at the cost of any good taste and any aesthetic considerations. Thus I make my VOW OF CHASTITY."

Copyrighting your script or film

There are two main entities who do this. The first is The Library of Congress Copyright Office. The second is the Writers Guild (WGA). There is a process involved for each which typically includes sending a copy of the work, a fee and a registration form. The WGA has set up a very convenient way to do this through their website.

Don't rely on mythical methods like sending a copy of your script to yourself in the mail, and not opening the envelope (and other dubious screenwriter myths). If you want to protect your work, do it properly.

At the end of production, when your film is sold, even if you have made it guerilla style, you will still need to prove it is your own work. Without such documentation, the sales agents and distributors simply won't touch your film.

Library of Congress Copyright Office
101 Independence Avenue, S.E. Washington, D.C. 20559-6000
www.loc.gov/copyright
go to the Performing Arts section.
202-707-3000
The fee is $30

The Writers Guild West
7000 West Third Street, Los Angeles, CA 90048
323-951-4000 or 800-548-4532. 323-782-4500 for Intellectual Property Registration office.
www.wga.org
Then go to "Registering Your Script Online" in the left hand sidebar. The fee is $20 non members, $10 members.

Keya - Every agency is different. A lot of times, the perception is that a younger writer will be better served by a smaller boutique agency, and a director or actor is better served by a bigger agency. That's a misperception because a lot of times, the information for projects will be concentrated with the larger agencies. Then again, some big agencies don't pool information so it ends up like being represented at a boutique agency. Also, there might be an agent at a boutique agency who is really stellar at representing writers and at helping get writers careers off the ground. It's a tough thing to generalize. It really comes back to relationships and what is good for you.

Q - Should a writer have both an agent and a manager?

Keya - If a manager and an agent work well together, it can be beneficial because they have two companies out there looking for opportunities. If a manager and an agent aren't clicking, then you're in a situation where your representation isn't working out for you.

Q - Do many writers end up going on set?

Keya - It's not guaranteed by the Writers Guild but, it's a good experience for the writer and can be helpful for the actors and the director, if they have questions about dialogue for instance. Sometimes a producer or studio director won't allow that, which is unfortunate. If a writer's getting their movie made and someone is bringing their project to life, sharing that with the writer is a good thing to do.

Q - What advice would you give new writers?

Keya - Always be writing. Get as many people as you can to read your work. Writing can be hard and isolating, yet it is the basis for every movie that comes out. It's a daunting process. Always be optimistic as you never know where that next script will head. For producers I would say don't take no for an answer. Be tenacious and believe in the projects you are pushing and the filmmakers you are shepherding. Be resourceful and leave no stone unturned when you are trying to get a project off the ground. Be fair, honest and realistic.

Chris Vogler

THE WRITERS JOURNEY

Q - How does a writer get their first break?

Chris - There are many pathways. But you can learn from general trends and extrapolate some principles out of it. It helps to know somebody in the system. It's not the only solution but it can help as it can get your stuff read. You need to have it read by a high level executive, but to do that you need a personal recommendation.

Q - What happens if you don't have an advocate in the system?

Chris - You have to be very good, persistent and lucky. They are all necessary elements. If it does get a personal recommendation, that can be a big break for you, but you have to be good. Another element is novelty. One of the most desirable elements about a script is the buzz that comes to it because people perceive it as new. If there's something shocking or remarkable, it can set you apart. You're trying to get yourself distinguished from this vast pool of scripts that are floating around all the time. What you want is people running down the hall of the studio going, '*you've got to read this!*' An example is *There's Something About Mary*. It had an outrageousness about it and it made people within the studio eager to call their friends and ask if they had read the script.

Q - What makes a great script?

Chris - They like to say that it's character, and that does drive a lot of the Oscars. One side of filmmaking is driven by character oriented movies and everyone who has an artistic feeling about themselves responds to those, but the majority of filmmaking is oriented around good plot and situations. Also, taking us to a world we haven't been to before is an important element. A movie that can convincingly create an alternative world is also an ingredient of success. That accounts for the success of *Harry Potter* and *Lord Of The Rings*. It's true of other movies too, such as *The Hours*. It creates a unique film universe that takes you outside of your time and place, and that's a valuable service.

Q - How do you create an original screenplay while adhering to the dramatic structure?

Chris - You have to observe the forms and be aware that the audience is programmed to accept things through certain filters. They have expectations which you can totally dismantle, but within the form, you can do things that are startling. *Adaptation* is conventional in certain ways, but it is almost breathtaking in the way it presents this inner reality of the writers experience. There's a contract with the audience and certain terms have to be fulfilled. Such as to entertain us and take us out of our normal reality. There are lots of other contracts too.

Q - Have any films worked outside of the contract?

Chris - I think there are films that work in spite of the story contract, where there may be some story there, but it's secondary to the experience. This trend started with *Flashdance*. It was a minimal story that was almost besides the point as the filmmakers were giving you the sensation of the dancers and the choreography. That's true of *Chicago* too. Nobody claims that's a complex story, but the film satisfies other contracts.

Q - What do you think about filmmakers like Robert Altman and Mike Leigh?

Chris - They have found another way to get at it. Rather than to have it scripted, they improvise a lot. It's more of a character driven emphasis.

Q - Is that less satisfying for an audience?

Chris - I think this alternative approach is more acceptable now because people are so inundated by standard techniques. It's a time where they are thirsty for new approaches. I'm thinking of a movie like *Bowling For Columbine,* which isn't trying to be a story, and it's bending some of the expectations of a doc too. You're always going to have the dance between the conservatives who play it safe, and those who applaud innovation when something new comes along.

Q - When reading scripts from new writers, what common mistakes do you see?

Chris - One of the most common problems is the failure to identify the main character and set them apart. Everyone is presented with more or less the same value, and the writer has made the assumption that you'll figure out who the hero is. I think you have to give us certain signals that let us know who the main character is. More emphasis on the character and more time spent describing the main character, or they may put the character in the initial position in the story. All these things are clues that the audience is used to reading.

Q - What have you learned from reading scripts?

Chris - Often the problems are in the beginning. When the story starts to unravel after 75 pages, there was something in the first ten pages that caused that collapse. By going back and making a slight adjustment in the beginning, you can often correct that. The set up is so important. The parameters you set are critical to later on in the story.

Q - Are there any books or courses you would recommend to new writers?

Chris - I would say it's useful to take John Truby's seminar, which is good for systematically laying out the options. It gives you all the logical options. It's also useful to take an acting class as it gives you the sense of what's a realistic mouthful of dialogue for an actor. Until you've had that experience I don't think you can write good dialogue.

Q - What do you think about Mckee or Syd Field's books?

Chris - I think all these books are terrific. I endorse having a good grounding in Syd Field's work as he was a pioneer. You can get great things out of *Making A Good Script Great* and out of Mckee's *Story.* It's really useful to absorb their techniques, language and the terms that they use. Then you go off and make your own and create your own language.

Q - How does a writer get an agent?

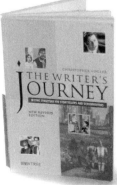

'The Writer's Journey' by Christopher Vogler is an endless source of inspiration that draws on the common rules and structures found in all forms of story. The author has a great deal of experience and stresses that his book is for guidance and is not a set of rules. Once you have grasped the concepts in this book, it's amazing how all great movies seem to adhere to the principles. Essential.

Chris - That's a mystery to me as well. There are certain areas that remain murky, but I think the answer is to be very good and to be committed to being a professional writer. You have to get beyond the idea of *'I'm going to write one script and sell it.'* You have to present yourself as a professional who works fast, who isn't distracted by other things, and who is there at the table to work. The agent is trying to sell not just your script, but you as a worker too.

Q - What do you do in the face of constant rejection?

Chris - To deal with that you have to distinguish yourself from the rest of the pack by doing things like entering local writing contests and apply for writing fellowships. Anything you can do that signals to the buyers that you are special is very important. Winning third place in a local writing contest sets you apart. When you win something like that, it opens the door for you for a short time, so you must be ready to step through that door.

Q - What single piece of advice would you give a new writer?

Chris - Do it every day. It has to become like grieving, part of your normal routine. It can't be a special thing you do when you have a vacation.

Q - Do a lot of people crave the success more than the writing itself?

Chris - I heard a writer say that *'you'd better enjoy the writing, as that will be your life'*. It's like you're a long distance truck driver and you're ass has to be in that chair for a certain number of hours a day or it isn't going to work.

Q - Any tips on how many pages a day and the time of day to write?

Chris - No. There are certain logical ideas you might apply. It makes sense to do it early in the day so you make sure it gets done every day. Either you don't go to bed until you've done it or do it first thing. Many people operate well on the morning idea because you're not quite awake yet so you're able to tap into your unconscious and that kind of writing can be very good. One of the biggest problems people have today is distractions. Some people like to write early in the morning because the rest of the world is asleep.

Q - Is there an acceptable amount of pages to aim for per day?

Chris - People are satisfied to do a couple of pages a day. But typically when you're in production, you're expected to get 5 or 10 pages down. 10 pages is a good days work. I learned a lot about this in the editing room on an independent feature I produced. My chief realization is that telling the story became like building a ship, and the basic structure of the story was the laying of the keel, and then the individual scenes became the planks that you attach to the keel. Then it was a case of smoothing the hull and sanding and refining and taking stuff out. Streamlining became an important principle to me. I recommend that for writers too. If you ever have the chance to edit a film, it will teach you volumes about what you should have done on paper. It's important to have good characters and ideas to support the structure.

Sometimes the scene is pages of talking. You can do that but it's always better if the scene is trying to achieve a specific reaction from the audience. Make them mad, make them care. You're trying to get something out of them rather than just moving on to the next scene. It may not be your destiny to have it made into a film, but it's important to tell the story anyway. It's little comfort, but every script has something to say to somebody. They have their impact even if the movie doesn't get made. There have been many times when I've read a script that I knew would never become a movie, but it gave me a piece of information that I needed at that moment. The writer had not failed.

Top Screenwriting Competitions

The Nicholl Screenwriting Fellowship
Academy Foundation,
8949 Wilshire Blvd.
Beverly Hills, CA 90211-1972
310 247 5059 (voice)
www.oscars.org/nicholl/
index.html
Contact: *Greg Beal,*
Deadline: *5/01*
Notification: *Late October*
Eligibility: *open to anyone*
Entry fee: *$20 before April 1st;*
Rules: *No applicant may have earned more than $5k for screenwriting.*
Awards: *5 x $30k fellowships.*

Filmmakers Magazine / The Radmin Company Screenwriting Competition
Screenplay Division,
P.O. Box 54050
Irvine, CA 92619
www.filmmakers.com
contest@filmmakers.com
Award: *Top 50 scripts read by The Radmin Company, 10 finalists will be read by the Radmin company, Industry professionals, production companies and literary agents. Plus tuition, pitching, readings, social events etc.*

Venice Arts Screenwriting Competition
3830 Valley Centre Dr.
#705-735, San Diego,
CA 92130
www.venicearts.com
Deadline: *April*
Entry Fee: *$30 (early), $40 (on-time), $50 (late)*
Award: *$5k*
Aim: *To pursue the development of innovative screenwriting programs to support the local community in LA and the worldwide community via the internet.*

American Zoetrope Screenplay Contest
916 Kearny St, San Francisco,
CA 94133
415 788 7500 (voice)
415 989 7910 (fax)
www.zoetrope.com/contests
contests@zoetrope.com
Contact: *Paul Kramer*
Deadline and entry fee: *$30 by early August and $40 by late September*
Eligibility: *open to all but no script earnings more than $5k*
Award: *$50k top prize and top 10 screenplays are considered for option and development by American Zoetrope and considered for representation by ICM, UTA, Paradigm and The Firm.*

The Hollywood Gateway Screenwriting Contest
2040 Westwood Blvd, LA,
CA 90025
www.hollywoodgateway.com
Submission forms online.
Deadline: *August 31st*
Entry Fee: *June 30th cost $35, September 30th costs $50.*
Notification: *Finalists in Dec and winner in Jan.*
Award: *$5k prize. An initial 12 month option agreement against a potential $100k purchase, one on one coaching on the art of pitching, script analysis by an experienced development executive, meetings with top agents and producers, transport to Hollywood and accommodation, copy of Final Draft, and the screenplay will be submitted to over 70 top agencies and production companies through the StudioNotes™ Weekend.*

Scriptalooza
7775 Sunset Blvd, PMB #200
Hollywood CA 90046
Tel: 323 654 5809
info@scriptapalooza.com
Entry fee: *Jan is $40, March is $45, April is $50*
Eligibility: *Open to all, with work not previously sold or made.*
Notification: *semifinalists June 15th, Finalists August 1st, Winner August 15th*
Award: *$10k to 1 winner. Top 13 scripts will be considered by Scriptalooza's participating production companies and literary agents.*

American Screenwriting Competition
c/o Flat Shoe Entertainment
311 N. Robertson Blvd., Ste.
172 Beverly Hills, CA 90311
Entry Fee: *$40 (by mid June), $50 (by end July), $60 (by mid-September)*
Award: *Grand prize of $11k, over $1k in screenwriting software, industry meetings, and more. Presented by Hollywood Scriptwriter Magazine.*

Final Draft's Big Break Contest
16000 Ventura Blvd. Ste # 800
Encino, CA 91436
Entry Fee: *$50*
Deadline: *June 30th*
Award: *1st prize $10k and roundtrip airfare to LA, 3 nights hotel accommodation to meet studio execs / agents. 2nd prize: $3k, 3rd prize: $1k To the top 10 finalists: all scripts submitted to a Hollywood literary agent, receive Final Draft software, 1 yr subscription to Creative Screenwriting Mag, ResMag and Script Mag, $50 gift card from the Writers Store and a copy of The Perfect Pitch by Ken Rotcop.*

The Chesterfield Writer's Film Project
PMB 544, 1158 26th St.
Santa Monica, CA 90403
213 683 3977
www.chesterfield-co.com
Eligibility: *open to anyone.*
To be submitted: *Two writing samples of fiction, play, script.*
Entry fee: *$39.50*
Award: *5 writers receive $20k over the year.*

Screenwriting Expo/ Screenwriting Expo 2
6404 Hollywood Blvd.,
Suite 415 LA, LA 90028
Phone: *323.957.1405*
Fax: *323.957.1406*
Deadline: *June 1 (early), August 1 (deadline), August 15 (late)*
Entry Fee: *$40 (early), $45 (deadline) ,$50 (late)*
Award: *$10,000 cash, trip to Expo 2, Final Draft Software, access to producers, agents and managers. To reward what Creative Screenwriting has been celebrating for the past 10 years: the art and craft of screenwriting.*

Walt Disney Studios and ABC Entertainment Fellowship Program
500 South Buena Vista Street
Burbank, CA 91521-4389
Telephone: (818) 560-6894
abc.fellowships@abc.com
Deadline: *From June*
Entry Fee: *Free*
Award: *Up to eleven fellowships in the feature film and television areas. Fellows will each be provided a salary of $50k for a one-year period. To seek out and employ culturally and ethnically diverse new writers.*

DEVELOPMENT

Dov S. S. Simens
www.hollywoodu.com

Q - What makes a successful low budget film?

Dov - The most important thing, without question, is the script. Since you don't have the ability to get any names or have enough money to do action or true adventure, it is totally story and script oriented. Every true, first timer that wants to launch a career had better read 200 scripts and understand what a story truly is. Not a one joke premise. In the no budget genre, if you want to succeed, take twelve kids to a classroom and chop them up! It's not that it has to be a slasher, but the genre that works in the low budget industry is dictated by how much money you have. So it's the dressed up stage play, the courtroom drama, the family reunion - always centered around one room or location, and then you're totally oriented towards the script. *Reservoir Dogs* did it, take twelve actors to a garage and chop them up! Spike Lee did his first film *She's Gotta Have It* where he took twelve actors to a house. Kevin Smith *Clerks* is in a video store. *Blair Witch* was three kids, one tent, and chop them up!

Q - How much can you do it for?

Dov - You can make your first feature for as little as $500. Get a digital camera, such as a Canon XL1S or a Sony PD150. To rent the camera for a weekend costs $150, and ninety minutes of Mini DV tape stock is about $10. So you've got the camera and tape stock, and now you get someone to come in with lights. You get someone to come over with a DAT for the sound, then you bring your twelve actors in and hit the record button… Tell them to talk for ninety minutes and you feed them. So let's stop talking about making films and *make one!*

Q - What common script mistakes do low budget filmmakers make?

Dov - They don't cut to the chase. For instance, men watching TV have attention spans of fifteen seconds before they hit the remote, so if one page of script is one minute running time, 15 seconds is usually line five on page one. Go out and read your script and tell me what happens on line 5 of page one. Is it something that grabs the reader and they don't want to switch? The problem with first time filmmakers is they write a novel but type it in script form, and they think it's a screenplay. It's not. It's a novel. You have things like 'fade in', 'exterior', 'park', 'day' and then you have four lines of exposition describing the park - trees, bushes, lovers holding hands and nothing has happened. In America, it goes, 'fade in', 'exterior, park, day', skip a space then there's the word, 'body', skip a space, 'penis, severed'. That's it. A lot of white space, cut to the chase and then on the bottom of page one, we have a grabber that holds you for another two minutes, and on every page we keep grabbing you and moving the story on with dialogue.

When it comes to actors, the biggest problem is new filmmakers treat the casting session as if its a fashion parade. They see the actors come in and the adrenaline goes to their head. The casting session is supposed to be five minutes with each person, and you'll go through 80 people a day. As the person walks in the door, within two minutes you have made a judgment call. But the key to casting is *can the actor act?* You spend four minutes with the actor reading their part. Let them read it their way the first time to see if they have creativity. Then tell the actor *'that was wonderful, I really liked it, now can you try it this way'*. Those are the key words to learning how to direct. If they take your direction and deliver on it, and they are creative, that's who you cast. It is not a modeling show.

Q - Is it worth going after stars?

Dov - No, let's get realistic. It's imperative to have a name in your movie, but the bottom line is you don't have enough money to get them on your first shoot. You need to stop living in fantasy land. So the answer is yes, it's important to have a name in your movie, but the reality is that you don't have the money on your first shoot to do it. First, make a low budget film that has a great script. Then if you do it with talent, you're going to find an interesting thing - the names will come to you. First you make the film, then you demonstrate your talent. You don't talk about it.

Q - How do you get your project to a name?

Dov - Get a list of the named actors that have development deals with the studios or networks. If they are a name, they are wealthy and will have their own production company. In that company there will be a development exec whose job it is to find and read scripts. Send your script to them. They throw most of it away after one page as nobody knows how to cut to the chase, and is still writing novels, but it's not a mystery how to get your script to the actor. Do your homework. Once a year in Variety, they publish a chart that lists the seven major distributors, Warner, Paramount, 20th Century Fox, MCA, Universal, Buena Vista, Sony, Disney etc. and the Mini Majors, Miramax, New Line, and under each one, it lists the thirty companies they have done development deals with. Of those companies that have development deals, half are owned by big name actors. There's the list of the companies. That's where there's $2billion of Hollywood finance.

Q - What common mistakes do filmmakers make on their first film?

Dov - They don't know what I call the 38 steps to filmmaking. When you make your feature film, you are going to write 38 bank checks from beginning to end. Buying film, renting a camera package, sound, lighting equipment, dolly, grip, insurance, ADR, foley, permits, M&E, catering. Most first time filmmakers have all this gobbledy gook about hiring talented people and let them do their job. No, you hire employees and you are the boss and you're supposed to know what everything costs. You create a budget and stick to it. The biggest problem with first time filmmakers is after falling in love with the mediocre script that they think is great, they then cannot seem to be cost effective. They don't know what anything really costs. They keep going to classes that talk about talent and they don't take any classes that talk about the business of making a film and how to buy film. If you are being cost effective, you are not going to buy the film from Kodak or Fuji at retail for instance, you are going to buy it from the White and Gray Market at discount prices.

Q - Everyone's first port of call is generally Kodak or Fuji isn't it?

Dov - It's either Kodak or Fuji, and I truly can't tell the difference between the two. So all I know is I would probably use Kodak because every kid that graduates from film school and wants to be a cinematographer, Kodak gives away some free cans. All these kids are used to Kodak and stick to it, although Fuji is 20% cheaper. So when I go in to buy Kodak, I tell them 'ooh, I can't afford that, I guess I'll have to buy Fuji'. As soon as I say that, they discount the price. But then I know how to buy factory sealed buy backs, re-cans and short ends and I can get even greater discounts.

Q - What is the minimum cost?

Dov has his own book out now, based on his two day course, called 'From Reel To Deal'. As you'd expect, it's typically no-nonsense kick ass kinda stuff that has a sense of 'can do, will do, try and stop me!' Post production is a little skipped over, as is the whole digital revolution. Still at under $20 it's a top buy.

Dov - $5k for 35mm. Film runs at the speed of 90ft per minute, so a 90 minute movie is 8,100ft. If you buy 8100ft of re-cans at 20c a foot, that's $1600. Now let's go get a 35mm film camera such as an Arri BL4, with a 10-100 zoom lens. You'll pick it up Friday, return it on Monday. That rental is $1k. You've paid $2k for film and $1k for the camera. Get your story that takes place in one room. Get your actors, rehearse for three days, go to the location on Saturday and rehearse there. Have the actors come in costume and make up on Sunday, give them each $100 that day and then Sunday afternoon, bring a light man over with four lights to do key, back and fill lighting, that'll be $200 for the afternoon. Bring a sound man that has a DAT, that's another $200 and shoot the movie in real time that afternoon. Load a 1000ft magazine and that's 11 minutes of running time, and then another 1000ft mag for the fluid master shot. Do it eight times and in 2 hours you've shot a 90 minute movie. Hitchcock's, *Rope* was done like that.

Q - Where do people get the money from?

Dov - There are people that put money into the ballet and opera and get nothing back from it, so why not movies? To get a group of dentists to finance your film for instance, get your cinematographers demo reel and your script and present it to them. Rent the local theater at 11:30 in the morning, give the projectionist $100 to come in early, then have the dentist meet you and your cinematographer in this exotic theater. Screen the reel and sell the sizzle. Turn to the investor and say '*how much money can I put you down for?*' And then shut up. You aren't going to get money unless you ask for it, so ask and then create silence, and you'll be amazed. Only talk to an investor in a movie theater.

Q - What do you do after making your film?

Dov - Get the word out there. Three weeks before you start shooting, get listed in the film production charts of *Variety* and the *Hollywood Reporter.* Who reads these charts? Acquisition executives. Every distributor in North America is looking for independent filmmakers. It has nothing to do with the love of filmmaking. It's because when you are an independent filmmaker, you are free to them. You spend your own money. They know you can make a film for 1/10th of the cost they can make films for. You have no overheads or development costs or union affiliations. When *they* make a film, *they* get the script and gamble money on not screwing it up, but *they* often do. With us, they don't gamble on a script, they see the final product! The next thing they love about us is that they know we're broke. Every independent filmmaker had better get ready for this. When you finish your first film, you are broke and it's not art. Now the distributors come out of the woodwork. They are not artists, they are vultures.

During the shoot, make sure you get photos for your press kit later on down the road. During post production, you make your press kit and send it to the acquisition executives. Then they will call you and ask 'when can I see your film?' You don't set up a private screening for any of them. You tell them you will set up a screening and sell tickets and they can come along to that. The acquisition execs come, and they rarely look at the film. They want to see the theater sold out, and if the audience loves the film when the credits roll, you will sell your film in the lobby 15 mins later. Hopefully you'll have 6-8 acquisition executives wanting to negotiate with you, and now you have entertainment attorneys that want to represent you, and you set up 8 lunches and negotiate a deal. If you fold, give up.

Q - If you can't get a theatrical deal, is it worth trying to make a TV sale?

Dov - If it doesn't get into movie theaters, it has little value to the video industry. So move on and go to dental school.

Q - Is there a key to survival?

Dov - Talent. I don't know how to teach talent though. Any teacher who says they can teach talent is lying. I can teach the mechanics of making a film and the business of showing the film, but not talent.

Q - Are there any common delusional concepts that new filmmakers have?

Top 10 Reasons script readers reject submissions

1. Unsolicited material hardly ever gets read. 'If the work is good, it will come through an agent...' is the thought process of most people in the business, which does not help you if you don't have an agent!

2. The story is not set in the United States or about Americans, and therefore does not directly serve the primary market.

3. The story and characters are familiar/unoriginal / unsympathetic. Or should we just cut the chase, IT'S BADLY WRITTEN AND DULL!

4. There is gratuitous sex, violence or drama.

5. The writing / dialogue does not have an original voice. Yes, you have written a clone. Get out and experience more life and stop copying your favorite movies.

6. The script does not produce an emotional response (not funny, scary, etc.). This is especially relevant to the first 30 pages of your script.

7. The story is poorly structured story. Often takes too long to get going then, er, goes nowhere!

8. The company has something similar in development.

9. The genre is not what the company currently wants to do.

10. The script is not commercial, for any combination of the above reasons.

Dov - One is that we're a filmmaking industry. We're not, we're a film marketing industry. We spend 2-3 times more on marketing than on the making of the film. That's the P&A budget. We need something to market so we're forced into making films. In Hollywood we know how to create a weekly event with our P&A money. We put the movie into theaters and place newspaper ads. We know that once we do the ads, the consumer reads them and will think it has a value. 19 out of 20 consumers won't go to the theater, but once they see the ads, 17 out of 20 will go to the video store later and rent it. Hollywood thinks about the world market. We think about revenues from Italy, England, Ecquador... each nation has revenue windows - theatrical, pay per view, video and broadcast revenues. We know how to take all those revenue streams and maximize profits. Hollywood treats filmmaking as a business.

Q - What single piece of advice would you offer?

Dov - Read 200 scripts this year. If you don't, you will fail. If you read lots, you will be in a better position to go forward to write a screenplay, or hire someone to write one for you. The best advice is career planning. The saying in Hollywood is *'first make a film, then you'll make a deal'*. What does that mean?

If you want $20m to make a film, there are only seven major companies that can finance it. They will give you $20m, but first they will ask you to go out and make a $2m film and get that film into theaters that makes money. How many of you have $2m to make a feature? Not many. How do you get it? First go out and make an excellent $200k feature, get that film into the theaters and making money. How many of you have $200k? Some do and can afford to spend that, but if you don't, you do the $20k feature...

Get the great script, but not a documentary and not a short. A short is short. You'll be amazed how many people make shorts that are 22 minutes long. That's not a short or a long. It's useless. With that same amount of money, you should have done a 90 minute feature. Make that dressed up stage play. If you think your film is low budget, and it's $2m, put it aside and make a $20k feature. If that gets out there, you make a $200k feature. And if it gets out there, now make the script. That's career planning.

John oBrien
Writer

THE SPEC SCRIPT MARKET

Q - How did you get started in the business?

John - I moved to LA as an actor, but soon realized I was never going to have a pension, so I decided to be a writer, which I'd never done before. I read everything I could on screenwriting and tried to digest the format. Then I started writing. I am blessed with a very common denominator taste in movies. I love *Indiana Jones* and *Beverly Hills Cop*. I like commercial movies, popcorn movies. So that's what I write. If you write a good script that the studio can market, you have a good chance of it being picked up.

Q - How easy was it to write and get out there?

John - I back doored into an agency through my then girlfriend, who was represented. I was encouraged to write a spec script so I wrote one that I thought had a good chance in the market. It got bought by Warner Brothers. When your agent sends out a spec script, it can go wide or narrow. As my stuff was commercial, it had wider distribution.

Q - Did Warner Brothers buy it through your agent?

John - Yes. The agent will get it together and talk to producers and tell them when the script is coming out. Some producers will send people over to pick it up. Then the lower levels of production companies will start reading the script and if they like it, they will take it to their boss. This can all happen within one working day, which is what happened with me. It went out on a Tuesday afternoon and on Wednesday afternoon, Warner Brothers called. An assistant had read it the night before and it went up to the head who said '*we need to put an offer in now so that we can avoid a bidding war*'. They called my agent to say '*this is our offer. You have an hour or we we'll take it off the table*'. Then your agent quickly calls the other studios who have not read it, and says '*we have an hour, do you want to put a bid in?*' It was my first spec script and I would have taken $1.50 and a cup of coffee, so it wasn't a difficult decision for me.

Q - Was it made?

John - No. It was a crazy experience and it got kicked back after the writers strike. Now I have to wait for the rights to come back to me, or somebody has to buy them from Warner Brothers. After five years I have the right to buy it back by paying what they paid for it. Before that, if Warner Brothers puts it into turnaround, other studios can purchase it for the same amount. It happens, but most of the studios don't like to sell scripts on because it's an opportunity for them to look stupid. So they keep their failures in a vault.

Q - How much did you get for the script?

John - $125k. $60k for the script, $40k for the first rewrite and $25k for the second.

Q - What happens if they give you a fee, agree payments for re-writes then decide to abandon the project before the rewrites are done?

John - Usually they will pay for the rewrites even if they decide not to make the movie. They will sometimes offer to 'buy you out' of the rewrites by paying you half of the rewrite fee, and then you don't have to do the rewrites as it's not going to get made.

Q - How long was the process?

John - It was very intense and I have learned that writers should bend over backwards to be accommodating. I was working directly with an experienced producer for eight months, as Warner Brothers were trying to rush it in before the writers strike. That collaboration was invaluable.

Your work doesn't count as the first draft until it goes to the studio. As I was working with a producer I would turn it into the producer, get notes, rewrite, turn it into the producer, get notes, rewrite... until everyone felt it was ready to go to the studios. So I ended up doing a lot of rewrites, mainly because I was still learning the tricks of the trade.

Q - What happened then?

John - The studio was happy with the rewrites, which to them says I can have an idea and put it on paper. I also went out of my way to be as easy going as I could, as well as being championed by my producer. They liked an idea I pitched and they signed me up to a two picture deal. I was still doing re-writes and had two pictures in front of me! It's one thing to get your first job, but having a career was a big thing for me.

Q - Do you think you were just lucky?

John - You can accidentally have a good idea, but I don't think you can accidentally write a good script.

Q - To get on in Hollywood, do you have to be flexible and be able to take criticism?

John - Yes, but there comes a time where there are compromises that you can't make and you have to protect yourself. Sometimes you get notes that you know could ruin your script, something I learned on my last script *Jack's Night*. The chairman, Alan Horn, gave me his entire notes which read *'make it PG 13'* and I was thrilled as that was easy. Then all the executives got

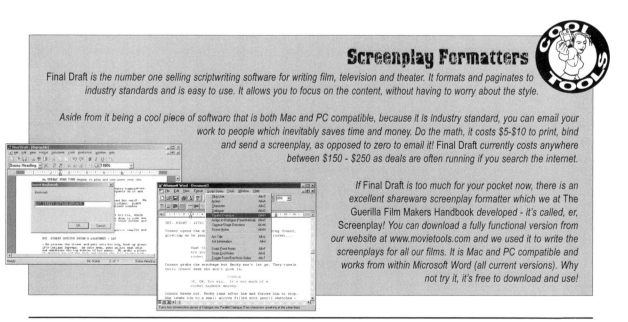

Screenplay Formatters

Final Draft is the number one selling scriptwriting software for writing film, television and theater. It formats and paginates to industry standards and is easy to use. It allows you to focus on the content, without having to worry about the style.

Aside from it being a cool piece of software that is both Mac and PC compatible, because it is industry standard, you can email your work to people which inevitably saves time and money. Do the math, it costs $5-$10 to print, bind and send a screenplay, as opposed to zero to email it! Final Draft currently costs anywhere between $150 - $250 as deals are often running if you search the internet.

If Final Draft is too much for your pocket now, there is an excellent shareware screenplay formatter which we at The Guerilla Film Makers Handbook developed - it's called, er, Screenplay! You can download a fully functional version from our website at www.movietools.com and we used it to write the screenplays for all our films. It is Mac and PC compatible and works from within Microsoft Word (all current versions). Why not try it, it's free to download and use!

together and read the script and gave me their notes, and then it came back to me for a redraft. Then you start getting way too many notes. In this case I think the problem was that they couldn't quite figure out how to market it if it was made. Now, when I'm thinking about writing, the first thing I think about are the poster and the trailer. If I can picture those two things clearly, I feel I have a good project. If the studio can't picture how they are going to sell the movies, that makes it hard to green light.

Q - Do you get pigeon holed into a genre?

John - Yes. My first movie happened to be Eddie Murphy inspired, so I started getting all of these projects that were not only that genre, but that voice. I was asked by Warner Brothers to write a script for someone like DMX. So I came in with a pitch for a movie, a simple action drama. I wrote it in 19 days, turned it in on a Friday, and on Monday morning I got a call to say that it's green lit. However, I was off the project after two quick rewrites and another writer was brought on.

Q - How much changed from your draft to what was on the screen?

John - 90%. I was amazed I actually got a credit on the movie. It was a valuable insight into the process, because those people just get things done. I pitched in December and they wanted to put the movie out in February. They really did, and it appealed to the people it was meant to appeal to.

Q - Does your agent push you to do what you want?

John - Yes. I feel completely comfortable with her speaking on my behalf, which is not true of a lot of people.

Q - Should you stay true to what you believe or give in to the studio and make their film?

John - There are always things that make you want to stay on a movie, such as an actor or director, but in general, you should consider if it is worth it. The goal for producers is getting the studio to say yes. Quality is irrelevant at this point if the studio is going to say no, so everything is geared to them. Then you can argue about the quality.

Q - Do you often pursue projects and then get told they will never get made?

John - When you come up with a take on a movie, you pretty much have to figure out the movie in your head, and that's the hardest part. Then you go in and pitch it to the producers, and if they're happy with it, you take it to the studio, who may make you jump through lots of hoops. Finally, you've done as much work as you can on the movie only to find that you don't get the job. I am working on a project now where I worked on the pitch with the producers, took it to the studio and they liked it, but then they

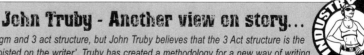

Public Domain

If the copyright on a work has expired, it falls into the public domain. You can then use that work in your film. So, what is in public domain? First, any work that was published, but never copyrighted, is in the public domain.

Any work that cannot be copyrighted, such as government publications, are in the public domain. However, government publications must have credited references to the agency that created them.

Work for which the copyright has expired is in the public domain. As a rule of thumb, any work published prior to 1923 is probably in the public domain. Check the copyright date on the work as the copyright may have been renewed and you must go by the most recent date. Always check as new laws state that a modern work does not have to be dated to still be copyrighted.

Works created outside of the USA should be checked with a copyright lawyer or the US Copyright Office for something that is public domain in the US might not be in another country.

How can you find out if a work is in the public domain? Contact the Library of Congress Copyright Office, and fill out a search form where you provide pertinent information like type of work (book, recording, etc.), title, author and your name and address. Submit the form with a search fee (around $80/hr.), and they will contact you with information on the copyright holder and whether the work is in the public domain or not.

Really old stuff, like Shakespeare or Dickens, is public domain, so there is no reason why you shouldn't contemporarize the work and remake it. As a rule, 75 years after the death of an author, their work is public domain throughout the world.

Check with the Library of Congress at www.loc.gov/copyright

hesitated. It's a high profile project and I know the reasons they are hesitating aren't the reasons they give. I'm not an 'A' list writer and the safe decision for the studio exec is to go with a proven name. If the name doesn't live up to the expectation, the studio executive will not be blamed. But if a lesser name doesn't live up to it, they will ask why they didn't hire the 'A' list person who would not have screwed it up. We pitched to the studio two weeks ago and they are still on the fence, so I said to the producers '*I don't think going back in and talking to them again is going to make any difference. Why don't I take the weekend to write act one and that way, I can put it on the page and make their decision easier.*'

Q - How important is act 1?

John - You should be able to sell any movie by page 20. If you can't, your script has something wrong with it.

Q - Do you get writers block?

John - I get stuck a lot of the time, sometimes for a day on the end of the sentence, but it's just a tough sentence. Sometimes it's the worst job in the world. Sometimes I will sit at the computer for twelve hours and not get anything down. I try to see and hear a movie in my head, so when I get stuck, I throw myself on my bed, close my eyes and picture the movie. I rewrite as I go, so if something is not right, it bothers me and I can't leave it. Other writers I know can just put stuff on the page, even if it is utter crap, and then they go back and correct it later. They are much better off as it gets done. I delay the whole process by working the way I do.

Q - Would you advise filmmakers to give their script to their friends or agent to read?

Script Tracking - The Film Executive's Info Network

What: Tracking is the process film executives use to monitor what, where and when properties (scripts, books, articles, etc.) are being placed on the market by writers' representation.

How: Through the executive's web of contacts at studios, production companies and agencies, he or she learns of what, where and when properties will be sent to market. This could be days for a script and months/years for a book. The executive calls the agent to make a plea to be allowed to read the material. If the agent thinks the company is a good fit for the material, or wants to service a relationship with the executive, he will send the property to the company for review.

Why Good: Tracking is good for the filmmaker because most of the executives in the Hollywood community will know your script exists and will try to get a look at it. If the script is good, it will create a buzz and a bidding war could start to purchase your work.

Why Bad: Tracking is bad for the filmmaker because if your script is perceived as not good, then word will get out and executives will pass the duty of reading the script to their underlings who will only read 30 pages or so to make sure the buzz is correct. Worse, a producer who might want your material if he actually read it, would hear the bad reviews and not bother to give it a read.

POTENTIAL TRACKERS: If you want to work as an executive and not as a filmmaker, here are some do's and dont's for script tracking to help you out.

DO create a network of friends (called a tracking group or circle) with one person who is affiliated with each of the main studios (Disney, MGM, Miramax, etc) and call or e-mail them all everyday to find out what material they are receiving.

DO go out to lunch, drinks, or dinner with these people either individually or in a group to keep the communication lines open. People do favors and share with those that they know.

DO read as many samples and submissions as possible so that you know which writers are good and which agencies tend to send out the higher quality material. This way when you hear one of these entities is releasing product, you can put your company on high alert.

DO call agents immediately upon hearing about a property that you are interested in. You are competing against all the other production companies in town, especially the ones based at your home studio. You want to be in the "first position" to get it.

DON'T share confidential information with anyone because everyone talks to cover their butt, and if you let out a secret about what your company does, it WILL come back to you. Ask your superiors if you can share it.

DON'T be afraid to call agents who might be out of your league in seniority. If you feel strange, get your superior to call with you and make an introduction.

John - It depends on your relationship with your agent. I give my work to my agent first, because I know she's not going to judge me if I was out of my mind when I wrote it. She's a good friend of mine, so I know I'll get good feedback. Give it to as many people as you want, and take the feedback you agree with. Unless everyone gives you the same feedback and you still don't believe it, then they're probably right. Be good at taking notes. Don't invest too much personally in people's response. If somebody says 'this scene sucks', then take a look at it, maybe it sucks. It doesn't mean you are a bad person. Don't get all touchy and upset.

Q - What precautions would you take when pitching ideas when nothing is contractual?

John - Register everything and don't assume people are stealing stuff from you. When you go to any meeting, people want you to excite them. They want it to be good. They just want to get through their day. However, I've been in meetings where I've thought the studio would steal my ideas. I've been in a couple of situations where I went in and said *'you stole my movie and made it and it's not cool'*. But you can't protect yourself from that. If you get that vibe from people, don't go back. A lot of people think they are getting ripped off when they're not.

Q - How did Starsky and Hutch come about?

John - Warner Brothers called me to tell me that I was done with *Cradle To Grave*. Almost every writer on every project is going to get fired. At that point, they had an outline, a director and Ben Stiller attached. So I went in and read this outline, and it was very different from the show I remembered as a kid. I met the director and said '*this is what I would do with this movie*' and he said 'great', and I had the job. It's helpful to have the studio be the people that want you involved! What I didn't understand at the time was there was a draft of it from years earlier that I never knew about. I thought I was writing an original script. After I wrote two drafts, the director and his writing partner wrote on it. They brought in people to polish as well. My point was I wanted to set it in the 70's, but when I started that was non-negotiable. That changed later, apparently, after I was done.

Q - When the film is in production, do they call you in?

John - If you are the writer, yes, but if the project has been moved onto other writers, usually you don't get called in. Nobody assumes when they hire you that you will be doing rewrites on set unless you're a big name. Your contract covers so many things, but you don't have any rights as a writer. Once you sell something, it's theirs and you just do the best job you can and don't get too attached.

Q - Is a spec script any different from a shooting script in terms of content?

John - If you're trying to sell a spec script, you have to realize that you're writing a script to be read, not a movie to be made. You're rewriting a reading experience they will buy based on a reading experience. The little tricks are true, such as... don't direct, but control the reader. If you have a whole page of action then break it up with dialogue. Keep your scripts to 113 pages, make it exciting to read. A lot of people are going to skim the action and just read the dialogue so it's a real bonus if your action writing is really good. There's a website (www.wordplayer.com) that's been helpful to me, and it's written by Terry Rossier and Ted Elliot who are a very successful writing team.

Q - Do you use script software?

John - I use Final Draft. However much time you would spend writing a script without a writing program is time better spent working somewhere to make the money to buy a script writing program. Find the $250 to buy Final Draft. Then you can also email scripts to people without worrying about messengers dropping them off.

Q - Should you be in LA if you want to write a Hollywood movie?

John - I plan to be in LA as long as it takes me to be able to sustain a career outside of LA, but I go to meetings at a moments notice. People like to know you're available. There's an energy in LA about movies that motivates you too.

Q - What advice would give new filmmakers?

John - Spend a lot of attention on your first twenty pages. It has all been seen before, so the secret is saying it in a different way. I read so many scripts that have the most predictable dialogue or situations, so you have to do the same situations but make it new. Don't be ashamed to try to think like the Hollywood executives. It doesn't make you any less to come up with a movie that Iowa wants to see. If you want to work in the studios, they've got to make movies they think people will want to see. I see way too many people that shun that. That's cool, but then you're not looking to work with the studios. Write a marketable script. To me, even if you feel it's hard to approach as a craft, write something that people are going to pay to see. Do that for a few years and then you can afford the luxury of writing what's meaningful to you, or what's going to be a harder sell.

Robin Schiff
Writer

Q - How did you get started in the film business?

Robin - I always wanted to be a writer and as a child I used imagination as a way of coping with life. My first job in the business was as a reader for a producer and soon realized that most screenplays were very bad, and I thought, '*I could do this better!*' At the same time, I wrote a couple of novels that were never published, but I felt that the best thing in the novels was the dialogue. I switched to screenplays and then my very first screenplay which I wrote on spec in 1979 was optioned for $2.5k! CAA, then a new agency, ended up signing me but the project never got made. I wrote a second screenplay that was also optioned for very little, but back then, I didn't need much to live and I could survive on the money. To make ends meet I used to go on gameshows and ended up winning several times. And not only money, I won a Chevy and a lifetime supply of drain cleaner! All the time I was getting encouragement from people who read my stuff, and I also did writing work on other stuff, but it was eight years before any of my work was produced.

Q - How long did it take you to write your first screenplay?

Robin - I wrote my first one in two weeks. I had raw talent but it wasn't until I did a series called *Almost Perfect* that I really learned how to tell stories. No matter how talented you are, there is a skill and a craft to it, and it took a really long time to get good at that part of it. I was always terrified because I didn't know how I did what I did. When you are trying to do something that isn't derivative or like anything else, but you still have to conform to certain demands of storytelling, it's really hard. I was working continuously during that time and getting better at it.

Q - How did you get that first screenplay optioned?

Robin - Someone I went to high school with tried to write a script with me. I didn't really want to do it, but she said she would do all the work and all I had to do is talk and she would write. I said 'ok', so we wrote this script. It was not good. She had friends all over the city, like secretaries and entry level people, so she would submit the script to all these people, but she didn't want to get rejected, so she used to put my return address on the envelopes. So I would get these manila envelopes in the post with the script and rejections from places I had never even heard of. I got a rejection letter from CAA and the letter said, '*are you the Robin Schiff from Palisades High School? This is Cheryl Peterson and we're not interested in this script, but give me a call, be great to meet.*' We met for drinks and it ended up with her taking my new screenplay. If that hadn't happened I'm sure I would have found another way to get an agent. The people who get agents have one thing in common and that is they figure it out.

Q - Did you look at screenwriting books?

Robin - Yeah. I took McKee's course. I have John Truby's books on tape. I read Syd Field's book when I started. And now I teach classes. I still take classes too, as there's nothing better if you're feeling stuck and it can often trigger stuff. Although I don't think you should adhere to the formula 'on page 27, there's a plot point etc. If you know how to tell a story, you can feel when something needs to happen. I also read the *Art of Dramatic Writing,* and *Writing From The Inside Out,* because I'm interested in the

DEVELOPMENT

psychology of being a writer. I'm obsessed with it and being a good writer. I always want to know if I can get better. There are a lot of writers who see all the money that's made on TV and most of them suck. I'm not interested in them. I'm only interested in the ones that have a real passion for it.

Q - What do you think about the three act structure?

Robin - It seems obvious that about twenty minutes into your movie you should know what the setup is and what should happen. That feels inevitable because what you set up is still a surprise. You don't tell a story that goes, '*I went to college, I did pretty well then I went back to college and I made the dean's list.*' But if you say, '*and then I got back to my apartment and the lock had been broken and I went in*', then you are interested in what is going to happen. You have to know it, then forget it. One of the worst structured movies of the last ten years is *Romey and Michele's High School Reunion* which I wrote. It has a twenty minute dream sequence that doesn't advance the plot. That is terrible story telling, but I had this idea in my mind that I wanted to have the same actors play the characters three different ways. High school, in the real, present day world, and imagined. And even though the structure isn't great, the movie still works!

Q - How would you advise a new writer to get started?

Robin - Write and write and write some more. There's a producer / director named Tony Bill and he used to say, '*if you've written a good screenplay, you could throw it out the window of your car and somebody would find it and make it*'. Don't worry about how you're going to get out, worry about finding your voice and that the material is good. Give the actors something good to play and learn what to leave out of your script. Find other people that are kindred spirits to start swapping your material with.

Q - Is it easy to get to respected writers for advice or mentoring?

Robin - I like the approach of '*how can I serve this person and get them to like me?*' I can't help but be drawn to people if they can worm their way in. If I'm going to hire a new writer, I want someone who has worked their ass off, even if it's in their own home. I'm not interested in someone who writes one spec script and then sits around and doesn't rewrite it.

Script Tips for a low budget movie

1. Characters should be kept to a minimum, and made quirky and unique. Look at your screenplay and start cutting or merging characters.

2. Design a story that can be told in a few contained, but not too claustrophobic, locations.

3. Design a story that can be told during the day rather than night as night = lights = time and money.

4. Set the story in the present. No fancy period costumes or futuristic settings. You will spend all your resources simply trying (and probably failing) to create a believable reality.

5. Keep your script length to under 100 pages. Aim for a 90 minute movie.

6. Set the story in a place that you can get free access to. For instance, if your uncle is the school janitor and you can get in on weekends, set your story in that environment.

7. Avoid visual effects unless you or your brother run your own VFX company!

8. Avoid explosions and car crashes etc., unless you are prepared to cut away instead of showing the action.

9. Production Value: Put the little money you have up on the screen.

10. Hook your audience with a great beginning and leave them with a great ending! Don't bore. Cut it out if any doubts.

11. And finally... Rewrite! Rewrite! Rewrite!

Q - What's the difference between writing for movies and TV?

Robin - In movies the writers are not treated very well. They want to pretend that you have died as soon as the script is done and then the director is king. In series television, the writer has more power. You are almost the director of the series! You go to a run through and if you don't like what they have done, you can talk directly to the actors. We also have the final cut. We do all the casting and the hiring and firing of the directors. It's one of the reasons why in sitcoms you don't necessarily get the top people, because they don't want to be in a world where they don't have the final say. In TV, writers are treated with more respect, you have more power because of the volume of material you have to generate.

Q - What's single camera, half hour?

Robin - Sex And The City is a single camera half hour, verses *Friends*, which is a four camera setup. Four camera is a more presentational style, partly because when you've got four cameras, you've also got to shoot so you don't see any of the other cameras. So what you're doing is getting a lot of coverage all at once and it feels different from a single camera show. As a rule, the dramas are single camera and most sitcoms are four camera.

Q - What are the creative benefits of writing for TV?

Robin - Every time you tell a movie story, you have to set up the world and conclude it at the end. With TV you can get into gray areas without ever wrapping it up. You can learn more about people and it often stirs up a lot of feelings. The best movies can involve you in that amount of time, but when they are not done in a skillful way, they're worse than the best of TV. I feel that the more a movie costs, the more idea driven it can become, and so characters can take a back seat. I like character driven work and there's more opportunity to do that in TV, especially in comedy.

Q - Is comedy one of the hardest things to write?

Robin - Only if it is for you! If you have the kind of brain where everything is refracted in some way then it's natural to write comedy. Gravitate towards what is most natural to you. It's hard enough to do anything well without setting some insane goal for yourself. It took me a really long time to figure out that I was a comedy writer.

Q - How long does it take to write an episode for TV?

Robin - The hardest part of it is breaking the story. You sit in a room with a bunch of people and you say 'I think a good episode would be such and such'. Then you just see if you can flesh it out into a story, and then a script. From start to finish it would be about a month. When you run out of time, you write in a week.

The great thing about television is that you learn to be a problem solver and roll with it. I've had a lot of problems with perfectionism and you just have to let that go. It's not that you don't try your hardest, but you recognize limits. The other thing that happens in production is that you start operating on a much higher level than you can in your regular life. Something kicks in and ideas beget ideas. You're having to solve problems. You get in this rhythm. I realized when I directed my first movie that I was calm because I had already written the script. I didn't have to worry about next week's script. My whole job was to film three pages today. Compared to running a show, it seemed like a vacation. Sure, I was exhausted at the end of the day, but it was more simple to wrap my mind around. One of things you can see by looking at Hollywood movies is that if the chosen solution is to throw money at it and not to

find a creative one, it's not necessarily going to get any better. When you problem solve, boundaries are good sometimes.

Q - Is it a different structure writing for TV than features?

Robin - With television, you're telling stories with dialogue and behavior, and not with pictures. In movies you want to tell the story visually. In TV comedy, the set up scene is usually the first scene, then there's an advance in the set up scene and a twist at the act break that is supposed to get you to come back. The first scene after the act break is the 'what to do' scene where they talk about what happened at the act break. Then there's a big comedy set piece and then there's the denouement. This is for a twenty-two minute show for instance.

Q - How should a new writer present a spec sit-com script?

Robin - Pick a show you love and study it. As an executive producer I hire writers and I look for a number of things - do they understand the conventions of the show? If a show starts with a cold open, have a cold open. If there's voice over in the show, have voice over. Is it a good story well told and does it make me laugh out loud? I'm looking for the thing that's going to wake me up. That's something you can't teach.

Q - How many writers are there generally on a sit-com?

Robin - I have worked with eight, but some shows have as many as sixteen, and they have three different rooms going at the same time. One room may be rewriting a script, while one is breaking stories, and the other is working on that week's episode. That's for a show that is up and running. The first year of a show, you usually work really long hours because no matter how well thought out the pilot is, you're still figuring out what the series is really about.

Q - How did 'Romy and Michele' come about?

Robin - *Romy and Michele* was in development for five years and when we first went into development, the teenage girl audience was viewed as pointless. Then *Clueless* and *Titanic* came out, and *Friends* got on air. I had written a play that was running and two female executives at TouchStone called me in and said, '*we think these minor characters in your play could be a female Wayne's World. Would you develop it?*' My answer was, '*I don't know if they're the center of a movie, let me think about it*'.

Then I came up with the idea of two girls who were perfectly happy until they fill out the questionnaire for the reunion and realize they've done nothing with the last ten years of their lives. I pitched it and the studio put it into development. They loved the first draft and then I spent the next five years, on and off, rewriting it. The typical development process.

In that time a new president of the studio was appointed and we ended up making the picture. We got along well, but I don't think he really understood the script. He kept giving me notes that I either didn't understand or just weren't right for what I was trying to do. So although I was an executive producer on the movie, at one point I did get fired. At that point I had Lisa Kudrow interested in a draft that was then rewritten by another writer and I thought it was awful. After a year of rewrites, they decided to come back to me. And because of the strong relationship with Lisa Kudrow, the script ended up being what I wanted to shoot, and it was amazing.

Q - Did you have control over the cast?

Robin - Not really. I had input but ultimately it was the studios call.

Q - Were those five intervening years frustrating?

Script Reader
Anonymous

SCRIPT READER

Q - How many scripts do you read and do the good ones really stick out?

Anon - I read ten scripts a week, and yes, the good ones always stick out. Of course, personal taste is a large part of it as it's an art form and subjective. But there are many universal factors that makes a screenplay good, such as is it easy to read, intriguing characters, great action, well thought out prose and sharp comedy and originality. One time at Thanksgiving I brought home two screenplays. I gave them both to my sister as an example af what I was reading. The first was a random submission that was poorly constructed, didn't flow well and was uninteresting. My sister, who was a novice, saw that right away. Then I gave her the second script and she was laughing in the first few pages, and had read the first 30 pages within 15 minutes. That turned out to be *American Pie.*

Q - How much do you charge and what do you get for the fee?

Anon - The basic rate varies, but it's usually $50 for a screenplay, with a turnaround of three days or so. If it's an overnight rush job, a company will tack on an extra $10. If we do a book, that usually can range between $75-$100 for 300 page book with extra money for every 50 pages after that. What you get for that is a cover sheet, which breaks down the basic detail of the script such as title, author, locale, genre, stuff like that. A log line which is basically a TV guide version of the work, a two or three sentence description of the whole story, a brief comment section, which is an overall view without going into detail about what you think of the script. Then the second section will be a synopsis of the script which is more or less a beat by beat description of the action of the script. What happens. Last is the comments section where you detail what works, what doesn't work, and do you think it should consider it for production - we could give it a *Pass*, which means it's not worth it. Then there is *Consider* which means the script is pretty good, strong in some areas and should be discussed. Then there is *Consider with Reservations,* which is the script has some good points but needs a fair amount of work to get it to a final form. And finally there is *Recommend*, which is the most rare of the lot. This entire document is referred to as *'coverage'.*

Q - What makes a script stand out as NOT professional?

Anon - First and foremost would be poor formatting, which is inexcusable. Typos and spellings, over describing action, not being economical with words.

Q - What makes a script stand out as being hot?

Anon - The most important thing is a fresh original voice. Characters that pop off the page with dialogue that crackles. Also the script needs to grab your attention almost immediately. Remember, this is something that should enthrall the audience right from the get go. So having a great action sequence, or a mysterious character doing something that you're not quite sure what he's doing or why, but it intrigues you, or it's in a beautiful locale, or it's a very funny humorous moment – all of these things will suck you into the screenplay and make you want to flick pages. Also important is that the screenplay appeals to people on a universal level, such as a universal theme as you can't go home again, is the good of one person worth the good of many etc. If a screenwriter can convey these themes through a personal story, it goes a long way to elevating that screenplay from the masses.

Q - What are the common mistakes that you encounter?

Anon - One mistake is writing a screenplay with a story that only happened to you, and is consequently only interesting to you and the people that it happened to. This is of course subjective, but for stories like that, stories of a personal nature, you have to use them as a kernel for a larger theme. Another trap that screenwriters fall into is writing scripts that are more suitable for television than film. These generally tend to be bio pics, women in peril, disease of the week type stories, which may be gripping and good stories, but are too small or narrow in focus to be considered a feature film. I should say that there is one way of getting around this and that is to get a major star interested in a role in your screenplay of this type. Then it'll elevate it out of movie of the week status to feature film. For example, *Erin Brokovich* is essentially a woman in peril bio pic movie of the week, but you add Julia Roberts and Steven Soderbergh and you have a feature film. Another major problem is over written dialogue and action. Screenwriters really need to learn the economy of words. If they can say a ten word sentence in three words, they should. Gratuitous sex and violence is a big problem too. Every scene in a screenplay should have something to do with the plot and the characters, anything that's thrown in that doesn't promote the story in any way and is just there for titillation needs to be cut. The only exception to this might be in broad comedies such as Austin Powers where the reality of the script is so bizarre it doesn't matter. You can do crazy things like taking Dr. Evil to psychotherapy with his son, and you go along with it just for the goofiness of it, even though it has nothing to do with the plot of the story.

Q - What advice would you give a new screenwriter wanting to break in?

Anon - Listen to how people talk. Notice how we tend to speak in short sentences and with simple words. This is how the bulk of your script's dialogue should read. As far as breaking in, once you've written your screenplay, it's gonna be difficult for you to get an agent, it always is and has been. Use any connection you have to get it to an agent or manager. It doesn't matter if it's a guy at the gym, your hairdresser – if you have an in, use it. I would also suggest that you enter your screenplay in as many screenwriting contests as you can, especially the larger ones such as the Nichol fellowship and the Fade In screenwriting competition. Agents and managers sometimes judge those competitions, but more importantly, everyone in Hollywood contacts the winners and runner ups. Frequently there are pitch sessions sponsored by writing magazines, and entertainment workshop groups where you pay a few hundred dollars and you can go to a hotel banquet room and pitch your story ideas to executives. If you have an idea that they like, they'll solicit a screenplay from you on the spot. However most ideas are poor, so make sure your ideas are clear, concise and will appeal to the general public, as that's what they're looking for.

STORY COVERAGE

TITLE: URBAN GHOST STORY

AUTHOR: Genevieve Jolliffe & Chris Jones
TIME: Present
LOCATION: Glasgow, Scotland
GENRE: Supernatural Thriller
ELEMENTS:

FORM: SP
PAGES: 95
PUBLISHER/DATE: N/A
SUBMITTED BY: Internal
SUBMITTED TO: S. Smith
RECIEVED:
ANALYST:
DATE:

Log Line: A young, teenage girl and her family are haunted by the spirit of her best friend who died in a car crash that she survived. Her mother seeks the help of a tabloid journalist to find out the truth, but his desire for a good story only makes matters worse.

Comments: Dark in tone and spare in dialogue, this chilling ghost tale brings with it a social angle that elevates it above the rest of the genre.

SCRIPT: CONSIDER
WRITER: CONSIDER

	Excellent	Good	Fair	Poor
Premise		X		
Story Line		X		
Structure		X		
Characterization	X			
Dialogue		X		

The coverage that we received for our third feature film, Urban Ghost Story… If you want to see what you think, you can download the full screenplay from our website at www.livingspirit.com. Hopefully by the time this book hits the streets, you will be also able to buy the DVD for further comparisons!

WGA

Margaret Grohne and Kay Schaber

WGA
Writers Guild of America

Q - What is the WGAw? How does it benefit new filmmakers?

Kay - The Writers Guild of America west, is a union, as well as a community of professional writers, founded to protect its members' interests, both financial and creative. As with other creative professional groups, writers often are not regularly employed. The Guild offers writers the security of knowing they will be paid if they work under a Guild contract, and you will enjoy other benefits - including credit protection, pension and health, and residuals. For instance, it's important to have a portable health plan so you don't have to worry about going to the doctor. We also offer a sense of community, that there are other people out there who share your concerns.

Q - What are the regular WGA Theatrical Basic Agreements?

Kay - The Minimum Basic Agreement (MBA) encompasses two budget levels - low, for films budgeted below $5m, and high, for those costing $5m and above. For low budgets, the purchase price for a screenplay is $34,740 (1.4 percent of a $2.5m budget) and for high budgets, $71,112 (1.4 percent of a $5m budget). There is a special Low Budget Agreement offering a partial or complete deferment of the $34,740 and the first rewrite for films budgeted at $1.2m and below.

Q - How does the Guild work with low budget films?

Margaret - The writers of low budget films need the Guild just as much as the writers of the big budget films. The Low Budget Agreement covers the purchase of an existing screenplay and the first rewrite, but it doesn't cover employment - you may not hire a writer to write original or adapted material without the payment of the applicable MBA minimums. In the Low Budget Agreement, the same MBA minimums are covered (i.e., the screenplay purchase minimum is $34,740), but the agreement has a different payment structure. With a budget between $0.5m and $1.2m, the minimum amount due the writer is $15,000 (1.25 percent of a $1.2m budget), $10,000 of the screenplay purchase is payable upon commencement of principal photography, and a $5,000 script publication fee is payable after the writing credit is determined. The remaining $19,740 ($34,740 minus $15,000) is deferred until the film realizes first revenues received after either the recoupment of production costs or commencement of commercial distribution, whichever occurs earlier. Then there's our ultra Low Budget Agreement level that covers budgets of $0.5m and below, where the minimums may be entirely deferred using the same backend terms.

In brief, for a film budgeted at $0.5m and below, one may defer all of the compensation; $1.2m and below, $10,000 of the screenplay purchase and the $5,000 publication fee is paid upfront, and the rest may be deferred. For $5m and below, standard minimums apply and are paid upfront, which is $34,740 for a screenplay purchase plus the $5,000 fee (again, the latter upon credit determination). Then for above $5m, you get into bigger money.

Kay - Writers may also negotiate for additional monies that are above our minimum payments, gross profits percentages, and enhanced creative rights. If a project is successful and it was written under a Guild agreement, there is a potential for residuals if the film or program is released in other media. Many writers new to the business are faced with the pressure to take whatever amount a company might offer, no matter how low, because they want to get the project produced. If writers don't have their work covered under a Guild agreement, they might see their hard work, sometimes taking years of effort, slipping through their hands with no recourse. Then if the projects are successful, everyone makes money but them! For screenplays covered under our Low Budget Agreement, the writer may take less upfront, but the deferred remainder is still owed to him or her, and, of course, residuals also ensure the writer receives money down the line should it have a life after theatrical distribution.

Margaret - Producers should bear in mind that if the film is not made within 18 months of signing the Low Budget Agreement, the writer is entitled to reacquire the literary material.

Q - Must the production company be a signatory of the Guild if they are to use these agreements?

Margaret - Yes. The production company would sign certain forms that basically say they're willing to follow all the requirements set out by the Guild, which enables the Guild to enforce contracts. There is no fee to the production company to become signatory, however, the writer must request the use of the Low Budget Agreement. A writer's application form can be found online on our website at www.wga.org.

Q - How much is it to join the Guild?

Margaret - If you meet the criteria for membership, it's a one-time fee of $2,500 and the dues are $25 per quarter plus 1.5 percent of your gross earnings for writing services. In some cases, arrangements can be made for paying in installments. It's $75 for the Associate membership, which is for writers who haven't reached the required number of 'writing units' to become a 'Current-Active' member.

Q - How many units of credit must you have to be a member?

Development Hell

Once you sell your screenplay, you now enter the development phase where the work is tailored to the studio's liking. Here is where many good projects get stuck for long periods of time, and here is why.

1. Sometimes the people who bought your script get fired or move on to other jobs while you are in the development phase. The new executives who come in may decide to shelve your project because it does not interest them or they wish to distance themselves from their predecessor.

2. Projects are frequently bought as favors to producers to give them something of their own to work on while they work on other things for the studio. This pacification can mean some projects were never intended to see the light of day.

3. Sometimes the subject matter of your script is at the mercy of current trends. A story about terrorist bombings immediately after an event like 9/11 will never get made.

4. You may have gotten your script to the point where everyone is happy. Now you just need a star or big time director to come on board. Their schedules are hectic and their personalities are fickle - waiting for them to make up their minds can take time.

5. If Tom Cruise, Mel Gibson, Julia Roberts, Steven Spielberg or some other major star(s) are attached to a script, it will take precedence over your low project without attachments.

6. The communication between filmmaker and executive is extremely important and frequently difficult. Many times, the notes of executives are vague and the filmmaker does not understand them, or the executive wants something done and the filmmaker cannot execute it properly. This may cause endless hiring and firing of rewriters.

7. Studios are businesses that are taxed. In order to offset those taxes, they will purposely leave projects in development in order to take business losses and expenses against them.

Margaret - You must earn 24 writing units within a three-year period to be eligible to join as a Current-Active member. Units are earned in different ways. A writer receives eight units when the Low Budget Agreement is signed, and if you're employed to do the first rewrite, you'll receive an additional 12 units. If you're employed to do a polish (here you must be paid Guild minimums because the Low Budget Agreement only allows deferral of the screenplay purchase and first rewrite compensation), you'll receive an additional six units - which makes it enough for you to join the Guild. If your screenplay is produced under the Low Budget Agreement, you will receive 24 units.

Q - What if the writer hasn't written before? Does the writer have to be a member of the Guild to receive benefits connected with the Low Budget Agreement?

Kay - No, not under the Low Budget Agreement. If the company is willing to sign this agreement and become signatory, the writer gets the protections of the agreement and earns writing units toward membership. Normally, using our other agreements, you would be covered only if you are deemed a 'professional writer' under the Guild's definition. Keep in mind that if you're not a Guild member, you can still include that you are to be considered a 'professional writer as defined by the WGA's MBA in your personal contract with a signatory company. By doing so, you will be allowed to earn writing units to join the Guild.

Q - Can you just write a script and become a member?

Margaret - No. But if your screenplay is to be produced through the Guild's Low Budget Agreement, you can begin that way, by earning units required to become a full member. However, if you've written a screenplay that's received recognition, such as at film festivals, you can apply to be a member of the Independent Writers Caucus.

Q - What is the Independent Writers Caucus?

Margaret - The Caucus was created as part of the Guild's outreach program for emerging and independent writers / filmmakers to address their needs and to advance their interests and careers. Becoming a member of the Caucus is a way to take advantage of being part of this community. It's a good first step and a great way to network.

Kay - Eligible non-members pay a $75 annual fee and get the equivalent of Associate membership benefits, including receiving Guild publications, being able to attend Guild and Caucus events, access to an alternate health plan, and using a reduced intellectual property registry fee, among others. The eligibility criteria vary - for instance, you may be eligible if the film you wrote screened at an industry-recognized film festival, if you are a recent graduate from an intensive screenwriting program connected with certain educational institutions, if you won or were nominated for a screenwriting award, or if you placed highly in certain screenplay competitions. Also, writers whose films are produced under the Low Budget Agreement qualify. The criteria must be fulfilled within a five-year period from the date the application is received and are subject to our Independent Film Writers Steering Committee review. You can also be a member of the Caucus for free if you are already a Guild member and meet the eligibility criteria. The application form is available at www.wga.org.

Top 10 screenwriting websites

Free information, files, tools and other stuff. Late night browsers paradise!

1.. www.wordplayer.com

2. www.moviebytes.com

3. www.whosbuyingwhat.com

4. www.script-o-rama.com

5. www.sydfield.com

6. www.scriptsales.com

7. www.wga.com

8. www.screenwritersutopia.com

9. www.write-brain.com

10. www.screenwriter.com

Q - What is the service you offer for registering scripts?

Kay - Our intellectual property registry is accessible from anywhere in the world for members and non-members. Registration provides a dated record of the writer's claim to authorship. We take your document and store it so we can, if needed, produce the material as evidence for a legal or official proceeding. It costs $20 for non-members, $10 for members, and documents authorship for five years. It's offered for scripts, treatments, synopses, outlines, books, stage plays, poems, lyrics, commercials, drawings, etc.

Q - Will the WGA notify the creator of the work when the five years is about to expire?

Kay - No. That is the responsibility of the writer. However, writers may renew their registration for additional five-year periods upon expiration.

Q - If you've registered copyright through the Library of Congress, should you register through the WGA too?

Kay - Yes, in that registering with the Guild's intellectual property registry creates a separate legal record for your material. In addition, you may consider registering drafts of your work-in-progress with our Registry, prior to registering your final draft with the Copyright Office. There are legal differences between the two, but generally, the idea is to secure the authorship. We recommend that you do both. The Library of Congress can take several months to finalize copyright, and the Writers Guild takes less than five minutes - you can either walk your screenplay into our registry offices or log on to www.wga.org.

Margaret - As a new filmmaker, it's important to register because you don't have much power in the business yet. You don't have attorneys or managers behind you helping protect your authorship. It's just $20 for added security.

Q - If there's a dispute, who can access the writer's work?

Margaret - We have to be subpoenaed by the court or asked by the writer who registered. No one else has access.

Q - Say a writer loses all copies of the script, but the WGA has the registered copy.

Kay - The writer can make the request in writing, accompanied by a photo I.D., such as a driver's license or passport. There is a $20 fee, and it will take a week to process.

WRITERS BLOCK

Can't seem to get the creative juices flowing? Try some of these tricks, drawn from a group of writer friends, to get going again or prevent yourself from getting blocked. Not all are recommended!

· *Exercise - go to the gym, for a long walk, run, bike ride, etc.*
· *Yoga positions are good for relaxation and sometimes rushing blood to the brain.*
· *Change the location in which you write. Get a different perspective.*
· *Cook something.*
· *Clean something.*
· *Take a shower to relax yourself.*
· *Take a nap to relax yourself.*
· *Watch other movies of the same genre to get ideas.*
· *Save an idea for the next day so you know where to start.*
· *Free-think ideas with another writer.*
· *Surf the internet, read on your idea so you are prepared with lots of potential plot points and character ideas.*
· *Write something other than a screenplay so you don't become stale (letters, poems, etc.)*
· *Keep more than one project going at a time. If one is not working, another will.*
· *Read your favorite authors for inspiration.*
· *Don't write sober.*
· *Use tools like The Observation Deck, a deck of cards which tell you to do a task such as build a history of a character to get you through tough spots.*
· *Keep a notebook of crazy words, colors, places or topics. Refer back to it for ideas.*
· *Some computer screenwriting programs ask you questions about the work in order to keep you from being blocked. Some complain that this creates "cookie cutter" screenplays.*

BEST TIP - KEEP WRITING!

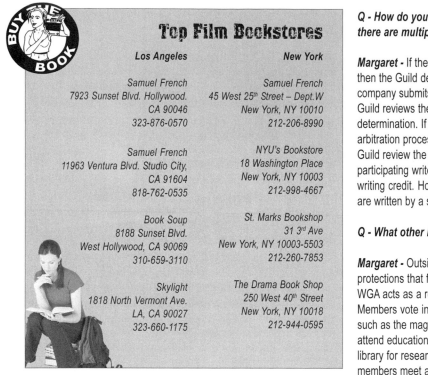

Top Film Bookstores

Los Angeles

Samuel French
7923 Sunset Blvd. Hollywood.
CA 90046
323-876-0570

Samuel French
11963 Ventura Blvd. Studio City,
CA 91604
818-762-0535

Book Soup
8188 Sunset Blvd.
West Hollywood, CA 90069
310-659-3110

Skylight
1818 North Vermont Ave.
LA, CA 90027
323-660-1175

New York

Samuel French
45 West 25th Street – Dept.W
New York, NY 10010
212-206-8990

NYU's Bookstore
18 Washington Place
New York, NY 10003
212-998-4667

St. Marks Bookshop
31 3rd Ave
New York, NY 10003-5503
212-260-7853

The Drama Book Shop
250 West 40th Street
New York, NY 10018
212-944-0595

Q - How do you determine who gets the credit if there are multiple writers?

Margaret - If the writers are under a Guild contract, then the Guild determines the credits. The production company submits tentative writing credits, and the Guild reviews the information and makes the final determination. If there's a dispute, there's an arbitration process. Under our rules, members of the Guild review the different drafts from all the participating writers and determine the appropriate writing credit. However, most produced screenplays are written by a sole writer or a writing team.

Q - What other benefits do you get?

Margaret - Outside of the creative and financial protections that form the backbone of the Guild, the WGA acts as a resource and advocate for writers. Members vote in elections, receive Guild publications such as the magazine, *Written By*; and are able to attend educational and social events. We have a library for research and archiving and a lounge where members meet and write. The Writers Guild Foundation sets up mentoring and craft programs. For instance, it sponsors a series of seminars by top writers - "Writers on Writing"- which anyone can attend.

Q - Who is eligible for the WGA awards?

Kay - Writers who have received credit for screenplays written for films that were exhibited theatrically in the Los Angeles area for at least a week and are under our contractual jurisdiction or the jurisdiction of an affiliated guild.

Q - What advice would you offer new writers?

Margaret - Protect your work, your ownership, and yourself. Do the best possible job you can on writing your screenplay, and make it as strong as possible. The most leverage you can have is by writing a good movie. Once you have finished that process, then try to get the movie made with your participation. To benefit your career, it's best to be wise about the contracts you enter into – take time to understand the Guild agreements.

Contact

Writers Guild of America, west, Inc.
7000 West Third Street, Los Angeles, CA 90048-4329
323-951-4000   www.wga.org

Writers Guild of American, East.
555 West 57th Street, New York, NY 10019
212-767-7800   www.wgaeast.org

Kay - Trying to get your film made is a balance of art and business. Make sure your voice is protected because that voice is where the film originates, and you should receive compensation and recognition for your contribution.

Literary Agents and Managers Contact Details

Literary Agents

Creative Artists Agency (CAA)
9830 Wilshire Boulevard
Beverly Hills, CA 90212
Phone: 310-288-4545
Fax: 310-288-4800
Web: www.caa.com

International Creative Management (ICM)
8942 Wilshire Boulevard
Beverly Hills, CA 90212
Phone: 310-550-4000
Fax: 310-550-4100
Web: www.icm.com

The William Morris Agency (WMA)
One William Morris Place
Beverly Hills, CA 90212
Phone: 310-859-4000
Fax: 310-959-4462
Web: www.wma.com

United Talent Agency (UTA)
9560 Wilshire Boulevard
Suite #500
Beverly Hills, CA 90212
Phone: 310-273-6700
Fax: 310-273-1111

Endeavor
9701 Wilshire Boulevard
10th Floor
Beverly Hills, CA 90212
Phone: 310-248-2000
Fax: 310-248-2020

The Gersh Agency
232 North Canon Drive
Beverly Hills, CA 90210
Phone: 310-274-6611
Fax: 310-278-6232

Paradigm
10100 Santa Monica Boulevard
25th Floor
Los Angeles, CA 90067
Phone: 310-277-4400
Fax: 310-277-7820

Writers & Artists
8383 Wilshire Boulevard
Suite #550,
Beverly Hills, CA 90211
Phone: 323-866-0900
Fax: 323-866-1899

Innovative Artists
1505 Tenth Street
Santa Monica, CA 90401
Phone: (310) 656-0400
Fax: (310) 656-0456

Broder, Webb, Chervin, Silbermann
9242 Beverly Boulevard
Suite #200
Beverly Hills, CA 90210
Phone: 310-281-3400
Fax: 310-276-3207

Original Artists
9465 Wilshire Boulevard
Beverly Hills, CA 90212
Phone: 310-275-6765
Fax: 310-275-6725

Hohman, Maybank & Lieb
9229 Sunset Boulevard
Suite #700
Los Angeles, CA 90069
Phone: 310-274-4600
Fax: 310-274-4741

Don Buchwald & Associates
6500 Wilshire Boulevard
Suite #2200, Los Angeles, CA 90048
Phone: 323-655-7400
Fax: 323-655-7470

Metropolitan
4526 Wilshire Boulevard
Los Angeles, CA 90010
Phone: 323-857-4500
Fax: 323-857-4599

Jon Klane Company
120 El Camino, Suite 112,
Beverly Hills, CA, United States, 90212
Phone: 310-278-0178
Fax: 310-278-0179

Literary Managers

BenderSpink
6735 Yucca St
Los Angeles, CA 90028
Tel: 323-856-5500

Gold-Miller
9200 Sunset Boulevard, 10th Floor
Los Angeles, CA 90069
310-786-4968

Brillstein-Grey
9150 Wilshire Blvd, Ste 350
Beverly Hills, CA 90212
310-275-6135

The Firm
9465 Wilshire Blvd., 6th Floor
Beverly Hills, CA 90212
310-860-8000

Industry Entertainment
955 S. Carrillo Dr., Ste. 300
Los Angeles, CA 90048
323-954-9000

Gail Silva
Film Arts Foundation

FILM ARTS FOUNDATION

Q - What benefits do you get as a member of the Film Arts Foundation?

Gail - We offer production and post-production equipment, film classes, and the opportunity for fiscal sponsorship. Unlike many undergraduate schools, we offer practical hands-on use of equipment - all we ask is our members take one of our orientation classes to familiarize themselves with the equipment before we sign it out to them for their own use. We still teach in Super 8 and we have equipment on Super 8, 16mm and Digital to rent. People that can afford to rent a 35mm camera should go to a commercial house! Within our education program now, we teach around 4000 individuals a year in somewhere between 250-300 classes. The classes aren't just technical, we also offer legal affairs classes, how to do your taxes, etc., and we have visiting lecturers such as theatrical distributors or presenters from PBS. We also provide a magazine, *Release Print*, where you can view all the seminars and workshops and work out what you want to do as a curriculum.

Q - With providing sponsorship, do you operate as a 501 (c)(3)?

Gail - Yes, we do. In the US, if you are trying to make an art film, experimental film, documentary or short narrative, the type of films that don't necessarily have a commercial value, we offer sponsorship through our non-profit educational institution. With this, you go out and look for money and any donors would then give money to the Film Arts Foundation, and we would then distribute the money to the individual. 501 (c) (3)'s are the way foundations in this country give money and many government agencies will only fund projects that way. The films that are funded are usually going to be social issue documentaries and short experimental works. However many of these documentaries do end up on public television or in movie theaters as well as Sundance and international festivals.

Q - Do you have to be a member to take part in your education program?

Gail - Yes. If you're not a member you can still take the classes, but you do pay more. Some classes are for members only, such as the orientations. We do this firstly because they're technical and you must know how to use the equipment, but also if we're going to let you check out a camera, we want to have all the information on you.

Q - How much is membership?

Gail - Memberships begin at $45 for a Supporter member. This is for people anywhere who love independent film. You receive ten issues a year of our *Release Print* magazine, access to our members-only web site, discounts on services and supplies, access to our videotape library and our resource library and discounts on the Film Arts Foundation screenings, which involve sneak previews and new documentaries. Then we have the Filmmaker member at $65. Most people have this. As well as the Supporter benefits, it offers discounts on over 250 of our seminars and workshops, access to our production and post-production facilities where you'll take an orientation course before you check out a camera, etc. You're also enrolled in our group legal plan and are able to apply for our fiscal sponsorship program. You have access to funding and distribution consultations with the staff. Then we have other levels, such as the Executive Producer and Alumnus memberships where a percentage of your membership dues are a tax-deductible donation and you receive some free tickets to screenings or a free t-shirt.

Q - Do you provide any film grants to filmmakers?

Gail - Yes, we do. We provide cash grants each year from $50k-$70k. We also have a lot of in-kind grants in terms of facility access. We have provided screenplay grants, and a scholarship so that the writers could take a month off to focus on perfecting their script. The grants tend to be small, and as we knew we would never be able to raise a lot of money, we tried to calculate the minimal sum that could help make a difference. We also provide development grants at around $5k. We realize that nobody wants to give you the first money, so we try and do that. Development could be research, putting your trailer together or even writing a script. We also give completion and distribution grants (usually with documentaries) which range between $7k-$10k. This could be after you've hit every resource you can, and you're just struggling to get that last bit. With The Robin Eickman Narrative Awards, we actually put in the $10k cash. Overall however, much of our grants are in kind donations, such as $50k or $60k worth of 16mm or 35mm camera rentals, location, sound, all of that kind of stuff.

Q - How much in total can you get a grant for?

Gail - Probably the largest cash grant we give to an individual is $10k. We can give out a total of $50-$70k and that could be a number of individual grants.

Q - What is the STAND program?

Gail - STAND is Support Training and Access for New Directors. It's part of the grants program for people who would like to make a short piece, but have never made anything before, yet have something they want to say which will represent their community. We select ten participants a year, and they get a working filmmaker mentor and $1,500 worth of access to the classes and all the post-production equipment to help them realize their small five to six-minute film. One STAND participant last year won an honorable mention in the Golden Gate Awards of The San Francisco International Film festival for an experimental piece. This year the oldest person in the program is a 58-year-old African / American man and the youngest is a 15 year old girl. Another recipient from '98, Veronica Majans, spent much of her life in the Mission, and after she completed the STAND program she and a friend got a little grant and went around to flea markets and bought Super 8mm cameras and taught a group of young women from the Mission how to use them. They all made films. Now, Veronica's been a mentor in our program and received a cash award aswell. So, sometimes there's a lot of nice synergy that happens.

Q - How do you choose the filmmakers who are to be paired up with mentors?

Gail - We're looking for people who essentially have been struggling financially to make a film, or who haven't had a chance.

Q - Do you offer grants for experimental works?

Gail - Yes. Not many people give awards for this type of work. We offer a grant of $5k, however, you have to do the whole thing for $5k. We don't want to give you $5k when you really have to raise $40k.

Q - Does your magazine give everyone access to different kinds of funding?

Gail - Yes, and now it's so much easier to find the information because everybody has a website. Funders may have different focuses, such as this one supports politically progressive projects and this one is sort of into film arts, or these will only fund if you film in New York and Minnesota. If you're a member, you can access our website and entire database of funding listings. You can even look up festivals and plan where you want to submit. What we're trying to do is give people the access and understanding of how to do it themselves.

Q - What kind of equipment do you have here for your members to access?

Gail - Unlike the video facilities of norm, we've never had high-end stuff here. Actually we still have flatbeds and we've had people from LA come up to use them. We also still have an optical printer for Super 8. We're the only place left in town where you can rent a Bolex. We have digital stuff up on the second floor in our six post-production rooms. We have Final Cut Pro and Pro Tools audio suites. Unlike going to a facility like a commercial company or even a non-profit organization such as The Bay Area Video Coalition (BAVC), there's very little that you can't do without an operator. Here, we show you how to do it and leave you alone. If you need an operator, we have a list of people.

Q - As any level of member, do you have access to the editing suites?

Gail - No. It has to be the $65 level to have access.

Q - I understand you also run a film festival?

Gail - Yes. Our whole point in doing a festival is not to just please filmmakers, as hopefully there are enough festivals here for their work to be shown, but to make a statement, saying that there are alternatives to mainstream film and television. The whole purpose of the festival is to make the public aware of these options. We also insist on paying the filmmakers for screening their films. Many other festivals around the country are not paying filmmakers to screen their films and we feel that that's wrong.

Q - I can imagine that political filmmaking here in San Francisco is huge considering the general area and the history?

Gail - Yes, and we've always been the maverick. It's a weird place, San Francisco. It's like we're an island because it's so not about mainstream politics or the rest of California. The rest of the state votes one way, and the Bay Area votes the opposite.

Q - How different is it for a filmmaker in the Bay Area than being in the major film hubs such as LA and New York?

Gail - It is very un-Hollywood up here. There's a certain regionalism. There is also more paying work in LA than NYC. If you had a chance to go anywhere else, I'd suggest Minneapolis and St. Paul. There is a chapter there of the IFP (Independent Featue Project) where they're more like Film Arts than anywhere else and they've been able to do incredible things, including funding films. They have a fund that they got through state legislature to fund features. There's a website called NAMAC (National Alliance of Media, Arts and Culture). It lists all the organizations like Film Arts and IFP, and you find descriptions and have contact information and descriptions of what all of us do.

Q - What are typical Bay Area filmmakers like?

Gail - In the Bay Area you have this real separation. You have the big majors. We've got Lucas, Coppola, Phil Kaufman and Saul Zaentz - a bunch of heavy hitters that live here, and then the people who are making larger documentaries. Then there are the people in the middle who aspire to something bigger, mostly in the feature realm. A lot of people write screenplays, and there are many screenwriting classes here.

Minority Filmmaking Sites

AFRICAN AMERICAN
www.uafw.org
www.dvrepublic.com
www.blackfilmmakers.net
www.blacktalentnews.com
www.blackfilm.com
www.blackflix.com

ASIAN
www.naatanet.org
www.asianamericanfilm.com
www.asianamericanfilm.com
www.theworkshop.org
www.asiancinevision,org
www.capeusa.org

LATINO
www.lasculturas.com
www.nalip.com
www.latinofilmnetwork.com
www.clnet.ucr.edu/community/nlcc
www.premiereweekend.org
www.golemi.org

NATIVE AMERICAN
www.nativenetworks.si.edu
www.nativetelecom.org
www.ableza.org
www.aifisf.com
www.piccom.org

Q - Do you have relationships with small, independent theaters in San Francisco?

Gail - We don't have a relationship per say with any specific theater but there are many alternative screening venues here. We do a lot of programming at the San Francisco Cinematech who do mostly experimental and avant-garde films. Dolby, who are out here, have a perfect sound screening room, and they will lend it to low budget filmmakers who finish their films and who want to show it to cast and crew. They don't advertise it, but we let people know that they do that.

Q - What common mistakes do you come across with new filmmakers?

Gail - People are caught off guard by the fact that it's going to be easier to raise the money than getting your movie screened. The filmmakers must consider the story and the audience. I don't care what kind of camera or editing system they use, it's still about the story and a consideration for your audience.

Top Short Film Festivals North America

Palm Springs International Short Film Festival
Ph: 760-322-2930 Toll Free: 800-898-7256
info@psfilmfest.org

Yorkton Short Film & Video Festival
Canada
Ph:306-782-7077
www.yorktonshortfilm.org

The Hollywood SHORTS Film Festival
Beverly Hills, CA
Ph: 310-288-1882
awards@hollywoodawards.com

Toronto World Short Film Festival
Canada
Ph: 416-535-8506
twsff@idirect.org

Crested Butte Reel Fest
Colorado
Ph: 970-349-2600
cbreelfest@webcom.com

One Reel Film Festival
Seattle, WA
Ph: 206 281 7788
info@onereel.org
http://onereel.org

Cinematexas International Short
Film Festival
Austin, TX
Ph: 512-471-6497
cinematexas@cinematexas.org

LA Shorts Fest
Studio City, CA
Ph: 323-851-9100
info@lashortsfest.com

Aspen Shortfest
Aspen, CO
Ph: 970-925-6882
www.aspen.org

Antimatter Festival of Underground Short
Film and Video
Victoria, BC, Canada
Ph: 250-385-3327 or 250-385-3339
info@antimatter.ws or
rogueart@islandnet.com

New York Expo
New York
Voice Mail: 212-505-7742
nyexpo@aol.com

ORGANIZATIONS

Q - What advice would you give new filmmakers?

Gail - Go for it. Use caution, but you don't know until you try. I've seen people come in here with no experience and have come out with incredible stuff that blew me away.

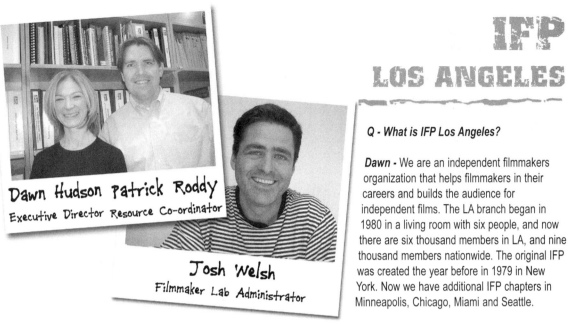

Dawn Hudson Patrick Roddy
Executive Director Resource Co-ordinator

Josh Welsh
Filmmaker Lab Administrator

IFP
LOS ANGELES

Q - What is IFP Los Angeles?

Dawn - We are an independent filmmakers organization that helps filmmakers in their careers and builds the audience for independent films. The LA branch began in 1980 in a living room with six people, and now there are six thousand members in LA, and nine thousand members nationwide. The original IFP was created the year before in 1979 in New York. Now we have additional IFP chapters in Minneapolis, Chicago, Miami and Seattle.

Q - What kind of services do you offer?

Dawn - Our services are varied and members receive a lot for their $85 a year dues. We have seminars, a screening series, camera rentals, lighting packages, casting rooms, Final Cut Pro editing, production offices and viewing rooms. We have a resource library that has sample business plans, box office reports, including ancillary, foreign and domestic sales. There are also books on filmmaking, art books, tons of scripts, tons of reels for cinematographers and directors. We have a resume bank, both in our library and online if you want to crew up or cast your film. Most of our programs are accessible to all our members. It works on a first come first served basis. There are a few mentorship programs for which we select talented filmmakers and try to help them one on one. *Project Involve* for example, is a mentorship program for young men and women of color. We train forty young people a year and about half of them have gone on to get paying jobs in the industry. We do a screenwriting lab, a directors lab, a producers lab for which we select ten applicants to participate. We also have consultation services which are available to all members. They sign up and can get advice from a line producer, an attorney, a foreign sales agent, a festival expert or post-production supervisor.

Q - Do you give grants?

Dawn - Yes. At the Spirit Awards, we give away $60k in three $20k grants. One for producers, one for documentary filmmakers and one for narrative filmmakers. At the LA Film Festival, we give away a $50k grant with the Filmmaker Award for the winning film and a $25k documentary award for the winner of the documentary section, both funded by Target stores.

Q - Do you have network evenings?

Patrick - We have a program called Indie Link, which happens eight times a year. It's only open to our members and the focus of that has been to get certain groups of our membership together. For example, last month we invited 25 cinematographers to bring in their reels to screen and network with a select group of directors and producers. Our programs at IFP are focused around writers, producers and directors. If we feel we service those groups then the art directors, the DP's and editors will benefit from that. So with Indie Link we aim to involve editors, actors and DP's, people that are a little outside of our focus.

Q - Do you have any seminar panels?

Patrick - Every year we have a producer series and a director series which deal with specific issues of the two professions. For example, the producer series always devotes a night to financing, and a night to distribution. People from within the industry will come in and talk on those topics.

Q - Once you're a member, can you then ring up for help and advice?

Patrick - Yes, even non-members can. That's essentially what I do all day, answer questions of where to get insurance, cameras, locations etc. and help with any technical questions. Locations are a big issue for people here in LA, because everybody's so savvy they want a lot of money to shoot somewhere. So, if somebody's looking for an office space, I might not direct them to a specific place but I will direct them somewhere where they can find those resources such as the California Film Commission which has free locations. The Commission has two programs. Film California First, which refunds location costs for certain locations and money that you pay to police or firemen. The other program is called the Star Program, where they will give you certain state owned properties for free.

Q - If filmmakers are members, can they come in and talk to someone about budgeting and scheduling?

Patrick - Yes. We have consultations with a Line Producer where he or she will read the filmmaker's script, and although they won't do the schedule and budget for them, their experience will give the filmmaker enough information to help them do it. If the member has already done a budget and schedule, the Line Producer will review it and give feedback. In the library, we have several budgets, so the members who are new to budgeting can come in and look at some samples. We have *Movie Magic Budgeting* and *Scheduling* software on the five computers in the library. They can use that anytime. We also offer classes on *Movie Magic*.

Q - How much are the camera and lighting packages, casting rooms and editing suite?

Patrick - The cameras that we rent are Canon XL-1, the Canon XL-1S and the Sony VX-2000, which go for $50 a day (check with us as these may have changed). We have accessories for the Canon cameras, like black and white viewfinders, battery belt packs, an assortment of lenses, field monitor, and tripods. If you get all the accessories with the camera, we call that our advanced package, and that goes for $150 a day. The lighting kits we have are two basic ENG light kits and they go for $40 a day. Casting rooms rent for $60 a day, or we can rent those for a half day rate of $30. Monday through to Thursday we're open from 10am to 10pm, so you can cast all day long, twelve hours for $60 or six hours for $30. We have our editing suite that goes for $70 a day, or $40 for a half day, or $325 for the week. We have vendors that give discounts on production insurance if you want to rent from outside IFP-West. That's also a reason people want to join. Though I've found we did have someone who was offering good rates to our members, for short term insurance for shorts and they stopped because they got too many claims. But, insurance perks are really important to members because it's so expensive. People don't realize how much production insurance will cost because you must get permits, if you go with SAG, you have to have it too and just to get a basic policy, just for a short or even the smallest kind of film, you still have to get workers comp and liability.

Q - Can members get a health plan with you?

Patrick - Yes. It's expensive to get health insurance as an individual, so to get a better rate, companies often have group plans. So we set this up with Progressive Benefits. They offered group rates to our members. It's fantastic for people who are freelancers and they can't afford to get individual insurance, and they might get better rates through us. They can also join a credit union through us. When you join, you set a subscription to *Filmmaker Magazine*. And you get the calendar, which is the monthly publication.

Q - When you join, do you get an information pack with all this in there?

Patrick - Yes. You get a membership package, which will give you information about the health plan, the credit union, consultation programs. You get the vendor discount list in there. We also do an orientation once a month. It takes me two hours to talk about everything IFP does and give an overview of everything.

Q - Do any of your other bases offer any programs?

Patrick - Minneapolis is the only one that offers grants (annually) and it's based on the screenplay. The Chicago branch has their financing conference that they do. New York and Los Angeles are the largest branches, and offer the most stuff. New York also has the Film Market. We do the LA Film Festival and the Independent Spirit Awards.

Q - What do you look for when people apply for the labs?

Josh - All the labs are project material driven, so the first thing we look at is the sreenplay – even before we look at people's background, history, qualifications. In terms of what type of scripts we're looking for, it's really open. We're looking for well written, original, independent screenplays. We're looking for scripts that really have an author's voice that's somehow distinctive. If it's in a traditional genre like Romantic Comedy or Sci-Fi, we're open, but we want to see that people are trying to do something new. We don't care about budget or genre, we want original voices.

Q - Does the background of the filmmakers matter?

Josh - No. We've had first time writers and we've also had people who are members of the Writers Guild. In our last director's lab, someone had sold several scripts and then became a staff writer on *The Sopranos*. In the directors lab, we've taken people who've never directed before and in those cases, the interview is important, as we are trying to see if they're serious. Even if they don't have previous experience, they need to demonstrate that they have creative vision and the ability to execute what they are talking about. We do tend to take people who have done previous work in the directors lab, either doing short films or people who have worked as writers or other key set positions who now want to move into directing. We have had a lot of people apply who have already directed features.

Q - What do you look for in applicants to the producer's lab?

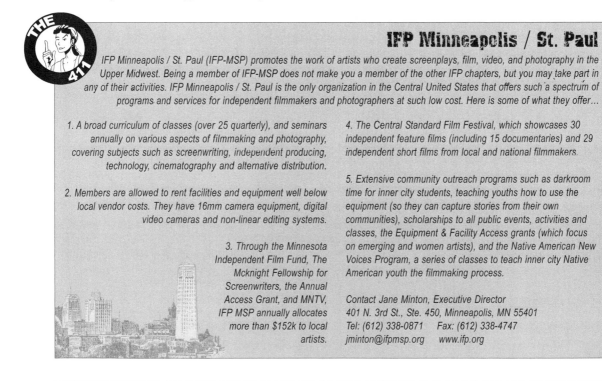

IFP Minneapolis / St. Paul

IFP Minneapolis / St. Paul (IFP-MSP) promotes the work of artists who create screenplays, film, video, and photography in the Upper Midwest. Being a member of IFP-MSP does not make you a member of the other IFP chapters, but you may take part in any of their activities. IFP Minneapolis / St. Paul is the only organization in the Central United States that offers such a spectrum of programs and services for independent filmmakers and photographers at such low cost. Here is some of what they offer...

1. A broad curriculum of classes (over 25 quarterly), and seminars annually on various aspects of filmmaking and photography, covering subjects such as screenwriting, independent producing, technology, cinematography and alternative distribution.

2. Members are allowed to rent facilities and equipment well below local vendor costs. They have 16mm camera equipment, digital video cameras and non-linear editing systems.

3. Through the Minnesota Independent Film Fund, The Mcknight Fellowship for Screenwriters, the Annual Access Grant, and MNTV, IFP MSP annually allocates more than $152k to local artists.

4. The Central Standard Film Festival, which showcases 30 independent feature films (including 15 documentaries) and 29 independent short films from local and national filmmakers.

5. Extensive community outreach programs such as darkroom time for inner city students, teaching youths how to use the equipment (so they can capture stories from their own communities), scholarships to all public events, activities and classes, the Equipment & Facility Access grants (which focus on emerging and women artists), and the Native American New Voices Program, a series of classes to teach inner city Native American youth the filmmaking process.

Contact Jane Minton, Executive Director
401 N. 3rd St., Ste. 450, Minneapolis, MN 55401
Tel: (612) 338-0871   Fax: (612) 338-4747
jminton@ifpmsp.org   www.ifp.org

Josh - We want someone who really wants to be an independent, creative producer. A lot of times, we get applicants who are directors or writers at heart, but they're applying to do the producers lab because no one else is making their movie, so they're going to do it. We do sometimes take those people if we like their material, but what we're really trying to do in that lab is find people who really want to produce and that's hard to find. Again, the first thing we look at is the script. Have they optioned or bought good material? We're open to people who are just starting out as well as people who are more experienced.

Q - How long are the labs?

Josh - Each lab runs for seven weeks. Participants meet three nights a week outside of those sessions. In the directors lab, we provide basic camera and sound packages and hook people up with key crew, like an editor, a line producer and a DP, and they go out and shoot scenes from their script. The director's lab takes eight people, in the producers it's twelve. In Project Involve it's twenty per semester, forty per year.

Q - Are people willing to be mentors?

Josh - People in the independent film community tend to be generous with their time. At the beginning of every lab, I ask people to come up with a dream list of mentors (sometimes they are unrealistic, like they want Steven Spielberg). I will go after anybody and my job is to match people up where I think there is an appropriate fit, and where the advisor would be helpful on a project. We've been lucky to have Alison Anders, Keith Gordon, The Polish brothers, Nicole Holofcener to mention just a few, who have been either guest speakers, mentors, lecturers etc.

Q - Are there any common mistakes people make during the labs?

Josh - Writers, directors and producers need to be able to speak articulately about their projects, so they can walk into a room, meet somebody, and tell them about the project in a way that's exciting and engaging. It's difficult and there are some people who are naturally good at it, but it's a skill you can learn, so informal pitching is good. When I interview people, if they seem completely inarticulate about their project, I won't see why they are excited about it.

Q - What mistakes have you noticed with new filmmakers?

Patrick - A lot of new filmmakers don't consider the legal issues that come up such as not getting the right music clearances. We see a lot of filmmakers ignore distribution and just concentrate on making their film, but then discover later that if only they had gone with the another actor, they could have been guaranteed a certain level of distribution. I think a lot of filmmakers here in LA don't realize how easy it is to get SAG actors, they think SAG is too daunting, but SAG does have some programs that work with low budget filmmakers. Yes, there are a lot of people you have to go through which can be a headache, but your film might benefit so much more from having a better quality actor. The majority of mistakes in independent films revolve around the screenplay, and people are not that knowledgeable about the costs of making a film. They come up with a number of how much they think it should cost and they don't understand how to get that money. For example, if you only have a budget of $1m, and you're going to Miramax, Miramax are not going to finance your $1m movie as they make larger budget films. That's another thing, filmmakers must remember that if the mini majors such as the Miramax's and Fox Searchlight's don't pick up their films, there are many other options available, whether it's self distribution or foreign sales. Know your audience. Planning is very important. Having the best script possible. Really look into all the possibilities and use all the resources you can. Doing just a little homework to find out whether or not your local film commission offers stuff will really help. Get tapped into your community and see what people you have there and what equipment there is. Some people think it's too daunting and that they need $10m to make a movie, but the reality is, it doesn't take $10m to make a movie. You can make a feature for $30k!

Michelle Byrd
IFP New York

IFP/NEW YORK

Q - What are the main programs of the New York IFP?

Michelle - The biggest program that we do is the Film Market, and then the international program. We are the only IFP that has an international presence. We have a relationship with the Rotterdam Film Festival, Berlin and Cannes. With Cannes we act as the US representative for the director's fortnight section and we help them set up screenings in NY and field questions from producers. They come to NY for five days looking at projects and that is a service to the community, not really a benefit to us. In Cannes and Berlin, we also do US stands for filmmakers and producers.

Q - Do members have to pay to do that?

Michelle - Members pay $200 to join the booth, and that is only if you're using our services. Some people just come and hang around the booth to meet people while they're at the festivals. In Berlin, we have a large stand that's divided between the IFP, Telefilm Canada and The UK Film Council, which helps extend our relationships between Canada and the UK. So if people are coming to talk to Telefilm because they have a screening in Berlin, they may also be able to connect with an American producer who might be there. It gives a better sense of being part of an international community, which I think is important for Americans. In Berlin, we put on a showcase of 8-10 films from our Market and give them a free screening in the market with advertising support.

Q - How did the Film Market start?

Michelle - The Film Market (September), started 1979 in NY as a companion to the NY Film Festival, and at the time, it was a market for completed narrative features. For first time American filmmakers, if they are going to receive distribution, most likely they have some sort of industry support from the outside. So, either there is some sort of distributor already involved or some producer of note who is going to help drive the financing. Or, there are actors in it that everybody knows so you can sell it. But, for us out of NY we sort of feel like the Film Market is a showcase for new talent. It's not so much about seeing a complete film. It's really more about showcasing an interesting writer / director that we would like producers, mangers and agents to sort of take an interest in.

Q - How many films are included in the Market?

Michelle - About 200, 100 of which are documentaries. The market place for documentaries in the US is extremely vibrant and it's a great way of getting your work out there. Generally 20 of the narrative projects are works in progress, and can be in very early stages. For instance, they may not have finished their principal photography - maybe they have only shot a few scenes. Some might actually be in post, but for the most part they are not. However people can get to the post stage much more quickly now than they used to, by doing everything in digital. Then we have around 20-25 shorts and scripts.

Q - Are their any restrictions, such as you mustn't have written a script before or never have directed before?

Michelle - No. It still remains one of the few open access markets. However, there is a $50 application fee for processing and then it is $200-$400 depending on the section you are placed in.

Q - With the IFP Market, what do you see as emerging trends from the buyers?

Michelle - There is a voracious hunger for documentaries at all stages of development. On the feature side I would say it's more difficult and buyers are only looking at projects that are fully financed. It is pretty rare that someone would get involved with something that's at the script stage. What most people get out of the market is a producer or someone who has access to some equity. Or, if they have a work in progress they frequently get festival invitation. There have been some instances where a short has lead to some work on HBO or the Sundance Channel, but it's not really a buyer and selling market. It is much more networking.

Q - What other programs do you offer?

Michelle - We do a screening series. Anyone who is a member of the IFP gets discounts on stock, camera equipment, production insurance, health insurance and other basic things that someone working independently would benefit from. We also have the Resource Program, which is a networking program that offers free advice such as from lawyers for example. We also do a monthly member mixer at the Museum of the Moving Image. We do a two day Screenwork Conference which includes a networking event with 8-10 panel discussions that covers TV and film. We also do screenings such as a monthly shorts series that's open to the public and free for members. We do a documentary series with the Lincoln Theater. We own *Filmmaker Magazine*, which is run by Scott Macaulay who produced *Raising Victor Vargas*.

Q - Do you offer any Labs like IFP West?

Michelle - We don't do the Labs for a variety of reasons, mostly because we focus on the Market.

Q - How do the various IFPs around the country differ?

Michelle - Pretty dramatically. There are different sized communities and differences in terms of what people need in each community. I'd say that the majority of our members in NY are writer / directors who haven't made a feature film yet but may have made several shorts. In LA, there is probably a wider cross section, such as many more actors. There are hardly any actors in IFP NY because in NY there are so many other things actors can be involved with.

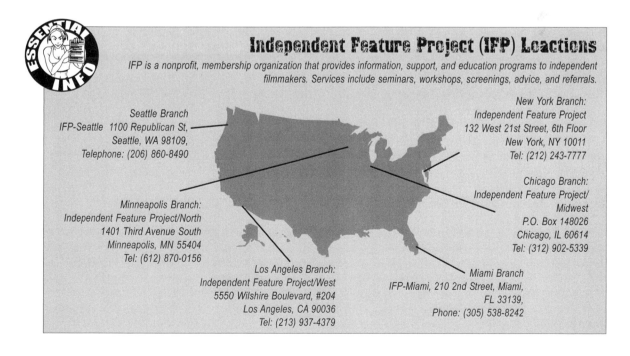

Independent Feature Project (IFP) Locations

IFP is a nonprofit, membership organization that provides information, support, and education programs to independent filmmakers. Services include seminars, workshops, screenings, advice, and referrals.

Seattle Branch
IFP-Seattle 1100 Republican St,
Seattle, WA 98109,
Telephone: (206) 860-8490

New York Branch:
Independent Feature Project
132 West 21st Street, 6th Floor
New York, NY 10011
Tel: (212) 243-7777

Chicago Branch:
Independent Feature Project/
Midwest
P.O. Box 148026
Chicago, IL 60614
Tel: (312) 902-5339

Minneapolis Branch:
Independent Feature Project/North
1401 Third Avenue South
Minneapolis, MN 55404
Tel: (612) 870-0156

Los Angeles Branch:
Independent Feature Project/West
5550 Wilshire Boulevard, #204
Los Angeles, CA 90036
Tel: (213) 937-4379

Miami Branch
IFP-Miami, 210 2nd Street, Miami,
FL 33139,
Phone: (305) 538-8242

Q - Do you notice a difference between East Coast and West Coast producers?

Michelle - The sense I have is that a lot of the NY producers don't have the same business infrastructure as some of their LA counterparts. For instance in LA, Susan Stover who produced Brad Anderson's film *Happy Accidents* and *Laurel Canyon* goes from project to project. Further, it seems like that in NY the larger film companies are not able to retain employees. People seem to work for a company for a couple of years and then once their own work takes off, they leave to form their own company. I think that is because it is so hard to find financing, and also because people are getting on planes and moving to LA with their projects, so ultimately it doesn't seem like there is as much equity money floating around in NY.

Q - Do you notice any difference in the type of film that gets made between NY and LA?

Michelle - *Raising Victor Vargas* is an interesting example. It is a beautiful film, no professional actors and in a way it is out of step with what people are doing as their first film. Just like *George Washington*, it wasn't commercially driven. It was an art house movie. I don't know whether people aspiring to make art house movies with people that you've never heard of and taking their time to develop slice of life stories, is specific to New York or LA. Contentfilm here in NY are doing a hybrid of independent films. They might have a first time director and then they have a very experienced producer or cast in the film, for instance, *The Guys* has Sigourney Weaver in it and was produced by Ed Pressman and John Schmidt.

Q - What about filmmakers in the middle of the country?

Michelle - I get the sense that those communities are challenged because more opportunities exist on the coast, but once somebody gets a certain amount of success or exposure, more opportunities come to those areas. The shining example would be Richard Linklater in Austin. He has galvanized that community by bringing jobs and opportunities to a bunch of different producers.

Q - What are some are the concerns that film lenders have about the film community in NY?

Michelle - The major concern is that some NY producers aren't treating filmmaking like a business. They have the passion for finding and developing projects, but it needs to be a business, otherwise you won't be doing that for very long. At IFP, we're looking at new programs we could offer which could help somehow line up the investor or business partner that looks after X, Y and Z while you look after the creative. Or, perhaps a company should create some component of it's business to go after television? In NY, a lot of the paying jobs are in TV. *Sex In The City, The Sopranos, Law & Order* and all their spins offs are keeping people employed.

Q - If you are a member of one IFP branch, are you a member of all of them?

Michelle - No, you are only a member of that one. You can join two, but there is a slightly higher fee for that. Typically people will join NY and LA, because they go back and forth. Or they will join Minneapolis / LA or Seattle / LA or Chicago / NY depending on where they go. However, we will honor each others memberships for programs that are less regional in scope, like our Cannes discounts.

Q - What advice would give a new filmmaker?

Michelle - I always tell people they need to make a decision about what kind of filmmaker they want to be. If you are interested in making art house films, then you need to develop certain types of resources to support that financially. Looking at a studio model of financing isn't really practical. Look at other people who are doing similar work and see how they do it. Remember that the people that you meet and connect with on the way up are the same people you are going to meet on your way down. It is important not to burn bridges and mistreat people. You need to have a database of contacts so you can keep your information organized. Keep track of things, which not everyone has the capacity to do - filmmakers don't usually work in offices. Don't gravitate to the cool. Everyone has something to offer. Spend time with people who aren't on your top hit list as you never know what they have to offer.

IFP NY
What you get when you join...

IFP Market - *a one week showcase held each fall for narrative, documentary works in progress, shorts and scripts, by independent filmmakers seeking financing, distribution or completion financing. Attracts over 2000 distributors and acquistion executives from around the world.*

No Borders International Co-Production Market - *this puts mid-career narrative and documentary filmmakers directly in front of potential financing partners through one-on-one pitch meetings, social events and workshops.*

Filmmakers Conference - *5 days of seminars and workshops during the IFP market.*

Virtual Doc Conference - *online conference held four times a year devoted to documentary filmmaking.*

Project Involve - *a 5 month mentorship program for filmmakers from cultural, ethnic and racial minorities. Four filmmakers receive a $10k stipend annually.*

Independents Night - *joint program by IFP/NY and the Film Society of Lincoln Center, to showcase new documentaries by IFP members that have yet to secure theatrical distribution. Free screenings and reception for IFP members are followed by Q&A with the director.*

IFP Buzz Cuts - *a showcase of short films by IFP members that share a unifying theme followed by a reception of free pizza and beer and filmmaker Q&A sessions.*

Independent Spirit Awards Showcase - *free member of films nominated for the Independent Spirit Awards.*

The Gordon Parks Independent Film Awards - *recognizes outstanding screenwriting and directing achievements by emerging Black/African-American independent filmmakers.*

Rough Cuts - *this provides a space and a forum to get the feedback that you need once your valuable work-in-progress is ready to be shown to a few valued colleagues.*

Workshops - *legal consultant workshop (15 private minutes with lawyers), quarterly networking sessions, Producers' POV workshop (private 15 minute consultations with industry experts).*

Resource Consultants Program - *invites members to contact the IFP for referrals to experts who offer advice on a whole range of issues.*

Canon XL-1 Rental Program - *$150 per week exclusively for IFP members.*

Other Benefits - *discounts on health and production insurance, legal fees, movie tickets to area theaters and a host of other valuable perks. Also members receive complimentary membership to the American Musuem of the Moving Image.*

IFP- NY
Michelle Byrd, Executive Director, 104 West 29th Street, 12th Floor, New York, NY 10001-5310
Tel: (212) 465-8200 Fax: (212) 465-8525

Fees - Individual Membership - $100, Associate Membership (outside Quad State Area) - $75,
Bi-Coastal Membership (both IFP and IFP West) - $150,
Student Membership - $65.

ORGANIZATIONS

Jacques Thelamaque
Filmmakers Alliance

FILMMAKERS ALLIANCE

Q - What is Filmmakers Alliance and why was it started?

Jacques - Filmmakers Alliance (FA) is a filmmaking collective that was created in 1993 by a small group of wannabe filmmakers, originally just to empower ourselves and get films made. It's daunting to make a movie on your own, so the idea was that if we shared energy, time, knowledge and resources, we could help each other make films. By starting on one production, we soon built resources that we could use on the next shoot and then on that shoot we acquired still more stuff for the third one, and so on. Over three hundred films and literally hundreds of filmmakers later, the structure of support is not quite as simplistic, but mutual support production is still the core of what we do, although many other things have been added to the mix. It's $125 a year and includes a subscription to *MovieMaker* magazine as well as our own in-house publication. Although you are not required to work on other people's productions, if you do so, you get barter dollars. You can bank those dollars and then turn them in for money to rent equipment. You can also solicit help from any of the members for your productions and use whatever equipment they are willing to provide. You can attend any of our discussion groups, writing programs, screenings and events for free. Work produced through FA is eligible to be programmed at our annual DGA screening/celebration or any events programmed by us. Also, features are eligible for distribution through our the FA Collection series on DVD. Finally, short films written by FA members are eligible for the Los Angeles Short Filmmaking Grant.

Q - How is the Filmmakers Alliance different from other organizations?

Jacques - We offer huge production (and now distribution) support that is managed by, and for, filmmakers.

Q - What kind of resources do you have?

Jacques - A lot of production equipment - sound equipment, lights, grip equipment, props, wardrobe racks, craft-service equipment, blue and green screens, etc. We have cameras, too, but they are mini DV, nothing fancy - although we have relationships with vendors like Panavision, Moviola and HSR for the high end stuff at very cheap rates. We have casting/rehearsal space and three post-production stations that include Final Cut Pro and tons of effects and design programs. We also have a book, script and VHS/DVD library which anyone can come in and use.

Q - What else do you offer?

Jacques - As a non-profit organization, we can offer fiscal sponsorship, which is not really relevant to features, but works great for shorts, documentaries or anything obviously non-commercial. How this works is that the filmmaker fills out some paperwork and provides us with background materials on the project, then people who want to donate to that project simply write a check to FA, and we turn around and grant it to the project so that the donator can get a tax deduction. And beyond fiscal sponsorship, there are the professional services, consultation as well as our educational component - the seminars, the writers programs and the discussion forums. And, finally, we are in the process of preparing to launch our distribution arm this year - both digital theatrical distribution and DVD distribution.

Q - What are the professional services and consultation?

Jacques - These are things we offer non-members for a fee or to members who need much more demanding support. Liam and I provide the consultations and set up the professional services ourselves. After years of production we have a thing or two to say to guide filmmakers not only through production, but through post and out into the festival and distribution landscape. Our professional services include things like equipment rental, production insurance, editing, digital effects and film emulation.

Q - How does the educational component of Filmmakers Alliance work?

Jacques - It's important to us that filmmakers are properly prepared in practical and aesthetic terms for the work they want to do through FA. To that end, we have a seminar series that we do about various filmmaking topics and issues. There is a seminar before every membership meeting, which is once a month (usually the first Sunday of every month - except for holidays). The writers programs consist of writers groups created and maintained by the members where ideas are developed and discussed and scripts are read and broken down. Frank Chindamo manages the Staged Readings, which are for scripts a little farther along in the process and it is more of a showcase that is cast with professional actors with people outside of FA, who can be helpful to the project, invited to attend. The discussion groups are a thing we call The Forums and include the Filmmakers Forum, where member-filmmakers come together monthly to discuss the aesthetics of filmmaking and critique each others' work. The other forums include the Experimental Film Forum, the Documentary Forum, the Post Production Forum and the Actors Forum. The forums are membership created and driven, so that new forums will emerge when enough members feel the necessity to come together to discuss some aspect of filmmaking on an on-going basis.

Q - What is the DGA event?

Jacques   It is our biggest event of the year, our annual fundraiser in mid-August held, of course, at The Directors Guild of America. It showcases a selection of the best short films made throughout the previous year. We also give the *Vision Award* to a filmmaker of note who agrees to be in attendance. Award recipients include Mike Figgis, Terry Gilliam, Wim Wenders and Allison Anders. The press comes, sponsors give us a bunch of money and we have a big party in the DGA lobby after the award presentation and screening. The DGA event is a great resource and filmmakers scratch and claw to get in because their work is show in front of a lot of people that can benefit their professional lives - agents, managers, producers, executives, festival programmers and others that we invite.

Q - What are the most common mistakes you see?

Jacques - People making films before they are ready to make them. Everyone thinks they know how to make a movie because they see what doesn't work in a movie. So they write a script without anyone outside of their circle of admirers seeing it and they are sure it is genius. Then they save up $10K or get it from their parents or friends. They haven't really tested the waters nor developed their craft but they make the film, anyway, and then are surprised that nobody is responding to it. Impatience is the word. Everybody has big dreams. They think their short or feature is going to be their ticket to a better life and they're in a hurry to get to that better life. But, in their impatience, they wind up really making it harder for themselves.

Q - What advice would you give to filmmakers?

Jacques - First, stay creatively active. Pick up a camera and shoot stuff and learn about your craft. Second, have fun, but take it seriously, too. Three, follow your vision. Don't try to make stuff you think will sell because it will always look like it. Try to challenge yourself in new directions or find stuff in you that is really unique. Whether you want to be a true artist or you want to make money, you need to find what is distinctive about you and make that compelling. This is the only way people will come to care about you as a filmmaker whether your goal is to do it for a living or just to do it for the rest of your life no matter how you make a living.

ORGANIZATIONS

Elizabeth Stanley
DGA

Q - What is the DGA?

Elizabeth - The Director's Guild of America is a professional organization that represents directors in film, television, commercials, documentaries and a whole variety of other areas, as well as unit production managers, assistant directors and technical co-ordinators in film and associate directors, stage managers and production associates in tape. We also represent technical co-ordinators in film.

We have low budget agreements that provide flexibility in staffing and salary levels. For the independent directors, they get their pension and health benefits that are very important in America, since we don't have a system of national health care. But, perhaps the most important is protection of the creative rights of the director, including the right to a designated period to put forward their own cut, and we will enforce those rights if necessary, on behalf of the filmmaker.

Q - What are the specific times a director has to produce his or her cut?

Elizabeth - The standard period is 10 weeks for your cut without any interference from the producers. On a low budget film up to $1m, it's reduced to 6 weeks. From $1m - $2.5m, it is 6 weeks plus 2 weeks which is 6 weeks to do your cut, then you show it to the producers, then you're given 2 more weeks. $2.5m - $3.5m, it's 8 weeks, and then above $3.5m it's 10 weeks. That's very important because a lot of times, indie filmmakers will invite the producers into the editing room at the beginning, and then they never really end up getting to show what their vision is. The other thing is, once you've shot 90% of the actual shooting days, *'your post-production rights vest'*. That means that you must then be consulted on all aspects of post-production after you've done your cut. Therefore it's not just a question of turning in your cut and being dismissed. It's about really protecting the director's vision, and giving him or her a voice. The other thing is that once you have these minimum rights established. Depending on your own strength and relationship to the project, you can always have a personal services agreement, which will negotiate better than that for you.

Q - What are the levels of the DGA's low budget agreements?

Elizabeth - There are four tiers. Up to $1m, and then $1m - $2.5m, $2.5 - $3.5m and $3 - $7m. They really both enable our existing members and those who want to join the DGA to do projects they're passionate about, under the protection of Guild agreements.

Q - How much does it cost to become a member of the guild?

Elizabeth - Generally speaking, there is an initiation fee of almost $8k for directors. However, if you join as a low budget filmmaker, a commercial director or a documentary director or on a basic cable show, we reduce it to $3.5k, and at a later date if and when you direct a film in a different category or project in a different category, you pay the difference. You also pay dues, which are the equivalent to 1.5% of your gross earnings (capped at $300k).

Q - If a new filmmaker was making a $1m film, could they come to you and say 'we would like to be a member of the guild'?

Elizabeth - In order to do that, they have to make the film under our low budget agreement and hire a DGA UPM and AD. To be perfectly honest, for a first time filmmaker (with all equity financing) making a film on a very, very low budget, it might not make sense for them initially. We don't want to be an organization of people who have only made one film as the guild's strength is rooted in the fact that we represent established working filmmakers, professional working filmmakers, and if we open the doors too wide and become an organization of people who have made one film and never make another one, then our bargaining power will be eroded. So, we really sit down with the filmmaker and evaluate on a case by case basis. On the other hand, if a first time filmmaker comes to us, and they're being hired by an established company, then that's a different matter.

Q - What other benefits do you get with the DGA?

Elizabeth - Residuals are a huge benefit. Every time your project migrates to an arena other than the original one, you receive monies. The residuals are not based on profitability. If they were, our members would never see anything. This is income that can enable our members to survive between one picture and another. It's our job to collect and distribute them. If the company refuses to pay, we have the legal basis to go after them because we require that any producer that signs our agreement get what's called 'a distributor's assumption agreement' from any distributor, and that gives us the legal standing to go after the distribution company if the fail to pay residuals. We have an International Department that has developed agreements with various collection societies abroad, like in France and Germany. The other great benefit with the DGA, is that we have a legal department. If you need to arbitrate certain issues, not just residuals, but if the company doesn't pay, or if the company abrogates your creative rights, we will go in and arbitrate it in an expedited fashion at no cost. There have been some really landmark cases we have taken up, such as one on behalf of Michael Apted and his film *Thunderheart*. One of the pledges he made to the Native American tribes was that he would show their way of life, and that was within the cut he did. When it went to television, the television company claimed their right to shorten it. He didn't like the cut that the company planned to show as he felt it made him renege on his commitment to the Sioux. So, he came to us and he wanted to take his name off the cut, and we took it all the way up to the Supreme Court and won.

Q - What about creative rights?

Elizabeth - We have a lot of negotiated creative rights that are guaranteed to directors for TV movies, features films and episodic TV. They range from talking about the guaranteed cutting time and the post production rights to the director having the absolute right to sign off on the budget before the film is shot and be a part of the casting decisions. We've all seen directors kicked out of the editing room before their cuts were complete and we just marched them back in. That doesn't happen too often. The director also has the bargained right to take his or her name off the film. Again, we hope that that isn't necessary, but these are all tools that we can use. We also have a code of preferred practices, which is not an absolute right but it's something else that we've negotiated with producers that they ought to follow. These rights are listed in our document, The Creative Rights Handbook (on the website).

Q - What else do you offer your members?

Elizabeth - We have screenings here at the DGA and an array of educational and cultural projects that we do through our Special Projects Department that are aimed at providing our members with ways to improve their art and craft. We have Independent Directors Committees in LA and New York where filmmakers like Steven Soderberg, Miguel Arteta, Neil Labute etc. are involved. The Committee have come up with programs and initiatives to better serve our independent members as well as to reach out to people who are not yet members. One of the great things they have done is establish a Director Finder series here at the Guild where every other Friday afternoon, Guild members view an independent features that do not yet have distribution in the United States. We invite our members and a list of distributors and the member invites whoever they want, cast, crew, distributors, whomever. We showed about 80

ORGANIZATIONS

films in the last four years and almost 50% have got some form of distribution. We do a series called *Under the Influence* where we show a film, usually of the 70's and we invite the director to talk about the movie with another director who was inspired by the film.

Q - Say for example, a new filmmaker comes out with a film and they're non-guild, do you contact them to join?

Elizabeth - There are really three ways you join the Guild. One is you're hired by one of our signatory companies to direct a commercial episode of a TV show, feature film, and you join on that project. Second, you bring us a low budget or indie film, and you say *'I want to sign this film'*, and then you join by virtue of being the director. We can also invite you to join if you've had a feature film released theatrically, and had significant critical or commercial success. So, for instance we invited Darren Aronofsky and James Gray. Then there are instances such as Patricia Cardoso who did *Real Women Have Curves*. She very much wanted to join, and we worked with Patricia to convince her producers to do so.

Q - Does the DGA do a lot of critical lobbying?

Elizabeth - In the last couple of years we've formed a Political Action Committee. The main thing it's been taking up are issues with a runaway production, which are film productions going out of the country. We have no problem with a production being made outside the US if it's in context with the story line. But if it's purely because of the exchange rate and economic incentives offered by other governments, then we really do want to keep that production here. We've also been concerned with intellectual property issues. There are issues before the US congress to do with the length of the copyright term. We've also been very interested in issues of violence in the media and censorship. We want to be sensitive to the concerns of consumers and parents, but at the same time we're interested in finding ways to make sure the rating system reflects the actual content of the films.

Q - What is the Assistant Director Training Program?

Elizabeth - The Assistant Director's Training Program was established in 1965. It's a way to strike a blow against the nepotism that controls hiring, and I would imagine there are probably about 400 people who have at least graduated that program since its conception. It trains Assistant Directors and in America, Assistant Directors generally don't move on to directing, they move up to production manager, line producer or physical production executive. It's a 2 year program set up much like a classical European apprenticeship program with a combination of on-the-job training paid by the employer and classes, and you can also get into the Guild by working as a non-union assistant director and gathering enough days of work so that you qualify and get placed on one of the Qualification Lists.

Q - Are there any other programs like that?

Elizabeth - We have a Women's Committee, an Asian-American Committee, an African-American Steering Committee, and a Latino Committee on the west coast, and an Ethnic Diversity committee in the East. We have some mentoring programs for women filmmakers and filmmakers of color who aren't members, because the statistics are dreadful for people being hired. Not only as directors, but as AD's and UPM's. So, we try to pair people with more established people in the category. We also have student film awards for women and directors of color where students can send in their short films, and they're judged. A lot of the people who win these awards end up going to be recognized in the Academy Awards for the student short films - like Patricia Cardoso with her Latina filmmaker award five years ago. The student film awards are really aimed at student filmmakers who are not yet in the guild, but it is part of our way to cultivate and bring recognition. We do a big screening of all the films that win, and then we invite the filmmaking community such as agents and producers, so that they get a chance to see the work.

Q - Are the seminars just for Guild members?

Elizabeth - Most are for members only, however, in certain circumstances we will also invite non-members, such as our annual film seminar. Steven Soderberg, who is the 3rd Vice President of the Guild, has helped create the East Coast Indie Directors

Committee along with other filmmakers. It's taken a number of years but you want to put together a group of people who inspire non-Guild members to say *'I want to be a part of that'.* Frankly, what we were dealing with four or five years ago is that people look at this building, and they think of it as part of the studio system and what we wanted to do was break down the belief that this was just for studios. We have had low budget agreements for quite a long time, and we wanted to bring a younger element into the leadership of the guild. I think we've had some success, and its a great committee and a great training ground for the future leadership of the guild. People tend to inspire each other.

Q - If somebody has a bunch of short films behind them, could they talk to the DGA about being a member?

Elizabeth - We don't invite people in based on a short film, but one of the great perks of my job is that I talk to filmmakers. I talk to others who want to get more involved, or people who are interested in coming in, and we have very frank and honest discussions. They're on radar and I try to stay in touch with them.

Q - Can non-guild members come and talk to you about your mentor program?

Elizabeth - Our mentoring program is really just for members. If we opened up a mentorship program for non-members, we'd be getting in over our heads. But, one of the things we do support is IFP's Project Involve. I'm on the board of that and we're also one of the sponsors. It's a wonderful mentoring program for filmmakers of color and gay and lesbian filmmakers.

AMPAS

Here are some of things the Academy of Motion Picture Arts and Sciences does for the film community...

Academy Players Directory - *A catalogue of actors and actresses used by casting directors.*

Exhibitions & Screenings of Motion Picture Artists - *Exhibitions are open to both Academy members and the general public at no charge. See Academy website for schedule.*

Grants to Film Festivals & Film Programs - *Two grants of $25k go to qualified and worthy applicants. Supports college-based internship programs which enable gifted students to work with prominent filmmakers. In 1999 the Academy Foundation further expanded its grant-making activities by extending support to film festivals.*

Lectures & Seminars - *The Academy offers many lectures and seminars on filmmaking by the experts of today. Open to the public. Check website for dates fees.*

Oscars Database - *Find out who won what, when on the Academy website.*

Samuel Goldwyn Theater Rental - *Open to anyone. Daytime rental: 9am - 5pm, 12 people max.) 2hr. minimum $600. Hourly rate after 2 hrs $150. Evening rental: Includes house manager, two theater staff, one security guard, parking and projectionist $3,500. With reception in Grand Lobby, includes same as above plus one more each theater staff and security guard $4,500.*

Student Academy Awards - *A national collegiate competition conducted by the Academy and the Academy Foundation. Participants compete for awards and cash grants ($3k-$5k), with films being judged in four categories: animation, documentary, narrative and alternative. An outstanding student filmmaker from outside the US is honored each year as well.*

Visting Arts Program - *The program assists colleges and media arts centers, as well as festivals, conferences and other film-related events, in sponsoring visits to their sites by leading film professionals.*

The Academy Awards - *Break out the golden men statues.*

The Nicholls Screenwriting Fellowship - *See screenwriting section.*

Academy of Motion Picture Arts and Sciences
Academy Foundation
8949 Wilshire Boulevard
Beverly Hills, California 90211
Phone: 310-247-3000
Fax: 310-859-9351
www.oscars.org
ampas@oscars.org

Q - What is the ABC/DGA Television Fellowship Directing Program?

Elizabeth - Each year three directors are chosen and are assigned to observe on a variety of episode TV shows. You don't have to be a DGA member to apply. The program was started to address problems in employment diversity. Generally speaking, the lower the budget, the lower the risk, the more likely they are to hand something to someone whose not part of the 'old boys' network.

Q - Is the 'old boys' attitude still a problem?

Elizabeth - First of all in America, making your second film is often harder than your first. You'll see more women producers than women directors, and my very simplistic theory is that the quarterback of a football team is almost always a white guy and that's what companies think of when they think about directors, while a producers role can be more like 'mom'. The producer may be a nurturer, but you're also the one that always says 'no' or 'choose'. In response, our various committees do a lot of mixers for members. At the beginning of each TV series, we get TV show runners to come meet and greet, but ultimately these show runners are saying its about money, and they want to hand the show off to someone they believe is going to deliver it on time and on budget. That isn't to say that minority and women filmmakers can't do it, they can, but they're not necessarily plugged into those networks. But we do what we can to plug them into the networks. It's been very slow in changing, and I think it will change more when those show runners and network executives and studio executives are more diverse themselves.

Q - As a producer, can you come to the DGA if you're looking for a director?

LA Screening Rooms

Universal City Studios
Samuel Goldwyn Theaters,
8949 Wilshire Blvd.
Beverly Hills, CA 90211
310 247 3000

Raleigh Studios,
5300 Melrose Ave.
Hollywood, CA 90038.
323 871 5649

Harmony Gold Screening
Room
7655 Sunset Blvd.
LA, CA 90046
323 436 7204

Los Angeles Film School
6363 Sunset Blvd. #400
Hollywood, CA 90028
323 860 0789 or
877.9LA.FILM

Sunset Screening Room, LA
8730 Sunset Blvd.
LA, CA 990069
310 652 1933

Charles Aidikoff Screening Room
150 S. Rodeo Drive
Suite 140
Beverly Hills, CA 90212
310 274 0866

Big Time Picture Company,
12210 Nebraska Avenue,
West LA, CA 90025
310 207 0921

The Culver Studios
9336 West Washington Blvd.
Culver City, CA 90232
Main: 310 202-1234
Screening: 310 202-3253

Ocean Avenue
1401 Ocean Avenue
Santa Monica, CA 90401
310 576-1831

DGA Screening rooms
7920 Sunset Boulevard
LA, CA 90046
310 289-2021

NY Screening Rooms
The Screening Room
54 Varick St
NY, NY 10013
212 334 2100

The Broadway Screening Room
1619 Broadway 5th Floor
NY, NY 10019
212-307-0990

Magno Sound & Video
729 7th Ave.
NY, NY 10019
212-302-2505

Millennium
66 East 4th Street
NY, NY 10003
212-673-0090

Planet Hollywood
1540 Broadway
NY, NY 10036
212-333-7822

Den of Cin
Avenue A at East 3rd Street
NY, NY 10009
212-254-0800

Pioneer Theatre
155 East 3rd Street
NY, NY 10009
212-254-3300

Tribeca Film Center
375 Greenwich St.
NY, NY 10013
212-941-3930

Elizabeth - We have an agency desk where we give out our representative information. We don't recommend one director over another because obviously we represent them all.

Q - You have a couple of theaters in LA and New York. Do you hire them out to non-members?

Elizabeth - We rent our theatres to any reputable client.

Q - What mistakes do you think new filmmakers make?

Elizabeth - Work on your script, whether you are writing yourself or working on it with a writer. Make sure that characters are developed and the story lines work. Once you've started shooting, if it's your own script, it's sometimes hard to leave your inner writer at home. Depending on where you come from, some filmmakers have a very strong technical grounding, and they don't know enough about working with actors. Whether its taking acting classes, you've got to really learn that - know how to talk to your actors. You have to find good people to work with, you should try to develop partnerships with producers, cinematographers and editors. I also think you have to be realistic about the budget of your film and how much you can spend on a film, and what that film is likely to be able to do. Is it a cable movie? a DVD movie? I also think a big mistake by first time filmmakers is that they don't 'study history, study literature and go out and have a life'. I think a lot of stuff is derivative. You have a generation of kids who have been raised on TV shows and movies and you see a lot of stuff that is very self-referential and doesn't really ring true. Get out and experience the world so you have something to say. Have a unique voice…don't just recycle the current hip, cool director. There's nothing wrong with retelling stories other people have told, but make sure your voice is your own.

Q - What advice would you offer a new filmmaker?

Elizabeth - I would say get every opportunity you can to practice your craft, whether that means putting on a play with actors or engaging in readings. Believe in yourself, do the projects you are passionate about, but also don't be afraid to figure out a way to support yourself - you can alternate your projects of passion with projects that make money, much like John Sayles does. Do that, be persistent and network like crazy. You have to have talent, and you have to network. You have to have a thick skin and be prepared to take a lot of rejection.

ORGANIZATIONS

Rich Hull
PGA

Q - The Emerging Producers Outreach Committee - why was that set up?

Rich - The Emerging Producers Outreach Committee is a committee of the Producer's Guild of America. It was set up to be an advocate and a source of support for Producers who are coming up through the ranks - for lack of a better word, emerging. The Outreach Committee is made up of a bunch of people who were emerging producers not too long ago who want to turn around, reach back and extend a helping hand. On the committee is Andrew Panay who did *Serendipity* and *Van Wilder*, Jonathan Treisman who did *Pay it Forward*, Shawna Brakefield and Michelle Jade Lee who come from physical production, Eric Watson who produced *Pi* and the latest Batman Movie, Chris Donnahue who won an Oscar for *Visas and Virtues*, Kevin Foxe, exec producer of *The Blair Witch Project* and myself.

Q - What does the Outreach Committee offer?

Rich - We offer seminars, networking events, mentoring etc. We just did a seminar in conjunction with the PGA Seminar Committee called *Producing the $500 Feature Film* which was awesome. You can get it on CD at the Producers Guild website. We host networking cocktail parties where you can just come and hang out with your peers. It's the equivalent of doing five lunches all in one night. We are also part of the PGA Mentoring Program which matches people who are less knowledgeable in one area of the business with people who are more knowledgeable. So for instance, if you're a tv exec and want to move into features, this is a great way for you to get in front of some of the biggest people in feature films and just pick their brains.

Q - So how can someone find a mentor?

Rich - If you are a PGA member you submit an application saying what kind of person you want to find, and who will be the most helpful to you for your next career step. Then the PGA goes and finds that person and matches you up with them. That person is obligated to give you three, four or five lunches which are one-on-one. It's a great opportunity.

Q - How big is the Guild?

Rich - The guild has almost two thousand members now. It had 400 this time two years ago. It used to be a bit of an old boy's club, but then it got a new executive director and then Kathleen Kennedy came on board as president and it's been growing ever since. To join, There's an initial non-refundable application fee of $25 and certain requirements that you must meet to join. You either have to have produced at least two feature films that have had a broad domestic or verifiable international theatrical release; or to have produced at least two long form TV programs (either TV movies or Movie of the Weeks) or to have had 13 weeks of episodic / non-episodic programs that have been marketed broadly in the domestic territory; or you must be recommended for membership by the Membership Committee, which will be judged on sufficient equivalent production experience that justifies membership as part of a producing team. Once you've qualified for that, there are two sets of fees required upon joining. Firstly there's an initiation fee of $725 for the Producers Council (which are producers who are responsible for the entire production of a project) or $350 for the Associate Producer Council (which are those who are on their way to becoming full producers). Secondly there are the annual dues of $300 for the Producers Council and $150 for the AP Council. It's less than SAG, DGA and WGA because they operate in a different sort of way. Producers are both employers and employees depending on what kind of movie they're making and where they're making it and how they got involved in it. Whereas a writer is definitely somebody who serves a very specific purpose in the process, same for the director, same for the actor.

Q - Must you be a member of the PGA to go to one of the panels that you offer?

Rich - No. If you're a PGA member you get in for free (if not it's $75). They're open to the public and we put on some great seminars, where you hear about other producers' experiences, how they learned the lessons the hard way so you don't have to.

Q - Do you act like a support group for new producers making their first movie?

Rich - One of the things the PGA has is a library of contracts. I use it myself. If you're trying to get your movie distribution and some distributor puts a contract infront of you and you say - *'is this what they look like, am I really giving up all these rights?'* You can look at other deals that have been done and say - *'ah right, this guy's screwing me'* or *'you know what, this is totally legit'.* We don't give legal services. There are plenty of lawyers in town that can give you great legal advice.

Q - I see that to be a member of the PGA you have to have at least two feature films under your belt - does the outreach committee provide advice/help to new producers who are embarking on their first film?

Rich - Absolutely. We do it on an informal basis, as well as formally through our seminars and mentoring programs. There's also the PGA's library of sample film and TV contracts to help first-timers with their various deals. And the Emerging Producers Outreach Committee provides guest speakers for various classes at UCLA Extension's Entertainment Studies Program, which are available to first time filmmakers.

Q - If you join the PGA, are there any health plans that you can join as exists with the DGA, WGA, SAG etc?

Rich - Yes, there are discounted rates for insurance. The PGA plans work a bit differently than they do at the DGA, WGA and SAG.

Q - Are there established pay rates or minimums for Producers?

Rich - No. Producers are different than other above-the-line people because, at the studio level, they're both boss and employee. However, in practice, the studios have a good conception for which sort of producer commands which sort of compensation package. On independent films, it's usually about more than just the paycheck.

Q - What other benefits are offered?

Rich - There are tons of great perks, and they're constantly evolving - from car leasing to great advance screenings (also special screenings of movies at Academy Award time) to production resources and a subscription to our quarterly magazine "Produced By". A good idea is to check the PGA website (www.producersguild.org) to learn about the perks at the time you decide to apply.

Q - What mistakes do new filmmakers often make?

Rich - Although you can't DO it all...you must LEARN it all. Although you have to be prepared, so much of this learning can only be done on-the-job. It's like running a restaurant. The restaurant manager doesn't wash the dishes or cook, but he definitely knows what's involved in both. If he can't oversee the people doing those jobs, he's not a good manager.

Q - What advice would you offer a new filmmaker embarking on their first film?

Rich - Don't be afraid to tell people that you don't have a clue. Don't make the same mistake twice. Learn to talk about yourself and your project in one minute or less. Check your ego at the door. Never have more than two screaming, yelling, freaking-out meltdown's per movie. Compliment people. Spend money on catering. Enjoy this experience, you never know how many more of these you might get to do. And above all...get lots of credit cards.

ORGANIZATIONS

Tom Bower
SAG Indie

SAG
The Screen Actors Guild

Q - What are the SAG agreements for low budgets?

Tom - There's five including the Affirmative Action which you can get if you have enough people of color, women, and people of age. There are five contracts below $2million. The first tier is the lowest perch, 0-$75k which we call Experimental. This was originally invented for student and short films. But now with new technology, a lot of films can be made for less than $75k. The limitations of that are that you can only use it for show at film festivals and if it gets sold, you must upgrade all of the talent to the highest level of scale. Then the next tier is Limited Exhibition, $75k-$200k. This is for films that are going to film festivals or are having a limited theatrical exhibition to qualify for Academy Awards. If it gets beyond a limited exhibition, then it has to be upgraded. What most people do now for low budget films is use the next level called the Modified Low Budget Agreement, which is up to $500k. They don't have to renegotiate with talent if they make a sale, and they don't have to pay more than their original agreement called for, which is drastically reduced. If you pay nothing on the Experimental, it's all deferred until you make a sale (then it is $100 a day which is 1/4 of scale). On the Limited Exhibition, you pay less than half of the regular scale. On the Modified Low Budget, its less than half of what the scale would cost and you'll never have to renegotiate that, so whatever you pay people, you're paid up. Then the next budget goes from $500k-$2m. That's the second Modified Low Budget and that's for less than half of what that scale would be. Anything above $2 million falls under the standard, basic agreement. Most people decide that rather than have any limitations on how they can release the film or what they have upgrade people for, just to go to the Modified Low Budget in the first place.

Q - How much is a day rate for an actor?

Tom - $100 a day, $500 a week or $600 for a six days on a Limited Experimental. For Modified Low Budget Agreements is $248 a day or $864 a week. It's also not consecutive days, so you don't have to pay for whole days unless it's overnight travel to a different location. Some companies making low budget films are now creating real ownership for the actors and the crew and all of the creative people. So if a sale is made, they have real points. Not phoney points based on net profits, but actual gross revenue sharing.

Q - Do you think actors generally don't want to do a low budget modified movie?

Tom - There has been a resistance to it, but it's also successful. Actors realize that they're probably going to do the work that they most want to do on the smaller films while they're waiting for their next big budget job to come along.

Q - There are benefits to becoming a SAG member, such as the health benefits...

Tom - Well this is huge for us. The low budget agreements create producer contributions to pension and health, which has become the foremost concern of the entire labor force of the industry. Runaway productions have depleted the pension and health plans with most of the memberships. So, whatever we've regained with Rule One, low budget agreements has been in the forefront of everything we do.

Q - With the low budget agreements, do you have to add money on for the health benefits?

Tom - Yes you do. It's 13.2% for pension and health. But, it's less then normal because the 13.2% comes from a smaller base amount.

Q - Would there be anything else you would have to add on top for SAG?

Tom - There's a bond, which is the guarantee that you're going to complete the project and pay the people. It is returned as soon as everything's in order and the movie is finished and you make your sale. It becomes kind of a pay request situation. The bond is a percentage of what you are going to pay your actors. It's on the basis of all your credentials and it's case by case, but it is based on some sort of a percentage. SAG reserves the final outcome on that, based on credit records etc. We make 1700 of these low budget movies a year, so people do find it affordable but it does become a part of whatever your budget concern is. It probably will cost less than $5k for a low budget film. And then there are certain guarantees for the payment of residuals. I don't know what part of the bond is used for that purpose. Anybody making a low budget film in New York or LA, should go to the Signatory Workshop, which happens the second Wednesday of every month at the guild. They walk you through all of these details so it becomes less of a mystery. They are free, but you must call a few weeks in advance and make a reservation.

Q - Does SAG cover stunt co-ordinators?

Tom - Yes. If you need stunts to be done, you have to have a stunt co-ordinator. Most low budget movies don't have one, and don't have a need for one but if you do, you pay them on a SAG scale. You pay them weekly or daily. The requirements for a stunt co-ordinator are much greater because it's such a specialized field.

Q - What happens with compensation in case of a fatal accident?

Tom - You have Worker's Comp. so between the SAG contract and that, you're covered.

Q - What is Station Twelve?

Tom - Station Twelve is when SAG members have not paid their dues and they're not legally qualified to work. Check with Station Twelve to ensure your actors are allowed to work. There's a twenty-four hour call line for that information.

Q - What is the standard work week schedule for a SAG member?

Tom - It's based on a six-day location work week. I think the seventh day becomes overtime and under most low budget agreements, you're not required to take consecutive days unless you're on an overnight location. Overtime has nine hours with one hour through lunch, this becomes time and a half up to ten hours and I think after twelve hours it becomes double time. I believe that applies to low budget as well as scale agreements.

Q - What are the different schedules in your agreements?

Tom - Yes. We have a theatrical, TV and DVD / home video schedule. You pay more for television and video rates, but you are given a greater window for the units that you sell. So it does breaks even. If you make a movie for theatrical release on the theatrical schedule but are then going to release on video, then you will have to convert the contract. There's no break or additional cost for going directly to a foreign release.

Q - If you plan to go theatrical but you only get picked up for video, you convert your agreement to video?

Tom - Yes. As soon as you're about to make that deal. Always stand back and see where you stand. See if everything is the same or has to be adjusted. In fact, you wouldn't be able to make the sale until you sign off with the guild anyway. You may have to pay more money, which becomes the assumption of the person buying as the adjustments have to be made with the performers.

Q - Can you do that up front?

Tom - No. If you know in advance you're working with a different contract, it either goes theatrical first or television first. You should do the same thing with AFTRA the other union for actors.

Q - Does having to deal with the two separate actors' unions cause problems for filmmakers?

Tom - No. We may create a problem for the members by saying, *'choose one union or the other, you can't be in both'.* That can be a problem. We failed to pass merger so the actors are caught in-between. AFTRA also represents musicians, recording artists, broadcasters, disc jockeys, but it also includes actors who do soap operas and there's always been confusion about who has jurisdiction. So in this current age of technology, if it's being shot on digital video, SAG may be entitled to the contract. If AFTRA offer a lower contract, filmmakers are going to take it of course.

Q -What if you were shooting a film that was set and shot in Russia and it had Americans in the cast?

Tom - Creative runaway is okay. We shouldn't be bringing work back here that is not shot in the place where the story is not set, anymore than we should allow things to leave.

Q - How can shooting in another country adversely affect an actor financially?

Tom - We want everybody brought up to the SAG standard. What is happening in the global world trade economy now where if someone's doing your job in Bangladesh for 30 cents an hour, then your job here becomes worth 30 cents an hour. We are striving for an international performers, international treaty or international performers contract.

Q - Is there a way that SAG can track a film in foreign territories?

Tom - We allow the distributor and end-user to go to the territory without tracking it because we know we can't track it. This is why studios get a much better deals than independents on residuals because they can track it. They distribute themselves and therefore they keep track of wherever they've distributed. But with independents, they sell it to a territory and its gone. So about all you can charge for is what you get up front. In the UK, Germany, France and certain other territories, there is a tracking system in place and if the distribution company is strong enough, they track and everybody benefits. When tracking the world-wide royalties, which all other countries collect and disperse amongst their citizens in all other countries, we have a strange situation here. The studios, rather than admit that we're entitled to any of these royalties as a participant, they choose not to collect the royalties themselves rather than have to share this participation with us saying that they've already provided residuals for us in the collective bargaining agreement and therefore not entitled to world-wide royalties in other territories. They remove the principle that we are subject to their collective bargaining agreement as opposed to some world royalty participation.

Q - What's Taft-Hartley?

Tom - The Taft-Hartley agreement states that someone is not required to become a member of the union the first time they work a job. The practical application of that is you can hire someone who is not a union member on the first movie they make and you would have to pay union security or preference of employment penalties. It is one way non-members can get enough union productions under their belt to join SAG. But it doesn't apply to low budget agreements. In that case, Limited Exhibition allows you to hire non-professionals. We call anybody not a member, a non- professional. Anything above that line requires membership.

TAFT HARTLEY and STATION 12

Taft Hartley - Named after Senator Robert Alphonso Taft and representative Fred Allan Hartley who passed the Taft-Hartley labor act in 1947. This covered the unions / guilds and the right to work policy, preventing unions from being closed off and enabling non-union / non-guild members to work for a limited period before becoming union members. Applied to the film business, Taft-Hartley allows non-SAG union members to work on a union show for a maximum of 30 days. At the end of that period, the non-union member must join the union to either continue working on that show, or for any other SAG film.

1. The producer can only hire a non-union member if they believe that the actor they require cannot be found, and only after having interviewed many SAG members, or when on set, a director may upgrade an extra or stand in to complete the scene.

2. If the reason to have hired a non-union performer (under the Taft Hartley rules) doesn't satisfactorily explain why a union member couldn't have be used, the production company is liable for a fine of $500.

3. A Taft Hartley form must be completed and, along with a photograph and resume, submitted to SAG 15 days before the performers first day of work.

4. In a right to work state (Alabama, Arizona, Arkansas, Florida, Georgia, Idaho, Iowa, Kansas, Louisiana, Mississippi, Nebraska, Nevada, North Carolina, North Dakota, South Carolina, South Dakota, Tennessee, Texas, Utah, Virginia and Wyoming), a performer may join the union after the 30 days, but unlike states such as California, doesn't have to in order to work on another show, union or non-union.

Station 12

This is a SAG procedure to ensure actors are in good standing with the guild.... ('yeah, OK Bernie, let's station 12 her') Generally, all casting directors will 'station 12' the chosen actors and the production office will 'station 12' stunt co-ordinators / performers or any actor who originates from the production office. Good standing would mean that the actors are up to date on their SAG dues, don't fall under having been Taft / Hartleyed once before. The fine for not clearing any actor who isn't in good standing with the Guild is $500.

The Taft Hartley Dept. of SAG is on 323 549 6866

Q - In the cases where minors are used, what's the issue with pay there?

Tom - You use them and pay them accordingly along with everybody else, but they wouldn't be forced to be members. They're allowed to do this one time in a principle role and next time they would have to join. Extras are allowed three vouchers before they have to join. The state governments are much more restrictive than we are. Each individual state has tougher terms than we do about that. And we enforce that. It requires tutoring and it requires a limitation of hours that they can work in a day and they have to have a certain break period. The producer has to get a work permit. It's a very strong department at the guild.

Q - How many Taft-Hartley people can you have on a film?

Tom - It depends. Usually you're allowed two or three but I do know of a case where a guy was doing a road movie with two professional actors and he didn't hire SAG actors for the other roles throughout the movie. I don't know if he had to pay them a speaking role according to the union pay scale, but they didn't have to become members.

Q - If you had somebody who was a walk on and had no speaking role, do they have to be a SAG member?

Tom - No, they're an extra. In most territories, they are not covered by extra union contracts, so whatever you get them to work for that's it. You may not have to pay them anything. There are however SAG union extras.

Q - If you were paying for a SAG union extra, on a modified low budget agreement, is it cheaper?

Tom - Yes.

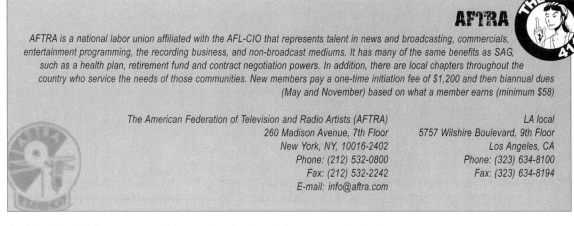

AFTRA is a national labor union affiliated with the AFL-CIO that represents talent in news and broadcasting, commercials, entertainment programming, the recording business, and non-broadcast mediums. It has many of the same benefits as SAG, such as a health plan, retirement fund and contract negotiation powers. In addition, there are local chapters throughout the country who service the needs of those communities. New members pay a one-time initiation fee of $1,200 and then biannual dues (May and November) based on what a member earns (minimum $58)

The American Federation of Television and Radio Artists (AFTRA)
260 Madison Avenue, 7th Floor
New York, NY, 10016-2402
Phone: (212) 532-0800
Fax: (212) 532-2242
E-mail: info@aftra.com

LA local
5757 Wilshire Boulevard, 9th Floor
Los Angeles, CA
Phone: (323) 634-8100
Fax: (323) 634-8194

Q - What about SAG agreements with regards to looping during post-production?

Tom - Looping is included in the SAG agreements.

Q - What are the rules and regulations for transportation?

Tom - I'm not sure that you have to travel first class when flying for low budget agreements. In our standard agreements, it has to be first class. In ground transportation, it's the same in all contracts and that covers transport.

Q - What about accommodation?

Tom - Everybody says first class, but what is that? I've been in lousy accommodations on huge budget movies and great locations on small budget movies. I think we want to educate actors and producers about making performers more of a partner in these low budget agreements. Treat them better wherever possible.

Q - If you're applying for a SAG low budget agreement, what's the procedure?

Tom - Call or go online to get the instructions of how to begin. You can download some of the paperwork off the net, but at some point you will have to go into the office to get all of the paperwork done.

Q - What information does SAG require?

Tom - Budget, most certainly. References of who you are, the probability that you are actually going to finish the movie, that the money is secured, any banking and bonding information - which most low budget movies don't have and we know that. They want to know if you have insurance. But when it comes time to sell your film, you will have everything in order from an accounting and administrative standpoint.

Q - Could you shut down a film?

Tom - If they were in violation of the agreement, we could. We've shut down films that failed to produce all of their agreements and security prior to shooting. Everything's got to be in order. We tell the members they can't show up.

Q - Are documentaries covered by SAG?

Method Acting & Classical Training

Method Acting
(also known as the Stanislavski System)
This technique uses relaxation techniques to allow actors to access their emotions. In this relaxed state, the actor can get their bodies and facial expressions to recreate to any situation the director wishes. In addition, method actors may use memories to stimulate the emotional response the director wants. Here, the actor recreates or relives a past experience they've had that elicits a similar emotional response to what is required in the scene. They will access their five senses to recall how things felt at that time in order to bring it to life in the present. They can become one with the character and may stay in character until they are done with the project. This method is quite internal and can be both rewarding and frustrating. Robert DeNiro, Al Pacino, Anne Bancroft, Marlon Brando and Dustin Hoffman all came out of this school of acting.

Classical Training
(sometimes called technical acting)
This technique is where the actor does not let the character envelop them, rather they rely on a planned performance using specific acting tools such as precise speech and movement to get the correct performance. In classical training, the actor uses external factors to analyze a character. A much older technique than Method Acting as it is the style Shakespeare and the Greek Classics used for their plays. Famously, Method and Classical acting came together in Marathon Man with Dustin Hoffman (method) and Laurence Olivier (classical). During one scene, Hoffman battled with Olivier, attempting to get him actually into the moment and character. After some time trying, the ill and aging Olivier gave up and asked Hoffman, 'why don't you just try acting darling?'

Tom - Only if you're using somebody to perform, otherwise not. AFTRA has a contract with documentaries I believe.

Q - What is schedule 'F'?

Tom - It means you are buying the actors for the run of the movie and you don't have to pay overtime. Darren Aronofsky, who directed *Requiem For A Dream* did this. He had $4m to make the film. He bought Ellen Burstyn and the other principle actors under schedule 'F'. It's not low budget, but it's a very low budget film. So, you're buying actors for $60k, which includes rehearsal time.

Q - Are there any other issues like that?

Tom - TV schedule 'F' is less. It would be something like $35k compared to $60k.

Q - What are the most common mistakes you've come across that filmmakers could avoid?

Tom - Not casting your movie well enough because you don't have the time as you're spending every moment scrounging for your budget. Also being forced by money into doing what is not right for the movie by casting the wrong person because they bring a name perhaps. It would be better to make your movie for less and not have so much interference. Make sure you give yourself enough time to properly prepare so that when all hell breaks loose and when the panic begins as the camera is turned on, you're ready.

Q - What advice would you give new filmmakers?

Tom - I love producer Peter Broderick's slogan, *'how much money do you have? It's enough. Make your movie'.* I would always encourage filmmakers to budget carefully enough so they can complete the movie they intend to make.

SAG CONTACTS

Main switchboard – 323 954 1600
Theatrical contracts – 323 549 6828
Production services – 323 549 6811
Residuals information and claims – 323 549 6505
Signatory Status – 323 549 6869
Station 12 – 323 549 6794
SAG extras – 323 549 6811
Actors to locate – 323 549 6737
Agent contracts – 323 549 6745
Legal Affairs – 323 549 6627

Matt Loeb
IATSE

Q - What is IATSE?

Matt - We represent in the motion picture industry, what are generally called 'below the line' workers, the artisans and crafts people. We also represent outside of the motion picture industry, stage hands, tradeshow workers and movie projectionists.

Q - How do members join?

Matt - There is a roster of up to 30,000 technicians in Hollywood and in order to get on the roster, you have to work for a signatory company for 30 days. Once you have 30 days under the contract, you can apply to the locals for membership. We have roughly 500 local unions that the IA oversees. Many of them have different policies on membership. Some of them only require the initial 30 days, while others may require an exam.

Q - What is the signatory company?

Matt - That's a union signatory, or a company that has signed our agreement. We have different kinds of agreements, regionally, as well as specific to the product, meaning low budget as opposed to big budget, and television as opposed to film and cable as opposed to network. There are subdivisions as to how the contracts are negotiated.

Q - What do the local numbers relate to?

Matt - Most of the international unions in the US have many local unions and they are chartered. I think it's just administrative. There is no relationship to the number 80 per se, and being a grip.

Q - What benefits does a crew member receive when joining a union?

Matt - The obvious benefit is the strength that you get by bargaining as a group. The skills and abilities are something that the filmmaker needs and the conditions will improve if they act collectively. The biggest benefits in the entertainment industry are health, pension and annuity benefit, so each person has full health coverage for them and their family, and a reasonable pension when they retire. They are the most important things. Other benefits include setting the terms and condition of employment, such as quality of life issues like penalties for working days that are too long, not being fed, or safety issues like being housed when you've worked a long day.

Q - Can a member of one local go and shoot in another state?

Matt - We have a couple of local, national unions, which have jurisdiction throughout the US. The camera local and the post-production locals have such jurisdiction. They have internal rules about how you travel. They do allow it, but you have to be housed and given a per diem. Internally, at international level, we also have rules about how people can go from one place to another. They have to abide by the rules of the local union where they are working. All of these other local unions have their own rules. When you become a member they brief you. We recognize that the industry needs to be accommodated so creative people can move from one location to another.

Q - Can a crew member who is a union member transfer to another job?

Matt - There are internal rules on how this works. Some of the locals allow you to hold a multitude of categories and others ask that you only hold one at a time. Regionally, to transfer to another local union there is a process. If a person moves from Texas to North Carolina, their community of interest is now in North Carolina so they apply for transfer.

Q - What would you determine as a low budget movie?

Matt - Our national agreement has a cap of $8.5m and that's for feature films only. Under that cap, there are three budget ranges: $0 - 3.5m, $3.5 - 6m and $6 - 8.5m. Our definitions vary from some of the other unions and guilds.

Q - What is the policy for $0 - 3m films?

Matt - We have quite a few agreements with companies covering that budget range. If a signatory company has $2m and they are making a movie, they pull out their contract and look up the rates for that tier and the benefits and conditions and the contract is applicable. If they are companies that haven't signed the signatory agreement, they may come in and negotiate with us in which case, the contract may look different, and our policy is to give those companies that have a long term agreement a better deal as they are buying in bulk. There are also companies that are trying to avoid the union.

Q - Do companies avoid the union as they can't afford to pay the guild?

Matt - I have a lot of theories on that, but we are very active in organizing and a lot of companies will pay someone above the line at disproportionate amounts and we don't accept subsidizing that kind of business plan. Our position has been, when you budget a movie, you should know that labor is a commodity and if you haven't got the money, don't make the movie. We've been very successful in approaching companies that try to avoid us and every time we get a contract, it's with a company that said they didn't have the money to sign the deal.

Q - Can you negotiate deferrals with the producer?

Matt - In NYC, we have a contract that has deferments, but it's an add on. When you get down to the lowest budget ranges, you're not saving salaries on deferment by avoiding a term agreement. For companies that can't sign a term agreement for whatever reason, we offer agreements with back end deals that are contingent on box office success.

Q - How long does a term agreement last for?

Matt - Generally, three years.

Q - Can it be negotiated per picture?

Matt - Right, but generally less favorable terms from the producers perspective.

Q - What is your policy on crew working on non-union films?

Matt - Those policies happen at a local level and vary. My philosophy is that if there is a production that, based on their circumstances, should sign an agreement, we may expect our people to support us in efforts to organize or strike. We would expect them to support the union should we try to organize it. However, if there's a job that's so low budget that it's outside the realm of us organizing it, I don't think that denying the member access to the work makes sense.

Q - Does the IA ever close productions?

Matt - That's what happens in some negotiations. We try to negotiate a contract, and if we're unable to reach terms, we instruct crews to cease rendering service.

Q - If members refused to stop working on the film, could they be expelled from the union?

Matt - There's a large number of disciplinary penalties, from being fined to suspension or expulsion. When you join a union, you become a voluntary member of an organization with rules, with mechanisms in place to enforce those rules.

Q - Are shows ever forced to become union and therefore certain non-members become members?

Matt - It used to happen more. We've done a lot of organizing in the past eight years or so. You have to work under a contract to get the 30 days, but you can't get the 30 days unless you are working under a contract. If you're a non-union person, the company is not allowed to hire you because if they are already signed to the union's agreement, they are subject to that roster. What people will do is say, *'well, let's call the union while we're working for a company that isn't subject to that roster and then when they come and sign, those days will count towards my 30'.* It certainly occurs that we approach non-union jobs with non union personnel and they get their days. I think that everybody who works in our crafts in the motion picture industry ought to be represented by us.

Q - If a producer signs with the IA, is there a certain number of crew members the production must employ?

Matt - No. The international contract, outside of the DP not operating cameras and things like that, has no staffing requirements. There are no minimum crewing requirements.

Q - So it's unlikely that someone coming right out of film school would get the job of a DP?

Matt - On the union jobs it depends on the relationships because some of those directors came out of film schools. They somehow get themselves connected through their reel or some acclaim that got. They get a little financing and bring their people with them, so it does happen.

Q - If you have a budget of $300k, would you advise a producer to talk to the IA?

IATSE Schemes and Contacts

IATSE (The International Alliance of Theater and Stage Employees) has several low budget pay schemes to help you hire union workers on your limited dollar. The three ranges are $0-$3 million, $3-$5 million and $5-$7 million. Each range has a different hourly rate for each crew position (which, in turn are all different from one another). Some positions, like Costume Designer and Scenic Artist are negotiable. You still have to pay for things like meal penalties, workers comp, etc. and the basic week is based on 56 hours. In addition, the New York local of IATSE has slightly different rules with only two levels, under $6 million and $6-$12 million. Contact the offices listed below for where you are going to work to obtain the pay scale chart for that region.

IATSE General Office
1430 Broadway
20th Floor
New York, NY 10018
Telephone: 212-730-1770
Office of the International President
Fax: 212-730-7809
Office of the General Secretary-Treasurer
Fax: 212-921-7699
Contact: Deborah Reid
www.iatse-intl.org
organizing@iatse-intl.org

IATSE West Coast Office
10045 Riverside Drive
Toluca Lake, CA 91602
818-980-3499
Fax: 818-980-3496

IATSE Canadian Office
258 Adelaide Street East
Suite 403
Toronto, Ontario, Canada M5A 1N1
416-362-3569
Fax: 416-362-3483

IATSE National Benefit Funds Office
55 West 39th Street
Fifth Floor
New York, NY 10018
Telephone: 212-580-9092
Toll-Free Telephone:
800-456-FUND
Fax: 212-787-3607

ORGANIZATIONS

Matt - I advise all producers to talk to us because if they don't, we don't know what their budget is. I can't tell without looking at the budget whether it's the kind of picture that should be under contract. If someone comes in and shows me the type of film that obviously shouldn't be under a contract, then at least I understand. In the lowest budget range, we would not be able to make a deal. We're flexible and learning as time goes on how to address lower budgets, but $300k is pretty low. I couldn't give you an actual cut off number because the number of shooting days, speaking roles, locations all need to be looked at.

Q - If a union agreement isn't feasible, do you give them your blessing to make the picture anyway?

Matt - Pretty much. The locals have different policies about that.

Q - Does the producer go to the locals separately or to the main organization?

Matt - It varies. There are a few larger cities, most notably New York where the locals sit down together even though they all have separate bargaining rights and do a one stop shopping negotiation for the employer. Most of the other areas use the international bargaining agent where we bargain jointly with the locals for contracts. In California, we have 20 unions but we are the bargaining agent there as well.

Q - What common mistakes do you come across?

Matt - Somebody will be an up and comer and think they know it all about productions, and they don't. The first thing a producer should do is get someone qualified who knows the lay of the land.

Q - What advice would you offer new producers?

Matt - Communicate and call us early. We have a real positive track record dealing with productions and there's nothing to be afraid of. Sooner or later you will be dealing with the union and so you are better off starting early on.

Joel Marrow
Transport Co-ordinator

WORKING WITH THE TEAMSTERS

Q - What is your job?

Joel - My job as a transportation co-ordinator is to service the company with all their transportation needs. That is, making sure all the equipment gets to locations. Trucks, actor's trailers and any kind of convenience we need. Making sure the crew gets there and also, in LA, the transportation co-ordinator is responsible for the picture cars too, which are all the vehicles that appear in the movie. And in the millennium of corporate America, we are the guys that are responsible for our budget. That is always the most important thing to the producers. How much does it cost? On a feature film the budget for transportation can be, depending on the size of the film, up to $5m, which is sometimes 5% of the cost of the movies depending on the set of circumstances.

Q - Do you also take care of driving the actors from one location to another?

Joel - Picking up the actors, also hiring all the drivers to drive the vehicles, renting the equipment. We're regulated by the Department of Transportation in respect to drug and alcohol testing so any piece of equipment that we rent has to be mechanically sound. We have to do 90 day inspections. The first inspection the vendor pays for, but if you have the vehicle longer than 90 days, the company pays for it. So there's a whole set of criteria that we have to know when it comes to complying to local, state and federal laws.

Q - Are catering wagons covered under transportation costs?

Joel - Generally, the caterer is hired by the producer, but on a day to day basis, we will work with them as to where to park, where we're going to set up and feed. Sometimes on a show, you might have 1000 extras, so when we go to scout a location, we are always thinking of the movie company like an army. You have to get them there and feed them, have a place for them to go to the bathroom and have a place to take care of the runs and pick ups. Once the location is chosen it's our job to analyze each location about where you're going to park your equipment - how you're going to get people from their houses to the set and back again.

Q - Do people tend to hire equipment through you as well?

Joel - Yes. They usually allow the transportation co-ordinator to rent equipment and we get competitive bids on people's equipment. When you work for a major studio, you use their equipment. But no one studio owns everything so it requires many different vendors.

Q - Do you cover the grip trucks and cranes?

Joel - Yes. We make the deals for them. I work with the DP and grip to find out what they what and then I lay out what's available to them.

Q - What are the Teamsters?

Joel - The Teamsters is a labor union that was founded in the late 1800's, that represents all the drivers. Unfortunately, Teamsters have a donut-eating, moron, stereotype because thirty years ago, it might have been that way. But we are professional transportation people and the Teamsters do make laws so we don't have to work seven days a week. A lot of times, the Teamsters get a bad rap, because on any one show there are more Teamsters on it than any other department because if we have thirty vehicles, there may be thirty Teamsters. A lot of times there is scrutiny there because of the cost.

Q - What if you have drivers going to locations and staying there? Are they hired for the entire day?

Joel - Yes, they are hired and again, once we get to the location, a lot of times there is shuttling of equipment. An efficient transportation co-ordinator will use his crew to do other things and prepare for the next day, move picture cars, prepare for what maybe coming up, plus you have a lot of different things that come up during the day. We send people to do pick ups, so we stay pretty busy.

Q - Do people double up at all?

Joel - Sure. A guy isn't just assigned to one truck. He may get to a location and then hop in a van, whereas some jurisdictions around the country, that's not so. In addition, Local 399 in LA, is strictly a studio driving company, whereas you go to New Mexico, or New York or Florida, you might be hiring a local there who not only does movies, but they do construction, warehouse work.

Q - Do the Teamsters have a lot of power on a non-union picture?

Joel - There have been times where the Teamsters stepped in. Generally, in today's market, on a $2m movie, it's obvious to the Teamsters that the market can't bear twenty Teamsters at Teamster wages, so they may have one or two big trucks that should be driven by Teamsters or people with the correct license. In the last five years, with low budget movies, there's a second wage scale that the Teamsters apply to those projects.

Q - Is it advisable to budget in Teamsters even on a low budget movie?

Joel - It's the producer's choice. If it's such a small thing where it's just small trucks, the Teamsters aren't going to be organizing anything on such a small level. But, on a larger budget movie, the producer may try not to hire Teamsters and that's where they will come in and try to organize it to get basic jobs.

Q - Could it be expensive to use the Teamsters on a low budget film?

Joel - It can be and there have been instances where the Teamsters have tried to take advantage of a situation, so there have been instances where they've tried to put more people on than the budget will bear. But in today's world, it's not like it used to be. Ten years ago, the moment they said non-union movie, the Teamsters would put up a picket line and there would be a laborer deal. It's not so much now. It's more of a negotiation and quite honestly, most producers want to hire professionals. We can save money, we can drive bigger trucks and put more departments in these trucks. It's interesting because when you say the producers, there's the physical producer that's doing your movie and then there's the producers Sony or whoever is supporting the picture. The hands on producer calls the transportation guy initially because we are the people that cross over. We fill in the cracks for the producers on things that don't necessarily come under our job jurisdiction and a lot of time you find that a harsh negotiation with the studio is done with attorney's that don't realize the contribution we can make.

Q - What would be an example of the things you do other than your job description?

Joel - I did the movie *Castaway*. This movie was a non-traditional movie as far as trucks and that kind of stuff was concerned, as we shot on a small island in the South Pacific. So, we had no vehicles per say, but they ended up hiring me and four others to provide an infrastructure, to make sure people got to the island everyday. One of our Teamsters also operates the generators, so we wired the island for power. I was responsible for all the shipping of equipment from the US to Fiji and that's a non-traditional way that we did it. We didn't hire the boats, as that was done by a marine co-ordinator, but I went on scouting trips with producers and we tried to figure out how we were going to get tons of equipment there.

Q - Was air freight a nightmare to deal with?

Joel - We don't do much of the air freight. Usually the production does. Air freight is a separate entity, and after 9/11 its more difficult to book your freight and making sure it gets there. Many times you film in LA one day and want to be filming in Denver the next. So you have to figure out which airplanes take air freight and you need knowledge of where your nearest airport is. That only comes through experience.

Q - If you're in California one days and Nevada the next, would have to hire different people from that state?

Joel - Yes. When you go in to Texas, they might only take four trucks from LA and then hire a local to supplement the rest of the labor force to drive the vans. In the last ten years, a lot of locals don't take people from the West Coast. What we do isn't so highly specialized that it can't be learned, so now a lot of times, there are people in each area that have the equipment and expertise to be the co-ordinator.

Q - If someone was making a $2m movie and was going to hire four members of transportation and a couple of union Teamsters, how much should they budget for that?

Joel - The basic rate for a Teamster is $24.37, which is a medium rate and you calculate straight time for the first eight hours. For the next six hours it's time and a half and after that it's double time. So, as I always say to the producer, *'I have a great way to keep the budget down, don't work so many hours'.* People always say to me, *'you guys make so much money'.* If a plumber or electrician worked sixteen hours a day, they would make more than us. We are one of the few industries where a twelve hour work day is a minimum and can be up to twenty hours a day.

Q - How early on are you hired by production?

Joel - Usually, between six to eight weeks and a bigger picture, ten to twelve weeks, especially if you are going scouting to different cities. I've been fortunate in my career. I've been all over the world and worked in 36 states and at least 7 foreign countries.

Q - Are action cars included in your job description?

Joel - Yes. We just did a movie called *Hollywood Homicide*, which is a contemporary LA police story featuring Harrison Ford and Josh Hartnett. It is throwback to the old days where we had a lot of car chases and stuff like that. We would have fifty cars to deal

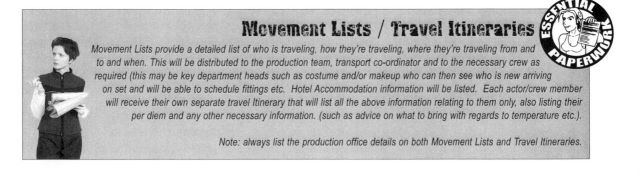

Movement Lists / Travel Itineraries

Movement Lists provide a detailed list of who is traveling, how they're traveling, where they're traveling from and to and when. This will be distributed to the production team, transport co-ordinator and to the necessary crew as required (this may be key department heads such as costume and/or makeup who can then see who is new arriving on set and will be able to schedule fittings etc. Hotel Accommodation information will be listed. Each actor/crew member will receive their own separate travel Itinerary that will list all the above information relating to them only, also listing their per diem and any other necessary information. (such as advice on what to bring with regards to temperature etc.).

Note: always list the production office details on both Movement Lists and Travel Itineraries.

with at one time. We had to find them, rent them and buy them. Also, there was a principal car where you have three of the same car so you can shoot simultaneously. We work with the director to get his concept to make the deals, plus we transport them, we have mechanics to maintain them.

Q - Do you work closely with the stunt co-ordinator?

Joel - Yes. We make sure that if you're going to do a stunt with a car, you have the proper seatbelts and they are the five point fuel cells. You go to safety meetings and talk about it over and over again to make sure no one gets hurt.

Q - Do you deal directly with the actors?

Joel - A lot of times. It can be frustrating to try to make actors happy. Some of them are unsatisfied with their trailers or whatever. Then there's great guys like Tom Hanks who's unassuming.

Q - Do you have a Teamster contract when you join?

Joel - Our Teamster contract comes in a manual. It covers what people do, what's expected, how they get paid, different provisions, night premiums, classification of wage scales and is basically a guide of how to calculate everything and what to expect. Whether its SAG, IA or Teamsters, it's spelled out in the book. You have to get hold of it through a member. The producer can call the union and get hold of a copy to help work out rates for budgeting. There are different contracts for what they call area standard, which would be standard for that area. If you went to New York it would be more than LA, so it depends on where you go.

Q - Are there any common mistakes that could have been avoided by new producers?

Joel - It takes a producer that hasn't been working with Teamsters, some time to build a relationship. I find most of the time, once a producer sees what you're doing, and I'm speaking for a transportation crew that's a good crew, the producer would be surprised because what we can do for them is really save them dollars in the long run. A lot of times, the producer will come and say to me, *'we have $1m transportation in this budget. How can we do that?'* and we sit and try to figure out a way.

Q - Any advice to new filmmakers?

Joel - I think that a new filmmaker shouldn't be scared by a transportation co-ordinator or Teamster because most of them will help as much as they can. They recognize what a show will bear in terms of cost and I get so many calls from smaller movies just wanting advice from me. My advice is don't be afraid to ask and don't think once you've talked to someone that immediately it's going to be a big nightmare, because a lot of times we can really help the producer do it for less money.

Mark Litwak
Entertainment Attorney

Q - What is the best type of company to set up to make your movie?

Mark - Different entities have different legal advantages and disadvantages. The best one to choose depends on the circumstances for each project and the needs of the individual producer. The primary concerns are taxes and liability. Generally, a corporation correctly established will be treated as an independent legal entity, separate from the people who own, control and manage it. But, in order to have the law consider your company a separate entity, you need to observe company formalities required by law, including holding and taking minutes of annual shareholder and director meetings, documenting important decisions and segregating company funds (i.e., not commingling them with your own personal funds).

One of the most important benefits of a corporation is its limited liability, meaning that the owners of the corporation are not personally responsible for the corporation's debts and contractual obligations. This means that creditors of the corporation cannot go after the owners' personal assets to collect what's owed to them by the company.

A corporation is taxed on income after deducting business expenses. The deductions may include salaries and the costs associated with medical and retirement plans for employees. Without a separate legal entity, some of these expenses might not be tax deductible. Sometimes the tax savings can offset the entire cost of setting up the company.

There are several types of entities including: the C Corporation, the S Corporation, the LLC and the Limited Partnership.

Q - Is there a benefit in setting up a C Corporation?

Mark - Yes, the benefits of limited liability and there may be some tax savings compared to operating as a sole proprietorship. Moreover, a C corporation does not have the restrictions imposed on an S corporation.

Q - What is an S Corporation?

Mark - A corporation can elect to be treated as a C or S corporation. It is the same type of legal entity as a C corporation, but when you file your taxes with the IRS you can elect to be treated as a subchapter S Corporation. An S Corporation lets you enjoy limited liability, but from an IRS point of view it is treated like a partnership or a sole proprietorship for calculating income tax. Therefore, the profits and losses are not taxed at the company level. Instead they pass through to the owners who report them on their personal tax returns. The S Corporation itself doesn't have to pay federal taxes. As an S Corporation shareholder, you pay tax on money you receive as a distribution from the corporation. Unlike a C Corporation, an S Corporation's profit is taxed once, at the individual shareholder's tax rate, rather than twice - first when the C Corporation pays tax on its income, and second when individual shareholders are taxed when their income.

If a company is not profitable there may be no taxes. Similarly, if the company pays reasonable compensation to its executives and at the end of the year has no net income, the company itself may not be liable for any taxes. You have to be careful not to pay an excessive amount in salaries, as that would be a red flag to the IRS. You can decide which type of corporation you want to establish after the corporation has been formed, and you can later change the status of C to S, or vice versa.

Q - What is an LLC?

Mark - An LLC is a Limited Liability Company that combines aspects of the corporation and partnership forms of businesses. You can elect to have the LLC treated for tax purposes like a partnership by the IRS. One of the advantages of a partnership is that the profits and losses flow through to the members avoiding the double taxation effect discussed above. In other words, there may be no federal taxation at company level.

There are two types of LLC. One is called a member-managed LLC, and the other is a manager-managed LLC. The member-managed LLC is a little democracy, where people run the company collaboratively and all have a voice in management. In a manager-managed LLC, some members are not managers of the business. They are investors who simply put money into the business. The good thing about an LLC is that it combines the limited liability of a corporation with the benefits of a partnership, in that the profits and losses pass through to the members. So, you can set up a member-managed or manager-managed LLC, and you can elect to have the IRS treat it (for tax purposes) like a partnership. The LLC won't have to pay any federal tax but may have to pay state income and other taxes.

Q - So why not a Limited Partnership?

Mark - In a limited partnership, the general partners are liable for partnership debts. In the past, before we had LLCs, the investors would be the limited partners with limited control, and the producers (who would run the business and make the movie) would be the general partners with complete control but also with personal liability. In order to give some insulation to the general partners, we would often set up a separate corporation to serve as the general partner of the limited partnership. That way they were protected, but it increased legal costs.

Q - What's the difference between an S Corporation and an LLC?

Mark - The LLC is less restrictive than the S Corporation. An LLC can have any number of members and there are few restrictions on who those members can be. An S corporation cannot have more than 75 shareholders. It can only have one class of stock, and shareholders cannot be non-resident aliens. Some states don't allow an LLC to be run with just one member, but you can do this with an S Corporation. The LLC often allows you to have the best of both worlds. For filmmakers who are trying to raise money and need a vehicle to produce the film and insulate themselves, I think an LLC is frequently, but not always, the best way to go. However, before making a decision, you need to talk to your accountant and lawyer as individual circumstances affect the choice of entity.

Q - What if you make three films?

Mark - It is possible to run all your films through one company. However, if you do so, all assets and liabilities are in one entity. Therefore, if you are

Exceptions to Limited Liability

Even if you have Limited Liability, there are times when an owner of a corporation or a member of an LLC can be held personally liable. Here are some of those instances…

1. If they personally and directly injure someone.

2. If they personally guarantee a bank loan or a business debt on which the corporation defaults.

3. If they fail to deposit taxes withheld from employee's wages.

4. If they are negligent in hiring or supervising their employees.

5. If they do something fraudulent or illegal so as to cause harm to the company or someone else.

6. If they treat the corporation as an extension of their personal affairs, rather than a separate legal entity. This might happen if you do not conduct your business in compliance with the formalities required of running a corporation or company.

FINANCE

Making a Contract

Contracts are often the only thing protecting the poor and downtrodden filmmaker. In its simplest terms, a contract is an agreement between two or more parties to do certain things for one another, and if one party should fail to live up to their end of the deal, the contract spells out the penalties that will be imposed. You should always consult a lawyer to help you sort out the legalese that is needed to make a contract ironclad and always get everything in writing. A verbal agreement can often be disputed and could ultimately be worthless. Here are some other things to think about when dealing with contracts.

1. Remember a contract is just a piece of paper and if someone is intent on doing something which breaks the contract, there is nothing you can do short of legal action, which is something that you may not be able to afford (particularly if you're an independent filmmaker).

2. If money is involved, get as much up front (on commencement of contract) as possible. If you can get it on the signing of the contract, even better. You don't know what might happen a little down the line - your investor or distributor might die, go bankrupt, get bored etc.

3. ALWAYS have a contract for everything, even if it's between friends and family. Many friendships have disintegrated because there was no partnership agreement in place defining the boundaries of each party. Pay the extra for a lawyer to draw up a contract to save your friendships.

4. When entering a deal with a company where they will supply you with goods or services, make sure they put the quote down on paper and fax it or email it to you. Many deals have fallen through because the company employee who struck the deal with the production company has left the company.

5. Follow your instincts - if something is too good to be true, it probably is.

6. ALWAYS sign a contract before work begins (especially with actors).

7. Read and understand all the text of the agreement, including the infamous fine print. Never sign right away, take the contract home with you and sleep on your decision. Beware of loop holes for in one section you may be given certain rights, but later on in the contract they may be taken away or nullified.

8. If in doubt, always consult your lawyer.

9. When you do consult your lawyer, make sure that both you and they absolutely understand how you will be charged (i.e. by the hour, by the half hour, a percentage of the movie). You want to make sure that each time you make a quick phone call with one simple question, that you're not going to be charged a half hour consultation etc.

10. If push comes to shove (and, by that we mean you are in DIRE STRAIGHTS – everyone has passed on you, and the rent is due, you're hungry and your cat is dying...), and it comes to the choice of either signing a bad contract and getting to make your film, OR not signing and not making your film, sign, take the money, make the movie and get ripped off. You will walk away with a very valuable experience and a show reel at someone else's expense. Remember, films do have a long shelf life - you may end up seeing some money back in the long run.

sued on a claim arising from one film, and the entity sued contains all your film assets, then revenues from other films may be vulnerable. For this reason, it's a better idea to form separate entities for each film.

Q - What would be the reason to choose an S Corporation over an LLC?

Mark - Often there is no advantage. But LLC's may be subject to more state income taxes than an S corporation, so that could be a factor. State taxation varies by state, so one should check the rates applicable before setting up a company.

Q - Is it best to go to an attorney to incorporate?

Mark - You can incorporate yourself. You are not required to use an attorney. However, if you are not knowledgeable about these matters, you can make poor decisions that might adversely affect your future dealings. Whether to incorporate on your own is also a function of how much risk you want to take, how much money you have for professional help and what's at stake. Some things are sufficiently complicated that unless you're experienced, it's not a good idea to do it yourself.

Q - Does it cost a lot of money to set up the relevant company?

Mark - Set up costs are modest, but vary by state and by the type of entity one establishes. Moreover, once you've set a company up, you may be subject to paying annual taxes. In California, for example, you must pay $800 a year for the privilege of doing business here. A lot of filmmakers think that they'll set up their company in another state, such as Delaware and operate in California and that will save them money. It may not, because you they may end up paying taxes in both Delaware and California. A little bit of knowledge is sometimes a dangerous thing and we often see filmmakers doing things they think are shrewd, which are not.

Q - Is there a limit on how many private investors you can have in the company?

Mark - Yes, in some situations there are. If you're seeking private investors and the investors are going to be passive, the interest they have is what's called a 'security' under American law. Securities are carefully regulated by the government through the Securities Exchange Commission (SEC). Remember the days when unscrupulous promoters sold worthless stocks to unsuspecting investors and caused the great stock market crash that resulted in the Depression. As a result, some very strong laws were passed. As we know, some of these shenanigans still go on ...think of Enron. But, abuses used to be more widespread. On the state level, these security laws are called 'blue sky laws', because some of these fraudulent promoters used to sell stock that had no worth more than the blue sky. The federal security laws apply when you have investors in more than one state. If all your investors are only in one state, you may only need to comply with that state's laws.

If you want to offer interests in your project to passive investors who are strangers to you, a so-called 'public offering', then you have to register with the SEC first. Registration and getting approval from the government is very time consuming and expensive and will cost a couple of hundred thousand dollars in legal expenses. This is not viable for most independent filmmakers. There are exemptions to registration at the state and federal levels, and the most useful are the so called private placement exemptions. There are some restrictions on private placements. First, you're only supposed to deal with

Company Pros and Cons

There are three types of company you could run. The 'C' corp, 'S' corp and LLC. Limited liability is the biggest reason for incorporation, whatever entity you choose, as this will protect you from financial disaster.

C corp

Pros:

1. Limited Liability
2. You may leave up to $250k in a business account with no tax penalty.
3. Capital generation - i.e. you may sell stock, issue bonds, borrow money, mortgage assets or contract for financing.
4. Taxed at corporate rates, which are lower than personal income rates.
5. The entity may live forever. No need to wind up corporation if an owner or manager dies.

Cons:

1. Possible Double Taxation.
2 Costly, formal ongoing documentation requirements.

S corp

Pros:

1. Limited Liability
2. Less complex management as there are fewer formalities than a 'C' corp.
3. Corporate income tax payments are not required. Taxed as a partnership.
4. Early loss benefit. Corporations may operate at a loss in their first 5 years. Shareholders may benefit from a reduction in personal taxable income by receiving their share of corporate losses.
5. Self employment tax is either reduced or eliminated.

Cons:

1. Shareholder restrictions – corporations, foreigners and partnerships disallowed.
2. Limited to a maximum of 75 shareholders.

LLC

Pros:

1. Limited Liability
2. Corporate income tax payments are not required. Taxed as a partnership.
3. Early loss benefit. LLC's may operate at a loss for the first 5 years. Members may benefit from a reduction in personal taxable income by receiving their share of corporate losses.
4. Shareholders can include corporations, foreigners & partnerships.
5. No limit on the amount of members.

Cons:

1. Life of corporation has a set ending date.
2. Some states will not allow an LLC to have only one member.

FINANCE

people you have some pre-existing relationship with. You can't take out ads for investors, but you can approach someone you know and ask if they would like to invest. Two, you'll be limited to 35 non-accredited investors, that is, investors who are not considered to be accredited investors. You can take an unlimited amount of accredited investors, which are basically wealthy people that have a net annual income of $300k or more. The government assumes that this type of investor is more capable of protecting themselves than non-accredited investors.

There are various categories of private placement that you can qualify for under the federal system. Often we rely on the Regulation D exemptions such as the Rule 504 offering, the Rule 505 offering and a Rule 506 offering. The 504 allows you to raise up to $1m, 505 up to $5m, and 506 doesn't have a monetary cap on how much you can raise. The 506 also pre-empts state law. You pick which category you want and are required to make full disclosure to your investors. This is usually done with a disclosure document called a PPM (Private Placement Memorandum), which looks something like a prospectus. The law requires you to inform the investor of all the risks involved in the endeavour before they invest. This document will explain your plans, who is involved, what you're trying to do, provide a synopsis, a budget summary and will include extensive sections covering all the risk factors. A filmmaker who doesn't comply with the security laws runs some risks. There are criminal penalties for non-compliance (jail), and a disenchanted investor could sue to get their money back.

Q - Can you do this document yourself?

Mark - If you're a person who thinks it would be okay to do your own brain surgery, then you're probably the kind of person who might want to do this on your own! This is very complicated, and should only be tackled by someone with considerable experience in both the movie business and securities laws.

Q - How much would it cost for a producer to put a PPM together?

Mark - If they're using a lawyer, it depends on how many state laws have to be complied with. Most filmmakers have their investors concentrated in a handful of states, maybe four or five. You rarely see a filmmaker who has investors in 40 states. It also depends on how much money you are raising and whether it will be a 504, 505, or 506 offering but you are probably looking at somewhere between $15 - $25k in various legal fees, filing fees and costs.

Q - Do you need a PPM if your family invests?

Mark - There is no special exemption if the investors are related to you. But, there's nothing that prevents your family from giving you a gift, something that's given with no expectation of compensation. If the money is truly a gift, you wouldn't have to comply.

Q - Is there a cap on a gift before they are taxed on it?

Mark - Yes. One may be subject to a gift tax in some circumstances.

Q - Once you're financed, do you have to put it in escrow until you have enough for principal photography?

Mark - You can to a large extent organize your company and plan to make your movie as you like, but you have to make full disclosure of this to your investors before they invest. If you give them a PPM and it says, *'we're not impounding the money and from day one we can start spending the money as we receive it'*, you can do that if your investors agree. But many investors may be reluctant to invest unless you put the money into escrow. Let's say you're trying to raise $1m, and an investor gives the first $50k. If you spend that on various operating expenses in pre-production and never raise the rest of the money your first investor will receive nothing back. In the film business, if you don't finish the film, you may have nothing left of any value. You might own the scripts, but they may be worth nothing. For this reason, a lot of investors are put off from investing until they are confident you can raise sufficient funds to make the movie. To encourage investors, often the filmmaker will need to set up an escrow account that is held by a third party like a bank. The money goes into the account and won't be released until an agreed minimum amount has been raised. That amount is usually the minimum amount needed to make the movie. When that sum has been raised, the money is released from the escrow account and goes into a production account. If the filmmaker is not able to raise the money, at some point the money will be returned to the investors, perhaps with interest.

Q - What advice would you give a new filmmaker when approaching investors?

Mark - Make sure you don't violate the law. If you want to find investors, understand that generally what motivates investors in film projects is not the financial aspects of the project as much as the glamour of being involved in the movie business or a sharing in the limelight. You'd have to be quite oblivious not to realize that investing in movies is a very risky investment. You could lose everything. The type of investor to approach is a middle class professional, someone who could afford to buy units in your project, and if they lose everything, it won't have any appreciable effect on their standard of living. A typical investor might be a successful doctor, lawyer or dentist. The investor you want to avoid is the retired school teacher who invests a big chunk of her savings into your film. If her investment is lost, this will cause her a great deal of economic hardship.

Q - Are there any tax benefits for investors?

Mark - There are no special federal tax benefits for film investors. Investors who suffer a loss can take that loss and offset other income depending on their personal income, whether it's a long-term loss or short term. There are some special tax incentives at the state level. Right now, there's a generous program in Hawaii, where if you structure the deal a certain way, the investors can get credit back on their Hawaii state income tax that can exceed what they invest, so their risk is minimal. Other states offer production incentives depending on how much money you spend in their community.

Q - Is giving a gift an incentive?

Mark - Gifts usually occur when someone is making a donation to fund the making of a picture, such as a documentary. If the money goes to a certain type of non-profit company, what's called a 501(c) (3) corporation, the donor may be able to take an income tax deduction for the gift.. If the filmmaker doesn't set up their own 501(c)(3), they can arrange to use another non-profit 501(c)(3) entity, like the International Documentary Association, to be the umbrella organization to receive the funds from investors. This organization will take out a small administrative fee of a few percent and pass the rest of the money on to the filmmaker to make the film. This way, the donors get to get a tax write-off and the non-profit gets a small fee and most of the money goes to make the film.

Private Investors

Private investors are simply individuals who want to invest in your film company personally, as opposed to investing in a company. These are typically friends, relatives and other wealthy people you meet (doctors, lawyers, car dealership owners, etc.) who either want to do you a favor or wish to be part of the glamour and adventure that is filmmaking. Some things to keep in mind, and that you must make clear, is that there is a good chance people will lose their investment due to the riskiness of filmmaking. Also, it's a legal requirement that you have a business plan (Private Placement Memorandum) containing resumes, attachments to the project, a budget, etc. to give to these potential investors. However, you can receive 'gifts' either directly from your friends or family (but they must check with their accountant on how much they can give as a 'gift' before they are taxed on it), or they can donate to a non-profit organization (501c3) that you have set up. Finally, be aware that when you take money from friends or relatives, personal relationships and emotions can come into play - make sure you have signed agreements clearly spelling out the terms of the deal with everyone! You don't want to be in a position where you dread catching up with family and friends at Christmas because you burnt their fingers very badly. They can't complain however, if they had ALL the facts before they parted with their cash.

Q - Can a lawyer help a producer find investors?

Mark - A lawyer can make introductions to potential investors, but most law firms are not oriented to be in the capital raising business.

Q - How important is a good lawyer to a film project?

Mark - It depends upon the project and what legal issues may arise. It also depends on the experience of the producer. There is no harm in having competent legal counsel. The only question is what will it cost? It is wise to educate yourself first so you have more knowledge about legal issues, and can avoid paying legal fees for basic information you learn on your own. I have written a dealmaking book specifically for non-lawyers. If you read my book you may gain a better idea of the different types of deals in the business, and when you go to a lawyer you may be able to make more efficient use of the lawyer's time.

Q - When you approach a distributor, should you be honest about your budget?

Mark - I think it's usually not to your advantage to disclose your budget while negotiating a deal with distributors. If you tell a distributor that you made a movie for $500k, it's going to be difficult to get an advance in excess of $500k. They'll say *'we're going to give you an advance and share the risk'*. From a filmmaker's point of view, it's best to get as large an advance as possible although it's not the only factor in choosing your distributor. What was spent on a film is not necessarily something you have to disclose to a third party. It's private and something you need to be candid about with only your investors and the IRS.

Q - How can you check the reputation of a distributor?

Mark - Word of mouth. I have a survey on my website of filmmakers' ratings of distributors, but it's limited. There are only 60 or 70 responses and some distributors aren't even mentioned. It's important to check out whom you are doing business with. The good news about distributors is that they are consistent and the ones who play games and cheat filmmakers tend to be consistently that way. They leave a long trail of disgruntled filmmakers in their wake, and it doesn't take a lot of research to find out who they are. You should ask potential distributors for their publicity packets. It will have information about the films they have distributed and the credits will disclose the names of the producers. So you can track down the filmmakers and get their opinions. Sometimes filmmakers dislike a distributor and bad mouth them for no good reason, so you need to take their opinion with a pinch of salt. Distributors can competently release a film only to discover that there may be no market for it. There are no distributors that consistently hit home runs. Not even the major studios, with all their resources, are able to consistently produce hits.

Q - What is cross-collateralization?

Mark - It is when expenses and revenue from two or more territories or countries are put in one pool. Say that a distributor distributes your film in France and it loses $500k and in England and Germany it makes $500k. If expenses from these three territories are cross-collateralized, the distributor would deduct the loss in France against your gain in Germany and England, leaving you with nothing. If the territories are not cross-collateralized, it means the distributor would take the $500k loss in France and you would share in the net gain in the UK and Germany. Cross-collateralization can also be applied in a situation where several different films are cross-collateralized. While that would make sense if the producer of each film were the same person, you would be unhappy as a filmmaker if your film was making money and the distributor was deducting expenses incurred on another film against your revenues.

A distributor that releases your film in theaters will almost always insist on cross-collaterising its losses against revenues from ancillary markets. You might want all the home video income and not cross-collaterise it with the theatrical expenses because a theatrical release is expensive. You've got to pay for the prints, pay for the advertising, ship the prints to and from theatres. In many

Finding money

Cash. You need it but where is it? This is the major hurdle to overcome. Without some cash you can't make your movie.

1. Film Production Companies - have deals with major US studios, may also have lines of credit with financial institutions to make their own films. There are also many stars who have their own production companies on the look out for their next project.

2. Foreign Pre-sales - sell your movie distribution rights to foreign territories (UK, Germany, Japan, etc.) to then get the bank to loan you the cash to make the film. (Gap financing). Not as prevalent anymore and you need big names to be attractive to these territories.

3. Studios/Mini-Studios (Disney/New Line) - as stated above, usually take projects from either production companies with deals with them, or independent producers who have a good property to sell.

4. Network/Cable companies (NBC/HBO) - similar to studios, but TV. Usually have smaller budgets and faster timescales.

5. Private investors - people with money who get a piece of your film for their investment. Must have a public offering that follows many SEC guidelines, which may cost upwards $10k.

6. Banks (gap, bridge, equity finance) - not as giving as they once were and more red tape than most of the others. More suited to a bigger budget film that seems like a more reliable financial investment to the bank.

7. Grant funding - best for socially oriented documentaries. Modest money from the NEH (National Endowment of the Humanities), the NEA (National Endowment for the Arts), and foundations with certain focuses, but lots of tedious grant writing and long decision making time.

8. Lawyers / Producer Reps - have contacts with producers and financiers and can put you in contact with them.

9. Foreign Equity - foreign private investors who may ask for some of the rights to the film, especially those for their country.

10. Co-Production – working with a foreign production company who may have access to monies or tax incentives that you cannot get in your home country.

11. Packaging – all of the large agencies have a packaging dept. where they create the entire 'package' of your movie by using their actors, writers, directors. They charge a packaging fee and will participate in profits. However this is highly unlikely to happen if you're a first time filmmaker.

12. Self-Financing – you have the most power because it is your money, but you have the most risk. Be careful of running up huge credit card debt.

13. Freebies - while not cash, get enough stuff for free and you are effectively raising money. If time is on your side and you have a good telephone manner, it is amazing what you can get for free or at massive discount. Get on that phone.

14. Rethink - the easiest way to make your numbers work is to slash your budget. We firmly believe that you should make your movie at whatever budget you can raise and not wait for that golden opportunity. When that amazing chance does appear, you will have experience behind you which will help you make better use of the opening.

15. Of course you could always rob a bank... Just kidding!

FINANCE

instances the distributor loses money on the theatrical release, and they want to recoup , these losses from the more lucrative ancillaries, such as home video and television.

Q - Is there a standard distribution fee?

Mark - In foreign sales, it's usually between 20 – 25%, but if you had a really high quality film, it may go down as low as 7-10%. The distributor can also recoup expenses from a film's revenue. What often happens is that a small foreign sales company takes on a low budget film, generates a few hundred thousand dollars of revenue and keeps all the revenue because there is no cap on their expenses. They will write off staff costs, travel, entertaining, and light bulbs for their office. One needs to cap expenses carefully. I cap expenses by category. We divide expenses into market, promotional and delivery categories. We allow distributors to recoup market expenses for one year only, and we have a cap per market. Distributors may release 20 new films a year and the cost of going to film and television markets should be shared and apportioned among those films. For promotional expenses, which are the expenses for creating a trailer, artwork, we limit those to direct out-of-pocket costs and require the distributor to provide receipts, if requested to confirm that the expenses were incurred. If there is no receipt, they don't get reimbursed. We specifically exclude overhead or staff reimbursements and legal fees. The other type of expenses are delivery expenses, which are out-of-pocket costs required to manufacture copies of the film and collateral material. Exclude reimbursement payments for materials received from territory licensees when you calculate the distribution fee, as these should not be considered gross revenues from the film. You also want to preclude the distributor from marking up delivery costs and charging these inflated costs to the territory licensees. Your distributor may purchase a 35mm print of your film from a laboratory, but when they deliver it to the buyer from Estonia, they charge him more, and pocket the profit.

Q - How are distribution fees calculated for domestic distribution?

Mark - Distribution fees vary by media. A distributor might take a 35% distribution fee for a theatrical release plus they get to recoup their print and advertising costs. For television, it might only be 25% and for home video there are two different schemes typically used. One is based upon a royalty that is often 20% or so of the wholesale price of each videocassette. No expenses are deducted. The other scheme is what's called the 50/50 net deal where the distributor gets to deduct their out-of-pocket expenses for video exploitation and then share the rest 50/50 with the filmmaker.

Q - Can you put a termination clause in your contract if the distributor is incompetent?

Mark - You can try to obtain a termination clause, but many distributors will resist such a provision, especially if the contract can be terminated for 'incompetence' which may be a subjective judgement. It is more likely that you can negotiate for performance milestones in a contract that allow a filmmaker to limit the term if performance doesn't meet certain standards. A contract where a distributor is asking for rights for 20 years makes me cringe. I prefer to negotiate an initial period that is short. For a foreign sales company that is not putting up a substantial advance, that means an initial term of maybe two or three years. If they do a good job, they can earn an automatic extension. The contract might say that if the distributor pays the filmmaker $200,000 as the filmmaker's share of revenue during the first two years of the term, then the term is automatically extended for another two years.

Q - What happens if a production company can't pay off its debts?

Mark - Bankruptcy is one option. You would need to take advice on what type is appropriate. You could also work out an installment plan with the people you own money to.

Q - Can a conversation over lunch be interpreted as a binding contract?

Mark - Yes, although certain agreements have to be written to be enforceable. For example, under copyright law, you can't assign an exclusive right orally. Another example is that you can't transfer a title to a piece of real estate orally. All states have a statute of frauds, which is a law that sets out which types of agreements have to be in writing to be enforceable. But, generally speaking, oral contracts can be perfectly valid and enforceable. The problem is if the parties don't sign a piece of paper setting forth what they are agreeing to, you have a big issue later proving what they have agreed on. It is always advantageous to put agreements in writing.

Q - How is a lawyer's time charged?

Mark - It depends. Some tasks may be charged on an hourly basis. Sometimes we agree on a flat fee for certain services. For instance, production legal services we often perform for a flat fee. Sometimes it's on a percentage basis of what the client receives.

Q - How much should be budgeted for a lawyer?

Mark - It varies depending on how the film is financed and distributed. A lot depends on whom you will be hiring. If you are making the movie for $1m, but you are hiring three stars and a director, and they all have agents and managers, the negotiations could be

The Business Plan / Private Placement Offering Memorandum

If you were going to invest in a project, the first thing you would ask is, 'do you have any paperwork I can study - I need details!' You might think it's easy to put such a prospectus together but...It is illegal under the Blue Sky Laws, to offer advertisement to potential investors, without having presented them with your business plan / private placement offering memorandum. This MUST list all the risks for the potential investor, and must also include all legal disclaimers for the owners/managers of the production company. So what is legally required to be in this document?

1. *The main disclaimer that must be listed on the front page:* This document if for informational purposes only. It is not a prospectus. It does not constitute a legal contract or offer information beyond the scope, such as tax advice or partnership documents. This document does not constitute an offer to sell or solicitation of an offer to buy any security. Neither does this document nor any other of the proprietary information herein be published, reproduced, copied, disclosed, or used for any purpose without the prior written consent of **(name of company)**. Filmmaking is a high risk business, and no guarantees are offered that investors will recoup any or all of their investment.

2. *The Executive Summary: which will include...*

A) An overview of what the production company's intention is i.e the film they intend to produce and distribute;

B) The production team; the product – i.e. a brief synopsis of the film;

C) The industry – a brief of the present industry & the particular genre that this film relates to;

D) The market i.e. of indie films, their successes and if cost effective;

E) Distribution – whether a distributor is presently interested or attached, or list the ways of attracting potential distributors;

F)The investment opportunity i.e. the budget of the movie, how it will be raised i.e. through 50 equity interests of $15k each, and when the investors should recoup their investment i.e. after distribution fees, expenses, repayment of any borrowed or advanced funds. Once investors have recouped 100% of their investment, any and all deferred payment compensation to cast and crew, and (if any) talent residuals have been paid – the

investors shall receive 50% and the Company shall receive 50% of any and all subsequent revenues.

3. *The Company:* When established, what type of company, the directors & managers: management and organization.

4. *The Film:* Who owns the screenplay rights, the target audience, when principal photography is scheduled, story synopsis, industry attachments.

5. *Industry Overview:* Explanation of motion picture production and its different phases, theatrical exhibition, non-theatrical, DVD/ video and ancillary including overseas distribution.

6. *The Independent Market:* A view on the present independent film market.

7. *Distribution:* Looking at the distribution of your project.

8. *The Investment:* The budget of the film, the equity opportunity offered, when the company may commence production of the film.

9. *Risk Factors:* Before the investor makes a decision to purchase the interests offered, prospective investors should consider the following factors, among the others set forth in the informational memorandum.

A) *Risk of motion picture financing* – explain the high risk and that it's only suitable for investors who are prepared to lose their entire investment;

B) *Risk of production* – explain that it's possible that the investor contributions may be expended without the completion of the motion picture and includes indemnities etc. i.e. the managers can't and don't guarantee that any of the key actors or production crew will fulfill their obligations under any contracts that they might have now or in the future – and that if certain key personnel cease to be associated with the project, it may be necessary to terminate the production;

FINANCE

C) *Risk of Distribution* – explain that there's no guarantee that the either contracted or not contracted distributors will undertake to distribute the film. And even if they do distribute, there's no guarantee that the marketing of the film will result in any financial returns.

D) *Lack of liquidity* – Investor's interests will be transferred w/o the consent of the managers. Holders of the interests may not be able to liquidate their investments.

E) *Tax Risks* – All tax risks depend on each individual investor's situation and prospective investors are advised to consult their own advisors as to all tax and legal consequences of an investment in a company. The managers cannot and do not make any representations, nor warranties, with regard to the tax treatment of any investment in the company.

F) *Lack of operating history* – The company is in the organizational stage and will not be formed until the capitalization of the Company occurs. As such, the Company is subject to all the risks incident to the creation and development of a new business, including the absence of a history of operations.

G) *Liability* – An investor's personal liability for obligations of the Company is limited to the loss of their original capital contribution and to any undistributed assets of the Company. The Managers shall only be liable to the Company or investors for losses, judgments, liabilities and expenses that result out of gross negligence, willful misconduct, or fraud. The Managers will not be liable to the Company or the investors for alleged errors or omissions. The Company will indemnify the managers for losses, judgments, liabilities, expenses and amounts paid in settlement of any claims sustained by it in connection with the Company other than those resulting from the Manager's gross negligence, willful misconduct, or fraud. Any indemnification payment could deplete the Company's cash available for investment in the motion picture or distribution to the investors.

H) *Loss on Dissolution* - Upon dissolution of the Company, the proceeds realized from the liquidation of assets, if any, will be distributed to the Investors only after the satisfaction of the claims of the Company, creditors, and the establishment of any reserves that the Managers deem necessary for any contingent or unforeseen liabilities or obligations to the Company. Accordingly the ability of an Investment Partner to recover all or any portion of his investment under such circumstances will depend upon the amount of funds so realized and claims to be satisfied.

10. *Schedules: Schedule A:* The Production Budget cover sheet and any notes. *Schedule B:* A list of recently independently produced features with reported budget and domestic box office returns.

11. *Biographies of the Managers.*

12. *Confidentiality Statement:* This Memorandum has been prepared by – Pictures, in regards to the production of the motion picture entitled **(name of film).** While the information herein is believed to be accurate, the Managers expressly disclaim any and all liability for representatives or warranties, express or implied, contained in, or for omissions from, this memorandum or any other written or oral information provided or made available by the Managers. Estimates and projections contained herein shall not be relied upon as a promise or representation as to future results. This memorandum is intended solely for the persons receiving it in connection with this offering and is not authorized for any reproduction or distribution to others whatsoever. The memorandum and other information provided to the persons receiving this memorandum shall be disclosed only to such employees, agents or other representatives of the recipient who shall reasonably need to know the same in connection with their evaluation of an investment in the Company. All copies of the memorandum and any other information given to persons receiving the memorandum shall be returned to the Company upon request if a transaction with the Company is not consummated. The information contained herein is proprietary, non-public information which may not be used other than for the purpose of evaluating this offering and must be kept strictly confidential. The recipient of this memorandum acknowledges compliance with the above.

FINANCE

protracted and time consuming. On the other hand, low budget films made without stars often don't require much negotiation. I would say, generally speaking, for a $1m film, your legal fees for production legal work would be $30-35k.

Q - Can a producer draw up their own contract and get the lawyer to check over it?

Mark - That doesn't necessarily save the lawyer time, indeed it may increase the work burden on the lawyer. When filmmakers draft their own agreements, it may take us longer to review and fix than if they just told us what their needs were, and let us pick out a template to start with. If clients want to save time, they need to educate themselves as to the basic principles, so the lawyer doesn't have to waste time telling them what their options are and explaining basic legal concepts. Filmmakers can also try to reduce their legal fees by handling some of the negotiations on their own. Clients can ask their lawyer to draft a contract that meets their needs, and then take care of any negotiations on their own. Filmmakers may be better off using my contract CD –ROM program, or the forms in my books, than writing contracts conceived on their own.

Q - In what areas do filmmakers have the most legal problems?

Mark - Three things are critical for filmmakers to secure in order for them to own their film. One, get a good depiction release for the actors that appear on your film. I wouldn't rely upon the release contained in the SAG model agreements, as they are drafted to protect the actors, not the producer. Make sure you have all the rights that you need, i.e., that you can edit the actors' performance, you have the rights forever, that it's for all media, worldwide. Two, have work-for-hire agreements with anyone on your crew that makes a creative contribution that could be copyrightable. The art designer, the cinematographer, the director all have to sign a contract that has the requisite work-for-hire language, which vests the copyright in the production company. Three, if there is any other copyrightable material such as music or still photos, you have to obtain a written license giving you rights to use that material. If you don't properly secure your chain of title and can't show through documents that you own everything in your film, you may spend a lot of money in making a film that is not releasable.

Q - Can somebody put an injunction on a film?

Mark - An injunction is a court order ceasing distribution of a film. Most distributors will insist that the filmmaker waive any right to ask for an injunction. Injunctions are not granted easily, but if you started distributing a film and hadn't secured the rights to use it on the soundtrack, the owner of that piece of music could go to court and ask the court to stop distribution of the film because it is violating their copyright. It could be very costly to you, and you could incur substantial legal costs to fight the request, and the damages assessed against you could be substantial.

Q - What would be your advice to new filmmakers?

Mark - You need to have some sense of what type of films can obtain distribution if distribution is important to you. Filmmakers often spend very little time thinking about how their film will be marketed. A filmmaker came to me a while ago with a family film about a boy who skateboards, and he has a dog. He made a film that would have been perfect for the Disney Channel. But, the filmmaker got it into his head that in order to be realistic, the characters had to use four letter words every other line. So, it couldn't

Top 10 Points to Look Out For in Any Agreement

Set out below are some very broad considerations which you should give to any agreement. Of course, each circumstance will require more specific attention. If your liabilities under the agreement could involve you in substantial expense, seek legal advice.

1. Ask yourself first what interests you need to protect and are they sufficiently protected.

2. Do you have any existing contractual obligations to other people and if you enter into this agreement are you going to be in breach of those existing contractual obligations?

3. What are your liabilities in this agreement and if things go wrong, what are you liable for? Look out for clauses which make you personally liable even though you may be contracting through a company i.e. are you being asked to give a personal guarantee for a loan which is being made to your company?

4. If you are required under the agreement to do something, ask to change any reference to your using your 'best endeavors' to 'reasonable endeavors'.

5. If you are providing your own original work or any intellectual property owned by you under the terms of the agreement, what happens if the project does not go ahead? Do you have the chance to regain or repurchase your property?

6. If you are due to receive any royalties or profit share under the agreement, make sure that the other party has an obligation to collect any revenue derived from the film or project, that they must show you their books and you have the right to audit those books. Check also your share of Net Profits (as defined in the agreement) as agreed i.e. are you receiving a share of the Producer's net profits or a share of all net profits?

7. What is the agreement asking you to do and is it reasonable and within your power to deliver or achieve?

8. What are the possible sources of income to you from the film or project and are all those sources being exploited? If so, are you getting a fair share of that income?

9. What sort of controls do you have over the conduct of the other party? Are the promises they are making under the agreement sufficient to cover your interests? What happens if they are in default of their promises?

10. Remember that if the agreement is being provided by the other side, the terms will be very much in their favor. This does not mean that they are necessarily trying to stitch you up, this is just business.

Production Budget

Your budget is a financial representation of everything you will need to make your film. There are many formats that you can use and several software programs like Movie Magic have built in templates that are easy to follow and do many of the calculations (including union fees and penalties) for you. You may end up making several versions of your budget, depending on whom you are talking to for financing. For example, your $1 million dollar budget that gets sent to foreign pre sales groups could be beefed up to $10 million if you are in discussions with a major studio.

1. Figure out how many days you are going to be shooting as it will effect how long you will need to rent equipment and retain actors.

2. Your first budget should be how much it costs to make the film properly, i.e. with a full union crew, a full compliment of days, proper visual effects, etc. This will give you a starting point from which to start cutting back.

3. When trying to find out prices, call several different vendors and get their rates. They will want to know the genre of the film, the number of days and the budget as it will effect their rates. Try to see if they will beat each other's prices.

4. Separate your budget into pre-production, production and post-production sections.

5. If you can swing it, include things like festival dues and delivery requires in the budget as well.

6. The easiest way to reduce your budget is to get rid of redundant or unnecessary crew members or actors.

7. If you can afford it, hire an experience line producer to read your script and come up with a budget in your price range.

8. Unions have different rates for low budget films. Find these out and plug the numbers into your budget.

9. Work out what you can get for free and then start working on it. Money you don't have to spend is almost as good as money in the bank.

go to the Disney Channel, and because the story was so soft, it couldn't get into theaters, as it would not appeal to adults. He made a good film that was totally unreleasable.

The major studios are increasingly in the blockbuster business. They want tent pole films like *Spiderman* that they can release in 3000 screens or more, bolstered by mass advertising campaigns. It's mass merchandise that appeals to common taste. It's very profitable if it's done right. The speciality companies are interested in art films or foreign films and the release pattern is different. They are interested in opening in cosmopolitan areas of the US to more selective moviegoers and they might distribute a film like *Run Lola Run*. They know their target audience. You have to understand what different types of distributors are seeking. Otherwise, you may produce a wonderful film that will only been seen by your family. Production is not the greatest obstacle to success nowadays. Distribution is the more difficult obstacle to surmount.

DeMille Halliburton
DeWitt Stern of Ca.

INSURANCE

Q - How much should a low budget movie producer put aside for insurance?

DeMille - That's a tricky question. There could be a producer who comes to me and says, *'I'm shooting this film over two weeks for $250k, I just need my permit to shoot and cover my equipment, vehicles that I rent, and I'm not even going to get workers compensation. I'm going to fly by the seat of my pants'.* Then there's another guy who wants to cover everything, even though it costs a lot. So, if they're shooting for two weeks and need General Liability to get a permit within the city of LA for instance, and insurance to rent equipment and for vehicles, it could cost $3k, and that's just the bare bones. Some people might even go less and say *'I own my digital camera, so I don't need equipment. We're using our own cars and I just need general liability just for those two weeks.'* Then it could be $1k.

Q - How does General Liability work?

DeMille - It covers third party property damage or bodily injury. So, if you're on the street shooting and you've got wires going on the sidewalk, and someone's walking a dog, trips and smacks their head on the sidewalk, you would be covered. In most locations, they will want to see that you have that general liability and they want to be named on that policy, so if anyone gets hurt there, they're covered. The minimum cover is up to $1m. One of the issues that people run into is when they're shooting at the airport, or a park or the beach, and the location requires more than the minimum $1m. They need say $5m, even if they are just shooting there for two hours. It can be done, but it costs a lot of money, maybe $1k per $1m. So they may have to scrap that location. When locking down locations, find out exactly what the insurance requirements are so there are no surprises.

Q - What are the other types of insurance to have?

DeMille - Equipment. Unless it's a $5k camera and you can use a credit card for the deposit. Most equipment houses want to have coverage for if their equipment is damaged or stolen, but also want to be named on that General Liability policy, in case someone gets injured because of their equipment. People sue everybody here in the US, and that includes the people who manufacture the wires, who own the cameras, who rented the camera.

Q - What's the Worker's Compensation insurance?

DeMille - It is coverage that's required by law, but not everyone gets it. It covers anyone employed by you in case they get injured. But a lot of people say *'He's not employed by me, I'm not paying him any money'* or *'I'm 1099ing them, they are self employed and I'm not taking out any taxes'.* It doesn't matter, they would still sue you. Some producers think if they 1099 employees, they're not responsible, but that's not true. No matter if they are volunteers, or '1099', if they are under your direction, you are responsible if they get injured.

Q - What is the difference between General Liability and Worker's Compensation?

DeMille - General Liability only covers the injuries of someone that is not employed by you. It's third party coverage. So, if someone's friend is on the set (or anyone who's not really involved in the production) and they are injured, their medical bills would be covered by the General Liability policy. Workers Compensation is for the people working for you.

Q - Would you recommend the producer buy Worker's Compensation?

DeMille - Definitely. If you're shooting everything in your buddy's apartment with a digital camera and it's just you and three other guys, then all the collaboratives in the film are doing it together and you know they're not going to sue, then you can weigh the options. But, if you have fifteen people in the street running around doing errands for you, the minimum amount that you'd have to pay for a premium is around $900. That's for fifteen people with a low payroll, or even volunteers. Many new producers don't have corporations set up, it's themselves out there. They're responsible and an injured person is going to go after them. So, if they can afford it, definitely get an LLC or corporation, and I would try your hardest to budget for Worker's Comp.

Q - What about auto insurance?

DeMille - If you're renting a truck that has equipment in it, you have to have it because they won't let it go out otherwise. If you're renting a truck by itself, often you can get cheaper insurance and lower deductibles through the actual truck rental company. Same goes for private passenger vehicles. As soon as the truck is carrying equipment though, you will need your own coverage.

Q - So the auto insuance covers everyone who's running errands for you too?

DeMille - It covers loans and rentals and so if a PA is using their own car, it would be considered a loan.

Q - What about cast insurance?

DeMille - As your budget goes up, you'd be looking at a Producers Package. It covers rented equipment, cast, camera negative, faulty stock, faulty camera, faulty processing, third party property damages (location), props and wardrobe etc. Cast insurance is expensive. It reimburses the production company for expenses incurred in the event of postponement, interruption or cancellation of a production due to the death of, illness of or accident to a scheduled performer or director. Accident-only coverage will apply to declared insured persons until a medical exam is completed and approved by the insurance company. Coverage usually begins two to four weeks prior to the start of principal photography. Extended term pre-production cast insurance is also available.

Q - How much is the basic cost for the Producers Package?

DeMille - It's based on your gross production costs for the whole budget minus insurance, legal fees, writer fees, music and post. That net number is then multiplied by a rate - say it's only $1m net and the rate is X - multiply it out, and that's what the premium is for that particular package. For a film that's in the low millions, like $1m to $5m, you could say 2-3% of the net budget, but that number is changing too, because the insurance companies can do whatever they want now. If they're writing Cast Insurance, and they're a little queasy about an actor, they nail you with a higher rate for cast insurance, and they may even demand that you to pay for the baby-sitter or the drug tests at the end of every day. There are hidden costs that you wouldn't ever think of. You have to really know what you're getting into when you're looking for your cast.

Q - Do you have to do a medical check on the cast?

DeMille - For them to get a full cast coverage where it covers sickness and illness, they would have to get a medical done. But, if you're covering for accident only, you don't have to get any medicals done. Most people want to cover everything.

Q - Do the various insurance companies have different rates?

DeMille - There are fewer insurance companies now that write entertainment then ever before, and of those few, some don't even look at budgets less than $5m. So if you're talking about someone who's doing a film for under $1m, there are maybe two insurance companies that could write it.

Q - What happens if you've written a low budget action movie with stunts?

DeMille - The best thing to do is hire someone who is from a stunt company, and then they're responsible for their own Worker's Comp. If you hire an individual stunt man, you may have to cover them under your Worker's Compensation. The insurer would also be particular about who they are and are not going to cover. So they may want to see that person's resume and look at the detail of what the stunt is that they're going to be involved with. The main concern of the insurance company is both that stunt person, AND it's also everybody else - the bystanders, other employees and equipment. So the overall insurance would be inflated because of the stunts.

Q - Would the insurance company insist on seeing the script to see if there's anything like fights or explosions?

DeMille - Yes. They will ask you to fill out a questionnaire and they'll want to see the storyboards. Not necessarily the details of what happens in the scene, but safety precautions that are being taken, how far away people are going to be from an explosion and how much safety material is in there.

Q - How are weapons covered?

DeMille - If it's a weapon that actually fires a blank, it's considered a stunt, because God forbid, somebody comes across a real bullet. If it's a prop gun where it doesn't shoot anything, it's different. But, think twice about anything out of the ordinary. Call your broker and say, *'We're thinking of using a hot air balloon, is that a problem?'* Anything that is out of the ordinary.

Q - What if you are shooting a film, had given the script to the insurance company, they know what's going on and then on set one day, the writer decides to change the ending?

DeMille - Worst-case scenario is to say, *'Listen, discussion closed, and it's not going to be covered'.* Worker's Compensation will be a battle, though. Legally, once the insurance company says they'll write Workers Compensation for you, they have to cover every employee that you have. So, if at the last minute you decide to hire a stunt guy to do something, they're responsible for it even though you didn't tell them. But, they could try to weasel their way out of it. As far as general liability, if a third party got injured due to a stunt that you didn't tell them about, then you're not covered. If you damaged a location, and knocked the power lines down, and the neighbouring companies were suing because they couldn't work, and the production line was shut down, there could be potentially millions of dollars that people could be suing you for and you could be totally excluded.

Q - What is Errors and Omissions?

DeMille - Basically in lay man terms, it covers what's in the film. What you see and what you hear. If there's a sculpture in the background and you don't get clearance for it and you get sued, that's Errors and Omissions. If someone says, *'that's my script!',* that's Errors and Omissions. If there's a crowd scene and there's a close up of someone you didn't get to sign their permission. That's errors and omissions. A lot of the time, low budget filmmakers don't get an E&O policy until they have a distribution deal secured. The distributor will want a three year term for a $1m minimum, it will be in the contract. When you actually get that policy, part of the questions are, do you have the proper music clearances? Do you have the proper clearances for people in there etc? If the answer is yes to the best of your knowledge, then you're covered.

I had a case where a reality TV show's producer actually produced an original feature that was an adaptation of a book. One of the characters in that book was a commonly known term that people use all the time. And, they were using that word for the title of this reality show. So, this producer (who happens to be a lawyer, too) wrote up a letter and told them to cease and desist using that name, which was almost impossible because it was derived from a European show. It was a big mess and a lot of money was spent on attorney fees. Luckily it had insurance to cover them, but they only had $1m, which was blown in four months. So we suggest you get your E&O before you even start shooting. A three year term for $1m coverage currently costs around $10k. The

Worst Case Scenario - Insurance?

Post 9/11, insurance is now expensive and a paranoid producer of a low budget movie could spend a large portion of their budget on helping them sleep at night. So how much do you buy? Well consider that you are making a high risk venture in all senses of the word, and so protection at every level is perhaps a little over compensating. Of course there are some instances where you MUST insure, to protect people and yourself. But beware of your paranoia and choose wisely.Remember, most insurance policies contain an 'excess' which often means that most items will not be covered as they are inexpensive.

Worker's Compensation
Covers anyone employed by you if they get injured. Includes 1099 (contractor) and W-2 (staff) employees. Pretty essential.

General Liability
Covers third party (people and things not employed, hired or owned by you) property damage or bodily injury. Essential if you are out and about with a crew.

Equipment Rental
Covers anything you have to rent from an equipment house (camera, lights, grip, etc.). You won't get equipment out of the door without this insurance!

Vehicles
Covers any production vehicle from a grip truck to a rental car. If you have a crash and your runner was not insured for commercial use it may invalidate the policy.

Errors and Omissions
Covers things you need clearances or rights for that you didn't get, which unintentionally end up in the finished film. You will need this when you deliver your film to the sales agent.

Producer's package
Bundle of insurance policies, which covers rented equipment, cast, negatives, faulty stock, faulty camera, faulty processing, office contents, money, security, props, sets, wardrobe and third party property damages for places you are responsible for. This is an all in deal that may be best in terms of value for money, BUT it may represent over insuring, especially on an ultra low budget cash conscious production.

FINANCE

first year is the most expensive part, one year now is $5k. They figure if you're going to get sued, that's when it's going to happen.

Q - Are there any other types of insurance?

DeMille - There's umbrella insurance, which increases your liability limits. For instance, if you have a $1m liability, and you're going to shoot at LAX, they will want a $5m limit, so you would get an umbrella of $4m to go on top of that $1m.

Q - What information would a producer have to supply you for insurance?

DeMille - It depends, but for a week, a brief synopsis of what they're doing, notes on any stunts or pyrotechnics, and the budget. But as soon as the numbers get higher, that's where you need more information. If there's cast, we need to know who it is, the number of days they're going to be performing and the medicals. If there are stunts and pyros, we need to get the resumes of the coordinators and questionnaires regarding the pyros. Regarding Workers Compensation, we need to know how many employees there are, what the total payroll will be for those employees. For vehicles coverage, we would need to know total vehicle rental costs. If it's a larger budget, we'll need full script, budget, day-out-of-days, resumes for producers...

Q - Who would be your liason on the film?

DeMille - The Line Producer or Production Manager.

Q - If you drop the camera and damaged it?

DeMille - Physical damage to equipment is covered. If it was a special camera and you did not have a backup and if you lost that day of shooting, the adjuster from the insurance company would liase with a production manager and they would have to give them a ton of information - the production costs for that day and what exactly happened. That day's shoot could be picked up another day and eventually the insurance company would pay for whatever that down time is, so that salaries, equipment rentals etc. A cast claim is even more complicated because the cast member could be near the end of the shoot and they come down with chicken pox. One of the ways to figure it out is *'Is there any way to digitally keep them in the last scene'* and what would that extra cost be? The insurance company would then pay for that extra cost.

Q - How do people make a claim?

DeMille - They call their broker who will get all the information needed, then it's submitted to the insurance company adjuster, and that's when the adjuster hooks up with the Line Producer to get any other details to expand on that.

Q - What about if your lead actor dies?

DeMille - You'd obviously be shut down. However, while everyone is figuring out whether they can find a replacement actor or if can they do it digitally, the clock is ticking and you're holding people so they don't go to another job. By holding them, you'd still have to pay those salaries. If you had cast insurance, you could ultimately get your costs back.

Q - How long would it take for an insurance claim to go through?

DeMille - It depends on how complicated it is. If it's just equipment, it could be a couple of weeks. But if it's cast insurance, where a lot of money could be involved, and where a lot of information has to exchange hands, it could take a longer period of time. It'll take even longer if the insurance company is not getting all the information they requested. There's always a case where we're waiting for that one little piece of information, or the Line Producer is waiting for someone else who is dragging their feet.

Q - What is the difference between an insurance policy and a completion bond?

DeMille - A completion bond is required by the investors or the bank who are loaning the finance for the film, and it's the responsibility of the Bond Company to make sure that the production is on budget and on time. The worst-case scenario is that sometimes the completion bond company takes over the film to finish it. So there are certain circumstances where we work hand in hand.

Q - What can a new filmmaker do to make your life easier?

DeMille - Think ahead. Sometimes it's impossible because they're getting favors here and there. They didn't know they were going to shoot there until yesterday, but to the best of their ability, they should do their homework. And, try to reduce the surprises.

Q - What are the common mistakes that you've experienced from new filmmakers in terms of insurance?

DeMille - Not thinking about insurance at all! And not thinking about the location deal. They are so happy that they've locked the location, and then a day or two before, they get the contract and it says *'...by the way, you need to name us on your general liability. It has to be this limit...'* It can cause a lot of problems if they don't get that stuff beforehand. So make sure you know exactly what the requirements are for your location, so either you know you can afford to do it, or you can just cross them off your list and find another location. A lot of the ultra low budget filmmakers think they can take their video camera and just go out on the streets and shoot and wonder why they're shut down, or they find out that they need a permit and to have a permit, they need general liability insurance. So, they call the day before saying, 'I need to get this now or else I can't get my permit, I didn't know'. Even if something's not required, they should still see if it's worth getting.

Top 25 things to do if you're shooting overseas

1 - Investigate the country's and it's individual region's relevant tax incentives/tax relief.

2 - Talk to the relevant Film commissions who can supply you free with photos, brochures, contacts (i.e. hotels, extra casting agencies, equipment etc.) and any necessary resource guides.

3 - Research other productions that have filmed in that country so to be aware of any problems.

4 - Contact the country's immigration departments to find out the policies for bringing in your cast and crew into the country.

·5 - Hire production managers or co-ordinators who've shot there before.

6 - Hire a local production or unit manager - that speak English.

7 - Hire a location manager who speaks English.

8 - Check whether the cast and crew will need any immunizations or vaccines before they visit the country. Contact the Center for Disease Control @ www.cdc.bov/travel

9 - Make sure everyone has a current passport and that it will not expire during the production (check also that it will also not expire within 6 months even if your shoot is for one month).

10 - Find out about the local country's unions and work with them to ensure their support.

11 - Meet with local authorities to find out if permits are required.

12 - Find a good freight company that specializes in the entertainment industry to handle all your shipping including necessary carnets etc.

13 - Find out if the country of production accepts carnets or if like Taiwan it accepts a different type of carnet.

14 - Inform your own insurers of your filming activities that take place out of the country making sure that you have proper coverage. Remember that foreign workers compensation will kick in if you're filming outside the U.S and bear in mind that you're not allowed more than four people on one international flight (Post 9/11 policy Flight Concentration).

15 - Being in a foreign country, you will need to get local insurance. Make sure you're fully covered. To find local insurance companies, check first with your insurance broker who may have relationships with companies in that country. Bear in mind that in certain countries, if you're not fully covered you can face different procedures e.g. in Spain, you must have the correct driving insurance as otherwise if you're pulled over for whatever reason, you could find yourself staying in jail until it's resolved.

16 - Find out what the local laws are in the country of your production and the procedures if you're pulled over for either speeding or drunk driving.

17 - Find out what the emergency medical procedures are (i.e. such as calling the country's equivalent of 911) and find out where the local emergency medical facilities are.

18 - Find a local doctor/dentist that speaks English.

19 - Secure the services of the necessary paramedics/doctors and fireman for your shoot.

20 - Calculate the local currency conversion and find out where the best bureaus of exchange are for your cast and crew.

21 - Find out if the country is NTSC or PAL - for either your own playback equipment or to recommend your cast/crew to bring their own necessary converters with them.

22 - Set up the equivalent of a Fedex/UPS/DHL account.

23 - Set up an account with an airline and the procedure for shipping dailies if necessary.

24 - Check to see whether you have to form a separate company in that country in order to operate.

25 - Set up bank accounts with the local bank in order to pay your local crew.

Lew Horwitz
Lewis Horwitz organization

FINANCE

Q - What is your job?

Lew - I am the president of a division of the Imperial Capital Bank called the Lewis Horwitz Organization. The division's core business is making motion picture and television production loans.

Q - How are the loans financed?

Lew - Banks loan money rather than invest it. This means that we need to get our money back, so we lend against the distribution and copyright as collateral (so if we have to, we could foreclose on the film). The one thing we do not do is lend against the potential success of the film. That would be an investment and if the film didn't fare well, we might never get our money back. The basic building block of a motion picture loan is pre-sales. We lend against contracts with worldwide distributors. These contracts have a minimum guarantee for the right to distribute that film in a territory. We also use bonding companies to ensure the film will be completed and is guaranteed for delivery.

We also do gap financing. We lend against the value of the unlicensed rights (those that have not been pre-sold). For example, if the film is budgeted for $3m and $2.5m was already in place with pre-sales, the other $500k is the 'gap', the difference between the collateral and the budget. Our limit is 20% of the budget. We have to estimate what those rights are worth and if we believe they are worth $1m, we will lend $500k. The reason we want that much coverage (200%) is because it's only a guess, and this is all discussed and agreed to *before* the film is made.

Currently, distributors aren't paying a lot of money with the world economy being what it is, so 80% of our loans are financed by using three different sources. One would be pre-sales. Two would be gap. And three would be some sort of investment. This could be a straight investment from an investor willing to take a chance, or a subsidy, tax arrangement or co-production. 80% of the films we finance have that third source.

Q - What is the state of pre-sales at the moment?

Lew - Terrible. Buyers are still buying as they need product, but they are paying much less than they have ever paid before.

Q - What are buyers looking for?

Lew - They are looking for theatrical motion pictures. Preferably one the US is distributing theatrically through a major studio. But they can't just buy those films, so they're looking for that type of film with a quality that could go theatrical. That means a good script that looks big on the screen, with more recognizable actors.

Q - How easy is it to sell low budget films of between $1 - $2m?

Lew - It's more difficult today than ever before. There are some distributors that do a wonderful job, but aside from a few companies, if an independent producer decides to produce a film, they will find it very tough to get financing because they will find it difficult to get enough pre-sales or investor money.

Q - Have you found a lot of actors taking pay cuts to work on movies?

Lew - Yes, not as often as is necessary, but there are some actors working for scale where they would usually want millions of dollars. In this case you will have a film that has great opportunity to get financed because the pre-sales should be more than sufficient to cover the budget.

Q - Do trends change from year to year?

Lew - Yes. I came home from Milan a couple of years ago and told my people that everybody wants family pictures. That lasted about a year and a half. By the time the films were made, nobody wanted them! We financed *My Big Fat Greek Wedding*. Nobody wanted that film but it took off because America is a country of immigrants, which is why so many people could relate to it. It was a miracle. Don't think you can do the same. We estimated what we thought the value of the ancillary rights would be and we thought it would be very small. At the time it came out on video, it had done about $240m. Video has added at least another $200m and it's not done yet.

Q - It's a business of unknowns isn't it?

Lew - Yes, and that's what keeps people investing in the film business.

Q - Did people call you with similar films after **My Big Fat Greek Wedding***?*

Lew - Yes and I kept telling them their films will probably not be *'Greek Wedding'*.

Q - How should producers approach you?

Lew - You need to approach a banker with a package - a budget, one or two actors in mind, a director, producer and all the rights that have been worked through with a sales agent. It's too early to talk to you unless you have a sales agent as we want the sales agent to give us estimates of what the value of the rights are, and make pre-sales.

Q - Do you read the screenplay and make creative comments?

Lew - No. We might read the screenplay out of interest, but I believe that's dangerous for a banker because if we love the film, we might make a loan we shouldn't make, or worse, we might dislike the film and look at it negatively rather than trying to find a way to finance it.

Q - If a new producer had everything in place, is there any common problem they may come up against?

Lew - We rely on the completion bond companies to make certain that the film is completed correctly. If the bond company feels comfortable with the producer, that's fine. The biggest problem is first time directors because they may end up with a dreadful film. That's not a problem if we're financing the film with all pre-sales and investments, but if we are financing any gap, we must believe the film will match the script and be commercial. Usually a first time director will have done a commercial or short film. If they've never directed a film, we would be very cautious before saying yes to the production loan.

Q - What is the 'notice of assignment and acknowledgment?'

Lew - That is an extremely important document required by the bank. The 'notice' part is signed by the production company and it goes to the distributor saying, *'I've assigned your contract to the bank, pay the money to the bank directly'*. The 'acknowledgment' part of it says, *'We're the distributor and we acknowledge we are going to send the money to you'*. That document will also request changes in the distribution agreement to provide the bank the most security in getting paid. There's a legal term called 'right of offset'. If producer A has sold a film to distributor B, but then it didn't work out well, and distributor B lost money, we don't want distributor B to withhold money from our film because producer A still owes him money, so the document says they have to waive their right to offset. We also state in the document that there can't be any subjective outs in the contract. In other words, if they don't like the film, they still have to pay for it. Everybody knows about these documents and prefers not to sign them, but they have to be done otherwise the lender has a great deal of risk.

Q - What are the 'inter creditor' and 'inter party' documents?

Lew - The 'inter creditor' is a relatively simple document, an agreement between all parties – say the investor, a UK sale and leaseback, and a bank loan - it would spell out who owns what rights and when money is paid to them. If everybody is in agreement, there isn't generally a problem. The 'inter party' agreement is about sixty pages long and is the same document as the 'notice and acknowledgment' except that it's for a distributor who wants possession of a film first, and it's quite complicated. The studio says *'too bad everybody, we want the film and its rights and then we'll decide what to do with it'* so we have a document that gives us various rights to protect ourselves.

Q - Does the film have to be commercial to be financed?

Lew - *My Big Fat Greek Wedding* was not a commercial film, but we were able to finance it because we had contracts for a sizable amount of the cost. There were no major actors and they kept the budget quite small. The amount they were willing to provide as an investment, and the few pre-sales they did have, allowed us to do a small gap, based upon what we thought the film might be worth. So between our little gap, a few contracts and a small investment, the film was financed, but it needed all those pieces.

Q - What are the most important territories?

Lew - Germany, Italy, Spain, UK, Japan and France. There are many more, but they are the biggest. If you can get a pre-sale for a good amount of money from one of these territories then we feel comfortable with the film because if they're still willing to pay a reasonable amount, then we know that the other territories will too.

Q - What is soft money?

Lew - Soft money is money that doesn't have to be paid back. That would be tax money. The UK sale leaseback, Canadian tax credits etc. None have to be paid back.

Q - Are there a lot of American films using co-productions?

Lew - Almost 80% of the films financed require that.

Q - Is it imperative to have a sales agent?

Lew - If a filmmaker doesn't have a sales agent, we won't look at the material. Sales agents are not easy to get because they want to make sure they are going to get paid which means they have to be able to sell the film.

Q - What should a film maker be looking for in a banker?

Lew - You should only work with a banker that you believe will respond positively to you in the event of a problem, rather than one that will turn around and say, *'sorry, you didn't meet this deadline, you're finished'.* So w hile the banker needs to check out the borrower, the borrower should definitely checkout the banker. The best thing to do is check around with other people in the

Grants and Finance for Feature Films

FINANCE

The AFI (American Film Institute)
2021 North Western Avenue
P.O. Box 279999, LA. CA 90027
Tel: 213 856 7600/7787
Indie Film and Videomaker Program with grants up to $20k.

New York State Council on the Arts (NYSCA)
915 Broadway, NY, NY 10010
Tel: 212 614 2900
Individual Artists Program: 212 614 3988
To provide support that allows artists to create, develop and present new work.
Eligibility: New York resident, no students, artist must find a sponsoring non profit organization to submit an application on their behalf.
Awards: up to $25k per project

The Center for New Television
912 South Wabash Avenue, Chicago, IL 60605
Tel: 312 427 5446
The NEA/AFI Great Lakes Regional Fellowship Program: To assist independent film and video artists whose personal work shows promise or excellence. **MUST be resident of Illinois, Indiana, Ohio or Michigan for 1 year.**
Awards: Up to $15k for total budgets up to $60k.

Texas Filmmakers Production Fund
Austin Film Society,1901 East 51st, Austin, TX 78723
Tel: 512-322-0145
www.austinfilm.org
Supports all genres and hybrids thereof but not television series or multimedia projects on budgets up to $200k. **Must be resident of Texas for 1 year.**
Awards: $1k-$5k cash award, up to $5k in Kodak film stock, $500 in video stock.

Corporation For Public Broadcasting (CPB)
901 E Street, NW, Washington, DC 20004-2006
Tel: 202 879 9740
General Program Review: To support television projects in the research and development, scripting, preproduction or post production stage, or any combination thereof. Emphasis on multicultural and children's programs as programs must be suitable for national PBS schedule.
Awards: up to $250k. One grant offered per quarter.

The Funding Exchange
666 Broadway, Room 500, New York, NY 10012
Tel: 212 529 5300
The Paul Robeson Fund: to support the production and distribution of independent film/videos that focus on social issues, reach a broad audience, respect the intelligence of the viewers, and combine intellectual clarity with creative use of the medium. Must be affiliated with a tax-exempt organization, priority to projects on issues where there are local or national organizing efforts and issues that have received minimal covereage. Write for guidelines and application, available after Sept. 1st.
Awards: $5k-$10k

International Film Financing Conference (IFFCON)
360 Ritch Street, San Francisco, CA 94107
Tel: (415) 495-2381   http://www.virtualfilm.com/iffcon
Matches 60 select indie projects-in-development with international buyers. North American filmmakers are given the opportunity to mix with potential overseas and domestic production partners over the course of the three days.

EQUIPMENT & SERVICES

The Roy W. Dean Grant
Provides goods and services from entertainment industry companies (equipment, editing, duplication, legal advice, etc.) for shorts and documentary films. Films must "be unique and make a contribution to society". You may live anywhere to enter the film and video grants. However, production benefits are only available in New York City and Los Angeles depending on which grant you win. Also offers several screenwriting grants.
From The Heart Productions, 1455 Mandalay Beach Road, Oxnard, California 93035-2845
Email: CaroleEDean@worldnet.att.net
www.fromtheheart.com

Panavision's New Filmmaker Program
Donates 16mm camera package to film projects, including graduate thesis films, of any genre. Highly competitive. Submit proposals 5-6 months before you intend to shoot. Film makers must secure equipment and liability insurance. Send S.A.S.E. to New Filmmaker Program, Panavision, 6219 DeSoto Ave., Woodland Hills, CA 91367-2602

FINANCE

IFP/Chicago Production Fund
Provides up to $85k of in-kind production equipment and services to an IFP/Chicago member with a narrative 16mm or 35mm film, 22 mins or less in length, to be shot in the Midwest. Artist must be a current resident of IL, IN, IA, KS, KY, MI, MO, NE, OH or WI. Projects seeking completion not eligible. Entry fee $25
www.ifp.org   Tel: 312 435 1825   Fax: 312 435 1828

The Oppenheimer Camera New Filmmaker Equipt. Grant
Aim: to support new filmmakers in producing their first serious film project (mainly SHORTS). FEATURE LENGTH FILM PROJECTS ARE DISCOURAGED. The grant awards the use of our Grant Program Arriflex 16SR camera package to senior and graduate thesis students and to independent filmmakers for a scheduled period of time. Proposed projects may be of any non-commercial nature: dramatic, narrative, documentary, experimental, etc. Our expectation is that you are working from your own vision, your own creativity and not for someone else (solely for a profit motive). The program does not support commercials, industrials, PSA's, music videos, or pornography. Please address questions/send proposals to:
New Filmmaker Equipment Grant Program
Oppenheimer Camera, 666 S. Plummer St., Seattle, WA 98134
Phone: (206) 467-8666 Fax: (206) 467-9165
e-mail: filmgrant@oppenheimercamera.com

DOCUMENTARIES

National Endowment For the Humanities (NEH)
1100 Pennsylvannia Ave, NW, Washington, D.C. 20506
Phone: 202-606-8269
www.neh.gov
Provides grants to media projects that present high quality programs that explore the humanities to public audiences. Grants offered for planning, scripting and production of film, television and digital media projects that address humanities themes. Also offers consultation grants to help conceive of new projects.
Planning grants: up to $30k over 6 months to facilitate advisory assistance, travel, research or other preparatory activity that will result in a detailed plan for full production.
Scripting grants: between $60k-$90k for 6-12 months to support the writing of a treatment or script for a 60 min or 90 min documentary.
Production grants: up to $800k for 2-3 years to support the completion of a single program, set of programs or pilot for a series. Fiscal sponsorship required.

California Council for the Humanities
312 Sutter Street, suite 601, San Francisco, CA 94108
Phone: 415 391 1474
www.calhum.org
An independent non-profit organization affiliated with the National Endowment for the Humanities.
Aims: to foster multicultural understanding and strengthen community life by sponsoring public humanities programs that provide Californians with access to the texts and insights of the humanities. Up to $20K grant.

ITVS – Independent Television Services
Phone: 415-356-8383 x232
www.itvs.org
LinCS (Local Independent Collaborating with Stations) a funding initiative that gives producers and local public stations the opportunity to work together. LinCS provides incentive or matching monies to collaborations between public television stations and independent producers. Funding ranges from $10k - $75k. Seeks regionally and culturally diverse projects.
Open Call Round: seeks provocative, compelling stories from diverse points of view an diverse communities. No finished works. Projects in any genre (animation, drama, documentary, experimental) and any stage of production will be considered.

Film Arts Foundation Grants Program
145 9th St, Suite #101, San Francisco, CA 94103
Phone: 415-552-8760   Fax: 415-552-0882
www.filmarts.org
Aim: to encourage new and diverse works by film and video artists who have little likelihood of being supported through traditional funding sources. These awards are targeted for film and videomakers in categories that are among the most difficult areas in which to raise money for media projects.

HBO Documentaries
1100 Avenue of Americas, New York, NY 10036
www.hbo.com/americaundercover.
Send in proposals via US Mail only.

The Pacific Pioneer Fund
P.O. Box 20504, Stanford, CA 94309
Phone: 650-996-3122
www.pacificpioneerfund.com
This fund supports emerging filmmakers from California, Washington and Oregon, which is a person committed to the craft of making documentaries, and has several years of practical film or video experience. The fund does not support instructional or performance documentaries or student film projects. Filmmakers are eligible for only one grant from the Pacific Pioneer Fund during their careers. $1K-10K.

business. It's a small industry. Every banker is known in some manner, whether they are good or bad, conservative or modern.

Q - What fees are involved for a low budget filmmaker?

Lew - Generally, fees are worked out so that the stronger the collateral, the less expensive the loan. As a rule, you'll find films under $3m usually pay 2% over the prime and a 2% loan fee and then the rates go down half a percent every million or so dollars. The gap fee is generally around 7%. Then the borrower will also pay the lenders attorney fees which are generally around $20k unless it's a complicated transaction, then it could be much more.

Q - How long can a filmmaker have the loan for?

Lew - We generally figure that our loans will run for fourteen months. We have an automatic extension for another four months. We charge a certain fee for fourteen months, but if it's necessary to extend it for a further four months, we'll charge a percentage of that fee. Generally we should be out of the loan in eighteen months. If the contracts get larger and the distributors put up some credit to back the contracts, that is the best collateral of all, and then we would give a much lower rate.

Q - What has been the lowest budget you have been approached with?

Lew - We are approached for all low budgets, but we won't do anything for under $1m.

Q - What piece of advice would you give a new filmmaker?

Lew - Talk to sales agents who will tell you what is selling today and what isn't. Unless you have your own money or an investor that is willing to let you do what you want, don't make your first film just because you like the subject. You've got to think about whether the film is commercial for the world, not just any one country. Never try to license the film yourself. Use professionals, whether it be attorneys, accountants, bonding companies or sales agents. Thrillers and action films usually do well but they have to be made with actors that are recognized. The budgets have to match the type of film you are making. To just say, *'I'm going to make a film tomorrow'* does not make sense. But if you can do it, God bless you, it's a miracle.

Creative Capital Foundation

*This national non-profit organization supports artists pursuing new approaches to film and other areas of the arts. Artists can receive grants up to $20,000 for purchasing equipment, attending film festivals, and other projecty related needs. Receiving a grant also places the artist with a mentor to provide advice on completing the project. The stipulation is that that a percentage of any proceeds from the sale of your project must be given to Creative Capital. **One note**, they tend to go for projects that are not intended for commercial purposes. For more info contact:*

Creative Capital, 65 Bleecker Street, 7th Floor, NY, 10012
Tel: 212-598-9900
Fax: 212-598-4934
info@creative-capital.org

Hal Sadoff
Financial Advisor

FINANCE

Q - What could you offer to a low-budget filmmaker with no track record in the $1 - 3 million range?

Hal - The finance companies that I work with deal with budgets ranging from $1m to $100m, and it's unlikely that they'd finance a low-budget, first-time effort along those lines. A track record is the most important criteria for us - we want to know that someone has been through the process before and has a good team around them. At $1m-$3m, it's difficult to finance in today's environment, especially if the project has no big-name stars attached - at that point it stops being a theatrical picture and becomes a television movie. The only way a theatrical movie in that range gets financed these days is through equity financing, or if HBO Films, ShowTime or one of the smaller, independent companies love the project and are willing to step up. Even then, it can still be difficult. Having Tom Hanks' production company behind *My Big Fat Greek Wedding* made it easier for the picture to get made, but they still had difficulties.

Q - What if a first time director has a great script and is working with a more expereinced director?

Hal - We would look to see what the director has done in the past - experience in music videos, commercials, short films or other related field and look at their reel, assess the team they have assembled, check out the DP (if one's on board), see if the producer has a track record of working with first time directors - all those things would be taken into account. A strong reel or short can be a great calling card.

Q - Do you see a lot of actors taking pay reductions to help make a movie?

Hal - Yes. People are realizing that in order to get films onto the screen, films in which they believe, they need to take a pay cut. This is the case now as actors and directors gain more control over their careers by producing as well.

Q - What are the more traditional ways of financing your film?

Hal - In the past, the traditional financing model was a negative pick up, where a studio would put up a payable-on-delivery contract for the whole amount of the film. They'd take the contract to a bank, who would then cashflow the film through to completion. Then the studio would pay the bank on delivery of the film. This then evolved into what's called a split rights deal, where the studio puts up a negative pick up agreement just for the domestic piece of the movie. In the simplest cases, an international sales company would then put up a guarantee for the entire foreign piece, and the bank would cashflow the film against these two contracts. But from there it gets more complex, and you have situations where the domestic backers cover the domestic piece, while the international sales company goes out and covers some of the international piece by making some pre-sales. These two amounts are then added together, and subtracted from the film's budget. The difference remaining then is called the gap. The filmmaker would then approach a financial institution, a bank or other lender, to cover this amount.

Q - What criteria do these institutions take into account when approached for Gap Financing?

Hal - They look at how large the gap is, the overall budget, who the sales agent is, what kind of film it is, the cast and film makers, which territories have been pre-sold and which remain. They will then lend against different aspects of collateral - the negative pick up piece, the pre-sales and the gap piece. Typically, the bank will be approached late in the process, once the film is fully packaged and most elements are in place.

Q - Do a lot of banks deal with media banking, and do any specialize in low-budget productions?

Hal - Yes. The Lew Horwitz Organization and Co-America Bank deal with lower-budget films. The Union Bank, JP Morgan Chase and NatExis Bank look for larger budgets. Producers approach them all the time.

Q - What can a filmmaker do to make the package more attractive to gap financiers?

Hal - Usually some equity in the production is required by gap financiers. Adding in a layer of equity underneath the bank allows them to lend more as they have an equity provider in position behind them. This would especially be the case with a $1-$3m budget, financiers would expect some form of equity in the equation in order to make it work. You'd also definitely need an international sales agent to try and make some pre-sales for you.

Q - What is the pre-sales market like at present?

Hal - It is difficult, you're lucky if you reach the 50% mark. Distributors are not as willing to pre-buy films as they were in the past, so it's a much more difficult state of affairs to get films financed in the traditional, split rights financing model. Pre-sales now happen primarily on films that have names attached, or independents where it's a passion project for a star who's doing it for much lower than normal fees. There are 7-10 major territories to sell - UK, France, Germany, Japan, Spain, Scandinavia and Italy. Buyers are always looking for good material - things that they believe people will go to movie theaters to see or that they'll turn on their Pay TV stations to watch.

Q - If you reach your target number of pre sales, should you allow for more in case you go over budget?

Hal - No, you wouldn't need to because you'll have a completion bond to take care of that. As financiers, we obviously have close relationships with all the bonding companies.

Q - Where do most producers go to raise equity and what form does it take?

Hal - For very low budget movies, you usually approach family, friends and associates. As you go up the scale, studios, indie film companies and financiers come into the picture. The equity itself would be cash or a guarantee by way of credit. The other element that adds into it, and which is especially relevant today, is soft money.

Q - What is soft money?

Hal - It's tax-based funding, subsidies or incentives for shooting in certain locations. For example, there are sale and leaseback incentives in the UK along with tax deals in certain other countries like Germany or Canada. This can amount to a significant portion of your budget - sometimes up to 50 percent. In practical terms, it's money that goes into a production which doesn't have to be fully repaid, or paid back at all. But that's over-simplifying things a little, because a number of the tax deals require a level of recoupment and those giving them do want to make sure they get their money back.

Q - Where can you get good deals on tax benefits?

Hal - Germany used to be massive. It's still massive but it's changing - they're making the deals more commercial. The UK seems to have a growth market for sale and leaseback and other types of tax deals. Hawaii has a tax deal that was used on *Blue Crush* and other films, but it's not that accessible because it's on a per project basis. New Orleans also has a tax deal that hasn't been accessed yet, but people are trying. Canada has incentives for producing there, but not really tax based deals. Australia and South Africa have some tax based deals. If you get a UK distributor involved, they can access all the UK subsidies and tax deals.

Q - How easy are co-productions for lower budget films?

Hal - It's difficult because a co-production means involving different countries, all of which will be looking for potentially different commercial things. It gets easier if it's a specific story related to that particular country or there's an actor or director involved who's local.

Q - How often does it happen that a film has a theatrical distributor attached?

Hal - Not often, and when it does, there are questions to ask - like whether they are contributing towards the production or the advertising costs? Or do they just want product to release? All those factors have to come into play.

Q - Is it difficult for quirky, eccentric independent films to find a place in the market?

Hal - I define an independent film as one that's not fully financed by a studio. Studios are looking more and more to outside sources of financing and for product that they can distribute, so as we move forward, making 'independent' films will become easier. I do think independent films are becoming more mainstream as a result, though.

Q - Should new filmmakers concentrate more on commercial movies?

Hal - I think if they want to attract finance they should do that, but 'art house' movies still have a place. There is a dividing line between art and commerce. I've always been on the financing side of the business and I always look towards commerce, but I think there still should be an art form and that shouldn't go away.

Q - How do you like to be approached by a producer?

Hal - The elements of a good package are a track record, a script, a budget and a potential cast list. If a script comes with two main people behind it, we can act in an executive producer role and help put the project together, and while we assume that the legal side is in place at this stage, if we decide to really get involved with it, then we do the full legal diligence. I like people to e-mail a summary or send a package with all the details of what they've put together, however we normally don't take on unsolicited projects. We respond to agents or managers that we know. We could spend all day looking at unsolicited projects from people we don't know.

Q - Do you read the screenplay and make creative comments?

Hal - It depends on the role we play in the project. When I was at the bank and we played a purely financial role, no, we wouldn't look at the script. But if you're investing in the movie, taking a role in international sales and putting the movie together, you are effectively acting as an executive producer, and in that case we would get involved creatively.

Q - What would your advice be for new filmmakers seeking private investment?

Hal - If you go out for a large private placement, it has to be sanctioned by the SEC and you need a formal document and proposal, but if you just ask a few people, you don't have to do that. For low budget movies, you need to approach people who you know, who believe in you and who have excess money that they are willing to put at risk when there's a chance they could lose it all. That's how a lot of fabulous independent movies have been made.

Q - What would your general advice be to new filmmakers?

Hal - Apprentice yourself to someone who has a track record in the industry. Learn from people who've done it before. Just coming in and doing it yourself is possible, and a lot of people have found success that way, but now so much money is involved, having experience is more important than ever.

Q - What common mistakes have you encountered?

Hal - Filmmaking has always been something you have to believe in - the dream. That's the excitement of it - but there are a lot of people who aren't realistic about the harsh environment of filmmaking today and don't realize how hard it is to get films made when you have no star and you're working with a small budget.

FINANCE

Greg Trattner, Maureen Duffy, Matt Warren
Film Finances, Inc

Q - What is a completion bond?

Greg - It is a guarantee to the finance provider that the film will be completed on time and on budget. If a film exceeds it's budget, we would pay any over budget costs or, if we fail to deliver and the distributor rejects the film because it's late, we would then have to pay the financier back whatever that distributor was going to pay for the movie. Banks rely on us to evaluate and to put our money where our mouth is. Studios do require them, but they mostly self bond on the bigger movies.

Q - How does it work?

Greg - We would hear about a project through either a producer or a bank who's considering financing a film. Assuming we sign off on a production basis, we would look at the legal documentation and negotiate with the producer's lawyers and the bank's lawyers. The producer's lawyers would look at the completion agreement that basically gives us our take-over rights, obligates the producer to film and produce the film according to the budget, script and other guarantees.

Matt - Our business is to help people make their films. We look at everything as something that we hope we can bond. But, we do ask if we feel confident that the script and the people involved in making the film can work with the limits of the schedule and budget to complete the delivery requirements. If yes, let's move forward.

Q - What is the lowest budget you've bonded?

Greg - Usually $1m. Our fee is a percentage of the budget and we need to charge a minimum of $30k. We don't really accept budgets lower because it is uneconomical, so although we can go as low as $600k, we don't recommend it.

Q - How is your fee calculated?

Maureen - There's a 10% contingency with a few exclusions; financing fees, overheads and our fee. Our fee averages at 2.5%.

Q - What do you need from the producer to start with?

Maureen - The script, the budget, the schedule and resumes of key personnel. Copies of everything they've got really makes it easier for us and more helpful to the production.

Greg - On a legal side we'd need to see the chain of title, the financing and distribution agreements and the agreements for the key talent and producer, actor and director and the general insurance production and confirmation that all the actors are covered for illness and accidents.

Q - What information do you require from the producer once the feature is up and running?

Matt - Everything that comes out of the production office such as updated schedules, call sheets, each day's production report and weekly cost reports. We have our own database here where we track all the films and their schedules. We talk to the line producer and accountant on a daily basis during the shoot, just to see what's going on. We visit the set at least once, and if it's a show in town, then we go several times. If they're in Bulgaria, then we go less often. It's important for us to know what's going on because in our business information is everything.

Q - When would a guarantee be called in? If an actor dies perhaps?

Greg - Our primary responsibility to the financiers is to get the film completed and delivered to the distributor. If there were some calamity such as an actor's death, that should be covered by production insurance. However, if the project was simply going over budget, we could exercise control over the film, eventually putting money in to get it finished.

Q - Would you bring in other people to finish the film – would you fire the director?

Matt - Ultimately, we have that right, but it would be in an unusual situation. Everyone goes to great lengths to make the film happen and not bring the bond in, and that should include the director.

Maureen - I've seen directors go pale when I've been introduced on set. Production relies on us as we've seen almost everything that can go wrong, so if you're smart, sensible and honest and tell us what you think the problems might be, we can try and catch you before you fall.

Greg - People know we have take-over rights, so they think we're cold-hearted, but as we do about 250 films a year, so we've seen almost every problem there is, and we have people who can help solve problems.

Q - Do you expect the crew to have worked on bonded films before?

Maureen - If they've never worked with us before then we try and surround them with people we have worked with so we have a safety factor. It's best if the key positions (line producer, production manager, accountant and 1st A.D.) are people that we have worked with. We would not bond a film if we had not worked with the crew before and the producers refused to bring in people we suggested.

Q - What else would ensure a refusal to bond a film?

Matt - Mostly if the plan itself is flawed and we don't think it's doable, given the budget and schedule and all those things we talked about earlier. Some people have unrealistic expectations of what they can do with a certain amount of money and that's when we say *'we've been down that road before, you're gonna need this, this and this'.*

Some producers have a finite amount of money so they either have to cut down what they want to do or they have to get more money. Usually it's easier for them to cut down. It is rare that we'd get to a point where we'd walk away. Everyone wants to be reasonable.

Q - Are there a lot of digital films?

Maureen - There was a flurry for a while but it's a small percentage with budgets between $1m and $5m. Everyone thought it would be the next big thing, but it hasn't really panned out that way.

Q - Has there been anything that's come up with digital films that hasn't come up before?

FINANCE

Finishing Fund Companies:

Frameline Film and Video Completion Fund
$2-3k grants for the completion of documentary, educational, narrative, animated and experimental media projects about or of interest to lesbian, gay, bisexual and transgendered people and their communities. No funds available for script development, research, pre-production. (Funded $15k for 'Hook By Crook')
www.frameline.org/fund   info@frameline.org
Phone: 415-703-8650   Fax: 415-861-1404

NAATA (National Asian American Telecommunications Association) Open Door Completion Fund
Awards post production funds to complete Asian Pacific American film and video projects that have the potential for national public television broadcast. A full length rough cut must be submitted. NAATA funds must be the last monies needed to deliver the broadcast master. Average award: $20k.
www.naatanet.org   mediafund@naatanet.org
Phone: 415-863-0814 ext.106

Women in Film Foundation Finishing Fund
Eligibility: All independent producers and non-profit corporations are eligible to submit proposals for completion funds as an existing film or video. Projects in development or pre production will not be considered. No student projects (graduate or undergraduate) will be considered. Los Angeles residency for CFI award only. A substantial number of the creative personnel involved must be women, project must be in progress and for the Loreen Arbus Award, must treat issues of disability. Grants: Unrestricted cash grants of up to $5k or furnished in-kind post-production services for the CFI Services Awards of up to $25k. For the Loreen Arbus Award – up to $5k in completion funding.
WIF Foundation, C/o Administrator/WIF, 6464 Sunset Blvd., Suite #1080, Los Angeles, CA 90028.
www.wif.org

Solaris Entertainment Finishing Fund
Set up by Greg and Gavin O'Connor (Tumbleweeds) to support fellow indie filmmakers who seek financial and technical resources necessary to complete their films. Solaris Completion Partners will provide capital to complete post-production on three to five independent features each year. They'll provide expertise and be instrumental in the film's promotion, festival strategy and sales strategy. Looking for: daring and original feature length fiction or non-fiction films that are told with strong distinctive voices.
144 Franklin Street suite #1, NYC, NY 10013
Phone: 212-343-7400   Fax: 212-343-2437
or
710 Wilshire Blvd, Suite 414, Santa Monica, CA 90401
Tel. 310-395-4588   Fax. 310-395-4083
funds@solarisentertainment.com
www.solarisentertainment.com

Hart Sharp Entertainment / True Film Fund
Past movies: You Can Count On Me / Boys Don't Cry. Does NOT accept unsolicited material.
380 Lafayette Street, Suite #304, New York, NY 10003
Phone: 212-475-7555   Fax: 212-475-1717
www.hartsharp.com

Echo Lake Productions
Funds films either on the production side or finance side (providing bridge, gap and finishing funds) for independent features for an arthouse, niche theatrical release. Directors must have directed before. For full funding, apply with summary first, then they will see the project's attachments (director and cast).
213 Rose Avenue, 2nd Floor, Venice. CA. 90291
Phone: 310 399 9164 Fax: 310 399 9278
contact@echolakeproductions.com
www.echolakeproductions.com

Maureen - Yes. The main thing is that the filmmakers don't seem to regard the digital tape as negative, which is very important. We've had quite a few debates with producers about storing that tape as negative. For us it's collateral.

Greg - The bank always wants to have the security of the negative and original elements. These are usually stored at the lab which gives a pledge holder agreement that states that nobody can remove those elements without the bank's permission.

Q - Is there anything in your agreement that producers or directors should be aware of?

Greg - The distribution agreement is often overlooked - if you're delivering a film to Disney by a certain day, there's a delivery schedule and various items that they require. Frequently those items aren't budgeted for, so when we're finalizing agreements with distributors, we have to double check for those things. You must get the cast insured and cleared medically before shooting. We run into that problem every time. The key issues with the talent would be to make sure that there aren't any stop dates or unreasonable approval - which allows the talent to walk away if they don't like the script or another aspect of production.

Maureen - It's a tough physical thing for a director so they should be in good shape before they start a film.

Matt - A lot of directors don't realize that their job is about making decisions all the time. Every person on the crew will ask for their opinion and it can be a little overwhelming. That's why it's important to have the experienced A.D. and DP with a first time director. Someone who can prep and help with their decision making process.

Maureen - Post production seems to be a black hole in pre-production. Nobody really prepares. We make them do a schedule and figure it all out. They never do. They're very optimistic.

Q - What advice can you offer new filmmakers?

Maureen - You can focus on making your movie if you have a first-rate accountant, production manager and line producer - they take care of the physical stuff and you can concentrate on what's going on behind the camera with the director. Hire experienced people that a bond company have used, or check the people out before you hire them, get three references. Physical production is so difficult and making deals is hard, so you really need somebody who knows what they're doing.

FINANCE

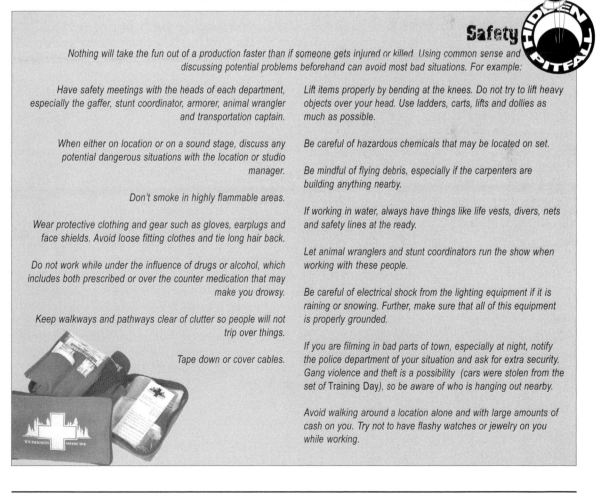

Safety

Nothing will take the fun out of a production faster than if someone gets injured or killed. Using common sense and discussing potential problems beforehand can avoid most bad situations. For example:

Have safety meetings with the heads of each department, especially the gaffer, stunt coordinator, armorer, animal wrangler and transportation captain.

When either on location or on a sound stage, discuss any potential dangerous situations with the location or studio manager.

Don't smoke in highly flammable areas.

Wear protective clothing and gear such as gloves, earplugs and face shields. Avoid loose fitting clothes and tie long hair back.

Do not work while under the influence of drugs or alcohol, which includes both prescribed or over the counter medication that may make you drowsy.

Keep walkways and pathways clear of clutter so people will not trip over things.

Tape down or cover cables.

Lift items properly by bending at the knees. Do not try to lift heavy objects over your head. Use ladders, carts, lifts and dollies as much as possible.

Be careful of hazardous chemicals that may be located on set.

Be mindful of flying debris, especially if the carpenters are building anything nearby.

If working in water, always have things like life vests, divers, nets and safety lines at the ready.

Let animal wranglers and stunt coordinators run the show when working with these people.

Be careful of electrical shock from the lighting equipment if it is raining or snowing. Further, make sure that all of this equipment is properly grounded.

If you are filming in bad parts of town, especially at night, notify the police department of your situation and ask for extra security. Gang violence and theft is a possibility (cars were stolen from the set of Training Day), so be aware of who is hanging out nearby.

Avoid walking around a location alone and with large amounts of cash on you. Try not to have flashy watches or jewelry on you while working.

John Manulis
Visionbox Pictures

ALTERNATE WAYS

Q - How did Visionbox start?

John - It was set up by a number of working filmmakers who felt there was something missing. Every time we worked, we felt like we needed a support system, expertise outside our own that we could tap into. There's a lot of knowledge out there, some people are good at some things and others are great at other things, and we wanted to take advantage of that knowledge and experience. I was a buyer at Samuel Goldwyn for six years, so I'd seen the business from the side of *what was* and *what was not* being made. There were some good films that were not getting made because the filmmakers had no clue of how the market worked. Often they thought they needed more money than they did to make the film, whether it was a lack of knowledge or ego I don't know, but I saw a lot of people coming in saying *'I've got $1.5m but I need $3m.'* I knew how to make their film for $1.5m, so I figured stop chasing money and start making films! That's where Visionbox started. Our motto is whether you deal with a $5k film, or a $5m film, most things are possible with the resources you have, if you know how to marshal your talents and resources. If you come at them with the right philosophy, limitations are opportunities, as long as you are not dogmatic about what you need and you are flexible and creative.

Q - How does a filmmaker submit their project to you?

John - Our website has information about that (www.visionboxpictures.com). We ask for a synopsis, and if we like it, then we solicit a script and go from there. Our goal is to keep it as open a process as possible. We don't run a development operation, so this is our solution for people who don't have agents to get to us.

Q - What are you looking for in the script?

John - A concept that feels marketable, a strong writing and directing voice, so that something about the piece will be distinctive. We're looking for voices that are film festival and critic friendly, strong and distinctive but buried within a commercial idea. I like to see films that have the body of a moviestar and the soul of an artist, metaphorically. *In The Bedroom* for instance, included a suspense genre element which raised it from being a small, but still potentially wonderful movie, to being commercially successful. The inclusion of a commercial element makes a big difference. I look for pieces that play to a niche audience - gay and lesbian, black, Latino or Filipino audiences for instance - where you can target a community so that a film without stars has something else to offer. I also look for films that have an elevating element, something that takes the basic story, changes it and raises it to another level. A small film came into me a couple of months ago from an established director who wanted help doing it as a $1m film. It was a fraternity film like *Porky's* and was very personal to the writer. It could be done, but I knew it would be more unique if, for instance, it was about the black fraternity as that story had not been told before. If he changed that, he would have something fresh and marketable. Because it was a personal story, he did not want it to go that way.

Q - What is the most important element?

John - It's all about the end game - distribution. You want the critics to love it and you're looking for free publicity, so we look for elements in a movie that are going to galvanize that free publicity. There's a lot of free publicity out there, but you need things that are note worthy, or things that people will want to write about - it could be an issue, a person or the filmmaker. The end game for me is getting the film seen. Why spend two years on a film if it's never going to be seen? Theatrical distribution is seen as the holy grail, but it isn't necessarily the case financially. We want people to see the work, whether that's through DVD, cable or another medium. Then the question becomes bringing some savvy to the risk reward ratio, so people are investing the amount they are likely to get out. If you hit a home run, you all make money, and you're happy and the film goes further, but you want to protect the down side in a practical way. I encourage people not to go into movies half funded, but at the same time I know people will. In order to sell your film, there are significant costs which may be more than the cost of actually making your film, costs everyone assumes distributors will pay for, and they may not. They don't think about delivery costs, marketing costs, the cost of taking a film to festivals and the cost of dealing with selling it there.

Q - Does shooting on DV make any difference to the quality of a movie?

John - The US is more accepting of digital films than the rest of the world right now. In terms of pre-sales, digital will either kill you or produce a 50% loss of value. When you've finished your film, it's not an issue at all. Audiences have proven over and over again that whether it's grainy black and white, 16mm or DV, as long as the story is strong, audiences will be there. Every one of our films has either gone theatrical or sold internationally, that's everything from MiniDV to HD productions.

Q - What format would you recommend now?

John - I choose camera platform based on the aesthetic needs of the movie, not on the budget - it's what will best serve your story. People always want the 'best' camera and it's not necessarily the best choice for their piece, so we try and help them find the medium that suits their needs best.

Q - When is HD appropriate to use?

John - If you're shooting vistas outdoors or in the daylight hours, HD has more capacity to work with those images. If you're shooting interiors, or untrained performers, the smaller camera systems might be better. However, it's all starting to blur as the HD camera systems are getting better and better. Hi Def produces a crisp image and, depending on the camera system, it can often produce a colder, less human image than film. As we do this every day, we can offer advice on camera systems to use. Often, the more important choice is not the specific camera but more the post production facility, and specifically, the colorist. This is the person who can create the 'look' that the film maker wants. You should 'cast' your post-production as you cast the actors in your movie, but most people don't do that and just take the cheapest route. Having the right post production team is going to seriously affect the look and sound of your movie.

Q - Isn't it more expensive than shooting on film?

John - Shooting HD is comparable to shooting 35mm, and more expensive than shooting on S16mm. We still find people saying *'I'm being given this camera for free so that's what we will shoot on'*, and yet that choice of camera is what will lock you into a post production route that may be expensive. For instance, if you shoot HD, you will need to down convert your work so that you can 'offline edit' it, and that's expensive. Most people don't realize that down conversion is one of the most critical parts of your puzzle. If it's not frame accurate, it can lead to disaster later on.

Q - Are there any film look processes that you can use when shooting on DV?

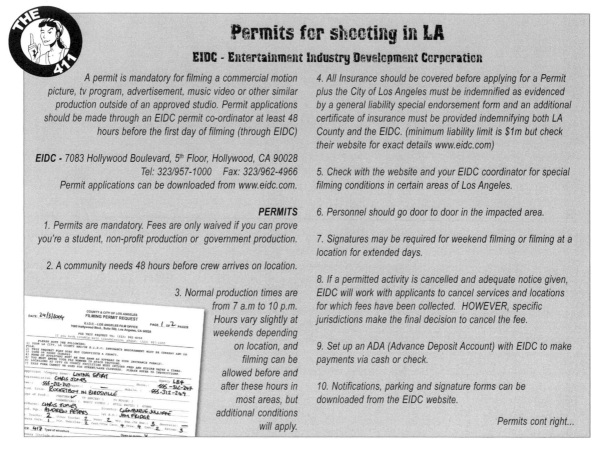

Permits for shooting in LA
EIDC - Entertainment Industry Development Corporation

A permit is mandatory for filming a commercial motion picture, tv program, advertisement, music video or other similar production outside of an approved studio. Permit applications should be made through an EIDC permit co-ordinator at least 48 hours before the first day of filming (through EIDC)

EIDC - 7083 Hollywood Boulevard, 5th Floor, Hollywood, CA 90028
Tel: 323/957-1000   Fax: 323/962-4966
Permit applications can be downloaded from www.eidc.com.

PERMITS

1. Permits are mandatory. Fees are only waived if you can prove you're a student, non-profit production or government production.

2. A community needs 48 hours before crew arrives on location.

3. Normal production times are from 7 a.m to 10 p.m. Hours vary slightly at weekends depending on location, and filming can be allowed before and after these hours in most areas, but additional conditions will apply.

4. All Insurance should be covered before applying for a Permit plus the City of Los Angeles must be indemnified as evidenced by a general liability special endorsement form and an additional certificate of insurance must be provided indemnifying both LA County and the EIDC. (minimum liability limit is $1m but check their website for exact details www.eidc.com)

5. Check with the website and your EIDC coordinator for special filming conditions in certain areas of Los Angeles.

6. Personnel should go door to door in the impacted area.

7. Signatures may be required for weekend filming or filming at a location for extended days.

8. If a permitted activity is cancelled and adequate notice given, EIDC will work with applicants to cancel services and locations for which fees have been collected. HOWEVER, specific jurisdictions make the final decision to cancel the fee.

9. Set up an ADA (Advance Deposit Account) with EIDC to make payments via cash or check.

10. Notifications, parking and signature forms can be downloaded from the EIDC website.

Permits cont right...

John - As independents, we don't know how our films will be distributed. But, the more you plan for the way you think your film is going to release, the better. If you're pretty sure you're going to have a theatrical release, you're going to get your film look by going to film anyway. If you think it'll sell straight to video or cable, you're going to want to start thinking about how you can achieve that 'look'. We don't do any of it in camera as we believe you should capture good, clean, neutral images. The tools that are available in post production are very powerful, even at the desktop level. So shoot clean images and create the 'look' in post. Digital may be inexpensive to capture, but it's expensive to fix as you're in a high tech world. We do tests throughout the entire process on every film. The filmmakers figure out what look they want for the film and we figure out how we want to get it there. Psychologically, because you're not going to see the film look for a year, we also do tests for the investors so they can see what it will look like. The last thing you want is your financiers to get nervous.

Q - Can you shoot on film and then post produce digitally?

John - Yes, you can shoot on 35mm or S16mm and then transfer that footage onto a HD medium. You never touch the negative again. You assemble the film in a HD world, you color correct and create the visual look of the film in a digital world and then do a digital to 35mm film transfer so that you end up with a 35mm neg from which you can make prints for theatrical release and festivals. We've started doing it on super 16mm now and it's very successful - 16mm is inexpensive, you're still shooting on film with a DP (so won't need to spend time and money mimicking film later), the cameras are small and portable, you can shoot a lot of footage. It's more expensive than shooting purely digital, but it's less expensive than shooting 35mm.

Q - Should you shoot 16:9?

John - In digital, we never shoot with a hard matte (letterbox) and we don't advocate shooting 16:9 anyway. Despite the many claims that you're wasting pixels, the truth is you are not wasting enough to matter. These films are going to spend the majority of their lifetime in a 3:4 format on television or video, and to get to a 3:4 format from 16:9 is a big blow up. So you'll be making a less attractive image for the bulk of the audience of your film if you shoot with a hard matte or in 16:9. I know that in the UK and Japan, TV is being filmed and broadcast in 16:9, but it's not a reality in the US at the moment, and probably not so for some time.

Q - Do you distribute films as well?

John - No. People bring us finished, or almost finished films, and they want help in accessing distribution rather than for us to distribute it.

Q - Is there a certain stage where you'll provide the finishing funds?

John - A finishing fund means you should be close to being finished, but for us, it is still investing in an incomplete and potentially unfocussed project. The further along you are, the more likely you are to be able to get funds. Instead of using our imaginations to figure out what this piece is going to be like and making that investment early, we come at it when people are up against the

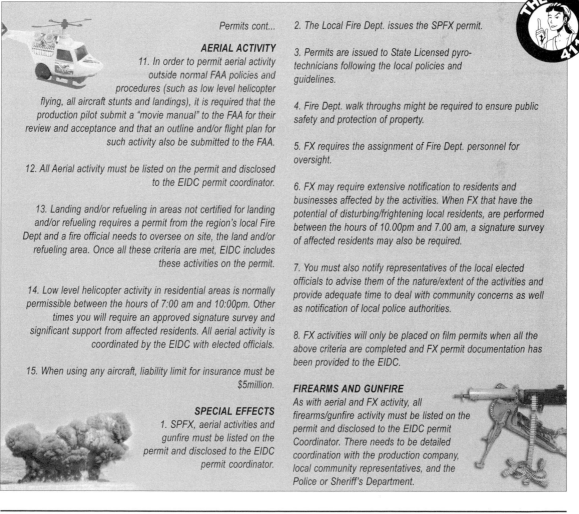

Permits cont...

AERIAL ACTIVITY

11. In order to permit aerial activity outside normal FAA policies and procedures (such as low level helicopter flying, all aircraft stunts and landings), it is required that the production pilot submit a "movie manual" to the FAA for their review and acceptance and that an outline and/or flight plan for such activity also be submitted to the FAA.

12. All Aerial activity must be listed on the permit and disclosed to the EIDC permit coordinator.

13. Landing and/or refueling in areas not certified for landing and/or refueling requires a permit from the region's local Fire Dept and a fire official needs to oversee on site, the land and/or refueling area. Once all these criteria are met, EIDC includes these activities on the permit.

14. Low level helicopter activity in residential areas is normally permissible between the hours of 7:00 am and 10:00pm. Other times you will require an approved signature survey and significant support from affected residents. All aerial activity is coordinated by the EIDC with elected officials.

15. When using any aircraft, liability limit for insurance must be $5million.

SPECIAL EFFECTS

1. SPFX, aerial activities and gunfire must be listed on the permit and disclosed to the EIDC permit coordinator.

2. The Local Fire Dept. issues the SPFX permit.

3. Permits are issued to State Licensed pyro-technicians following the local policies and guidelines.

4. Fire Dept. walk throughs might be required to ensure public safety and protection of property.

5. FX requires the assignment of Fire Dept. personnel for oversight.

6. FX may require extensive notification to residents and businesses affected by the activities. When FX that have the potential of disturbing/frightening local residents, are performed between the hours of 10.00pm and 7.00 am, a signature survey of affected residents may also be required.

7. You must also notify representatives of the local elected officials to advise them of the nature/extent of the activities and provide adequate time to deal with community concerns as well as notification of local police authorities.

8. FX activities will only be placed on film permits when all the above criteria are completed and FX permit documentation has been provided to the EIDC.

FIREARMS AND GUNFIRE

As with aerial and FX activity, all firearms/gunfire activity must be listed on the permit and disclosed to the EIDC permit Coordinator. There needs to be detailed coordination with the production company, local community representatives, and the Police or Sheriff's Department.

FINANCE

THE 411

wall, but they can show something of what it's going to be - sometimes just scenes, but now with desktop editing, we tend to see full assemblies. For the most part, people tend to need help going beyond the rough cut stage, whether they need an editor or support with sound and picture finishing. I am a fan of directors doing some of the heavy lifting of editing, digitizing, assembling, logging, even if they are not an editor, but they are investing in their own work that way. One of the nice things about the desktop systems is that we can spend time with it. A director can work with us for six to eight months and not feel pressured to get it done too quickly. We recommend that the director walk away from the project for a little time and then come back to it with a new perspective, a luxury that's not available in the studio world.

Q - Do you deal with documentaries at all?

John - Certainly on a service basis. But in terms of producing, only if we think it has award caliber. Unless you are going to be nominated for an Academy Award, it's very difficult to find a profit path in the US.

Q - What is Visionbox's Lab?

John - Michael Kastenbaum established the lab as a discovery zone for new talent to test their boundaries and nurture cool ideas. Our intention was to explore all subjects and formats, such as live action, animation or shorts as inventive personal films shot with micro budgets, giving the filmmakers creative freedom and basic resources and consultancy. The filmmakers would be their own driving force on their own projects. However, fewer vendors are giving stuff away any more so it's becoming much harder to do these cheaply now.

Q - What do you think about writer/directors, and actor/directors?

John - I'm a big believer in writer/directors as you can judge them from their script. I am open to actor/directors because they can bring in their 'known' friends, the talent. Again, it's about relationships. It's important to have someone feel like it's their baby, who's driving forward and writer/directors tend to be more invested in it. Producers are very suspect in LA, they are treated like the enemy.

Q - How much do you charge to get involved?

John - It's a sliding scale based on the budget, the smaller the budget, the more profit participation we get as we're basically an investor in the film. We can be involved at all stages, even through sales and distribution.

Q - If you were dealing with a filmmaker who was making a $15k movie, could you still do it?

John - It takes the same energy to make a $15k film as it does a $50m film. So we look very seriously at all projects, especially the small ones. We consider how much time we have, and then decide if we can take it on. It often depends on if we really love it. We also look at the market and decide what we're going to be able to do with that film, and how the investment will be paid off.

The main pitfall new filmmakers fall into is neglecting to figure out the structure *after* you've finished your film. We have the advantage of being able to evaluate our participation based on what happens after the film is completed.

Q - What are the common mistakes you have encountered?

John - Buying into the marketing hype which is *'pick up a camera and make a film'*. It's a great copy line for marketing and for the camera manufacturers, but it's just not true. It's a complicated process and the technology is changing every day. The pieces don't fit together smoothly - camera, editing, post, sound, film - all are different aspects.

NORTH OF THE BORDER - SHOOTING IN CANADA

Many US film productions have been lured to Canada primarily for financial reasons as producers can save tens of thousands (and, in big budget films, hundreds of thousands) of dollars. One contributor is the favorable exchange rate between the US and Canadian dollar. The other involves substantial tax credits offered by the Canadian government once the production is completed. Creatively, most of Canada can double as a US city (Toronto for New York City) or areas of the United States and Mexico (Western provinces look like Midwestern US and central Mexico) so that the film does not lose much aesthetically. Here are some things to know before you venture north.

Canadian content

A tax credit can be offered at the federal and provincial level if a film has a certain percentage of Canadians working on the project in all areas. Structuring a production so that it meets Canadian content guidelines requires extra effort and legal cost, so get a good lawyer who can get it right the first time. Also, if the film is Canadian content or a co-production with a treaty country, then some post-production must be done in Canada. You can do it elsewhere, but you will not get the full benefit. Contact Canadian Audio Visual Certification Office (CAVCO) for more details.

Production Service

If you do not qualify for Canadian content (usually this is for foreign producers), you can still get some budgetary relief for using Canadian labor (16% of labor costs returned). Contact CAVCO for more details.

Union versus Non-union

The Canadian unions are not as strong as they are in the United States, so making non-union films there is easier. Although SAG and AFTRA operate in Canada.

Deals

Summer is the busiest time in Canada because the weather is the best. If you can get away with it, try shooting in the fall or winter and you will be able to get better deals.

Film Festivals

These are great places to meet Canadian producers who can guide you to the best resources. Toronto International Film Festival, Banff Television Festival, Montreal World Film Festival and the Vancouver Film Festival are some of the top ones.

Telefilm Canada

Offers Canadian producers financing and certification of treaty co-productions as well as networking opportunities.

Canadian Film Commissions

Each province has its own film commission who can assist you with resources and guide you in many areas such as financing referrals, selecting locations, securing permits, finding crew, dealing with police and the military, etc.

Information provided by:
Laura Polley, Independent Film Financing, The Balfour Building, 119 Spadina Avenue, Suite #304, Toronto, ONT M5V 2L1
phone - 416-598-3270   fax - 416-598-5045   email - film@iff.ca

FINANCE

Be aware of the market and how it works. Get a mentor who doesn't have to give you a huge amount of time, but someone who's active in the business, who can give you a sense of perspective, of market reality, not just about budgeting, acting, cameras and editing etc. but the things that really make a difference, about finding your audience and therefore a distributor. Things that must be thought of early on in the process. Of course, everyone wants to be in production as it is fun, but the rush to production can be damaging and you often regret that a year and a half later.

What new filmmakers don't realize is that out of 3,000 submissions to Sundance, 125 get accepted, and out of those 125, only 5 or 6 get bought. And of those, one sells for $1.5m, another couple sell for $500k and the other one doesn't sell for any advance, it just gets distribution. So the market realities are very intense. They can be depressing, but you can be forewarned and therefore forearmed. The more you know the better off you are. Knowledge is power.

One of the pitfalls on low budget films is that a great deal of the process is not glamorous and therefore it's hard to get people to do it for free. It's easy to get people to show up on set for two weeks, three weeks is harder, four weeks and you'll probably have to switch crews. It's even harder to get experienced people to do it for free. It's also hard to get people to edit and to do sound. They are the only people you can't get on freebie deals and they are the most critical people.

Q - Sound is often ignored on a low budget movies?

SOUTH OF THE BORDER - SHOOTING IN MEXICO

Our neighbor to the south has attracted some major productions recently - Titanic, Deep Blue Sea and The Mexican are just a few of the many high profile projects that have been shot in Mexico. One reason for this is that he cost of labor in Mexico, combined with the strength of the peso and some tax benefits, allow a production to save up to 35% of its budget. In addition, Mexico's varied terrain can substitute for just about anywhere on Earth! The Mexican Film Commission can help you with the necessary info on locations and permits (they even offer a CD of locales for $40). Here are some facts to know in advance:

When shooting in government buildings and premises, it is necessary to obtain the appropriate permits in advance.

Permits for archaeological and historical sites(like Mayan ruins) are under the supervision of the National Institute of Anthropology and History.

Shooting on federal highways and roads requires a permit from the Federal Highway Police. They are able to block or divert either vehicle or pedestrian traffic, or temporarily remove any road sign.

For filming in natural areas you must have a permit issued by the Ministry of the Environment, Natural Resources and Fishing (Secretaria del Medio Ambiente, Recursos Naturales y

Pesca - SEMARNAP), through the Coordinating Unit for Protected Natural Areas (Unidad Coordinadora de Areas Protegidas) of the National Ecology Institute (Instituto Nacional de Ecologia).

Mexico´s beaches and territorial waters are under the jurisdiction of the Ministry of the Navy (Secretaria de Marina, SM). You must also notify the Port Authority and Naval Zone of where you wish to shoot.

One downside of shooting in Mexico is that the main language is Spanish (although many Mexicans are bilingual), which can cause problems. Consider partnering with an experienced Mexican producer or a domestic production company (or, find a friend who speaks fluent Spanish) to help when negotiating deals with workers, unions and cooperatives. Mexican legislation obliges film production companies to hire personnel of unions registered in the Ministry of Labor and Social Welfare, STPC and STIC. Contact the Mexican Film Commission for more information.

National Film Commission Mexico - Ave. Division del Norte 2462 - 5th. Floor, Mexico City 03300
phone (5255) 56 88 78 13
fax (5255) 56 88 70 27
conafilm@prodigy.net.mx
www.conafilm.org.mx

John - Yes, and sound is more important than the image. Unless you're doing a very particular type of film, the image quality is not what's going to make a difference. The film could be out of focus in parts, but if you can't hear it, you can't sell it. And low budget films are mostly talkie movies. Inevitably, I see people burning up tremendous angst and creative energy micro managing issues about the quality of their image, their problems 'in the frame', none of which matter in the world of distribution. The story, the heart, and the sound will matter.

Q - What advice would you give new filmmakers?

John - Think about your audience. Everyone you're asking to get involved with later on is going to be thinking about the audience, so identify an audience that is inclined to pay attention to this film for one reason or another, as opposed to just hoping they're going to like it. Audiences need to step out of their way because of something in this film. You need to know how to address your package to accomplish that.

Secondly, don't be shy about going after people with experience to be involved, whether you're hiring them or for a flexible relationship. If you can bring together some sort of mentors or advisors, or a combination of technical experts, they will stand you in good stead. And lastly, get an attorney on your team early to make sure you're protected!

Production Books

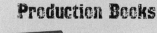

The Industry Labor Guide
by Jette Sorensen

A 1st AD staple, this is a compilation of rates and working conditions for union and guilds in the film, television and commercial production industries in the United States and Canada. Gives you a great idea of how much to budget for every possible crew member, just about anywhere in North America.

The Complete Film Production Handbook
by Eve Light Honthener

Focuses on the day-by-day details of film production. The author developed this book from her own professional notes from working on many films over the years. Includes information on pre-production tasks, establishing company policy, insurance, dealing with actors, music clearance, visas and customs, and much more. Includes reproducible forms for just about every situation.

Independent Feature Film Production
by Gregory Goodell

A straightforward account of what it takes to make a feature film. Thoroughly researched and expertly compiled information on all aspects of filmmaking, from financing to production to post-production to distribution and marketing

The Filmmaker's Handbook
by Steven Ascher & Edward Pincus

An excellent resource and an extremely in depth book on the technical side of making your movie. A must for any filmmaker - a great tool.

FINANCE

John Schmidt
ContentFilm

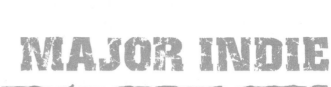

Q - What is ContentFilm and what was it set up to do?

John - We're an independent film production company, based in New York City, created by myself and Ed Pressman, with a focus on high quality, independent films at the lower end of the budget spectrum, that is around $5m and under. We have a head of production in NYC and in LA, and we have one in London. We have a network of friends and colleagues across the business who know who we are and what we stand for, and they send us stuff all the time.

Q - How do you like to be approached by a producer?

John - We like to look at projects that are as close to ready to go as possible. We are not into development or multiple rewrites. We like to find scripts that are not just polished but have a director attached. In each case in terms of the films we have green lit and how that dovetails into our philosophy, we've bought into both a script and a director's vision of how to get this film made, with what elements and in what kind of style. They have to approach our production folks with as much ammunition as they can muster. Honestly, a cold submission is hardly going to be noticed. The projects that get our interest are those that have a filmmaker attached that sparks our interest because he or she has done some kind of outstanding work, if not in film, then some kind of other medium. Or if it has somebody else attached in the form of talent that we find provocative. We're very eclectic. So far we have done comedies, dramas, romance, psychological horror. We're interested in everything. Currently we make 5-8 films a year.

Q - Do you like to have cast attached or can that be a hindrance?

John - We're delighted if there is cast attached that we're excited about, and if there is no cast attached, then we're pro active in helping to bring the right people to the project. At the budgets that we work with, we have greater freedom to cast our roles as perfectly as we can, rather than with the most bankable star.

Q - How did The Hebrew Hammer come about?

John - John Kesselman made a short film at USC that was quite successful and the script came to our office here where it was read, liked and then passed on to me and Ed. We thought it was hilarious and unique. We sat down with John to explore whether he wanted to option it and go the high budget Hollywood route, or if he wanted to cast this with us, and make it with us at a price which he was excited about doing, and we were excited about doing with him.

Q - With your film The Cooler, the producers managed to get big stars attached, how was that achievable?

John - William H. Macy had read *The Cooler* and loved it, but he declined to commit to it because he was doing some bigger projects and was moving in a different direction. We were fortunate to be able to sit down and talk to Bill and his managers and, I wouldn't say we convinced him to do the project because he was very attracted to it, but I'd say we got him across the hump because he knows Ed well from earlier films and we told him we're going to finance this, we'll make sure that you're treated well economically and that we're going to put all our energy and expertise into making it as good as it can be and get the best distribution deal it can. One of the great benefits of having a strong financial underpinning like we do at Content is that when you say you're going to make a movie, people actually realize that you are, and that has a lot to do with actors such as Bill Macy and Alec Baldwin saying *'if you need me for four weeks in May, okay, I can do it'*, rather than saying *'if we get the money together we'd like to have you.'*

Q - Does it matter to you what format you shoot your movies on - either film or DV?

John - No, we're interested in allowing the director to use the tools that are right for the film. We did start as a digitally focused company but found that the savings are focused in post production, and that's available whether you shoot on 35mm or DV. So *The Cooler* was S35mm, *The Guys* was 35mm, *Love Object* was S16mm, *Hebrew Hammer* was 24P and *Party Monster* was DV. So it's all over the map.

Q - Can first time filmmakers approach you?

John - Yes, a first time filmmaker who at least has a track record of short films, perhaps commercials or music videos, particularly strong film school work, those are important. We worked with Wayne Kramer, then a first time filmmaker who did a brilliant job on *The Cooler*. Wayne was an established writer and a tremendously knowledgeable follower of cinema. He had an articulate grasp on how he wanted to direct the film. He had story boarded scene by scene, walked us through that and convinced us that he was not just capable, but was very talented. We also worked with John Kessleman, another first time filmmaker who did a brilliant job on *The Hebrew Hammer.*

Q - Did the decision to shoot The Cooler on Super 35mm cause more problems?

John - No, we decided three weeks before shooting when Wayne came to us and said, *'this is why I want to go S35mm'*. He talked about shooting in the casino and having Macy and Baldwin two shots and having a great deal of the casino atmosphere in the background because of the aspect ratio. He cited other films that I didn't know were Super 35mm, like *Reservoir Dogs, In the Bedroom* and *The Usual Suspects,* not what you'd think as high budget films but very well crafted independent films. The impact on the budget was $150k and given the stars we had attached, and the sense that we thought we'd have a film that broke out of its budget bracket in terms of how it looked, it seemed reasonable.

Q - What was the budget?

John - Just under $5m, but it looks like a $15m movie. All of this stemmed from the classic high quality approach that Wayne took in making it, and was captured in the decision to shoot it S35mm. Whereas in a film like *Party Monster*, DV was perfect. It's a pop, bright, colorful look that is appropriate. The lowest budget film we have is $750k.

Q - Do you have any tips for filmmakers on how to keep their budgets down? For instance, if you have a $1m movie, where do you find that most of the money ends up going?

John - Most of it needs to go into the physical production and post production. You've got to minimize everything you can above the line through striking the best deals you can. The other cost items such as story and rights from a first time filmmaker should somehow be absorbed into the back end, then you've got as much money as you can for the shoot and post production to get a good, well mixed product out the other end.

Q - Making a film on a budget of $750k, is it union or non-union? Have the unions ever been a problem?

John - No, they haven't, because our philosophy is to talk to the unions and tell them what we're doing, and tell them what our cash budget is, and in that context, there's usually some work for people. Union crews are the best crews around so it's not a factor of union or non-union.

Q - Do you think it's easier to make more of a hard hitting drama when shooting DV than on film because there's less risk as you're spending less money?

John - No. I think that you might be making projects that otherwise might not get made, but those films might just as quickly be forgotten. The ability to do something adventurous and original and exciting is just as often accompanied by a directors desire to do it on film than it is by having a iconoclastic belief that it has to be done on DV.

Q - Is it hard to compete with exhibitors who deal with higher budget films if you've shot on DV?

John - It is. We're not in the distribution business, we're in the production business. We make our films as best as we can and bring them to the market. My previous business was in sales and distribution so I know it well, and it's an extremely crowded and difficult market. P&A and publicity is expensive. Holding screens is expensive. But when a movie comes along that people want to see, it's the same old story. You can't keep them away. Films that come out of left field without a great deal of hype and catch a critical wave, then catch an audience wave.

Q - Do you believe that with DVD distribution there are more outlets for the independent filmmaker?

John - Yes. I think independent filmmakers should take comfort and be conscious of watching how the home entertainment and DVD market continues to evolve, because there's a tremendous direct to consumer video business that is thriving. It is mostly dominated by obvious niche players like children's video and exercise videos for instance, but the high quality independent film audience can also be reached this way. It's not yet obvious as to how this will happen but I think it's going to become more and more viable.

Q - Would you say there is more of a market for the lower budget Digital movies on the East Coast? Are there any distinct differences between the two coasts?

John - New York's film community benefits from New York's center as a theater community, and also it's a diverse and politically minded city. It's appreciation for European film is decades old. Everyone knows that when you have an independent film that works, it'll do more business in New York than in any other market in the country.

Q - What are the common mistakes you've come across with new filmmakers?

John - They'll do anything to get their film made and I can't find fault. There's so much blood, sweat and tears, so much sacrifice that when it comes to first time filmmakers and getting these films made and what they go through, I have nothing but admiration for them. It's so tough and so many films get made each year against all odds.

Q - Any advice to new filmmakers?

John - Don't give up.

Shooting in NY - The MOFTB

The Mayor's Office of Film, Theatre & Broadcasting (MOFTB) is the central clearinghouse for production in New York. All productions, must go through them to obtain free permits and services to assist them in public locations throughout most of the city's five counties. When your project is shooting at an exterior location and requires traffic control, re-routing, work in the street, or a scene with guns or uniformed police, you must have the special NY Police Movie and TV Unit on the location. The police unit will assign its officers at NO CHARGE to you. All decisions on what is permitted are made by MOFTB, working in close consultation with the Police Movie & TV Unit, and other key city agencies as necessary. Filming in city parks, interiors within city buildings, bridges or tunnels will require additional permissions from the controlling entities. Please call the MOFTB to obtain specific contact information.

To be Eligible

You must present to the MOFTB, an original certificate of insurance (check http://www.nyc.gov/film for details about insurance amounts, language and other requirements). Students working on student films must obtain a letter from their school, on the school's letterhead, stating the student's name, status as a student (i.e. full-time, in good standing,) date(s) of the shoot and the signature of the appropriate representative from the school.

Permit Time Schedule

1. Very simple shoots of 1 or 2 days, or shoots of longer duration which are walk-and-talk, and are not working in the street, do not require police assistance. It is possible to get a permit for this type of project 24 hours before shooting, providing the insurance certificate and permit application are presented in good order before NOON of the day before shooting.

2. All feature films, television movies, series or specials, elaborate exterior commercial shoots and music videos doing exteriors with celebrities, multiple locations and/or playback, must have a pre-production meeting with the MOFTB. It's recommended that this meeting be scheduled with the MOFTB about 3 weeks before shooting, but must be scheduled no later than 5 business days before shoot begins.

3. The outside deadline for all permit issuance is by noon of the day before any shoot on a Tuesday through Friday and by 5 p.m. on the Thursday before a shoot on Sat/Sun/Mon.

4. The agency is as flexible as possible when emergencies requiring a schedule change on the day before a shoot, but emergency changes should always be called into both MOFTB and the Police Unit as the first priority.

5. The permit provides special parking privileges at working locations for vehicles essential to your shoot, such as equipment trucks, lifts, cranes, campers and honeywagons. Crew or personal cars are not covered by the permit. You must follow the MOFTB regulations that are given for this process. You may also be eligible for a scouting permit during pre-production.

Special Permissions

1. Any children under the age of 16 years must, by New York State law, have a Permit to work in a film or television production from the Child Performer Permits Unit, a division of the city's Administration for Children's Services agency. A minimum lead time of 48 hours is required. The parent or legal guardian is responsible for obtaining the child's permit.

2. Pyrotechnics, fire effects and explosions, including simulated and other smoke effects, at both ext and int locations, require prior inspection and supervision by the NYC Fire Department.

3. Exceptional requests (i.e. removing a lamppost, building a stage) may require additional permits from another city agency. MOFTB will advise you as to who to contact in these cases.

Special Jurisdictions

There are a few frequently requested locations within the city which are under the jurisdiction of other governmental bodies and are NOT available on the MOFTB permit, and require special permits.

Subway Stations, Trains and Buses

In order to film scenes involving the use of subway stations, trains or buses, you must make arrangements well in advance, from 1 to 5 weeks or more, with the Metropolitan Transit Authority. The Transit Authority's Special Events Unit will provide you with an estimated cost for your request. Other divisions of the MTA provide access to Grand Central Station and the Metro North and Long Island train lines. Also the Port Authority arranges all shoots at all airports, the PATH trains to New Jersey, certain piers and the Lincoln and Holland Tunnels to New Jersey.

For any location sites not directly available through the MOFTB permit, the agency has extensive contacts and will support your requests. This includes the MTA, the Port Authority, government buildings, parks and landmarks under state or federal jurisdiction, as well as many, key privately owned locations such as the Rockefeller Center and most non-profit institutions which have relationships to city government such as the American Museum of Natural History and Lincoln Center. When you start pre-production, they will provide additional details, and will work with you to anticipate and resolve any problems that may arise.

MOFTB - Mayor's Office Of Film, Theater & Broadcasting, 1697 Broadway, Suite #602, New York, NY 10019 Phone: 212-489-6710 Fax: 212-307-6236 www.nyc.gov/html/filmcom

FINANCE

Chris Hanley
Muse Productions Inc.

MAJOR INDIE

Q - What is your background?

Chris - I was always interested in photography, music and art dealing in New York City. The movies that I was into were considered to be fiercely independent, like Fellini's *Satiricon* or Bergman's *Seventh Seal*, and later John Waters' *Pink Flamingoes*. I didn't really separate an art house film from an independent film from a studio film. When *Star Wars* came out, it was cool. I liked *Blade Runner*, Fritz Lang's *Metropolis*, these appealed to me as much as *Casablanca* and *The Wizard of Oz*. I came out to LA in '92 with Vincent Gallo, when there was a recession and everybody was depressed in New York. You could meet anyone in California if they thought you had money, unlike New York. Films like *The Crying Game* that brought Miramax into the forefront were just starting. I knew all about competing for book rights from my literature and philosophy degrees so I ended up with the more controversial movies, like *Secret History, The Killer Inside Me, American Psycho,* and Jeff Eugenide's *The Virgin Suicides*. The studios wouldn't touch *American Psycho* which to me was interesting and available.

Q - How quickly can you break into the industry as a producer?

Chris - I think it takes about five years if you're just starting out as a producer. If you're a young director that captures reality in a certain way you could end up being recognized overnight. In my business I get a reasonable property at a reasonable price, go out and find the director, actors and get it financed. I'm not always trying to figure out what's going to multiply the investment and the negative cost, but I try to fill the cast up with highly recognizable names so that I can get the movies financed. That's not the only way to make a movie, but our budgets aren't $200k. The lowest I've done is $800k. We shot that digitally. That was called *This Girl's Life*. James Woods plays the Parkinson's disease inflicted father of a web cam porn girl. We just did one with Adam Goldberg directing called, *I Love Your Work* and he rounded up Giovanni Ribisi and Christina Ricci. We managed to get Famke Potente, Vince Vaughn, Josh Jackson from *Dawson's Creek* and Jason Lee - so some great names.

Q - Was the last film you did on digital also the first film you had done on digital?

Chris - Yes, however we do shoot behind-the-scenes on digital. It is nothing new, but this one was Hi Def and we could shoot slow motion in camera with the two Panasonic cameras we had, unlike the current Sony cameras. You can do it digitally afterwards, but the resolution isn't quite as sharp. We didn't save much money shooting HD digitally though, unlike if you shoot DV.

Q - Does it make any difference to the actors whether you shoot digitally or 35mm?

Chris - Some actors are more aware of the difference between digital and 35mm than others. If they look at the dailies they get the aesthetic and their acting is pretty consistent.

Q - Is there much shooting on Super 16mm here in NYC?

Chris - You can shoot more film on 16mm as the cameras are smaller, although if you're shooting in LA above $1.5m, it really should be union, so 16mm v 35mm v digital become irrelevant. I grew up with TV so to me, digital looks like reality. To others it might look psychedelic, because of the colors.

Q - Is it hard to get recognition after making your first movie?

Chris - You can shoot a movie and send it into festivals to get recognition from the film community or the public. I thought *Freeway* was going to launch director Matt Bright in the exact same arc as Tarantino. He did fine, but didn't become Tarantino as a director.

Q - What is the studios' attitude to the small independents?

Chris - The studio system was set up to track what's popular in terms of the demographics, so it has to filter everything. The kind of criteria the studios use to determine whether or not they are going to green light a project is the value of the cast and director. This tends to go completely against low budget filmmaking and upstart filmmakers. They keep them at the bottom of the pyramid. However, at a certain point, the value of directors like Baz Lurhman or Paul Thomas Anderson, or actors like Kirstin Dunst or Reese Witherspoon becomes so significant that the studios have to take advantage of it. There's a balance of having to accommodate new filmmaking just to make the major stuff work. Ultimately, that's where the big directors come from. Some, like David Fincher, just jump right through. Plenty of times, a first time director will get a $40m movie. PT Anderson's first movie was called *Sydney* and was maybe one of his best films. It wasn't expensive, but the next thing was *Boogie Nights*.

Q - If you have an idea that's off the wall, will the studios tend to disregard it?

Chris - Guys like Harvey Keitel and Terrence Malick can do anything at any level. Todd Solondz has a project that is proving very hard to finance, but as it depicts the sexual life of a woman in her early teens, it's just not something that will be financed and it won't ever be a studio picture.

Q - It seems that everyone is looking for fresh talent these days?

Chris - People in Cannes said *The Pianist* was 'okay'. These films get a half baked reception in Cannes, then blow up when they get released and the public take over. *Secretary* was in Sundance, there was a bit of a buzz on it, then it got three independent Spirit Award nominations and the director is suddenly recognized. It didn't explode into some big huge thing, but it was very solid and it shows how powerful the buzz at the festivals can be.

Q - Some new filmmakers try to make studio movies for money rather than films they are passionate about?

Chris - Yes, I believe that it's better to have a story that tells something about real life, or depicts something deep, passionate, interesting, captivating from your own life experience that is worth spending time on. I can't imagine why anybody would sit there, like an ad agent, and try and figure out what should be made in order to succeed. One would hope you have a story that you're passionate about and want to tell. Some people try to do a studio movie and 99 out of 100 fail. You could try to do a few cool movies and get a great reception. Vincent Gallo knew what he wanted to do on *Buffalo 66*. A lot of it was drawn from his own life. His mother really did only have one photo of him and was obsessed by the Buffalo Bills and he hadn't spoken to her in 6 years and Steve Buscemi really did drive an ice cream truck and had been in the fire department. Now he wants to do *Queer*, one of the Lynne Burrows' books. He's got the screenplay going and I don't think he's thinking about whether the studios are going to think of it as a genre movie.

Q - Did you have the book Virgin Suicides?

Chris - We bought the rights to make the motion picture from the novel. Originally, we had Nick Gomez directing who did *Lawsuit for Gravity* and he put together a screenplay, but we just weren't getting the actors. Then Sofia Coppola put together her own screenplay without even knowing who owned the rights to the book, she just felt like doing it. Then she came over and said *'I really, really want to do it'* so I said, *'well, if you want to split the development with me, I guess we can cast it between you and me',* so that's what we did. No one else wanted to split it with me. We were pretty happy with the result. We were lucky that we had Kirsten Dunst and Josh Hartnett when no-one knew that their careers would be so illustrious. It's budget was about $4.1m.

Q - What would you say about the independent market today?

Chris - It's as difficult as it's been in ten years because most economies are not that strong. The United States is having the best box office years they've ever had but almost none of that is independent filmmaking. There are very few established producers. When I go to the studios, I get a lot of *'no's',* but that's not because there's lots of people before me. I feel that this independent work that we do doesn't really fit into the system. The advantage we have is that we are some of the only people that get their calls returned. It's just hard to get the green light on projects.

Q - Can a new filmmaker approach you directly?

Chris - We get 100 emails and five scripts a day. I can't read them all but I read every draft of screenplays that we're financing. If an email just says *'query',* I delete it. I get four or five an hour during business hours and they are just screenplay synopsis and I have no idea what they are. I have a tendency to go for people that already have a following. I know Vincent Gallo can get me the actress I need, but even Vincent or Steve Buscemi started somewhere with nothing at all. Wilder La Sanchez who wrote *Spun* made it. He was just a methadone addict from Portland who had a crumpled up, completely non-standard format screenplay in his hand. The garage door was open and Tim Pedenel, who works with us, was standing there and Wilder said, *'Hey, is this Muse?'* and somehow got Tim to read it and then I read it and it was like real life - you don't see real life very much. Everybody else is trying to figure out how to write a screenplay that's some kind of genre.

Q - Do they never send an e-mail with a pitch?

Chris - They do but I can't read them all. Some people say, *'I'm not really a screenwriter',* but they want to draw my attention to their story. If it's some hot shot film student guy with a genre thing, he's going to get recommended by somebody. I don't have rules for getting me to read something. There was this guy, Eric Fieg, who called me up and said he wanted some advice. He said, *'I've got this little project and I've got a good writer and we're going to shoot in Wilmington and I wondered if you could help me out'.* I gave him a couple of names. So he shot the movie and it was, *I Know What You Did Last Summer,* so suddenly Eric Fieg is a bigger producer than I am!

Q - Is it hard to get independent films into theaters?

Chris - New Line, Fox Searchlight, Miramax, Newmarket, they do it for sure. But they wait until you've finished the movie - they truly hit the independent theaters. We have the US rights for the French film *Irreversible,* and Lion's Gate is putting it in theatres in thirty-five cities. I don't know that many people that can do that.

Q - Would you recommend new filmmakers tie the distribution end up to begin with?

Chris - No, they won't be able to. We can't set up the North America deal until the film is cut and has music. They won't buy it in advance as it costs too much to put it in the theaters, so if it looks like something they can only make money on video, they won't buy.

Q - Are the unions ever a problem on low budget films?

Chris - I know that the chairman of the East Coast council knows my name really well. Sometimes we sneak productions through without them being union, but there are times when we just can't make the budgets work. The biggest problem is that the crews have to be bigger than you want them to be. I have to have a five person art department, a five person camera department and so on, and I don't need it. Vincent Gallo just made a movie with three or four people. He has his own camera, his own truck and Nagras and microphones and he pays them well. My lowest budget movie, the $800k one, we filled up an entire block with trucks. The police had to block the roads and this was super low budget. If you have a train of trucks, the union has every right to ask what you're doing.

Q - Is it easy for a new filmmaker to get hold of an actor like Steve Buscemi?

Chris - No. It's hard. Christina Ricci and Steve Buscemi have been in lots of movies but they've turned me down on three or four movies. It depends if Tim Burton or the Coen Brothers are about to use them.

Q - Any advice for new producers looking for finance?

Chris - There are professional people who want to get into the film business and have money to invest. Also look for subsidies - Louisiana, Puerto Rico, London, Canada, anywhere where there are tax breaks. But, that tends not to work where the budget is $1m. It's better if it's above that.

Q - What common mistakes do you notice with new filmmakers?

Making movies on Credit Cards

Robert Townsend did it with 'Hollywood Shuffle'. Spike Lee did it with 'She's Gotta Have It'. Even Kevin Smith's 'Clerks' was financed primarily on plastic. Seems like a good way to go - especially with all those pre-approved, low/no interest rate, free balance transfer applications in your mailbox. And, if you sell your film (which, we all hope you do) you might escape the daunting possibility of owing $15k at 18% APR. However, the majority of low budget filmmakers who do go down this route of financing will find themselves in just this predicament. So, a word of warning: one thing you really don't ever want to do is destroy your credit rating. This will take years to correct and not only damage any chances of raising money for the next film, but also make it difficult for you to rent that apartment you need to move into when the production office or set closes and they take your cot away.

Chris - You have to have a talent to visually present the drama. A lot of great cinematographers start with documentaries. Mary Harring who did *American Psycho* did BBC documentaries and is known for her knowledge in music, which is one of the reasons she handled the music side of *American Psycho*, kind of merging it with some of the murders. My advice is just to write the dialogue or story. It doesn't matter if it's in the right format. There was this stripper in a club who told me she had written a screenplay based on her experiences of making her way up from Miami to New York stripping, and I said, 'wow, what an amazing story that would be. Here's my card'. It never arrived. My advice is just do it. Don't talk about it. It helps if you're a real person and not trying to figure out how to be one.

Michael Nilon
CAA

THE AGENT

Q - What is an agent's job?

Mike - To get actors jobs in motion pictures and film and negotiate their contract.

Q - Do you act as a buffer between the performer and production company?

Mike - Yes. I am the liaison between the two.

Q - What are the benefits for the producer to come to an agency?

Mike - You can get better deals as there's a common goal. I don't think *The Hours* would have been made in the same way if we hadn't represented Stephen Daldry and all three of the actresses, so it made it much easier. However it makes sense not to limit yourself to one agency. There might be someone perfect somewhere else.

Q - What would be the best way for a producer to approach you about hiring one of your clients?

Mike - Call me up. I prefer to talk to someone rather than just receive a script with an offer without notice.

Q - How soon before principal photography would you expect to be approached?

Mike - Anywhere from a few days to as much as a year. There are a lot of people we represent that help make the movie happen, so a lot of the time we would be approached early on.

Q - What's the typical turnaround for a decision?

Mike - Sometimes they need an answer in 24 hours and they make that perfectly clear. On average, a week to two weeks, depending on where the actor is and whether he is working. At certain points when actors are working, they won't read other scripts because they want to focus on what they are doing. Sometimes production companies are okay to wait indefinitely for the actor.

Q - Do you read the script before handing it on?

Mike - Typically, I won't give a script to a client until I can give them an opinion on it, usually that opinion has come from having read it, or from someone I trust who has read it.

Q - If you don't like it, do you still have to pass it on?

Mike - Yes. We're paid for our opinions and if it's something that we don't respond to, we have to say so and why. There are times when clients have arrangements with agents where they say, *'you read it first and if you don't like it, don't send it to me'*, because they are swamped, but in general it's your responsibility to pass it on.

Q - What's your usual response if a film is low budget?

Mike - There are many elements that will convince an actor to do a low budget film. How much will they get paid? Who is the director? Who are the other actors? What is the quality of the script? When and where does it shoot? Budget is just one factor.

Q - What are the main concerns of an actor on a low budget production?

Mike - On a larger budget production they will have a degree of comfort and stability. They tend not to be as well cared for on smaller budgets, although this is movie specific as some people have had wonderful experiences on low budget films.

Q - If the budget is very low, what can a producer do to make it more appealing?

Mike - Sell the strengths of it. If you have a director that has done something before, (it doesn't have to be features, it could be theatrical direction), use that as a selling point and don't publicize the weaknesses.

Q - What are the main problems with low budget productions?

Mike - Inexperienced producers usually have a tough time through no fault of their own. It's difficult to get people to pay attention and take you seriously. What I want is someone to give me the straight scoop - *'we don't have all our money'*, or *'we're not sure where we're shooting'* and do it in a way that's clear, focused and easy to deal with. Some people are under the impression that they should play fast and loose and say, *'we have all of our money together'* or *'this person is doing the movie'*. That happens far too often and helps no-one.

Q - Would it be a good idea for producers to come down and meet you?

Mike - Absolutely. Producers should say, *'I want to come up to the office to sit down with you for five minutes'*. If they just want to sell themselves and the project, that's a good idea.

Q - What is your bad experience of a low budget production?

Mike - I've been in situations where the clients have worked hard preparing for a movie that collapses because the producers weren't playing it straight.

Q - Do you handle the contract negotiations yourself?

Mike - Yes, but it's usually with business affairs executive here or with the client's outside attorney.

Q - How do you determine your client's quote?

Mike - Agents try and base it on the most the client has ever been paid and producers try and refute that.

Q - How are payments made to the actors?

Mike - In equal, weekly installments.

Q - Does the producer have to put it into escrow?

Mike - On independent films, that's what we prefer. I have a client who's doing an independent now. We asked the producers to put all the money in escrow before he got on the plane. It turned out a portion of the money went into escrow and gets paid out every week in advance, but the main danger is that he may not get paid on time.

Q - What is a per diem?

Mike - That's what an actor gets per day in terms of spending money on set. It's usually anywhere from $53 a day which is the SAG minimum up to thousands a week.

Actor Deals

1. Actors Fee - Union SAG minimums are dependent on budget, and on a no quote, favored nations deal. Some agents/actors may request a Pay or Play Deal once a shooting date is established. With this deal, you MUST pay the actor, in full, for his or her services whether the project is either delayed or never shoots at all. You don't want this!

2. Points - Many agents/actors will request points, that is a percentage of the gross or net of the movie. Make sure this is based on NET receipts i.e. after repayment to investors and any taxes etc. If there's a chance to get a huge star / director attached to your project, you can offer them gross points. They will then get a percentage of first dollar monies.

3. Looping / ADR / Pick ups – Make sure your actors are contractually obliged to do these.

4. Nudity - There may be a no nudity clause in actors' contracts. If nudity is called for in the role, it's important to let the actor know before any audition / interview. There may be certain requests or demands if nudity is required, i.e. a closed set, no photography, whether body doubles are used etc.

5. Credit billing - Who gets top billing? What order is your billing? Do you get an upfront credit? What about poster billing? Alphabetical is always the best.

6. Editorial approval - Some agents / actors may request this, however unless it is a huge star, don't give it up.

7. Rest Periods - SAG has requirements concerning breaks for your actors, which are different for adults and children, and different for shooting on sound stages and on location. Also there are regulations to bear in mind, such as if your actors are traveling to the location by air. Consult SAG first.

8. Publicity - Make sure that your actors are contracted to do the press junkets when the film is released, which could be years after the shoot!

9. Perks - An actor may request certain items, such as their own trailer, their own staff, special meals etc. This will obviously increase your budget but you must weigh whether the actor is worth it to your film. Per Diems (daily pocket money), although a perk, are common.

10. Title - Some actors may agree to do your film if you give them a producing credit, either as executive producer or co-producer or producer.

Q - What are the main areas in a contract you'll be looking to nail down?

Mike - The main areas are pay, the work period and the billing. Then there is the perk package - how many plane tickets will they get, do they get an assistant? What's their trailer going to be like?

Q - Can actors request their own make up artist?

Mike - Absolutely. I would consider that part of the perk package, especially if it's a woman who stars in a movie where she has to look particularly pretty.

Q - What is a pay or play deal?

Mike - If a deal is unconditionally pay or play, they have to pay the client even if the movie doesn't happen.

Q - Do you solely represent actors or do you work with directors too?

Mike - It's almost primarily actors. I work with a couple of directors and some writers as their talent contact. I don't get them jobs.

Q - How does your commission work?

Mike - It is 10%.

Q - What is your response to non-union films?

Mike - Not good. I don't know if there are any exceptions, but that's one of the first questions we ask. One of the guilds has to acknowledge it and then we try and get a pay or play. Those are the first two things we address.

Q - There are so many Guild low budget agreements available now, it must be possible to find one to suit an ultra low budget film?

Mike - Sure. If you wanted to be a SAG signatory, I believe it wouldn't be all that difficult. You can make SAG movies for hundreds of thousands or less. It is something you should do just in terms of dealing with agents.

Q - What is favored nations?

Mike - It means no person's deal is better or worse than anyone else's. It is used a lot in low budget films.

Q - What can a producer do to make your life easier?

Agent or Manager? Large or Small?

Getting representation is the golden fleece for the filmmaker in Hollywood. But, what kind and how large of a company to go with can be confusing. Here are some pointers to help you refine your decision.

AGENCIES

Large agencies (ICM, CAA, William Morris) have a lot of power and a lot of clients. That is good because your agent can get your work to any producer anywhere, get you a meeting with almost anyone, get your project to their major talent and fight for you to get paid fairly. The downside is that you are one of many and unless you are a marquee client, you will not get all the attention of one who is. Also, you may get placed with a servicing (younger) agent, who has less clout and experience. These agencies usually will not take chances with first time filmmakers unless they have major heat such as doing well at Sundance.

Smaller agencies (Gersh, Paradigm, Innovative) have less power and fewer clients. You will get more attention from your agent, but they might not be able to get your script to as many producers, actors or directors as the larger ones. However, they will fight just as hard for your compensation. They are more open to first timers, but still wary.

Boutique agencies are very small and only have a handful of clients. They take chances on first time writers and directors hoping that they will stay with them if they break big. You will get plenty of attention, but the larger players in town know that their clients are inexperienced or of a lesser quality and don't take them as seriously as the larger agencies.

MANAGERS

Managers are another way to go. They come in large, small, and boutique varieties and the good and bad points of those types are the same as the agencies. However, there is one key difference between the two.

Managers can be producers, agents cannot by law. As such, managers tend to collaborate with their clients more, thereby potentially making a stronger piece of work. They become personally involved in your project and will fight for it harder.

Finally, because agents want to package projects with clients from their agency, you might want to consider a manager who is not tied to such thinking.

Both managers and producers take commissions from what you earn. Both take 10%.

Mike - Have all of the information and give it to me straight. It's good to know how to speak to agents, hopefully the agents know how to speak to producers as well. You don't need to pitch the movie or over hype it, just be smart and respectful.

Q - Would you tell a producer not to be put off approaching named actors with low budget projects?

Mike - You have to realize that a lot of times it's a very hard sell. You shouldn't be put off by it. There are certain actors that won't do them, but if you really believe in your project and your director, you should make your case. Paul Thomas Anderson got Tom Cruise in *Magnolia*.

Q - What advice would you offer a new filmmaker?

Mike - If you're making a low budget film with an actor who will take little money, try and involve them in the process early. A lot of them have production companies and they like to be part of the process. I've had clients benefit tremendously from doing independent films and it's launched their careers. If you really have something that's worthwhile, don't go into it with a defensive position, go into it with full confidence and if it is that good, you will get noticed.

Rosalie Swedlin
Industry Entertainment

THE MANAGER

Q - What is your job?

Rosalie - I'm a manager/producer at Industry Entertainment and my job involves managing my clients' careers as well as opportunities to produce. I work with writers and directors in partnership with their agents. There's a lot of overlap between the work of an agent and that of a manager, but in a market place that is increasingly fragmented, where very few films are financed by a single source and fewer films get made, many clients have gravitated towards adding a manager to the mix of their representation. What we try to do is fill in the gaps that agents are increasingly unable to fill because of the pressure and workload that comes with handling a large client list. In the same way as an agent, a manager will formulate a long-term strategy for her client according to the direction that the client wishes her career to take. I was a slow convert to the idea of management at first. I was at Creative Artists Agency (CAA) for ten years, then formed my own production company. After 4 years, I went back to the agency world at ICM. In that intervening period, the business had shifted and I found I was hearing my colleagues talking about managers and thinking why does the client need them, if I'm doing everything I'm supposed to be doing? But it became apparent that the work of an agent had become much more transactional: deal making, booking, and signing. The pressure to sign is so great that if you're handling sixty clients - which a lot of the top agents handle - you can't possibly provide the hands-on attention needed for the client. The way I like to work with clients is something that I can do more effectively as a manager.

Q - Would you recommend new filmmakers to look for a manager or agent?

Rosalie - That depends on the individual. Sometimes, an agency is reluctant to take on someone at an early stage in their career, although things go in cycles and sometimes it depends upon whether it is the chic thing of the moment for an agency to look at a short film or a commercial director's reel. Working as a manager and having been inside two large agencies, I think if you choose the right, well connected manager at an early stage in your career, you will benefit from the attention and focus that you will be given. If you are a filmmaker who intends to be self-generating, someone who will consider external assignments, but prefers to create your own material, a manager can be of use whether it's instead of, or in addition to, an agent. If a writer intends to be purely an assignment writer with no ambitions to produce, direct, or crossover from one medium to another, then they may be better off with just an agent. As managers, we try not to put ourselves in a competitive position with agencies. We are a different kind of representation that's complimentary to agency representation. There are all kinds of advantages of having both a manager and an agent but in the end, every commission a client pays is money out of her pocket. Nevertheless, I've rarely been in a situation where the client didn't feel that there was added value to my involvement with her career.

Q - What would you be looking for in a new filmmaker?

Rosalie - An original voice, a distinctive way of telling a story, a style that feels unique. Everybody's looking for a style that's very showy, but I've seen some very remarkable filmmaking where you don't see the director's hand at work. I always look for something that is either visually arresting or that moves me. With writers, I tend to look for someone who can tell a story in a distinctive way. When I pick up the phone and say I really want you to meet this writer, someone you've never heard of, I hope my credibility is such that I can get people to pay attention.

Q - If somebody comes to you with an idea for a low budget film, what is the usual response?

Rosalie - If it's somebody who's never directed, I would say go and get a script! In the independent world, very little is commissioned from the ground up. Usually the process starts because somebody has a script. Even if it's an aspiring filmmaker who has done something in another area (i.e. written a book, been a journalist, etc.), my first piece of advice is to go write a script or get someone to write it for you, because until there's a script, you can't get anybody to read anything, whether it's a financier or an actor. If you're an unknown factor, representation can really make a difference, especially if your manager or agent has credibility. Sometimes it's also knowing how to work an agency. There are a handful of senior agents who handle the clients that make a movie happen, but because they are getting so many firm offers from studios on fully financed films, a producer and/or director of a small, independent (and probably unfinanced) film would be better off finding someone within the agency who will be an advocate and whose taste is trusted. I like to think that what we as representatives can do is help somebody help get their film or project recognized by understanding what the politics and who the playmakers are within each of these agencies.

The production side of our company has had partnerships with television and film studios. Currently, we have a first look feature deal with Warner's. In the past, we've had television deals at Fox and Columbia TriStar. If a client wishes to make use of our production capabilities, our production and management personnel, and our relationships with the studios, then we are happy to work closely with them if we believe that we can add value to the project (i.e., that we are the best producers for the client's project). However, as managers we also have access to many different kinds of financing relationships and the ability to provide introductions for our clients to both the talent and the financing that get movies made. We don't have the capability to fully finance films or spend a lot of money to develop them. Occasionally, if a client brings us a book or a script or something that requires just a small investment, we can provide a modest amount to either take it off the market or develop it further. We charge 10% commission. However, if we are the producers on a project, then we take our producing fee and return the commission.

Q - As agents have a reputation for being competitive, would you say it would be better to get a manager?

Rosalie - It's hard to make generalizations. Having said that, you don't need to be franchised by the guilds to be a manager so anyone can claim to be a manager without necessarily bringing any experience or credibility to the job. I would say that any manager at this or any of the top companies would add value. When a director client of mine is casting a movie, I can pick up the phone to the agents of the actors he wants more easily than his agents can, just because agents are competitive and don't like to help each other, whereas I am neutral.

Q - Would you say a manager tends to focus on one assignment while an agent puts forward many more?

Rosalie - Focus is a big part of it. Like most agencies, we receive scripts from different sources and sort through all the opportunities that are presented. Often we read a lot of the scripts, talk them through, and when a client decides she likes something I, along with the client's agent, will look at all the people involved with the project, (the producer, studio executive, any actors attached etc.) and then between us we will strategize as to how to get the client the job. An important part of my job is to discriminate and to be sure the choices are in synch with the client's long term goals.

Q - Do you think it gets to the stage where you don't need the agent?

Rosalie - I like to believe that if everybody is doing her job, the client is well served by having the team. Sometimes the client will form other close relationships which become another form of a partnership. For example, if you're making most of your movies for one entity, then you feel those people are also part of your team. There probably is an optimum number of advisers but it varies from individual to individual.

Q - What if you are a new filmmaker, looking for a manager, and you only have a short film to back you up?

Rosalie - I've got a couple of clients who are real babies in the field. I believe in them and I will continue to work with them in addition to the successfully established clients that I have. When you first take someone on, it has to be about your enthusiasm for their work, but also your belief that you know how to sell them in a way that it is in line with what they want to achieve. One client I'm working with now, I signed on the strength of her first British film. She has just done her second film, another small British movie, but this time it's much more accessible to an American audience. One of the things I say to this client is that, as a result of this second film, there will be a lot of new assignments which could giver her a career in the US. Even if her long-term goal is to make films closer to the sensibilities of her British films, she will need to find a way to work within the Hollywood system unless she wants to remain an independent filmmaker. There are certain filmmakers who always make their films outside the system. John Sayles is an interesting example because he will write for hire, making significant amounts of money that enable him to finance his own small movies which he then directs. If you want to stay an independent filmmaker, you have to accept the realities and practicalities of making films independently, but once you've established yourself, there will always be someone to finance you because you've established a 'brand' that filmgoers will follow.

Q - What makes a new filmmaker stand out?

Rosalie - Their work - on screen and on the page. But it also helps to be compelling and articulate in a room. It's a competitive marketplace, in which it can still be difficult to survive, even with a body of work which should speak for itself. It's heartbreaking, but the reality is that there's something beyond the work itself that needs to be present. It's like a college interview - you got good grades in school but you go to meet somebody from the university and during that interview something doesn't come across. Personal interaction makes a difference. So much depends upon perception, first impressions, and image etc. How you present yourself is critical.

Q - How important is a filmmaker's relationship with their manager?

Rosalie - Your rapport with someone you choose to be your representative is crucial. You need someone who understands who you are, someone who you'll look forward to speaking with, someone who will take your phone calls and be accessible to you. It tends to be a one on one relationship: you are signing with a particular manager more than a management company. On the other hand, when you choose an agent, you also choose an agency and there's a greater consciousness that other people will be a part of your life, influenced by the agency and what it's known for. ICM, for example, has always been known for excellence in the independent world. They have taken this very seriously and they encourage their actors to do interesting work. If you've been at a big agency and felt lost, you'll next choose an agent at a smaller agency. Or if you've been at an agency specializing in TV and you want a movie career, you'll find agents at an agency that can service both desires.

Q - What kind of mistakes have you noticed with filmmakers?

Rosalie - One of the biggest pitfalls is not knowing when to say forget it, it's not working. Given the way that movies are financed today, with a lot of people influencing the development of the script and casting - factors which may not work in the best interests of the project - it's important to know when you've crossed the line with all those little compromises that you've made. You have to know when that moment comes and it takes courage to pull the plug and walk away. When you've been struggling to get your movie made and someone comes along with the possibility of financing your movie, you have to know when some casting or script decision is going to make it something which is not what you set out to do. You need to find the ability to assess each specific thing being asked of you, based upon whether that decision will enhance or damage your vision. It is also vital to be able to step back and see if the overall vision that you set out to incorporate in your project remains intact, that the end result will be something you'll be proud of. I can apply the lessons that I have learnt from being a filmmaker myself when advising my clients.

Q - What advice would you offer a new filmmaker?

Q - What is Quality Filmed Entertainment?

Steve - We're a literary management agency and production company for new talent. We try to be as filmmaker friendly as possible by being more practical to help their careers. Rather than just putting in phonecalls, we invest time into development and if possible, production and distribution. This might mean producing a short film to use as a sales tool for the filmmaker to get them into the room to pitch projects.

Steve Hein
Quality Filmed Entertainment

Q - Do you provide funds for filmmakers?

Steve – No but there's always some sort of tit for tat relationship that we have access to i.e. producers who can give $x to shoot your short but with the proviso that they get to be attached to your stuff for a year etc. Nine of the twelve shorts we've done to date are financed by the filmmakers themselves. They either had some sort of success as writers, had trust fund money at their disposal, or had been scraping the money together over the years. When guys are putting in their own money, we're there to try and make sure that you only have to do that once and that the film made will do it's job. Don't underestimate the power of shorts. One of our clients got a two picture deal with Dreamworks on the strength of two shorts.

Q - How easy is it to get attention from the studios with a first time filmmaker?

Steve - It's challenging if you're just out of film school and all you have is a short shot on 8mm. If you have a feature that's won awards at festivals or you're a screenwriter who's sold a screenplay and you want to change your career, then you're going to be far more attractive to them. Everyone gets a little nervous if there's no track record.

Q - What is Branded Entertainment?

Steve - It's basically entertainment plus marketing. We're doing a series of five minute shorts that are sponsored by Reebok, similar to the BMW films that were out a year back. We'll be producing the short films for the writer and creator of the series who's a first time filmmaker. Reebok's paying for it and they're going to put them on TV, websites, DVD. It's something new and innovative and hopefully we will keep it going on. We're doing this in association with Hypnotic with whom we have a good relationship as we represent some of their filmmakers and they represent our library of short films.

Q - What advice do you give?

Steve - It's tough being a filmmaker, it's a highly competitive business and it's important to have as many people on your team as possible. I also think it's important to try and expand your career into as many different directions as possible. It's all about trying to build careers together and to climb the ranks together.

TALENT

Rosalie - In a world where marketing is such an important factor in success, you have to know how to market yourself. When I was first looking for a job in Hollywood, because I had worked in publishing, publicity, and as an agent, I said I can do all these things. I then realized that I was confusing people. For filmmakers, what financiers want to hear is who you are, what you want to make and why you have a burning passion to do it. If you're a writer, go and write your ideas down. The more you write, the more work you will have to show potential representatives. There are a lot of screenwriting competitions to enter. I recently took on someone who was a semi-finalist in a number of different screenwriting contests. I don't do it often but this particularly impressed me. If you're a filmmaker, and you've made a movie, find ways to get people to see it. Create screenings, send out postcards, get hold of lists and utilise all available resources. Try to find ways to stand out from the crowd.

Paul Petersen
A Minor Consideration

CHILD ACTORS

Q - What are some of the differences between working with young children, pre-teens and teenagers?

Paul - There are many rules and regulations when using kids. The younger the kid, the stricter the rules. There are different categories from the age of 15 days to 18 years. These deal with number of hours activity, maximum hours at employment site, rest and recreation. Infants under 6 months need a nurse on hand, and *work* should be treated as *play* for all pre-schoolers. This means plenty of rest breaks, finger food for snacks and time for recreation. Grade school children need education breaks of at least 20 minutes at a time. The older children, from roughly 12 to 17, certainly know where they are and what they're about, and they can handle the pressure of production within limits.

Q - When do you need a tutor on set? How much should a producer budget for them?

Paul - In California you must always have a teacher/welfare worker. Other states are not so careful, and there are provisions within the union contracts that allow for up to three days without a teacher, depending on circumstances. In many jurisdictions a working child is considered absent from school when they work, and that can result in Incomplete Fails at the end of the school year. We urge producers to supply a teacher on all school days, but that's not mandatory in some situations. An experienced teacher has room to maneuver for schooling requirements, but at the end of the day they are responsible for time and the child's welfare. You should budget from $200-$350 per day.

An unescorted minor is seldom a good idea. You are guarding against the unexpected, so it is wise to have on-set first aid as well as a teacher. If the parent does not accompany the child, the guardian must be over 18 and in possession of a letter giving authority to act as the guardian, including a medical release form. 16 and 17 year-olds can work without a parent/guardian present, but if they're in school they'll need a teacher for three hours.

Q - Any advice for dealing with parents of child actors?

Paul - Parents should be brought into the process as early and as often as possible. They are NOT a necessary evil! Law and contract language calls for them to 'be within sight and hearing of their child at all times'. Smart filmmakers know that this unpaid parent can be an important addition to the crew.

Q - How long can a child actor work before a mandatory break must occur?

Paul - The guidelines call for mandatory meal breaks at specific times, 5½ to 6 hours depending on the meal, (lunch or dinner), but it is the unrelieved stress of the work continuum that must be watched. Breaks for rest and snacks should follow the commonsense principles of getting a child through the day. Fluids and sugar-free snacks should always be available. Schooling is not a break.

Q - Do you have to have any special meals planned for minors?

Paul - This is one of those areas where the co-operation of the parent and teacher is important. Breakfast, for example, can help make the morning more productive. In the work environment, children need energy and periodic breaks to refuel, nap or just kick a ball around.

Q - How long can you shoot with a minor each day? Per week?

Paul - Little kids have shorter work days. Infants have as little as two hours; 16 year-olds, in New York for example, can work adult hours, but the federal 'cap' says no more than 48 hours per week. Beware of overtime. It can be illegal, and anytime a 9 to 17 year-old goes past 8½ hours you are at the edges of permissible conduct. The 'turn-around' (time from dismissal to the next day's call) is always 12 hours. Shooting schedules should always be arranged with these time limits in mind.

Q - Does a film production company need to obtain a license to hire minors?

Paul - In California, a company must apply for and receive a *Permit to Employ Minors* from the Department of Labor. This is a simple, no cost process. Other states rarely have such rules. Make sure that all children who are employed have a valid work permit for that jurisdiction. You can check with the Department of Labor or the Local Authority of the nearest Film Commission office.

Q - Does the state that you are working in send out inspectors to ensure that regulations are being followed?

Paul - Most states assume the studio teacher will enforce the pertinent regulations which may be stricter by contract, rather than in law or regulation. The unions have field reps, and in Canada there are *On Set Liason Officers* (OSLO's) that watch the work place. Always let your conscience be your guide as kids and their parents have recourse when common sense boundaries are exceeded. This is work, not slavery.

Q - How do you get real emotion reactions from a child actor?

Paul - Kid actors are actors, and don't forget that. Bending fingers, telling a child that their dog is dead, or poking an infant with a pin is beyond stupid. Tell the child what you want, explain the context to them and their parents and hire the ones who can give you what you need. Children have a far richer interior emotional life than we suspect. Take care to let the child 'decompress' after an emotional scene and make time to explain to them that the emotional scene they just witnessed is 'pretend'. Arrange scenes and coverage so the kids do not have to participate in frightening moments if at all possible. There are several 'right ways' to film a scene.

Q - Should filmmakers shoot rehearsals with the children?

Paul - It's all too easy for a child to grow stale with over rehearsing. They generally come better prepared than adults. The younger children are often more 'real' the first time round, and if you're looking for a genuine reaction to a surprising situation set things up that way and let the cameras roll. As a general rule the kids above the age of nine will give you what you need time after time, especially if you take the time to explain the scene's requirements.

Q - Are there specific companies that handle minors?

Paul - Yes, there are talent agencies that specialize in Minors, and the good ones know who their best actors are. Don't just pick kids off the street. That's a demeaning way to look at children, especially the ones who are already in the

Free info!

Check out http://www.sag.org/ young_performers an all important site for filmmakers with regards to hiring child actors. This site will eventually contain all the state regulations and laws for the employment of minors in entertainment. There are nine states currently posted and the SAG basic agreement. The critical factor for filmmakers (who often think they are exempt from reality) is that child labor laws are always in force. ALWAYS!

TALENT

business. Experience is always helpful. Children who look younger than their years are almost always an advantage. If you need special skills like horseback riding, skate boarding, etc. make sure the child actually has those skills. If you are even contemplating a stunt that puts a child at risk talk to the professional stunt community and take their advice, which may require hiring a little person to double as the child. Be mindful that the child comes with a parent/guardian and as I mentioned earlier, the sooner the parent is included in the casting process the better. Savvy producers often take the time to interview parents when they get deeper into the casting process.

Q - How do you keep a child from being bored during set ups?

Paul - Children are affected by the total work environment, which means that the entire crew should be mindful of their conduct. A game of catch with a crew member can relieve boredom and stress in equal measure. The time spent 'in school' should always be treated with respect. Kids are full of questions and the whole crew must be patient, but this is still a work environment and the kids must know the rules. Temper tantrums can be a problem. For babies, have a stand-by. For pre-schoolers you must sometimes exercise patience and the skills of a parent. A major disruption means a 'time out'. Care in the casting process can prevent a host of problems.

Q - What kind of consent forms does a filmmaker need to have signed when working with minors?

Paul - Work permits, certainly. Medical release forms for an unaccompanied 16 or 17 year-old. Permits to Employ if called for by the state. Talk to the theatrical unions and become a signatory if at all possible. For those 'edgy scenes', particularly of a sexual nature, be certain you know the laws against the sexual exploitation of a minor, because even simulated behavior may be illegal.

Q - Can a teacher remove the child from set if unhappy with the working conditions?

Paul - Yes, if in the judgment of the teacher, the working conditions are such that there is danger to the health, safety or morals of the minor; they can remove the child from the set or location. Studio teachers are responsible for the health, safety and morals of the minor.

Q - What are some of the most common mistakes filmmakers make when working with minors?

Paul - The most common mistake is thinking the young actor is just another actor. They are not. If it's not safe for your child, it's not safe for the child you employ. Look for the kids who are not raw rookies, because they already have a feel for the process. Yes, the rules for employing a child are restrictive, so deal with it, don't ignore it. Arrange shooting schedules to accommodate the needs of your performer (school, rest periods and all the rest). Don't be shy about calling the Young Performers Committee at AFTRA or SAG (323) 549 6619 to ask for advice, even if this is a student film or non-union. Expert advice should not be ignored.

Q - What advice can you give new filmmakers for dealing with child actors?

Paul - First, remember that kids have always been a part of the filmmaking process. Second, common sense and age appropriate behavior are important for everyone involved. Third, children are not props or plot devices, but real people who will have to deal with the consequences of early employment. Fourth, and probably the most important, graciously resign yourself to the creative limitations imposed when you are working with children. They can be exasperating, true, but when they are good they are very, very good.

Work Time For Kids

These are the general guidelines for hiring a minor for the entertainment industry in the state of California. Rules vary from state to state, so check with the relevant state film commission to get exact details.

Age: 15 days to 6 months
Work time when school is not in session is 20 minutes work activity, 2 hours max at employment site. May not be exposed to light exceeding 100 footcandles for more than 30 seconds. May only be employed between 9:30am and 11:30am or between 2:30pm and 4.30pm. 1 studio teacher and 1 nurse must be present for each 3 or fewer infants 15 days to 6 weeks old. 1 studio teacher and 1 nurse must be present for each 10 or fewer infants 6 weeks to 6 months old. Parent and Guardian must be present. Exceptions to the work time rules are possible with parent and teacher approval.

Age: 6 months to 2 years
Work time when school is not in session is 2 hours work activity, 4 hours max at employment site. Balance for rest and recreation. May only be employed between 5am and 12.30am. Parent or guardian must be present.

Age: 2 years to 6 years
Work time when school is not in session is 3 hours work activity, 6 hours max at employment site. Balance for rest and recreation. May only be employed between 5am and 12:30am. Studio teacher must be present. Parent or guardian must be present.

Age: 6 years to 9 years
Work time when school in session is 4 hours work activity, 3 hours school, 1 hour rest and recreation, 8 hours max at employment site. Work time when school is not in session is 6 hours work activity, 1 hour rest and recreation. May only be employed between 5am and 12:30am (to 10pm preceding schooldays). Parent or Guardian must be present.

Age: 9 years to 16 years
Work time when school is in session is 5 hours work activity, 3 hours school, 1 hour rest and recreation, 9 hours max at employment site. Work time when school is not in session is 7 hours work activity, 1 hour rest and recreation. May only be employed between 5 am and 12.30am (to 10pm preceding school days). Permits to work and employ required, unless a high school graduate or equivalent. High school graduates may be employed as adults.

Age: 16 years to 18 years
Work time when school is in session is 6 hours work activity, 3 hours school, 1 hour rest and recreation, 10 hours max at employment site. Work time when school is not in session is 8 hours work activity, 1 hour rest and recreation. May only be employed between 5AM and 12:30AM(to 10PM preceding school days). A parent or Guardian need not be present.

Pertaining to all Minors
Permits to work and employ are required unless the minor is a high school graduate or equivalent. High school graduates may be employed as adults. Studio teacher need only be present for minors' schooling if minor still required to attend school. Minors in grades 1 thru 6 must be tutored between the hours of 7AM and 4PM. Minors in grades 7 thru 12 must be tutored between the hours of 7AM and 7PM. 1 studio teacher per 20 minors on weekends, holidays and school breaks and vacations. 1 studio teacher required per 10 minors.

Exceptions
Minors under 16 do not require the presence of a studio teacher for up to one hour for wardrobe, make up, hairdressing, promotional publicity, personal appearances, or audio recording if these activities are not on set, if school is not in session and if the parent or guardian is present.

TALENT

Michelle Morris Gertz
C.S.A.

GET THE CAST

Q - What is the job of a casting director?

Michelle - A casting director works with the director and producer, collaborating on casting the roles and bringing in the actors. That's everybody from Julia Roberts to the waiter that says 'May I help you?' Basically anyone that speaks. People that don't speak and that are in the background are extras casting, which we don't do.

Q - Why have a casting director? Why not cast yourself?

Michelle - You're paying for knowledge, expertise and relationships and with casting, there's a lot of phone calls, paperwork, pictures and files to go through, it's busy work. The producer has too much on their plate already and most don't have the time, inclination or even the knowledge to hold full casting sessions and to see all the actors that are out there. That's why it needs to be collaborative. Sure, if the producer is passionate about casting he or she can be part of the process, but to not have a casting director on a project, even if the casting director isn't paid and only gets credit like on a short film or student film, I think is doing it a disservice.

Q - Can you give me the basics of how it all works?

Michelle - You're sent a script and invited to a meeting with the director and producers, quite similar to an audition, and you share your thoughts about the characters. You discuss how you would approach the whole process. Based on that meeting and previous experience, that's how they choose you. Once that's out of the way and you've negotiated your deal, you find out who they think are the best people for the roles and you share your ideas and start to marry it all together. Obviously for the larger roles, you're going to be going through a list of names. You look at how much money you have in the budget and who you can afford for those roles, and who is actually available when are you shooting. You would probably start by meeting some actors and making some offers. Once you get down to the supporting roles and the day player roles, you can have casting sessions. Sometimes you may want to put out a breakdown or have casting calls. The casting director does pre-screens or pre-reads and brings in a bunch of actors that they want to try out and also introduce to the director. So, let's say I meet 150 people for a role, I'd probably bring a good mix of 20 back for the director and producer. Some might be very strong for the part, some might have a certain 'something' but not particularly right for the role, however if they have a certain 'something' then the director should see them. A lot of times I'll bring someone in for an audition because his or her reading has something magical in it that even if the person who is cast might not bring. It's amazing, you can go through 100 readings and each person interprets it differently. The best part of my job is when something unexpected and wonderful happens, when you find something special... that spark. You bring someone in as a favor or you bring someone in at the end of a day and you're exhausted and they read and it's unbelievable. It's like, that's how it was meant to be said all along and it's wonderful to see. It's a fun process.

Q - How can the director help you with casting?

Michelle - If the director has a vision and is able to share that with the casting director, it helps. If at the onset you know what you're looking for, you can bring him things that he's looking for, and on the flip side you can also bring him things he's not looking for. A good casting director will try to expand their vision and try to make him see things that originally weren't there. Trying to make all the characters sit together, whether it's a character or a family or a town so that the story is cohesive.

Q - If you were reading a low budget script and there were superfluous characters that didn't need to be there ...would you advise cutting them out?

Michelle - Absolutely. Anything that drags the story, whether it's a character or a set piece should be taken out, particularly on a low budget movie. I read a script the other day that had 85 parts and they want to make it for $1m and there's no way, even if you pay everybody low budget scale. It's a lot of people to wrangle!

Q - There's a myth that on low budget movies, you can't get big name actors. Is that true?

Michelle - It boils down to the script and relationships. If you have a director / producer / casting director, someone who has a personal relationship with the actor or agent or manager and is able to get a script to somebody who wouldn't normally take it off the street, it is possible. You should have realistic expectations knowing that you can shoot for names, but you're not always going to get them and there are a lot of actors out there and only so many good scripts. If you really believe in your material and you wrote it for Julianne Moore then absolutely approach Julianne Moore, but do it in a smart way. Take your best shot, don't just send it randomly. Write a personal note. Have a meeting with her first if you can. Explain the script and how you wrote it for her. Include info about the project, people involved and complete your packet so that when you do present it to that star that it's the best package that it can be. You only have one shot. If you have good relationships with the agents and managers, they'll do their best to get the material to heir client. On the other hand, they work for the client, not for you. So, they might be your best friends but if it's not good material they're not going to pass it on. I've worked on projects where people have passed and I couldn't believe it. Months later I'd see them for something else and I'd say *'Oh, you passed on that'* and it turns out they never even heard about it. Take your best shot. If you know their best friend and can get them a script that way, whatever works.

Q - Is there a directory of actors?

Michelle - Yes, the Academy Player's Guide. Agents and managers put their clients in. It has their headshots and contact information. If I'm really stuck for a role or I want to get ideas, I'll refer to it.

Q - Do the actors pay to put themselves in the directory?

Michelle - Agents and managers pay to put them in. If you don't have representation, I believe you can put yourself in because there are people who just have direct contact numbers. There are four volumes. It's men, women, children and character actors. They also have a portion there for everyone nominated for Academy Awards.

Q - Do you think it's worthwhile for producers to get hold of those books?

Michelle - Absolutely, to familiarize themselves with people. A producer should not cast from it solely, but a casting director will always be open if a producer says 'Hey, I saw this picture of this girl, I think she looks really great, can you check her out?' You can also get it on CD. There are also some acting websites and Breakdown Services has a website where they post what's currently being cast and they also have something for actors to post their pictures and resumes.

Q - Would you recommend people going to Breakdown Services?

Michelle - Casting directors put in what they're casting and agents and managers get it every day. It's the main source and pretty much everybody uses it but it is a monopoly. The casting director would put out a breakdown (if you don't have a casting director, the producer can put out a breakdown) of the project, whether it's a student film, short film, independent, TV, commercials... It's a wonderful way to reach everybody. Breakdowns are immediate, you put it out at 6pm at night, and you're getting calls at 8am!

TALENT

Getting a work permit for a kid

1. Obtain the 'Application for Permission to Work in the Entertainment Industry' from any Division of Labor Standards Enforcement Officer or online.

2. The minor's parent or legal guardian must complete all of the requested information on the application and print / sign their name.

3. If the minor is of school age, an authorized school official must complete the 'School Record' portion of the application, sign his or her name, print their title or position and affix the school's seal or stamp.

4. If the minor is not of school age (15 days old thru kindergarten), the minor's parent or legal guardian must provide one of the following: A certified copy of the minor's birth certificate; the minor's baptismal certificate; a letter on the hospital's letterhead attesting to the birth of the minor; the minor's passport. The completed application with original signatures and the school's seal or stamp affixed should be mailed or presented in person to any Division of Labor Standards Enforcement Office for issuance of the minor's entertainment work permit. No infant under the age of 1 month may be employed without a licensed pediatrician's certificate.

There is even a commercial breakdown which is immediate. I thought people would start to submit their head shot and resume online, but it hasn't really taken off as there's something about having a picture and resume in your hand.

Q - What would you say if a low budget filmmaker wanted you to cast a friend as a favor?

Michelle - I'm not often asked to cast someone as a favor. I think everybody in the business understands that actors work hard and they train and all they really want is a shot, so I'm asked to see people all the time which no casting director should ever mind. When you're asked to cast somebody as a favor it depends on the role. I like a film to be seamless and so if you're asking me to cast your grandmother as a security guard, it's not going to work. But if she is playing a part, sitting in a restaurant, drinking coffee and talking to the waiter, why not? Ultimately, the director is the one who's going to have to direct them. Above all, you want them to be professional and a team player.

Q - What would you say if they wanted to cast their actor friends to keep costs down?

Michelle - You have to be careful about mixing business with friends and family. It doesn't mean it can't be done, just be careful when doing it. If your friend is the best person for the role then cast them. But don't do it out of being lazy or cheap, because if your friend will work for scale, so will a lot of actors. Why not say 'I'm considering my friend for this role... But I want to see who else is out there...' That's how I would approach it. I would never demand that we cast anybody because in the end you're doing a disservice to the film.

Q - Are you are a buffer between the producer, the filmmaker and the agent?

Michelle - Yes. casting directors have stronger and more frequent relationships with managers/agents than producers. Unless you are at a top agency, you're not talking to producers or directors regularly. Your allegiance is to the film, the producer and director, so sometimes you end up upsetting some of your agent and manager friends.

Q - What's the attitude to low budget movies in the industry?

Michelle - Since Sundance and othe film festivals have exploded, and Hilary Swank won the Academy Award for *Boys Don't Cry*, independent films are respected more. Independents are like theater, actors try to prove themselves by doing independents. Maybe somebody will leave a TV series and do a really low budget independent as it's a much more free environment for them to work in. At the end of the day, it's about the script.

Q - Once the roles are all cast and the deals made, is that the end of your job?

Michelle - Yes and no. You hope that you're done with the cast by the time you start shooting but that is rarely the case. You're usually casting while filming is going on. Often we are around for most of the shoot, particularly the first few weeks, and if they add roles they might call you, if they end up doing re-shoots they might call you, or if somebody falls out because of scheduling conflicts etc. so you're never really done. At the beginning of the casting process the director is totally yours. There's very few distractions. Then the closer they get to shooting, the busier they become and it's hard to get the directors attention when he's on set all day and he's dealing with other issues. The best scenario is to have major roles cast well in advance while casting is still the focus.

Q - Are there any problems that the actors might come to you about when working on a low budget shoot?

Michelle - You hope that everyone has been truthful from the outset so that you don't have too many problems. But, you always get little things. Sometimes the actors aren't happy with their dressing rooms or they weren't clear during the negotiations about what they were getting into. We try to please them, because no one wants an unhappy actor. A lot of time, the producers don't have time, or don't want to listen. Our relationships with agents and managers are friendly, so they'll call us to complain and see if we can do anything and work a little magic. Sometimes we can, sometimes we can't. It's important to have everything documented and written down, memos and contracts. Always have a contract signed before an actor starts work. What happens is if they start working without that is that they can come back and say 'I didn't know....x' and you're sort of cornered into giving them what they want or they'll walk off and ruin your movie. Make sure it's clear how much money they are getting. The fee, plus the commission; and what is their wage? How much overtime are they getting? How much rehearsal time is there? How much post do they have to do? (ADR) How much press are they going to have to do? What's expected of them? Anything that's not written down and not part of that deal, believe me, the agents are going to ask for money to get them to do it.

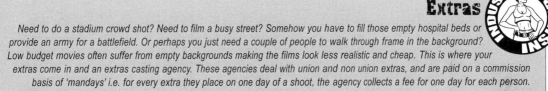

Extras

Need to do a stadium crowd shot? Need to film a busy street? Somehow you have to fill those empty hospital beds or provide an army for a battlefield. Or perhaps you just need a couple of people to walk through frame in the background? Low budget movies often suffer from empty backgrounds making the films look less realistic and cheap. This is where your extras come in and an extras casting agency. These agencies deal with union and non union extras, and are paid on a commission basis of 'mandays' i.e. for every extra they place on one day of a shoot, the agency collects a fee for one day for each person.

1. If you're on a union film, you must use a certain amount of SAG extras. Generally it's 40 with 5 stand-ins, but on low budget indies, SAG is willing to negotiate and grant you a waiver to lower the numbers. There are SAG vouchers that must be filled in and even Taft Hartley applies here, with separate forms for extras.

2. Extras casting agencies also have a list of non union extras plus access to the 'right looking' people for your shoot i.e. school kids, medical professionals, professional musicians, actual firemen, actual police officers etc. People who genuinely look the part and therefore make your film look more 'real'.

3. Production companies can help look for their own extras by either placing ads, radio spots or contacting certain groups, schools, community groups etc. as well as collaborating with the production's publicist.

4. Before securing your extras, make sure they've been informed of how long you anticipate them to be on set.

5. If there are a large number of extras from one source, try to provide transport to move them to and from the location.

6. Make sure there are enough restroom facilities, and that food and water is on hand at all times.

7. Remember that your extras are going to have to do a lot of waiting around and will get bored easily. Advise them to bring a book.

8. Your extras might not show up, so be prepared to have a backup plan.

9. Make sure you have at least one, but preferably more, designated production crew members to take care of all the extras, providing them with call times, what to wear, what to bring etc.

10. Provide your extras with release forms and make sure they sign this before they leave.

Q - How much does it cost to get a casting director on a say $1m low budget movie?

Michelle - Casting directors are paid independently per film just like actors. They have quotes that they made for their last film. Obviously like an actor, they will work for below their quote if they're passionate about the material, or if it's a director or producer they really want to work with. For $1m movie for a very good casting director, you may have to pay them between $20-30k, some a little more, some a little less. Maybe give them a co-producer credit instead of money. A lot of casting is producing because you're trying to attach talent that's going to get you more money and more exposure, making your film bigger. So those first few roles that you attach are important.

One producer I'm working with thinks casting is the most important part and so he allocates a large percentage of his budget. There are a lot of producers and directors that don't feel it's as important. Just like when chasing an actor to hire, don't go too far over your head. If you're only doing a $2m movie and you aim for the biggest casting director, you're not going to get that person and even if you did get them, you'll probably get their assistant doing the work. Meanwhile, an up and coming or younger casting director will want to work hard for you. A producer with guts could approach a huge casting director with a $1m movie in hope that they would find something or identify with then. So it's never out of the realm, just like it's never out of the realm to make an offer to a big star. They might say no, but you should try. In my opinion it's not always the biggest name and the biggest casting director that's going to do the best job. Filmmakers have to be smart about their decision with their casting director. They should know that theirs might not have the biggest name and best credits but if he or she works hard, is passionate about the material, that's what is important. You want someone who's going to feel the same about your material as you do, shares a vision, work toward that vision and will make the package what you hoped it would be.

Q - Are auditions included in the fee?

Michelle - Independent casting directors generally don't have a permanent office, so we are usually based at the production office. You'd need to provide them with office space or provide them with the money to rent office space. If you're working on a big movie and a studio gives you an offer, you may be able to do an independent on the side, then the low budget one's in luck because they get to use all the things you have.

Q - What happens if people come to you without being fully financed?

Michelle - A lot of times, people call up and say 'I have a project that's not put together yet. Would you be interested in consulting or helping me attach people?' and it depends on the casting director. It's time consuming and there's not a lot of money involved so I'm not sure that a casting director that is busy on other projects is going to do it. On the other hand, if it's great material and the casting director believes in it , make them a producer and they're more involved from the start.

Q - What about fixed fee consulting?

Michelle - A lot of people do $5k for a month of consulting, doing lists, availability checks. It doesn't necessarily mean that at the end of the consulting they're going to cast your film. It is considered a step deal.

Q - Does the casting director negotiate budget agreements and actually do the deals?

Michelle - The casting director negotiates all deals up to schedule F, which is $65k. So if you're paying someone more than $65k, that's when your studio's business affairs take over because then the attorney's need to do legal contracts. With an independent or low budget film, the casting director might work with the producer to do it, but once it gets over a certain amount, there are other things that come into play according to SAG rules, such as actor scheduling, rehearsal time is built in. It's not just a straightforward SAG contract. But, on most low budget films, it's going to be favored nations, and that's the smartest way to do it. Favored nations is basically that everybody in the cast gets the same amount. Most of the time when I do favored nations, it's favored nations scale.

Casting and Audition Tips

1. No one is out of reach. Make a list of people who could play the parts in your picture and approach their agents. Actors can often have a bad year and be eager for feature work, or may have a soft spot for the edginess of low budget filmmaking. If you don't ask, you'll never know – and they might say yes.

2. Agents are all difficult. Their sole job is to protect their client, hustle as much money as they can and moan and groan about conditions. Agents can neglect to inform their clients of the potential job if the money is likely to be bad. They also can take forever to get back to you. Agents' salaries are based on how much money they bring into the agency. Why spend time and energy on negotiations if there isn't a pot of money at the end?

3. The flip side is that if you have an exciting project and you are honest and upfront, then they may see your movie as a positive opportunity. Deals can be struck. For instance, the actor can become an executive producer or, you get the actor, but must use several of the agency's clients as well.

4. If you have a way in to an actor, bypass the agent and get the script to him. No agent will be able to stop an actor who is determined to be involved in a project. Be aware that some actors hate this approach and enjoy the protection that their agent gives them from a barrage of wannabe filmmakers.

5. Get a copy of The Academy Players Directory, a book of US actors, to find potential players. Contact Breakdown Services who release character descriptions to actors.

6. You can get international casting information from www.spotlightcd.com and the various links on it – including the UK, Australia and Canada.

7. There are several casting services and trade magazines where ads can be placed very cheaply, such as Backstage / Backstage West.

8. If you can afford it, hire a casting director. They usually have ideas for casting that you never thought of, and more importantly, have relationships with their agents and the actors themselves. If you cannot afford the casting director, try approaching their assistant - they are usually aching for a chance to prove themselves.

9. Videotape auditions. It will help you put a face to the hundreds of hopefuls you will undoubtedly see.

10. Allow yourself enough time to cast properly. 3-4 months is optimal. Remember to allow for costume fittings and rehearsals.

11. Be honest and up front about money and conditions - preferably on the phone when arranging an audition. It's better to know upfront if there are going to be any problems, rather than on set.

12. If you are questioning whether you can pay SAG minimums, call them. SAG has several programs, such as Limited Exhibition and Low Budget Independent Feature, which are geared toward low-budget filmmaking. In the end, it may end up saving you money.

13. Where should you hold auditions? Many studios and casting facilities have rooms for this purpose. If your day job is in an office building, try using a conference room, after hours or on the weekend. Some apartment complexes have reception rooms, which work well too. You can even hold them in the front room of your house as long as the atmosphere is clean and professional.

14. Once you have cast a part, sort out ALL financial agreements in a contract, before you shoot.

TALENT

So if you work a day, you get scale. If you work a week you get a weekly scale. It works well for smaller films.

I worked on a studio film where it was mostly favored nations scale because the top three people were paid and everybody else was favored nations. Even when you have auditions, on the breakdown, you can put 'scale' so that you're not getting submissions of actors that are more expensive. It is the casting director's job not to bring you Meg Ryan when you can't afford her.

The actor has to know the budget of the film. That's why agents and managers always ask before auditions. 'What's the budget?' 'Who's producing it?' 'When's it going?' 'What kind of film are you shooting on?' 'What's the anticipated release date?' They want to know what they're getting into. With favored nations, often credit comes into play. Alphabetical is always the best way to go. People understand that certain actors are name value and certain actors bring in an audience. You can organize your own credit structure and say 'The three main actors we're going to do in this structure and then the rest will be alphabetical'.

Q - Have any big actors agreed to do favored nations on a low budget indie?

Michelle - Sure. What happens is they do a no quote deal. They do it for less than their price or they do it for favored nations. With certain directors, like Woody Allen, actors want to work with them so they'll work for favored nations. They can do it because they make a lot of money on their other films. After all, acting is an art and craft and unfortunately, what we do is a business, so money comes into play, but at the heart of it, it's an art form so those that are really passionate about it find something that they want to work on and that makes it worthwhile.

Q - What can a producer do to make your life easier?

Michelle - Be realistic, collaborative, and organized. That doesn't mean you can't call someone at home to bounce ideas off them, and you can ask them to come in on the weekends if you need a special person. But be respectful. My two best experiences were with Chris and Paul Weitz on *American Pie* and Shawn Levy on *Big Fat Liar* because they're wonderful human beings and they treat their actors with respect. They work hard during the day and they get their work done and they don't second-guess their casting director, producers or anyone else around them. They trust that the people they hired are doing a good job and that's important. To be a good filmmaker you have to do that. There's no one person that can do everything alone.

Q - What advice would you offer new filmmakers?

Michelle - Besides appreciating your crew and cast, just be respectful of people. It's so important. Understand that everyone has a family and a life and we love what we do and we're all creative people. It's an art form but at the end of the day we're all human. I love what I do but I go home to my husband and daughter. A director that doesn't understand that he's working with human beings is not someone I want to work with. Be realistic and don't be stubborn. Know your material and know what you're going after. Don't waste your time going after people who won't do it, who aren't interested or if they do end up doing it, it's like they're doing you a favor. If you get lots of agents who read your script saying *'The relationship doesn't work, and it's not believable'*, take a second look at it. Sometimes you are way too close to the material, particularly writers/ directors or producers who have been on projects for a year or two trying to get it going. It's important to listen to people you trust and listen to the feedback you get.

Using Friends As Actors

Actors cost money. Even if they offer to work for free they will at some point probably ask for money for subway or cab fare. It is almost essential that your principal cast be pros, but if push comes to shove, friends and relatives are an option.

1. Always make a contract with everyone that appears in front of the camera - carry release forms that can be filled in on the spot. Not only will this protect you legally, but the sales agent will require these documents.

2. Unless you are sure of their skills, don't give a friend an important role. Be aware that they could be spectacularly awful. They may also be unprofessional.

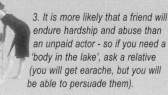

3. It is more likely that a friend will endure hardship and abuse than an unpaid actor - so if you need a 'body in the lake', ask a relative (you will get earache, but you will be able to persuade them).

4. If you are making a SAG film, they will not like that you are using non-union players.

5. Friends and relatives are great if you need a crowd - they will even come in costume (but, be careful of damaged egos when a costume is horrible).

6. Always consider an actor over a non-actor, even if the actor in question has little or no experience. They want to be there and will have some training. There are thousands of actors just waiting for any work or a break. Place an ad in Backstage, Backstage West or contact Breakdown Services and watch the headshots roll in.

Another common mistake is rushing through the process. On a low budget movie you think *'I don't have a lot of money so I must shoot soon so I will give the casting director one month!'* That's a huge mistake. If anything, usually it takes 3-4 months. It's going to take time for people to read the material. What are they going to read over the weekend? The script for the $1m movie or $50m movie?

Enjoy the process, don't rush through it because you are going to learn things from each actor that comes in, you're going to learn from your casting director, you're going to learn from everybody so don't be so egocentric that you don't realize that. A common mistake is not looking at the project as a collaboration. New filmmakers look at it as a dictatorship. That's reflective in your film. When you have the captain of the boat thanking everybody, being appreciative, laughing at the jokes in the film and enjoying the process, everybody enjoys their job and everybody does better work.

Casting - The Directories

Academy Players Directory
1313 N. Vine St., Hollywood, California 90028
P: (310) 247-3058   players@oscars.org
www.acadpd.org   www.playersdirectory.com

Started in 1930's by The Academy of Motion Picture Arts and Sciences to be "the bible" of casting. That first issue of the Players Directory included photos and information on about 1,200 actors. 60 years later, more than 16,000 actors are listed. In 1997, the Academy and Breakdown Services, Ltd., which supplies the entertainment industry with daily information about available acting roles, created The Link (www.submitlink.com) - an online service where Breakdown Services electronically transmits its daily breakdowns of available acting roles to its agent clients. Using the photos and resumes from the Players Directory, those agents may then electronically transmit to casting directors the names of talent that they would like to see considered for the roles described in the breakdowns. The website also has lists of talent agents and casting directors.

The Players Guide New York
123 West 44th Street, #2J, New York, NY 10036
P: (212) 302-9474   www.playersguideny.com

This is the largest and most respected directory of actors on the East Coast. An actor appearing in The Players Guide will automatically appear in searches done on the West Coast on-line Academy Player's Directory so casting directors on both coasts can find you via the internet. All Players Guide members with agency and manager contacts are automatically in The Link.

The Union of British Colombia Performers Talent Online
#300-856 Homer Street, Vancouver, B.C., V6B 2W5
P: (604) 689-0727   info@ubcp.com
www.ubcponline.com

The Union of B.C. Performers (UBCP) is a trade union in the Province of British Colombia and the B.C. Branch of the ACTRA (Alliance of Canadian Cinema, Television and Radio Artists). They supply an online directory of Canadian actors who are members of the UBCP. As a member you will automatically be registered in the west coast on-line Academy Player's Directory, so again casting directors around North America can find you via the internet. All UBCP members with agency and manager contacts are automatically in The Link, and the web site also has a list of talent agents and a production list.

TALENT

Gary Marsh
Breakdown Services

HOW, WHERE & WHEN?

Q - What is a cast breakdown?

Gary - A Breakdown is a complete synopsis of the characters contained within the scripts. We have staff writers who read the scripts who then create the breakdown. The breakdown is instantly uploaded to our website so that agents and mangers can view the casting information. Our breakdowns include episodics, pilots, feature films, movies for television, theater, student films, industrials and commercials. Casting directors mostly request submissions electronically via our online Breakdown Express site at www.breakdownexpress.com. We cover union and non union, although the majority of projects we release are union. Union Projects are released at no charge, whereas non-union projects are charged a fee of $75.00. Our clients are primarily interested in union projects since they represent union actors. However, we release non-union projects to agents and managers since some of our clients are developing non-union talent.

Q - How does the electronic casting system you referred to as Breakdown Express work?

Gary - Most casting directors request Electronic Submissions through our Breakdown Express system. This allows agents and managers to instantly submit actors pictures and resumes online. By using Breakdown Express, filmmakers can instantly view actors pictures and resumes and then create auditions for selected actors and notify agents and managers with a click of a button. Filmmakers can also send out global notes for the agents with the venue. This system also works for actors that have submitted themselves through Actors Access. It saves everyone an enormous amount of time and expense. Using Breakdown Express is probably the most efficient way for producers and casting directors to receive submissions instantly. Actors can go to www.actorsaccess.com for Actors Access. Projects that casting directors want actors submissions are listed at this web address. Actors can register and view breakdowns at no charge. They can also upload two pictures and a resume for free and use it to email. If they want to add more than two pictures the cost is $10.00 per picture. If they want to use our Internet submissions system to make a submission then the cost is $2.00. We also provide Showfax for actors. This is a service that gives the actor the ability to download a portion of a script to prepare for an audition - we call them 'sides'. A filmmaker, at no charge, posts all the 'sides' with us and the actor can download them as a member of Showfax. The cost of membership is $68.00 per year. The other alternative is to just pay $1.00 per page if the actor doesn't think they will use $68.00 'Sides' in a year. The whole point is that actors have access to audition material 24/7.

Q - What is Screenplay Online?

Gary - This is where an agent can download a complete screenplay from our website at www.gobetween.com. Instead of having to Xerox many scripts, and messenger them out, the filmmaker gives us the script, we digitize it (no charge), we give the filmmaker the code and then when anybody can call up and ask for the script, the filmmaker tells them to go to Screenplay online and tells them the code and they download it. When the agent wants to purchase access to it, they can buy $500 tickets for $500, so in essence, it's a dollar a download for an entire script (a ticket is one download). To get a script to or from an agent can cost $20 to messenger, so the agents love this because it is so much cheaper. The benefit of this is if a filmmaker is in Ohio or LA or London and they want LA agents to have their script, they can email that code to anywhere in the world. We did a reverse thing like that for the second *Tomb Raider* movie, where Paramount paid us to put the *Tomb Raider* script in the system and we gave them the code and they emailed that code to all the designers and the people working on it around the world. Instead of trying to email scripts where problems can be had by all, the crew went into the site and typed in the code and accessed it. We are in the process of taking this service online. For the low budget filmmaker this is great because they can get resumes as well as suppliers of craft services and the like. It's a subscription service paid weekly, monthly, yearly. It's just like a magazine. All crew members pay $75 for the first two months and they get discounts after that.

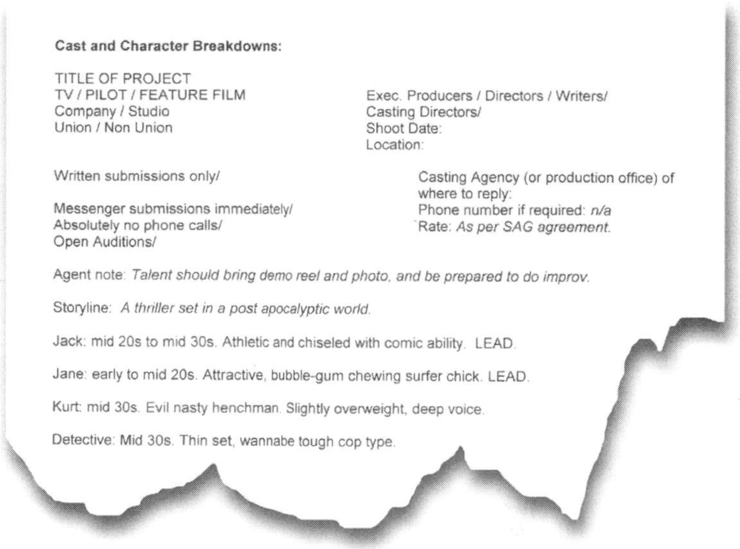

Q - What other services do you offer?

Gary - We also have a music department that takes care of the needs of the music supervisors too.

Cast and Character Breakdowns:

TITLE OF PROJECT
TV / PILOT / FEATURE FILM
Company / Studio
Union / Non Union

Exec. Producers / Directors / Writers/
Casting Directors/
Shoot Date:
Location:

Written submissions only/

Messenger submissions immediately/
Absolutely no phone calls/
Open Auditions/

Casting Agency (or production office) of where to reply:
Phone number if required: n/a
Rate: As per SAG agreement.

Agent note: Talent should bring demo reel and photo, and be prepared to do improv.

Storyline: A thriller set in a post apocalyptic world.

Jack: mid 20s to mid 30s. Athletic and chiseled with comic ability. LEAD.

Jane: early to mid 20s. Attractive, bubble-gum chewing surfer chick. LEAD.

Kurt: mid 30s. Evil nasty henchman. Slightly overweight, deep voice.

Detective: Mid 30s. Thin set, wannabe tough cop type.

Q - Is there a standard method for independent producers to do a breakdown themselves?

Gary - Yes. The form guides them through it. They can go to Actor Access and see what happens. The information we need is online along with the casting information.

Q - Is there any advice you would give to new producers?

Gary - When they release a project, it become their calling card as to who they are and what they are about. Be up front and honest and don't hide things. If they have any budget at all, get an assistant to work as a casting director as agents will submit to someone they know far more readily than someone they've never heard of. If your project has nudity in it, let the agents know that. You'll be respected for it. We get complaints if producers aren't honest.

Contact
LA: 310 276 9166 / NY: 212 869 2003 / Vancouver: 604 943 7100
www.breakdownservices.com
www.showfax.com 310-385-6920 - sides service.
www.gobetween.com - delivers packages digitally.
Tune Data – 310 276 9166 – music breakdown service
www.playersdirectory.com - Academy Players Directory. LA
www.playgersguide.com - The Players Guide. NY
www.ubcptalentonline.com - Union of British Colombia Performers. Canada

TALENT

Gilly Ruben
Line Producer / UPM

Q - What is your background?

Gilly - Since I was seven years I wanted to be in the film business. I met a DP at the National Film School who asked me to work on a film school film in the UK. The Director of the film had Alan Parker as his tutor, whose assistant had just quit. So I went to work for Alan Parker and slaved for 9 years. When we were doing *Mississippi Burning*, I became very friendly with Frances McDormand. Frances introduced me to her boyfriend, a gentleman called Joel Coen. When I left Alan, I went on to commercials and documentaries when Joel Coen called me and said *'we're making this little film called The Hudsucker Proxy. Do you want to come and production manage the second unit with this guy called Sam Raimi?'* And that's how it began. And because of working with the Coen brothers, the phone just kept ringing and ringing.

Q - What is your role as a Unit Production Manager (UPM)?

Gilly - I'm one of the first people to be hired. I employ every person and make every deal, though I tend not to do the Screen Actors Guild deals, they are done by the producer, but I hire everybody, and I fire people if need be. I get every piece of equipment for the show and I look after the budget on a daily basis. Call sheets, production reports, how we made the day, how much did we spend that day? Was that within our budget? Are we over or under? Where in the budget are we going to take the money from if a particular department is over budget?

Q - What would be the first things to do on a low budget film?

Gilly - The budget is the most important thing - get everything in order with that. Then make sure you have your insurance and that you're bonded. In terms of getting a production going, find your key people and start planning what's to be done.

Q - Is a large part of being a UPM having negotiating skills, especially on a low budget movie, getting stuff for free?

Gilly - I recently helped on a feature film for a production cost of $241k. A friend of mine came up with the finance himself, along with a couple of investors. If someone has worked on a lot of movies in production, you build up relationships with vendors so it's easier to ask for favors. So I called in every single favor. We got free lights, free grip stuff, in fact most of everything was free, which was why it only cost $241k. The way it works with your vendors is if they consider you an investment and they do you a favor, then you'll bring them your next financed job. People are clever with their words in this town and everybody knows somebody who knows somebody. I don't think its difficult to get deals, especially if you can utilize time when their equipment is not being rented. What are they losing by investing something?

Q - What advice could you give on negotiating skills?

Gilly - Be honest and fair. Treat people nicely and with respect and then people are nice to you back. You don't get anywhere by shouting at people.

Q - What would your advice be to using friends on a low budget movie?

Gilly - First of all, you do need to use your friends because they're the people who are going to do you favors. But use friends that are qualified for that particular position. However, it's not always in one's best interest to pull in one's friends because you can ruin a lot of friendships that way. It can become too personal.

Q - What kind of rates are there in terms of a producer hiring a production manager?

Gilly - Well if you're in the DGA there are set negotiated rates. But if you're like me, and aren't actually a member of the DGA, the producer can offer you diddly-squat and you'd accept it because you need a job and you don't have a leg to stand on. The IA covers all the crew, the Director's Guild covers the director, the unit production manager, and all the Assistant Director's.

Q - Any tips on scheduling? What pitfalls can you fall into?

Gilly - If it's a first time director, you need to allow more time. Unfortunately, that constitutes more money but you have to make allowances otherwise you get screwed. You have to have a very strong 1st AD to help the director through that. Most first time directors write their script with no idea of the cost. You need to think of creative ways to make something less complicated than what has been written.

Q - Have you ever been able to sneak in shots, guerilla style, without anyone knowing that you're filming?

Gilly - Yes, but not recently. It's just too risky. The unions will shut you down if you don't tell them that you're making a movie because you've only got something ridiculous like seventy dollars. The unions are very strong here and have a lot of power.

Q - Des the UPM deal with permits?

Gilly - No. The location manager deals with that. I deal with approving the permits or the amount of money the locations cost.

Q - Do you deal with the Teamsters?

Gilly - Yes. For instance on a low budget film I did recently, I hired a transportation co-ordinator who had a good relationship with the Teamsters. I found him through recommendations from people who have done lower budget stuff. We got *'Movie Of The Week'* rates, which we were told would be the last time they would ever do this. Transportation (Teamsters & the equipment vehicles) and locations are the two largest numbers you'll see below the line on a budget.

Q - If you had a low budget movie, under $500k, would you mention that to the unions?

When To Shoot

1. Traditionally, late summer and January are slow times for rental companies.

2. If your film is set at night, it will take longer to shoot, as every shot will need to be lit. If you shoot during the day, it's possible to get away with little or no lighting. Shooting from the hip during daylight is the best way to cover a lot of ground when you don't have much time and money.

3. Find out how often and when it is likely to rain or snow where you are filming. Avoid those times, or shoot in the Southwest where you have little chance of either, great light and the days last longer.

4. Crews and actors (especially) don't like being cold and wet. Try and work around bad weather, or if the script calls for it, control the weather by creating it with wind, rain or snow machines. Better still, cut it out of the script!

5. In the fall and winter, it gets dark earlier. Conversely, you can really take advantage of mid June when we have maximum daylight. On a similar note, try to shoot as far west in a time zone as you can, as you will get up to an hour or so more light in the day than if you shoot at the eastern edge of it.

6. Avoid the Christmas/New Year weeks as people are not in the mood to work and everyone will be with their families.

Gilly - It's around $1m you start worrying. I don't think they would do anything at $500k. It's a double-edged sword. Would they rather have their members be working and not be paying benefits into their union?

Q - Do they blacklist and how long do you get black listed?

Gilly - Yes, they blacklist individuals. I know that a gaffer friend of mine (who works for a big time D.P, but lives on the East Coast), every time Production puts his name up to say that the D.P would like to hire him and that he wants to come and work out in LA, they'd say *'no way'*. They just won't let him work in LA.

Q - So crew members from one state may not be allowed to work in others?

Gilly - Correct.

Q - Could you join each state's individual union so you could work anywhere in the States?

Gilly - You could, but you'd have to pay a lot of money and in some cases, you're not allowed to join. Again, you'd also have to make sure you have a certain number of days working in each locality and you have an address in that particular state

Q - So even though he is very experienced, they're still funny about it?

Gilly - Yes. They'll say *'why are you employing somebody who's a member of the New York local, when there's so many people unemployed in LA? Why not hire one of the people in the union here?'*

Q - You can't say 'I'll hire every other single person from the state, just let me hire him'?

Union v Non-Union

Should you or shouldn't you use union crews and talent?

1. If Non-Union, you face the possibility of one of your crew members wanting to become a union member and the best way of them doing that is to ring the union and inform on you. The union turns up and shuts down the entire production, forcing the show to go union. The crew member then unscrupulously becomes a union member.

2. If Union, you may have to have more crew than you need, particularly on a low budget production.

3. If Union, you're more likely to get better and more experienced crew members.

4. If non-Union, some companies may not want to help as they have been burned by non-union productions in the past.

5. SAG offers low budget agreements that are very reasonable. Many agents do not take non-union productions seriously when trying to provide work for their clients.

6. The Union takes the view that if you don't have the money to properly budget for labor, you shouldn't be making the movie, and they may expel any of their members who decide to work on your show.

7. The Union also states that they if you can't afford their upfront rates, you can negotiate with them. This may also include back end deals that are contingent on box office success.

8. Confusingly, unions have said that if your budget is so low that you cannot use their members, they may give you their blessing to do the show non-union (this is up to each local union).

9. On a non union show, it's likely that less experienced crew members will get a career break - a clapper loader gets to be DP, an assistant editor gets to edit for instance.

10. If you go Non-Union don't list your production in any trade magazines as the Unions will know that you exist, and potentially cause you problems because you did not approach them first. If you cleared your show with the Unions, then you have nothing to worry about.

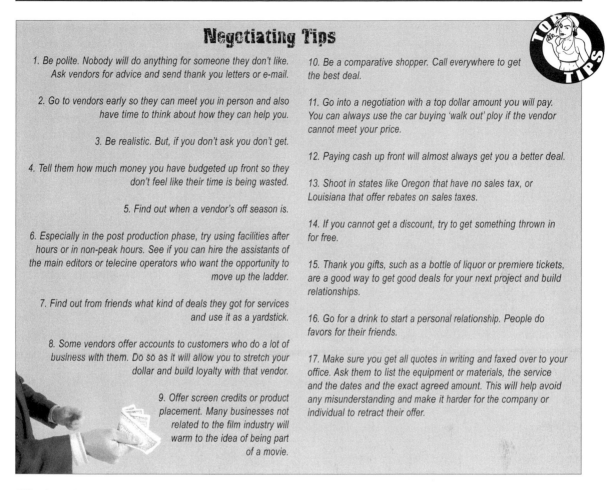

Negotiating Tips

1. Be polite. Nobody will do anything for someone they don't like. Ask vendors for advice and send thank you letters or e-mail.

2. Go to vendors early so they can meet you in person and also have time to think about how they can help you.

3. Be realistic. But, if you don't ask you don't get.

4. Tell them how much money you have budgeted up front so they don't feel like their time is being wasted.

5. Find out when a vendor's off season is.

6. Especially in the post production phase, try using facilities after hours or in non-peak hours. See if you can hire the assistants of the main editors or telecine operators who want the opportunity to move up the ladder.

7. Find out from friends what kind of deals they got for services and use it as a yardstick.

8. Some vendors offer accounts to customers who do a lot of business with them. Do so as it will allow you to stretch your dollar and build loyalty with that vendor.

9. Offer screen credits or product placement. Many businesses not related to the film industry will warm to the idea of being part of a movie.

10. Be a comparative shopper. Call everywhere to get the best deal.

11. Go into a negotiation with a top dollar amount you will pay. You can always use the car buying 'walk out' ploy if the vendor cannot meet your price.

12. Paying cash up front will almost always get you a better deal.

13. Shoot in states like Oregon that have no sales tax, or Louisiana that offer rebates on sales taxes.

14. If you cannot get a discount, try to get something thrown in for free.

15. Thank you gifts, such as a bottle of liquor or premiere tickets, are a good way to get good deals for your next project and build relationships.

16. Go for a drink to start a personal relationship. People do favors for their friends.

17. Make sure you get all quotes in writing and faxed over to your office. Ask them to list the equipment or materials, the service and the dates and the exact agreed amount. This will help avoid any misunderstanding and make it harder for the company or individual to retract their offer.

PRODUCTION

Gilly - It can depend on whom you talk to at the union and how much of a bee in their bonnet you are with that particular person you're trying to get in. It can get ugly.

Q - So all the locals are controlled by the IA?

Gilly - The IA overall, is run by one particular individual. However, each local has its own representative. Even though this man (who runs the I.A) is like the Godfather to the whole structure, each local has their own representative. And many times on movies, you'll find reps from each of the different locals coming out to visit the set to make sure that everything's in order.

Q - It's shocking to think that when you're trying to make a movie for $1m, that the unions are so powerful?

Gilly - Yes, but where there's a will there's a way. I saw the cast and crew screening of this movie last night, which we did for $241k and it's a proper, full-length feature film. We weren't union, we weren't DGA. We were Writer's Guild because the director was in a writer's guild and we were SAG on their very low budget agreement. But we saved a lot of money by shooting it on video.

Q - If the IA found out about the film, would they do anything?

Gilly - I don't think they'd bat an eyelid because of the amount of money that it cost.

Production Binders

The key to saving time and money is to be organized. A production binder (or several!) will help you find important information quickly when the heat is on full blast. Get yourself a 3-inch D-ring binder from an office supply store along with some dividers that can be labeled. Label the dividers into sections relevant to your film. Here are some suggestions:

Blocking / Shot selection, Breakdown sheets, Call sheets, Camera reports, Sound reports, Camera/Grip information, Cast list (inc. contacts, credits and headshots), Correspondence, Crew list (inc. contacts), Day out of Days sheets, Deal points / Legal, Film safety and security (local hospital, police, etc.), Hair / Make Up, Script notes, Production schedule, Production Design (art direction, set design, etc.), Props, Special effects, Shooting script.

Q - What has been your worst experience on a movie?

Gilly - I was on a movie where the producers doctored the budget to get all the low budget rates. They said *'of course we're going to spend the contingency. We don't have enough money to make the movie.'* So they did. It had a first time feature director from very visual video commercials. Our call times on a Monday morning were 7am, by Wednesday, we had shot so many hours they had moved it to 5pm. It was very difficult, just running the crew absolutely ragged. I'm from a school where you never spend a contingency, as it is your safety net. They spent the contingency, which usually means the bond company will come and take it over. They didn't on this one because the producer was close friends with our rep. from the bond company.

Q - If you spend half your contingency, and you're on a bonded film, are you at risk of having the Bond Company come in and take over?

Gilly - Yes, it's possible. If you're making a low budget movie with private investors, it doesn't necessarily demand a bond though. But anything that has any other kind of financing, even if it's over a couple of million, they will demand a completion bond. And if you spend half of the contingency, then the bond company will come and investigate, possibly take over and replace key members of the crew. A lot of people will go over budget a little, but they save in other areas so it doesn't eat into the contingency. But if you've done all the juggling you can and you're still going into contingency, then you're in trouble.

Q - How often do you supply the bond company with progress reports?

Gilly - They get faxed through to the insurance and bond company daily. With most movies, you fax the studio your call sheet, production reports, daily costs and hot costs too.

Q - What about the DGA?

Gilly - You give them other reports on a daily basis, but not your hot costs.

Q - Do you do that at the end of the day when you've completed the day's shooting?

Gilly - Yes. Most production co-ordinators have programmed into the fax machine all the companies that need to have the hot costs and production reports.

Q - Is overtime with the unions a set fee?

Gilly - Yes. With the low budget rate you don't hit overtime until twelve hours, as opposed to on a

Office Stuff

Aside from the obvious stuff, such as a computer, printer and a desk, here's a list of other stuff you will need in your production office. You may also consider networking your computers. It's easier than you may think and will mean you can share resources such as your printer and internet connection.

Refrigerator	Office supplies (lots of paper and toner)
Coffee maker	Courier service account
Water cooler	Recycling bins
Microwave	Extra keys to office
Radio	Paper shredder
DSL connection	Filing cabinet
Heavy duty punch (for scripts)	Stamps
Spare cellphone charger	Petty cash box (lockable)
Photocopier	TV / VCR / DVD (for reels)
Good chairs	Backup device (Zip disk or CDR)
Fax	

normal agreement where it's straight time until eight, time and a half from eight to twelve and double time after twelve. On low budget it's time and a half from twelve onwards. So in fact, the crew actually quite enjoyed working on it, because if they did that amount of hours, they would get a semi-decent pay check. However, I don't feel you can do that to a crew. What kind of benefit is it if everybody is so exhausted all the time?

Q - What are the things to look out for when hiring crew?

Gilly - One of the most important things when you're crewing up is to make sure that all the personalities gel. You want it to be one big happy family, and as a production manager, I try and find the right people to gel.

Q - Who is the main person you hire and what is your relationship with them?

Gilly - The two most important people for me are the accountant and the production coordinator. The co-ordinator is my eyes, ears and right hand. I rely on the accountant to let me know how we're doing on a daily / hourly basis as I'm dealing with every department and there's no way I could know where I'm at financially every second, but the accountant does because they plug it all into a computer. Not one piece of paper involving spending money gets approved without me signing off on it, and I rely on the accountant to record it. I will never work on a budget line by line by line. It's just one big sum of money. I know my guidelines and I know where I can take money to compensate elsewhere. I have a specific production co-ordinator that I work with, although my accountant is now a very happy professional dog-walker as she was fed up after fifteen years of the movie business!

Q - Your production coordinator is literally your right hand?

Gilly - Yes. What I need is a production coordinator who is also confident in the SAG rules and regulations, and can station twelve an actor. Station twelve is where you find out if all the actors are actually SAG eligible - if they have paid their dues, if they can work and if they are indeed a member of SAG.

Q - What if they're not a member of SAG?

Gilly – Then you need to Taft-Hartley that actor. You're only allowed one or two on a production. You can Taft-Hartley someone who is not SAG - you have to write in the form that you've done an extensive search for a SAG actor and say that this non union actor fits the role exactly and the director wants this person and no other. It helps them to become SAG later.

UPM Checklist

- ☐ Set up your office space.
- ☐ Set up your office stationery. Letterhead, business cards etc.
- ☐ Organize your insurance and completion bond.
- ☐ Check through the preliminary budget.
- ☐ Hire the production accountant and production co-ordinator.
- ☐ Become signatory to bank accounts.
- ☐ Hire the key department heads.
- ☐ Refine the budget with your key crew, getting good deals with vendors etc.
- ☐ Make sure all clearances have been acquired for the script (if necessary).
- ☐ Become signatory to the Unions/Guilds.
- ☐ Prepare all contracts, releases, permits and necessary paperwork for crew, cast, locations etc.
- ☐ Order film and equipment.
- ☐ Create production binder with contact lists.
- ☐ Distribute necessary paperwork.
- ☐ Arrange rehearsals.
- ☐ Secure police, fire officers etc.
- ☐ Approve all check requests/invoices/PO's etc.
- ☐ Arrange hotel accommodation/travel accommodation.
- ☐ Head production meetings.
- ☐ Oversee day to day production including overseeing call sheets, production reports etc.
- ☐ Secure wrap of shoot.
- ☐ Make sure all equipment has been returned.
- ☐ Handle all insurance claims.
- ☐ Create screen credit list.
- ☐ Turn over files etc. to Producer.

Catering

A film crew looks forward to only one thing - lunch. There is no better way to create crew ill will than to give them either poor quality to too little food. Catering often becomes a major problem for the production team on low budget films.

1. A film crew works better on a full stomach - especially if they are out in the cold. Coffee, tea and cold drinks should always be made available, with someone making sure that the key personnel (who are working harder than the others) have their drinks brought to them.

2. Feed a crew as much food as you can. Have snacks such as fruit, pastries, candies, pretzels, peanuts, bread etc., all constantly available.

3. Film caterers are expensive but they do provide a wonderful service. Try negotiating them down to a price per head that you can afford.

4. If you can't afford a film caterer, find someone who is used to catering for large groups and employ them for the duration of the shoot. They may bring their own equipment and will certainly have good ideas. Catering students can also be a good option, but they will be inexperienced and unprepared for the barrage to which they will be subjected.

5. Large sandwiches are a good lunchtime filler - easy to prepare and distribute. However, beware of crew boredom with this culinary treat. Try and make up a simple menu (also catering for vegetarians) and give people an option. This will prevent arguments, and give them something to look forward to.

6. Actors are fussier than crew and often expect to be treated better than you can afford. Be aware of this very important factor.

7. Candy and beers after a hard weeks shoot can offer a good emotional bribe to get back in favor with a disgruntled cast and crew.

8. Concentrate on foods that are easy to prepare, cheap to produce, and fast to distribute and clear. Draw up a list of meals and outline them in a schedule. This will allow certain meals to be rotated.

9. If possible, give your crew a small amount of money each day and ask them to feed themselves. This works well if you are close to shops, a cafeteria or a diner. This way they get a choice, and you get zero catering problems.

10. Product placement is always a good source for a couple of boxes of chips, chocolate bars, etc.

11. Some cast and crew will expect breakfast. It's your choice, but as soon as you give it to them, you will have to cater for this extra meal every day. Ask them to eat their cereal or bagels before they leave home.

12. If cast and crew are away from home for a location shoot, you will need to cater for all their needs, breakfast, lunch, dinner and hearty snacks for night shoots. This quickly becomes VERY expensive.

13. Make sure that food is not left out too long, in the sun or uncovered. You don't want your crew coming down with salmonella.

14. It's obvious, but if you are shooting in a confined place, avoid farty foods for lunch!

Q - Does being a member of the DGA benefit crew members?

*Gilly –*Yes, most definitely financially if you are a member of the DGA. On *The Hudsucker Proxy*, which was not a DGA film, the First Assistant Director was a DGA member. Then *Fargo* came around and the DGA said to him *'we'll throw you out because you did a non DGA film as a first AD.'* So on their next movie *Fargo*, he became Joel and Ethan Coen's producer.

Q - Why is it so difficult to be in the DGA, especially after having worked on such high profile movies?

Gilly - I was nominated for a Directors Guild Award and they still won't let me in. However, if the director is nominated for a DGA award then so is the 1st AD and the UPM. You have to have enough days working on a DGA film, and if not, they won't let you join. It's the usual catch-22. I'm often credited as a production supervisor rather than unit production manager on the films which are

DGA signatory. The problem I have is that I'm never going to get enough days, because producers keep hiring me as a production supervisor, mainly because they want to take the DGA benefits and the money. It's cheaper labor. Production Supervisor is not a DGA category. The only way I can be a member of the DGA is to work out of town on DGA movies and make up the rest of my days. There's only one job that I did get paid the full DGA rate working as a Production Supervisor on a DGA film and that was on *Being John Malkovich*.

Q - You've worked on documentaries as well as features. What are the fundamental differences?

Gilly - Documentaries are the perfect example of not getting any permits, which is more the Guerrilla style of filmmaking, shooting from the hip. I did additional shooting on a small documentary-style movie where we shot on Sunset Boulevard outside the clubs and we didn't have any permits and nobody stopped us. With documentaries, you're not looking after the budget by the day. You do the call sheets, but you don't have to necessarily have to do the production reports so there is less paperwork.

Derek Roberto
Production Co-ordinator

Q - What is the job of the Production Coordinator?

Derek - The Production Coordinator works hand in hand with the Production Manager and line producer. Our primary responsibilities are to hire the crew and equipment necessary to make a film, TV show or commercial and to do so within the budget assigned to us. We typically hire people that we have either worked with before or have gotten a glowing review from someone we trust. In addition, the production coordinator helps the Production Manager set up schedules for and facilitate pre-production, such as organizing location scouting, casting, tech scouts, travel, permits, shoot days and the wrap. We make rental agreements with vendors for the production's equipment - from motion picture cameras and cranes or helicopters to roles of camera tape for the camera department. I end up making lots of call sheets and lists of things in order to keep the production organized. We also cater to the director, producers, and other executives (who are either part of the production company or affiliated with a studio/executive producer) when they come one set, making sure they have what they need while visiting.

Q - What are common problems that you encounter?

Derek - The problems I often come across are not enough money, too small a budget, a producer wanting to do to much for too little, not enough time and too little light (not enough money for a lighting package that could reproduce full daylight on a desert landscape). Most of these come directly from not having enough cash on hand, but then again, you can throw all the money you want at something, but it won't necessarily make it good. I've worked on more things that can easily be forgotten or haven't and won't see the light of day because the script was bad. But the memorable ones are those that were good ideas to begin with. With a good script, you can shoot it on Hi-8 and it could be a piece of art.

Q - What advice would you give a novice filmmakers?

Derek - Take a job, any job and work hard. Work as if it's your last job. The PA position may seem bad, but you get to see more and interact with the production process. Most PAs on features do lock downs (confirmation of people and equipment hire) or paper work a la the 2nd AD Department. On commercials, they get to be there at the beginning (if they are in the office) when scripts and boards are prepared, when cast and locations are chosen, and calls to the crew are made; also during the shoot, if there's a moment, they can shadow any of the key positions that might interest them (as long as they don't become a pest). Don't PA too long as it's easy to get pigeonholed. Let people know what you want to do, then DO IT. Overall, working in production is a good way to make contacts and get to know people who may help you with your future projects.

PRODUCTION

Amy Hansen
Production Accountant

ACCOUNTANT

Q - What is your job as a production accountant?

Amy - Overseeing the day to day expenditures, which include the payroll, petty cash and paying for all equipment and purchases. I make sure that everything is reflected in our computer software.

Q - How early on in the process are you hired?

Amy - Accountants should be taken on as early as possible to process the payroll, the expenses already incurred and often to look over the budgets. Since production accountants are really the only people who know the software, on a low budget, I would say three or four weeks ahead of time as they need to get the information into the computer as quickly as possible.

Q - Would you bring in a payroll company or does it depend on the budget?

Amy - A production accountant will have a payroll company to provide payroll services and the software for the computer as a package deal. Usually, I can select the payroll company myself but sometimes the producers will have a company that they use. Sometimes they already have the software installed and everything is ready to go.

Q - What's the first thing you do on day one of your job?

Amy - Day one is usually just getting the offices in order, setting up forms as people always need checks right away. It's important to get everything set up in the computer, particularly the chart of accounts, so I can translate the complete budget into computer terms. Until the approved budget is input into the accounting system, everything show up as negative. The cost report is the most important accounting report that we generate. We issue one just before shooting which reflects the entire pre-production costs. Once we begin shooting, we put out a cost report once a week - this is especially important, even on low budgets, because you really need to see where you are and make sure that nothing is out of place.

Q - Does that literally list everything that you've spent?

Amy - Everything. There's a number of different ways to present the numbers. The cost report itself only lists categories like office supplies or key grip. You can also print a transaction report, which shows every single name that's in the computer, so you can check whether something has been coded incorrectly or when you present your cost report to the UPM (unit production manager) and they flip out over something you can give them the a detailed report. Some just ask for a summary cost report.

Q - Is your closest crew relationship with the UPM?

Amy - Most definitely.

Q - Do you also manage the individual key personnel budgets?

Amy - Usually the UPM prefers to do this because they make most of the deals. They'll tell each department how much they have to spend, they would then be expected to come up with a budget and that's something they would review with the UPM. The UPM has to okay it, and that's when it is presented to me. If somebody were to submit a department budget and I thought something was not right then I might mention it to the UPM.

Q - So, you would go straight to the UPM. Would you go to the producers as well?

Amy - Not generally. There are so many different types of producers. There are the producers who really get involved and those you never meet that just provide money and everything in between. I have worked on projects with producers I've known and they say, *'please come and tell me if something isn't right'* because they want to be in the loop.

Q - Do you have to report to the bond company if it's a bonded film?

Amy - If you are working on a bonded film then yes, you report to the bond company. I don't think I've done a low budget film that's been involved with a bond company though. I used to work on a lot of movies which were budgeted at about $3.5m and bonded. But some films don't have money for a bond or contingency and there's nothing illegal about that, it's just a choice they make.

Q - If you were going to be with a production company that had a bond, what kind of rules would you have to follow?

Amy - Once the budget is locked, you can't change it. You can show your overages and underages and do changes for the estimated final cost, but you can't actually change that budget number. Sometimes when the UPM does the budgets themselves, they realize in the first week of shooting they've made an estimation error and they'll say *'let's change the budget amount'*. You can't do that with a bond company at all. I don't like to change the budget amounts once we start shooting because I think it's good to have it as a guide. There certainly isn't any reason you can't go over or under an amount because that's what happens all through the process of filmmaking.

Q - What other reports do you have to put forward?

Amy - There is also the 'Hotcost' which is generated daily from the previous day's production report. It'll tell you approximately where you are day to day. When there is a one person accounting department there generally isn't time to do a hotcost because you're going fourteen hours a day.

Q - Does the UPM do the production report?

Amy - No, the AD's do it on set. Sometimes they are so overwhelmed that you don't get them for a few days which makes hotcosts impossible, another reason that on low budget films we don't do them. Most other reports I generate would be for my own use, because I like to keep track of things on a day to day basis. Oftentimes, the producers and the funding source request those too.

Q - On a low budget film where they are still writing through the shoot and making changes, would they ask you to look at potential budget changes?

Amy - By the time I'm hired the budget is already started, although there are always little changes during the prep period. I think that accountants are considered watchdogs. We're not necessarily considered to have an idea of how much things cost, so I think that most times those decisions are made apart from accounting. Changes to the script can affect many budgetary items, and must be incorporated into the budget ASAP.

Q - How does the dispersal of petty cash operate?

Amy - The petty cash is a major element of low budget. We can have trouble getting credit accounts from vendors so we have to write checks or use cash right away. I encourage checks because it leaves a much better audit trail for taxes, but there are certain things that you always do pay by cash. Usually it's the head of department that will get the petty cash. We open up a float of petty cash at the beginning and give them an amount which is negotiated with the UPM and based on their total budget. We make sure they don't have more money in cash than their total budget would allow for. So, they spend their cash, get an envelope, fill out a form listing each item they purchased with the receipt for it and turn it in. On a low budget film I try to turn around petty cash as quickly as possible. They will ask for twenty-four hour turnaround, which can leave you wondering how many envelopes are you going to get and how much cash you have in your safe.

Q - What about things like cell phones and mileage?

Amy - Cellphones have always been a problem as the costs can spiral out of control. The UPM is the only person who can authorize an employee to use their cellphone, but I've seen people put cell phones through their petty cash which I pay as a reimbursement. Mileage is almost never granted. The people who get mileage, because of the union SAG, put it on their time card.

Q - Do the transportation guys get reimbursed?

Amy - No, because they are driving company vehicles and the production company pays for all the gas. Almost nobody gets mileage on a low budget show, not even the PA's, and they do a lot of driving. On a larger budget show sometimes they'll get mileage, at about 32c a mile.

Q - What about a per diem, do you take care of that?

Amy - Yes. That's only for when you're out of town. It goes to everybody and there's a certain amount based on how much money they think it costs to be in a particular city. So, if you were to go to New York, it would certainly be much higher than if you were shooting in a small town in Arkansas. There's a set amount for SAG, but the crew is negotiable. The IRS determines taxable and non taxable rates for each city.

Q - What is the per diem for?

Amy - You have to wonder as the hotels are paid for and you eat your meals on set. People figure if you have to go out of town, you have to buy incidentals.

Q - What else do you deal with other than the per diem and petty cash?

Amy - Mostly the payroll and making sure vendor checks are ready for departments like set dressing, wardrobe and locations. Locations in particular spend so much money; you can't just give them petty cash. Besides, for tax laws, that wouldn't work. We try to get purchase orders from as many people as we can. They are very important for accounting. Every time someone buys or rents something and we haven't actually paid for it, it needs a purchase order. Otherwise, if somebody wants to rent something from Panavision that's very expensive, and forgets to do a purchase order, the office has no idea they rented anything. Weeks could go by before Panavision sends us a big, ugly surprise bill which we haven't budgeted for.

Q - Do you deal with union rates?

Amy - Most of the low budget shows that I do are DGA and SAG, but they're not union for the below the line crew, although the unions are getting tougher and tougher here in California.

Q - So, they turn up and say, 'Let's do a deal or we'll close you down'.

Petty Cash

All receipts MUST HAVE the vendor's name, address, telephone number either stamped or attached with a business card. If you spend petty cash on items where there are no receipts (i.e gratuities, parking meters, pay phones), you must make up a receipt, listing the expense and the date. Any last minute petty cash items, such as location receipts, MUST HAVE the name of the vendor, their address, telephone number, tax ID number or social security number and a signature for receipt of the cash. At the end of each week, petty cash receipts must be handed in for payment the following week.

Per Diems

An allowance given to actors prior to the day or week of work. This is to cover any 'out of pocket' costs that might be required. Per Diems are now seen more as a perk, but are standard throughout the industry. There are scheduled minimum rates and Per Diems are subject to tax.

Cell phones

Cell phones are always needed on a film set, however if the production company has agreed to reimburse the use of cell phones, then it's a difficult task to keep under control. Try and restrict cell phone use to certain crew members and cap the usage. Request that the crew members submit their bills containing all work related calls (circled) to the production office, for reimbursement.

Mileage/Gas reimbursement

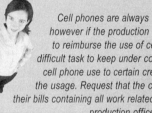

This can be done either by paying an agreed rate per mile (i.e. 32 cents per mile) OR through reimbursement of gas receipts, BUT NOT BOTH. Drive To's can be arranged for rural locations where mileage is determined by calculating the mileage from the production office to the location and back, and multiplied by 32 c per mile. This is usually required by the unions and would be filled in on the weekly time cards. The IRS has a set allowance, and if the reimbursement exceeds this, anything over is considered taxable income.

Restaurant meals

The IRS require charges over $25 to be submitted on credit card receipts along with what was ordered from the menu, and a list of all crew who ate with you. If you paid by another method other than credit card, then you must have an itemized receipt with a business card of the establishment.

Car Allowance

Sometimes, key crew who will be using their own cars on production, can request car allowance. Car allowance is paid through the payroll service for IRS and is listed on the crew time cards. Car allowance is considered taxable income.

Kit/Box Rental

Certain crew members may have negotiated kit with the production. i.e. a make up artist may include her own make up equipment under kit/box rental. Again this is listed on the crew time cards and is considered taxable income, but will be declared in a 1099 at the end of the year.

Meal Penalties

If shooting more than 6 hours in a row, you must give your crew a meal. If you don't, you're be liable for meal penalties which occur every 15 minutes, and if you're not watching, they can escalate out of control. Time of Lunch and Dinners are listed on the time cards.

Amy - Yeah, we used to see that a lot with TV movies, but not so much now with reality TV shows and things like those. On low budget shows we can be so small that the unions don't even care.

Q - How large do you have to be before the unions start to care?

Amy - I have been on shows that have started out non-union and changed, but it depends on how much is going on in town. Somebody calls the union and says they're on a non-union show, sometimes the union will show up.

Q - Are you, as a production accountant, in a union?

Amy - Most of the time I'm non-union, although my rate is usually negotiated.

Q - Do you find that people in production companies are more likely to hire people that are non-union because they don't have to pay union rates?

Amy - Definitely. Especially on low budget because not only are union rates so much higher, but union members additionally receive PH&W (pension health and welfare), vacation and holiday pay, and meal penalties.

Q - What are meal penalties?

Amy - There's a rule that states that if you're shooting more than six hours, you have to give the crew a meal. If you don't give them their food after six hours, then every thirty minutes you start to incur a penalty. It currently starts at $7.50. If you're in the middle of a shot, you get a twelve minute grace on that. If you exceed that twelve minute grace period, by another fifteen minutes it's another $10 and it keeps on going up.

Q - Who is the person on set who controls that?

Amy - That's the AD's, they run around like crazy trying to make sure that everyone eats. SAG also gets meal penalties. The first one is $25. If you have a show that's non-union except for SAG and DGA, you have to make sure everyone sits down after their six hours or else. And, then the overtime of course spirals wildly. In California, the first eight hours you work are based at straight time. The next four are paid at time and a half, so instead of it being four, it's six. So a twelve-hour day is actually fourteen pay hours. When you're working out a person's rate, you have to take their daily rate and divide it by fourteen. After that it is overtime.

Q - With low budget, non-union shoots, do you find it's a flat fee for below the line?

Amy - Actually, it's illegal to do flat fees. You have to do hourly. It's California state law. So that's what we do. We say *'if you work twelve hours a day, this is how much money you're going to make'*. If they work over twelve hours they get overtime. This protects people from working eighteen hours and only getting $100. Some departments are exempt, production accountant being one. It's basically a flat rate based on a weekly rate, but it only works for heads of department. Exempt employers are generally paid a good enough rate to start with though.

Q - Would you need their contracts to know what their hours are?

Amy - Exactly. The first thing that we do for an employer is to create a start packet. It has memos explaining the production and the deal memo. This is usually generated by the payroll company and it has all the information that they need in order to pay each employee - their name and address, their social security, their rate and the signatures of the employer, the UPM and sometimes the signature of the accountant. It also has their I-9 in there.

Q - What is the I-9?

Amy - The I-9 is verification of the employee's name and address and they have to check a little box to say either 'I'm a citizen of the United States' or 'I'm not a citizen but I have a permanent residency'. Then you check their ID, like a passport, drivers license or social security card. This is mandatory for every employee, as it's illegal to pay them without it.

Q - Who do you give that to?

Amy - That goes to the payroll company. It also has the information on each employee so you can figure out how many tax exemptions they want. The top half will list who they are and how much they make and then the second sheet might list how many exemptions they want for their taxes.

Q - Why would they be able to tick off their tax exemptions?

Money Matters

W-4 Forms

This is used to calculate the proper federal and state withholding deductions. All employees must fill these out before they are paid. IRS regulations require that an individual be taxed as Single with zero exemptions if the W-4 is NOT filled out properly.

I-9 Forms

An absolute requirement of the Federal Immigration and Naturalization Service, where all employers must fill out upon hiring an individual, and must be updated every 3 years. Instruct all personnel to fill these out accurately.

W-2 Forms

Employees receive this from their employer at the end of year end by January 31st. This shows your entire wages for the year, how much tax has been deducted, how much pre tax has been taken out for medical plans etc.

EXPLANATION OF TAXES and DEDUCTIONS FROM YOUR WAGE CHECK

Federal Tax information is for any US resident. State tax information is only for residents of the State of California (or your appropriate state).

Employer Paid Taxes:
FUI (Federal Unemployment Insurance)

The employer must pay taxes to the Federal Government to fund services and benefits for temporarily unemployed workers.

SUI (State Unemployment Insurance)

The employer must pay taxes to the State Government to fund services and benefits for temporarily unemployed workers.

Workers Compensation

This is a legally required insurance which employers usually purchase from insurance companies to help sick or disabled employees whose injury or illness is caused by their jobs.

Employee Paid Taxes:
FIT (Federal Income Tax)

Employers are required to subtract estimated taxes from employee's taxable earnings and pay this to the IRS (Internal Revenue Service). These estimated income taxes are called withholdings. An employees taxable earnings are affected by marital status and withholding allowances. A withholding allowance, or personal exemption, is the amount of money by which someone can reduce the amount of earnings subject to income tax. Everyone is allowed one allowance plus an additional allowance for each dependent. The employee informs the employer how many exemptions they can claim by filing a W-4 when they're hired.

SIT (State Income Tax)

This is based on the same parameters as the FIT, however this tax is paid to the State.

FOR BOTH EMPLOYER AND EMPLOYEE:
OASDI (Old Age, Survivors, and Disability Insurance) commonly known as Social Security:

This provides pensions to retired persons aged 62 or older, payments to disabled persons, and benefits of dependents of insured workers who have died or become disabled.

Medi-Care is a health insurance program for persons 65 or older and/or disabled.

UNION OR GUILD

Any Union or Guild charges (Pension, Health and Welfare etc.) would be at the current contracted rate in effect for that union or guild.

Amy - You can control the amount of tax you pay on every check. At the end of the year when you turn in your tax forms, either you owe the government more money or they owe you money back.

Q - Does the payroll company deal with that too?

Amy - Yeah and each employee usually knows and you usually choose the same thing every year. It really has to do with how much money you earn, how often you work, because as freelancers you don't really know. The higher the number you select, the less tax they take. You send it to payroll and they input it.

Q - Would you use things like Movie Magic?

Accountant Show Reports

Provided by production accountant Nancy Ramey.

All of the standard software programs for the entertainment industry provide you with the following reports:

COA (Chart of Accounts)
This report prints out your COA so that you can have an account listing. On some systems, you have the ability of choosing whether to print balance sheet accounts, cost accounts or all. An account will usually consist of a location number, a production number, a major account (i.e.: 1100 – Script) and a minor account number (i.e. 01 - Script Costs). Sometimes a sub account number (i.e. 01 - Writer #1, 02 - Writer #2) is used and will be included.

Example:
1100 – Script
01 - Script Costs   0.00
01 - Writer #1   0.00
02 - Writer #2   0.00

Set numbers are usually printed in a separate report. Set numbers are used in the Art Department and sometimes locations.

Edits (audits or transaction) reports
These are used to check your input entry in accounts payable, petty cash and journal entries. This enables you to make account or description changes before posting your work to the general ledger. This is also available in payroll to correct coding only.

In the check printing module your will have the option of printing a pre-check register. This lets you see how much each check will be and how many checks you will be printing. After you print your checks you should print a Check Register, this will give you a record of the checks numbers you printed, the print date, to who the check was written and the amount of the check.

Posting Reports
Accounts Payable, Journal Entries, Petty Cash and Payroll all can give you posting reports. These reports are your permanent record of the work that you have done and maybe accessed during an audit.

G/L Inquiry (also may be called a transaction report)
You can print out by transaction number or account number everything that has been entered into you accounting system. Note that there may be a large variety of ways to print out your transactions depending on the system that you are using.

Trial Balance
This is a summary report of ALL of your show accounts. This will show your balance sheet account amounts (Bank accounts, petty cash accounts, deposits, accounts receivable, accounts payable, clearing accounts, accruals and cost accounts. This report is important because it not only shows how much money is in each account but at the end of it there is a total line that should equal zero. If there is any other number at the end of this report, you are out of balance and should call your software support person.

Cost Reports
This report compares the cost to date (actual costs plus purchase orders) with your budget. You will make changes to the Estimated Final Cost column to keep track of the current status of the show (over, under or in budget)

Bible Report
This is printed out after the show has been completed. It lists each account by number in order (both balance sheet accounts and cost accounts) and shows all the transactions that were entered into each account.

PO Log
This is a manual log indicating which department was given each purchase order and then when they come back in to accounting, the date the PO was assigned a vendor, who the vendor is, a description of what was ordered and the cost of the item(s).

Hot Costs
These are mini reports that a producer may want to see each morning of a shoot. To do a Hot Cost you will need the production report from the previous days shoot and a daily shooting cost number for each item in your budget. Most often you are asked to keep track of crew and actor overtime, meal penalties (if they apply), forced calls, film footage shot (over or under the amount allocated) and any thing else that cost the show money not allocated in the budget.

In each accounting system, there are other reports that may be printed. Examples are vendor reports that show every thing paid to a specific vendor, a complete check register report, a purchase order report and an unposted transaction report. These are you keep track of what you have or have not done.

Amy - That's something that people use before accountants show up because they don't have the accounting software. They use it to create their budgets and get their funding.

Q - Have you ever worked with the UPM on a preliminary budget? Or, have they always had the budget and then brought you on board?

Amy - They've always had them. On bigger films, oftentimes the accountant does do the budget because the funding is so different. It might be a studio funded project where the budget is based on the script or the stars of the movie.

Q - Do you ever have to put cash flow charts together for investors?

Amy - These are usually done before I show up because individuals who are interested in giving us the money to get a film made are understandably a little nervous.On some films I have done cash flows.

Q - If a sound recordist has personal equipment and wants to be reimbursed, would that go through you?

Amy - Yes. We call those box rentals or kit rentals. I almost always get one because I use my own computer. You almost always see them for the DP, the gaffer, the key grip and wardrobe. Oftentimes there are multiples for car rentals.

Q - Do you find that producers have put a contingency in the budget, and do they use it?

Amy - About half of them have put a contingency in. I have been lucky. On the films that have been real shoestring budgets we've come in under budget. The budgeting is almost easiest during the shoot and prep periods because you do know what is going to happen. The serious unknowns can come in post.

Q - Do you do accounting for post?

Amy - Yeah. Somebody has to generate checks and do payroll for the couple of people that are left - usually just the editor and the post production supervisor. Low budget sometimes do it themselves, which is tricky because only the accountants know the software and you will lose the ability to get reports, so they might ask the accountant to work through post. This could be eight to sixteen weeks. Another option is that the payroll companies will deal with post on the same software, but it can be a bit pricey.

Q - Would you have to deal with insurance claims if the camera broke for example?

Amy - No. It's handled by the production staff. If an employee is injured and there's a workers comp issue, it's initially handled through the production co-ordinator. We do, however, sometimes help by doing insurance claims, doing spreadsheets etc.

Q - Who handles the workers compensation?

Amy - The payroll company gives us forms for our workers comp. We usually pick it up with our starters packets. If there is an injury, record it immediately, usually from set. Workers comp is never put in the accountants hands.

Q - Would it be the production accountant's name on the check or would it be a joint signature with the producer?

Amy - They always put the production company name on it, but the check signer is debatable. I think it's important to have two signatures as a matter of control. The sensible combination is the accountant and UPM because every invoice, contract and deal I get, needs UPM approval. Sometimes a producer will be the signer, and on some shows I haven't been a signer at all. It is useful to have the accountant as the signer as we're always in the office if somebody needs an emergency check.

Q - Are the budgets padded in each section?

Amy - I think that it's a good idea, especially if there's not a contingency, because there's that great fear of going over. As we get to the end of the shoot, we'll start transferring any overages we know we have into post because post is very unpredictable.

Q - Do you know of any tax incentives?

Amy - We do get a percentage back for using certain people and places, like the California fire and police departments. There are certain locations where we can get some back. It isn't as much as it should be, which is why many of our films are now being shot outside California. Many crew are upset because a lot of films have gone to Canada and Australia.

Q - If you are using the police or fire departments do you need contingency for safety as well as paying them?

Amy - Yeah, you have to have security in certain locations, sometimes from a specific company to protect the trucks or the police for traffic control. We pay the police directly, rather than the department as they're part of our crew at that point. We pay their motorcycle rental, which is about $50 a day.

Q - Would it be the location manager who organizes the police and firemen?

Amy - Yeah, locations give them all their times and releases them when the day is over.

Q - What is the 401K?

Amy - We don't have that because we're freelancers. When you work for a company you give a percentage towards retirement, which the company matches. If freelancers want a retirement fund, you have to do it yourself.

Q - What about health benefits for people who work on the shoot?

Amy - There's a health plan system called Motion Picture Industry Health and Welfare. You have to earn 300 union hours per qualifying period to get benefits and you have to qualify with 600-700 hours. The best thing is work on a union show at 56 hours a week, which is what you generally accumulate on a picture. Once you get 600-700 hours you qualify and you get the benefits.

Q - So, if you're non-union, you have to sort out your own health benefits?

Amy - Yeah. People try to get a good pay rate because they know that they're going to be paying their own insurance. Typically, on low budget you don't get paid as much as a union film nor do you get benefits. This means that people often split from shoots if they are offered a union show and to some degree you can't blame them.

Q - How do you set up a bank account?

Amy - Usually I set up the bank, a regular checking account for our day to day stuff and another with high interest for our funding. You establish a rapport with a certain bank and use them regularly so they don't mind if you suddenly walk in and ask for $10k worth of petty cash. We get special checks that work with the software, so we have to order blank check stock with the name of the company printed on it.

Q - Do you find banks in LA are film friendly?

Amy - They are definitely film friendly to the big films. Low budget films do have problems sometimes, as no one wants to give us credit as they don't know if we're good for our money. So, they'll ask for enormous deposits or COD only.

Q - Would you have to set up an Escrow account for SAG members?

Amy - I have had to set one up specifically for a SAG member. SAG usually requires a bond. It's based on how many people they have and what their rates are, so it's like a percentage of what we'll be paying SAG altogether. Usually it's quite large which can be tricky as you have to have the money up front.

Q - The bond is a deposit?

Amy - Exactly. Sometimes they'll ask for close to what these people salaries are because they want to ensure that you're paying all their people. When your show finishes, SAG sends you some forms for you to fill out listing how much you have paid each SAG member and the hours they worked. SAG then contacts each person and says, *'have you been paid properly? Is everything finished?'* and once they've figured all that out, they give you your money back. You can't start shooting without this bond. It's just scrounging together that cash that can be tricky. You just have to hope that your investors are willing to put it up for you.

Q - Is it a Catch-22 for crewmembers trying to get into unions but can't as they have not worked on union films?

Amy - If you're working in film, you do make pretty good money. Even a production assistant, which is the lowest paid scale on a film, makes good money, so I think people are happy to be working. Once you've done one union show you have to keep doing union shows, otherwise you lose your benefits as I did a couple of months ago, but now I'll get them back as I start a union show on Monday. I think says something about the state of our health care system because it is so expensive for people to have their own health insurance. The health and welfare plan is very good in the motion picture industry. The coverages are excellent.

Q - What are the most common mistakes?

Amy - From an accounting standpoint, one of them is poor budgeting. You can really find yourself in a terrible state of affairs if your budget isn't correct. We joke that it would be a good idea if everyone from the office worked on set and everyone on set worked in the office for a day. It's really important to understand how the production functions as a whole unit.

The Wrap

Preparing for the end of a production is just as important as being organized for the beginning of one. This is where hidden costs, damaged properties and forgotten items can come back to bite you if you are not thorough. So, make sure you budget enough time to do it properly. Also, it is time when you should be thanking all those people who helped you through those glorious days on set and in the office - and who could make your post-production life easy or a living hell if you don't take care of them now. Here are some things to think about when going into the wrap.

Leave enough time to strike sets completely and thoroughly (could be several hours or a few days). This includes making sure all utilities are turned off and the property is clean. If you are on a sound stage, a good stage manager can make your life easy here.

Return all rentals to their houses ASAP so you don't get charged for extra days or late fees.

Pay all Loss and Damage claims to those who are owed them and then file insurance claims to recoup your losses.

Collect release forms from everyone so that you are covered from certain liability.

Collect all keys, cell phones, computers, PDA's and any other office or mobile equipment that you can be charged for.

Do all your exit paperwork, such as final paychecks, camera reports, lab reports, petty cash reports, etc.

Make sure to have contact numbers for everyone just in case you need to get in touch with them at some point.

Take a cast and crew photo for publicity and to give to your hard working cast and crew.

Throw a wrap party. Many local restaurants will cut you deals on food, drink and hospitality/dining rooms if you bring a lot of people.

401k & IRAs

The 401k

401k is a tax code that refers to a retirement plan offered by employers to employees. The company has control over the choices for investing the money within the 401k plan. These could include a combination of mutual funds (a group of small pieces of many stocks to reduce investment risk), stock funds (singular company stock) and bond funds (i.e. treasury bonds, state of California bonds etc). As the employee you have the choice of how much free (pre) tax you want them to take out of your money.

For example, say you make $1k a week and you want them to take 10% of your money. That 10% will not be taxed and your weekly taxable income would then be $900. That $100 is now being invested automatically into the selection that I have chosen. You won't be taxed on this 401k money, until you withdraw it, which by that time should have grown significantly. If you take the monies out before the official 401k retirement age of 59½, you'll face a 10% penalty (except for certain loan options). Another option for when you leave a company is that you can transfer it into a rollover IRA account.

A matching plan

Some companies have another benefit where they offer to match a part of your contribution. They can match up to a maximum of 20% of what you put in, depending on the company policy. It's a good idea to find out the maximum amount that your company will match (generally this is around 6 or 7%). If you can afford it, it's in your best interest to match that amount because then you're getting the maximum amount of what your company can give you. Effectively it's free money that they're giving you. Most companies will allow you to take out more than this amount, if you could afford to, but the company won't match it. There's also another wrinkle which is mostly for corporations. You only earn a percentage of what they match for every year you work at the company. For instance, if you work at the company 1 year, you get to keep a percentage of all the money that they've matched for that year. That percentage increases each year. It's an incentive to stay with the company.

IRAs, 401k solos and SEPs

Firstly there's the IRA, an Individual Retirement Account. This is a non employer offered retirement account. Just like the 401k there are certain penalties if you take out monies before the official retirement age of 59½. There are many types of IRAs, tax deductible and non tax deductible and a Roth IRA. There's also a 401k solo for the self employed individual, and several other self employed retirement plans, known as SEPs - Simplified Employee Pensions. It's best to talk to a financial advisor to work out the best one for you.

Q - Are the deductions the same country wide?

Steven - Each state sets their levels of the baseline rate, workers comp. and SUI. Media Services insurance pays out the state mandated benefits and our carrier will administer those. Every employer has an account for state unemployment with the state and that will determine the following year's rate for SUI based on the number of claims they "experience".

Q - Isn't it too expensive for a low-budget production to use a payroll service?

Steven - I get calls from filmmakers saying they're doing their first movie for $100k and want to run everyone through our payroll service. Pretty quickly they'll be asking us to just pay the SAG portion of their film under their low budget schemes, and the rest of the crew they'll pay as independent contractors. Everyone should do it, but I'm realistic, and some just don't have the budget for it.

Q - How much is deducted from the checks if you're paying SAG rates?

Steven - It's almost 33%. That's 13.3% for the SAG fringes, pension, health and welfare, then there's the standard 20% on top.

Q - So producers could come to you with just the actors and the key crewmembers attached?

Steven - Yes, that happens all the time. There are companies that won't, because there's very little profit in it. My feeling is that these people didn't start out making $100m movies and you hope that one day the relationship is going to pay off. We're not totally altruistic as it's a business, but it's really rewarding to help people too.

Q - If a production company couldn't afford a payroll service, would they be liable to have to pay all these individual fringes themselves?

Steven – A lot of people pay everyone as an independent contractor, basically writing checks with no fringes. So if you get paid over $600, you're responsible for paying your own fringes. We advise against them doing this. There are extensive rules as to whether someone is considered an independent contractor or not.

Q - Union and non-union. If a production company came to you and they're non-union...?

Steven - There are many indie production companies that shoot projects non-union because they don't have the budget for it. Nowadays it is much harder to get away with it. If you're doing $100k movie, then people are unlikely to bother you. But if you're doing a $1m movie, you're going to have to be union and the unions want their people working, and they can shut you down. You're foolish if you think you can get away with it.

Q - So it's better to tell them how much money you've got and to see if you can make it work?

Steven - Absolutely. Work with them to establish a rate, and SAG has modified low budget, a low budget and experimental categories too.

Q - Do you handle anything in addition to the payroll, such as the per diems or mileage?

Steven - The production accountant handles the per diems, which are non-taxable if they don't exceed the IRS guidelines. The time cards we provide deal with mileage reimbursement, which isn't taxable if it doesn't exceed $0.365 per mile. We can also deal with kit rental, so where you're a make-up artist with your own make-up products, the production company is essentially paying you to rent your own equipment. So, on your time card, if you make $500 a week, you can also add on your kit rental which might be for $100 a week. The kit rental is non-taxable. You can obviously do the same thing in other areas, for instance, if you're an accountant and you have your own computer, a sound recordist who has his own equipment, etc.

Q - Are the crew paid weekly?

Steven - Yes, if it's a union project it will be weekly on a Thursday or Friday. It seems so archaic in this day and age to have the old time cards. Everyone's working towards an electronic time card which you would sign, it goes to the accounting office, gets zipped over to us and goes right into our payroll system.

Q - Are crew paid on a 12 hour day and then overtime if they go beyond that?

Steven - Although they shouldn't as they must have an hourly rate, the industry is used to paying people a flat rate. In other words, you're working a ten hour day for $200. We can't see that on a time card. You should have to figure out what the hourly rate is, and on the time card you have to have the start time, lunch breaks, when you come back from lunch and when you leave for the day. That rate has to match what you put on the deal memo as the hourly rate.

Q - Do you ask for the payroll monies upfront before you pay the crew?

Steven - Many of our competitors require money on deposit, but we realize that a low budget filmmaker can't do that. It's very difficult for them to provide us with two weeks of payroll up front. However, if we release twenty checks for your crew, I'm going to make sure I get a check for the total amount before I release the payroll. The first two invoices we do are done by cashier's check. It's inconvenient I realize, but we do this so that after two weeks we'll know a little more about your company, check you out and most likely you'll have a good record and be okay.

PRODUCTION

Q - So if you're a member of a union, your health, insurance and pension plans are covered?

Steven - Yes, but you need a certain amount of hours working on union projects to be able to get the benefits as well as continuing to work those sort of hours. People call me and say *'I have to work, but don't give me a project unless it's a union project.'* It's fantastic insurance if you're a union member.

Q - What would you advise an independent contractor to do in these circumstances?

Steven - You're basically going to be looking for the lowest insurance you can find, which is unlikely to offer you the benefits that a union package would.

Q - Do you cover residuals?

Steven - Yes. Residuals are extremely complex. It depends if the film is shown on a plane, or which run it is, etc. Sometimes we do residuals for projects that we didn't do the payroll for, so that's another fee we would charge. Our department would need the time cards, the deal memo and all the paperwork from the initial payroll. It could be from one of our competitors, but we all work together on that basis and they'll give us all the information that we need.

Q - How do you keep track of residuals?

Steven - We have a huge department dedicated to it. Residuals can be a real problem for a low budget filmmaker who's finally sold their film, which had deferrals and depending on the deals, they have to pay residuals to the actors or possibly the crew. Using a payroll company to handle this five years after the film has been sold takes the burden off the filmmaker.

Q - What is the fee to handle the residuals?

Steven - On average it's 2.5%, but it can go up to 5%. It depends on what type of project it is as if it is only a cable run we might decide we're going to charge a flat dollar rate. Obviously as the product gets older, it degrades. TV programs like *The Tonight Show* have to report the runs to us. It's on our list of projects in development to be able to track the runs. Our system keeps track of what has been paid so nothing gets paid twice.

Q - How do you keep track of a film that's say sold to Thailand?

Steven - It's very difficult to do that, so we don't. We rely on the distributor telling us where they've sold it.

Q - So the distributor has to be honest and inform you so that you can then chase up the monies from the production company and pay the residuals?

Steven - Yes.

Q - Can you also be hired for post payroll?

Steven - Yes. There is little accounting to be done when a project is completely finished but there are still cost reports to do and invoices coming in. For a fee, our staff can also do it in house here which may be cheaper for the production company and it works well for the accountant as they're working on numerous shows in the same capacity.

Q - How can a filmmaker keep costs down?

Steven - One is to join the IFP, or they can negotiate with the unions. A good thing to do is to pick everyone's brains. We have a Movie Magic Budgeting and Scheduling training course every month, and it's free. It goes over the screenwriting, scheduling and budgeting programs. We also have a 'safety on set' team who'll show up on set and advise you of safety requirements. It's completely free and saves you money as you won't have injuries or loss of productivity with days where you can't shoot due to accidents. You can bounce ideas for stunts and question them on safety on set. When you use our services and your film has stunts in it, they'll give you a call.

Q - If you worked on an action movie and had stunts most days, would you really want them there everyday?

Steven - Most low budget film makers know that stunts are an expensive proposition so they try to avoid them. Our safety on the set team is not antagonistic, they are there as a presence and so you can bounce ideas off them.

**California Feature
2003 Rate Schedule**

FRINGES:

OASDI	6.20%	$87,000 CEILING
MEDICARE	1.45%	NO CEILING
FUI	.80%	$7,000 CEILING
SUI	5.40%	$7,000 CEILING

WORKERS= COMPENSATION:

TALENT	5.89%	$1,525.00 /WK CEILING
CREW	5.89%	
EDITORIAL	4.33%	
CLERICAL	1.81%	

HANDLING FEES per check:

INDIVIDUALS	0.25%
CORPORATIONS	$7.50
ABOVE THE LINE	$7.50

Rates valid to 12/31/2003, subject to government changes to payroll taxes and insurance carrier changes to workers' compensation rates.
Note: Rates do not include Union Pension, Health & Welfare, Vacation or Holiday.

Q - It's a free service?

Steven - Yes, we're the ones that pay them. Keeping workers comp incidents to a minimum helps us maintain our low workers comp rates. This allows us to be more competitive. I find it worrying when filmmakers call me with a $200k movie with plans to shoot underwater, or work with animals and helicopters. And I'm not going to take on the payroll of a $1m film that has lots of stunts. If there is a stunt sequence, we may charge them a flat fee per stunt, just for us to be able to cover the people that are involved.

Q - Can production companies be audited at any point?

Steven - Yes and if you're running the payroll through us, we will assist you with the audit. Generally, the audit comes from the IA. The unions police themselves regularly. It's not an audit regulated by the government unless you're under serious investigation for fraud!

Q - What are the most common mistakes that you've encountered from producers?

Steven - Some people don't know the union rules at all. They often don't know how to properly fill out deal memos and time cards; this means that our payroll co-ordinators have a difficult time dealing with the production's accounting department. We will always try to have our co-ordinators meet with the production accounting team so they can 'train' on the proper way to fill out and submit timecards, etc. We don't like to say no to any project so you can help us and yourself by learning as much as you can about the process.

Q - What advice would you offer a new filmmaker?

Steven - Use every free resource you can find, and there's an awful lot of them. You should network through the IFP, Women in Film and numerous other organizations in LA. You can always bounce ideas off us. I don't know one hundredth of what the people around me know, and if I don't know that answer, they'll find it for you and there's no charge for that. So, take advantage of what you can.

Paul Sessum
The Skouras Agency

BELOW THE LINE AGENT

Q - What do you do and what is your function?

Paul - I have a small agency that represents Below the Line department heads, such as cinematographers, production designers, costume designers, film editors etc. I introduce my clients to new producers and directors, help them nurture their current and future relationships, negotiate their contracts and try to find the next job or film that will take them to a new level.

Q - When is it a good time for a producer to approach you? I presume when they are crewing up?

Paul - When they know who their director's going to be, then you know the needs of the director and film and you can look for who's available and who is right for the project, and set up interviews.

Q - What would your response be when someone comes to you with a low budget independent film?

Paul - I'm always open to that as I find independent filmmakers usually have an interesting voice, that they have something to say. If the client responds to a script, it's not about the money, it's about the story.

Q - So if a new indie filmmaker is looking for somebody that has a lot of experience it depends on the script?

Paul - Yes, it depends on the script and what the client's looking for. I believe that everyone is accessible to anything. It's a matter of creative taste. Some agents are more concerned about the profile of the film, the exposure it's going to get and the financial step for the clients. If the film has got something to say, the rest will follow.

Q - What can a producer do to make your life easier when they come to you with a low budget, indie film?

Paul - Be clear about the situation and the circumstances in which the film is going to be made. I would like to see a prepared schedule or that they have a reasonable schedule in mind. I need to know what they're planning to pay for these services and whether they have thought through the full staffing requirements for the film.

Q - What are the main problems that your clients have had while working with a first time filmmakers?

Paul - Mostly it's communication. The director oftentimes doesn't anticipate the demands that are put on them, how quickly decisions have to be made and committing to those decisions, because they are hard to undo without costing the production company time and/or money. Directors get myopic and devoted to their vision so they get trapped inside the box. When you bring someone with a great deal of experience into that, two things happen. That person either picks up the ball and everybody follows, or the director starts to feel threatened by the knowledge that their direction of the film is slipping away. Somebody with a great deal of experience may be less inclined to experiment.

Q - Do you deal with more general crew as well or is that left to the department heads?

Paul - They work with the line producer to bring in the crew. If my client has someone that they really require, it's not part of the deal, but it's certainly something we'd talk about. You can negotiate that people have right of refusal for their crew. Ultimately, the company pays the bill so has the final decision. But mostly, everyone works together on it.

Q - Particularly the camera team?

Paul - That is often where the problems are. If you're doing a $1m film and you're hiring a $20k a week cinematographer for $5k, the crew can't necessarily take that much of a cut in pay, and they don't get the creative rewards from it. It's finding the balance. We shift money around to get the people that we need and keep the balance.

Q - But I suppose it's an underlying thing. Once they hear...

Paul - Yes. The seed is planted and they start going *'oh, there was more money'* and start feeling bad about their own situation. They made a deal and they have to live with it.

Q - What is your attitude towards non-union films?

Paul - I don't really worry about whether a film is union or non-union. Locally the unions have been really aggressive and very good about working out arrangements with low budget production companies. They've strayed away from the actual pay rate but it depends on health and welfare. Clients want to do interesting projects so they have flexible rates to prevent them being ruled out because there isn't enough money, but they still want their benefits paid. However, if a film needs every penny and makes a clear effort to put the money on the screen, you inform the client's what the situation is, they can determine if they want to get involved or not. I try not to divide between *'is this a union or non-union job'*. You have a producer doing a $2m picture who hasn't spoken to the union to say *'hey, we're doing this, what sort of deal can we work out?'*, inevitably the union feels a little bit slighted, especially when they've been so good lately about trying to work out deals. For instance, in Vermont, I had a client producing a film there for only $1m and the union showed up. But they worked out a deal with the union, production continued, everyone was happy, the health and welfare was paid, the rates remained the same.

Q - Do you ever go to festivals looking for new clients?

Paul - Film festivals are a great resource for finding up and coming talent. We're marketers basically, so we have to have something we can sell. It needs to be extraordinarily provocative and outstanding. I look at ten cinematographers a week and maybe find two a year that have something. Otherwise it's not beneficial for them to have an agent. The agent's not going to be able to accomplish much, they're going to feel frustrated with that situation so the best thing for a new up and coming person to do is to work, work and work. Generate a reel, try to be selective so when you're taking something to an agent for representation, it's a solid package of quality work. It doesn't mean it can't be low budget, but really focus in on the material. Once you get enough good work, you can develop a reel or a book that shows your experience and the agent has something to work with and can start introducing you to various different filmmakers.

Q - If people don't come to agents, where are the other places that they could go to for Below the Line crew? What are the other resources available

Paul - Talk to the unions to get their roster, see who's available. Go to the cinema and see who's doing what and how to reach these people. Directors go and see other people's films and they love someone's work then they'll call to find out who these people are.

Crew Websites

www.av-scene.com
www.crew.net
www.crew-list.net
www.debbiesbook.com
www.indieclub.com
www.mandy.com
www.media-match.com
www.nowbeyond.com
www.panix.com
www.reelcontact.com
www.filmstaff.com
Check film commissions of where you will be shooting.

PRODUCTION

Greg Jacobs
First A.D

1st AD AND SCHEDULE

Q - What is your background?

Greg - I started as a production assistant and then worked on a lot of non-union, low budget independent films in New York with John Sayles, the Coen Brothers and Hal Hartley.

Q - What does your job demand?

Greg - My job is to organize things for the director so they can focus on working with the actors and figuring out their shots. I break down every aspect of every scene, separating out all the elements. This involves organizing each day, working out how many days the movie will take to shoot, analyzing the script and figuring out what actors, props and wardrobe are required, and working out how many extras are needed for the scenes.

Q - How early on would you be hired?

Greg - It varies. On *Ocean's Eleven* I came on board four months before we started shooting, but on a smaller movie like *The Limey* I only had six weeks in pre-production. It just depends on how complicated the scale of the movie is, since *Traffic* and *Ocean's Eleven* shot in several different cities, it required co-coordinating the locations so I came on earlier.

Q - Do you bring your own team on board?

Greg - Yes, I bring a 2nd AD and a 2nd 2nd AD. They both help run the set so that I can be next to the camera. They keep the crew informed, deal with things like crowd scenes and complicated choreography, and they also help keep the set quiet and locked so that the public doesn't walk through frame. The 2nd AD helps do the call sheet by inputting the information. I work with the same people most of the time.

Q - Do you do the scheduling with the production manager?

Greg - I'll get input from the production manager, then I'll run it by the director.

Q - What order do the considerations for the schedule go in?

Greg - The actors are top priority, because if X actor is hired for the movie, the schedule has to accommodate him or her. I also try to take the dramatics of the script into consideration and try not to shoot the climax of the movie in the first week. It's helpful within the confines of location and actor availability to shoot as much as you can in chronological order, since characters develop during the course of shooting, which can pay off at the end of the movie. We did this on Richard Linklater's *'Before Sunrise'*, a 20-day shoot about a boy and a girl meeting on a train and spending the night in Vienna together. It was a big help to the director and the actors, but it was unusual that we were able to do that.

Q - What do you use to schedule?

Greg - It's easier for me to organize on a laptop rather than using stripboards. I always use a program called Movie Magic, which gives me a template on which to schedule the film.

Q - Do you do the breakdown sheets?

Greg - We do a shooting schedule, which shows the elements needed for each day; cast, location, props, and extras. That information is distributed to crewmembers in pre-production, so they know what to prepare for. Call sheets for the next day's work are prepared by the 2nd AD and me during lunch and reviewed by the production manager.

Q - Is there any other paperwork that you deal with?

Greg - Production reports giving a detailed account of the day's shooting are filled out by the 2nd AD and given to the studio, the financier, or the producer. It tells them how many set ups were done that day, and if all work was completed, and gives a detailed account of "which crewmember worked which day", so it also goes to the accountant.

Q - How would you describe the relationship between the 1st AD and the director?

Greg - My job is to support the director as their right hand man so they can make the movie they want to make. I'm there to give them everything they need and guide them through each day. Sometimes it's as simple as reminding them what time it is and what still needs to be done to complete the work that's scheduled for the remainder of the day. I make sure all the elements are in place so that when the director shows up, everything they need to help accomplish the shots they need is at their disposal.

Q - What is the 1st AD's relationship with the crew like?

Greg - Nearly all of the crews I have worked with have done their jobs professionally, so it's really about making sure everybody is informed about what's going on and what's coming up, so that myself, the gaffer, the key grip and production designer can make informed decisions about what's needed to stay one step ahead. I've always found the drill sergeant approach is the wrong way to go because I don't think you get the best from people under duress or by screaming at them.

Q - Is it always the 1st AD who says, 'quiet on set' and that kind of thing?

Greg - Usually. When there are big crowd scenes, I'll call background action, and then once the background starts moving, I'll call action.

Q - Is it your responsibility to run production meetings each day?

Greg - I have weekly meetings during pre-production as crew comes onboard to let them know what's going on and what's planned, especially if it's a complicated production. Before shooting begins, I have a big production meeting to walk the department heads through every day of shooting. I don't have meetings on the set, but I go around as needed and inform the crew as to what's going on. At the end of the

Final Script Rewrite

Before you lock your script, consider these changes to save time and money. In essence they will not change the story, but they will make it easier to shoot.

Kids
Cut 'em, or change to teenagers, for obvious reasons.

Animals
Cut 'em. Outside of movies actually about animals, you just don't need the headaches.

Atmospheres
If it says... 'Rain pours...' in your screenplay. Cut it...! Rain is a nightmare. Does it really make a difference if it isn't raining?

Night Exteriors
Rewrite and either move the scene indoors or into daytime.

Too many characters
Overwritten screenplays often contain too many characters. Merge two or there where you can, or cut if possible.

Stunts and action
Figure out how to tell the story without seeing the actual action and write it into your script. It can be as simple as a character explaining what happened.

PRODUCTION

Greg - I try to keep it as relaxed as possible. If they walk onto a set that feels chaotic and tense, it's going to be hard for them to give their best performance.

Q - Are there any differences between working on a low budget and bigger budget films?

Greg - On the bigger budget movies, the issues or problems are just more expensive. Sometimes the lower budget movies are harder because you have to make fifty extras look like five hundred, and obviously there is less time to shoot.

Q - Is your job finished on the last day of shooting?

Greg - Yes. It finishes on the last day of shooting.

Q - What are the common mistakes you've encountered with new filmmakers?

Greg - Sometimes there's a tendency to think they can do too much within one day of shooting. I'll sit down with the cinematographer, production designer and director and figure out how to do it more simply when there are only thirty days to shoot a 150 page script. Do we find as many locations as we can in one building or around the block from each other, or can we make that huge night scene a day scene?

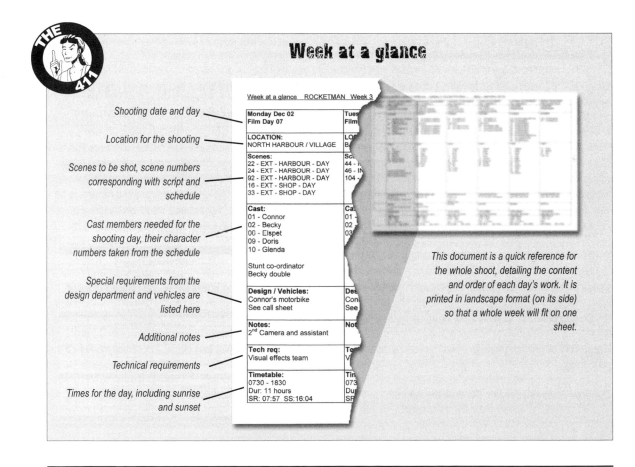

Week at a glance

Week at a glance   ROCKETMAN   Week 3

Monday Dec 02 **Film Day 07**	**Tues** **Film**
LOCATION: NORTH HARBOUR / VILLAGE	**LO** BA
Scenes: 22 - EXT - HARBOUR - DAY 24 - EXT - HARBOUR - DAY 92 - EXT - HARBOUR - DAY 16 - EXT - SHOP - DAY 33 - EXT - SHOP - DAY	**Sc** 44 - 46 - I 104 -
Cast: 01 - Connor 02 - Becky 06 - Elspet 09 - Doris 10 - Glenda Stunt co-ordinator Becky double	**Ca** 01 - 02 03
Design / Vehicles: Connor's motorbike See call sheet	**Des** Con See
Notes: 2nd Camera and assistant	**Not**
Tech req: Visual effects team	**Te** V
Timetable: 0730 - 1830 Dur: 11 hours SR: 07:57 SS:16:04	**Tin** 073 Du SR

Shooting date and day

Location for the shooting

Scenes to be shot, scene numbers corresponding with script and schedule

Cast members needed for the shooting day, their character numbers taken from the schedule

Special requirements from the design department and vehicles are listed here

Additional notes

Technical requirements

Times for the day, including sunrise and sunset

This document is a quick reference for the whole shoot, detailing the content and order of each day's work. It is printed in landscape format (on its side) so that a whole week will fit on one sheet.

Ready, Set, GO!

Procedure for shooting a take

When going for a take the 1st AD yells 'Quiet Please! We're going for a take!' making sure all is quiet on set...Then... The 1st AD yells 'Roll Sound!' (this is because sound stock is cheaper than film stock)... The Sound Recordist rolls sound and yells, 'Sound Rolling', and then 'Speed' when the sound is up and running to speed...Then the Sound Assistant / Camera Assistant places the Slate in front of the camera and reads the pertinent info off the slate, such as 'Slate 356, take 3!'... The 1st AD then yells 'Roll Camera'... The camera operator rolls camera and yells 'Running', then 'Speed' when the camera is running. The 1st AD yells 'Mark it' and the sound assistant claps the slate. Then if there're is any background extras required, the 1st AD calls 'Background Action' and the extras do their stuff. Then either the 1st AD or the Director yells 'ACTION' to cue the actors' action. When the scene is over, WAIT a few seconds (to give yourself a bit of space for editing) and then the Director yells 'CUT!'

SCENE 24 TAKE 4

After yelling CUT...!

1. Check with your camera and sound crew that all went well technically.

2. Check with your actors, explaining what you thought of the take, and asking how they felt.

3. Decide whether to go for another take or not, and if not to make sure you have a safety take.

4. If happy with take, then tell the camera operator to 'check the gate', where the camera operator will take the lens off the camera and look into the gate, checking for hairs etc. If something is found, you need to clean the gate and perhaps reshoot. If the gate is clear, the camera operator shouts 'clear' and you can move on to the next take.

Note - If shooting digital, the process is much the same, but because tape stock is so much cheaper than film stock, there is a tendency to leave the camera rolling. Do this and you will pay for it in post production as you will have endless hours of material to trawl. Be disciplined, no matter the medium you choose to shoot.

Q - Any tips for new filmmakers?

Greg - Wear comfortable shoes. I think the best advice would be to surround yourself with people whose personalities are compatible with yours and are the most talented people in their craft. LA is a huge talent pool and I can't imagine a new director going out and not finding the cream of the crop. There's no excuse, even on a low budget movie, because the unions are so flexible. Be open to ideas and suggestions and don't be defensive about accepting input. Remember, filmmaking is a collaborative medium.

Prop Problems

Not all props are easy to get hold of inanimate objects. Some are a real problem... Think ice cubes under hot lights for instance. Television and computer screens cannot just be filmed, you need clearance to use what is on the screen (if you didn't create it) AND then you need special equipment to allow the camera to film the screen itself. Who will take care of vehicles? Do the characters drive? Can the actors actually drive? Are there any animals and where are they coming from? Who will look after them? Most common problems relate to special props within the story, a newspaper headline that was forgotten etc. Remember, a poor prop can destroy audience 'suspension of belief'. Food is always a problem, especially if an actor is expected to eat it! And then there's the stunts, action and FX stuff, a whole department unto itself. Consider all these problems and props before you get to set. Often they can be modified in the screenplay, removing a production problem without compromising the drama.

PRODUCTION

Ken Lavet
Location Manager

LOCATION

Q - How do you approach your job?

Ken - When I get the script, I break it down by locations. I sit down with the director and production designer discuss their concept, what they would like to see, and then, depending on the size of the project, I spend anywhere from two weeks to three months scouting for locations. I try to find six different choices for each location. The production designer and I are usually the first ones hired.

First we try to figure out what's going to be a set and what's going to be a practical location. It has become more complicated in the last few years, because there are so many computer generated graphics and visual effects. It's hard to know where the physical ends and the computer generated begins. You try to sketch that out and map some kind of a strategy. Then I'm usually on the road, driving around LA, or I'm on a plane somewhere. I can spend several weeks in any part of the country. I photograph and document everything and usually e-mail photos back, but I prefer face to face meetings with the director and production designer. It could be three to four months of searching and it's the most enjoyable part for me. It's hard to find anything new in LA because it's been shot so much. I try to avoid location services because their files are often over used. The California Film Office, which is state run, has a digital film library with a list of locations. People can call in and register their properties so it's a good resource.

Q - What are the main considerations?

Ken - The first consideration is how it looks. You can film anywhere with enough resources and time. The sound mixers will need you to think in terms of noise, and the DP in terms of lighting for example. If you can't light your tenth floor loft, then it's no good. After that, you consider the logistics, especially in a city like LA where it's crowded and overshot. Think about parking and access to the location. Night filming in residential areas is probably the most difficult. The more affluent an area is, the more empowered and politically connected people are, the more difficult it becomes. They don't need money, although I've found that almost everybody has a price. If two weeks earlier some Schwarzenegger film was in the neighborhood and they paid $5k, the neighborhood's not going to do it for $1.5k.

Q - So filming on location can be very expensive?

Ken - It depends if you are doing anything on the street, any type of driving, you do need police and that becomes expensive. If you're in somebody's house, that's ok. The EIDC have a certain pay scale for student films, where they'll waive their fees, but for any commercial film, there's a certain amount you have to pay. Also adjacent cities like Santa Monica have their own prices and you can get those from the California Film Office. I find that small communities around LA tend to be more restricted and take more time to process permits, so when you're out looking you really need to know where you are and who the authorities are before you start showing pictures to the director.

Q - Can a low budget filmmaker get a location for free?

Ken - If they have friends and family that want to help.

Q - If you find a house you like that has never been shot in before, what fees would you be looking at?

Ken - A little Valley house with three bedrooms could be between $500 and $1500 a day. It's a personal thing. I want the people to feel good about what's going on. Inevitably, you find some family that's never been approached before and don't work in the film business, but they have a brother-in-law that either works in the film business, or has had filming done. You walk away having got it for $750 a day and when you come back they say *'my sister-in-law had filming done at her house and it was $2500 a day'.* I like to give them a fair price to begin with, but it can be anywhere between $2k a day for a Valley house to $10k a day. A Brentwood house or Santa Monica house can be $5-10k a day. It can start at $5k and by the time I come back, it can be $10k. We were looking at a house in Malibu and the guy who owned it was a tough customer. We had two days of filming and eight days of prep there and I had just managed to grind the price down. So when the director walks in, he stands next to the owner and says *'I've got to have this place. It's perfect.'* And of course, the price went through the roof. People are going to get the value for their houses as it's connected to the real estate market. When house prices are up, or when filming is strong in LA, people can make a lot of money. But there's a limit of how many days per quarter they can have their house filmed.

Q - Is that because of the disruption to residents in the street?

Ken - Exactly. Somebody could be making $100k a year on location rentals and their neighbours are making next to nothing.

Q - So in order to shoot on a residential street, you have to have permission by all the residents?

Ken - In real trouble areas, it can be up to 95% compliance, but you do need to get everyone to sign. If you're in a commercial area, and you want to do any road closures, depending on the time of day, you need to get the merchants to sign off if it will affect them adversely. In LA it's a standard form, some of the smaller communities have us draft something because they haven't generated forms. It's always better to lay it out for them so that problems don't crop up the day before filming.

Q - So would you recommend new filmmakers shoot in the suburbs?

Ken - Yeah and although I don't promote it, if they only have $100k budget and twelve people they might not call the permit office. On a low budget film, the trick is to find a house that is perfect as it is, and then you're able to keep the expenses down. One of the conditions for filming in a residential area is that you can only park essential equipment in the street. The rest has to be parked on designated parking lots. The parking is outrageous, especially in downtown LA or any urban area. We spend almost as much a day on parking as we do on locations. If you're spending $12k a day on various locations, you're going to spend half to 70% of that on parking. They say, *'$12 dollars a day, but for four cars in the same spot, it's going to be $48 a day'.*

Q - Is it cheaper to shoot in a studio or on location?

Ken - The back lot of Universal is around $10k a day, not including dressing time, or staff and crew expenses. You have to use in-house people. If you are a small film, it's cheaper to shoot on location.

Q - How much would you be looking at for a permit on a small street - are permits expensive?

Ken - It varies from city to city, anywhere from $500 to $1,250. It depends on whether its day or night filming. The city and county of LA allows filming between 7am and 10pm without getting signatures from the residents. There are certain trouble spots, places have been overshot or people raise objections and you need to get signatures to shoot there any time. Permits in LA are expensive. I think its $500 to film in a small residential street; you'd have to check the prices. It depends on the areas. If you're in the hills, you need a uniformed fire safety officer, which I think is about $600 for twelve hours. Street filming will require police officers. It's retired police officers in the city and they're not part of that permit, so you pay them separately. They can be $600 each. I looked today at *Charlie's Angels* to see what we spent on permits. It was $111k including fire. In LA they distribute what you pay to the fire department and the transportation department. People complain about the EIDC and shooting in LA, but considering how much filming is done here, I think it's easy. They'll go all out for you.

Q - Are the prices doubled if you shoot at night?

Ken - The permit prices don't double but if you shoot in Brentwood, and move some guy out of his $5m house, he'll want a suite at the Beverly Hills Hotel and expenses. You can go anywhere from $150 to $500 a night.

Q - Does the California Film Commission have places where you can shoot and get the money back?

Ken - If your location is state property then it's free, with the exception of staffing costs and parking fees. Individual film commissions offer deals on permits. California has California First, which is really a way of people getting reimbursed for any kind of governmental expense, as a tax benefit. They designated $35m for a pool of money, so it's a case of who gets there first, including the studios. It's a lot of paperwork but it's worth doing. We got a considerable amount of money back on *Charlie's Angels*.

Q - Do any states entice filmmakers with deals?

Ken - New York offers free police. I've heard that if a production hires local crew members in certain states, they get a huge tax break, because hiring local crew members keeps the industry in the area.

Q - What forms do location managers have to organize?

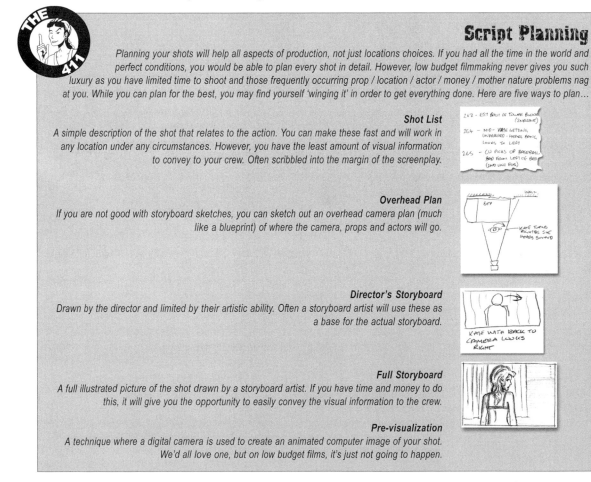

Script Planning

Planning your shots will help all aspects of production, not just locations choices. If you had all the time in the world and perfect conditions, you would be able to plan every shot in detail. However, low budget filmmaking never gives you such luxury as you have limited time to shoot and those frequently occurring prop / location / actor / money / mother nature problems nag at you. While you can plan for the best, you may find yourself 'winging it' in order to get everything done. Here are five ways to plan...

Shot List

A simple description of the shot that relates to the action. You can make these fast and will work in any location under any circumstances. However, you have the least amount of visual information to convey to your crew. Often scribbled into the margin of the screenplay.

Overhead Plan

If you are not good with storyboard sketches, you can sketch out an overhead camera plan (much like a blueprint) of where the camera, props and actors will go.

Director's Storyboard

Drawn by the director and limited by their artistic ability. Often a storyboard artist will use these as a base for the actual storyboard.

Full Storyboard

A full illustrated picture of the shot drawn by a storyboard artist. If you have time and money to do this, it will give you the opportunity to easily convey the visual information to the crew.

Pre-visualization

A technique where a digital camera is used to create an animated computer image of your shot. We'd all love one, but on low budget films, it's just not going to happen.

Location! Location! Location!

Finding that perfect location spot can be a difficult task, involving many questions. When you go out on your location scout, it's advisable to take with you several of your key crew members (i.e. sound mixer, DP, production designer, location manager) who can help field out any potential problems. Here are some suggestions of what you should be on the look out for:-

Aesthetics - Is this the right location for your film? Is it big enough bearing in mind the movement of equipment and crew? Are there power cables in the way for your 16th century movie?

Costs - How expensive is it? What permits are required?

Noise - Is it too close to a busy highway? Is it on a flight path? Any construction about to commence? Listen for hums and buzzes

Accessibility - Is it easy to find and to get equipment in and out?

Parking - Is there parking nearby, is there enough, is it expensive?

Power - Is there electricity on site or will you have to bring your own generator? Is there enough electricity? Are there plenty of outlets?

Facilities - Are there enough bathrooms or are you going to have to bring in portapotties? Is there a green room for your actors? Is there storage room? A room for craft services? A large room for everyone to sit and eat?

Safety - Is it safe? Check the fire regulations

Water - Is there access to water?

Insurance - You're going to need insurance but check that it's not ridiculously expensive

Cell phone coverage - Is there telephone access? Will your cell phone work?

Wet Weather Cover - If the weather turns, is there a place to be out of the rain?

Convenience - Is it close to your other locations?

Availability - Is it available at all hours of the day? Are there too many restrictions?

Point of Contact - Who is your main point of contact if there are any problems when shooting?

How to keep your location owners happy?
Other than the Filmmakers code of conduct that all your cast and crew should adhere to, here are some other suggestions to keep everyone happy:

Provide some local press coverage. Keep them informed. Introduce them to your lead actors. Make sure all damages are paid for. Always be respectful and polite whatever the situation. Send out thank you letters with small gifts (like a bottle of wine or a gift basket). Thank them in the end credits.

Most of all, when you've finished filming, always leave the location in a state better than that you found it in!

PRODUCTION

Ken - Liability. It's proof of Workers Comp, liability and property damage. That's the first thing. The next is a permit application. If there are special effects, your special effects co-ordinator will have their own separate permits that are referenced by your filming permit. If you're doing any after hours in LA, the forms need to be distributed to the community within 300ft of any filming activity. You need to get signatures, and depending on the area, it's anywhere between 80-100% compliance.

Q - What is the basic location paperwork you prepare for the crew?

Ken - Maps. We do itineraries for the scout, listing everybody, the times and the places. We do permits, letters to neighbors in addition to the county forms, location agreements, parking agreements and lighting agreements.

Q - Can you post road signs for your crew?

Ken - It's not legal, you're not supposed to post anything on any city property. I get little barricades and attach them the signs. In Santa Monica, if you put up signs, they'll be removed twenty minutes later.

A Carnet

Also known as an ATA Carnet, the initials are an acronym of the French and English words 'Admission Temporaire/Temporary Admission'. This is a simple international customs document that is accepted in well over seventy participating countries. It is implemented to ease custom procedures when shipping your film equipment. They are valid for one year, allow unlimited exits and entries in the US, and ensure that your shipment is tax free. On your carnet, you must list your approximate date of departure from the US, and all the countries that you anticipate visiting within that year, including any in-transit countries, and the number of times you expect to leave and re-enter the US. There are basic processing fees (up to $250), determined by the value of your shipment, and they require a security bond which varies from country to country (generally around 40% of the value of the goods). This is paid to the US Council for International Business (USCIB) who are the National Guaranteeing Association. Generally it takes 5 working days to process a carnet, however, it is recommended to do your carnet months in advance and ship your equipment with plenty of time, allowing for customs delays. Carnets DO NOT cover consumable goods (food and agriculture products), disposable and hazardous items, or postal traffic.

U.S Council for International Business: Carnet Headquarters, 1212 Avenue of the Americas, 18th Floor, New York, NY 10036. tel: 212 703 5078/5087 fax: 212 944 0012 e: atacarnet@uscib.org

To better serve its Carnet Holders, the USCIB works with two Service Providers, Roanoke Trade Services and the Corporation for International Business. All Carnet offices can issue a Carnet.
www.carnetsonline.com

Q - Do you get fined if you're caught?

Ken - No. They just take them down. The city of LA does the posting themselves, but in some cities, you have to do it yourself.

Q - Is it expensive to cut off traffic?

Ken - Yeah. If you walk into a restaurant and said, *'we're going to shut this block down for a day'.* You have to pay them. The city and the police are part of the permit fee in LA, that was one reason why *Charlie's Angels* was so expensive. We shot three blocks downtown and a couple of blocks of Hollywood Boulevard and we needed to get traffic cops out there, the ones with the barricades who know where the closures are and they help direct traffic. That's very expensive.

Q - Is it the job of the location manager to work out things like emergency facilities and safety?

Ken - The major studios have safety officers and they're involved from the beginning. They come to the production meetings and give a little talk at the beginning. They talk about safety, and for me, when I'm looking at a location, I'm looking for asbestos, lead pain etc. The whole new thing now is the issue of mildew or spores growing in the walls and ceilings. I showed a director the whole of the Queen Mary and everything was great until we found out there was an asbestos problem. It was only $1.5k to fix it, so you have to think what's best for the crew's safety in those situations.

Q - Do stunts come under a separate permit?

Ken - You just have to tell the city what you're doing. In addition to pyrotechnics, it's restrictive. If you use gunfire, you have to warn people within a mile radius. If you want to build a set on the coast of Florida for example, there are all sorts of mitigation arrangements you have to do.

Q - What are the major considerations when shooting overseas?

Ken - You may need a broker to bring your equipment in, which is all documented and they make sure that it's all taken out of the country again, but that's more of a production question. Sometimes if you are there a few months in advance you can look for the best crew accommodation, construction warehouses, wardrobe and a main parking point for transportation for instance.

Q - Do you deal with product placement agencies?

Ken - As far as product placement goes, the studios have it all in house with their own people. People used to make a living doing product placement, but I don't think that's the case anymore. Part of my job is making sure the products, signs and billboards, such as a Smirnoff bottle in the background, is cleared. The question is, is it the background or is it going to be featured? You run the risk of asking if you can use their sign and them saying 'no'. Then you have to take it out during post production. If you get some promotional offers, like from Coca-Cola, then you will have to watch out for the big Pepsi sign in the background.

Q - What common mistakes have you encountered?

Ken - When we were doing *Out Of Sight*, we went to a California prison. We had meetings with the warden and three weeks before we were due to shoot, they called us and said they couldn't do it. Unlike most other trades in the film business, you're always dealing with non film industry people as a location manager. The thing that's fun is you don't have to sit in an office all day and you can be out, always seeing new things and meeting new people, and that makes it interesting and different.

I heard about a Jack Nicholson film down in Texas, with this LA based location manager. He had the whole town in Texas lined up for a shoot lasting several days. He had everything taken care of and made deals with the home owners and merchants. On the first day of filming some guy rolls up in a Cadillac and says, 'Who the hell do you think you are? I own this town!' and the location manager said, 'I've got all the paperwork. It's back in the office'. He drove away and never came back.

Q - What advice would you give new filmmakers?

Ken - Go through your script. Make sure when you're writing a scene in a location, consider how expensive it's going to be and try to work out who owes you favors. If it's a residential location, find a friend. If it's a commercial enterprise so try to accommodate them in terms of hours. You could suggest promotional exchanges, so if you're shooting at a little drugstore, show the name. Try to avoid shooting a lot of night / exteriors in neighborhoods. Keep it out of the public way as much as possible. You don't want to be on the streets in downtown LA when you could be in some small suburb somewhere else.

Filmmakers Code Of Conduct

(courtesy of the EIDC)

Commercial Filmmakers' Code of Conduct for filming on public lands permitted by the Bureau of Land Management and National Parks Service.

To the Public: We are pleased to be filming in this location and appreciate your cooperation. If you find this production company is not adhering to this Code, please call (name and title) at (telephone and beeper numbers with explanation about how to call a beeper).

To our Company: You are guests and should treat this location, as well as the public, with courtesy. Please adhere to the following guidelines:

1. Removing, trimming and/or cutting of vegetation or trees is prohibited unless approved by the permit authority.
2. All signs erected or removed for filming purposes will be removed or replaced upon completion of the use of that location unless otherwise stipulated by the location agreement or permit. Also, remember to remove all signs posted to direct the company to the location.
3. All sets and props will be removed upon completion of their use.
4. Production, cast and crew vehicles shall observe designated parking areas.
5. Cast and crew meals shall be confined to the area designated in the location agreement of permit. Individuals shall eat within their designated meal area, during scheduled crew meals. All trash must be disposed of properly upon completion of the meal... All catering, craft service, construction, strike and personal trash must be removed from the location.
6. Remember to use the proper recycling receptacles for disposal of all paper goods, cans, bottles and plastic items that you may use in the course of the working day.
7. Do not wear clothing that lacks common sense and good taste. Shoes and shirts must be worn at all times, unless otherwise directed.
8. Crew members shall not display signs, posters or pictures on vehicles that do not reflect common sense or good taste.
9. Do not trespass onto adjoining property that is not within the boundaries of the property that has been permitted for filming.
10. The cast and crew shall not bring guests or pets to the location, unless expressly authorized in advance by the company.
11. Any animals to be used in the filming process shall be under the control of qualified personnel at all times.
12. All catering, craft service, construction, strike and personal trash must be removed from the location.
13. Observe designated smoking areas and always extinguish cigarettes in butt cans.
14. Cast and crew will refrain from the use of lewd or improper language.
15. The company will comply at all times with the provisions of the filming permit.
16. Members of the film community have a long-standing record of supporting the goals of the environmental community. At the conclusion of the filming process, it is the desire and the intention of this company to leave the location as it was found prior to the start of the production.
17. Be advised that any violation of the above may result in the cancellation of the permit and the closing down of the shoot. – (name of company) appreciates your cooperation and assistance in upholding the Filmmakers' Code of Professional Responsibility.

Tracey Wilson
Storyboard Artist

STORYBOARDS

Q - What is your background?

Tracey - I went to art college, and then worked as an illustrator, doing children's books, advertising, that kind of work. Gradually I got interested in doing film work but wasn't sure how to get into it. I always had a fascination with film. The first time I ever heard that they used artists was when I picked up a book about ILM and saw the drawings by Ralph McQuarrie. I realized they actually used sketch artists, and so I began to pursue that. I started doing pop promos and commercials and got into it that way, and then got onto a feature film.

Q - What was the first feature film you worked on?

Tracey - The first film I did was *Dragonheart,* but just before that I did work as an illustrator on a film called *Crusade,* which fell through. On *Dragonheart* I had to learn as I went along. I couldn't tell anyone that I hadn't done it before, but the director knew apparently. They told me it would be for three and a half weeks in Slovakia, but it ended up being for four months.

Q - What is the job of a storyboard artist?

Tracey - Storyboards are like a map to help the rest of the crew know what the director wants, and to inspire everybody. It's a series of drawings that represent that shots that the director wants. I would of course work closely with the director to create them. It's like a map that enables people to tie everything together. Storyboards are the first visualization of the screenplay. A lot of the job is thinking, I'd say only 20% of it is drawing. The rest of it you've got to sit down and construct a sequence and think about what's going to work. When you're short of time, you are often forced to draw quick *line work*, but if you have more time, it's nice to render the story boards so they have more of a feeling rather than just the actions.

Q - What is a concept artist?

Tracey - A concept artist works for the production designer, and they draw how the set is going to look, and design everything to do with the set. Whereas the story board artist draws the action. You work primarily for the director. We all collaborate of course, but the director would be the one to hire the story board artist and the production designer would choose the concept artists. Sometimes they overlap, if they can't afford a concept artist, the story board artist may be asked to do concepts as well.

Q - How soon are you brought in?

Tracey - Usually, just after the producer and the director are on board. Often you're the first person to be hired.

Q - Are you the first person to be hired so they can present it to the studio?

Tracey - Yes, if the project isn't green lit.

Q - Is there a certain style to doing the storyboards?

Tracey - No, everyone's got their own style. Some people will do more action films, other people will do more romantic comedies. It depends on what your illustration style suits.

Q - Are there certain illustrations or words you use for different actions and shots?

Tracey - Yeah, you'll abbreviate certain words like POV for point of view and MS for a medium shot. There are direction arrows which help too. I have worked for a couple of directors who refuse to have arrows on their drawings, which I think is a bad idea, as it doesn't help people see which way something's moving. By the time the boards are locked and you get to set, the boards are turned into a kind of flick book for quick reference.

Q - Do you literally do every shot the director wants?

Tracey - It depends on the director. Usually to begin with, we start on the big sequences that they know are definitely in the script and will cost a lot of money. Some directors just want the main effects sequences story boarding, and some want to lock down all the dialogue sequences as it's like a security blanket for them, so they've got something on paper and they can say *'well this is what I asked for'*. If they don't get it, they can prove it.

Q - Are they always just black and white sketches?

Tracey - Usually, but if it's an important scene, we can do color key frames as well. But usually, for speed reasons, we do them in black and white. Also you get a lot more drama from black and white, as there's a lot of light and dark. When you want to pick something out and show more detail, then it's nice to do those key frames in color, so they can work out how everything's going to look and work with the art and design departments as well.

Q - How big do you end up drawing them?

Tracey - We usually do three frames on an 8.5" x 11" page. On average, you're likely to do about ten or twelve pages a day, that's pages, not frames. Then you may also rough out more frames too.

Q - Does it go onto the computer at all?

Tracey - Often they make 'animatics' from the storyboards, but some people have started storyboarding on the computer using software. They look pretty good, but I find it's often quicker to draw something than do it on the computer.

Q - Have you worked on low budget movies?

Tracey - Yes. There tends to be more work to do on the smaller ones because you're the only one on it. On bigger projects there's usually two of you minimum, maybe more. Often you work harder as they expect you to do a lot more in terms of character design as well, whereas if you're on a bigger film, that's usually handled by concept artists. When you're working for an independent director, they'll often call you at nine in the evening, or they'll try to get you to work a weekend without realizing you don't get paid for weekends. It's just a bit more loose.

Q - How long do you think it would take to board a low budget drama?

Tracey - With smaller projects I've done it in six weeks. There's a lot of it that doesn't get covered, but pretty much all the big sequences do. I've also worked with people who've had a spec project that they want to present and I've just done a few boards for them in two weeks.

Q - Have you ever found that the location is different to what you had drawn, and so the story boards are abandoned?

Tracey - Yes, you can do all these boards and then see the film and it's nothing like what you drew. On the other hand, it's nice when you see the film and it is shot for shot what you have drawn.

Q - Would you work with the stunt co-ordinator?

Tracey - I've worked with stunt co-ordinators. On *Die Another Day*, we had to work closely with the 2nd unit director and the stunt coordinator on some scenes. I had to draw a sword fight, so that was tied in with the stunt co-ordinator and various fencing moves.

Q - Do you find action sequences hard to story board?

Tracey - It depends on the sequence. For example, with a fight scene you tend to just do a few key frames as the scene needs to be properly choreographed and this involves the stunt coordinator. I worked on a project where they wanted all the fight sequences storyboarded shot by shot. So the stunt guys did rehearsals which we taped and then the story board artists drew them up from the tapes. Action sequences, in general, are fun to draw.

Q - Are there differences doing story boards on films laden with effects?

Directing - Basic Tips

1. The simplest way of covering a scene is to shoot a wide shot (master) first, and then move in to do your medium shots, close ups and cutaways. The wide shots usually require the most lighting and set dressing and therefore the most time setting up. When you move in, you will of course see less in the frame and therefore need to make minimal adjustments.

2. Keep consistent direction of movement. If a person walks out of frame from right to left, then they must enter the next shot entering from right to left. You may change the camera angle to make it appear that they have switched sides, but in fact, the on screen movement remains constant.

3. Do not cross the 'line of action' (see box in Script Supervisor).

4. Allow the action to end before calling 'cut!' as this will give the editor flexibility and often vital options when cutting the film.

5. Shoot plenty of cutaways, inserts and transitional shots so your editor has plenty of options to 'cut away' from the actor when needed, perhaps to help with a fluffed line.

6. Move the camera. If appropriate, tracking shots usually make the film more kinetic.

7. Change your angles. High and low shots can help create mood.

8. Establish geography. Especially with actions sequences (fights, primarily), shoot enough wide shots so the audience can see where everything is. When you cut in to the action it will have more impact.

9. Watch your dailies. You will see what is working and what isn't.

10. Learn to edit. Cutting your own work, or someone else's, is one of the best way to learn about what to get, what isn't needed.

Storyboard Abbreviations

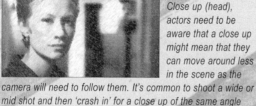

MCU
Medium close up,
(head and shoulders).

MS
Medium shot, head and
upper torso, versatile
and basic shot.

CU
Close up (head),
actors need to be
aware that a close up
might mean that they
can move around less
in the scene as the
camera will need to follow them. It's common to shoot a wide or
mid shot and then 'crash in' for a close up of the same angle
(there may be minimal relighting), and the camera may not even
be moved. Either a zoom lens would be zoomed in or a prime
lens will be swapped for a longer lens to get the close up shot.

LS
Long shot, a wide shot
which is generally
includes a character's
whole body and
immediate
surroundings.

ELS
Extreme long shot, a
very wide shot where a
character's would
seem tiny in the frame.
Great for establishing
shots.

BCU
Big close up. Any
movement will be
exaggerated, so an
actor opening his
eye's wide will seem
like a surprise, or an
extreme shock has occurred. Actors will not be able to move
around too much as they will quickly move out of shot.

MLS
Medium long shot, in
between a LS and an
ELS, character is
relatively small in the
frame and you see
much more of their
surroundings.

ECU
Extreme close up
(eyes or anything
extremely close), This
is more of an effect
shot, the actor's eyes
as a killer approaches
for instance, the bullet going in the gun chamber, the number
flashing on the cell phone for instance.

High angle/Low Angle
Camera is looking up at
the subject or looking
down at the subject.
High angles looking
down can dominate
and low angles looking
up can imply power. Beware of production problems when using
these shots - looking up might shoot 'off the set' etc.

EST
Establishing shot or
master shot, often
used to introduce a
scene or location to
the audience.
Generally, this is a
wide shot of a building or landscape or an introduction to the
location in which the scene is set.

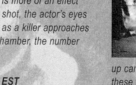

Dutch Angle
An extreme tilt of the
camera. Used to make
things look weird or
crazy.

Storyboard Abbreviations cont...

Pan and Tilt
Moving the camera horizontally or vertically.

Dolly
Moving on the camera in or out, or alongside (crabbing). Dolly shots are effective but take a lot of time to set up. Dolly shots can be enhanced by using a little zoom at the same time (which means your track could be shorter).

Zoom
A zoom lens is used to zoom in (closer to the subject) or out (away from the subject). The advantage of a zoom lens is that the camera does not move and so there is no need to refocus. To get a smooth zoom you will need to hire a special zoom control unit. Zoom shots can look a little odd because we cannot zoom our eyes and so our brain knows that this is a trick effect. NEVER allow an operator to perform a zoom manually, it must always be motorized.

Other abbreviations include ...
OS - Over shoulder, the camera is looking over someone's shoulder. Often used in conversation coverage.
OC - Off camera, this refers to dialogue / sounds off camera.
VO - Voice over.
POV - Point of view, shot from your main character's point of view, such as looking down the dark corridor.

Tracey - Yes. They like you to establish, in the storyboards, what could be a matte painting or what could be CG or a model. We write a note by each frame saying, 'this would be model,' or 'this would be 2nd unit'. That helps them to break down the sequences.

Q - Does the director sit with you and say, 'I want that shot here?'

Tracey - It depends on the director. I've worked on projects where I've been given shot lists, where the director's said, 'I want this shot, this shot and this shot', and figured it all out. But often the director doesn't really know what he wants until he sees it. He has an idea, but he likes you to be a catalyst for new ideas. So they give you the script and you go away and come up with a couple of ideas. I find it takes about three weeks to get into their head, to get to know what they like and don't like. There have also been cases where you work with a director who didn't like what you were doing, it wasn't that you are doing anything wrong, it was just the fact that you didn't really fit. Often the director doesn't want to hire a storyboard artist, and it's the producer's that make them. Then again, I've worked with some lovely directors who are very open to ideas, and if you come up with a good idea, they will let everyone know it was yours.

Q - Do you need to understand what look different lenses will give?

Tracey - Yes, it's good to know about lenses. If the director wants a certain lens, like a 50mm lens, then you'll know what he's going to be seeing through that lens and you can draw it accordingly.

Q - You must have a lot of directors referring to specific shots from movies as well?

Tracey - Yes, more than people realize. A lot of stuff's repeated in an indirect way. They never want the same shot, but they'll say they like that shot in that movie. So you have to think of something that's similar, but is also as good as that. You're often asked to draw a character to look like an actor. If there's someone who's a big box office hit, they like the boards to look like him or her.

Q - How do you present storyboards?

Tracey - If you're at a production meeting, everyone is handed a copy of the sequence or they are pinned on the wall, and you go through them. Often the director doesn't want anyone to see the boards until they're approved.

Q - What happens in those meetings?

Tracey - It's with all department heads. They want to make sure everybody's clear about their tasks and what the director wants. It's at that point an effects guy will say *'You can't have it explode that way, you've got to do it this way'*, and so we'll change the boards accordingly. This meeting would be pretty far in advance of the shoot. If you have a four month prep period, you'd probably have a big meeting at least once a month, and then more frequently in the last few weeks. It just helps to figure out as much as you can before the first day of shooting. At least have the first few weeks of shooting boarded and settled and sorted out. Obviously it's going to change from day to day, but if you can have a more or less clear idea of the basics, that usually helps.

Q - Would you recommend all directors use story boards?

Tracey - Whatever they're comfortable withI do believe, however, that storyboards are an essential talking point when you begin a project. Not only do they help with budgeting and storytelling, but they capture the mood and emotion of a script, and are a good visual representation of the directors ideas.

Q - What are thumb nails?

Tracey - The director will give you a little sketch, and you'll go away and produce something much better. I worked with one director who had a white board and would quickly draw up, shot by shot, what he wanted. Of course there were bits missing and I'd go away and fill in the spaces too. If the shots have already been figured out, it makes my job a lot easier. It's nice to know what's going on in a directors head, if they can put pen to paper and do something, it doesn't mater how scribbly, it will help.

Q - Can you recommend any storyboard books?

Tracey - There's a good book called, *Shot by Shot*. There's a couple of film editing books which are good too. It helps to read up on stuff like that, so you know when to cut stuff, like if you're doing a comedy scene, it's good to know when to cut in comedy rather than an action scene. When I started I didn't have any film training, and it's something that the more you do, the more of an instinct you get for it. It's hard to teach, because it's something that you learn by being thrown in at the deep end and learning from your mistakes.

Q - Do you have any advice for new film makers?

Tracey - Watch as many films as you can. That helps with regard to story boarding, and directing as well. Keep a library in your head. As a story board artist you are often asked to pull up a certain shot from a certain film and it's good if you know that film, and when you're drawing a sequence, it's nice to remember how they did angles in various scenes. The more you see, the more you remember. A lot of people don't know what they want until they see it, or they know only what they don't. That's not unusual. Then they change their minds a lot too. That is part of the creative process too. But it helps, especially if you have little time and money, to have some initial idea of what you want.

PRODUCTION

Eric Stoltz
The Indie Actor

ACTING

Q - What attracts you to certain projects?

Eric - The criteria shifts constantly, but it's usually the script above all... an idea or character or genre that captures my attention and curiosity. That being said, sometimes it's the director, or an actor who is involved, or even a far off location. Above all there's got to be some hope that it can turn out to be good, or have a shot at meaning something, otherwise it's hard to get up in the morning.

Q - What do you experience on smaller Indies that you don't on studio films?

Eric - There's much more creative freedom on an indie film, for the most part. Without so much money riding on the outcome, people are much more trusting of the creative force that galvanized the whole production. There are less fingers in the pie, so to speak, and consequently you get a much more immediate feeling on the set. If the director wants to ad-lib a scene, or change something that may not be working so well, you can try it. There's no need to call up the producers at the studio for permission, find the writer and have him or her put something in writing to be approved. If a director gets an idea, you're able to try it right there in the moment, and that's a lot of fun as well as being very satisfying.

Q - What are the common problems you encounter when working on low budget films?

Eric - A lack of preparation. Quite often a director will come to the set not really knowing how he's going to put the scene on film, and thinking he can wing it. Winging it is great if you're Arthur Penn or Jonathon Demme, but most directors don't have that wealth of experience to draw on. Also the food can be very bad on an Indie. This may sound like a trivial problem, but I find that after week two of lousy food, the crew and cast really hate coming to work. Keeping a company excited about the work is not an easy thing to do, especially if they're not being paid very much. I think a good caterer is far more important than people realize.

Q - How do directors differ from big budget studio movies to low budget Indie films?

Eric - It depends on the power and status of the director, but it seems that for the most part on a studio film, the director is much more beholden to the producers and the studio itself. Which is understandable, if you're talking about twenty to fifty million dollars. Consequently, there is a much more profound sense of *'give them what they want to see'* that I don't often find on an Indie. Indie directors usually have much more of a *'this would be a lot of fun to try'* attitude. Also studio directors tend to have all the great toys - the cranes, the dollies, the lens package - that enable them to do practically any shot they can dream of. Indie directors have skateboards, grocery carts, and operators with large shoulders for all the handheld shots.

Q - What can a production team do to make your life easier?

Eric - Hire a great transportation department. Good map drawing is essential. I can't tell you the number of times I've got lost on the way to work because of a bad map. Putting the corresponding Thomas Guide Map page on the call sheet helps. If an actor needs 30 minutes in hair and makeup, an AD should not give him or her one hour *'just in case'*. Wasting peoples' time to cover your butt results in a lack of trust. Go over the schedule with the actors as well as the department heads. Is it going to help or hurt the film to have the big love scene up on day one? Is convenience for the location department more important than the connection the actors will naturally develop for their characters and each other over the course of filming? Hire a good caterer.

Q - On some low budget films there can unfortunately be an element of crew vs. cast. Have you experienced this?

Eric - I've lived through 'Director vs. Crew' - a director I was working with on day one of filming accused the crew of 'being against him' and 'conspiring to screw up his shots'. It was not a nice way to start a shoot. I asked that he apologize to them, and told him they were trying their best and that this was not a good way to get them to work long hours. I've also experienced 'Director vs. D.P.', in which a director had only one way to shoot the scenes, and the D.P. had many ideas to share about how to possibly improve his ideas. The director shut the D.P. down, refusing to listen or consider anything other than what he had in mind. Consequently, the DP gave up trying to contribute, and the film ended up rather bland looking. I've also had 'Director vs. Everyone', in which the director was a tyrant who thought he knew more than everyone else, even though he had absolutely no experience, and his crew had done literally hundreds of films. And his refusal to listen to anyone else's ideas - be it the DP, the producers, the actors, the designers or the writer - made him alienated on his own set, with the camera department going so far as to put the monitor as far away from the scene as possible so no one had to deal with him. All of these experiences were easily preventable, if the director had a, been in therapy and b, actually listened to the people that he hired! There's no point in hiring good professional people to do a job and then disregard everything they suggest. I believe a good director should be focused on getting his vision on film, yes, but also open to others ideas and opinions. You never know when or where or how a good idea that may help elevate your film may arrive, but usually it comes from the great people that you surround yourself with. In my experience, the best directors are the most secure, the least threatened by an idea they may not have considered, and the first to admit that their original idea might not be the best.

Q - On an Indie film do you recommend rehearsal time, and if so, how much time should be allocated?

Eric - I absolutely recommend rehearsal time, I think it's one of the best things you can do in prep. I love at least two weeks, and If possible on the sets with the DP and the first AD present. Now no one is going to give two solid weeks to rehearse, but if you can schedule it simultaneously with your prep for instance, rehearse in the mornings, so that you can have your production meetings etc. in the afternoons, it will really save your ass once you're shooting. You can arrive on the set with your key players knowing how the scene is blocked, how you're going to shoot it, and most importantly you've worked out with the actors beforehand most of their questions about the scene. That's not to say that more questions won't arise, they always do, but you'll be so far ahead of the game that they won't slow down your day.

Q - What can a low budget Indie filmmaker do to encourage you to participate in their film?

Eric - First of all have a great script, but know that it can and should change and take on a life of its own as people contribute their ideas. Be open to a collaboration, ask your key players *'What is it about this script that you love'* and *'what is it about this script that you don't think works, and what do you see as potential solutions?'* Everyone likes to be included and invited in to the process as a partner rather than as someone who simply takes orders.

Q - What advice would you offer a new filmmaker?

Eric - Travel around the world, experience different cultures. Fall in love. Break up. Get into therapy. Read books. Go to museums and concerts and plays. Take the subway and the bus and interact with people who are not *'in the business'*. Get a job and support yourself. Watch older great films and find the filmmakers that move you. Go to revival houses and see films on a big screen, turn off your television. Find the scripts of great films and read them, then watch them to see how they made the leap from page to screen.

Blocking

Blocking a scene refers to the process of figuring out how the actors and camera will physically move through a scene, and it is done on set. Blocking allows the director, heads of departments, as well as the actors, to see where potential problems might arise. For instance, the camera team may realize that a light is in their shot during a tracking move, or an actor may not feel comfortable delivering a certain line at a specific spot on the set. Blocking also allows for the camera team to mark on the floor (with white camera tape) points where actors stand, or the camera moves to, and these are used as focus points (this is where the phrase 'hitting your mark' comes from). Resist the temptation to drop blocking. Five minutes blocking may save an hour trying to figure it out on the fly.

PRODUCTION

Lorette Bayle
Kodak

Q - What different gauges are available for filmmakers to make a feature film, to be shot on film as opposed to a video or digital format?

Lorette - Everything that's manufactured from Super 8, 16mm, Super 16mm, 35mm and 65mm. Those are all origination formats. Super 16mm production has definitely risen. Kodak released a new range of stocks called Vision 2 which dramatically reduced the appearance of grain. There's an HBO project called *Conspiracy* that Stephen Goldblatt recently shot on S16mm, then it went through a digital intermediate at a 4k resolution and was outputted onto 35mm and you could not see any grain, it was like it had been shot on 35mm because that process doesn't increase the grain, whereas the regular photochemical post-production route does. There's quite a number of independents and people doing shorts that are opting to shoot on S16mm and then blow up to 35mm later. Often, they don't do the blow up as they will wait to see if they get distribution and then do the blow up. At Sundance last year, there were a number of S16mm projects that were finished on HD or DigiBeta for the film festival. When you shoot on film, you have this amazing resolution and color depth, and the image has more life to it, plus dynamic range (highlights do not blow out like video) so no matter what you shoot on, S16mm or 35mm, you have that quality to it.

Q - Is shooting on S16mm a cost saving issue?

Lorette - Yes. There was this mentality that S16mm was not any better than shooting on digital video, but it's clear that it is better. It is comparable to HD, which is a very nice format and viable, but the problem is that 24P HD is expensive, more expensive to shoot than S16mm, so why would you shoot on that? Of course, by the time you publish this book, all that may have changed, but Kodak is raising the bar with new film stocks that will once again improve image quality. The new stocks are better in post production, especially in digital post production. You have images that have the appearance of less grain and the image is just amazing.

Q - What length is 35mm delivered in?

Lorette - It comes in several lengths, depending on the stock. It can be as little as 100ft on a daylight spool, through 200ft, 400ft and 1000ft. In some of the stocks, there's also 2000ft used for television shows. 16mm is supplied on a special flexible 200ft core for the Aaton A-Minima camera, 100ft daylight spools, 400ft rolls and 1200ft rolls which is usually used in television.

Q - What is film speed?

Lorette - Film speed can mean two things - either the speed at which the film passes through the camera, that is frames per second, or it could be the sensitivity of the film stock to light, that's the EI (exposure index). Feature films are usually shot at 24fps here in American and Canada. The Exposure Index for Kodak film stocks goes from IE50D D all the way up to EI800T. The lower the EI, the finer the grain, the higher the EI the more grain. But the lower the EI the more light is needed to expose correctly.

Q - What is the best stock for a low budget film?

Lorette - I would hesitate to make a recommendation, but there are obvious choices for 35mm stocks. If you have a low light interior, you'd shoot on 500 Tungsten. If you have *really* low light situations, you'd shoot on 800 Tungsten. 800 Tungsten is a really good choice if you are in night time exteriors where there is some practical lighting but you can't bring in a lot of film lighting. If you want to have low grain, you would shoot 200 Tungsten, which is considered the workhorse of film stocks. The Vision 500T 5218 is the highest seller that Kodak currently has, and then if you're in daytime exterior, bright sunlight, EXR 50 Daylight is the obvious choice. If you're shooting all day long outside, Vision 250 Daylight would be a better choice because you could shoot in a low lit morning and the evening. That's what Allan Davieu used on Spielberg's *Empire of the Sun*. There is a morning shot where everything is quiet, but then you see the ships firing bombs onto the city - that was EXR 250 5297 shot at 4am. There's a low contrast stock, 320 Tungsten and a lower contrast 500 Tungsten, that gives you a particular look. Vision 2 200T can be used for blue/green screen work as it is specifically designed to reduce the red line or fringing that occurs around objects when compositing.

Q - What does the color balance of the film mean?

Lorette - Tungsten is a film stock that's made for tungsten balance lights that have an orange color cast, whereas the daylight film is made for blue white light. In the earth's atmosphere, when you're outside during the day, you have an enormous amount of blue light and the daylight stock is made to absorb that light. But light does change throughout the day and does not remain the same color temperature. For instance at noon, the bright sunlight can produce super saturated colors and very black blacks. But that same stock shot early in the morning or late at night will look like low contrast stock with de-saturated colors.

Q - If you were shooting inside and you had loaded your camera with Tungsten film and then you wanted to shoot outside but could not reload the camera with daylight stock... what could you do?

Lorette - There are two choices. The best choice is to shoot with a Wratten 85 correction filter in front of the camera lens (which is orangey colored). This will convert the daylight into tungsten balanced light. Alternatively, you could correct it in telecine or when you do an actual final print and correct it in the lab.

Q - What's the color chart?

Lorette - At the head of each roll, the camera team will shoot a small amount of color chart and gray chart. This is used at the lab or telecine to 'line up' the image, to ensure blacks are black, whites are white, and colors are accurate.

Q - What are Key Kodes?

Lorette - Film stock has information built into the edge of stock that can be used in post production. Every 20 frames on 35mm, you get a Key Kode number that gives you all kinds of information - it tells you the number of frames you're at, plus the emulsion, the year it was made etc., both in human readable characters and machine readable barcode.

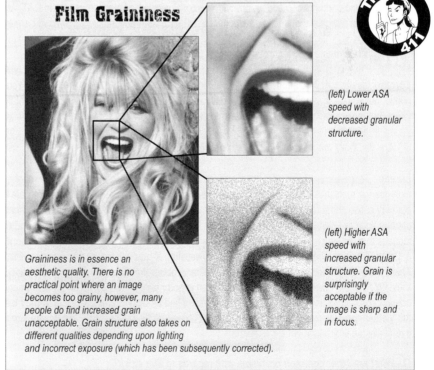

Film Graininess

(left) Lower ASA speed with decreased granular structure.

(left) Higher ASA speed with increased granular structure. Grain is surprisingly acceptable if the image is sharp and in focus.

Graininess is in essence an aesthetic quality. There is no practical point where an image becomes too grainy, however, many people do find increased grain unacceptable. Grain structure also takes on different qualities depending upon lighting and incorrect exposure (which has been subsequently corrected).

Camera Kit... cont

PHASE ADJUSTER

Used to alter the frame rate of the camera so that it can be used to film television screens. Without this device it is possible a dark band or bar will appear on the TV.

EYEPIECE EXTENSION

Useful for when the camera is mounted high or low, or in an awkward position.

CHANGING BAG

Used to load and unload magazines with the film. Remember you will need empty cans when shooting so that you can unload film, perhaps with short ends being re-canned.

HIGH SPEED CAMERA

If you want to do slow motion shots of up to 150fps, you will need to hire a special high speed camera body. Note that this HSRII is grey in color. You can use your existing lenses and tripod/head with this body.

TAPE MEASURE

Used to measure the distance between the focal point on the camera and the subject. Aids in focusing to ensure the image is sharp. Don't make the common error of mixing up feet and inches with centimeters and meters on the tape measure or the lenses.

CONSUMABLE STUFF

Compressed air for cleaning, torch for checking the gate, camera tape, gaffer tape, clapper board, camera report sheets, dulling spray (to reduce reflected highlights), empty cans, stickers for the cans etc.

VIDEO TAP

Device that connects to the camera so that the director can watch the shot on a small TV monitor. The quality is as good as the kit and can be recorded for instant 'playback'. Don't expect too much out of old kit.

BARNEY

A blimp that covers the camera body and deadens some of the sound. Leather coats draped over the camera will also help.

HEAD

The camera sits on the head. The better the head, the smoother the action. Rent the best head you can afford. Ensure you have the right bracket to connect the camera to the head.

LEGS

The tripod - comes in two sets, tall and short.

SPREADER

Connects the base of the tripod for use in places where the tripod spikes will damage the floor, or just won't hold fast.

TRANSPORT

You will need a large station wagon or truck to drive all this kit around. Ensure one person is responsible for all the kit being packed away and checked so that no equipment is accidentally left. Think about where you are going to park overnight and if the equipment will be loaded and unloaded at the end of each day.

THE CAMERA ASSISTANT KIT

This will include all manner of bits, including tape, compressed air, WD-40, filters, lens cloths, pens, scissors, screwdrivers etc. Most of this kit usually lives in a bag that hangs of the hip of most camera team members.

Shooting Formats

Standard 16mm	**Super 16mm**	**35mm (open gate)**	**35mm (anamorphic 1:2.35)**	**Super 35mm**
Shoots a 4:3 shaped image, ideal for standard TV, but not good for cinema or widescreen DVD as the top and bottom will need to be cropped off.	Shoots a 1:1.85 shaped image by dropping the right hand, redundant, sprocket hole. Ideal for blowing up to 35mm (1:1.85 cinema prints) and for widescreen DVD. Super 16mm gives 40% more definition than standard 16mm (when blowing up to 1:1.85). Blow up is expensive though the stock is much cheaper than 35mm.	Shoots a 4:3 shaped image. This negative has two purposes. The whole frame is often telecinied for 4:3 TV versions of the finished film, and the top and bottom are cropped off, to create a 1:1.85 aspect cinema print and widescreen DVD version. No blow up is needed, so money is saved in post, though the stock is more expensive than all 16mm formats.	A format which 'squeezes' the image using a special lens on the camera (anamorphic lens). When projected the images is passed through another anamorphic lens which 'unsqueezes' it, giving a much wider picture (think Gladiator, Armageddon etc.) This format has special shooting requirements, due to the additional lens, and is not ideal for low budget filmmakers. No blow up is needed in post.	This format takes the centre of the standard open gate 35mm film. It is used for a blow up at the lab where the 'squeeze' is added to create an anamorphic 1:2.35 image. You can also use the original unsqueezed version for 4:3 TV versions. This requires optical blow up stages at the lab which are expensive.

NOTE - All blow up stages can now be done both optically and digitally. Digital blow ups should produce better results and are ideal for archiving for future use.

Q - What do you require from the producer with regards to insurance?

Charlie - In common with most equipment rental companies, CSC requires the production company to produce evidence of comprehensive insurance cover in advance. The cover must insure not only the equipment chosen (valued in US$) but, any additional requirements, and any consequential liability and loss of rental.

Q - If a filmmaker offers payment on day one, would you give them a better deal?

Charlie - We will always try to achieve the best possible price for the film-maker, and we are always open to discussion about the budget and the specific requirements. However payment will be required in advance.

Q - What are the common mistakes producers make?

Charlie - Insufficient budget for the equipment required, and little or no allowance for the inevitable additional items.

Q - What advice would you give a new filmmaker?

Charlie - Always call and discuss your requirements with your potential supplier well in advance. At CSC our sales representatives are eager to make it work for our clients. Production should clarify the needs of the D.P, and consequently allow the final budget to be accurate and to avoid any unpleasant shocks! If in doubt, call in advance and discuss. If you don't, it's almost inevitable that your crew will request additional items once they start to check the equipment out, so get ahead of them and work with your rental house. That's what we are there for.

Lighting Books

The Camera Assistant: A Complete Professional Handbook by D. C. Hart
If you plan on being a camera assistant, this is the book for you. It details the various duties of these positions, from pre-production equipment checkout through the actual shooting to the equipment wrap. It also discusses how these jobs differ depending on whether you work in feature films, television, documentaries etc. There are lots of helpful tips on various topics such as film formats and aspect ratios, testing equipment, blocking, set etiquette and finding work.

Cinematography by Kris Malkiewicz
This book deals with the various aspects of cinematography (cameras and their internal workings, filters, film stocks, lenses, and framing) in a non-technical way, so that those unfamiliar with cameras can have a working knowledge of the terms and principles of shooting film. In addition, there are sections about shooting with digital cameras and videotape, if you decided to go that route with your project.

Film Lighting by Kris Malkiewicz
Contains informal, but knowledgeable interviews with some of the top gaffers and cinematographers in the film business, such as Conrad Hall, James Wong Howe, Haskell Wexler, Robert Wise, and Vilmos Zsigmond. There are also sections discussing principles of cinematography, various kinds of lighting equipment, methods of image manipulation, and the ins and outs of studio and location lighting.

The American Cinematographers Manual by
The technical bible of cinematography published by the American Cinematographers Society (ASC) since 1933. Thick and rich, each section of the book is authored by an expert of that subject. It covers everything you need to know about shooting, lighting, lab procedures, digital film mastering and computer graphics. Essential.

Q - Does grip equipment differ between 16mm and 35mm?

Xavier - No, but I've noticed that digital packages have become smaller. People don't seem to want that much light anymore, so they get away with small tungsten lighting that they can plug into the wall.

Q - Who do you deal with most on the crew?

Xavier - Sometimes it's a key grip, a DP or a gaffer. Often, they'll bring us business, and then when they have a personal project, they'll ask for help and we are happy to help. Over the years we've made many friends, grips, gaffers and DP's. With students, we help them out and we hope they won't forget us.

Q - Are there any times of year where there's not much filmmaking going on, so you can get better deals?

Xavier - There is never one time that is busier than another. When it's supposed to be busy, it's dead and vice versa.

Q - What are the hours in terms of picking up and dropping off equipment?

Xavier - It's 9am to 6pm Monday to Friday, We are not open on weekends.

Q - What sort of day rates do you arrange?

Xavier - Everything is negotiable, but sometimes we just can't do a deal. There are so many rental houses so it's difficult.

Q - Do productions ever hire out electricians via you?

Xavier - Yes. We'll get a crew from out of town, and they have their DP, and then they'll get the grips and gaffers locally. They'll call and say, *'these are the lights I need, and can you get me a truck, a driver and two grips?'*

Q - What is the process if equipment is damaged on set?

Xavier - A lot of times the damages aren't that much, but it's always deductible. It's usually under $1k, so they just pay it. People walk off with stuff, but then we know that crew is not a good crew to work with.

Q - What are your considerations when hiring equipment out?

Xavier - You want it to be in good shape and complete when it goes out and when it comes back in. We require general liability insurance for $1m, miscellaneous equipment for $250k, if you rent a grip truck you have to have auto liability for $1m, and then physical damage as well. Sometimes if you are getting a couple of things and you don't have insurance, we are able to do a waver where you sign off, saying that if anyone gets hurt, we are not liable. I find it's not about the equipment, it's about injuries. With students, their schools cover all the insurance's so we are okay with that.

Q - What are the most common problems you have to sort out?

Xavier - Budget. Sometimes you have a DP or gaffer that wants all these new lights and they can't afford them. So we suggest lights that are comparable, but they insist on a certain light, even though they cannot afford it. As far as equipment problems, Kino Flos and fluorescent lighting is fickle and it doesn't work all the time. The little 46 amp generators are supposed to hold a certain amount of wattage, and yet when you attach an HMI you may find they don't hold it. We can't explain it and that's a problem. Communication is an issue - them not knowing what they want or what they need.

Q - What can a producer do to make your life easier?

Xavier - To know what they want. Treat people with respect and dignity and don't complain. If people yell at me I'm going to work slower. We pick up the phone and decide whether we want the job based on the way we are spoken to. A lot of customers come here and they are excited about movie making and we are happy to help them out, but we aren't interested in people with attitude.

Q - What are the common mistakes made by the production company?

Xavier - Miscommunication with their crew as far as what they need. They may say *'we need a 4k'* and expect to be able to plug it into a wall without a generator. Also people wanting to do big productions without insurance. We can't release equipment until we get that insurance.

Q - What advice would you offer a new filmmaker?

Xavier - Plan out your shoot and don't wait until the last minute as you run into problems. We have people here that have shoots in two months from now and they are already arranging insurance and lighting list. You have to know what you want because I can't choose it for you.

Track and Dolly is one of the most versatile and popular tools for moving the camera smoothly. It's not too expensive and deals can always be made, but you do need a large vehicle, at least two strong people (dolly grips), and you need to allow time for set-up.

Richard Pilla and Jeremy Ramsaur
Hollywood Rentals

LIGHTING RENTAL

Q - What would you recommend as a lighting kit for a low budget movie?

Richard - It's difficult because when we do end up recommending a list to a producer who's in the process of putting their numbers together, they end up falling in love with the price and list we've given them. When their cameraman and director come on board, they usually have a whole different plan and the producer can want their crew to make the picture with that list. What we normally see on a small budget film is a couple of tungsten units, 2 to 4 HMI's, a little bit of kino flos (which are fluorescent lights), and you'd have all the different colored tubes so you can use the same fixtures for both tungsten or daylight. Lastly I'd recommend a small grip package. You don't see a lot of big stuff, no big 18k or 12k PARs on that list, as that would eat up the entire budget. We try and be more flexible with the low budgets because we understand that people are tight, yet are trying to be creative. We try and find out what they're doing and then we'll try and package it to stay inside their budget. Like we could supply you with a 3 ton grip truck that's pre loaded and that might work out as better value for you than by hiring piecemeal.

Q - If it's scaled down further, what kind of lighting kit would you suggest to keep the costs down?

Jeremy - The ultimate basic kit would be two redheads, 2 or 3 kino flos, a bounceboard, 2 or 3 C-stands. That's key, backlight and fill. With those two lights and a fill light, you can light almost anything (small scale). If everything you're shooting is interiors, then you'll be using tungsten, which is cheaper than daylight lamps.

Q - What's the best way to get a better deal on your lighting package?

Richard - Go with what the rental company has on the shelf. A producer should start with a wish list, but we won't have everything in at any given moment, so to avoid expensive sub rentals, take what is on the shelf and compromise. So communicate with the rental company, ask what they have, and you'll get a better deal.

Q - Are there certain times of year that's a better time for filmmakers to get good deals?

Richard - Yeah, when it's slow, usually around the holidays. The Summer is usually busy. At the end of the Summer, TV comes up and we get busy again, straight through to February. February, March, April and May are the times you may get better deals.

Q - Are all rentals calculated on a three day week?

Jeremy - That used to be standard but now everything is negotiated per job. There are list prices on things, but the bottom line is how much do you have to spend and can we take that money and afford to give you what you want.

Q - What grip trucks do you have?

Richard - We have one ton grip trucks at $150 a day on a three day week, all the way up to ten ton preloaded grip trucks which are $550 a day on a three day week. Of course we will negotiate. We don't like to put the preloaded trucks on low budget features because they're commercial trucks and a commercial rate is a lot more than a feature rate. The amount of gear you get on those grip trucks make them a bargain - you get all your stands, overheads, ladders, tools, preloaded expendable package on an *'as used'* basis. For low budget features you'll want to take off the expendable package so the crew guys don't cut into them and knock up your bill. We give the driver from the production a road test out in the back, even if it's a one ton, three ton or five ton truck - we make sure that at least they know how to drive the truck. But when you get into the bigger ten ton trucks, those are class A's so you'll need a union driver. If we get a bad feeling from your driver, we will tell the production absolutely not, this person cannot drive our truck. The vans are sensitive pieces of gear, they are expensive and need to be operated by a perfectionist, so we're picky.

Q - Do you hire out generators and do you supply anyone to service it?

Richard - Yes. Generators are going to cost you $700-$1000 a week. Sometimes the transportation co-ordinator services the generator. He does all the refueling, changes the oil, filters etc. and the production takes care of the costs and arranging it. We can send out people too to refuel and we charge $50-$75 for them to show up, plus the fuel. We service 24 hours a day, 7 days a week. We can send a 40 (union local number) guy out there because to be a generator operator, you have to be certified.

Q - What about damaged equipment?

Richard - If a generator comes back and it's broken, then that's the productions responsibility. It's just like if a light falls into a lake and is ruined, it needs to be paid for. That's why we have you guys sign out the gear in *'operating condition'* and we get a certificate of insurance to protect ourselves, because if you're leaving this place for a low budget feature with a couple of hundred thousand dollars worth of gear, we want to feel comfortable. The proper paperwork on a low budget feature is crucial to us, because they tend to be erratic and pressed for time. We will need a signed contract, a good insurance certificate (for general liability for $1m), and the gear release document (where the crew signs out the gear in working order).

Q - Does insurance cover blown bulbs?

Richard - There's no charge on burnt out globes as they have a life. But if your guys are misusing it, they're touching the globe with wet hands, or they drop them - then will charge. If you get hit with $800 worth of *'missing and damaged'* on your show, is that enough to go to your insurance policy? It's usually not worth it. I rarely see productions go to their insurance, as insurance usually covers things like a truck that gets into a smash, or a couple of lights and generator that gets stolen.

Q - How much would a replacement HMI bulb cost, if it were dropped by a crew member?

Richard - They run from a couple of hundred bucks to a couple of thousand dollars. 12k PAR globes are very expensive so you don't want to damage them.

Q - How many crew would you recommend that the lighting dept. has for working on set with a basic lighting kit?

Richard - You could have a two person crew, the Gaffer plus a Best Boy. A six person crew would be best, the Gaffer, Best Boy and four electricians.

Q - Why do you get flicker when using HMI?

Jeremy - Most HMI's produce a pulse light that looks continuous to the human eye, but could result in flicker on film. The main culprit is the magnetic ballast that are used to control the current on HMI lights. A way to avoid this is to use Flicker Free HMI's which have electric ballasts and allow filming of up to 10,000fps. Everyone wants flicker free because it weighs a third of what the old ballasts weighed, so they can manhandle them more easily, and also because you lose the flicker problem. However it's more expensive as a rental. The old magnetic ballast comes free with the light, and if they want flicker free, it's additional. With tungsten lights, flicker isn't an issue. Flicker applies to all AC lamps, including fluorescents, although it can be less severe than HMIs.

Richard - One thing to bear in mind if you do go with non-flicker free on a low budget film is that you are taking a risk. More than likely you'll be working with low end crew guys and you might find yourselves looking at your dailies where there is flickering because nobody realized that could happen.

Q - How can you eliminate the flicker if not using flicker free ballasts?

Jeremy - If you are using the old magnetic ballasts, you can eliminate flicker by using a crystal controlled camera (which most are nowadays), however you will still come across the problem if you're shooting slow motion. Even on some of the digital cameras, that have a faster shutter, you can see a strobe from a light flickering. You can also change the camera shutter angle or, on film cameras, you could use a frame rate that's divisible into the AC frequency - so in the US where the AC power is at 60Hz, frame rates of 12, 15, 20, 24, 30, 40 or 60 can be used without flicker problems. If you're on location make sure that your AC current is stable and that if you're using a generator, that it's a crystal controlled one. In countries with 50Hz power, such as the UK, you can film at 10,12.5, 16.666, 20, 25, 33.3 or 50fps without any danger of flicker. Shooting at 25fps for a low budget film is common in the UK. For video, if shooting in 60Hz countries, a standard NTSC camera shooting at 30fps (60 fields) can be used without flicker. In 50Hz countries, a standard PAL camera shooting at 25fps (50 fields) can be used without flicker.

Q - What if you want to shoot slow motion but don't have flicker free HMI's?

Jeremy - You can use tungsten lights as tungsten doesn't flicker, but it really only works if you're indoors or it's at night. You could use magnetic ballasts for the majority of the shoot, and we could supply you with the electric flicker free ballasts for the days you need them. You could also shoot with kino flos which are a good bang for your buck. They also draw very little power compared to other lights, and so good for situations where power consumption is an issue, or for when you have no generator. A lot of times

Gels

A common way to change the color of light, other than a color correction filter on the front of the camera, is to use gels on the lights (as well as windows and other light sources). Gels are made of flexible, transparent heat resistant plastic, that comes in small sheets and large rolls. They're reusable and fairly durable, but crease easily, can be noisy in windy locations and will need replacing if they become paler due to the heat of the lights. Gels are mounted on lights in gel frames or can just be attached to barndoors with clothespins.

CTB (Color Temperature Blue)
Converts tungsten light to daylight. These can also be referred to as booster gels as they boost the color temperature. The gel will cut out about 1 1/3 stops of light. Also available are 'dikes' (dichroic filters). These are blue glass filters that correct tungsten light to match daylight. These cut about 1 stop and must be fitted to a particular light.

CTO (Color Temperature Orange)
Warms daylight to tungsten light. 3/4 CTO gels are roughly equivalent to an Wratten 85 camera filter, and will cut out 2/3 of a stop of light. Both come in fractions ranging from 1/8 to one full f-stop. These gels are also available as a combination with Neutral Density filters which can be extremely useful when you want to diminish window light.

Other colored gels are available for creating a variety of effects. For instance... Green - This can be used to create fluorescent lighting. Yellow - This can be used to create light coming from a street lamp. Pale yellow can be used to warm up a HMI that is too blue. Blue Frost - This changes tungsten to daylight while adding diffusion, therefore preventing further loss of light by having to add a camera filter.

They can be purchased in full, 3/4, 1/2, 1/4, and 1/8 gradation, from deep color to pale, to make large or slight changes in color for matching the light sources. Remember, the deeper the gel color, the less light is emitted.

Gels are expensive and big productions tend to use it and discard it, so if you are around the bins on the studio backlot, you my be able to save your self some cash by operating midnight raids.

Lighting Equipment

Gels
Put over the front of lights to change their color balance - orange to turn day-light into tungsten balance, blue to turn tungsten-light day-light balanced. Also trace and spun to diffuse light.

Spare Lamps
Keep lots of spare bulbs. You should not be responsible for bulbs that blow, unless your crew was negligent.

Flashlights
If you want a flashlight in shot, your normal one won't do, you need to hire an extremely powerful one from an effects or lighting company.

Extension Cables
Can't get enough. Make sure that the cables you get can handle the power. Rent extra.

Expendables, Gloves, Clothes pins & Gaffer Tape
Pins are used to attach gels to barn doors, gloves are a necessity with hot heavy lights, and gaffer tape will stick pretty much anything to anything.

Stands
Used to mount lights. You'll also need various poles and C stands. Make sure you have enough for your lights.

Bounce Boards
Used to reflect light. Some are small and hand held, used to fill actors faces in daylig Large sheets of foam core are ideal and cheap. Use nets to reduce the amount of light emitting from the lamp.

Grip Truck
A 3 ton grip truck is ideal as comes with loads of extras.

Practical Light
A light that usually lives within a scene and is usually tungsten blanched, table lamps, desk lamp, ceiling lights – loaded with a standard bulb from 100-275 watt (beware of melting lights at 275 watts!) Beware of fluorescent lights as they have an odd color balance and may turn out green or pink on film.

Tungsten Units
Also called quartz due to a tungsten filament in a quartz glass bulb that encases halogen gas. There are all types ranging from baby 1k, 2k redheads and blondes, to 20ks.

Fresnels (pronounced freh-nels)
Incandescent spotlights and floodlights. Range from 20-12,000 watts and come in many sizes. The lens has circular concentric rings that throw out soft light. Has light adjustment that changes intensity of the light. Inky dinks are 50-200 watt Fresnels. HMI's can be fitted with Fresnel lenses as well.

Open Faced Lights
Lights with no lens on the bulb. Less controllable than fresnels and come in a variety with various names, mickeys, blondes, scoops.

HMIs
An arc light that contains gas enclosed in a glass envelope. Produces matching daylight at 5,600k or 6000k. Very efficient, give off less heat than tungsten and can be run off a smaller power supply than tungsten. Come flicker free and non-flicker free types and requires a ballast.

PARs
Sealed beam lights that project light forward in straight lines. Used to illuminate space. Various types of PARs have different traits of color temperature, wattage, voltage and some without lenses. They are more efficient that Fresnels but not as controllable.

Lighting Equipment ...cont

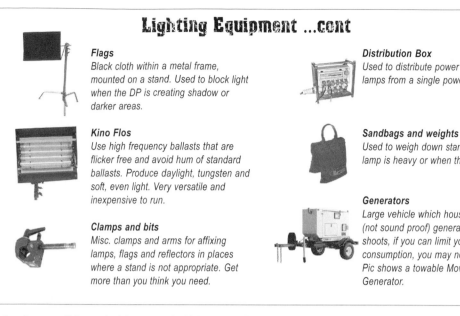

Flags
Black cloth within a metal frame, mounted on a stand. Used to block light when the DP is creating shadow or darker areas.

Kino Flos
Use high frequency ballasts that are flicker free and avoid hum of standard ballasts. Produce daylight, tungsten and soft, even light. Very versatile and inexpensive to run.

Clamps and bits
Misc. clamps and arms for affixing lamps, flags and reflectors in places where a stand is not appropriate. Get more than you think you need.

Distribution Box
Used to distribute power to several lamps from a single power source.

Sandbags and weights
Used to weigh down stands for safety, when the lamp is heavy or when there is wind.

Generators
Large vehicle which houses a sound deadened (not sound proof) generator. For low budget shoots, if you can limit your power consumption, you may not need a generator. Pic shows a towable Movie Quiet®20KW Generator.

---

when I've seen flicker make it into a movie, it's because of an already existing desk lamp that has a tiny fluorescent lamp in it. Second to that, it's a crew member making a mistake, which is also common because everything has adjustment switches, between flicker free and magnetic. One problem with flicker free is the sound, as the ballast makes a buzzing noise.

Q - Can you hire anything to prevent the flicker on TV or computer screens that appear in a shot?

Jeremy - Film cameras run at a different frequency to that of a TV, so when you see a TV in the background of a shot you will see dark lines on the TV screen - that's because the film camera is shooting 24fps and the TV is running at 60 fields a second. Some TV props have been designed to display a video image compatible with 24fps but you will need to hire that from a specialist.

Q - What are the most widely used lights on productions?

Jeremy - An HMI 6k PAR and tungsten 5ks, 10ks, 2ks.

Q - What is the most convenient light when shooting on location?

Richard - Kino flo. It's plastic, it's light, and it's durable. Also a small tungsten unit which you can set up on a stand somewhere. With both lights you don't need to worry about flickering, or power as you can plug them into the wall. Power is always an issue for low budget film makers - we have lights that would drain the juice from three houses just to turn it on! Flashlights are the best light and candles! The most convenient light is daylight and a bounce board. Really good film makers don't have to use us!

Jeremy - I've seen people who'll crumble when they can't get a huge amount of equipment and lots of electricians, and then there's the other guy who can do anything with nothing and it'll look fantastic.

Q - Is there any method to stop the heat build up on lights?

Jeremy - Use less lights and ventilate or use air conditioning between takes. Also, to minimize the heat on actors faces you can use a heat shield filter, which just looks like clear plastic filter, but it's expensive. Lights such as 6k, 12k and 18k PARS can create so much heat and UV, it's just like the sun, and they'll take the color out of stuff - so the gel that is placed in front of the light and is used to balance colors, can fade. Nobody thought we'd be taking 18kw and pointing it down onto a piece of plastic, and it will burn the color out in hours, so they put a heat shield in front of it and the heat shield takes the beating, the color lasts longer and the actors might be slightly cooler.

Q - What are practical lights?

Jeremy - Practicals are lights that are part of the story world, such as a household lamp. It's good to use either photofloods or reflector foods. Photofloods look just like normal household bulbs and can be used on normal household fixtures, however as they are so bright they do become very hot and their lifespan is only around an hour. Reflector floods are the same but have a reflecting surface that projects a more directed beam of light. Sometimes in hospitals, there will be overhead fluorescent lights and the lighting team have a choice of whether to change the three hundred fixtures or to filter the camera. Sometimes productions might order five hundred four foot tubes for a hallway or office.

Q - What are barn doors and why are they used?

Jeremy - A barn door is a ring that goes on the front of a light- you can close in the barn doors, making your own cone, so as to control the light. It's adjustable.

Q - What is the purpose of scrims?

Richard - Scrim is a cloth like, heat resistant, material that is used to cut the intensity of light. You can put on a single, a double layer, though we don't recommend many more layers because it puts more heat on the globe and the lens. We've had problems with that, especially when the lights are facing down. A single layer relates to one 'stop' on the camera, a double is a two 'stops' etc.

Q - What about reflectors?

Jeremy - It's a cheap way to light. People I know who know how to deal with sunlight, use reflectors and it's the easiest way to actually get really good looking light for nothing. You can use a mirror bouncing sunlight in from outside. The brightest of our lights that cost a $1k a day will just compete with the sunlight, and the sun is free.

Q - Do you sell expendables?

Richard - We have an expendable supply store yes, and we supply everything from gels to batteries. Everything the camera team needs. Gels are one expensive expendable, as a roll costs anywhere between $49 to $200m depending on where you buy it. You need to encourage your crew to re-use gel as much as possible.

Q - What are the main problems that you encounter with filmmakers?

Richard - Planning. If you don't take the time to pay people to plan, you end up paying quadruple down the road. For instance, you're filming in Utah and all of sudden you want additional lights from us, lights which you hadn't thought about, so now you've now incurred shipping costs. Even if you do plan, directors do change their mind in the middle of the shoot - now rather than shooting the end zone of a football field, the director wants to shoot the entire football field and at night!

Richard - We have a saying here, '*champagne taste on a beer budget!*' We talk to those producers every day, producers who aren't realistic. You've got the script and come up with $500k for a $3m movie, and they try to behave as though they have that $3m. If you are good at what you do, you can do almost anything with hardly anything, you just need to know how to use it.

Color Temperature

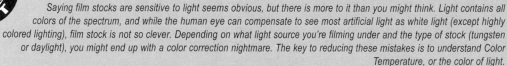

Saying film stocks are sensitive to light seems obvious, but there is more to it than you might think. Light contains all colors of the spectrum, and while the human eye can compensate to see most artificial light as white light (except highly colored lighting), film stock is not so clever. Depending on what light source you're filming under and the type of stock (tungsten or daylight), you might end up with a color correction nightmare. The key to reducing these mistakes is to understand Color Temperature, or the color of light.

When light is at given intensities, it gives off a different colors. This is measured in degrees Kelvin (named after the British scientist who devised a way to measure the amount of red and blue in a light source by comparing it to the color of what is called a 'black body' – an instrument that is dead black when it's cold but changes color when it's heated to various temperatures.) At one end of the scale is 'warm light', which oddly enough has a lower temperature reading (2,900-3,400 degrees K) and gives off a red orange hue. Tungsten lights and household incandescent lights fit into this category. At the other end of the scale, light is said to be 'cool' or 'blue' and has a higher color temperature. Daylight at noon is around 5,600 degrees K as are H.M.I lights (Halogen-Metal-Iodide). Here a bluish tint colors all objects. Just as a visual for these two concepts, imagine heating up a piece of metal – as it starts to get hot it glows red, then as the heat increases, it glows white.

Light in the early morning and at sunset have a 'warm' color temperature, HOWEVER you still need to treat it as daylight because all light from the sun is daylight. Lights can also be between red and blue. For example fluorescent lights tend to give off a greenish hue. As an example of a possible problem area, imagine you have found a great office location with huge windows - it may be a great location but it's also a DP nightmare. What if you have tungsten lights being mixed with daylight through those HUGE windows? The solutions would be... black the windows and frame them out, gel the windows to rebalance the daylight as tungsten balance, or gel the lights to rebalance them as daylight balanced.

*Film stocks are balanced for either **DAYLIGHT** or **TUNGSTEN**. Using daylight film under 'blue' lights (the higher color temperature) or using tungsten film under 'warm' lights (the lower color temperature) will create normal colored objects. If you were to shoot daylight film with 'warm' lights, everything will look orange. Conversely shooting tungsten film stock under 'blue' lights will make everything look blue. This can be corrected by placing filters over the camera lens or gels over the lights (see filters and gels for more info).*

Video. *On video cameras, there is the white balance - an electronic way of telling the camera what kind of lighting is being used. Always ensure that all light sources in a shot are balanced the same, either all daylight or all tungsten.*

Q - So sit down with your DP and plan exactly what you're gonna need?

Jeremy - Yes, and make sure they have time to plan as it will save you money.

Q - Any money saving tips?

Jeremy - Pay up front. Some people draw the bill out over time, which costs us time and money to chase. Some new filmmakers walk in with a lot of attitude saying *'we've never done anything with you before and we want 30 days to pay 'cos we're bringing you a job!'* We've got 500 jobs and most of them don't have their attitude. If you *'work with us'*, we will *'work with you'.* If you don't work with us, then we work by the rules. So it generally boils down to how nice you can be. Don't have an attitude.

Q - Should an inexperienced producer keep a tight reign on everything, especially if their crew is inexperienced too?

Jeremy - Absolutely. You should know everything, especially if you're a line producer, production manager or producer. If you hiring quality people, and you plan and listen to their advice, you're going to spend 10% more out of the gate, but you're going to save 30% over the whole shoot. But producers never see that. We've had shows where they even forget to call us to come and pick it up. We'll check and no one will know, so it'll stay out and we end up billing for two weeks because nobody would figure out whether they needed it or not. That's another thing about Hollywood, nobody really wants to make a decision because they're scared it's going to come back to them.

Q - Is it a good idea for the producer to come to you first to meet you?

Richard - Anybody who meets us in person is likely to get a better deal. Meeting face to face is always better than over the phone.

Q - How far in advance of a film shoot do you like to be approached?

Jeremy - As soon as you know you're filming, call us.

Q - What happens about getting equipment back to you?

Jeremy - It's their responsibility to ship it back. This is another common mistake - they don't pay the crew to come in and wrap the equipment.

Q - What are the common mistakes that you come across when dealing with low budget filmmakers?

Richard - First, the film crew load out of here without enough equipment and end up paying more over the long run. Secondly, people who really don't have enough money to start the movie that they're trying to do in the first place, come back to us and start trying to exchange the freebies we've given them for another freebie. That's when it starts affecting our ability to be nice. Trust your crew. You hired the DP to be the DP, you hired the gaffer to be your chief lighting technician and the key grip to be the donkey. Trust them. If you don't trust them, then light it yourself, shoot it yourself and do everything yourself and you'll see that you can't.

Q - How do you feel about giving good deals when it's a low budget movie?

Richard - If we try to set a price with a producer who's a new filmmaker we usually forecasts that there's going to be at least $3k damage on the job. The reason being that they won't be hiring professionals who've been in the business for years. And so we may not want to give away the equipment because we expect that the producer is probably going to fight over the damages. Not only that, but on low budget films, the crew don't usually know how to fix certain problems that they might come across. For instance, flicker. They don't know what to do about it and so we have to get a guy on the phone with the young filmmaker who thinks it's faulty equipment but actually it's the crew member. Nine times out of ten, these crew members are donating their time and they're half as dedicated as a pro. They walk off set early, miss days, ten times more than they would on a paying job, and that leads to missing, stolen and damaged equipment. When the producers return the equipment they feel like it's not their fault. In one week, we'll hire out equipment to a student film and equipment to $6m feature. At the end of the week, the student guys will come back and owe us $1800 in damages whereas the $6m feature would come back and owe us nothing, even though they took twenty times as much equipment. They just hired people who were paid to look after the equipment and check it when they signed for it. If an experienced DP comes to us, who's used us several times, and he's about to do a low budget feature, then we would extend ourselves because we've built up a history, and we know that he's going to get good guys to look after the equipment and not rip us off. We do realize it's a rat race out there and it's very hard to pull off a low budget feature.

Q - What's your advice to low budget filmmakers?

Jeremy - Everybody's got these ideas that it's going to be grand. But grand takes time and money. Everyone thinks they have to go big to make it work, because it's Hollywood. There's no reason to. Some movies look like they've been made for $30m, but were made for a $1m because they got the right DP, director and producer. Money isn't always the answer. Money makes things go real smooth, but it's also a waste if you can do it by planning instead of just dropping it out of your back pocket.

Eric Alan Edwards
Director of Photography

THE DIRECTOR OF PHOTOGRAPHY

Q - What's your background?

Eric - Gus van Sant (dir. *Good Will Hunting* / *My Own Private Idaho)* and I both went to Rhode Island School of Design where I studied photography and filmmaking. My influences were Scorcese and Kubrik (in particular, *Clockwork Orange* and *Dr Strangelove*) and I continually watched *The Graduate.*

Q - How do you approach the look of a film?

Eric - It always has to do with the subject and the material at hand. In the beginning, I'm describing fantasies and fetishes. I look at a whole list of films and try to learn all I can about what the director's fetishes are. Then I'll look at print material, photography and paintings, while talking with the director about light. All the movies that I rent and look at during the first week of talking to the director have to do with visual style and I try to nail it down as much as I can by using examples.

Q - How important is the relationship with the lab?

Eric - It's important now that there are more processes. They're all hard to control beyond just getting the dailies, or trying to establish the tonality of the film. You need a language with your timer. For example, I'll say, *'This is going to be a hot summer movie, so it needs to swelter'* or *'this is an overcast day, so push it a stop and make it with more contrast but still keep the yellow in'* and *'when it's night-time, it's supposed to be a warm night-time not a cold night-time'.* So, with your color timer, you're trying to lock in one or two shots that your movie is about. It can get complicated when you do special effects or you're doing a bleach bypass or other processes like infrared.

Q - What's the most important technical aspect of cinematography?

Eric - For me, it's identifying my film stock and lighting techniques and that makes up about 95% of my craft these days. There are so few choices now because everything's being replaced by digital manipulation. For example, *Oh Brother, Where Art Thou* broke a mould by going straight to digital post for the entire movie, and once that happens, it's a completely different form of manipulation. If the money isn't available to go digital in post, then the contrast of the film becomes extremely important because the only controls you have are coloration and density, or light and dark.

Q - In the UK, low budget filmmakers will shoot on Super 16mm because it's so much cheaper. Is that the case here?

Eric - The difference between 16mm and 35mm is that you're shooting on a smaller negative and you then have to do a blow-up to 35mm for theatrical projection. That's how we shot *The Slaughter Rule.* It was an enormous headache. You save yourself $50k of film stock costs up front, but then you've got to spend $50-$70k in post blowing it up. I have done two films in 16mm and when blown up the focus, lens, scratches and dust problems are magnified and will need dealing with in post. Your film is never as sharp as you want it to be, and you end up spending the same money. There are certain film projects that 16mm is appropriate for. The advantage of Super16 is that the equipment is literally one third of the size of 35mm equipment and the speed of working with the gear is attractive.

There are films that make sense to shoot in Super 16mm and let the grain happen. The funny thing about that film is it was actually shot on 35mm but then they went back and used old short ends from an earlier Nicolas Roeg film and it was grainier. It looked like Super 8mm. There's a recent example of that with *Traffic* where he took 35mm and kept degrading it, and he went through five generations of film to get that opening sequence which was astounding, so it makes absolute sense.

Q - With Super 16mm would you need less light than 35mm?

Eric - No, because you have the same high-speed lenses like F1.4 and the film emulsions are all the same. You can use less light with digital cameras.

Q - Can you explain Anamorphic?

Eric - In Anamorphic, you have the lens on the camera that squeezes the image and a similar lens on the projector that un-squeezes it. The result is a very wide image (1:2.35 aspect ratio).

Q - How noisy are cameras in general?

Eric - That's always been a problem. The smallest cameras are the noisiest, such as the Arri IIC and IIIC, which are hand held. The Aäton was the first 35 to come out that actually had a chance of contending with studio cameras. Attempts at making quiet cameras are the Moviecam SL (super light). With hand held cameras you're always trying to do a close up and that's when the noise is most critical. Movie Cam is quiet and Panavision is extremely quiet.

Q - How long does it take to change a roll of film?

Eric - For an experienced person, it takes a minute and a half. You could get it down to a minute.

Q - Why would you shoot on Super 35?

Eric - The beauty of Super 35 is that you don't have to carry large lenses around with you (anamorphic) and yet still shoot a widescreen image (1:2.35). You can carry conventional lenses, conventional equipment. It can also be shot at two perf or three perf and protect television. You can get 16:9, 1:1.66, 1:1.85 1:2.35, the whole gamut.

Q - What are gels and filters used for?

Eric - Filters are usually what goes on the lens. Gels just technically go on the lights.

Basic Film Camera Package

This is an Arriflex SRII, one of the standard Super 16mm workhorses. The camera department can become awash with equipment, and often, many new filmmakers forget that it's what is in front of the camera that is important and not the 'toys' or 'shots' in of themselves. There isn't too much cosmetic difference between S16mm and 35mm cameras beyond the fact that the cameras and magazines are a little bigger. And the main difference between film kit and video/digital kit is ruggedness and weight. Film kit is almost all metal, so it's damn tough and very heavy. The camera will be stored in a large aluminium flight case. On the whole, there is less 'stuff' with film, than there is with video.

PRODUCTION

Depth Of Field

This refers to the area in the frame that will appear to be in focus. If you have very little (shallow) depth of field, then not much is in focus, whereas a lot of depth of field means almost everything is in focus. Shallow depth of field generally is effective for close ups for the subject seems pulled out of the background forcing the audience to concentrate on it. However, in these situations focus is critical for you can lose it very easily. Large depth of field is great for establishing shots. Two main items affect depth of field, the length of the lens and aperture setting. Here are some rules of thumb to follow…

Length *The shorter the lens (wide angle) the more depth of field you will have, and conversely, the longer the lens (telephoto) the less depth of field you will have.*
Aperture *The more light you let through the lens, the more depth of field you will have. So, at F-2 you will lose almost all of your depth of field while at F-22 you will have great depth of field.*

By combining a different focal length lenses and changing the amount of light reaching the lenses either through lighting or with filters you can manipulate the depth of field for creative purposes. In addition, the type of film you are using can effect depth of field. Small format films stocks like Super 8mm and Super 16mm tend to have greater depth of field, while larger formats like 35mm and 70mm have less depth of field.

Q - So filters are used because of things like tungsten film and shooting in daylight then?

Eric - That's correction gels and they are used to match your lamps with your particular emulsions. There are two types of film stock - tungsten emulsion (for use with tungsten balanced lights) and daylight emulsion (for use with daylight or daylight balanced lights). You can use an 85 filter on the camera if you have tungsten film and are shooting in daylight conditions, but you will rarely take a daylight emulsion and shoot indoors with it using an 81 correction filter. There's so much loss in exposure when you do that that you just choose to use a tungsten emulsion indoors. When I was growing up, there was a cinematographer named Robbie Muller, who started using mixed illumination (I call it hybrid illumination). You welcome in all the accents that occur with fluorescence, neon, candlelight, incandescence, daylight and you just let it happen. Once you learn what all those things do and combine them on the same palette, you can start to use them and have fun with them. It's all about mixing. So often you're trying to control just the fluorescence, like in the film *Se7en*. That's both a bleach-bypass film and a tightly controlled fluorescent lighting film - they kept it green / cyanic and it worked.

Q - If you were a low budget independent filmmaker, what would you include in your basic lighting package?

Eric - The first film I shot I brought my own lights and the highest priced items were the quartz tungsten bulbs that cost $18 a piece. I went to a machine shop and I took a bunch of aluminium parts from a local factory and I made lights. You can light it with fluorescent; you can light it with sunlight. One thing I've gotten bolder with in my work is taking a single photo bulb and placing it in the centre of the room, if that's what the scene calls for. The other thing we had in *My Private Idaho* is practical lights, and often I'd hold them in my hand next to the camera.

Q - Could you explain what 'practicals' are?

Eric - A practical lamp is an on-camera light - examples are a desk light, torch light, standing light, a floor lamp or a table lamp etc. I often replace normal light bulbs with photofloods in a practical light. You can easily blow them out so I use dimmers. The photofloods only last for three hours and get extraordinarily hot. There's 250watt, there's daylight (which are never really daylight), Tungsten and 500watts - they're fire starters. I go down to these 7.5-watt lights that look like golf balls. I've had so many directors say *'I love the way you lit 'My Private Idaho', weren't there scenes in that film where you just had practicals?'* I say, *'yeah, there were'* and they say, *'well can we do that for the whole movie?'* They know how long it takes to light scenes and they don't want to spend all the time doing that. It's really about whether or not you want to see the actors eyes or to address the concerns of female faces, because regardless of what is said, stars don't want to have a camera pointed up their nose and don't want to look ugly. They don't want to have a face in shadow for 35% of the movie. You can design a film to light with practicals and there are famous examples. The most recent one I've seen is *Eyes Wide Shut*. Kubrik pretty much lit that film and he was his own gaffer from what I could see. Often, when you see a 360° shot, you have to light it so that you can just go in there and shoot in all directions, but there is a price - do you get to see into a woman's eyes? Eyes are the windows to the soul and if they're dark, especially actresses with dark eyes, you have to get in there and light them.

Q - What are the basic elements of lighting?

Eric - There's the key-light, the fill-light and the backlight and those are the three elements which can be widely interpreted. For me, it gets down to cosmetics and the emotionality of light. There are a couple of things I keep going back to in terms of lighting which are really simple. A key light predominantly lights the scene and is usually the strongest light on the subject. It can come from the front, side or behind and usually has a direction. The fill light wants to have some direction but it's generally a more diffused light and will fill in harsh shadows. The backlight is often a hard light because you can be trying to separate black hair from a dark background, so you need to have these hot hits on the hair. That's the classical three point source lighting.

Q - So you can be working with that as a basic, but then also do everything else on top of that?

Lenses

Prime Lens

This is a lens of a fixed focal length. They are usually sharper than Zoom lenses, have a lower f-stop and are better for low light interior scenes. However, depth of field can be very shallow when the lens is wide open and focusing can become critical. These are often referred to as FAST lenses. 16mm, 25mm, 50mm and 75mm are the standard primes for Super 16mm and 35mm. On 16mm, the 25mm lens is reproduces a perspective similar to that seen by the human eye. On 35mm, the 50mm lens does the same job. For 16mm, Zeiss-Distagon Super speed lenses are recommended, which come in focal lengths of 9.5mm, 12mm, 16mm and 25mm. These lenses are faster than the standard primes and are therefore sharp even when you're shooting wide open. Depth of field can be very shallow when the lens is wide open and focusing can become difficult.

Wide Angle (left)

Lenses shorter than 25mm are considered wide angle. Wide angle lenses have a greater depth of field, but can distort the subject if it is too close to the camera.

Telephoto / Long Lens (left)

Those that are two or more times longer than 25mm are considered telephoto, or a long lens. These can keep your subject large in frame at greater distances - great for dangerous stunt work where you don't want the cameras on top of the action. Long lenses have a shallow depth of field and can create an out of focus background. Telephoto lenses can be used to photograph the sun setting and heat hazes. Bear in mind that long lenses are extremely vulnerable to camera vibration.

Close up or Plus Diopters

Also used to film close up objects. They are mounted in front of the lens like a filter. They enable closer focusing with all lenses and require no exposure compensation. The higher the number of a plus diopter, the closer you can focus. Conversely, as power increases, the quality of the image deteriorates. With a close up diopter you can no longer focus on infinity. Great for shots of eyeballs, the phone book or postage stamps. (pix - above without close up diopter, below with close up diopter).

Zoom Lens

These lenses do not have fixed focal length as you can move between wide angle and telephoto. The most popular Zoom lens for Super 16mm is the Angenoux 12-120mm and the 10-150 Angenoux. All zoom lenses require the same procedure for setting up a shot - open the aperture fully, zoom all the way in on the subject and examine the sharpness. After focusing, REMEMBER to return to the proper T stop. For smoother zooming, you can use a motorized zoom control.

Coverage

A good director knows what they want to shoot, before they get on set. If they know that in the final edit of the film, 'the monologue scene' will always be in close up, then they will not waste time and money shooting a wide master for coverage. However, should you find yourself working on a studio film, you may be required to shoot much more than you think you need so that the executives feel comfortable with the amount of coverage the editor will have to use in order to tell the story properly. If you are working on a low budget film, you have to be much more economic with your shots, yet still have enough to tell the story powerfully and effectively.

1. Always shoot a master shot of the scene. This establishes location and always gives you something to cut back to.

2. Shoot singles (either medium wide or close up) of the actors in the scene. This way you can edit their performance to improve dramatic impact.

3. Get as many cutaways and insert shots as possible. This will help tell the story and give the editor more options.

4. Even if you are happy with your first take, always do a second take for safety. You never know what can happen, such as the lab screwing up the processing or the film getting torn.

5. When you go to a new location, shoot an establishing shot. This orients the audience to location and gives your scene a jumping off point.

6. Never cross the parallel line of action to the camera. Doing so will make the actors seem to flip flop location on the screen, and it will disorient your audience.

7. Ensure reverse shots match one another. For example, if you are shooting two 'over the shoulder singles' of two people talking, the two actors' eye lines should appear as if they are looking at one another and not off at some weird angle.

8. Get all your shots on one object or actor (master, medium shot, close up) at the same time. This will reduce relighting time.

9. If part of a take is good, but the rest is bad, you may not have to do the whole shot over again. You can 'pick up' from just before the mistake and continue through to the end, but you will need a bridging shot (insert), such as a reaction from another character to cover the join.

10. Shooting lots of coverage can wear down a crew. Keep your eye on their fatigue level so you know when to call it a day.

11. Learn to work within your budget and schedule. Neither are limitless and on low budgets, they are VERY limited. Extra takes could mean you have to drop scenes. Always be aware of the longer term impact of your choices.

12. Learn how to edit and work on other peoples films. You quickly learn what you need and don't need.

13. Know the rules before you break them. Oh and just to confuse you more, there are no rules!

Eric - Yes but the rules do stray. Some cameraman believe that 'when in doubt, backlight' because it makes everything golden. Sunshine is a prime example - you don't want that key light from the front, it should be behind or from the side.

Q - For an independent filmmaker working on a film with a budget of $1m, what sort of basic lighting kit could you get?

Eric - Start with the basics. When I used to shoot news, my lighting kit consisted of a photoflood, a Lowel Tota-light, a polarizing filter and groundbreakers / groundlifters.

Q - What are the 'groundlifters'?

Eric - Groundlifters allow you to attach a three prong plug into a two prong outlet (domestic). If you are doing a film for $1m, you can afford two 18ks, a couple of 12ks, a couple of 4ks, one 575 and a small Tungsten package. I'm always inclined to work with less equipment and try and shoot with as few technicians as possible - not easy to do in Hollywood!

Q - What is 'day for night'?

Eric - Day for night is achieved by under exposing the shot by approximately two stops and then use a filter to accomplish the coloration. Filters used are blue, green, magenta and ND (neutral density). The secret is not to get the sky in the shot because that gives away the day for night. If you need to get the sky, then use a ND and hide the transition in the horizon or buildings.

Q - What's 'magic hour'?

Eric - Magic hour is lovely - it's dusk. *Days Of Heaven* was shot at magic hour for the entire film, and it took them two years. There's another wonderful film called *The Sheltering Sky* that was shot in Tunisia, North Africa. In the wintertime in North Africa the light is amazing. There's an age-old axiom that when you're shooting in the desert, it's only good for the first hour or two before and after sunrise / sunset and the rest of the day you just eat lunch and have a siesta.

Q - What is 'trace and spun'?

Eric - Tracing paper is used on windows with a camera on the interior and 'blow out' lights on the exterior so it looks like daylight. You'll need to put blinds or curtains inside or it can look unreal. Trace is the most heavily diffused material used on lights, there's tough spun, grid cloth, quarter grid, half grid, double grid and 216 diffusion. Tough spun is fibreglass - it's like matted hair and is very handy for low budget filming because it goes anywhere.

Q - What about mixing stock?

Eric - You can mix high and low speed stocks no problem, but I'd advise against mixing brands.

Q - What speed are the general stocks?

Eric - They start at ASA50 and go to ASA100, 200 and 500. The 200 is a wonderful stock with the Vision 200T being the most beautiful thing around, the blacks are really black.

Q - What are the major bugbears for lighting?

Eric - A woman's face in a convertible at noon in the desert! You have to remove the sunlight with an overhead black and then come out with an 18K on the camera to reconstruct the desert light. Night time and lighting architecture is hard. When we shot *Copland* we had to light the George Washington Bridge, which was extremely challenging and fun because we had to strategically place the lights.

Q - How long does it take to set up a basic shot?

Eric - The time it takes to light is about two minutes longer than it takes to make-up the actors and dress the set. In Sydney Lumet's book *Making Movies*, he says that for every hour you take to direct an actor, you need an hour and a half to light him. I try and stay within that because time is money, but basically,

Lens & Focal Length

Telephoto
The background is crushed and the figure appears more normal. There is less spillage of 'set and props' to the left and right.

Wide
The background is more distant and the figure appears more distorted - depth is enhanced with objects closer to the camera appearing much larger than those slightly further away.

PRODUCTION

Simple Lighting Setup

Even the simplest of shots needs to be lit properly, or it will look like your average home movie. This simple mid shot of an actress required four lights - key light, fill light, rim light and a background light. The overhead diagram to the left illustrates where each light was positioned.

Key Light

The key light 'models' the subject and is often the most important light in the scene. It is often the foundation on which all other lights are based. In this case it is a light placed to the front left of the actress, perhaps representing a window light source (in the story of the shot).

Fill Light

This light is designed to 'fill' the harsh shadows created by the Key light, to create a more natural and rounded look. It will pick out detail and texture where otherwise there would be only dark shadows. In this case, it is placed close to the camera.

Back Light

To add another dimension, in this case, a light source is mounted behind and above the subject. It hits the back of objects and the actress and gives a nice impression of three dimensionality.

Background Light

This light has been positioned to illuminate the background of the scene to create a more natural look. Without it, there would be a fully lit actress sitting against a very dark background.

the larger the shot is then the longer it takes to light. Usually, you don't get one shot in less than half an hour so if your day is twelve hours then twenty-four shots is extremely ambitious.

Q - What is video playback?

Eric - There was a time when you had the director standing next to the cameraman to watch the performances. They were so close that they didn't need earphones. Now, there are video monitors that have a digital feed from the camera and the director looks at that for framing and camera movement and the have a sound feed from the sound recordist so they can hear the performance too.

Q - Do you find that the director often watches the video playback rather than the performance?

Eric - They're often watching the performance on the monitor, but I think the monitor becomes a security blanket and directors can become dependent on the playback and they start talking about what takes they're going to use. They're analyzing a performance as opposed to creating it. Filmmakers today has grown up with a camcorder and therefore a monitor in their hand.

Q - We never used playback on our three features, as it slowed the process down. We always got what we wanted too.

Eric - There's a beauty in that simplicity. There is less involvement by other parties, and it is a director's medium.

Q - What is 'color temperature'?

Eric - Color temperature is based on the heating of a 'black body'. For example, a blacksmith would take a piece of metal, put it in the fire and it would heat up to red-hot. That is a certain temperature and so is the incandescent filament in a lamp as it's charged, like on a dimmer, as it goes up to line voltage. It has a core temperature conventionally of (if it's a practical bulb that you buy at your hardware store) about 2900°. So, if you took your blacksmith and his horseshoe and you heated that horseshoe up to 2900°, the light that the horseshoe gave off would be the same color as your practical bulb. In quartz film labs, it's 3100°, so the blacksmith would have to go in there and heat it up even hotter to 3100°. Sunlight is 5500° so if you heated that black body up to 5500°, it would be as blue as the sun - it would be the same color as the sun.

Q - What is 'white balance'?

Eric - White balance refers to video cameras. You take their three color signals and equalize the output so when they are pointed at a white object, that object is represented on the TV monitor as white. If you're using tungsten light, everything is going to look too yellow, so you'll take a white card and point the camera at it, push a button and it will calibrate electronically all the tubes to white. So, white balance is calibrating the video signal to different lighting conditions. It goes for tungsten, fluorescent, daylight, sunlight and firelight.

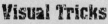

Visual Tricks

Day for Night
Although not done often these days, mainly because it is tricky to do effectively, there may be occasions when you have to shoot day for night. When shooting day for night exterior, the best place to have the sun is behind and above the subject or behind and to the side. This is because you want to create as many dark areas (shadows) you can. If the sunlight is 90° from the optical axis, grad filters are helpful in darkening the skies. Underexpose 1½ to 2 stops on the wide shots and 1-1½ on close ups. Make sure you inform the laboratory on the camera report that you have shot day for night. Day for night is much better when shooting at dusk as the low angle of the sun creates longer shadows. Day for night interiors are much easier to control, but require a lot of grip work to block out the natural daylight. Black out windows slightly in front of the actual window and then throw some green light on the window from the outside.

Shiny Streets
Wetting down the streets can enrich night exteriors, creating high contrast textures that reflect the lights, whether or not it's supposed to be raining in your scene. But it can be expensive if you need large areas wetting down.

The Magic Hour
This is the time of day when the sun is below the horizon (pre-dawn and post-sunset), but there is still light in the sky. The light is soft and golden and cam make your subjects look amazing. Magic hour is very short, so be ready to work very quickly.

Sunset
Long lenses, anything between 500mm-1000mm, are used to capture a perfect sunset. The lower the sun in the sky, the more atmosphere you're shooting through, and the richer it will look. The same can be said for shooting the sunset on a smoggy day. This will give you a beautiful orange orb. Shooting a blazing sun in a clear sky can be too hot and therefore not pleasing on film. Graduated filters can be used to create more of the orange glow. Make sure to balance the light in the background and foreground, as they will change as the sun goes down and changes color temperature.

No. 12519

LABORATORIES COPY

The Camera Report Sheet

| CONTINUED FROM SHEET No. | — | SHEET NUMBER | 1 | CONTINUED ON SHEET No. | — |

THE SHEET NUMBERS MUST BE QUOTED ON ALL DELIVERY NOTES, INVOICES AND OTHER COMMUNICATIONS RELATING THERETO

PRODUCING COMPANY	ARRI MEDIA	STUDIOS OR LOCATION	LOCATION
PRODUCTION	"FILM TEST"	PRODUCTION No.	
DIRECTOR	P. COOPER	CAMERAMEN	S. NELSON	DATE	14/07/02

STATE IF COLOUR OR B & W: COLOUR

PICTURE NEGATIVE REPORT

ORDER TO	TECHNICOLOR		LABORATORIES
STOCK AND CODE No.	5246 2508	LABORATORY INSTRUCTIONS RE INVOICING, DELIVERY, ETC.	CAMERA AND NUMBER: ARRICAM ST
EMULSION AND ROLL No.	513,014 (1)	NEG DEV + CLEAN, RUSH PRINT TO LOCATION AS ARRANGED	CAMERA OPERATOR: S. NELSON

MAG No.	LENGTH LOADED	SLATE No.	TAKE No.	COUNTER READING	TAKE LENGTH	'P' for Print B&W COL'R	LENS F/L & STOP	ESSENTIAL INFORMATION	CAN No.
1	400'	1	1	0'	30'	P	T2.8½ 25mm	EXT. DAY	1
			2	30'	30'	P		ND 0.6	
			3	60'	10'			81 EF	
			4	70'	30'	P		¼ BLACK PROMIST	
		2	1	100'	25'	P	T4 85mm		
			2	125'	25'	P			
			3	150'	30'	P			
		3	1	180'	50'	P	T4 18mm		
			2	230'	50'	P			
		4	1	280'	30'	P	T2.8½ 25mm		
			2	310'	30'	P			
			3	340'	20'				
			4	360'	30'	P			
				390'				10' WASTE	
2	400'	5	1	0'	40'	P	T4 35mm		2
			2	40'	40'	P			
			3	80'	50'	P			
			4	130'	20'				
			5	150'	30'	P			
				180'				220' S/E	

FOR OFFICE USE ONLY | TOTAL CANS | 2

TOTAL EXPOSED	550	TOTAL EXPOSED	550	TOTAL PRINTED		TOTAL FOOTAGE PREVIOUSLY DRAWN	0'
SHORT ENDS	220	HELD OR NOT SENT	—		FOOTAGE DRAWN TODAY	800'
WASTE	10'	TOTAL DEVELOPED			PREVIOUSLY EXPOSED	—
FOOTAGE LOADED	800'	SIGNED			EXPOSED TODAY	550'

This document is usually filled out by the assistant camera person. This one is for a movie shot on film, opposed to video/digital (which would differ slightly), and is used by the laboratory and editor later on down the line. Each night, a copy of this document will be taped to the exposed film cans and sent to the lab (or if shooting on tape, a copy will be sent with the tapes to the cutting room). You will get a pad of these triplicate sheets from the hire company when you hire your cameras.

The sheet details shots, takes and notes on what is expected from the lab. It also details information like roll numbers, stock types and contact details etc.

Q - What is the chart you put at the beginning of the film, in front of the camera?

Eric - The color chart. It's an accepted form of color chips so that the laboratory can faithfully represent what the cinematographer has captured. The colorist who is printing your dailies will then have a reference for correct color.

Q - Could you explain 'color grading' and 'color timing'?

Eric - Color grading is controlling the three axes of color, i.e. cyan, magenta and yellow, in order to shift the film print to a colder or warmer tone. Lightness and darkness can also be controlled but contrast can't.

Q - When you've shot and you take your dailies to the lab, do they do a general 'one light' with the color grading?

Eric - You can do a one light, which means you've shot everything at the same exposure, but each camera set up usually involves a slight difference in shift. Generally I ask for 'timed dailies' which are color shifted to evenly match all the shots we didn't see. They're trying to match the color, light and dark of many shots within the same scene.

Q - What can you do in advance of shooting to make sure that certain problems are ironed out?

Eric - Tests are something you should always do - especially when you go through the digital process. If you're trying to do something you haven't, or have seen done, then you need to shoot tests, otherwise you don't know what you're doing.

Q - Film is extremely sensitive, so is what we see with our eye going to be like that?

Eric - It's actually the other way round - eyes are more sensitive than film. Your eyes see more degrees of darkness than film does. You have to come to terms with what a camera sees because it's a mechanical device and, equally, you have to come to terms with what film sees. I always like to say that filmmaking is stupidly easy, but, in fact, you have to go through a lot of trial and error with emulsions to see what light does. The big problem for filmmaking is that as you sit in a room and you have a vision, you'll see something that is beautiful but too dark for film to record it, so you're trying to do something with effects that involves lights, time and money to recreate that look. Video is different as you start discovering these wonderful accidents as you see them on the screen in front of you, but with film, you have to shoot it, get it back from the lab and then it's going to be wrong, so its a dialectic which is very long and slow. The actual understanding of the aesthetics of color and film is the hard part.

Q - What is a 'spot meter'?

Eric - A spot meter reads reflected light as opposed to an incident meter which reads the light hitting a subject. It's used to selectively measure each individual value in a scene. They're handy for measuring the moon, sun or practical lights to

Film Frame Rates (slower and faster)

A major drawback of digital formats is thay they can't handle slow motion very well. What few cameras can do it, don't offer very high frame rates, which means slow motion must be 'created' in post production, which is never as good as if it were shot in slow motion on set. In this area, film is still king. On any action, especially things like a glass being dropped and breaking, or a stone being thrown through a window, shoot slow motion as the action happens so fast in reality, that it can be almost unseen in shot.

Slow Motion

True slow motion (also known as over-cranking) is where you run the camera at a faster frame rate than the normal 24 fps, such as 48fps. When projected at 24fps, the action would run at half speed - slow motion. While most cameras can do some slow motion (often up to 50fps or 75fps), high speed cameras are needed to capture dramatic shots.

Ramping

This is where the camera ramps from one speed to another, in shot. For instance, 24fps to 100fps. The effect is that the shot begins in normal speed, then slows down and turns into a slow motion shot. The catch is that as you speed up or slow down you need to adjust the exposure to compensate, so you will need to have an Iris Control Unit (ICU) too.

Post Slo-mo

The other way to create slow motion is to film at regular speed and then to slow it down in post-production. The effect can be jerky or even slightly blurry if done digitally. Where possible, always shoot in slow motion on set if you want it in slow motion in your movie. This will save money in post too. Of course if you shoot DV or HD, this may be impossible.

Fast Motion

The opposite of overcranking, undercranking, refers to running the camera at a slower frame rate than the normal speed of 24fps, such as 12fps, which produces fast motion when replayed at 24fps. In the old days, chase sequences would often by under cranked so to make the cars move faster than they were actually going (the trick still works as long as you don't undercrank too much, say 21fps to slightly speed up some action).

Time Lapse

This is a technique where single frame exposures are taken over a prolonged period, at say 1fsp or 1 frame per minute. It's used to film subjects that move too slowly to be seen with the naked eye, for instance, a flower bud opening, buildings demolished and rebuilt, or the sun rising and setting, hours in real time, seconds when played back on film. There are a variety of gadgets that enable you to do this, but the most common is to use an intervalometer, which allows you to set the frame rate for a given time period.

see if they are too bright. They're great for when you cannot use an incident meter. The incident meter is the one you use the most. It tells you the base amount of light and your mind knows the rest from experience.

Q - What would you do if you had a scene where you had an actor in front chatting away and in the background there was a TV set and you didn't want to see the line go through?

Eric - You have to convert the signal to 24fps. Or, alternatively, shoot at 24fps with a 144° shutter. There's always a little white line that showws up and it slowly rolls up, but it's not too bothersome.

Q - What are the most common mistakes that you've come across by new filmmakers?

Eric - There's a million. From understanding what it takes technically to set up the filmmaking process, to what their expectations are of how fast or how slow something will take to do, and what the camera is capable of doing. Some directors have trouble with point of view objective camera verses subjective camera is a very difficult concept for directors to understand. Screen directions

The Light Meter

The light meter is the primary tool of the DP when placing lights. It is used to measure the amount of light in a given hitting or reflecting an object or scene. This reading is then used to set the camera aperture to expose the film correctly. It looks scary when you see a DP doing it, but it's actually quite simple. So go on, have a go. As a director, you may never light a film, but if you know how to, your DP will certainly treat you with greater respect.

First off, on the light meter, set the ASA to match the ASA of the film in the camera. Then set the frame rate at which your camera will be running (shutter speed). Depending on the light meter, this may be 24fps or 25fps (both will produce almost the same result). Now hold the light meter close to the subject and take the reading, Then calibrate the aperture ring on the camera to match the reading. That's it! Of course, it takes a great deal of experience, trail and error and downright talent to produce consistently stunning images.

There are two types of light meter readings... Incident and Reflected.

Incident Light Reading
This measures the amount of light hitting the subject, rather than the light reflecting off the subject. Your light meter will have a white hemispherical light collector (lumisphere) which represents the general curvature of a human face. This is pointed from the subject's POV to the camera, so that the same light hitting the subject is hitting this sphere. This sphere can also be 'flat' (recessed) which can help measure illumination contrast, levels or brightness differences by aiming the meter at one light at a time.

Reflective Light Reading
This measures the amount of light bouncing / reflecting off the subject. The meter is pointed at the subject so to read only the light bouncing off the subject.

There are two types of Reflective light meters... The Standard Meter and the Spot Meter.

The Standard reflective light meter
Has a wide angle of acceptance (up to 60 degrees). Here all the light in this angle of acceptance is averaged together to give a reading.

The Spot Meter
This gives a narrow angle of acceptance (1 degree or less). Looking through the meter, the DP can see the exact spot they're measuring. These are used to read the light from smaller areas at a greater distance, measuring backlight, highly reflective surfaces, when the main subject is moving or to measure an extreme brightness range (the sun or the moon etc.). They're also very handy for measuring practical lights to see if they are too bright and great for where you can't get your incident meter. Spot meter readings can be useful for fine tuning a reflective and/or an incident reading.

The Gray Card

Light meters presume all subjects are of average reflectance, or a neutral gray—often called 'middle' or 'medium' gray because it falls between pure black and pure white. The use of the neutral gray standard allows a reflected light meter to render correct readings for 'average' subjects in 'average' lighting situations. Using an 18% reflectance gray card, you can get a reflected light reading, which is the same as reading an incident light (18% gray tone is the averaged out light in an average scene and film, either color or B&W, is formulated to produce a proper exposure when it's exposed to produce an 18% gray tone).

When to use a Gray Card

Use a gray card when lighting situations fool the typical camera light meter. This could be when there's back lighting, such as a bright sky or window behind the subject, when there's a light source such as a bulb or light fixture in front of your camera, when a large part of the scene has a very light tone like snow, or a large part has a very dark tone. If you get the same reading with the gray card as without it, you didn't need it. If the gray card gives a different reading you should generally use the gray card recommendation or do several exposures (bracketing) to see which negative comes out best.

When to use Color Scales

Filmed at the time of the slate to help the color timer at the lab. The color timer can then check for any changes in color balance that might occur because of mixed stocks or different baths during the developing process.

are tough as well, and the ability to implicitly understand what the lengths of lenses do is important. It's important to learn how to use cameras without a zoom lens so that you physically have to move the camera to come to know the different lenses. Whereas with a zoom, it takes longer to understand that a telephoto lens throws the background out of focus. And a wide lens requires you to hold the camera close. You go through film school, but you still have to learn how to make movies. Everything you learn as a cameraman you learn in the field.

Q - What are the main problems for a DP?

Eric - Getting good scripts!

Q - What advice would you give a new filmmaker?

Eric - Make a short film before you make a feature film. And don't be afraid.

Q - You've got to learn your craft?

Eric - Shoot with prime lenses, and it doesn't have to be film verses video, you can shoot video, but shoot with prime lenses and edit. And learn when to use sound and when not to use sound.

Q - What is your opinion of digital filmmaking?

Eric - There's a whole lot of things going on, for example the whole question of *Dogme 95*. It was all done in the 70's, we just repackaged it and put a new piece of cellophane on it. They were saying, *'what if'*. Soderberg is championing small filmmaking, saying once you get into the Hollywood system of guilds and equipment and methodology, it's hard to fight the number of people you have on set. I mean Soderberg got rid of the cameraman, what a hero! He said, 'No, I'm not going to do it by the system, I'm going to try to make films as an author of films.' I did it with *Kids* to some degree, where we reduced the equipment way back to nothing and there's something to be said about that. That's good advice to new filmmakers.

PRODUCTION

M. David Mullen
Shooting Hi Def

THE DIGITAL DP

Q - What is your background?

David - I've been making Super 8 films since I was a teenager and tried to get into film school, but didn't manage, so instead got an English degree at UCLA while making short films on the weekends. I went to film school in California for three years and got a masters in filmmaking, and started making the transition from making my own films to shooting for other people, partly because I could shoot more often if it was for other people. Then I started shooting low budget features and have shot 27 so far, seventeen on 35mm, one in super 16mm and recently five in Hi-Def. On average, their budgets ranged from $500k - $2m. I've done a couple as low as $100k, but nothing lower than that, and recently I did a film that was 24P Hi Def on a $300k budget, followed by one budgeted at $4m.

Q - What are your thoughts on shooting Hi-Def v Film?

David - 24P Hi Def is pretty high quality. It's not technically as high quality as film, and it doesn't have as much resolution or latitude, and the color is compressed, but it doesn't have much grain either, so even though it is softer, it's not grainy so holds up very well. I tend to think of it as a different looking film stock. It has certain qualities that are different and can have a shiny, plastic look. If you transfer Hi Def to film, it picks up a layer of film texture. There is debate as to whether Hi Def saves money. LA is a big production city, so there are a lot of deals to be made on both video and film equipment, but if I were a filmmaker in Milwaukee or somewhere that didn't have Hi Def post facilities, then I would have a harder time saying 'you're going to save money' because Hi Def equipment is more expensive to rent than the film equipment. The rates are often double that of film equipment, but you have to offset that with the much cheaper cost of the tape stock over film stock. The trouble is if your end result has to go back out to film, the cost of transferring any digital master to film using a laser recorder is very expensive, and negates any savings you made by shooting Hi Def in the first place. So I'd say it's cheaper to get a film made in Hi Def, compared to 35mm, but once you have to transfer it back to film again, most of those cost savings are lost. A lot of people never need to make a print as they sell it straight to home video or cable television, and so they get to keep those savings (not needing a 35mm print). There are costs with online mastering with Hi Def, but on the other hand, even for the home video market, it's starting to become more common to need a Hi Def master as some cable channels now show movies in Hi Def. Now there is a trend to master to Hi Def (whether you shoot on film or Hi Def) so that you can make all the different video tape versions for sales - you'd make a 4:3 NTSC, 16:9 NTSC, letter boxed NTSC and then all that again in PAL. All this from one master Hi Def tape, so there is a potential saving there too.

Q - How much do the shooting tapes cost?

David - A fifty minute Hi Def tape is around $70, that's equivalent to 5000ft of 35mm stock which would cost around $2,500. Most of the 35mm films I have worked on spend about $70k for film stock, processing and telecine costs for editing purposes. On Hi Def video, you have tape stock costs and the cost to down convert those tapes to NTSC or PAL for off line editing. But then the cost to laser record a Hi Def digital master back to 35mm is currently about $70k, but the costs are dropping.

Q - Does it take longer to shoot on Hi Def?

David - I think for the most part, it's the same as shooting film. Lighting is often not related to the format, but defined by what you're trying to do in the scene dramatically. If you have to add five lights to get the right look, those five lights are necessary whether it's video or film. Occasionally, when using a lot of natural light, the advantage of video is that you can see whether something works or doesn't work immediately. There are slight time savings that come from re-loading Hi Def less often but it's nothing significant (on Hi Def you might re-load once or twice a day at the most). I found Hi Def makes shooting car scenes easier because you're not pulling off to the side of the road to re-load the camera. You can for shoot fifty minutes straight without stopping.

Q - Are Hi Def cameras as big as the film camera?

David - A Hi Def camera is a little bigger than a Digital Betacam camera, but it's very long once you put a zoom lens on one end and the batteries on the other end, and then you start to include accessories. With a film camera, you often have the option of top or back loading. So it's a bit bulky either way, but you can strip the camera down to its basics, which is more or less like a news camera, with just a battery on the back and a lens on the front and a clip on matte box. Once it's stripped to that level, it's much lighter. I haven't used the ultra light 35mm cameras, like the Aaton 353 or the MovieCam Light as they are usually out of my budget.

Q - A lot of filmmakers are under the impression that video cameras are lightweight and easy to move around...

David - The advantage with film equipment is there's more variety. In film you have everything from an Eyemo, all the way up to huge cameras. You can have cameras that run 1000 fps. Digital is more limiting in terms of frame rates and size of the cameras.

Q - Are there any Hi-Def high speed cameras?

David - Panasonic has a Hi Def camera that does multiple frame rates. It records from 2 fps up to 60 fps and can do true slow motion shots. The camera is slightly smaller and lighter than the Sony Hi Def camera and uses slightly smaller tapes - DVC Pro HD. The trouble with the Panasonic camera is that there is less resolution than the Sony camera. It's a 1280 by 720 pixel camera, not a 1920 by 1080 pixel camera. Its CCDs have slightly less than 1 million pixels each, whereas the Sony camera has 2.2 million pixels per CCD. That doesn't mean it looks like it has half the resolution, in theory it does but in practice, other factors affect whether a shot looks sharp or not. I haven't seen a feature transferred out to film that was shot with a Panasonic camera, but I'm sure for the right project, the resolution is fine. There are people now who are shooting with the new Sony 25P MPEG IMX camera, which has the resolution of 720 by 576 pixels. It records to an MPEG compression format and it's in true 25P, it has more resolution for moving objects than regular interlace scan has.

T-stops and F-stops

A camera lens has an iris, or aperture, just like your eye. The aperture, mechanically controlled by a ring on the lens (and sometimes electronically on digital cameras) is used to control the amount of light passing through the lens to hit the negative on a film camera, or CCD on a digital camera. The markings that are used to set the iris are called F-stops, and on some lenses, T-stops, and they directly relate to the readings on the DPs light meter.

F-stops

F-stops are referenced by numbers (always white markings etched into the ring of the lens) with F-2, F-4, F-5.6, F-8, F-11, F-16, and F-22 being the most common. The lower the number (toward F-2), the more 'wide open' the lens is said to be (with less available light). The higher the number (toward F-22) and the lens is said to be 'stopped down' (with more available light). The amount of light entering the camera between adjacent F-stops is either halved (going toward F-22) or doubled (going toward F-2). For example, F-8 allows twice the amount of light into the camera that F-11 does. Likewise, F-5.6 would let in four times as much light as F-11. F-stops are calculated by a general mathematical equation that is the same for all lenses, no matter what type.

T-stops

T-stops are similar to F-stops and even have the same reference numbers - except that they start with a T (T-2, T-4, T-5.6, etc. and are also etched onto the ring, but in color). The difference is that T-stops are calibrated for each individual lens as opposed to a general mathematical formula, thereby creating a more accurate reading for the specific lens you are using. This takes into account light loss from it passing through the lens itself. Also, zoom lenses and long prime lenses will have T-stops, but short prime lenses will usually have only F-stops.

Q - Is 25P easier when it comes to post?

David - When you shoot 24P and you cut it in an NTSC environment, you're dealing with 3:2 pull down that's embedded in the NTSC recording. But even if you shot film at 24 frames and transferred to NTSC for editing, you'd have to deal with that and most editing systems that deal with film cutting, like the Avid Film Composer or Final Cut Pro, can deal with 24 frame rate. But PAL is easier in the sense that there is no pull down to deal with, just a frame to frame transfer back to film.

Q - What is the pull down?

David - NTSC video runs at 60 fields per second interlaced scan, which is 30 fps. Film runs at 24fps, and in order to convert 24 frames into 60 fields, certain fields have to be repeated - because if you simply convert 24 frames into 2 fields you'd end up with 48 fields. You have to convert 48 fields to 60 fields and that is done by repeating certain fields with a redundant field. That's called a 3:2 pull down. It's something you don't have to deal with in PAL. There's a new 24p Mini DV camera, the Panasonic DVX100, that captures in 24p and records it to NTSC so it has 3:2 pull down fields. There is software coming out that allows you to pull that out again, so you can edit it as if it were NTSC footage or edit it in a true 24P environment and add it back in. The trouble with editing it as NTSC is your 3:2 pull down cadence is not always in the same spot once you start editing the footage. Unless you edit on the A

Shooting Ratio

Shooting Ratio is the ratio of how much film you shoot to the amount of time on screen. For example, if you're going to make your film on a 3:1 shooting ratio means that for every minute of film that makes it into your movie, you're going to shoot 3 minutes of footage - throw away 2 and keep 1. A 400' can of Super16mm = about 10 minutes. Therefore, to make a 90 minute film you need 9 cans multiplied by 3 (if shooting ratio is 3:1) which equals 27 rolls, which equals 10,800'. The same ratio applies to 35mm except that a 1000' roll of film runs for approximately 10 minutes. Here you would need 27,000 feet for a 90 minute film an a 3:1 cutting ratio. Of course, the lower you plan your shooting ratio, the less expensive it is for stock and processing. The downside is that you have less of a chance to compensate for bad takes, technical problems, cutaways and experimentation. It's going to be hard to shoot at 3:1, even 5:1 is tough. Most low budget films end up somewhere near 8:1 cutting ratio.

1. Save stock wherever possible. It's expensive to purchase, and expensive to process.

2. Work out your system between sound, camera and clapper loader/cam assistant so the camera starts turning over at the last possible moment. Just a couple of seconds wasted at the head of every shot will accumulate on a feature shoot.

3. Don't get too anxious to call cut. Often in the cutting room, you will need that extra second on the end of a shot. When you feel the shot has ended, wait a beat before calling cut.

4. Know in your heart if you have got what you need in your first take. Takes that are not needed waste time as well as stock.

5. If you get a hair in the gate, you should re-shoot. If stock is very short and you are having to get everything in one take, don't bother to re-shoot, (unless the hair is massive - many major features go out with hairs in the gate.) In the cutting room you will always use the best take, regardless of technical problems that camera operators will moan about, such as hairs, flare, soft shots and wobbly camerawork.

6. Rehearse as much as possible. Block the scene for the cameraman so he knows what is going to happen and when. If the scene could be spontaneous in terms of performance from the actor, allow the cameraman to widen the lens so there is more space in frame to accommodate the unexpected. This will avoid losing the frame or focus, forcing a retake (which will probably be wider anyway).

7. If you are shooting 35mm, you will only develop and print the shots you want. If you shoot 16mm or Super 16mm, you will print everything.

8. Storyboards will help, but it is likely that too many shots will be boarded and that when it comes to shooting, not all shots will be possible due to the location being different, a script rewrite or simply a lack of resources.

9. Shooting on tape formats such as DV or HD often means that directors will say 'leave it running while I just...' This can mean hours and hours of wasted footage that doesn't cost much in terms of tape, but will cost you severely in the cutting room in wasted time and frustration. Whatever the format, remain disciplined about shooting absolutely no more than is needed.

Over or Under Exposing

Just because your light meter says one thing, it doesn't mean you have to shoot it that way. You can intentionally over and under expose a scene in order to create a certain mood or effect. If you do this, know that film reacts differently from video.

Shooting on Film
Overexposure is good, under exposure is bad, because with overexposure you will still have an image on the negative, which you can manipulate in post if you decide to change your mind.

Shooting on video
Underexposure is good, over exposure is bad, because video cannot recover as well from 'blown out' images.

frame on a film composer. Even if you're cutting an NTSC transfer of film footage, you only cut on the correct frame so that your 3:2 pull down is always happening at the same spot, so you're cutting on a true film print, not a fake video print which has the extra field. Again, this is a good reason to seriously consider shooting in PAL.

Q - Do you need less light for video?

David - I don't believe you need less lighting for video. People have done lots of video shoots recently with extremely low light levels, but that's also possible in film. The 24P Sony camera is roughly rated at 320 ASA, which is comparable to film stock. If you turn off the shutter and go down to 1/24th of a second, you gain a stock which is near to 640 ASA. If you boost the gain by 6DB, you gain another stock which gets you up to 1280 ASA, but there are 800 ASA film stocks that can be pushed to 1600 ASA or higher, so it's all roughly equivalent in terms of sensitivity. It's just that more people seem to be working with less light for video, but it's nothing to do with film verses video.

Q - Should you process your video to look like film if you plan to scan back to film at the end?

David - No. if you're transferring anything to film, you want to avoid film look processing. You don't need to do it as the process of transferring back to film will do it for you. I heard that on *Star Wars Episode 2*, they tried to emulate certain looks of film stocks using software, but I can't imagine it's doing anything radical to the image other than adding a texture and contrast. The only thing that I notice is that digital transfers to film tend to lose some color and look less saturated on film once they go out from a digital master. So you have to do certain things to counteract that. It might mean color timing the film digitally with a little more saturation. or it might mean printing the final transfer onto a more saturated print stock, like Vision Premier.

Q - Should you shoot tests?

David - There's a lot of looks you can create digitally, with digital color correction tools, and one could test those things, but it's expensive to transfer those tests to film. On *Jackpot*, we were limited to one minute of footage that we could afford to transfer out to film before we shot the movie. I knew normal scenes with normal lighting would transfer more or less the way I saw them, and I was more concerned about extreme lighting effects. So I shot an African-American actor and a White actor and put extreme hot back light, or extreme under exposures to see how those shots looked on video, and then on a film print. I wanted to know how over exposure was going to look once transferred onto film, because video tends to clip things that are too bright. Once they exceed a maximum level, they get cut off and you lose information.

Follow Focus

Camera assistants have their hands on the focus control at all times, ready to compensate for any subject movement. When the camera to subject distance changes during the shot, the focus will have to be readjusted, especially when the depth of field is shallow. This is called 'following' or 'pulling' focus. Prior to shooting, the movement of the scene will have been 'blocked out' and markings will have been made on the floor at the point where an actor will stop their motion. Measurements are made from that point to the camera lens, so that the focus puller will know exactly how much to adjust focus to keep this crystal clear. Depending on the actors and the type of shot (i.e. the camera on a dolly), this can be very complex.

PRODUCTION

Cheap Special Effects Filters

If you can't afford to hire expensive effects filters, gelatin filters can be used. Stills photographers use them with a special plastic holder which snaps onto the front of the lens. Split diopters, graduated, star, close up, diffusion - all can add to the image if used in a subtle manner. Best of all, they're cheap.

Polarizing

Much like your polarizing sunglasses, if you place the camera at a right angle, this filter can radically reduce reflections in a window. Obviously useful when shooting through glass on sunny days.

Split Diopter

This is essentially half a close up lens. It allows the extreme foreground and backgrounds to be in focus at the same time. It's a weird effect, but very pleasing in the right circumstances. Often a vertical object such as a door, tree or wall is used to disguise the transition from one focus plane to the other.

Graduated

Used to create heavier skies, for that Ridley Scott look. Many colors are available, including neutral density which can be used to simply darken the sky so that it does not over expose and burn out, thereby losing detail in the clouds.

Close-Up

Most camera lenses don't get very close to a subject. So if you want that extreme close up, you are going to need a close up filter. They look a bit like a large magnifying glass, and come in different strengths. Buy the strongest.

Mask

Binoculars and a keyhole are perhaps the most common type of mask. They work best on the longer end of the lens and can be done in the lab instead, although that will cost significantly more. Mask shots tend to look cheesy.

Q - Are there any issues with shooting on Hi Def in the rain or desert?

David - Since the cameras are electronic, they are more prone to overheating than a film camera. They have a lot of intake and exhaust vents to keep the camera cool and can be hard to seal if you are trying to protect it from dust. I would say the camera would have more problems in a hot and dusty environment than in a cold, wet environment. You want to watch sealing the camera too well, as then there's no fresh air circulating into the camera and it will shut itself of once it gets too hot. One problem with video is the lenses seem to lose their back focus more easily than film cameras. This has to do with the temperature inside the camera. I learned the hard way on *Jackpot* that we had to check the back focus on the lens regularly, at least twice a day, and any time we changed lenses, or when we moved from a hot to a cold environment. With video, the light has to go through the lens, through a prism block where it gets split three ways and has to focus on the three different CCDs, so there's more chance for focus to drift. That's why professional video cameras all have back focus adjustment knobs at the back of the lens. With MiniDV cameras, there is no way to adjust the back focus.

Q - What advice would you give new filmmakers shooting Hi Def?

David - They have to be concerned about focus. The cameras have more depth of field on average than 35mm, similar to Super 16mm depth of field, but because you don't have an optical viewfinder, you have the camera's video viewfinder and that makes it hard to judge focus, especially on a wider shot. But the Hi Def format has enough resolution so that if you're off on your focus, you'll see it on a big screen or on a Hi Def monitor. It's not practical to operate and look at a big 24 inch monitor to judge focus, although you can, in a critical situation, wheel the monitor over to the camera so the focus puller can see it. Some people who come from a video background have a cavalier attitude to

The Rule of Thirds

If you look at an object, your eye is automatically drawn to points on it one third of the way in from the left or right and one third from the top or bottom. For this reason, when you frame your shots it is best to place objects on these points, or along the lines themselves. This makes for attractive framing. The easiest way to do this is imagine a tic tac toe board drawn across the frame. Where the lines intersect is where you put the object. For example, if you have a person holding a gun looking left to right, put the person one third of the way in from the left hand portion of the screen with their head (or, eyes if it is a close up) one third of the way from the top. Place the gun one third of the way in from the right and one third of the way from the top or bottom depending on which way they are looking. This is also why when you have one character talking to another that is off screen, they are always slightly off center.

focus pulling because you can get away with sloppier focus as it's only seen on a standard definition monitor. If you transfer something to film and then put it on a 50ft screen, you're going to know if the focus isn't sharp, so you have to be diligent. You have to watch over-exposure as it's down to how much information you can record on the tape. You shouldn't under expose everything to the point where there's nothing clipped because then you have the opposite problem where if the image is too dark, you have to bring it up in post, and then you can have noise problems. You have to make a judgment call as to how much clipping is acceptable - a light bulb, a bare fluorescent tube, a car headlight, a lens flare - all these things can clip and it's okay.

Q - Is there anything you can do in post if you have problems?

David - People say you can fix focus, but I don't believe it, though it's easy to soften an image in post. Some people have done tricks where if there's too much depth of field, they'll draw a window round the person and draw the background out of focus.

Q - What cameras would you recommend?

David - There's not much choice, the only two in use are the Panasonic Varicam and the Sony Cine Alta / HDCAM range. There's the Viper, which is made by Thomson, which doesn't have a deck in it, but sends out raw, RGB, unprocessed Hi Def data down two cables into a hard drive system. So it's better quality Hi Def than the Sony and Panasonic cameras because all the luminance and color information is uncompressed, giving more latitude in post to color-correct. The reason it hasn't taken off yet is because it's very new and people haven't worked out all the data storage problems. The only tape format that records uncompressed Hi Def data is the D6 Voodoo Format by Phillips, and it's very hard to find those decks, and they are expensive to use and don't record uncompressed data in real time - they do it in half speed. So if you shoot six hours of material, it will take you twelve hours to copy it from D6 uncompressed, so I don't see that as a solution either. There are now some field data recorders by a company called S-Two, and there is the Sony HDCam-SR format, all of which might be the solution if the costs are reasonable.

Q - Have you encountered any problems shooting on DV?

David - There are problems generated by the design of these consumer DV cameras. It's not a DV issue, but a consumer design verses a professional video design. Professional DV cameras, like the Sony DSR 500, which is a great camera, takes standard video lenses and is designed like a Betacam unit. Every low budget filmmaker is looking for a true 16:9 Mini DV camera that has an interchangeable lens. If the Canon XL1 had 16:9 CCDs and a 24P option it would be the next big thing, but jumping to 16:9 CCDs would raise the cost of the camera by a couple of $thousand.

Q - Would you recommend people rent or buy cameras?

HD vs. FILM

Robert Rodriguez said 'film is like painting on a canvas in the dark - you don't get to see what you did until the next day when the dailies arrive.' This has always been a downsides to shooting film, for despite its beauty, you don't know if you have problems until it later. With the cost of film stock, processing and telecine, HD seems to be more and more attractive. Or, is it?

Film

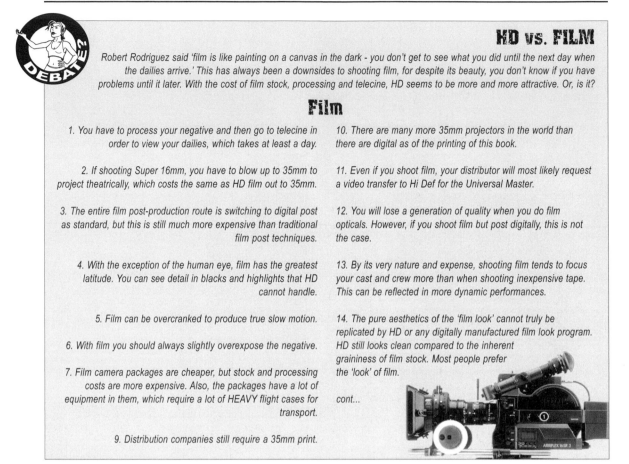

1. You have to process your negative and then go to telecine in order to view your dailies, which takes at least a day.

2. If shooting Super 16mm, you have to blow up to 35mm to project theatrically, which costs the same as HD film out to 35mm.

3. The entire film post-production route is switching to digital post as standard, but this is still much more expensive than traditional film post techniques.

4. With the exception of the human eye, film has the greatest latitude. You can see detail in blacks and highlights that HD cannot handle.

5. Film can be overcranked to produce true slow motion.

6. With film you should always slightly overexpose the negative.

7. Film camera packages are cheaper, but stock and processing costs are more expensive. Also, the packages have a lot of equipment in them, which require a lot of HEAVY flight cases for transport.

9. Distribution companies still require a 35mm print.

10. There are many more 35mm projectors in the world than there are digital as of the printing of this book.

11. Even if you shoot film, your distributor will most likely request a video transfer to Hi Def for the Universal Master.

12. You will lose a generation of quality when you do film opticals. However, if you shoot film but post digitally, this is not the case.

13. By its very nature and expense, shooting film tends to focus your cast and crew more than when shooting inexpensive tape. This can be reflected in more dynamic performances.

14. The pure aesthetics of the 'film look' cannot truly be replicated by HD or any digitally manufactured film look program. HD still looks clean compared to the inherent graininess of film stock. Most people prefer the 'look' of film.

cont...

David - You should rent if it's a limited length production, because you can afford to rent something better than you can afford to buy. A lot of beginners don't realize they can rent, and many people think in order to make their feature, they have to invest $20k in gear, then they start thinking they can't afford to make their movie as they have to save up to buy the equipment and then rent lights. If your shoot is only eighteen days long, your budget might allow you to shoot in Hi Def for the amount you're going to spend on buying DV gear.

Q - How do you find shooting 35mm anamorphic?

David - I didn't find anamorphic to be as hard as people say it is, as we were shooting day interior and day exterior where I had plenty of light. Anamorphic lenses are only tricky when you start working with low light because the distortions that are built into them start getting obvious, with flares, wierd backgrounds and going out of focus. We dealt with that by not pulling focus too much (we had enough light for a good depth of field). If you were doing a lot of long lens night photography in anamorphic, it would be complicated.

Q - Is it more expensive to shoot anamorphic?

David - We got a great deal with Panavision for our package. I asked for the cheapest lenses as they are small, light and cheaper. It turns out they are harder to get hold of as their light weight and size make them popular with Steadicam operators. So all the action movies use the C series lenses. All that was left were the biggest, most expensive, primo anamorphic lenses, which is great except for their size. Since we weren't doing Steadicam, I figured that wouldn't be a problem. The lens package itself costs roughly

HD vs. FILM cont...

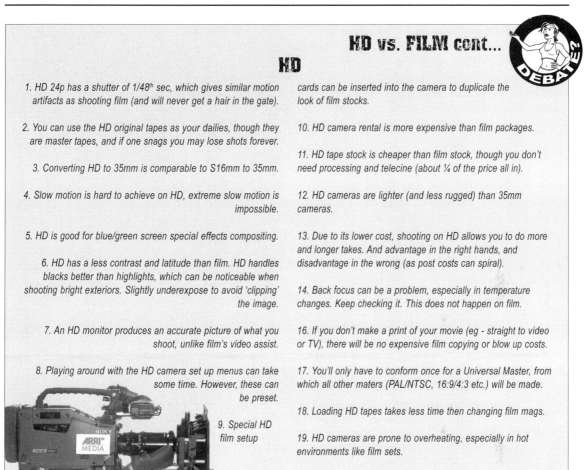

HD

1. HD 24p has a shutter of 1/48th sec, which gives similar motion artifacts as shooting film (and will never get a hair in the gate).

2. You can use the HD original tapes as your dailies, though they are master tapes, and if one snags you may lose shots forever.

3. Converting HD to 35mm is comparable to S16mm to 35mm.

4. Slow motion is hard to achieve on HD, extreme slow motion is impossible.

5. HD is good for blue/green screen special effects compositing.

6. HD has a less contrast and latitude than film. HD handles blacks better than highlights, which can be noticeable when shooting bright exteriors. Slightly underexpose to avoid 'clipping' the image.

7. An HD monitor produces an accurate picture of what you shoot, unlike film's video assist.

8. Playing around with the HD camera set up menus can take some time. However, these can be preset.

9. Special HD film setup

cards can be inserted into the camera to duplicate the look of film stocks.

10. HD camera rental is more expensive than film packages.

11. HD tape stock is cheaper than film stock, though you don't need processing and telecine (about ¼ of the price all in).

12. HD cameras are lighter (and less rugged) than 35mm cameras.

13. Due to its lower cost, shooting on HD allows you to do more and longer takes. And advantage in the right hands, and disadvantage in the wrong (as post costs can spiral).

14. Back focus can be a problem, especially in temperature changes. Keep checking it. This does not happen on film.

16. If you don't make a print of your movie (eg - straight to video or TV), there will be no expensive film copying or blow up costs.

17. You'll only have to conform once for a Universal Master, from which all other maters (PAL/NTSC, 16:9/4:3 etc.) will be made.

18. Loading HD tapes takes less time then changing film mags.

19. HD cameras are prone to overheating, especially in hot environments like film sets.

---

twice as much if you shoot anamorphic. If you want a 2.35 image on 35mm, your other option is to shoot super 35mm, which uses normal lenses and the anamorphic squeeze is created in post, which is an expensive process, but it means you do not need special anamorphic lenses on set.

Q - Is there a loss in resolution?

David - There's an increase in grain and a loss in sharpness. Anamorphic has a more detailed look, but also a more distorted look, as you use a bigger part of the negative. Whereas super 35mm uses a bigger negative, but you chop off half of it just to get it to scope, so you get more grain. Our recent trend has been to do the blow up to Scope digitally, with digital color correction. So when you scan it to film you do it as an anamorphic image, so you don't have to do an optical conversion to scope. On *O Brother Where Art Thou*, they shot on super 35mm and converted it to scope digitally when they did their color correction. The final prints seemed less grainy than a lot of super 35mm films, but it seems slightly soft to my eye. Roger Deakins said in an interview there

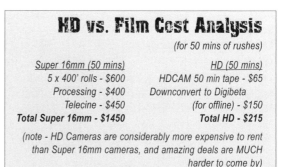

HD vs. Film Cost Analysis

(for 50 mins of rushes)

Super 16mm (50 mins)	HD (50 mins)
5 x 400' rolls - $600	HDCAM 50 min tape - $65
Processing - $400	Downconvert to Digibeta
Telecine - $450	(for offline) - $150
Total Super 16mm - $1450	**Total HD - $215**

(note - HD Cameras are considerably more expensive to rent than Super 16mm cameras, and amazing deals are MUCH harder to come by)

was a little softness from the digital intermediate stuff, but since it was a period movie, it wasn't necessarily a problem. It's still cheaper to do the blow up conventionally, but the advantage of actually shooting anamorphically for the independent film makers is that often, they only want to get as far as the first print so that they could take it to a film festival. If you shot anamorphically, or in 1.85, you can make a contact print off your negative, put an optical track on it and you have a print ready for projection. If you shoot super 35mm, you have to do an expensive blow it up to anamorphic. So it makes sense to me to use a format that keeps post production simple. When you consider the visual design of the movie, plan the post production path all the way to where you want to end up, if you don't, you're going to trip yourself up somewhere.

Q - So many filmmakers make excuses not to make their film because they haven't got $2m...

David - Sometimes it takes more experience to make films on small budget and with less equipment, because you know what you need and don't need, and what you can get away with. I tell people they should shoot on better equipment and they say, 'you're a big budget DP' and I say 'no, not really'. I tell people to make the best of their budget. If you have $10k, I'm not going to tell you to shoot on 35mm or Hi Def, but I'm not going to tell you to shoot on the cheapest camera either. There are ways of getting the most for very little by careful spending. The other argument I don't buy is if you shoot on DV, you can spend more on production value. To me, that only works sometimes because what's the definition of production value? Surely the camera, the film stock and the processing is sometimes part of the production value? Other times it isn't. Sometimes you shouldn't spend your money shooting on 35mm, when the look of the film could be done on another format and will suit the story perfectly well. I've read scripts where there's not much plot or dramatic scenery, but it's about life in a specific location. The whole mood and texture of the movie is in the script and you know if they don't shoot it right, that aspect won't be carried through. If you have a low resolution format, it will only work when you shoot close ups of actors talking and if their script is that, that's great, but if the script is not that, it won't suit it.

Q - How much do filmmakers need to put aside for the lighting package for a Hi Def film?

David - The lighting packages are based on budget and the script needs. Are you shooting a night exterior or just day interiors etc? The advantages of having a small package is that they are small, light and quick to set up and break down every night. The disadvantage is that you have less flexibility when things go wrong. The biggest problem on a low budget film is the loss of natural light. You're in a room with a lot of daylight windows and you lose the light. On a big show, you can turn on some huge lights and keep shooting. On a small budget, if I'm given a small handful of lights and the natural light has gone, there's not much I can do other than to shoot close-ups against a wall. I also use Kinoflos which are low wattage fluorescent lights with naturally soft light, I can light the daylight Kinos with HMIs and tungsten Kinos with tungsten lights. You tell directors what the limitations are with smaller packages and you need to schedule your shooting days around the fact that if daylight is needed, you shoot it while it's available. The cheapest lights to rent are tungsten lights. The trouble with those is if you need them in a daylight situation and you don't want to gel windows, you're going to put the blue gel on a tungsten light and cut its output by two stops.

Q - What would you recommend as a basic lighting package for a film of $500k?

David - You might have a basic package but then you would have items just for one day so it is tailored to the story needs. Generally you would always have a collection of small tungsten units, usually from 2k down to smaller, with a lot of 650w lamps. That range gets used a lot and are common for night interiors. I also find you need one or two really bright lamps because you don't want to be limited to just small lamps. You might occasionally want a really strong light coming through a window creating a shaft in a room. My typical package on the smaller films tends to be a suitcase of tungsten lights, a Dedolight kit and then a couple of punchy lights like a 1200 watt HMI Par, or maybe a 2k baby junior, which is still under 20 amps, and then Kinoflos. Anything above that requires a generator anyway. The only other lights I would recommend are Xenons. A 1k Xenon puts out a perfect beam of light and looks like sunlight. If you have a small enough window in a room, and you put a Xenon outside it, you can get a powerful shaft of light coming through and still be using very little electricity, but they are expensive lights to rent.

Q - Do you have problems with flicker?

HD vs. DV

The DV format has, arguably, had its day, and is beginning to be replaced by HD technology. However, this does not mean that DV is not a viable format for the seriously broke new film maker.

1. HD has 6 times more lines of resolution than DV, and therefore is MUCH sharper.

2. Hiring quality DP's are more important when shooting HD because the cameras can 'see more'. While good lighting can always help any shoot, low-end DV camera lenses are harder to focus and the white balance capabilities are less precise. You will end up wasting time trying to get a perfect picture with a device that really cannot give you something superior.

3. If your movie is accepted into a film festival, the DV image generally falls apart when bumped up to HD for projection. HD can be very successfully projected in a large theater.

4. The cost of transferring a movie from HD or DV to 35mm is about the same.

5. DV has poor audio functions (often no manual levels or poor metering), so frequently you will end up renting a DAT recorder and pay more for synchronization in post. With HD, this is not such a problem.

6. Lower end miniDV cameras don't have the ability to record continuous time code if the camera is stopped and the video reviewed. This is essential for editing because there can be errors introduced in the EDL that may not show up until the final conform, and that by this stage, any corrections will be time consuming and possibly expensive. Some DV cameras might also reset the timecode to zero when changing batteries, causing more editor nightmares. HD cameras do not have these problems.

7. Distributors know that HD24p is a good alternative to 35mm. The novelty of shooting DV has worn off and they're now more critical of quality issues.

8. DV cameras and tape stock cost significantly less to rent and buy than HD cameras and tape stock. There are also more DV cameras readily available to buy and rent, and more technical people with enough experience to help you troubleshoot when things go wrong.

9. Shooting PAL DV is MUCH better than NTSC, as it's frame rate can be converted to 24fps without having to perform and image manipulation (aside from de-interlacing if you did not shoot with a progressive camera). PAL is also higher resolution than NTSC.

10. The major advantage to DV is that for a modest investment you can set up with a camera and edit suite and complete your movie in your bedroom.

11. Arguably, audiences do not see the difference between 35mm and DV, as long as the DV is shot and lit professionally. We conducted a straw poll after 28 Days Later and of the people we asked, NO ONE had an issue, or even noticed, image quality. SCARY! However, these people are not sales agents or distributors.

David - It's getting more common to have flicker free lights. Low budget people can sometimes get the cheapest HMI stuff, but the danger is if the bulbs are old and the wires are bad, you may get flicker. Then again, most of the problem with HMI flicker is from the generator because the generator is not running in sync. With video, if there's a flicker problem, you might see it but on the monitor, but with film it's usually invisible until it's processed and viewed.

Q - Do you recommend using a lot of practical lights?

David - It's important to work with the art director to ensure that you have more than enough practicals. I want to have twice as many household lamps as one could normally have, so I can turn them on or off. A lot of times I'll go through the scenes with the art director and say, *'I need a tungsten lamp that takes ordinary bulbs and not some little unusual light bulb'*. They'll bring stuff that looks good as a lamp but doesn't give out enough light to shoot by or isn't flexible in adjusting its level, or puts out some weird light pattern that looks terrible on faces. Nowadays the look of movies is much more natural and part of that is they use many more natural lighting sources. It makes things go quicker when practicals are doing more of the lighting, in particular for wide shots.

Q - Is screening digitally more accessible now?

David - Yes although there is so much unevenness at festivals in terms of digital projection because they'll tell you they they're doing Hi Def projection one minute and then they'll tell you there wasn't enough call for it and so they only rented a Betacam deck and you don't know the quality of the projector or the decks. Sometimes you can get screwed, you have a great looking movie but can't find a decent projector to show it on. It's hard to be too positive about the state of digital cinemas because the trouble is the cost of implementation has to be born by the exhibitors and not the distributors so their incentive to convert is low, and unless they are going to be subsidized by the distributors, it's not going to happen. Some of these theaters own film projectors they bought thirty years ago and have paid for them decades ago. Now the Hi Def system might cost them $100k, and in three years it may be replaced by a better system. I would like to see some of the smaller art house cinema chains invest in a Hi Def theater. If independent filmmakers get a distribution deal, they are only going to go to those theater chains that project digitally. They are not going to go to big chains, they'll go to ones that specialize in independent cinema. All the push towards digital projection has been towards big Hollywood films like *Harry Potter* and *Star Wars* when it is the smaller films that would benefit.

Viable Shooting Formats

So many new filmmakers get stuck in the seemingly endless debates over which format to shoot. Film or video? DV or Hi Def? Super 16mm or 35mm? Here are a few simple answers as to when you should shoot which formats.

Video Formats

DV (be it miniDV, DVcam, DVCPro etc.)

Shoot only when the story suits the format. These would be stories that are small, low key and intimate, where the insertion of a small, innocuous DV camera would not impact either the performances or the world. It may also be that the directorial style of shooting from the hip suits the story. Also, use DV when you have absolutely no budget. If you have some cash, strive for AND ACHIEVE a higher quality format such as DigiBeta. Many new filmmakers make the deeply regretted mistake of starting their project on miniDV only to realize the limitations of the format too late in the day.

DigiBeta

This is a fantastic, professional format that is ideal for shooting micro budget films, especially when the plan is to stay on videotape only (for sale to TV, DVD and video but NOT to play on a cinema screen). You can shoot in true 16:9 and the quality of images achievable is quite startling. You also have the benefit of cheap and reusable stock and a simple, tried and tested post production path. It is also possible to master your movie and blow up to 35mm and maintain visual excellence, which is much more questionable when having shot on DV.

Hi-Def

Essentially it's just high quality (definition) video, but it can be shot in progressive scan, which mimics the look of a film frame quite accurately. Hi-Def is probably the smartest option for the cash strapped filmmaker as you get the benefits of cheap and reusable stock, simple post production routes, and still maintain a very high resolution, future proof image. The downside is that there are few cameras out there and therefore getting a deal can be tough.

Film formats

Super 16mm

The lowest quality professional film format that you should consider is Super16mm. It has all the benefits of really looking like a movie because it is film, it's lightweight, robust and relatively cheap to shoot. Most importantly, it has that magic that you don't find on any video format, which is the 'f' word - film. All film formats create a sense of focus and urgency in everyone involved, which simply makes for better filmmaking. On the downside, S16mm is not suited to post production special effects (because the image can weave from side to side slightly, although this is not noticeable to the viewer in normal shots) and in order to produce a 35mm blow up, you will need a 'fat cheque' at the very end of post production. The real strength of S16mm is that you do not need that 'fat cheque' in order to get the movie in-the-can and all the way through post production.

35mm

This is where you DO need that 'fat check' up front. The format is hellishly expensive to shoot, but it carries all the advantages of shooting on film and the images acquired are truly second to none. If you can afford to shoot on 35mm, then I would strongly recommend it. The cameras are bigger and heavier than S16mm and most often, have only small magazines, which carry around 2½ minutes of film at a time.

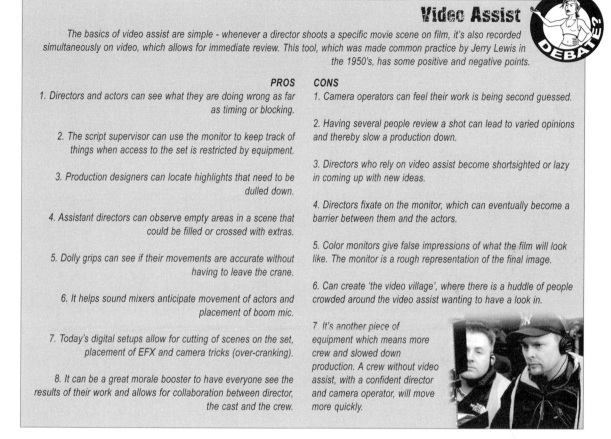

Video Assist

The basics of video assist are simple - whenever a director shoots a specific movie scene on film, it's also recorded simultaneously on video, which allows for immediate review. This tool, which was made common practice by Jerry Lewis in the 1950's, has some positive and negative points.

PROS	CONS
1. Directors and actors can see what they are doing wrong as far as timing or blocking.	1. Camera operators can feel their work is being second guessed.
2. The script supervisor can use the monitor to keep track of things when access to the set is restricted by equipment.	2. Having several people review a shot can lead to varied opinions and thereby slow a production down.
3. Production designers can locate highlights that need to be dulled down.	3. Directors who rely on video assist become shortsighted or lazy in coming up with new ideas.
4. Assistant directors can observe empty areas in a scene that could be filled or crossed with extras.	4. Directors fixate on the monitor, which can eventually become a barrier between them and the actors.
5. Dolly grips can see if their movements are accurate without having to leave the crane.	5. Color monitors give false impressions of what the film will look like. The monitor is a rough representation of the final image.
6. It helps sound mixers anticipate movement of actors and placement of boom mic.	6. Can create 'the video village', where there is a huddle of people crowded around the video assist wanting to have a look in.
7. Today's digital setups allow for cutting of scenes on the set, placement of EFX and camera tricks (over-cranking).	7. It's another piece of equipment which means more crew and slowed down production. A crew without video assist, with a confident director and camera operator, will move more quickly.
8. It can be a great morale booster to have everyone see the results of their work and allows for collaboration between director, the cast and the crew.	

Q - What common mistakes have you come across with new filmmakers? What advice would you offer?

David - Often their priorities can be skewed. I've interviewed many directors who say, *'in my films, the camera never stops moving'* and I say, *'why?'* To me, camera movement has to be tied to the story. You can't just apply style externally over the material. I have had directors say, *'this scene is boring so I want to shoot it in an exciting manner'.* To me, an exciting style doesn't make a boring scene less boring. My attitude is why don't you go out and re-write the scene so it's not boring anymore? The mistake is to think style can save weak material. Another mistake is that people are unrealistic about their schedule. One attitude is, *'we'll plan for a lot and if we only get half of it, that's great'.* My attitude is, *'I'd rather plan realistically'* and if I have more time to do more stuff, that's great. It never helps to go into a shooting day with an unrealistic idea of what you can accomplish. You need a good AD to pre plan carefully and to make sure actors are on set on time.

And advice? Dream big. There's a tendency for people to say, *'I want to be the next Kevin Smith'* and it's not because they think Kevin Smith's films are the best films ever made. It's because they think that's the level they can aspire to and I've never found that to be a good idea. And I love Kevin Smith's films! Anyone who's a good artist should aspire to be as good as the artists they admire. If you want to learn to light, you have to study good lighting, period, not just lighting in other DV movies. Study photography, paintings and movies with great cinematography, study nature and the light around you. I had three lights on my Super8 films. That's how I learnt to light. On a bigger film, they light sets from a farther distance and light more space. But when you come down to lighting a face, which most cameramen have to master, it's pretty basic. It's having an eye for people's faces, color and direction. It doesn't have to involve expensive equipment. People can learn a lot by studying *The Godfather* or *Citizen Kane*.

Jim Plannette
Gaffer

THE GAFFER

Q - What is the job of the gaffer?

Jim - The gaffer is the person who supervises the lighting that is agreed upon with the DP. The gaffer should be present during pre-production, the scouting of locations, the planning of the sets and the lighting of the sets. When you get to set or location and you are going to shoot, there is some discussion after the rehearsal as to how the lighting is going to be done. And then the gaffer executes those choices and later fine-tunes it with the DP. He is sort of the DP's right hand man.

Q - How do you train as a gaffer?

Jim - Pretty much on the job. You start as a set electrician and try to figure out what is going on, ask questions and then move up.

Q - What do you do to ensure the safety of the crew since you are working with electricity?

Jim - The person in charge of safety for the department would be the gaffer. He must ensure that hazards aren't present and all the work is done safely. There is a tendency to rush, but you cannot allow that to cause you to do unsafe things. There's a really good safety program now that trains people on how to use AC power.

Q - Do you go on location scouts?

Jim - Yes, I should go on all the location scouts and be present at production meetings. Many times the DP and I will go back to locations and talk again about how we might handle this particular location. Often, the goal is to make the lighting invisible, to make it look real. So you can look at the location in its reality and then figure out how to make it look like that when lit and being photographed. You would consider where to put the lights, whether you need to have the lights on some sort platform or on a scissor lift, whether there needs to be pre-rigging etc.

Q - How do you calculate how much power you need?

Jim - Generally, you would have a portable generator with you and its size would be determined by the lights you anticipate using. You know how much power each light will draw and so you can calculate how much that's going to be.

Q - If you were not going to have a generator, and were shooting in a house with normal power?

Jim - If you were going to use house power, on the location scout you would go to the panel and see how much service there is to the house. In newer homes, there is probably a 200 Amp service, and you can actually tie in and go ahead of the breakers and clamp onto the cable of the house and theoretically pull 200 amps of light and plug in that way. You need a permit to do that in LA, and you need a breaker panel so that if there is short it doesn't start a fire. Often, if you are on the 20th floor of an office building, you will find a panel that doesn't have much on it and you can tie into that panel. It is actually done pretty quickly. If you are plugging into the wall of a house, try to isolate the circuits and know that each circuit is probably good for 20 amps, so you could plug in something up to 20 Amps but no more. That would be fine if you were using small HMIs or Kinoflos.

Q - How many electricians does a gaffer usually have?

Jim - It depends on the size of a movie. Usually it is a gaffer, a best boy and three or four crew.

Q - What is the best boy?

Jim - It is an unfortunate term that came about years ago when you chose as your assistant the *best man available* - called a boy in those days. He is really in charge of men and equipment. He is hopefully right by my side for the master set ups and organizes the crew and the lights that are necessary for it. Then he can do his paperwork, and things like that, during the coverage of the scene because that doesn't require as many people. And, then the next big shot comes back in and he helps with that. It's pretty much men and equipment. He is also very involved with the safety aspects.

Q - What is the most important trait to have as a gaffer?

Jim - This goes for the movie business in general, but it is not to have too big an ego, because every job requires collaboration. This includes the director. If you get so invested in your ideas because you think that they are so brilliant, and you can't adapt, it's really unpleasant. So a healthy ego, but not too big an ego, is important. The ability to communicate is important.

Q - How do you work with the grips and what is the line between the grips and the electricians?

Jim - They key grip should also be present on location scouts and production meetings. Often the DP speaks with the gaffer about what the lighting is going to be, and then the gaffer conveys all that information to the grip as the grip is often off doing something at the time of this discussion. All three people are communicating all the time about what's going on and what's been done and what's coming up. I try to be a step or two ahead, and if we are moving to a different part of the location or set, I try to get that prepared ahead of time so that when the company moves in there is something to look at. If you set a few lights prior to the rehearsal, frequently the actors will gravitate towards those lights, which is a good thing.

Q - Do the grips rig the lights?

Jim - If there is a frame in front of the light that has gel or diffusion on it, they set it. They use all the century stands (C-stands). If there are solids needed to stop the light from hitting something, they are in charge of setting those too. When you are outside and you are using large 12x12 or 20x20 frames, they are in charge of those, either to bounce the light or to provide negative fill. Everything that is not actually attached to the light that adjusts the light is a grip responsibility.

Q - Do you bring your own equipment to a production?

Jim - I don't but some gaffers do. When I write out of list of equipment I need for the movie, I don't have to take into consideration what I own, I just write down what I need. If the equipment fails, it's not my fault.

How much power?

Now for the physics lesson! There is simple formula that all filmmakers should know, which will keep you from blowing circuit breakers in a house when you shoot!

Watts = Amps x Volts.

But what dies this mean? OK lets take an example. First off, US power runs at 110 volts, so that's the volts part of the equation. Watts, well that's down to the lights, say a Red Head at 750 watts, and a small HMI at 2kw - so that's 2,750 watts total. Divide your watts by 110 and you will know how many amps that you'll need (in this case, 2,750watts divided by 110v = 25 amps). Most houses have 20 amp breakers, so you'll need at least two dedicated breakers for your lights. Make sure that either your gaffer, your producer, your 1st AD or the best boy communicates with the location manager of where you are shooting and knows exactly how many breaker they have to play with. Ironically, most times a fuse or circuit blows is not due to over powered lighting, but by a crew member inadvertently turning on a 2kw heater or the most common culprit, the kettle. REMOVE THE KETTLE FROM THE LOCATION!

PRODUCTION

Q - What would you say are some of the most indispensable lights and rigging for a low budget film?

Jim - Regardless of the budget, I try to order lights that have more than one use, so you have fewer lights. I think that my lighting budgets are lower than most because of that. There are some lights that I just don't order because they only do one thing. And, they do it pretty well, but other lights do it almost as well and do other things too. If we are doing a low budget movie, it would depend on whether it would be on a sound stage or on a location. If it was on a location, then you would have HMI's, so you would order as many large HMI's as your budget can stand. And I think you would order a lot of Kino Flos that are daylight balanced, because they are very versatile and you can do a lot with them.

Q - What would be the most common problems facing a lower budget shoot?

Jim - Not having enough lights, especially to balance with the background. For instance, if you are shooting inside, the windows might blow out because you don't have enough to compete with the daylight outside. But that is a look in itself. The biggest problem is not enough time and equipment to do it properly.

Q - What is the difference between hard and soft lights?

Jim - In lighting a movie, you use a combination of hard and soft light. A hard light would be light probably from a Fresnel unit (Fresnel is a lens on the light). It makes a hard shadow that doesn't look real. It looks like a movie light. In order to make it look a little less theatrical, you add some sort of diffusion material, and there are many types. I only carry three because it makes it easier to decide. You can put a light grid in front of the light and it softens the shadow a bit, but it diminishes the light as well, so that means you need a little bit bigger light. One of the things in low budget movies is that there is a lot of hard light because they can't afford to soften it because they need that much intensity. But, it's good if you can. Another way to make soft light is to bounce it. So you can take that same unit and bounce it off a wall, even a bed sheet, and that will make a really soft light. And, you can shine the light through the sheet, again it takes a bigger light, but that makes a soft light. If you put the diffusion in a big frame and you put it even further from the light, that's even softer. When you put it through two frames, softer still. When you bounce it, softer still. If you bounce it and then have it go through diffusion, ah, it's softer still. It seems to me that in any frame, it is important to have things that are underexposed, but it is also important to have things that are over exposed. Highlights are very important. If everything is within a normal range, it gets to be boring.

Q - And, if you are overexposed you have more latitude to play with?

Jim - Yes. When shooting film (not video), it is better to be overexposed than under as the negative will hold more information and you can always print it down - then your blacks get blacker and you have better contrast. If you have to print up then you pick up grain and it isn't very attractive. What's called a 'thick negative' is important, and the way to get a thick negative is to overexpose.

Q - What are some differences between lighting on a sound stage and on locations?

Jim - One of the advantages of a sound stage is that you have total control, and if necessary you can move a wall. But, you have to be careful that all of this control does not make it look like a movie. You still need to think of the reality of where the light could be, so that it doesn't look to theatrical, so you don't distract the audience who will read it as false. The idea is to pull them into the story and make them forget that they are watching a movie.

Q - Is there an order to which you put up the lights?

Jim - I start with the back and move forward. Then I balance the foreground to the background.

Q - If you are on location in a house, how do you deal with natural light sources?

Lighting Types

One way to create the 'look' of your film is to play around with the lighting. Moody film noir will have harder shadows and higher contrast, whereas a docudrama would have low contrast (flatter) lighting. Get together with your DP and Gaffer to discuss ways to come up with interesting lighting schemes using the items below.

Hard Light

Hard lights, such as a Fresnel, produce an intense, bright light that creates hard shadows that tend to be dark and sharp edged and can be used to emphasize more depth in the texture such as the wrinkles on a face. These lights tend to be uses as key or back lighting.

Soft Light

A gentle, subtle light that's non-directional and produces a scattered light that creates softer shadows and is typically used as fill lighting. One way to make soft lighting is to use a hard light and bounce the light off, or through, diffusion such as silk, bed sheet. Soft light doesn't necessarily mean that it's a flat light, which refers to a low contrast ratio throughout the scene.

Bounce Light

Bounce light is a type of a soft light that is great for softening shadows and subtly filling in areas of an actor's face. You can bounce light off of anything reflective, such as foam-core, silks, a bed sheet, wall or ceiling. Overhead bounce is 'safe' in that ceilings are more frequently color-neutral and lighter than walls.

Umbrellas

Umbrellas with a reflective surface on the inside are used for quick conversion of hard and broad light sources into softer ones.

Reflectors

These add sparkle to people, products and props that are back-lit, in deep shade, or that have an excessively bright background. Similar to bounce boards but used in exteriors, reflectors provide fill. One example would be shiny boards, mirror like, aluminum surfaced reflectors that are used primarily for lighting dark or distant backgrounds, such as tree foliage, where uneven light won't be noticed.

Chimeras

A wireframe, cloth box with diffusion at one end that attaches to a light and helps soften it. Originally used in still photography.

Nets & Scrims

Both are used to control the intensity of light. Nets are netting stretched between a metal frame that is attached to a C-stand and placed in front of a light. Scrims are usually round metal screens placed on the light itself. Both come in singles, which reduce the light one stop, and doubles, which reduce it by two stops.

Gels

Used for coloring or color correcting light. Comes in full, ½ and ¼ strengths.

Silks, Spuns and Muslin

Various types of diffusion. Silks are large white sheets. Spun and muslin are cottony, cloth-like substances. All are usually hung within square or rectangular metal frames and soften light.

Flags

Used for stopping light from getting onto the subject. They are generally made of black cloth held within a metal frame and are attached to a C-stand.

Barndoors

Metal flaps that attach to the light itself for directing the light in a certain direction.

China Balls

A paper lantern light that creates a soft light like candlelight. They can be very beautiful, but are hard to control.

Cheating

Tricks used on set to help make the lighting look more realistic. For example, raising a table on blocks to bring it closer to an actor's face in order to tighten the composition or moving people and furniture away from the walls to reduce shadow on background problems and make it easier to use back light.

PRODUCTION

Jim - It depends on how long you expect to be in that particular part of the house because the problem with the real light is that it is constantly changing. If it is a sunny day, the sun is moving or it will go behind a cloud. It will change. So sometimes you actually block out the real light, which is a fairly elaborate grip job. But, then it gives you the control that nothing is going to change over the course of day. And, if you are in one room for 12 hours, it's probably a good idea to do that.

Q - What precautions do you take when dealing with wet, snowy or really hot conditions?

Jim - There always has to be a good grounding system to the portable generators. If it's raining you ensure that the distribution boxes don't get wet. Cover them with something waterproof. At times, the crew will have to wear rubber gloves instead of leather gloves so that they can prevent themselves from getting a shock. You just have to be more careful if it is damp. I haven't really had any problems with heat.

Q - Does the gaffer deal with the lighting companies?

Jim - The gaffer puts in the list of equipment that is going to be needed. Often you use the same company because you find one who's equipment is good and well maintained and you develop a certain relationship and loyalty. So if you are doing a job where there is plenty of money, that's fine. But, if you are doing one where there is not very much money, you can say, '*I need help with this one…*' and often you'll get it.

Q - Do you have any tips for dealing with practicals?

Jim - If you shoot in a building that has a lot of fluorescents, there are two ways to handle it. Normal fluorescents don't photograph accurately as they have green in them that the eye doesn't see, but the film does. So, if you didn't have enough money to change all the tubes, which is expensive, what you can do is supplement the lights with Kino Flos, and you put the same tubes in the Kino Flos as you have in the building, and then the lab can correct the green. If you are doing a night scene and using practical lamps in a house, often it is good to use larger globes, but put them on a Variac, so you can adjust the voltage. A Variac is a unit that not only increases voltage, but decreases it as well. I have built some little light boxes that simulate practical lamps so you can use a practical lamp as kind of a visual source, but another light actually does the lighting. Practicals work really well.

Q - What would you say are the problems that you encounter with new directors?

Jim - Often directors, and not just new ones, don't have a clear sense of what's possible. They are not realistic. Part of the pre-production process is getting them to accept the reality of what you are doing. No matter how big the budget is, the movie that they are trying to make is always bigger. A friend of mine just did a movie with $100m budget. Unfortunately, they were trying to make a $120m film! So, they were having the same problems that people at $50m have, that people at $40m have, that people at $10m have. During the pre-production process, hopefully the director can understand the reality and make adjustments because if he doesn't, the movie will suffer. You try to work too fast and don't do a good job. Also, they often think they can do more work in a day than they really can. More setups. Sometimes they attempt to make the master shot perfect when in fact they are only going to be in it for a brief period of time (in the edit). And, by the time they get to the coverage, the actors are quite often burned out. So the part of the scene that is really important isn't as good as it could have been because they spent so much time on the master. It's also priorities. Some directors think that every shot in the movie is the important shot, when in fact that is not true. You have to realize that this scene is really important, and that the other scene is important too, but not as important. You rate them, this scene is the A scene, this is B…so, we will spend a lot of time on the A scene, but on the B scene, let's just get it done.

Q - Have you any tips for new directors?

Jim - For any director, an effort should be made to be realistic about what's possible in terms of time and equipment. It seems better to do fewer shots well than many shots rushed.

Q - On a big Hollywood movie, say between $60-$100m, how much goes toward the lighting budget?

Jim - The overall budget is often a reflection of cast and not the lighting. I think the lighting equipment that I order is maybe $10k per week, and so a twelve-week movie will be $120k. As a percentage of the budget it is pittance but $10k per week to a low budget movie is a huge amount.

Q - Any recommendations when filming moonlight? For example, a lot of DPs like to use a blue filter?

Jim - I don't believe in blue moonlight. When you go outside at night in the moonlight, it doesn't look blue because your eye color corrects the sunlight reflecting off the moon. So, if you recreate a shot in the moonlight that looks blue, the audience will think it looks odd. There are other ways to achieve a moonlight look. For instance, if you have a house with lights on inside, you can make those warm and then the light outside neutral and then by contrast it looks cool (like moonlight) without looking blue.

Q - Do you have any tips for shooting sunsets?

Jim - Shoot a little too early and a little too late, and everywhere in between, because the early stuff turns out to be not too early and the stuff that you thought was too late turns out not to be late at all. The most important thing is to balance the foreground to the background, so as it gets darker, whatever light you have on the people on the foreground will get darker as well. It is tricky to do and the exposure is always determined by the sky and the sun. The balance is usually determined by your eye. You look either through the camera, which is the best way, or right next to the camera and see what the background looks like in relation to the foreground. Magic hour is the time of day when the sun is below the horizon, but there is still light in the sky. It is not necessarily an hour, but in some latitudes on the planet it is. It is a beautiful soft, quite often cool light. You can sometimes underexpose it and make it look like night although that is problematic I think. It's tricky and again, you should shoot a little too soon and a little to long and somewhere in between you get it right.

Q - Does shooting day for night still happen a lot now?

Jim - No. Day for night exterior is difficult because you need to avoid the sky to make it work, and it is hard to avoid the sky. If you have the sky in the shot and you don't move the camera, you can use a grad filter to help darken the sky. It is something to avoid if at all possible. Certainly shooting interior day for night is possible - you black out the windows, keeping the black a little distance away, then you put some plants outside and light them so that you see something. Sometimes it is necessary because children cannot work at night.

Q - Some lighting guys will wet down streets, why do they do this?

Jim - Wet streets pick up the reflections of all the lights and signs and it is very visual, and very Hollywood. It can cost a lot.

Q - Do you think all the world's problems can be solved with gaffer tape?

Jim - I know a movie could not be made without gaffer tape. I have some at home!

Q - What advice would you give to a first time filmmaker?

Jim - Surround yourself with as many experienced people as you can find. Even experienced people will, on the right project, work for nothing. It's more about the project and the passion you have for your work than it is about money. You can make your money on *Oceans 12*, but that doesn't mean you don't want to do something smaller too. Actors will do movies where they love the script, and so will crew members. So, surround yourself with as many experienced people as you can.

Liz Ziegler
Steadicam operator

Q - What is a Steadicam?

Liz - It's a stabilized camera platform that enables an operator to move around places where a dolly couldn't go. For example, up and down stairs and over rough terrain.

Q - Is it feasible to strap a Steadicam onto any camera operator?

Liz - I wouldn't recommend just putting it on anyone because it's like riding a bike - it becomes better with practice. Also, a seasoned operator has all the knowledge and instincts of framing that allows them to film, but they too would need to build the skill of using a Steadicam as well as having the strength and endurance needed to maintain the shot. I spend a lot of time working out and practising. I know a lot of instances where people have crumbled because, depending on the lenses, it can all get really heavy.

Q - Do you look through the eyepiece when shooting with a Steadicam?

Liz - No, you look into a high intensity green monitor.

Q - If somebody is hiring a Steadicam operator, would you bring your own equipment?

Liz - Most of the full time Steadicam operators have their own equipment. In the beginning, the major rental companies all bought Steadicams, but it's really not a *'strap it on and go'* instrument, so they don't have them anymore. You need to own one and continually practice. I have the luxury of having my own SL (Moviecam SL – 35mm camera especially designed for Steadicam) so, in general, it's an owner/operator kind of deal.

Q - Can you use Steadicam for shooting with DV cameras?

Liz - Yes. Although it can be too heavy for an apprentice, there are all sorts of combinations of camera and Steadicam models available. You can buy any of them. Most places that have them don't rent them anymore.

Q - How much does it cost for a Steadicam operator?

Liz - Roughly $1k for the Steadicam and $1k for the operator for ten hours. It works out at $100/$200 an hour. Sometimes I rent out my camera too. At the beginning of my career I spent hours trying to make things work because people would change the electronics, plugs and hardware and I didn't want to show up unprepared. These days, so that I don't have to go through that again, I'll do anything to get my own camera on even if it's practically given away!

Q - Is it possible to shoot a whole film on Steadicam?

Liz - Somebody just did! A guy in Germany shot a whole movie on Steadicam in one take. It's also possible to shoot, say, a whole *ER* episode on Steadicam but I believe it would need a lot of practice.

Q - Do you do a lot of rehearsing?

Liz - It depends on the director. I did a shot on *Charlie's Angels* where it seemed we rehearsed it forever, but some people want you to shoot with no rehearsal. For me, guidelines are preferable - I like to know the game plan. I watch the actors and the director blocking the shot so as to get an idea of what they want.

Q - How do the actors respond to the Steadicam?

Liz - Amazingly well. I'm always amazed that actors can zone things out. I couldn't do that. I'm in the front line with the actor and sometimes I'll see footage or a still and there's an army of cable pullers, boom operators, the camera assistants focusing and these actors are doing their thing with this horror going on. It's impressive. Actors are a breed!

Q - Do they ever hire you as a backup?

Liz - Some people want you there as they think they're going to get lots of toys! Commonly, though, a Steadicam operator is available anytime but they are not paying for it everyday. You have a minimum for the equipment and when you put it on you get a bump.

Q - Should you watch lots of movies that use Steadicam to get a feel of it?

Liz - Yeah, but there are good and bad things about that because you can watch incredible shots like in *Goodfellas* or *Magnolia* but creating your own ideas is something else. There are certainly areas that haven't been explored and it's too easy to get wrapped into the warm blanket of what's been done before. Picasso was brilliant because he first learnt the technique and then expanded. It's great to understand the routine but certainly aspire to more.

Q - What is the most common mistake you have come across?

Liz - Thinking that you can run with the Steadicam - it looks horrible. The best example I've seen of running was Larry McConkey on *Basic Instinct*. Ideally though, you should be on a vehicle because it's designed to take out a certain frequency of movement. With new filmmakers, commona mistakes are screen direction and mechanical solutions. For example, if the camera is wobbling on a dolly then you put an apple box under the dolly head. When I first started out I'd get called on things for no movement or *'I want to move two inches from here to here'* and it was almost like they wanted the Steadicam but didn't know how to use it. People nowadays are becoming more savvy because it's a commonplace tool, but I must have made $1m for jobs where there was no reason for me to be there!

Q - What advice would you give a new filmmaker?

Liz - Keep shooting your vision. Take in everybody's comments but come up with your own conclusion. People are always wanting to do it for you, and it's rare that someone is giving you a solution - It's good to keep that in mind.

(right) Steadicam operator John Ward on location.

THE SOUND MIXER

Mark Weingarten
Production Sound

Q - What is your job?

Mark - I record all dialogue in sync with the picture on set. On a low budget film I will do more sound effects and room tone on set because there will be a smaller budget for them in post production. On a bigger budget film I will often let the sound effects go because there is such a large crew and it's too expensive to make them wait around just for sound effects.

Q - Do you have time to do that when everyone wants to move forward?

Mark - Sound is very important. Sometimes situations are difficult and you have to be forceful, you have to say *'this is no good-we have to fix this'*. Directors should listen carefully to the sound. It's great if at the end of the take where there has been a problem, without cutting they can say *'let's go back to this line and get it again clean'*.

Q - When does the producer hire the sound mixer?

Mark - Traditionally one to two months before the start of principle photography, sometimes if they are really scrambling it can be a week or two before they start.

Q - Do you bring your own crew with you?

Mark - Yes I almost always work with the same boom operator. I have two cable people I like very much and I try to bring one of them on every film, but often on location we are asked to hire a local cable person.

Q - Do people pay for the use of your equipment?

Mark - Yes they pay my salary and box rental separately.

Q - Do you check out locations as well?

Mark - Yes I go on scouts, pre-production meetings and I talk with the post production people about what the editors will want. Sometimes there is a sound editor already hired, or they know who it's going to be, so I can talk to them about how they will want the sound delivered.

Q - If you have a great location but it's awful for sound, what do you do?

Mark - A lot of times, I'll say *'if there is a location that you are concerned about, just pay me to go there and I'll check it out'*. I'll go and sit there for a few hours and just listen to how bad the sound is over the course of a day. How frequent are the planes? How bad is the traffic? Is there nearby major construction? Is there a pre-school down the road the block? And then I'll say, 'OK or No'. I just finished a Christopher Guest movie called *A Mighty Wind*. Chris is very concerned about sound, because his movies are all ad libbed and there really is no possibility for looping so the production sound is the sound without question. On *A Mighty Wind* we also were recording all the music live so that added another element to be protected. There was a house that they wanted to use, but Chris was concerned about a nearby freeway. I asked them where in the house we were going to shoot interior / exterior / front / back. They said that there was a big scene in the back yard with music and lot's of characters with lot's of potential dialog. So I

The Blimp and Barney

Film cameras make noise when running, which sensitive microphones can pick up. In order to eliminate or reduce this problem, try using blimps and barneys. Beware though, a lot of camera noise escapes via the lens, which obviously cannot be covered.

Blimp
A soundproof, fiberglass enclosure that entirely covers the camera and keeps noise from escaping. While very effective, blimps can be bulky and make camera operation more difficult. They also cost a little more money to rent.

Barney
A lightweight padded covering that generally performs the same task as a blimp and can have a heating feature for filming in cold conditions. A less traditional, but equally effective technique is to tie a blanket or jacket around the camera. Generally, barneys only work on cameras that are fairly quiet to begin with.

went out there in the morning and sat in the back yard for a few hours and listened to how the freeway sounded as it went from rush hour into the regular day. It was fine. I told them 'it won't be a problem', but I did notice that on the ground there were a lot of dry leaves and nuts that crunched when you walked on them, so I had them rake out the entire yard.

Q - What is the most basic kit for a sound recordist?

Mark - The basic kit is a recorder, some cables, a boom pole, boom mic, a zepplin and a windjammer. The Sennheiser 416 and 816 mics are both very directional mics, but a bit heavy and it helps to have an experienced boom operator to deal with that. For that reason I would recommend Schoeps hypercardiods for a lower budget film where you probably have an inexperienced PA as your boom operator. The Schoeps are lighter and have a bit wider pattern which is more forgiving if you miss your target a little. I believe you should have more than one boom mic. Almost everything I do is with two booms, but on a lower budget you may not have the luxury of an additional boom operator. But you will still need an additional mic to hide behind a flower vase or table leg, and of course you need one in case the first one breaks. As far as wireless goes, that's an issue for low budget. It's great to have one wireless for each speaking actor, because you never know what you going to encounter. How they light and shoot a scene may prohibit you from being able to boom. But of course, it's cost prohibitive to have that many radio mics if you are renting them, so it's great if you can discuss with the director and DP beforehand, just how they intend to light and shoot a given scene to determine if you need to have that many wireless mics or not. The first thing to buy, equipment wise, when you are starting out, are two high quality boom mics (Sennheiser, Schoeps, Neumann etc.) a boom pole, a recorder, two wireless mics and a small mixer (in that order). If someone calls you at midnight and says 'can you come do this shoot tomorrow?' You can say 'yeah', but if you say 'I could but I don't have a mic' it will complicate things. A high percentage of film sound can be done with one mic on a boom pole.

Q - What different recording formats are there?

Mark - I record whatever format the picture editor wants, usually DAT. I record for the sound editor on a multi-track recorder, which records at 24 bits, so the sound quality is better. On the multi-track there is a copy of my mono mix that went to the DAT as well as all the mics, isolated so that if they don't like the mix I made, they can redo it in post. A lot of times I will have all the actors wired, but only use the boom for the DAT mix. If they don't like the boom they can listen to the wireless and see if they can improve things. Chris Guest usually shoots everything hand held on 16mm and everything's improvised. We are never really sure what is going to happen, so we usually divide the room in two pieces - front / back, left / right, this side of the kitchen cabinet / that side of the kitchen cabinet etc. Whatever seems appropriate to the room, and we put a boom in each section. Knowing the situation the DP usually lights in a way to give us the freedom to swing the booms anywhere, so that we can follow the actors wherever they go. When that kind of lighting is not possible, we break out the wiresless mics and hope for the best.

Ultra low-budget feature productions can buy a cheap DAT recorder onto which they can record their sound in the knowledge that they should get excellent quality and rock solid sync.

Getting Good Sound

It has been said that sound can be up to 80% of the movie going experience, so it should not be neglected. Unfortunately, many inexperienced filmmakers forget to properly budget or prepare for recording sound, stating that they will 'fix it in post'. Thinking this way usually means many $thousands in post-production time, versus a moment of cast and crew time on set.

1. Hire the best sound recordist you can. Inexperienced sound recordists may be paranoid and request further takes when they are not needed, or not know how to fix problems.

2. Everyone is a perfectionist. Learn to recognize when the sound is good enough.

3. When looking for locations, bear the sound in mind. Traffic and planes are usually the biggest culprits, as are air conditioning units. Most natural sounds can be covered up and disguised in post-production.

4. Blimps and barneys are good at filtering out most camera noise, but they will not get rid of everything.

5. Always get at least 30 seconds of room tone at each location so your dub mixer can lay down a decent ambient track.

6. Post sync dialogue (looping / ADR) is a pain and expensive. Try to avoid it by either getting it right during the take or wild without the camera rolling, so it can be dropped in during post.

7. If you cannot use a boom mic due to space constraints, try using lavaliere mics hidden within the set (like a flowerpot or table lamp).

8. If you can afford it, try using more than one boom mic to record the sound so that you are completely covered. Also, get as many wireless lavaliere mics as possible for your actors.

Q - Do you think on bigger budget shoots, the sound guy gets a rough deal?

Mark - Sometimes, but it's a real pick your fight situation. If everything's fine I don't say much, but every once in a while I do say something positive like, 'that take was really good for me', because I feel that too often the sound guy only says negative stuff. Sometimes I get a hard time, but I accept what's out of my control. If I don't say much, I find that when I do say something, they'll say 'okay the guy hardly ever complains, so this must be important'.

Q - Have you found your requests being ignored on set?

Mark - I make sure the director knows when there's a problem. I always say let's at least get one right and if you like it you have it, and if not, you can possibly use the sound from the one good take over the picture from one of the other takes.

Q - What's a PNO?

Mark - Every time you start the DAT, it prints a number for that section of tape. For example, scene 2, take 5, might have a PNO number 22. In post, all they have to do is hit 22 and it automatically finds it. Always note the PNO numbers it helps post production find things and makes post much easier.

Q - Are there any specific DAT machines that you would recommend?

Mark - The three main machines are HHB, Fostex and Stelladat. My personal preference is for the HHB, which they don't make anymore. Most DAT machines don't have the greatest mic inputs, so it's better to go into a mixer that has good preamps.

Q - What is an overlap?

Mark - When two people speak at the same time, it's called an overlap. To propel the drama, the director often likes the actors to talk on top of each other, but that can lead to problems in the edit. Ideally, this means the person on screen has to make sure that they are clean when they speak and the person off screen has to make sure that the person on screen can have those gaps. Some directors feel that this hurts the performance, and it's a fine line between getting it clean and potentially impacting the performance.

The Slate/ Clapperboard

Slates mark the beginning of each filmed take and allow the editor to synchronize the sound track with the picture. The slate displays the scene number, take number, director's name, DP's name, name of production company and name of film. Each shot is given a slate number, and each slate can have any number of takes. Scene numbers are NOT used on the slate. When shooting a take, the clapper loader reads aloud the slate number, then the take number, before clapping down the hinged part of the slate at the beginning of each take - 'the clap', making sure that the slate is in frame. If using the traditional clapperboard, numbers can be written on camera tape and stuck to the back of the slate which can be used quickly when needed.Remember to give as much pre roll as possible before each slate (7 seconds is the minimum) and to number sound rolls consecutively.

'Timecode Slate ' or 'Digislate'

This is when a timecode generator feeds code to the sound recording device (usually a DAT machine) as well as feeding an identical code to the time code slate (which is connected to the sound recording device). The time code slate has an LED screen comprised of hours, minutes, seconds and frames. When the slate is clapped, the time code at that instant is held for a few frames on the display. This time code is usually read visually in the telecine and entered into the computer. The system then locates the same time code number in the audio and the shot is then 'in sync'.

A **'Smart Slate'** has it's own built in timecode generator and is better because there's no need for a connection between the slate and the DAT recorder. A **'Dumb Slate'** is an older method that has no internal time code generator so it receives it's time code from another machine, most likely the sound recording device (the DAT) via a cable or preferably through a wireless transmitter. Make sure that the time code numbers are easy to read, particularly in bright sunlight. Always record the 'clap' just in case there's a problem with the timecode.

The Smart Slate has 5 running modes for generating time code.

1.Free Run/Time of Day: here the internal time code generator works like a clock with the actual time of day. It runs continuously whether the audio is recording or not.

2. Free Run/User Set: here the user chooses the starting time for the time code generator and it doesn't correlate to the time of day. The hour digits are used to signify sound roll number.

3. Record Run: this is when the generator stops when the audio recorder does i.e numbers work like a tape counter and pauses during pause or stop. Again the hour digits are used to signify sound roll number.

4.External Mode: a continuous time code from an external source that's being regenerated on to the tape.

5. Jam Sync: the recorder synchronizes it's internal time code generator to match the starting numbers from an external source. When the external is triggered the internal time code will keep in step with it. Always Jam Sync every few hours to make sure sync isn't drifting.

In-camera Time Code

When filming with time code capable cameras, the camera and the audio recorder record the identical time code. This enables the telecine machines during telecine to read the time code and automatically sync it to the audio code.

Head Slate

Slates that are done as normal, at the beginning of each shot.

Tail Slate

This is a slate done at the end of the shot, which may be used when you need to be less disruptive with actors etc. Traditional clapperboards are done upside down to indicate a tail slate. The assistant also yells out 'tail slate' when marking the slate.

M.O.S Slate

(originated when a German director in Hollywood asked for the shot 'mit out sound' and the camera assistant wrote M.O.S on the slate). When recording without sound, write M.O.S. on the slate and do NOT raise the hinged bar.

Voice Slate/Voice I.D

At the beginning of each tape, the sound recordist or assistant will record the necessary technical information such as the roll number, the title of the film, the production company, the director's name and any other useful information.

The Tone

After having recorded the voice I.d., the sound recordist will record 30 seconds of tone (minus 8db for analogue / minus 18db for DAT) from the built-in tone generator of their audio recorder or mixer. This tone is used to calibrate the level of the playback machine in the transfer process. Every recording MUST be slated whether sync sound or not. Ie. such as 'spot effect for scene 25, car idling, take one' or 'wild track for scene 12'.

Shooting Film - If shooting at 24fps, use 30fps timecode NON DROP FRAME. If shooting at any other frame rate consult your transfer lab.

Shooting Video - If shooting video, use 29.97 timecode.

Shooting Hi Def - Should you shoot at 30fps or 23.976? Shooting on hi def is currently a nightmare for any sound guy!

Sound Equipment for Low Budget Shoots

Recording device
DAT, Digital Audio Tape, is now the defacto. For low budget productions, cheap semi-pro machines are affordable to buy, never mind rent. Beware of distortion and of non professional connectors that don't deal with the rigours of film making very well. Resist the urge to use ¼" tape.

Recording device
MiniDisc isn't ideal, especially when DAT is so affordable. However, it may be used at a push, especially for weekend re-shoots where only a few lines of dialogue may be used.

Headphones
Essential to use high quality 'cans'. Enclosed earpeices mean you hear more of what is going down onto tape, although some recordists prefer the open type.

Microphones
Undeniably the most important part of the sound recordists kit. They include...

Tie Clip Mic (powered)
Can be concealed on an actor when a normal mic isn't appropriate. Radio mics are expensive and excellent, but beware of radio interference with cheaper ones.

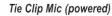

Directional Mic (powered)
Several mics produce excellent results and a nominal hire charge will get you the best mic available. Rent. Sennheiser 416 is a good workhorse.

Large Diaphragm Mic
Ideal for recording foley sessions or close mic. singing. No use on a film set.

Omni-directional Mic (unpowered)
Cheap and cheerful and pretty much no use except in emergencies for guide tracks. Avoid.

Camera Mic
If shooting digital you may have a camera with a mic. This mic is useless for production sound but ideal for recording guide tracks for sync.

Jammer / Baffle
Fits over the mic to protect it from wind. Usually comes with a 'furry' jacket that reduces wind noise even more. Essential.

Cables
Must be high quality and shielded. XLR cables are the professional norm and cheap semi-pro cables should be avoided and one short cable just isn't enough.

Batteries
Batteries must be replaced regularly. You can't wait for the battery to go down as quality might be compromised. Buy in bulk before shooting.

Stock
Whatever format you record sound, make sure you have enough stock for the shoot, plus a few extras. Work on recording a one hour tape a day and always label clearly.

Connectors
Most cheap semi pro equipment will use ¼" jack plugs which are unbalanced. Pro kit will use XLR connectors which are balanced and more suited to the job. If you have both, you will need an adapter to convert between the two. Before you shoot, make sure you can connect everything up as needed.

Leather Jacket
Used to put over the camera in order to help deaden noisy cameras.

Sound Equipment for Low Budget Shoots ...cont

Telescopic Mic Boom Pole
Used by the assistant sound recordist to place the mic over the actors, getting the mic as close as possible. Must use lightweight pro kit, fishing rods and clothes poles just don't cut it.

Mixing Desk
On complicated jobs where multiple mics may be used, you may need a small portable mixing desk. This does add headaches though and isn't ideal for low budget productions.

For that reason, I double boom everything, so I boom the off screen actors as well as the onscreen ones. Then if the dialogue overlaps, it sounds good on both sides and it's usable. However, it is still harder to cut than clean dialogue.

Q - Do you find the actors disturbed by that?

Mark - Yes, but you try to work it out before you shoot. On a film I did with Billy Bob Thornton, he didn't like anybody speaking during is close ups. He'd do his own close up with no-one, and react as though someone was saying the other lines, he did them completely clean. He'll also do multiple line readings over and over again in the same close ups. This is fantastic for the editors.

Q - Does he do that to keep it clean?

Mark - I don't know. It's just the way he worked on that film. Some actors say *'you don't need to bring the another actor I can read with the script supervisor or by myself'*.

Q - How involved are you in post-production sound?

Mark - On every movie I try to sit down with the sound editor once they've locked the picture and watch the cut on the Avid, and then talk about the sound in every scene. If there's a problem scene, then I'll tell him where he can find the material on the multi-track to repair it or that there is no alternative and that's the best we have. I like to go through that process, but my favorite part is in the mix - this is when everything comes together. It's where I learn where I could have done better, what I should have done and what I did that was good. I would recommend all production mixers go to at least one final mix. If the production mixer and sound editor can get involved before they start shooting it's great. I've done a lot of movies where they don't hire the sound editor until after the production is done, so in that case, you have to do what you feel is the best thing and then explain it later. I did a Robert Altman movie a couple of years ago and he's the king of the multi track - I recorded it that way for him and I thought it was ingenious. People's fear of the multi track is that there's so much to sort out and how are they going to deal with all that information. For Robert's movie, I gave him a two-track mix for dailies but there were occasions where they wanted to pull things out which were additional. Because I ran the multi-track simultaneously, they could go back to it and take whatever they wanted. Generally, though we use the DAT in post production, which is two track. When I sit down with a sound editor, I explain to them what the multi tracks are for and then I watch the movie and I say, *'this scene is worth going to the multi-track, because we can fix this'*. Usually it's only a couple of isolated incidents where they need to go back to the multi-track or not at all.

Q - At the end of each day, would you supply them with the DAT's and the multi track?

Mark - I give them one DAT, which is the master, and I keep the multi tracks until the very end of the movie. This is because two months into shooting, the director might say, *'you remember that phone call we recorded on day 3? We're going to do the other side of that call today. Can you give us the recording of the other actor?'* and I'll say, *'yeah'* and I'll go back to the multi-track and ask the script supervisor what the preferred take was for perfomance and I'll make a dub of that take and use it for playback on set.

PRODUCTION

SOUND REPORT SHEET

Production Company - LIVING SPIRIT

Production - ROCKETBOY

Roll Number
12

Recordist - JOHN HAY

Production Number -

Date 22/3/2004

Speed	3.75	7.5	15

Format 35mm 16mm Video

Recording format -
DAT

Pilot Hz	50	60

Cam. speed 24 25 30 PAL NTSC

Sample rate	44.1	48

TC 24 25 29.97 30

Transfer notes - AS PER INSTRUCTIONS FROM PRODUCTION OFFICE - CLONE DATS

SCENE	SLATE	TAKE	TIMECODE	M/S	Channel 1	Channel 2	Comments
102	92	1		M	DLG		OK
102	93	1		M	DLG		OK
102	93	2		M	DLG		RADIO MIC BUZZ
102	93	3		M	DLG		OK
138	14	1		S	DLG JOHN	DLG JANE	CRACKLE ON TRACK ONE
138	94	2		S	DLG JOHN	DL	OK
12	95	1		M	MUTE (GUIDE)		TRAFFIC
12	96	1		M	GUIDE		TRAFFIC
12	96	2		M	GUIDE		TRAFFIC
12	97	1		M	DLG		

Sound Report Sheet

The sound report sheet is the document used by the sound recordist team to tell the lab or editor what is recorded on which tapes, and other bits of information. It's printed on a letter sized paper and filled out by hand. It will go to the labs with the negative, or the editing room with the video tapes later on.

Q - How important is documentation?

Mark - You should write as much information on the tape and your sound reports as you can think of. On the reports note if a particular line is good in a particular take especially if it has been a problem in other set ups.

Q - What about shooting HD?

Mark - Any sound person will tell you that shooting on HD is a nightmare. I think the sound you put in the DAT should be the sound you use to cut with. HD has inputs to put sound right into the camera and I initially said, *'let's not put any sound on the camera'* thinking they'd be forced to sync it to me, but because there was so much question about the time code, I said, *'alright, we'll feed the camera'.* We sent a line up tone to each camera, set the level and tried to tape the knobs down. There were cables running to all the cameras - you'd have the video cable, two audio cables and possible time code cables. Ultimately, they'll figure it out and HD will be fine. I think sound people should do as much research as they can about unfamiliar technology. There's nothing wrong with calling everyone you know and finding out what they know about it.

Q - What are the common mistakes you have encountered with sound?

Mark - They say people don't notice sound unless it's bad sound. Even my relatives who are very attuned to sound will never tell me *'that movie sounded great'*, but they will tell me if the sound is bad. It's tough for sound people because it's a fine line between doing a good job and interfering with people's performances. I try to find a solution that accomplishes both. A lot of times, it's dictated by the cinematographer. If you're having a lighting problem that's preventing you from booming, and the cinematographer tells you to take a hike and you go to the director and tell him the problem, it's really important for the director to say, *'hey dude, why don't you step up and help the sound guy out'.* Some cinematographers are so lovely and they support the sound department, but some have a real attitude and aspire to sabotage the sound guy. In those cases, you need a lot of support from the director and producer. Sometimes you have a location that everybody loves but the sound is impossible. I never get upset about airplanes as nobody can control that stuff, but what upsets me is when you get somewhere where you could control the sound but no one wants to. They say, *'we don't want to pay $50 for a guy to turn off his lawn mower'*, but that's the difference between getting good sound and bad sound.

Q - What Guerrilla tactics can be used? What advice would you offer?

Mark - A lot of times, you can record things on set. If there's a scene where someone is listening to an answering machine, I see no reason why you can't record whatever he or she are listening to on set so long as it's not overlapping any dialogue. You can play it for the actor to react to and you may use it in post. I'm a big fan of shooting a couple of takes with it on, and then turning it off so that everybody has a sense of what it is. Every time you see a bar scene in a movie where there's loud music, you have the actors at an unnaturally low level. You need the actors to speak up, to make up for the music. To achieve that, you might want to play the music in rehearsal or in one or two takes so the actors can get used to it. If sound is poor for some reason, after the take, re-record it wild as often it will just drop in during the edit. Advice? Care about sound. Go to a movie, close your eyes and listen to the dialogue, then, put your hands over your ears and watch them talking without being able to hear it. If you can't hear what they are saying, it's bad sound. Whatever you can do to make the sound better is good. Consider your locations in terms of sound. If the location's right but the sound's not great, consider how much dialogue you have there. If it's a lot, it will be a problem. If not, then fine. Any interior that you could shoot elsewhere - shoot it somewhere quiet instead. There are a lot of creative solutions. If you can get everyone on set to care about the sound, then the sound will be the best it can be, which is all anyone can ask for.

Microphone Patterns

Different microphones respond in different ways, and not all are suitable for recording actors' voices on set or location. Microphones that are used in film and TV tend to be very directional, or they can be hidden very close to the actor (radio tie clip mics for instance). Remember the golden rule though, if you heard a sound, the sound recordist probably did too.

The Camera

Through the lens of a camera, there is a definite cut off at the edge of the frame. It's the nature of the medium. Therefore all manner of things can be happening just 'out of shot' and as long as it doesn't interfere with the actors' performance, there is no problem. Except of course, possibly for the sound... There is no definitive cut off with sound, so the acoustics of the entire environment will need to be considered closely.

Tie Clip or Lavaliere Mic

Tiny omni-directional mics that can be hidden on the actor or (very nearby), often attached to a transmitter and battery pack that is hidden in the actor's back pocket (watch out for actresses in skin tight dresses, where does the battery pack go?). Radio versions are most common as they need no direct cable connection to the recorder, but the cheaper ones can be subject to interference. An excellent choice but can produce bass heavy, even nasal sounding recordings.

Omni-directional Mic

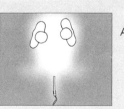

These mics pick up sound equally in all directions. Because of this lack of directionality, they are not suited for film use (except as tie clip or lavaliere mics). They are most often seen in radio stations or board rooms for conference calls.

Shotgun Mic

A directional mic that is the primary weapon of the sound recordist. Due to its directionality it is great for capturing dialogue when the mic needs to stay just out of shot. An older but still excellent mic to rent is a Sennheiser 416 (and 816 for ultra directionality). Most often seen on the end of the sound assistants boom pole. Beware though, they can pick up sound from the sides and behind in unexpected ways.

Uni-directional Mic

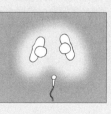

Also known as a Cardoid mic, and are generally not suited for drama as it picks up so much sound around the set. These mics are often seen in the hands of TV reporters or rock singers, rarely on a film set.

Jeff Blauvelt
HD Cinema

RENTING HI-DEF

Q - What is Hi Def?

Jeff - High Definition is the latest video format that has superseded the quality of standard definition video. It's a resolution, measured in pixels, is 920x1080 (one SMPTE standard), and the minimum to be considered HD is 1280x720 pixels (another SMPTE standard). Within these two resolutions there are additional frame rate variations and choices of interlace or progressive scanning. In addition there's a range of technical applications for Hi-Def, from production, post-production through broadcast. If you're going to shoot HD, my advice would be to stick with what we call 24p for convenience (you actually shoot 23.98 progressive frames per second).

Q - What do the different versions of HD relate to?

Jeff - 1280 x 720 relates to the number of pixels horizontally, (1280) by the number of pixels vertically, (720). 1920 by 1080 is another format that is even more common and that has double the pixels - 2 million rather than 1 million, so it's higher resolution (five times the resolution of PAL). For television, that increase isn't important, but for large screen presentation, the number of pixels does matter and experience says that if you want a good theatrical screening, you need the higher resolution.

Q - What is the difference between the different variations of progressive and interlaced?

Jeff - A progressive image allows the use of all of the computer processing power that has recently been blasting through to us at cheaper prices and with more memory and more disk space. An interlaced image is a leftover specification from broadcast television that's not necessary and is actually bad for production and post.

Q - When you're shooting Hi Def, what aspect ratio should you end up with?

Jeff - 16:9 widescreen. Some filmmakers frame their picture to be cropped later, into either 1:1.85 or 1:2.35 aspect ratios, but it's wise to protect your full 16:9 frame because sales and distribution deliverables will require a nice 4:3 image (center cut out of a 16:9 picture), so you need your tops and bottoms, therefore you can't have a mic descending into that area of frame. In film, you have a little safe area, whereas there's no safe area in digital video. If you can protect your image top and bottom and side to side, even if your primary input is going to be 1:1.85, it helps.

Q - What would you say is the standard Hi Def package to use?

Jeff - The Sony HDWF-900 has become the industry standard for 24P HD production. The camera package is enough to go out and shoot a movie with - it includes batteries, charger, matte box, follow focus, lens (wide angle zoom - the Canon 4.7 which goes to 52mm). Those are the essentials. Many DP's like to use filters, particularly graduated filters, neutral density (ND) filters, which are a real problem solver for shooting exteriors. Pro Mist filters are also popular as they can often soften the image and can give a more filmic look. Monitoring is where the greatest variety in the packages comes in. Hi-Def monitors are expensive. Now you have a choice between CRT and LCD monitors. CRT's have a tube in them, are heavier and use more power, but the image is sharper, the color is more accurate and there's no lag or blurring for high-speed action. So CRT is preferred for the quality of the image.

Q - Do you see exactly what you end up with through the monitor?

Jeff - With a CRT, it's pretty close. You are far closer to the final look than video assist on film can offer.

Q - How much would a basic camera package cost to rent?

Jeff - The advertised prices could be as high as $2k a day for a whole package. But most offer 30% off, so it's $1.4k per day, and then individual owner operators can go down to $1k. LA is pretty much a three day week, whereas New York is a three and a half day week. We've seen a lot of features shot in three weeks, some in four or five and very few shot in two weeks, so a three-week camera package could be had for around $9k. To purchase this camera package would probably cost around $150k.

Q - What's the running time of an HD tape?

Jeff - Shooting 24 frames on a BCT 40 HD tape will last 50 minutes. That's the longest tape a portable camera can take and they cost around $60. You can later transfer onto 2.5 hour HD cam master tapes for editing and backup.

Q - How many tapes would you get through on a HD shoot?

Jeff - People would shoot less film than tape, but for those three week shoots, I would say 30-35 tapes on average.

Q - Isn't DV cheaper to shoot your low budget movie than HD?

Jeff - It's much harder to shoot a production with a low cost digital camera (DV) because the camera can't handle the dynamic range that HD can. The F900 makes you look a genius, where with DVCAM, you have to agonize over lighting and gelling windows. You can save money by shooting HD. You also have to look at post-production costs. As much as I believe that filmmaking is primarily about the story, and that what's on the screen is more important than the camera, that's only true to a point. In reaching a mass audience, you have to make a decision about international distribution. I would always suggest shoot HD or film. The DV era has ended for filmmaking.

Q - What are the benefits of shooting HD or DV rather than film?

Jeff - There are new formats that are standard def but that are 24 progressive, an interesting alternative and I would recommend those highly for new filmmakers with a budget under $50k for feature. It's a wonderful tool that looks good and you might be able to take the finished product direct to video. But if you want a true international distribution where distributors in the hard to please countries insist on certain standards, you need to shoot in HD or film. HD over film is a long discussion. In terms of actors' performances, the ability to get greater coverage without increasing your costs for the performances of the actors is significant. They are more relaxed knowing it's video, not film. They are willing to take more chances on it and can be more spontaneous and improvised. There are slight differences in the temporal, visual experience. However, if you shoot HD and you really want that film look, you can transfer to film and you get the extra softness. Another film v HD factor is the price to blow up to 35mm is the same or less, than blowing up S16mm to 35mm in the traditional optical way. So to get to 35mm, there is no advantage in shooting S16mm, and I would make the case that your HD blown up to 35mm will look better than S16mm because of the grain and the resolution of 16mm. The last thing about film v HD is the post-production process. People are now scanning film negative to a digital intermediate that is higher resolution than the current HD Cam. The new HD Cam SR format will soon become a useful standard for high res digital intermediates for feature film production. Now your whole post-production process, even if you shoot film, is digital, until it is finally scanned back onto 35mm for theatrical distribution.

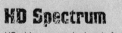

HD Spectrum

HD video comes in 4 main formats.

Resolution	Aspect ratio	Interlaced (i) or Progressive (p)
1. 1920 x 1080	16:9	60i/30p/24p
2. 1280 x 720	16:9	60p/30p/24p
3. 704 x 480	16:9/4:3	60p/60i/30p/24p
4. 640 x 480	4:3	60p/60i/30p/24p

Q - What about dirtying down the image of HD to make it look more like film?

Jeff - A few people do that and it's a mistake to add noise in the production process, you can do that at the end of the post-production process but you really shouldn't do it as you're shooting.

Q - If you shoot HD and transfer to film, does it have a natural film look?

Jeff - If it's properly shot and exposed, most viewers won't be able to tell it wasn't shot on film, but you do need to take care not to over-expose and clip the image.

Q - You can record the audio to the camera, but what are the advantages of also recording to a DAT ?

Jeff - The good thing about using a DAT is that the soundman can check his recordings and double check for clothing rustle and ambient sounds, without having to bother the camera operator asking him to rewind. You should always record audio to the camera as well. It takes 2-3 times real time to audio sync, so if you shoot 30 tapes and 20 hours of material, you're going to have 48 hours of synching. So even at $50 per hour, you're looking at a fee of around $2.5k - so if you've not thought ahead and don't have audio cable running from the DAT to the camera, you're going to be paying extra. In the indie film world, nobody in their Final Cut Pro or Avid Xpress suites has a time code DAT machine, so the first thing every filmmaker does is take their DATs and pay another $1k to get those DATs onto a DVCAM tape, or manually sync themselves. So why not take a portable DV recorder onset and record sound onto that, as well as picture?

Q - What time code should you run your DAT at?

Jeff - If you're shooting 23.98 or 24P, you should run your DAT at 29.97 and you MUST use non-drop frame. Sometimes people think that 23.98 is drop frame and 24P is non-drop frame - they are both non-drop frame rates and your DAT should always record non-drop frame and you should always do your downconverts as non-drop frame!

Q - Any tips on recording sound when shooting on HD?

Jeff - If you use an analogue mixer which is 0db when you set your tone, it's not a big deal if your peaks go above zero a little bit as long as you can't hear distortion. However on a camera that records audio digitally, it's important that your zero is set at -20db, and while peaks can go above -20db, if they go above zero, there's a good chance they will break up. The meters on the camera do not always show the short peaks, so even though your meters are not peaking above zero, you could end up with unusable audio. That's why you need a dedicated and experienced sound recordist.

HD AUDIO

HD Cam tape has four digital recordable audio tracks (though cameras may not access all four tracks without additional hardware). Dolby E is the preferred digital audio signal for HD TV transmission, allowing for eight channels - six channels of 5.1 surround and two of stereo. HDTV transmission uses a digital surround compression system called Dolby Digital. For HD mastering, you must create a Dolby Digital 5.1 mix which will be encoded on the HD master. It's likely that you will also have to supply a stereo mix in the normal way for broadcasters.

Q - How many audio channels are there on an HD camera?

Jeff - A typical HD camera has access to two analogue audio inputs. With an HDSDI 50 pin adapter that costs about $600 a week to rent, you can get two additional digital audio channels. It's a little cumbersome because most people have analogue mixers on the set, not digital, so you'd have to convert your analogue mics to a digital signal to then put into the digital channel.

Q - Can you do slow mo on HD cameras?

Jeff - This is *the* major feature set of the Panasonic Varicam camera - it allows true variable frame rates. For feature film production, we would say you should shoot a higher resolution format, and any shots that you want to be in slow motion, shoot them at 60 interlaced and create the slow motion in post. You'd capture the 60i footage as Quicktime data, copy to a firewire drive, then import into a software program such as After Effects for slow motion creation. You can also deinterlace (throw away one field per frame) creating a 1920x540 res image, then line double with interpolation to get to a 1920x1080 resolution progressive 60p frame that you then slow to 24. Software in post such as Real Viz or other morphing techniques can create in-between frames that can create a smoother slow mo in post. Our recommendation is actually to bring along a super 16mm camera and shoot film for slow mo, particularly if you want to do any cool effects such as ramping.

Q - Is there a big quality difference if you cut your slow mo effect on Super 16mm into your HD tape?

Jeff - You can cut very well with the HD footage if you use noise reduction and grain reduction in your telecine transfer. When you shoot a high frame rate then slow it down, it will look different from your normal footage, but it cuts very well with HD video and has the intended effect. Shoot it both ways if you are worried. Definitely roll your HD camera while you shoot film so that if it doesn't work, you have a choice.

Q - Is HD tungsten or daylight based?

Jeff - HD is tungsten based but there are ND and Color Correction filters built into the camera.

Q - Can you do any color adjustments in camera?

Jeff - Yes and you must ensure that you get the best exposure. Some DPs might use an HD camera control unit with a waveform monitor, or an oscilloscope, to monitor and control the clipping of black and white levels and adjust the gamma curves to optimize the final images. The unit allows the operator to dial in detail in the highlights and dark areas and create images with incredibly dynamic range within a dramatically lit scene. If ever in doubt about the exposure, a DP should slightly underexpose by 1/4 to a 1/2 stop, to avoid blowing out the bright highlights. Details in the darker areas, if not clipped, can be brought out later in post. There is a huge range of color correction that can be done in post.

Q - Are there any tips for shooting on HD, knowing you are going to end up on film?

Jeff - Don't over expose your highlights, and turn the enhancement down to -35/-50. Conventional wisdom is to not turn detail off entirely, however some people argue you can and should. If you turn it off completely, your HD footage isn't as crisp as it should be. If you want to have a good image to show your client, you should add the detail on set rather than in post.

Q - What is downconverting?

Jeff - Downconversion merely means taking the HD video and reducing its resolution to that of standard definition video. We

HD RATES

One major drawback of HD for indie filmmakers is that the technology is new, therefore the equipment is new. Anyone who rents it, it going to have recently made a major investment. Unlike film cameras where the investment may have been repaid many years ago. The upshot is that HD deals are MUCH harder to get, and completely free equipment, almost unheard of. In comparison, film cameras are much easier to get for free. Here's one company's rate card to give you a ball park idea of costs.

Price for HD capture / HD editing: *$350 an hour with one hour minimum. The HD digital video capture is done in real time, the data transfer out to firewire is about 5 times real time.*

HDCAM to DIGIBETA
30 tapes to Digibeta @$105 each = $3150
30 60min Digibeta tapes @$38 each = $1140
Rent DVW-500 Digibeta deck to load the off line non linear system – 3 days @ $500 per day = $1500
Rent DVW – 500 Digibeta deck to output from the off line non linear system - 1day @$500 = $500
Total $6,280

HDCAM to DVCAM
30 tapes to DVCAM @$75 each = $2250
30 60min DVCAM tapes @$18 each = $540
rent DSR-1500 DVCAM to load the off line nls 3 days @$100 per day = $300
rent DSR-1500 DVCAm to output from the off line nls – 1 day @$100 per day = $100
Total $3,190

call it 24p but most of the time we mean 23.98p. Even if you shoot actual 24 frames per second, it has to be played at 23.98 frames per second to do a downconversion. During the downconversion process, the time code is changed from 24 frames (23.98) to 30 frames (29.97). This is really a very important step because now the video can be recorded, screened, logged, off-line edited on standard Avids and Final Cut Pro using the familiar formats of Digital Betacam, BetaSP, DV, mini-DV, and VHS.

Q - What format is it best to work with offline?

Jeff - Digibeta is the best choice if money is no object, but the tape and VTR rental are expensive. For lower budgets, you may be better off going to DVCAM and applying the significant savings to an HD online, or give it back to your production budget. DVCAM has 2 tracks of digital audio that are the same quality as Digibeta and DAT. An exception to this would be if you plan to finish in Digibeta. If you know you never will do an HD online, you will probably want to downconvert to Digibeta. Beta SP is not a good option, unless you or your editor owns his system and VTR already, even then you may reconsider. This is because Beta SP downconverts require outboard delay processing and are harder to do to get accurate video, timecode and audio sync.

Q - What types of decks can you use to transfer DVCAM?

Jeff - DVCAM must be transferred using a Sony DSR-1500, 1800 or 2000 using the SDI serial digital input option. The older DSR-40, 60 or 80 VTRs will not have proper video, timecode and audio sync even with serial digital input. Once recorded, the DVCAM tapes can be loaded into the non-linear system using any DVCAM VTR or even a camera via Firewire.

Q - Any basic tips for shooting or recording HD?

Jeff - Always shoot REC Run time code, not free run or time of day. With two cameras near each other it is easy to slave one to the other and just start your primary camera first every time. With multiple cameras shooting recordings of live events, you can then use free run time code. You should ALWAYS record your downconverts as non-drop frame (NDF), and edit your project in NDF if you ever want to online with that list in HD. As for terminology, it is confusing but 30 frame, and 29.97 usually means the same as 60i (60 or 59.94 interlaced frames). High Def video can be shot at 23.98, 24, 25 and even 30p progressive frames per second, and it can be shot at 50i, 59.94i and 60i interlaced frames per second.

Q - Are there any sync difficulties if you shoot in 24p and downconvert?

Jeff - Even if you shoot actual 24 frames per second it has to be played at 23.98 frames per second to do a downconversion so for audio purposes especially it's better to shoot 23.98 and record your DAT with 29.97 NDF time code.

Q - Are there any problems with time code?

Jeff - Cinema Tools is now included in Final Cut Pro 4.0 software, and this enables an EDL (edit list) import from Avid or other standard non-linear systems and subsequent conversion of the 30 frame cut list to 24. So there's no problem converting if the time code on the tape is continuous. However, it can be one frame off if there are time code breaks. If you spot a one-frame error, it is very affordable and easy to fix if you catch it right away and the HD video is still on the non-linear system. The editor will know which cuts he agonized over and he can check those easily. If he can't tell, probably the audience can't tell either.

Q - What happens if you want to intercut conventional 4:3 NTSC or PAL material into your HD24p project?

Jeff - It's a mess, don't do it!

Q - If you shoot on film, why post in HD, especially if you're going to release on film?

Jeff - You do it primarily for the distributor deliverables. The HD24p format is becoming known as the Universal Master. From this single master, a variety of deliverables can be derived. An HD 1080/60i interlaced program master is required for some broadcast networks, others require 720/60p progressive program masters. These can be in 16x9 format, but also may be in 1.85 or even 2.35 letterboxed formats. For standard definition broadcasts Digibeta, D1, D2 dubs may be made in 16x9 widescreen, letterbox or cropped to 4:3. This can be done for both PAL and NTSC, again from the same HD Universal Master. PAL conversions from 24p originated material look fantastic, much better than the usual NTSC to PAL conversions many producers have been forced to accept. In the past, if budget limitations did not allow a producer to shoot on film, better quality was achieved by shooting and editing in the hard-to-find analog PAL format if there was going to be worldwide television distribution. Now for the same price range as Digibeta PAL gear and post, you can get full HD cameras and HD post.

Q - What are the 'digital dailies'?

Jeff - The digital dailies refer to the overnight transfer of film or HD to a digital tape format that is of high enough image quality to make decisions regarding the quality of the original. Several companies are using real time HD MPEG-2 encoders to heavily compress the originals but still have HD resolution. JVC has a new D-VHS VCR that will play these tapes. However, these are for screening and logging, but not for off-line editing. Digibeta and DVCAM downconverts can be considered digital dailies and can be used for off-line editing.

Q - Should you do HD clones or back ups of your HD universal master?

Jeff - Having HD clones is a good idea and doing the HD clone with the downconverts together is cheaper, although it can be expensive. We have seen some producers use Digibeta as a back up to their original HD.

Q - Are there problems with multiple generations on HD?

Jeff - Up to 17 generations of HDCAM and up to 30 generations of HD D5 looks good. It doesn't hurt to playback HD tapes up to 4 or 5 times, but I would avoid more than that on camera originals.

Q - Can you use film lenses for HD cameras, and can you get the same depth of field with an HD camera?

Jeff - Yes, the P+S Technik adapter allows the same depth of field of 35mm primes as they look on a 35mm camera. But, you lose two stops of exposure, and therefore that can be an issue in low light situations. For indie filmmakers, zooms are the most popular. Canon HJ11x4.7 ENG style and Canon HJ 21x7.5 Cinestyle are our most popular lenses.

Q - Does HD have an electronic shutter speed in camera?

Jeff - Yes. It has a variable shutter, which is most often set at 1/48th sec at 23.98 (24 fps), which gives you the same motion blur as shooting film with a 180 degree shutter. You lose one stop with this shutter, so often it is turned off in low light.

Q - So what is the financial difference for shooting a low budget movie between hiring a S16mm film camera, which you might even be able to get for free and shooting on HD?

Jeff - The numbers show that the film processing, telecine transfer, audio synching with that compared to HD, HD is way ahead of the film. You might be paying a little extra up front, but not in the back end. We will gladly take the cost of your film stock and processing, and telecine transfer from your budget and give you a free camera.

Phil Messina
Production Design

THE PRODUCTION DESIGNER

Q - What is your job?

Phil - I am a production designer for feature films. I began as a draughtsman, moved up to art director and about a dozen films later was given my first opportunity to design a film, *Erin Brockovich*. There is no one path to becoming a production designer, but many designers have an architecture, theater or art background.

Q - What is the role of a production designer?

Phil - In collaboration with the director, the cinematographer and the costume designer, I am part of the creative team that determines the physical *'look'* and dramatic visual feeling of the film. I translate the script and the director's vision into the physical world that's captured on film. By doing this, I place the characters in environments that help drive the visual storytelling. I also work very closely with the DP (and costume designer) to create a coherent visual palette - how the set will be lit and framed and how the costumed characters will look in the sets is all extremely important to the final product. I work closely with the DP as far as light sources, wall textures and colors - even down to the density and tone of lampshades and window dressing (curtains) - it all affects the way my sets finally look on film.

Q - Who makes up the art department?

Phil - The production designer is the head of the art department. The art director and the set decorator are my left and right arms. The art director is responsible for turning my sketches and photographic research into drafted construction drawings and completed sets. He supervises the draughts people who produce the construction drawings, and also is responsible for both scheduling and budgeting of the sets. The set decorator is responsible for all the sets' furnishings - from window dressing to furniture to light fixtures, etc. Assisting the decorator is the leadperson who is responsible for keeping track of the pick up, dressing and then return of all the items as well as supervising the dressing (swing) crew. The art director and the decorator work together to determine how the dressing fits with the built set and when the construction will be completed and the sets ready to dress; on a tight schedule there's often a lot of overlap that happens there - several crews working at once. You want to try to avoid that, but sometimes it's inevitable so it's important that you structure a department that works well together.

Q - How do you structure each project and what's the first job you tackle?

Phil - After I read the script (often several times) I try to gather images that I think begin to capture some aspect of the visual storytelling. They usually are photographs or paintings and their relevance may be very abstract or quite literal - initially I try to capture a feeling more than a specific detail. I then try to determine whether the sets should be built on stage or shot on location. This decision is often made with the director and producers. Sometimes this is very obvious - as with the space station in *Solaris* - and sometimes it is determined by shooting schedule, being able to control the lighting in a specific way, how the set will physically be shot or simply script page count. On *Erin Brockovich* we had 32 pages scripted for the law office, so it was a good bet up front that it would be built on stage. I then begin scouting locations with a location scout - my favorite part - as it's here that you begin to put the big pieces of the film together. It's like a treasure hunt in that you never know what you'll find out there. I try at first to be open to a range of solutions as sometimes a location will hatch an idea that I never would have though of otherwise. If something looks even a bit interesting in location photos, I'll try to get a look at it because I never know where it will lead. I also try to keep the larger interests of the company in mind and take into account not only how great the location will look on film, but physically how are we going to shoot it? Is it uncontrollably noisy for a lot of dialog? What's the direction of the sun? How will you get a dolly into the space? If it really is perfect I'll do my best to sell it to the director, but be honest up front about the limitations of the location. I try to think like the gaffer as well as the sound person and the AD, so we end up with a location that works for everyone. Sometimes though, a place is so perfect you just say "It's difficult but worth it - we'll figure out some way to make it work".

Q - What else is important as far as location scouting goes?

Phil - As far as scouting goes, I try to be the person who knows the city and location options better than anyone - even the scout - so when the director comes up with an idea I can offer a creative solution. I will sometimes suggest a location that I scouted three films prior but for one reason or another never used, and for this situation, it's perfect. Sometimes I'll see a location that isn't scripted - as in that great theater turned parking garage in *8 Mile* - and tell the director 'I don't know what this could be used for, but you have to see it'. Curtis Hanson loved it too, and ended up rewriting the scene to fit the location. In my experience, it's not uncommon for the script to adjust to take advantage of the strengths of a particular location.

Q - What does the term 'wilding' mean?

Phil - 'Wilding' means removing pieces of the set - usually walls - to accommodate the camera or lighting. It's easier to consider this early on in the design process so the grips aren't forced to saw out a piece of the set while the whole crew looks on. It's always preferable to know about specific camera moves up front, but as you gain more experience a lot of it becomes intuitive. Still sometimes the director will come up with a great idea that involves taking out a chunk of the set and it's here that I will try to suggest a smart way to remove a wall knowing that the less damage done the quicker it can be repaired for the next shot.

Q - How important is attention to detail to you?

Phil - Extremely - that's where the fun is. Not only to provide what's scripted, but go the extra mile to provide the director and actors with options that add a layer of realism or help to define their characters. Things like filling dressers and closets with things that you think the character would have. Often this level of detail isn't seen on screen, but I feel it helps the actors to establish a believable environment and has a non-quantifiable effect. Seemingly small items such as food, personal effects or items in cabinets all add up. I love it when an actor responds to an unscripted piece of set dressing - it really makes me feel as though I've contributed in some small way to the performance. While filming one of the final scenes in *Erin* for example, we were shooting Albert Finney on the phone triumphant from winning a major lawsuit. Without telling either Albert or Steven we put Albert's picture on a copy of "LA Lawyer Weekly" for his desk. Well, Albert played the whole scene while reading the article in the magazine - it was wonderful!

Concept Art

The concept artist will, after having sat down with the director and production designer, create the first visualization or 'look' of the film. They provide a series of images that can capture the essence of what the film will 'look' like, whether it's an alien world, a representation of medieval England or a dazzling theatrical world of Paris in the twenties. The images will help the director stay focused and can also be shown to financiers to keep them happy or to help persuade them to invest. It also provides a look for the set designers, set builders, and costume designers to follow. It helps give reality to what is otherwise simple words on paper. Pictured is an image by Alex Fort for Rocketman *and Vampire Girl, a Living Spirit Pictures project in development.*

Accurate details also give the director freedom to improvise. Another example from *Erin* is the water board set where Julia's character sifts through plans and documents searching for clues. The location was an empty sheriff's office that we dressed for the film. The set decorator and the leadman actually found real documents - even from the right region in California - that were being thrown away by a neighboring real water board. So we had a truckload of authentic documents, which we filled the location with. It was great, because it was one of the first scenes that Steven shot with Julia, so after the set was lit he closed the door and the two of them played the scene alone and I knew that they had the freedom to pick up and feature anything in the entire set.

Q - What is the relationship between the production designer and the DP?

Phil - It truly changes with every project. Often I'm brought on before the DP, and I have to make decisions with their best interest in mind. On *Solaris* for example, all of the lighting for the space station was integrated into the design. Steven Soderbergh was the DP and we discussed the lighting concepts at length - mostly we referenced other films and talked about what we thought worked and what didn't. I then worked closely with the gaffer to incorporate these ideas into the design from the very beginning. Another example is *8 Mile* where Curtis Hanson, the director, suggested that he, the DP and myself start the conversation about the visual approach to the project by all bringing images to the table. We all sat around a large conference table and laid out and discussed the various images and how they might be relevant to the film. This was a great thing to do early on because by the end of the meeting we all had an idea of what the approach would be, albeit in broad strokes, but we were all on the same page.

Q - How do you create a color palette for a film?

Props and Set Dressing

Just about everything you see on the screen, barring the actors and SPFX, fall into the categories of props and set dressing. Props (short for 'properties') refers to all objects that are handled by the actors or featured in the script, such as a cigarette, a car, food, coffee cups, candles, newspaper headlines etc. Set Dressing refers to background decoration of a scene i.e. furniture, paintings etc. Props and set dressing may cross over, and may even include wardrobe when referring to something specific. i.e. sun glasses. The person in charge of props is called the Props Master. They handle the selection, cataloging and maintenance of the props. The Set Dressing is overseen by the Set Decorator who is responsible for physically creating the vision of the Production Designer and the Director from the drawings created by the Art Director. The set decorator's next in command is the Lead Person who supervisors the Set Dressers (called the Swing Gang). If sets aren't dressed on time, it can put the whole movie behind schedule.

1. Make a list of all props and potential set dressing from your script as early as possible. This will give you enough time to gather or create them cheaply or for free.

2. Be aware of TV programs or web sites that will appear in the script as these may either require you to get the rights to the show / site, or to hire someone to generate them.

3. Likewise, photographs, newspaper headlines, magazine articles and books etc. will need ample prep time for their creation.

4. If there is a prop that is prominent in a scene, such as a box of cereal, try to get product placement to fill this need. However, if you can't get this because you have put the product in a negative light, you will need to create a fictitious brand.

5. Make sure everything is as realistic as possible. Use authentic props and set dressing. Actors often need this reality.

6. Be well organized and have a choice of each prop ready in case it doesn't fit the production designer or director's vision - also, you might need multiple props for multiple takes, or for if one is damaged. This is especially true for food and stunt props.

7. Make sure that each prop is always readily at hand.

8. If you have an action vehicle in your script, ensure it's properly insured. It may be more cost effective to rent a vehicle from an actual place of business than a specialized action prop house. i.e. rent an armored car from Brinks instead of Warner Bros. This obviously depends upon the use of the vehicle within the film.

9. Keep an eye on your props so that they don't go home with your crew.

10. Return your props and dressings on time to avoid late fees.

Low Budget Production Value

1. Fill the scene with as many props as possible without it looking cluttered. The common low budget problem is shots with sparse detail.

2. Do not use cheap wigs and costumes unless you are doing so for comedic reasons. They never look good.

3. Try to use practical lights in a scene to highlight props and set decorations. This can be anything from a desk lamp to buttons and dials that light up on a submarine control console.

4. Reduce or control the amount of light to create mood. Candles are always a good, cheap way to do this.

5. In exterior situations, shoot during 'golden hour' to get the best light.

6. Always shoot wide shots of your locations as it makes your film look bigger.

7. Cast people of different ages in your film, if appropriate, so it does not look like a student filmmaker using his friends.

8. Find creative ways of moving the camera to make the film more dynamic. Examples include mounting the camera to a skateboard or shopping cart as a dolly.

9. Stunts can be a lot cheaper than you think, and make a film pop with excitement. Brainstorm with a good stunt coordinator on how to get more bang for your buck.

10. Make sure you have enough close ups and cutaways. Eye light in close ups always looks good.

11. Reality is better if you have no money, so get permission to use the real thing. A genuine convenience store will look better than one you build as a set.

12. Try to get as many extras as possible for crowd shots and public location (like a parking lot or train station) in order to make the scene look bigger and more real.

13. Wet down streets with a hose in order to make a scene shimmer on film.

14. Avoid shooting in noisy areas so you can use as much location sound as possible.

15. If a shot looks empty, tighten the angle so you see more actor and less emptiness.

16. Avoid elements you cannot do effectively. Anything that does not look real or authentic will destroy the suspension of belief for your audience.

Phil - Each project's visual style tends to express itself in a different way for me. Larger budget films and ones where I build sets on stage are obviously easier to control. Lower budget films and 'location shows' are a bit more challenging. The color palette on *8 Mile* for example, was generated by my initial scouts to Detroit. The city really is a character in the film and we tried to let its voice come across on screen. There were a lot of rusts and earth tones - both in decayed metals, but also in the colors of the fall, which is when we shot. We tried to keep the tones of the sets in muted colors, browns, reds, oranges and darker greens, but with a sense of life underneath. The films characters were in more vibrant and saturated colors, reds, blues, blacks and even white, to stand in stark contrast to their surroundings. During the last battle on stage, Eminem's character takes off his sweatshirt to reveal a bright white t-shirt and the effect is luminous. The hard part is when locations fall through at the last minute and you are forced to replace a carefully made decision with a sometimes hasty one. Actors also play a part if they have specific ideas about their costumes or sets that differ from yours. It's a delicate dance to make them feel comfortable while being true to the original vision of the film.

Q - What have been your greatest challenges?

Phil - Having the set ready to shoot is always a challenge - its not so much a question of it being done sometimes as it is running against a deadline - especially when the due date moves up on you. There are always things you'd like to change or finesse, but I think that's the nature of the art form. The most important challenge for me is to keep my vision clear throughout the design process as it is being translated through the ranks of all the people that I rely on to follow it through. By successfully translating the ideas and keeping them clear, my team is able to build upon and enhance them, not dilute them. It's all about keeping people focused on that vision, but also not being dogmatic to the point that you miss an unforeseen opportunity. You have art directors and draught people interpreting renderings and research, a set decorating department that's out shopping in the real world trying to find pieces that preserve and build upon the design concepts. Without constant vigilance, things can start to subtly veer off track, so it's my job

Production Design

If there's no consideration for production design, your film can look uninspired, messy and unfocused. By stylizing the look of your film, you can make it stand out. Even on a low budget, spending more time and money on what goes up on the screen, will go a long way.

1. Allow your production designer and concept artists the freedom to use their own ideas. They're generally experienced at this and can take your vision to new levels.

2. Building models of your set can help with the communication between the director and the production design team as to what needs to be changed or added. It can also help the director and DP envision where the camera and lights will go, so the set builders can compensate with removable walls etc.

3. It may be advantageous to create a maquette (a small model) of certain people, creatures or objects, in order to fully visualize what they look like. This is especially true if you're working in a fantasy world. On a side note, bringing these objects into a finance or studio meeting, can help enhance your vision.

4. Consider the color palette of your film with the Production Designer, the DP and Director. The locale and tone of your story will affect this choice. For instance, if your movie is a comedy set in the Caribbean, you might want to use saturated colors. Changing the color palette throughout the film can be an effective way of creating mood.

6. Keep a consistent color theme in order to avoid a jarring mish mash of hues that make no sense. This applies to everything in the movie, from props to costumes to locations etc.

7. Get everyone on the same page. Often, production designers may come up against costume designers or the DP over the choice of colors. Help everyone see the importance of this. This most often occurs when budgets are very tight and time is short as filming can turn into 'just get it shot now!'

to keep it all together and focused while letting talented people do their jobs. The finished set may not always turn out exactly the way you initially conceived of it, but it it conveys the essence of the concept I'd say it's a success.

Q - What are the specific challenges when working on a low budget film?

Phil - Designing a lower budget film is often much harder and can be more frustrating because of limited resources. On a larger film you have more options and you can throw resources at a problem when things go awry or to change a flaw in an otherwise great locale. On lower budget film, you have to be more calculated - again it's always great to be as specific as possible as to what the camera is going to see, especially on period films. When choosing locations, they have to go a longer way toward working as they are, as you often are limited in how you can alter them. On these films locations fees, ease of lighting, being able to use multiple spaces within one location and actors schedules will drive the decision to shoot there as much as how great the place looks.

Q - If you have to choose between shooting on location or on stage, which would you rather?

Phil - It really depends on the specifics of each project. Sometimes a great location offers you something that would be tough and/or expensive to achieve on stage like a great view, background movement or traffic, or a space with a large scale or ornate detailing. In some instances, the decision to build or shoot on location can change due to circumstances beyond your control. The club that holds the rap battles in *8 Mile* was originally to be a location. We found fantastic spaces but always for one reason or another we couldn't make them work. We had over 400 extras in these scenes and safety considerations such as fire exits became very important. We almost went with one space that we were going to have to build more exits and install a sprinkler system into, but at that point it became a wash expense-wise to just go ahead and build a set. I only had a day to design it and we had about two weeks to build, paint, dress and light it, so it was tough, but it's times like those that the production really appreciates the designer and what he can do to help get them out of a problematic situation.

Q - What are some of the unique qualities of the directors that you've worked with?

Production Design Books

The Filmmakers Guide To Production Design
by Vincent LoBrutto
A rich book that covers the essentials of storyboarding, set decoration, budgeting, props, and wardrobe and tips on how different genres effect them. Each chapter has practice exercises at the end so that students, and professionals, can stay sharp.

What An Art Director Does
by Ward Preston
This book lays out the procedure and the challenges in becoming a motion picture art director or a production designer. It covers the basics, but also has some first hand stories of the difficulties working in the film industry.

Art Direction for Film and Video
by Robert Olson
A practical, thorough look at the duties and skills of art directors and production designers. It provides lessons on script analyzing and concept developing that will help you develop sketches drawings to bring sets to life. It also details how to work with directors and producers, and operate within budget limitations.

Phil - I've been lucky as a designer to work with two extremely knowledgeable and talented directors. Both Steven Soderbergh and Curtis Hanson possess an incredible breadth of knowledge not only about filmmaking, but about the history of film. When you can access such a range of films as examples, I think it makes for a more informed decision making process for the particular project that you're collaborating on. Both can cite moments, shots, sets and performances from the most obscure films past and present, I often find myself making lists of them to research when I go home. During the prep for *8 Mile* for example, Curtis held a series of screenings that were open to the entire crew - films that he thought had something relevant to our project; we saw *Hoop Dreams*, *Midnight Cowboy* and *A Killer of Sheep* to name a few. It's a wonderful experience, like being in an advanced film school program, to be able to discuss these films with someone like Curtis. You realize that there's always more to learn, not just about creating beautiful sets, but about design as one integral piece of the entire storytelling art form.

One aspect of Steven's filmmaking process which continually amazes me is that he shoots the film as though he's editing it in 'real time' in his head. There's an efficiency to his shooting style that's very inspiring to both the crew and the actors. The actors really seem to respond to him in a special way, I believe because they know that there aren't going to be a lot of takes and a high percentage of what is shot will be used. There's a momentum that he builds up that really pays off in terms of energy and how it's captured on film.

Q - What advice would you give to new designers?

Phil - It's important to choose material that you have some connection to. To build and sustain a career over the long haul, I feel that it's more important to choose great stories and to work with inspiring directors than to make choices to go for the big splashy (often empty) design opportunities. Achieving great design on an otherwise terrible film I think would be of little consolation. I know that the reality of someone just starting out though, is that often there aren't a lot of choices, but still it pays to be selective about what you choose to contribute your talents to. At this point, if I get offered a fantastic script for a $3M film, I'll take it. You never know who the next Wes Anderson or Quentin Tarantino will be. You also have to make choices that will complement the work you've already done. Although I had done gritty, reality based films such as *Traffic* and *Erin Brockovich*, I chose to do another, *8 Mile*, because I had always dreamed of working with Curtis. So associating yourself with talented directors, I feel, will always pay off.

Susie - If you need them, then yes, specifically if a character going to get shot or wet or has a stunt double, or if they have to wear something delicate for a long time. When we did *What Lies Beneath,* Michelle had to wear that nightgown for so many months, and there was so much water and stunt doubles, we had 20 of everything.

Q - Is it possible to make a movie with period costumes for $1m?

Susie - Yes. One of the main things about budget is most things are possible as long as everybody's making the same film, and expectation levels are the same. You can't dress 1000 extras, but if you have a story that is contained, then it's fine.

Q - If you hire costumes, do you need insurance?

Susie - Yeah. The production usually has a certificate of insurance. It's for everything, all the equipment, props etc. It's an overall insurance policy that the production buys to insure everything they rent.

Q - What would you recommend for a costume designer to always have on hand?

Susie - A good attitude. Always have steamers, ironing boards and irons, and things to make clothes dirty and clean. Ageing clothes can be a difficult process as you want to make them look old but, you can't ruin them. Most of the clothes people wear every day are not brand new and when you're creating a character, they need to look washed, especially shoes, they need to look dirty and have the soles worn down.

Q - Do actors ever get to keep their clothes?

Susie - Yes. Especially the big actors. They have it in their contract that they can take whatever they want. Props, watches, furniture. If they have been helpful and good to work with, a lot of times, the actors will get clothes as a gift from the producers.

Q - Is there anything in your contract with the production company that they should provide you with?

Susie - In my contract, a car for myself and I like to have control of who works in my department. If we have to travel, I ask for first class travel and accommodations, screen credit, paid advertising credit. The terms of contract (in terms of over time), and a per diem if I'm on location.

Q - Is there anything a producer can do to make your life easier?

Susie - Get the film cast. Late casting is challenging. It's a working relationship and some producers are in tune with what a costume department needs and what they require. Others are less so, but every relationship you have with people is a whole other set of conditions.

Q - How is continuity dealt with?

Susie - People take pictures and make detailed notes after a sequence is shot. You have to remember how everything is worn. How did she wear the scarf? Which shoulder did she carry the bag on? Getting it right is crucial so that the audience isn't distracted by a mistake and also so there's a consistency with the takes when they're cut together.

Q - Do you discuss with the Director and actor if a character has specific clothes, like Sean Penn in 'I Am Sam'?

Susie - Yes, once again, that came from research. I went to this place called LA Goal in which the director did a lot of her work. I interviewed a lot of guys there who were developmentally handicapped and I asked one guy *'how do you feel about your clothes?'*

Costume Continuity Sheets

The backbone of the Costume department are the continuity sheets for each and every character in the film. It outlines what each character is wearing, small modifications which might occur in the performance (loosening a tie for instance) and many other aspects. It will be planned out in pencil then overwritten in pen when it actually takes place. These notes will be cross referenced with the Polaroid shots that will also be filed in the costume department's 'bible'.

Character Name
Each character in the story will have their own individual continuity sheets.

Drawings
Use quick sketches to help, such as this one which shows the way the actor has re-tied the scarf around their neck.

Story Day
Should be outlined in the script but Story Days may need to be allocated by Costume/Makeup depts.

Scene numbers
Taken from the shooting script.

Set or location
Interior or Exterior plus location, taken from shooting script.

Notes
Anything that is important to remember about the scene - 'removes glasses' or 'unbuttons shirt' for instance.

Costume
A complete list of all the clothing worn by the actor in the scene, which may also include the whole story day.

Scene Break
A break in scenes, but not Story Day. When the character reappears in later scenes they may or may not be wearing the same costume.

Story Day Break
A hard story break which will almost certainly denote a costume change unless your character does not change clothes (uniforms for instance)

Note - These sheets will almost always be prepared by hand due to last minute changes on set.

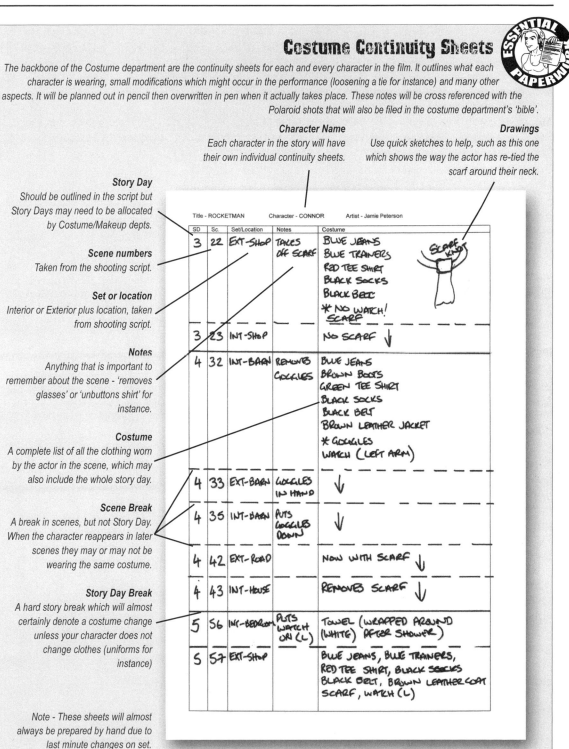

Title - ROCKETMAN   Character - CONNOR   Artist - Jamie Peterson

SD	Sc.	Set/Location	Notes	Costume
3	22	EXT-SHOP	TAKES OFF SCARF	BLUE JEANS / BLUE TRAINERS / RED TEE SHIRT / BLACK SOCKS / BLACK BELT / ✱ NO WATCH! / SCARF
3	23	INT-SHOP		NO SCARF ↓
4	32	INT-BARN	REMOVES GOGGLES	BLUE JEANS / BROWN BOOTS / GREEN TEE SHIRT / BLACK SOCKS / BLACK BELT / BROWN LEATHER JACKET / ✱ GOGGLES / WATCH (LEFT ARM)
4	33	EXT-BARN	GOGGLES IN HAND	↓
4	35	INT-BARN	PUTS GOGGLES DOWN	↓
4	42	EXT-ROAD		NOW WITH SCARF ↓
4	43	INT-HOUSE		REMOVES SCARF ↓
5	56	INT-BEDROOM	PUTS WATCH ON (L)	TOWEL (WRAPPED AROUND (WHITE) AFTER SHOWER)
5	57	EXT-SHOP		BLUE JEANS, BLUE TRAINERS, RED TEE SHIRT, BLACK SOCKS BLACK BELT, BROWN LEATHER COAT SCARF, WATCH (L)

SCARF KNOT

He said, *'I don't like to wear anything bright. I don't want to wear anything that attracts any attention'*. He said people stare at him because of his handicap. When I took this information to Sean, he seized on it and I said, *'I think you should always wear these pants and this coat'*. He was completely there with it. Sean is very much an actor who completely transforms himself.

Q - Is there a problem with actresses wanting to look good all the time?

Susie - Sometimes. Some actresses don't realize that people can identify more with you if you look real. I've worked with Drew Barrymore and Sandra Bullock who, and although they are both pretty and powerful, they are also unafraid to carry a look that is self-deprecating. I think this endears them to the audience.

Q - Have you come across a lot of filmmakers with ego problems?

Susie - Sometimes people think things are more precious than they actually are. I'm guilty of this myself if I really love something, but sometimes if the director doesn't like it, let go of it because that's your job.

Q- Do you ever get pigeon-holed as a costume designer?

Susie - Lots of times, you get stuck doing one thing. The period movie people are dying to do contemporary movies and vice versa. Yeah I think you do and that's hard to break out of. If you're good and do your research, you can do anything, but especially in the period thing, if you haven't done a lot of it, they think you can't do it and that's just not true.

Q - What route would you recommend for somebody who wants to be a costume designer?

Susie - The best designers are people that have done all the other jobs on a wardrobe crew as it helps you understand what everybody else does. A lot of people decide that they are costume designers but they're not educated in terms of experience. That's the one good thing about working on low budget movies - you have the opportunity to learn about filmmaking. You become more of a filmmaker rather than someone who just does the clothes.

Q - Is it hard for wardrobe assistants to break out?

Susie - I had worked for a long time as a wardrobe assistant and I wanted to design and so I finally put my foot down. Producer friends would ask me to assist again but I had to say no. A friend recommended me to a guy who was doing a period movie and they took a chance and hired me. It's just a case of collecting enough credits and relationships to get noticed.

Q - Would a well established costume designer consider working on a low budget movie if they liked the script?

Susie - Absolutely. The low budget movie I was going to work on that just fell apart had a great script. The scripts I had been reading before, although they were bigger budget movies, were not that good. Producers shouldn't have any qualms about sending their scripts to more established designers.

Q - What would be the best way to approach you?

Susie - If you see someone's work you like, you can find them through the guild or through agents.

Q - What advice would you offer a new filmmaker?

Susie - Stay open and be flexible and roll with the punches. Don't let your ego get the better of you. Work hard. Remember everybody's job is valuable.

Costume Design Books

**Costume Design 101
by Richard La Motte**
A well-written 'how to' for someone wanting to know more about what it takes to make the costumes in a movie come together.

The Costume Designers Handbook: A Complete Guide for Amateur and Professional Costume Designers by Liz Covey & Rosemary Ingham
The bible of theatrical costumers, this book follows the process from script to production, also containing a chapter on the profession.

Costume Design: Techniques of Modern Masters by Lynn Pecktal and Tony Walton
A combination of great interviews conducted with 18 leading contemporary costume designers, explaining how to go from sketch to costume, with stunning illustrations of the finished products.

Make up Artist Books

Grande Illusions by Tom Savini
For those who love special make up effects, especially from the horror genre, this book is for you. It teaches you how the effects Savini has done in movies, such as The Burning, The Prowler, Dawn of the Dead, Friday the 13th, and Creepshow all came together. There are two volumes, Books I and II.

The Complete Make Up Artist, 2nd Edition by Penny Delamar
An essential for anyone who wants to become a successful make-up artist in film and TV. Written for those learning about media make-up, this book provides a wealth of information, activities and advice.

The Technique of the Professional Make Up Artist by Vincent J. R. Kehoe
Covers all of the current studio make-up methods and lab techniques, with text and art contributions from some of the leading experts in the industry. Kehoe clearly explains the differences between applying make up for TV verses film, interior versus exterior and studio lighting versus natural daylight.

PRODUCTION

Judy Lovell
Make Up Supervisor

MAKE-UP

Q - What is your job?

Judy - I'm a make up artist. I had an excellent apprenticeship with the BBC in London, and was lucky enough to work on a variety of shows, some with extravagant budgets, as well as lower budget projects, where I learnt many tricks - one needs to know how to use Guerrilla tactics!

Q - How early on in a production are you hired?

Judy - It varies and depends on factors like if it's a period piece and the length of pre-production.

Q - How important is the communication between actor and make up artist?

Judy - I can help put the actor in the right frame of mind, which is important. Sometimes you get actors wanting to get into character, and if they're going to be screaming and shouting, they can start being a little snappy towards you. That's where a healthy sense of humor is needed. I've never minded that when I've respected the actor. I try to understand and learn their part, and help with the continuity for it as well as I can. When they are on set, I want them to know my full attention is on them.

Q - Do you work alongside the production designer and costume designer to sort out problems?

Judy - When we are filming, my boss is the director, though I work most closely with the actors. I believe hiccups should be sorted out in pre production. You don't want to do things that can upset an actors train of thought, and once we start filming, I'm very loyal to the actor because he is having to put the goods on the table and create. There are always re-writes, so one needs to go with the flow, and have lateral thinking.

Q - Are things like spectacles part of the make up artists remit?

Judy - I work in conjunction with costume or stand by props who would normally supply spectacles, but it is negotiable. I carry a large supply of beards, mustaches, wigs etc.

Q - Does make-up include bruises and cuts?

Judy - Yes, although as it becomes more complex, it starts to move toward a special make-up effect. I regularly deal with cuts, noses, ears and of course wigs and beards etc., which takes time to research and get right, and you will need to factor that in.

Q - Do you have contact with the script supervisor?

Judy - Yes. I do my own script breakdown and make sure I get the information from the script supervisor about the day breakdowns. I'll read it, and sometimes it's very straightforward to work out. Other times the director may say *'the next scene is a little while later'* - and a little while later in the story may mean two hours, two weeks, two months, two years - of course I must know exactly when that scene takes place, and my breakdown will tell me that.

Q - Do you take lots of continuity stills?

Judy - If you're on low budget, Polaroid stock/digital supplies may cut severely into the budget. However you do need pictures for continuity. I often do a sketch.

Q - What can be done to speed up the process of make up?

Judy - I like to get a shooting schedule before shooting starts. I co-ordinate with the AD team with actors call times and meet up with actors, or at least communicate with them before. And I am always early!

Q - After the film has wrapped completely, are you called back?

Judy - Yes. You have to be prepared for that.

Q - How do you do old age make up?

Judy - First I should be involved in the casting as people 'age' differently. It's easy to over use prosthetic pieces in such a way that it destroys the look of the actor and it looks too much like a mask. People tend to forget about contrast and think of pretty colors and make the face look ordinary, instead of remembering light and shade.

Q - Do you do hair as well?

Judy - Yes, if there's enough time for me to do it. I enjoy working with wigs, beards, mustaches, gents hair. Hair coloring and perming I don't get involved with as you need a salon for that. I should have an assistant to help with hair.

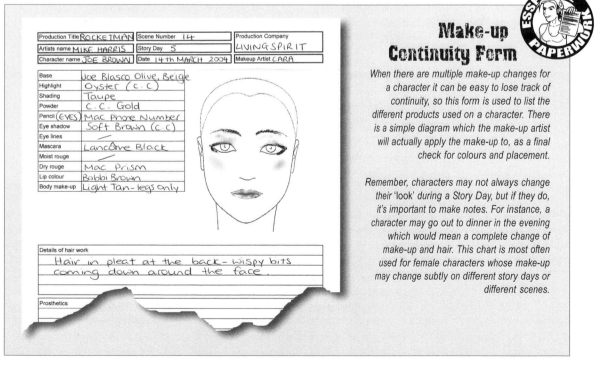

Make-up Continuity Form

When there are multiple make-up changes for a character it can be easy to lose track of continuity, so this form is used to list the different products used on a character. There is a simple diagram which the make-up artist will actually apply the make-up to, as a final check for colours and placement.

Remember, characters may not always change their 'look' during a Story Day, but if they do, it's important to make notes. For instance, a character may go out to dinner in the evening which would mean a complete change of make-up and hair. This chart is most often used for female characters whose make-up may change subtly on different story days or different scenes.

Q - What tricks are used to keep actors fresh in the heat?

Judy - It's all about making sure they don't get sunburnt, keeping them in the shade, using umbrellas, dressing them in cool clothes, and giving them the right food and drink. I get the actors onto various foods that mosquitoes hate, garlic for instance. Mosquitoes go to the pulse points (wrists, ankles). Make sure that no products have any perfume on them, and put citronella or tea tree lotions on the body. You need to keep the skin in good condition and that means getting the make up off at the end of the day, and giving the person a deep cleanse.

Q - How does one go about finding a make up artist?

Judy - Phone the make up union to see who's available. There are also non union make up artists and make up artists with agents.

Make Up & Hair

The Make up artist is just that - an artist. Likewise a hair stylist has style. It takes special skills and experience to know how to apply cosmetics and sculpt hair for film. If you put this in the hands of amateurs, what may look okay for a Saturday night out on the town will look garish on a 40 foot screen.

1. Often on low budget movies, the Make up designer and Hairstylist are the same person. If you can separate the two, do so, because one doesn't necessarily have the skills of the other.

2. Don't assume your make up artist can do all make up, such as special make - blood, cuts, bruises, prosthetics etc., Ask what they can do before you hire them.

3. If working on a low budget, ask your hair stylist or make up artist to be creative with the actor's natural hair to avoid unnecessary wigs or facial hair.

4. Some cosmetic companies will offer free or discounted make up in exchange for a mention in the film itself. Get your product placement person on this ASAP.

5. If dealing with gore, special make up or complicated wigs, it's a good idea to do camera and make up tests. What you might consider looks realistic in real life can look really fake on screen and vice versa.

6. Remember that make up is where your actors start their day. If they're made up in a relaxing fashion, then will leave feeling good and ready for their shots.

7. Your make up artist can keep an eye on the actor's deeper feelings and fears and report back to the producer if they are concerned about the shoot in anyway.

8. Make sure you have enough time allotted for your actors before they go on set. Depending on the complexity of the make up this could take anywhere from 15 minutes to several hours.

9. Make sure that the hairstyle is not too 'over the top' for each character. You don't want your hairstylist trying out a new design if it's for a working class mom living in a housing project.

10. Consider hiring extra help on days when you have a lot of extras or principals in a scene. It may save you considerable time.

11. Make sure your actors remove their make up each day and their skin cleansed. You don't want to be giving them acne.

12. Make sure to have enough room for your make up and hair departments to work freely.

13. Schedule time during prep for your make up and hair people to meet the actors to discuss any issues or ideas.

14. Make sure the 1st AD has make up and hair check for imperfections just prior to the first take, and also to keep an eye on sweating and degradation in the make up under the hot lights.

15. Polaroids or digital photos of the actors should be taken from all angles at the end of each shot to ensure continuity.

16. The make up department will create a character breakdown for make up notes, a make up story order (i.e. how many changes there will be not just from day to day but within each day), their own continuity sheets which they will use throughout the shoot.

Make Up Continuity

As with the Costume department, make-up will crunch their way through a terrifying number of Polaroid photos. Possibly even more than the Costume department, as continuity is so important, actresses playing with their hair being a prime example. These photos will also be very useful if you work your way through several make-up artists during your shoot (as is often the case) as many pros will give you a few days or even a week for free, but not six weeks!

These Polaroids will be filed alongside the continuity notes on a folder, or sometimes they will be stuck into the screenplay on the blank side of the script page (the scene from which it is taken then faces the Polaroid). Notes will be made on the actual photo about scene numbers and characters as well as information that may not be clear on the picture (such as sweat etc.)The make-up artists may also take several shots, from the front, side and even back, as hair continuity is always a potential problem.

It may seem like a good idea to ask both Make-up and Costume departments to share a single camera, but this regularly causes problems. Considering how cheap the cameras are (and you can always ask around to borrow one), you should get a second one.

Q - Do the unions allow you to work on non union films?

Judy - If it's a non union production, I tell the union I'm working on it, and so far, there hasn't been a problem.

Q - What are the things a director can do to make your job easier?

Judy - Let make up know what they want. Also, give the make up artist time in his schedule so the make up artist can 'input', or listen to what the director wants, and come back with research, suggestions and to work as a team.

Q - What common mistakes have you come across with new filmmakers?

Judy - The most common mistake is not using everyone's talent. Also, time keeping. Any hold up is time not shooting film. Thinking ahead too. I've had a writer give me a script who said, 'can you read it and give me any information that might reduce the cost from your point of view'. That's smart. There's no life after the daily wrap when you're on a film, so everything else needs to go on hold when you are shooting. You can pace yourself on commercials, but not films as they take up all your time. I have to believe in the film script so the actors know I'm behind what they're doing. There have been a couple of films that I didn't want to do but did them for money, which was much harder.

Q - What advice would you give new filmmakers?

Judy - Love your work. However long you've been in the business, when you stop learning something new each day, it's worth re-thinking what you are doing. Luck is important in life, but more important is taking advantage of those lucky opportunities when they arise. Working on a film is like being in an orchestra. Depending on what is taking place, sometimes certain instruments have a solo, and when it's your solo you need to be ready. The conductor is the person you have to keep an eye on and that is the director.

PRODUCTION

Annie Wells
Script Supervisor

Q - What is your job?

Annie - I am a script supervisor. I break down the script for the ADs to generate the shooting schedule. I also take that breakdown to wardrobe, hair and make up for their continuity. Then I break the script into eighths (of a page) for the producers. In pre-production I note all the props, the changes, when there's a gun shot or someone gets injured for instance, so that when the shoot starts I'm aware of which scene the actor needs bruises for. This also means that I can indicate the age of the bruising.

Q - When are you hired?

Annie - Two weeks before shooting, by the director. In that time, I break down the script and go over it with him to see if he sees it the way I do. Then I go over it with the art department, hair, make-up, costume and props because it affects everybody.

Q - Do you time the script?

Annie - I do, although it is kind of arbitrary. You can give basic timings, but you can only guess when the director may choose to do a pan, or use a dolly or crane to get into the shot, which is not in the script. You have an idea how long it would take someone to walk down a street on film, and it won't be for five minutes, that never happens. You say to yourself, *'that's about a 15 second shot'*. From experience and shooting movies, you get an idea of how long a movie will be on screen.

Q - Does the 'one page equals one minute' rule generally work?

Annie - Yes. Every time I add it up it comes out as a minute a page. Sometimes a script says 124 pages, and I say 122 minutes.

Q - Do you have to watch for actors' ad libbing?

Annie - I try and get it. Sometimes it's impossible. I ask the director if they want the actors to keep to the script. Dialogue changes are the hardest thing to keep track of. Actors can change the sense of a script.

Q - Do you note the continuity for shots?

Annie - Yes. The continuity is one aspect. Each department should be a responsible for their own continuity, but the script supervisor oversees it all. Make-up would work out how the hair is going to be, and costume would work out when they are going to put their jacket on or not for instance. When shooting starts, the script supervisor oversees that and has a constant dialogue with those departments. They'll let you know if something changes. It is the same level of detail whether I am on location or in a studio.

The other part of the script supervisor's job is the action. I have to watch that the actor picks up the drink with the same hand, sits down on the same chair. That's why dialogue is important, because if they say, *'today, he picks up the cup'*, you remember it's today. In one take they may say *'hello'* with their hand in one position and it's different in the next shot. You then would have to decide which you want to do when you go to cut.

Q - Do you give the editor all your continuity notes?

Annie - No. The editor doesn't care about the continuity notes. I keep two scripts, one for me with all my notes, and another one for the editor. The editor only wants to know whether they were wide shots, close up or medium shots. I line the script for the editor to show which take the director liked. I make a straight line if the dialogue or action is on film and a wiggly line if it's not, for example when lines are being said by someone who is not in shot.

Q - How many scripts do you do that with?

Annie - I do it with the script I'm working on while we're shooting and then for the editor I'll make it neat.

Q - How do you separate it?

Annie - You don't do the takes. You do the lines per setup. When it's scene five of the master - the wide shot - is called '5' for instance. Then you do a close up of one person in the same scene, which would be '5a'. A close up of another would then be '5b'. Each letter gets a line. '5' is the master you made. So on the side of the script, (called the facing page) you write down what the shot was. That's for the editor. The continuity is the other departments.

Production needs various details from me, such as how much was shot, how many minutes, what time was the production report - what time was lunch? What time did you call 'roll'? How much is left to be shot? Did we shoot everything on the call sheet?

Q - Does the production send the sheets on to the studio?

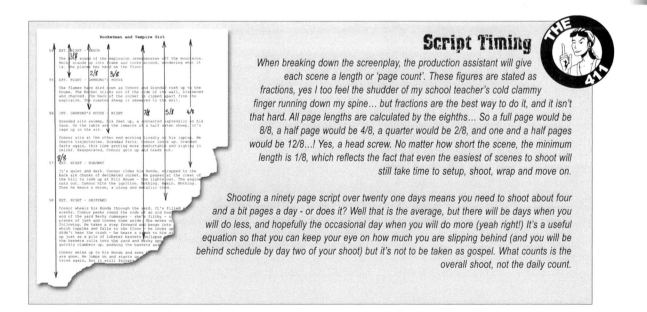

Script Timing

When breaking down the screenplay, the production assistant will give each scene a length or 'page count'. These figures are stated as fractions, yes I too feel the shudder of my school teacher's cold clammy finger running down my spine... but fractions are the best way to do it, and it isn't that hard. All page lengths are calculated by the eighths... So a full page would be 8/8, a half page would be 4/8, a quarter would be 2/8, and one and a half pages would be 12/8...! Yes, a head screw. No matter how short the scene, the minimum length is 1/8, which reflects the fact that even the easiest of scenes to shoot will still take time to setup, shoot, wrap and move on.

Shooting a ninety page script over twenty one days means you need to shoot about four and a bit pages a day - or does it? Well that is the average, but there will be days when you will do less, and hopefully the occasional day when you will do more (yeah right!) It's a useful equation so that you can keep your eye on how much you are slipping behind (and you will be behind schedule by day two of your shoot) but it's not to be taken as gospel. What counts is the overall shoot, not the daily count.

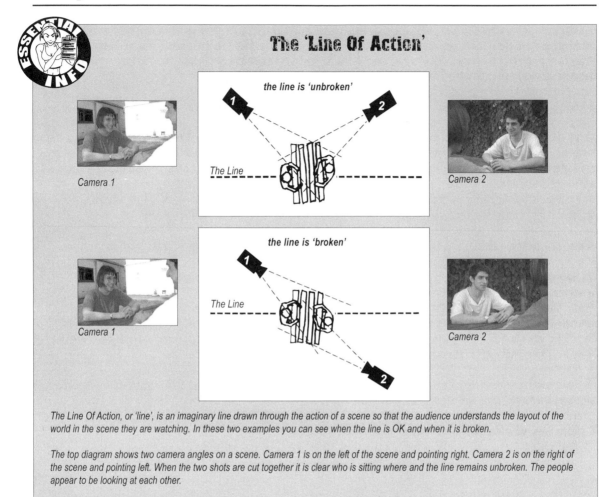

The 'Line Of Action'

Camera 1

the line is 'unbroken'

The Line

Camera 2

Camera 1

the line is 'broken'

The Line

Camera 2

The Line Of Action, or 'line', is an imaginary line drawn through the action of a scene so that the audience understands the layout of the world in the scene they are watching. In these two examples you can see when the line is OK and when it is broken.

The top diagram shows two camera angles on a scene. Camera 1 is on the left of the scene and pointing right. Camera 2 is on the right of the scene and pointing left. When the two shots are cut together it is clear who is sitting where and the line remains unbroken. The people appear to be looking at each other.

The lower diagram shows the same scene with cameras on the left and right, but this time, camera 2 has moved across the line of action. Note how the two resulting shots show the characters sitting on the right of frame and looking left. Cutting these two shots together will jar. In this instance the line is 'broken'. The people don't appear to be looking at each other.

The 'line' is a very simple concept but desperately easy to break. If in doubt, make short video movies and practice by actively breaking the line and examining just how awkward the shots will look when cut.

Annie - They put my information into the main report that goes to the studio every day. They sometimes send them my reports as they say how many set ups were used, if the day was completed, when the camera wrapped. Their report is mostly mine with camera (how many rolls of film they shot) and sound.

Q - Do you take Polaroids?

Annie - I don't like to rely on somebody else, so I take my own digitals. Every department takes their own. If I don't get a picture, I'll go to hair and make up and say, *'do you have a picture of so and so'*, but I try and get a picture of everything I know I'll need.

Q - When do you take those pictures?

Annie - I have to look at the situation and work out when the best time is. Sometimes hair and make up don't get a picture and they'll ask if I did. A lot of actors don't want to sit still for a picture, so you get it while they are talking to someone. Others are wonderful, such as Julia Roberts, who respects everyone else's craft more than any other actor I know, knows that we need pictures. If I can't get pictures, I'll make notes of what they are wearing in my script.

Q - Is eyeline something you have to be aware of?

Annie - Yes, although good DP's are very good with eyelines, we now have a lot of first time directors who don't understand it. I always note which way the actor is looking, camera right or camera left. Crossing the line is okay if it is deliberate and if you know where the cut is going to come. The script supervisor, DP and the cameraman will often get into a discussion about it, but it is the script supervisor that notes the eyeline. In the facing page, you will put 'medium shot, Bill looks camera left'. You may need to shoot it so they could be looking camera left and camera right, depending where you want to cut, which means you have two masters. So you'll ask *'which master are you going to match to?'* and sometimes they're not sure so they do both.

Q - Do you have to note down where the camera is?

Annie - No, but I do note the lens, in case of pick-ups. The script supervisor's script is the bible. It has every shot, every take and the more information you can put down there, the better it is for you. You have no idea how many questions you are asked during the day.

When I break down the script, I number the days so when the camera team asks, *'is this day 4?'* I check my notes. I also do a chart of all the characters so I know what scenes they are in. The actors will ask what scenes they were in last, which is very useful as I can give them a quick rundown of what happened previously in their character's story. *Solaris* was a complicated script

Script Revisions - The Rainbow Effect

When production starts, the script continues to change due to rewrites, deleted scenes, production issues, actors requesting new dialogue etc. In order to keep track of the changes from draft to draft, a paper color coding system is used, which states where the editing occurred and on what date. Only the changed pages are printed, each revision onto a specific colored paper, before they are slipped into the script - creating a rainbow effect. The old pages are removed, but should be saved for reference and legal reasons. The color order can be altered depending on preference or paper availability, but here is the most common way it is done. Find a good paper supplier now to avoid buying in a panic at the last minute.

White (the original shooting script), Blue, Pink, Yellow, Green, Goldenrod, Buff, Cherry, Salmon... The colors then restart and are referred to as Double white, Double Blue, Double Pink, etc.

Page Count Timing Sheet

Scene No.	Length (mins)	Length (pages)	Description
			Rocketman - Timing Sheet Sheet 2 of 9
22	0' 15"	1/8	Connor rides up Hill House driveway
23	0' 40"	4/8	Connor and Davey talk outside house
24	DEL	DEL	DELETED SCENE
25	0' 30"	5/8	Becky and Jospeh argue about going out
26	3' 00"	12/8	Connor and Becky meet on the fire escape
27	0' 15"	1/8	Connor and Becky ride away on bike
28	0' 15"	1/8	Connor and Becky approach barn on bike
29	1' 15"	4/8	er and Becky enter the barn and talk abou

The old industry convention of a page of screenplay equals a minute of screen time does work as an average, but some pages can run to a couple of minutes on screen, where others can be very quick, well under a minute. When doing the schedule, the AD will have timed the script and created a report like this one, detailing the page lengths and associated estimated timings for each scene. This will help better estimate how long will be needed for each scene during the shoot.

full of flashbacks and flash-forwards, so breaking it down was very complicated. I color coded it on my computer so I could look at it quickly. I could see one block is a flashback. I find breakdowns invaluable - to really know the script and the characters, as once you start shooting you have to concentrate on the action and the editing.

I just finished a pilot where there was a scene and everybody was rushing and not thinking. An actor walked out the room, with this teddy bear in his hand, which he has taken out of his case. I said, 'wait a minute, a dog tears up the bear in the room when he's gone'. Everyone said, 'oh yes'. Even the actor forgot. You have to be organized. You have to devise your own system of organization. I have a grid with the characters crossed with every scene they are in. I'll color code every scene where a character is injured, until it would have gone so I can see it quickly.

When it comes to actors not matching shots, I will always say to the director, *'do you want me to go in and tell them if they're not matching?'* and sometimes they'll say yes. Other times, directors will say, *'no, tell me and I'll tell them'*. Generally, the director will want to be told first as it's a control issue. Some actors are not good at matching and if you go in and tell them, you upset them. You tell the director and suggest he has a close up in case it doesn't work - we call it 'the clock on the wall.

Q - Do the directors also keep an eye out for this stuff?

Annie - A lot of directors don't. We have a lot of actors directing first time, so I have to get to know the AD and production designer. A DP might be trying to do a two shot set up in a car and a mirror is in the way, so he'll take it off as it looks ugly in the shot. I have to check how much that mirror has been seen previously and then a decision has to be made.

Q - What happens on films when the studio doesn't think that the director has shot enough coverage?

Annie - It depends on the power of the director, but they will often meddle more with the young, first time directors. Studios keep repeating what has worked, so it's hard to be creative and take chances, especially in TV. I tell the director, *'it's your vision. It's okay to listen to other people's ideas, because it might help'* but the director should keep his vision. Once everybody starts saying, *'let's do this, let's do that'* it's generally a disaster as the essence of the film gets lost.

Q - What common mistakes do you come across with new filmmakers?

Annie - Eyelines, letting the actor change the dialogue too much, and often, they don't understand the editing process. They may spend too much time on a master which may be used for a cross, when the meat of the scene is in the close up. Some directors shoot scenes three different ways as they don't know how they want the scene to go.

Story Days

Story Days are the number of days that your script (film) encompasses on screen. It could either be a matter of 1 Story Day as in Training Day, 7 Story Days as in Seven Days and Seven Nights, or over a period of 25 years (although only visiting particular days out of those 25 years) as in Ghandi. A story day is indicated by an obvious change of time in the storyline, or by literally moving on to the next day. Your department heads need to know the story days, but in particular, costume and make up. It's essential that your Story Days are calculated when breaking down the script for scheduling as, with most shoots, you will be shooting out of sequence. Therefore, if in an action movie there's a big fight scene halfway in the film, which results in your lead actor having a big noticeable scar for the rest of the movie, it's important that you don't forget the scar. In this case, the Story Day (that will now be on breakdown sheets and continuity sheets) will notify your make up department to what condition your lead actor is in so that mistakes are not made. On a low budget movie, it's advisable to minimize your story days, so that your actors are not spending time changing costumes and wasting valuable production shooting time.

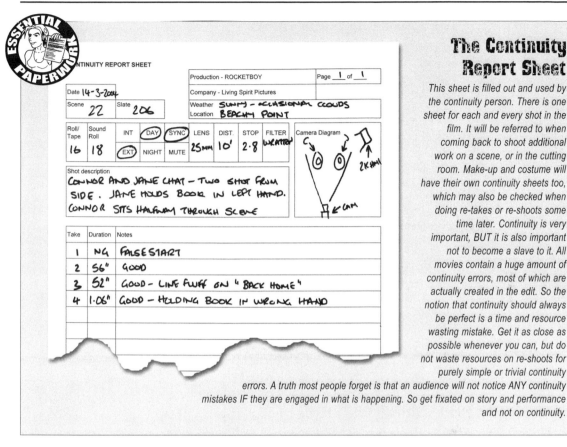

ESSENTIAL PAPERWORK

CONTINUITY REPORT SHEET

Production - ROCKETBOY		Page __1__ of __1__
Company - Living Spirit Pictures		

Date 14-3-2004

Scene 22   Slate 206

Weather SUNNY - OCCASIONAL CLOUDS
Location BEACHY POINT

Roll/ Tape	Sound Roll	INT	(DAY)	(SYNC)	LENS	DIST.	STOP	FILTER	Camera Diagram
16	18	(EXT)	NIGHT	MUTE	25mm	10'	2·8	WRATTEN	2K HMI, CAM

Shot description
CONNOR AND JANE CHAT - TWO SHOT FROM
SIDE. JANE HOLDS BOOK IN LEFT HAND.
CONNOR SITS HALFWAY THROUGH SCENE

Take	Duration	Notes
1	NG	FALSE START
2	56"	GOOD
3	52"	GOOD - LINE FLUFF ON "BACK HOME"
4	1.06"	GOOD - HOLDING BOOK IN WRONG HAND

The Continuity Report Sheet

This sheet is filled out and used by the continuity person. There is one sheet for each and every shot in the film. It will be referred to when coming back to shoot additional work on a scene, or in the cutting room. Make-up and costume will have their own continuity sheets too, which may also be checked when doing re-takes or re-shoots some time later. Continuity is very important, BUT it is also important not to become a slave to it. All movies contain a huge amount of continuity errors, most of which are actually created in the edit. So the notion that continuity should always be perfect is a time and resource wasting mistake. Get it as close as possible whenever you can, but do not waste resources on re-shoots for purely simple or trivial continuity errors. A truth most people forget is that an audience will not notice ANY continuity mistakes IF they are engaged in what is happening. So get fixated on story and performance and not on continuity.

Q - What advice would you offer new filmmakers?

Annie - Be flexible. No situation is ever the same. Every film is different. So you can't go in and say *'this is the way I do it'*. I have to look at the situation, get to know the director and get to know his needs and wants and the actors and you have to work accordingly. If you don't, you'll have a miserable time. I never throw myself at an actor, as it is easy to turn them off and then they'll never help you. There are actors that make a script supervisor's life hell. So for the first week you gauge the situation and change accordingly.

Q - Is this because the actor doesn't want to be bothered?

Annie - It's usually because they are in character and don't want to be distracted. The first time I worked with Denzel Washington I sensed that in him, so I backed right off. He knew what I was doing and in the third week he approached me. Then on his last movie, he asked me to work with him. A lot of people say he's difficult, but he's not. You just need to know how to work with them. Be low key until you get to know how everything works.

Julie Weinhouse
Hero Product Placement Inc.

PLACE THAT PRODUCT

Q - What do you need from a producer to see if their film is suitable for any of your clients?

Julie - We'd require a copy of the script and basic information like cast, distributor, director, start date, budget, a synopsis and a wish list (what the production company wants).

Q - What does the term 'hero' mean when referring to product placement?

Julie - Hero is an industry term, which refers to a featured prop. For example, the featured watch of the lead actor is a 'hero watch' whether it performs a heroic stunt or not.

Q - How many filmmakers have financed a large chunk of their movie through product placement?

Julie - It's a myth that you can get your film funded though product placement. However you could possibly receive some product for free and therefore wouldn't have to pay a weekly loan on that particular product, but this isn't going to heavily reduce your budget.

Q - How much could be available through product placement?

Julie - It depends. If your budget is under $5m, some agencies won't do anything with you. We handled *Monster's Ball*, which was around $5m, but it had Halle Berry in it and so we had a clear commercial placement within that. If you have a low budget with no distributor and an unknown cast, you're not going to receive a lot of support because it's not known whether your film will ever see the light of day. We have to deliver to our clients. If I deliver a bunch of indies that don't have distributors, I'm not going to have that client anymore.

Q - What kind of exposure do companies ask you for?

Julie - Some companies want blatant exposure. I strive for natural exposure, which would be a minimum number of seconds but it is something that shows up as scripted in the final theatrical release of the film. If it's a 'nothing' item such as a background cereal packet, I'm hoping that they use it and try and work it into the shot. I dislike seeing really obvious product placement in films. Product needs to be integrated. When you shoot your film you're trying to recreate a reality. What I look for is a positive association of that brand within a context. However all depends on the amount of product that we're offering or if we're paying a fee and discussing a promotion.

Q - If something is gratuitous, are there regulations?

Julie - TV has heavy regulations but with film there are none. If your objective is to make a film that you're going to distribute through video or TV, you should realize that if Coke is featured prominently, it's not likely that the broadcaster who's bought the product, will get Pepsi to pay the thirty second slot. Pilots generally avoid putting any logo brands in, so that when they show it to the big ad agencies that spend millions of dollars, they won't see a competitive brand.

Q - Can companies such as Ryder Truck Rental give you a free truck if you feature them?

Julie - Definitely. That's referred to as barter. This also works if you feature a specific hotel in your film (where nothing inappropriate happens). You show the exterior of the façade and in exchange you want the cast and crew to stay at that hotel. A hotel can make their own decision on what they can or can't give away based on the content of the film, the distribution and the talent along with their own factors - what time of year is it? How many people are they putting up? How much revenue would they lose? You can negotiate and suggest a lower rent or ask *'If I rent ten rooms, will you give me the eleventh free?'* This will always be more successful than if you ask for 100% for free.

Q - Can you verbally name a brand?

Julie - If it's not integral to the script and you can't afford an attorney to look at it, just modify it (McBurgers for instance). If you're trying to make the dialogue glib, be more creative or chance it. If you're stating a fact, it is your right and freedom of speech to do so.

Q - How important is it to credit sponsors?

Julie - To some companies end credits matter, and to some they don't. However, it's a nice thank you.

Q - What are the common mistakes that you come across?

E.R.M.A -
Entertainment Resources & Marketing Assoc.
www.erma.org

If you wish to do some product placement in your film to reduce negative cost or feed your crew, E.R.M.A. can help you get on the right path. Their website provides lists of agencies that handle product placement and their respective specialties (airlines, soft drinks, etc.). When looking for an agency E.R.M.A. suggests that you...

1. Determine what kind of service you require, full or partial. That will help determine which agency you hire.

2. Contact as many agencies as possible and ask questions about what they do.

3. Find out who their clients are and talk to them about their experiences with the company.

4. Visit the company and meet the employees to see if you like them.

5. Get a credit report on the company and check to see if they have any litigation against them.

6. Try to find companies that want a long-term relationship over many films. Get a written contract with the agency for a specific number of placements during a defined time period. Refunds for poor performance should be included.

7. Get a monthly written status report on your project from the agency.

8. Do not pay the full retainer fee in advance. Get on a payment schedule (quarterly is most common).

PRODUCTION

Julie - I've received script pages where it looks as though something has been covered up. Being deceptive is bad. Secondly, don't rely on product placement for helping you fund your movie.

Q - What advice would you give?

Julie - Be charming, respectful and realistic and don't bully or pressure people. Give them as much material as possible, like the synopsis and your expectations. Get pictures taken of the product in the film and keep people up to date. If you're asking for a favor, think about what is the best way for you to obtain your objective.

Mic Rogers
Stunt Co-ordinator

STUNTS AND ACTION

Q - What is the job of the stunt coordinator?

Mic - My job is to choreograph the stunt sequences and give production a budget for all the action in the story. Independent films often think they can't afford a stunt coordinator but it can be cheaper than you might expect and good value for the money.

Q - Do you deal with hiring the other stunt guys?

Mic - Absolutely. The stunt coordinator is the person who says *'This guy is a good double for this actor'* and *'You need three stunt people to be cops'*. I make sure production has the information to make their deals and that wardrobe, hair and makeup are all aware of their sizes, hair colors, etc.

Q - What is the best way to find the best stunt coordinator?

Mic - Look at a film you're trying to emulate and call their stunt coordinator. Ask around who the best stunt guys are? Most people will give you a name. You have to be careful though. Just because a guy has a lot of credits, it may only be because he worked for a day on each show. I'm lucky to get a credit a year because I work on one picture for seven months. The number of credits don't necessarily equal talent. Here's what you can do if you call me and decide you can't afford me? Take my suggestions seriously. I'll give you the names of three people who can do your job. Send them the script and they'll read it. You need to get together the money they should get, but it's worth your effort because they'll be capable people, hungry for the credit. Every guy who has taken this advice has rung me and said *'I'm so grateful you introduced me to that guy'*. I know young stunt coordinators who now have relationships with young producer/directors and they are going to continue down the road together.

Q - What basic preparations does a filmmaker need to make for stunts?

Mic - Take the time to get someone to work on the action as there are ways to get around the money problems. Unfortunately, filmmakers tend to prep on the day with the stunt guys.

Q - How early on do you like to be approached?

Mic - As soon as the director is hired, and he gets his executive staff together. Even if the script has one car chase in it, a director should be asking the question, 'how are we going to do it?

Q - What are the most common stunts for low budget films?

Mic - Car chases, flights, crashes through windows, car hits - it's common stuff in any picture. The low budget stunts are generally the ones that are done badly as they don't want to spend any money on them.

Q - Can a stunt coordinator advise as to the best ways to achieve the drama in the script?

Mic - Yes, a good one can. Some directors say I want to bring the car around the corner and jump it and land it in this backyard down the hill and round the corner all in one take. But that's not going to look any good. No one camera can get all the action. You're going to have multiple cameras on it, which means you're going to edit it. Big stunts come in editing, the drama is created in the editing room. A good stunt coordinator knows about editing and how the action should be cut together for maximum effect. Some stunt guys aren't smart. They just want to fall down and pick up a check. There are also guys who are overly 'I'll teach you and I'll set the cameras' and they want to direct your show for you! There's a fine line. A good coordinator will tell you the ways to achieve what you want and then step back and let the director do his job.

Q - Are there any camera techniques that enhance the look of the stunts?

Mic - Sure. A good example is picture-fighting, where no one actually hits anyone. It's all camera angles. Good angles like in *The Fast and The Furious* make the car turnover near the end of the picture look great. If the camera is over there and I can't see the shot in my head, I'm in the wrong business. You need a coordinator who can do that.

Q - Have you got any ways of cheating stunts to keep the budget down?

Mic - Yes. Typically, a 100 foot high fall will cost around $20k in today's market. Throw a good $500 dummy out the window and we'll do our best to make it look good. With a car crash, you can have a car coming down the street, cut inside to a POV, a ball bounces across the road, back to the panicked driver, the swerve, cut around the corner to your wrecked car. So much goes into production in Hollywood right now that is not being planned. Stuff isn't even written. Still, I haven't been on a show yet where they've shot the shooting script.

Q - Is that because of constant rewrites?

Mic - Yes. There's all these people handing notes down the chain. The director gets tapped on the shoulder and it's the studio boss who says *'we don't think scene 82 is working'*. The director says but we've already built the sets and the boss says, *'instead of a bar room fight, we think it should be a tea room scene'*, and then everyone down the line, art department, stunts, wardrobe, has to start scrambling and you lose time and money. I shot stuff on *Charlie's Angels: Full Throttle* and three days later we'd get script revisions for those scenes. When I'd bring it up that we'd already done the sequence, I'd be told It's okay, disregard those notes. The more you can plan in advance, the more money you'll save. And if you've got good people, you can still be flexible creatively on the day.

Q - Does it work out worse to film in this way?

Mic - Not always. Some films, like the *Lethal Weapon* series, were very organic. You've got Mel Gibson and Danny Glover and their action derives straight from their characters. If say, something wasn't working I could ask if it really did anything for Rigg's character? Do we really need this fight? Shall we jump to something else and Dick (Donner, the director) might say *'yeah, you're right and we'd throw out the schedule and put the 20 guys from the scene in the big fight at the end'*.

Stunts

Stunt performers are part of SAG, so most of the rules that apply to actors apply to them as well.

There are a few ways to find stunt performers. You can contact SAG, you can contact filmmakers who used stunt people in the past to get a recommendation, or you can contact a stunt person directly and see if they are up for the job. The bigger names may not do your low budget film, but they will almost always refer you to someone who will. The basic minimum SAG pay for stunt performers is $2,525 per week. However, if your stunt person is also coordinating or second unit directing, then they will negotiate for higher rates. You will also need to purchase more insurance if you have a lot of stunts. This only covers the rate of pay for the stunt performer but there will also be a raise for each stunt adjustment (stunt) that you require your stunt performer to do.

In addition to SAG, check out:
www.stuntmen.com
www.stuntwomen.com
www.v10stunts.com

Q - How many cameras would you recommend for a simple action sequence?

Mic - It depends on how simple. Without being facetious, I'd say as many as you can get. On *The Fast and The Furious*, we had eight cameras on the big car turnover. The more you get on it, the less takes you have to do. It's the second time that people get hurt. Get it right on the first take to minimize risk.

Q - Is it possible to achieve really good stunts on a low budget movie?

Mic - Sure, you just can't spend any money on wardrobe! If the action is the centerpiece of your movie, be on it early and spend the dough. You can carve the budgets of other departments. If you're shooting a musical, you don't cheap out on the music and musicians. Same with action - spend the money on what's really important.

Q - Do actors tend to do a lot of their own stunts on a low budget films?

Mic - Actors on low budget pictures often feel this is their big chance and that they can't say no to anything they're asked to do. But you can't expect an actor to drive fast through city streets just because he or she has a driver's license. There's a way to do it , not just for impact but for safety.

Q - Are there any stunts that filmmakers don't regard as stunts?

Mic - Sure. Some of them say, *'the guy's only falling over a table'*. Well sure, but how big is the table? Is it glass? Is it curvey or sharp? How old is this person? How far are they falling? How are they going down? Little things like that slip through and people get hurt, and then you get sued. Or they bang themselves up and think *'it's no big deal'*, but two years later, the actor has a bad elbow or wrist and their quality of life is affected, which could have been prevented if someone had just spent a little bit of time and money. A stunt coordinator can work with your actors; lots of things can be actor action. It's our job to know what the actor can or should do and where you'll need a stunt double.

Q - What stunts are a particular problem?

Mic - The problem is usually the expense. Fire stuff, water stuff, finding special doubles for children all come to mind.

Q - Are there any stunts that take a lot longer to prepare?

Mic - Yes. High falls and car wrecks. If you're going to do a high fall, you have to consider where they are falling from. Is there a place to put a catcher? Do you want to do a high fall or a descender? If you do a descender, you need a special effects rig. That means you need a special effects guy. Is he qualified? Plus there is testing involved, actor location, stunt adjustments. With car wrecks, you have to prep the cars, cages and location.

Q - How long can the preparation take for stunt sequences?

Mic - It can take months, writing it, getting approvals, budgeting it, getting approvals, finding locations, getting everyone to agree on it, getting approvals, designing sets, getting approvals, building sets, building rigs, finding specialists, rigging, rehearsing and on and on. Or it can be as simple as a guy saying *'I want a car chase'* and me suggesting three cars, this crash, this many guys, this much money. Done. I've seen guys do deals that easily. You're out of the office in twenty minutes and preparing.

Q - Does it become more complicated on a bigger picture?

Mic - Sometimes. The bigger, the more expensive the picture, and the more expensive the stunts can be.

Stunts and Pyrotechnics

Although stuntmen and SPFX guys may seem a bit cavalier about their craft, rest assured they are fully aware of how easily their work can turn fatal. Many have migrated to stunt work from other dangerous professions, such as Navy Seals, and they know exactly how to avoid or minimize injury, while still making the effect look like the real thing.

1. Approach a stunt coordinator as soon as you can so that they have the maximum amount of time to come up with ideas for your stunts or SPFX, and more importantly, enough time to figure out the safest way to do them.

2. To find a stunt coordinator, ask other filmmakers for recommendations and then call those people to talk about your film. Call the biggest people in the field, they might not do it, but they will turn you over to a respected colleague who will. Also, there are a few stunt person agencies you can solicit as well.

3. Stunts are dangerous. Don't push a stuntman to do his job quicker, or with less safety equipment. Remember, they are putting their life on the line for you.

4. Stunts aren't as expensive as you may think. A good stunt can make the film look like it cost much more than it actually did.

5. If a stuntman or pyrotechnician is eager or very willing to reduce safety standards, be wary. They may not be fully qualified and therefore a liability. Don't mess, get a qualified person to do the job.

6. Be careful with blank firing weapons. Metal fragments can become stuck in the barrel of the gun (from previous firings because someone did not check or clean it properly). The power of firing a blank round is more than enough to shoot this object at a deadly speed. The last thing anyone wants is a repeat of the Brandon Lee tragedy on the set of The Crow.

7. Try and organize all your stunts into one shooting block. This will minimize time wastage by dedicating the production to stunts and effects during this period.

8. There are many books on the subject of homemade (safe) effects and cheats, some of which are excellent, safe and could save you lots of money. For example, to simulate a helicopter flying over at dusk can be achieved by panning a bright light over the set and mixing the sound effect over it.

9. Sound is a major consideration with stunts and effects. A good 'whack' sound in a fist fight can hide a dodgy stunt. Track lay these sequences with extra care and attention.

10. Digital effects are now very cost effective, and techniques such as wire removal for high falls may well be within your budget. Ask for a quote.

11. For large stunts, you will have to provide a fire engine and paramedics on the scene. You will need costly stunt insurance as well.

12. Actors are comforted when a stuntman is around for potentially dangerous scenes. It says to them that they are protected, that you take their safety seriously, and that you are a professional. If the situation is relatively low impact and merely involves a degree of physical acting, try a trainee stuntman to lend a hand on set.

13. Always ask for advice. Stuntmen and pyro technicians know many cheap ways to achieve what may seem impossible to you as a new filmmaker.

14. Before embarking on an expensive and time consuming stunt or effect, ask yourself if you could actually cut away from it or cut out of the scene, just as it is about to happen. For instance, see the lead up to a car crash, then hear the impact over a shot of the face of a grieving relative at the funeral. It's a lot cheaper if you don't have to film it, but if you do go down this route, make sure it's done cleverly and that you're not cheating and disappointing your audience out of something they might expect.

15. If you get the stunt right the first time, DO NOT go for a second take. Two reasons. You will be undermining your stunt co-ordinator's authority and you will be unnecessarily exposing them to additional risk. The latter is what happened to Harry O'Connor, a master stuntman in the filming of XXX where he died repeating a stunt.

Q - If a filmmaker has an action film, do you help them out and find the appropriate crew?

Mic - Every coordinator will know who the safe effects guys are, who the great horse wranglers are, who's a good armorer.

Q - Do the armorers need a license?

Mic - Yes, because prop masters don't use replica guns. They use real guns that are plugged, but the guns are still dangerous.

Q - Are they props if you're going to fire them?

Mic - Weapons are props. The prop department will rent them and according to the standards that are set down for safety, the barrels are plugged so nothing comes out. They have to use blanks. Still, they are dangerous, because any gun with a full or blank is introducing an invisible bullet which goes out at full speed. He will bring the gun; he will charge it and make it hot, safety off. The AD says *'we're ready to roll'*, the props guys will hand the gun to the actor. I have trained the actor to keep his finger off the trigger and on the frame and then when they say *'action'*, he can do his thing and be aware. So we have a safety protocol. But just because a stunt guy is a stunt guy, it doesn't mean he's good with weapons. You have to know who you're dealing with.

Q - How does stunt insurance work?

Mic - Health insurance for individual stunt people is through the Screen Actors Guild. And then there's Workers Comp. But the filmmaker is liable for anything that happens to the stunt person.

Q - Do they have to have a certain amount on their insurance to cover stunts?

Mic - That's a question for a producer or production manager. I start with *'is the company signatory with SAG?'*

Q - What are adjustments?

Mic - Adjustments are when you pay the stunt person an amount above the daily rate based on the difficulty and danger of the stunt they're doing. There's no set amount; a coordinator determines how much it will cost to have his person do a certain stunt. If producers don't take the deal, they need to negotiate quickly. But you often get what you pay for, and this isn't bad wigs, this is people's lives. Any added stunts once the deal has been sorted out will cost more money. Adjustments are usually per take. If a camera person screws up and you have to do it again, you pay the adjustment again. It's something that should be discussed and agreed on beforehand.

Q - A high fall can't be real time, so how are they shot?

Mic - They're shot at high speed with different angles and different frame rates. New filmmakers should ask me about frame rates so that it comes out well. When edited, the fall can be extended to look longer and more spectacular.

Q - What's your relationship with the first AD, the second unit director and the director?

Mic - Stunt coordinators service the whole show and if there's a second unit director, I supply a deputy to that unit. It depends on which has got the heavier action. As a stunt coordinator, I will be where the hard action is that day. If it was a big show, I would have a 1st unit coordinator, a 2nd unit coordinator and I'd bounce back and forth overseeing everything. I work with the 1st AD on the schedule at the beginning and after that with the 2nd AD.

Q - Are a lot of stunt coordinators also second unit directors?

Mic - Many are. Second unit directors are generally stunt people because second units generally shoot action shots. But right now a lot of people are trying to use it as a stepping stone into directing, so you might get a producer or cameraman who doesn't know how to shoot action.

Q - How important are storyboards for stunt sequences?

Mic - They are and they aren't. I don't need them, but they are a way for me to communicate with other departments. The storyboard artist should just draw the images the way they're written in the script, in consultation with the director and the stunt coordinator, so we can narrow stuff down. Some artists like to embellish and add their ideas and the more they embellish, the more they add to the budget and to the confusion.

Q - Are there many directors who know exactly what they want?

Mic - Sure. And a few of those don't want anyone's input. But the best directors are usually getting input from their DPs, stunt coordinator and ADs. Why hire the best people and not take advantage of their expertise and experience?

Q - How much should a producer put aside to cover a car crash on an ultra low budget movie?

Mic - This is it. It depends on the crash. If you're doing a *Fast and Furious* style crash, you need a good car and a good roll cage. A good cage is around $8,500. The problem is directors want to do *Fast and Furious* with insufficient budget. Do it safely and work with someone who can be creative within your budget. Action is like horror, in that a lot can be implied.

Q - If you were preparing a car to go up a ramp and turn over, how would you do that?

Mic - I can roll the car over on its top without a full cage. I'll put a hoop in it to protect my guy. Special effects or construction builds the ramp to our specifications.

Q - How long do you leave it before the paramedics come in after a car roll?

Mic - Our policy is that everyone stays away from the scene until the stunt guys move in and see if the driver is okay. He either is or isn't. If not, then the paramedics come in. If you want lingering shots, we cut, take the stunt person out of the car, put some dust in and you can shoot as long as you want.

Q - What common mistakes do you encounter?

Mic - Not getting involved with stunt guys early enough, by waiting until there's only one week to prep.

Q - What basic advice would you offer a new filmmaker?

Mic - Trust our vision and be willing to take advice from professionals. We want to give the filmmaker what she or he wants. If action is the centerpiece of your film, make sure you have your prep time. The best piece of advice is approach the big stunt guy and if you can't get him, ask him who the next up-and-coming guys are. If you work well together, that person become a loyal member of your team.

Q - So new filmmakers shouldn't be afraid of approaching you for advice?

Mic - No, not at all. Do yourself a favor and listen to the advice of a professional stunt coordinator.

Matt Sweeney
Special Effects

Q - What is the job of the special effects person?

Matt - We do any special effect that actually appears in front off the camera in real time, and then we also work with the visual effects people to help them create elements. So we do rain, wind, fire, snow, action props, explosives, water effects, fog, smoke. A lot of prop shop work and large action sets.

Q - How early on should a producer approach you?

Matt - It depends on the show. If there's a lot of special effects, the effects person should be in as early as possible. Especially for guerrilla filmmaking, so your costs can be minimized. So we could say, *'this effect for that sentence in the script is going to cost you $30k to do!'* So it's helpful for budgeting purposes and also to consider rewrites.

Q - Do you work closely with the stunt co-ordinators?

Matt - We do a lot of rigging for the stunt people. Some of the rigging they do themselves and some we do some. They mainly do ratchets, where you yank someone through a wall, or an air ramp where they are launched through the air. We rig the cars to do a canon roll, put a roll cage in them, deal with explosions etc. I love explosions, but they have become more difficult since the crack down on terrorism. They have increased all of the regulations in the US. You used to be able to handle explosives under the direction of somebody without a license and now you have to have a license.

Q - Do you collaborate with the special effects make up at all?

Matt - We help those guys out somewhat, but those make-up guys are all part of a separate team of people. They are closely aligned with the make-up guys. A good friend of mine Matthew Mungel, is a make-up guy. He'll do wounds, prosthetics, but he also does regular make up. If he needs to have a little squib put in, then he'll talk to us.

Q - How easy and safe are bullet squibs?

Matt - They're very safe if they're properly done. A body hit is not that expensive by itself, but you've got to bring in a guy for a day to do it, get a permit - even if it's just one body hit, it's still going to cost. The actual hit itself is about eight dollars but you've got to have a licensed guy to put it in.

Q - Do you ever get paid per adjustment like the stunt guy?

Matt - Stuntmen get paid depending on the risk or amount of pain they have to go through. It's not the same with special effects guys. If we're going to have an effects guy in a car to set off some effects at the same time the stunt guy is going to do a car crash, then he's going to get paid the same adjustment as the stunt guy. But if we have to rig something on top of a 150 ft radio tower, we're not getting anything more. There are various union issues when working in water though.

Q - If you've got water in your script, how does that alter the payment?

Carlos - Anything taking place on the water, your production time is going to double or triple. Tempers will grow short.

Q - What's more expensive, doing an explosion, or a blue screen model shot?

Matt - It depends on the difficulty of building the model. How long is it going to take you to build the model? You figure you'll spend a day doing it on blue screen, plus whatever effects are required with it. The blue screen model could be either way less or way more, depending on how many effects the model has to do and how detailed its got to be and what action its going to do in front of the blue screen. If you take a hanging spaceship and do it all with camera moves, then obviously it's cheaper than having it on some remote control gimble.

Q - Is there a special way to shoot models and miniatures?

Matt - Take more care than shooting regular footage because you have to make sure that it's not revealed as a miniature as you're shooting. One of the problems with shooting miniatures is the size of the effects. If you have a miniature boat, the smaller the boat is, the water is going to look crappy because of the surface tension, the water droplet size. Flames in miniature are difficult too.

Q - What kind of effects can be done cheaply and effectively?

Matt - Smoke is cheap. Wind is inexpensive and that kind of thing adds quite a bit. If you're inside a set you've built and you're looking out of the window and there's a tree out there - motionless, it adds nothing to the scene, but if you've got someone out there with a fan, it adds quite a bit. That's why you notice a lot of camera men will do a wet down at night. They feel it looks better. There are other tricks you can do. For instance, we tell them to keep the camera away from the car when we are exploding it and the talent even further away and use the longest lens you've got and it will stack them close together. Lens selection really does a lot. You can put people in the action or take them out of the action.

Q - Is fire safe to use?

Matt - The safety aspect is the biggest thing, even with something like a candle. In the past, people have done stupid stuff and the authorities have reacted. They say, *'you guys knocked over candles and set the caught fire. You've got to have a licensed effects guy from here on in'*. The problem with fire is the safety aspect, it's very labor intensive. If you wanted to be in a small room and have a fire start, you have to build a special set for it with non flammable materials and you've got to open the top to let the heat out. If you're doing it on a stage, you have to protect the sprinklers from going off, then you have to have it all on propane. As soon as you get into using flammable liquids, your danger is increased ten fold as then you have a vapor problem.

Q - Is it very expensive to use fire?

Matt - There are cheats. If you want to see somebody through the fire, you do the long lens shot with a flame bar between the actor and the camera - they are a distance apart so safe, yet through the lens, the actor looks as though they're in the flames.

Q - What are the common mistakes that producers are not aware of?

Matt - The most common problem we have is producers not thinking enough ahead of time. If they tell us in pre-production stages, what they want to see, then we could prepare that in a cost effective way. If they go, *'tomorrow can we shoot this and this'*, then, we've got to work all night and it's not going to look as good as if we'd had a month to work on it. It's all time frame stuff, and lack of decision making that screws us up. You can say, *'okay cameraman, move your camera over here'*. That doesn't cost them anything, but if they change their mind about what we're doing or can't make up their mind in time, that's what screws it up.

PRODUCTION

Q - Are there problems with directors who haven't prepared shot lists?

Matt - Yes, if they haven't thought out properly what they want to see. I had a talk with a young director a while ago and I said, *'you're hurting yourself on this film as you can't make up your mind on what you need to say right off the bat'*. The studio then said *'you can't do that effect, it's too expensive'*. And I said to the director *'if you'd figured all that out in pre production, then I could have taken the expense out of that one scene and buried it in all the other scenes and the studio would have been unaware!'*

Q - Do you work with storyboard artists?

Matt - Yes. With us, it's more like, *'here's the first cut, here's what has to happen here. The next cut is this and the next cut is this'*. If you break it down into pieces, it will be cheaper to do than trying to do it all at once, and will give you a better chance of success.

Q - If you're working on a $1-$3m movie with a car crash, how much would a producer put aside for that?

Matt - If it's very simple crash, then all it is, is a stunt guy and some good seat belts. If you have to turn it over, then you're getting into more money. If two cars crash, you've got the cost of both cars, the cost of the stunt layers and that's it. Let's say the next level is that a car runs off the road and rolls. Now you have the added expense of building a roll cage into the car. That's probably $3k-$5k. You still have to pay the stunt guy, but now you have to pay him a little more. You also have to prepare some way to make it rollover, which would be a ramp that they go up and flip off. That takes a little bit more of prep. The next level is if you need a canon roll shot, where you shoot a big piece of telephone pole out of a car which makes the car flip and go through the air. That's a roll cage plus a canon, plus pyrotechnics, plus a big adjustment for the stunt guy. So there's an escalation with complexity.

Q - What else is covered by you?

Matt - All atmospheric effects, water, rain, wind. The snow dressing can be very expensive.

Q - Are there instances when you develop a new machine for a new effect?

Matt - Yes. I've got 11 overseas containers down the street full of equipment that we've built. I have a lot of strange equipment. We built the time machine for the movie which is sitting downstairs. That cost $750k to build. If you'd have done this by conventional methods, you'd never have done it in time, or you would have spent $2m! It took two and half months to build. A lot of work.

Q - Do you supply weapons?

Matt - No. It's the property department that does the weapons. But now if the prop guy needs some work done on the weapon, to have it modified, that's frequently us.

Urban Ghost Story, the third feature film made by the authors, employed a forced perspective model - a small sign six inches long, suspended on fishing wire in such a way that from the camera viewpoint, it appears to be much larger and attached to the side of the building. Note operator's hand holding the sign in the right picture.

Special Effects - Rough Guide

If your film calls for something to enhance the reality of a scene or requires you to create the illusion that the impossible or improbable really occurs, then a cool special effect may be what you need. While special effects may be costly and dangerous, careful planning and a seasoned SPFX man can alleviate those concerns while adding a huge about of production value to your project. Here is a list of special effect types you can use to make your film pop. But beware, if it goes wrong, you could waste a huge amount of time and effort on something that, if it just isn't good enough, you will need to cut. Nothing destroys the audiences suspension of belief like a dreadful special effect.

Pyrotechnics
Fire, smoke, flares, fireworks, explosions, debris - anything which burns, smolders or explodes, such as a campfire that burns at the same rate for continuity, and is smokeless and safe.

Models & Miniatures
Small versions of a real object, i.e. the Whitehouse in Independence Day. Also forced perspective models, hanging miniatures, objects that are difficult to film or control, like a virus or an atom.

Mechanics
Anything from a rig to control milk pouring out of a jug on cue and at just the right rate to a massive rig to knock down a wall (if it needs to be done mechanically rather than pyrotechnically).

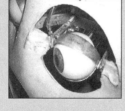

Action Prop/Animatronics
Making creatures up which have realistic movement, operated by radio control servos, cables, or computer operated these days.Also, any object to be constructed that must perform movement.

Breakaways
Glass (bottles, windows), and crockery, hand props and furniture (balsa wood is used for those chairs that are to be broken or thrown) and structural breakaways (walls collapsing, a roof cave-in etc.)

Prosthetics
A latex piece that is attached to an actor that sometimes requires body and face casting enabling artists to sculpt 'onto' actors faces and bodies.

Water
Anything taking place on or in water i.e. water flooding a submarine or a sinking ship, shooting in water tanks, miniature damns.

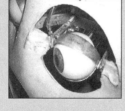

Firearms
Weapons, firing blanks, bullet impacts, bullet squibs, bullet hits, bullet holes, arrows, knives.

Atmospheric
Rain, mist, wind, snow (falling and dress), hail, wind, fog, smoke, ice, dust storms etc.

Miscellaneous
Rocker units (i.e. a boat in heavy seas), earthquakes, cobwebs, volcanic lava, quicksand etc. Anything else you can imagine!

PRODUCTION

Q - There was the terrible tragedy on the film The Crow – what was the problem there?

Matt - That's one of the problems you can get into when you don't have a large body of knowledge on a subject. It was a very low budget film and they had a new guy for the props. They needed to have a shot of a guy putting the bullet into the gun, so this new prop guy pulled the bullet out of the shell and poured out all the powder. But he left the primer in there. So they did the shot of putting the bullet into the gun and shot that. Now the bullets sitting in the gun. I think they changed the prop man and went to another location, so here's the gun with one bullet in it. Some actor then fiddled with it, click, click, click, and in that process, the hammer fell down on the primer, which usually initiates the powder in the thing, but it was just strong enough to send the bullet out and jammed it in the barrel. Whoever unloaded the gun just pulled this case out, didn't think anything of it, then the next shot was the shooting of Brandon Lee. The gun was filled with blanks, but there was more power in the blanks than there was in the original powder, and a bullet head is now sitting in the chamber, so when the blank was shot, it propelled the bullet out and unfortunately it hit Brandon Lee. And that's what killed him. There were a whole bunch of mistakes made there. The first thing was no-one checked the barrel for obstructions when they loaded it with blanks. The second thing was the prop master on that shoot was not knowledgeable enough to know that when you shoot somebody that close, you shoot a little off centre so you don't blow powder in their face and hide it with camera angles. That's why all the gun / stunt stuff and special effects stuff is better being handled by someone who knows this stuff and who's been doing it a long time.

When I go on a set and want to be working with a prop master, I really want to see Mike Gibbons or Mike Papac or Chuck Stuart, some guy about my age who I know has been doing it for thirty years and is not going to do anything like that. My friend and I were on a low budget show and it was a new prop guy and the shot was the bad guys come in and they terrorize this market, and this guy takes a gun and shoots a woman on the floor. So we had this gun loaded up with bullet heads and the prop guy comes in and has this 44 magnum. They are almost ready to do it, and my friend John came in who is a smart special effects guy says, *'there's something wrong with that gun, lets take it to the truck and take a look at it'*. So we went out and the props guy unloads it and it had full load blanks in it and at that range, it was enough to hurt that woman. It would blow the wad right through her clothing and puncture her skin. So we said, *'hey man, just so you should know, we're doing this just amongst us. We'll fix this'*. So we picked the wad out, poured out the powder and they did it on the primer and they could add the sound in post.

Q - Is it possible for new filmmakers to make any of these props at home?

Matt - You don't want to make your own explosives. You can get hurt, hurt somebody else and everywhere in the civilized world you will get into trouble without having a license. Great Britain is more intense than here. Germany, even more intense than Great Britain. Blood is easily done, there are some good recipes for blood. We sell blood by the gallon and ship it all over the world.

Q - Have you come across a lot of filmmakers who are more interested into the toys than the story?

Matt - Yes. I gave the director on *Charlie's Angels* the button for a test and said, *'hey man, press that button and that set will explode'* and he practically wet himself! I tried to get them to do a full scale explosion rather than visual effects and the visual effects guy was behind me on that as he didn't want the visual effects either. I wanted to take the whole roof top of a building, take it out on a dry lake and do a huge gasoline explosion. I tried to convince them, but we were never able to do it in the end!

Q - What advice would you give a new filmmaker?

Matt - The guerrilla filmmaker should seek out friendly people and throw themselves on their mercy and say, *'hey look, I want to do this effect. We have no money. Give me some suggestions'*. Some of them will go *'ha, ha'* but some of them will say, *'if you do this and this, that will work, or call this guy...'* If you want to do rain and you don't have any money, narrow the shot, you still get the same effect but don't need to do anywhere near as much work. You have two lovers kissing underneath the light on a door on a building, if you just have someone holding a rain wand over them it would work. If you want to show the whole building, you have show rain towers and a water truck and a bunch of guys. If we're looking down the street and the whole building, we're now talking a crane and a rain bar – now you're up to $15k. Instead, you could send your PA out there, hire a water hose put the sprinkler on, hold that, look through the lens - always look through the lens, to make sure it looks right. Think about the effect itself. If you've got two sources of rain, how do they come across? Make sure it all comes from the same angle. Lowering the scope of these things, cutting down the shot - it'll be cheaper.

Q - Of course you could just cut the rain from the scene! Any other tips?

Matt - Say I'm going to cut you with a knife. You can get a really expensive knife, hollow it out and fill it with blood and get somebody to squirt blood out of it, or you can make some blood paste. You show the clean side of the blade, the actor comes in and wipes the blood on them. Or you can rent one that's already set up, like a collapsing knife.

Q - For something like a collapsing knife, would you rent from a special effects place or from the props house?

Matt - Try both. We have got collapsing knives sitting on the shelves from shows going back ten years, and so does the prop house. There are new prop ideas all the time being asked to be made. We had this shot where a guy would have to stab someone with a sword. You have two levels of expense on that. Here's the shot - you have a half hollow, half solid blade and half of it pushes in. If it's got to come out again right in that same shot, then it's expensive, because then you have to figure out a complicated rig to make the blade shoot back out after you've done that, so the cheaper way to do that is to have one shot of the knife coming towards the guy and then the next shot, the reaction and then the knife coming out. All you need a chest plate with a tab on it to hold the tip as you pull it out and have it coated in blood. Or you could do it the really expensive way and do it all digitally. Or see it come out the back of the guy. There are lots of levels of expense.

Q - So you suggest new filmmakers should sit down with their special effects guy and work out the most cost effective way of handling the special effects?

Matt - If you're a low budget filmmaker, ideally, you should have some friendships or contacts among people that do all these things where you can call them up and pick their brain. The bigger the quantity of special effects guys you have in a given area, the more willing they will be to share information. Here in LA, there are a ton of us and there's not that dog eat dog competition. If you went to Madrid, Spain, where there are only two special effects guys, so as they are so busy, neither one of them is going to help you on your low budget film. If there's an effect that I haven't done before and it's just been done in the latest movie, I'll ring up the effects guy and ask how it was done and he'll tell me. There're no secrets.

Q - Any final tips?

Matt - We've done a lot of stuff for low budget films and they'll call and say, *'we need someone to come up and do a bullet hit'*, so I'll recommend someone who's lower on the food chain that charges less to do a couple of bullet hits or something and then there are a couple of books that are good that filmmakers can read and learn a lot from.

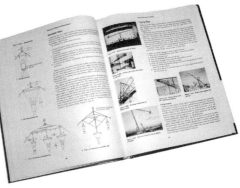

Secrets Of Hollywood Special Effects by Robert E McCarthy is a great, hardback book for new film makers and aspiring special effects technicians producing a low budget film. It is incredibly detailed and covers a huge amount of effects. It's so detailed in fact, that often new film makers could be put off as it looks more like a physics manual than a film making book.

Boone Narr
Animal Trainer

ANIMALS

Q - What does your company do?

Boone - We train and supply animals for motion pictures and television. For the past 3 decades our company and its trainers have worked with every major studio on hundreds of films, TV shows and commercials. We have experience with difficult animal work, stunts and cutting edge computer enhanced film making technology. Animal training is a non-specific term used for anyone training an animal a behavior described in a script (e.g. teaching a dog to retrieve the newspaper). Animal wrangling is a term used for cowboys who handle livestock.

Q - What animals do you train and which are the easiest / hardest to work with?

Boone - We train everything from the cats, dogs and birds that you would find in any home, to the wilder animals in nature such as primates, lions, tigers, elephants and more. In the last 30 years, we've trained just about every animal there is. You would think the easiest to train would be cats and dogs because they've been domesticated for so many years, but because of computer generated images and visual effects where animals talk as well as act, working with these animals has gotten more challenging. The body language has to coincide with the dialogue. Training is much more precise than it was years ago. I'm often asked, 'What's the hardest thing to do with an animal?' I believe it is to make the animal's relationship with the actor appear natural. Nothing upsets me more than when I see an animal looking at his trainer off-camera. However, the hardest animal to work with is the 2 legged kind - humans! Our 4 legged friends are eager and willing to please, they don't deceive. Animals are truly who they are, no disguises.

Q - What are the laws when using animals in a production?

Boone - Deal with a reputable animal company who will have the right permits and licenses - USDA (United States Department of Agriculture), Fish & Game, CDC (Center for Disease Control), as well as local city and county Animal Control Department permits. When filming out of the country, you would also need USDI (United States Department of the Interior) and Import / Export licenses. Always check with local agencies regarding quarantine restrictions when filming in foreign countries. The animal company should also be in good standing with the American Humane Association. This organization governs the use of animals in the motion picture business and sets guidelines for to keep animals safe from inhumane treatment. It is a must that the AHA is on set when an animal is working.

Q - Does the production company need a license?

Boone - The production company must notify the American Humane Association whenever an animal is to appear on set (any reputable animal company will also notify AHA). If the animal is working on location, a location permit may be needed which allows an animal onto that location. If the production is traveling, a health certificate will be required.

Q - How much extra time should a filmmaker add to a shoot when dealing with animals?

Boone - As long as an animal has adequate prep time, there is no extra time needed on set *provided* the learned behavior is within the capabilities of the animal. For instance, I was once asked to have a chimp ride a bicycle under a giraffe while juggling three bowling balls! I don't know if Tom Cruise could have pulled that one off. It is during the prep time that an animal learns their behaviors, much like an actor uses prep time to get into character. Storyboards can also be of great assistance.

Q - How much does a trainer cost? What do you get for your money?

Boone - Animal trainers are members of Local 399 – International Brotherhood of Teamsters, the same union that employs transportation drivers, captains and co-ordinators and animal wranglers. As with all unions, there are restrictions that must be followed regarding minimum pay and hours worked. The rate range can be anywhere from $25 / hour for a beginner trainer to $40 / hour for an experienced trainer. Animals are rented out separately from the trainer and are rented on a daily or weekly basis. Rates can run anywhere from $25 to $5k per day, depending upon the rarity of the animal and what it is expected to do. Prep rates are 50% less. There is also a fee for transporting the animal to location. A backup dog would be around $150 per day, whereas an elephant would obviously be much more. 95% of our business is generated through referrals and repeat clients.

Q - Do you need an animal trainer for background players / practical props (dog walking behind main players or a goldfish in a bowl) or just for principle players?

Boone - It is recommended by the American Humane Association that a professional animal trainer be on set whenever an animal is used - goldfish or dog. We've supplied everything from dogs being walked by background players, to flies and ants to enhance scenes. No job is too small, nor is the animal.

Q - What should producers know about animal casting? Would they go to a company like yours for this?

Boone - Cast the animal trainer first who will then assist you in finding the right animal for your project. This might entail looking through pictures so the filmmakers can decide on the look and type of animal. The trainer will then do research to find the right animal and show perspective animals to the filmmakers. It's much like casting actors.

Q - What kind of insurance should a filmmaker get when dealing with animals?

Boone - If the animals are a predominant element in the motion picture, productions are encouraged to cover the animal under their insurance policy, just as they would an actor. This is in case the animal is injured or gets sick. The production's costs are covered for the day they could not shoot with the animal.

Q - What advice would you give filmmakers who are intending to use animals in their films?

Boone - Be creative but realistic with your needs. Do your homework. Allow ample prep time. Take time to do it right because you may not have time to do it over. They say 'never work with animals or kids', but it's not because it takes more time, it's because they are scene stealers.

American Humane Association

AHA maintains comprehensive guidelines that address all aspects of production and every animal species imaginable - from the largest elephant to the tiniest spider. For the realm of entertainment, the AH define an animal as any 'sentient creature'. They ensure that stunts, safety measures, camera angles, special effects and even lighting, make-up and costumes for animal actors receive pre-production planning and consideration. Approach the AHA as early in pre-production as possible, so they can help solve potential problems before any harm occurs.

American Humane Association, Film & Television Unit Office, 13266 Dickens Street, Sherman Oaks, California 91403
Tel: 818 501 0123   Fax: 818 501 8725
www.AHAfilm.org   info@americanhumane.org
AH also operates a 24 hour 7 day-a-week ANIMAL SAFETY HOTLINE (800) 677 3420
AH ensures callers complete confidentiality

Jim Hanna

Hanna Bros Extreme Motion Picture Catering

CATERING

Q - What are some of the best kind of foods to have on a movie set?

Jim - It depends on weather, time, locale and type of crew personnel. In general, hotter weather dictates lighter fare (i.e. fresh fruits, salads, smoothies and fish), cold weather (night shoots and early mornings) requires heartier foods (soups, stews, steaks, biscuits and gravy, hot chocolate). The part of the country you're in also plays a role in what you feed your crew. On a standard set in the South, a caterer will go through 10–20 gallons of sweet tea per day, while the same caterer will do well to go through one gallon of sweet tea on set in Los Angeles.

Q - What kind of foods / snacks / beverages do you have available between meals?

Jim - This depends on how much money has been assigned. The crew should always have cold water, fruit punch and a variety of sodas available between meals. Drinks will cost a production approximately $1.50 to $3.00 per person per day (based on a shooting crew of 100). Snacks can range from crackers and fruit at $1.00 per person per day to hot sandwiches, smoothies and espressos being patrolled around the set by crafts service personnel at $8.00 per person per day.

Q - Do you bring a whole kitchen to the set, or do you have a mobile truck / van?

Jim - Our company only uses mobile kitchens, which we only send out if the number being fed is over 75 per day.

Q - What are the differences between a Studio movie and a low budget independent feature from a catering point of view?

Jim - It's not always the catering budget. I've been on low budget shows where the UPM really took care of their crew when it came to catering, and I've been on big shows where catering isn't anywhere near the top on the list of priorities. One of the real differences is the crew size, the majors bring a lot of people. Another is the speed with which you get paid, that has been problematic with independents.

Q - What should a producer budget for catering / craft service on a low budget movie?

Jim - You must ask yourself, how well do you want to take care of your crew? An easy way to put your crew in a good mood is to feed them well, and a good caterer can make a world of difference and save you a lot of headaches. Most people are more agreeable and happier when they have something in their stomach. I know I am. Questions to ask are is the caterer local or not? Housing can become an issue, although this can be negotiated, as well as travel costs to and from location. Just the bare minimum catering, with no frills, for a crew of around 100 people, would be $12.25 - $13.75 per head. A nice meal and selection, without a lot of fluff or pricey foods (i.e. lobster or filets) would be $13.75 - $15.75, shellfish and higher priced commodities on a regular basis $15.75 - $18.25. Really spoiling your crew would be from $18.25. However, this does not include additional expenses such as catering labor, water, ice, coffee, chili, soup, propane, gasoline, canned fuel, charcoal and props food - this is when the catering department works with the props dept. Sales tax is added to the catering invoice too. Prices vary a great deal all over the country, but if you let your caterer know how you want to take care of your crew, the above prices should be a pretty good place to start. If crew size is smaller, prices can be higher because volume purchasing from food purveyors is no longer possible for the caterer.

Q - Is the catering fee always calculated per head of cast and crew?

Jim - Yes, with a minimum guaranteed per day. It doesn't make sense for a company to send a catering truck out to feed less than 75 people - you'd be much better off (from a cost perspective) having a local restaurant drop off lunch.

Q - Is the catering labor fee built into the cost per head, or is it separate?

Jim - Cost per head is for food only. Catering labor varies tremendously across the country, as do catering employees. As with most things, you get what you pay for. Our employees only work on an hourly basis. Some companies have their employees work on flats, which is unfair on the employee and leads to high turnover, which in turn leads to having inexperienced personnel on your set. Crew size and extra counts will dictate how many catering employees the caterer needs to service them properly. The following should give you a reasonable idea of what to expect: A crew size of up to 60, 2 caterers are needed; a crew size of 60-110, 3 caterers needed; 110-160, 4 caterers needed; 160-210, 5 caterers needed; and so forth. Basically, you need another employee for every 50 people being serviced after the first 60. If your crew (or more likely your extra counts) gets very large, the increment then changes to one employee per 100 people served over the first 500.

Q - Do you have any suggestions or tricks for how a low budget producer can stretch his catering / craft service dollar?

Jim - I would suggest getting catering dropped off to the producer, either at the office or the location, as this will save you a bundle in labor, although this will sacrifice the service. Any crew member that can't eat breakfast or lunch within the one hour window (and believe me, there is ALWAYS someone) will have to eat something that has been left out too long or has already been trashed. Having the food dropped off also drastically reduces your flexibility when it comes to changing your location, or at a time other than what you had originally anticipated (this also happens a lot). If drop off is not an option then I would suggest just being forthright with the caterer upfront about your budget and needs.

Q - How would you know if you're getting a good caterer?

Jim - Specifically check the references of the chef that is going to be on the catering truck for your job. I always hear crew saying, *'I've had this catering company before and chef Y was good but the other time we had chef Z and it wasn't so good'.* The chef on the truck interacts with your crew, so make sure they've worked on some films and that their work was acceptable. Don't hire a caterer because they are the cheapest, as they will bring something to eat, but you're probably not going to like it. There are a lot of corners that can be cut in the food business. Maybe their equipment isn't good, maybe they plan on buying inferior products, maybe their employees have never been on a film before, or maybe they don't pay their taxes and insurance. When you're trying to lowball the catering department you're essentially cutting your own throat.

Q - What advice would you give a new producer / filmmaker on how to make your job easier?

Jim - We always like it when a producer / filmmaker is upfront with us about what they have to spend. There are a lot of variable costs associated with catering, and they can be altered. We like it when a producer has done some homework on us, and has checked references as we put a great deal of effort into our reputation. Treat the catering department like crew, because that's what we are - so don't ask ONLY the catering department to double up in rooms when on location, and if the rest of the crew is getting per diems, so should we. Then we have the things that make me as a caterer happy when we're on site. These are having tables and chairs already set up and a room that's air-conditioned. It's ideal when I can keep the kitchen parked in the same spot the entire day and that the kitchen location is close to where the crew is to be fed, preferably with electricity and water on site. We also welcome feedback from everyone. Tell us how we're doing, and if you'd like to see anything different, and then we can adapt. Finally, once the job is complete, what makes us even happier is that you spread the word, as we all know this is a very tight knit business and a good word goes a long way. A nice credit at the end of a film is always appreciated and so does paying us in a timely manner. We too have to pay the bills incurred as a result of the production and our creditors keep us on tight leashes. My final bit of advice is to hire us again on your next film! Loyalty works both ways.

PRODUCTION

Mike Munson
CFI Technicolor

THE LAB

Q - What is the job of the lab?

Mike - The lab processes the camera negative to produce dailies, then to either create telecine dailies or print them, then deal with post-production all the way up to the answer print and the bulk release prints.

Q - Can you take me through the process if I shot 35mm?

Mike - You shoot your negative during the day, it comes to the lab at night. Most of the negative is developed at night for telecine or print, so we process the negative however they want it. We add a head leader and a foot leader, then we clean it and it will be ready to go to the lab. We log in the amount of cans we receive, so we can keep an inventory of what's going in and out. Negative developing does the same thing, where they'll write in how many cans come in and they check what kind of processing has been requested. If it is a print show, the circled takes from the camera report will be printed onto a roll which they will build up to 1000ft. What's ever left over will be stored away as B roll. From there the print rolls will go to the timer. The timer will put a printer light on it depending on whether they want to do scene to scene (3 light color correction) or if they want to give it a one light (an average color correction for the entire roll). From there it will go to printing, where they will clean the roll, and will print a positive print off that negative. The positive roll will go to positive developing and once finished it is viewed by our contact people. The contact people will discuss the results with the DP's. If everything looks good, it goes to the post-production facility used by the producer.

Q - Is it just on 35mm that you print only the circled takes?

Mike - Yes and any larger format. By circling the scenes on your camera reports, you are telling us to print those scenes. We don't do this with Super 16mm.

Q - What is pushing and pulling?

Mike - You pull process if the negative was overexposed as it decreases the exposure index of the film, and you push if the negative was underexposed as it increases the exposure index of the film.

Q - What is flashing?

Mike - It's where they put it on a printer, strike it with a bit of light and it gives the negative a uniform exposure. This slight exposure lowers the film's contrast.

Q - What is one light?

Mike - One light is grading/timing for the whole roll - we keep the same adjustment for the entire roll without changing it much. We usually do a one light, unless the negative is really bad then they will do it by scene by scene, or three light transfer. An exception to this would be if there were a day scene and a night scene side by side. They will need to be timed differently.

Q - What are edge numbers?

Mike - These are numbers printed along the edge of a strip of film by the manufacturer. They are also called Keykodes (Keykode is the trademark name for Kodak edge numbers). They are for cutting purposes. You have a bar code and a numerical code. It gives you a location on the negative and for Kodak purposes, it tells you type of stock, emulsion, when and where it was made. It can tell the Kodak reps that information too.

Q - How important is it for the production team to meet the lab contact person?

Mike - It's really important. You want to create a rapport with the lab so that we know what kind of look you are trying to achieve. By knowing this, we can advise you of ways to shoot and what stocks to use. Also, if there are any problems, such as hairs in the gate or scratches, we will be able to quickly contact you and try to fix the issue. Remember, we are with you all the way through to the answer print, so it's advantageous for us all to be on the same page.

Q - What's the lab TONICS sheet?

Mike - It contains a list of all the footage, roll by roll. It show the scenes, takes with key numbers and printing lights, which is the measure of the amount of red, green and blue emulsion layers. We send this report out to the production team so that if they're any problems, the DP can call their lab contact and discuss the issue.

Q - What is the camera report sheet?

Mike - The camera team generates this report, and it basically gives us all the information about the exposed negative. They list the stock, emulsion number, magazine and roll number. It has all the details such as the company, address, the title of the movie etc. But, most importantly, it tells us which takes they want printed and how. The camera team circles the takes to be printed and then lists the processing details such as to flash, push, pull or whatever and moreover, how many stops they want it. The key though, is to make sure every can is listed and taped shut so it's impossible to open without tearing the seal.

Q - Are all dailies prepped for telecine these days?

Mike - Not all but most. We will assemble the rolls of the processed original camera negative into laboratory rolls of 1000', give it leaders and clean it so it's ready for the telecine. I would say more than 50% of the dailies are prepped, but at Technicolor, because

Choosing a Lab

1. Lab contacts are usually very friendly. It's a good idea to go and look around a lab just so that you know roughly how everything is done.

2. Make sure that you will have a lab contact. This will be one person who will be your point of contact when discussing issues through pre production to final print.

3. Keep in contact with the lab and try not to run up a serious debt. When the film is ready for delivery, the lab could withhold the neg until payment is made. This is a big problem and should be avoided. Find out who the accounts person is and keep them happy.

4. Try and get an all in deal where you agree to a fixed price for a fixed amount of footage, including all sound transfers, stock, and even courier charges for dropping off the stock and dailies.

5. Double check what the lab tells you with regard to any processing issues. Your cameraman can be a useful source of information here.

6. Get some figures from other production companies to see if the deal is competitive.

7. You will probably edit on a non-linear system. Make sure the lab telecines your footage with ALL the technical information onscreen such as roll number, keykode, time code, etc. Ensure they know what film speed you shoot at (24fps), the sound sample rate and your aspect ratio (film format).

8. While going to a bigger lab with the latest equipment gives you more latitude for what you can do to in the processing or telecine stage, they will charge more. Smaller labs using older equipment will often be more than adequate for your low budget needs.

Super 16mm to 35mm Blow Up

Stage 1 - Super 16mm Cut Negative - Once an answer print of this cut negative is agreed from a grading point of view, it moves on to Stage 2.

Stage 2 - Super 16mm Interpositive is made from the Cut Negative - this Interpos is low contrast and contains ALL the gradings agreed by the production company.

Stage 3 - Super 16mm Interpositive is blown up to 35mm Internegative. Notice The Super 16mm aspect ratio (1:1.66) has been cropped down with a mask to 1:1.85 for cinema release (optional).

Stage 4 - Check Print is made and agreed by the production.

Stage 5 - Optical Sound Negative is made from master sound mix. This will be combined with Stage 4 to produce a combined, optical and picture Check Print. Note the digital sound encoded between sprockets on the left of the negative.

a lot of the stuff is going to become a feature, someone will still print the film so they're going to see the image they'll actually have. It's better in the long run to do this, to see what you're doing, but I think cost prevents it.

Q - If you're printing it and viewing it here, is there any problem you would notice that you probably wouldn't notice if it went straight to telecine?

Mike - Unless there's an issue like HMI flicker, it will be something you're going to pick up in telecine. A lot of times even if they have a telecine, people will probably print the roll anyway so they can see what they have to deal with. If there are scratch issues, they might want to see how it falls in the format. A lot of times in HD, you're going to see the whole thing, whereas when it's a printed image it might matte out.

Q - What sort of problems do you commonly come across?

Mike - HMI flicker, camera scratches, magazine scratches.

Q - How would you tell if a scratch happened in camera rather than later on down the line in post?

Mike - Your telecine scratches and camera scratches tend to be straight, but sometimes camera scratches have a hook that comes down and sometimes you can see it, sometimes you can't. Sometimes you can put it under a microscope and see it. Your lab scratches tend to have a little movement and magazine scratches have that also.

Q - Can you get rid of the scratches?

Mike - Some you can, some you can't. A lot of times, pre-developed scratches will be blue. Those you can't wet gate, so they have to be eliminated after the lab.

Q - What is wet gate printing?

Mike - Wet gate is used at the answer print stage and will cover up by coating cell scratches that are after developing and some white emulsion scratching. Wet gate can do a good job on negatives. If someone has something with a cell scratch, we might print it wet gate so they have an example of what it will look like. The actual process is a chamber in the printing machine that fills with fluid prior to printing and ensures safety to the original.

Q - Are there any other problems that happen in camera?

Mike - X ray fog. It doesn't happen often but you have to be careful when you're shipping internationally. You see a pulse (almost like HMI flicker), the outside will have a slow pulse to it and as you go further into the roll, it gets smaller, so it'll go faster.

Q - What is the procedure should the master neg be damaged by the lab?

Mike - If the damage is on the inter-negative, we would go back to the inter-positive and make a new inter-negative. If it's the master negative, then it gets dicey. We would be totally honest with the production company and apologize for the damage. We have commercial protection in the terms and conditions of our contracts, which protects us from claims due to accidental damage. But, we wouldn't hide behind that. We would be talk to you about how we can fix the problem. This is exactly why producers should insure their negative right up to the time you get your inter-positive made.

Q - What problems do you come across with new DP's?

Mike - Exposure problems.

Q - What is the line that goes all the way down the camera when shooting Super 16mm at 150fps?

Super 35mm - Widescreen without anamorphics

Stage 1 - Super 35mm negative is cut - notice the aspect ratio (not on negative but in camera viewfinder). Notice also that more negative is exposed than on flat 35mm.

Stage 2 - Answer print is made to check and confirm grading.

Stage 3 - Super 35mm Interpositive is made from Super 35mm cut negative.

Stage 4 - 35mm Internegative is made up - The image is now optically squeezed, freeing up the area on the left of the frame for the optical sound track. This interneg now conforms to standard 35mm formats and includes the anamorphic squeeze.

Stage 5 - Optical Sound negative is made from master sound mix. It can be combined with Stage 6 to produce a combined, optical and picture, print. (Com Opt). Note the digital sound encoded between sprockets on the left of the negative.

Stage 6 - Combined Optical and Picture print (a check print will be produced before show prints). Note how the image is squeezed, and the optical sound on the left.

Stage 7 - Theatrical Projection - when the print is projected in the cinema, the projectionist uses an anamorphic lens to 'unsqueeze' the image, giving a very wide image.

Mike - At S16mm, your left side is where your key code is. On a monitor it is on the left hand side. It could be a gate problem particularly if it's straight. If it's a roller, it will have some kind of movement. It could be something to do with the speed of the camera, too. That's something that comes up; I used to get camera oil or lubricant on the cameras from high-speed cameras. The processors, because there was nothing touching the film, would not take it off on the first pass. What it is where the lubricant goes on, it would be on the base side of the negative and the first chemical that comes into the developer is to loosen up the backing. The lubricant would be there and it wouldn't be able to do its job and would leave little dots.

Q - Do you do telecine here?

Mike - Yes, at our Technicolor Creative Services division. That's where filmmakers go if they need or want to keep it all in house.

Q - Can your dailies be viewed at the lab and if you're on location, how will the dailies be viewed and how quickly is the turnaround on the dailies?

Mike - It depends on the workload at the lab and how quickly the production wants the dailies processed, but usually it's about a four to six hour time frame. The lab gets hit between nine and midnight. We have facilities for dailies to be viewed here, but we need some advance warning to set up our viewing theater. As for how do you watch dailies on location, you can use anything from a standard TV and VCR to a professional monitor and Mini DV tapes. One of the problems of viewing dailies for a feature off VHS copy of the Beta in a hotel room with a hired TV and video is that you can't see much. The focus puller is probably tearing his hair out trying to work out if he got the focus he wanted. A better way to do that is to view in a slightly higher format, such as SVHS or MiniDV. The VHS that they are supplied with has a gray scale, framing reference and color bars, so that the DP can line up the monitor properly.

Q - What happens with the sound process?

ACME MOVIES

Acme Films, 123 Any Road, Anytown, Somewhere, London

To - The Chosen Labs
Somewhere
London W11 5NP
21/4/2003

Dear Sirs,

We have granted to ANY DISTRIBUTOR, hereinafter called "The Distributor" the rights of Film Distribution, video, and television in TERRITORY on the following Film:-

YOUR MOVIE

This communication is your authority to allow the Distributor access to the following materials in your possession, for the purpose of manufacturing the Film and Trailer requirements:

LIST MATERIALS (Negative & SOUND for example)

It is to be understood that all costs in connection with the manufacture of their requirements are at the sole cost of the Distributor.

Also you will not impose any lien upon or against the materials by reason of any charge or obligations incurred by the Distributor. Three copies of this letter are enclosed for signature and return two copies to this office.

Signed
Acme Film

Countersigned
Laboratories

Counter signed
Distributor

Mike - DATs will come in or Nagras or whatever they use. As far as prep for telecine, we will hold it and send it with the negative to the transfer house. The sound tapes are transferred at an audio facility and then a separate mag track can be produced.

Q - If the master sound mix has been done, is it possible for that mag to be synched up and the film screened with sound?

Mike - Yes. However, preferably, if the optical sound transfers have taken place, we would produce a married print for the first screening. Remember though, on first answer prints, neither Super 35mm or Super 16mm can have a married optical sound track, but you can run with separate magnetic sound.

Q - What about the optical sound at the final stage?

Mike - It depends if we process it or not, but if it comes back to us, we leader it up and sync it from a work print. We'll sync the negative with

The Lab Access Letter - A vital document for international sales, giving access to your materials held at the lab. But what if you have not paid your bill? They won't give you the letter, and so you can't sell your film! Just hang in there, they will give it you eventually, though you may have to sign your life away first!

The Lab Report Sheet

This is the report you will get back from the lab when they have processed your neg. It will often be faxed to the production office before the rushes are delivered so the DP can check for problems such as excessive dust and sparkle, negative scratches and that the printer lights are all as expected (implying that the exposure has been correct).

Lab Roll No.
All the camera rolls are spliced together by the lab into larger rolls. These rolls replace camera rolls for identification purposes during post production, now there is one video tape for each roll for example.

Printer Lights
These tell the DP what exposure the operator used to print the rushes. The lab technician will aim to produce a neutral look to the rushes. A scene with average lighting, shot with and average exposure will be printed with average printer lights (25Red 25Green 25Blue) to produce average looking rushes. So if the rushes look ok, but the printer lights read 18R 18G 18B you'll know that the original negative was underexposed by 1 stop (7 points are about 1 stop). Printer lights range from 0 to 50 but getting too close to either end would be worrying. This report shows excellent printer lights.

Camera Roll No.
The editor still relies on any continuity and camera reports that will still refer to the original camera rolls numbers

ACME LABORATORIES

DATE	12/04/2004	PRODUCTION COMPANY		LIVING SPIRIT		
PRODUCTION	ROCKETBOY		CAMERA REPORT		12050	
CAMERAMAN	JOHN DOE	STOCK 7248+74	LAB ROLL 5	TIMECODE 5	USER BITS 5	

VIEWING REPORT

COLOUR X   B/W

LAB ROLL NO.	SOUND ROLL NO	CAMERA ROLL NO	SLATE	TAKE	PRINTER LIGHTS* R	G	B	AVERAGE EXPOSURE	REMARKS
5		1	1	1-3	29	27	25	27	ALL OK GOOD EXPOSURE
			2	1-3					THROUGHOUT.
			3	1					ALL OK
			4	1-2					ALL OK
			5	1-4					ALL OK
			6	1-3					ALL OK
		2	6	4					ALL OK
			7	1-2					SLIGHT FLARE RHS
			GVR	1					ALL OK
		3	14	1-3	30	28	26	28	ALL OK
			15	1-3					SMALL HAIR IN GATE, MASKS OUT
									ALL OK

Remarks
Lab technicians are extremely good at spotting problems which may not later be apparent on an Avid at lower resolutions.

Slate information
The telecine operator will note the information from the clapperboard.

POST

the track. The master is transferred onto film as an optical representation of the sound. That optical sound can then be printed alongside the picture for a married print. This analogue signal is always there, even if a digital format such as DTS or Dolby Digital placed on it as well. Should the digital track fail or the theater not be equipped to handle it, and then the optical track would kick in. Everybody would love to get rid of it though!

Q - Are there differences in the way you handle 16mm and 35mm?

Mike - 16mm is harder to deal with but it's actually not handled that much differently. We treat the negatives the same but they're separated into different machines super 16mm and 35mm. The machines we use are identical. 16mm takes more handling ability as it can act weirdly at times, but it goes through the same process. 16mm is generally one light graded roll by roll. With 35mm, you print and transfer the circled takes on the camera report sheet, which are extracted from the negative roll. The portion that you don't use (B roll) is stored until you need to pull something from it. One thing is to be sure to tell use whether you are using regular 16mm or Super 16mm as the machines we use handle them differently. We do Super 16mm here at Technicolor but NOT standard 16mm. When we handle standard 16mm at the lab, it is just prep for telecine.

Q - What is skip bleach (bleach by-pass)?

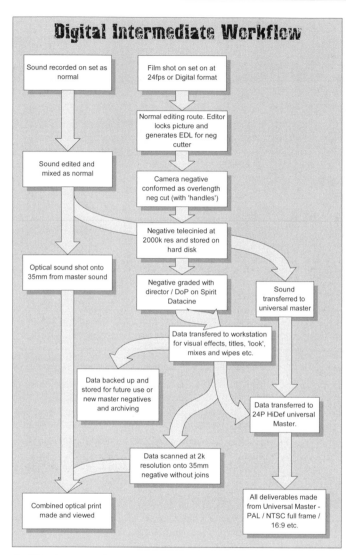

Digital Intermediate Workflow

Sound recorded on set as normal

Film shot on set on at 24fps or Digital format

Normal editing route. Editor locks picture and generates EDL for neg cutter

Sound edited and mixed as normal

Camera negative conformed as overlength neg cut (with 'handles')

Negative telecinied at 2000k res and stored on hard disk

Optical sound shot onto 35mm from master sound

Negative graded with director / DoP on Spirit Datacine

Sound transferred to universal master

Data transfered to workstation for visual effects, titles, 'look', mixes and wipes etc.

Data backed up and stored for future use or new master negatives and archiving

Data transferred to 24P HiDef universal Master.

Data scanned at 2k resolution onto 35mm negative without joins

Combined optical print made and viewed

All deliverables made from Universal Master - PAL / NTSC full frame / 16:9 etc.

Mike - It's a boutique look. It increases the contrast, darkening shadows and reduction of color saturation color. We take the negative and during processing we 'skip' the bleach process and fill a tank with water, which leaves a lot of exposed silver on the film. It's processed that way and Kodak has always said they don't know what the long-term effects are to do it that way. It costs slightly more than the normal processing costs.

Q - Are there any other effects like that?

Mike - People talk about cross processing, which also affects the colors. That's where they take the reversal neg and put it through the positive soup but we are concerned about what damage it does to the chemicals so we don't do it.

Q - Can you achieve artistic effects in the lab, like make S16mm color neg, black and white?

Mike - Yes. Although, if you want black and white, you should just shoot that stock in the first place. However, if it's a decision that has been made after shooting, the lab can produce a new B&W neg. looks softer on screen than an original black and white negative. Then there are the softening and mood effects which can be created by controlled negative exposure, that is underexposing the films a couple of stops on purpose. It gives a harsh, grainy, appearance. You should always do tests when trying these things so you don't end up ruining your neg when time and money are really on the line.

Q - What happens after the master neg is printed?

Mike - My term would be cut negative. It would be re-cleaned back to heads and ready to be printed again. Once you're completely finished with it, it will be vaulted. It's best to keep it here as opposed to taking it home and sticking it in a closet.

Q - How does the process work once you've got your answer print?

Mike - A check print would be made from a dupe. An answer print is from the original. You sit in with the timer and they will take the print and adjust the colors from scene to scene. By that time, they have every splice where the scene begins and ends, it has a footage counter and from there they will give each scene its individual printer lights. Once that is done, we'll make an IP (inter-positive), and a dupe (inter-negative) and a check print from that. Well create the release prints from the inter-negative.

Q - So you do all the necessary amendments to the check print?

Digital Intermediates

Many films now use digital intermediates (DI), opposed to the traditional optical methods that have been used for the last 100 years. The process means that you shoot film, do your offline edit, then scan the shots, at a very high resolution, add special effects, titles, color correction etc, then store on tape as well as transferring back onto negative to make your prints. This new technology saves loads of time, allows you to alter your film in an almost infinite number of ways, plus the master is digital and therefore will never degrade (although you do need to consider long term data storage issues).

Sounds good, huh? Well, the one downside to DI is the cost - $180k -$240k all in (2004), though this will drop as the technology becomes less expensive. DI substantially reduces the cost to create HD, SD & DVD deliverables. A 16mm blowup to 35mm can be done with no additional cost. Other cost savings can come from the ability to combine digital dailies and 3 perforation 35mm in the camera reducing by 25% the amount of film used on the set.

If you do go down the DI road, the first thing to do is for you and your DP to find a digital post house so they can guide you through the various stages. Once you find a place that works for you, and you have your negative cut, you (and perhaps your DP) will spend about two weeks with a colorist, scanning (Thompson Spirit Data Cine and Imagica are the most common scanners) and color correcting the film (usually on a DiVinci or Pandora machine) and setting the overall final look for the project. Once completed, the color corrected data is moved onto a powerful workstation for the final conform. Here things like dust busting, scratch removal, speed changes, transitions, title graphics and end credits are added. Additionally, simple effects, wire and boom removal can be performed. Also, visual effects and other digital elements can be imported into the project. Generally, the conforming and cleanup stages only take a day or two.

You can check your work by creating a digital answer print and playing it back in a digital cinema. You then have the choice of creating an inter-negative or an inter-positive, depending on how your release prints will be generated (though most people skip over the inter-positive step). There are tons of different film stocks with different grain and look characteristics you can select, and the output from the film recorder creates a master that requires only one light printing with no further color or printer light changes.

Mike - You should do all your timing corrections in the answer print stage because you want the dupe to be a one light, because if its going to go into mass production, they want it to be a one light. That print is usually 2500ft a minute, so they want to stay at one light and keep going. We up here have CCP's which are big loopers, the negative will be in a loop and continuously running, so the machine is going so fast, you don't want it doing a lot of light changes.

Q - So if you do the one light, then to get to your final once you've timed it, you do that on your answer print stage...

Mike - We make an IP so its locked into the IP and then the IP is going to put it onto the dupe.

Q - Once you've done your answer print, is the release print a lot cheaper?

Mike - Yes they are. Any print from the original neg is going to be expensive by comparison with a print from an inter-negative (the dupe). Your answer print is built into your front-end costs, as this is the final print that has had the most work done to it with color timing. Release prints are dupes of the answer print and the price is calculated on a sliding scale of discount, depending on how many prints you are ordering on that dupe.

Q - What is a low contrast print?

Mike - A Low Con print is produced by using the same color timing of your answer print but output on stock that has a much lower contrast. They are used for telecine transfers because the contrast levels on regular print stock are too high.

Q - Are there limitations of timing?

Mike - With the Hazletine timers you can do quite a lot. You can change your reds and greens, make them hotter and colder, and change the density, making it lighter or brighter.

Q - Are there any differences in developing Super 35mm?

Mike - The dailies print; grading and neg cutting are the same as normal 35mm. However, at the inter-negative stage, on an optical printer, you put an anamorphic squeeze in. Then when you make the final projection print, it has the anamorphic squeeze and when it goes to the theater, they unsqueeze it on projection and put it back to widescreen format.

Q - Is the optical process with Super 35mm very expensive?

Mike - Yes, but you get more frame area for the picture and the cost of an anamorphic lens for regular 35mm can be costly as well.

Q - What is the lab access letter?

Mike - This gives us the OK to release negatives to specific people. Typically sales and distributors will need a lab access letter. With the bleach bypass we also ask for a letter to confirm that's what they want.

Q - What is the Tonics system?

Mike - When a daily is done, the edge code is stored, so if a negative comes back to the lab, it'll have a printer light. Tonics (Total Original Negative Information Collection System) is a computerized system that will record information so you can always find it.

Q - Do you get a lot of HD now coming to you?

Mike - A lot of the TV shows are going to HD or 24P, which is not what we want to see. That's the non-film route. Technique, which is part of our company at Technicolor, actually download negatives through a process called digital intermediates. They can take your digital image and put it into an IP or dupe. They did that with *Panic Room*.

Time / Footage Chart

Time/Mins	35mm @ 24 fps	16mm @ 24 fps	16mm @ 25 fps
1 mins	90ft	36ft	37.5ft
5 mins	450ft	80ft	187.5ft
10 mins	900ft	360ft	375ft
15 mins	1350ft	540ft	562.5ft
25 mins	2250ft	900ft	937ft
30 mins	2700ft	1080ft	1125ft
60 mins	5400ft	2160ft	2250ft
90 mins	8100ft	3240ft	3375ft
120 mins	10800ft	4320ft	4500ft

NOTE - 16 frames 35mm = 1ft   40 frames 16mm = 1ft

Q - What are the most common mistakes you come across?

Mike - The exposure problem is the most common one as it builds a lot of flexibility. Insufficient information on the camera report sheets, making sure messages and comments are received, particularly with regard to cutting negative or moving the negative about. Also people don't shoot enough tests and end up wasting time and money.

Q - What advice would you give a new filmmaker or DP?

Mike - Get involved with the contact person as they will be your eyes and will point you in the right direction.

Glossary of Lab Terms:

A & B Cutting - A method of assembling original material in two separate rolls, allowing optical effects to be made by double printing.

A or B Wind - The two forms of winding used for rolls of film perforated on one edge only.

Anamorphic - An optical system having different magnifications in the horizontal and vertical dimensions of the image (used for cinemascope style effect.)

Answer Print - The first Answer print is the first combined (action and sound) print produced by the laboratory from a cut negative for further customer grading comments. The final Answer print is a print which has been fully graded and accepted by the customer.

ASA or EI - Exposure Index or Speed Rating to denote film sensitivity.

Aspect Ratio (AR) - The proportion of picture width to height.

Bleach Bypass - A technique where, by skipping the bleach stage in the color processing sequence, silver is retained in the image along with the color dyes. The result is effectively a black and white image superimposed on a color image. Bleach Bypass images have increased contrast, reduced saturation, often giving a pastel effect.

Blow Up - An optical enlargement of a film from one gauge to another, such as 16mm up to 35mm. The opposite of a blow up is a Reduction Print.

Checker Board Cutting - A method of assembling alternate scenes of negative in A & B rolls, used fro 16mm, which allows prints to be made without visible splices.

Cinemascope - A system of anamorphic widescreen presentation (Trade name).

Clone - An identical copy, usually referring to a digital tape.

Combined Print - A motion picture print with both picture and sound on the same strip of film. Also, referred to as COMPOSITE PRINT/ MARRIED PRINT.

Dailies/Rushes - Daily rush prints. The first positive prints made by the laboratory overnight from the negative photographed on the previous day. Used to see if there are any mistakes in the filmmaking process that need to be fixed immediately.

Density - A factor which indicates the light stopping power of a photographic image.

Developing - The chemical process which converts a photographic exposure into a visible image.

Dissolve - A transition between two scenes where the first merges with the second.

Dupe - A copy negative, short for duplicate negative.

Edge Numbers - Coded numbers printed along the edge of a strip of film for identification.

Edge Fog - Exposure along the edge of the film from raw light, in most cases from a lightleak, due to the camera door not being taped. Edge Fog can sometimes be visible in the frame or sometimes outside of the frame effecting the clarity of the latent edge numbers.

Fade - An optical effect in which the image of a scene is gradually replaced by a uniform dark area, or vice versa.

Flop-Over - An optical effect in which the picture is shown reversed from right to left.

Grading (Timing) - The process of selecting the printing values for color and density of successive scenes in a complete film in order to produce the desired visual effect.

Intermediates - General term for color masters and dupes.

Interpositive - A color master positive used as protection for the original neg and as a printing master from which the internegative is made.

Liquid Gate - A printing system in which the original is immersed in a suitable liquid at the moment of exposure to reduce the effect of surface scratches and abrasions.

Mag-Opt - A motion picture print with both magnetic and optical (photographic) sound track records.

Optical Sound - A sound track in which the record takes the form of variations of a photographic image.

Pull Processing - A special type of processing where the film is developed for a shorter time than normal, usually to make up for intended overexposure.

Push Processing - Lab technique where the film is developed for a longer time than normal, usually to make up for intended underexposure. It should be noted that only entire rolls can be pushed, not individual scenes. Pushing film will add some contrast and graininess.

Pitch - The distance between two successive perforations along a strip of film.

Reversal - The processing of certain types of film to give a positive image on film exposed in the camera.

Skip Frames/Step Printing - An optical printing effect eliminating selected frames of the original scene to speed up the action.

Unsqueezed Print - A print in which the distorted image of an anamorphic negative has been corrected for normal projection.

Wet Printing - (See Liquid Gate). A system of printing in which the original is temporarily coated with a layer of liquid at the moment of exposure to reduce the effect of surface faults.

POST

Jeff Betancourt
Editor

THE EDITOR

Q - What is a film editor's job?

Jeff - An editor helps the director put the film together. On a basic level, I utilize the footage that was captured on set and assemble the film, from beginning to end. Creativity really comes into play as I make adjustments to the film. I talk to the director about what he or she wants from the material, and together we consider each performance and shot, and decide how best to tell the story. The director and the editor have to put their egos aside when working together. Editing is a long process, more akin to a marathon than the sprint of production, and rarely does the first idea, regardless of where it originated, ever work. We try different line readings, new angles and new shades of performance until a scene feels real and true.

Q - What makes you decide to do a film?

Jeff - The characters. It's so hard to make a movie and it absorbs so much of my life - it takes six months to a year - so I have to love them! Even if the script isn't perfect, there has to be something I respond to on a gut level that says, *'I want to see this movie, I want to be a part of this'*.

Q - When do you come on board?

Jeff - I begin on the first day of principle photography. Ideally I would have been in contact with the director during pre-production, giving him my thoughts and listening to ideas as they plan the shoot. During production, I'm in constant communication with the director and I act as a second set of eyes and ears in the editing room. I evaluate the footage in terms of focus and continuity. I also evaluate footage in terms of performance and storytelling. I start editing scenes as soon as possible and send rough cuts to the director so we can discuss which scenes and performances are working and which ones aren't.

Q - Would you do that on a low budget film too?

Jeff - Yes. Even on a micro-budget film like *Chuck & Buck,* I was cutting from the beginning. Some producers assume that it's too expensive to hire an editor during production, but it's important for editors to see the movie come together as the film is being shot. Because schedules are so intense for the director and producer, I'm often the only one who is able to watch all the dailies. If I feel there's a shot missing, they can try and get it before they strike a set, as opposed to having to build the set again months later. Seeing scenes quickly also allows the director to see performances coming together and to make adjustments. In the end, I believe the editor can save the production money and make the film better by being there from the beginning.

Q - What makes a movie work?

Jeff - I think films work when they convey some kind of emotional truth. As filmmakers, our best tool for achieving this connection is a good story. If we tell a story well, people forget themselves and become deeply involved, making it a satisfying and complete experience. Whenever the film is screened and the audience isn't responding the way the director and I intended, it's my job to ask 'what can we do to make it better?' One way I have found is by constantly making sure that the characters' goals are clear and that the audience understands what stands between the characters and their goals. As editors, we have to string little emotional moments together in a way that appears seamless and natural, hopefully providing the audience with emotional continuity. Sometimes that means restructuring the film so that it makes more sense on this emotional level. Additional photography can also be critical in completing a film. It's often those little pieces of story that make the film complete. Maybe it's just an extra look between a couple of characters, or a scene that allows a character to express feelings that may have been hinted at in an earlier cut. Those moments are what make a scene resonate with an audience.

Q - What makes a good edit? What makes two shots cut together?

Jeff - I've always felt that the best editing is the editing that you don't notice. I suppose that goes back to that sense of emotional truth. Each shot in a film has an energy and emotional element. In putting shots together, we want to make sure there is some continuity of that energy. My first impulse is to cut on an action. I like there to be some movement at the beginning of cut because of the forward momentum that it creates. This energy is liberating because, if I do it right, you're not bound to physical continuity as much as emotional continuity. Sound is important too. If the sound is smooth and you don't *'hear'* the cut, you'd be amazed what people will buy visually. I can have a complete jump in action, but a smooth soundtrack can carry you through. All that being said, sometimes the best cut is the one we don't make. My favorite scene in any film I've done, comes at the end of *The Good Girl*. There was a scene between Jennifer Aniston and John C. Reilly that was covered from every angle. They both gave amazing performances take after take, from the wide shots to the close-ups. I saw the dailies and there was this one master shot that spoke to me deeply. I put it in and said, 'that's it'. The director and I cut other versions of the scene, but we kept coming back to that awesome master shot. In it, we really got a chance to see these two people emotionally naked with each other. When we cut from close up to close up, I always felt like we were forcing the audience to see the scene in a certain way.

Q - Do you have any tips for editing dialogue scenes?

Jeff - Every time I think I've developed a set of rules for cutting dialogue, the next movie turns everything on its head. Every scene and every actor is different, so I end up depending on my instincts. I watch the dailies over and over, until bits of life shine through, and then I string together my favorite pieces from multiple takes. I start the process of shaping the scene and I ask myself *'how am I going to make this work and get it all to seem real?'*

The Editor's Job

1. Label the tapes as they're returned from the lab, or from the set (if digital). Organization is your best friend.

2. Digitize the material onto the editing system. It's very important to ensure that you digitize timecode and that the timecode on the tapes is accurate. Check, check and check again.

3. Break down the footage into the various shots and takes and sort them into bins for easy access. Make sure you can read and easily understand the labels for the bins.

4. Once digitized, store the original in a safe place. Your exposed negative film should be stored at the lab until you decide to cut your neg. If shooting digitally, consider cloning your camera tapes and send them to a relative for safe keeping.

5. For your first assembly, order the scenes the same way as the screenplay had planned. If there is a scene that is missing or contains visual effects that will be added later, place a title card in those areas stating what should be there.

6. Don't worry about your first assembly being overly long, badly paced, or tonally off. These will be fixed in the next passes.

7. Re-edit, reorder, screen, then help with the reshoots... Keep doing this until you truly have the best edit of the film. Export and EDL for final neg cut or digital conform.

8. Tidy the sound and co-ordinate with the sound editors.

9. Visit the labs for viewings of test prints, visit the final mix to advise on sound, visit the final conform to advise on color correction.

INDUSTRY INSIDER

POST

I also have to ask myself, *'what are the characters are saying emotionally as opposed to what they are saying verbally?'* A character can be saying, *'I love you'*, but because of the context, they might really be saying, *'I hate you'.* It's important that I show that moment in a way that conveys the hidden meaning. Maybe I'll hold on a close up of the other character for a long time, or maybe I'll try cutting away later than what seems natural. I keep playing with the footage until something connects with the director and I emotionally. I strive to convey those emotions in as unique and truthful a way as possible. There are really no rules.

Q - Any tips for action sequences?

Jeff - You can get away with more in action sequences because they can be fast and kinetic. However, you can't get lazy. You have to make sure the action and energy of each shot is clear and precise and the sequence has internal rhythm that keeps the energy going. I hate when action scenes are cut too quickly and chaotically. I like to know where the protagonist is, and feel like I'm in the middle of the action. The only way I know to accomplish that is to make the action and the goals clear. Steven Spielberg and James Cameron are masters at this and I'd advise anyone to watch their action sequences to see how amazing they can be.Sound effects are also important for action scenes. They help establish the rhythm and often give a scene a great deal of emotional impact. When I show an action scene to the director for the first time, I always clean up the production sound and add sound effects.

Q - Are fight scenes hard to cut?

Jeff - A lot happens in a fight, but to make it special, I try to give it real emotional weight and to make sure the violence has impact. Inevitably, we have a ton of footage and no matter how well the fight was covered, you always feel like you need more. I end up trying to stretch what footage I have and often have to reuse shots or overlap action in order to give the scene enough energy.

Q - How long do you work?

Jeff - During production, I try to keep it nine to five, because I know that once production wraps, the hours are going to get a lot longer. Eventually, we end up working 12 hours a day, six days a week. When the budget is low, we work longer hours because the deadlines are constantly looming. Every day of renting the editing equipment and the editing space eats up the budget, so we all work long hours to ensure the film is getting all the attention it needs before the money runs out.

Q - How soon after shooting ends would you have a first assembly to view?

Jeff - I try to show the director an assembled cut one week after production wraps. This week gives the director some much needed time off and it's my time to sort of play with all the footage. I work really hard and as fast as I can to get a complete and presentable version of the film done. Unfortunately, the first cut is never very good. It's often called 'the editor's cut,' but it's really a rough assembly. It has a beginning, middle and an end, but it rarely has life and colour. That takes more time and patience.

Pickups and Reshoots

For the most part, it's best get all your shots during principal photography. However, there might be some that you can't get due to time constraints, some that you realize after viewing your first assembly or a test screening that you now need, or some that were screwed up the first time around and need to be redone. Going back to 'pick up' or 'reshoot' is extremely common, and should be budgeted for both in cost and time. Some pickups, such as close ups of fingers on a keyboard, a wide establishing shot of a location, a match igniting, or a coffee mug being placed down are very simple and can be done over a long weekend with a minimal crew. Even getting a certain look from an actor that resolves a loose end is fairly easy, only complicated by time schedules and continuity issues (making sure they are wearing the same shirt they wore the day of the original shoot and make-up is consistent). Larger reshoots of whole scenes or sequences can be more complex (even though you'll need a larger crew, it's still not that difficult or expensive to organize). Getting your film right is so much more important both creatively and psychologically.

Editing Tips

Whether you hire and editor or cut your project yourself, the cutting process can be both rewarding and frustrating. You will love seeing your film come to life, but may cringe at shots or sequences that don't work, or at bad acting that you let go on set (at the time you blamed the actors, but now you suspect it's more to do with your script and you now regret not spending time on that extra script rewrite!) The key here is to keep going to your first cut, then have a few unbiased people watch it so that you make changes or schedule reshoots to fix problems you could not see as you. Then repeat these two steps over and over until you get it right. While the length of editing varies by budget and time constraints (one month to a year), a general rule of thumb for a low budget picture is to allow 12-16 weeks for picture lock. Remember that the editor hasn't been on set and therefore isn't aware of how painstakingly long it took to set up a certain shot, or how difficult it was to get that perfect take.

1. Hire your editor during production and have them begin editing from day one of shooting. The editor will see your movie come together and can inform you of problems as you go along (such as needing more coverage or cutaways), problems that will then be simple to fix and far more economical than fixing them in post.

2. Establish a relationship with the lab (this goes for the director and the DP as well) prior to shooting and have meetings with them as necessary. This will iron out problems that may arise, such as what to do if the footage comes back dirty.

3. Whether shooting film or digital, make sure the sound and picture are synched together before sending the dailies to the editor. You are paying him to cut, not to sync sound for weeks.

4. Make sure your editor has all the necessary post paperwork - camera reports, continuity reports, sound reports, lab reports, etc.

5. Generally, it's a good idea to keep the actors out of the cutting room. Scenes may not have gone as planned, and insecurities may flare up which may adversely effect future performances.

6. Kill your babies. That scene, the one that looked beautiful, with amazing acting... If it doesn't advance the story, then you need to leave it on the cutting room floor.

7. If you're not sure about a scene, take it out and see if you miss it. You can always put it back in.

8. If you have to make major changes, note the scenes on index cards and stick them to the wall. This will keep you from getting lost.

9. Music and sound effects will enhance a scene that is tedious, but they will not fix the heart of the problem.

10. Dropping the ends of scenes sometimes helps, it can create a question in the audience's mind - what's going to happen next?

11. Don't be afraid of inventing new scenes, or lines of dialogue, getting the actors back and having a mini reshoot. If the audience doesn't understand something fundamental, you can fall back on the blunt instrument of explanatory dialogue.

12. Take a break before locking picture. When you come back to it, you will see the movie with new eyes and increased energy.

13. If you are faced with a long dull scene or a shot that you can't cut away from, try hacking it with an unusual cut. It might work.

14. Listen to the people who view your rough cuts. While they might not know exactly what is wrong, they know what is working for them and what isn't. Don't fall into the mistaken position of believing you know better because you are the filmmaker

15. Don't take anything personally. Whatever opinions you or your editor express, you are both just trying to make the film better. It isn't worth losing a friendship over.

16. Most Important! Sort out your entire planned post-production route before you shoot. Both FCP and Avid Xpress Pro can handle the job. Don't get sucked into the 'Avid is better than FCP' and vice versa devate. They are both excellent tools. What is important is the cuts the editor makes, not the software used. (Avid Film Composer is pictured below).

POST

SOMETHING [REDACTED] SCREENING SURVEY

Please take a moment to let us know how you feel about the movie. Thank you.

1. What is your gut reaction to the movie overall (PLEASE check only one).

| Excellent ( ) | Very Good ( ) | Good (X) | Fair ( ) | Poor ( ) |

2. What is the *first thing that comes to mind* to describe how you feel about this movie.

Felt like a cheap made-for-TV movie. Maybe it was the cheesy music, but some of the acting was so-so and the script felt it clicked.

3. Would you recommend this movie to your friends? (PLEASE check only one).

| Yes definitely ( ) | Yes probably ( ) | No probably not (X) | No definitely not ( ) |

4. What would you tell your friends about this movie? Not just whether you liked it or not, but how would you describe it to them?

See above. Also, it wasn't funny enough to be a comedy or serious enough to be a drama — it didn't seem to know what it was

5. Please tell us all the things you liked about the movie. (Please be as specific as possible).

Jill was likeable.

6. Please tell us all the things you didn't like about the movie. (Please be as specific as possible).

Cheesy music, Brian wasn't believable, con was too telegraphed, some of the locations looked cheesy.

7. Please list which scenes you liked most and least, if any. (Please be as specific as possible).

Scenes Liked Most	Scenes Liked Least
1. End - Jill confronts Brian	1. Carter beats up Brian in bathroom.
2.	2. Brian + Jill w/ Dad in hospital
3.	3.
4.	4.

8. How would you rate each of the following performances and elements of the movie? (Please mark one answer for each performance and element).

PERFORMANCE ELEMENT	Excellent	Very good	Good	Fair	Poor
Jill, played by Kari Keegan		X			
Brian, played by James Wilder			X		
Carter, played by Richard Norton		X			
Chester, played by Joe Estevez		X			
Harlan, played by Adam Caine		X			
Michelle, played by Heather Marie Marsden		X			
Elizabeth, played by Elizabeth Jarosz	X				
The Dad, played by Geoffrey Lewis			X		
The story			X		
The understanding of the con		X			
The comedy			X		
The drama			X		
The plot twist				X	
The ending				X	

Test Screenings

Even if a festival deadline is fast approaching, you should have a test screening of your film. Showing your movie to an impartial audience is a good way to tell if all the mechanics of your story are working. While the opinions of the people watching your film are just that, opinions, for the most part, if a problem keeps being raised, you should attend to it. Hold a test screening with a VHS deck, pair of speakers and video projector.

1. Pure human emotion is always the best indicator of how things are going, so watch and listen to your audience. See if they're shifting in their seats, are they fidgeting or looking visually bored? Has anyone fallen asleep? Are they laughing in the right spots? Looking at their watch?

2. Have your editor copy the whole movie with all the sound, sound effects, temp music onto VHS, DV or DVD. Where titles or scenes are missing, put up a card explaining what should be there.

3. You may have several test screenings. A small one with people whose opinions you respect would be a good starter, to fix immediate problems. These can be people in the industry who can see technical problems that a general audience may not get. Once you make these changes, then have a larger test screening. Invite friends of friends who aren't in the industry. Avoid family as viewers as they won't tell you the truth.

Q - How do you go about test screenings?

Jeff - We start with family and friends, to keep it intimate among people we trust. Also, having the first screening on VHS in someone's home makes a potentially traumatic event as casual and comfortable as possible. Ideally, they haven't read the script so we can ask them questions about issues we might take for granted. Their response can help us make story and character beats clearer. After working so intensely on a film, it's difficult to see it objectively, and these screenings help me gain some perspective. Just sitting there with all these people in the seats, I can see the film in a new way. I begin to see it through their eyes one scene at a time, and it really makes me focus on every little beat. It's an extremely difficult but rewarding process. Sometimes I know all the changes I want to make by the time the lights come up

Q - As James Cameron says, 'a film is never completed, it's just abandoned.' Do you agree?

Jeff - Definitely. I always feel like there is more I could have done, but it's the nature of the process. Films can be delicate, and when you realize that a few frames can make a big difference in how a scene is perceived, you want to make sure you've tried everything. Eventually, however, you have to let go and trust that if you've worked hard enough, and put in the emotional energy, it will be a success. Independent films don't have release dates like studio films, but festival deadlines act as a cut off. If you're going

Test Screenings cont...

4. Remember a test screening is all about finding the problems. Don't expect anyone to praise your film, and if they do, ask them what they hated about it. Invite them to be as harsh as possible.

5. If you can't afford a video projection venue, then find someone with a huge TV and buy everyone pizza. Try to create as much of a theatrical experience as possible, so take the phone off the hook and switch off cell phones.

6. Draw up a questionnaire and ask them to fill it in (pictures). Do this before you get into a general discussion in order to reduce 'group think'. Have a big box of pens at the ready.

7. Have a freeform discussion at the end of the screening, and ask questions about the things you suspect may be a problem.

8. Your distributor or studio may require a test screening of their own so they know how to market your film, and how much to budget. This will be with a completely unknown group in your target audience, and from all walks of life, to hopefully represent the audience who will eventually be viewing your movie.

9. This can be a harsh environment for actors and directors. Don't let actors attend, and warn the director that it's going to be rough.

to make an independent film and you want to find a distributor, it's important to work around these dates. They provide an incredibly positive and supportive environment, and you want your potential distributor to see the film there with an enthusiastic audience, as opposed to seeing it on tape or alone in a screening room.

Q - Were the studios intrusive with the studio films that you did?

Jeff - Intrusive isn't really the right word because the studio's relationship with the film can differ from project to project. I've been fortunate that the studios have always been supportive and have believed in the talent of those involved in the projects I've worked on. In the best circumstances, everyone agrees on what kind of movie is being made. In those situations, there are ways to make the process work for everyone involved. However, if the studio has a different vision, then it can be an extremely painful process. At times like this, you want to address as many of the studio's concerns as possible, while still retaining the integrity of the film. As always, communication is critical, and as the editor, I can help the director express his or her position. There are often ways to address the studio's concerns if you understand the root of what they're asking. It's easy to make drastic changes but miss the mark. I find if I listen carefully, I can address their notes and still retain the heart of the film we've set out to make.

Q - Obviously once you've finished editing, you go into the sound mix, so do you stay right to the end of the whole film?

What is the 3:2 Pulldown?

Film runs at 24 frames per second. In North America, NTSC (National Television Standards Committee) video runs at about 29.97fps (commonly thought to be 30fps). If you did a straight transfer from film to video, the motion would appear too fast and the audio would quickly become out of sync. In order to fix this problem, the 3:2 pulldown process is used. In general terms, what occurs is that four film frames are distributed over five video frames, which over one second gives six additional film frames which will mean the film will run in real time again. The term pulldown refers to the idea of an intermittent shutter mechanism that 'pulls down' a frame of film, holds it for a certain amount of time and then advances on to the next frame. Because NTSC runs at 29.97 fps, or 0.1% slower than 30 fps, the telecine house doing the 3:2 pulldown must slow the picture and audio on the film side down by 0.1%. In non NTSC parts of the world, the 3:2 pulldown is less of a problem. Both the PAL (Phase Alternating Line) and SEACAM (Sequential Color With Memory) standards operate at 25fps. In PAL world, low budget films often shoot at 25fps (film and Digital), post at 25fps, transfer to tape for broadcast / DVD at the correct speed, but theatrically, the film is projected at 24fps, effectively slowing the movie down by 4%. This is unnoticeable to all but the director, editor and composer.

Jeff - Yes. To me the mix is one of the great perks of the job. As the editor, I go to the final mix because I've done so much preliminary sound work in the Avid and because I've worked so closely with the director and material. By this point in the process, the director has put a lot of trust in me, and I'm often the first sounding board for new ideas. My understanding of the film can also help in music discussions such as, which score cues work and which ones do not.

Q - Do you work with sound editors? How does that work?

Jeff - Because sound is so important to me, and because the director and I have spent so much time selecting effects during the editing process, we usually ask the sound effects editor to use our work as a template. I hand over all the elements I've used in the Avid temp tracks and all the editing I've done to the production tracks. Talking about sound is difficult and I usually find giving them this material is better than having hours of discussion. An observant sound editor uses our basic tracks to get a sense of what works for our story. From there, he can go in any number of directions but it's a good starting place.

Q - What common mistakes are made by new filmmakers?

Jeff - New directors tend to be really hard on themselves and take it very personally when a scene or a film doesn't work as well as they'd planned. They blame themselves and think they've failed somehow. Nothing could be further from the truth. As much planning as is put into a project, the truth is that things rarely work out as planned. It's a difficult lesson to learn, but the plus side is that you can always work and make things better. I'm a firm believer that every film can be made better in the editing process and that even the most difficult film can be brought to life through careful and creative editing.

Q - Are new filmmakers precious about removing scenes?

Jeff - Sometimes. Part of the editing process entails removing scenes and seeing what that does to the pace of the film. It can be painful when we try to take a scene out, but we try to remember that it can always be but back in. Ideally, every scene should have to prove in some way that it needs to be a part of the film. The process is really about being able to let go of preconceived ideas and listening to what the film is telling you. If your favorite scene really belongs in the movie, it'll find it's way back in. For first time directors, it may take a little while to build this confidence, but when they do, the process becomes very liberating.

Q - Do you ever let the actors in to the cutting room to see scenes?

Jeff - Initially, I like to keep them out of the editing room. I want to make sure the director is comfortable with the footage before anyone sees it. It is important for an actor to trust the director that I always want to protect that relationship. Once the director has had a chance to play with the scene, and it has reached a point we are satisfied with, we will let them see certain scenes. It's such an emotional process for actors. I have a great deal of respect for them and want to serve their performances as much as possible.

Q - On a studio film you would have every angle covered, but not so on a low budget film. Any tips?

Jeff - I'm a big proponent of digital filmmaking. As much as I love film, digital video is an amazing tool and offers low budget filmmakers a great deal. The biggest advantage of shooting on digital video is that you can shoot much more footage. You get a lot more coverage, and the actors and crew aren't under as much pressure. We shot over 80 hours of footage for *Chuck & Buck*. It was such a delicate film that I really feel we needed all that footage in order to capture the nuance that was so important to the story. If digital video isn't for you and you choose film you have to prepare more. You will have to work hard with your actors and crew, often working things out with them before you get to set. You just won't be able to afford as much coverage, which will put more limitations on the editing.

Q - How do you become an editor?

Jeff - Anyone who wants to be an editor needs to cut as much as possible. Cut anything and everything you can - music videos, short films, and especially documentaries. It's the only way to learn the process and to develop your own methods. This is also a great way to develop relationships with other filmmakers and to establish creative ties that will serve you throughout your career.

Q - Any technical tips? What advice would you give?

Jeff - I use note cards when I work - one card per scene in the movie and then put it up on the wall. I end up with a nice outline of the film that is helpful in charting the movie's progress - it's flow and pace. It's like having a battle plan, so the director and I can sit there, look at the wall and talk through scenes before I sit at the Avid. New directors are always

Final Cut

At some point you may get involved with another company who may demand 'final cut', meaning that they will have the last say on what ends up as the final edited version of your film.

1. Although it would be great to NOT give up final cut, you may find this extremely difficult because the other company is putting up money for your film.

2. If you do have to give up your right to final cut, fight for your version in the diplomatic way. If you don't and things get nasty, you'll be sure your opinion will never be heard.

3. If you hate the final cut, don't worry. Five years down the line you'll never think about it, and if you then see the picture, you may agree with the re-edit!

4. The final cut isn't an attempt to ruin the film. Everyone has the film's best interest at heart. Remember this, and don't let things get out of hand.

5. If the worst comes to the worst, then take action if you have to. James Cameron allegedly crept into the neg cutting rooms on 'Piranha 2 - The Flying Killers' and re-cut the movie AFTER the executives had agreed on the final cut.

6. As a director or producer, it is likely that you have less objectivity and more emotional investment in the film than anyone. As such, you may cling to scenes when they need to go. Listen to other people's comments.

surprised about how much we move scenes around, but it's common to rearrange scenes for clarity and pace. Having note cards really helps us see how the structure can shift and be made stronger. When I drop scenes, I move them to another wall of the editing room so that we can always keep track of what has been removed. There are no set rules, but I find the first third of the movie is where scenes are usually cut. Inevitably, there is set-up or character development that is unnecessary and I can feel the audience aching to get to the story. On a related note, I'd also recommend looking through old takes every once in a while. One never knows what little gems may have been overlooked in an actors performance.

Be open to the material's potential and try everything. In order to make the film the best that it can be, I always experiment and try new things. I see so many movies that feel unfinished. I can't help but feel that if they had put in more time and effort in the editing room they could have accomplished so much more. No matter how hopeless it seems, I keep reworking it, cutting and recutting. I'm always amazed at what I can get out of the material. *Star Maps*, the first film I edited, is a great example of this. The director had an initial cut of the film that wasn't connecting with the audience but he and his producer raised money to do some additional photography. It was at this time that I got involved. We started restructuring the film and reworking performances to clarify the goals of each character. I learned a great deal in those few months about structure and story. We kept working right up to, and beyond, the submission deadline for Sundance, and in the end, the film ended up connecting with the audience much more than we could have ever hoped. It was an amazing experience for all of us because it really taught us the value of perseverance and hard work.

David Gray
Dolby

Q - What is Dolby Stereo, Dolby SR? Dolby Surround?

David - Dolby Stereo is the trade name for an analog film format developed by Dolby Laboratories that uses four channels of audio (Left, Center, Right and Surround) and utilizes 'A' type noise reduction. The format also involves matrix technology that encodes the four channels of audio to two channels (Lt and Rt), which is printed on the film. In the theatre the two channels are decoded back into the 4 original channels. Dolby Stereo SR is the same as Dolby Stereo, with the exception that it utilizes SR noise reduction thus allowing more dynamic range and more headroom. Dolby Surround is the name given to Dolby Stereo in the consumer marketplace.

Q - What is Dolby Digital?

David - Dolby Digital is the trade name for a film audio format developed by Dolby Laboratories that incorporates six channels of discrete digital audio. Dolby Digital is the most popular digital soundtrack being utilized by all the major studios and independents as well. In the US, there are over 40,000 Dolby Digital equipped theatres.

Q - How is Dolby Digital encoded on the film?

David - Dolby Digital is optically printed between the sprocket holes on 35mm film, as this area offered robustness in terms of wear and tear, making the format more reliable. Each perf area holds approximately 10 milliseconds of six channel audio.

Q - What is meant by 5.1?

David - The numbers refer to the number of channels in the format or system. The .1 refers to the sub woofer channel because of its low frequency only characteristics. These identifiers also generally have channel locations associated with them. 5.1 is Left, Center, Right, Left Surround, Right Surround & Sub (LFE). There's also 6.1 and 7.1 (generally not used by low budget film makers).

Q - What is Dolby Pro Logic? What is Dolby Pro Logic II?

David - Both Dolby Pro Logic and Dolby Pro Logic II are matrix-decoding technologies for transforming two-channel matrix encoded (Lt Rt) material to either four channels or five channels. Pro Logic II also has user adjustments for width of the soundstage and can be optimized for music or film. Generally speaking Pro Logic or Pro Logic II is used for two channel mediums such as VHS and CD. Most DVD's use a 5.1 or 6.1 channel Dolby Digital soundtrack.

Q - What does it cost a filmmaker to license Dolby?

David - Dolby requires a Motion Picture Service Agreement (MPSA) which is an agreement between you the film maker and Dolby. The fees vary by region and release pattern. Pricing does not vary depending on which format or formats you choose, as all Dolby formats are included. Contact the Dolby office for pricing.

Q - Is a representative of Dolby present at every film mix?

David - Dolby endeavors to attend every mix at least at the mastering stage, but that is not always possible.

Q - What is Dolby Digital Surround Ex and what are its advantages?

David - Dolby Digital Surround Ex is an extension of the Dolby Digital format, adding a seventh audio channel. This channel is designated as the rear wall of the theatre. This additional channel allows full around the room panning with the center rear really being behind your head. Ambiances also benefit in having the third plane with which to work, giving more depth and envelopment. All films can benefit from Dolby Digital Surround Ex, although films where surround panning is prevalent will be more obvious (i.e. action movies). Dolby Laboratories does not have additional charges for Dolby Digital Surround Ex. Dolby Digital Surround Ex is best accomplished utilizing special encoding hardware that we supply during the mastering, and as part of the Motion Picture Service Agreement.

Q - What is the difference between Dolby Digital, DTS, and SDDS?

David - Dolby Digital is an *on film* six channel digital audio film format. Audio is placed in between the sprocket holes. DTS is a double system six-channel digital audio film format. The audio is on a separate CD-Rom that is then synchronized with the picture. SDDS is an *on film* eight channel digital audio film format. Audio is placed on the film edges outside the sprocket holes.

Q - What is THX?

David - THX is a set of specifications for theatrical playback of movies. If a theatre meets or exceeds these specifications, they can then display the THX logo. THX is not an audio format nor do they make theatrical audio processing equipment.

Q - How does a filmmaker go about getting an agreement with Dolby?

David - Two documents are necessary via contacting Dolby Laboratories. Firstly, the MPSA - Motion Picture Service Agreement which specifies the obligations and responsibilities of both parties, and there is a fee for the MPSA. Secondly, the TSA, that's the Trademark Service Agreement, which grants rights and usage requirements to the filmmaker / production. The TSA also has the required technical specifications that must be met in order to use the Dolby logos. The logos themselves can be obtained in camera-ready artwork or electronically from Dolby Laboratories. Most title houses will have the current logos. No deviation from the official logos is allowed.

Q - How much does the MPSA cost?

David - Dolby Laboratories has a multiple level fee structure (the highest published amount is $12.5k) that takes into account the region in which post-production is being done and release pattern. Contact the nearest Dolby Laboratories office.

CONTACTS

Dolby Laboratories, Inc.
3601 Alameda Ave. Burbank,
CA 91505
818-823-2800

Dolby Laboratories, Inc.
1350 Ave. of the Americas,
28th Floor,
New York, New York 10019
212-767-1700

Dolby Laboratories, Inc.
Wooten Bassett, Wiltshire
SN4 8QJ England
(44) 1793-842100

Jonathan McHugh
Jive Records

Q - What is the job of a music supervisor?

Jonathan - A music supervisor handles the finding and clearing of music and helping director's realize their musical vision.

Q - What kind of rights do you need to clear to use music in film?

Jonathan - There are two main rights needed. The synchronization rights, which are the publishing rights to have their music synchronized against the picture. The other right is the master rights and that is the recording that the song comes from.

Q - How do you find out who owns particular rights?

Jonathan - Most copyrights are handled by three performance rights societies, BMI, ASCAP and CSAC. You can go to their websites and type in the copyright name and you'll find out whose copyright it is, the publisher and some other information.

Q - With film, is the music licensed for a certain number of years?

Jonathan - When you license a piece of music, you want it in perpetuity because once you finish your film that music is locked in and it costs a lot of money to go back in and pull it out.

Q - What do you need to be aware of in terms of royalties?

Jonathan - Royalties only become a factor on the soundtrack front, and are not determined by the number of plays of the film. As for the soundtrack, the royalty is based on the number of tracks on the record and how high a royalty rate that artist gets. It would be highly unusual for a producer to deal with these issues as it's the record company who creates the soundtrack.

Q - Can you get good deals with record companies?

Jonathan - Unfortunately, the majority of songs are owned by record conglomerates who get thousands of licensing requests a week. A music supervisor is paid for their musical knowledge and relationships. they can save you a lot of money as oppossed to if you are Joe Nobody approaching a record company for their music. The labels may grant 'festival licenses' where they charge a small amount of money to let the film use their music. If the film gets distribution sometimes a 'step deal' can be negotiated record companies and publishers. Here, the rights holders will take a chance on the film and give the producer the rights for a small amount of money up front. Then if the film makes money at the box office, the music rights holder will receive some of the profits.

A good supervisor is essential, as they can get you reduced prices that you can't get on your own. They can get to artists managers and convince them to put their artist in the film even if the label sometimes doesn't think the use is enough money

Q - If you want an original score, how do you go about getting a composer?

Jonathan - A music supervisor can recommend composers to you in your price range. Occasionally if you have made a great film, a composer may wave their normal fee if they identify with the subject matter of the film.

Q - At what stage should you bring in a music supervisor and/or composer?

Jonathan - Sometimes a music supervisor will come in at the beginning of the process if there is pre-recorded music that needs to be done. Sometimes they'll come in during production and watch dailies. Composers don't usually come in until at least some of the film is shot so they have something to score to. The director/composer relationship is a very interesting one. They need to gel because a lot of times a director doesn't speak the music language and it's interesting watching them communicate and struggle for the right words. In the independent world, a first time director will sometimes bring in a composer and the studio will want a bigger composer. Then it becomes incumbent on how much power and the director has, and how well the score is working in the film.

Q - Is it generally a flat fee for the composer?

Jonathan - Composers can sometimes offer filmmakers packages, which can be inclusive depending on what type of music is needed. An electronic package where the composer just uses sync, and a straight up fee depending on what level of music the composer is doing, such as just a guitar, piano score, or is a full orchestra needed?

Q - What should you budget on a $1m movie for a composer?

Jonathan - I did a movie last year $1m budget and we had $15k for source and $15k for score. That's low, but if it's all you got, you can find people to work for that and you get music for the price.

Q - If the composer attains the rights to music and the producer sells the film to Thailand for instance, does the producer then have to pay the composer royalties?

Jonathan - It depends on the deal between the producer and composer. Sometimes will do films for a reduced fee, in return for a percentage of the profits. On a movie I just did, they split ownership of the publishing. The film company kept 50% and the composer kept 50%, so whatever monies that are accumulated throughout the world, that composer will receive his share in those different territories.

Q - How is that controlled?

Jonathan - With difficulty. Each territory has what's called 'black boxes', where if the cue sheets aren't done correctly and it's confusing as to who owns what, the country will keep all the performance money. In America, there's no performance royalties for songs or music in a movie, but there is performance royalties in TV. Overseas when it plays theatrically, there are performance income That's why it's important to pay a good publishing administrator as they'll collect money on your behalf. If the cue sheets are not filled out properly, the money goes into these black boxes and its split up amongst the musicians in that country. Publishers usually do the administration deal like a 90/10 split. You own 90% of the copyright and you have to give the administrator 10% of any revenue that's pulled in.

Q - Is it expensive to hire an orchestra?

Jonathan - The big orchestras here are unionized and what happens a lot of times is films will go to Europe, or a right to work states like Washington. If you record a unionized score, you will have to pay reuse fee just to put the score on a soundtrack. The more pieces of an orchestra you want the more you'll pay.

Q - Do a lot of new filmmakers use their friends who are in bands?

Jonathan - That happens a lot. Filmmakers want to use a bands songs, and the band wants to give it away but the record company may want to make some money on it. That's where it helps to have a music supervisor put all the pieces together.

Q - Does a music supervisor have any involvement with the contracts?

Jonathan - They look them over, but unless they are also lawyers they shouldn't really. They can suggest language and then hand it off to the attorneys involved.

POST

Music Rights

To use music in your film, there are three distinct legal rights you MUST acquire before locking and mixing the sound. Failing to do this could result in a film that no one will sell, buy or even screen in a festival.

RECORD / MASTER RIGHTS

Copyright in the recording of a song or composition owned by either a record company or the entity that has paid for the recording and thus owns the master tape. Different record companies may hold the copyright to a recording in each separate country.

PUBLISHING RIGHTS

Copyright owned by the author or composer of the work, literally the notes on the page. These become public domain 50-75 years after the death of the composer dependent on the country. These rights are controlled by a music publisher on behalf of the composer or author. Where there is more than one writer, then two or more publishing companies may own a share of the work.

SYNCHRONIZATION RIGHTS

Rights granted to a filmmaker to 'synchronize' the copyrighted music in conjunction with the film. Publishing rights granted for the composition or song by a music publisher on behalf of the composer or author. Record / Master rights granted by the record company to use a recording of that song or composition.

Q - Is there a place where producers can get a list of record companies?

Jonathan - Billboard Magazine is a good place. There's a thing called Floor11, which is an A&R directory. There are websites, like allmusic.com. Variety and The Reporter will have bi-yearly listings of all the music companies that license music and composers.

Q - When is the best time to talk to the record company?

Jonathan - You can pitch them in script form but today, most record companies want to see rough cuts of films and know, who the distributor is, how many screens it will be released on, and who the stars are.

Q - Do new bands generally do film scores for free for exposure?

Jonathan - Not for free but for a small fee to cover costs and time. Artists want to because, it's so hard to break into the film music industry and the visual medium of commercials, film and TV. It can be a very lucrative 2nd career.

Q - How does library music work?

Jonathan - You buy the music outright. there are all types and flavors like Cha Cha, bluegrass or disco. If You want a style or want wallpaper music, library music can be great AND cheap. First Come library is one of the biggest As is APM and Killer Tracks.

Q - Do they have set rates?

Jonathan - They do but sometimes they are flexible

Q - Could you release a sound track based on library music?

Jonathan - Never say never, but it's not likely.

Q - What is the music cue sheet?

Jonathan - It is a list of the music from the film. It tells who owns the publishing and the masters. It tells the order of where the music in the film is used so each piece of music can be tracked.

Q - Who should you give the cue sheet to after its finished?

Jonathan - The film's distributor, or the films rights owner. Every distributor in every country is going to want a copy of the cue sheet attached to the film as they are the ones responsible for getting it out there and figuring out the collections.

Q - What's the difference between background and featured music?

Jonathan - Featured music is heard out front that's not over film dialogue. It's played in montages, whereas background music is usually under conversation. This is where library comes in handy because you may want some music for a bar scene but you don't want it to interfere with the dialogue in the scene.

Q - Are there any other rights you need to clear?

Jonathan - Reproduction sync rights are needed if you cover a song, rights. The version you use in the film has to be cleared by the original

Q - If you want to use the lyrics of a song within your script, can you do that without clearance?

Jonathan - No, you have to get clearance from the publisher.

Q - Can the title of a song be used as the title of a movie?

Jonathan - It may but you have to have permission from the songwriter to use it as a title. This is an issue called 'broad rights' which can be a little nebulous.

Q - If you use a film clip in your movie that has music in it, do you need clearance?

Jonathan - Yes that's a clearance from the film studio that owns the clip. This should be cleared in production.

Q - What is needle drop?

Jonathan - Needle drops are a brief use of music. Again, that is where libraries are great. Why spend $5k on a pop song when you can get a reproduction of a country station?

Q - If you had an actor singing in a film, do they get the musical performing rights?

Jonathan - They could because it's a recorded performance, so they should receive a share of the song. For example, the actors in *Chicago* will get all the performer royalties for foreign territories and TV.

Q - What mistakes have you encountered with new filmmakers?

Jonathan - Filmmakers can be too egotistical at times. Producers have to trust their music supervisors and be collaborative. Music can enhance a film so much, and bad music especially can hurt it. To me, the biggest problem I see is that music is the last thing that's budgeted and if you put more money into it and think about it, you can win by allowing music to enhance your picture.

Q - What advice would you give new filmmakers?

Jonathan - Be adventurous. The concept of having music from a new band and taking a chance on them is something that could pay off if the band becomes big. Think about different ways to look at things. Music is a very subjective thing. So listen to new ideas and remember film making is a collaborative process.

POST

Harry Gregson Williams
Music Composer

THE COMPOSER

Q - When does a composer first get involved in a film?

Harry - That varies. I've done a lot of animation. I'm just completing my fourth animation for Dreamworks, *Sinbad* having done *Antz, Chicken Run* and *Shrek*. Often one's involved much earlier than in a live action film, mainly because they like to animate to your music and that doesn't happen in live action films, unless it's *Moulin Rouge* or something where the music is driving the film. In a straight up and down live action film, I would get involved during the last couple of weeks of the director's cut in post-production, not in pre-production or shooting.

Q - Has it ever got to the stage where they've said, 'we need the score in two weeks time?'

Harry - Only on a re-score. I re-scored *Phone Booth*. The director had the movie scored and the studio and the director started to get uneasy that the score wasn't quite doing what it might have done, so I was brought in. I desperately wanted to do it as it was a really good film but I was pulled in with four weeks to go.

Q - How long would you like to have to prepare the score for a low budget movie?

Harry - Low budget or high budget doesn't make a difference. If I wanted to do a good job, then the more time the better. On *White Angel* we had a couple of months, and that was fine at the time. If I were to do it now, I would want longer. With *Shrek*, it was only forty five minutes of score and thirty five minutes of songs, which I didn't look after, so I could have done that standing on my head in four months.

Q - Do you always look at the script?

Harry - If someone's trying to get you involved early, before the shoot, then that's the only way you can judge whether you'd be the right person to do it - by looking at the script and at the talent involved.

Q - How important is it for you to meet the director / producer to ensure you are chosen for a film?

Harry - I always think it's like putting together a basketball team. You don't want some weirdo even if he's talented. You may as well have someone who has a bit of charisma and who will bring something to the party. By the same token, you don't want some belligerent person who's going to say, *'this is the music and this is what it's going to be'*. I think you earn that place. So much of composing is about repeat business, and I don't mean that from a bank account point of view. If you have a standing with a director and a history with them, it works. From a composer's point of view, it's all about meetings. If someone's not going to see you face to face, it's not going to happen. You can send out as many CD's as you like but they want to see who you are.

Q - What do you need from the production team as the composer?

Harry - I need communication. They will have already temped the film which will give me some indication of where they're up to (temp music is music from other films used a guide, to give a feel to the edit). There's got to be something to learn from the temp track. Thereafter, constant communication is vital and the way I like to work is in a collaborative way. I expect the director to come and direct me through the process. I'll be throwing ideas at his film and he'll be pretty much on the spot listening to the music. I then make suggestions and react and read his body language and see. Danny Ireland (the director I worked with on a couple of movies) burst into tears when he heard the music, and I knew that was a good thing. Tony Scott starts flailing around with his arms, indicating he wanted more drum beat.

Q - What is the role of the editor in this process?

Harry - The editor is always someone the composer should stay in close touch with. We are mixing *Sinbad* at the moment and the music editor came into the room and said, *'they've cut five seconds out of this huge sequence at the end where the crowds are cheering and 'Sinbad' is pronounced a hero'.* It's good to know that. Sometimes they're so busy, they think, *'Oh well the composer will just cut out six bars'*, but that could really wreck your music and not be good for the film. So we've got a mole in the editorial department, and there's nothing clandestine going on, but it's like, *'for God's sake, let us know what's going on and send us over a tape of the change and, if we've time, we'll make the change in the music'* rather than someone having to cut it on the final dub. I always see the editor as a very important person. Some editors have great influence with the directors. They shape the film for the director. Some directors edit their films themselves, even if they hire an editor. They are there really saying, *'go from this shot to this shot'*, but some directors are a bit more distant and let the editor do their thing. Whichever way you look at it, they are very powerful people in the process and they need watching.

Q - Are there any instances where directors have temp scores and they can't let go of them?

Harry - Yes, often. I understand the process of using temp music. There are some composers who refuse to listen to temp music. I don't mind either way, but quite often I'm hoping it isn't any good and that I can beat it. Once they find some music that totally nails the feel of the movie, it's best to listen to that once only. The worst that can happen is that you try to emulate the temp score.

Q - Does a film have to have memorable themes?

Harry - I don't think it's necessarily about that. I can't think of a score that I've done that doesn't have some tangible theme. Otherwise music can become just drifting sounds. However, I really like the score to *Traffic*. If you listen to it, it's pretty dull, but I remember thinking how effective it was in the film. I don't think there was a theme. It's possible to be very effective without having a theme, but then a theme doesn't necessarily mean something an audience will be able to walk away humming. In *Sinbad*, you will definitely know the tune by the end. Not because I've banged it out so many times, but because it becomes synonymous with *Sinbad*. It's his theme. There are a million instances of film scores, where as their theme, the composer doesn't use a tune but maybe uses a motif or an atmosphere. In *Phone Booth*, there's very little melodic content in that score, but when you heard a certain sound which was a low, synth, throbbing sound, it meant something. If you can call that a theme, then it was. When

Temp Music

While you are editing, and before your original score has been written, you will want to put some music tracks down to help set a tone and find the pace of scenes and your overall movie. You will find yourself browsing the soundtrack section in music shops and plundering the collections of music score collectors, in search of the appropriate feeling score to use as a guide. Music editors sometimes call this 'tracking'. At this point ANY music is fair game as you do not have to pay royalties (as the film will never be screened publicly in this unfinished form). Many film festivals will accept temp music in your submission for entry, with the stipulation that you will have permanent score in place should you get into their event.

However, beware when it comes to temp music. On one hand, it can be very helpful to your composer to have famous music tracks as temp music in order to give them an example of what you want from the score. On the other hand, you may grow too attached to that style of music and not open yourself up to alternative ideas. All too often, new filmmakers lay in some temporary John Williams or Jerry Goldsmith, and not surprisingly, it improves their film. BUT, neither John Williams or Jerry Goldsmith, nor the London Symphony Orchestra, is likely to do a low budget indie film.

POST

that happened in certain spots of the film, you get a sinking feeling in the pit of your stomach.

Q - How do you approach scoring a movie?

Harry - Hopefully, a pattern starts to emerge in one's own composition. I don't mean that you're repeating yourself all the time, but for example, I hear elements of *White Angel* in some things that I do now. I surprise myself, as I'm not intentionally going there. I probably couldn't sing you the theme of *White Angel* now but sometimes I hear it. Harmonically, there are certain chord sequences that please me personally. You'll find them in my music through and through. I'm striving towards the same thing each time and trying to make it the best it can ever be. The tunes are different, the films are different, but I don't see myself as a bottomless pit of ideas. The trick is to keep it fresh for a composer, to make sure you move between genres and filmmakers. So I won't be doing too many more animations after *Shrek 2*.

Q - When you start, what do you physically require from the filmmaker?

Harry - A half-inch tape and a Super VHS tape, split into dialogue on hi-fi channel one and effects on hi-fi channel two. Sometimes we split up the dialogue and effects. Then we have a 29.97 non-drop frame SMPTE time code.

Q - When you return the score, what format do you return it in?

Harry - It depends on what people ask for. Mostly I deliver a Pro Tools session and a music editor that can operate it. Also, on a lot of Hollywood films, with the advent of Avid, you get to the dubbing stage and the picture isn't the same as when you last looked at it two days ago and the music editor's got to be able to make effective cuts on the fly to help the music make sense again.

Q - What is 'spotting' the picture?

Harry - 'Spotting' refers to a meeting where the director shows the composer his film. It's a process where everyone decides where music will go. For practical reasons, you need to spot a movie and it can be very insightful, other times it can be a bore because a director might have worked out so clearly in his head where he wants the music to start and finish, he's put it on a temp track so we're listening to a temp track. He'll say, *'I like the way this goes here and there and how it rises at the end'*. So you can make notes, but it leaves no room for your input.

Q - Why do directors 'spot' films?

Harry - The practical reasons are that they then have something to hold you to. *'I spotted music for that scene, where is it?'* I'm not hired to write a certain amount of minutes. I'm required to write the score, so who's to say what the score is? It's only happened

Spotting and Timing

After the temp track has been cut, the director and composer figure out where and how the real score will be placed in the film. The first part of this process is called spotting and second part is called timing.

Spotting
Literally the 'spots' where you want the score to be. Written down as spotting notes which contain very general 'in' and 'out' cues as well as any specific instructions about the score such as when certain themes are to come in, or if there is to be an absence of score. The final version of these notes is called the master cue list.

Timing
A precise (to the 1/100 of a second) list of the music cues that is given to the composer to execute. In addition, this 'cue sheet' contains descriptions of each shot, which includes its cuts and lines of dialogue. This is rarely done for low budget or indie films.

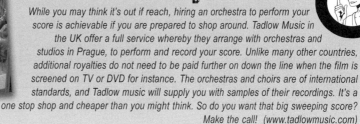

Hiring an Orchestra

While you may think it's out if reach, hiring an orchestra to perform your score is achievable if you are prepared to shop around. Tadlow Music in the UK offer a full service whereby they arrange with orchestras and studios in Prague, to perform and record your score. Unlike many other countries, additional royalties do not need to be paid further on down the line when the film is screened on TV or DVD for instance. The orchestras and choirs are of international standards, and Tadlow music will supply you with samples of their recordings. It's a one stop shop and cheaper than you might think. So do you want that big sweeping score? Make the call! (www.tadlowmusic.com)

once in eight years of doing this thing, that I forgot to do a cue. I looked back and thought it didn't need music, although the director did ask for music there. He made it known in no uncertain terms that he wanted music there as it was on the 'spotting' notes.

Q - Do you sit down and watch the movie together?

Harry - Yes. We do and keep stopping the tape. For instance on *Sinbad*, there was a good temp score with John Williams, Hans Zimmer, and a bit of James Newton Howard. It had been done by the music editor and it really flowed well. However, at one point, Jeffrey said, 'what you're going to hear is quite a nice temp score, but its 25% too dark and 25% not fun enough'. *Sinbad* is a hero. He's not going to die. He might live like he's going to die, but he's not going to. He can get himself out of anything. So when he's in a perilous position, never make the audience feel that he's in jeopardy. The temp score was verging on scary and we didn't want that. People are so set in their ways that once they've got a temp track, they can have trouble letting go of it.

Q - When does the composer get paid?

Harry - They never pay you the money up front which is a good thing. It is normally paid in four instalments. First, on spotting, which is the beginning of the process anyhow. Secondly, on any scoring, when musicians come in. Thirdly, sometime in the middle / distant future and fourthly, when everyone's signed the contract and the film is being released.

Q - What is a click track?

Harry - It is a preset tempo 'map' of a given part of the film that is going to be scored, and it is laid down to allow musicians (perhaps even on different days or locations) to have something rock solid to depend on. I work out the tempo of a piece for a given cue. Just like in speech, there's a rhythm to everything and that is one of the first things one does with composition, is to work out what pace the music will be. That doesn't mean to say it's going to be a constant pace. There can be gaps and rests. But it has to feel right according to what is going on in a given scene. Once one has got that, a click can be laid down and so that anything that happens can happen at any given time, but around that click track - the centre of gravity. In fact, my click track is hooked up to time code, which is hooked up to the time code of the film. Some of the old timers don't use click tracks, they just instinctively know.

Q - How expensive is it for a filmmaker to use an orchestra?

Harry - It depends. Orchestral rates are similar in America, but all the animated movies I've done, I've been sent to London to do. If we made a movie in Hollywood and it was a union film, we'd have to pay them the same rate as we'd pay someone in Budapest. However, in Budapest we could get away with just paying them once. You can't do that here. You'd be paying for them to play it on the score to by synched up to the theatrical movie. So when that movie moves to video and TV and DVD, the musicians are paid again and again. The musicians have a strong union. On a recent film I did for which I think the total budget was $1.8m, the music budget was $65k and it was a package - that meant the Producer wrote a check and didn't want to hear from me again, expecting ALL expenses, including the orchestral fees, to be picked up by me. For *Sinbad*, I got a fee and that's my fee and out of that I pay my assistants and the running of my studio, but I don't have to pay for the orchestra.

The Music Cue Sheet

The music cue sheet is a document that lists all the music cues in your film, including the title of each music segment, the duration of each segment, who the composer is, who the publisher is, who the record company is, the main use of the music (whether it's background or featured), and the Performing Rights Organization that the performer is affiliated with. The Performing Rights Organizations such as ASCAP/BMI/SESEC determine from the music cue sheets how the royalties get split and paid to it's members, and they take responsibility for it's collection, both domestically and internationally. Your sales agent and distributor will insist on a copy of the music cue sheet to be included in your delivery requirements. They will pass this on to buyers around the world, who will determine the fees they must pay the relevant collection societies. If the producer is paying the appropriate composer's fee upfront, they usually retain the publisher share of the music while the composer retains the writer share. If this is the case, the producer needs to set up a publishing company so that they will recoup the publishing royalties. However, if the producer is unable to pay the composer an appropriate fee upfront, a composer will often negotiate to keep the publisher's share of the music. It's recommended as a producer try to retain at least 50% of the publishing rights, but it depends on the cache of the composer. If the producer does manage to hold on to a share, the music cue sheet will then ensure that some time down the line, unexpected checks may appear in the mail.

If Music cue sheets aren't filled in correctly, the countries to which the film has been sold will keep all the performance monies and split it amongst their own members.

Music cue sheets should be sent to these following organizations...
ASCAP - American Society of Composers, Authors and Publishers. www.ascap.com
BMI - Broadcast Music Incorporated. www.bmi.com
SESAC - Performing Rights Organization for Songwriters and Publishers. www.sesac.com
MRI - Music Reports Inc. www.musicreports.com

Q - If you were going to have a 40 piece orchestra, how would that be split into instruments?

Harry - We might have twenty violins. On *The Magic of Marciano* I just wanted a string orchestra and four woodwinds - flute, oboe, clarinet and bassoon and strings. The fewer strings you have, the more you hear the individual scratchings. In a big sweeping John Williams score like *Superman*, there's an eighty or one hundred piece orchestra playing there. Also, it matters where you choose to record. On *Marciano,* not only did I have the musician's costs but someone had to orchestrate my music. When I say orchestrate, I mean actually transcribe the parts and do the orchestration (notes on the paper for the musicians to read). I wasn't going to write out each violin part myself.

Q - So when you do the orchestration, you write the score?

Harry - I write the score, and from that score, people then make the individual parts. So that's an expense and obviously the recording studio itself is an expense and these days studios don't come with much. When I did *White Angel*, I didn't have any gear but my mate owned a recording studio and you could go into a room and there would be a few keyboards you could borrow, or there would be a bit of gear lying around. These days there's nothing, *'you want a Pro Tools rig, you hire it in!'* They provide very little except the space.

Q - Would you take care of the fixing of the orchestra and studio where you're going to record?

Harry - There is a music contractor who looks after the booking of the musicians and takes 10% of the overall Orchestral fee. Booking the studio is easily done with one phone call, so I do that.

Q - When are the orchestra given their parts?

MUSIC CUE SHEET		Sheet No...1	Of...5

Film Title - **MY MOVIE**	Director - **JANE DOE**	Film Duration - **92'35"**
Prod. Company - **MY COMPANY**	Producer - **JOHN DOE**	Music Duration (total) - **28'12"**
Alternative Title -	Production Year – **2003**	Trailer / Promo / Programme - (T/P/F) - **F**
Country of Origin – USA		

Music Cue Title and ISWC No.
This is the name of the track. You will also use the codes that you created in your spotting session with the composer to list the tracks - so 1M1 refers to the first music cue in reel 1, where 2M4 refers to the fourth music cue in reel 2. The ISWC is like the ISBN number used for books and you'll find one on most commercial recordings (usually on the spine of the CD for instance). If your music has been written specially, you obviously won't have an ISWC number. If you can't find the ISWC number, leave it blank.

Performer(s)
Simply a list of the various performers who actually performed / sang the music. On a low budget film, this will most often be the composer.

Publisher / CAE No.
The Publishing Company that represents the composer / arranger / author and its respective CAE number. If you have used music that comes from a source that doesn't have a Publishing Company (such as an actor singing or unsigned band) then you should list it as Unpublished.

ISRC
ISRC is not yet used in the industry so you can ignore it for now.

Video Clip Duration
This won't really factor into your work so ignore it for now.

Catalogue Number
This is the number you will find on commercial recordings so that it becomes easier to track down the specific recording. Often found on the spine of a CD for instance.

Music Cue Duration
This lists the length of each cue in minutes and seconds.

Cue No.	Music Cue Title and ISWC No. (if known)	Composer / Author / Arranger / CAE No.	Publisher / CAE No.	Performer(s) Video / Record title	Catalogue Number	ISRC No.	Music Orig. Code	Music Use Code	Music Cue Dur.	Video Clip Dur.
01	1M1 - Opening titles	Jeff Davies (C) CAE: 555 121 335	Acme Music Publisher Ltd. CAE: 555 289 895	Jeff Davies	-	-	X	F	1"12'	-
02	"Running on empty"	Pete Stevens / Dave Jones (C) CAE – None	Unpublished	Thundercracker	-	-	C	F	0"22'	-
03	1M2 - The Chase (Incidental Music)	Jeff Davies (C) CAE: 555 121 335	Acme Music Publisher Ltd. CAE: 555 289 895	Jeff Davies	-	-	X	B	2"39'	-
04	Water Music	Handel CAE - N/A (Public domain)	Public domain	London Symphony Orchestra	AcmeLibray 22512	-	L	F	0' 6"	-
05	"Here Comes The Drizzle"	Jane Aston (C) CAE: 555 125 245	EMZ Music Ltd. CAE: 555 552 378	Monotones, The	AcmeDisc 2135431	-	C	F	0' 22"	-
06	Nightclub Beat	John Dingle (C) CAE - 555 112 489	Computer Music Ltd CAE - 555 569 872	Boston Orchestra	-	-	L	B	1'56"	-
07	1M3 - Say Goodbye (Incidental Music)	Jeff Davies (C) CAE: 555 121 335	Acme Music Publisher Ltd. CAE: 555 289 895	Jeff Davies	-	-	X	B	3' 36"	-
08	Beethovens Fifth	Beethoven CAE - N/A (Public domain)	Public domain	Steven Sanderson	-	-	P	F	1'36"	-
09	1M3 - Say Goodbye	Jeff Davies (C) CAE: 555 121 335	Acme Music Publisher Ltd. CAE: 555 289 895	Jeff Davies	-	-	X	B	3' 36"	-

Composer / Author / Arranger / CAE No.
The name of the composer and their CAE number. The CAE number is a unique code used in the music business which helps collection agencies around the world identify individuals and companies. The Composer writes the music, the Author writes the lyrics and the Arranger is a composer who adapts an existing work (only required if the music being reworked is in copyright). Composers dead for over 75 years are out of copyright and should be listed as Public Domain.

(C) = Composer (Music)
(A) = Author (Lyrics)
(C/A) = Composer/Author (music & lyrics)
(AR) – Arranger

Music Origin Code
Where the music came from.

L = Live Performance *(maybe your characters are watching a band, listening to the opera. Remember an actor singing a song in your film is a performance and you will need both performers and compositional rights cleared before using).*
C = Commercially Recorded Music, *such as a band.*
L = Library Music, *which in some instances may include music that you have used software like Sonic Edit Pro to create (check the install disks).*
X = Specially Commissioned Music, *essentially the music that has been written for your film by the composer.*

Music Use Code
The Music Use Code can be either F for Featured Music, or B for Background Music.

F = Featured music, *music that the characters can hear. A jukebox, the opera, a nightclub, the radio, a group of friends singing a greeting for instance. It also includes the composers opening and closing tracks.*
B = Background music, *the music that the characters do not hear. Essentially the composer's music and any other tracks you have used to accompany the drama.*

POST

Harry - At the recording session. These session players who play film music are astonishingly good at sight-reading. That's what they do. There's a three hour session in the morning. It starts at 10am. Everybody tunes up, you tell them a bit about the film and what their role is, maybe get then to play some of these through first. Then they put headphones on, and listen to the click track that I have designed. I can conduct, but if I have a click track, they follow that.

Q - Who is it that prints out the scores for the musicians?

Harry - The copyist. It would go, composer, orchestrator, copyist, player's music stand.

Q - Would you be the person who hires the music contractor (also known as the fixer)?

Harry - No. That is to say I would let the producers know who I wanted to use as my fixer and they would then look after hiring that person. I would then suggest key players that I would like hired or have the fixer recommend appropriate players for the project.

Q - How good are synths?

Harry - To use pretend violins and flutes is still as cheesy and cheap as it always was. However, if you do your research and have about $3K to spare, drum beats and synth sounds can sound good.

Q - Do filmmakers have a tendency to want to over-score the movie?

Harry - Yes. I think it's anxiety. *'Does that scene really play without music?'* There is a tendency to over-score.

Q - What is it like when you have directors and producers who are knowledgeable about music?

Harry - With Tony Scott, he's very much a non-musical person but he's an artist and is very good at painting pictures with his words, so he can tell when I get stuck. In a way it's more comfortable, so he doesn't start going into, *'second inversion C sharp minor please'*, because it would start getting weird. The director of *Sinbad* is a guitar player and a very knowledgeable musician, and we used that to our advantage. I don't find it threatening. He knows what he's talking about, so it works both ways.

Q - Do you go to the final mix?

Harry - Yes, I have to otherwise they'll not do it right. I don't go just to say, *'push the music up'.* This is where it comes together.

Q - Are there instances where scenes can work with just sound effects?

Harry - In *Castaway* the music didn't come in until he was on the raft and got away from the island, so that's about two-thirds of the way through the movie, and when it came in and one wasn't aware that it had been missing, it has such an effect, it was amazing.

Q - Do you have any control over the soundtrack album?

Harry - A score soundtrack, yes. A song soundtrack, no. That's where a Music Supervisor earns his keep.

Q - Some companies don't release soundtrack albums anymore, just albums of songs from and inspired by the film?

Harry - Yes, but Hans Zimmer sold two million copies of *Gladiator* and there was no song on that. Most artists don't sell two million records. He had a very good record company who were behind him. It was an Oscar-winning film, an Oscar-nominated score. That all helps.

Q - What are the common mistakes producers and directors make when it comes to music?

Harry - Over-scoring and under estimating the creative process and conditions that are necessary to write a great score.

Q - What advice would you offer a new filmmaker?

Harry - Look at the market place. There are a few people who are visibly successful and they are lucky. There are a lot of people with oodles of talent. I've got three assistants who are well equipped to score a film and haven't yet. There is always a perfect composer for any film and music budget, and it's up to the filmmaker to make sure he is in early enough to get hold of him. There's no excuse for getting a shitty score.

Q - Should a low budget filmmaker approach a successful composer?

Harry - Absolutely.

Q - What are the qualities that make a great film composer?

Harry - Hans Zimmer once said to me he thought that composing was only 50% of the job. I agree. There's a lot that makes up the other 50%. It has to do with diplomacy and holding things together. You have to present yourself as keen and knowledgeable, hungry, flexible and collaborative.

Q - What do you think makes a great score?

Harry - Music that supplies an otherwise missing dimension to a movie, music that seeks out something beyond what is literally up there on the screen.

POST

Doreen Ringer Ross
BMI

Q - What is BMI?

Doreen - BMI is a performing rights society. The company licenses broadcasters, radio, television and so forth to use music. We collect money from them and pay it back out, through an elaborate accounting and distribution system to the creators, who are the songwriters, music publishers and composers. There are multiple Performing Rights Societies in America, ASCAP, BMI and CISAC. Due to this competition, we promote other ancillary activities, such as being involved in the Sundance Composer Lab introducing filmmakers to composers, music supervisors and publishers. It's in our best interests to have our songwriters and composers thriving. The more they thrive, the more market share they possess and the more we can charge for the deals we cut with the broadcasters.

Q - Does the creator of the music pay to subscribe to BMI?

Doreen - No. They just put their art in. We are protectors of the copyright law.

Q - Is there performance income if the film is released theatrically?

Doreen - There's no performance income off theatrical performances in the US (there is when those films get sold to cable and tv).

Q - If a filmmaker sells their film to NBC, do you collect the royalties from NBC or the producers?

Doreen - NBC. All the producers need to do is make sure all their licenses are in place and that a music cue sheet is filed. There are samples of these on our website. This shows who wrote the piece of music, who owns the publishing, how it was used and its duration. If that document doesn't make it into the system, no one will get paid. If you've generated original music, you can collect on the publishing and part of your deal is that you can get paid. Often on low budget films, you'll give the publishing royalties to your composer to sweeten the incentive because there's not enough money in it on the front end.

Q - What is the difference between you and ASCAP?

Doreen - It divides up in terms of the creators' affiliation. Harry Gregson-Williams is a member of BMI, so the studio would have to put his publishing through their BMI company and Hans Zimmer is at ASCAP at the moment, so they would have to put his publishing through their ASCAP company. The composers are contractually affiliated, they can switch back and forth at the end of their contracts, but most of them don't.

Q - Can producers come to you and ask for advice?

Doreen - We have all kinds of solicitation brochures out there as we're trying to encourage filmmakers to call us and say, *'help'*. It's so difficult and convoluted when you're talking about clearance and who needs to call who and what you can and can't use. We want to help filmmakers get it right to start with, rather than having to clean up the mess that ends up in our administrative office when cue sheets are not right. There's a whole system that is involved in how to deal with music that isn't readily known, so I'm here to facilitate that and encourage filmmakers to reach out to us. We have a website, bmi.com where we provide information on who owns what song etc. The more personalized way we get involved is through recommendations. Music supervisors are looking for work and the filmmakers are looking for music supervisors, so we're facilitators. If there's a film, we'll make creative recommendations on the music supervisors that may be appropriate, based on their budget, personality and the type of music they are looking for. We work with all the agents who represent the composers and with composers who are underrepresented. It's the same with songwriters or bands. We're really artist development oriented here and deal in all strata of people working in this area.

Q - How do filmmakers get a soundtrack deal?

Doreen - Ten years ago every film seemed to want a soundtrack. Record labels were feverishly picking up them up, throwing money at the films to get the score and the songs. This has dried up now and I'm happy we've gotten back to a place where the music is about serving the film and less about being some huge tool to be exploited by the marketing department. . In a reciprocal way, we collect money for the various overseas societies in the US and send it to them so they can pay their members, who may just be licensing through us in the US.

Q - What are the various music clearances?

Doreen - If you're going to try to license a song that already exists, you need a synchronization license, which you secure from the owner of the copyright who is the publisher. You will also need the master use license, which is the license you would obtain from the record label of that particular recorded version. If there's a song that you love and you can't afford an already recorded version of it, you can record your own master, bypassing the master use license. You'd still need the sync license because you are using the song though. This is where we are most useful. In addition to talking about the specific licensing issues, we can step in to recommend alternatives to the normal process. Filmmakers need to know that you need these licenses, as it will come back to bite you after the fact if you don't. Sure, you can do it guerrilla style. Todd Haynes made a film years ago about Karen Carpenter, called *Super Star,* and he used Barbie Dolls to tell her story and used her entire catalogue of music. I was watching it, with the guy who owns those songs, at Sundance, and I don't think Todd was ever allowed to release that film beyond festival screenings. You can do it that way, but you can then never sell the project. That's a problem with only having festival licenses, if you haven't negotiated the step deal that attaches to the back of that, it can kill your sales potential.

Q - Can producers come to you to be put in touch with record labels with unknown bands?

Doreen - There are indie labels out there as well as people who represent groups of unsigned masters. There are a lot of creative options. You need to be open and informed about what your vision is musically. If it was hip hop that somebody was looking for, I would be hooking them up to different people than if it was a country soundtrack. We can recommend everybody that's in the mainstream of this business, but it'll then become a case of sniffing out the sub-culture, which is what we do.

Q - At what stage should a producer come to you?

Doreen - They can use us as an ally all the way through the process. If they're trying to figure out how to budget a film, we can help or hook them up with people who have a clearer idea. If they're in post and looking for a replacement track we can help there too.

Q - What common mistakes have you come across with new filmmakers? What advice would you offer?

Doreen - It's a common mistake to think you can use music for free. Also to become too emotionally enraptured with a musical idea. That's called temp love and it's undone some of the best filmmakers. They fall in love with a particular piece of music that they cannot afford or they use it until it stifles everyone's creativity. You're pushing the composer into a place that is robbing them of the creative process and what they might be able to contribute to your film. As for advice. Follow your vision. People love to jump up and tell you can't do things and I love to say *'yes you can'*. You just have to persevere and figure out how you can get it done. There are people out there who will find your energy infectious and help you if you shine with it.

Dlana Szyszkiewicz and Kevin Coogan
ASCAP

Q - As well as being a member owned performing rights society, what other services does ASCAP offer?

Kevin - We offer career development services to members who are creators (lyricists/writers/composers) and owners (publishers) of musical works - including workshops, showcases, seminars, panels and various networking events. We also offer networking receptions and mixers for filmmakers and musicians, and we attend festivals such as South by Southwest where we host a reception for all filmmakers. We have a huge talent pool of ready, willing and able, to score independent film. A lot of what we do is to help facilitate new relationships and give people alternative resources and career tools from the novice student filmmaker to those who have several productions under their belt. There is no fee to join ASCAP.

Q - Can independent producers become members and what are the benefits?

Kevin - If, as a producer you form a publishing company and there is some public performance of your work or of a potential public performance, you can become a member. I recommend the producer going into partnership with the composer and forming a publishing group so you can split the back end of the publishing rights. If the producer/composer is not a member, then they are missing out on PRS money. It's also a common scenario on low budgets to perhaps pay the composer less up front but give them the publishing rights. The composer could also keep the soundtrack and re-use rights so that they could take the score and re-use it in another project. We're happy to help producers sign up and get their publishing companies when needed.

Q - What on-line resources are available for filmmakers trying to clear music?

Kevin - ASCAP.com offers a wide range of valuable information for music users and creators. 'The ACE Title Search' database allows you to search ASCAP's repertory by title, writer, performer or publisher for contact information for music clearance purposes. The ASCAP membership offices in LA, NY, Miami, Chicago, Atlanta, Nashville, Puerto Rico and London are also valuable resources for finding just the right music for your project.

Q - What is the difference between you and BMI?

Kevin - ASCAP is a membership organization. We're run by our members and by a board made up of twelve writers and twelve publishers that are elected by the membership. BMI stands for Broadcast, Music Incorporated. Their board is made up of broadcasters - the same people we collect money from.

Q - Does ASCAP collect international royalties as well?

Diana - We have reciprocal agreements with our sister societies throughout the world, who are run similarly to ASCAP as membership organizations, rather than privately held companies or corporations. Nearly one-forth of our license fees come from the performance of ASCAP repertory abroad so we're aggressive about having good relations with the international area. We collect and distribute royalties to foreign societies for the performance of their repertory here in the USA, reciprocally, they send royalties to ASCAP members who have had performances in their country; the only difference is that in the US, the filmmaker does not get a percentage of box office. The only money a composer earns in the US from a theatrical release will be their upfront, creative fee as a composer. They get points on the back end, or points on the soundtrack, but not on public performances in a movie theater. In Europe there's a 1% tariff that is taken from the box office that is then divided amongst the songwriters, composers or publishers that have music within the film. We're a not-for-profit organization but we do have operating expenses. Our operating expenses from 2002 were around 14.6% of the gross revenues that we received. We became the first performing rights organization to distribute more than a half a billion dollars in 2001, and 2002 we distributed over $587 million.

Kevin - The monies collected from television and cable are huge. When you combine cable and broadcast television, it is the largest license area for music. For an independent filmmaker, a lot of times you're going to have a limited theatrical release. You'll do the festivals and then a lot of these films get multiple performances on cable television and it can generate a nice amount of money for people who have music in it. Independent filmmakers should look at this as a potential back end if they do end up forming publishing companies.

Q - How important is the music cue sheet?

Diana - Very. Without a music cue sheet, you will not get any money. For a major film, we circulate the music cue sheet to all the major societies through out the world, otherwise we use something called the Audio Visual Index. It's a listing of all the cue sheets and where they are housed throughout the world. For example, *Titanic*, James Horner is ASCAP. ASCAP has the *Titanic* cue sheet, although it's been circulating as it was a huge film. If someone needs it, they can request it from us and we will forward it to them. The music cue sheet is the foundation of a composer's payment. The production company generally submits the cue sheet. But we suggest that the composer needs to get a copy of it, as they can then make sure it's correct.

Q - What is title registration?

Diana - A title registration is a form that is filed with ASCAP to identify the writers and publishers of a song, the percentage of their contribution, the song title, the album name or film production and the affiliations of the creators of the song. The title registration is as important for a songwriter, as the music cue sheet is for the composer to insure accurate and timely payment for their work.

Q - If a film is screened in a remote island, is there a way of tracking it?

Diana - Yes, if that remote island has a performing rights licensing organization. If not, then it would be difficult. We would rely on that territory to report to us that the performance occurred. Also, if a member happens to know that a performance occurred in certain territories and they didn't get paid for it or they'd like to forewarn us of it, we'd be more than happy to advise the society that the performance occurred and request payment.

Q - What would NBC pay for an underscore roughly?

Diana - There are several factors to consider including musical duration, and time of day. For example, an NBC prime time performance of one minute of underscore for 100% writer's share may be $200.00, and the publisher would also receive $200.00 for their share of the use. If the performance occurred in the afternoon it may only be worth $150.00 or so per minute. The performance royalty overall is calculated using a weighting formula that takes into account the economic significance of the station relative to other stations in that media. For television, as well as the time of day being taken into account, so is the 'use' of the work (underscore, commercial, theme).

Q - What advice would you give?

Kevin - The filmmaker should not be afraid to contact ASCAP or give the composer the rights to the music because this money is not coming out of their pocket. This is money that we're going to be collecting from the broadcasters.

Diana - The more specific a producer is about the type of music they're looking for, the better we are able to provide them with a composer or song that fits their needs.

Debbi Datz-Pyle
Music Contractor

Q - What is a music contractor?

Debbi - A music contractor hires and organizes the orchestra for movie scores and for CD's, jingles, concerts, award shows and even video games.

Q - As well as organizing the musicians, do you hire the studio?

Debbi - Contractors are not required to do any more than hire, supervise and prepare AFM (American Federation of Music) contracts. But for me, good contracting is a lot more than just hiring musicians. I get involved with every aspect of the project. Once I am hired I coordinate the entire team which consists of orchestrators, engineers, copyists and agents. I work closely with the music production departments of the various film studios to co-ordinate scoring dates, booking studios, and preparing budgets. Being a good contractor requires balancing the needs of your composer, the musicians and the filmmakers. Once everyone is on board I send out a contact sheet with our schedule and the orchestra breakdown so we are all on the same page.

Q - How do you know which musicians to hire for the various films?

Debbi - The criteria for hiring the musicians is based on the composer's requests and the type of score he or she is writing. First and foremost is the music itself. Is it a jazz score or orchestral? Is it hip hop, pop or rock and roll? With that in mind, composers will ask me to either hire the musicians I feel would be best, or ask me to hire specific musicians they have worked with in the past or were recommended. I will always honor a composer's request and admire their loyalty. I am blessed to record in Los Angeles where most session musicians can play any type of music you put in front of them, which amazes me each and every time I do a session. However, there are times when specific musicians are needed. For example, for the movie *Chicago*, Danny Elfman's score was based on jazz from the '20's and 30's. Although there are many great jazz players here, finding the players that I felt would emulate that period was important. Many times I will speak directly with musicians about a specific style we are trying to create. I enjoy working with the musicians personally and encourage their input. Having a mutual respect between the orchestra and myself brings a better vibe to all of my sessions.

Q - How long is each session and is a musician hired per session or in a block of sessions?

Debbi - The minimum call for a film is three hours. Musicians can be called for one three hour session or many days of double sessions which are six hours. Let us say I am doing a film which would require 5 days of double sessions with 90 musicians required per day. All 90 musicians are called for each day but they are not required to take all 5 days. They accept only the days they are available. I then continue on with my list or call the composer to discuss alternates until each day is booked.

Q - How much music would you be able to record in each session?

Debbi - Each composer goes at his own pace. Anywhere from 2 minutes to 5 minutes an hour. If we are on a low budget project the composer will try to move at a much faster pace and can even get 30 minutes recorded in a 6 hour day. Composers will present mock-ups of the score for the director prior to scoring, so once we get to the actual scoring sessions we can move quickly with very few changes made by the director.

Q - If you overrun a session how is this calculated?

Debbi - Overtime is always charged in fifteen minute increments.

Q - How much is a player paid for each session?

Debbi - Scale for a three hour session is $243.34 plus 10% pension and $15.54 for health and welfare benefits. If a motion picture's production costs are under $25 million they can qualify for the low budget recording rate of $169.36 plus benefits.

Q - Are there standard contracts for each musician?

Debbi - The music contractor does not pay the musicians directly. At the scoring sessions, I keep track of the hours worked and collect all the paperwork I have given each musician to fill out. I calculate their wages based on the length of the session, the instruments they played and the specific chair they filled. I will then transfer this information onto a standard union contract applicable to the type of session I did. There are specific union contracts for film, records, commercials, live engagements etc.

Q - How much should a filmmaker budget for a music contractor?

Debbi My fee is based on the same scales the musicians are working under. Union scale for a contractor is double scale. Most contractors including me charge triple scale. We are on union contracts along with the orchestra. If I am dealing with a low budget project or a composer with a package deal (which means they are responsible for all costs) I try to help by lowering my rate to the standard double scale.

Q - What is the smallest orchestra that a film producer could hire giving them a good orchestral sound?

Debbi - It is hard to say what size small orchestra can give you a large orchestral sound. This depends on the composer, their style of writing as well as the engineer and studio. I have heard 20 strings sound like 50. Many composers with smaller budgets use smaller orchestras to enhance the synth tracks they have done themselves.

Q - What would a 40 piece orchestra consist of or does it depend on each score?

Debbi - The composition of the orchestra totally depends on the score. A 40 piece orchestra can be mostly strings or a combination of instruments. This of course is a creative choice that the composer and his orchestrators make.

Q - How much would a filmmaker need to budget for a 40 piece orchestra? And how many sessions might this entail?

Debbi - I would estimate wages with benefits for a forty piece orchestra at $30k for one day or 6 hrs. Not including any other recording costs. The amount of sessions depends on how many minutes there are to record.

Q - Could you record for a 40 piece orchestra twice, therefore doubling up and creating an 80 piece orchestra for your score?

Debbi - If a player or players are asked to double, it would cost the company double. 40 players doubled would cost as much as having 80 players being there. One way to avoid this payment would be to record a cue in the first three hours of a six hour session and overdub them in the afternoon.

Music Libraries

You can either order CD's from these places or download MP3/AIFF files from their websites. You must pay for licenses (synch, mechanical, performance rights) depending on what you plan to do with the music - rates vary based on what territories you want and what you plan to do with it (TV, feature film etc.) It's not especially cheap to use library music, but if you want a blast of Wagner or Beethoven, it's much cheaper than hiring an orchestra. You pay per 30 seconds or part of.

FirstCom Music, Inc.
Contact: Stephanie Lovick
e: info@firstcom.com
9000 Sunset Blvd. # 300
West Hollywood CA 90069
www.firstcom.com

Global Graffiti
Contact: Skip Adams or
Jacqueline Woolf
e: ggmusic@globalgraffiti.com
22-30th Ave #A
Venice CA 90291
Phone: 310-577-8940
Fax: 310-821-1734

Killer Tracks
6534 Sunset Boulevard
Hollywood, CA 90028 USA
Toll Free: 800.4.KILLER
Phone: 323.957.4455
Fax: 323.957.4470
www.killertracks.com

Promusic, Inc.
Contact: Dana Ferandelli
dferandelli@promusic-inc.com
11846 Ventura Blvd, Ste 304
Studio City CA 91604
Phone: 888-600-8988
Fax: 818-506-8580

Sonic Licensing
Contact: Cameron Peebles
cameron@sonicLicensing.com
11301 West Olympic Blvd.
Suite 336,
LA CA 90064
Phone: 1-866-286-9307
Fax: 1-866-286-9307

Who Did That Music?
12211 West Washington Blvd.
Los Angeles, CA 90066
US/Canada 1.800.400.6767
Phone: 1.310.572.4646
Fax: 1.310.572.4647

JRT Music
Post Production Services/
Music Libraries
e: jrtmusic@earthlink.net
648 Broadway, Suite 911
New York NY 10012
Phone: 212-253-8908
Fax: 212-353-9317

Manhattan Production Music
355 West 52nd Street 6th Floor
New York, NY 10019
Toll Free: 800.227.1954
Phone: 212.333.5766
Fax: 212.262.0814

**Corelli-Jacobs Music &
Recording**
25 W. 45th St. New York,
NY 10036?4902
Phone: 212 382-0220
Fax: 212 382-0278

DeWolfe Music Library, Inc.
25 West 45th St.
New York, NY 10036-4902
Toll Free: 800 221-6713
Phone: 212 382-0220
Fax: 212 382-0278

Sound Shop
321 West 44th St.
New York, NY 10019-5818
Phone: 212 757-5700

Q - How much would you expect to for a recording studio with a 40 piece orchestra? Does this include the recording engineers?

Debbi - A recording studio that would fit 40 players is about $3k a day. If your orchestra is larger than that you would need to record at one of our scoring stages which can hold over 80 players and cost anywhere from $6k–$15k, depending on hours and recording equipment needed. The engineers are independent and are not included in the studio fees.

Q - Once the producer has paid monies to the musicians, is this considered a world buyout or will the producer have to pay any more monies in the future?

Debbi - We have no such thing as a buy out here. If a music score is released on any other medium such as a soundtrack, an additional payment is paid to each musician. Producers also make a payment equal to 1% of their gross receipts form the release of the film into other markets being DVD, television , pay cable etc. This 1% of monies are distributed to all the musicians who worked on the film for the life of the film.

Q - I understand that many scores are recorded overseas in England or in Prague?

Debbi - I believe costs are the main reason scores are being done overseas. Some countries receive help from the government, others simply have lower rates and some offer a buy out. To fight these issues we have developed lower rates for film scores as well as soundtracks. For me, you get what you pay for, meaning there is no comparison to the quality of work found here in the States. From the musicians to the studios to the engineers I truly believe we have the best in the world. Certainly the most versatile.

Q - Are there any other fees that the producer ought to be aware of? For instance transferring large instruments?

Debbi - That is called cartage. This cost is based on the size of the instrument.

Q - What is the master recording recorded on to?

Debbi - The master recording is recorded on to Protools , digital or analog multi track.

Q - Do you have any advice for a new filmmaker in relation to scoring the movie?

Debbi - Since new filmmakers usually have budget restrictions I think it is a good idea to ask a contractor ways of keeping costs down. We all have one goal in mind, to make a great film without spending a billion dollars!

Mark Graham
Music Copyist

EXPERT OPINION

Q - What is a music copyist?

Mark - The copyist prepares the parts for each musician to play from. In addition to music skills, the copyist must have good organizational skills to make sure all the parts are prepared correctly, and the required scores and sketches have been prepared. Part of the job is to make sure the project is managed so that all aspects of it are completed within the prescribed time frame. You need a copyist who understands how music needs to be written for each instrument in the orchestra, how the layout of the music is essential for page turns, how to edit for enharmonic changes, how to put in dynamics and other information that pertains to specific sections of the orchestra. Budgets vary widely, based on factors such as orchestra size, style of music, type of music, delivery times, last minute changes etc. There are also differing agreements with different scales, including ones to accommodate low budget films and video games. These have been very successful in accommodating composers and producers who have limited budgets, but still want to use a live orchestra as an element of their soundtrack.

Q - How do you fit into the music team?

Mark - Relationships based on similar values, open communications, artistic integrity and mutual respect can lead to success in any area of the film business, and relationships with composer, contractor and orchestrator are all very important to the copyist. It's all about feel and relationships, which in turn affect the practical stuff. If there's trust then they can say 'take care of it' and know that you will. Every composer and team are different and we deal with them each in a different way, sometimes in completely different ways.

Q - What software do copyists use? Do you deal will all types of music?

Mark - Specialist music notation software, but also the leading sequencer and audio programs if we're dealing with MIDI and audio material. The main programs we use are Finale, Sibelius, Mosaic, Digital Performer, Logic, Cubase, and Pro Tools. The style and approach to layout of a part for an opera, a musical, a movie or live performance can be quite different, but the basic skills and the attention to accuracy, clarity and detail are important no matter what style of music.

Q - What kind of turnaround time do you need?

Mark - What we want, what we need, and what we actually get are very different. Deadlines in post production are tight and getting tighter. There is no industry standard time. Some composers would be happy with 4 weeks to write the score, others would be horrified.

Q - What do you think makes a good composer?

Mark - One whose primary interest is to serve the film.

POST

Phil Ayling
RMA

Q - What is the RMA and what does it offer its members?

Phil - The RMA is a non-profit organization that functions as an advocacy group for musicians. It was formed in 1982 when musicians in Los Angeles felt that the AFM (The American Federation of Musicians) was not combating a non-democratic atmosphere within the union, enforcing contacts rights, or effectively lobbying general rights of musicians such as anti-piracy legislation. Now, the RMA works across the entire music community as a legislative representative with the musicians best interests at heart. LA is the biggest chapter of RMA, but there are growing locals in New York, San Antonio, Nashville and Northern California. You may be a member of more than one, but being a member of one does not mean you are a member of all or another. A basic membership in the Los Angeles chapter runs you $120 per year. Many musicians choose higher levels of support at the Contributing, Sustaining and Patron levels and are individually acknowledged in a special section of the annual RMALA Directory - which has become a major reference source for the recording industry. In addition, all of our members are listed in the Directory by Instrument and by name.

Q - Do you receive royalties for your members and how are they collected?

Phil - The only royalties we collect and disperse come from Japanese CD rentals. The amount of money a performer receives is based on the frequency of rental. A Japanese company called Geidankyo accumulates these figures and sends us a list of who is due funds. However, we can only pay out to performers who have given us power of attorney to do so. Once this paperwork is filled out, then we can release their monies. We provide this service for members and non-members.

Q - What type of information can a producer get from your website?

Phil - You can get tons of information on where and how to hire musicians and the union regulations that go along with hiring them. You can find scoring stages, recording studios, and support services such as companies that do payroll, cartage and schedule rehearsal halls. But probably the most important thing is that you can find out the pay scales of the musicians, so you can budget accordingly. Go to www.rmaweb.org

Q - What films fall under your Low Budget Motion Pictures and Cable Movies category?

Phil - Any theatrical motion pictures whose final costs are estimated to be no more than $29.5m. Also, any TV movie made for the networks (NBC, ABC, CBS, FOX), basic cable (USA, FX) or pay TV (HBO, Showtime) budgeted at $2.652m per program hour fall into this area. Straight to video films that exceed this threshold may be considered on a case-by-case basis.

Q - Do you have to notify the musician if he performs within the Low Budget rate scale?

Phil - Yes. You have to tell them right up front. The day you hire them.

Q - How do you go about getting the Low Budget rates?

Phil - Once you have your estimated budget in hand, your head of production (which could be an executive, a UPM, a producer or anyone else handling this function) must contact the AFM or have your contractor do so. After they review the budget, they certify you Low Budget and then you can contact our members under those auspices. However, should your film go over budget and break into the Full Budget category, you have to pay all your musicians the Full Budget rate. You have 30 days within the release of your film to make up this difference. Now, while this can technically happen, it is highly unlikely that it would for the picture is usually locked and you are deep into post-production at this point, so your numbers shouldn't fluctuate much. This really is to prevent producers from submitting fraudulent budgets in order to get the lower rates.

Q - What is the rate for Low Budget musicians?

Phil - Currently, it is $169.36 per three-hour session plus 10% of scale wages for their pension. You have to pay for their Health & Welfare package as well, which is tied to the IATSE plan. Currently, that rate is $17.94 per day per musician. You do not have to pay for their vacation time as you would in the Full Budget. There is also a special rate for music preparation for low budget films and that is done on a page rate, which is based on the amount of music and the number of musicians. Since this varies from project to project, there is no standard rate to quote here.

Q - Do you offer any discounts on the soundtrack?

Phil - All films that have the required AFM credits on the CD jacket are allowed to release albums under a Low-Budget Film Soundtrack provision. The specifics are any albums with pressings of 25,000 Units or less pay only 25% of the Sound Recording Labor Agreement scale upon release. Also, an additional 25% of basic regular phonograph scale for pressings in excess of 25,000. When sales go over 50,000 units, then the soundtrack becomes Full Budget and requires additional payments. If the CD contains 45 minutes or more of music originally intended for the film and 80 or side musicians are due payment, then you get a 15% discount. All of these monies are paid to the musician. The AFM also receives 75 copies of the soundtrack from the producer. The benefit of this provision to producer is that it keeps the cost of producing a soundtrack down, and we make additional money only if the recording is more successful. Further, the lower cost keeps the production in the local US or Canadian city instead of running off to a cheaper locale.

Q - What is Electronic Multi-Tracking and what is the rate you offer to the Low Budget category?

Phil - This takes into account music created through electronic means such as keyboards, synthesizers or sampling as it is normally one person creating the score, as opposed to a group of musicians. Currently, the rate for these players is $213.25 per hour for one person and $188.18 per hour per person for two or more people.

Q - What advice would you give for a new filmmaker in order to make his dealing with musicians easier?

Phil - Generally speaking, the filmmaker does not have much contact with the musicians save for spotting sessions and the odd visit when the composer is working with them. However, there are some things a filmmaker should be aware of when hiring a composer that could make the musicians time more effective. Everyone has someone they went to college with or a friend or a relative that can produce music through a home studio or synth program. This can produce some entertaining and interesting stuff that sounds great in a club or in the car. However, there is a good chance that it does not add anything to a film. A filmmaker should look for a composer with experience in creating music for films. Or, if they are first timers, look for someone whose music has meaning in the film as opposed to just sounding cool. The other main thing to be aware of is whom the composer has around them. Make sure that the music prep team, such as the contractor and supervising copier, are experienced and organized. The composer should not be looking at anything other than the music and his team should make sure he has nothing but creative worries to think about. Efficiency is the key. For example, on *My Big, Fat Greek Wedding*, the producers did not have a lot of money for a score, but they knew what they were doing and no time was wasted having musicians sit around waiting to be used. They knew when to record certain portions of the music so that it was cost effective. Lastly, pay for the talent and you will save in the product. Most producers have enough money to do a score once, but not twice, so hire the best musicians possible and you will ultimately save time and money.

POST

Peter Brown
Sound Design

SOUND DESIGN

Q - What is your job?

Peter - As a Supervising Sound Editor, I help the director and picture editor combine their dialogue, ADR, Sound Effects, Backgrounds, Foley and Sound Design into a final mix. Those are the principle audio elements in a mix, except for music, which usually has a separate supervisor.

Q - What did you do at USC?

Peter - I was in the film production program, which trains you to be a director, cinematographer, editor, or sound engineer. I tried all of the disciplines and found I had a real penchant for sound.

Q - What happened after you were graduated?

Peter - During the summer following my graduation, I called sound guru Steve Flick every week until he finally asked me to come over to Sony and observe a mix. The following week he called me to his shop, the Creative Café, showed me this whole roomful of 35mm mag short ends, and said, *'Spool all this stuff up.'* It was something akin to cleaning out the Aegean stables, but like a man possessed, I emptied the room in a day and a half, and stayed on for six years.

Q - How did you rise up the ladder?

Peter - I made myself useful, and worked like a dog. I would work for Steve all day in his library and then on student films at night and on weekends. After about a year and a half, I landed my first feature-supervising gig through an assistant editor who had been a comrade at USC. I saw it as my first break and dumped all my energy into it. I think my fervor impressed Steve, and he hired me as an actual editor after that. Being a workaholic is very helpful if you're a sound person.

Q - How important is production sound on a movie?

Peter - Very. Filmmakers on both big and small films make a big mistake when they choose locations that are terrible for sound. Good sound design accesses the subconscious mind with subtlety and force. In a low budget film it can provide many layers of atmosphere and detail far beyond what is actually seen on screen. In a big budget film it makes the drama larger than life, gives the action its hyper-realistic edge.

Q - As a sound designer, do you get many thanks from the public?

Peter - Not really. I think being in the sound field requires a pretty healthy ego.

Q - Do you find that you recognize standard sound effects in movies?

Peter - Yeah. The other day, I popped in the DVD of *One Flew Over the Cuckoo's Nest* and there's this pastoral opening scene with beautiful images, music, and then - screeeeeeeeeee - That red-tailed hawk scream I hear in every film whenever there is a lonely wide-angle establishing shot. My first reaction is revulsion at such a cliché, but then I step back and reflect that though it may seem overused to most sound professionals, it still works magic for the general public, maybe even *because* it is such a cliché.

Q - How do you work with the director and editor?

Peter - On low to mid-budget films sound editors often communicate one on one with the director throughout post. As the budget increases, the director's entourage increases and her available time decreases; the responsibilities of working with the sound team falls increasingly into the editor's realm, unless the director has a particular interest in sound.

Q - What is the first step when they come to you?

Peter - I look at the script or a rough-cut of the film and start to assemble a library of sound specific to the needs of the project. I will spot the film - make a list of all the effects needed with specific attention to the moments that require new recordings or sound design. On large films, I may start collecting and creating sounds before the film is even shot. If a film features humpback whales, horses galloping on the beach, a pygmy nuthatch or a prototype car engine, you may have to do some original recordings in remote locations. It is best to get these recordings done as soon as possible because they don't always work out on the first try.

Q - What's the difference between working on a $1m movie and a $100m movie?

Peter - A good sound job on a low budget film requires economy and simplicity. You must think through your schedule and budget meticulously because you are probably working for a flat rate and only have enough resources to do things right the first time. On a $1m movie you should only begin the sound editorial once the film is locked. With high budgets, it's a whole different approach; the filmmakers now have the option to experiment, reject, rework, rewrite, and even re-shoot! Every time the picture changes, the sound budget increases to pay for the additional work it generates. On a $100m film, you can spend over half your time conforming old sound tracks to match the new picture.

Q - Do you come across the same mistakes with big Hollywood movies as low budget movies?

Peter - While both suffer from a number of the same maladies such as bad stories, poor production sound, or wall to wall music, only large budgets need fear the affliction of 'overwork'. During long post schedules, I have actually seen a few decent films get worse and worse through incessant trimming, tweaking, previewing, note-taking, and re-shooting, until they are altogether ruined.

Q - What would be the first step in building a soundtrack?

Peter - With any film, dialogue legibility is your number one priority, so sit down with a viewing copy of the film, watch and listen. Figure out what is illegible and in need of ADR (re-voicing). On a small budget, this may be a significant expense, and planning around actor's schedules is always difficult, so start early. Next find a stage for your final mix, this may take almost half of your

Track Laying Yourself?

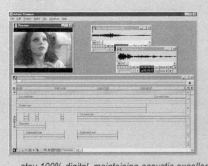

Sound is an area where low budget films often fail, yet they need not. The technology is cheap and all it really requires is a little know how and a lot of time consuming work. Sound Effects CDs are an excellent source for of high quality stereo recordings of pretty much everything you could imagine. These are the same recordings as used by multi million dollar productions. And you can use them too! If you can't afford to buy the disks, try asking the studio where you plan to do your final mix and see if you can use their CD library. Be creative with sound and try and fill your soundtrack. You can track lay the sound in your film with a number of semi-pro and domestic computer tools such as Adobe Premier, Avid Xpress and Final Cut Pro. Using either SPDIF digital input / output, and by pulling effects directly off CD, you can stay 100% digital, maintaining acoustic excellence without a silly price tag. You will need a good computer, large and quiet space, good amplifier and speakers and high quality microphone.

budget, so you need to find a facility that can deliver an excellent mix, but still leave room in your budget for Sound Design, Foley, Dialogue, ADR, FX, backgrounds, and music editing.

Q - On a budget of $1M, what percentage should you devote to the sound department?

Peter - 4-6%

Q - Can you remove camera noise?

Peter - You can do a lot with filtration and equalization tools to decrease camera noise. There are even special filters designed to attack the unique frequencies created by camera shutters such as the Dolby CAT 43 and more recent CAT 430. Of course these tools are limited if the noise in the original recording is very loud. It is always best to prevent the noise from getting there in the first place by blimping the camera or using other sound absorption techniques on the set.

Q - What do equalizers do?

Peter - They are audio filters that shape the sound for you, boosting or lowering specific frequencies. The bass and treble knobs on your stereo are types of equalizers.

Q - Do they include tools like reverb?

Peter - Not really. A reverb unit is an effects processor used to simulate various acoustic spaces like a large hall, cathedral or a canyon with an echo.

Q - How do you work out what sound effects you need for a movie?

Peter - I make a chronological list while I'm watching the film. It's very helpful to have window burns (burnt in time code) so you know what time in the film it is because everything is going to be time related. I prefer to do my first spotting session with a film that's broken up into editorial reels. You start to make a pull list. Once you start to work, you're going to have a continuity for the film that says what happens in each scene. Underneath the continuity, you start to write in what the effects are - your spots. You write in all the backgrounds and effects you need for each scene, and you start to write in the specific sounds from your library that you're going to use. You've got a big book that has all the different scenes and all the different pulls.

Q - What is a pull?

Peter - It's all the different sounds that you're going to use. They call it *'pull'* because they used to have to send someone to the vault where the ¼ inch tape was, and they'd have to pull the tapes out and transfer them to mag.

Q - How long do you spend doing the sound on a movie?

Peter - With *Spiderman*, the crew was on it for 6 weeks, then nothing happened for most of the fall while they finished the shooting. They had to re-shoot some scenes because of the Twin Towers. Then there was another temp in the fall so there was another month or so there, and then it really started up sound wise in January for about four months. It wasn't too long actually, considering the scope of the film. With *All The Pretty Horses*, I was on that for pretty much a year from start to finish, although there was a big break in the spring.

Q - Is there a limit on building layers of sound?

Post-Production Sound

1. Make sure that you previously recorded the best production sound you could - especially when it comes to dialogue. This will reduce the amount of ADR (it never sounds as good and it gets expensive) and other post tricks you will have to do. If an actor blows a line, or you are not sure, have them record it wild without the camera running and drop it in later.

2. Put your actors' voices on separate tracks so your re-recording mixer can set their levels once for each track instead of having to move faders up and down as each person talks.

3. Put your effects on different tracks from your dialogue and music so you can adjust them separately.

4. A good ambience track (atmosphere / environment) will act like filler in the cracks, smoothing over your edits. Choose your atmospheres with care.

5. Think of sound effects that might occur offscreen, such as a dog barking or a ship's foghorn, which could fill out your soundscape and perhaps help add tension or mood to your film.

6. A heavy ambient / atmosphere track can cover many natural sound problems.

7. If you decide to record your own sound effects, don't do it in an apartment that is noisy or located on a busy street.

8. Many household items can be used for creating sound effects. Slapping a raw steak on a counter makes a great punch sound.

9. Your various tracks should compliment each other, not compete, so don't have important sound effects and a really loud music score at the same time.

10. Too much music can make the audience 'music deaf' and so your score ends up having no impact. A rough guide is no more than 30 minutes of music in a 90 minute movie.

11. If you need to edit some music, cut on the beat. In some instances, you can just crossfade your music and it will be fine.

12. Always do a foley track as it really helps fill out your soundscape. It's also vital for your M&E mix for international sales.

13. Get to know your dubbing mixer before you start working so that you can talk about what kind of sound and effects you want. Also, defer to his or her expert opinion when you are in doubt. They do this day in and day out and know what will and won't work.

14. Your final mix should be done in a studio that handles feature films as opposed to TV programs or news. While these other studios may be cheaper, you will not get the best-shaped sound and end up in the more expensive suite anyway. Most of all you are paying for the person whose fingers are on the faders, not the cool kit.

15. Make sure to save enough money to pay the recording studio / dubbing studio so that they will not keep your tapes hostage.

16. Appreciate the power of silence. Sometimes the best tension is created when nothing is being heard.

17. If you plan to track lay yourself, don't underestimate how much time it will take. Six to ten weeks is a good guide. You are not experienced and don't have a huge SFX library to hand.

18. Work out how you are going to get your audio to the mix. Avid can export an OMFI file which is often the best way, but do tests as without them, it won't work on the day.

Peter - There's always some type of limit with the machines you're using, but you have to narrow it down. You start with a zillion tracks, which might be one tenth of a zillion tracks for dialogue, and a tenth of a zillion for music and you do what are called pre-dubs. You take eighty effects tracks for a certain event and you mix them down, so if it's a SDDS film, there'll be eight channels that the audience will eventually hear in the theater. You take that pre-dub and you set it aside and you do the same thing with the foley, and then you do the same thing with the dialogue, so that when you get to your final mix, you've got all these pre-dubs. You're not dealing with the original elements any more. As the sound guy, you've got to sit on the stage and know where all those elements are in case they want them back.

Q - Do you find that less experienced directors are not prepared with all their effects?

Peter - That always happens. The dumbest things come up. I was talking with a guy today and he asked me, *'how is the wine pouring?'* It could have been a situation with that particular wine pour when everybody thought it was everybody else's to do and I could go to stage tomorrow and find out that nobody's covered it. That situation doesn't scare me though because I've been preparing for the last six years by recording. I still try to record something every week, master it, and keep cataloguing it to make my library bigger. It's not enough to just go out and grab commercial sound libraries. You need to have it in your brain and you want to make stuff as unique as possible. A good gunshot for somebody might be awful to somebody else. One of my best experiences sound wise was working on *Hellraiser V* with Addison and Byron Miller and the director, Scott Erikson. It really felt like a team was making this film. Scott loved sound and knew what an important part of the film it was. The only way to get what you want is to sit there and audition different sounds and hear different things - you need patience. If you've got a good rapport, spending time with the sound guys is really helpful. You can't just say, *'I want a hawk screech there'.* You've got to be there to hear all the different hawks and figure out which one is the right one.

Q - Have you ever found that new filmmakers use sound inappropriately or take their creativity too far?

Peter - Yes, but the opposite is more common.

Q - Have you ever been in a situation where somebody has wanted a silent moment in a film to stress a point?

Peter - There's a scene in *Copland* where Sylvester Stallone gets shot. He's already deaf in one ear and he gets shot in the other and you just hear this low hum and it's all in silence. It creates tension. It's fantastic.

Q - What do you need from a filmmaker if you're doing the sound on their film?

Peter - First of all, tapes, but this will probably change in a couple of years as people are figuring out how to export digital files directly from Avid's. The reigning method is to make a videotape output, which is then digitized into your computer. You break your film into editorial reels and hand those over with the sound matching the picture on the reels, putting the dialogue on track one and M&E on track two (these are guide tracks only), so that the dialogue editor can hear the dialogue without all the other noise. Then you'll need an EDL (Edit Decision List) that says where all the audio cuts were made and what sound takes were used. You'll need the original production audio on DAT or ¼ inch tape along with the sound rolls. If it's an independent film and you're doing the music cutting, you're going to want all the music CD's.

Q - Have you encountered any issues with time code?

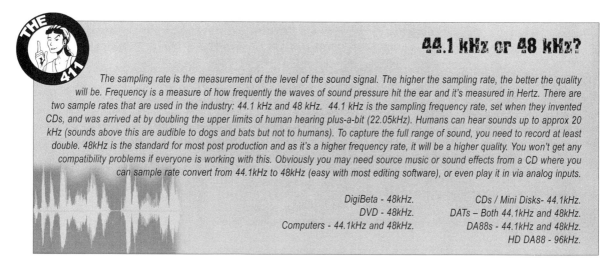

44.1 kHz or 48 kHz?

The sampling rate is the measurement of the level of the sound signal. The higher the sampling rate, the better the quality will be. Frequency is a measure of how frequently the waves of sound pressure hit the ear and it's measured in Hertz. There are two sample rates that are used in the industry: 44.1 kHz and 48 kHz. 44.1 kHz is the sampling frequency rate, set when they invented CDs, and was arrived at by doubling the upper limits of human hearing plus-a-bit (22.05kHz). Humans can hear sounds up to approx 20 kHz (sounds above this are audible to dogs and bats but not to humans). To capture the full range of sound, you need to record at least double. 48kHz is the standard for most post production and as it's a higher frequency rate, it will be a higher quality. You won't get any compatibility problems if everyone is working with this. Obviously you may need source music or sound effects from a CD where you can sample rate convert from 44.1kHz to 48kHz (easy with most editing software), or even play it in via analog inputs.

DigiBeta - 48kHz.
DVD - 48kHz.
Computers - 44.1kHz and 48kHz.

CDs / Mini Disks- 44.1kHz.
DATs – Both 44.1kHz and 48kHz.
DA88s - 44.1kHz and 48kHz.
HD DA88 - 96kHz.

Track Groups And What They Mean

Dialogue Tracks *(mono)*
Keep dialogue tracks clean and bright, where needed use ADR (dialogue replacement), but be mindful that ADR can sound pretty bad.

Sound Effects Tracks *(mono and stereo)*
Track lay an effect for as many things as you can. Differentiate between effects that will stay mono and are from the perspective of the characters (such as doors and switches), and effects that will be in stereo and add acoustic punch (such as police sirens and thunder claps).

Atmosphere Tracks *(stereo)*
Don't be afraid to lay several thick atmosphere tracks and mix them as they can provide a very attractive stereo image. Use atmospheres to help create continuity during a scene, and also to help illustrate that a scene has changed by switching to a different atmos track.

Foley Tracks *(mono)*
The movement of the actors in the scene need to be brightened by a foley artist, a person who will add these with expert precision and clarity. Don't be afraid of going a little over the top, very rarely do you make a loud swishing sound when turning your head, but you do in the movies.

Music *(stereo and mono)*
Always in stereo (except when it comes from a prop in a scene such as a TV) and sparingly placed. Avoid drowning out your sound mix with music and use it only when you really need it.

Tools
A mixer will have tools like echo and reverb (used for churches, canyons etc.), a noise gate (that can kill sound below a certain level, excellent if you have too much reverb), a notch filter (to help get rid of continuous sounds such as a fridge or the camera). Don't let these tools lull you into a false sense of security, get it right in the track laying.

Peter - Yes, with OMF sessions exported from other software, such as Avid. You've digitized your picture but when you play your sound with your picture, it seems to be drifting. Drift is usually some kind of time code issue. It's when things start out the same and get further and further out of sync. The problems arise because there are different ways to count time code, drop frame or non-drop frame. Drop frame allows you to have the time code on the screen equal the time on the clock. Non-drop frame counts all the little numbers and frames that go by. Then there's 30FPS verses 29.97FPS. We call 30 frames film speed and 29.97 FPS pull down.

Q - What other time code issues have you come across?

Peter - Problems can arise for a number of reasons, and the time code has to be done just right, or it's not effective. One of the most common problems is a bad transfer, so when you put the tape in your machine, it doesn't read the code and it's never apparent what's wrong. It takes a lot of time to figure out, and it's going to cost you money to have it redone, so you want to make sure you get it done right, first time. Another problem is having the wrong time code on there. You can have the right level, on the right channel and everything can be good, but it's just the wrong kind, so when Pro Tools listens to that code and figures out how fast to run, it drifts out of sync with the material that was loaded in, because it's at the wrong speed. That's probably the easiest way to get into trouble. The second easiest way is use error when the sound guy has turned on his system and forgotten to reset something or flicked a switch and now you're pulling down your session and you shouldn't be.

Q - What differences have you noticed with the introduction of digital formats?

Peter - I don't get all excited about the differences between 96k and 24 bit. I think all those things are technical issues and what attracts me to making films is the story. I try to think about how sound serves the story and I try to recognize when you're wasting time playing with sound, like when you're trying to showcase this great sound effect you just came up with, but you've completely lost sight of the fact that it's a scene about a boy meeting a girl.

Q - What is a Gear Box?

Peter - A Gear Box allows you to convert sounds from whatever wrong rate they're at, to the one that you want. If, for example, you've got a sound that's at 30fps and you need it to be at 29.97fps, you just feed it into the Gear Box and it feeds it out correctly.

Q - When you digitize your sound into your machine, do you do that at 44.1kHz or 48kHz?

Peter - I've always used 48k but lots of DV projects come in at 44.1k. On DV films I would encourage the film makers to boom whenever they could, recording onto one channel, but also to have another channel with either a backup mic or just the same mic at a different level, just in case someone was too loud and over modulated. DV can also work at 32kHz which is awful. That's not a standard format so I have had to covert it up to 44.1k using Session Browser, an awesome program, which can convert an entire Pro Tools session to a different frame rate. It's an emergency procedure for a screw up that shouldn't have happened in the first place, but in this imperfect world we live in, these things happen.

Q - What is a tail pop and what does it do?

Peter - It's a friendly little reminder that tells you when you're in sync at the end of a reel. Because you have so many different tracks of sound that you're trying to mix down into your final elements, there are zillions of opportunities for those things to get out of sync, and when you only have a pop at the beginning, that's only so helpful. The head pop is pretty easy to keep in sync. The tail pop goes all over the place with only small errors, so that's why you need one at the beginning and one at the end. It helps you start to track down, troubleshoot and figure out what's gone wrong if you've got that head pop and tail pop.

Q - Have you found a lot of new filmmakers don't have that tail pop?

Peter - All the time. People just don't have academy leaders on the head and tail of their film. I don't know why.

Q - What must you have for the final sound mix?

Peter - Well organized tracks that are going to work at the chosen studio or mixing stage. It's good to start a day early, especially on low budget stuff, to test things out and to make sure they work.

Q - So you'll have mixed your sound effects down to eight tracks at this stage, and in the final mix, you do the pre-mixes of these tracks to one track, is that right?

Peter - The eight-track example is one track. It would be the final soundtrack, made up of eight different elements; far left, left, center, right, far right, left surround, right surround and boom. Most people would use Dolby Digital which has six tracks (left, center, right, left surround, right surround and sub).

Q - If you are working on a low budget movie, how much time should you leave for your final mix?

There is some confusion over THX. It is NOT a mixing format, therefore you cannot mix in THX. It is a rigid set of quality control standards setup up by George Lucas, to ensure that any THX theatre or equipment meets their exacting standards. So you can mix in a THX certified theatre, or playback on a THX certified amp, but all it really means is that the guys at THX say, 'yep, it's good enough for our stamp of approval.'

Peter - It's usually based on how much money you have for the sound.

Q - Is it possible to do it in a week?

Peter - Yes. Some low budget features have been mixed in a week. If I had $100k to do a sound job on a film, I'd get a dialogue mixer, as good as I could afford, and do three or four days of dialogue pre-dubbing. I would go through the entire film and smooth out all the dialogue because that's the most important part of our sound. Then I might spend a day pre-dubbing and assembling all the foley and effects. So, that's four days for your dialogue pre-dub, three - four days for your final mix, and then two days for your print master and versions (M&E). I'd like a little bit more for a fix day, so maybe eleven or twelve, but there is a certain economy. People usually allow one day for print master and versions at low budget level, but that never seems to work.

Q - Do you pay Dolby for a license?

Peter - Yes. The Dolby mix is made during your print master process, and Dolby have their own proprietary computer equipment to make a magneto optical disk. A lot of studios have a Dolby box to matrix and un-matrix the stereo sound track. The MO disk is then to your negative house where the shoot the optical sound negative that's going to get married to your print.

Q - When you walk out of that mix, do you have your M&E as well?

Peter - If you're lucky enough to have a distributor, it's based on what the distributor demands, but as standard, it's an M&E. A DM&E, is a separate, usually three channel mono dialogue, music and effects.

Q - What do people use the DM&E for?

Peter - The DM&E is needed for the discreet elements, so if you're cutting a trailer, the first thing they're going to want is the 'D' track. They want to access the clean dialogue so they can cut it up. They're not going to want the effects and music married to it as they will mix their own music and effects in. The M&E is for international distribution. It allows them to dub in foreign languages.

Q - What are cue sheets?

Peter - Cue sheets are indicators of where the sounds are in your sessions. Every sound has got a little time marker on it. It tells you the key frame or the time code where the sound is. I use the TAPE program and if you do it all correctly, you just open up the tape, tell it to reference your session and it goes directly to your printer and prints out.

Q - What are the main concerns of a recording mixer?

Peter - Balance and figuring out how to best tell the story through sound. There are usually two mixers, a dialogue mixer who handles the music as well, and an effects mixer. The first job for the dialogue mixer is to go through, clean up and sweeten the track, so that every word is legible. Once that is laid down and the dialogue is legible, you start squirting in all the other sounds and making a nice, realistic bed. You want the music to carry you and take you on that emotional roller coaster, but you never want it to over power the dialogue. So they've got to deal with all the tracks in front of them, deal with the technical issues and then deal with all the personalities in the room who are vying for attention, like the picture editor and director.

Q - Any tips for getting the best sound on a low budget movie?

Peter - Location is the biggest thing, but it's generally the thing you can't do anything about. On the last film I worked on we had great mixers, editors, a great director, we did great ADR with great actors, but it still had all kinds of problems because the initial recording was poor. You must make sure you've got the best production sound guy you can get and you must make some really hard decisions about getting a nice, quiet location. Do your ADR on the set and shoot rehearsals, with sound, not with picture. If a take goes bad, try to get the actors to redo some of those lines. If the sound on a low budget film is unusable and you have to go to an ADR studio later, it's going to cost you a lot of money to try to replace those lines and it's also going to annoy the actors. I've worked on some student films where, instead of booking ADR time, we'd go with the actors out to the location with my sound rig and we'd record the ADR there. That's been pretty effective. Completion anxiety always sucks and that's more of a problem with first time filmmakers. Let it go and move on.

Nerses Gezalyan
Foley Mixer

Q - What is foley?

Nerses - It was named after Jack Foley, who was an editor, and he created the idea of foley. Foley is a collection of sounds that enhance the soundtrack. It's usually footsteps and clothes rustles, whatever the actor touches and does we cover.

Q - How much time should a producer budget for foley?

Nerses - It depends on how much foley is required. At one extreme we can help with everything - explosions, wind, anything you could possibly think of, we will come up with a sound. At the other extreme would be a drama with a few characters in a house - but even then, those sounds are the hardest things to do because you are trying to make sounds organic and not make them stand out or feel mass produced, and that's hard, and it's where the craft comes in. We ask for three weeks, but most of the time they try to have it done in ten days. Technology has changed and producers think it will take less time to do the job, which is not necessarily the case. You need to really know what you're doing to do it in that short a period of time. If you don't, you'll do the job but it tends to stand out a lot more than it should. To me, sound shouldn't just fill the scene, it should be more specific. The sound should help the movie rather than be a separate entity.

Q - Is there anything a filmmaker can do to help save foley time?

Nerses - Absolutely. Some filmmakers carpet the floors of interior sets so the dialogue will not be polluted by live footsteps (actors walking around). I would always say get dialogue as clean as possible and add footsteps in foley. If you want to sell you film abroad then you will have to do a special sound mix called an M&E mix (music and effects) which is all the sound, minus the dialogue. It will be used to re-voice the film in non English speaking territories. In that case you will need to cover everything in either sound effects editing or foley.

Q - On a low budget movie, could you do the foley in less than ten days?

Nerses - It's possible. We've had instances where the filmmaker doesn't have enough budget and we've tried to do the best we can. You have to deal with whatever budget is thrown at you. If you have three days, you have to do it in three days.

Q - How much do you charge?

Nerses - That's hard to say, but our normal fee (inc. studio etc.) goes from between $400 - $550 an hour. More or less, I would say $50 - $60k is the average budgeting for foley. Some major movies can go further than that. For *Starship Troopers*, we had nine weeks of foley and that went beyond $50k. So if it's a busy action movie, it can be $60 - $70k and for low budget movies, $30k is not unusual. There is a standard rate which is close to $500 per day (feature films) for a foley artist and TV is $400 per day.

Q - How many foley artists should you have for a low budget, non action movie?

Nerses - Most of the time, you have two foley artists. If you have two, the pace is faster and you accomplish more, and you'll finish sooner. Not to say that one foley artist couldn't do it, but you would end taking longer. For example, when we are doing group movements with one foley artist, you would need to do a couple of passes to make it sound as busy. With two foley artists, one pass would be sufficient.

Q - What does a foley studio have equipment wise?

Nerses - Aside from the recording equipment, projector and screen and mixing desk, the stage will also have props - and lots of them! In fact anything you can imagine. There are pots and pans, different kinds of shoes, car doors, cables, everything you have in your house the stage will have. A lot of times, foley artists are able to understand the sound, and if the artist doesn't have the correct prop, he can come up with a sound using alternative props.

Q - Do you have lots of doors on the walls?

Nerses - Yes. We have a closet that has a door and inside there are lots of doors.

Q - What do you do for surfaces?

Nerses - I would say there are four different surfaces for footsteps - wooden floors, concrete, sand, gravel and dirt. With that combination you can pretty much make every surface, except for metal. That would be for sci-fi movies, and that's where the mixer is helpful for the foley artists with the limited surfaces they have. For example, if you have a metal surface and you need to make a heavy sound, you can change the pitch to help the foley artist.

Q - Do foley artists watch the scene and do it there and then?

Nerses - Yes, although with technology these days, it's not that critical because with Pro Tools, I can physically sync tracks. The saying used to be that *'a good foley artist is three frames off'*, so the editors used to move the whole track three frames and see what works out, but that was what happened before Pro Tools and other technologies.

Q - How many foley artists are there?

Nerses - There is a core of about 20 people, and all of us know each other. We do the bulk of the work and a further 75 fill in and do TV and low budget movies. The big budget movies are done by a few because of their experience.

The Props Room

To the side of the foley studio there is often a room that is filled with all manner of props. A great foley artist will take items and use them to recreate sounds - and not just the sounds appropriate to the item. There is a famous story about The Exorcist and a foley artist who recreated the famous head turn scene sound effect using a leather wallet filled with credit cards. Remember, it doesn't need to be real, just sound real.

Q - Is there a quieter time of year to get a better studio deal?

Nerses - Usually the summer is slow, and in winter and spring, things pick up. We always try and accommodate new filmmakers, because they don't know who they will be in the future, so we have done a lot of low budget movies ourselves.

Q - What can a filmmaker do to make a foley artists life easier?

Nerses - It's always nice to have enough time to do things. Unfortunately, stars take half of the budget and producers have no other choice but to cut back somewhere and, so we suffer.

Q - What is ADR?

Nerses - ADR is Automatic Dialogue Replacement, and it's also called looping. This is where if there is a problem with a line of dialogue and the actor will re-voice that line in a theatre some time after the shoot ends. Some artists have a problem delivering the lines the same way as they did during the shoot, where others don't. To be involved in ADR you should have the personality to deal with huge egos. This is not the job of the foley artist, but sometimes, foley studios are used for ADR.

Q - What do you want material wise from the filmmaker?

Nerses - If there is anything unusual in the movie you should let us know, such as snow.

Q - Do you have any advice on preparation for recording foley?

Nerses - New foley artists can be worried about doing the 'proper' thing, but you should not have that fear. Our job is to match the production sound and that doesn't necessarily mean coming up with the best sound, it means do everything that is possible to make it fit the movie. Often this can be as simple as moving the mic a little further away to add a certain amount of *'room'* to the sound, so you are not necessarily recording the best, cleanest sound, but you're doing something that works with the movie.

Cinema Surround Layout

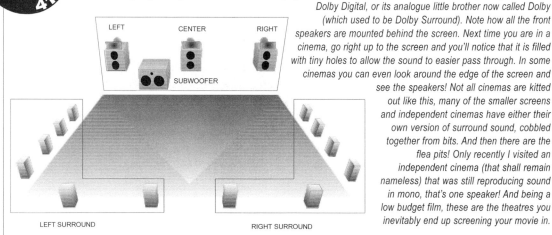

This is a pretty average 'small theater' that will playback surround sound encoded soundtracks. Usually this means Dolby Digital, or its analogue little brother now called Dolby (which used to be Dolby Surround). Note how all the front speakers are mounted behind the screen. Next time you are in a cinema, go right up to the screen and you'll notice that it is filled with tiny holes to allow the sound to easier pass through. In some cinemas you can even look around the edge of the screen and see the speakers! Not all cinemas are kitted out like this, many of the smaller screens and independent cinemas have either their own version of surround sound, cobbled together from bits. And then there are the flea pits! Only recently I visited an independent cinema (that shall remain nameless) that was still reproducing sound in mono, that's one speaker! And being a low budget film, these are the theatres you inevitably end up screening your movie in.

Tom Lalley
Foley Engineer

Q - What are the most common technical problems you encounter?

Tom - From an audio post production standpoint, it's so important to have your ducks in a row when you start out, because you have less compatibility than you once had. We work with Pro Tools and Digi Design own Avid, and yet even Pro Tools and Avid and not completely compatible! So plan your post production route meticulously. On a budget, you don't want to do things more than once, and when you have to have stuff copied or transferred, it takes longer to do, so it's important to pay attention to those aspects before entering the studio.

Q - What is the standard format that you record onto?

Tom - Here we record on Pro Tools, and then they take it and post it on a server. It depends on who's doing the dub for the show. I would advise you have meetings beforehand and be meticulous - if you are working with Pro Tools, check what version as not all versions are fully compatible for instance. A lot of the higher end consoles have sample rate conversion built in, but some people don't like it from an esoteric standpoint, so it is best to try and get everything prepared in the same sample rate that your final dub will be using (probably 48kHz). You want to minimize any conversion or compatibility issues before you get into the studio. We try and have as high a sample rate as we can for audio quality and 48kHz is probably the best choice for a low budget film. There is a difference between 44.1kHz and 48kHz. You also get fuller sound with 24 bit. There are so many steps between 0 and 1000 at 16 bit, and it's even more than that when you're dealing with 24 bit. Everything in the analogue world is valueless, whereas digitally, you have to assign a value to it, so if you are in-between values, it's going to gravitate off to one of those values and you will lose accuracy. The more steps you have between 0 and 1000, the more accurate it will be and the better it will sound.

Q - Do you pass the sound through a compressor when you record foley?

Tom - Things like swords are very dynamic, and the impact is spiked, but there's also resonance from it that you want to catch. We do use a compressor, but more than, we limitors to the extent that they do the compressors job. The compressors will bring out some of the frequencies that with a normal recording you would not hear. It heightens them. When you go to the dubbing stage, they have to treat it again. There are so many choices of what to emphasize, music, effects, foley? They make choices and say, 'well use the foley here as it works in this section' or 'we're not going to use the foley here, we'll highlight the effects instead.' When a foley is done right, it's customized and is never part of someone's library. We did 'Saving Private Ryan' and one of our foley guys went to a place in Georgia where they have WW2 guns and recorded all the different ones, plus bullet bites. When you do all that stuff, it gives the film it's own sound and that makes it unique.

Q - How many tracks can Pro Tools take?

Tom - As many as you want. Technology helps out new filmmakers tremendously you can mix an entire movie in Pro Tools now.

Q - What common mistakes do you come across from new filmmakers?

Nerses - It's always the fear element, and many new filmmakers try to prove something. If you try to make Hollywood movies, you need technology and money, and if you don't have those, you can forget about it. It's easy to use technology and come up with a good looking film. It's hard to find good filmmakers who are creative with limited resources. To me, that's more important. There are so many craftspeople who can help you make it look good, but to make it creative is down to the filmmaker.

POST

Mike Minkler
Re-recording Mixer

RE-RECORDING MIXER

Q - What is the job of the re-recording mixer?

Mike - The term 're-recording mixer' is ambiguous, and was created many years ago to differentiate between recording and taking recorded material and re-recording it (mixing). When you shoot the movie, the goal of the production sound mixer is to get the best dialogue recording he can from the actors - he's not interested in getting movement or background sound effects. So you should end up with a production track that is at best, 99% usable and, at worst, 0% usable. The average is somewhere around 80% usable with 20% being replaced by ADR. That's just the quality of the voice on a technical level.

The goal for the production mixer is to get the best technical recordings of the actors voice that they can, and what they miss is everything else, so that has to be supplemented later with foley, sound effects, environment or anything that is part of the fabric of the reality to the story. Then there's another layer, the hyper reality that the sound effects can bring to the soundtrack. The re-recording mixer has to take the production recordings that were made over a period of three months and match them up, clean them and make them sound like they came out of the actors mouths during the same time period. They also need to incorporate the ADR (or looping recordings) to make those sound like they were recorded at the same time too. That's on a technical level. Artistically, we can change performances drastically, and actors rarely understand this. I tell them, *'buddy, we used pieces from 10 production takes and 10 ADR takes just to make one paragraph and make you look really good'*. I've had words cut up into syllables from different takes, sentences cut into words and paragraphs cut up. Performances are changed drastically to optimize what they have, and that's one of the great things film can offer over stage or television. Not that those things are not good, but on stage as it's live, you cannot go back and re-edit. It is what it is. On television, they are shooting in such a hurry that the actors don't get much more than one or two takes. The editorial process in television is such that they only get to edit for three or four days, so it's more of an assembly than anything else. In dialogue re-recording, we do a lot of performance enhancement. The editors bring me a lot of material to work with and I have to sew it together.

With the sound effects, you supplement and create an acoustic fabric. To heighten the reality, you dramatically motivate things and accent things. You try to cultivate the movie, even if it's a little talky movie. Give it clothing. On some movies you can dress it up so much that you take away from the visuals though. Our job is to enhance the visuals, to help the performances and create an environment that feels true, to enhance moments with sound effects and music that carries the audience through the journey the characters are going on. That's part of the story telling. If you start using sound that is contrary to that, don't put it in. If it's going in another direction, it will dramatically change the way the scene feels and that's a mistake. Some movies need a lot of sound and work, others need a little and it's not dependent on budget or genre, they are all individual cases. Some directors know how to use sound, where others think of sound as music and slop it over the scenes. They haven't experienced cleaning it up and enhancing it.

Q - What materials do you need for the final mix?

Mike - Good tracks. We don't use cue sheets anymore as I have input meters on all my channels and can see all things coming in to me at all times. What I need is really good material that was thought out. Somebody needs to have a sense of how to put the blocks together.

Q - Do new film makers ignore sounds, or use the wrong sounds?

Mike - Both. They can ignore the sound, use an inappropriate effect or don't think about how one sound effect impacts on the next. They walk in with a bunch of stuff that they didn't think out. We can mix it that way and make the best we can, but it'll be garbage. I don't like to work that way. If I have time, I can re-construct where possible as we have a server connected to our console where we have over a million sound effects that we can bring in.

Q - Are there times when the sound editor didn't lay the right sound effects?

Mike - All the time. Sound effects editors do a great job. It's a big job. They have to come in with a great composition of sound material, something that was well thought through. If anything is missing or not good enough we can embellish it, or go to our libraries and grab new effects. They can go to our server too and do the same as we continue mixing, so we are not held up.

Q - Who and how many people are present in the mix?

Mike - The picture editor, sound effects editor, supervising sound editor, music editor and two mixers. The producer never comes in. They show up for one playback, and the directors generally show up an hour here and there.

Q - Do any directors want to be there all the time?

Mike - Yes. Some want to be part of every decision which is wonderful.

The Final Mix

This is when all your sound effects, music and dialogue are mixed into one. It's the most exciting moment of the whole process, as your movie seems to leap to life.

1. Mixing studios are expensive. Make sure you are prepared, your charts are clear and any or all creative decisions have been made.

2. Mix in stereo at the least. You can opt for analog Dolby, which is a surround sound system, free for TV, video and festivals, but you pay for cinema. There are other digital formats, each with a fee for use. Dolby Digital is the most widely used format and the preferred format.

3. Get to know your dubbing mixer. Push them to be satisfied with 90% and don't waste time trying to get that last little effect absolutely perfect. Often a film will mix itself, so avoid trying to get that last 10% out of the mix, it will cost you 90% of your time.

4. If you are on a tight budget, it's possible to mix a feature film in 3-5 days (with M&E). Don't let the mixers persuade you into 3 weeks.

5. If camera noise is a problem, most of it can be filtered out, but not all. Either post sync the dialogue or lay in a heavy ambient track over it, e.g. a plane flying over, or a printing press.

6. A good foley artist will work wonders. A foley artist is a person who adds the clothing rustles, footsteps, keys jangling in pocket etc. Spend a good two-day session here and you will have a much livelier sound track.

7. Cheap computer software and hardware can be used. Most PC's/Macs can record in 16 bit digital stereo. Sound effects can be recorded and cleaned up in programs like Cool Edit Pro (free download from the web) and editing systems like Premiere / FCP / Avid Xpress can be used to track lay sound effects. This isn't ideal and presents the few technical headaches, but it is possible, especially if you are technically minded.

8. Produce a Music and Effects mix (M&E) at the same time as your master mix. The M&E is a mix of the film without any dialogue, to be used for re-voicing in foreign territories. This is essential and you will be unable to sell your film without it.

9. Work out what of stock you need for your master mix and buy it before you go to the studio. They will try to sell you their tapes / disks at an increased price. Alternatively, do a deal including stock. Don't underestimate how these charges can add up.

10. The Dubbing Theater is the best environment you will ever hear your film. What may seem like an over the top sound effect may be too subtle on a TV speaker. Make sure all plot sound effects or dialogue are clear and correctly emphasized.

Q - For me, being at the final mix is the biggest part of the process as you see it all coming together.

Mike - It's gratifying and it's the only place where you can instantly change your mind. The earlier stages of pre-mixing the dialogue, ADR, foley, backgrounds and overall sound design is boring, even for the director, so they usually end up leaving.

Q - What is a pre-mix?

Mike - It is where groups of tracks, such as the dialogues or the foley, are EQued, balanced and processed before being mixed together into a final group, or a pre-mix. Every single track of the dialogue needs attention, to remove unwanted noise, to match the EQ, to match the reverberation. Every single line and word has to be gone through. Essentially you want to make all the dialogue sound natural and as if it was recorded at the same time, in real time. It's amazing how hard that is and it's a slow process. We have to pre-mix that to where it works really nicely. With sound effects, there is a lot of material that comes in. We have to decide on panning (left, center right or surround speakers etc.), reverb, EQ decisions, how does it match up, how does it blend into the next sound effect? Maybe it takes 30 sound effects to create one huge sound effect. That takes a lot of trial and error to get it to work. You need all that busy work and decision making done in a pre-mix session, to get it down to a manageable and artistic level, so that you can take the pre-mixes and fine tune how they interact.

Q - How many tracks might you need to pre-mix?

Mike - Hundreds, with possibly two hundred thousand pieces of sound going to make up the movie, especially in action films. For a low budget picture, cut it by 90%, because they don't have the time or money, or maybe they don't need it. Many independent films are centered around the story and characters where to embellish the sound is not so important.

Q - When you get to the final mix, you want to have done as much track laying as possible?

Premix to Final Mix (for a low budget film)

Dialogue Track 1 (m)
Dialogue Track 2 (m)
Dialogue Track 3 (m) → Dialogue Premix (s)
Effects 1 (s)
Effects 2 (s)
Effects 3 (s) → Effects Premix (s)
Effects 4 (s)
Effects 5 (s)
Music 1 (s)
Music 2 (s)
Atmospheres 1 (s)
Atmospheres 2 (s) → Atmos Premix (s)
Atmospheres 3 (s)
Foley 1 (m)
Foley 2 (m) → Foley Premix (m)

Final Mix (s)

m = mono   s = stereo

Magneto Optical Disk with Dolby Digital Mix.

35mm Optical Sound (made at lab)

Note the two optical analogue sound tracks to the left of frame, and digital information between sprocket holes on the left of frame.

When completing your mix, it can all get a bit confusing as there are so many different mixes and formats. In essence, you will deliver a Magneto Optical disk of the Dolby Digital mix to the labs (that's the surround mix), who will use that to make the optical sound for the 35mm prints. This mix will later be used on your DVD too. You will also have another disk or tape (DA88 format if tape) that will have a stereo mix for broadcast TV, and an M&E mix for foreign sales. You may also have a 'stem' mix, which is a disk or tape that has the mix but in all its separate channels, should you or anyone else, wish to go back and change it. Deliver on disk is becoming more popular, usually as a Pro Tools session.

Audio Tracks In Detail

Even a low budget film should have excellent sound. As long as you spend time selecting good effects, laying them in, acoustically annotating everything on screen (and some things off screen), then adding good ambience tracks, detailed foley and finally a considered and rich score, you are in for a great sounding movie. We spent a great deal of time on the sound for our third feature film, Urban Ghost Story, but at the same time, knew we didn't have limitless resources. This example below is all the tracks from reel five of the movie

1. Dialogue Tracks (mono) - The sound of actors' voices that was recorded on the set. It important to get this as clear and crisp as you can so that less sweetening or ADR will be needed later. In this instance there are three mono checkerboarded dialogue tracks. Note how each track is for an individual character so the mixer can easily access each.

2. Set FX (mono) - These are sounds that we recorded live on set, broken apart from the dialogue so that they can be used in the M&E mix. This is stuff like footsteps, a door slamming, or water running. There are two tracks of set effects here.

3. Panic (mono) - This is a single 'just in case' track. Used for audio you probably won't use, but might have to in case of an emergency or creative epiphany.

4. ADR (mono) - Also known as looping. Re-recording of actor's lines that were not properly picked up on the production. Two tracks here. All our ADR was recorded wild, mostly on-set after the shooting finished, but sometimes in the actors apartment.

5. Foley (mono) - A recreation of all the actors' movements in a film, from their footsteps to clothes rustling. Will also be a large part of the M&E mix. In this instance there are two foley tracks.

6. Spot Effects (mono) - These are all the character and story driven sounds. Door slams, car tire screech, telephone ring etc. Two mono tracks here.

7. Spot Effects (stereo) - Used for wider sounds such as a gunshot, police siren or a sword being swung etc. We had four stereo tracks as many effects needed building from several layers.

8. Ambiance (stereo) - Continuous 'background' sound that appears throughout the film. Not usually recorded on set, but pulled off of library CD's. A full atmosphere track can really make your film sound rich. Spend time and get these right. We had four tracks as it was a spooky ghost story.

9. Music (stereo) - Either composed, taken from a library or some other source. Can be in the background or foreground. Too much music can be really annoying. One track here but you would normally have at least two or more.

REEL5.EDL

Dialog 1	
Dialog 2	"Ho, w
Dialog 3	
Set FX 1	Carry)
Set FX 2	
Panic	
ADR 1	ADI
ADR 2	
Foley 1	Roll 5 footsteps
Foley 2	Roll 5 clothes
SpotFX 1	Baby c
SpotFX 2	Rummaging
SpotFX 3	Police siren / Police siren
SpotFX 4	
SpotFX 5	
SpotFX 6	Jabba' / Lift r
Atmos 1	cor-l2 / cor-l2
Atmos 2	cistern / cor-l / winc
Atmos 3	drips(s) / windy / western
Atmos 4	office; / wind-b
Music 1	THE MUSIC

05:04:19:21:00

POST

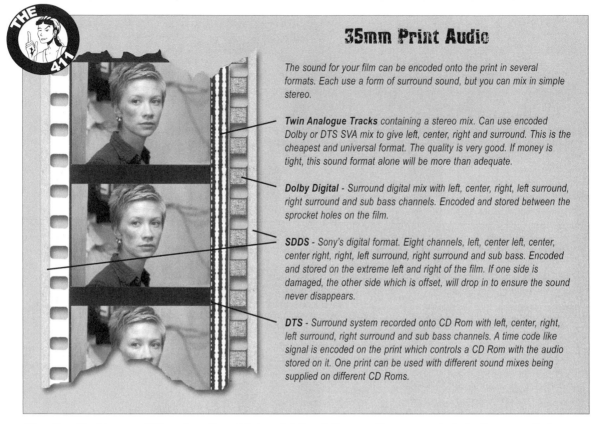

35mm Print Audio

The sound for your film can be encoded onto the print in several formats. Each use a form of surround sound, but you can mix in simple stereo.

Twin Analogue Tracks containing a stereo mix. Can use encoded Dolby or DTS SVA mix to give left, center, right and surround. This is the cheapest and universal format. The quality is very good. If money is tight, this sound format alone will be more than adequate.

Dolby Digital - Surround digital mix with left, center, right, left surround, right surround and sub bass channels. Encoded and stored between the sprocket holes on the film.

SDDS - Sony's digital format. Eight channels, left, center left, center, center right, right, left surround, right surround and sub bass. Encoded and stored on the extreme left and right of the film. If one side is damaged, the other side which is offset, will drop in to ensure the sound never disappears.

DTS - Surround system recorded onto CD Rom with left, center, right, left surround, right surround and sub bass channels. A time code like signal is encoded on the print which controls a CD Rom with the audio stored on it. One print can be used with different sound mixes being supplied on different CD Roms.

Mike - On a big picture, we still have five editors at their workstations in the room. They are constantly feeding us re-edited material, reconceived material. It never stops. On a low budget film you might not have that resource, so you should have all your effects track layed and you should know what you want from the final mix. The sound systems used today are multi channel - left channel, center channel, right channel, (all at full range), and a left and right surround channel (that are not full range because they are smaller speakers), and then there is the sub-woofer for that chest thumping bass. Aesthetically, it works really well. It can also be used on DVD where many low budget films will inevitably be seen (though a separate less dynamic mix may be needed for this).

Q - How much should you use surround sound?

Mike - For me, the image is in front of me, and sound can enhance that image and the storytelling. The surrounds can be used as an enhancement too, but should never remove you from the screen in front of you. You need to be careful and ensure that whatever you chose to mix into the surrounds is not disembodied. All the sounds should feel a part of a whole.

Q - Is it common for new filmmakers to over score their movies? Do composers come to the mix?

Mike - It can be. Filmmakers can overuse music because they don't have the right emotion on the screen within the acting or composition or writing. So, they try to cover it up with some music or sound effects. Composers used to come to the mix, but when sound effects became so important in the late 70's, they would show up and freak, *'where's my 270 piece orchestra? I don't hear it!'* They have gotten smarter and know that the music may compete with jets and helicopters.

Q - What tools do you have available to you?

Mike - There are hundreds of software programs you can use, but you need an understanding of what those tools are. You can over process things so easily and make things sound bad. I try to use very little processing. Typically you might use a little reverb to add space around a sound effect, or a noise gate to remove a little background sound.

Q - What is the best sound mastering format?

Mike - They all have their good and bad points. I prefer Dolby Digital as it's a reliable system, and the most widely used.

Q - Do you do the M&E mix?

Mike - Yes. This is a mix used for foreign sales which is essentially the whole sound track, minus the dialogue. It's used when dubbing into different languages. I try to put every ounce of the original feel into the M&E mix. We are usually only given two days to do the M&E, but some may take longer. When I'm pre-mixing and final mixing, I keep it in mind that I will do an M&E mix and make sure I separate things at that point, so they will fold together nicely and I won't have to find them later.

Q - Is there anything filmmakers can do to help with the final mix?

Mike - All the technology you have at home to use is wonderful - Avid and Pro Tools. Can you mix something for a theatrical release with those tools? Not really. But you can assemble your soundtrack with them. You can add things, balance a little bit here and there but that is not a mix. There are a lot of filmmakers who are looking for cheaper ways of doing things and they all have this misconception that the mix can be done in this domestic environment.

Q - What is the final mix recorded on?

Mike - We do everything to hard drives on a Pro Tools format because it's popular.

Q - How much time should a producer budget for the final mix?

Mike - I would say the average movie would be 300 hours. That's not a low budget guerrilla film. They will want to do it in 50 hours. A big budget movie could go up to 2000 hours. So what's the difference between 50 and 2000 hours? It simply makes it a better sounding movie. So you should budget as much as you can and give special attention to the dialogue pre-mixes.

Q - Are there certain times better than others to approach you?

Mike - Anybody will do something if it's down time. I've done student films and things for free. If I'm sitting around doing nothing and I like the project and people, I'll do it. If not, I may push it onto someone else.

Q - What are the most common mistakes you have come across and what advice would you offer a new filmmaker?

Mike - The common mistake in sound are just not using it well. But everyone tries as they know they can get a lot of bang for their buck these days. It is a commodity you should use just like a good actor. Then there are guys that don't have any taste and don't know how to use sound. Bad taste pulls something back from the film. Many people want to be filmmakers because of the fame and fortune. If that's what drives you, the really ambitious ones will get there. Then there's those who have a lot of ambition and no talent. They won't get there. They'll be making small films but will never get the fame and fortune. It's what motivates you? If you're going to be a filmmaker, make a movie. Everything has been done before. It's how you do it, so don't look for gimmicks. Don't rely on being weird to make it different. You can tell the same story 10,000 different ways. Just tell it honestly with a lot of heart and soul and purpose. Every director has a crutch he leans on. Some have two or three. Find your style, and you won't find it with your first film.

POST

Tim West
Pop Sound

Q - What do you do?

Tim - I'm a sound mixer, which involves recording, editing music, editing voiceovers and effects, sound design, mixing and putting it to picture.

Q - What could someone do in their home with their editing software?

Tim - A great deal. There's no longer a great divide between high end professional equipment and cheap(ish) consumer equipment. Pro Tools has a free version, for example, which you can do most sound design and editing at home with. There's some very good competitors such as Nuendo, which is excellent. There is a lot of cheap and even free software out there, but then it is important to get something that is OMF and EDL compatible. In order to use an EDL, you need a machine with nine-pin control so the computer can control the DAT machine and look for the places and load in the audio automatically. Both Final Cut Pro and Avid Xpress allow you to export OMF (open media format) files which you can then import into Pro-Tools in a studio, so you could track lay your film in those programs. OMF's have become a pretty standard way of moving sessions between different systems.

Q - What is the most important factor for a low budget filmmaker coming to you?

Tim - The more preparation you do, the more it will save you money. There's this attitude that I've heard people on set say, *'we can fix it in post'* and anyone who says that has never been in post production to see it. I would tell any director, treat your sound person as well as you do your cameraperson. If you think the sound was bad, then do another take. A lot of time can be saved in the mix if you get a dialog editor to assemble, clean and premix the dialog tracks before going into the mix - the same goes for effects. Think about premixing the music with the composer. Don't go into a mix with the intention of endlessly experimenting, especially if you are trying to save money. If you have a really precise idea of what you want and you're not going to be doing any experimenting, then you'll save a lot of time. Prepared, with all the different elements carefully organised and the final picture on a useable format. Billing usually starts when you walk through the door, and rummaging in boxes looking for that lost DAT is lost mixing time!

Q - What about problems with camera noise?

Tim - It is a lot easier getting rid of unwanted sound nowadays, especially if it's constant. Say there's a generator running constantly in the background, in the last couple of years there's some amazing and cheap software that we use everyday in the studio that can do incredible things by sampling the noise you want to take out - which it does very effectively. We've even got a distortion taker-outer plug-in that looks for the gaps in the sound and fills them in. Being asked to take out distortion used to be a joke!

Q - What about dubbing charts?

Tim - It's always a good idea to have clearly laid out charts, detailed paperwork for anything, as everybody can have the same information. If a director has a clear idea of what they want, there's no better way to convey that.

Q - If you've forgotten a sound that you really want in, can you add it at the last minute?

Tim - Most stages are equipped with a sound effects server, so that shouldn't be a problem. Again, it is wise to go through everything before you get to the mix stage - it depends on the room and the mixer how equipped they are to make last minute changes to the editing.

Q - Who attends the final mix?

Tim - It varies. It is sometimes just the Director. Other times you get the Composer, editors, the director, the producer, the entire cast and crew, the directors mother, and some strippers the producer met in Hollywood.

Q - Does it ever get ridiculous with too many people?

Tim - Yes. As a director, the fundamental decision would be to think, why would it benefit me having certain people there? It would speed things up, because you might be mixing away and the composer will say, 'my music's too low' and get all picky about it. You might not want to have to justify your decisions. One of my colleagues worked out that when mixing a 30 second commercial, which would normally take 2 hours, each additional person in the room adds 1 hour.

Q - How would you get the best deals at your company?

Tim - That could get me in trouble! Lets just say that approaching a commercial facility over the summer wouldn't hurt.

Q - What common sound mistakes do you come across?

Tim - Trying too hard to tell the story with sound. For example, you're in a room, and there's something outside the room, maybe a car has crashed outside the room, but you don't see it on film. I find that annoying, because it's like a play. As a rule with sound design, if don't you see it, or its not referred to in the script, don't put the sound in. If there's a kettle boiling sound, make sure you see the kettle. Don't have it whistling in another room unless it's relevant to the story. Many directors try to over sound design things. At the end of the day, the rules governing the editing should govern the sound - which is to say that it shouldn't detract from the story.

Q - What advice would you offer new filmmakers?

Tim - Have some budget left over for your sound. There are certain things you do to save some money. Buy your stock, DAT's, DA88's, and CD-Roms, before you go to the studio. A DAT in an average post-production place will be $70 as opposed to $5 from a consumer store. Then are things you cannot skimp on. You will need money for Dolby / DTS licenses - there's no way around that. If you make a glorious 35mm film, don't skimp and do a stereo mix, do a good surround mix. And get the dialogue right. Pander to the sound guys on set and listen to them. Wear headphones. Try and get a feed from the DAT machine and listen yourself as to whether something is usable. Within reason, tell the sound people they can re-take but on the other hand, listening to whether something performance wise is usable and if that plane flew over head misses the dialogue, say, 'no, that's going to be fine'. Be decisive. Watch films and decide what you like sound wise out of them. Whether you like the David Lynch dark, oppressive sound design, or lots of score - decide what elements you like, put them on VHS and give them to the relevant people. If you can temp score and sound design your film, that's a good idea. Otherwise you can just hand it over to people and say you want their influence on it. But then it might turn out completely differently to what you imagine.

Sheena Duggal
Sony Imageworks

Q - What is your job?

Sheena - As a VFX supervisor I work with the director and advise him on how best to use visual effects to achieve his vision. When a shot in the movie cannot be photographed, or created practically, we use visual effects to augment or create entirely new digital elements. We also design shots specifically to utilize the VFX in effects driven movies. I am responsible for designing and supervising the shooting of these elements or plates during principal photography, and also for the creative supervision of the digital artists and animators during the post production phase.

Q - What is the role of visual effects and what do visual effects entail?

Sheena - The role of VFX has evolved enormously over the last few years. While in the past, visual effects have primarily been applied to projects that were more or less classified as effects driven, nowadays pretty much everything from feature films of every genre and budget, to music videos, TV shows and computer games utilize visual effects in some form. A film with 200 visual effects was considered a big show less than 10 years ago. Nowadays we are working on projects with up to 1,000 shots. This omnipresence of visual effects has created a much higher awareness of our work. Unfortunately, this is also slowly causing the demise of several admirable art forms at the same time. These days, you will rarely see a matte painting that has not been created in a computer, cloud tank effects are used rarely and artists working in the fields of animatronics and prosthetic makeup may fear that their working days are numbered, prompting many to diversify by enhancing their computer skills. I personally believe that the marriage of all existing techniques, from miniature models to make up appliances and all other in-camera effects, with CGI, would be most beneficial to filmmaking today. Each discipline, applied in their most advantageous situations, would ultimately create the most cost efficient solution as well. It is hard to define the role of VFX as this is very dependant on the content of the movie - is it an effects driven movie or are the effects invisible and driven by story and vision? The type of effects we create range from simple wire removals, paint fixes, 2d composites, digital matte paintings, particle effects (rain, smoke), simulated lighting applied to 3D elements, texture painting, to the addition of digitally animated 3D characters, both realistic and stylized, which can interact with fully simulated digital environments (CG Spiderman flying through CG NY City). Given the resources there is hardly anything that can't be created digitally.

Q - What is digital compositing and the job of a compositor?

Sheena - Digital Compositing is what we call the job of artists who are experts in seamlessly combining elements together. These can be 2 dimensional elements, like a blue-screen shot on a stage combined with an outdoor background plate, or 3 dimensional elements which have been generated entirely on the computer, like the mouse in *Stuart Little*. Digital compositors require an artistic eye and the ability to add the nuances to a shot which make it feel more believable, a shadow or light kick in the right place can be important in sealing a reality, as well as perfectly color balanced elements which live in the same world. Digital compositors have many skills and are able to, rotoscope, track, paint, color correct, color and light 3d elements and create simple matte painting work. These are all skills, which when combined, create the final composite.

Q - What is blue screen / green screen and the difference between the two?

Sheena - A blue / green screen is a backing used to shoot foreground elements which will later be digitally extracted from the blue or green screen backing, creating a matte which can easily be separated from the foreground elements in post production in order to insert the desired background (i.e. a matte painting, cg-generated background or to composite a separately photographed plate element). The digital blue / green screens are designed to reflect light back at the camera, which, when correctly exposed gives us the most separation between our foreground element and the blue / green screens. The decision to shoot blue or green is somewhat subjective. Experts usually have a preference for one or the other. DP's usually like to shoot blue when working with actors as it gives the most pleasing flesh tones and is better suited for outdoor screens. Green screen requires less light than blue screen to get it's best separation exposure, and there is less film grain in the green channel than the blue channel so we can achieve cleaner edges when we extract a matte. These days the digital technology we use works equally well for either and the decision on which to shoot will depend on the color of the set, wardrobe and the preference of the DP. On *Spiderman* for instance, all FX shots (that required background replacement) featuring Spiderman, were shot on green screen, as his costume contains blue fabric (although it is not the same blue tone as in the blue screen, using a green screen instead simplifies the process.)

Q - What is motion control, motion capture, rotoscoping and can you explain briefly how these work together?

Sheena - Motion control allows us to record camera data and gives us the ability to have an exact repetition of any given camera move as many times as required, in different environments, and with different subject matter. Motion capture allows us to record the exact movements of a real object and apply it to a computer-generated object. The technology was originally designed for orthopedic surgeons to monitor the abnormalities in human posture and gait. In the example of a person, motion capture points are placed on the person and their motions and expressions are digitally recorded as data, which is stored so that we can later apply those movements to our synthetic character. (movement is very hard to animate so motion capture is preferable). The advantages of motion capture include real time visualization and realistic looking cg animation. Although we are using it extensively on many upcoming movies, it is worth noting that the animation for *Spiderman* is comprised of almost entirely key frame animation, which animated frame by frame by an animator working on the computer. In VFX terminology, rotoscoping describes the frame-by-frame painting of an element or tracing of an image. Typically a matte is created that allows us to separate elements within the same image and manipulate them independently of each other. It is a time consuming and labor intensive process, as we are required to hand articulate fine detail within an image.

Q - What are the most important issues to be considered in advance when you know something is going to involve some kind of digital manipulation?

Sheena - It is important to plan, storyboard and discuss with the VFX supervisor the options available. There are often a number of approaches that can be taken when shooting VFX shots, for example motion control can be avoided if you shoot locked off Vistavision plates (8perf) and then add a camera move in post. Finding a vendor to do the work should not be based on who can give you the lowest price, look at their work and if possible talk to other directors who have worked with them.

Q - Must a filmmaker storyboard the sections of the movie with the effects?

Sheena - Ideally a filmmaker would storyboard the VFX shots, this way we can anticipate the complexity of the shot and specify the equipment needs and the technical approach. This also allows us to advise on the most cost effective way to shoot the shot as it is designed. If we don't have storyboards we then often need to be prepared for anything to happen on the day of the shoot and have all the potentially required equipment available - which is more expensive.

Q - VFX don't have to be kept to big VFX Hollywood blockbusters?

Sheena - Visual effects are no longer confined to 'big effects' movies, but instead show up in almost every film today. We created 120 Visual effects for *Anger Management*, a romantic comedy, ranging from complex computer generated crowds with 3d people in Yankee Stadium, to matte paintings and simple blue screen composites.

Q - Technicians also spend time fixing problems, what kind of problems do they fix?

Sheena - A blemish on an actors face, removing unwanted film equipment in the frame, changing the color of the skies, removing an unwanted cloud - you name it and we have removed or altered it. We often do work to fix technical issues like a wobble in the camera, scratches on the film negative, light spillage, hairs in the gate, water spots on the lens, slowing down or speeding up a camera move etc.

Q - How does the process work?

Sheena - Visual effects editorial receives film negative from the production with editorial counts for the VFX shot. VFX editorial prepares the film for scanning and it's sonically cleaned. The film and notes on format and how it should be scanned, go to the scanning department where the film is digitized into the computer. Technical assistants create a location for the scanned data on the computer and the digitized images are placed here. The shot then goes through a color correction pipeline where it is color matched to a timed clip supplied by the production. The supervisors have usually already determined software requirements, assigned tasks and chosen an approach to complete the shot. The shot goes through the hands of many artists before it's completed - dust busting, match moving, modeling, animation, lighting, texture painting, matte painting and compositing. This is a sample of a possible pipeline for a shot; the actual pipeline would depend on what we are creating. Artists work on the shots, digital production managers track all data and notes relating to the shots and daily production meetings are held in a screening room. The VFX supervisor and the crew review the daily shot progress at 'dailies' for which the shots are recorded onto video or film. The shot is often revised multiple times, shown to the Director for approval, and then recorded back onto film. The film is sent to the VFX editor and delivered to the production editorial to be cut with the non VFX principal photography.

Q - How much do visual effects cost?

Sheena - A stationery shot costs less than a moving shot as the amount of work is simplified by not having a moving camera. Elements don't need to be animated to track the camera motion in order for us to apply them to a shot. If the shot is moving we may use motion control to match the movement of the elements. There are fixed rates for film scanning and recording. In the case of a simple blue / green screen composite, it is possible to get a fairly accurate approximation of costs, but we usually bid based on the experience we have, and compare similar shot costs to what we have done in the past.

Q - Is the line between high-end visual effects and low-end visual effects merging?

Sheena - VFX software packages for both the high and low end, filmmaking and video games, are converging. The high-end tools are becoming less expensive in line with the price of the hardware platform, and the low-end tools are providing more performance as the hardware costs drop, making memory and processing power more affordable. It is inevitable that the two will converge and the distinction between the high and low end will be determined by the skill level of the artists.

Q - If doing effects on HD, do you need to be more careful with visual effects?

Sheena - Working with HD is comparable with working at feature film resolution, but the digital compression used in HD causes a lot of issues, particularly for blue / green screen shots. The smaller contrast range of HD may also be a problem. In addition there are many formats in HD that can lead to confusion. HD is becoming very popular with production as a way to look at dailies. Recent movies I've worked on have not printed film dailies and this simplifies the process, when VFX create shots for temp screenings as we do not have to scan and film record the material.

Q - Does the VFX Supervisor, Stunt Co-ordinator, Special FX Supervisor and production Designer congregate in pre-production to calculate where the crossovers between the different fields occur?

VISUAL EFFECTS

Visual effects seem like they would be very expensive, and they can be. However, you can do a lot of interesting things with relatively inexpensive software, that can enhance your film - such as removing a boom microphone, stabilizing a shaky camera move or animation. Preparation is your biggest cost cutter, so plan ahead by storyboarding your VFX shots and talking to a visual effects company or supervisor as soon as possible.

Motion Control

A technique where a camera is placed on a motorized head / dolly that is computer controlled. It enables you to perform a camera move over and over again in exactly the same way. The camera move co-ordinates can then be imported into a 3D program so the software can generate new elements that perfectly match the on-set camera move. The 3D elements and on-set footage can then be composited together. (pictured is the Juno from www.mrmoco.com)

Motion Capture

A technique used to record the exact movements of a real object and translate them to a digital character. Most common is an actor in a specially designed suit with motion capture sensors attached to it, which the computer can capture to record the movement. This data is then applied to a computer generated 3D object which will then inherit the real world and life like moves that animators find so difficult and time consuming to imitate (pic www.metamotion.com).

Animatics (previsualization/'previz')

Animated video story-boards for visual effects, which make a more accurate representation of what will eventually be filmed or created in the computer. It helps everyone understand 'the shot' and can be used in the edit as a temp shot for timing.

Rotoscoping

The frame-by-frame painting or tracing of an image. A matte is created for separate elements within the same image, so that they can be manipulated independently of each other. It is very time consuming and labor intensive process as it has to be done by hand. Famously used to animate Snow White.

Blue/green screen

A blue/green screen is used when shooting an object where the background is going to made transparent and a new background inserted digitally. Backgrounds are often matte paintings or cg-generated landscapes. Used because it's cheaper than taking a crew to a location, or because the location does not exist. The digital blue/green screens are designed to reflect light back at the camera, which, when correctly exposed gives the most separation between our foreground element and the

blue/green screens. DP's usually like to shoot blue when working with actors as it gives the most pleasing flesh tones. Green screen requires less light to best separation exposure and there is less film grain in the green channel, which makes for cleaner edges. Make sure actors are not wearing the similar tones to the blue / green screen. The key with shooting blue / green screen is even lighting and as much distance between the screen and subject as possible (to avoid light spilling from the screen and onto the back of the actors). This means you will need a big space to shoot in.

2D compositing

Two-dimensional (flat) image creating where no shading is used, like blue/green screen techniques. Generally, this takes less time to create and is therefore less expensive.

3D compositing

Three-dimensional image creation where the objects appear to be alive within the film, such as animation like 'Spiderman' or the mouse in 'Stuart Little'. Large use of shading and simulated light sources to create this effect, which takes longer and costs more.

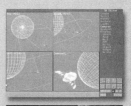

Sheena - We have pre-production meetings with all department heads and stay in constant communication with regard to how each of our requirements affects the other departments.

Q - With Gollum as an example, CGI characters are becoming more realistic. How important is the marriage between the traditional disciplines such as miniatures and mechanical fx rather than doing everything CGI?

Sheena - Although I work in the field of computer related VFX, my opinion is that the combination of the various existing techniques is highly beneficial to most productions, both financially and artistically. You name *Lord of the Rings* as an example, and I think it is in fact a very good one to illustrate that CG is not the answer to everything. While Gollum is indeed 100% computer generated character, brought to life via motion capture, the overall production is comprised of the entire gamut of FX, from miniatures (such as the Isengard towers), to elaborate prosthetics on the Orcs and Uruk-Hais, the volcanic like matte paintings for Mordor, all the way to traditional stop motion used for the troll in the cave sequence. While some films, such as the *Matrix* films, lend themselves to a higher degree of CG use, I believe it to be a question of individual approach to the sequence at hand, rather than seeing a general answer for the question.

Visual Effects Quote Procedures

1. Look through your script and locate all the scenes that may require visual effects. For low budget films, reconsider if you can rewrite to avoid the effects.

2. Create a breakdown sheet that lists the scene, effect and the priority of how crucial the effect is to the story.

3. Research visual effects houses. Most visual effects houses have the same equipment - the major creative differences will be the ingenuity of the visual effects artists. Try to find facilities that have done effects that are similar to yours. Call them and ask for demo reels. Be careful here for smaller houses may have done work on big films, but may only have done small portions of the scenes they show. Ask them specifically what they did on each shot.

4. Find four or five visual effects houses that you like and ask them for a quote. Do not tell them what your visual effects budget is, as they will try to make their work fit that number as opposed to just giving you a bid. It's OK to tell them what the overall budget of the film is, however. Send a copy of the breakdown sheet and the script for their review.

5. Get their bid and have them send a breakdown on how they would do each shot. Be wary of houses that significantly underbid all the others for they may not be able to deliver on time and on budget.

6. Once the bids are in, if they are excessive, find ways to cut, change or alter your visual effects so that they are less expensive. For example, CGI animals may be more expensive than hiring an animal wrangler and the real thing and shooting green screen. Change 3D effects to 2D, or try to find a way to make them mechanical effects that you can do on set. The cheapest of course is cut! How much you really need that effect?

7. Once you choose a facility, take them on, or have them either become or work with your visual effects supervisor.

8. When doing effects, you will need to be available to check work in progress. The more you do this, the less chance there is of them doing work that is either inappropriate or unneeded.

9. Remember, visual effects people are artists, not just people who press keys and move a mouse. Treat them as such.

Q - Who does the VFX supervisor keep in closest contact with from a production?

Sheena - The director, but she will also work closely with the DP, and all department heads. The VFX producer will work closely with the Unit Production Manager and producer on the production side. If the principal actors are in the scenes with visual effects shots then this will be shot by the 1st unit. If we are shooting stunt doubles or inserts, plates etc, then this will be shot be 2nd unit or the VFX unit.

Q - What advice would you have about film stock when shooting visual effect elements?

Sheena - Some of the Kodak vision film stocks cause problems in terms of edge artifacts and cross talk once digitized, so Kodak designed a film stock called SFX 200 specifically to counteract the problems encountered when shooting blue / green screen footage for matte extraction in VFX. The elements can be shot on this stock even though the background plates are shot on a different stock. There are

VFX Shooting Formats
Bad   Good

DV

All variants of DV, miniDV, DVcam etc., use image compression, which in turn adds 'noise' to the image, which is not too noticeable by a viewer, but the computer will see it. To make matters worse, the way DV encodes colors is quite poor, so it is not very good at blue / green screen. Best avoided for VFX.

Hi Def

The image is rock solid, no chance of camera weave. HD can also shoot progressive scan, opposed to interlaced, which is better for VFX. The image is also very high resolution, making for sharp pictures and good mattes.

Super 16mm

The film frame of Super 16mm is quite small, and therefore grain can become an issue. Due to the fact that Super 16mm has only one sprocket hole, the image can suffer from weave, a gentle rocking movement. The viewer doesn't see this, until you try to composite an image, at which point the foreground 'wobbles' and the background is static. Image stabilisation can be used, but this is yet another costly process.

35mm

Special film stocks are produced on 35mm for blue/green screen work, which is ideal. The image is rock solid (as long as the camera is not faulty or the mag has been badly loaded). Film grain is usually not an issue too. The incredible resolution of 35mm means that you can often 'zoom' into an image digitally and pull elements, or even create entirely new shots without too much noticeable loss of quality.

some Kodak vision 2 film stocks which work very well for VFX and are probably less expensive than the SFX 200.

Q - When should a producer approach a VFX Supervisor?

Sheena - During pre-production. Introduce him/her to the director so they can discuss creative approaches to the VFX shots.

Q - If the budget on a movie was low, would you be able advise the producer of certain elements to avoid?

Sheena - Avoid multiple moving cameras, try to design the VFX shots as lock offs and consider digital camera moves. Don't shoot anamorphic, as the optical squeeze creates a multitude of problems for the VFX experts in post due to the distortion artifacts, there is also a lack of extra negative area to move around within which limits what can be done. Both these issues make the shots more expensive. Shoot as much of the effects work as you can practically. Storyboard VFX sequences and spend a lot of time during pre-production planning your shots. Be aware of what will increase the expense of a shot in post-production if it is not shot as required during principal photography. If the VFX Supervisor advises you to spend money on more expensive digital screens and asks for specific video or camera equipment during principal photography, it will often save you money in post production to supply them with it and shoot the VFX elements as expertly as possible. VFX can often slow down the shoot as they need to get accurate data in order to create the CG elements, be prepared for this and let them document what you need.

Q - New filmmakers might think that visual effects are too expensive. Is that true?

Sheena - It really depends on what the visual effects are. Usually 2d composites are less expensive than full on computer generated effects. I would recommend bidding out the VFX before making any commitment to having them in the movie, it is standard for effects houses to bid against each other on upcoming projects.

VFX are not confined to big effects houses like Sony Imageworks or ILM, there are many small boutique companies that also create excellent feature film VFX. Find a supervisor / artist to work with that understands your vision and the budget constraints that you're operating within.

John Knowles
Fotokem

Q - What is a telecine?

John - A telecine is a device that takes motion picture film and transfers it onto video tape, and now that can also be directly onto hard drives.

Q - What materials do you need from the filmmaker?

John - You can transfer off any element, but typically we get the original negative. On some films, where they want a certain look, they'll make a print and transfer from that, which also protects the negative from additional handling.

Q - Tell me about the dailies transfer process.

John - Initially we would get the exposed and developed camera negative (dailies) from the lab and transfer them onto a format that the editor can load into his system (Avid / FCP etc.), whether it's a DigiBeta, BetaSP or a hard drive. The editor would then edit the film, and at an appropriate time, and subject to budget, the picture would be conformed to HiDef for test screenings (on a low budget feature, BetaSP would be fine). This could be screened to 300 people in a digital theatre so the marketing people can start getting their data on how the movie plays, too short, too long and that stuff. This replaces the traditional work print preview.

At the highest end of the independent features, they'll make a DigiBeta of their rushes, usually clean with no window timecodes burnt into the picture. They can then use that to assemble a version for sales promotional things and it allows them the option of finishing digitally in a nice video environment before they have the funds to cut the negative. If there is not enough money for the DigiBeta transfer, the next step would be to transfer onto BetaSP for editing purposes only.

Q - Is it during the telecine session that the audio and picture are put into sync?

John - Yes that is typical. Synching in the telecine takes a little more time as you have to stop working on the picture and sync the sound. Some independent film makers choose to synch on their Avid to save money. They transfer their dailies MOS (without sound) and then synch up themselves in the Avid. The two things that does is delay the time that the dailies are seen with synchronized sound, and the other thing is the editor has to enter in all of the time code from the audio that was not captured in the telecine session, and that list management may be more complicated, but that's the job of the editor. The other thing is that any audio problems, such as drift or bad microphones, are caught at a later time rather than early in the morning, if we were synching, and then we could make a phone call to get the problem fixed. You can do telecine faster when you are not stopping down to sync, so you save some money if you do synch yourself. Most features do sync sound at the telecine though.

Q - What would a filmmaker leave the telecine with?

John - The tapes for the editorial staff and any additional tapes for any other pertinent people (VHS sceeners of dailies etc).

Q - What form of video tape is the best to use as your master?

John - For normal resolution television, DVD and video, Digital Betacam is the best. With the work tapes for the editor, either BetaSP or DVCam, which will be loaded into Avid or Final Cut Pro. In the Hi Def world, it's either HD cam or D5?

Q - What are key codes?

John - In 1990, Kodak, AGFA and Fuji all put a machine readable bar code on their camera negative stocks (in addition to the printed numbers on the edge of their film). In 35mm, every foot (16 frames), there's a new, fresh number that counts the feet, and those numbers are read by a sophisticated device in the telecine machine, along with the time code from the audio and the time code you are laying down onto the video tape you are recording to. It correlates all of those three lists so that at any point on the video tape, you know the exact time code for the audio and the exact key code or edge numbers on the film, which as we know, are now machine readable, so that later, a negative cutter can go in and off of the video cut list, with some verification, cut the negative.

Q - How important is the relationship between the key code numbers, the time code that the dailies are transferred with?

John - It's critical. It has to be frame accurate as that's what the negative cutter is going to cut by.

Q - What is color grading?

John - The color correction process can be as sophisticated as you want, even in the dailies. We still try to present to the DP, dailies that have the look of the film. There's a great deal of responsibility on the dailies color timer to make sure they balance out the shots, even though from day to day, their shots are in different environments. One day it's cloudy, another day is sunny. The telecine colorist will be introduced to the DP before shooting so they can communicate, to ensure the feel of the film is right from day one. That's important as we have a phrase, *'death by dailies'*, which is where in a facility that doesn't have good communication, the DP is left to the mercy of the telecine house, doing dailies that represents his work. So it's important that we don't misinterpret the DP and his work.

Q - How would you deal with color timing in the dailies?

John - We would normally do a *'best light' t*elecine. We will start at an agreed point (color balance/contrast etc) and make modifications if needed - for instance, a dailies colorist will look at the camera reports and it tells him that *'a coffee filter was used on this shot'.* He then knows not to eliminate that look it's the look they wanted. So it's a matter of balancing the images to what the DP and director are looking for, with a little modification from shot to shot, if it gets a little darker in the evening for instance.

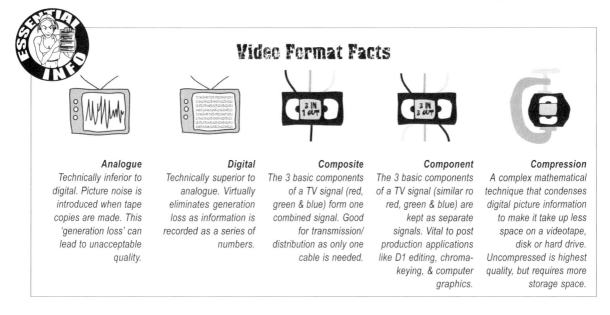

Video Format Facts

Analogue
Technically inferior to digital. Picture noise is introduced when tape copies are made. This 'generation loss' can lead to unacceptable quality.

Digital
Technically superior to analogue. Virtually eliminates generation loss as information is recorded as a series of numbers.

Composite
The 3 basic components of a TV signal (red, green & blue) form one combined signal. Good for transmission/ distribution as only one cable is needed.

Component
The 3 basic components of a TV signal (similar ro red, green & blue) are kept as separate signals. Vital to post production applications like D1 editing, chroma-keying, & computer graphics.

Compression
A complex mathematical technique that condenses digital picture information to make it take up less space on a videotape, disk or hard drive. Uncompressed is highest quality, but requires more storage space.

Q - What is TV safe?

John - The way the tubes are set up in a domestic TV is such that there is always some cut off around the image, and some cut of a bit more off the picture than others. TV safe is a general electronic area, measured by the number of lines from the top, bottom and sides of the picture, so if you were to put the image in there, you know everybody will see it. If there's critical action on the edge of frame, in telecine, they will make sure it's pulled over in the Pan and Scan process. There's also title safe which is inside TV safe. It is important to keep all your titles within the title safe area.

Q - What are the different TV standards you use for international sales?

John - The biggest thing nowadays is most films are being mastered in HD. From HD you can make pure PAL or NTSC tapes with the correct frame rates. International sales will require a number of tapes, both widescreen and full screen pan and scan, NTSC and PAL. If you do a HD master, making all these tapes for your sales agent becomes easier, and ensures the best possible quality.

Q - What is the 3:2 pull down?

John - It's a process that is used when you're transferring (on a telecine machine) material that was shot at 24 fps, but you're transferring to NTSC video. The way you get from 24 fps to 30 fps is every other film frame gives 3 video fields. What happens in one second of 24 fps film information, is every other film frame creates an extra video field, so at the end of 24 frames, giving you 12 of those film frames, created an extra 12 fields, divided by 2, you've gotten from 24 fps to 30 fps on video. It goes 3:2, 2:2, 3:2 as a sequence.

Q - Can the 3:2 process cause any problems?

John - Yes, if they don't know which film frame they are actually on, they could end up cutting the negative one frame off. But negative cutters know to watch for this stuff and there are all kinds of checks and balances. The negative cutter hole punches the negative for verification, so the cutter knows where the starting point was in telecine to verify these things.

Sound and Your Dailies

For projects with sync sound, provide your telecine house with your original source tapes. Make sure the sound has been recorded with 30fps non drop frame timecode. Each sync take must have 8 seconds of continuous time code pre-roll prior to the slate closure (the camera does not have to run during the sound pre-roll). Takes with short audio pre-roll and/or tail slates take longer to transfer and will lead to a more expensive telecine session. Digital slates are recommended for efficient, cost effective synching. Slates must be readable (not too far away), in focus, angled towards the camera with all the numbers visible, and stationery for at least 3 seconds. Illuminate the face of the slate and use the 'dim' LED setting when shooting in dark conditions; use the 'bright' LED setting outdoors. Unless there is a specific request to do so, the telecine house will not transfer wild sound during the telecine. Wild track should be circled on the sound reports if needed.

Q - Where do they make the hole punch?

John - At the beginning of each roll, or at any point a splice has been made within a roll. The negative cutter uses the punch hole as a reference for all the other cuts he is going to make in the raw camera footage. They can look at the cutting list (EDL) and the negative cutter will know then that if he goes down 45 feet and 3 frames that it's in the right place. Plus they have eye matching from the abacus sets.

Q - What is the difference between drop frame timecode and non drop frame timecode?

John - Non-drop frame puts a consecutive number on every single frame of video. Non drop frame is not true to the clock as it doesn't run at 30fps, it runs at 29.97fps, so that at the end of one full hour of video, it will be about 3 seconds short of the clock on the wall. They decided they needed a better timing process, so they came up with drop frame time code so networks could time everything to the clock on the wall. The way they do drop frame

Mastering Tips

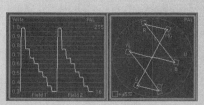

The waveform monitor and vectorscope
These used to measure the video on a technical level. The video level must not peak over 1v or under 0.3v or it will be rejected. Many software editing tools come with software scopes, like this one from an Avid. Generally, these are a guide and are not as accurate as a dedicated scope.

Bars
There are 30 seconds of bars before your picture starts, which are used to line up the video levels on the scope. The white to the left is just under 1v, the black to the right is just over 0.3volt. Essential to get right or your movie will be rejected.

Clock
This is needed so that the tape can be cued up for broadcast or duplication. Normally the clock will countdown from 30 seconds to 0 (the start of the show) and will fade to black at 3 seconds before the start of the show.

TV Safe and Title Safe
The TV safe area, the outer box, is used as a guide and your drama must stay within it. Many TV's will crop off right up to TV safe. Title Safe, the inner box, is a guide for the maximum extent to which you should place your titles onscreen.

time code is that at the end of every minute for the first nine minutes, if you were to stop on a window burn and look at it, it skips two numbers, but it doesn't skip frames. When it gets to the last second of the minute, it goes 28 and then not number 29 or 00, it goes to 02 and that's a cumulative thing. They figured if they skipped eighteen numbers in ten minutes, that would be a consistent calculation and would keep the timing of an episodic TV show with the commercials integrated true to the clock on the wall, so at the end of the hour, they don't sit there with 3 seconds of extra black.

Q - In the feature film world, is it drop frame or non-drop frame?

John - In sophisticated editing systems, it doesn't matter as long as you aren't mixing the two. When budgets are tight and you may not have a sophisticated editing system I would recommend non-drop frame.

Q - If you're on location, how can you view your dailies?

John - They can put up a portable satellite dish and we beam it to you, but that would cost $2k a week! In spite of all the high tech stuff now, people just deliver cassettes as it's reliable, inexpensive and it works.

Q - What happens if there is a technical problem with the dailies?

John - We have emergency numbers and that's also part of the job of the lab, to communicate to the production if there is a problem. Maybe there is a camera magazine that we think is causing camera scratches, or a microphone has a problem, or the

The Recording Report

Whenever you produce a tape at a professional facility, they will create a Recording Report, a letter sized sheet which will live in the box with the tape. This is a log of everything on the tape, where it came from, what was done to it, who did it, when it was done, even the machinery used. This is an essential piece of paperwork that is invaluable when attempting to track down faults that happened some time in the past.

Sub title
A brief description of what it actually is, in this case a telecine of a 35mm print.

Format
The type of tape used.

Tape Number
Facilities will sell you a tape at a massive mark up, so take your own stock. But if there is a problem with the tape they will say, 'well you didn't use our tapes, so it's not our problem...'

Audio layout
DigiBeta has four audio tracks. In this case the stereo mix has been recorded to tracks one and two (left on track one and right on track two) and the Music and Effects Mix has been recorded to tracks three and four (music on track three and effects on track four).

Standard
The TV standard, essentially PAL, NTSC or SCEAM.

Picture Source
Where did the pictures actually come from? In this case a low contrast 35mm print, but it could also be another source, such as DigiBeta camera tapes for instance.

Tape Content
Description of what's on the tape.

Audio Source
Where did the sound actually come from? In this case a time coded DAT tape.

Notes
Some things will need to be noted for QC (Quality Control). Things like black and white footage, super 8 like footage, degraded footage, odd sounds... anything that could be interpreted as a mistake, even though it's a creative decision, should be noted here to avoid misunderstanding.

In Timecode
The timecode where this particular element begins.

Out Timecode
The timecode where this particular element ends.

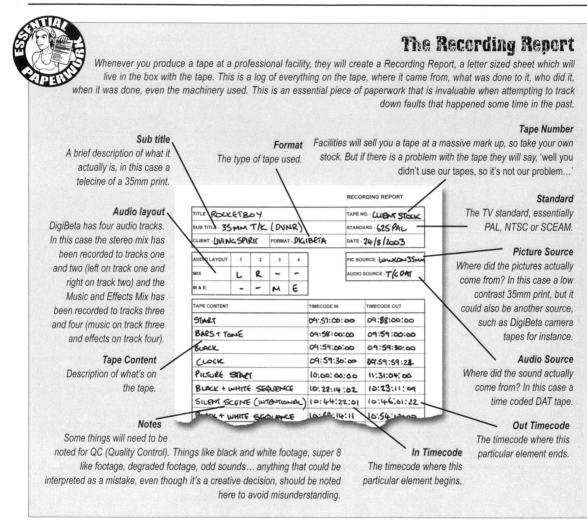

RECORDING REPORT

TITLE ROCKETBOY	TAPE NO. CLIENT STOCK
SUB TITLE - 35MM T/K (DVNR)	STANDARD - 625 PAL
CLIENT - LIVING SPIRIT	FORMAT - DIGIBETA	DATE - 24/8/2003

AUDIO LAYOUT	1	2	3	4
MIX	L	R	–	–
M & E	–	–	M	E

PIC SOURCE - LOWCON35MM
AUDIO SOURCE - T/C DAT

TAPE CONTENT	TIMECODE IN	TIMECODE OUT
START	09:57:00:00	09:88:00:00
BARS + TONE	09:58:00:00	09:59:00:00
BLACK	09:59:00:00	09:59:30:00
CLOCK	09:59:30:00	09:59:59:24
PICTURE START	10:00:00:00	11:31:04:00
BLACK + WHITE SEQUENCE	10:22:14:02	10:23:11:09
SILENT SCENE (INTENTIONAL)	10:44:22:01	10:46:01:22
BLACK + WHITE SEQUENCE	10:69:14:11	10:54:12:00

time code is not working, so the synching process in the telecine is taking longer. It's a huge responsibility.

Q - Do you come across a lot of exposure problems?

John - Yes, because it's a learning curve. Some people have the advantage of being able to shoot tests. We try to work with them to fix the under exposure or grain. It's not our job to be critical. Our job is to convey information. A lot of people push the envelope and end up pushing it too far. Film has a greater range than any other medium. Hi Def is great, but film is still the best.

Q - Any advice for filmmakers with regards to slates?

John - Make sure you get good clean slates on every shot, in focus, exposed and clear (both vocally and visually). Otherwise you may waste a lot of money in the telecine as shots need to be eye matched. Tail slating is necessary sometimes, so let us know there is a tail slate by writing it on the camera report sheet, or again, we can waste a lot of time and money. Try and be organized with your report sheets, they should always be detailed and readable.

World Distribution Of the Three Major TV standards

- ☐ NTSC
- ☐ PAL
- ■ SECAM

Abu Dhabi - 625 PAL
Afghanistan - 625 PAL/ SECAM
Albania - 625 SECAM
Algeria - 625 PAL
Andorra - 625 PAL
Angola - 625 PAL
Antigua - 525 NTSC
Argentina - 625 PAL N
Australia - 625 PAL
Austria - 625 PAL
The Azores - 625 PAL
Bahamas - 525 NTSC
Bahrain - 625 PAL
Bangladesh - 625 PAL
Barbados - 525 NTSC
Belgium - 625 PAL
Belize - 525 NTSC
Benin - 625 SECAM
Bermuda - 525 NTSC
Bolivia - 525 NTSC
Bophuthatswana - 625 PAL
Bosnia/Herzegovina - 625 PAL
Botswana - 625 PAL
Brazil - 525 PAL M
British Virgin Isles - 525 NTSC
Brunei - 625 PAL
Bulgaria - 625 SECAM
Bukina Faso - 625 SECAM
Burma - 525 NTSC
Burundi - 625 SECAM
Cameroon - 625 PAL
Canada - 525 NTSC
Canary Islands - 625 PAL
Central African Republic - 625 SECAM
Chad - 625 SECAM
Chile - 525 NTSC
China - 625 PAL
Colombia - 525 NTSC
Congo - 625 SECAM
Cook Islands - 625 PAL
Croatia - 625 PAL
Cuba - 525 NTSC
Curacao - 525 NTSC
Cyprus - 625 PAL/ SECAM
Czechoslovakia - 625 SECAM
Denmark - 625 PAL

Djibouti - 625 SECAM
Dominican Republic - 525 NTSC
Dubai - 625 PAL
Ecuador - 525 NTSC
Eire - 625 PAL
Egypt - 625 PAL/ SECAM
El Salvador - 525 NTSC
Equatorial Guinea - 625 SECAM
Ethiopia - 625 PAL
Faeroe Islands - 625 PAL
Fiji - 625 PAL
Finland - 625 PAL
France - 625 SECAM
French Polynesia - 625 SECAM
Gabon - 625 SECAM
Galapagos Isles - 525 NTSC
Germany - 625 PAL
Ghana - 625 PAL
Gibraltar - 625 PAL
Greece - 625 SECAM
Greenland - 625 PAL
Grenada - 525 NTSC
Guadalope - 625 SECAM
Guam - 525 NTSC
Guatemala - 525 NTSC
Guinea (French) - 625 SECAM
Guinea - 625 SECAM
Guyana Republic - 625 SECAM
Haiti - 625 SECAM
Honduras - 525 NTSC
Hong Kong - 625 PAL
Hungary - 625 SECAM/ PAL
Iceland - 625 PAL
India - 625 PAL
Indonesia - 625 PAL
Iran - 625 SECAM/ PAL
Iraq - 625 SECAM
Israel - 625 PAL
Italy - 625 PAL
Ivory Coast - 625 SECAM
Jamaica - 525 NTSC
Japan - 525 NTSC
Jordan - 625 PAL
Kampuchea - 525 NTSC
Kenya - 625 PAL
Korea (North) - 625 SECAM/ 525 NTSC

Korea (South) - 525 NTSC
Kuwait - 625 PAL
Laos - 625 SECAM/ PAL
Lebanon - 625 SECAM
Leeward Isles - 525 NTSC
Lesotho - 625 PAL
Liberia - 625 PAL
Libya - 625 SECAM
Luxembourg - 625 SECAM/ PAL
Macedonia - 625 PAL
Madagascar - 625 SECAM
Madeira - 625 PAL
Malawi - 625 PAL
Malaysia - 625 PAL
Maldives - 625 PAL
Mali - 625 SECAM
Malta - 625 PAL
Martinique - 625 SECAM
Mauritius - 625 SECAM
Mexico - 525 NTSC
Monaco - 625 PAL/SECAM
Mongolia - 625 SECAM
Morocco - 625 SECAM
Mozambique - 625 PAL
Namibia - 625 PAL
Nepal - 625 PAL
Netherlands - 625 PAL
Netherlands Antilles - 525 NTSC
New Caledonia - 625 SECAM
New Zealand - 625 PAL
Nicaragua - 525 NTSC
Niger - 625 SECAM
Nigeria - 625 PAL
Norway - 625 PAL
Oman - 625 PAL
Pakistan - 625 PAL
Panama - 525 NTSC
Papua New Guinea - 625 PAL
Paraguay - 625 PAL M
Peru - 525 NTSC
Philippines - 525 NTSC
Poland - 625 PAL
Polynesia - 625 SECAM
Portugal - 625 PAL
Puerto Rico - 525 NTSC
Qatar - 625 PAL

Reunion - 625 SECAM
Romania - 625 SECAM
Rwanda - 625 SECAM
Sarawak - 625 PAL
Samoa (Eastern) - 525 NTSC
San Marino - 625 PAL
Saudi Arabia - 625 SECAM
Senegal - 625 SECAM
Seychelles - 625 PAL
Sierra Leone - 625 PAL
Singapore - 625 PAL
South Africa - 625 PAL
South West Africa - 625 PAL
Spain - 625 PAL
Sri Lanka - 625 PAL
St. Kitts & Nevis - 525 NTSC
Sudan - 625 PAL
Surinam - 525 NTSC
Swaziland - 625 PAL
Sweden - 625 PAL
Switzerland - 625 PAL
Syria - 625 SECAM
Tahiti - 625 SECAM
Taiwan - 525 NTSC
Thailand - 625 PAL
Togo - 625 SECAM
Trinidad & Tobago - 525 NTSC
Tunisia - 625 SECAM
Turkey - 625 PAL
Uganda - 625 PAL
United Arab Emirates - 625 PAL
United Kingdom - 625 PAL
Uruguay - 625 PAL M
USA - 525 NTSC
Former USSR - 625 SECAM
Vatican City - 625 PAL
Venezuala - 525 NTSC
Vietnam - 625 SECAM/ NTSC
Virgin Isles - 525 NTSC
Yemen - 625 PAL/ SECAM
Former Yugoslavia - 625 PAL
Zaire - 625 SECAM
Zambia - 625 PAL
Zanzibar (Tanzania) - 625 PAL
Zimbabwe - 625 PAL

POST

Flex files

A flex file is a text file that is created in your telecine session and has all the necessary information for you to input into your non-linear editing system. The Flex file is delivered to you on a floppy disk and lists all timecodes and key code numbers associated with the scene and take numbers and any other information that the telecine operator thinks is relevant to your production. You can load this file into your Avid / FCP and automatically create a bin with all the time codes for the slates. You can then batch digitize all the shots without having to break them down yourself, though you will still need to name them. You can save money by not having flex files, and some editors don't use them as they are only as good as the telecine operator and can sometimes be slightly inaccurate. However, for NTSC projects, they can be invaluable. On the whole, worth doing, but if mistakes are made, shout about it.

Q - What is the Spirit Datacine?

John - It's a machine that transfers film at a very high resolution, usually onto HD. It can do lower resolutions too, but that would be uneconomic. The machine costs about $1.2m, where a Rank Cintel, loaded with standard definition (not HD), is about $650k. So right away, there's more than $0.5m just in hardware. The DaVinci 2k color corrector costs twice as much as a standard def color corrector, and the monitor alone is $50k! So the room costs around $2.5m to build! There is a amazing color correction, you can even slow down and speed up footage. But nothing is better than shooting it at the correct speed on set. You have to be careful using slo mo in an electronic environment, because bear in mind, 24P is not what you're going to broadcast, you're going to need to down convert and when you do that, you're going to create 30 fps NTSC masters and 25 fps PAL masters, and if you've done some odd vario speed on the master, there may be some other side effects and weird artifacts that occur in the down conversion. Any time you change the speed of the picture, you have to change the speed of the sound. Anything more than 4% is going to sound like chipmunks or really slow. You can't correct that.

Q - How much is a standard telecine suite to hire?

John - Perhaps $250 an hour, depending on the configuration. Approach us as early as possible. Many people talk to us months before a project begins.

Q - What information would the telecine operator want from the filmmaker?

John - Just enough to make sure they fully understand the project. We usually ask for spec sheets, a detailed list of all the specifications such as aspect ratio, time code, what information is to be burnt in, position of the key code window etc.

Q - What are the most common mistakes you come across?

John - Most frustrating is when a problem or error occurs, and then it happens again and again. For instance, you're paying by the hour, and someone is in here trying to synch dailies by eye because they didn't get good clean slates, it isn't economical. Also remember to start the audio at least five seconds before the clapper so that we have a good run in for sound and timecode.

Q - What advice would you offer?

John - The more knowledge you have about post-production, the more you will be able to save money an be more efficient. Call the facilities and talk through your proposed post-production route.

Video Terms Glossary

BITC - *Burnt In Time Code. Time code numbers recorded from camera tapes and visually displayed on screen giving a frame-by-frame picture reference. BITC is used on reference copies of dailies, which in turn will be used for the off-line edit.*

BLUE (GREEN) SCREEN - *Foreground subject is shot against a plain blue screen, on film or video, so that background images can be added electronically in post-production. Blue is chosen as it is the least naturally occurring color in flesh tones. Green screens are also used these days as images on green blend with the foreground images better.*

CHROMAKEY - *Technique which allows a vision mixer to substitute a saturated color (usually blue or green) in a picture for another picture source.*

DEINTERLACING - *Broadcasting or recording a video signal with only one of the fields of a frame. Gives the picture a grainer, and therefore, more filmic look.*

DVE - *Digital Video Effect. Devices such as ADO, A53, Encore and Kaleidoscope for picture manipulation.*

DVTR - *Digital Video Tape Recorder. Multiple generations or passes on DVTR's do not suffer from tape noise degradation associated with analogue formats.*

DROP OUT - *Momentary loss of signal on a video tape, showing up as randomly occurring white spots on the picture, present in worm or poor quality tape.*

525 - *This is the standard, specifying the number of horizontal lines that makes up the TV picture. 625 being the standard in the UK and 525 being the American version.*

FIELD - *Area of a TV screen covered by alternative lines. Two fields are equal to one frame (picture).*

FRAME - *Single television frame or film image. In the US, 30 frames per second are scanned to give the illusion of continuous motion. Each frame is composed of two fields.*

HUE - *Color tone of a picture.*

KEY - *Effect that allows a picture to be superimposed over a background.*

LUMINANCE - *The black and white information of a video signal.*

MATTE - *An area blanked off within a frame in order to include additional material or remove unwanted material.*

MOTION CONTROL - *A computer assisted camera and rig with multiple moving axies, enabling high precision, repeatable camera moves.*

N.T.S.C. - *National Television Standards Committee. Color standard used in the USA, Canada and Japan.*

OFF-LINE - *A pre-edit used to establish edit points for the on-line edit, usually on non-broadcast standard equipment.*

ON-LINE - *The main edit during which mixes, effects and audio are brought together using broadcast standard equipment in order to create a "master" edit.*

PAL - *Phase Alternate Line. Color standard used in Western Europe (except France), Scandinavia, China, India, Australia, South Africa, etc.*

PAL M - *A version of PAL standard, but using a 525 line 60 field structure. Used only in South America.*

PIXEL - *The smallest picture element on a television display.*

Q-LOCK - *Device for synchronizing audio with video machines.*

R.G.B. - *Red, Green, Blue. Primary television colors before encoding to a composite signal if required.*

RESOLUTION - *The definition (clarity) of a television picture, and the ability to determine small objects or the detail in objects.*

625 - *This is the standard, specifying the number of horizontal lines that makes up the TV picture. 625 being the standard in the UK and 525 being the American version.*

SECAM - *French, Eastern Europe and African color television standard. Stands for Sequential Color with Memory.*

STANDARDS CONVERSION - *The process of converting between different TV transmission signals. Usually refers to and from NTSC and PAL.*

T.B.C. - *Time Based Corrector. A device required to correct time base errors of a VTR, which build up during operation. Needed in dubbing, particularly for poor quality material.*

TELECINE - *A device for transferring film to video tape. Film can be color graded during this process.*

TIME CODE - *Binary Code recorded on video and audio tape recorders which uniquely indentifies frames. Used for synchronizing recorders and editing.*

POST

David Hays
E-Film

TAPE TO FILM

Q - What is tape to film?

David - The tape to film process is taking images captured on film or video (digital) and manipulating and storing on digital tape. These digital images are then transferred to 35mm film. Tape to film is used by many different types of productions. Independent producers sought the digital capture mediums (DV, DigiBeta HiDef etc.) as a less expensive way of telling their stories without the cost of film. Others captured on 16mm and 35mm and use digital post production to off line the film, create visual effects, and for color timing the film using video post production tools.

Q - How do you transfer to film?

David - At E-Film we evaluate the Master tape, frame by frame, to ensure you are within your aspect ratios and verify there are no dropouts or other anomalies that may affect the transfer process. The shooting computer up-rez's the files (if they are PAL or NTSC) to 2K (approximately four times the resolution) , and then an Arri Laser Film Recorder shoots a red, green, and blue pinpoint laser to expose the 5242 film (fine grain intermediate stock). The negative is then processed as you would a normal negative and a daily print is made.

Q - What happens to the sound in the transfer?

David - Sound is treated as a separate element, usually mixed to a DA88 tape format based on cut reels of less than 20 minutes. If a digital sound master is needed ie: SDDS, SRD, DTS, then an MO disk needs to be created prior to shooting the optical sound track. This optical track is actually a piece of film that only has the soundtrack on it and looks like squiggly lines on the left hand side of the screen. Yes, 'squiggly lines' is a technical term! Other information that is on the optical track is what looks to be a bar code in between the perforations. This is the digital sound which is read by a device also attached to the projector. When the optical track negative is married to the picture negative you have a release print for theaters.

Q - Are there different processes of transferring to film?

David - There are 3 types of recording devices used in tape to film transfers - Laser, CRT and EBR. EFILM uses the Arri laser film recorder. This is the latest and most widely used recording device which writes with pinpoint accuracy a red, green and blue laser onto an intermediate film stock giving you the best possible image and color rendition. It can also write to an ESTAR negative which, when doing a tape to film project and you need many festival prints, can save you a generation printing from the original digital negative. The CRT recorder exposes a camera negative stock by turning electrons into photons to expose the film. The main concern is when the electrons excite the single phosphor, it can then excite the surrounding phosphors as well. This can over expose the blacks leaving them milky and the contrast and colors can be difficult to achieve. There have been modifications to later models of CRT that have minimized the problem with mechanical adjustments and newer shooting software, so this is still a viable means of film recording. The EBR it is a method of using an Electron Beam Recorder to expose layers of 16mm or 35mm film which are then composited by an optical printer to an intermediate negative. The problems with this method are that because the images need to go through the traditional optical process they can be subject to composite misalignment, and more handling equals more dirt on the negative. This is one of the older methods of recording digital images to film and not used very much anymore because the equipment is pretty scarce and the result of the newer technologies is much better.

Q - Could a filmmaker shoot their DV film off a TV monitor themselves with a 35mm camera?

David - They could as long as they kept in mind the sync issues inherent to shooting monitors with film cameras. It's not the best way to get digital images back to film because new technology for transfers can be much better and cost effective.

Q - What is the quality of Tape to Film transfers?

David - Everything makes a difference, from choice of cameras through to the final print stock. Getting the film maker's vision to a final film out is a combination of testing the cameras and filters, the post color processes, and the final film stock you print to.

Q - What are the best formats to shoot on if you're going to transfer to film later?

David - You should match the type of format to the type of film you want to make, or the type of equipment that is available to you at the time. I have had dozens of film makers come through our facility and have looked at Mini DV through HD and 35mm prints from a negative and each one has reacted differently to what they feel works best for their production. Some choose the Mini DV because it is more suited to their film or they might actually own the camera and some choose HD because of visual effects and need the resolution for certain shots. It is also feasible that you can use multiple formats in your film to get a story point across.

Q - How does High Definition compare to Standard Definition when transferring to film?

David - High Definition can significantly change the look of a film. It is a much higher resolution than Standard Definition which captures 720X486 for NTSC and 720X576 for PAL, but HD captures information at 1920X1080 lines of resolution. Just in terms of pixels transferred to 35mm film HD is better quality.

Q - Is HD more or less flexible to work with than film?

David - The film negative can capture a much wider and more resolute range of image than any type of digital capture. So when working with a film negative you may have more latitude when color timing, either in the laboratory, or in the digital environment than you have with Hi Definition. HD has a great deal of information but you must expose this image properly and cleanly to be able to manipulate these digital images to their fullest. Some film makers have been able to create looks using filtration in the matrices of the camera as well as filtration on the lens, with great results. Keep in mind that this can 'lock' you into a look that you may not like on final color correction or film record out.

Q - Is exposing for HD the same as film?

David - Exposing HD is different to film (you expose for the highlights). If you lose information in the highlights by over exposing you can't get that information back. When you expose for the highlights you will still have quite a bit of latitude in your low lights.

Q - Is it better to shoot on PAL video rather than NTSC?

David - NTSC is a 60 fields 30fps and to transfer this to film at 24fps you will have to lose 12 fields per second or 6fps to get to 24fps. That is almost 20% of the information captured on tape and can cause strobing artifacts, objects stepping across the screen, aliasing horizontal lines and jagged edges. New developments in equipment and software makes field and frame removal easier and creates less artifacts. I strongly suggest you test each facility to see what their techniques are for cine compressing (going from 30fps to 24fps) and see which can give you the best results on film. PAL is usually transferred on a frame for frame basis back to film, so a frame of video is recorded to a frame of film. This means you are not removing any information in the form of fields or frames from the images and avoid most artifacts associated with NTSC. Software can convert the 25fps to 24fps by separating and reblending the fields to create new frames.

POST

Q - Are there sound problems transferring PAL or NTSC to film?

The sound issues going from 30fps to 24fps are that since you have removed information from your picture you may experience 'rubber' type sync during dialogue scenes. By transferring PAL to film and projecting at 24fps there is a 4% slow down. To keep in sync you can slow down the audio 4% with a sound device, which can have a slight effect on performances.

Q - Should you avoid anything in particular when shooting on video?

David - Avoid fast camera movement when the subject is stationery. If you know you have a certain look you want to achieve or there will be situations that may affect the outcome when transferring to film then definitely shoot tests.

Q - If you want to manipulate the speed of a shot, is this best to do in camera or in post?

David - Manipulation of speed can create artifacts when applied in post (on the final film), but the process is getting better. New variable speed digital cameras can offer an alternative to shooting on film. If shooting film you can shoot slow motion. It is always better to shoot what you want rather than trying to create it in post.

Q - Which cameras would you say have the best quality for tape to film transfer?

David - Use the camera that suits you, your film or your budget. Cameras that shoot in 24fps MiniDV should be looked at as they correspond with the 24fps of film projection and may eliminate some common issues and artifacts.

Q - What should a filmmaker supply for the transfer?

David - It is best to break all of your reels out into separate reels 20 minutes or less. The reel breaks are creative and a part of the editorial process. The reels usually come to us on digital beta for NTSC and PAL and on HDCAM or D-5 for High Definition and in some cases can arrive on firewire as well. The sound should be delivered on an MOdisk or DA88 also corresponding to the image reel breaks.

Q - If CGI elements need transferring to film, what is the best format to provide them in?

David - Typically the CG elements are usually incorporated in the online process. If you are going to have CG in your film create the elements in 24fps and on a frame basis. One technique is to have your NTSC converted to 24fps then create the graphics and composite them as 24fps elements. This should give you a cleaner look.

Q - Should all color correction happen on the tape before the film transfer rather than grading the actual film print?

David - Yes, as this alleviates the necessity to try to color time the film in the laboratory process. You want to have the balance of the images done in the digital realm and any other special color timing should be done at this time. The idea with tape to film is to have the transfer facility replicate what you have created in your digital timing. This also helps with your lab process as you should not have to time the film as extensively at that stage.

Q - Is that why people sometimes use Video Post- Production Tools even when shooting on film?

David - Final Cut Pro, in both Standard Def and Hi Def, allows the on-set offline as well as the final online. Color Correction on a DaVinci system can give you the option of Power Windows and overall color correction and balance of the images that can save time in the film lab when going to release print.

Q - If elements were originally shot on film and transferred to tape for post production, does the transfer back to film deconstruct any 3:2 pulldown and restore the original 24fps before printing onto film?

David - In the EFILM process this is done as part of the tape to film services offered. It can be done in a variety of ways with different looks resulting.

Q - If not, can this cause problems?

David - It is not so much that it causes problems as it could make your film look bad.

Q - Are rolling titles created in video suitable for transfer to film?

David - No because usually they are created on a field updating basis to create the roll causing strobing and double images on each credit. To create titles effectively use traditional film opticals or as single frame digital card created in software.

Q - How long does the transfer process take?

David - A 30 second commercial delivered with sound takes 3-4 days while a 90 minute feature with sound takes 14-18 days.

Q - How expensive is it? For instance how much would 10 minutes of video with sound cost to transfer to film?

David - Our rates vary based on the total project. A 10 minute short would in SD would be $550 per minute in HD it would be $750.00 per minute. 60 minutes plus the rates are 395.00 for SD and $550.00 for HD. These rates include the following Technical Evaluation (1) negative (1) work print (1) Optical Track (1) First Trial Print. We are open to working with all types of film makers and we evaluate projects and budgets as they come in, and we try to work with in those budgets as best we can with all.

Q - Do you have any tips or recommendations you can give for filmmakers who want to do this process?

David - The best method for all film makers is to test. If you need to build into your budget or need to beg and borrow, testing is the best possible way of realizing how to get what is in your mind's eye onto film.

Q - Can filmmakers do tests at your facility?

David - Yes, we encourage it and offer discounted pricing. It will save time and money in the production, post production and final film.

Q - How is E-film different to its competitors?

David - E-Film is the pioneer of the digital laboratory services. We have concentrated on tape to film since our inception and we feel we provide the best quality of images available to the tape to film marketplace. Our proprietary up-rezing software coupled with the laser film recorders are constantly being evaluated and updated to provide high quality images at competitive pricing. We have been working with filmmakers for over 10 years doing tape to film transfers that include thousands of commercials, independent shorts and major motion pictures that have been shot DV, HD and film.

Q - What final advice would you offer a filmmaker contemplating shooting on video and transferring to film?

David - I would say that the story is the key. If you feel you have the story, and if the tape to film process is available to you, by all means use it. The best thing anyone can do is translate a story to the rest of the world no matter what format it is used.

POST

TITLES AND OPTICALS

Pacific Title
Kevin Braun   Rick Sparr   Jimmy Zelinger

Q - What does a producer supply you with in order to make the titles?

Jimmy - Sometimes they supply us with ideas, sometimes they have ideas of what they want to incorporate. Sometimes they say, *'Here's the basis of the movie, design something for us'.*

Q - What is the process?

Jimmy - We type up the titles on the computer (or the titles are supplied by the company on disk) and we make a video for them, or we can make kodaliths, which is the old way. We shoot it in the camera department and then it's married optically with the background. Or we can do it digitally, whereby we render it out with the background and record it onto film.

Kevin - If you want to do an animated title, you want to do it in the digital realm now, because it's cheaper than optically and you wont need expensive tests. If Jimmy creates it digitally, the client can come in and take a look at it, make some changes, look at it again, record it out to film and it's done. We are doing a lot more digital main title work and end credits now. If the design is at all intricate we are just telling the client to go ahead and do it digitally as it saves money in the long run.

Q - Do you still do traditional optical titles?

Rick – Yes. We still do basic opticals and simple main titles and end titles in the traditional manner.

Jimmy - We do some of the end credit crawls optically, but that is becoming a thing of the past, because digitally, we can do it more cost-effectively since *'redoes'* are rarely needed.

Q - Is there a price difference between digital and optical?

Rick - Yes. Do to the fact that you have to digitally record out the entire end crawl on film, and depending on the rate that the client is paying it could be a substantial difference.

Q - If a producer just wanted a white on black end crawl, what do they need to supply you with?

Jimmy - A hard copy of all the names of everybody in order, and we've got a system of how a roll up should look if it's just plain white on black. We also have to go through each name to proof read, and then send it through legal and the cutting rooms.

Kevin - We lay it out and the client can come in and take a look at the proof to get an idea of what it's going to look like. Once it bounces back between legal and us, legal signs off on it and we take it down to camera and they shoot it optically on the animation stand.

Q - Are there any colors you should avoid putting on black?

Jimmy - Red. People always come in and say *'we want this shade of red'*, but red looks bad on film and it looks worse when it goes to video.

Q - What can you do with the desktop packages like Avid, FCP, After Effects and Photoshop?

Kevin - You could make a darn good prototype. If you love the idea you came up with, you can give it to someone like Jimmy and say, *'we want this on film'*. If the client fancies themselves as a designer and want to do their own titles, they can do that in some desktop package, render out files and we can make it to film.

Jimmy - That's happened with cutting rooms and the Avid. They have access to designs and they come up with some ideas and say, *'replicate this, but better'*.

Q - How do you super-impose titles over picure?

Kevin - We are sent the original negative from the negative cutter, and if we are doing it optically, we make IP's (interpositive) here and then we wedge those IP's. At the same time we're doing that, Jimmy is working with the titles, he designs the main title card, and the fonts for the rest of the cards. Once we got all the backgrounds wedged, the colors picked and Jimmy has all the artwork done, Jimmy will make lithos from them, take them down to the camera department and shoot what's called the Hi Con. Later, the background and titles are married on an optical printer.

Q - What is the 'Hi Con'?

Kevin - It's high contrast black and white film stock designed for shooting titles.

Jimmy - If you want to do animated titles, you're better off doing them digitally, as it takes time to plot all those moves in camera. You're eating up all this valuable time in camera. Whereas in digital, you can animate the moves on the computer, render out a Quicktime movie, and view it instantly to make sure everything is correct.

Q - What are the cheapest titles?

Kevin - Simple white titles on black backgrounds that fade up and down (shot optically).

Q - What are the common problems you encounter when doing titles?

Kevin - Getting the client to decide on what they want. Often they have a certain thing in their head and you keep showing them samples, but they still have a hard time making a decision.

Q - How long is the process if you want basic titles and the end crawl?

Kevin - A couple of weeks if everything goes smoothly.

Q - When would you like to be approached by the producer?

Kevin - During the director's cut at some point.

Q - What about sub-titling and backgrounds without text?

Picture Clearance

Like music, if you want to use a film, video, picture or any other visual media clip in your project, and the item is not in the public domain, you will have to get the rights to use it from the owner. This process is called clearing or licensing, and can be very expensive. For the most part, you may not edit or manipulate the media in any way, with the exception of cutting from the clip to another object and then back again (such as a show on a TV screen). The sure fire way to find out who owns the copyright to media is to contact The Library of Congress in Washington, D.C. and do a search.

Film clips

You must get the rights from the copyright holder, which is usually the studio that distributed the film. Generally, the cost of the clip depends on how many minutes you need, where you plan to show your project and for how long you want the rights for. The longer a scene you want and the longer you want the rights for, the more expensive it will be. As for where, if you only plan on showing your project at festivals, you may be able to negotiate a lower rate than if you expect to have your film broadcast on television or shown theatrically.

Television and video clips

Follows the same process and stipulations as film clips, but you will contact the network, broadcaster or copyright holder in these situations.

News Footage

Contact the news organization that broadcasted the clip to get the rates for the clip. The same factors apply here as in film and television clips. Figures, either public or private, who appear in news footage, such as a general news story, do not need to be contacted for clearance.

Still photographs

Publicity photos and one-sheets (movie theater lobby posters) generally do not have to be cleared because they are for this specific reason. Production stills from a film or television show must be cleared by the studio or network that created them. Paparazzi or art photos must be cleared with the photographer. Magazine and book covers must be cleared by both the publisher and the photographer of the picture.

Stock footage

This is usually purchased from a stock video library and the clearance rights are given to you as part of the sale.

Kevin - We do textless backgrounds (for international sales). In the textless version, we take the same counts we used to shoot the main title, but don't use the Hi Con title elements and just shoot the textless backgrounds on the optical printer or render them out for the film recorder (you will not need to do this if you don't have any titles over picture).

Q - Do you do foreign sub titles?

Rick - We do foreign over lays. Certain companies want their titles redone in a foreign language and it's the key ones - Italian, French, and Spanish. The studio tells us what they want and depending on what the requirements are, we might have to do multiple foreign versions.

Q - Once the titles are complete, what does the filmmaker walk away with?

Jimmy - Once they approve it, we shoot it, send it to the lab where it's developed and printed, and we get back a print and a negative. The neg is sent to the neg cutter and the print is given to the cutting room to screen.

Q - What are the digital effects you deal with?

Jimmy - We have a 3-D department here and a huge 2-D department. Effects are blue screen and green screen shots and the whole gamut of visual effects. We can add effects to titles too, like glows, animation, highlights, matte paintings.

Q - Do you have to do any optical zooms?

Kevin - Yes, all the time. They are going digital as well. Every time we do a push in optically, we shoot it two times as I know they are not going to buy the first one. If you do it digitally, they can come in and see where it's going to end up, record it once and it's done. It's so much easier.

Q - If you wanted slow-mo but you didn't do it in camera, is it effective in digital?

Kevin - Yes. Optically, we have formulas to use to get it to a set speed, print so many frames, and skip so many. Digitally, we can do the same thing and more. The next level is you can blend neighbouring frames or just compute new frames and tell the computer, *'I only have eight frames but I need to make it twelve.'* The computer will chew on it and make the new frames. That is time intensive, but the results can be amazing.

Q - Can the results be as good as if you had shot it in camera?

Kevin - I've done some testing with a car going through woodland, doing an S curve, and as it approached the camera, I wanted to slow it right down. The result was very good and you could almost believe that it was shot that way, but there are some artefacts, which is indicative of some of these speed changes. It usually looks very good, but there are areas that will need painting out. Once you are done, it will look as if it was shot at that speed.

Rick - Take your time and do it the way you want it on set, because it's going to save you down the line.

Q - Can you alter facial features?

Rick - We can do bodily enhancements such as removing bags from under the eyes, removing wrinkles etc. Sometimes they don't have the time to light properly because of schedules. So we have to enhance the look of face and soften the features a lot.

Q - Are there a difference between independent films and big budget features?

Jimmy - Yeah, huge. Independents often don't know what they're doing! They don't do enough prep work and sometimes have attitude too. We're here to help but a lot of people have a hard time saying, *'we don't understand this...'*

Kevin - Everybody wants everything tomorrow, but sometimes they are not organized, which makes it much harder to give them what they want. I just finished working with one independent client who was very organized, which helped them a great deal because we were able to spend our time trying ideas, instead of cleaning up any mess.

Q - What advice would you give new filmmakers?

Rick - The more prep work you can do before you start shooting, the more money you will save in post.

Jimmy - A lot of times guys will come in here with a film that's been shot, but it isn't working, and they try to optically enhance it to make it work. Now you're doing so many shots to try and make something work that just isn't there. I think storyboarding the whole picture is crucial and the proof of the pudding is Spielberg. He storyboards every one of his movies from start to finish. He cuts on film and doesn't use Avid. His stuff goes through on time and budget. He does his homework. Also, they should come talk to us about the process so we can find the most cost effective way to do stuff.

Kevin - It can be hard to come up with a compelling title for a new filmmaker, but it can be done. The last low budget title that shook me was *Pi*. Some people view the title as a few minutes of information that's thrown at you to tell you who's involved with the picture. Other people see those first few minutes as an encapsulation of the film, a synopsis or flavor of what is to come. Being passionate about each project is very important, we aren't in a factory making widgets, we are telling stories.

POST

Dan o'Grady
J and G Films

NEGATIVE CUTTING

Q - What is negative cutting?

Dan - Negative cutting is where your original camera negative is cut up and spliced together, using the cutting list supplied by the editor, so that he lab can make prints. We will need the original camera negative, which will probably have been held at the lab. Independent filmmakers will more than likely cut using Avid, Final Cut Pro or other computer based edit system, which will create an EDL (Edit Decision List), which we can import into our system. That EDL will tell us where every single shot begins and ends, where it comes from and where it will go. We are then able to conform that original camera negative to match exactly the edit that the filmmakers had locked in the cutting room.

Q - Would you recommend having a work print?

Dan - That's a money issue, but we recommend doing a test print of a scene or two so that you can really get a sense of what it will look in a theatrical environment, not just on a TV monitor in the edit suite.

Q - What is the process when the neg arrives?

Dan - We get the negative in from the transfer facility, usually in 1000ft rolls. We then log it using a bar code reader (using the bar codes on the edge of the negative), and that information is fed into a computer system called 'Osc/r'. We would then break it down into smaller rolls, usually about 400ft, so they are manageable. Then we log the key numbers into a computer and if it's a video daily, we verify the source time code so we're able to input the head key number of the footage and the start time code, roll it down to the reader, log it in and the computer tells us what the time code has to be on that last frame and we verify that it is correct. If its not, we know we have a problem either with the time code generator or a break in the negative. Once that's all catalogued, it sits on the shelf until they start calling up and pressuring us to pull for opticals or giving us the final cut, in which case they give us the cut and EDL's. We convert that over and start cutting.

Q - What is the key code?

Dan - It is a numbering system they have for each roll of film. In the past ten years they've added bar code to it so that readers can scan in the numbers, which is fine, but we verify it as we're cutting the negative. For instance, a lot of people get their video dailies with a key code burn in and while they are accurate 99% of the time, it's that 1% we worry about. Problems occur when things aren't verified at this stage, so we physically look at the negative and know what numbers are going in the computer and that's the verification to double check.

Q - Can you re-join a cut once it's been neg cut?

Dan - That's tricky. What happens is in the process of initially making the initial cut, you lose a frame as you need two perfs to make the overlap for the splice. We have recut a lot of films where we happily splice over a splice. It's not a recommended method as it's not as strong as the original splice and there's still that one splice that is lost. If you had a close up of two people talking and you only used 10 frames of it originally and now you want to make it longer, there will be something missing.

Q - That is quite a serious problem.

Dan - Yeah, but you have to deal with it. The basic rules of recuts are that you can't make anything longer. You can neg cut anything you want, but you can't make anything longer. That's why it's important with independent filmmakers that they don't rush into this aspect. You have to give us the final cut.

Q - What advice would you give the film editor?

Dan - We only need one film frame either side of the cut, but when you're doing a video edit, the two video frames are needed as you can convert over one or two depending on the field he's on. But two is a good rule. I've had editors that work with the director to try to minimize costs, but some editors consider the Avid to be such a good tool that they use it as they want. Some editors use a lot of opticals, like slowing shots down, and do it because the Avid can do that. They are cool tools to use and work with some films, but by the time the film gets to us, the filmmaker is out of time and money, and we don't take responsibility for the editing of the film.

Q - What is the most common EDL system to use?

Dan - Almost all our EDL's are in CMX3600 format. We can deal with a lot of EDL's but the most common out of the Avid's is that.

Q - Is the EDL in the same format if the feature is cut on Final Cut Pro?

Dan - We only deal with EDL's. There are negative cutters that will accept cut lists out of some of these systems. The reason we don't do it is because those key numbers are not verified. What happens is if there is any kind of error at all, it turns out to be a disaster.

Q - How does the neg cutter handle the opticals?

Dan - The EDL is the biggest clue as it tells you what to do as far as motion effects. So we convert it over and isolate the events, print them out, pull the neg base accordingly and give that to whomever is shooting the opticals. Sometimes we're very involved with it, sometimes not. When it's the film work print end, we're not involved at all. The editor takes care of it.

Q - Are there a lot of over length neg cuts with the digital process?

Dan - We're finishing a film at the moment where over the past ten years, the filmmaker shot eleven ten minute or so short films that he's putting together into one long film. Three of them have been done over the ten years and he has masters so there's no

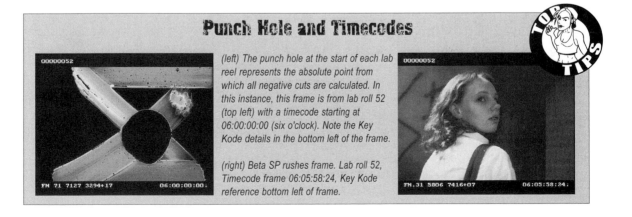

Punch Hole and Timecodes

(left) The punch hole at the start of each lab reel represents the absolute point from which all negative cuts are calculated. In this instance, this frame is from lab roll 52 (top left) with a timecode starting at 06:00:00:00 (six o'clock). Note the Key Kode details in the bottom left of the frame.

(right) Beta SP rushes frame. Lab roll 52, Timecode frame 06:05:58:24, Key Kode reference bottom left of frame.

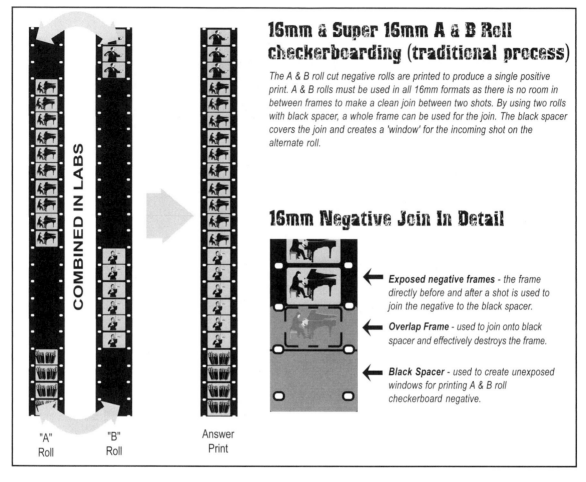

16mm & Super 16mm A & B Roll checkerboarding (traditional process)

The A & B roll cut negative rolls are printed to produce a single positive print. A & B rolls must be used in all 16mm formats as there is no room in between frames to make a clean join between two shots. By using two rolls with black spacer, a whole frame can be used for the join. The black spacer covers the join and creates a 'window' for the incoming shot on the alternate roll.

COMBINED IN LABS

16mm Negative Join In Detail

Exposed negative frames - *the frame directly before and after a shot is used to join the negative to the black spacer.*

Overlap Frame - *used to join onto black spacer and effectively destroys the frame.*

Black Spacer - *used to create unexposed windows for printing A & B roll checkerboard negative.*

"A" Roll

"B" Roll

Answer Print

neg cutting involved. But quite a few of them were shots that came to us and their decision was to pull all the scenes needed for these shorts and transfer them to HD and record out. So you pull it in a single strand format with extra frames and the Osc/r can pull any shots that are in the bumper together. They ask for a 40-frame handle, so we gave them select rolls of 40 frame handles and they transferred them. The reason for the handles is you've got to get the splice away from the transfer gate to avoid jumps. It also gives them margin for re-editing, and again, that's a double-edged sword, as we've done features where they pull flash to flash, like we do for commercials and then they never stop editing.

Q - What's flash to flash?

Dan - That is camera start to camera stop on a shot. We do negative cutting for commercials where they shoot a lot of footage and they don't want to retransfer everything so we pull selected shots for them, from slate to slate or flash to flash. So technically, the negative is cut, but its not cut. There is still some integrity to it.

Q - Do you find you're asked to pull out a lot of shots for dupes?

Dan - Yeah. Because of the digital stuff and the way they edit now, there are a lot of advantages. The biggest thing you find is films are cuttier, and the simple reason for that is they transfer everything. There aren't out takes anymore. Where there used to be out

35mm Negative Cutting

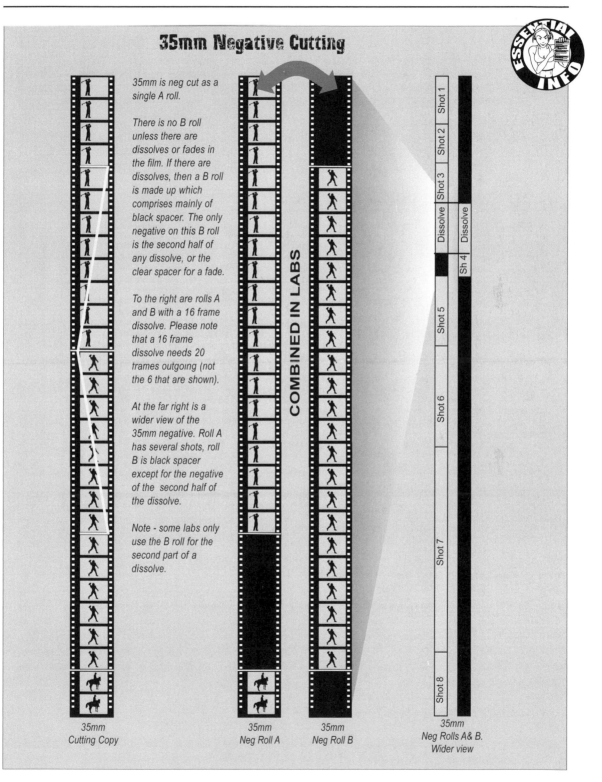

35mm is neg cut as a single A roll.

There is no B roll unless there are dissolves or fades in the film. If there are dissolves, then a B roll is made up which comprises mainly of black spacer. The only negative on this B roll is the second half of any dissolve, or the clear spacer for a fade.

To the right are rolls A and B with a 16 frame dissolve. Please note that a 16 frame dissolve needs 20 frames outgoing (not the 6 that are shown).

At the far right is a wider view of the 35mm negative. Roll A has several shots, roll B is black spacer except for the negative of the second half of the dissolve.

Note - some labs only use the B roll for the second part of a dissolve.

COMBINED IN LABS

35mm
Cutting Copy

35mm
Neg Roll A

35mm
Neg Roll B

Shot 1
Shot 2
Shot 3
Dissolve
Shot 5
Shot 6
Shot 7
Shot 8

Dissolve
Sh 4

35mm
Neg Rolls A& B.
Wider view

Anatomy Of An EDL

CMX 3600 is the most common and robust cross platform EDL that we have come across. Make sure that when you supply your EDL it is on the correct format disk, most cutters use DOS format. Note also that a CMX 3600 can only handle 999 cuts. You will probably never see your EDL in this format as it's almost always electronic… But then if it can go wrong… Better to at least understand the process when you consider that sharp blades are about to come into contact with your master negative!

Edit Number - this is the chronological number given to each and every cut.

Video - As it's a picture only EDL, each of these will be V for video.

The Lab Reel / Beta SP source in point column - the time code where a shot actually begins.

The point on the assembled master negative time line where the shot begins.

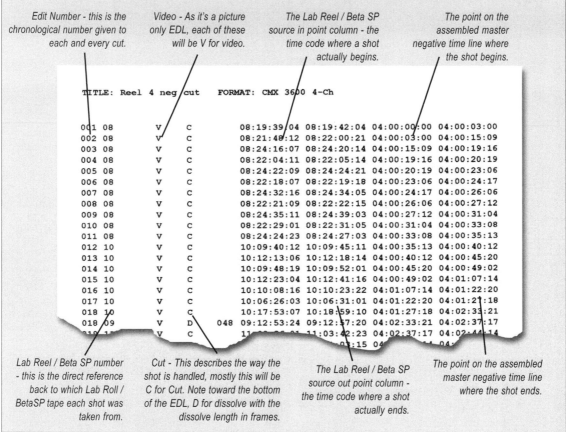

```
TITLE: Reel 4 neg cut    FORMAT: CMX 3600 4-Ch

001 08      V    C         08:19:39:04 08:19:42:04 04:00:00:00 04:00:03:00
002 08      V    C         08:21:48:12 08:22:00:21 04:00:03:00 04:00:15:09
003 08      V    C         08:24:16:07 08:24:20:14 04:00:15:09 04:00:19:16
004 08      V    C         08:22:04:11 08:22:05:14 04:00:19:16 04:00:20:19
005 08      V    C         08:24:22:09 08:24:24:21 04:00:20:19 04:00:23:06
006 08      V    C         08:22:18:07 08:22:19:18 04:00:23:06 04:00:24:17
007 08      V    C         08:24:32:16 08:24:34:05 04:00:24:17 04:00:26:06
008 08      V    C         08:22:21:09 08:22:22:15 04:00:26:06 04:00:27:12
009 08      V    C         08:24:35:11 08:24:39:03 04:00:27:12 04:00:31:04
010 08      V    C         08:22:29:01 08:22:31:05 04:00:31:04 04:00:33:08
011 08      V    C         08:24:24:23 08:24:27:03 04:00:33:08 04:00:35:13
012 10      V    C         10:09:40:12 10:09:45:11 04:00:35:13 04:00:40:12
013 10      V    C         10:12:13:06 10:12:18:14 04:00:40:12 04:00:45:20
014 10      V    C         10:09:48:19 10:09:52:01 04:00:45:20 04:00:49:02
015 10      V    C         10:12:23:04 10:12:41:16 04:00:49:02 04:01:07:14
016 10      V    C         10:10:08:16 10:10:23:22 04:01:07:14 04:01:22:20
017 10      V    C         10:06:26:03 10:06:31:01 04:01:22:20 04:01:27:18
018 10      V    C         10:17:53:07 10:18:59:10 04:01:27:18 04:02:33:21
018 09      V    D    048  09:12:53:24 09:12:57:20 04:02:33:21 04:02:37:17
                          11:03:42:23 04:02:37:17 04:02:44:14
                     :15 04          04:
```

Lab Reel / Beta SP number - this is the direct reference back to which Lab Roll / BetaSP tape each shot was taken from.

Cut - This describes the way the shot is handled, mostly this will be C for Cut. Note toward the bottom of the EDL, D for dissolve with the dissolve length in frames.

The Lab Reel / Beta SP source out point column - the time code where a shot actually ends.

The point on the assembled master negative time line where the shot ends.

takes, an editor wouldn't have access to certain scenes and takes. Now they have everything. Even if they need ten frames, they borrow ten frames from a shot that wasn't printed originally.

Q - Are there any special requirements when shooting Super 16mm and is there much Super 16mm going on?

Dan - There is. Super16mm is cheaper to shoot than 35mm and you get a lot more footage. It's perfect for the widescreen TV (DVD) as it's the right aspect ratio, and for HD too. For people that want to blow it up, there is special handling with the way we cut the A and B rolls with extra frames for blow up. When we know someone is going to do a blow up, we warn them about the extra frames we need for the editing process.

Q - Is it all A and B for 35mm and Super 16mm?

Dan - 16mm, yes, it has to be A and B because that's the only way you can hide a splice. In 35mm, its more single strand as they'll do their fades and dissolves optically. It depends on how many effects you have. The more effects you have in a film, the more cost effective the A and B 35 method will become. If you have ten dissolves in a reel, those ten dissolves can cost a lot to make optically, but it only costs 10c more a foot to print the B roll each time. That's something you have to weigh out at the beginning.

Q - How do you charge as a neg cutter?

Dan - With video editing we have two charges. We charge for the logging of the negative, and then we also charge per event in the EDL. Normally, to a film work print, with 35mm, we charge by the ten minute reel and with 16mm, we charge by the cut.

Q - What happens to all the unused negative?

Dan - We hope to get rid of it sooner or later. A lot of it winds up on our shelves. But when the job wraps up we try to get them to put it in storage. In the independent film world especially, there's a good chance they will be going back into it for something.

Q - What do you supply to the lab?

Dan - We supply the cut negative and that's it.

Q - When you do the cut? What is the process?

Dan - We do it in two stages. We stand at a table with a synchronizer, negative and scissors and make the cut. Then we sit at a splicer and splice it together. We scrape off the emulsion, we use Kodak cement and bind it together. It's a good idea to get the negative cutter involved early in the process. Unfortunately with some projects, they wait until the last minute and things aren't set up properly. We like to get involved at an early stage when they are starting to telecine stuff so we can verify it early on, but definitely by the time the editor is brought in, we should be in there. A negative cutter doesn't charge to get involved in the early stages. The more you communicate, the less problems there are down the road.

Q - Are the problems with down converting?

Dan - You can't trust that a telecine operator is paying attention to the time codes and Key Kodes early in the morning. So it's attention to detail to verify, as once you've cut the negative, you can't go back. So if we make a mistake for a reason like not verifying something, we only have ourselves to blame. Video people don't have that, they just transfer it and say, *'we'll do it again'* if there's a problem. We don't have that option so we never trust anyone else's work.

Q - What are your thoughts about digital post and the way it's moving?

Dan - I'm hoping to still be here! New filmmakers are not even shooting negative anymore, just going out with DV cameras, though the quality is not the same.

Q - What common mistakes do you encounter made by the editor?

Dan - Mostly it's doing stuff that wasn't done on the film. Sometimes they get into weird variations of speed changes that don't correlate equally over the film rate. They might do a 76.2 reverse action on the Avid and then you have to figure out how to get that done on film. One of the most common mistakes is when they use video sources, which are at 30 fps and they edit them into a 24 fps project. They have to account for things, but again that's stuff we bring up when we check the EDL.

Q - What advice would you give a filmmaker?

Dan - Make the film the way you want it.

POST

Matt Lian
Global Doghouse

TRAILERS

Q - What is your job?

Matt - I'm a creative director at a trailer production company. I oversee every aspect of the creation of movie advertising and take the project from start to finish, from script to execution.

Q - How do you go about creating a good trailer?

Matt - We don't often deal with filmmakers. By the time a film gets to us, it's with a distribution company, so we're dealing with the marketing departments. What we need is a completed film, although that's not always the case, and any ideas they have about their 'vision'. If we're lucky, we'll get specifics on how they're looking to position the film, ideas about scenes, or if there's an actor they want to push. Anything that narrows our approach is great.

Q - So you have to work out what this movie is about?

Matt - We watch the film a number of times and write a positioning statement that deals with the films strengths and weaknesses. We deal with the brass tack issues in terms of the difficulties we're going to face making it appeal to women, or making a narrative out of what's a difficult film to follow. I like to think that by the end of it all, the film has a voice of its own, and through the process of making the trailer, it speaks louder and louder as you try different things with varying degrees of success. It would seem you could have some formulaic approach to making a good trailer and it seems that every step of the way, each film defies the last experience you had making a trailer.

Q - Is it important to latch onto a single concept for the trailer?

Matt - Sometimes a simplistic approach is the most effective way to market something, but it depends on the movie. A film is oftentimes a complicated endeavor, and trailers that are successful to me are ones that make me want to see the film, and not because I think, *'oh that's an action film!',* or 'that has Bruce Willis!' There's something more ephemeral about the appeal of certain trailers that defies a simplistic kind of *'there's one thing about this movie'* that makes me want to see it. The single concept to me that makes a trailer effective is when it conveys the essence of the film in a way that seems interesting and unique. But if you talk to any studio marketing head, they would say that the more familiar devices that can be employed and the more comfortable a trailer is, the better. Part of my job is to reconcile the competing ideas of the marketing execs at the studio and what I, and the filmmakers want. I try to infuse what we do with a bit of a unique voice.

Q - Why do some trailers contain all the best parts of a movie?

Matt - I think the significance of the opening box office numbers is the holy grail of movie releasing now and the studios will do whatever is going to put more people in theatres during that opening weekend. Sometimes with comedies, the jokes are funnier in short form. It's literally whatever jokes get the most laughs, they will include in the trailer. They are not going to give away the killer in a *'whodunnit',* but by the same token, it's all fair game to try and get people see the movie.

Q - Some independents can be downer movies. How do you market a depressing movie?

Matt - That's difficult. If the subject matter is so bleak, you can wonder how willing people are going to be to sit through it. We marketed a film called *Lilya Forever* about a fourteen year old Russian girl that gets sold into prostitution in Sweden, and is a very bleak picture. There as a glimmer of hope, but essentially it's downtrodden, yet it's beautiful and amazingly acted, there are so many fine qualities and it was positively reviewed. Our first trailer, which was a little over two minutes, was a pretty honest approach to the subject and dealt with the bleakness and sexual violence of it. The distribution company was like, *'who's going to see this?'* It's not the feel good movie of the year, but the campaign we ended up going with did deal with what was happening in the film in an oblique way, that didn't alienate anybody from a marketing stand point with people thinking, *'this is too sad, I don't want to go watch it'*. It was review driven and pedigreed, but there are times where you're required to take a more oblique approach to serve the film.

Q - What are the key aspects that you're looking for when making a movie trailer?

Matt - If it's an action movie, you gravitate towards the big set pieces, try and distill the plot down in a way that is clear, looking for specific dialogue that is expository and concise and gives people enough to latch onto, to feel like they have some idea of the story. That cuts across all genres. I'm always keen on finding a laugh as I find people are more willing to go see a film if they are invited to laugh a bit. Even action movies lean towards the humorous scenes to make it seem fun as well as expensive and exciting. I also gravitate towards any strong moments of performance or anything that is self contained and emotionally evocative. That has a lot of currency in trailers. Pretty, big shots that show production value and show that the director has an eye help too.

Q - Why do some trailers include shots that aren't in the final film?

Matt - We worked on *About A Boy* and one of the bits we used from that film didn't make the final cut. It's a scene where Hugh Grant goes into a baby store and has concocted a story that he has had a baby, and we ended up using that just to get butts on seats. The mentality is *'whatever is going to make the film appeal to whoever is going to see the trailer - it's fair game!'* You hope that it's because you believe in the product that you are willing to take those deceptive steps. People rarely complain about material that is not in the film or stuff that is created specifically to market the film. In *Legally Blonde 2* there was a teaser trailer that is just Reese Witherspoon talking straight to the camera. Within reason, the studios are willing to employ any gag to get people to watch their movies. There are lines that are drawn though, for instance if something has been cut that's significant in terms of plot and it's a complete misdirection, it would not be used.

Q - How many trailers would a company make?

Matt - Usually one. *Bend It Like Beckham* created two trailers though, but normally, the smaller films have one trailer. The films that they may anticipate a broader audience for, that the smaller companies rarely get, may create a teaser trailer too.

Q - Have any trailers failed to have any impact and forced them to make a new trailer?

Matt - It depends on how soon they get the trailer in theaters. You aim to get it in a couple of months before release, but if it's a couple of weeks into the campaign and they realize it's not doing well, even if you put a trailer on the fast track, to create prints, you are looking at 7-10 days minimum, and that's not including the creative work. That rarely happens.

Q - Could they do it for TV spots as well?

Matt - With TV spots there's much more agility as you can create that in a day and finish it. For instance, when *Spirited Away* won the best animated film for the Academy Awards, Disney called us and said 'we want to do an academy award spot'. They did it three days before the Academy Awards, anticipating it was going to win, and had it on air four days later.

Q - What's the difference between a theatrical trailer and a TV trailer?

Matt - Length. Although there are 60 second TV spots, 30 seconds is most common. There are certain things you can get away with content wise on film that you may not be able to for television. Two and a half minutes is generally the limit for theatrical

POST

trailers, depending on which companies release it. The small companies aim to get the trailer positioned well, and in order to do that, they have to be conscious of how long the trailer takes - the longer the trailer, the less likely they are to get it in front of a big film because they vie for time for those movies. We created a trailer for *Whale Rider,* a film that has won a couple of awards and hopefully it will get a big audience, but we had to shave time off the trailer because the distribution company was concerned about where they could place it if it were two minutes thirty. So we cut thirty seconds off so now it may play in front of bigger films.

Q - If there is a bigger film, is it a fight to get the trailer on?

Matt - Absolutely. Some films come with trailers attached, that come from the distributors. On *Harry Potter,* they told the distributors they already had five minutes of trailers attached to the prints, and there was some wrangling about that.

Q - Do you get the billing information at the end of the trailer?

Matt - Yes, you have that checked off. It has to go through legal checks first. Sometimes there's contention about who's names you have to mention and in what order, there are those legal considerations, but they happen through the distribution company mostly.

Q - Have you ever retitled a film as it doesn't work?

Matt - No, because by the time it comes to us, the film is so far down line that it's not really possible to retitle. We're working on a small film now that doesn't have distribution yet. The producer is not crazy about the title and has made it clear that she doesn't want the marketing to be super specific to that title because she fears when distribution is secure that they'll want to change it.

Q - Do you want stills with the print as well?

Matt - No. But you hope that there is some cohesiveness between the trailers and what appears in print. Sometimes the font they use for the title is the font they use in the graphics and trailer. In a perfect world, if there is consistency between the print campaign and trailer campaign, you have a brand for a film that people recognize.

Q - Do you show the trailer to the MPAA after it's done?

Matt - Yeah, and they approve it. There's green band trailers, which is what everybody wants as they are suitable for all audiences. A red band trailer is restricted to adult audiences only. You can choose to not submit to the MPAA, which is rarely done because most theater chains won't play trailers that haven't been approved by the MPAA. A film called *Spun* which just came out didn't submit the trailer for approval, but they did submit it to the theater chain and said, 'this is what we're aiming for with our trailer, is it okay?' We had to conform to the limitations that the theatre chains imposed on us and tone it down a little.

Q - Why did the Spun guys not go to the MPAA?

Matt - There's so much to avoid in that film that if you try and stay away from everything that is going to be objectionable to the MPAA, you're going to be left with nothing. The essence of the movie is a bunch of people getting spun out, and there's some bondage stuff too. The jokes aren't going to work unless you have some material that is never going to pass the censors. So I think a determination was made that the audience for this film wasn't a mass audience, it was a specific demographic that wouldn't mind the material being slightly offensive or risqué, at the very least, and they decided to go after that segment of the audience. On a side note, if you have a smaller art house division distributing a film and you submit a trailer to them, you'll get away with nothing. You can't even have a gun on screen, and yet you have a studio film submitting a film to the MPAA and they get away with murder, and the get a green band on their trailer!

Q - What percentage of the budget should a filmmaker set aside for the trailer?

Matt - Typically, it will take three to four weeks to make a trailer. It also depends on what stage in post production they are at too. Sometimes you have a rough assembly and get more material as the process continues and it can drag on endlessly. Inclusion of graphics will depend on how much money you set aside. Typically you'll spend anywhere between $30k and $40k on creative work, and then another $30k to technically finish the trailer and make prints. That number wildly fluctuates though.

Q - Are there any common mistakes you've encountered?

Matt - It's difficult for directors and producers to separate themselves from their perceptions of the movie, scenes and shots. There's a lack of understanding that even though the director hates a specific scene, in the trailer it's something different as it has been re-cut and works for the film. There's baggage that they bring into the process, and that can work against the campaign. It depends on who's producing the film, and who has approval.

Q - What advice would you give an indie filmmaker who is cutting their trailer on Final Cut Pro or Avid Xpress?

Matt - Bringing a fresh set of eyes to the material is important, as is knowing who your audience is. I think the more thought that's put into the commerce part of filmmaking, the better. Try and get as far away from the mentality that helped you put the film together, and ensure the material is going to put butts in seats.

Q - Any advice for new filmmakers?

Matt - More often than not, problems making a trailer are a reflection of the deficiencies at script level. I started as an editor, so I have very specific ideas as to how to make a scene and tell a story. Sometimes bad movies make good trailers, so it's hard to say. I just think that the more attention that is placed on the writing, the more likely you are the have a good film that is easy to market.

Your Negative and Master Tapes

All your efforts as a film maker are sealed in the neg / master tapes which is exposed on set. It's therefore a good idea to treat your neg as though it were gold dust.

Negative

1. Make sure film is processed as soon as possible.

2. Neg doesn't last forever and should be stored someplace cool and dry. For a small fee the lab will store your neg in a vault at the correct temperature and humidity.

3. Don't ever throw away or erase your Beta SP telecine masters if you have chosen to cut non linear. They are the only way back to your master negative edge numbers.

4. Don't underestimate just how much stuff a feature film generates.... Usually at least 100 rolls of unused cut neg, 5 rolls of A&B roll cut neg, 5 rolls of S16 Interpos, 5 rolls of 35mm Internegative, 5 rolls on 35mm negative, prints, 50 master sound tapes, 50 master BetaSP tapes, 5 rolls of 35mm optical sound, master sound mix tapes, optical effects and titles negs and internegs... You get the picture. Where is it going to go? Is it safe? Do you need it all?

Tapes

1. Your mater tapes are just that, masters. If you have shot digitally, consider making clones and using those as your work tapes. Ensure the correct time codes are transferred at the time of making the clones.

2. Minimize wear and tear on your tapes. Don't keep rewinding and fast forwarding just to watch a favorite shot.

3. Always completely rewind tapes before storage. This will avoid kinks in the tape forming over long term storage.

4. Tapes should be fast forwarded and rewound every five years or so.

5. In due course, you may consider cloning your tapes to a future technology, such as solid state chips or disks. Only time will tell here.

6. Your sound is as important as your neg. Store your tapes or DATs in a safe place.

Derek Hildebrandt
30h!s Creative Inc.

DVD PRODUCTION

Q - What services can you offer?

Derek - We produce DVDs. We offer still and animated menu design, bonus feature development and production. This includes interactive games, bios, and commentary tracks, behind the scenes, trivia tracks, subtitling and any unique DVD features, which are custom to a particular title. We offer video compression to MPEG-2 and audio compression to Dolby Digital Stereo or 5.1 Surround. We do the actual DVD authoring (custom DVD navigation and programming) and DVD Mastering to either DLT (digital linear tape) or DVD-R for replication.

Q - What is the actual process of authoring your movie on to DVD?

Derek - Authoring encapsulates three stages. Encoding, authoring and pre-mastering. For encoding, you must have a clean, color corrected broadcast safe transfer of your film on either Digibeta or HD. The actual authoring is the stage where all the video, audio, still graphics, and subtitles are combined to create a working DVD disc. This includes the order in which videos and / or menus play, what buttons are active on a menu, what happens when buttons are activated, what audio track / subtitle stream should be played, etc. This is also where region coding (ie. where geographically this disc will be permitted to play) and copy-protection flags are set.

Pre-mastering which includes replication, is the process of 'pressing discs' in production lines that spit out a new disc every few seconds. This is done by large plants who have spent thousands on the necessary hardware required for this service. Most replication plants do offer 'one off' or 'check disc' services where one to a hundred discs are made for testing before mass replication. Companies such as Technicolor, Future Media, SF Video and Disctronics can handle the mass replication. For projects requiring less than 50 copies, it may be cheaper to use recordable discs. This is called duplication not replication.

Q - Can a producer create their own menu using programs on their home desktop and then go to a replication house?

Derek - Any graphics application (ie. Adobe Photoshop) can be used to create still menus, while any piece of video can be used as a menu, as long as it is designed with this purpose in mind. These elements could then be compressed / encoded, and handed over to an authoring house for use on any DVD. Applications like Apple's DVD Studio Pro, Adobe Encore DVD and Sonic are authoring packages, which allow you to combine your different assets (video, audio, stills, and subtitles) into a functional DVD that complies with the DVD-Video specification. This disc could then be output to a DLT for mass replication or to DVD-R if a small number of discs are needed. DLT seems to remain the preferred method of transfer to the replication facility, though more and more facilities are beginning to accept DVD-R discs as a master for replication. DVD Studio Pro also integrates with Final Cut Pro, Photoshop and After Effects and lets you use layered Photoshop files to create menus. However there are limitations with these programs. For instance, you might find that you can set the Bit rate but not on a scene by scene basis, or you might find that it supports subtitles but not closed captioning.

DVD is targeted at the home user, who will not require mass duplication from a replication facility. Its strength lies in its user friendly conversion of Quicktime movies into playable DVD-Video discs, with simple menu navigation. It also doesn't have the option of setting the bit rate for encoding, which can affect the image quality.

Q - How much would it cost from having a basic menu system created for your independent movie on DVD to an animated menu system similar to the 'Hollywood style'?

Derek - Budgets vary significantly from place to place, so get your specs nailed down and simply pick up the phone and call a number of places to get quotes. The additional cost of an animated menu system would come from additional design time, animation, compositing, and editing of your video source. Then there is the additional need to encode the video source, since still graphics are typically imported straight into the authoring package (which handles the encoding of still graphics).

Q - What is the typical presentation of a DVD?

Derek - DVD presentation varies greatly, depending on who is making the decisions, and the type of disc being created. A typical 'Hollywood-style' DVD would open with legal disclaimers, followed by logos, trailers / advertising (you've got a captured audience, after all), and a transition to a main menu. From the main menu, you have access to the different features on the disc, from playing the program in its entirety, to accessing specific scenes, setting up alternate audio streams and subtitles, and viewing any of the additional bonus features or interactive features on the disc. Most DVDs are a variation of this structure, but tailored to the specific needs of the disc.

Q - What special features are a good idea to have on your DVD?

Derek - The best special features on a DVD are always those that provide extra entertainment and information for the viewer. Behind the scenes, director's commentary, and deleted scenes are great for fans. Trivia challenges, interactive games, and any attempt at making the DVD a more interactive experience where the user gets to control what they see makes the DVD a more useful tool for entertainment and education. Basically, the more additional features that you can include on a disc, that are relevant to the movie, the better.

Q - Is there anything to avoid when designing the menus ?

Derek - It is important to design DVD graphics knowing that they will be viewed on a television set. The same rules that are applied when creating graphics for broadcast work well when applied to DVD graphics. One should avoid fonts with thin lines, use drop shadows to separate titles from the background and keep type at a size that will be legible at a typical view distance. Avoid extreme contrasts such as white on black or black on white. Remember that if you have animated menus, this movement could impede the usability of your menu interface.

Q - Can a DVD be authored to play in all regions - region free?

Derek - If desired, a DVD-Video disc can have flags set that would make it unplayable in different regions of the world. It is typical to make discs that are unrestricted, unless they are being created for different markets around the world and might have different release dates, or even different sets of features. Unfortunately, a DVD cannot be authored for presentation in both NTSC and PAL. However, it is said that most PAL DVD players have no problem playing NTSC discs. A producer could also put NTSC on one side and PAL on the other. Most studios put Dolby Digital audio tracks on their PAL discs instead of MPEG audio tracks. Because of PAL's higher resolution, the movie generally takes up more space on the disc than the NTSC version.

Q - What is the difference between +RW and –RW DVDS?

Derek - DVD+RW and DVD-RW are two competing re-writeable DVD standards. There are many claims that one or the other format is better, but they're actually very similar. A DVD+R/RW drive can't write a DVD-R/ RW disc and vice versa, unless it's a combination drive that writes both formats.

POST

449

Q - Does this difference cause problems for your DVD playing on all players?

Derek - Yes, not all players and drives can read recorded discs. The problem being that recordable discs have different reflectivity than pressed discs i.e the ones that you'd find in a store. DVD-R and DVD+R discs work in about 85% of existing drives and players, while DVD-RW and DVD+RW discs work in about 70%. There are a few companies here in LA that will test compatibility on a matrix of DVD players and give you a report but there are also several sites online that you can check the compatibility issues of your player with DVD-R and DVD-RW discs. Customflix (www.customflix.com/customer/compatibility/jsp), DVDmadeEasy, DVDRHelp, YesVideo.com, Homemovie.com and Apple. DVD-R (pronounced dash R not minus R) is compatible with most DVD drives and players so is the best choice if you are going to makeyour own discs.

Q - What are DVD 5 and DVD 9?

Derek - DVD 5 is used to refer to a single layer DVD disc. DVD 9 is used to refer to a dual-layer DVD disc. This means that there are actually 2 layers of data on the one side of a DVD 9 disc. The laser that reads the data from the disc can change its focus to read from the two separate layers that are stacked on the same side of the disc. This allows almost twice as much information to be stored on a DVD 9 disc compared to a DVD 5 disc.

Q - How many hours can a DVD store of your movie?

Derek - Dual layer technology allows for over four hours of continuous playback on one side. There used to be a 'flipper' disc where movies were split over two sides of a disc, but with the compression rate nowadays being much higher that shouldn't exist.

Q - What is that pause that certain movies on DVD have half way throughout the movie?

Derek - The pause that occurs in some movies is due to the dual-layer format (DVD 9) where the laser that is reading the data from the disc needs to change its focus in order to read the data on the other layer. This causes a disruption in the flow of data being read from the disc, and results in a short pause on most set-top DVD players.

Q - What is the Dolby Digital 5.1 sound on your DVD and is it best to have this rather than stereo sound?

DIY DVD

If you want a great DVD for your movie, and you do, then that means YOU will need to oversee the production. Leave it to the distributor or anyone else and you will no doubt get an uninspired collection of extras. We would all like out films to be seen on the big screen, but the way technology is going, it's likely that this DVD is going to be where many agents and studio executives see your movie. So make it special.

You can produce all the extra bits on miniDV - 'The Making Of...', 'Directors Commentary', 'Deleted Scenes' etc. So get interviewing yourself, and make it snappy and entertaining. Get a great 16:9 transfer of your movie, clean it up and remove dust and sparkle. Make sure you have a great Dolby Digital mix (the licence is free for DVD), create some great menus in Photoshop etc. If you feel so inclined, you could master the whole thing yourself, though in practice, we would recommend letting a dedicated company with a track record do this. If you give them detailed notes (ideally a flowchart), all menus and backgrounds on disk, and all the video elements on tape (clearly labelled with in and out timecodes), then you should be able to cut a GREAT deal. Maybe as little as $500, even less.

They will burn you a DVD-R for you to test (if it's a dual layer DVD9 disk then they will burn two DVD-R's as there are no DVD9 recordable disks yet), and when you are happy with the job, they will export it all to a DLT tape which will go the factory that will press your disks.

Derek - Surround sound comes in several formats. Dolby Digital 5.1 is a standard format for surround sound. The term 5.1 refers to the 5 channels of audio (Left, Center, Right, Left Rear, Right Rear) plus 1 channel for a sub-woofer. If you have a multi-channel sound system, you will benefit by listening to soundtracks that are available in surround format. A popular option is to have both 5.1 and 2 channel stereo soundtracks available on a DVD. This will allow you to have the best mix available for those with surround sound systems, and an optimized mix with standard stereo systems.

Q - What kind of turnaround would you require to produce a DVD and duplication?

Derek - DVDs can be made in one day or several months depending upon the content and budget. Duplication usually takes 2 to 4 weeks depending upon quantities and schedules.

Q - Should a filmmaker have a letterbox and a standard (pan and scan) version of their movie on the DVD?

Derek - It isn't necessary but one can do so if the disc space permits and there is room in the budget. I personally buy DVD movies in the widescreen format, as I like watching the movie the way the filmmaker originally intended it to be seen.

Q - Do you have to have closed captioning / subtitles on your DVD and copyright protection?

Derek - Closed Captioning (CC) is a standard method of encoding text onto an NTSC signal. The text can be displayed by a TV with a built in decoder. Captions commonly refer to on screen text designed for hearing impaired viewers (i.e it includes a description of sounds and music) and they are not visible until the viewer activates them. Subtitles are straight transcriptions or translations of the dialogue. Copyright protection can be in the form of CSS (Content scrambling system) which is an encryption and authentication scheme intended to prevent DVD movies from being digitally captured. Some DVDs are also encoded with Macrovision to prevent you from recording the image on to a VHS tape.

Q - What are the D codes that you can see printed on a disk?

Derek - D1 relates to the US NTSC, D2 is a UK PAL release, D3, European dvds not sold in UK and Ireland and D4 relates to Australia and New Zealand and the rest of Europe.

Q - What about artwork?

Derek - Print work such as the artwork required for the DVD labels etc. would be handled by another company as we deal only with the creation of the audio visual.

Q - What can a producer do to make your life easier? And any advice for authoring your movie on to DVD?

Derek - Start planning your DVD before making your movie. Are there things you can shoot concurrently with your movie to help save money or create a unique bonus feature? Also, think about how involved you want to be in the DVD process after you've made your film. Do you want to spend the time and effort to learn about the actual process? If you do and /or don't have the budget to use an outside production company, consider making your DVD simple and logical to execute. If you do use a creative production company to help create your DVD, it's helpful to be well organized, available, and open to suggestions. Good luck!

POST

Tom Ortenberg
Lion's Gate

DOMESTIC DISTRIBUTION

Q - What is your job?

Tom - I am the President of Lion's Gate Films releasing, which means I'm in charge of the marketing, distribution and acquisition of all our theatrical motion pictures. Lion's Gate is an independent producer and distributor of motion pictures. We release around 15 movies a year, theatrically sourced from producing about 6-8 movies and acquiring another 8-10 movies a year (through the festival circuit). For example, *American Psycho* and *Monster's Ball* are in-house productions. *Gods and Monsters*, *Affliction*, and *The Red Violin* are all pictures we acquired at film festivals.

Q - Does Lion's Gate champion independent films?

Tom - We do the kinds of pictures that studios either can't or won't do. The studios do the *'boy meets girl'* films better than we would, so we don't compete on that level. We look for pictures with independent credibility and some level of commercial sensibility, as we are putting up our own cash. Some of our most edgy movies are picked up at the festivals, and we pride ourselves on being the kind of company that would release certain movies, like *Irreversible* with Monica Belluci, or *Dogma*, for which we had to take on some members of the Catholic Church. Here at Lion's Gate we take our charge as an independent very seriously.

Q - When should a producer come to you if they have a story?

Tom - The easiest way to break through the clutter at Lion's Gate is with a completed script including an attachment, whether it's a director, some casting or a producer who has a successful track record. That really helps get a project noticed. We're looking for movies that are ready to be made. A good script that needs a lot of work makes the process more difficult because we don't have the money to do a lot of development. That is better left to the majors, who have bigger budgets and can afford to sink a few million in the development of projects which may not get made.

Q - If a first feature producer came to you with a great director or well known cast, you'd be more likely to take it on?

Tom - There has to be something. *Monster's Ball* was one of those great unmade scripts circulating Hollywood. It had a director attached to it, Mark Forrester, whose only previous work was a low budget indie that had never got picked up called *Everything Put Together*. We all read the *Monster's Ball* script and although Billy Bob Thornton was attached to it, it was at a much too high a budget and the producer of the film had no track record. We believed in Mark's vision and the material was so strong that we collectively decided this was too good a script to not get made. Thankfully people responded to it and all worked for virtually nothing to help get it made, which paid off for everybody.

There are success stories that come to us with nothing attached. James Cox brought us *Wonderland*. He had made a couple of terrific shorts and one disastrous feature. We believed that James' vision spoke volumes and we weren't deterred by one commercial failure. Sure enough, James' vision attracted Val Kilmer, Josh Lucas, Lisa Kudrow and Christina Applegate. Tim Blake Nelson had a new baby at home but we sent him the script and he flew out for a couple of weeks, leaving an agitated wife and new born baby back home, as we knew Tim couldn't help but respond to the material. The film cost remarkably little to make in 23 18-hour crazy days.

The material is the thing. If it's a great script, Lion's Gate is a great place to come to, and we'll help you find everything else.

Q - Would you prefer people go through an agent to get their work to you?

Tom - Ideally yes. Businesses want everything done through the proper channels to protect themselves from getting sued. I would encourage any independent producer / writer to network at seminars and panels. When I talk about marketing, distribution, finance and production on these panels, I am always being given scripts. You can't be an asshole when somebody's begging you to read their script.

Q - How important are film festivals to independent film makers?

Tom - The major festivals - Sundance, Toronto and Cannes - are extremely important in terms of getting your completed film picked up. There are other festivals that are gaining in importance, like Berlin and Venice, but they still pale in comparison. A couple of other North American festivals are trying to assert themselves. *Kissing Jessica Stein* was picked up by Fox Searchlight out of the LA film festival. *Roger Dodger* was picked up out of Tribeca last year. If you're a filmmaker who has been rejected from a film festival, there's no shame in that. There's no accounting for taste at any film festival. *Gods and Monsters* and *Affliction* were both rejected by the Toronto Film Festival, which combined were nominated for five Academy Awards and each won an Academy Award. Every major festival in the country rejected *My Big, Fat Greek Wedding*. Never take rejection by any film festival as a setback.

Q - How easy is it to make money from a theatrical release in America?

Tom - Generally speaking, theatrical is a loss leader for the rest of the distribution channels and ancillary markets. We try not to lose too much money theatrically, but recoup on home video, DVD, pay per view, VOD, pay TV and all those channels. If you manage to get a small release in New York and LA you should be able to get some national reviews that will be worth taking around. It's extremely rare for anybody to pick up a picture that has already opened theatrically, but at least you've started the process of a calling card for your next picture. If you have a really good little movie, you can help get it released by setting up a couple of press screenings, getting reviewed in the LA Times and the New York Times, so you create a portfolio for yourself. You can hand some production guy a folder with a New York Times review in it to really help make a career or help with the process of getting the next picture.

If we release a film that doesn't do that well theatrically, it helps to be able to hand to the director a couple of good reviews and say, *'I'm sorry the picture didn't do more business, but here's a love letter from the New York Times or the LA Times that you can take with you on the next film'.*

Q - Is it difficult to release films in LA?

Tom - It's hard to do it successfully as there's so much clutter in the marketplace. You need a good movie, a great marketing campaign, a passionate distributor with good marketing instincts, money and determination.

I worked with one filmmaker who made a small, indie romantic comedy, and until *My Big Fat Greek Wedding*, nothing was tougher to distribute successfully than an independent romantic comedy without cast. Those types of pictures only work when they have Tom Hanks and Meg Ryan in them. This guy was a showman, a salesman; he wrote, directed and financed it himself. Ultimately he ended up distributing it himself. He booked the Laemmle Monica in Santa Monica and set up his own press screening. I saw him in Santa Monica handing out flyers on the street, *'please come see my movie'*. As hard as it is to get a picture open in New York and LA, it's even harder to do it around the country. There are fewer independent theatres, so generally only the biggest and best of the indie films get out there. You need to meet with some initial success and if you don't, the odds of turning it around later are pretty much insurmountable. Lion's Gate home entertainment releases about 70 movies a year on video and DVD so we're looking for a lot more than we release theatrically. So our home entertainment division picks up a lot of movies straight for video. There is no shame in bypassing theatrical if the pay cable premiere allows you to pay your investors back, or gets you exposure for the next one. We release a lot of movies on video that other people took out theatrically. *Diamond Men* was one that was out theatrically just over a year ago. It did zero business, got some good reviews, disappeared, we picked it up for home video where everybody will make some money out of it.

Q - If Lion's Gate picks up a film, what happens in terms of commission afterwards?

Tom - When we buy a film, it's usually from a sales agent, or the producer, and there are several producer / sales agents that handle many independent pictures too. We usually make a deal in which we will define all of our terms. The basics are the minimum guarantee, the level of theatrical commitment, the fee structure and the length of term. The minimum guarantee is how much we are going to pay for the movie up front. Will we make a dollar amount P&A commitment? Will we make a commitment to a certain broad release where we promise to open the movie in at least X number of cities? Will we promise to release it by a certain date? Those are all things that are part of the negotiation and the answer could be 'no' to all of them. We're going to pick up your movie for $1m, but we're not promising a theatrical. Maybe we will, maybe we won't. It's subject to negotiation. Our distribution fees can go from 15% to 50%. The more we pay up front for a movie, the higher our fees are going to be. Generally, we won't pick up the movie for less than 15 years and often will insist on 25 years as we need to recoup through TV cycles work. How many years does HBO have the rights for? There are still significant revenue streams that we insist on being in a position to capitalise on. I'm constantly amazed at how many different ways there are to cut a deal. Seventeen years later, we're still making new deals. We're always looking to make things work. We see Lion's Gate as being a filmmaker friendly company. We pride ourselves on being the kind of company that filmmakers and actors like to work with and will speak kindly of. We pride ourselves on paying the back end and paying it quickly. Being able to do that on pictures like *Monster's Ball*, where everybody worked for next to nothing, there were a lot of people that we paid a lot of money to. If it's a more commercial proposition, where we're planning to spend $15m on P&A and plan on going out on 1500 screens, we might get a more involved in tweaking what we would consider to be the commercial sensibilities of the picture. But in general, we pride ourselves on honouring the artistic vision of the filmmakers and we think that makes us a better company to do business with.

Q - How did Secretary *do?*

Tom - Secretary did terrific. We did about $4m at the box office, which on the Art House circuit is great. At Sundance some people thought that young women would be offended by it. What they didn't get is that young, professional women were the main audience for this movie. They were the ones who liked it most. It stunned me that most people didn't see that. We did word of mouth screenings for young, professional women and they loved it because it was a female empowerment movie and although the lead character may have been submissive, she was the one that held all the cards.

Q - What is the time scale between theatrical and home entertainment releases?

Tom - If we pick up the film at a festival, we endeavor to get the film out theatrically inside of 12 months. Sometimes we do it in 6 months, sometimes 14 months. Film rental comes in about 90 days after we release it. Video will follow somewhere between 4 to 6 later. TV will start generally 6 months after video. It takes a while for those cycles to catch up with our fees and P&A expenses so it can be some time after the first year that the producers start seeing net back end. HBO might be the gravy at the end of the train, but you might not get your overage until that, so sometimes we will pay a percentage of back end up front and call it a day. People are always receptive to that. We send out quarterly statements. Do negotiate to get your statements quarterly or semi-annually.

Q - What is P&A?

Tom - P&A stands for prints and advertising, but is essentially the marketing dollars you are spending to release the movie. That is the cost of making the prints, trailers, posters and television, radio and newspaper ads.

Distribution Pointers

1. An advance. Rarely given, usually only if the film needs completion money, in which case the distributor/agent might take a higher commission.

2. Number of Years for the rights to be licensed to the Distributor/Sales Agent: From 5-35, standard is 5-10 years. NOT in perpetuity. Try to have the initial term be relatively short (say 2 years) with automatic rollovers should the distributor deliver a certain amount of revenue in that time and/or a specified slate of theatrical releases occur, which should include New York and Los Angeles screenings. If those performance requirements are not met, all rights would automatically return to the filmmaker.

3. Extent of Rights being requested by Distributor/Sales Agent: i.e worldwide, worldwide excluding domestic to be negotiated between the parties.

4. Fees/rate of commission: Usually between 20-25%. Sometimes 30% depending on the extent of input by Distributor/Sales Agent and this should be limited so that the Distributor takes only one commission per country.

5. Ownership: Make sure you, the producer, will still own the copyright to the Film – not applicable if you are selling the film to the Distributor. If you are licensing the rights to certain territories you will remain the copyright owner.

6. CAP on expenses: Make sure there is a maximum limit (a ceiling) on expenses and that you are notified in writing of any large expenses i.e. over a specified amount, that you are able to refute if necessary.

7. Direct Expenses: Make sure that overhead of the Distributor and the staff expenses are not included in Distribution expenses and will not be added as a further expense.

8. Sub Distributor Fees: Make sure that these fees are paid by the Distributor/Sales Agent out of its fees and not in addition to the Distribution expenses.

9. Consider your position on Net Receipts: i.e. monies after Distributor has deducted their commission and fees subject to any sales agreements you enter into with a Distributor. Make sure this is clearly delineated in the contract with no loopholes. Remember that taxes should be taken out of gross receipts not net receipts.

10. Errors and Omissions Policy: See if this is to be included in the delivery requirements as this could be an added unexpected expense. Distributors are often willing to absorb this cost and recoup from gross profits. It is important that you as the filmmaker are added as an additional named insured on the policy.

11. Cross Collaterization: Where the Distributor will offset expenses and losses on their other films against yours. You don't want this.

12. P&A (Prints and Advertising) commitment from the Distributor: Negotiate total expenses that will be used on P&A in the contract i.e. a fixed sum. Include a Floor and a ceiling.

13. Domestic Theatrical Release: Negotiate what print run is expected, and in what locations. Specify what locations so that you don't find a clause in your contract such as 'your film will be released in three of the top one hundred markets'.

14. Distribution Editing Rights: Limit for only censorship requirements although if you are dealing with a major Distributor this will not be acceptable.

15. Producer's input in the marketing campaign.

16. Trailer commitment: will this be another hidden additional cost? Make sure theaters have this in plenty of time.

17. Release Window: Get Distributor to commit to release the film within a time frame after delivery of film to Distributor.

18. Audit Rights: The Producer has the rights to inspect the books with a ten-day notice re: the distribution of the film. The Filmmaker should receive statements (either quarterly or monthly) from the distributor with any payment due to the filmmaker.

19. LIMITATION ON ACTION: You want to make sure that you have enough time to act on any accounting irregularity that you may discover. Fight to have at least a three- year period from receipt of a questionable financial statement, or discovery of any accounting irregularity, whichever is later, in which to file a demand for arbitration.

20. If the Sales Agent intends to group your film with other titles to produce an attractive package for buyers, ensure that your film is not unfairly supporting other films or that you are receiving a disproportionate or unfair percentage.

cont...

DISTRIBUTION

Distribution Pointers... Cont

21. Make sure that the rights revert back to the Producer in case of any type of insolvency or if the Agent is in material breach of the agreement.

22. Check the Delivery requirements very carefully.

23. Indemnity: Make sure you receive reimbursement for losses incurred by you as a result of distributor's breach of the terms of the agreement, violation of third party rights, and for any changes or additions made to the film.

24. Lab Access Letter: Distributor should not be permitted to remove masters from the lab nor take possession of the original negative and any other original materials. They may have a lab access for supervised use of the negative and other materials for duplication or promotional purposes.

25. Termination Clause: If the distributor defaults on any of its contractual obligations, the filmmaker should have the right to terminate the contract, and regain rights to license the film in unsold territories as well as obtain money damages for the default. Filmmaker should give distributor 14 days prior written notice of default before exercising the right to termination.

26. Filmmaker Warranties: Filmmaker's warranties in regard to infringement of third party rights should be to the best of the Filmmaker's knowledge and belief, not absolute.

27. Arbitration Clause: This ensures that any contractual disputes may be solved through binding arbitration with the prevailing party entitled to reimbursement of legal fees and cost by the losing party. For the best results, the parties should submit such action to binding arbitration with the AFMA (American Film Market Association) arbitration division. The Distributor will fight for Arbitration to take place near them locally. If they're not local to you, either fight for arbitration to occur locally to you or in a place of equidistance to the two of you.

28. LATE PAYMENTS/LIEN: All monies due and payable to the filmmaker should be held in trust by the distributor for the filmmaker, and the filmmaker should be deemed to have a lien on filmmaker's share of revenue. The distributor should pay the filmmaker interest on any amounts past due.

29. SCHEDULE OF MINIMUMS: For each foreign territory for which a distributors or foreign sales agent who licenses foreign sales rights, there should be a schedule of minimum acceptable license fees per territory. The distributor is not permitted to license the film in each territory for less than the minimum without the filmmaker's approval.

30. FILMMAKER DEFAULT: The distributor should give filmmaker 14 days written notice of any alleged default by filmmaker, and an additional 10 days to cure such a default, before taking any action to enforce it's rights.

Q - How much would you spend on P&A for a $1m movie?

Tom - To construct your material, screen it, make some prints and take out some ads could cost $200k. Could you do it for less? Absolutely. Could you spend more? Easily. Lion's Gate can't do it for less, because we put out theatrical marketing materials that are polished, we're not going to cheat on it. You can technically open a picture without a trailer. Not advisable if you're looking to maximise box office, but in a Guerilla sense of trying to get your picture out there, yes, you can remove that expense.

Q - How much would be spent on P&A for home entertainment?

Tom - It depends on what the expectations are. The video P&A should never be more than 25% of the total video gross. I insist on capping the video marketing and duplication costs at no more than 30% of the total gross. If the picture ends up grossing $1m on video, you won't mind if they spent a couple of hundred thousand dollars on video P&A to get there.

Q - What mistakes do you see regularly with new filmmakers?

Tom - They think they have all the answers. The ability to listen is as or more important than their ability to pitch.

Q - What advice would you offer new filmmakers?

Tom - It takes persistence, hard work and if you're not prepared to fight the good fight it's better not to start. When you're told, *'no'*, find a different door to knock on. If the major festivals say no, go to the minor festivals. You have to plan on getting your hands dirty.

The MPAA

The Motion Picture Association of America (MPAA) rate films for content so parents know how much violence, sexual content and bad language are contained within. All seven major studios are members of the MPAA. Independent producers don't have to submit their film for a rating, although usually they do to be consumer friendly and also because theater owners may require it.

Who decides?

An 8-13 member board in Los Angeles who's biggest requirement is that they are parents.

What are the ratings?

G - General Audience: All ages admitted, no sex, violence or profanity that most parents would find offensive to their children.

PG - Parental Guidance Suggested: There may be some profanity, violence, brief nudity but no drug use. It's advised that parents examine the film before they let their children see it.

PG-13 - Parents Strongly Cautioned. Material may be inappropriate for children under 13: Stronger violence, nudity, sensuality, language or other contents. Any drug use content will initially require at least a PG-13 rating.

R - Restricted, Under 17 Requires Accompanying Parent Or Adult Guardian. If nudity is sexually oriented, if violence is too rough or persistent, if there are constant uses of hard language and expletives, the film goes into the R category.

NC-17 - No One 17 And Under Admitted. It doesn't necessarily mean 'obscene or pornographic' in the oft-accepted or legal meaning of those words. The Board does not and cannot mark films with those words. These are legal terms and for courts to decide. The reasons for the application of an NC-17 rating can be violence or sex or aberrational behavior or drug abuse or anything else, when present, most parents would consider too strong and therefore off-limits for viewing by children.

NC-17 used to be entitled 'X'. However, 'X' was never trademarked by the MPAA. The MPAA believed that parents should be able to take their children to any film they see fit, but the National Association of Theater Owners (NATO) wanted a rating to mark films of adult nature. Therefore, 'X' was created, but not trademarked. Because of this, producers of adult entertainment took the 'X' rating and used it to brand their films. So, something that is XXX would mean three times as titillating in their eyes. XXX is not part of the rating system. It is a marketing tool only.

How do you get a rating?

Submit an application form for certification with a print of the film to be reviewed and a fee. The fee is variable and is based on the length and negative cost of the film. The Board will then call the filmmaker and tell them when the film will be reviewed and when a decision will be made. All of the screenings are done in a closed room fashion so as to preserve the reviewers' anonymity. If you don't like the rating that you're given, you have two choices. You may either recut your film and go through the process again or appeal the initial rating through an appeal's board. If you're worried about certain scenes contact the MPAA and they're more than happy to guide you towards the rating you want to achieve.

Are trailers rated?

Trailers are approved for 'all audiences', which means they may be shown with all feature films, or 'restricted audiences', which limits their use to feature films rated R or NC-17. There will be, in 'all audience' trailers, no scenes that caused the feature to be rated PG, PG-13, R or NC-17. Each trailer carries at the front a tag, which tells two things, first the audience for which the trailer has been approved, and second, the rating of the picture being advertised. The tag for 'all audience' trailers will have a green background whereas the tag for 'restricted' trailers will have a red background.

www.mpaa.com

DISTRIBUTION

Andy Gruenberg
Mac Releasing

THEATRICAL RELEASING

Q - What is the job of a theatrical booker?

Andy - We call exhibitors, tell them about our movies and then pick the right theaters for the films. The guy who manages the prints and tracks them during the release is called the booker. All theaters want the same thing and that's an audience to turn up. Some theaters care about certain types of movies and the majority want relationships with studios. They want to be in a position where they can have all the movies rather than choose specific ones. People have learned over the years if you have to pick movies, you can be as right as you can be wrong. That's why you see big megaplexes being built.

Q - Is there a bad time to book a film?

Andy - There used to be, there isn't anymore. The month of May used to be terrible, now May is the best. When I first started in the business, you could tell how good a movie was by its release schedule. You want to make sure you book far enough in advance that you get all your accessories sorted like your trailer playing .We recommend eight weeks minimum.

Q - How do you calculate the house allaowance?

Andy - The exhibitor requests a house allowance and the distributor either accepts it or negotiates. This covers the running of the theater, and then they break it down by seat. After a certain amount of seats being sold, the theater will hit the house nut and a much greater percentage of the box office will start to flow back to the distributor. It is rare for independent and low budget films to hit the house nut though. The distributor takes a fee from that revenue. Usually the advertising is taken care of before the producer gets any money. The marketing has become so expensive that nobody plans on making their money back theatrically, but producers look at it as a business of entertainment, which includes television and DVD and home entertainment and pay per view, where you will make your money back.

Q - When do you pull a movie from a theater?

Andy - It's different each week. If you have a good relationship with an exhibitor and the movie is not doing well, but reviews are good, they may stay with you for a couple of weeks. But generally, the lowest gross is pulled.

Q - What would be a good gross for an average movie?

Andy - $10k in a couple of theaters would be good, not great, but you wouldn't get pulled. If you did $5k, it would be piecemeal, if it did $25k that would be great.

Q - Should you choose a smaller theater if you have an indie film?

Andy - If you choose a smaller theater, less people will go. The genre comes into that.

Q - What are your thoughts on self-distribution?

Andy - It depends. If they know the right theaters, they can place the advertising and do all the things that are necessary to get their trailers played as well create a marketing plan that will get people in a movie theater and keep them coming, then they should do it. There are very few people that can do that. It's the marketing that's the hard part. The distribution is not easy but it's the marketing that gets people in.

Q - How do you get paid?

Andy - Directly through the exhibitor. As a simple example, let's say you make $10k. House expenses are $5k. So you have $5k left. $4.5k goes to the distributor and the exhibitor keeps $500. The distributor will then recoup expenses such as trailers, posters, advertising and shipping prints.

Q - What do you request from the producer?

Andy - We take a look at the movie and decide which markets in the US each movie would be best suited for. At this point in time, Mac Releasing doesn't go on a national basis. We pick our spots. We have a Hispanic movie coming out called *Washington Heights*, which is an area in New York between Harlem and the Bronx. What we do is go to New York City, book 20 runs theatrically with some niche marketing. We will go in areas that cater to Hispanic clientele. Rather than a full run in Manhattan, we are taking three runs in Greenwich Village, Midtown and the Upper West Side.

Q - How much do you need to put aside for the P&A for a $1m film?

Andy - 'P' is the cheaper part, (the prints). You buy as many prints as film festivals you want to attend. They cost $2k each. The 'A' is a huge number. New York is the most expensive market. An ad in the New York Times is $900 an inch compared to Syracuse where it's $90 for that same space. Then you are making television ads, buying television time and making trailers followed by the duplications and shipping. A lot more people get to know about it from television ads but the budget increases dramatically.

Q - What do TV costs start at?

Andy - You can buy as little as you want while the studios buy a couple $million on the New York market. There's no sense in buying $5k of television time. But if you buy cable and be specific about what you want out of it all, maybe $90k.

Q - Where is best to platform your independent film?

Andy - New York. I think to release on one print is enough and it is smart if you have a limited budget because you can use your money more effectively and efficiently and you get a good read in New York City.

Q - Are there 100 top markets?

Andy - It's the same list that television people use and is called the ADI. New York is one, LA is two and then Chicago or San Francisco are three and four, but usually people say the top three rather than the top ten.

Q - What common mistakes have you noticed by filmmakers? What advice would you give a new filmmaker?

Andy - You want to meet smart people that are doing a good job. When you make a movie it's not just a one person job. Someone's got to write it, someone's got to invest in it, someone's got to buy it after it's been made. There are a lot of people involved, but generally once it gets to the point where there should be a sale, something's gone right rather than wrong. As for advice, have it sold before it's made. Movies are very expensive to make. Digital video is making it cheaper, but if you get an actor, that costs and that means the director costs and the sets cost and the insurance costs and before you know it, those costs add up.

Carole Curb
Curb Entertainment

INTERNATIONAL SALES

Q - Is there a type of film that sells the most?

Carole - Yes, the action thriller. Ever since I've been in distribution since 1988 that has always been the tried and true genre. For independent filmmaking however, lots of action is very costly. So it tends to be a thriller with some action in it, and that's what we seem to have had a lot of success with over the years.

Q - What do you need from a producer to sell a movie?

Carole - A good film! With good production stills and quality sound. I welcome producers working with us because it all helps to build the movie for the buyer. For instance, if they're out there on the streets talking up their film, that only enhances what we're doing behind the scenes with the buyers. Also, with the screenings, we can only get so many distributors to fill the room, so filmmakers can help enhance it with their friends who will laugh or cry at the appropriate moments. A buyer doesn't know if it's another buyer or a friend. It's a matter of building heat. Fundamentally though, you have to have a good product.

Q - Do you find with low budget movies that sound is often ignored?

Carole - Sound is an area where I often find poor quality. You want people to be able to hear your actors. You can fix a lot of problems through ADR, but it costs more money to fix the sound after the movie is shot.

Q - Can a filmmaker come to you early on with their screenplay seeking finance?

Carole - Yes we do co-invest. If we do come on board as a producer, I find that other investors are more prone to put in money. I have either matched funds previously or I've put in a third and they put in two thirds. But we're talking about independent movies, so it's not huge amounts of money.

Q - Can filmmakers also come to you for pre-sales?

Carole - Yes, but we haven't done a lot of pre-sales. What the filmmakers usually do is show us their script, tell us who the director is and if there are any stars attached, and ask us if we can do a list of minimums and asking prices, and then ask us to come onboard. It's difficult to come onboard before the film is made because you don't know what your end product is going to be. It's easier to get onboard at with the principle photography done, or the finished film. Then you can make more accurate estimates.

Q - Is there a standard list of minimums?

Carole - There's a standard list, swinging from minimums to asking prices, territory by territory, but a lot of it will depend on if it's theatrical or not. So frequently they'll have theatrical prices and then another set of prices if it goes to video and television. Let's say that with a good thriller we'll know it's going to go for somewhere between X and Y in certain countries such as Malaysia, Singapore, Turkey etc., so, when we see a film, we take another film we have sold that we think it's comparable to and then we plug in those numbers and come up with an estimate of prices.

Q - What technical elements do you need for delivery?

Carole - If it is a theatrical release, you'll need your IP (inter-positive) and IN (inter-negative) and then your video master, your sound elements and your E&O insurance and of course your delivery stills, etc.. We have a list of delivery items.

Q - How expensive is it to obtain an E&O insurance policy?

Carole - Now it's about $12k.

Q - Is there anything on the delivery list that regularly causes problems that the filmmaker never considers?

Carole - Stills are the one place where people don't spend much money. They're so anxious to get their film made, they're not thinking of the marketing side of it. Second time filmmakers are thinking of it but first time filmmakers are so in to getting their film made and making sure they survive, that stills can go by the wayside. But you can do photo shoots afterwards and catch up but then you're paying more.

Q - So filmmakers should be aware of the extra monies required for delivery expenses?

Carole - That's a common problem for a first time filmmaker. They have their budget to make their movie, they finish the film and they think their job is done. Then they find out they have $50k delivery items that they didn't even budget for. If I really think the film is good, I will pay for the delivery costs, along with the distribution expenses and recoup it from sales. Often, when filmmakers see the royalty statements that show what's been earned, they don't realize that we as their distributor have to now recoup the $50k for the delivery items, then the distribution expenses which is the trailer, the flyers, screenings, posters and then on top of that we have our distribution fee! So when they see what they end up with, they get a shock. It takes a lot of money to get your film out there. It's hard. Independent filmmakers have been very careful on how they've budgeted their money, so I try to be careful on how we budget ours, as ultimately, we're spending money that has to be recouped from them.

Q - Are the expenses capped?

Carole - Yes, distributors should definitely cap their distribution expenses.

Q - Do these expenses include going to the three major film markets?

Carole - Yes the three major film markets (Cannes, AFM and MIFED) and the two TV markets (MIPCOM and MIPTV). We take a major presence at those markets and only take market expenses for the first year. It's pro-rated with all the films that are in their first year cycle. So let's say you have three new films which we acquire for AFM, three for Cannes and three for MIFED. We'd try and make sure that they're not competitive, so you'd have a romantic comedy, a thriller and a drama, or say a romantic comedy, thriller and a family movie. There would be nine films in the first year cycle, so each film would pay a ninth of the market expense.

Q - How much could that end up being?

Carole - For those five markets for the year, it's usually around $35k, and I try to keep it down and watch our costs. There are some companies who charge a set amount, like $15k for each of the three film markets, well that's $45k for the year for just 3 markets. We get five markets and the last time I looked, I don't know any case where it exceeded $40k. These are approximations of course.

Q - Do you give any kind of guaranteed marketing expense commitment?

Carole - Filmmakers are more interested in me limiting my expenses than making me commit to putting up the money. We can put up to $100k in marketing expenses but that's our lid. Sometimes if I see that the advertising isn't paying off, then it's not worth spending the money. I try not to get to that $100k, but still try to get the same value, and it's usually closer to $75k. That includes the $40k market expenses, then your trailer and flyer (lean and mean) for say $20k, and then you've got your screenings and

DISTRIBUTION

advertising to do. We have the first double page ad in Variety and Hollywood Reporter, so they're usually taking a third of a page in each trade that costs $7k in Hollywood Reporter, $7k in Variety, and then some dailies in Screen and Moving Pictures. So the advertising works out to be about $20k. Then you still have to do your screenings and any other special screenings during the year, and anything that's specifically devoted to your film. So the total comes up to somewhere between $80k and $100k. I find the better the picture is selling, the more you spend, because you have to do more. Ironically it's actually good news if you're spending more!

Q - Is there anything that a producer can do to help it be more economical?

Carole - I've thought a lot about this, and I've tried to be lean and mean. Sometimes the trailer turns out to be $12 and the art $8k. Yes we can probably get the art for $5k but invariably you have to do reprints, which will cost $1500 to do one reprint and then over the longevity, it's still about $20k no matter how you slice it. It's very hard to get it down. You could probably stay closer to $75k if you really limit your advertising by sharing a page with other films.

Q - What if the filmmaker wants to be involved in the trailer and artwork?

Carole - I like having the filmmaker involved in the trailer and artwork, because they've been living with it for years. It's their vision, their child, and you want to hear their thoughts. I like to hear their ideas first, then go and get some different choices, show them and listen to their feedback. The same goes with the trailer. We've managed to get some great trailers and flyers by working closely with the producer. However by the same token, I don't like them to do it, especially with the trailer, because they are too close to it and cutting a trailer is very different to cutting a movie.

Q - Is there a different type of trailer that you need for the markets than the one you'd generally see in the theaters?

Carole - Yes. Ours is more a promo reel and it goes for about two minutes, whereas the ones in the theater are much shorter. Sometimes you can use part of your promo reel for the domestic trailer but I find that because not everyone speaks English overseas, we have to hit the foreign market harder, faster and more to the point. Whereas the domestic trailer can be subtler, edgier, with maybe more writing than voices because people can read English quickly.

Q - What kind of a deal does a producer get with a sales agent?

Carole - Depending on the heat of the picture, the standard distribution fee for foreign is 25%. If there's a bidding war, you can go down to 20% depending on the term, advance etc. Sometimes it can be as low as 15% depending on other factors.

Q - You mention an advance, is there likelihood that producers can get an advance?

Carole - Yes. It can be in many forms. It could be that a distributor gives an advance to deal with delivery items, or it can be upon delivery that they're paid a certain amount. As a rule, advances are going down, because the economy is down and the prices we're getting are lower, so people aren't anxious to take a chance. If all delivery items are in order, you could be looking at a token advance of $10k to $300k, but that being said, I rarely give $300k! But we have been close. Even if you have all the stars and planets lined up it's still difficult! You have to have the right genre. One of the films we acquired had the right genre, played in Sundance, had a fabulous title, had a fabulous domestic company releasing it, was a true story, had names - it's only then, with all these hooks, that the buyers started to get it. If you don't have like ten hooks to beat them over the head with, it's hard. I'm not talking about the little countries like Greece and Turkey. They will come to us as they know that they're going to get a certain type of film from us, and they know they're going to get it delivered correctly as they've been working with us for years. They'll buy our whole slate as a package and we have key countries that do that. But the bigger countries that pay the big money, they will want to screen the film as they don't want your whole slate, they just want to pick out one or two.

Q - How does packaging work?

Sales Agent Deliverables

Not all of these items will be needed by a sales agent, but most will. The cost of making up this extensive list of items could feasibly cost more than the production costs of an ultra low budget film. Speak to your sales agent and negotiate an exact list, with a budget for making up that list, BEFORE you sign any sales agreement. This is a LOT OF STUFF!

Release Print
35mm com/opt print (Combined optical print). This is used by the sales agent to screen the film at markets in a cinema environment.A 90 minute film will be 5 reels long.

35mm Interpositive and 35mm Internegative
Made from the original negative. You have already made this in order to produce your final print, and will be held at the lab. (90 mins is 5 reels)

35mm Optical Sound Negative
Made from master sound mix. You have already made this in order to produce your final print, and will be held at the lab.(90 mins is 5 reels)

Sound Master
Master sound mix, probably supplied on either DA88, time coded DAT, hard drive or MO disk. Some agents may request a 35mm sound master which you should avoid. This sound mix will also be on the DigiBeta on tracks 1 and 2.

Music & Effect Mix (M&E)
Master M&E sound mix used for foreign territories to re-voice the film. Supplied on either DA88 or time coded DAT. Some agents may request a 35mm sound master which you should avoid. This sound mix will also be on the DigiBeta on tracks 3 and 4.

Textless Title Background
35mm Interneg / Interpos / print of sequences without title elements. Used by territories to re-title in their native language. Video versions of the textless backgrounds will also be needed.

35mm Trailer
Including access to interneg, interpos, optical sound, magnetic sound master and M&E mix. It is common now to produce the trailer on DigiBeta and digitally copy the video onto film. The quality isn't as good but it may be adequate and certainly cheaper and easier to produce.

Video Tape
Full screen (not widescreen) perfect quality Digital Betacam of the film, including stereo sound (on tracks 1&2) and M&E (on tracks 3&4). You may want to make widescreen versions and 16-9 versions too, but these will probably be subsequent to the full screen version. You may need to supply a BetaSP so that the sales agent can make VHS copies.Should also include the trailer, in full screen (not widescreen) perfect quality, including stereo sound (on tracks 1&2) and M&E (on tracks 3&4). You will also need a trailer with textless backgrounds too.

Video Tape Textless Backgrounds
Full screen (not widescreen) perfect quality Digital Betacam of textless background sequences, including stereo sound (on tracks 1&2) and M&E (on tracks 3&4).

Universal Master
24P HD transfer of your film, fully graded and cleaned. Hi res and true 16:9 image, means it can be used to make ALL the different tapes required for international sales. Also includes all audio versions, Dolby Digital (for DVD), stereo (for broadcast TV) and M&E (for revoicing). This would replace ALL other video tapes required in this list. All textless backgrounds can be included at the end of the tape.

Stills set
100 full color transparencies will be requested but you can get away with 20 as long as they are good. May be possible to supply these on CD / DVD now, but they must be very high quality scans professionally done.

Screenplay transcript
Final cut including all music cues. This isn't your shooting script, but an accurate and detailed transcription of all the dialogue and action. You will need to sit down with your PC and a VHS and do it from scratch.

Sales Agent Deliverables... cont

Press Kit and reviews

Copies of the press kit, on paper and disk, and copies of all press and reviews. Don't give them the bad reviews.

EPK- Electronic Press Kit

BetaSP of interviews with actors and principal crew. Shots of crew at work, plus clips from film and trailer. You will also need a split M&E version so that interviewees voices can be dipped down allowing a translation to be spoken over the top. cont...

Music Cue Sheet

An accurate list of all the music cues, rights etc. See the music cue sheet later in the book. Used by collection agencies to distribute music royalties.

Distribution restrictions

Statement of any restrictions or obligations such as the order in which the cast are credited etc.

US Copyright Notice

Available from The Registrar of Copyright, Library of Congress, Washington DC, 20559, USA.

Miscellaneous Paperwork

Chain of Title

Information and copy contracts with all parties involved with production and distribution of the film. This is needed to prove that you have the right to sell the film to another party. Usually the writer, director, producer, musician, cast and release forms from all other parties involved.

Certificate of Origin and Certificate of Authorship

Available from lawyer. You go in, pay a small fee, swear that the information is correct, they witness it and you have your certificates.

Certificate of Nationality

Available from the Department of Culture Media and Sport, Dept., of National Heritage, Media Division (Film), 2/4 Cockspur Street, London, SW1Y 5DH.

Credit List

A complete cast and crew list, plus any other credits.

Errors and Omissions Insurance Policy (E&O) - A policy that

indemnifies distributors and sales agents internationally. Available from specialised Insurers (approx. cost $10k). You may be able to negotiate around this, agreeing to supply it if and when it is needed by any specific distributor.

Lab Access Letter

A letter giving access to materials held at the lab to the sales agent. Remember, if you haven't paid your lab bill yet, they may not give you this letter.

Carole - Technically we sell each film on it's own. We don't cross collateralize. But we have our standard buyers who need product and they come to us to buy all their films. We don't like to refer to it as a package. They will give us the prices, they'll say we want to pay this for that, and that for that. Or they'll say we want three films at $10k each. They know our taste and each sales company has its own identity. Our identity over the years is that we've done a lot of romantic comedies, family films and thrillers, but we don't do anything that has too much drugs, eroticism or is too horroresque. A little horror and sci fi is fine though.

Q - Generally, new filmmakers can't afford to get stars in their low budget movies.

Carole - More than ever, stars are important. I like to think that it's better to have a movie that works with no stars than having one that doesn't work with stars, but that being said, people really want stars. Your picture has to be really good to sell without stars.

Q - How long does it take to see returns on a film?

Carole - Distribution is a sluggish business and I try and tighten it up to make the money flow through as fast as possible. You sign your deal memos, then you come back and sign long form contracts and then theoretically, 20% is due, and then upon notice of delivery 80% is due. I have noticed that by the time we go to a market, a lot of times the filmmakers have been unable to fully deliver for about three months, so I say to filmmakers, the faster you can deliver to us, the quicker you'll get your money. The ideal scenario would be that if we took the film to the first market we could actually say to the buyer that we can give them notice of delivery immediately. The filmmakers don't understand that it's predicated sometimes on them delivering to us because we can't give notice of delivery to the buyers until the filmmaker delivers to us. And on top of that you've got to get it QC'd (quality controlled) and that takes time. I've had deliveries that took a year and the filmmaker then wonders where his money is.

Q - Territories pick up a license for a certain amount of time. How long is that usually for?

Carole - It can be all different things. Five to seven years is standard though a lot of the territories are now asking for more. It can be up to twenty five years. When the movie expires, they sometimes extend for an additional amount of time. They buy the rights they want, either theatrical, video and TV, or all. We try and get a backend deal where we get a portion of the theatrical, a video royalty and a split on television. But the smaller countries who aren't paying a lot of money will ask for flat deals, which we usually grant to them because it's very hard to track their accounting. How can you track what's going on in Singapore or Budapest?

Q - What is the shelf life of a film before you've exhausted everything?

Carole - That depends on the film because sometimes now, we're even selling older films. But if you're talking top dollar, I would say the first three years is where you're going to get the optimum price. First year really important, first two years very important, and then after three years you'll start getting smaller amounts.

Q - What else do you require from the producer to help you?

Carole - Their feedback to help with the trailer and flyers. Having them give us the delivery items right away. If they do come to the market, that they work the crowds. They go to the screenings, they make sure that the sound is nice and loud, that the film is in focus. We have someone doing that too, but the filmmaker is picky about things like that. I like having them there at the screenings, maybe introducing the picture, filling in the empty seats with appropriate people. Sometimes we hire people to hand out flyers on say Third Street Promenade during the AFM, or on the Croisette during Cannes. You've got to build the heat and the filmmaker working the crowds, while we're in the booth selling and showing the trailer and flyer, can be really important. Or over cocktails at night, talking about the film, telling anecdotes. Sometimes we do small dinners with key buyers who love to hear stories of the actors and actresses, and the trials and tribulations of making films. I think the filmmaker can be really instrumental.

Q - Having a filmmaker introducing the picture helps?

Carole - I find that by having the director or the producer there to introduce it makes it special. The buyers might be less likely to leave early if the producer or director are sitting right there, because they feel maybe they should stay. I like that. But be aware that a buyer might be watching your movie and walk out after five minutes, and then he'll go and buy it! It's terrible because the other buyers might think he hates it, and sometimes a person will do it because he wants to cool down his competition. He walks out and everybody thinks it's no good, but he's actually only doing it to kill the competition. Your first impulse is to lock the doors!!!

Q - In between markets, do you send out tapes of the movies?

Carole - We're very proactive and you have to follow up and send out screeners (VHS / DVD), follow up calls, set screenings, send publicity, send what's happening in the United States, say if you've just closed with Blockbuster on a film. Quickly get that news over to video buyers all over the world. It all helps to build up your film. You can't let up after a market and come to a screeching halt and wait until the next market.

Q - Is there an even flow with the sales throughout the year?

Carole - No, you still get your kick at the markets. But, there's a lot of interim sales going on.

Q - What are pre-sales and how do they work?

Carole - Pre-sales are where you'd sell your movie to a buyer before it's even been made, and would go to the bank for a loan to provide the money to make your film until your movie was completed and delivery of the movie was made. This used to help a lot with the financing of movies. It can either be a pre-sale off a script, which I've virtually never done, or it can be a pre-sale off a picture in production. The only thing I have done pre-sales on, but it's not really a pre-sale, is if the film is already in the can and in post production, I've taken a flyer and a trailer to the markets and sold it. There's no screening, but they've seen the script, seen the trailer, seen the flyer, so they have a pretty good idea of what they're buying. I really don't like pre-sales because when the movie doesn't meet their expectations, they invariably come back and renegotiate. Whereas if it's better than their expectations, they're never going to come back and pay you more. I want to make sure that they want the picture and it's going to stick. I encourage people to see the movie before any deal is signed. People aren't pre-buying so it's hard to pre-sell. I'm amazed that filmmakers would actually go into production without all their financing in place and this is where problems can occur. Say they had to raise $1.8 million for the total budget of the film but their pre-sales were $1.5. They'd end up losing the picture to the bank because they couldn't sell that last $300k. There would then be no territory left open as their profit margin. In addition to that, what if one of the countries reneges, are you going to go over there and sue them? What if they say their economy has taken a nose dive and they only want to pay half. Who comes up with the other half? I think that's why we've stayed in business all this time as we never did gap financing with pre-sales. If we went into production we had the money in the bank to complete the film, or we didn't go into production. And pre-sales only really happen with bankable stars and directors, and as I say, we've never done it.

Q - How does a first time filmmaker find a sales agent?

Carole - You do screenings and invite the various companies to come. Or you can call them and send screeners, and go and meet with them. There's a list of buyers. Usually you'd do a couple of screenings, one in NY and one in LA. Sometimes they get a producers rep, which is becoming more prevalent, because the producers rep will also help them negotiate the contract and field all the offers. I think filmmakers should have someone like that to work with.

Q - How important is it to launch a film at the film festivals?

Carole - If you can get one of the big festivals, like Sundance, Cannes, Venice or Toronto, that's magical. If you go into Sundance, and get good notices, and then go to a market such as AFM, that's heaven, because you're capitalizing on the exposure in January right into the AFM market in February. Or if you have a picture in the festival in Cannes in either Un Certain Regards, Critic's Week, Palm D'Or or Directors Fortnight, and then you are also selling it at the same time, then it's like a trump card, it's wonderful. If you're winning awards in the smaller ones, that can be meaningful. Anything you can do to build a portfolio, especially if the picture is not an obvious genre, or doesn't have stars. If you can build it through the festivals, people take note, but it's a slower build.

Q - Is there any kind of reference book where you're able to look for the right sales agent / distributor?

Carole - The trades bumper issues for the markets always carry a list. You should look at their ads and see what kind of films they're doing. If you see those that look like they're selling the same type of genre as your movie, then they might be right for you.

Q - Do you sit down with the producers and work out a strategy for their movie? How often do you report to producers?

Carole - I usually lay out what we're going to do, show them our advertising, show them the direction we're taking in order to sell it. We make sure that they like that idea because it is important how you launch a film. I wouldn't want to do it without laying it out as I wouldn't want them to be disappointed with what we're doing. I have an open door policy. I like to treat producers how I would like to be treated, so as soon as I'm back from the market, I call them and let them know what we've sold, who we're trying to close with who is interested, here's what I didn't think worked with the campaign, here's what I think did, maybe we can tweak the back of the flyer as now we've got some good reviews etc. We're constantly figuring this out, not only for the new films, but also for the ones

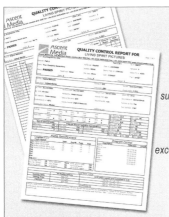

The QC Report

Quality Control is used by sales agents, distributors and broadcasters, to ensure your film reaches the rigid technical standards required for international sales. The QC report (quality control) is usually two or even three sheets long. The first page is a very detailed list of what is on the tape, it's format and technical information in excrutiating detail. It also lists problems in a summary... and it's these problems that you need to deal with. They will be detailed on the second sheet. Problems are listed, with timecodes, and they are rated in severity. 5 is considered Imperceptible, 1 is considered Very Annoying. Most frustrating is the fact that much of the QC process is subjective. With one company it could pass, yet with another it could fail. Only excellence all round will guarantee a pass. Not all companies use the same paperwork, although it's likely to be very similar to this example here.

QC Failure Reasons

Video blanking (rare)
Problem - this is where a border has been put on the master, either at the top and bottom or on the sides. If it extends too far into the picture area it will fail.
Solution - don't put any video bars on your master.

Crushed blacks (common)
Problem - the video levels drop below 0.3v and picture information. is lost.
Solution - the video signal can be boosted, but this should never have happened if you had kept an eye on the waveform monitor.

Crushed whites (common)
Problem - the video signal has peaked over 1v and so picture information in the whites is lost.
Solution - the video signal can be clamped down, but this should never have happened if you'd kept an eye on the waveform monitor.

High error rates (rare)
Problem - the DigiBeta machine used to master the tape produced too many digital errors for it to play back on other machines, although it would play back the tape itself.
Solution - either clone onto a new tape from the original machine or re-master!

Picture drop-out (medium)
Problem - distortion & errors, caused by dust or tape problems.
Solution - most commonly this will mean transferring to a new tape and cleaning up the errors, either in a paint program or by going back to the source material for the problem shots.

Audio dropout / spikes etc. (common)
Problem - there can be errors on the sound which means it may spike or pop, or disappear all together.
Solution - go to the original mix and check it. If it's OK then re-lay onto master. If not, you may need to re-mix the audio for that part.

Audio peaking (medium)
Problem - the audio peaks and potentially distorts on transmission or duplication.
Solution - re-lay the sound pulling the levels down at that point, or pass the sound through a compressor / limitor box.

Weave (rare)
Problem - the image weaves from side to side. Only a problem on film, usually S16mm, and most noticeable on titles or static shots. Rare to be a real problem.
Solution - not much can be done, short of major digital stabilization. Get your checkbook out!

Joins kick in gate (rare)
Problem - the physical edit on film jumps on screen. Caused by a cheap neg cut and most common on S16mm.
Solution - do your neg cut with a good company in the first place!

Audio too low (medium)
Problem - the audio is too low. As well as a technical problem, this may also be because you have a very dynamic mix, or it may be a creative choice.
Solution - remix , or pass the mix through a compressor limitor to make the quieter bits louder.

Too dark (subjective)
Problem - the picture is deemed consistently too dark. Even if you have made a 'dark' film, this can be a problem.
Solution - re-grade the picture brighter.

Too grainy (common for S16mm without DVNR)
Problem - the picture contains too much grain, usually a problem from Super 16mm only.
Solution - re-telecine, passing the image through a DVNR box, which will dynamically process the image and reduce the effects of grain (as well as dust and sparkle).

Dust and sparkle (common)
Problem - Image contains dust & sparkle. Only a problem for film.
Solution - passing the telecine through DVNR may help, but most likely you will need a de-spotting session where a technician manually 'paints out' the blemishes.

Hairs in gate (medium)
Problem - a hair was trapped in the camera gate when shooting. Only a problem with film.
Solution - either replace the shot OR manually paint it out. Any foreign object can cause a similar problem (such as a boom in shot etc.)

Audio hiss (common)
Problem - the audio is poorly mixed and has a lot of hiss.
Solution - possible to filter some, but you may need to re-mix properly.

from the last market. They've been building their portfolio so it's good to then do a quick sales sheet that announces all the things that have been happening since the last market, that they now have a US theatrical release, they now have this review, they now have this festival etc. I'll do an update blurb sheet that goes with the flyer to bring people up to date on the film that we sold at the last market. Just constantly keeping things alive and looking for opportunities. For instance, when DVD came in, all those pictures that we didn't have DVD releases become valuable again. Suddenly they were re-buying packages on DVD.

Q - What would you advise a new filmmaker to look for when seeking a distribution company?

Carole - I would attend the markets and go and watch the sales agents in action, see who's there, see if they take long lunches at the beach or if they're at their selling booth eating a sandwich. Get to know the person you're dealing with. Lots of times though, they might be taking lunches on the beach to sell a buyer so that's not necessarily bad, but just do as much due diligence as you can. Go to the market that's nearest you, look at them in action, listen to word of mouth and get references from other.

Q - Looking at a distribution contract, is there anything producers should really look out for?

Carole - I recommend everybody have a very knowledgeable producers rep do it, or an attorney. Sometimes producers are knowledgeable, but usually they're not. I'd prefer to negotiate with someone who knows the business because you can be fair then, and they know you're being fair, whereas someone who doesn't know the business wouldn't know when you're being fair or when you're not.

The Major Sales Markets

MIPTV
Television market for world buyers.
Cannes, France
Mid April
www.miptv.com

MIPCOM
Television market for world buyers.
Milan, Italy
Mid October

NATPE
Primarily US market, but some international.
Host city changes (New Orleans most recent)
Late January
www.napte.org

London Screenings
London, England
Designed to catch traffic for MIFED and serves primarly European and US buyers.
Late October
www.londonscreenings.com

LA Screenings
Los Angeles, USA
Cannes competitor primarily for USA based sellers.
Mid May
www.videoageinternational.com

AFM - American Film Market
Los Angeles, USA
Primary feature film US market for world buyers.
Late February
www.afma.com

MIFED
Milan, Italy
Feature Euro market for world buyers.
Early November
www.mifed.com

Cannes Film Market and Festival
Cannes, France
Primary feature film Euro market for world buyers.
Mid May
www.cannesmarket.com

Sundance Film Festival
Utah, USA
Festival, not a market but attended by buyers.
Late January
www.sundance.org

Berlin Film Festival
Berlin, Germany
Festival, not a market but attended by buyers.
Early February
www.berlinale.de

Toronto Film Festival
Toronto, Canada
Festival, not a market but attended by buyers.
Early September
www.e.bell.ca/filmfest

Q - What happens if nothing happens at any of the three markets?

Carole - You have to either come to grips with the fact that your film is not good, or that your campaign is not good. The first thing you'd do is tweak your campaign and see if you can't go in with another slant. If I see a film that's not selling, then I say, how can we breathe some life into this? I try and see if either we or whoever is handling domestic, can close a domestic deal, because that helps enormously. If it's a drama see if you can make it a family drama, if it's a thriller, see if you can make it more an erotic thriller. Come to it with a different slant. We can get buyers in the screening room, we can send out screeners, we can pitch it over the phone, we can do amazing trailers and flyers but we can't put a gun to the buyer's head - the film has to sell itself. Sometimes the film is very good, but it's just it's not what they're looking for. They can't slot it on a television time period, it doesn't fit any of their

Surviving Cannes

Oui, it is May. It is time to go to the French Riviera and see who will win the Palme D'or! Champagne, croissants, caviar! Cannes is a rollicking good time, full of decadence and luxury for those who can afford it, or those can schmooze their way into the hot spots. Even if you can't or don't, Cannes is a spectacle unto itself, with hundreds of screenings, a full fledged film market and so many stars buzzing around it will make your head spin. (see map on page590)

The first thing you need to do to prepare for going to Cannes is to get accreditation (your pass) to the Festival. There are three types of passes you can get:

Professional Pass

This is available to all practicing film industry professionals (producers, directors, writers, actors, agents, technicians, composers, film lawyers, film accountants and facility houses) and is FREE. This gives you access to the Palais and the Riviera complexes enabling you to attend all the screenings in the official program and sidebar and enabling you to enter the major hotels where companies reside. For this pass apply to Unifrance, 4 villa Bosquet, F-75007 Paris Tel: 47-53-95-80 Fax: 47-05-96-55 (you must provide evidence of industry qualifications of at least 3 films that you have worked upon - flyers, posters, business cards etc).

Market

This is only available to companies and there are registration fees attached. You receive a blue badge that will give you access to market screenings and events. For this pass apply to Marche du Film Service des Accreditations, 3, rue Amelie. F-75007. Paris. Tel: 53-59-61-41 Fax: 53-59-61-51. www.cannesmarket.com

Press

If you can get this, then you have free range of the festival. It's hard to get, unless you're company has been accredited by the Festival press office and you hold a national press card, or you have been specially commissioned by a media organization. For this pass apply to Press Office of the Festival de Cannes, 3, rue Amelie. F-75007. Paris. Tel: 33(0) 1-53-59-61-85 Fax: 33 (0) 1-53-59-61-84 email: press@festival-cannes.fr Press Relations Applications for accreditation are available from mid January each year from the accreditation department of the festival. The Deadline is generally early April. Although applying for accreditation used to be completely free, there is now an administration charge.

Getting Tickets for films

If you're a festival attendee, you can get tickets for films in and out of competition. Tickets are released each morning for films screening that day and the following morning. The ticket office is run by Unifrance and can be found in the Village International France area, located at Espace Pantiero (by the Ferry Port). Ticket office opens 10-12am and 2-4pm every day. You need to get in line from 8.30am at the latest each day to guarantee a ticket,

For films screening in other sidebars (Un Certain Regard, Directors' Fortnight, Critics Week), you need to line up outside the venue approximately an hour before screening. You need either a festival, market or press accreditation to get in. For Market Screenings, you need market or press Accreditation for entry, although sometimes you can talk your way in.

It might be in your best interest to stay outside of Cannes so that you can take a breather from the chaos. You will have to rent a car, but they are not that expensive, neither is parking in Cannes. Visit Cannes Festival Virgin Guide at www.cannesguide.com for a list of hotels and immediate online access to Hotels in or on the outskirts of Cannes, as well as bus, train and taxi phone numbers. For additional information, such as screening times, go to the festival's website at www.festival-cannes.com.

Once at the festival, go around to all the hotels and meet with as many companies as you can, to find out who does what. Your next script sale might be a few feet away. Hang out at the American Pavilion, which is a great place to meet people and to find out where all the parties will be held. If you have a film in the festival, be prepared for a media assault. It is hard work because of the time difference. Lack of sleep and repetitive question answering will wear you down. If you are advertising or marketing your film, be aware that posting flyers is illegal and they will be torn down immediately. If you decide to do this anyway, don't put anyone's name, the company name or any contact information on the flyer. Try and find alternative methods of creating a buzz, such as one filmmaking team who wrote screening times of their project in crayon on the sidewalk.

Cannes - A Festival Virgin's Guide

Buy this book! It's cheap, small and has just enough information to not scare you too much, but keep you out of trouble too. Essential for any first timer to Cannes!
ISBN: 0-9541737-1-6
By Benjamin Craig (www.cannesguide.com)
Cinemagine Media Publishing
www.cinemagine.com
Photo courtesy of www.cannesguide.com

slots, it's not a video title, because perhaps it's a little slow moving and doesn't have any stars, and it just misses being a theatrical because it doesn't have any names and it's a little bit too low budget. Sometimes you just miss and then you've got to try and put it together and sell it in packages with other films. Ultimately the filmmaker has to have confidence in their sales agent, see that they're advertising it on the first pages in the trades, that they have screenings when all the buyers are there, that they're sending out screening cassettes, and they've done a good campaign. Then if the picture doesn't sell then they have to take responsibility for it which is sometimes hard.

Q - How long would you take a film on for?

Carole - 15 to 25 years. People have done 10 to 12.

Q - Any advice for a new filmmaker?

Carole - Get a great story, develop it so it makes sense and then put the best cast you can get in it. I have seen so many films where I'm amazed that somebody has wanted to spend money on it. Develop your project so that all the questions are answered. Don't leave story ends unresolved, and make sure your story makes sense, not just to you, but to everybody. Keep it simple. You can do twists and turns but make it make sense. Don't be afraid to be mainstream and commercial. You can be independent and still be commercial, you don't have to be edgy. You CAN be corny! It doesn't matter because there's a variety of people out there.

Sales Agents Tips

1. Consider the viability of your film as a salesman - would I want this film, and if not, why not?

2. First films are usually the fruit of a long held dream. From that perspective, if you feel the desire to make it, don't worry about commercial viability. As long as the film isn't awful, and you don't spend too much money, you should get it screened somewhere. Plus you will learn sooooo much.

3. Sales agents are tough to deal with - they are professional hardcore negotiators. If they sign your film, they will more than likely want 15 years, 25% of sales, plus expenses and refuse a cash advance. The upshot is that you will probably never get paid. You MUST try to get a cash advance, and one large enough to cover your costs, but be aware that this is unlikely.

4. Keep some territories for yourself. If your sales agent messes you around, this will mean you can approach distributors in a different country and make a direct sale. You will get a lesser fee because you are not a sales agent, but it's better to get 100% of a $10k than 100% of nothing.

5. Alongside your film, you will have to supply a huge amount of delivery items (see the Delivery List elsewhere in the book). These are important and often overlooked. Without these items, no sales agent will touch the film, or they will fulfil the delivery list and charge you for doing so. Take care of it yourself. Study this list and make sure you know what each thing is, how much it will cost, and where you will get it.

6. Think about whether you want to shout about how little you shot the film for. Other films have used this tactic successfully but it could damage sales. In the eyes of a buyer, a film is worth what it cost.

7. Attending one of the big film markets like Cannes, MIFED or the AFM will broaden your outlook of sales agents and of how films are marketed and sold. GO TO THE NEXT ONE!

9. Get a performance clause in your contract, if they don't do a certain amount of sales, you can get the film back.

10. Cap expenses so that they have to get written permission to spend more than you agreed initially. Otherwise they could be free to charge you whatever they want.

11. Be tough from day one. Insist on reports as agreed, prompt payment, accurate information. Make them understand that you will not tolerate complacency. If you make yourself a nuisance, which is well within your rights, they might actually give you what you want.

12. We are moving into a global marketplace. Consider very seriously selling your film yourself. You might not have the contacts or the budget, but ANY sales made will mean cash in your pocket and not the pocket of a sales agent.

Estimated Sales Breakdown

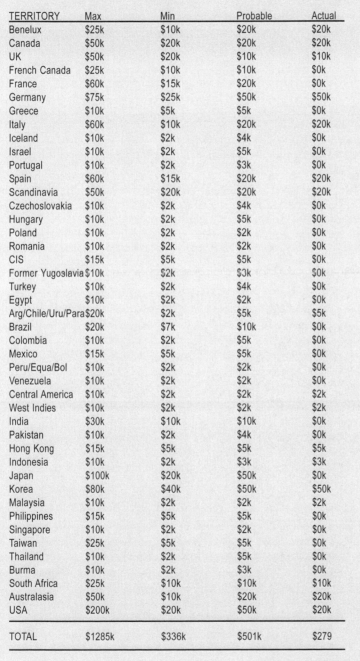

All sales are negotiated and calculated in US$

TERRITORY	Max	Min	Probable	Actual
Benelux	$25k	$10k	$20k	$20k
Canada	$50k	$20k	$20k	$20k
UK	$50k	$20k	$10k	$10k
French Canada	$25k	$10k	$10k	$0k
France	$60k	$15k	$20k	$0k
Germany	$75k	$25k	$50k	$50k
Greece	$10k	$5k	$5k	$0k
Italy	$60k	$10k	$20k	$20k
Iceland	$10k	$2k	$4k	$0k
Israel	$10k	$2k	$5k	$0k
Portugal	$10k	$2k	$3k	$0k
Spain	$60k	$15k	$20k	$20k
Scandinavia	$50k	$20k	$20k	$20k
Czechoslovakia	$10k	$2k	$4k	$0k
Hungary	$10k	$2k	$5k	$0k
Poland	$10k	$2k	$2k	$0k
Romania	$10k	$2k	$2k	$0k
CIS	$15k	$5k	$5k	$0k
Former Yugoslavia	$10k	$2k	$3k	$0k
Turkey	$10k	$2k	$4k	$0k
Egypt	$10k	$2k	$2k	$0k
Arg/Chile/Uru/Para	$20k	$2k	$5k	$5k
Brazil	$20k	$7k	$10k	$0k
Colombia	$10k	$2k	$5k	$0k
Mexico	$15k	$5k	$5k	$0k
Peru/Equa/Bol	$10k	$2k	$2k	$0k
Venezuela	$10k	$2k	$2k	$0k
Central America	$10k	$2k	$2k	$2k
West Indies	$10k	$2k	$2k	$2k
India	$30k	$10k	$10k	$0k
Pakistan	$10k	$2k	$4k	$0k
Hong Kong	$15k	$5k	$5k	$5k
Indonesia	$10k	$2k	$3k	$3k
Japan	$100k	$20k	$50k	$0k
Korea	$80k	$40k	$50k	$50k
Malaysia	$10k	$2k	$2k	$2k
Philippines	$15k	$5k	$5k	$0k
Singapore	$10k	$2k	$2k	$0k
Taiwan	$25k	$5k	$5k	$0k
Thailand	$10k	$2k	$5k	$0k
Burma	$10k	$2k	$3k	$0k
South Africa	$25k	$10k	$10k	$10k
Australasia	$50k	$10k	$20k	$20k
USA	$200k	$20k	$50k	$20k
TOTAL	$1285k	$336k	$501k	$279

It is almost impossible to give sales estimates for a film that does not exist, so we based thes figures on a genre driven film, shot on S16mm, with no real stars. It looks pretty good and is OK. It's not going to win any Oscars, that's for sure. We came to these figures after talking with sales agents and other film makers. Of course the sales agents talk it up, the film makers inject reality.

The figures quoted in the first three columns represent Max., Min. and Probable sales based on the assumption that film is actually sold in a given territory. The fourth column, Actual, is based on what sales are likely to be achieved in total (that's the film makers talking there!) Genre films also sell more consistently.

Remember, it is very possible that you may only achieve two or three sales, say the US, Germany and Korea. Treat any more sales as a bonus. Remember also, these sales are not what go to the filmmaker, the sales agent will slice their commission off the top, then their expenses. And to make matters worse, the money will come in over a five year period in dribs and drabs.

DISTRIBUTION

Holly Becker
IFC

INDEPENDENT FILM CHANNEL

Q - What is your job?

*Holly -*I am the director of production and development for IFC Productions, the division of IFC Entertainment that makes films for theatrical release.

Q - How is the IFC channel different from its competitors?

Holly - The Sundance Channel is probably our major competitor and they tend to be more issues oreintated in their programming, where IFC is more focussed on the art of filmmaking. We both show uncut, commercial free films but they have different personalities.

Q - Is IFC connected with InDiGent?

Holly - Yes. InDiGent is a division of IFC Productions and we fully finance it InDiGent stands for Independent Digital Entertainment and the division is focussed on digital filmmaking in particular. IFC Productions is budgeted to make 6 films a year, including InDiGent films. We sometimes work with first time filmmakers, but they're backed up by experienced producers. In general, we're looking for more established directors. Our division was set up to perpetuate the dream projects of more established independent filmmakers. We've had success with those projects. For example, *Boys Don't Cry* had a first time director, but Killer Films were the producers and they are experienced. *Camp* was also a first time director and the producers were Jersey/Killer. InDiGent is also director driven but those projects must be made on an extremely low budget. We're talking about movies that can be made in twenty days or less on video. We have a great casting director named Ellen Lewis. When she gets talent for films, it gives them a reputation. They tend to be actors based in New York, and they can do it when they are on a break from other projects. That's what makes it possible and attractive for them.

Q - Is $300k the cap budget for InDiGent?

Holly - It's roughly around that, give or take a little with deliveries. Certainly less than $350k.

Q - What kind of films do you develop?

Holly - We're looking for budgets beginning at $300k with $5m as our ceiling. Normally we partner on films in the $5m range. We sometimes finance documentary films and don't like to be pinned down to any genre. IFC Originals, which is the programming division for the channel, does documentary film. They've done some great ones. Their mandate is to make films about filmmaking. We tend to do original films with original voices, and films that people feel passionately about.

Q - How do you advise producers to approach you?

Holly - I meet a lot of people at IFC markets, that's a good place. Also Sundance, in a festival context. I always like it when people send e-mails introducing their project as I get a lot of cold calls which are not a good way to introduce yourself. If there's someone who is already a friend of mine and can introduce me, that's a way to get more attention. That also happens in reverse. Sometimes filmmakers say to us, *'will you look at this person's project?'* and we will.

Q - Can a first time director approach you with a script?

Holly - It's unlikely that we would get involved with a project that way. Projects are originated by producers with whom we have relationships with already or alternatively, films originate with directors who already know us. We tend to get approached by agents.

Q - If films are produced by IFC, are they also distributed by IFC?

Holly - IFC Productions has been in existence since 1997; IFC Films is the releasing division and has been around for two years. There are a few movies in the history of IFC that we have produced and also distributed. In the future we are going to be picking up fewer films and putting more energy into our tentpole productions, more like a mini studio.

Q - Do you welcome new filmmakers showing you new films for distributing on the television channel?

Holly - All the movies we produce or distribute eventually play on IFC. That's part of our deal. We get financing through Cablevision and we are in business to build a library for them. Now we sell things to HBO or other cable companies that have bigger budgets, but as our channel grows, it would make more sense that we will premiere films on our channel. We also go to all the major film markets looking to buy.

Q - Does IFC provide any services to help keep the budget down?

Holly - Yes. InDiGent has camera and editing facilities. We have Avid suites and we are developing a theater downtown into an IFC cinema that will have production capacity with editing suites and screening rooms. We have limited lighting equipment and deals with production houses all over town that have sizable reductions.

Q - What sort of films should new filmmakers make?

Holly - You just need to tell a story from the heart, in as personal and original way as possible. Be bold with your first film, as that is where your reputation will stem from. Nobody cares if there is someone out there who is able to copy an established filmmaker's style, you need to be distinctive.

Q - Would it help if the director has the script packaged with an actor on board?

Holly - Absolutely. You need to have as strong a package as you can as this is a director medium and is a risky business in terms of investment. We're as bold as anyone I know out there in terms of financing, but we still need that.

Q - What mistakes do you encounter with new filmmakers?

Holly - One mistake is to micro manage and be super controlling. Get a director with a capacity to delegate and wisely pick your peers. That was one of the first pieces of advice I ever got, and it's the best advice. Filmmaking is a collaborative medium and you will rise because of your partners. You can't do every job, although there are some established directors who are their own DP's and editors, but I personally think it's best to split those jobs. You're working in contained circumstances and people try to stretch a dollar too far, and it doesn't work. You need to match your movie to your circumstances. You can be wildly inventive even on a small scale. Go out of your way to single out people who can mentor you. See a lot of movies. You would be surprised how many filmmakers have a limited film vocabulary. They come in with ideas they think are so original, when they've actually been done fifteen times. You need humility and have realistic expectations. You shouldn't assume you will be in a position to get stars in your movie or make even a $2m film. You should network like crazy to find someone for your movie who is experienced and can bring other experienced people on.

Aaron Ryder
Newmarket

INDIE DISTRIBUTION

Q - What is Newmarket and what is your job?

Aaron - Newmarket is a film financing, production and distribution company. In the early 90's it was a financial institution which dealt with cash flow and pre-sales for foreign sales companies and relatively low risk investment in films. We fully financed our first film in 1998, a movie called *Cruel Intentions,* which worked out really well. With the success of *Memento*, we are basically an entire theatrical distribution company. We also have a video distribution company that we co-own called Silver Nitrate which is the final component and we can use to mitigate on any investment. I run the production side of things.

Q - Do you have a set number of films that you would produce each year?

Aaron - The companies that have set a quota in the past have failed miserably. We could just go out and produce three or four films a year, but Chris Ball and Will Tyrer, the two principals of Newmarket, are conservative with their appetite. I think that's the reason this company is stable and successful, because we choose films that have strong material and come with strong packages. We won't pursue anything that is mediocre. Ideally we like the idea of distributing six to ten films a year.

Q - And that started off with Real Women?

Aaron - *Real Women Have Curves* and *The Whale Rider,* a beautiful New Zealand film which we picked up in Toronto.

Q - What's the budget range on these films?

Aaron - We've done films for well under $1m. We probably shouldn't be doing anything over $12m because of the risk. If it doesn't work out, we cannot just write it off. The films that we produce and fully finance tend to be in that $1m-$8m range. Newmarket can fully finance a film and package it. We can do the bigger stuff, we just can't do it alone. *The Mexican* was something we developed and then partnered with the studio. This is a very successful method, it's called split-rates financing. We put together the material and we had Brad Pitt on board. We chose the studio we thought would handle the film best and we made ourselves a great deal. So it became a DreamWorks / Newmarket movie, even though it was completely developed through Newmarket. It was conceived as a $10m movie, but we knew that Brad Pitt wanted to do a cooler film because he'd met with us on *Memento* and took that very seriously. So when we got *The Mexican,* which was a little more accessible, he jumped on board. His agent and Julia Roberts' agent had dinner one night and then she was reading it and wanted to do it with Brad. It turned into a very, very big studio vehicle and more than $10m. It was a very successful film. It would have been a very different movie if it had a different cast.

Q - What kind of common problems do you encounter with first time filmmakers?

Aaron - Director's often think *'this is my movie'* and it's not. It's Newmarket's movie or Tristar's movie, or Fox Searchlight's. It's not your movie. You have the job to direct it for them, because they are paying for it. It's their film now and no matter how close you are to the material, at the end of the day you have to understand that any company that's financing the movie is taking a tremendous amount of financial risk for your vision. The vision is yours, but the film is not.

First time filmmakers are very proprietary which can make a difficult situation worse when the finances become stressed. They have this misunderstanding that there's a set way of doing things. There's not. The industry changes every twenty minutes. The way *Memento* came together is not the way *Donnie Darko* did. Each film is different, there is no set way and the actor that was really hot a year ago is now unemployed and unemployable. If you have the right timing, you're able to trigger the financing with the right people at the right time and you can turn out with a great film. If you put the wrong elements together and the timing's off, you can come up with a disaster.

Q - Do you find that a lot of new filmmakers expect final cuts?

Aaron - No. I've never met anybody who expects that. We're a very filmmaker friendly company, I guarantee you that. But to give final cut, it's impossible for a company like us to do. Newmarket is versatile and can work in several ways - as a purchase for hire, as a finance company, as a distributor, or we can work as all three, or a combination of.

Q - Does it help when the filmmakers come to you with a package?

Aaron - I'd rather see stuff that isn't packaged. If it's packaged, they've already gone to the studio and it's been around. I'm not vain enough to think they would come to us first but the chances are that they're looking for an alternative source of financing, because they can't find a studio that wants to do it.

Q - If a new filmmaker was going to come to you, would you be looking for experience?

Aaron - It would be difficult for us to get involved with first time filmmakers who have done very little. That might change. It's a difficult time in the industry and for now, I'd rather not take a lot of risk on a first timer.

Q - If somebody comes to you with a screenplay and you love it, what happens then?

Aaron - It's getting me to read something that's the problem. There's a certain line of defense here. Scripts that are solicited usually go out for coverage and if the coverage is good, it's read by one of the in-house story editors and if it passes that, I read it. I'm reading a significant amount a week, on top of all the production stuff that I'm working on. So at the end of the day, if I read a script and love it, I'll do everything I can to put that movie together because it's so rare that you read something you really fall in love with.

Q - What happens when people hand you scripts at panels?

Aaron - I'm probably not going to read it. Do I pay the $50-$60 to have it covered? I usually ask them *'what is it about?'* as I'm not going to burden one of the other guys who have ten other scripts on their backlog. I don't appreciate the bullshit advice to do whatever you can to get someone to read your script. It is better to find somebody reputable to read your script or somebody you know. Every time I do a panel I get given fifteen to twenty of them. That's two hours per script to read. Why should I give you two hours of my life to read your script if I don't know you? I might be saying the unpolitically correct thing, I'm just trying to be honest.

Q - If you're doing a deal, what can a producer do to make your life easier?

Aaron - Understand the process. Some producers just don't want to know. They say *'just tell me what to do and I'll do it'*, and that makes things really difficult for me because it's not that simple. You might as well do it yourself and remove them from the process. We work as a partnership, we're not going to throw in money and hope the movie's good.

Q - What about production companies who come to you from the indie world with a great script and a director you like?

Aaron - That's the best way to do business with Newmarket. There are a lot of great, young production companies out there.

Q - Do you guys go the major markets with the films?

Aaron - We are now distributors looking to buy movies. It's important for us to have relationships with foreign entities, to know what they want. It's important to see the films that are being sold. My first year in Cannes was just amazing. I remember walking down one street and saw all the film posters and thought *'My God, what do they do with all these movies?'*

Q - If you have an independent, low budget film to distribute, is it good to play at the major film festivals?

Aaron - It's difficult, but definitely worth going through because if you have a film that's in competition at Sundance, and you're looking for a buyer, you are in the best position to have your film sold. They are very helpful for filmmakers, especially for features, as you need to get an audience for your movie. There are three big festivals here in North America each year and you're competing with other filmmakers and the studios. Film festivals are inundated with so much material and I wonder how they can pick which ones go into them. If you have a finished film, the best thing you can do is get yourself a producer's rep. Have someone on board to help you, or you will have to try to do it yourself. Work out a strategy. If you are a filmmaker with no distribution, the most important thing is making sure that the right people see your film. You should hire somebody that believes in the film and is able to do that for you and take a cut of the finished product. There are a couple of really good guys out there, it's what they do for a living.

Q - Are there any particular types of films you're interested in picking up?

Aaron - I gravitate to things like *Memento* and *Donnie Darko*; smaller, more intelligent films that could be considered challenging in some respect. However, it doesn't always make good business sense to do films like that. So we're also very much involved with *American Pie*. We bought the foreign rights to that movie and it made this company a tremendous amount of money. I'm also proud of it and it's done very, very well, but it's obviously different creatively.

Q - How did Memento come about?

Aaron - I'd known Chris Nolan for years and we talked about the idea. He gave me the most innovative script I had ever seen. I had just started at Newmarket when I optioned it. We needed another producer, as I was new and Newmarket wasn't prolific as a production company. Jennifer and Suzanne Todd, Team Todd came on board. That was the first film that I made here and it worked out pretty well. You spend twenty minutes with this Chris and you know he's in command of what he wants to do with his career. He can just give a sense of his talent by simple conversation. That was made evident by watching *Following*. There are directors whose talent I've recognized, so I continue to look for things to do together. Sometimes you might not find it. It's often been the case that a young director can never really get it going. To go out and just look for talented people is difficult. Richard Kelly is a good example. *Donnie Darko* was a script that I had seen probably half a dozen times when they were looking for financing. It was always a really interesting script, but you just didn't know that the kid had the goods to pull it off as a film, because the story is ambitious and they were talking about shooting it for under $5m. I believe he is a very talented filmmaker but he didn't have anything to show for it. It would have been Newmarket taking a risk.

Q - Did you intend on distributing Memento yourselves?

Aaron – No. We showed the film to all the studios, but everyone passed. So we decided that we should distribute it ourselves and together with Bob Berney, we were all involved with the marketing of the film. It was a really interesting, fun experience because none of us had ever done it before and we had a significant amount of control - such as the poster, the ads, the website, when it would be released and how. We were all very involved, Chris, Emma (his wife and associate producer), Bob and the folks at Newmarket.

Q - Did you expect it to take off like it did?

Aaron - No. We would have been ecstatic for it to make $5m, let alone $25m.

Q – So when did you come on board with Donnie Darko?

Aaron - Pandora financed the film and handled the foreign sales themselves, with Flower Films producing. It was then in Sundance 2001, the same year that *Memento* was there. We saw the movie and we really liked it. Everybody thought *'it's a good film but it's going to be hard to market. It's too long and it's got problems'*. So we didn't buy it at Sundance, nobody did. At this time we hadn't yet released *Memento*. However our aspirations were to build our distribution company so we put an offer on it saying that we needed to talk about re-cutting the film with the director as it was well over two hours. We spent six months editing, allowing Richard to have the cut he was proud of. The cut that they showed at Sundance wasn't finished, they had rushed to get it in. We went back and did a couple of pick-up shots and cleared the music rights. So we were very involved but definitely at the later stages.

Q – How did the distribution do?

Aaron - We put it out at the wrong time as it was just after 9/11. We thought we could make an alternative Halloween movie, which is a bad idea. I think that we learned a lesson. If you have a film starring a young protagonist or young people in it, it doesn't necessarily mean that film will attract a younger audience. The core audience for *Donnie Darko* is the same as *Memento,* which is an older audience. We probably should have released the film in February. There were just too many films out at the time and people weren't going to the movies at that time. For Newmarket to release a movie, putting it in theaters and to pay for the P&A can cost us approximately $2m. We only see about 38% of the money that the film makes at the box office and that comes back to us over a long period of time. So we lost money on *Donnie Darko*, but that's the financial risk that we take. So for a filmmaker to say *'we've got a shitty deal because of the pecking order,'* how much are you going to pay us? We'll gladly share that risk with you, but if you want to put your own money in the P&A, we'll give you a much better deal. We can do that, we have done that. You can share in the upside but you also have to share in the risk. When it works, it's like *Memento* and *My Big Fat Greek Wedding*, everybody wins. And if it's only mediocre, everybody wins at the end of the day. If it just fails, the distributor loses. Everybody loved that movie and they think *'wow, he's such a good filmmaker, but boy did they fuck up the distribution of that movie'*.

Q - How many theaters did it play at?

Aaron - It opened on fifty-eight screens, which again was probably a mistake. We should have opened it on fewer screens. It took $45k at the end of the day. On video it hasn't been huge. Video directly ties to performance at the box office. So *My Big Fat Greek Wedding* should be massive on video whereas *Donnie Darko* will be mediocre. It'll do better than a lot of other films that made that little at the box office because its got Drew Barrymore and Patrick Swayze on the cover. That makes it a little easier but it's not a dramatic amount of money. People look at it and don't know quite what it is, but I do believe that it's a film that will build as the years go by.

Q - Can any filmmaker come to you - is there a process?

Aaron - We are a financing institute and considered a buyer, so we receive a tremendous amount of material. There are certain days where we'll see fifteen scripts. With so much material out there, it's difficult to process it all so I tend to solicit certain directors and I don't just read scripts cold, I have to have a conversation with somebody about them first. I have accepted things from filmmakers and writers. I tend to find most material through producers and my relationships with writers as opposed to agents.

Q - Is Newmarket mainly domestic distribution?

Aaron – Yes, we don't distribute overseas. What we've traditionally done is finance the film against foreign pre-sales. There's a company called Summit that is arguably the best foreign sales company out there. They'd say *'ok, with a movie like this at $5m, with that kind of cast, we can cover you for XX foreign'*. And then we make an assessment of the risk against domestic. So we would then sell it piecemeal to the various distributors with Summit doing the sales overseas.

Q – How does the finance structure generally work?

Aaron - Newmarket would dictate what the budget of the film would be. Summit would say *'we can cover you for $8m out of foreign sales'*. So Newmarket would say *'ok, let's make the movie for $10m taking a $2m risk'*. So Chris Nolan made *Memento* for $10m. Meanwhile, Summit are doing the foreign, getting as much as they can on a piecemeal, territory by territory basis, to get as close to that $10m as they can.

Q – Does the filmmaker ever see any monies from the foreign sales?

Aaron - Very few filmmakers would see any of that foreign money. They usually have a net percentage of the proceeds. I can think of very few filmmakers that would be able to take a gross position out of foreign.

Q – What about after once budget monies have been recouped?

Aaron – Remember, the foreign side is sold on a pre-sale basis so Japan will buy *Memento* for $500k. It's theirs. They've bought that territory. It could be months after the film is released that that money comes back into Newmarket. The filmmakers deal is with Newmarket, not the foreign distributors, so they will see percentages based on the proceeds Newmarket receives.

Q – Can you put 'bumps' into the contract?

Aaron – Yes, but usually only for domestic as the bumps are based on US box office. You can't really base it on foreign sales because you'll spend years of your life trying to chase foreign money.

Q – How long, generally, are the foreign licenses?

Aaron - Fifteen years is usually a good deal and can be up to 30 years. So the Japanese distributors buying *Memento* for X amount of dollars for X amount of time will exploit all those markets in Japan. If there's any excess money, it goes back to the pot at Newmarket.

Q - Can you give me a rough idea of an approximate deal that a director would receive as a percentage from say, a $5m movie?

Aaron - Chances are if you're making a $5m movie, you're doing it with a younger, less established director and the company that's paying $5m for this movie is taking a financial risk. They are going to want a significant reward, and at times, all of the reward. For a director its usually 5%.

Q - What budget should a new filmmaker aim for?

Aaron - Make a film for under $3m. You're going to have to convince somebody you know what you're doing and you've got to be able to talk through how you're going to do it. The way people are able to mitigate that, is by attaching cast, which is hard because you are a first time filmmaker. Newmarket has had success with first time filmmakers.

Q - Do you find there are more independent's rising up at this time?

Aaron - Quite the opposite. We are in a drought as far as independent films are concerned. It's as if a bomb went off and nobody heard it, but the effects are going to be felt for some time. Everybody's running around trying to make movies but they're not doing it without taking a significant amount of risk.

Q - And that's because of the financial market?

Aaron - It's a really tough time. The foreign distributors are really hurting. The ancillary markets are really hurting and they have nothing to mitigate their down side with. It seems to be the US smaller independent market that is surviving, which is why we've begun this distribution company.

Filmmaking is so accessible now. All it takes is a couple of friends and a camera and we have successful films that are shot on digital. There are so many new digital films - what's going to happen with them? Are they ever going to find an audience? I'm not a huge fan of digital films. I heard more negative things about the way *Tadpole* looked than I heard positive about the movie itself, and that's a good movie.

At the end of the day, if you can only shoot your movie on video, then shoot your movie on digital. The story is the most important thing. I've seen 400 movies this year and a lot of them are on digital and some of them are spectacular. But it's so satisfying to shoot film.

Q - If somebody came to you with a short that you loved, would you then be willing to look at their feature screenplay that they're hoping to do for $5m?

Aaron - Absolutely. There's a director in New York called David Von Ancken, who directed a short film called *Bullet in the Brain*. It's my favorite short film in years. I'm desperately trying to find a feature to do with this guy. Short films are such a tough medium because there are so many and how do you stand out? David's film stood out to me.

Q - What advice would you offer new filmmakers?

Aaron - I don't think enough filmmakers ask *'who's going to go and see this movie?'* There are some films where the scripts are good but I have no clue who would go and see those films. If the filmmakers can answer that when they're conceiving and working towards the idea, they'll be able to sell the film to the production company or the financiers. These people have to sell it to the studios or to the marketing people and at the end of that day, how are you going to get butts in the seats? So you're either doing it with a reputable filmmaker or you're able to make a film that's easily marketed. The other choice is to make a really good film and it's a creative endeavor every time out of the gate, but that doesn't always happen.

In pre-production, I ask filmmakers to do me a favor. On the way home, go to Blockbuster, go to the new release section and look at all the new movies. Write down the name of every movie you've never heard of. Tell me who's in it. They're shocked every time they do this. *'I had no idea XXXXX was in this movie. Why didn't it come out?'* No filmmaker signs up anticipating seeing their movie premiering on the third shelf of a video store. It's how you rise above that.

Bob Berney
Marketing

MARKETING

Q - What is your job?

Bob - I am president of an independent distribution company called Newmarket Films. I'm involved in the acquisition of projects. We normally buy completed films so we work all the film festivals, sales agents and producers' reps. We budget the release and do the strategic planning which includes publicity, marketing, sales, distribution, collections and manage the ancillary rights as well.

Q - What do you look for when you are viewing films for acquisition and distribution?

Bob - We look for quality films that are a mixture of genre and something a bit out of the ordinary, we don't like formulaic studio films. We try to find a niche group to market the film to. *Memento* was in many ways a genre thriller, but it had interesting elements underneath its commercial surface.

Q - What type of movie is easiest to get into theatres?

Bob - Nothing is easy. It can be any number of things. In the indie world, it might be director driven, an actor or a critical reaction.

Q - Is word of mouth the best source of advertising for low budget films?

Bob - Marketing independent films is risky and very expensive as you have to compete with everything else, so doing it on the cheap is not viable. The playing field is too high. That does limit the number of films acquired and released.

Q - Are there any pre marketing ploys to finance movies?

Bob - If you have the elements lined up, like a name or director who's done a good promo reel, it can help close a deal.

Q - It's become difficult to get films financed in the last couple of years?

Bob - Yeah. With all the consolidation and closing of European TV stations, it's become really tough to pre-sell. It's daunting for a first time filmmaker to go that route. Even if the sales agent likes the script, it's hard for them to put it together.

Q - How early on should you start considering marketing a movie?

Bob - The minimum time is four months, and the real time is seven months, less than four is pushing it.

Q - What should a new filmmaker know about marketing their film?

Bob - The platform release becomes risky and word of mouth is a fragile thing. There has to be a comprehensive plan because you can't wait to see what happens when you see the initial openings of the film. The Friday night 'look at the numbers' mentality of the studios has filtered down to the independent world's theatres and distributors, so you are still expected to do well immediately. Most films are platform, which means opening in New York and LA, then expanding. You have to do so much planning for the other markets in case the film does take off, although that becomes risky, as you need to spend money on the publicity for all of them too. Part of it is to determine if you can reach the audience within your overall budget. If it's a conventional or studio film that has qualities that rely on television advertising, you then have to question the marketing plan or acquisition of the film. Should you have intense word of mouth screenings or is it something that is purely review driven? You have to analyze each film. You get a bit more of a break in independent distribution. The theater owners are sensitive to the plea that it's going to take a while and word of mouth has to build. They'll give you some slack, but you have to demonstrate that fairly quickly. Their leash is tight. You have to be pretty confident and believe in your film or it's a pretty quick exercise in failure.

Q - What is required from the producer for the marketing campaign?

Bob - The best thing is a brilliant set of production stills, other than that, good notes or ideas. If the film has come from a novel, you have to access the elements that will help you make the film.

Q - How many stills would you suggest they deliver?

Bob - A lot of the contracts will ask for a couple of hundred, but it's usually the quality that matters. New filmmakers should get sample delivery schedules from the studios, because they are extremely scary. If you suddenly sell your film, you'll have to spend a lot of money to complete the delivery list to make the sale complete, so it's really worth building the requirements into your production. Even independents like us have to sub license to home entertainment companies and their restrictions are going to be very studio orientated. We have to have to live up to those expectations, so then our schedules become strict.

Q - Should they provide you with trailers as well?

Bob - It's better to work together to make something. If they have a particular way to do it inexpensively, it's helpful.

Q - Would you tell the filmmaker what your distribution plans are?

Bob - Yeah. I find that most filmmakers are interested in that, dependent on their time and what they are doing. Usually I find the organic way to market the film is within its creation and why they've made it. If you have filmmakers that have the communication skills to help you do that, it's fantastic.

Q - Do you work out the poster with them as well?

Bob - I usually do. It's dependent on the project, the level of interest and ability of the filmmaker. Some are really good and some only want something that isn't possible. For the most part, I try to include the filmmakers in every level of the process.

Q - What kind of deal could a new filmmaker expect with a distributor?

Bob - It could be any deal. It's usually a small advance and maybe commitment to release the film theatrically, either in a number of cities or on a minimum number of prints. Usually it's weighted towards the commitment to release the film. They have the costs of guarantee. In most of these cases, the release commitment and marketing campaign are much more than the movie campaign. To do it right, that money is the first money that comes back to the distributor and if it doesn't work, it will be recouped on the other rights. So the filmmaker will have the film released, but will never see money. You have to go into that together.

Q - Should a filmmaker put a minimum commitment on the contract with the distributor?

Bob - If possible, yes. I don't know if it's the filmmaker of the agent or the lawyer, but often too much of a guarantee is asked for, which is going to limit the distributor's willingness to put the money into marketing. You want to try and get a release commitment, but you have to decide if theatrical is what you want as many movies are forced into a theatrical market that could have been successful in cable.

Q - Is there a standard agreement with the percentage split?

Bob - No, it's all over the place. It can be scaled on different levels of gross and be wildly varying in terms of fee. The distributor may split the remainder in different ways. If filmmakers bring their own marketing money, sometimes the fee will be lower. All the sub licensers can have fee structures that may be similar to the overall one, but they may not be. If there are overages, there can be different fees with different sub licensers, like home video or Pay TV.

Q - Is the festival route a good way to go to gather publicity?

Bob - I think the festival route is a good route to take. It exposes the film to critics, distributors and audience reactions.

Q - How much does it cost to advertise with TV and radio spots?

Bob - The costs vary, from $20 up to $0.5m! If you're talking about regional cable deals for independent films, they can be $10k for the first week.

Q - Is radio a lot cheaper?

Bob - No. Radio in the big markets is very expensive, although we do a lot of sponsorship radio, where programs are 'brought to you by so and so'. In LA, the big radio stations are very expensive and expect huge buys to do promotions. Anywhere you go with independent films, you are faced with different expensive options, but you have to narrow it down to the core audience, and if you reach that core, you can then expand and broaden out. You can do this after the first week, if you are kept on and then you might change the look of the television or newspaper ads.

Q - How much should you take on your opening weekend to guarantee you stay on another week?

Bob - Every theatre has a different level. Generally, if you're opening in a few theatres, you need something in the $10k plus weekend numbers for New York and LA openings to make a difference. If it's below that, you're in trouble.

Q - Is there a bad time to open?

Bob - The only time I get nervous about is between Thanksgiving and the end of the year. The end of the year is tough, unless you believe you have an Oscar performance in your independent film. You're going up against very expensive competition.

Q - Why is it that some movies are marketed in a way that is misleading?

Bob - You can secure a campaign a certain way to get people in, but ultimately it can backfire.

Q - Did you use any special tactics to market My Big Fat Greek Wedding?

Bob - We did a lot of advance screenings and community support, but we did have famous producers and were able to make entrées to television. Once the film got word of mouth, it became a television publicity campaign. I anticipated it would do really well, but I don't think anyone thought it would make $200m.

Q - Are there any traps that indie filmmakers should be aware of?

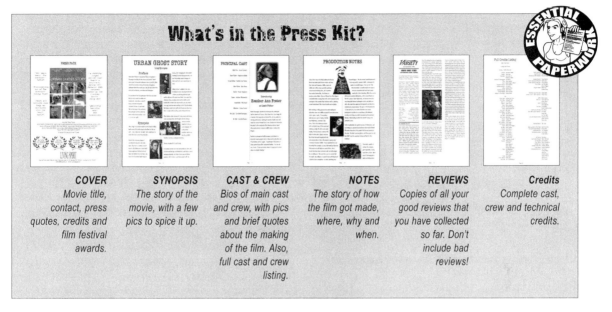

What's in the Press Kit?

COVER	SYNOPSIS	CAST & CREW	NOTES	REVIEWS	Credits
Movie title, contact, press quotes, credits and film festival awards.	The story of the movie, with a few pics to spice it up.	Bios of main cast and crew, with pics and brief quotes about the making of the film. Also, full cast and crew listing.	The story of how the film got made, where, why and when.	Copies of all your good reviews that you have collected so far. Don't include bad reviews!	Complete cast, crew and technical credits.

Bob - Generally, it's been pretty bad if you do a romantic comedy without a star. It's a tough genre.

Q - What is four walling?

Bob - It's renting the theatres directly, using your own money for the ads and managing the release. It's hard to do because even if you have enough money to get it open, you rarely have any plans beyond that. Usually a distributor will come in if it goes through the roof, but that's rare. It might be a way to get attention for a small, DVD deal, as you'd get your money back, so it's a way if you have no other options. Four walling is more effective for documentaries and short films to fulfill their Academy qualifications.

Q - How much would you have to put in to make it work?

Bob - If you four walled a theatre in downtown New York, you'd have to spend at least $10k to make any impact, plus you'd have to hire your own publicist and make your own poster. You budget would suddenly be $100k.

Q - Have you ever passed on a film that went on to become huge?

Bob - Probably many. It may not be that you passed on it, but the timing may not have been right or you couldn't afford it. Everyone loved the Michael Moore film but no one wanted to buy it. There are always films that you try to get and they fail and you're glad you didn't get them. You make your best judgement and it can go either way.

Q - What are the most common mistakes you have come across by new filmmakers?

Bob - You do need help. If you're a filmmaker, you should get a lawyer and producers rep. The big mistake is to not have any counsel and taking a big slot in a festival without thinking about it. You have to think it through and moving too quickly is a mistake.

Q - What advice would you give new filmmakers?

Bob - Make a film you're passionate about. You should be smart about the distribution world, but you can't formalize it to fit a schedule or a trend. Make the film based on your inner artistic sense and desire and balance that with your business side.

Laura Kim
'Warner Brothers Independent

Q - What is your job as a publicist?

Laura - It's about generating the right exposure for the right purpose, such as, by helping a film at a festival raise it's profile for a better chance of a theatrical sale, or if a film is about to open, generating awareness timed to the release of the film. If it's for a film company, it's to establish a profile for them to help them conduct their business.

Q - How early would you like to be involved on a film?

Laura - With a release, I'd say six months would be perfect as it would give me the time to really build a campaign. Four months would be more realistic for most independent films.

Q - Do you help with creating the image for a film?

Laura - Yes, that's important - it impacts what the press and the public think, and hopefully convinces the public to see the movie.

Q - How do publicists choose which films they'll represent at festivals?

Laura - You should know that publicists watch a lot of the films that have a good indication of being chosen by festivals, often before the selections have been made. They want to work on movies they like, so they try not to commit to anything until they get a chance to see as much as they can that's out there. Start early. The truth is, you may well have found the perfect rep (publicist, producers rep etc.) but most of them are making their own selections too.

Q - Is the festival fee for a publicist a flat fee?

Laura - It varies. Try to set up a flat fee including expenses to simplify your life and avoid suprises.

Q - What is the value of a publicist?

Laura - A lot of low-budget independent films which don't have 'name' cast or profile, don't need to spend much money on publicity. They should just concentrate on making a good movie. Find a great friend who's a good writer who'll do it for a small fee. Make sure that the photography and the broadcast footage is good and that you have interviews with the cast and crew. To hire a full-time publicist may cost you $1.5k a week, so when budgets are tight, set a fee and only have them on set when you need to.

Q - What is the main advantage of hiring a unit publicist?

Laura - The filmmakers can be freed from considering marketplace issues so they can concentrate on making a better movie.

Q - Would you sit down with the new filmmaker and work out a strategy?

Laura - Yes. Every film is different as is every relationship. It's a different kind of language depending on whether you're describing how you see it unfolding, or what the plan will be, or what the trouble will be and where you can fix it. I talk about their film, what they hope to do with it, what seems likely for them, what they aspire to and what their realities are.

Q - What materials would you need from the production?

Laura - I would want a full cast, crew and contact lists. I would like any footage that was shot during the production that could be used for broadcast material later (with transcripts). I like to know what the production is legally bound to by their actors in terms of the photo approvals. I need to make sure that my interpretation of the film is the same as, or aligned with, the filmmakers.

Q - How many photographs would you suggest were taken?

Laura - As many as possible. I think that around 200-300 useable color slides or digital images is good. The US distributor may want access to all of them so they have plenty to select from (including shots of the director, producer and writer). The photos should be compelling and really capture the film. If your cast have the right to approve images, you'll want to shoot twice as many. When it comes time to release your film, and a photo editor is looking for art, if you don't have it, you may lose that slot or page. When people ask for exclusives, they will want an image that is selected for them.

Q - Is it a good idea to set up the actors in a studio and take shots?

Laura - It can be. If the film already has a distributor involved, this request will come from their marketing department. They're called special photo shoots and are either done in the studio or on the set somewhere. They set up a place to make it as convenient as possible for the actors, with hair and make-up there. During production is ideal as they are already there. This can be very expensive and difficult to do later.

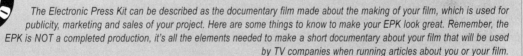

The EPK

The Electronic Press Kit can be described as the documentary film made about the making of your film, which is used for publicity, marketing and sales of your project. Here are some things to know to make your EPK look great. Remember, the EPK is NOT a completed production, it's all the elements needed to make a short documentary about your film that will be used by TV companies when running articles about you or your film.

1. Shoot on DV or BetaSP. The EPK doesn't have to look like your film, but it should look like a network news interview.

2. Find a quiet room with a nice background to shooting interviews. You can use simple three point lighting schemes and a lavaliere microphone. Interview the director, writer, producers and all principal actors. If you have a cameo by a major star, make sure to schedule five minutes to get a sound bite from them. Ask why the filmmakers and actors wanted to do the film and what it was like working with each other. If there is a theme or topic germane to the film (such as firefighters) ask everyone his or her opinion about it.

3. Make sure your interviewees repeat the question in their answer for easier editing. (What is your role in BATMAN? My role is BATMAN is...) Ask interviewees not to refer to 'the movie...' in their answers, but to refer to it by name.

4. Shoot material of the crew setting up shots, the director in action, the actors working in a scene, and writers and producers doing their thing. This will spice up the EPK. Roughly edit these shots but leave them loose.

5. Exciting action sequences or complicated stunts look really cool in EPKs.

6. Include three cut scenes that represent the film as a whole. These should be completed scenes with full soundtrack. Also include the trailer.

7. You could also include a CD of the score to use, as long as you have the rights from the composer.

8. Shoot everything 4:3 so that there are no problems when broadcasting the EPK. This of course does not include any film clips that you use which will be in widescreen format.

DISTRIBUTION

Setting Up Press Screenings

1. Give yourself enough lead time. Magazines, television and newspapers can start thinking about stories several months before they appear in their publications or on air. Remember, you only get one story out of them, so make it count.

2. Create a press release. This is usually a one sheet, 2-3 paragraph statement that tells the press the basic details of your film, when the film will screen along with an RSVP contact number. Contact the publications that you want to show up and ask for the fax number or e-mail to their news desk.

3. Book a theater. Make sure they can screen whatever format you are going to show your film on and make certain there are enough seats for the amount of people you invited. Not everyone will come, so you may consider over booking, but it is a risk.

4. Have press packs made for the screening. This should contain all the basic information that the press needs to write a review about your film. This consists of production information, a synopsis, bios of the key cast and crew and still photographs of the director and key cast members. You can include statements from other people who may have been crucial for the inspiration for the film, such as the author of a book on which it was based.

5. Have a hospitality area set up. The press love free food and alcohol, and putting them in a good mood before they see your film can't hurt.

6. While not necessary, having the director, producer, writer or actors around for a Q&A session can be beneficial.

7. Try to get a few 'ringers' in the audience (friends, relatives) who will laugh or clap to create a positive atmosphere.

8. Don't worry too much about getting your film shown on the big screen for journalists. Many won't make it, so have DVD's available (don't offer VHS now as DVD is far better). Some important film critics may want to screen the film alone.

9. Find the hook that sets your film apart from others, and then use it to catch the imagination of the press.

10. Follow up your press screenings with phone calls to the journalists to thank them for watching the film, ask if they have any further questions, and to see if they enjoyed the film. Don't push or attempt to coerce them.

11. Remember that your low budget film is being judged the same as Hollywood blockbusters. Expect criticism.

12. Remember that there is no bad publicity. Invite as many publications as you can for the smaller organizations are just as passionate about film as the larger ones, and they may give you more favorable notices as they will empathize with the David and Goliath angle.

Q - During production, if a filmmaker has a budget of roughly $1m, what percentage should they spend on the publicity?

Laura - It could cost $20k. If you also hire a crew to shoot the EPK, the costs will vary depending on how many days you shoot.

Q - How important are EPK's?

Laura - They're pretty important if you care about broadcast coverage during your theatrical release. An EPK is a set of clips, footage of the director interacting with the actors and other assorted behind the scenes footage. You should also include interviews with the main cast members and key crew. You will need to supply broadcast clips for any festival you go to and most broadcast outlets won't even cover your film if you don't have supplemental information they can air with the package.

Q - What is a press kit and what would it contain?

Laura - The press pack is all the basic information that the press need to be able to write about and understand your film. It usually contains information about the production, a synopsis and any sort of biographical information. It can include statements by the director, and other people who may have been crucial for the inspiration for the film, or the author of the novel on which the film was based. I recommend a directors statement because not everybody's going to sit down and talk to the director. It's your way of responding to issues that might come up, but it's basically positioning a film before, during or after a journalist sees it, so they can understand what the filmmaker was trying to do.

Q - Do a lot of journalists just take information from the press kit?

Laura - Yes, they will pull what they want from it. That's the reason you interview people for the press kit, so that if journalists don't have time to interview the talent themselves, they can write or edit from those materials.

Q - Can you ever have too much publicity at the wrong time?

Laura - Yes. Managing expectations has become a huge component of what we do. I think that for any film that's theatrically available at a festival, too much press can be damaging. Remember, newspapers are unlikely to write about your film more than once. The market place is competitive as there are twelve to fifteen movies opening every weekend, and if you get written about too early on, you may not get another story for your release.

Q - How much does it cost to have a publicist at a festival?

Laura - It depends on the festival. $4k for one festival may be fine but $4k for Sundance may not cut it. The filmmaker has to cover a portion of the publicist's travel, hotel, faxing, FedExing and pay their fee on top of that. There are also materials to produce, screening venues etc. It's expensive to go to most of the important film festivals. Festivals like the LA Film Festival are great for sales purposes because the buyers live there, and you can always find a sofa to crash on.

Q - Have you gotten more mileage out of a low budget film than you thought possible?

Laura - *Real Women Have Curves*, *Chuck & Buck* and *In the Bedroom* are all good examples. *In the Bedroom* was a beautiful, challenging movie that was successfully launched out of Sundance. It was one of the best-executed, strategic campaigns, because that film is a difficult movie.

Q - Is that because of the quality of the film?

Laura - It has to do with the passion of Miramax, the filmmakers, from all of us. It certainly helps if we are all in love with the movie.

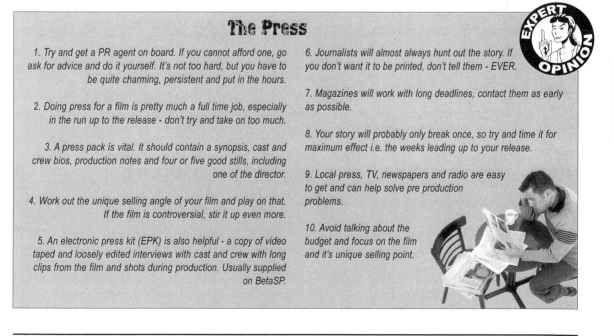

The Press

1. Try and get a PR agent on board. If you cannot afford one, go ask for advice and do it yourself. It's not too hard, but you have to be quite charming, persistent and put in the hours.

2. Doing press for a film is pretty much a full time job, especially in the run up to the release - don't try and take on too much.

3. A press pack is vital. It should contain a synopsis, cast and crew bios, production notes and four or five good stills, including one of the director.

4. Work out the unique selling angle of your film and play on that. If the film is controversial, stir it up even more.

5. An electronic press kit (EPK) is also helpful - a copy of video taped and loosely edited interviews with cast and crew with long clips from the film and shots during production. Usually supplied on BetaSP.

6. Journalists will almost always hunt out the story. If you don't want it to be printed, don't tell them - EVER.

7. Magazines will work with long deadlines, contact them as early as possible.

8. Your story will probably only break once, so try and time it for maximum effect i.e. the weeks leading up to your release.

9. Local press, TV, newspapers and radio are easy to get and can help solve pre production problems.

10. Avoid talking about the budget and focus on the film and it's unique selling point.

EXPERT OPINION

Q - Was Chuck & Buck *a difficult film to market?*

Laura - Yes. The problem was it's dark subject matter, shot digitally, with no stars. If it was misunderstood, it had some potentially dangerous or challenging issues. It's a film about arrested development rather than sexuality, but it's funny, human, warm and heartbreaking.

Q - What role does buzz play?

Laura - If a film has not screened to any buyers, they're anxious to see that, which creates one level of buzz. If you have pedigree - a prominent producer or name cast involved – then you lift that buzz factor even more. I wouldn't recommend trying to get the buzz or publicity until you're finished with post. There's no film to see. Publicity during that period, when you don't have an actual festival date, is wasted. You're one of hundreds of thousands of films that are at that stage. If you are a low budget film, that money should be spent on post. There are listing services like *Film Finders* that all the buyers subscribe to so they know what's out there and they can contact you directly. At festivals, buzz, I find, can be a dangerous thing.

Q - What about gimmicks?

Laura - They have to really suit the film.

Q - Is it a good idea to put a listing of your film in Variety and Hollywood Reporter?

Laura - If you want the industry, press and others to know about your film, yes.

Q - What tips could you give an independent filmmaker that could maximize the impact and minimize the damage during the festival process?

Laura - Do not send tapes out and do not make the film available until you have gotten sound advice from someone who understand festivals and the sales process. Distributors are going to hear about your movie through some sort of listing and they'll call you. Know it's their job to call everybody so don't be flattered. They're going to want to see the film first. Wait and get a couple of people that you trust to give you a real, honest opinion about whether your film is ready to be seen by these distributors. Don't give away your world premiere to a festival that's not going to further your objective. If you're looking to get bought, submit to the festivals that buyers attend. Be strategic.

Q - What common mistakes have you come across?

Laura - I think a big mistake is when filmmakers spend too much time and energy thinking about all of the publicity, buzz, and all of the machinery, before they've even finished the film. The truth is that the best thing you can do for your film and future is to make

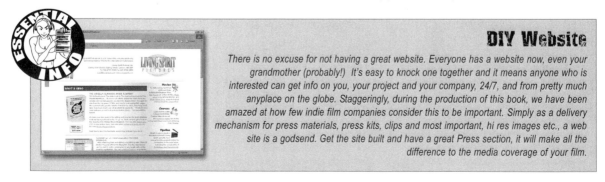

DIY Website

There is no excuse for not having a great website. Everyone has a website now, even your grandmother (probably!) It's easy to knock one together and it means anyone who is interested can get info on you, your project and your company, 24/7, and from pretty much anyplace on the globe. Staggeringly, during the production of this book, we have been amazed at how few indie film companies consider this to be important. Simply as a delivery mechanism for press materials, press kits, clips and most important, hi res images etc., a web site is a godsend. Get the site built and have a great Press section, it will make all the difference to the media coverage of your film.

Q - How many screening rooms do you have and what are the rates?

Chris - We have three THX certified theatres that are Dolby Digital and can handle almost any sound format. One seats 70, another one seats 118 and we have a small executive room. We rent them out at a per hour cost and the rates change. During the day (9am - 6pm) it's $150 an hour. In the evenings after 6pm its a flat fee of $900 (for the evening). We do 50/50 film (35mm) and digital video. Most people rent out the theaters during the week but we do let them out at weekends occasionally. As we have to bring in staff for those days, it's more expensive at around $1400 for the weekend. If you're looking to do an evening screening the lead time is usually three weeks to a month. If you're looking for daytime, probably a couple of days notice is enough.

Chris Wilson
Culver Studios

Q - What time is best to get distributors to see movies?

Chris - Evenings, between 7pm and 8pm. Sometimes we do a 4pm start too. But in the evening, filmmakers can get a crowd and it's better then. Remember to allow at least 15 mins extra for people to arrive and get through security at the gates. We can make arrangements to provide food and drinks or producer can bring it in. We don't charge for the space itself as that's part of the theater rental. The only other thing is clean up charge, but we're pretty flexible.

Q - Do you encounter problems with prints that have been on the festival circuit?

Chris - Yes. Most of the films that make those circuits are not taken care of, so sometimes when we get films back, we have to put them back together. They never come back as good as they went out. There's not much you can do about it as the people who handle your film often aren't trained to take care of the print. We've had films come back to us that are falling apart.

Q - Can people negotiate deals with you?

Chris - Depending on the nature of the project, I can give a lower rate. It depends on how much time you will take and what kind of work you are doing.

Q - What are the common technical mistakes you encounter?

Chris - We have a wide variety of equipment due to the nature of the work. The most common mistake is people assuming you have what they need. Due to the evolving nature of technology, not everybody has everything. Security at the theaters has been tightened and most theaters are asking for peoples names in advance which is difficult, but you should be prepared to deal with these issues.

sure it's the best film it can be. Make sure your script is really ready. Focus on making the film, getting the performances you need, and telling the story you want to tell. Do what you need to do publicity-wise during production - bare minimum, get good photography, and if you can, some on set footage and interviews for your EPK. Almost all independent films are a challenge to market and publicize, but if it's received really well by audiences and the press, that's half your battle. And if the distributors really love your film, they will find a way to get it out there.

Q - Any basic advice for new filmmakers?

Laura - Now, more than ever, it's important to make the movie you want to make. Don't worry about your responsibility to any communities or investors. When you try to please too many people, it's disastrous for the film. Only be responsible to yourself, really telling the story you want to tell.

Lesli Lawrence
Pulse Advertising

THE IMAGE

Q - What is your job?

Lesli - Pulse Advertising's primary focus is the key art for motion pictures and home entertainment. I am the Senior VP and I work with the clients and our creative director. Filmmakers can come to us for a visual print image for the film, to stimulate the imagination and desire of people to see the film.

Q - Do most people come to you before they start production?

Lesli - Our primary clients are the marketing executives in studios. The studios can start the creative process at any time. When a project is green lit or when it is already in production or when the film is wrapped. Each studio works differently and has different timetables. We are grateful when we are brought in early on a project so that we can be part of the strategy and also have the time to immerse ourselves in the material. It also gives us the opportunity to shoot things in production that may be unavailable afterwards. We also do work with independent producers and since this handbook is focused on that area of filmmaking I will address it. Independent producers come to us at all stages. We have created the key art for films which are only in the script stage so that the marketing materials can help sell the film. We have created key art for films for film festivals. Of course as I said before, the earlier we are brought in the better.

Q - Is it important to latch onto a single concept when you are designing the poster?

Lesli - Any idea that is reinforced over and over again helps give a film its identity. If you keep changing that concept, it can be detrimental to people remembering or understanding the film.

Q - Would you sit down and discuss the image of the film with the producers?

Lesli - We get a script before it's been cast; sometimes when it's still in rewrites. We'll read it and then we'll have a discussion with the studio, producers or director about their ideas. We'll tell them what we think is the most saleable angle, and work out what their icon is, or if there are stars that are going to push the movie - we'll come up with a direction for it to go. We come up with thumbnail sketches and concepts, copy ideas and title designs. We might say the title is going to hurt rather than help the film and so we'll come up with alternate titles. The interpretation from the script to the finished film can be totally different. We have been surprised in the past when all along we thought it was a one genre and when we saw the film it was something else.

Q - How do you design the poster?

Lesli - We do research based on whether it's a period piece, science fiction or any other genre. If we can sell one idea we proceed with the design and photography. Then we design comprehensives, which are shown to the studios, which run tests by showing them to focus groups and saying *'what do you think this movie is about?'* I don't believe in testing because if print does what it's supposed to do, it's memorable. From there, the studio will approve it and we'll do the finished art, created at a high resolution so that it can be printed for billboards, bus-sides and outdoor / indoor theatre banners. That one image will reinforce the identity of the movie. We've done things that take a week and others that take a year. It depends on the film and how much time there is. It's a creative process so the more time you can give an agency the better, although sometimes people work really well under pressure.

Q - What do you require from the producer?

Lesli - If the film has started production it really helps us if we can look at the unit photography, because that gives an idea of its texture. Otherwise we have to guess the feel of the film. You can also find shots in the photography that you can use in the poster. There are many great posters that were just pulled from a shot.

Q - Is the service you offer as important as the lawyer, DP etc?

Lesli - I believe that what we do is as important as other elements of the film process. If you can't market a film properly and do it justice it will never be seen. A lot of good films that went unnoticed because the advertising was counter productive or invisible.

Q - What causes problems on posters?

Lesli - There are tremendous restrictions and they are different internationally than they are here. It's fun to work on international advertising because there are fewer restrictions as far as sex and showing body parts. The contracts have certain written stipulations. For example, there are equal likeness clauses that make designing a challenge. The other things is that key art starts as a vertical format and then is adapted into a horizontal format such as billboards. Then there's the billing block which over the years has become a design challenge in itself. Just look at old billing blocks and what they've become today. All of the guilds have approval over the billing block and there is a tremendous amount of approvals the studios have to go through - it's amazing that any poster ever gets made. We do not arrange these approvals, the studio gets them from everyone. It's an enormous job.

Q - What are the things a producer should bear in mind for a low budget campaign?

Lesli - You want to forge a relationship with an agency, work out how they'll be compensated. We're all artists, we love films and print. Let the experts do what they are good at. If you're paying expenses only, the hard costs, it's crucial that you make them think that you believe in their work, enough for them to get excited about it and not question it.

Q - Is Pulse accessible to new filmmakers who have a low / no budget?

Lesli - Sure, because a new filmmaker who says, *'I made this movie, I want to show it to you, I want you to help me with the main titles, the poster and key art'*, is likely to be the decision maker. If a filmmaker comes in and says, *'I have five people who need to approve it'*, we would be trapped in a no win situation. One decision maker that deals with the agency, that communicates and gets along with them, will get much further than if they have an entourage of people where everyone has a different opinion.

Q - How much should a new filmmaker budget for the advertising?

Lesli - If it's one person approving everything, you really get along, and they loved everything you did, it could be reasonable. We negotiate for independent people because we love independent movies. With the bigger studios, the approvals are so long and so hard and there are so many revisions, it becomes. It also depends if the filmmaker has materials. They may they have a unit photographer, or they may need a special shoot with our photographers. This can be expensive, but there is a range of photographers, you don't need Annie Leibowitz or the higher end photographers to do this kind of work.

Q - For a $1m movie, can you give a rough idea of how much they need to put aside?

Lesli - I'm just talking about print. Trailers and TV spots are a whole different thing. If the filmmaker is distributing the film they will need a poster and ad slicks for newspaper. It would be great to set aside for creation and printing of these materials about $35-40,000. Of course it depends on quantities and number of markets. These are very rough numbers.

Q - How much is it to advertise on a billboard?

Lesli - We supply them with the artwork and then they either paint them or have them printed on big sheets. That's one part of the cost. Then there's the actual space. It can be more than $20k a month.

Q - What other publicity material is there?

Lesli - There's the internet, where you can get e-mail lists and chat rooms. You might do fly postering and invitations to screenings, small posters you can send to the press and also press kits that have the image on the front and a synopsis of the film inside. You can hand out cards in malls, saying, 'come to a screening' or think of cheap promotional things to get people excited. Look at *The Blair Witch Project*. That was backed by a big studio, but they did start out promotionally small, but impressive. If your movie's really good, there are always free promotional things to think of.

Q - What are the common mistakes you've experienced from producers?

Lesli - Having too many decision makers when it comes to the advertising. There's nothing worse than presenting a great poster and having it revised so many times that it loses it's power. Independent producers need to be brave and have a strong point of view and not be influenced by every random opinion coming their way. Another mistake is not having a unit photographer shooting on the set. It's really worth the investment. Those shots will save them money in the long run for publicity and advertising.

Q - How many photographs would you recommend they have?

Lesli - That's hard to say, it's all in contact sheets. It's not like they are doing big prints of everything, so it isn't as expensive. They should cover the actors, the sets, you'd be surprised what you could use and what ends up being in the poster and publicity.

Q - Are producers willing to accept criticism when you tell them the name doesn't suit the movie?

Lesli - A good producer would be open to making their film the best that it can be, but they fall in love with something that no one else can understand. We are working on a movie called *Old School* for DreamWorks and I heard in the translation of *Old School* in different countries is *Little Old School House*. It's not what the movie's about at all. So they'll change titles all over the world because the original doesn't translate. If you have a great title, it makes you want to check it out.

Q - The image of Julia Roberts holding the baby in Erin Brochovich was memorable...

Lesli - Yes. Steven Soderbergh took that shot and gave it to us, he has very good taste. If you look through our portfolio, a lot of pictures are just taken right out of the story. They capture the essence of the character, of what the story's about, they touch people. I've always said some of the best images are the ones you drive by at 40mph and say *'oh, what was that?'* The best kind of advertising is when you can catch someone's attention and break through the clutter.

DIY Poster

If you find yourself invited to a festival and you still don't have all your sales materials in place, you can get away with most things, but it's always best to have a poster. You can easily design your own on your computer, and making a print is very cost effective. The best and cheapest are companies are online, where you upload your artwork (usually as a JPEG) and they return you a tube in the mail with your poster! There seems to be a new, better and cheaper company every week, so get over to Google and get searching! Your presence at the festival will be greatly enhanced by having a poster. Think bold design too, maybe black and white, or just two color. You want an image that catches the eye and makes the viewer remember the name of the film.

Photo courtesy of www.cannesguide.com

Q - Does it work differently depending on where the film is being shown?

Lesli - Yes it does for example it's darker in England so posters need to be lighter. There are certain actors that are well known in certain parts of the world and they don't play other places at all. The lead actress in *Braveheart* is very popular in France so the French poster had her in it, whereas the domestic poster just had Mel Gibson.

Q - How do you handle low budgets?

Lesli - Everybody has to be really clear, honest and up front. We'll say, *'this is what you're going to get for the money that you're paying. You're going to get three ideas; you've got to pick one'.* We have to keep it limited so we don't go out of business and they can get what they need.

Q - Is there a difference between working on an independent film and a Hollywood film?

Lesli - Sometimes the story gets lost in the big blockbusters because they're so busy selling the big star, stunts and their big explosions. You're like, *'where's the story?'* That's why I love independent movies, because they are surprising and I love international films because they aren't formulaic. I don't want to know what the end is when I'm watching the beginning. Do we approach then differently? The challenge is to make them interesting every time.

Q - Do you have any advice for new filmmakers' trailers?

Lesli - Some of them show the entire movie and you're like, *'I've seen the whole movie now. I don't need to pay for ticket.'* Do you know why they do that? It's because they test the best. The people they are testing go 'oh yeah, it's about this and that' and they'll like it because the audience understood it. It is not necessarily good advertising. I've sat in theatres where it's one trailer after the next and they all blend in - this is the kiss of death, mediocrity, blending in. Don't be afraid to stand out.

Q - What advice would you give a new filmmaker?

Lesli - Have a grasp of your budget, have an idea of what kind of movie you're making and make sure you can communicate it. We're running with what you say so later on if you say *'I've made a drama not a comedy'*, then that's a waste of money. Invest in the unit photographer and hire an agency of people you believe in, *and then believe in them!* You're allowed to second guess, but you've hired them because they are the experts, so try to not sit there and undermine them. We have a famous director who has taken our poster, painted over it and designed it himself. It's bad and what's sad is the movie probably won't do well. He didn't believe in us. You should believe in the people you've hired, let them do their job and take risks. Safe advertising is not going to get you visibility. So nerves are a good thing. You can't afford to just have things blend into the background. Be bold.

Jeanette Volturno and Trey Wilkins
Catchlight Films

Jeanette and Trey of Catchlight Films put finishing funds into Amy's O which was written and directed by Julie Davis. They then self distributed the film theatrically.

Q - What was the budget of Amy's O and how many theaters did you play?

Jeanette - The film was shot on 35mm on a budget of $750k. We opened in one theater, The Angelica in New York and five theaters including Laemmle's Fairfax in LA. We ran in both cities for about seven weeks.

Q - Did you plan the theatrical first or did you have a DVD release lined up too?

Jeanette - Showtime had made us an offer for a great cable premiere, which was tied to Blockbuster Video who wanted to release that November. We organized the theatrical with only 2 months lead time releasing at the end of August.

Q - Did the short lead time cause any problems?

Trey - Only in terms of us not being eligible for any of the long lead magazine articles.

Q - Did you make any money from the theatrical?

Jeanette - We made money in LA but not in New York as it costs so much money just to buy the ads in papers there. Once you have a release it's then another hurdle to build on that release. If you don't have a good screen average on day one, you're taken out of the theater immediately. Also, to keep the momentum, you need to add another theater and get that first screen average to be the same as the one you were in without there being any drop in percentage.

Q - Did you deliberately choose to screen in New York first?

Jeanette - It's kind of an unspoken rule and it's how you're measured. If you survive in New York, you can make it anywhere in the States. It really helped us in LA, we would hear *'oh, you had a really good opening weekend in the Angelica'*, and that would get us in the LA theaters and raise awareness in the press.

Q - Did you hire a booker and how much was that? How did you get your film in the Angelica?

Trey - Yes, we paid a flat fee of $10k to release in LA and New York. We got in The Angelica and the Laemmle through our booker and his relationship with those theaters. You're hiring their relationships and it's the biggest benefit. However, it's not always guaranteed that their experience is going to be most effective for your project as every project is different.

Q - Did you have a publicity company on board?

Jeanette - Yes. We hired a company for four weeks and paid about $5k. They handled New York and LA and made a lot of contact with larger TV and radio shows that we wouldn't have been able to get to.

Q - What about P&A?

Trey - We spent $75k in New York and $30k in LA. Advertising in LA is much cheaper, The New York Times ads are literally ten times more expensive than any other city, for something the size of your thumb. We also did 50 trailers and cut a very expensive tv spot and talked Adelphia into some ridiculous rate to get some spots for us on TV and cable in total we must have had about 165 spots and we spent a little over $4k which was amazing…usually packages start at $15k. We even got a great spot on the Emmy's!

Q - What deal did you get from the theaters?

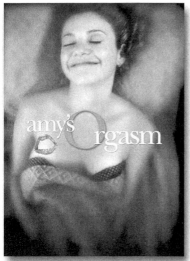

Trey - 10/90 deal which is 10% to the distributor after the house nut and 90% to you. Usually there's an option of taking this kind of deal or 25% of the total. The 10/90 only really makes sense if the film does really well, so for the most part, you're better off taking the 25%.

Q - Is there a particular weekend or certain time of the year that's the worse to open?

Trey - We were always told that one of the best times to release is around August and to try not to release after late September, to avoid the summer blockbusters and the contenders for the Oscars. Our DVD release of Thanksgiving was one of the three best dates that you could possibly have.

Q - How did your DVD release do? Have you and the director managed to see any returns?

Trey - It's been four months since the DVD release and it's done quite well. We haven't as yet made our investment back but we have been receiving checks quarterly. Julie hasn't seen any money back either as yet, except for an amount that she personally invested in P&A in the Los Angeles market. It takes awhile for all the markets to be exploited and we are still working on foreign.

Q - I understand that the title was originally Amy's Orgasm?

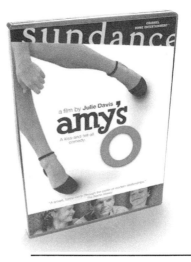

Trey - Yes. Blockbuster refused to release it under that title so we changed it.

Greg Laemmle
Laemmle Theaters

INDIE THEATRES

Q - What type of films do you show?

Greg - Films that differ from the standard Hollywood fare. Even if they're based on a standard form, they should contain something new, whether it's cast, tone, style or content.

Q - And who do you deal with?

Greg - Distributors. We don't often work with the producers, they sell their movie to a distributor who deals with us, the exhibitor.

Q - What percentage does the distributor get?

Greg - On average, they receive between 40-55% of the box office receipts. However, they also pay for 95-100% of the advertising.

Q - Are there any other monies you have to pay out?

Greg - No, not really. The film rental covers almost everything. We may have to pay additional fees for intermission music, and sometimes we contribute a small amount to the ad campaign. Our concession deals (popcorn and drinks etc.) are separate and provide us with another source of income.

Q - What is the house nut?

Greg - It's a figure, usually calculated on the number of seats in an auditorium, which represents the cost of running that auditorium. Another way of calculating film rental is to base it on a net amount above the house nut, as opposed to a percentage of gross. This can be a way for the distributor to achieve greater sums, but it still generally falls between 40 - 55%.

Q - If a film is performing badly after the weekend, do you pull it?

Greg - Not usually, as we're not opening our next film until the following Friday, so it has to finish out the week. Although, if we have something opening on a Wednesday or Thursday, and the film in question is the lowest gross, then it could disappear sooner.

Q - Who controls the movie bookings?

Greg - Booking conversations take place between the theater owner or their booking agent and the distributor. The distributor ultimately determines which theater the film will play in, but they can't unilaterally place a film in a certain theater. There's a certain amount of negotiation. We would usually want to see the film and the reviews. In some cases we might not need to see the film because of its reputation, we may just want to see the ad campaign. The distributor works with us to determine the theatre, the dates etc. That happens months in advance, but is finalized on what we call *'Monday for Friday'*. This is when you come in Monday morning and see what theaters and films are available and make sure there's something for every screen. Whenever a film opens, it does so at the expense of another film closing. Occasionally something surprises us with the amount of business it did and we may delay the release of another film.

Q - What's the time scale between agreeing a release and the actual release?

Greg - In prime locations three months, but I also have conversations well beyond that.

Q - Do distributors have checking services?

Greg - I'm assuming some do, and we welcome it. I'm not at the theater myself selling tickets, so it is possible there are problems. If we're made aware of them, we'll look into it. There's never going to be an exact correlation between the number of people in a multiplex and the number of tickets that are sold. People switch auditoriums or stay over to see a movie a second time.

Q - What is 'four walling'?

Greg - It's a different kind of rental deal, where we are dealing directly with a producer. The producer rents the auditorium, (the four walls), pays a fee in advance then collects all of the box office receipts. If they are successful, they may achieve a higher percentage of revenue than they would under a normal situation. But it guarantees our share of the receipts. The flat fee is roughly $4k a week. Advertising is their expense, but we don't charge for handling the box office or a projectionist fee. We try to treat the film as one of our own. It happens regularly and we believe we owe it to the filmmaking community to give people an opportunity to have their films screened, particularly in LA. The reviews here are important for people's careers and so they can set up sales of ancillary and foreign rights.

Q - Would you recommend that route to indie producers?

Greg - If the deals you're being offered aren't financially viable, I would. If you have a service deal, where a producer is paying a distributor to release their film, at a certain point you may be better off controlling the release yourself than paying some joker who has no vested interest apart from his fee. As long as you understand that a theatrical release is labor intensive, and it's not a pot of gold. A case in point would be the release of *The Debut*, which was a Fillipino / American film. They weren't happy with the deals they were being offered, but they knew their core audience and how to reach that audience, and they were ultimately prepared to make the investment of time and dollars. They went market by market and four walled the theatres they felt were appropriate, and went around the country. The film ended up grossing $2m, which for a small, independent American film is quite a lot.

Q - What are your publicity requirements?

Greg - We don't have any. Some people who four wall say, *'we're going to spend $50k on ads'* and then the film does no business as they don't do any grass roots work. Some films have a very active e-mail or postcard campaign and do a lot of business.

Q - What is an average box office take for a low budget film on an opening weekend?

Greg - A good estimate is $7k, that's something that you sit up and take notice of. But even if you have a good opening weekend in a four wall booking you may not be able to extend the release beyond what was originally booked.

Q - Are there any particular dates that aren't recommended to open on?

Greg - Academy Awards weekend is not a good weekend, although because there are fewer films opening it's not that bad. If you have a small film, I would try to avoid year end as there are too many other big films opening, but otherwise, it's fine.

Q - How do you promote a film in your theater?

Greg - Trailers and posters are very important. It's crucial to have good materials, but otherwise the most important thing is elbow grease - making sure flyers and postcards are being distributed properly. You need to mail all your friends, cast and crew and make sure they know about it. Those things are very simple but very important.

Q - Have you come across any strange publicity campaigns?

Greg - We had a midnight movie that ended up playing for almost half a year on weekends. The filmmakers went to midnight screenings of other films with hand held DVD players and showed their trailer to the people in line. Little stunts are valuable. Some people have decorated their cars and driven through the city, even getting TV coverage, but it had no impact on the box office. It's nice to build name recognition, but ultimately nothing beats that personal touch, especially when you're working on the small end of things.

Q - What is the EDI and does it relate to the movie theaters?

Greg - AC Neilson EDI is a box office tracking service. There's another called Rentrak and they give people access to box office information.

Q - How can people find out what the top ten or top hundred markets are?

Greg - If you're talking about a contract situation, you need to find out what the top ten markets are. If you only find seven, it could mean they don't release the film in LA or New York.

Q - What sound formats do you have and what are your theaters equipped with?

Greg - In the art house world, DTS, SDDS and Dolby Digital are all common, also Dolby SR as analogue. You'd be surprised how many theaters are not equipped with digital sound. You have to consider if it is an important part of your release.

Q - When the reels come in, are they spliced together onto one reel?

Greg - Yes.

Q - What do you think of everything turning digital?

Greg - It'll happen, but right now the cost is ridiculous. The lion's share of the savings is to the distributor and producer not having to make prints, but if they're not willing to bear any of the cost there's no reason for the exhibitor to promote the shift. If someone were building a new theater and the costs were roughly the same, you might as well put it in, but right now, it's too costly.

Q - When do you start putting trailers in theaters?

Greg - It can start on a spot basis. The distributors have greater access to trailer placement and that's an advantage of being with a distributor, but for a heavy run, four to five weeks out. We have a lot of repeat customers, so you don't want to show the trailer too many times or they'll get tired of it.

Q - What is the length of trailers?

Greg - Two and a half minutes.

Q - What do you think a filmmaker should look for in a distributor?

Greg - Passion and a good track record in terms of releasing films and what other people say about working with them. They are going to live with your film so they need to be committed beyond the financial side. The acquisitions manager can be passionate about it, but if they show it to the other people at their company and the team throws their hands up and says, 'forget it', they are not going to get their company behind the film.

Q - What common mistakes have you encountered with new filmmakers?

Greg - Aside from the fact that they didn't make quality films, it's the mistake of the budget getting out of proportion to the reasonable market return. When films can and are made cheaply enough, it gives greater flexibility in releasing the picture. When the budget gets out of proportion everyone's hands are tied. There's no way to win. You have to release it in a fashion that's bigger than the potential return and you can't nurture the film. From the beginning, you have to turn it into something it isn't. There are so few films in the independent world that gross over $2m, so if your budget is based on the film grossing $10m, you're starting out in rough territory. A distributor thinks *'I don't know if I want to pay $5m to acquire this film because I'm going to have to gross $10 - 15m after all these other things are covered and that's not going to happen.'*

Q - Does it make a difference to the paying public whether a film is shot on DV and blown up or just shot on 35mm?

Greg - No. As long as the quality is there.

Q - If a low budget movie is having a good run, how long can it run for?

Greg - There are situations where you achieve that perfect release and it succeeds, especially if the competition isn't that great. We played a film last year and gave it a week as a favor. It ended up playing six weeks, midnight shows and a couple of suburban locations. It went on to receive some Spirit Award nominations and had a huge ancillary life. Its theatrical life was curtailed as the video release date had already been set and they weren't able to push it back. It grossed $250k, but that's two to three times what they were expecting.

Q - Is there anything a filmmaker can do for the theater?

Greg - Being available on the weekend to do Q&A to personalize the experience as much as possible. It doesn't necessarily attract more people to the theater, but if they like the movie it can help with word of mouth, and that's the number one tool of the independent filmmaker.

Q - How do you see the state of the independent movie world?

Greg - I understand production money is drying up, but the potential for films to break out of the $2m box office range is greater than ever. There are more screens available, and if films cross over to a broader audience, the distributor can expand the release more easily. Films like *The Good Girl, Kissing Jessica Stein* and *Bowling For Columbine* have all benefited from the potential to go from two runs to two hundred relatively quickly.

Q - What advice would you offer a new filmmaker?

Greg - Don't make your film for a market, but be aware of the market. Don't spend $5m making your film if you can do it for $500k and still come out with the right film. It's important to get your film out there, and you'll help yourself by having funds reserved for the release of your film.

DISTRIBUTION

Jeff 'the dude' Dowd
Producers Rep

PRODUCERS REP

Q - What is your job?

Jeff - I am involved in financing films, producing and executive producing. I consult on script and on initial business plans in terms of packaging actors, directors, distribution, financing. I also consult on the marketing of films. As a producer's rep, I represent films and help them find distribution, sometimes following through to help on the marketing. I help build bridges from the artists to the audiences.

Q - How did you get into that business?

Jeff - I came out of a background of political organizing against the war in Vietnam which taught me all types of grass root skills that could later be applied to marketing of movies. It also taught me how to listen to the public. In the 1970s, we had 28 movie screens in Seattle where we could listen to the public and try new and innovative ways of marketing specialized films. For example, United Artist had a film called *The Black Stallion* produced by Francis Coppola and Fred Roos. The first time that I realized this was a useful job was with United Artists and *The Black Stallion*. They didn't think the film would play because it was too arty for kids and too kiddie for adults. They made the mistake of showing it to a New York Times critic alone in a room and he said *'this film has 28 minutes without dialogue and kids won't sit through that'*. So the producers asked me to do a full test screening of it, with about 500 people. During the part without any dialogue, a little girl obviously needed to go to the bathroom really badly, so she stood in the aisle, her legs wobbling, but she was so transfixed, mesmerized by the screen she just stood there for 5 minutes and then sat back down. All the other kids in the audience were enthralled, proving that kids could indeed sit through 28 minutes without dialogue. It's a wonderful story of how the public taught us a lesson.

Q - If a new filmmaker wants to come to you, how should they be prepared? Obviously they need a good script?

Jeff - You can throw a great script onto the Hollywood Freeway and it'll get made. You will be able to get producers to help you build a team, actors that want to be part of it, financiers and distributors. But it all starts with the script. And if you can't write it yourself, find a writer you can work with and work together.

Most scripts that aren't re-written five to ten times over are just not going to work. You get closer when you're into double digits. You should hire someone who can give you the most critical and helpful feedback. I think you can probably go to any known writer in the world and say *'I'm a first time filmmaker; I'd like to pay you $10k to work through my script with me'* and you'll get them. Pay me, pay other people. There are people that are good at this, that do this kind of work and do it well.

When Frank Daniel took over USC, he told all the directors, *'this is how it's going to work. I'm going to teach you about writing, and then I'm going to teach you about acting. Then you'll understand something about directing.'* The key to success is making sure it's written well, that you're writing great parts. If you write great parts, you can get great actors for nothing. I was in the same office at Sundance for years and I'd watch these guys come home at night carrying ten, fifteen, twenty-five films. Even if these Sundance people are a bunch of cracked-up vampires and never sleep as I did the math on taking fifteen films home at night and being back at work at nine in the morning. Your first ten-fifteen minutes had better be real good. As Frank would say *'entrance is everything'*, and you'll notice in all the movies you like, the characters have great entrances in the beginning.

The question you have to ask yourself is this, *'are there 200 people that will want to come and see this movie opening on Friday night?'* It only has to be 200. Will they tell their friends *'you've got to see this?'* If that's not the case, you're conning people out of their money.

Q - As well as being aware of the marketplace, filmmakers must be careful not to fall into the trap of copycatting?

Jeff - Festivals are full of copycat movies. Don't do a mockumentary, particularly about the film business. There are 200 of them sitting out there right now. I think that it's a very risky thing to do an ensemble piece. Where's the emotional focus of the film? There have been great ensemble pieces like *Swingers* or *Usual Suspects,* but the *'bunch of people sitting around talking'* movies are not that interesting and they don't have the emotional depth. The point is we're selling emotions at the end of the day, and the emotions had better be real and true.

Q - What would you advise a first time director with a great script who has some well known producer come on board – and the director is then told 'okay, I'll just buy the script off you?'

Jeff - That's a dilemma. Do you sell it to somebody? On the one hand, you can make yourself a producer and stick by your guns and say *'look, I'll step back from this as a director, but I want to learn from this process. I want to be right there in the middle. If you're going to bring in a better director then I want that to apprentice that better director. If you're going to re-write it, I want to apprentice that re-write. I want to experience the whole process'.* And if you're able to deal emotionally with that, you're going to come out as a winner. Your movie's going to get made, you're going to get a credit, you're going to get relationships out of it and there are lots of cases of people who've done that. Written something and then gotten it made and moved up.

Festival Do's and Don'ts

Do research on as many festivals as you can before you start to submit. Find out what kind of films they program, when they program, who attends and what resources they have available to entrants.

Do be mindful of entry fees. Sometimes you will find one that is free, but most likely they will be between $25 and $50. Don't enter a festival that is over this amount. Sundance is $50 so why should anyone else be more expensive?

Do budget for your stay at a festival. This may not be in the budget of your film, but put some money aside for hotel, food and transportation as most festivals provide none of these things for entrants. You can always get a bunch of friends together and pack one hotel room. Makes for great stories.

Do advertise your film as much as possible yourself. Bring press kits, VHS tapes, flyers, posters (some festivals forbid postering buildings and passing out flyers), hats and anything else you can slap the name of your film on. Be creative as well. If your film is about cowboys, dress one of your friends up as a cowboy and have him walk through the festival handing out flyers.

Do get a press agent, but ONLY if you are going to be at one of the larger festivals were there will be a lot of press. It also may be helpful for foreign country festivals as the agents will be more familiar with the press agencies.

Do make sure that your print is in a format that the festival can handle and that any special requests, such as HD players, are taken care of two weeks in advance.

Do schmooze with the festival operators to find out where the free food, booze and best parties are. If you are cunning, you can survive on this free food. Pack doggy bags.

Do not freak out if the projector blows up or the sound drops out of your film. Remain calm and professional. Usually it is a volunteer running the projector with very little training. Don't blame them. Also, an agent or producer may be in the audience and if he sees you go ballistic here, they may think this is how you will be on the set of a major job when things go south.

Do not stay too far away from the festival center. The pace of most film festivals, especially the larger ones, is draining. Having to drive half and hour or more to your hotel at the end of the night just sucks.

There are some producers that will help out a first time director and help build that team. You get a cinematographer, an agent or lawyer, an editor and actors. If an actor commits to this, it adds a level of credibility. If you have a really good script with a couple of good parts, you will get an actor. It's different than it was, much more conservative. Why? Because it's harder to get people to promote the movie. I worked on a movie with David Arquette, *Dream with the Fishes*, two or three years ago. He can get on TV shows. It helps to have somebody willing to promote your film, so you have the good parts, you will get the actor. So don't think the agents are your enemy. A good producer can figure out how to work with the agent.

Q - Do you find there are more people using digital now because they can go out, shoot and then make it work when cutting it together in the edit?

Jeff - That's no excuse to not have the highest quality films. You can only talk about the potential of digital. The digital theaters aren't all set up but in some time, we'll have them. I'm hoping there will be digital theaters on college campuses. It's no harder to set up a digital theater than putting in 120 seats and a speaker system. That's all it takes. There's a guy who's just made a wonderful, but not perfect, film for $500k. When that starts to happen, you have the equivalent of college radio, which sustained REM, Pearl Jam, Nirvana. I hope this will happen in the next couple of years, so you can have alternate, less capital intensive ways to release films.

I'm not sure Joel and Ethan Coen, John Sayles or people like that I worked with on their first films would necessarily get out there today. Keep in mind, *Blood Simple* got passed on three times by every distributor before it was picked up. I think for some films, the answer may lie in expanded television or people are playing with new kinds of DVD clubs. The Internet, obviously there's a great future there with broadband. There are technological things that are happening that could really lead to some of the deserving films having more of a chance to get watched.

Q - Low budget movies have to come up with a lot of marketing gimmicks just to get the attention of the distributors. With Blair Witch for example, it was the marketing of the film that made the film...?

Jeff - Two things about *Blair Witch*. One is for X amount of people the film totally delivered. I viewed it, before Sundance, with my ex who was not enthusiastic and said, *'oh, another independent film we've got to view'*. I put the film on, and this is at night, you know and my ex didn't say after ten minutes, *'let's turn this thing off'*. It worked as a genuine horror film for us. Some people it didn't scare at all, and others didn't want to see it, but a very large number of people went to watch it as a date film. And they gave it very strong word of mouth. Second, there are other people who saw it as an inventive low budget way of experimenting with form. The media were saying this was a *'fuck you'* to the studio systems, and a call for revolution. Then you have the Internet site, which was brilliant marketing. One of my mentors used to say *'you want a film that becomes a cocktail party conversation piece'*.

Q - How accessible is the business if you are starting out?

Jeff - How do you break down the studio walls? You start with actors. A lot of actors have companies and the people in the companies are often closer to them than their agents or managers. You can access them by phone, they're all listed. You can write a compelling short note that catches people's attention. Even in a pitch, you should tell a story that is well told as a joke. You can approach people like me who can provide various functions, open doors and help people. Worst case scenario, you can always get a Hollywood lawyer, who can open up doors to the agents and the managers, because they all work together. I don't think the question of access is the biggest problem. I think it's an excuse.

Q - What are the common problems you encounter with new filmmakers?

Jeff - It all starts with the movie. Most independent filmmakers under budget post, they barely get the film finished. You need to do screenings and have enough left over for marketing. You should do lots of test screenings with twenty to thirty people with a TV set or a digital projector. You don't need to do it in a theater. Talk to them and get feedback. You can get the kind of audiences you want

The Art Of The Schmooze

Getting information from tight lipped sources, having hard to reach talent to read your work, persuading nay saying studio execs to put your project into production and working deals to keep the budget down are the main chores of a Hollywood producer. Here are some tips on how to talk your way to the top. This may seem predatory or sleazy, but unfortunately, it is the way it works. The ability to get what you want when others cannot achieve it is what will set you apart. Talent is both common and cheap, but the ability to make it happen is rare. Hone these skills, read books on the subject, even do courses!

1. Form as many contacts as possible. This can be people you do business with daily, or through social events like industry mixers. People do favors for those that they know.

2. Get on the phone and stay on the phone. Find out the latest news and gossip about projects, talent and the needs of the studios. The more in the know you are, the better game you can talk.

3. Set breakfasts, lunches, drinks and dinners with people you want to meet. Pick fun places to go so that you are associated with an upbeat, friendly feeling.

4. Research the person that you want to talk to and their company/clients, and try to fit their strengths to your needs and vice versa.

5. Have a plan when you talk to people. Know what you want to get out of a meeting or phone call so that the other person does not feel like you are wasting their time.

6. Use connections that you have already made to get introductions to new people. A phone call placed on your behalf can make a stranger more open to you.

7. Do activities outside of work with your contacts (some of which will hopefully become your friends), such as going to sporting events, movies, parties, camping/skiing trips. Not only fun, but you have something to bond over.

8. Create customer loyalty by using the same vendors over and over again. They are more likely to cut deals with people that they know personally.

9. Join organizations like IFP/ STEP-UP/Filmmakers Alliance.

10. Do charity events. The major players all participate in several - probably to ease their souls from all the schmoozing.

11. Be respectful to assistants. They have crappy jobs at low pay, but are the gatekeepers to their bosses. Further, they may soon be the next person in power that can help you.

by going to theaters and inviting the people who have just been to see a movie that is similar to yours. You'll get both creative ideas that you'd rather hear from them than critics and you'll get marketing ideas that you never would have though about yourself. You don't need the Sundance Institute to do this. You can do your own Sundance.

One of the reasons Redford started Sundance Institute and a lot of us got involved was because we saw that potentially great voices might not be in the Hollywood system, they might not be living in LA. We felt that people like that had great vision but they weren't doing as much as they should on the script. The first message of Sundance was *'Stop. Do not make your film. Please stop. You're not ready.'* Sundance wanted to take these artists, bring them up to the Institute and let them work with some of the best and the brightest writers, directors, editors, marketing people and production designers. If we could bring those people together and help them and re-write the script, then they could get to the point where their movie might actually work

Do you know how much it will cost to attend the Sundance Festival? Between $15-40k to show up there properly. Why? Because it's a hostile winter environment. You are not allowed on the road without a four wheel drive vehicle. You have to be in a condo. You're nuts if you don't bring your actors in and some of them will insist on flying first class. There's 700-1000 press there. Are you going to go all the way up there, and not have a publicist? Publicists charge from $5k to $15k.

What are distributors looking for? A picture they can personally get really passionate about. The primary objective, particularly at the studios, believe it or not, is not necessarily trying to make money on any given picture. That's a shocking statement. Their top priority is to survive, to keep their jobs. If you work at Warner Brothers, you don't get a piece of the action. The guys at Fox Searchlight have green lit nine or ten films that have cost $50-80m. Now they're only going to be able to pick up maybe one or two movies a year. What's going to be the key thing when they pick it up? The key thing is going to be whether they love it.

Then they want to know, *'are the critics going to get behind it?'* Those of us that know critics will know pretty early on what they're going to support and what they're not, and they kind of tell us in their own way. Or if they don't tell us, we learn pretty quickly, through the publicist, through a wrap up article or they talk amongst themselves. That's what they're looking for, which is another reason filmmakers had better ask themselves, *'is this something they think the critics will support? What's special about it for critics?'* But the primary thing is somebody in their company, usually the head of marketing, is eventually going to come down to that. Regardless of how much the acquisitions people champion it, the head of marketing has to decide at distribution, *'Do we have the time and do we want to do it?'*

Q - If somebody's come to you with their finished film, would you then sit down with them and work out a strategy?

Jeff - Yes, and I help build the team. We start with publicist, then the lawyers, as I'm not an attorney. You hear the marketing plans. Now that's a big discussion between the producers, publicists, myself, lawyers and agents. You weigh things, what the playing field is and how the critics feel. You discuss when you plan to show it to the distributors, and how you plan to get people to see it at Sundance or how you'll get the critics to sit down with the filmmaker, because that can often help. I've often ended up doing deals with a company that might be the best company for the end amount of money, and the best for people's careers, although that company may not be the highest bidder.

The documentary *Scratch* was a film about turntable people, who are truly artists. We felt critics would like it, so we showed it to some before the festival. It was definitely a gamble. You're not going to show it with an audience and they might need a private screening, but you might then be able to walk into Sundance with some good press. I've done that a number of times. What other ways are there of drawing attention? Sometimes a good party can make a world of difference.

Q - What can new filmmakers do to help with the press?

Jeff - Don't think you turn it over to the distributors and they take it from there. Your film is your baby and the rest of us, we're just the good aunts and uncles. This is your child. Everybody knows that somebody on the team is the ultimate guardian of the film. I didn't need to help the guys with *Kissing Jessica Stein*, I didn't need to pick up the phone and help them. Heather Juergensen and Jennifer Westfeldt were doing Q&A for the audience on a Friday night in the fourth week. There wasn't any bad politics or bad marketing because Heather and Jennifer went to twenty-six cities. They were saying, *'look, we want to go to these cities, we want to do these extra shows, put us to work.'* A lot of people don't know whether the filmmakers really want to do it that much, they're afraid to ask, so you have to say *'I'm ready to work with you.'* You have to be pro-active.

I'll give you an example. There was a critic in San Francisco who didn't like *Blood Simple* that much. We sent Joel and Ethan there to have lunch with her. Her review said everything good she could possibly say about the film and nothing bad. That pro-active nature can make a big difference. If you meet the reviewer, your film will most likely end up being on the front page or close to it. You do that twenty times, it makes a huge difference. It's very important for someone on the filmmaking team to be able to get the actors to do extra work. I'm not afraid to ask them. Most actors, (if asked by the director, not the distributor) *'please show up'*, will do, because they get along with the director.

Q - How did Kissing Jessica Stein *evolve?*

Jeff - One of the reasons *Kissing Jessica Stein* was so good was that it was written by two actresses, Heather and Jennifer. It started as a workshop thing, then it was an off-Broadway play and then they brought it out here. It was a studio development deal, then they said *'let's make it independently'* and they shot the whole movie for a little over $1m. I came to the LA Film Festival screening with a publicist, Laura Kim, one of the best publicists in the world. I was introduced to the first time producer, and when some people made a few comments I said *'you should listen to this stuff'* with his editor standing behind him going *'yeah, yeah, yeah'*. He said *'we can't do anything now, we don't have enough time, it's only five weeks away and we don't have any money'*. Years ago, I would have said, *'okay'*. However, I've seen too many films being questioned by distributors and audiences who read the festival reviews in Variety, Hollywood Reporter and Screen International. At the Toronto Film Festival I had dinner with some prestigious directors and a first time American director. They all like this guy's movie but they said to him *'it was all good except for this in the first act'*. And he said it was too late and wouldn't change it. So I decided a few years ago, it's important to speak up. So for *Kissing Jessica Stein*'s first time producer I made it really clear. I said *'you want to destroy these women's careers? You want to make sure this movie never sells? If so, don't do anything'*.

Over a couple of days they did some editorial changes with Heather and Jennifer. We had another screening and people said some brilliant things and we ended up answering three or four questions. They thought there was an abrupt ending, that there was a problem with the gay relationship as certain people thought it looked like Jessica might have been a *'lipstick lesbian'*, so if they broke up, it might suggest that being gay was not a lifestyle but just something you might fool around with. Then there were some marketing questions and a terrible scene at the end of the movie. Two days later, in one day of shooting, they did three or four things that put the break up in the minds of the other characters, to make it clear the break was coming. They re-shot the last scene, which was of Jessica pandering to her old boyfriend, and changed it to much better one where they ran into each other at a bookstore.

That movie was the biggest independent movie seller that year at Cannes, MiFED, Sundance, London, you name it. It didn't have a star in it nor was it a big genre picture. Could they have done those changes earlier? Yeah, and it would have been easier. That was an emergency room operation that worked.

Q - What is your opinion of low budget independent filmmakers?

Jeff – I love them but much of the time I'm disappointed that they don't take advantage of the rare opportunity that they have to make films because they do not do their homework especially when it comes to story telling and script. There's a huge support system for films. There are festivals, there are critics, and there are organizations like the IFP and Sundance etc. that are there to support independent films. But they have to be worthy of support and there has to be something special about them. It's very important that you make something special and not just okay. The converse of this is there are 4000 independent films from Canada, America, Britain and Australia that are never going to see the light of day because they never did their homework and they shot too soon. I think many of those filmmakers are cinematic con artists, they're almost criminals. They're not going to get a theatrical release, they're not going to get a video release and they're not even going to get a cable release. I think those filmmakers that did those 4000 films are con artists. They are almost criminals. I think they con the actors to work for nothing, their parents, their parent's friends, their investors, I think that people who stick up banks to put food on the table have a much higher moral level because it's a victimless crime. It's a tragic misuse of money and human resources when filmmakers con people out of money when they haven't done their homework. Let's say those films average $100k a piece. Multiply $100k by 4000. That's $4bn. $4bn is a lot of money to burn. And marriages have been destroyed, relationships have been destroyed, people have entrusted the filmmakers with certain things, they're all pointing to the *Blair Witch* and the success stories but they didn't do the homework. Some arrogant people, who like to call themselves artists, will say *'ah, he's just being commercial.'* That's not what I'm saying about the marketplace. I'm saying to new filmmakers *'hey, come down to the deep end of the pool where audiences are instead of doing shallow end movies and calling it deep. And calling it art'*. Saying pick up a camera and *'let's make a movie'* does not make you an artist. It's harder to write a book than it is to pick up a camera. On a positive note we live at a time when we need visionary movies now more than ever. There's a huge support system to help build a bridge to audiences and audiences will embrace great films but it's up to the filmmaker to make nothing less than a great film. That's the challenge. Are you ready?

Peter Belsito Sydney Levine
Film Finders

Q - What is Film Finders?

Sydney - Film Finders is a consulting service and publisher with the most comprehensive database for film rights tracking in the world. We provide accurate, updated information on who is buying and selling and which territories and rights are available in the current market. We list the various stages of development of each project i.e. whether they're completed, available for acquisition, or seeking equity investment. Titles can be retrieved according to genre, stage of production, rights available and through the above-the-line cast and crew.

Q - How much is it to subscribe?

Sydney - We have different services and different rates which range from $350 for the basic annual website subscription to $15k for more in-depth reports that studios may require. The basic annual subscription gives you access to the listings of all films, buyers and producers by event. It doesn't however give you access to project comments or to rights availabilities. That would cost you $5k per year and that's only available prior to, during and after each of the three major festivals of Cannes, Berlin/AFM and London/MIFED. However these can be purchased for $2k for each market. There are other services are listed on our website.

Q - How can Film Finders help low budget independent Filmmakers?

Sydney - We have a free submission service for independent filmmakers to list their films in the database and to be included in reports. Our data reaches film buyers and festivals, which producers might not otherwise have access to. Film buyers and festival programmers may then consider whether or not to contact the producers from that list requesting more information. For now the website only lists films in the market. For free, filmmakers can also access Sydney's Buzz online and the services page, which details the further reports and their respective fees.

Q - Can you help put producers in contact with attorneys, reps, agents and distributors for their films?

Sydney - If you've submitted your film to our database then it will be included in relevant reports which subscribers receive. This enables sales agents, US distributors, attorneys, producer reps and festival programmers to read about the film and call you. If the producer has an international sales agent, the sales agent will list the film in our Market Preminder report before the major international markets so distributors around the world can know about the film. Our consulting service is where we become more actively involved in getting producers meetings with all industry people relevant to the project, be it either attorneys, reps, distributors, sales agents or agents. We do this for finished films as well as for screenplays. We make sure that all relevant sales agents are contacted and given the chance to pick up films for the film markets. We also take these filmmakers to the markets and introduce them to the players which opens doors and opens their eyes to the inside workings of markets/or festivals.

Q - How much would a consultancy fee be and how is this calculated? Is this service affordable and therefore feasible for a low budget filmmaker say whose made their movie for $1m?

Peter - It is difficult to answer that question as our fee varies from project to project. This is because we may have to do more services and consulting on one film than on another. In fact, we don't even quote prices to the producing team without meeting them and finding out what their needs are. We feel that the producer is the most important part of the filmmaking process because they create the value of the film. They are the ones who turn the lights on in the morning and shut them off at night. So, we talk with the producer and see how we can help them before we talk price. For example, if they have a small indie film and they want an Oscar, we probably can't help them, or if they have a low budget, walking and talking, slasher movie with no stars and they want to get into Sundance, we can't help them. Not that we wouldn't try if they really wanted this as we aim to help, but we try to be realistic with our clients so that they get the most out of their film. This whole process could cost a few thousand to tens of thousands of dollars depending on what we see is the level of the workload. One thing I should mention is that we are paid on retainer and we do not take anything on the back end. And, yes, low budget movies, even those less than $1 million can afford us. *Cabin Fever* was our baby a year ago when we got it into Toronto. This year we have handled several low budget Academy Award contenders.

We are not a funding agency nor are we a source of funds for filmmaking. What we can do in this area is put out clients in contact with the people who can finance projects, be it equity investors or studios or production companies. Further, we can consult our clients on matters of finance, such as looking into international co-productions and international tax shelter deals.

Q - How can you help independent filmmakers at film festivals?

Peter - We actually start helping them beforehand. The first thing we do is tell them that not all film festivals are created equal. Not that any festival is bad, but certain ones have certain criteria and demographics that they are looking for. We talk to our clients and find out what they want out of their project and then guide them to the festivals that would serve them best. Ultimately it is about leveraging their current project to get the next one made, so we want our clients to be in the best position possible to do that. Once we are at the festival, we coach our clients on how the festival operates and how to act while there. For example, we teach them how to engage the press and how to get the most out of their screenings. Additionally, although we are not reps ourselves, we can introduce our clients to producer's reps and international sales agents - most of whom are our friends.

Q - What advice would you offer new filmmakers?

Peter - Talk to people like us, festival coordinators, festival programmers and distributors before you even start production. If you find out what we are looking for, then you can have a great point of reference for making decisions when casting, location scouting, developing the story and whatever other choices you need to make when producing the film. Also be sure to remember to take photographs of the action on the set as these are the basis of your marketing campaign and of the sales agents' and distributors' marketing campaign. Without photos there are no posters. If music is part of the film, find a music supervisor early on and never use music without prior clearances. Put some of the budget money aside for post-production and sound as well as for consultants, producer reps and attorneys. Remember the point of all of this is to get you to the next film, so arm yourself with as much knowledge as you can to do that.

Phone: 310 300 2190   Fax: 310 300 2220
Email: filmfinders@filmfinders.com   Contact Peter Belsito for questions re: subscription services.

TRADE MAGAZINES

The Hollywood Reporter
www.hollywoodreporter.com

Daily Variety
www.variety.com

Cinefex
www.cinefex.com

Filmmaker - IFP/West
www.filmmakermagazine.com

Creative Screenwriting
www.creativescreenwriting.com

Script Magazine
www.scriptmag.com

American Cinematographer
www.theasc.com/magazine

Moviemaker
www.moviemaker.com

Backstage & Backstage West
www.backstage.com

Film Threat
www.filmthreat.com

DISTRIBUTION

*Geoffrey Gilmore
Sundance Film Festival*

SUNDANCE

Q - What is your job?

Geoffrey - I am the director of the Sundance Film Festival. I'm responsible for the creative direction of the festival. We play about 125 features at the festival and this year we played close to 90 shorts. The digital impetus has lead to a massive increase in the number of shorts submitted to us. We get a couple of thousand features submitted to us, and double that in shorts.

Q - How are the films chosen?

Geoffrey - Every film gets seen by one or more screeners who give a score and a condensation. All films above a certain score are seen by one of the core staff of five people. It's a collective decision although the buck stops with me. The big myth about the Sundance Film Festival is that it's a political selection process, that Harvey Weinstein calls me up and tells me what to put in, which is not the way it operates at all. The presumption is that you need connections in order to get to us. In fact, discovering things that nobody's heard about is much more gratifying than having someone call you up saying, *'Geoffrey, you have to see this'*. I take those phone calls and would be a fool not to, but we don't have large committees or a lot of different advisory mechanisms.

Q - Do you see all the films that come through?

Geoffrey - I see almost everything that's in the festival, except for the shorts. I don't have the time. There's a range of different people who watch things and with everything that has a quality to it, someone says, *'we should give this to Geoffrey'*. So that's where the hundreds of films that I watch come from. It's not a narrow choice. That said, with a couple of thousand features out there, I can't watch everything.

Q - If a film doesn't grab your attention after ten minutes, is that it?

Geoffrey - It usually takes half an hour or more. If a film has been given to me I watch a pretty good part of it, it doesn't make sense to turn it off after ten minutes.

Q - What do you look for in a film?

Geoffrey - We look for originality, films that have an edge to them. We're not scared off by much. A lot of people say that they aren't, but they are. People are scared off by the politics and sexuality, by the edginess or the kind of production qualities of things. Another argument I often make is that we're very much a festival of discovery, for new films and new directors, but we're also trying to showcase the full spectrum of independent work. Since that's changing all the time, we continue to change.

Q - So originality is important when choosing films?

Geoffrey - It's certainly one of the major characteristics. You're always looking for something that you feel is fresh, but it hardly makes sense to argue that you're looking for one thing. If someone gives me a genre film and says, 'this is something that I never thought you'd take', I say, 'why not? It's beautifully done and has the greatest love story I've seen in a long time'.

Q - As a programmer, where does personal taste come into the selection process?

Geoffrey - A good programmer is a person who knows the difference between weird and bad. There's a lot of people who don't. When I look at films for freshness and originality and a sense of discovery, I'm really trying to look at a very broad category of work.

Q - A lot of Hollywood executives attend Sundance don't they?

Geoffrey - It's one of three festivals that attracts the American film industry. The market that takes place at Sundance is one of the biggest in the world, there's an awful lot of deal making and relationships formed and networking that comes out of it. Because of its proximity to Hollywood and NY, it's one place where both attend. But if you look at the spectrum of work that we do, it's really serving a lot of different communities, not just the film industry out of Hollywood or NY per say. The media tends to write about what gets bought and not about what's the best work at the festival. At what point was the standard for evaluation of a festival how many films got sold? That's ridiculous.

What we've been willing to do is expand the sense of what is possible in the marketplace. The kind of films that people used to argue aren't commercial, we disproved that and put those films on a platform that allowed them to be received. That goes from gay and lesbian work that was stigmatised at the beginning of the 90's, to different kinds of low budget and works with unknowns in them. In some ways it's a *'nobody knows nothing'* business. If you had come to me and told me that in the last three sessions of Sundance, that the top three independent films box office wise would have been *Memento, In The Bedroom* and *My Big Fat Greek Wedding*, I dare say nobody in the business would have signed onto them. They would have looked at those three films and said, *'these are the films that aren't going to break out'* and it shows you that despite the intensity of knowledge necessary to do this work, it's very hard to make predictions. Sundance is also a place where people come to find talent. I know a lot of the major actors in the world right now, simply because they came out of Sundance in the last decade and a half.

Surviving Sundance

If you are reading this book, the chances are your trip to the Sundance Film Festival will not be subsidized by a studio, agency or production company (if you are, buy us a drink, will ya?) Here are some tips for making your life easier and a little less expensive while still having a good time in Park City.

No one needs to register to attend the festival, but you should try to buy as many tickets to films before you leave (buy online). If you cannot, then you can get them at several kiosks around Park City, but you will have to get them a few days in advance as they sell out quick. You an also queue in a 'stand by' line for seats where people don't show up to a screening.

If you can drive to Park City, do so. But, if you have to fly, you must go into Salt Lake City and then rent a car for the 40 minute or so journey into Park City. There are some shuttles that go back and forth from the airport as well. It snows in Utah in January, so think about a 4 wheel drive vehicle if you can afford it.

Staying in Park City is a lot of fun. If you want a hotel in the town, book it as soon as you can as they go fast. Also, many people rent out their homes and apartments to festival goers. They are not cheap, but if you can get 10 friends to all go in on a house together, then it's not that expensive. If you have a film in the festival, Sundance will be able to put you in contact with other entrees who want to split a place.

Every night there are a myriad of parties in and around Park City. The big ones that are sponsored by companies like Miramax or talent agencies are tough to get into. But, if you keep your ears open and talk to enough people, you may be able to schmooze a pass. Other parties happen in people's hotels or rented houses. These are also great ways to get free food and drink. If you are lucky, you might end up in a hot tub at 3am with a bottle of champagne!

If you do have a film in the festival, be prepared for a lot of work on the days leading up to your screenings. You will have to do some publicity - hopefully a lot of interviews with media. You should be prepared to personally publicize your film somehow. Posting flyers is illegal in the town, but you can pass them out at other screenings and parties. If you can think of a cheap stunt, to get people into the theater, go for it!

If you have any major problems or concerns, go to the Sundance main office and they can sort you out. They usually have free cookies, water and other goodies there as well.

letf - Photo courtesy of www.sundanceguide.net

DISTRIBUTION

Q - The foreign films that are showcased, are they independent or have had they had more financial backing than the American independents?

Geoffrey - You have to show commercial work in order to get the idea that international work is going to sell out of Sundance. *The Full Monty* and *Four Weddings and a Funeral* came out of Sundance, not very many people know that. That's not to say that that's my objective. A major producer in the UK may want to take his film to Cannes, Toronto and Sundance but I'm not necessarily committed to doing that as I want to show something that's new. I have shown works that have done that route, but they have to be pretty exceptional. Or I sometimes make an argument to someone, *'hey, why don't you give us a chance at it, to really do it well at Sundance, and see what kind of platform we can establish for you?'* and people have been very pleased about that as well. Most of my programming for my festival isn't done out of other film festivals.

The international section of the festival is actually quite large, with almost a third of the films shown being international. But I don't pretend to be a comprehensive film festival in the sense of a really big festival like Toronto, showing 300 features covering the world. We're very selective and to some degree I would argue we're always going to be showcasing a very representative but not necessarily comprehensive range of work every year. We may have one year with four films from China and the next year, none. We have a commitment to showing English language work from international sources and there's always a lot of Australian and New Zealand and UK work. That's not to say that the distributors from those places see us as the place to come. I'm looking to showcase brand new filmmakers from around the world and I've done that over the years and will continue to do that. That said, the presumption about Sundance from the international side is that the foreign side is not as invested with visibility as the American side, as that is where all the media attention is directed. We've spent a lot of times in the last couple of years with our sales office trying to develop strategies for getting visibility to international films. A film like *Whale Rider* which had already showcased at major festivals before it got to us nevertheless had such an enormous reaction at Sundance that the filmmakers told me how significant Sundance was for them. I don't want to be the world's dominant sales market, I'm trying to showcase a range of different filmmakers and a range of different kinds of filmmaking and to me that independent ethos has evolved in the world. One criticism of Sundance that you might hear from filmmakers is 'my work wasn't commercial enough for Sundance to show it'. I find myself being defensive when I'm told that as the last thing I'm going to do is to say, *'the only reason I'm selecting you is because your work has some market possibilities.'* But that continues the argument that the international work went to Sundance and it didn't get sold, and you're in a catch 22 situation.

Q - How involved is Robert Redford in the festival?

Geoffrey - He's not a figure head. Does he actually have a role? Absolutely. A week from now, he's coming in and we'll do a review. He tears everything apart and we think about it. Does he sit and watch films with us? He's a filmmaker, he doesn't have the time to do that. The greatest attribute he brings to the process is that he's a filmmaker and understands filmmaking and has a lot of ideas about filmmaking that he can share with people. He has been instrumental in the way the festival is structured and how the festival thinks of itself as a filmmaker oriented festival. He is also the man that can sell work too, as he's been in the media spotlight for a long time and knows how to deal with it. He's at ease with that. He's been the person who has been the biggest advocate of restraining our growth, of making sure we reign it in and don't grow topsy turvy. We get a lot of people saying, *'why don't you do this or that?'* but we are slow about how we want to develop. We don't want to completely change the nature of what the festival is. He's the guy that has the vision, who supplies the sense of what this has been since he begun Sundance in 1981. He's not the only leader and doesn't try to be, but he certainly has a creative sensibility that informs a lot of what Sundance is.

Q - What other programs does Sundance offer?

Geoffrey - There's a theater program and a documentary program that my colleague runs which is very well established in the international realm. This year we augmented the festival by showing a program of international documentaries. My colleague Michelle Satter runs the writing and directing labs, I run a producers program and Peter Golub runs the composers lab. These are selective and small educational programs that take place up at the Sundance village during the summer from late May to early August, and, except for the producers program, which is a program you can pay your way into, it's an open avenue.

Film Festival Necessities

Things to do to prepare and for when you are there.

PREPARE...

Get your airfare, accommodations and rental car (if necessary) squared away early. See if the festival has some deals worked out for filmmakers.

Save some cash so you can have a good time and relax.

Get business cards printed to pass out.

Create a website to promote your movie online.

Create stickers, flyers, a press kit (b&w, color and digital photos), posters and postcards to pass out, with times and locations of your screenings. The press kit is the most important, followed by flyers and postcards.

Take several copies of the film's EPK (electronic press kit) to pass out to distributors.

Pack some fancy clothes for parties.

Don't forget your cell phone. If you are going far away, call your wireless company to see if you can get a good long distance rate.

Have a next project to talk about!

If you can afford it, get a publicist to help you create a media strategy (do this only for the big festivals like Sundance or Toronto)

WHEN THERE...

Meet as many people as possible - filmmakers, distributors, journalists, agents... Get their business cards and pass them yours!

Create a buzz for your film - pass out your flyers and postcards. Do a cheap (or, not so cheap) publicity stunt. Get your actors and friends to go and help you and do as many interviews with the media as possible.

If you can afford it, throw a party for your film. Team up with other films to reduce the cost. Find out where other parties are - then crash them!

If you are on a budget, hang out at the film festival office. Everyone goes there and they usually have free food.

Hand out your movie / promo items to journalists and distributors.

Follow up with everyone you meet, there or when you get home.

Talk about your next project and try to get as many people to read it as possible.

Don't sign any contracts with representation while you are there, unless you have your attorney present.

Collect ALL press and reviews

Go support other filmmakers by watching their work and cheering!

HAVE FUN!

Q - How do you get onto the labs?

Geoffrey - You submit by making a proposal. We keep it limited, you're dealing with thousands of scripts that are coming to you and you're taking a dozen of them. That goes beyond selective and there's a very complicated and specific set of criteria that are used to make those judgements. I've always viewed it not as a place to learn about screenwriting or directing, but as a process of taking good stuff and trying to make it great.

Q - Are there any funding programs?

Geoffrey - We have a process where the documentary program funds internationally and has become part of Sundance. There are some other possibilities for Sundance funding of films that we have been discussing that haven't been established yet.

Q - What is the Sundance on-line film festival?

Geoffrey - It's only four years in operation and I think the quality of work we have gotten continues to jump enormously each year. We are seeing things now that are being made for us from different places in the world and we're doing something that's getting millions of hits. We're still dealing with broadband technologies which only allow certain works to be showcased, but there is a kind of investigation of experimental, animation, narrative work that I think is really starting to take off. I can't tell you that it's great yet as I don't think it is, but I am impressed by the changes in the work that we have shown and the quality of film that has been produced now opens up possibilities for different forms of thinking. None of the work that we have in the Sundance festival is part of the online festival. It's limited and determined by the forms that the medium should be developed in. It's a different medium.

Q - Do movies that get picked up at Sundance go on the movie channel?

Geoffrey - Some. The Sundance Channel has to license things just like any other channel. The channel doesn't necessarily compete at a theatrical level, so it has to find works that in some ways get passed by major companies. I consult with The Sundance Channel and help them buy stuff, particularly international stuff. It's a three part owned enterprise with Universal, Viacom and Redford, and its growth has been tremendous. It's now in 40 million homes and has 16 million subscribers. It's a profit enterprise, as opposed to the institute which is a non-profit. The channel is one of two independent channels in the US (along with the Independent Film Channel) that showcase a lot of both distributed and non distributed work, and that has broadened the view for people who don't have a chance to see films in theaters.

Q - Do you think the market fluctuates for independents?

Geoffrey - If you define independent filmmaking as films which are in 600 or less theaters, the grosses are increasing and the competition in the marketplace is increasing. On the other hand, breakout performances of films vary from year to year. This year there were a number of breakout performances and I would argue that this year in America has been the strongest year for quality art cinema since 96'. It's tough in the independent world from a financial point of view, because the funding basis has gone. That didn't cause a huge drop in the number of films sent to us and I'm not sure it's caused a huge drop in the number of films being made. What it has done is lower the prices that films are being made for, and the prices people are willing to pay for them. That's something people are going to be cautious of, as too many people have been burnt at too high a level.

Q - How would you recommend filmmakers prepare for Sundance?

Geoffrey - It depends on the nature of the film. If you want to sell it, you need representation, people to help get the buyers there. It's not that you can't do this by yourself, but it's hard. People say they can't afford representation, well you can. Depending on the quality of the film, you'd be surprised at the number of people who are willing to do something with you for little money up front, based on anticipation. If you think selling your film is only a possibility, you showcase the film for all it's worth. Ideally, you're also talking about the next job, how to develop yourself, asking about opportunities, making contacts. Sometimes people come to a festival where they get into an entourage of people and never leave it. You never meet anybody that way. You need to take the festival for what it is, an opportunity to meet people and see things and learn and advance yourself. Sundance will probably be one of the more memorable experiences of your young life, but not if you haven't done what the festival is about. Reconsider what it is you want to do as a filmmaker. People don't tend to do this. The truth is, the best films surface and have an interest. Very rarely have good films slipped through the festival without getting noticed.

Q - Do you believe that Sundance can make a career?

Geoffrey - The truth is that there are filmmakers who didn't get into Sundance, who did very well for themselves. I believe that the cream rises to the top, regardless of where it comes from.

Q - What mistakes do you see with first time filmmakers?

Geoffrey - Developing the script. You don't have to make a good film, you have to make a great film. People think that if they make a good film, they should get accolades and I say, *'unfortunately, it's not that kind of a game'.* If you really want to get visibility, you have to get a standard that is much higher than sufficient. I'm not sure that people start off with that kind of determination. You also have to work in order to improve yourself. You can't sit there saying, *'I'm going to make a film five years from now'.* You can't become a director by not directing and you can't sit in a classroom and be taught what direction is. You can learn about it and understand things but you become a director of incredible quality by making films. Now in the industry, by your second feature, you're told you're washed up. You've got to work. You've got to find ways to work to develop yourself, whether that's a feature film or commercials or videos or whatever it is you're shooting.

I don't think this last decade of filmmaking is going to be recognized as one of the great decades of film. In fact a lot of the work has a degree of mediocrity to it and a lot of twenty something angst based on a limited life experience. People need to make what they know, but there has been an insularity for a long time about a certain generation who's naval gazing was getting to the point where it was boring. So you want to encourage people to understand things about the world and to have references that they make points to, and to know something beyond pop culture. If you can tell me who won American Idol last night, that's great. If you don't know anything about anything else, you're in trouble. I know I'm being obnoxious, but I argue for people to learn things. People need to be able to understand that as filmmakers, there are so many different hurdles to overcome. It's easy for me to say things like, 'save money for post production' but 90% of people spend their money unwisely, they don't use it for sound and music when they really should.

Above all, what I want to encourage people to do is become great filmmakers and see themselves as someone who has stories to tell, ideas to communicate and aesthetics to show. One of the things I tell people is that if you're a filmmaker, you've got to watch a lot of film. How else can you do it? There's only a handful of filmmakers who don't watch film who become great filmmakers. Fellini's are very rare. They brag that they never saw anything, but there are not many of these guys around. I'm amazed at the number of filmmakers I talk to who don't know anything about film. There's a range of experience that they don't get that I'm really pedantic about. I tell people to read stuff and watch stuff. You've got a long way to develop yourself.

Dan Mirvish
Slamdance

SLAMDANCE

Q - What is Slamdance and how did it come about?

Dan - Slamdance is a film festival in the US that happens pretty much every year in the 3rd week of January. Our specific niche is that we are the alternative to Sundance. In 1995, I made a feature film called *Omaha* and knew a whole bunch of other filmmakers who had made features. A lot of us had met at the IFP Film Market in New York and traditionally, Sundance had always picked up a lot of films from them. But, this particular year they didn't, which was very disappointing because it was becoming clear that Sundance, which was this great festival of discovery in America for new filmmakers such as Soderberg and Linklater, were no longer interested in first time filmmakers working with low budgets, without distribution and no stars. They seemed more interested in second and third time directors with distribution with Miramax and bigger budgets with stars. So, that wrecked this whole niche that we are in which is ironic because we are the niche that they started. I don't think they were doing that intentionally, but they grew fast and they didn't realize that they were leaving anyone behind.

We knew that Sundance was still the preeminent film festival in the US and the reality from what distributors were telling us was that if you don't get into Sundance, you won't get distribution. So, you are really stuck if you don't get into Sundance. Philosophically, we thought that when you are making these indie films, you have a lot of control over them. You've raised the money, you've finished the film and then all of a sudden you are at a point where you have lost control. You are at the whim of the festival programmer, and in the US, that is Geoff Gilmore. And, we thought that is a shame. And, we had heard of a couple filmmakers that had not gotten into Sundance the year before had done renegade screenings of their own films in back rooms or their own hotel rooms. We found out later that James Merendino with his film *The Upstairs Neighbor* and Matt Stone and Trey Parker the *South Park* guys, did *Cannibal: The Musical* this way. We didn't know them, but we thought it is not such a stretch to say that if a couple individual filmmakers can do this, why can't a group of filmmakers do this collectively? Get together, stick a logo over it and make a big splash.

The name was a take off on Sundance. That was the first year they were getting some negative backlash press, and we were the perfect antidote for that. For every critic of Sundance, they would say, but there are these other guys who still have that spirit. It was clear that we were filling that niche, not only from the filmmakers' perspective, but from the audience perspective - they wanted to see what the next new thing was.

Q - They were coming to see you guys?

Dan - Yeah. We are media whores. And, that is what I brought to the table most. I worked at a press office in Washington, working for a senator, and I knew someone at Variety and I had an agent at that time. And we used their mailroom to sort of spread the word - free postage. And, we were getting front page Variety stories a month before the festival started. New York filmmakers were hearing about it and contacting us. So the first year we ended up with about 40 submissions. At the time, I was working at an electronics store in LA, and in that first Variety story, they didn't give a contact number or anything, but they did say that I was working at this strore, so, people would come in, look for me and submit their films to me! We would watch their films on the big screen TV's in the store!

Q - As the years have gone by, other festivals have picked up on the idea, like No Dance?

Dan - Exactly. We opened Pandora's box. If we hadn't done it, someone else would have within a year or two. That same year, there were several other underground guerilla film festivals starting in the US as well. The New York Underground started, a counter to the New York Film Festival. Chicago Underground, which was in response to the Chicago Film Festival. South by Southwest, which had been a music festival for 20 years, but they started a film component which became a big deal. And, what was called the LA Independent Film Festival, which is now called the LA Film Festival, which was in response to the AFI. And, as far as Park City goes, two years after we started the first alternative festival started, then Slamdunk, No Dance, Lap Dance, Digidance all started their own thing. The key thing that we did very consciously was to be nice to everybody. Every year our submissions go up by 400, so last year we had 2400. Even in our second year we had 400. Venues in Park City are very hard to get, and we wanted something small. The first year we had a dozen features and a dozen shorts. We have grown a little bit and we show more shorts, but the same number of features. This year we may have a completely separate documentary section. But we keep it small. That was part of the problem with Sundance, they had gotten so big, that unless you were one of the hot buzz films, you get kind of left behind.

Q - So, basically you wanted to keep it as you set it up?

Dan - Yes. We stuck to our mantra of first time directors, no US theatrical distribution and low budget, which means under $1m.

Q - Did you set up in Park City from the beginning?

Dan - Yes. One of our venues was 20 feet down the hall from one of Sundance's venues. So people were in line for one of their screenings and went past one of our screenings. But, by keeping the number of filmmakers small and by keeping the expectations of distribution low, it makes Slamdance more fun. The level of expectation is so much higher at Sundance - everyone thinks they are going to get distribution, so if you don't you are just miserable. But, with Slamdance, everyone knows that they might get picked up for distribution, but if you do, it will probably not happen during the festival. So come to it and have a good time, and don't worry about distribution, just meet the other filmmakers. We want to bring filmmakers together because that is the best part of festivals - meeting other directors. Those are the bonds that will see you through the next few years.

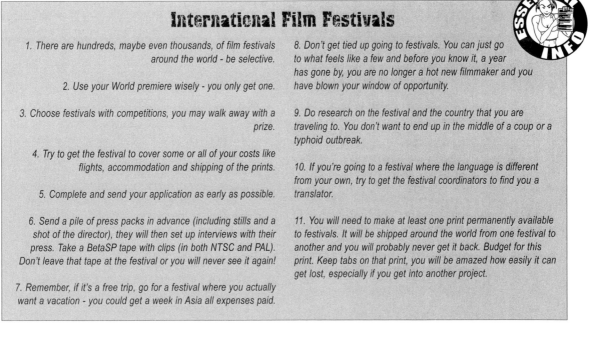

International Film Festivals

1. There are hundreds, maybe even thousands, of film festivals around the world - be selective.

2. Use your World premiere wisely - you only get one.

3. Choose festivals with competitions, you may walk away with a prize.

4. Try to get the festival to cover some or all of your costs like flights, accommodation and shipping of the prints.

5. Complete and send your application as early as possible.

6. Send a pile of press packs in advance (including stills and a shot of the director), they will then set up interviews with their press. Take a BetaSP tape with clips (in both NTSC and PAL). Don't leave that tape at the festival or you will never see it again!

7. Remember, if it's a free trip, go for a festival where you actually want a vacation - you could get a week in Asia all expenses paid.

8. Don't get tied up going to festivals. You can just go to what feels like a few and before you know it, a year has gone by, you are no longer a hot new filmmaker and you have blown your window of opportunity.

9. Do research on the festival and the country that you are traveling to. You don't want to end up in the middle of a coup or a typhoid outbreak.

10. If you're going to a festival where the language is different from your own, try to get the festival coordinators to find you a translator.

11. You will need to make at least one print permanently available to festivals. It will be shipped around the world from one festival to another and you will probably never get it back. Budget for this print. Keep tabs on that print, you will be amazed how easily it can get lost, especially if you get into another project.

Q - How is Slamdance organized?

Dan - Technically there are four of us who own Slamdance. Me, Peter Baxter, Shane Kuhn and Jon Fitzgerald. We have had a lot of other people, like our guy in NY, this guy named Paul Rachman who was also one of the very first people involved. I like to say, *'It's more than a festival and slightly less than a movement and bordering on cult at various times'*. Once you are in the family, you can't get out! If you are in the festival one year, we make you a programmer the next year. If you are a programmer one year, we will make you a juror the next year. If you are in New York, guess what? You are part of our New York office. And, because we are so strict about that first time director thing, it's not like we are showing the same alumni's films every year. We are constantly rejecting alumni films. My own film got rejected!

Q - Are the programmers people who work for you or are they volunteers?

Dan - They are all volunteers and they are mostly alumni of Slamdance. We are very much an alumni based organization when it comes to programming. People submit a film to our office and it gets seen by two different people. We have a scoring system of 1 through 10. If a film gets two bad scores initially, then we sort of eliminate it from contention. If it gets two good scores or just one good score, it goes on to a third watch. Then when it comes down through the process of elimination to about 100 or 200 films, we sit down and have meetings. It doesn't go by numbers anymore, now we are talking about each film and why we liked it and they are getting watched six or seven times. With the shorts there will be group viewings. Eventually we come up with a consensus of the top 12 films. The key thing that distinguishes us is that we don't make any early invitations, and that is a real difference between us and Sundance as well as other festivals. If Geoff Gilmore or one of the other top programmers sees a film that they like at Toronto, they can say on the spot, *'I love your film, it's in the festival!'* Well, the problem with that is that is one slot that is no longer available. What we do is we keep all the slots open until the last minute. And, the other thing is that it is completely non-hierarchical. I have no more say than anyone else. And, as far as what we look for, other than the director / budget / distribution thing, there's no real criteria.

The documentary criteria is different and it must be interesting and original content, but it must also be in an original and interesting form. And, that is tough for documentaries because it may be great subject matter, but if it's shot like other documentaries, then pick another festival. The other thing we do, which other people may not realize, is that we call the filmmakers right before we make the final decision, in that last weekend. We sort of try as best as we can to feel out the filmmakers a little bit over the phone to see if they are interesting people. See if they have a good attitude, see if they really want to be in the festival, see if they have gotten distribution since they submitted the film. For us, it is more about the filmmaker than it is about the film itself.

Q - Do you offer other programs throughout the year or during the festival?

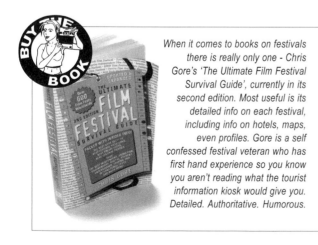

When it comes to books on festivals there is really only one - Chris Gore's 'The Ultimate Film Festival Survival Guide', currently in its second edition. Most useful is its detailed info on each festival, including info on hotels, maps, even profiles. Gore is a self confessed festival veteran who has first hand experience so you know you aren't reading what the tourist information kiosk would give you. Detailed. Authoritative. Humorous.

Dan - We started a screenplay competition, and that has become a big deal in itself. We got 1500 submissions last year. We do that in the off-season, spring and summer. We have had success stories from that as well. The unique thing that we do, compared to other screenplay competitions is, win or lose, everyone gets constructive criticism coverage. We also do On the Road Screenings. And, then we do screenings in LA, NY, and now we have a regular screening in New York every other month. We've done events in Cannes for the last 5 years. We've also done things in Stockholm, Amsterdam, Santiago, Chile, China, India and South Africa. Sometimes they are done in conjunction with other film festivals, like Stockholm who invited to do a bunch of Slamdance things apart from what they do.

Q - So, once a filmmaker gets into Slamdance, they have the opportunity of a full year of screenings?

Dan - We don't call ourselves a traveling film festival, but, we do have ties with other festivals, and even if there is no official Slamdance event, we will put them in touch with South By Southwest or the Atlanta Film Festival or Maryland. We also have an online film festival year round which is called Anarchy, and that happens once every other month. We show three short films and we are in our third year of that, and the winners are selected by the online audience. Then we show all the winners in Park City in a special section.

Q - Do you have to pay for any of these?

Dan - Yeah, that's how we raise funds. It is around $50, but look online to be sure. With the screenplay competition and the festival, if people submit early or late, we have staggered deadlines, and different fees.

Q - What are the great success stories of Slamdance?

Dan - Marc Forsters won the audience award in our second year for his feature *Loungers*. He went on to direct *Monster's Ball*, which did quite well. We were one of the first festivals to spot Chris Nolan's talent when we screened his debut *Following*. Ray McKinnon won the Oscar for best live-action short for his film *The Accountant*, which we'd premiered and he has directed *Chrystal* starring Billy Bob Thornton. The same year we showed Ray's film, we also premiered David Greenspan's *Bean Cake* which went on to win the Palm D'Or for best short in Cannes. Mike Mitchell who directed *Duece Bigalow* is a great example of a guy who does well with a short at Slamdance and because of that gets a studio film.

Q - If there are mistakes for new filmmakers to avoid, what would it be?

Dan - The biggest mistake new filmmakers make is to copy or pay homage to whatever the hottest new indie film was the year before. After *Reservoir Dogs* and *Pulp Fiction*, it was like five years of Tarantino films one after another. And, if a film has four of the following six things, it doesn't work for us - If it's about a group of twenty-somethings sitting around a bar, smoking, taking drugs and talking about how they are going to film themselves robbing a bank, stay away from it.

Like *Clerks*, there were a lot of those things in there. Anything that is about twentysomethings, any film that is about filmmakers that is self referential about making films, cut it out. You will get that response from every festival director, every festival programmers, every distribution person. It may be an absolutely brilliant film, but the bar is so much higher. Another big mistake is to copy Hollywood films. So when people are making light romantic comedies, which if they star Tom Hanks and Meg Ryan they do great. But, they work because they have big time actors in them. If you cannot afford big name actors, don't make a big name genre film. It won't succeed on the festival level because festivals are not that interested in modern Hollywood films. And, they will not work in the commercial world because you don't have big name actors in it. To succeed in the indie arena, you have to be original.

Q - What about any technical points that comes up?

Dan - Editing is one of the poorest things. People have a way of focusing on cinematography when they are in production, they will get fixated on perfect lighting, especially now when they are deciding on doing film or digital. Where as at the end of the day, editing is far more important. That is how I can spot a bad film right away is if it is not cut tightly. If you are submitting a film to a festival, and a lot of people ask me this, at what point can you submit a film? Can it be in rough-cut stage? As long as you can hear the dialogue, that should determine when you can start submitting the film.

Q - Is it detrimental to submit a film that does not have the final music to it?

Dan - It's got to feel like a real movie, so even if it's temp music, as long it's not big temp sound. With my own film, I had to take the final cut of the picture, but with big temp sound, and you could see all the cuts in it. And, I submitted that to 15 festivals and didn't get into a single one. As soon as I had a completely finished version of the film on tape, all of a sudden I got into a lot more places. Festival directors will lie and say, *'we will look at anything at any stage'.* We say that too. But the reality is that we are more interested in the film, the more finished it is.

Q - So if you can wait, then it is best to wait?

Dan - Everyone is concerned about the schedule, *'I have to finish it by Sundance'.* The most important thing is to take your time with it. Don't rush it for an arbitrary deadline of a festival. You don't have to premiere the film at Sundance, you can premiere at other festivals at other times of the year, which will make the filmmaker happy. At the end of the day, you start to realize that you will have to live with this film for the rest of your life. And, you have to sell it, so you better damn well be happy with it. If you make cuts because someone else tells you to do it…if it's a good idea, then you should do it…but, if you do it to please a festival director or a distributor, especially if you don't get distribution, then you are going to be stuck with an ugly stepchild that you don't want to look at for the rest of your life.

Q - What general advice would you give a filmmaker who is starting up?

Dan -Take the time to know what you are doing first. Whether that is by making a bunch of short films, going to film school, or working on other people's films. So when you are ready to make your first feature or serious short, and you are about to spend your Mom's money or grandmother's inheritance, you know what you are doing. Not only how to make the film, but just as importantly what is going to happen next. Read the book I wrote the intro for, Bret Stern's *How To Make A Film For Under $10,000 And Not Go To Jail,* Read Chris Gore's book, *The Ultimate Film Festival Survival Guide.* People don't even think about film festivals until after they have made their film, which is the last time you want to think about it. Go to film festivals so you can see what is out there. All festivals have great panel discussions that you can learn tons from. Go to the Independent Feature Film Market in New York. Not necessarily the best market to sell your film, but it is a really great seminar.

Q - What would you say to filmmakers about all of these film festivals out there around the world?

Dan - Pick and choose carefully because there are so many and you can't afford to submit to all of them. Ask yourself why you are submitting to each of them. Slamdance is reasonably obvious, if I go to Slamdance I will get some attention. But, a lot of people will not go to a lot of mid sized festivals because the Hollywood people won't be there. In a mid sized American festival you could get a great review from a local critic which you can use, and if they are bad reviews, no one sees them. And, some of those festivals are great for meeting other filmmakers and meeting the jurors. Or, they may be at a great resort location and you get a good vacation - they may fly you there. There are a lot of festivals that people may have not heard of that are completely worth going to. Also, think about location. Even if it is a crappy festival in LA or New York, you can turn the screening into something bigger than it is, then it may be worth it.

Nancy Schafer of the Tribeca Film Festival

EXPERT OPINION

Q - How did the Tribeca Film Festival start and when does it take place?

Nancy - The Tribeca Film Festival was founded by Jane Rosenthal and Robert De Niro to bring art and commerce to downtown Manhattan in the wake of September 11th, and to celebrate New York City as a major filmmaking center. The Festival is an eclectic mix of independent American and international films as well as various panels, one-on-one discussions with influential filmmakers, workshops, and the Tribeca Family Festival. It takes place for nine days in early May at theaters and venues around downtown Manhattan. We look for narrative, documentary and short films from all over the United States and the world. We choose work that catches our eye, surprises us, startles us, and reminds us of why we love filmmaking. The submission window begins in early October and ends in early January. For the most complete information, please refer to our website - www.tribecafilmfestival.org - where you can also sign up for our mailing list to get submission details via email. We notify by mid March 1st. Last year we had 2400 applications and we screened 300. We have a pre-screening committee, but all the final decisions are made by the three programmers: Peter Scarlet, Executive Director, David Kwok and myself.

Q - What is the Tribeca Family Festival?

Nancy - The Tribeca Family Festival is comprised of film screenings and panels for children and their parents as well as the Tribeca Family Festival Street Fair, which last year had over 300,000 attendees. Events at the street fair include jugglers, puppeteers and storytellers. It takes place during the main festival.

Q - What is the Tribeca Film Institute? What does it offer to filmmakers?

Nancy - The Tribeca Film Institute develops year round screening and panel content. In conjunction with the Tribeca Film Festival and the Alfred P. Sloan Foundation, it offers an annual screenwriting contest where the winners are offered expert industry advice and financial support to develop their scripts for the screen. The writers each receive $48k over the 8 month period while they are participating in the program. They each have writing advisors and science advisors who meet with them and provide advice about content and style during the re-write process. The Institute showcases at least one of the scripts at a reading during the Festival. Members of the film industry, including agents, producers and directors, are invited to the reception that follows. The Institute also makes efforts to introduce the writers to agents and producers who may be interested in the projects, when possible. For more information on this program, please visit 'Tribeca/Sloan Film Program' on the website.

Q - What is the Tribeca Film Center?

Nancy - The Tribeca Film Center is a building that is home to many entertainment companies. Robert De Niro and Jane Rosenthal partnered many years ago to establish a place in New York City where filmmakers, writers, and other creative people could work and create an environment to enhance their businesses. The building rents executive offices, a screening room, conference rooms and reception areas. Many of the tenants help each other with production services and advice on such things as editing, music, legal and more. The Tribeca Film Institute is a non-profit organization and is not the same company as the Tribeca Film Center, however, its founders are the same and much of the Institute and Festival executives are housed in the Film Center.

DISTRIBUTION

Kenneth Turan
LA Times

FILM CRITIC

Q - What is your job?

Kenneth - My job is to look at a film and offer an intelligent opinion, with an eye towards helping people understand what they are going to look at and if they want to see it or not.

Q - What is unique to low budget films from your perspective?

Kenneth - Low budget films have the luxury of being personal. They don't have to conform to the demands of the market place and that's a wonderful thing. They can be original and daring, and take chances and do all the things that expensive studio films have a much harder time doing.

Q - Would you say low budget movies are on a level playing field with bigger films once they hit the screen?

Kenneth - Absolutely. Frankly, most critics are desperate for the sort of satisfaction a really good independent film can offer.

Q - What should a filmmaker give to you to make your job easier?

Kenneth - Accurate information. Names of the actors and names of the people they play. A little bit about each member of the cast. It's always helpful to have information about what they've done previously and it helps to have information about how this project came to be - how this film got made. All standard stuff.

Q - Is it a good idea to get the press involved early on in the film?

Kenneth - As a critic, I do not want to be involved until the film is finished. It's my job to look at the film and if I get too personally connected with it, it's harder for me to look at it with any degree of objectivity. But as a film journalist, if the film is of interest, you'd rather write about it sooner rather than later. It's worth trying to be in touch with a journalist while the film is being made if you have an interesting story that you think would lend itself to a feature article. When I deal with independent filmmakers, some of them mistakenly think I can review the film before it is in theaters and they want me to do a blurb. The more you know about how journalism works, the better off you'll be when you attempt to deal with journalists.

Q - So you should know what the journalist wants?

Kenneth - Yes and what people do at what publications. For instance, I don't do feature stories and so to pitch one to me is a waste of time. The more time you put into it, the better the results will be. Invest time into reading the publication you want to pitch to, knowing who does what, what they will and will not do, so you can call and say, *'look, I think this is what you want to be doing'*. This isn't brain surgery. What it takes though, is putting in some time. I know its very time consuming to make a film, but there's no way around it. The more time you put into understanding the media, the better the response you will get from the media.

Q - Would a film journalist prefer to be approached early on?

Kenneth - Sure, but what everyone has to realize is everyone gets bombarded by a lot of things, so you should devote as much time as you can to thinking about this and trying to come up with an angle that will interest the journalist. If you have a journalistic sense and develop a sense of what makes something a story, if you read a lot of film journalists and see what they are interested in, then it's much easier when you come to the journalist and say, *'this is the angle, this is what I think you should be writing about my film'*. Journalists are looking for things to write about, but it has to be interesting.

Q - Is it a good idea to have a hook?

Kenneth - Yes. You have to.

Q - Is it a good idea to put an anecdotal story in your press pack?

Kenneth - Yes. Any background to the film is always of interest. Different critics do this differently. I do not read press material until after I've seen the film. I don't want to have anything in my mind besides the film. At that point, I'm interested in anything that might shed some light on the film, that might help me understand it better.

Q - Is it the distributor that invites you to the screenings?

Kenneth - Usually what happens if people can afford it, is they will hire a publicist. But this is not essential. I've been invited by filmmakers themselves and by distributors.

Q - What advice would you give a self distributing filmmaker?

Kenneth - Understand that we can't review something until it has a release date. I don't just write about films that are out there. This is not a blanket rule, but for me and most major publications, there has to be a release date. The second thing is, because we tend to be swamped, the more in advance you can call us, the better. If you call us and say, *'my film is opening tomorrow'*, it makes it harder.

Q - How far in advance should they call you?

Kenneth - If the film has a firm release date, I would say a month in advance. The critic may not be able to get to it for a week or so after you call.

Q - Do you prefer seeing the film projected properly or have a tape sent to you?

Kenneth - I won't review off of a tape. I could do it, but I prefer not to. We have done it at the paper at times, if the filmmaker cannot afford to rent a screening room, but we all prefer screening rooms.

Q - Do you prefer to have coffee, tea, general hospitalities available?

Kenneth - That stuff is nice, but not essential. Most of the screenings I go to, there's no coffee or tea. It's nothing you need to worry about. If the room you have provides it, that's fine. What's important is that things are run in a professional manner - that the film starts roughly on time and someone is there to start it. Try and have it in a professional room.

Q - Do you like it if the filmmaker is there to introduce the film?

Kenneth - It's interesting to see who made this film, but it can be awkward too. I would discourage the filmmaker from watching the film with you. We are there to judge the film and it sets a whole other dynamic in play if the person who made the film is sitting there with you.

Q - Is there a particular time of day that is best to invite reviewers to see the film?

DISTRIBUTION

Handling Interviews

If you wanted to be in front of the camera, you would have been an actor. However, as the filmmaker or producer, you will have to do interviews in order to publicize your project. It's unavoidable.

1. Have a list of questions prepared which you can offer the interviewer who might not be prepared.

2. You will be asked the same questions over and over again. Be prepared with responses that are concise, intelligent, humorous or profound. Ask the interviewer to show you the questions in advance.

3. If you are being recorded, pause before answering. This will give the editor a clear editing point.

4. Try to answer the question with the question in the answer. For example, 'What was it like, working with an elephant?', answered, 'Working with the elephant was amazing...'

5. Say the name of your film as many times as you can without becoming annoying. Try to avoid referring to it as the 'film', 'movie' or 'project'. If people don't know what it is called, they won't go see it.

6. Wear something interesting so that at the very least you will stand out.

7. It is not a bad thing to avoid answering confrontational questions, especially if the reporter has an axe to grind, or you suspect a hidden agenda. Politely decline to answer or shift the conversation back to the film itself. Remember, controversy equals free publicity.

8. Always have your publicity stuff on you - press pack, EPK, stills, posters, etc.

9. Telling good, relevant stories is always better than giving boring standard information. Be entertaining.

10. Make sure you know how long the interview will last so you can organize yourself to get the maximum amount of information out in the allotted time.

11. Have business cards printed up and give one to the interviewer so that they can always contact you and spell your name correctly.

12. The interviewer may want you to say something particular, or in a particular way. Try to be flexible here and let them put words in your mouth - as long as they are accurate!

13. If you don't want something to get into the press, don't say it to them.

14. Always be complimentary of other filmmakers, actors and their work. If you have nothing nice to say, don't say anything at all.

15. Try to avoid talking about the budget of your film unless it was truly a remarkable feat such as you made it for $7k from a lottery win.

16. Do any and all interviews, local radio and TV, newspapers, magazines etc. Not just because it's free press, but it's good training for when you have to do the kind of live interviews that will scare the s**t out of you!

Kenneth - No. It varies, depending on how busy we are. Most critics like to see a film during the five working days, but if circumstances demand it, people will go on the weekend, but there has to be a good reason for it. Every critic likes different times of the day. Most screenings are at night which I'm happy with.

Q - How many screenings would you suggest?

Kenneth - It depends. One reason you hire a publicist is that they understand how this is all done. For most critics, if you give them a choice of three or four screenings, it's probably good enough, but with the critics from larger publications, who's schedules are hectic and they have to see a lot more films, you should keep it in the back of your mind that you may need to set up screenings around their schedule. Find out what the key media are in whatever city you are in and make sure they can make one of your screenings.

Q - Is one advantage of having a publicist that they know who's out there and who works for who?

Kenneth - Absolutely. There's no question that it helps to have a publicist, but not everyone can afford one, especially these days where people are making films for almost no money.

Q - If you can't afford one, is there any advice you'd offer?

Kenneth - The quality of the reviews depend on the quality of the film. The amount of journalistic attention you get depends, in part, on how smart you are in coming up with hooks or angles or stratagems that will interest an editor or reporter. The movie business is a business that seems to thrive on excess. What the *Blair Witch* People did was draw on the audience's response to the film, and what drove the audiences response was an extremely shrewd web campaign, and the campaign got the people out. Once the people were out, the journalists noticed. So initially, the focus was not on the journalists. It was a better campaign than the film was.

Q - Would you recommend new filmmakers use the Internet as a marketing tool?

Kenneth - It seems to help. The majority of movie goers (people in their 20's and 30's) are big Internet users, so this is a great thing to do, and if you're good at it, it can't hurt.

Q - What is positioning?

Kenneth - These things are devil's bargains. Most people don't want to feel if they take their film seriously that it's pigeon holeable and you can boil their film down to a sentence or one sheet for a marketing concept. But if a film is really good, it is true. You can do a film justice with that kind of campaign. On the other hand, there are so many films out there. We are in a world in LA where in a given week, a dozen films will open. You must, as a filmmaker, find a way to make yourself heard. You cant just say *'I've got an interesting film'*. That may be true, but you won't reach your audience that way. Other films are yelling too loudly. You must have some other way to differentiate your film. One way to help is to get the movie into a festivals, where, if it is good, the film critics will see it and the critics will create the hook for you. That's what happened with *Whale Rider* - it's been a huge festival success, starting with Toronto, and that became the strength of the film, that people loved it in festivals. That was enough of a hook to get people to write about it in newspapers and get critics interested.

Q - Do festival awards help?

Kenneth - Sure. But there are many festivals and the more obscure the festival, the less important the award is.

Q - Is it worth putting the smaller film festival awards in your press pack?

Kenneth - Yes. It can't hurt.

Q - Do you see all the films that have a release date, or do you select certain ones?

Kenneth - We have three critics at the LA Times so we divide up the films. It's personal as to what we choose to review. Every critic has films where when they hear about it, their ears perk up. Among the three of us at the Times, sometimes there are films we all want to se, other times only one of us is interested.

Q - Do journalists talk to each other with regards to the films they review?

Kenneth - To a certain extent. Once I've seen a film, I don't want to talk to anyone until I've written about it. You want to keep your focus. There are critics who's taste I share and if they've gone to a festival and they've seen something, I'm always interested in being tipped off by them, saying, *'this is a film I think you'll find interesting'*.

Q - Should you approach ALL journalists with your film?

Kenneth - You should do your homework and be selective.

Q - If there are certain publications that cover the same thing, should you approach them all, or pick out the ones you think are best?

Kenneth - On a given publication, you should only contact one person, because if you contact two people and they both want to do the story, you may end up with no story. Often, you are better off contacting the editor or whoever it is that's responsible for assigning stories, and let him or her figure out whether they want to report on it.

Q - If there are several publications in the same vein, would you suggest going to the one that best suits your film or talking to each?

Kenneth - Often these publications overlap in what they write about. When you're talking about *Time* and *Newsweek* and *The Matrix*, you're only going to get one of them. When you're talking about a small, independent film, several magazines might write about that. I don't think you have to contact just one of them. The editor involved should let you know if they have exclusivity concerns.

Q - Is there a long lead time with magazines?

Kenneth - It's months and months. It depends on the magazine. If you have magazines you're interested in, you should write them or call them and find out what their lead time is and make sure that you've given them plenty of time to have the story finished by

Publicity on Set

People get a buzz from being on a film set. This includes the press, which you can use to your advantage while you are still in production.

1. Invite local newspaper, TV and radio reporters down to the set for a first hand look at moviemaking in action. It will get them excited, especially if you are shooting in a small community that does not get a dose of Hollywood every day. This can result in unexpected favors from interested locals. Movie making is magical and interesting to most people outside of NY and LA.

2. While you have them, use your cast for interviews. It is much easier than trying to wrangle them later, when they are on another project. Make sure you shoot your own interviews for your EPK at the same time.

3. Create slides or CD-ROMS of still photographs of the director and principle cast in action. Hand these out to the visiting reporters to make their lives easier.

4. Having a constant flow of press coverage will make your investors happy.

5. Don't blow the big publicity yet, you want to keep that for when the film is released.

6. Collect and archive of all articles that occur on your project. It will come in handy later for promotional purposes and future project fundraising. There are some professional clipping services like Burrelles, who track TV, radio and magazines around the country for stories, that you can approach to get hard to find reviews. These organizations tend to be expensive.

7. Build a dedicated section on your website for press. You will be amazed how few filmmakers do this. Get some great photos and allow them to be used for free. You will soon find your pictures appearing in newspapers and magazines. Make sure the are high resolution and if you use JPEG compression, don't apply too much as it make the image look poor.

the time the film comes out. Some film publications will write about a film if they really love it, even if it doesn't have distribution. Some publications like to discover smaller films and maybe help the film get distribution. But most publications will want to tie their story to a release date.

Q - If an article can get into the paper on the opening weekend, is that beneficial?

Kenneth - If you have an interview with an actor or yourself it is good press. It all depends on how interesting you make the film sound.

Q - Are there any cases where the film isn't that great, but the story behind it is intriguing and makes good press?

Kenneth - Absolutely. It's often not a factor in determining whether a story is written or not. The quality of the film, or whether the papers film critic likes it or not is often not a factor in assigning a story. A film can have an interesting story that can fascinate the readers and not be a film that the critics like. Those things don't, and shouldn't, go together.

Q - Are there any organizations that co-ordinate times and screenings for journalists?

Kenneth - No. It's pretty much catch as catch can. That's another reason why you need multiple screenings, otherwise your film may be going up against *The Matrix* and most critics will have to go to *The Matrix*.

Q - What final piece of advice would you give?

Kenneth - Be as professional as possible when dealing with the media, and put the time in to understand what we do, how we do it and who does what. That's why you hire a publicist, because as a filmmaker, you often don't have the time or energy leftover to do that. It is universally hard to make a small film so that can't be your hook to a journalist. A lot of filmmakers think it can be, *'I made this ultra low budget movie'* - there are a lot of people saying that and you need to have a little more.

DISTRIBUTION

Renee Tab
ICM

Q - What is your job?

Renée - I'm a motion picture literary agent and my core business is representing writers, directors and producers.

Q - How do filmmakers get an agent?

Renée - It's about making a great product - write a great script, make a great movie and then utilize the relationships you have, and make to find the right representative.

Q - Do you go to festivals to find talent?

Renée - Yes it's a great source of discovering new talent and seeing filmmakers reinvent themselves as well. Agents cover festivals of all sizes.

Q - Do you sign people up when you see their showreel?

Renée - Yes, it's based on the quality of the work.

Q - Do you ever pick up talent from film schools?

Renée - I haven't yet but would be open to it. I think it's exciting to find young talent, nurture their careers and help them grow.

Q - Are the studio's looking for new wave filmmakers?

Renée - I believe studios are always looking for a new point of view in storytelling. Of course that also means new filmmakers must be extra prepared and put in the work to get the job.

Q - What kind of agent would you recommend to new filmmakers?

Renée - Someone who truly believes in your talent. Somebody you like on a personal level, but you don't need your agent to be your friend. Your agent needs to be inspired by your work, to live, breath and sleep your business.

Q - How does the commission work?

Renée - Generally the agency receives a commission of 10% and manager relationships vary.

Q - Can producers have agents?

Renée - A lot of producers have agents, as they are fed more material and their deals are looked after. The bigger producers don't need agents because they want material and commissions from everybody.

Q - Could a new producer get an agent?

Renée - Yes and the need for agency representation depends on the specific producer, but to have an agency working for you on a daily basis can only be a positive.

Q - What are the advantages and disadvantages to having an agent?

Renée - In my opinion you are at a disadvantage without an agent. Agencies provide so much information and have access to so many more opportunities that are just physically impossible to monitor without the group working on your behalf. Additionally, it's best to let the agent focus on the business side of your career so your energy can be spent on the creative.

Q - Is it common for new filmmakers to have unrealistic expectations and then become disillusioned with the agent?

Renée - It is common for all human beings to have unrealistic expectations but you must set goals and visualize what you are striving for. It's important for the filmmaker to be realistic about where they stand in the market place. If they are a first time filmmaker, they shouldn't expect to direct a $100m movie. It is my job, as an agent, to explain this to my client and to work out a strategy that will eventually get them to directing a movie of that size.

Q - What kind of projects could a new filmmaker get after being signed to an agency?

Renée - It's all relative to the filmmaker. There isn't one perfect answer because it varies from filmmaker to filmmaker, however studios like to keep filmmakers working within the same genre so first time filmmakers are most likely to get a film within the genre of their first film but at greater a budget. The other major possibility is that they will get one of their own projects made.

Getting An Agent

1. Invite agents to screenings of your film and explain that you are seeking representation. The big film festivals and those in NY and LA are great for this.

2. Don't sign with the first agent. Make sure you go with a person you like, who understands your tastes and what you want to do with your potential career.

3. Don't necessarily go for the biggest or most glamorous agency, as you will be the small fish in a pond, alongside very BIG FISH who make a lot more money for the agency, and therefore get the most attention.

4. The agent won't get you work, they will just get you into a room with the people who can offer you work. Then it is up to you to sell yourself.

5. Arm your agent with press clippings, copies of your film and showreels.

6. Listen to your agent. If you have chosen wisely they will mentor you and help you through the new world of the film business. It is not the same world as the low budget one - it is much more political. So, open your mind and learn.

7. If you have made a well-received first film, everyone will be watching the second to see if you are a fluke. A good agent will minimize this risk by steering you toward projects that will showcase your strengths.

8. Keep in touch and find that fine line between proactive and pestering. If you haven't spoken to your agent for several weeks, give them a call to remind them you exist, and to think of you for any projects. You can also remind them to follow up on any meetings that you've had or want.

9. If you are partnered (producer with director or writer with director for example), discuss how you will deal with an imbalance of power / opportunity when success comes. And, remember that even if only one of you gets representation, it will still open doors for the other, which may lead to that person getting their own agent down the road.

10. Make contact with as many writers, producers and actors as you can from within and outside the agency and form alliances. Nothing gets an agent more excited than a packaged project that they can sell.

AFTERMATH

Q - What kind of income would a new filmmaker expect on a studio film and what other ways can they earn money?

Renee - If you're coming from some hot, little indie movie, you're not going to be making a lot of money on a studio picture as a director. However it depends on the budget. As a writer, the most common ways to earn money are writing a spec (a new screenplay) or getting a rewrite job.

Q - What's the likelihood that you would have control on a studio picture?

Renée - Control on any picture, studio or independently financed, will be more likely if you work with producers and executives who share your vision and will support you during the process. Typically, writers, directors who bring the material have an advantage of maintaining control.

Q - Do film festivals and awards help?

Renée - Additional exposure always helps, especially from film festivals. It's also important to surround yourself in a community of other filmmakers.

Q - You surround yourself with other filmmakers as you never know where it's going to lead...?

Renée - Yes and no, it's easy to get lost in the noise, but you never know where a great opportunity will come from. My answer is to network but stay focused on the ultimate goal.

Q - A lot of writers have to pitch after writing alone for a long time. Is that difficult?

Renée - It can be difficult and I would suggest practicing a lot, such as in front of your friends or the mirror, and even taking an acting or public speaking class. You should be able to communicate your vision with energy, vibrancy and with the tone the story is going to be in. You want the executives to be excited to be working with you.

Q - Do you have any advice for a new filmmaker, who's made a hit DV movie and has then gone on to make a $15m movie?

Renée - Be prepared and ask the people you respect for advice. A great film to see is Terry Gilliam's documentary *Lost in La Mancha*, because it portrays everything that can possibly go wrong making a film.

Q - If you have a $20m movie, with a new director, how do you ensure he or she is comfortable?

Renée - We believe in our clients ability to handle such a budget otherwise we wouldn't guide them in that direction. Once they go into pre-production we encourage them to surround themselves with a great cast and crew.

Q - What are the open writing assignments?

Renée -Typically they are projects at studios that need writers to adapt novels, rewrite existing scripts, develop original ideas and remake a film.

Q - Are these projects sent out to all the agencies?

Renée - No, but through relationships we have with the studios we obtain the information.

Q - Is it a good idea to have a screenplay ready after completing your first film?

Shaun Redick
ICM

Q - What is your job?

Shaun - I work in International Operations at ICM. We act as consultants to our clients in regards to independent feature film packaging, finance and distribution.

Q - How does the packaging process work?

Shaun - My hope is that it starts with a really great book or script. Usually a client, either a producer, actor, director, or writer will have a concept, or material, that they are very passionate about and will bring this to our international packaging group for consultation in terms of what actors are available and will spark to the script. If we are in need of a director, then based on the subject matter, we will put together some ideas. The trick is to build value into the feature package throughout the process, because in most situations with packaging a feature, the financing and distribution comes after the actors and director are attached. Financing for an indie feature, 9 times out of 10, is not based on passion but profit potential that is based on the actors and filmmaker attached to your feature. Distribution works in the same direction, but is by far the hardest point to achieve in the packaging process.

Q - What do you look for in projects for packaging?

Shaun - Mostly, a very passionate client. Rarely do we stray outside of our client's needs. However, often a senior agent will bring to us a major actor or director's feature that has a personal element to it and that will give us incentive to start putting the film together because our starting point is at the top level already. Many of these type of personal, potentially low budget films, end up with the most awards and kudos at the end of the year.

Q - How do you choose which festivals to go to with regards to both your clients and looking for projects to package?

Shaun - Seriously, it's all about Sundance, Cannes and the Toronto Film Festivals. Sundance and Toronto are set up to sell your finished product. Cannes is both to showcase a feature in need of media attention and world wide distribution, and also to meet with international financiers and distributors to pitch your feature package, in hopes of securing your financing to cover the budget.

Q - Do you deal with any of the distribution aspects of a film? i.e. marketing etc.

Shaun - We stay in the game throughout all aspects - packaging, raising financing, film festivals, markets, world wide distribution, and once a studio or independent distributor buys the rights, we try as much as possible to consult on the marketing that we feel the film needs to succeed. More than that we expect and want our clients opinions and needs to be heard.

Renée - It's a great idea to be proactive as this town moves quickly. It's important to move on to the next 'right' feature when you feel ready. However you don't want to spend too much time in between as then you'll have to reintroduce yourself to the town.

Q - What common mistakes do you find with new filmmakers?

Renée - It's relative to each individual and circumstance, but my overall advice would be to trust your representatives and maintain a sense of humility.

Q - What advice would you offer new filmmakers?

Renée - It's impressive when you go into a room really prepared. Don't go if you're having an off day. Do your homework, know who you're talking to, know why you're talking to them, know what they like. Love what you do and don't sell yourself short. Don't go after something just because you want to make a movie, but make sure it's what you want to make. Keep a great attitude and be positive. Try and stay grounded and surround yourself with great people.

AFTERMATH

Carlos Goodman
Entertainment Attorney

Q - What do you do as an entertainment lawyer?

Carlos - I represent talent in their dealings with the studios and independents. That may involve development deals with the studios where the studios pay for a writer or filmmaker to develop a script, or it may involve a financing deal where there is no development and instead a commitment to finance the movie, subject maybe to casting the film in a way that the financier wants. In the independent context, an important thing for me to do is structure the deal in a way that makes sure that the film either happens or if it doesn't that the filmmaker can walk away and not get stuck in 'development hell' as it's called.

Q - What is the best way to find a good lawyer?

Carlos - Most people find their lawyers through their agents or managers. Networking is a good way, too.

Q - Do most people have an agent and a lawyer and not a manager?

Carlos - Mostly an agent and lawyer. You pay the agent 10% and the lawyer 5%. Some people also have personal managers at another 10%, or even business managers at another 5% - it can be a bit too much help for an independent director.

Q - Are there any problems that can arise between independent producers and directors should an external entity take over the project?

Carlos - If you don't formalize an agreement between a producer and a director, you can get into a lot of trouble if things don't work out later. The issues that would come about in that situation would be the producer's protection that if they're about to commit themselves to work hard for a writer/director, that they have some protection for the situation in which the writer/director gets a better deal if they choose to work with someone else. For example, if a big producer comes along and says *'this is fantastic, forget about your little producer, let's make the movie together'*. So the young producer might insist upon some sort of exclusive right to produce the movie, and they might enter into an agreement that would be called an attachment agreement. That would typically provide the producer with a legal attachment to the picture for some specified period of time.

For the writer/director, if they are willing to limit themselves to this producer, they would also want to make sure that the producer makes a grant of all rights back to the writer/director of any creative contributions the director makes to the script or the project. This is because a period of time could go by and the young producer is never able to get anything happening and then the director says, *'Sorry, it hasn't worked out, I'm going to move on and find a new producer'*. Then the first producer says, *'Wait a minute. I gave you that idea that you're using in act three and I was the one that worked with you to make the script better while we were trying to get the movie made and I had all these ideas in there. You can't use those ideas without compensating me'*. That's a worst case scenario, but that's something that you want to have clarified in advance.

Q - Is a verbal agreement binding?

Carlos - By and large, yes - although copyright can only be transferred by written agreement. But in the area of ideas, which are not copyrightable, verbal agreements can have force and effect. However, the person who's depending on the verbal agreement can be in a weak position - and the law is shifting in the direction of limiting claims based on idea theft. The problem can happen when two people have a verbal understanding and one person goes off and starts doing something without the other person. The other person might claim that they should have had some entitlement to be involved in the project. The problem is financiers don't want to step into a lawsuit, so the person claiming to be excluded can really muck up the works simply by writing a letter claiming to be involved. The claim won't be covered by insurance and the financier will look to the individual against whom the claim is made to indemnify the financier. It gets very tricky.

Q - What would the case be if someone had a great idea and asked you to flesh it out and after you did, they didn't like it?

Carlos - It happens all the time and this is an area of law that is in flux a bit. The person who has the idea could never stop the person who went ahead and developed it and wrote it from exploiting that material, but they might have a claim that they have the right to be involved in that project because they expressed the idea to the person with the understanding that they would involve each other if this idea was used somehow. That creates a contractual relationship of sorts that is shared on the basis that one party knows the other party is involved. Unfortunately for the person that has the idea, ideas are not protected by copyright law and so the nature of the claim is different and could be claimed for damages.

Q - What's the likelihood of a new filmmaker getting final cut when working with a studio?

Carlos - That very rarely happens on a first time basis. There are situations in which a filmmaker has done a small film that's not a studio movie, but its so highly regarded and well received that the studio wants to be in business with that filmmaker at all costs and maybe they will give a final cut deal to that person. That would typically be something the director wrote to direct themselves, not a piece of material the studio has.

Q - What should an independent filmmaker look for in a studio/distributor?

Carlos - You want to know that if you make a movie, that this is a studio that has been successful distributing films like the one you have and that the studio has a track record of doing a good job with small films via festivals, Academy approaches or tasteful marketing. Creatively, some studios have reputations for being filmmaker friendly and hands off. Other studios have reputations for being very hands on and you need to know what the personality is of each of these studios.

Q - What should new filmmakers look for in a sales agent?

Carlos - In the deal, you want to pay attention to the sales fee. It might be bigger for smaller films without stars because the sales involved are smaller and the sales agent will have trouble selling those movies. Also, the fee for selling international rights should not be the same for selling the US rights. The fee for the 'domestic sale' should be smaller, so you want to have one fee for international and a smaller fee for domestic. You also want to put a cap on the expenses that can be charged by the sales agent for marketing and attending film festivals etc where they sell the film.

Q - Is it a good idea to play the buyers off against one another?

Carlos - Absolutely. You have to play people off against each other to drive the excitement. Don't show the movie to any buyer before the festival. That's a huge thing. A lot of the buyers plea with the filmmakers to take a peek at the film so that they can say, *'if we buy it, it'll be better for you. We'll go to the festival together and we'll make it a big event for you.'* That's just letting the fix into the henhouse and I suppose there have been some cases where that has been done, but it's not recommended. Also, never tell them the cost of the film as it may negatively affect the amount of money you could get offered.

The Next Project

Now that you've finished your first film and are either enjoying the film festival circuit, a great distribution deal or both, you should remember that people are going to be asking the all important question… 'so, what's next?' You have been through hell, need a rest, and have probably forgotten that one of the main reasons to make you first film, is to get you to a second film! This is your calling card, and you are hot for a limited period, SO TAKE ADVANTAGE!

1. Have a second screenplay ready to go, ideally BETTER than the movie you just made, and in roughly the same genre. This is always the best thing to have because it is tangible. Agents like this as well because they know you will have product to sell.

2. Have five to ten ideas for a film that you can pitch to executives. If you have treatments, even better.

3. Try to stay within the genre of your first film. This builds a track record for you and makes studios and financiers more likely to trust you with their cash. If you want to start moving in a different direction, write a screenplay that consists of your old genre and the new one. So, if you made a ghost story first and want to go action next, write a supernatural thriller with lots of chases and gunplay.

4. Get an agent and get into meetings. Make contacts and build relationships. Your agent will get you into the meeting, your movie will make the people you meet take you seriously. You are now in the running for serious and bigger things. Be ready emotionally, psychologically and physically. You are no longer a wannabe, you are a has done and want to do bigger and better.

5. It takes a good year to write a screenplay, so if you are not ready, it could be twelve months before you are ready for that meeting, by which time you are no longer hot, at best you are luke warm. Get writing that second screenplay NOW!

6. Hook up with bigger and more established producers. They may exploit you, but they will take your 'hot' statues and talent, marry it with their contacts and experience, and things can happen VERY quickly. Once your second movie is done, you are in a very strong position.

7. Don't get high on your own supply! For years you have been telling people how talented you are, just to get them to invest / get involved / help. You will have won some festivals, gotten some great reviews and your new agent will tell you just how amazing you are! STOP NOW! You are not that good! Keep your feet on the ground at all times.

Q - Can lawyers help raise finance?

Carlos - Some do. Frequently, lawyers will become involved in sending a script to independent distributors to try to find financing. Some lawyers help to find money from private financing sources, particularly in New York. If the script is good enough, I may introduce the filmmaker to a producer client who can help get the project made. We also represent many executives so we might submit the project directly to a studio.

Q - How would your time be charged?

Carlos - Most talent lawyers charge 5%. However, in the indie context, the producers also have to budget a line item for production legal (the work involved in hiring the actors, dealing with location agreements, etc.) and that work typically is done on a flat fee basis.

Q - How much should a filmmaker budget for a lawyer?

Carlos - Typically, people doing really small films budget about $20k to $30k for production legal, but that's a very small sum for the amount of work involve - in other words, just because the film is small doesn't mean there's any less legal work - sometimes, the small picture involves more work. So, the number of lawyers willing to do that work for a number close to $20k is limited.

Q - Does the lawyer read the script to check for legal problems?

Carlos - There's a service that you send the script to and they read it and identify clearance issues. One is a company called Truman Van Dyke.

Q - What happens when someone puts an injunction on a film and how much does it cost?

Carlos - I've never seen it happen. The person who obtains the injunction must put a very significant bond to get the court to order a stoppage on a film. A gross example of a possible injunction would be if someone found a script on a table and went and made it without buying the script first and the script was copyrighted and registered - the person who owns the script could say, *'I own this script, therefore I'm entitled to an injunction to stop you from infringing my copyright'*. I suppose there may be some scene where you're using someone's likeness without authorization - like taking a clip of an actor without their permission and using it in a film. Sometimes there could be an injunction if you sold a movie to a distributor and someone claimed that they own the movie. But generally, it's very hard to get an injunction.

Q - What are the common mistakes you have come across?

Carlos - In the sale of indie films, music problems can be the most frequent problem area. Young filmmakers often just get festival rights for the music, but they fail to pre-negotiate a specific price to purchase the music for general exploitation. That's a killer because it gives the people who gave the festival rights a lot of leverage if they hear that a distributor bought the film for a large amount of money. Another problem is maybe the filmmakers got a name actor to do the film and agreed to give that actor a first dollar gross on the picture. When you go to sell the movie, the distributor doesn't necessarily want to assume that first dollar gross so you have to go back to the actor and renegotiate. Sometimes you make a movie with a name actor and they say you can't use their name in the advertising, so the distributor that wants to buy the picture isn't willing to buy the picture without the right to market that star. Of course, clear chain of title is a must. For example, maybe someone made a deal with a third party a while ago in which that third party had approval that conflicts in some way with the sale - that kind of thing can be a big problem obviously.

Dealing With Debt

Now that you've maxed out those credit cards to make your film, or to survive while making your film, you've got to pay it back. It can be daunting especially if you have rent, car loans, school loans, health insurance and other bills coming at you, as well as labs, camera rental companies and actors screaming at you because you failed to pay them, as you went over budget!

Get a job - *Seems easy enough, pays the most, but takes up a lot of time when you should be working on projects. Of course, the old standbys of waitrering and bartending still exist.*

Temping - *Takes up a lot of time, pays not that great, but you have flexibility to choose the gigs you want. Plus you meet a lot of people going to different companies.*

Script Reading - *Great for that little bit of extra cash - you can get around $50 for writing coverage on the screenplays that the executives don't want to read. Contact production companies, agencies and studios to see if they are hiring.*

Medical Research - *Robert Rodriquez did it to make El Mariachi. Donate your body to research clinics and you can earn some cash for testing drugs and the like. You can get some good free medical care if you have something nagging like asthma.*

Extra Work - *Doesn't pay very well and you stand around a lot, but you are on a film set and if you are smart enough, you can network.*

Production Work - *Visit websites like www.crewnet.com to find freelance gigs on films, TV shows and commercials and put your new found skills to use. If you have just made a low budget film you are probably used to dealing with problems and achieving the impossible on an hourly basis.*

Wedding Videos - *These days everyone wants their wedding filmed. Capitalize on this and make some money by shooting and editing nuptials. Works for bar mitzvahs, births and just about any other celebration. If you are smart, you will easily outshine the competition.*

AFTERMATH

David Berke
Entertainment Attorney

Stephen Israel
Producer

WHEN DISASTER STRIKES

Q - What are the most common traps that filmmakers can fall into?

Stephen - The independent producer is working with a limited budget and thus, an even more limited budget when it comes to legal. It's been my experience that people tend to leave taking legal advice to the last minute or cut corners or ignore the issue altogether.

David - A common example is happening to client of mine. He took a standard form agreement and then, without the help of a lawyer, doctored it up to approximate what he believed the agreement should say. I'm not just saying this out of self-interest. I know that attorneys are expensive and it may be difficult for some people to employ them. But the consequences can be tenfold in terms of the problems that are caused. With all my experience as an advocate, when looking objectively at the contract, I can't tell what my client thought he was trying to say and I can see how the other side would like to interpret it. The price of an attorney would have been so much less than the loss that my client has now suffered. He has effectively lost his movie. Filmmakers often think they can get away without legal advice and they are usually wrong.

Stephen - Contracts are all very well and good if you know who you're getting into business with. They are wonderful things if the other party is acting in good faith and intends to follow through with the contract. It doesn't matter how big your contract is, a contract will not force a performance out of someone. But the contract can give you remedy. I experienced a production company that mismanaged a film, they went massively over budget, were dishonest and did things that were outside the bounds of the contract. What the contract allowed me to do was take back control of the film, even though they got away with a certain amount of the dishonest activities. Your best defence is to be in business with good people. A good contract has to take second place to that.

David - I agree. A contract is only as good as the intentions behind it. However, even the best contracts between people of good faith can run into circumstances that weren't contemplated, can contain ambiguities that were the result of honest mistakes, and not ill intent. A great contract is not the solution, but invariably it's always the tail wagging the dog. If you don't have the money to negotiate or get proper advice, then you don't have the bargaining power and you might encounter terms that in the perfect world you wouldn't agree to, but you don't have the ability to say no. There isn't a filmmaker on earth who doesn't believe that their film is worth something, they wouldn't have made it otherwise. Consequently, if push comes to shove, the impetus to have the film distributed tends to overwhelm most people and they will think, *'it'll work out'*.

Q - Aside from contractual issues, what other problems do filmmakers encounter?

Stephen - Problems can be divided into three broad categories - pre-production and development problems, production problems and distribution problems. If you're talking about pre-production and development problems, a lot of inexperienced producers will make promises that they can't fulfil with the expectation that *'it'll work out'*. By that I mean they make promises and statements about who's committed and the financing they have. They claim that the financing is in place and a certain actor is attached. If you finesse those issues in pre-production and development, they can come back and bite you hard. In the case of an independent producer it's often the case that the producer tells the director that the money is there, tells the money that the actors are contracted and tells the actors that the money is secured in the hopes that if these three things were true at the same time, the film would get made.

As an independent producer you want to put the best possible face on the situation, because you're trying to attract someone like Nicole Kidman. I know this independent producer who had a $1.5m movie and she made pay or play commitments to the tune of a couple of hundred thousand dollars, but until it's all signed, it's not definite. In the end, she got some bridge financing from her family to the tune of $250k to fund pre production based upon the actors saying they would be there, and at some point or other, the mere fact that she had embellished the truth gave the actors cold feet and they pulled out. The film then fell apart like a house of cards, landing the producer with a family bill of $250k - no recourse whatsoever. It was all because she embellished the truth about how committed people really were to the project. The actor's response was not completely unreasonable.

David - The are two pitfalls to avoid in pre production. First is making promises you can't keep and second is to make sure the rights are attached to the project contractually, because if you don't, a terrible situation may result.

Q - We've made three independent features in the UK, and we have encountered distributor problems with all of them...

Stephen - It's the Wild West! Independent filmmaking is the last bastion of completely free market capitalism. There are no rules.

Q - If you're a new filmmaker, how do you find out who isn't going to screw you?

Stephen - *'It's not what you know, but who you know?'* Well, this is the film business and it's true. Your job is now to know people. So get out there and know people. The bigger your network, the more references you can get, and that's the only real way to find out who you want to be in business with. Other people will give you a fair assessment of what they're like.

David - It's due diligence. You have to take things with a grain of salt to a certain extent. If you say, but *'I would have had the next Gone With The Wind and the distributor just didn't do it right'*, I'm going to think twice. When someone gives me an example of how the distributor jacked up expenses, I'd take that seriously. Producers tend to be self-deluding. It's not said with insult, but with affection. But if you hear of someone else who's having a bad experience with a company and you sit there and think, *'it's not going to happen to me, I'm going to be smart about it,'* then you're in trouble.

Stephen - The production company I mentioned before, I had heard at the beginning of the process that they were a bad company to be in business with and I thought, *'you know what? I'll write a really tight contract'*. When I finally got the film back and I won, I was lucky that the film was worth something. I have subsequently heard from numerous people that have been in business with them, who have been screwed badly. One person lost his home. I look back with a certain sense of regret that I didn't send these guys to jail, because I had the ammunition to do that, but it was more important to me to get the rights back to my project with my own skin intact.

Bankruptcy

When everything goes wrong and you cannot pay your bills, you can resolve your debts by filing for bankruptcy. The good news is that you will be able to satisfy your creditors even if you do not pay them fully, however the bad news is that it will show up on your personal credit report for 10 years. While not a necessity, it's best to contact an attorney who handles bankruptcy in order to save money and headaches in the long run. There are two basic types of bankruptcy proceedings in the United States, Chapter 7 and Chapter 11. Chapter 7 is called Liquidation, and it is the most common type of bankruptcy proceeding. Here an appointed trustee collects all your non-exempt property (like an editing system or production vehicle), sells it and distributes the proceeds to your creditors. You cannot transfer any of your equipment to a non-exempt status, and anything that you did move or tried to move will come back into play. You are out of business in this proceeding.

Chapter 11 is called Reorganization. Here a trustee is appointed to oversee the rehabilitation of your company to allow you to use your future earnings to pay off your creditors. You are allowed to keep your possessions and stay in business. The trustee will make the decision for Chapter 7 or Chapter 11 based on the amount of debt, the future projections of the company and the number of assets on hand. You may set up another company even if you file for bankruptcy, however, getting loans and credit cards may be more difficult or impossible.

AFTERMATH

Q - If there were a breach of contract, an indie producer won't have the money to sue them, which the distributor knows...

David - I have no magic bullets. There are little things I would like to see in an agreement - if I was representing a distributor, and one thing I would not like to see is an arbitration clause. Arbitration favors the rich and not the little guy. If I was a foreign company or a distributor, I'd be much more afraid of a good old-fashioned law suit than I would an arbitration. I would also want the term of the agreement as short as possible.

Stephen - When you're finding a distributor, they hold all the cards. They have long gotten out of the responsibility for properly distributing their films, as they are not fiduciaries. They don't have a responsibility to look after your financial best interests.

David - Beyond their contractual obligation, that's right. From a small distributor's standpoint, you'd think that in terms of simple economics, they would have a great incentive to distribute your film properly. I think distributors probably make quick decisions as to where they are going to place their energies and where they're not, and invariably some films will suffer.

Q - How do you prevent distributors running up expenses?

Stephen - With small distributors, the thing to do is cap their expenses. I got in a situation with a major foreign sales agent, where we capped their sales expenses and they said *'hey, we've hit the caps and the kind of deals we are doing are relatively small, so we are going to have to either financially curtail our deal with the film, or come to some other arrangement.'* We came up with a fair and equitable arrangement of how they could recoup expenses above their cap. We effectively came up with a new cap.

Q - Are there any issues to be wary of on the domestic / DVD distribution side of things?

David - You need to have some contingency in the agreement defining for what sub-distribution. If you don't specify sub distribution as some other form of revenue generation, they are just going to throw it away.

Q - Should it be normal for a domestic distributors to have a cap on their expenses?

Stephen - Without knowing the specifics, it's hard to say, because what makes a reasonable cap? If they are going to put a film in every single store in the country, the cap may not be enough. But bear in mind, if you're dealing with a sub-distribution deal and you have a distributor, presumably they only get paid some portion of the money coming in, so there should be some assumption of good faith there. I have a better history with foreign sales agents than I do with domestic distributors, so I tend to trust what the foreign sales agents tell me. There is more transparency in foreign sales as the actual accounting is very simple. The foreign distributor pays X amount of dollars to the foreign sales agent. They have very clear accounting issues.

David - It seems possible to me that you can have an agreement with a distributor that says, *'I own this film, you're going to distribute it for three years, you're going to pay me 25% of everything you take in except your reasonable expenses which you'll disclose'.* Sign it, date it and you might have a more enforceable agreement than a 20 page long form agreement.

Q - What would you say are the most common reasons that independent producers sue their distributors?

David - I've taken cases where the distributor has admitted they owe the producer money and don't pay. What can you do? There's a practical reality to it. In one case, we sued the distributor, and I went to visit him in his rat hole of an office. His wife and two small children were playing in the same room. They were babysitting. He wasn't impressed with my client's problems. He had his own and it's like, *'I owe you money? Line up'.* If you're not dealing with of reputable distributors, they may lie, cheat and steal. One thing you can do, and I guess this is more applicable to foreign sales contracts, is that you can have the contracts in your company name, which can protect you from potential bankruptcy problems, but payment is supposed to go to you, unless it's through the sales agent. That can make things a lot clearer in the event of bankruptcy, who owns the underlying copyright and payments.

Q - Is it likely that a production company could claim the underlying copyright and payments?

David - Yes. The practicality of that situation was that I never saw those contracts, but if you ever have to go backwards and figure out who owns the title, then you have a fairly clear paper trail as to who the copyright is owned by and the situation with payment. Again, the good contract can't protect you from everything, but it can give you something to do when things go wrong. When I say bankruptcy, it could be as simple as a $750 filing and you'll never see or hear of them again until they pop up with a different name.

Stephen - By and large, you should have a bankruptcy contingency clause.

Q - What are chapter 7, 11 and 13?

David - Chapter 11 is receivership and reorganization by a trustee. Chapter 7 is liquidation. If it's a small company, you only see 7, not 11. Chapter 13 is another form of reorganization. You can come out of 13.

Q - How would those different chapters be decided?

Stephen - It's decided by the bankruptcy courts.

David - Practically speaking, the chances of you ending up with anything are minimal. The thing is, if you go chapter 11, then theoretically trade debts have greater priority than personal debts.

Stephen - Yours is technically a secure kind of debt. Theoretically, they are holding money in trust for you so it is never theirs to begin with, so theoretically the money should come back out again. The practice is, if your debts exceed your assets, you're buggered. As a trade creditor, you can also end up on the creditors committee.

David - This is esoteric, because certainly if you're in a position where the bankruptcy is that significant, then you're in a whole different situation. I was talking about bankruptcy as a method of escape for the little fish.

Q - So they can liquidate and then completely start up again?

David - Reappear as somebody else. If they are a corporation and there are no personal guarantees involved, they can liquidate and start trading under a different name a week later.

Stephen - But not with your film! The key thing is to have a clause in your contract so that all the rights revert to you.

Q - If a production company is unhappy with their distributor and believe that they've breached contract, what is the best course of action for a producer to take?

David - It depends on what your resources are as to what you should do. At a minimum, write a letter. Document everything. Creating a paper trail is critical.

Stephen - The one thing you shouldn't do is nothing.

Q - If all your assets are tied up in the company but you are unsatisfied, what should you do?

Stephen - You don't have to be threatening, that's the first thing. It's probably worth trying to be nice first. You can be nice, even when putting things in writing.

David - If you're going to use a step approach, which is often a good one, a little used literary device is the cc. Rather than getting a nasty letter from the attorney, which already means the heats on, write your letter and cc the attorney.

Stephen - Another case I was involved with. I was pissed off with a foreign sales agent over an accounting issue. I delayed legal action until I went to Sundance when I knew I could find the president of this company to have a quiet conversation. I bumped into him at a party and said, *'Hey, I wanted you to know there's going to be a really nasty looking letter coming across your desk in the next couple of weeks. I have to write it because my lawyer's telling me, but just so you know, I'm perfectly amenable to a reasonable negotiated settlement'.* So what you are doing is sending a two-fold message - you are asserting your rights in the letter, but you're prepping them to not be quite so pissed about it, because there's two approaches. They can say, *'Okay, there's a problem, we can up with a negotiated settlement',* or they can say, *'screw you'.* The thing is, you look to assert your rights. You don't want to say, *'I'm going to court'.*

Q - What if you're being nice and nothing happens?

Stephen - Unfortunately in this town, filing a lawsuit is often about just getting people to return a phone call anyway.

David - Some lawyers like a device which is to send a letter that says, *'Here's all the things you've done wrong, attached to it is the complaint we're going to file if you don't come to terms'.* The bad news is mostly there's nothing you can do and here's why. You probably can't afford to pay a lawyer an hourly fee unless the lawyer is drunk or incompetent, you can't induce him or her to take out a contingency, because there's no pot at the end of the rainbow. The accounting may show that you have no money or that you are $3k in debt, so they aren't going to take the case.

Q - How much would it cost to get a lawyer involved?

David - Often more than what's at stake. The bad guys know that and you don't even know what's at stake.

Q - What does a production company do then?

David - I knew a guy who was in a situation where he was dealing with bad folks and bad folks often hire bad lawyers. He couldn't do the audit to verify how much he was owed. He had family investors, and he couldn't pay me, and I don't work for free. There are charities and causes that I find much more worthy than his that I could devote my time to. So what he's facing is simply riding out the term. He had a five-year agreement and a year and a half left, he bit the bullet and ran out the term. Is it going to be good for the film? No. Is he going to have a clean reversion of ownership? Yeah. The deal's over. That is sometimes the only recourse.

Q - So you need to make sure you don't get a twenty-year term?

Stephen - You don't get those from smaller distributors anyway.

David - As far as the distributor is concerned, limit the terms as best as you are able. If you have so many bells and whistles going off that tell you this is not a good thing, then it's better to walk away.

Stephen - Part of the thing you learn here is the system is kind of broken and I don't see a fix in the near future. There are more new distributors and exhibition outlets coming up in the US, which may change the way the business is, but it really boils down to being happy with the people you're in business with.

David - In an objective world, if you know that this is a bad situation for you, don't be seduced by the possibility of getting your film distributed, matched against the possibility of your project being tied up for ten years in the hands of people that will do it no good. Isn't it better not to sign the deal?

Q - What if you sign and you think they are good people?

David - Be a thorn in their side. That's the best thing you can do. Make yourself intolerable and get your film back. If you make yourself enough of a problem, the chances are that someone's going to say, *'You're not worth it and your film's not worth it'.* Enlist the aid of attorneys who are friends who, if they are not going to do the work for you, at least they will lend their name or cc them. That's not a foolproof answer, but it might work.

Q - When should a producer know when to quit the fight against the distributor?

David - When they're 67, and they still live with Mommy!

Stephen - An important perspective to have as a producer is that being right is not always what it's cracked up to be. Winning is important. As a general rule, I try not to pick fights unless I know I've won them *beforehand.* If you don't have the evidence up front for malfeasance then you have to investigate to try and find the evidence that says they are bad people. That gets expensive very fast. If you already know what you're looking for, then you've won before you started.

David - As a lawsuit, that becomes a basis for negotiation. Sometimes you need to sue somebody in order for them to take you seriously, because if you're just pissing and moaning, and it's not costing them anything, then you're just pissing and moaning. A lawsuit comes with deadlines and court appearances, and there is an end game. If you file one at some point, there's going to be a trial. All of a sudden, the other side realizes they're in a fight, and it becomes a basis for negotiation. Unless the other side thinks they are right, in which case you are in big trouble.

Stephen - In the absence of information, we assume the worst, which is why I go back to the attitude that says, *'I'd rather only pick the fight if I've already won it'.*

David - I represent a studio and there's a case where for a short period of time, they had two films with the same working title. The producer of one of them is absolutely convinced that the studio only had one film. It doesn't matter that the other one didn't make any money either. That's a perfect example of something that seems dodgy, but isn't. One of the things I've realized about conspiracy theorists is that most people who are conspiracy theorists have never worked in large organizations. The fact of the matter is that large organizations are comprised of several hundred individuals all going in different directions. So the idea that there are criminal conspiracies operating in distribution companies is farfetched, but there are some practices they routinely engage in. Take expenses; the attitude is, *'I've got this expense here, I have to assign it to something'.* It's clearly in the company's best interests to assign it to a film and preferably a film that they would otherwise have to pay money out for. That's not a criminal conspiracy; it's just business.

Stephen - That goes back to the brokenness thing. It's systemic. It's a function of what they do. If they can reduce expenses and pay out, that's a good thing for them. They are in an adversarial relationship with you. I'm not saying distributors are bad by any means, but they are going in looking to maximize their profits just like you are.

Q - How does a film producer deal with the collapse of a company because the film has failed?

Stephen - I come from a long, ugly corporate career, but so far I've done a little better than break even, but the thing is, I'd advise people not to be in the business. If you are determined to be in film, you have to get used to failure and rejection as it is 95% of the producing business. The number of people that **can** say 'yes' are few and far between.

Credit Report Companies

Experian Consumer Assistance (formerly TRW)
PO Box 2002
Allen, TX 75013
(888) 397-3742
www.experian.com

Equifax Credit Services
PO Box 740256
Atlanta, GA 30374
(800) 685-1111
www.equifax.com

Trans Union
2 Baldwin Place
PO Box 1000
Chester, PA 19022
(800) 888-4213
www.transunion.com

AFTERMATH

David - Imagine yourself the pimply faced kid in school and getting rejected every single time.

Stephen - Success is always relative. If you get a film made, that's a success. If you get it into a festival, that's good, but did you get it into Sundance? Okay it's in Sundance, but did it win an award? Okay you won, but did you get a distributor? Okay you got a distributor but did it make money? It might have made money, but did the investors get all their money back? At some level, your film can be branded a failure, but the point is that up until the last two parts, which are did you make money? And was it critically well acclaimed? But until that point you haven't made your money back. The number of films that make their money back is substantially less than 50%.

David - One thing that I see from people that have failed is the broken bodies of their families. If there's no place other than your family's mortgage or your grandparents retirement fund to make your film, maybe you should do something else. You don't see people in other businesses playing with money that they can't walk away from. Investors are investors. They should not be 'guaranteed' success. You've sold them a product, hopefully honestly, they understand there's a risk, maybe they'll get a return, maybe they won't, and if your film goes belly up, guess what, they've made a bad investment. People have made bad investments in better companies - look at the stock market. With family, however, you are playing with money you cannot walk away from, because you're going to have turkey dinner with them or not for the rest of your life. So that may be a line I would draw.

Q - How would you deal with a distributor who goes under, taking your profits with them?

David - You need to monitor the person's bankruptcy proceedings. Unmonitored, people will try and get away with anything they can, but if you're a creditor in a bankruptcy, then the bankruptcy court and lawyers are obligated to disclose what's going on. The only people who really make money in bankruptcies are lawyers, but it's still worth keeping an eye on the progress of the case because somewhere buried in that is a settlement, which is paying the trade creditors. But pay attention.

Q - What are the pitfalls of making a movie with credit cards?

Stephen - I would prefer it to your family money, but then you have to be prepared for the fact that your credit is non-existent, which could make your future filmmaking efforts a little more difficult. The risks are huge.

Q - What are the long term issues of bankruptcy?

David - The long term ramifications on a personal level are what was always understood as seven years of bad luck has just gone up to ten years of bad luck in terms of credit reporting agencies. It will seriously affect the way you do business.

Q - What do you do if an actor or crew member removes themselves from the picture after being signed?

David - Generally speaking, if they want their name off the picture, you need to ask yourself, *'Why do I care?'* You can substitute. Why would you want somebody on your film who doesn't want to be there?

Stephen - Actors can't ask for that. They can contractually, from the outset, limit how much you use their name. It's generally contractually set up from the beginning.

Q - Do you find a lot of legal problems with copyright?

Stephen - Not so much. I'm not involved with music, where I think it's more prevalent. You don't hear of films getting held up because the chain of title was messed up. You do hear routinely about films where the film can't be released because the underlying rights to the music weren't cleared.

David - To get an injunction to hold up a film, you need $100k just to get the lawyer serious about taking it on. For the injunction, you need a bond. The bond is to protect the person that's being enjoined from the damages that they will suffer in the event that the injunction was improperly granted, and that's a function of the value of what it is you're enjoining. It could be an astronomical sum that you have no idea of. The bond is to stop morons from stopping commerce in its track, so the bond needs to be substantial.

Q - What should people be aware of during production?

Stephen - Getting releases signed is important. One thing I've learned is, don't run away from problems thinking they will go away. Take location permits as an example: If you get caught, you're going to have to make a decision as to whether you are going to give up the location, or pay fees and do it fast. It's a bad thing to lose a location halfway through. We were shooting a picture in San Marino. I wasn't aware that San Marino was very film unfriendly and the permit fees run to over $1k a day. We were open with the city but the city sent us a fax with some pages missing, so we thought the permit was a flat $500. The thing was we were totally up front with them, we told them where we were and then halfway through the first day, they came and shut us down. We asked why and they were like 'you haven't paid your fee'. That cost us about $9k on a film with a budget under $50k. So don't duck problems.

Q - What advice would you give new filmmakers?

Stephen - If you are not committed to film, follow this advice - don't do it!

What to do if you're arrested

Some times problems occur on a film set such as not having a permit for special effects, weapons, animals etc., upsetting a local merchant or damaging a location. Or can come out of the blue, like the dawn raid we received for being suspected international money laundering drug dealers (we kid you not!) If you find yourself being taken 'downtown', here's a few tips...

1. Never admit guilt, in fact don't say anything while being arrested. You must speak to a lawyer first. Remember your Miranda Rights - 'anything you say can and will be used against you in a court of law...'

2. DO NOT piss off the police officer. They're just doing their job. Be as courteous and accommodating as possible.

3. When you get to the station, you are allowed one phone call. Use it to either call an attorney or your most responsible relative/friend/producer who will either come to bail you out or hire an attorney. NOTE: Make sure before production that a system is always in place for someone to take control of the production if you are detained for unexpected reasons (such as this or the death of a relative etc).

4. If you don't have any money or do not know an attorney, the court will appoint one for you. They're usually not as good as a private one, but are better than nothing. Plus, it's unlikely you are in serious trouble. It's most likely a misunderstanding. You will know yourself now much hot water your in. Let's hope you haven't funded your film through illegal Colombian imports!

5. STAY CALM! DO NOT say anything until your attorney arrives. You don't know what angle the police are looking for, even if they appear to be nice to you, so keep quiet.

6. You have the right for your attorney to be present during your interview and remember, you can stop the interview at any point to talk to your attorney.

7. Assuming you are innocent, or at least relatively innocent (!), co-operate as much as you can, but always with the attorney's 'say so'.

8. Unless you are charged, they cannot take your photo or prints.

9. Make sure you find out all the charges against you and discuss with your lawyer whether they are criminal or civil charges, and further, if they are felonies or misdemeanors.

10. Unless you've killed somebody, absconded with the entire production budget or funded your film through drug dealing, you should be out of jail within 24-48 hours.

12. The police are not out to get you. They are doing their job and they want you out of their hair as soon as they can. As long as you know their agenda, you can help them as long as it does not incriminate you.

13. Expect the unexpected!

SS94-45464-BB64566
JONES, C. J. 2298

TS23-56708-BB50234
JOLLIFFE

AFTERMATH

Josh Deighton
Fox Searchlight

THE STUDIO EXEC

Q - What is your job?

Josh - Director of production. I am responsible for bringing new projects into the company and overseeing the development, attaching writers, directors and producers. We do everything you do before getting into production. We oversee the film through production and post-production. There are other executives who support the film as far as they can. They are in charge of post-production, physical production, sound and music etc. Another part of my job at Searchlight is that a quarter of our releases are acquisitions, so I go to festivals - Sundance, Cannes and Toronto every year, to look for new product. We look for compelling, distinctive, intelligent, sophisticated, but also commercial material. We are looking for the two or three films that come out of Sundance every year that are both aesthetically challenging and have a point of connection with audiences. Films that justify making it into movie theatres as they are emotionally moving. There's a lot of fine, independent films that are too small for us. We're looking for comedies, thrillers, horror movies, teen movies, pretty standard genres, but films that have something about them that's elevated. We like risky films.

Q - Why doesn't Fox take on the smaller films?

Josh - There are companies that make their living making films that make $500k, that never have more than 20 prints around the country, but we can't. Other companies do it better, maybe they don't belong in theaters, but on cable or video. Our budgets are typically at the $8-$12m range.

Q - What kind of turnaround is it from the first meeting to the finished product?

Josh - It is always a very very long process. I've never seen anything happen in less than two years.

Q - Do you look at the track history of directors?

Josh - Definitely. We've made a lot of films with first time feature filmmakers, but they have a large body of work in music videos, short films or as a writer. It doesn't have to be as a feature filmmaker, but a track record of some sort is required. If its a first time filmmaker, we want them to take ten minutes from their movie and make it, shoot it digitally to show you can do it.

Q - What are the pros and cons of hiring an indie filmamker?

Josh - There is a culture clash between the indies and the pros, and a filmmaker who has made a couple of short films will come to work for the studio and feel there is a conflict between our way of working verses the way that they have worked all along. Their way of working is fine, but doesn't always fit within the system. Because a director has always edited his own films and I've gone ahead and hired an editor, and there's a very tight post production schedule, I expect the director to work through that editor. It can be hard to take people who are really talented and get them to get their heads around working in a different style.

Q - Is it a benefit if the filmmaker has made an ultra low budget movie?

Josh - It's less a benefit for me in evaluating a director then it is a producer. Just because I work for Fox, we can't make movies below a certain number. If we try to rent a location, *'what's it for...? A Fox movie...?'*, there's no way around it, you're paying top dollar. Some young guerrilla producer who has made small movies, I'm dying to work with them.

Q - Do you require a lot of extra coverage from the filmmakers?

Josh - I have never had a conversation with a filmmaker that said, I didn't think they were getting enough coverage. If I started getting dailies where the scenes were only being covered from one angle, one take, I would have a problem with that. I feel that a director's vision is important and they should have an idea what shots they are going to cover each day. Just going out and collecting the shots you storyboarded three months ago is going to be problematic. Having back doors and other ways to cut around something is necessary.

Q - What is the difference between Fox Searchlight and Twentieth Century Fox and Fox Animation?

Josh - Fox and Fox 2000 and Fox Animation make films who's target audience is the world of movie goers. We are focused on specific niche audiences. We make movies for arthouse audiences and if the arthouse audiences go to see it, we can do really well on that movie. We make films for African/American audiences or teen audiences with the same idea.

Q - Can you afford to be more original in that case?

Josh - I hope so. That's the idea.

Q - What do you look for when acquiring movies?

Josh - When we go to festivals, we take the head of marketing and distribution with us. We're looking for a movie that can be sold. Is it too small to catch an audiences mind? Are there hooks to it? Would we have picked up *The Good Girl* if Jennifer Aniston hadn't been in it? I don't know. But you see that movie and understand how you're going to market it, and what the story is behind it. For acquisitions, it's so much about how the critics will respond to it.

Q - Are there any films that Searchlight wouldn't go for?

Josh - A horror film that is really satisfying for a hard core horror audience is not going to be for us, but a horror film like *The Others* or *The Ring* which was really satisfying to that core horror audience but also beyond that, is more appealing. We don't do romantic comedies as they are so cast specific. We can't afford to make action movies satisfying. So there are genres that we can't make work because of our budgetary restraints.

Q - Do you make any movies abroad?

Josh - We've made movies in Australia, France, Ireland, England... When we budget, we are looking for the cheapest way to make it. That being said, there are genres for which being set overseas would be a creative problem. A teen movie about teens in France would be hard for us.

Q - How did The Dish *fit into the niche market?*

Josh - *The Dish* is in the grand tradition of *The Full Monty* - a quaint, heart warming, emotionally satisfying comedy. There's always a place for those. Domestic audiences will eat that with a spoon. But that's different from an American-style broad comedy made in Australia. Those don't work. The smaller, character driven comedies do work.

Q - Are those films you would produce or acquire?

AFTERMATH

Josh - Acquire. We made *The Full Monty*, but some of these little 'commonwealth comedies' are so magical that trying to guess which one is best to bet on in production is not the way to go.

Q - Is there a lot of communication between the different divisions within Fox?

Josh - Yeah. I sometimes get scripts from an executive at 20th Century who says it isn't right for them but it might be for me.

Q - If a filmmaker has gone through the Searchlab, do they have a better chance of getting their film made?

Josh - Yeah. That's what Searchlab is for.

Q - What is your opinion about digital movies?

Josh - I think there are beautiful digital films and ugly digital films. The beautiful ones can be dark and be about sad, depressing issues. I don't work for a cable channel or a video distributor, I work for a film distributor. We put films on 200ft wide screens. There has to be a reason to put that film in front of 300 people. I'm not worried about dark stories, but it has to be cinematic.

Q - Would **28 Days Later** *have been better served if it was shot on film ?*

Josh - It couldn't have been made on the budget if it was shot on film. There are parts of the film where the center of London is empty. You have a film crew and you had to get everything ready and lock everything down and close up, you're talking about $millions in location fees. This story captures the immediacy of the situation.

Q - If people come to you with cast attached, does that help?

Josh - The nearer it is to a movie, the better. If someone comes through with a cast and a director and a DP and budget, it's much easier for me to make. If there's an actor you know that will help me market the film, but can't attach them right away, it is helpful. Casting is very subjective. It's a magic you feel when you put a movie together.

Q - Do you find there are trends each year?

Josh - The theme of Sundance two years ago was flossing. There were eight movies with characters flossing their teeth. I'm not sure if there are themes as such, but there are things that are over done, like gritty, urban gangster stories, which we would pass on unless there is something distinctive about them. There are so few comedies and smart, entertaining movies. Last year, Sundance was all about issues of sexual identity and sex change. There are waves but it is down to the programmers. At the LA festival, they have great programmers.

Q - What mistakes do you come across with new filmmakers?

Josh - I can often rule a film out for acquisition in the first three minutes. If it doesn't look like a pro movie, with a directorial point of view, and the image doesn't take me away, it's not going to work. Sound design is so important too. This is before we get into the story and the actors. Hiring a DP is important. As a first time filmmaker, hire the most experienced DP you can, the most experienced editor and mixers. They will catch a lot of the problems.

Q - What advice would you give new filmmakers?

Josh - You need to have magic. Get a terrific script, a good actor and a great director.

Donna Langley
Exec Vice President of Production

UNIVERSAL STUDIOS

Q - What is your job?

Donna - Executive Vice President of Production at Universal Studios, and I find material that is viable for feature films that fit within the Universal slate, and then to work with the writer to develop the script to the point where we can begin to package it with the filmmaker and actors, getting it to a place where it's ready to go into production.

Q - What size projects do you deal with?

Donna - It depends. The great thing about being at a studio like Universal is that the slate is very eclectic and varied, in both size and genre. While I've been here I've worked on everything from $23m movie to a $100m movie.

Q - What is considered low budget for a studio like Universal?

Donna - It changes year to year, but within the studio system, low budget is between $8-$12m. To do anything under that is difficult as a studio movie. We did a film called *How High* which was shot on digital that was in the $8-$10m range.

Q - What do you look for in new filmmakers?

Donna - A few things. I look for work that is clearly accomplished. It doesn't have to be a big budget, but if there's a clear narrative, good performances from the actors, a good story, those are the things that get you excited about finding new talent. Once you get into a position to work with a new filmmaker, it's about listening to what the filmmaker is going to bring to a project and how they will approach making another movie.

Q - Are studios looking for new filmmakers all the time?

Donna - Absolutely, though it depends on the project, size and circumstances. If you work with a new filmmaker, as opposed to a seasoned filmmaker, you're looking for a comfort level as a studio, and for ways to create an environment with the filmmaker that will allow them to do their best work in the most responsible way.

Q - If you've heard good things about a filmmaker, how do you see their films?

Donna - If a film screens in a film festival, (even if it's a tiny one), you can go through the production company. The great thing about being in a studio is we have resources. We have a story department with researchers that can put feelers out there. We also have an acquisitions department that is very well connected with the independent film world. It depends if the filmmaker is someone who has not yet found representation for themselves, usually through either a distribution company or the production entity that's involved in their film.

Q - What mistakes do you come across with new filmmakers?

AFTERMATH

Donna - There's two categories. One is personality defects. Young filmmakers can have a tendency to be suspicious of the hierarchy in the studio system. If a filmmaker comes to the table with that attitude, and it's born out of experience, that's fine, but I would advise young filmmakers to have an open mind in terms of the people that they are working with. Every film is different and has it's own set of problems and personalities. And while filmmaking is all about achieving the filmmakers vision, it's a collaboration across the board. That's just my way of looking at it. Everyone involved in the making of a movie is involved in the collaboration and it's key. That's not to say give up your artistic integrity or your single mindedness as a filmmaker. The good thing about working with experienced filmmakers is there's a confidence level there, and experience brings a lot to the table. Knowing when and when not to pick your battles is also key. The other is in a technical area. It depends what the background of the filmmaker is. I've worked with a number of first time filmmakers that have come from videos and commercials and sometimes I find that those directors have not experienced working with actors, so they tend to be a bit afraid of the performance aspect, and it can be a difficult for them to connect with the actors. Also it can be not understanding how to transition the scenes if you're used to short films. There's usually one or two things, but with the help of a good producer and technical team, issues can be resolved.

Q - Are there any casting issues?

Donna - With first time filmmakers, the major casting issues we'd have is that we would want a name actor in at least one of the main roles. There are very few times in the studio system where the studio will be making a film with a new filmmaker and an unknown actress. The only time that the cast might be unknown is when we pick up a low budget film in acquisitions or it's a negative pick up deal.

Q - What are the pros of hiring a new filmmaker to direct a studio film?

Donna - Broadening the talent pool is a great thing. The studio system is just that - a system - and it can bottle neck at the top if you haven't had an influx of new and exciting filmmakers. There's nothing more exciting than when you go to a film festival and find new talent. Keeping that cycle going is important. Having a new voice is exciting and its rare that it happens.

Q - Are you also looking for original material and edginess?

Donna - It depends. There are filmmakers who are just auteurs. That's not to say that they can't fit within the studio system because Paul Thomas Anderson, to name but one, can and has. His voice has found a way to become an important part of the fabric of modern American cinema so there will always be people who want to finance his films. I think in terms of other filmmakers who are breaking into the field, it goes back to that thing of how you feel when you sit down and talk. There's a lot of people who make edgy films for their first film, that may feel uncommercial simply because they are low budget. When they are out of film school, they are flexing their directorial muscles for the first time. You can sit in a room with someone who has directed a piece of material like that and be blown away by it. They can walk in and say, *'I know I directed that, but for my next film I'd love to direct a romantic comedy'.* It depends on the individual. As a studio executive, my comfort level depends on conversations with that individual. You can tell if someone wants to stay in their indie world or branch out and make bigger movies. A lot of the movie makers coming out now are not interested in making small, arthouse films. They want to graduate to make commercial, mainstream movies.

Q - Should a new filmmaker pitch a film in the same genre as their indie film?

Donna - It's much easier to try and stay within reach of the genre you made your student film or first film.

Q - Do filmmakers tend to get branded in a certain genre when they do a studio picture?

Donna - It's easy to be categorized within the studio system. I think it goes across the board, filmmakers / writers / actors, even producers. I have a friend who's a director who has always directed thrillers because he directed one to great success as that's where the work was, and he's now on his fifth movie, looking to get out of that genre. It's difficult and he's had to choose a thriller that is much more character based in order to segue out, and hopefully that will help him move into more serious drama which is where he wants to be. You have to be sure of where you want your career to end up once you get into the mill of the studio system because it's very easy to get on a certain path. There are filmmakers that have gone from one genre to another, so it's a lot about the material and making careful choices.

Q - Is it a good idea for a producer to come to the studio with the film already packaged?

Donna - It depends. There are a few instances where that's helpful. If it's a more commercial piece of material, then no, sometimes the packaging can be a hindrance.

Q - Do any studio directors use short cuts to save money and time and do the studios dictate how much coverage is needed?

Donna - Yes they use shortcuts. There are the seasoned directors who you don't have to watch for coverage. They know when they have a scene in the can which gives us a comfort level. Independent filmmakers tend to cut through it getting only the shots they need and then getting on to the next scene. However, that might not be what we need as we are in the business of making popular entertainment which means that there is a formula of the kind of shots we require. We insist on this because we know that it works. There are a number of variables that go into that formula but in terms of using DP's for example, I could never see a situation of a first time director dictating who they would use. For a first time studio filmmaker, you want a DP who has a body of work under their belt, as we would want to surround the first time filmmaker with as much experience as possible.

Q - What advice would you offer new filmmakers?

Donna - In terms of finding representation, if you have a good piece of material that you believe in and has gotten you some good attention, the most important thing about choosing an agent is about who you gel with. Each agency has its own persona and then there are agents within that agency who do certain things better than others, so doing you homework on agencies and agents is good. Look at the people who are doing the things you respect, and that way you can narrow it down a bit. If you have the opportunity to meet with several agents, meet with them as many times as you can. Remember you are the commodity and they would be lucky to have you. Oftentimes, people jump into situations with an agent because they're fresh and new and they are grateful they are wanted. If you are talented, you want to be with an agent who believes in you. With regards to approaching a studio, you need to do your homework, because each studio has its own persona and branding. It's about looking at your material and matching it to the best place. If you don't think you have the experience or connections to produce it yourself or enter it through the studio system, think about partnering with another producer who has a good relationship with a studio, or someone who's career you admire and has got similar movies made through the system. Be realistic about what the material is, verses what the studio makes. Oftentimes, I find people get frustrated as they come to the table with something that a studio can't make. The studio is a business and you hope to be able to marry the commerce with the art somewhere along the line, but first and foremost, the material has to make sense and you have to be able to sit back and say, *'how can I put this together in a way that people are going to go see it?'*

AFTERMATH

The Film Makers Compromise

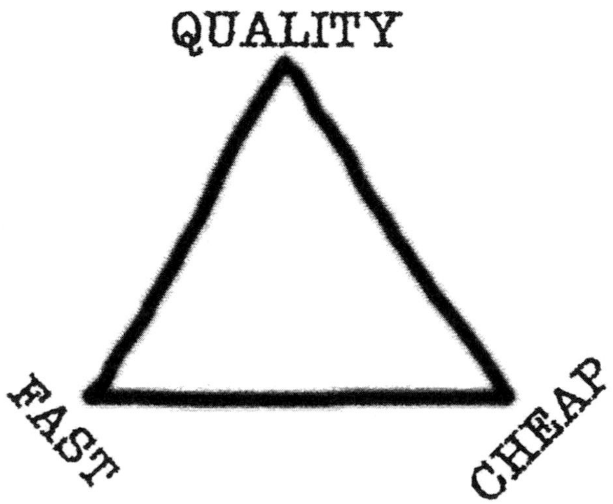

QUALITY

FAST

CHEAP

Study this simple triangle. Whatever film making discipline you apply, you can only ever have two corners, and always at the expense of the third corner.

2

CASE STUDIES

THE LIVING SPIRIT STORY

PROLOGUE

SS94-45464-BB64566
JONES, C. J. 2298

TS23-56708-BB50234
JOLLIFFE, G. A. 3434

Note - The interviews in this section were performed between 1994 and 2004. While their film making endeavours are UK-centric, the spirit of what they have done, and the hard lessons learned, are universal.

British filmmakers and authors of this book, Chris Jones and Genevieve Jolliffe met at Bournemouth Film School in 1989. Chris, born and bred in the North of England, had started making amateur horror films on Super 8mm many years earlier. His first triumph, an unashamed homage to the films of George Romero and the *Evil Dead*, an immense success at his college. After 'bluffing' his way into film school, he began work on what he believed would be his greatest film yet, *Rundown*, a sci-fi thriller. Genevieve was inspired and terrified at an early age, by the black & white classic, *Dracula*. *Star Wars* quickly followed and she knew that she wanted to make movies. She started out working in the industry, attending markets such as the Cannes Film Festival and dabbling in animation before travelling the world with her Nikon and Super 8mm camera. When she attended film school, she quickly became frustrated by the lack of inspired leadership and was eager to make a movie. After meeting, Chris and Gen decided to make *Rundown*, Chris' graduation film, but too many obstacles were put in their way. They decided to leave the film school, Chris after two and a half years, Gen after only six months. Neither of them made a movie or shot a single frame of film while at the film school.

ACT 1
THE RUNNER

Q - How did Living Spirit Pictures come about?

Gen - Film School, at the time, was about making depressing TV style drama, full of pessimism, about minority issues - anything that involved a social problem. They didn't want to do anything that strayed from that formula, there was no variety, just one particular kind of film and if you didn't fit into that, then you didn't get a film made. When we came out of film school we just wanted to do something that was BIG. The frustration of film school had built up in us to such a degree that when we considered what to make, there was one thing we really wanted to do - blow everything up! We were both fans of *Aliens* and *Die Hard*, so we knew that we wanted to make an action thriller.

Chris - I was in my third year at film school, Gen was in her first. We teamed up and decided to make a film school project together. I was taken onto the film school course as a director and I was supposed to be directing a film that year. I put forward a script that I had written in my first year and had been developing ever since, about a game show in which contestants were killed. After endless script development meetings with the staff, it became apparent that this was not going to happen in the form that I wanted. It wasn't going to be the sci-fi action-adventure that I wanted to make. Gen felt the same.

One night we sat down and thought - What would happen if we didn't actually make this movie at film school? We'd worked out a budget of around $20k, went down the list and calculated that the film school offered us a crew (which in any case we could persuade to work with us) and equipment (which would cost us $6k if we had to hire it). So, in reality, all the film school could offer was a quarter of the budget in equipment hire and some serious headaches (and they got to retain the copyright!)

We still had to raise $15k and if we could raise that, we could raise $20k and make the film outside the film school. We decided to leave film school, set up our own company and make the film the way we wanted. London was out of the question as it would just be too expensive to live there so we decided to set up in the North of England, in Cheshire, so that we would be a big fish in a small pond.

Q - Is that when you approached the 'Princes' Trust'?

Chris - We found that we were eligible for the PYBT (The Princes' Youth Business Trust, an organization headed by HRH Prince Charles which helps young people with big ideas but no money). We put our application through and got a soft loan of $4k and a further $3k a year later. This

First Assistant Director, Lisa Harney on 'The Runner'... after 5 weeks shooting at 3 a.m. in a Manchester ghetto. It's all a bit much.

enabled us to get all our business equipment, computer, fax, letterheads, all that kind of stuff. And so Living Spirit was born.

Q - Why the name Living Spirit Pictures?

Gen - We wanted a name to express the way we planned to run our business and make movies. Everyone seemed to like it, even the strange people who still ring us and ask if they can join our religious cult!

Q - Did you start a formal company?

Gen - Yes, we were no longer in the playground. We took an accountant's advice and started a Limited Company (US laws differ here). There is so much to running a company and it is very expensive. Read some books on starting a company, they're a lot cheaper than advice from a solicitor or accountant.

Q - After you began trading, what was at the top of the agenda?

Image Copyright Jon English

(above) A production sketch for Rundown, *a game show on which contestants are hunted and killed - the script was very developed when Chris and Gen left the film school. Due to problems with special effects, the project was eventually binned in favor of* The Runner

Gen - The movie. We were at home, planning the film, looking at the reality of the project. We had a script for a forty-five minute film costing about $20K and had sent off details to potential investors. We weren't sure what to expect, maybe one or two replies. Every single one wrote back and offered finance, saying - *'if you make a movie, we will put in some money... but why a short?'* we were also asked. We started thinking, maybe they're right. $20k is a lot of money for a short - why don't we double it to make a 90 minute film costing $40k. Naively we believed that to be the equation. We're not going to sell a forty five minute film. But we could sell a ninety minute film and suddenly, a much larger market was opened up to us. No longer would we be confined to tv - but now the feature market, including cinema, video, tv, satellite and cable, and now DVD.

Q - Were you nervous about skipping the short film stage?

Chris - Yes of course, but we were no longer in film school, we had to pay the rent and put food on the table. I have spoken to many filmmakers who say - *'I'll make a feature film next but I've got to do another short and learn a bit more'.* And I say *'What do you need to learn?'* You'll learn three times more if you make a feature film and regardless of how much you mess up, you'll still be able to sell it. More than likely you'll make some money back too. If you don't, so what! Make another one'. You've just got to go for it!

Gen - I think you've got to be prepared to take the risk - we were prepared to do that, to plunge in head first. We realized that if we wanted things to happen, we couldn't wait in the hope that Hollywood would give us a call and offer us *Jurassic Park 9.*

Q - Have you chosen the projects you have undertaken on commercial viability?

Chris - We've talked a lot about how we choose the stories we make into a film. Anyone who has seen *The Runner, White Angel* and *Urban Ghost Story* would agree that they are all very different. And you can see a linear progression in our experience, each one gets substantially better than the previous. We're aware of commerciality, we have to be. However, no matter how much we ever thought we were being hard nosed business people, it all boiled down to one thing - *'what did we want to make?'*

(left) In order to convince investors, some pretty dodgy artwork was created. We couldn't afford a model, so Gen had to step into the role for these shots.

When we made *The Runner* we were into movies with serious muzzle flash, semi automatic weapons and lots of explosions - and we did just that. It turned out to be a pretty dreadful movie but we blew a lot of things up. I guess in context, *The Runner* is a knee jerk reaction to the inhibitions of film school. It felt VERY decadent.

Q - Did you have problems talking to people at the top?

Gen - To begin with we did - it depends on your approach. Many young filmmakers, particularly those fresh out of film school, are arrogant, and assume that they have an unwritten right to freebies, discounts and will get offered the best projects. We didn't feel that way and chose not to be arrogant and reasoned that we were more likely to get help if we asked politely.

(above) To prove to EGM that Living Spirit had what it takes, they produced a short two minute action packed trailer. This was a very successful course of action to take as it convinced everyone the picture was going to happen.

Q - How did people in the industry react to these two young upstarts?

Chris - At the time the industry was depressed and didn't seem to understand what we were doing, we were so far removed, we were almost a cottage industry. It was obvious that if we wanted to make movies in the UK then it was up to ourselves to generate our own projects. We've just had to do it with the limited means at our disposal, with whatever talent that we had, and on a micro budget. Risk it all and hopefully at the end of the day it will all come together. We were in a *need-to* situation.

Q - Are there any filmmakers who have been a source of inspiration?

Gen - We knew the story of Sam Raimi and *The Evil Dead* and after we saw a documentary on its making... about how he shot a promo on S8mm, then would visit doctors and dentists etc., get out his 8mm projector, pin a bedsheet to the wall, and show these potential investors what he wanted to make - and these people put money in. He was only eighteen. We thought *'Wow! Maybe we could do this!'*

Q - You tried to get investment for **The Runner** *from several sources, but because you had no real track record, you didn't get very far. How did you eventually get things going?*

Chris - We met a company called EGM Film International based in Cardiff, Wales. We said, *'Hey! We're young filmmakers and we've got this idea for a film.'* We showed them a promo tape of films (made by other people) and they were very impressed. We had a one page synopsis which we had written the night before because we thought that we should look like we knew what we were doing. And they said, *'We'll make this but we need to shoot in three weeks time. If you're not going to be ready then the whole show is off.'* We said *'Of course, we're poised'* and we walked out of the office thinking, *'great, we've got this chance to make a feature, but what are we going to do? We're shooting in three weeks time and we don't even have a script!'*

Like most things on *The Runner*, the script was written on a need-to basis. We'd been floundering about, trying to make this great movie and just never got around to putting words on paper. Now we had a real big problem.

(above) Screen hero Jack Slater as portrayed by Terence Ford... The Man, The Myth, The Legend, The Brother...

(below) Ford in action...

(below) Paris Jefferson and Andrew Mitchell - Heroine and Villain. Andrew gave such a psychotic interview that Living Spirit nearly rejected him - as it happened, he turned out to be one of the best things about the film.

Gen - We said we'd fax them the budget, so we had to go out and buy a fax machine! EGM had said, *'we don't want to spend over $60k'*, but we knew it would cost more. We said, *'we need $200k'* and they said, *'we'll give you $70k'.* We said *'Okay, we'll send you the budget tomorrow'.* We consulted our figures and saw that we really had to spend at least $150k. They said - *'No! No! We'll give you $100k.'* We knew that once they committed funds, they would have to finish the film. So we just agreed. We didn't waste much but it actually costs a certain amount of money to blow up half of North Wales, so we spent a lot on pyro's, bullets and all sorts of things - the budget escalated to $200k, exactly what we thought!

Q - With only three weeks pre-production, no money and no script, how did you manage to get everything going?

Chris - We rang a few friends and asked *'What are you doing for the next couple of months? Do you want to come and live at our house and make a movie?'* Everybody said yes and moved in. About thirty people in all. It was great. There were very few problems. Lots of relationships sprung up between various crew members, perhaps because the work was so crisis ridden, everyone needed a shoulder to cry on and it all got rather steamy at various points. I am really surprised there were no *Runner* babies!

I suppose there was a tremendous sense of camaraderie, that no matter what was asked of anyone, they would do it. I've often felt as if I now know what kind of team spirit troops must feel before they go into battle for the first time (not that our job is anywhere near as demanding).

Q - The screenplay usually takes months of development?

Chris - Yes, we had to write a script, good, bad or indifferent. We had to have ninety pages of words to give the actors, to say on the day. Neither Gen nor myself could afford the time to divorce ourselves completely from the much needed three weeks of pre-production. Mark Talbot-Butler, the editor of the film, seemed to be capable of writing a screenplay, so we commandeered him. He did a commendable job when you consider that this was his first screenplay, and the timescale involved. There was simply no development process. When it came to the point where we were shooting, I would walk on set, be given my pages of the script, hot from the photocopier, and read it for the first time. I'd think *'Oh!, so that's what we're doing!'* and Gen would read it and see that there were three helicopters needed and she'd say to me, *'Give me three hours',* and off she would go and come back with three helicopters. Really, she did get three helicopters. It was incredible.

There were so many screw-ups because we were totally unprepared. It was a serious crash course, and I emphasize the word crash, in how not to make films. We learned so much. At the end of the day the film was pretty bad. It looked and sounded great and consequently sold, but it's many years on and we still haven't nor expect to receive a penny.

Q - How did you get a cast crazy enough to be involved in this movie?

Gen - We put an ad in the actors newspaper *The Stage* and received sack loads of CV's and photos. It really was sackfuls. The postman once brought three sacks up to the front door and then he informed us that he wouldn't deliver to the door but would leave it all at the back gate. We sifted through these replies and thought, there can't be this many actors in the world, let alone the UK - we sorted them into two piles, *Looks OK, Doesn't look OK*. Then sorted the *Looks OK* into two piles, *Done Film Work, Haven't Done Film Work*. It still took a few hours to short-list, and the list wasn't very short, but it did cut down our work load.

Q - So what did you do about the lead actor?

Chris - Tough man Jack Slater had to be played by a star - but we couldn't afford a star - so we got the brother of a star.

Gen - We rang up a few agents and told them who we were and what we were doing. One agent came back to us and said *'What about Terence Ford?'* We'd not heard of him. *'Well he's done some TV and a movie.'* Still we weren't impressed. Then she said, *'he's the brother of Harrison Ford'.* We thought great! Apparently Terence had read the treatment and liked it, so he rang up and Chris spoke to him (we couldn't afford to fly out to audition him). *'He sounds cool'* said Chris.

Chris - They sent us his CV which was pretty unimpressive with regard to feature film work, but his photo was good. He looked like a younger, more rugged version of his brother. We felt we had found our lead actor. He was Harrison Ford on a budget. We offered Ford a fee of five grand. EGM took over at that point. We said Harrison Ford's brother's interested. Their ears pricked up and they gave him the job. Gen picked him up from the airport and brought him to the studio (which was actually our garage). When we first met, I feared we might have problems as he had lost a lot of weight and his hair had silvered. His photo had portrayed him as a much more rugged and tough looking actor. As he was Harrison Ford's *younger* brother, we all imagined someone like Harrison Ford ten years ago. In fact, they were only separated by a few years so looked about the same age.

Gen - We didn't have much choice. We'd spent loads of money on his flight and were about to start shooting. We'd have to change him a bit. Dye his hair for a start.

Chris - We had cast another guy in the role of the villain, he was an American living in the UK. A week into shooting, he didn't turn up. We thought *'where is our villain?'* Gen got on the phone to his agent and found out that he was on holiday in Turkey and didn't want to come back. So, here we were, I was on set and Genevieve came up to me and said, *'we have a problem with shooting McBain tomorrow* (the villain), *well, he's on holiday in Turkey and he's not coming home.'* I said *'fine, OK',* because I had become used to this kind of crisis every twenty minutes. I relied on the company slogan - *'Gen'll fix it!'* Anyway, that night I returned to the production office and there were two photographs on the production office wall, one of this rather delicate looking actor from Amsterdam and the second, slightly less delicate, living in London.

Gen - They both looked like models.

The blind leading the blind! (above) Cameraman Jon Walker, who had never shot a film before The Runner, *was one of the most experienced crew members!*

Chris - The one in London was a friend of the lead actress and she suggested him as he could play American, so we decided to interview him. We asked him to take the train up to Cheshire and we gave him an interview. This is an interview that took place at two-thirty in the morning after a long day's shooting, with the whole crew asleep in this house. We had twenty bunk beds in our living room and there I was in one of the bedrooms with fourteen people farting and snoring giving and interview to this guy who must have thought, '*Oh my God! What am I doing here?*'

Gen - The other actor from Amsterdam had said, '*whatever happens, I will come over from Holland for an audition*' and I said, '*we can't afford to pay for you to come over, and if you don't get it, then I'm sorry, it's your tough luck!*' And he said '*that's fine, I'll get it! I'll get it!*' So I drove to pick him up from Manchester - he didn't have enough money to fly, so he had spent thirty hours on a ferry and train. It was maybe three o'clock in the morning when we got back and it's straight upstairs to do the audition.

Chris - He was quite good looking and very pleasant. We took him into a room full of bunk beds and asked, '*what would you like to read for us?*' He replied in a strong Dutch American drawl, '*Okay man. I don't want to read no words. I've prepared my own interpretation of the part. Do you want to hear it?*' We agreed. A pause before he suddenly exploded into this incredible, violent, one-man play about killing babies in Vietnam. I was sitting on the bed thinking '*we cannot employ this guy, he will murder us in our beds. In fact, I'm going to double lock my bedroom door tonight!*' Mark, the editor and writer, was sitting next to me, and he was equally terrified while watching this performance with dinner plate eyes. We left the room.

'*Oh my God. What are we going to do? This guy's completely insane*' I said and Genevieve is hyper, saying '*He's great. He's so energetic!*' The other actor, the one from London was more bankable, a little more secure. We knew he would at least read the words on the page (when they were eventually written). Then there was the method maniac who might have been a little more exciting on the screen, but I just couldn't get over the paranoid thought that he might actually kill us all. We couldn't decide so we promised to tell them in the morning after sleeping on it. So, the Dutch actor had to sleep on the kitchen floor, since there was no space anywhere else. In the morning, we decided not to give him the part. We said '*We're going with the other actor*' - he was devastated.

Gen - You shouldn't admit this.

Chris - It's fine now - but for some reason, something said '*this man's not as loony as I thought he was.*' It was something he was projecting in the hope of getting the role, and I had this gut feeling, '*hire him quick!*' I dragged Gen out of the room and said '*I think we should take him*'. She said '*you spent all night saying we can't*' and so we had another debate and decided to go with the psycho Dutchman. I went out and said '*you've got the part! That was just a test to see how you'd react!*' And he bought it. He really believed me.

(left) Endless paperwork, contracts, accounts - the bane of every guerilla producers life.

Q - What happened with the crew?

Gen - Most of the crew were very young, and everyone was inexperienced. I suppose we were all cheap labor. The crew got nothing but a $10 donation from EGM, halfway through the film. One day, Geoff, one of the partners in EGM, came in with a brown envelope of used notes and handed them out. Actually, he ran out, so a few crew members didn't even get their ten bucks.

Q - With thirty five people living in your house, what was it like?

Chris - We lived in this one cottage, at least eight people to a room, mixed accommodation. We sectioned off half of the main room. That was the office. The other half was the bunking quarters. One bathroom, one toilet, no shower, no washing machine and we shot

(above) Windmill Cottage - Living Spirits' base in Cheshire. Served as hotel, kitchens, locations, studios, indeed everything for the thirty strong crew and production of The Runner. "We were evicted three weeks after shooting, but at least we got the movie in the can."

like this for over a month. We ran out of locations, so we built a lot of them in the garage, in our back garden. And it was hell on earth. But it was great and everybody loved it. We could ring every one of those crew members and say *'there's a reunion',* and everyone would be there. The only way I can explain it is like this. Sometime during the shoot I remember being driven around North Wales, I'm not entirely sure where and I'm not entirely sure how many hours we'd been out there, I just sat in the van, looking across this dark landscape and tried to remember what it was like to sit down in front of the TV at night and relax. I had completely lost contact with that side of my life. And it felt that we could do anything we wanted to. Really, seriously weird.

Q - How did you deal with preparing locations with so little time?

Gen - The general order of business was *'what are we going to do today? We've got to do this or that scene and we'd better do this tomorrow...'* And so we'd sort out the locations a day in advance, two days if we were lucky. The money situation just made things worse - on the first day of principal photography the backers didn't turn up. We had to carry on without them but we didn't have any money to get the food. Occasionally, we ended up in deep trouble - I remember one time, we drove for hours, a whole crew and cast in convoy, to a mine in the middle of Wales. When we got there, they wouldn't let us in. And that was one of the times when we had actually *got* permission!

Chris - That's right. We were about to do the final scene in the film - the climax of the movie. As usual we were trying to set up the shoot the day before and Gen was zooming across North Wales to find a mine in which to shoot. She found a brilliant one in Llan-something. We got to the mine/power station and took all the kit in. It was like driving into a Bond set. The middle of this mountain had been quarried out. There were houses, office buildings, everything *inside* the mine. Roadways, traffic lights and cars parked inside the mountain. We shot for two days without any problems, and on the third day we had to film in another location. Come the morning of the fourth day, we returned to the mine and there was a new guard on the gate who said *'You can't go in'.* We protested... *'We have clearance'.* But we weren't going to get in, no amount of bribery could budge this guy. It transpired that the original guard had been sacked for letting us in as part of the mine was a top secret Ministry Of Defense nuclear air raid shelter. It was so high level that even the guard who had let us in didn't know it was there!

Gen thinks *'Okay we've been filming in a high security establishment and we're not getting back in. We've got to finish our movie. What are we going to do?'* So, she gets back into the car and zooms off to find another mine - and she did! The next day the convoy drove 100 miles into what seemed like the heart of darkness. It's raining like a waterfall and all

we can see is wet black slate. It's so depressing. We arrive at the mine entrance and unload the gear. Everyone is soaked. We check out where we can film and it is a half mile walk underground with the equipment. We have twelve hours to shoot the last 15 pages of the script for our action-packed adventure, the most action-packed sequence in the whole film. And I'm thinking - *'Let's go for it. Lets go for it! We're going to finish it!'*

(above left) Things got pretty nasty on set.... A good rule was, 'Never argue with the director when he has a gun...'

(above right) The mine in Wales - a great location, but unfortunately, it turned out to be a secret Ministry Of Defence Nuclear Air Raid Bunker.

Five hours later, we're still lugging *IN* all the gear. Eventually it's all in. We're about to go for the first shot. It's taken five hours to set up. Terence is there. Lead actress, Paris is there. I rehearsed. I called for silence... Then we realized there were no guns. This was the big shoot out. The armorer says *'I'll go and get them.'* Fifteen minutes later the guy comes back looking kind of sheepish and says *'I don't know how to tell you this, but the guns are in the back of the prop girl's car.'* And I said *'fine, then get them.'* Then he says *'But the prop girl has gone back to Cheshire twenty minutes ago.'* The props are on a four hundred mile drive, with no cell phone, and we have got six hours to shoot the climax to our movie! The next thing I can remember is being woken up by Jon Walker, the DP. Apparently, I'd just fallen asleep on a large rock. Both body and mind had gone into retirement - for a short time I was in a vegetative state.

Gen - Then it got worse. We had a massive argument with the cast. It became apparent that we weren't going to finish the film that night. Also we had been rushing to finish the film because the lead actress, Paris Jefferson, had said she had to fly off in the morning so that she could get to another shoot somewhere in Europe.

We knew this was the last day we had with her and we were running out of time, and we'd lost the guns - it was absolute hell. Then Paris says *'well, why don't we all come back tomorrow?'* - *'But you're not going to be here tomorrow!'* I reply. *'Oh, no. I can be here if you want me to be.'* Shocked, we blew up at her and had a massive argument with all the actors. Everyone took sides, mainly against us. It all got pretty heavy and enemies were made. Most of us made up later, but there were still a few grudges floating around. In retrospect, Paris was quite within her rights, it's just the insanity of low-budget filmmaking creates a crazy atmosphere. Our executive producers, John and Geoff, had gone off to America by then and were out of contact. So, we decided to pack it all in and come back in a month when we had the guns, the mine and the actors. Then we'd finish *The Runner*.

Chris - Tensions between cast and crew always ran high. It has to be said that a lot of the time the actors were quite right. There was such hell going on, they couldn't help but snap, because they spent ninety percent of the time just waiting for

(left) Three choppers for free in as many hours...

us to decide what to do. And everybody was ill with flu. However, one day we had a real medical shock. I was shooting on set and Gen came up to me and says...

'...Have you heard? Terence is dead. He's just been air lifted to Bangor Hospital. He's dead. What are we going to do? Can we write around it? It was like something out of Fawlty Towers!*'*

We'd got so used to problems that the concept of our leading man being dead was simply another obstacle to overcome. What had actually happened is that Terence was ill, the doctor had given him a sick note and sent him to bed. By the time we heard about it, the rumor mill had changed it to *'Terence is dead!'* The entire production was thinking *'What is going to happen?'* while Terence is wrapped up in his bed with a hot water bottle and a dose of aspirin. That was a bad day.

Gen - I remember my state of mind at that time. I had been told that Terence was in the morgue - it was some kind of Welsh joke by the hotel owner. So I was racing through the narrow winding roads at a hundred miles an hour, thinking of ways we could write him out of the story without it looking too crazy. I wasn't bothered that he might be dead - all I wanted was to make sure that the film didn't suffer! That is the degree to which we were all affected by the insanity of low-budget filmmaking. It gets into your blood and takes over your soul, I guess that's why it feels a little like going to war.

We were staying in a tiny Welsh village, where the villagers thought that this kind of joke was really funny. The other joke they played on us was potentially more serious. Someone rang the hotel telling them that they had planted a bomb. So we had the police round, searching everyone's room. I remember being in dreaded fear that the police were going to check my room, because that morning I had just taken delivery of a crateful of semi automatic weapons from our armorer, AND a fake bomb for the bomb scene. Luckily they didn't check my room.

Q - The Runner *has many action sequences with one breathtaking highfall. How did you get stuntmen involved?*

Gen - The week before filming, we received lots of phone calls because we were trying to find actors and crew. I got a call from a guy called Terry Forrestal who said he was a stunt man and wanted to help. I said *'Yeah, great, great'* thinking he was another karate expert from down the road who wanted to get into the business.

Terry said *'I've been working on Indiana Jones, this, that and the other and I used to do James Bond'*. He reeled off a list of a hundred A list movies. I asked for his CV and said I'd get back to him. You have to understand that we had taken so many weird phone calls from so many wacky people that we were cautious. Then his CV arrived, and I looked at his list of movies - it looked like my video collection! I realized - this guy's for real! Immediately, we rang him up and arranged to meet. He was so keen and wanted to do everything he could to help us out. Everything was possible. In fact, he was so enthusiastic that he wanted to do more stunts than were in the script!

Chris - Terry had read the script and saw the bit about the high fall, *'how are you going to do this? Well, we'll probably dress the actor up and jump off a low point onto some cardboard boxes. Ten feet or so. You know, we'll cheat it. It'll look all right...'* And he said *'No, no. You need a proper stunt. I'll do a high fall for you.'*

(above left) Stuntman, Terry Forrestal, considers the jump he is about to make. (below left) The crew, roped off above, prepare for the final shot as the sun sets.

And I said *'How high is high? 15 or 20 feet?'* - *'Oh no'* he said, *'I'll do a ninety foot high fall for you'* He pointed to this house in the distance which seemed pretty big and explained, *'it's about that, and a half again'.*

I was stunned. So we went on this location scout in North Wales to find a cliff from which he could jump without killing himself. Finally we found a cliff. On the day he just turned up with his airbag man, blew the bag up and jumped off the cliff. Well, in fact there were two high falls. We co-ordinated this with Terry. The first one was off the cliff into the airbag. The second, the more dangerous was off the cliff into the water. On each stunt attempt we had three cameras. Two would have done the job but we really wanted three.

So we had three cameras set up and shot each stunt twice. We ended up with six separate shots, all in slow motion so that they would cut together to make it look like the fall lasted for ever. Well, the actual high fall lasts for nine seconds in the movie - a serious amount of screen time for somebody to be hurling towards earth at two hundred and thirty five feet per second. So it gave the impression of an immense fall which really did get gasps in the theater.

To be honest, one of the best things about *The Runner* is that stunt and even Terry considered it one of the best falls he's ever done. I think he meant in the way it comes across on screen. He'd done other, more dangerous falls, much higher but somehow they don't look as dangerous. Perhaps the circumstances were never quite as wild as on this shoot. We were totally into Sam Peckinpah and action movies, so we wound the slow motion dial until it wouldn't go any further - no matter how fast the film was whizzing through the gate, Terry still went flying through frame.

Gen - And there was, as with all stunts, a real sense of danger. When Terry jumped into the lake he said *'If I don't come up after five seconds, either I've hit my head on the bottom or I'm dead'.* It was a very long five seconds.

Q - Once you had the film in the can, was it all down hill?

Chris - Not really, we had to fix all the problems we had given ourselves during the shoot. A good example is the firing range scene - there are shots in that sequence from five different locations, shot at seven different times, with up to seven months separation - piecing it together was a logistical nightmare. Mark Talbot-Butler edited the film after we finished shooting. Unfortunately, we were evicted from our house for having thirty five people living there which broke the terms of our tenancy. This meant that we had to put most of the work in Mark's court - he had to go off and do a lot of the cutting on his own, locked in his attic. It was all very rushed.

The International Sales booth for The Runner *at the Milan Film Market 1991. Visiting a sales market is an invaluable experience.*

EGM wanted the film ready for the MIFED film market in Milan which took place in October and we therefore made sure it was done. This really compromised the movie. We only had about seven weeks post-production. A great deal of energy was spent getting the picture to look good, the audio to be full and rich, and to make sure the cuts flowed. But at no point do I remember sitting down to ask whether the story was actually working. This neglect meant we had a good looking, great sounding, boring movie. And even then, the sound was rushed with effects still being edited while we began dubbing. Mark didn't even have an assistant. He was in his Mum's attic with a Steenbeck (editing machine) working eighteen hours a day. No pay, no nothing. Each time I saw him, he began to look a little weirder - not surprising really.

(above) Cast and Crew of The Runner at the London Premiere - A great night!

While Mark was cutting away, we were working on the score with an old school friend who had done the music for my amateur Super 8mm Zombie films. He had gone on to play in a local band and was excited by the prospects of being involved in a *real* film. He had to fake an illness and take time off work to spend seven days at his keyboard. There was no music budget, so we had to create that big orchestra sound with some synths and an Atari computer locking it all together. It worked out really well, the music was pacey and dynamic - and recorded in our front room. When John Eyres (one of the Exec producers) came to view the final cut, he wasn't particularly happy. He wanted some stuff cut out. We agreed but never cut the scenes out. He wanted to remove the helicopter rescue at the end of the film, because it said RAF on the choppers (giving away the fact that the film was shot in the UK and not in the USA as claimed).

(above) The Living Spirit team for The Runner - *Left to right, Chris Jones - Director, Genevieve Jolliffe - Producer, Mark Talbot Butler - Screenplay & Editor, Andrew Mitchell - Actor and Jon Walker - Cameraman.*

Q - How was the premiere?

Chris - Everyone clapped, but it was hollow polite clapping. I think people were amazed that we had managed to get it made, a film that looked and sounded good. But what a dreadful story.

Gen - It was the achievement, rather than the actual film that was applauded. The audience were saying well done for getting this far. We were caught up with it all. We didn't get nervous. We just enjoyed it.

Chris - At the time we thought that it was the best movie ever made. We talked like we were old time movie moguls. It was terrific! Sadly though, we were not yet aware that we had actually made a really crap film. But at the time, that didn't matter - it was OUR premiere!

Gen - However, we do have people coming up to us who saw *The Runner*, saying how much they like the movie, how they've gone out and bought their own personal copy of the film. *The Runner* aspires to big budget movies and isn't like the majority of low budget 'quirky' movies that get made.

Q - How much did The Runner make you?

Chris - To date, not a single penny. Living Spirit did not make the proverbial 'fortune' out of *The Runner.* What happened to us, and what happens to most first time feature makers, is that we got caught with a standard distribution deal. Basically, EGM financed the film and acted as the sales agents. They received thirty five percent commission plus all expenses before they started to recoup their investment. This meant that they got all their money back, plus thirty five percent commission, plus expenses, before we would even see a penny. It means we will never get paid, never ever, which means that we'll never be able to pay our cast and crew which means it's a bit of a downer really. This is a very common story that many filmmakers tell.

Gen - We were very naive when we took the film on. Our attitude was - *'Let's do the film, We've got three weeks. Let's just do it, get our foot in the door rather than just sit on our butts'.* So, when the contract came, we had a lawyer go through it, and he advised us not to sign it. But at the end of the day, we thought, well, we have a choice here. If we sign it, there is a possibility that we could get ripped off. If we don't, the film may never happen. So we went with it. I am very glad we did, it gave us a track record and a showreel. Most important was the experience, *that* was invaluable. If you have nothing to lose, just go for it.

(top) The final poster for The Runner, complete with splendid action movie style chromed logo and blazing background. (above) Living Spirit are presented to HRH Prince Charles after receiving their award.

Q - How do you feel about it all now that it is ancient history?

Chris - We went with it and got the chance to make a film. We got to go mad in North Wales, with Hollywood stuntmen, bombs, guns and a bunch of actors - it was a fair trade off. My only regret is that nobody got paid - I guess and hope that everyone was rather philosophical about it. For many of the crew, the experience was worth more than the money.

Gen - A lot of the crew members were either still at film school or had just left and had never worked professionally on any kind of film. I remember at the first production meeting, Chris asked who had worked on a film before. It was quite a shock when only two people put their hands up. The average age was 19/20. There was even a 14 year old - I felt old at 19.

Q - Can you protect your rights as filmmakers on the first film?

Gen - The main problem you're facing is that it IS your first film. You are so desperate to make it that you will sign anything. If it comes to the crunch, I would advise anyone to sign because what is important is that you make the film. Just make sure you invest none of your own money

The Runner is available in the US under the title Escape from… Survival Zone *(often on eBay). If you get the chance to view it, we would recommend you don't! It really isn't worth an hour and a half of your life! Check out the trailer at www.livingspirit.com instead, you'll see everything worth looking at in under 90 seconds then.*

or money that you are responsible for and therefore reduce your losses. If you can make your first movie without losing anything, then go for it because nobody is going to give you free money and nobody's going to invest in you because you've never made a film before. It is easy to be completely shafted, everyone from Tobe Hooper to Steven Spielberg has been ripped off, and not just on their first films. I think it is the nature of the business. Once we had finished *The Runner*, we had a lot less trouble making *White Angel*. We had more control and simply refused to sign anything unless we had total control.

Q - I believe you are in the Guinness Book of Records.

Gen - Yes, as Britain's youngest producer for *The Runner*. I was 20, not so young when compared with American filmmakers.

Q - Because of your connections with the Princes Trust, did you invite the Prince of Wales to the screening?

Chris - We actually won an award - the PYBT award for Most Tenacious Business Of The Year. There was a special award ceremony with a screening of *The Runner* at the BAFTA theater in Piccadilly. HRH came along and presented the award.

Q - Did HRH see the film?

Chris - He saw some of it but he couldn't watch it all because he had other appointments on the schedule. He said it looked a little too violent for him.

Q - How did your second film, White Angel, come about?

Chris - Obviously, after *The Runner*, we wanted to make another film. *The Runner* had crippled us so much that we didn't have any funds left. The only way we could possibly get out of the great financial hole we were in was to make another movie! We decided to make what we considered to be the most commercial film possible, shooting with the least amount of money. *White Angel* was conceived the same day that we saw *Henry, Portrait of a Serial Killer* (in a grimy cinema) We thought it was a great movie but it was too offensive for a wider audience. However, we thought we could make something with the same feel, but not quite so graphic - and turn it into a taut thriller.

Gen - We also saw *Silence of the Lambs* and felt that we could do something similar, that was more contained, and not awash with gore. Also we didn't think that Hannibal Lecter gave a true portrayal of a serial killer - sure, he was a terrific character which the audience had a love hate relationship with - but he had been glamorized for the movie. We researched real serial killers, reading lots of books, for example Dennis Nielson's biography, *Killing For Company* by Brian Masters. We became fascinated by the British serial killer and his peculiarities. Admittedly, most of our research was very lightweight, we didn't want to start making psychological assumptions, merely chart the actions of a killer. The closest that we came to real research was through my uncle who worked at a top security prison and he would tell us of his encounters with the infamous Yorkshire Ripper. We also saw some home movie footage of Dennis Nielson which gave us the idea of using video taped interviews.

Ellen Carter fights Steckler in the climactic scenes of White Angel.

Chris - Many people appear to have a morbid fascination with the serial killer. The motivation seems so meaningless, and it's now a cliché, but it could be the person next door. Audiences like to dip into horror, to experience the shocks and come out of the other side unharmed and emotionally purged.

Q - What are you looking for in a no-budget script?

Gen - We knew the limitations of our location, so we developed our story from that single point. We were looking for containment, to keep the majority of the story in one place. The production office would be there, all the facilities such as makeshift changing and make-up rooms, a kitchen and equipment store. The location was inside the M25 (the major freeway around London), at the end of the tube (underground line), we could even see the station from the front door of the house! This meant that the cast and crew could be given a monthly underground pass, and therefore their travelling expenses were minimal. The location was also close to shops, parks etc., and all the other locations required in the screenplay were within five minutes walking distance. It worked quite well.

Chris - Where we went wrong with *The Runner* is that the production was sprawling, shooting in locations that were hundreds of miles apart. That would eat up our shooting time. We had to put people up and pay for hotel rooms, catering, travelling etc. The number of principal cast was five, far too high. This in itself was very expensive which is why we limited the principal cast in *White Angel* to two, with Don Henderson (a well known TV actor in the UK) bobbing in and out (we actually only shot for two days with Don).

Q - So The Runner *was a good exercise in how NOT to make a low-budget film?*

Chris - Yes, after *The Runner* we sat and looked at the budget to see where the money went. A lot was spent on American actors, flying them over, making them comfortable and getting them in front of the camera. So, we said, *'what has Britain got to offer?'* We have great actors and we knew that if we could find one, who was willing to do it for virtually nothing, on the assumption that they will get paid eventually (and also receive a percentage), then we were onto a winner. We made a conscious decision to try and get a really good, classical actor, and Peter Firth filled that bill.

On the other hand we felt that we had to have a North American in the film, or we would be in the position where the

Americans may not want the film because it doesn't have that American feel. And we had heard stories about other British films like *Gregory's Girl, Trainspotting* and even *Mad Max* from Australia, being dubbed for the American market. We knew that *White Angel* had to sell in the US as in financial terms, the American market represented a huge slice of world

(left) The house used for the primary location in White Angel *had to double up as both production office and set. Ruislip outside central London was the perfect location and was steeped in suburbia.*

sales. In retrospect, we were being over cautious. If we could have persuaded a great British actress like Helen Mirren to play Carter, it may have improved sales and I think it would have been a better film. The Americanization of the lead female character (Ellen Carter who was played by Harriet Robinson) felt inserted into the story. Having said that, Harriet does have a quality that people like - I don't think we could have made a better choice with a North American.

Q - Why genre subjects?

Chris - Most low-budget filmmakers don't choose a genre because they've sat down and clinically thought, *'now if we make a sci-fi thriller, the Japanese market is going to like it'.* I think most first time filmmakers make the kind of film that they really want to make. Either that works or it doesn't. With *The Runner* we wanted to blow as much up as we could - we wanted to throw as many people off cliffs as possible - we wanted to create mayhem because we loved *Die Hard* and similar Hollywood movies. Low-budget filmmakers story choices seem to be a product of their youth. More than anything, on your first film you get the chance to do whatever you want. More than likely, the money will come from someone who knows nothing about filmmaking. You've got so little money at risk that you can go out on a limb, and in retrospect, we could have been more daring with some aspects of *White Angel* - to arouse much more controversy.

Peter Firth as the mild mannered serial killer, Leslie Steckler. Peter's experience brought a new dimension to an otherwise run of the mill screen killer.

Q - The script idea is rooted in the idea of a very British murder?

Chris - We said let's make this film British. As British as *The Long Good Friday*. The intrinsic Britishness emerged during script development. We didn't start off saying, let's make a film about a VERY British serial killer. We said let's make a film about a serial killer in Britain, and the true British angle came out when we started on the research, and also with the involvement of Peter Firth. He manipulated the script in the way that we wanted him to. The scripts that we've produced are functional. They get from A to B without showing too many of the footprints in the wet paint (we hope!). Peter Firth took the screenplay and changed Steckler from this mid Atlantic, generic psychopath and brought the character into the English home. Many of the mannerisms in the film were invented by Peter. A number of people have been surprised by this. They think everything in the film comes from the director or writer, when in essence, the director, writer and producer are merely the people managing the creative talent. Actors have the last say by virtue of their own performance. We felt Peter's ideas were good. You know on set whether something is working or not. For instance, we agreed with Peter to use the recurrent theme of *'would you like a cup of tea?'* as one of the main angles in the film. It was there in the script, but Peter made much more of. Each murder was followed by a *'cup of tea'*. Even the way Steckler dresses, the top button of his shirt being fastened was Peter's idea. There was a conscious decision to make Peter this out of date character, in so much as the film is set in the nineties, but everything about him is stuck in the seventies. He wears those trousers and that neck tie that only weird people still wear. He was very much stuck in that vein, and of course, clothing charity shops were the best place for him to shop. This is what people of quality bring to a production. An experienced and talented actor will bring so much to any story, and it's worth moving heaven and earth to engage their services. From a marketing point, everyone always thinks that big actors cost big bucks. This isn't necessarily so, and their mere presence in a film will enhance it's value.

CASE STUDIES

Peter Firth and Don Henderson - great British actors are worth every penny or percentage you pay them. They will bring quality and experience to any production.

Gen - We had seen so many movies about serial killers, but nothing that really explained why they do what they do. We wanted a more realistic approach, looking into what urges these people to do it - movies had shown these killers in a kind of glamorous light, rarely exploring why. We thought that the British serial killers were more interesting. The frightening thing, was how these killers really blended into society - how normal they looked... what fascinated us most was, *could it be the guy living next door to you?*

Q - The killer next door seems to be a concept which keeps coming up?

Chris - Yes, we decided that the screenplay should take the serial killer living next door right to its logical conclusion, to create a killer who is actually very likeable as a human being. We never see him murder except in small details*, and when it does happen, it has a kind of humour to it rather than horror. Therefore, apart from his memories of various crimes, we never experience Steckler, the serial killer. But we do see Carter kill and she is not the serial killer, which in turn is an interesting slant. Several people have mentioned that Carter was a bit of a cold character and that they liked Steckler. This is exactly what we wanted. Some people seem to like this different slant on the killers. At the end of the day if you get two killers together in a house and get them to talk about killing it's going to be strange, it's going to be funny, it's going to be horrifying and it could get very nasty. We wanted to get that seething atmosphere into the house, *lock the doors and see what happens...* Some of the elements from the screenplay we lost in the shoot. For instance, the heating was supposed to have gone insane during the film so that it was always hot in the house. We wanted a pressure cooker. We wanted claustrophobia. That is something that harks back to the needs of a low-budget film. You need to look at what you've got and turn that into an advantage. We had a small location, so we thought, let's make it claustrophobic.

Q - Had you seen the British serial kiler film 10 Rillington Place?

Chris - Yes, a long time before we made *White Angel*. After *White Angel* was completed, we saw the film again and were pleased, and to some extent shocked, by the similarities. There weren't any conscious similarities when we were making it. I don't know whether Peter had seen it but he had done research into serial killers. I remember Harriet asking Peter whether he had a defined idea of how he was going to play the character and he said *No, I don't have a clue, I'll tell you how I'm going to play it on the last day of photography.* And you could see it sometimes when he was unsure how Steckler would react. He had in him that ability to say, *I'll try this out and if it doesn't work, then fine.* This was a very valuable asset to have.

Q - A serial killer moves in with an undiscovered murderer. Where did that idea come from?

Polaroid photos are one of the only times we see Steckler's victims. It is amazing how multi talented your crew can be when pushed.

* In order to secure deals later, extra scenes of sex and violence were shot and added.

Chris - I don't know really, I guess by a process of development from a single concept. What we did is play around with this single concept. For example, we want to make a film about a serial killer. We have to make it in one house. We can't have him just going out and killing people because that would be tough to shoot, so we introduce a woman to get a male / female thing going and keep it in the one place. What could she be? Well, if she knows he's a serial killer, maybe it's his wife, but then it's obvious. Maybe she can be a crime writer, an expert on serial killers and he wants her to write his story. That's good. But why would she do it? Well, maybe she murdered her husband, bricked him up in the wall of the house and got away with it. Maybe the serial killer finds the body and blackmails her? Then, they're both murderers. Hey! That's a good idea. Before you know it you have a rough hook on which to hang your structure.

In a scene cut from the final film, Ellen Carter has recurring nightmares about her husband's body trying to escape from it's living room wall tomb.

Gen - Then you write the first one page synopsis, give it to your mates and ask what they think - *well, this is good, this is bad - OK*. Turn it into a two page synopsis. You keep building and building. What we like to do is to write it as a novella first, or at least a thirty page short story. When that reads well, then you've got something. It is structured very heavily. We have two plot points which come thirty minutes from the beginning, thirty minutes from the end and we have a sixty minute centre section. So, we have act one at thirty minutes, act two which is sixty minutes and act three at thirty minutes. And in addition, in the middle of act two we have a mid point. If you watch any good Hollywood feature, you'll see that they often stick to this common structure. When editing, what usually happens is that you end up cutting some of the junk out of the middle where it gets too wordy and slow. You also trim stuff from the start of the movie so you get going much faster. Then the movie should end up at around ninety minutes.

Q - What are the plot points in White Angel?

Chris - We spend the first ten minutes setting up the various stories which combine to form the main plot and characters. Ellen Carter has killed her husband and hidden the body - she has *'got away with murder'*. She is a crime writer who studies mass murderers. There is a serial killer in London killing women who wear white, and the killer may also be a woman. Mild mannered Steckler is probably the serial killer, he cuts up newspapers and has dead bodies in his living room after all! He moves in with Carter as a tenant. And all the time, the police are closing in as they have a fingerprint on a hammer that was left at the last murder scene...

The plot is completely set up in the first ten minutes or so, and then we had a framework in which to work. The fingerprint on the hammer is the time bomb waiting to go off which gives the movie a sense of impending doom and momentum.

Plot point one is where Steckler says *'I am the White Angel and I want you to write my story'*. Up until that point he has been getting on with his life, Carter has been getting on with hers. We've been setting up various parts of the story. But at that point, the film changes direction. It sheers off at ninety degrees. Carter's life is totally destroyed. Steckler's is totally fulfilled because he's got the writer he wanted to do his book. We then spend the next forty minutes of the movie exploring this theme of writing the book and what Carter is interested in. The mid-point of the film is where Carter interviews Steckler and he says about his wife, *'she deserved to die, the world is a better place without her'*. In the same scene, Steckler turns the interview around to Carter and she says of killing her husband, *'he deserved to die... the world's a better place without him'*. And she realizes that she has said the same thing as Steckler, therefore it questions the

(above) The hammer in White Angel *was the device which provided the plot and twists. This evidence would eventually lead the police back to the killer, and straight back to Ellen Carter for the final twist.*

(left) The original premise for White Angel *explored the differences between murder and manslaughter through the eyes of two killers.*

differences between them. It's a subtle mid-point but it is a character point when Carter suddenly realizes that she is essentially the same creature, a human being with the ability to kill. The rest of act two develops this theme - her attempts to poison him etc. Plot point two is where Carter finds out (wrongly) that her friend, Mik, has been killed by Steckler. She finds the glasses covered in blood - that's a pinch point - just before plot point two.

The exact position of plot point two is where she sees the blood and the knife in Mik's flat and comes home to find Steckler burying the body in the garden. Again, at this point, the film sheers off at an angle. Carter is no longer interested in writing the book. She has one thing on her mind and one thing only. To kill Steckler. To get him off the face of the planet. She can't turn him in to the police because she'll go down for murder. So she plots an elaborate plan which the audience discovers as it happens. This leads us to the climax and twist in the tail. Most people like a good twist, it lets them leave the theater feeling fulfilled in a strange sort of way. However, it can often backfire and make the audience feel cheated. We are not saying *White Angel* is the greatest screenplay ever written, but it does work as a thriller. Some people say the story was *'gripping'*, which is a real compliment when you consider the constraints under which the film was made.

Q - So the treatment was extremely detailed before you wrote the script?

Gen - Absolutely. *White Angel* wasn't a short treatment. I think that the final version was twenty five pages. It is important that you can write this kind of treatment and you know the structure (page eight is plot point one and on page twenty two you have plot point two, with the mid point on page fifteen). We structure everything, so when writing, you don't lose control of your characters, nor will the story lose its direction. Every scene has got to move the story onward to its final conclusion - otherwise you may be boring your audience. You have around two hours to get everything across, and leave no loose ends.

Chris - Screenplays and stories are all about mystery and exploration. Many fim makers are obsessed by character, *'let's stop the movie and have a talky scene where the character confesses that he's shot a kid in a back alley ten years ago'* - this is often resolved later in the film, and I find it divisive and obvious. For me, a movie is about getting on to the next scene. One of the interesting things that we did on *White Angel* was when we finished the first rough cut we went back and started to cut the end out of many scenes, and some of the middle. What originally was a well structured scene now felt unbalanced, not finished. The audience felt there was more, that they were not being told everything. This is not a hard and fast rule but it is a good guide - *don't tell your audience everything!* It keeps them wanting more.

Q - There is a great deal of video footage used. Was this in the script?

Chris - Yes. There were two reasons for the inclusion of video tape footage. I'm from the amateur filmmaking scene and while I started on Super 8mm, VHS soon became a medium that was very accessible. I loved the way that in science fiction movies of the eighties, video footage was heavily used, (eg. *Aliens*). It always looked grainy and really gaudy and I thought it was great. What an image. So, wouldn't it be great to get Steckler's monologues on video tape because that is a format that is much more *'real'*. People understand that film is drama but the news is *'real'*. People believe video images. In the film, Steckler gives interviews, and I thought, if we can do the interview on tape, then we have a five minute take in one. Five minutes of the film translates to about six percent of the final product. We had fifty five rolls on which to shoot this film. I was fully aware that to get a five minute monologue in one film take, which is what I wanted, was going to be difficult. So we shot it several times on video tape and then transferred the final result to film (by filming it off a TV screen). So you have a chunk of your film finished with a cutting ratio of one to one which is pretty damn good. The cutting ratio is how much stock you shoot in comparison with how long your film is. If the film is to be one hundred minutes long and you shoot one thousand minutes of stock, then you would have a cutting ratio of ten to one. Most low budget feature work is between eight and twelve to one. I think we shot *White Angel* on four and a half to one. It's all about preventing waste. Don't do endless takes. I learned on *The Runner* that take one is often very similar to take fifteen. Often in the editing room your can hear your voice calling *'Take four. Loved it darlings!'* and you wonder why you got that far - there was nothing wrong with takes one to three. If you've got the shot and your cameraman says that it's fine and the gate's clear - go with it. It saves you time and it saves you *stock and it saves you money.*

Gen - We had seen the effect of video images in films like *Henry - Portrait of a Serial Killer* - where it was pretty nasty - and the reason it was more horrific than seeing the other killings on film, was simply because it was shot on video tape. It was real. It's like seeing the news - the images can be shocking.

Q - Some writers chose an imaginary cast when working on a script, to give characters life. Did you do this?

Chris - Yes. When Steckler's character was formed I had Jeremy Irons in mind. For Carter, the female lead, I only had one person in mind. No chance of getting her, of course. A 1970's Jane Fonda! It helps you 'see' them in the scene when writing.

Q - When you started pre-production you had very little money, why didn't you wait until you had your full budget in place?

Chris - Mainly because we would have had to wait forever. We had worked out that it was possible to make a feature film for less than fifteen thousand dollars and we looked at how we made *The Runner* and where the money went. There were obvious things like film stock, processing, camera gear, things that you cannot avoid. You can get a good deal, you can get discounts, you can get some things for free, but there is always going to be an expense. There are however, other expenses that you can avoid or minimize. The reason why *The Runner* went over budget was that it was set in lots of locations, so out of a twelve hour shooting day, you'd spend a quarter of it driving between A and B, and then another quarter loading and unloading the vans... We lost thirty to forty percent of our time through location changes. *The Runner* was filled with events that just wasted time through ignorance or lack of forward planning. *White Angel* was going to be different.

When creating a character it helped a great deal to visualize a certain actor playing that part.

Food is always an issue. More than likely, you won't be able to afford a food wagon. On top of good food, remember cast and crew will need tea, coffee and water at all times, and a warm dry place to sit down and eat.

Gen - The rules for low-budget scripts are all cost related. Money is the one thing you have little control of because on a no-budget film, you don't have it. The big expense we had on *The Runner* was crew and accommodation expenses. That took $20k of our budget. On *White Angel* we decided to shoot in London and buy everyone an undergrounf pass. It cost $30 a week to get cast and crew to and from location.

White Angel was based in one house and there are very few scene changes - this minimized time wastage and allowed us to finish the film in eighteen shooting days as compared with nearly forty on *The Runner*. From *White Angel's* point of view the two golden rules we had were, minimize locations AND shoot where the cast and crew can spend the night at home and not at our expense. This saves money in other ways. For example, if we wrapped early, we may not have needed to provide a meal in the evening. So, we'd not need catering that night. Catering is one of the areas where basic expenses can't be avoided, and it is actually a bad idea to skimp on it. If you feed your cast and crew well, you'll get twenty percent more out of them. You have to feed them something so why not make it good! A low-budget shoot needs good food to look forward to. Out in the rain, or the cold, good food keeps the spirits up.

Q - What would be an average menu?

Gen - We didn't supply breakfast because everyone lived in London and we looked at it as coming to work. Lunchtime, we would provide sandwiches, easy food that could be served from a cardboard box anywhere. For the evening meal, we'd always do something hot, baked potatoes, stews etc. Warm, stodgy food with plenty of carbohydrates to keep people going. We'd also send out chocolate bars to break up the times between meals and even persuaded a local bakery to give us all their cakes that were left unsold at the end of the day. Once a week, we provided beers. It is the same idea as getting chocolates etc. You give people beer and they think, this isn't so bad and it holds the team together.

Q - Where were all the meals prepared?

Gen - There just wasn't room in the kitchen, so Mark Sutherland, the set constructor, found a skip outside a pub which was being refitted. He pinched the old bar and set up 'Steckler's Diner' in the garage. Meals were prepared and con-sumed in the garage and it was pretty squalid - the caterer had a simple gas fired stove, but still managed to feed thirty mouths, twice a day. I guess the crew named it 'Steckler's Diner' because sometimes we just didn't know what was in the stew!

Q - From a production point, what advantages did White Angel present?

Gen - We had a film set in suburbia, a location that would be cheap to shoot in, which would be near central London so that we could get the cast and crew to it easily. It was set in the present, so actors could wear their own clothes, or we could buy stuff from the charity shop, down the road. I'm not joking. We had a deal with Oxfam (UK charity shop). It cost us a hundred dollars for all our costumes in the film. And it worked. At the end of the day, when you have $15k to make a film, three and a half goes on film stock, two on cast and crew because you've got to give them something.... and before you know it, the whole budget has gone on essentials. Therefore, $100 for costumes. At each production meeting, Mark

Sutherland, our production designer, would proudly announce that out of his total budget of $150, he was going to spend another 60 cents on nails. He couldn't get them for free and was quite distressed about this.

Chris - He became notorious for going around dumpsters. The dumpster is a production designer's supply base on a low-budget shoot. Another man's junk is a production designer's dream.

Q - How detailed was the budget?

Gen - Very. We had to know where every penny was going to go. We worked out what we thought the entire production was going to cost - everything - even down to the gas and phone bills. Then we started to work out what things we actually needed to pay for to get the movie in the can - we just couldn't raise the entire budget before we shot, so we concentrated on getting the movie shot. Eventually, we narrowed our list of essentials down to around $15k. We knew we might need more than this, but once the snowball is rolling down the hill, it is difficult to stop it.

Chris - You spend months just trying to get this thing going, and then a few days before the first day of principal photography, the production runs itself - it's as if you have built a huge machine, and all you need to do is maintain it to ensure it doesn't stop working. If you get to the first day of shooting, you'll probably make it all the way to the finish line.

Gen - First of all, we concentrated on getting the right house that was cheap. Then we could start sorting out everything else. We rented the house in Ruislip, West London, and based the production there. Most of the film would be shot there and the production office would also operate from one of the upstairs bedrooms. Then we visited all the hire companies and I spoke to them about the film, and of course, getting free deals. I told them who we were and that were trying to... *'make a career for ourselves, we are young filmmakers, the film is very low-budget, and we need the best deal ever - please, please, pretty please...'*

Remember that any initial deal is the quote they probably give anyone. No one pays full price. Tell them how little you have. Get a quote. Look at your budget and decide what you can afford. Then ring them back and try to make a deal. They can only say no. I used to ring up, say a lighting company and say, *'look, I've got five hundred, can you do it for that?'* It is also important to pick a time to shoot your movie when you know that there is less work around in the industry. Then you will receive better discounts. You must make sure that you tell them exactly what you want and for how much. This is all I can afford, and I need an all in deal, all the equipment, all the accessories, all the gel, all the spun - ask if there are any hidden extras, or if you pay extra if you go overtime, what about broken bulbs. And get a quote that lays everything out in detail. The best deal to get is always an *'all in'* deal.

Q - And what about cast and crew?

Gen - You've most probably started thinking about who would be an ideal cast for your film, and you may have been speaking to agents who have been asking for the kind of money that is completely impossible - ask for their help and support. Again, it is best to be straight with these people and not to attempt to deceive them. If an actor likes the script and wants to do it, their agent will probably be unable to stop them.

Q - How did you budget for crew wages?

Gen - We put the crew on deferred payments. We agreed to pay their expenses so that they wouldn't be out of pocket. The film was shooting in London so we concentrated on people who could get the tube (subway) rather than paying fuel expenses which are harder to estimate before shooting. Also, we always over budget for expenses because there are

(left) All the night-time sequences for White Angel *were shot during the day with the windows covered by black trash bags. A routine is very important if the cast and crew are going to perform to the best of their abilities with limited resources.*

If money is tight, the basic Super 16mm Camera, Tripod, Lens, DAT, Mic and stock is all that is needed to make a cinematic quality feature film... And of course there are many new digital options. Oh you will also need and a script and cast and... (below left) Jane Rousseau, camera operator for White Angel.

tiny elements that you just don't expect. Somebody can't get the tube. The shoot runs after tube hours or someone rings up and has to get a taxi for some reason. That money has to come from somewhere so it is best to over budget on transport.

Q - Crew members need to eat and pay the rent, how do you deal with these very serious problems?

Chris - What we did on *The Runner* was very different from *White Angel*. On *The Runner*, we couldn't pay anybody anything and we didn't want to do this again, because people have to live. So, what we did on *White Angel* was to cover everyone's expenses, a tube ticket everyday and everyone received $75 a week, to keep them in beer and cigarettes. On top, we offered a deferred payment so that when the film was sold, they would receive their wages. This would be more than they would have got since they have to wait years for it - and don't kid yourself by promising money in two weeks. There is also a very good chance that they will *never* get paid. Selling a film is a long process. You've got to be straight with people. This is the money we've got - they can say *yes* or *no*. And make sure you pay it to them and reward them with good catering.

Q - What's in it for them?

Chris - Mainly experience at your expense. Many UK pro filmmakers earn money through commercials, television etc. but they usually want to make movies. There are also a lot of new students being turned out from film schools - take advantage of their enthusiasm and give them responsibility. In my experience, most people will deliver if you give them the opportunity to do so. There is a debate about deferred films - *are they ethical?* Well, almost all big budget features take advantage of free labor by taking on free runners or office assistants - we are doing the same, but giving them greater opportunity and experience, and a possible fee if it all works out. At the end of the day, everyone can say no. As a rule, if you can pay someone, do it, you will get a better worker, and no nasty phone calls two years down the line if you were not able to pay as promised.

Q - What shooting elements proved a problem later?

Gen - Something hit us when we were doing the effects on *The Runner*. The sheer quantity of stock needed to shoot action and effects. So on *White Angel*, we deliberately had very little stunt work or effects. By remaining in London, there was another saving. Because we were near the facilities houses, anything could be dealt with by a phone call and a quick trip in the truck. For example, if a camera went down, it was easy to get a replacement without costing much time or money. Also, we were close to the labs and could view rushes every day. When we were shooting *The Runner* up in North Wales, the camera did go down and it was a serious problem. We had to call London to get a new camera delivered, and then wait for them to courrier it up to us. With transport on location, always expect your trucks to break down - they always will! They'll get stuck in mud, stuck in snow, completely fail or crash. We had a few crashes - no-one was hurt, seriously at least. People get in too much of a hurry. This is one of the problems of low-budget filmmaking. Safety. Everybody knows there is a limited time scale. The production team is rushing to and from the set. Props must get to the set or the crew is sitting about waiting - so the foot goes on the accelerator and you speed along winding roads. On *The Runner*, I remember nearly losing my life when I was driving at 100 mph on a busy winding road on my way to the set. A truck pulled out in front of me at the last minute and the brakes made a horrific noise - luckily I am still around. It is incidents like this, when you realize that although it's important, is it really worth losing your life for a movie?

Q - What was the total you needed to make White Angel?

Gen - The grand total was about $125k. We didn't raise all the money at once. Initially we could only raise $15k and we thought, either we hang around waiting for all the rest or we take a risk and shoot it with what we have. The cast and crew were working on deferments and we could just about do it if we shot for eighteen days. Once we had the movie shot, we could show investors what they would be investing in, and it worked, it was much easier to get people to part with money when they could see where the other money had been spent. A lot of people think they need the full budget to make the movie but I would say, if you can't raise it all, and it's your first movie, just go for it. Once you've got something there, then people are more likely to put money behind you because they see you are not just talking about it but actually doing it. We both know a lot of people who have been waiting years to get their first movie off the ground because they haven't managed to get their two million budget yet - *dream on!*

Q - How did you approach investors?

Gen - We approached people who we thought might have a bit of money stashed away, and asked if they were interested in investing it. We also approached people who might be specifically interested in investing in films. Lots of people want to be a part of the film business, it's something to talk about over drinks. Starting with the local area, we made a list of doctors, dentists, lawyers etc. and sent letters off to them, working our way from A-Z. Obviously this can cost a lot of money, sending out letters etc., so we decided to make a short-list of firm contacts, people who we'd met or people to whom we could get an introduction. Also, news of *White Angel* travelled by word of mouth. We would meet a lawyer and he would be really keen so we'd send a full package of information. We'd have a second meeting and he'd say '*I've got this friend and she's interested, would you like the number?*' We had more success that way, rather than by cold calling.

Q - What's in an investment proposal?

Gen - We put a package together that would include a synopsis of the film, a brief of the budget, a breakdown of their investment and the returns that they could expect. The returns were calculated on the cost budget rather than the total budget. For example, if we were making a movie for $200k but only needed $100k to cover all immediate cash costs on the film (the remaining $100k would be on deferred payments) the investment percentages would be calculated from $100k. This meant the deal was even more interesting and showed we didn't want to waste a penny. Once initial investment monies are recouped

During the shooting of The Runner it became obvious that special effects and stunts cost time which translates to money. White Angel was tailored to contain as few effects as possible. Even the body in the wall of the house was created by a (at the time) non professional, Phil Mathews, who is destined to go on to greater things.

(left) The original artwork on the cover of the White Angel investment proposal. With virtually no material, we tried to make it look as much like a shocker of a movie as possible.

(below) The involvement of TV and Film faces such as Don Henderson help solidify the project in the eyes of potential investors.

i.e. all investors get their money back, deferments are then paid (cast, crew, facility houses etc.) Once the film has broken even (paying back the total budget of $200k) then all monies received from that point are deemed to be profit. Monies are returned and are split 50/50 between the production company and the investors. Therefore, the investors provide $100k and the deferred cast and crew provide the other $100k. The first sales would repay the investors back their $100k, then the deferred $100k would follow. The remainder would be split 50/50 between the production company and investors - an investor who put in $10k would receive 10% of the 50% split (5% of total profits).

Q - How did you confirm an investment?

Gen - We provided a simple contract, two or three pages and as long as they were happy, they would sign it. We had all the control. The only thing that they would be doing is putting their money in and receiving reports from us on the progress of the film. For them it was a risky investment but they knew it, and wanted to do it. There are many payments that must be met while in the sales process, all of which eat into any potential returns, such as making delivery and marketing. These figures need to be nailed down wherever possible. Obviously, they are deducted from any sales and that will push the investors profits further away, but there is nothing that can be done about this. Without your delivery items, you won't be able to give your film away - it's like a car without an engine.

Q - Did investors give the money up front?

Gen - We didn't cash flow the payments because our budget was so small, but if someone wished to invest a larger amount, say $100k, then we would have linked that in with a cash flow prediction. We didn't do this on *White Angel* because the money was raised in instalments anyway, so there was no need. We were almost doing a cash flow without knowing it. As soon as we had shot something we invited the investors down to the set, showed them around to prove that we were filming something and they met the lead actors. It creates the buzz and raises more money in itself. Once the filming finished we then concentrated on raising money to finish the film. We cut a trailer and showed that to investors - we kept the trailer short and punchy, left them wanting more.

Q - How long did it take to raise all the money?

Gen - One of the big problems with no-budget filmmaking is that if you raise money in instalments you often take time off from finishing the film, so the film takes longer to produce. We were still raising money nearly a year after we shot it.

Q - So, you must finish shooting?

WHITE ANGEL Schedule Breakdown

1991

October
Commence writing screenplay. Begin to attract finance.

November
First Draft Complete.

1992

January
Approx. $15k raised. Decision to shoot in February is made. Casting and pre-production move into top gear.

February
Principal photography begins and lasts 21 days.

March
Begin editing, continue day jobs and continue raising production finance.

May & June
Several small reshoots to patch some of the holes left in the main shoot. More investment comes in.

September
First fine cut complete.

December
Fine cut complete. Begin track laying sound and music.

1993

February
Final mix at dubbing theater. Negative is cut and labs begin very long process of printing.

March
Labs damage the master negative. Living Spirit recall cast for reshoot of damaged stock. Re-mix quickly.

April
First Prints viewed. Publicity gearing up for Cannes. London based sales agents view the film. No one bites.

May
Cannes - meet several companies who all express an interest.

July
Re-edit film and remix as it needs tightening and there are some sound problems.

August
Pilgrim Entertainment signed as sales agents for one year.

September
Premiere at the Montreal Film Festival. Goes down well. German, Korean and US companies express interest and negotiations start.

October
UK premiere at London Film Festival. Plan for an April theatrical release funded with money expected from Germany, Korea and US.

December
Korean and German deposits paid.

1994

Jan - March
Publicity for theatrical release.

April
Theatrical release. Film performs badly due to opening on bad weekend. Deals with US and Korea fall through. PANIC.

June - December
Pilgrim fail to deliver any deals. Publicity works a bit too well and Chris and Gen spend short time in police cells. Chris and Gen lose home.

1995

January
Labs threaten court for monies owed. Living Spirit sack Pilgrim. Feature Film comes on board to handle the video release.

Feb - March
Video release begins publicity. New version with more sex and violence is edited to help bolster sales.

April
A song, performed by local band, is included in the new edit. It's later discovered to be owned by the Elvis Presley estate and carries a price tag of $1.5m. Re-edit - AGAIN!

May
Video release.... Film performs poorly.

September
Living Spirit approach and secure new sales agent, Stranger Than Fiction. They are confident of making sales.

1996

February
White Angel is sold to Benelux, Italy and several far Eastern territories. Monies as yet have not been received.

1999

January
White Angel is recut after the experience of 'Urban Ghost Story', taking out seven minutes of 'nothing', tightening the action and drama. The first director's cut in history to be shorter than the original!

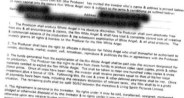

Investors in White Angel were given simple contracts that were one page long. Good for us and good for them.

Gen - Yes. It's vital to cover the screenplay as thoroughly as you can. You don't know if your lead actor could die, get awkward, move out if town... This could cause major problems. Even if you have to drop *close up cut-aways* during the shoot, do it in order to cover the main action and the screenplay. I know several other movies that were shot over, say ten consecutive weekends, but I guess the cast must have been made up from either friends or actors who lived locally. I wouldn't like to do it that way, but it is an option. Once we had completed shooting *White Angel*, we had no problem raising money for post- production. People could see what was there. They could watch it to see how it was working, see it was working well and put more money in. Not rushing the film allowed us to have a few test screenings, reshoot the ending and polish the feature as a whole. To check that everything was in place and that the story was going as planned - and that people were going to be gripped. It's better to do this than rush the post production only to discover your problems when you are sitting in a cinema with a crowd of two hundred people on the day the movie opens.

Q - Control is important. Why?

Gen - On *The Runner* we had given the final cut to the distribution company, they had a lot of say in the picture because they had put all the money in, in one lump sum. At the end of the day the film was not the film we wanted to make. The producers kept changing the film, trying to force the material to be more commercial, sacrificing the characters and the story, and they rushed post to get the film to the Milan film market - we ended up with a film that we felt didn't make too much sense. With *White Angel* we didn't want a situation to arise where people whose opinions we didn't agree with had a creative say in the process - *wouldn't it be a good idea if her head exploded?* etc. We wanted to keep control so that it would end up as the movie we wanted. That's not being possessive. It comes back to the writing stage where we will involve quite a few people to discuss the project, and screenings where we ask the audience to criticise the final result.

Q - What were your main legal questions?

Gen - The main contracts are for your actors and your crew. Especially, with the actors, you have to make sure that everything is in there. You have to have total control, to make certain that you can do anything that you want with the picture, reshoots and with the publicity afterwards. You do not want an actor refusing to do something because it's not contractual and they then request more money. The price that you have agreed to pay includes everything. The music

contract is also very important to nail down. The composer composes the music and you have permission to use it in the film. You think everything is fine, however, there are other hidden problems. There are mechanical and synchronisation rights along with publishing/performing rights that all have to be cleared. Mechanical reproduction is perhaps the most important for low-budget films since a good deal of money is recovered through video. If a buyout is not agreed, money is payable on every single copy of the video reproduced worldwide and it comes out of the producer's pocket. On *White Angel* we covered all such rights and no further payments are to be made. Anyone buying this film will ask to see these contracts and not having them in place might prevent any sales occurring.

White Angel publicity shot - Sexy girl, big gun, blue light - this kind of image is about as far removed as possible from the attitude of many (but not all) UK based production companies and institutions. This was a problem for Living Spirit as we couldn't afford to hire a model, so Louise Ryan, from the set construction team, kicked off her overalls and boots, and slipped into something slinky...

Q - Did you use a lawyer?

Gen - We used a lawyer on *The Runner,* but not an entertainment lawyer. This was a problem because the film industry is very specialized and needs a legal expert, which is expensive. In the US, with it being such a litigious society I recommend that you have an attorney look over any and all contracts. Yes, it may be expensive but many organizations offer free or cheap counseling. In the end you'll end up saving money and a lot of headaches.

Q - What did the schedule for White Angel look like?

Gen - The schedule was 20 days, with a day off each week, so that gave us 17 shooting days. We made sure we never had more than a 12 hour day. If you start running into long hours because you are trying to cover ground, you will pay for it further down the line. A crew can only work *so long*, and we said, no more than twelve hours a day. Only the producer works longer. In fact, the producer never sleeps! When I schedule, I look at locations first, making sure I shoot all the scenes around a certain location at the same time. This saves time getting in and out of a location. Try to bunch an actor's scenes together so you use them for the least possible time. It's not possible to make everything work, but minimizing waste will save money. It's like putting a massive jigsaw together when you don't have the cover of the box to tell you what the picture looks like. If you have a star who is costing you money, there is no doubt that they should become the priority. We also decided to shoot in February as this was a lean time for rental companies in the UK and we were able to get great deals.

Q - What was the worst day?

Gen - I can't think of a *'worst day'* on *White Angel*. I can think of several on *The Runner* but you see, *White Angel* profited from the disasters on the first film. We learned from our considerable mistakes. On *White Angel*, we knew the ropes, we knew how to shoot a movie for little or no money. In a way it was quite dull because, from a production point of view, we got it right. We did lose one location and had to make a bank out of absolutely nothing. There is a scene in the film where Carter goes to a bank where all the evidence against her is locked in a safety deposit box. So Carter gets through the reception and into the bank vault. We had planned to use a real bank which was agreed, but they pulled out at the last minute. Someone found a gutted bank that we could use. There was nothing in there, and it was like a warehouse, but it did have the vault door intact. We decided to paint deposit boxes on the wall and we all worked on it, painting away through the night and half an hour before shooting in the morning it was finished. The paint was still wet in the shot! To be honest, that was not a real disaster. Filmmaking breeds this kind of situation. If you can't handle that, you shouldn't be making films.

Q - Were there any problems shooting on location?

(above) The bank vault was nothing more than a metal door with cardboard security boxes painted grey. Little white stickers were added to give the impression of key holes.

(below) After producing The Runner, the production of White Angel ran smoothly and without hiccup.

Gen - Nothing above the run of the mill stuff like weird people hassling the cast and crew, or the weather. One thing to consider when looking for locations is the sound. Filmmaking is always biased toward the image, but we had real problems with one or two scenes because we shot near an airport. We also had real problems in an apartment where kids were running about upstairs - this really held us up.

Q - How did you find working with the actors?

Gen - Actors tend to flock together, as do the crew, and sometimes this can generate a *them and us* situation which can be unhealthy. There were a couple of incidents that proved problematic for the production team. For example the lighting for the scene might take longer than expected and the actor might have gone for a walk or something. We did lose all our actors on one occasion. We had told them that the set up was going to take a little time so they decided to go off together. We had a room for them but they weren't there. The whole crew had to search the town, and they were found having an dinner in the local restaurant. It was a bit of a heart stopper at the time. On *White Angel*, none of the actors really put pressure on us, they were all great. But on *The Runner*, we had terrible problems with the cast, clashes of interest, egos, impatience, frustration (from both them and us of course) - it was a volatile pot of angry energy.

Q - How did you go about casting the movie?

Chris - We never finished the screenplay to our satisfaction and were still rewriting the script on the set, but when it was in a position where we felt - this will work, and we had our $15k in the bank, we had to start casting. First, we put ads in *The Stage* and *PCR* (UK casting papers and newsletters). As usual, we received sackfuls of mail. The ad said *'Wanted. Sophisticated Psychopath'.* We got some very strange letters back! One was from a guy who had pasted his reply from pieces of newspaper and enclosed a photograph of himself, hooded in black, holding a carving knife. It read *'Give me the role or I will kill you!'* I looked quite hard for the sophisticated angle in this guy's approach but I couldn't quite see it. We also had photos of naked girls saying *'give me the role and I'll make your dreams come true!'* It's very strange. A few people are either very determined or very desperate. I even had one woman come to the house and offer to take a shower with me in exchange for the lead role. Deadly serious.

So, you have to be careful how you deal with actors and be as fair as possible. We broke the replies down into a short list of fifty, then to twenty five and initially interviewed them all. We found a church hall in West London, which cost ten dollars for the day, and was heated by a thermonuclear burner in the centre of the room. It had two settings. Off and meltdown. You couldn't hear yourself shout when it was on. So, we spent the day alternating between ice and fire. We ran through the actors and they were all slightly inexperienced professionals. We realized that no-one had what it took to fill the role so we started thinking about classic, British actors.

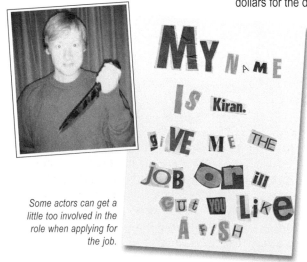

Some actors can get a little too involved in the role when applying for the job.

We knew that we needed someone with quality and ability. So, we went to the top. We approached top British agents. We liked the idea of Michael Caine but he wasn't available or interested, and another famous actor we approached seemed to warm to the idea. We said that we were young filmmakers trying to make British movies, we needed support. He liked the idea so we sent him the script. Two days later we received a phonecall and he absolutely destroyed us, *'the script is complete crap! What you are doing is immoral. You're destroying the British film industry by making this sort of crap!'* He just decimated us. We were shattered. This great British actor who I'm not going to name, poured cold water over our entire concept. Eventually I said, *'well, it's obvious that we're not going to be working together* - and he said - *why don't you make something beautiful and wonderful like* Baghdad Cafe?*'* and I said *'what's* Baghdad Cafe?*'* I'd no idea what he was talking about. I wanted to make *The Fog* or *Halloween* or *Return of the Living Dead Part IV.* He asked *'why are you making this kind of film?'* I replied, *'because I like it!'* We went around in circles.

Peter Firth liked the screenplay very much and had experience of low budget films - he accepted with little hesitation. Harriet Robinson was a little more unsure - she had no experience of low budget film making, but once she heard Peter was involved, it tipped her mental scales in our favour.

Q - Can an agent stop an actor from doing a low-budget film?

Chris - By virtue of not even telling an actor a film is being cast, an agent can stop an actor getting involved. However, the bottom line is that if the actor wishes to do a film, then they will do it regardless. You have an advantage as a no-budget filmmaker. Your screenplay should be different from typical scripts that are going around - more than likely it will be rough around the edges, maybe contain some clichés, but it will hopefully have a bit of energy about it and originality. At the end of the day, actors want to work, to stretch themselves artistically, even experiment. They like to do things that are different, that might win awards or get some attention, and low-budget productions are famous for this.

Q - What about approaching the top actors?

Chris - Always start at the top. Do not start at the bottom because you will undersell yourself. We tried Michael Caine and got a resounding NO, but at least we tried.

Q - And how did Peter Firth get involved?

Chris - His agent was helpful, although we never told anyone what the budget was. We always said that it was under a million. The fact that we had $15k in the bank was a closely guarded secret. I'd seen *Lifeforce*, possibly one of the worst movies ever made (although I loved it!), where Peter Firth runs through the streets of London and saves the world from a plague of space vampires! I was aware of his Oscar nomination for *Equus* and his work on *Tess*. We also knew of the Brit low-budget film *Letter to Brezhnev* that was a huge success here in the UK. We were interested. His agent offered us the usual $30k per week deal and I said *would it be possible for Peter to just read the screenplay?* He was sent the script and he called me - he liked it - he understood what low-budget meant, and after a discussion over the treatment of the violence in the film, he agreed that he would like to be involved. I filled the agent in on the fact that we didn't have any money. A certain chill entered the negotiations. She said, *I have to say that this is not what we are in to.* Then I got this phone call from Peter who said, *whatever my agent says, I do want to do this movie. You guys just work it out with my agent and come to an agreement. I just want to do it.* We paid him what we could afford and gave him a deferred payment and a percentage so he might get more once the movie was sold - his agent was fine (as with all the cast and crew, no extra payments were ever made as the film never broke even).

Don Henderson was originally thought of as the gangster, Alan Smith, from whom Carter gets the gun. The role of Inspector Taylor was available and one night I suggested to Gen that Don should be Inspector Taylor. Now, we paid Don more than we could really afford but his agent was being a real stick in the mud and we ran out of time. But Don was a great chap. He's the best. I never really had to direct Peter, he just hit his mark and delivered the goods. Occasionally he would look to me to see if he was going down the right alley, or I would ask him to emphasise something, but that's about it. There was one scene with Peter and Don. What a dream it was. One take. Perfect. It was that simple.

Q - So, it's a false economy to use method actors?

Chris - It can be. If time is short and there just isn't money to get it right, it's better to get a scene covered than half the script covered electrifyingly well - half a script doesn't make a feature film. Peter didn't need to immerse himself in the character to play Steckler - he didn't need to keep a knife in his inside pocket, or follow women home from work, just to see how it felt. It's great if you're Daniel Day-Lewis in a multi-million dollar movie. Time is a luxury we did not have. People who have lots of experience in front of the camera know what it takes to play the lead in a film, they know about pacing a character, knowing when to say - no, we don't need another take. I remember a scene with Don Henderson - I ummed after a shot and he said - *'no, that was fine'*. I'd never come across an actor who didn't want more screen time. Don knew that he couldn't give any more so why waste time and money doing another take.

Q - Stars often won't sign until the last minute?

Chris - We were shooting before Peter actually signed. Principal photography had started. Peter only became involved two days before we began his scenes. It was very tight. That is a problem but it is one of the burdens of having no money. You have to keep a reserve in mind in case your star can't or won't do it.

Q - Did you have to wait until the last minute?

Chris - If an actor says *'I want to do this film',* there are usually a couple of provisos. They might want the dialogue altered to suit them, or a say in the co-star. You have a choice then, to say yes or no. They will only sign at the last moment, just to make sure they don't get that call from Spielberg after they are signed to some low-budget thing. As you get close to shooting the chances become more remote of that call coming and *your* chances get better.

Q - Main cast professionals. Minor cast are friends?

Chris - Every crew member of *White Angel* appears in the film. Genevieve actually plays four different characters. A classic example - we were shooting a late night scene with an actress who was to play a prostitute, but she didn't turn up so Gen put on the wig etc and did the scene. I'm in it as a forensic expert. It's

When trying to attract a star cast on a low budget film, the screenplay is without doubt the most valuable asset a production company can offer an actor

unavoidable, but it makes the film very personal and saves you a whole heap of money. Why employ the services of a professional *'extra'* to stand around. When you've got $15k, you're not going to waste a single dollar when anyone can do it. Get friends and relatives. Get them to pay to be in it. Get them to invest money in the film and you'll give them a role. One guy paid a $2k to play one part in *White Angel* (unfortunately, we had to cut him out). But be aware that they might be crap, although this guy was pretty good, so audition them and see if they can act. Have a backup plan, don't rely on non professional actors to be able to deliver.

Q - Did you give him back his thousand dollars?

Chris - No.

Q - What about crew. How do you get the best people possible people?

Chris - The initial crew was myself (the director), and Genevieve (the producer). Jon Walker, the DP who shot *The Runner*, and he was also involved with the script for *White Angel* and we have a very good working relationship. For the rest of the crew we sent the feelers out - people who knew people who knew people. We had some experienced professionals come in. They said how much they wanted. Then, we'd say *'I'm sorry - Can you do it for this?'* Sometimes we got a yes, but mostly a no. We had very few industry names involved. What we did get was intense dedication from a crew of relatively inexperienced people. Everyone who was there, wanted to be there, and that got us through the rough stuff. Our experience in production pacing also saved the production from disaster.

On a film school project, the crew could work anywhere between three and seven days, and for 18 hours a day. That's fine for film school, but you can't work people like that for anywhere near as long as it takes to shoot a feature film. You can run a film crew into the ground in the first week but by the third week you will pay severely.

A classic example is the production designer on *White Angel*, Mark Sutherland. He'd never been near a movie in his life but he became famous for getting the job done. Sometimes he'd have stupid deadlines. The house where we shot White Angel had three bedrooms upstairs, and two small rooms downstairs. One of the upstairs bedrooms was the production office, another was a

(above) Not all performances require highly skilled thespian abilities...

(right) This isn't a desperate attempt to raise much needed funds, it's the multi talented crew helping out as the cast!

bedroom for the production team and the other was make-up and wardrobe. So, no bedroom scenes could be shot upstairs. Downstairs there was a living room and a back room. The backroom became the store room. So, apart from the hall and kitchen, we had one room in which to shoot - this room would have to change, when required, into the front room, backroom, all three bedrooms and anything else that was needed.

Day one - it was dressed as Steckler's bedroom. Overnight, Mark tore that down and built Carter's bedroom. Day two - we shot Carter's bedroom. It was torn down overnight and replaced with the living room including one huge hole in the wall. Virtually, the entire film was shot in that one room and we never waited for the set to be finished. Mark always got the job done on time and under budget. Everybody would pitch in and pick up a paintbrush. Once a film begins shooting, it's like a rolling ball - difficult to stop - It's just a matter of how quickly and how well it will be done.

Another example of Mark's flexibility came when we had finished the film and we had a test screening where the audience offered suggestions. The one thing that was clear is that the ending was wrong. In the original ending, Steckler shuffles in after being stabbed, shot, bashed etc, straps Carter into a chair and starts drilling into her head with a dentist drill. It was a great bit of *Friday 13th* style movie hokum, but everyone seemed to feel that it was the end of a different movie - it just didn't fit. So we decided to re-shoot the end. We returned to the house where we shot the original footage. Unfortunately, in the interim, drug dealers had taken over this house and wouldn't let us within a thousand yards of it! So, Mark Sutherland came up with the idea of a set. But where could we build it? In our garage of course. So, we built the hallway and part of the living room in the garage at the front of our house. We painted the walls, put wallpaper up, built false windows and re-shot the whole end section of the film. The actors were very good and never said anything, I guess they were used to our peculiar ways. I must admit that when I said to Peter *'let's go to the studio.'* I think he was expecting something different from our garage. I remember him walking in - he was very impressed and said this is fine. But he did say it was one of the strangest places he'd ever had to shoot. No-one ever knew and we got away with the cheat.

Q - Everyone seems to do a bit of everything?

Chris - People like to put filmmakers in boxes. This person is an editor, that person is a designer. Most filmmakers are just that. People who love making films.

Because the location where White Angel was shot appeared to have been taken over by drug dealers, the house had to be rebuilt in minute detail - in the garage! - (right) how the garage looked in the final film.

Everyone would like to direct but most don't expect to be doing that to start with. So, you get this crossover where everyone can do everyone else's job. One day the sound man was ill so Jon Walker took over and recorded sound as well as lighting the film. That's a tremendous asset. Whatever shit happens (and it always does) you can deal with it.

Q - Did you ever overcrew?

Chris - We just made sure there was enough crew to do the job. For instance, we had two make-up artists which was a conscious decision. The film is about two characters who were needed for shooting almost every day - with two make-up artists we were ready to shoot half an hour earlier every day. That was worth it.

Q - You say it was a small crew, but the credits do seem to be quite extensive?

Gen - Yes, if you have a low-budget picture it's a good idea to make up about fifty fictitious names in your titles, especially if you only have 15 or maybe 20 people working on the team - it makes your movie look more expensive. A few extra credits can also stretch the length of your film if it is a little on the short side. Chris edited the film and I edited the sound. We chose to use pseudonyms to make it look as if we could afford an editor and sound editor.

The crew for White Angel *looks large when everyone is standing together, but every department was honed down to the absolute minimum required to get the job done quickly and efficiently.*

Q - Was the main reason for editing the film yourselves financial?

Gen - Yes, it was mainly because we couldn't afford to get anyone to cut it for us, so we thought why not do it ourselves. Plus we wanted to learn the process of editing.

Q - What were the main difficulties in editing?

Chris - Objectivity. Staying objective on something that firstly, you wrote, then directed, saw the rushes, sunk up, rough cut, fine cut - It's like the third part of a triathlon. Just being objective about material, *'should that scene have gone or should it have stayed?'* - and keeping the energy up while being wracked by paranoia. Technically, we didn't know what we were doing, we'd never cut anything before, so we just had to start on day one, with *oops how do we edit film?* and learn by our errors.

Q - Did you find there was trouble keeping the story-line running through it?

Gen - No, it was obvious when things either weren't working or when the pace was slow. We actually didn't shoot too much, our cutting ratio was 4 or 5 to 1 so we didn't have too much material with which to go crazy.

Q - Did you storyboard?

Gen - No. At the time we thought it to be a waste of resources for a low-budget picture, although our next picture, *Urban Ghost Story,* utilized storyboards. *White Angel* was also restricted by the locations and many times, the rough shooting script that Chris had worked out had to be scrapped because it just couldn't be done in the location we found, or because we just ran out of time and money and ended up shooting the scene in a single wide shot just to cover the action and plot.

Q - How did you decide the final cut for White Angel?

Chris - We had about 95 million different final cuts - this is going back to being objective, because you're so damn close to the thing. We were really happy with our first final cut and had begun track laying and getting ready for the dub when our cameraman, Jon Walker, came round and took a look at it. We were saying *'Isn't it brilliant...!'* but he reckoned we could lose some stuff. We went through the film slowly and Jon's point of view made us sit up and think about it differently. We ended up cutting about 12 minutes out of what we thought was our final cut - we neg cut, printed it at a running time of 100 minutes and we went to the Montreal Film Festival and watched it with a full audience - they enjoyed it but it was quite obvious more needed to come out.

When we returned to the UK, we thought let's have another fine cut - we went back and cut another 6 minutes out, called that the final movie - re-premiered it at the London Film Festival and everything was going swimmingly. Then only 5 to 6 months later, we decided that we had to do yet another re-cut for the international market, to make the film more sexy and violent. We cut out 10 minutes, put some other stuff back in - all this is about 3 years after the film was shot in the first place! We needed more *'oomph'* so we re-shot stuff, got Harriet back, with a completely different hair cut and reconstructed the film yet again. All the new stuff was shot on Hi8 video and helped give it a much more seedy and voyeuristic look - we are kind of pleased with it now.

Gen - We also had an audience test with our first rough cut. We arranged a screening at some offices where the staff agreed to stop behind to watch the film - they were all complete strangers and we wanted to see what effect it had. They came back with - *'well we thought it was great in this part, but maybe too slow in the middle'*, so we decided we could chop out more in the middle. That was also the dreaded point when we discovered that the ending of the film was wrong and we had to go back and reshoot that.

Q - The music is a strong part of White Angel. How did you decide on a theme?

Gen - There were certain composers whose music we liked a lot, for instance Bernard Hermann who did some of Hitchcocks' most famous movies, and we felt that *White Angel* needed a Bernard Herman type score, with mystery, intrigue, suspense and a big orchestra feel. When we initially started out, we were going to have computer synthesised sounding music - then we found Harry Gregson-Williams who could pull off a brilliant *'orchestral sounding'* theme and we jumped on him. He could take a few musicians and turn them into what sounded like the London Symphony Orchestra.

Chris - At various stages during the editing, we cut a lot of music from other films into *White Angel* in order to make it feel more like a finished movie. We used a lot of *Basic Instinct* - that had the right tone and pace. When it came to the music being composed by Harry, we said, listen to this, this is kind of what we want - and then he took all of what that music was *'saying'* and regenerated it in his own original way and worked in his own theme and composition. At the end of the day the music doesn't sound anything like what we originally wanted, it sounds better as it is a completely original interpretation of the film. Dubbing on other music just helped everyone focus on what we were aiming at. We also

considered using out of copyright music because it's free. You don't pay copyright on the musical notes, only on the performance and recording. There were loads of music libraries and we could have used anything, from Brahms to Beethoven with a full orchestra for about $350 per thirty seconds. That's world-wide rights. The problem was finding the right music to fit the scenes. If you're doing *Amadeus Part 2*, then you're fine, but not a serial killer thriller.

Harry Gregson-Williams wrote the score for White Angel. *He then went on to write the scores for* Antz, Armageddon *and* Enemy of The State!

Q - Sound mixing is where it all comes together, how did that go?

Chris - Most of the sound in *White Angel,* apart from the dialogue, has been recreated in the studio, and by the studio, I mean our front room, not a $3k an day studio. Most low-budget films suffer from poor sound and we were determined that *White Angel* was at least going to sound good.

Q - How does the sound mixing process work?

The final mix can be a harrowing event and there is no space for perfection. Make all creative decisions in advance as a five minute discussion about a bird sound effect could cost you $60!

Chris - We ran through the whole movie and we added an effect for every single little thing that happened, be it somebody putting a cup down, somebody scratching their face, whatever it was, we add an effect - all those sound effects were then track laid into place. We ended up with I guess about 12 - 15 tracks of sound - 2 music tracks, 2 dialogue tracks, 3 or 4 effects tracks which would be stereo as would be the music, 2 Foley tracks, 2 or 3 atmosphere tracks - which would be background sound, and then on occasion 1 or 2 extra tracks for when we had problems or when there was a heavy sequence. All those tracks are then premixed, we mixed the 2 dialogues into one, the 2 music into one, the effects into 1, the atmos into 1 - we end up with 4 or 5 different pre-mixed tracks being atmos, music, dialogue, effects whatever, and those were finally mixed into one Dolby mix master, which is when it sounds great.

Q - How did you prepare for the final mix?

Chris - We had a hell of a time as we weren't ready for it. We had a new computer system on which the sound was laid and three days before the mix we found out that it was all out of sync! We had to start from scratch and re sync every effect. We worked solidly for three days and nights, I had never done that before and I hope never to do so again. We were still cutting hours before the mix but we got there. Fortunately we had been good about track laying and everything was pretty much covered so there weren't any panicked cover up jobs.

Q - What was it like in the theater?

Chris - Great, it's where everything comes together. It's dark, it's loud and there are lots of plush sofas and free coffee. The only down side is that it's so expensive and there is always this urgency to get to the end of the picture. There is absolutely NO room for perfection in a low-budget mix. We paid about $300 per hour and mixed for two days, the second day we went late into the night. Big overtime, so I guess we needed three days. I would recommend a minimum of three days and five is better, that would give you time to cover the M&E mix as well. If you're not prepared, you're going to have a terrible time, so have everything track laid, know your movie inside out, and just go for it.

We had some pretty bad camera noise which the mixer managed to filter out - not all of it though, so we added a loud mechanical printing press sound over the top. Don't believe that you can get rid of 100% of a noise, unless you're prepared to cut it out completely (dialogue and all). There are amazing things possible at the dub but it all takes time, if you have a 2 hour movie, it takes you 2 hours just to go through it, and you have to go through it at least twice, once for pre-mixes and then your final mix, so you've lost 4 hours just in screen time, never mind changing tapes. All this and there's still only 8 hours in the working day.

Q - What is the M&E mix?

Gen - The M&E is the Music and Effects Mix. When you're selling overseas, the buyer will want a copy of the soundtrack without the dialogue so that they can dub over in their own language. To do the M&E mix is quite easy, all the mixer has to do is to pull the dialogue tracks out - if you've properly track-laid it and there's good foley, there shouldn't be any problems. The problems with the M&E mix come when you're deciding on what format to mix. Full M&E in stereo or split Music and Effects? We did both in the end but the one we use most, if not all the time is the traditional split Music and Effects, music on track one, everything else on track two.

We also ran headlong into a problem at the telecine. While the video format we chose (DigiBeta) could take four tracks of sound, (the full stereo mix on tracks 1 & 2, the M&E mix on tracks 3 & 4), we couldn't lay it all down at the same time - we had two separate mixes, two tapes. We ended up having to telecine it once and then re-run the whole lot for the M&E mix - that added a huge amount to our telecine budget straight away, and like the dub, it's damn expensive to start with.

Probably the easiest way to deal with this now is to separate everything. Get the telecine down onto DigiBeta and just concentrate on getting the picture right. Then go to a sound facility, or even the sound department at the telecine house, and get them to transfer your full stereo mix to tracks 1&2 of the DigiBeta, then the M&E to tracks 3&4 of the DigiBeta. You'll also need to ask them to pass both mixes through a compressor limiter as the mix you have may well be too dynamic for TV and video. Just make sure they keep the audio levels legal. If you have mixed in Dolby Digital that complicates things even more as you will be dealing with Magneto Optical disks.

Q - By the time you do the dub do you have a sales agent?

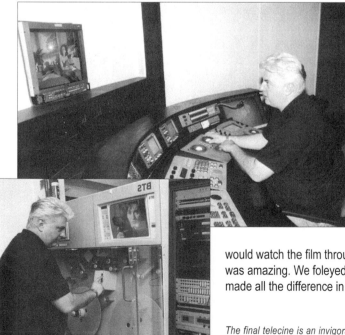

Gen - We didn't, but we did speak to a sales agent to see what they would want. By that time you should have sales agents interested enough for them to explain to you what they would require.

Q - What happened about foley?

Gen - We had an amazing woman called Diane Greaves do the foley - the foley is where someone adds all the sounds that an actor makes just moving around. She would add the leather creak in a jacket, the footsteps on gravel, the sitting on sofas. Diane would make a sound for pretty much everything that happened on screen. She would watch the film through and then do all the foley in one pass! She truly was amazing. We foleyed the whole picture in one very long day and it made all the difference in both the full dub and especially the M&E mix.

The final telecine is an invigorating yet terrifying experience. It is the very last stage of production and once traversed, the film is technically completed. However, it is hellishly expensive and fraught with potential technical errors.

Q - What was the first print like?

Chris - The first 35mm print we saw wasn't great - the sound disappeared half way through, it was really dirty and it was a bit of a nightmare as some cast members were present. At the very last stage there was an accident in the lab and our neg was ripped. We didn't have any insurance so had to go back and reshoot! Thank goodness there were no actors in any of the shots that were damaged or that could have turned into a nightmare.

Q - Did you have any problems with the telecine?

Gen - Yes, firstly we produced a widescreen telecine which no distributor could use, so we had to do another. We mastered to D1 and the film was supposed to fit, but the tape ended fifteen seconds before the final end credit, so we had to recompile on another D1 tape! We would master to DigiBeta now. The sound was not compressed in advance so we had to do another sound dub and lay the M&E down at the same time. The first print we got out of the lab was too dark so we had a battle with the lab to make up a new S16mm print with the printer lights increased to give a brighter image. So yes, we had some problems, it all got fixed eventually but it cost an arm and a leg in both time and money. This seems to be very common. Every new filmmakers has some horror story about the labs.

Q - What was the first thing you did once you completed the film?

Gen - Slept for a week.

Chris - Yeah but when we got our own VHS of the film we literally drove home at 100mph ran into the living room, put it on the telly and watched it. We'd spent the past two years seeing this film in bits (as it was cut on film and not an Avid) and we didn't know what it looked like all strung together with full sound

Q - What was it like?

Gen - Quick, it seemed to fly through. It was brilliant.

Q - How did you approach selling the film once it was completed?

Chris - We didn't have a sales agent or a UK distributor on board. Miramax had made a few phone calls to ask what this strange film called *White Angel* was about, and a few of the big players like Paramount and 20th Century Fox faxed us at three in the morning (UK time), which was quite fun, but essentially we had to start from scratch. We set up meetings with five sales agents and sat them down to watch *White Angel* - the idea was that we would then field the offers from those meetings.

Gen - We couldn't afford screenings at a theater where everyone would sit down and watch together, so we decided it would be better to give everyone

ORION PICTURES CORPORATION

VIA FAX: #011-44-

September 13,

Genevieve Jol
Living Spirit
The Old Pict
Througham,
Stroud, Glo
England

Dear Ms.

SENT BY: JOHN FERRARO : 6- 7-93 : 2:17PM : PARAMOUNT PICTURES- 0285 82 843 :# 1/ 1

Paramount Pictures

JOHN E. FERRARO
Vice President
Acquisitions

MOTION PICTURE GROUP

June 7, 1993

Ms. Genevieve Jolliffe
Living Spirit Pictures
FAX: (44-285) 821-843

Dear Ms. Jolliffe:

I recently read about your film WHITE ANGEL and would like to discuss it with you at your earliest convenience.

Would you have a print of the film available for me to screen here at Paramount in Los Angeles?

I look forward to hearing from you soon.

Kind regards,

JF/dm

A Paramount Communications Company

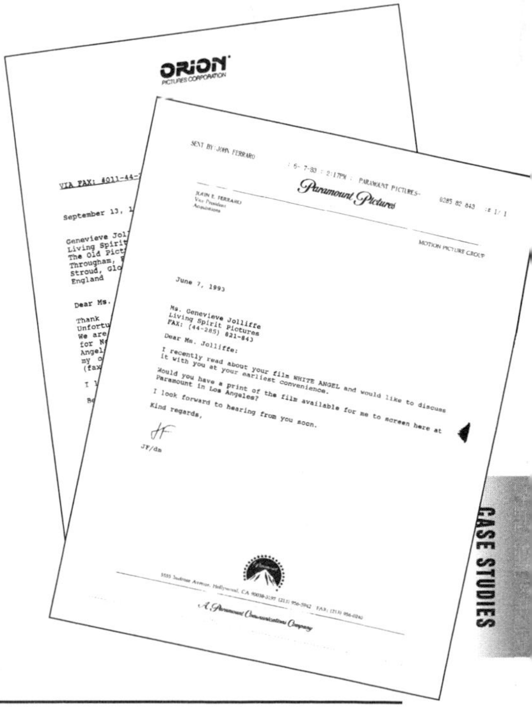

(right) Midnight faxes from Hollywood did prove to be a tremendous giggle and ego boost, but ultimately bore no sales. However, it was good to establish contacts and worth noting that even small obscure British productions do get noticed by the major players.

CASE STUDIES

The Haymarket in central London on the wet Friday morning of the theatrical release for White Angel. *How cool is that!*

their own individual screening in a small studio - we set up a really good sound system and monitor, dimmed the lights and let the film do the job. We sat outside, between the door and the elevator so there was no chance of them making a swift exit.

Chris - The reactions we got were mixed. First of all, one company didn't turn up and we had to drop a tape off with them. Another watched it and left 5 minutes before the end saying it was too long and didn't have enough scope for them. Another said they would get back to us (they didn't). The Feature Film Company saw it and liked it but ummed and aahed. Finally, Miramax saw it and visibly liked it a lot - obviously Miramax is THE biggest distributor and sales agent of low-budget independent features in the world, and the fact they were interested was very exciting.

Gen - Their UK acquisitions rep thoroughly enjoyed it. She told us that she believed *White Angel* could be a hit at the upcoming Cannes Film Festival - Peter could win awards and we would win Best Film. She was sure Miramax could do a great deal with it. We talked about advances etc.

Chris - We were very specific about what we wanted - a big cash advance to cover the budget and to pay the cast and crew, and that was all we wanted. We said we needed an advance of $600k against all rights, which was double what we needed, and that we wanted an answer quickly. She said, *'No problem, I think we can probably do that and I can give you an answer in 48 hours!'*

Gen - She told us that she was flying to New York for the weekend to see Bob and Harvey, and that she would like to take a copy of the film, and get back to us on Monday. She did get back to us, telling us that they had seen it but they hadn't got an exact answer yet, *'but we're all really positive about it'.* However, as we ran up to Cannes the channels of communication dried up, even after this amazing amount of interest and promises. When we tried to contact her, our calls would either be directed somewhere or she was *'out of the office'.* This was a little weird after she had been so positive. Then we got a letter in the post, saying *'thanks very much, but we're not interested...'* And it was pp'd by somebody else! Remember, this was after the intimation that we were going to get a very large cash advance with world-wide distribution, and we would pretty much win the Palm D'Or!

Chris - The basic message is to take everything you hear with a pinch of salt, keep your options open, hassle for the money, and don't let the situation rest, pursue it. If you can't speak to the person, and they say they are still thinking about it, then you are in an awkward situation - they may still be thinking about it, or they may be giving you the run-around. However, if they really are interested, they will come up with an offer within 7 days, and anything over 7 days, then I think you have to say, well thank you for the interest but really we want to show it to somebody else now.

Q - Six weeks later you went to Cannes - did you take a print with you?

(right) Glossy sales brochures were out of the question so a full color A3 sheet was pasted up with photos and a synopsis of the film - the torn paper effect was in keeping with the serial killer theme. The results were color laser copied and laminated. They turned out to be both cheap and effective. Go crazy with your color printer. But remember, it's GOT TO LOOK GREAT!

Chris - No, we didn't have a print then as we had shot on S16mm and making the 35mm blow up was going to be costly. We didn't want to incur any extra costs yet. We took 40 tapes of the film (telecinied from the S16mm answer print) and 40 tapes of the trailer that we had cut the night before. We also put together some sales literature that was literally cut and pasted together and printed on a colour laser photocopier before being laminated - it cost us about $150 to do 50 of these brochures, but they looked really good. When we got to Cannes, people were impressed and thought we had spent thousands on the marketing!

Q - How did you gain entrance to the festival?

Gen - The easiest way at that time to gain access to the market was to turn up with a business card and two passport photos, calling yourself a producer. We waited in a hot sweaty line at festival accreditation to get our pass that got us into everywhere we needed to go. It now costs about $50 to enter if you have not applied in advance – so do it in advance!

Q - If you had to sum up Cannes in one sentence what would it be?

Gen - Hot, blisters, hard work, expensive, bullshit, pornography, free drinks, little pieces of strange food on plates which you eat lots of because you can't afford the to eat properly.

Q - Did anyone show an active interest in the film?

Chris - Yes, we rented an apartment outside Cannes and drove in every day, which worked out quite well as it was quite cheap to do that. We targeted every single world sales agent, visited all the hotels and every stand and told them that we had made this feature film called *White Angel* which was *terribly good*, and would they want to see the trailer, and would they like to keep a copy, and would they like a copy of the sales literature, here you are and thank you very much, gave them a business card and took one of theirs.

Gen - We felt we had to see who was who, and what kind of films they did, so that we would know who to target. It was difficult to see the top people like Fox, Paramount or Universal etc., but everybody else who would have been impossible to see if you walked into their offices in LA, would be willing to see you in Cannes, especially if you have a film.

CASE STUDIES

Q - So Cannes is a great place if you have a film to sell?

Chris - Cannes is an experience which brings the film sales business into sharp focus.

Gen - It is also about finding out which companies do what, learning the marketplace, meeting people either in their sales suites or at parties.

Q - What happened when they saw your trailer?

Gen - We would walk in to their suites, chat to them about the film, show them the trailer and get some feedback - yes, no or maybe. Those who were interested asked to know if we were going to have a screening back in LA after Cannes. No company made an offer there and then.

Chris - The problem is that sales agents are not at the market to acquire product but to sell their product, so it's one of the worst places to go to get a sales agent. Cannes is about the only place a filmmaker can go, and know that anyone who is anyone in the film industry is within one mile from where they are standing. That in itself can make getting a meeting doubly difficult, and you have to be very persistent - most people are booked up before they even leave for the airport!

Gen - Out of the 100 people we saw, 80 of them were not the type of people who would pick up *White Angel* - they would go for schlock horror, movie rip offs, ninjas, family drama, porno - it can be pretty sleazy, but hey *'it's all product!'* Films of quality seem to be sold independently, behind closed doors or not at the market at all.

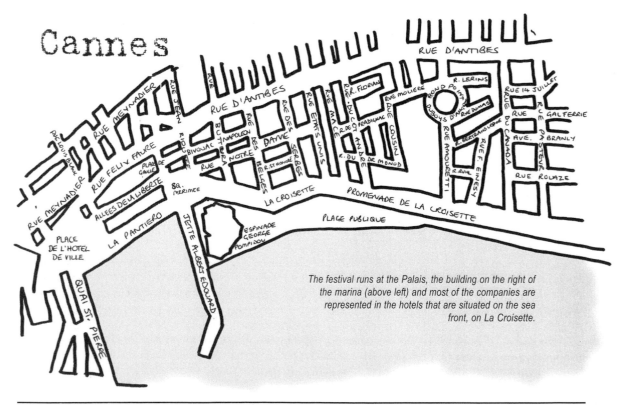

The festival runs at the Palais, the building on the right of the marina (above left) and most of the companies are represented in the hotels that are situated on the sea front, on La Croisette.

(right) The British Pavilion at the Cannes Film Market - a hotbed of moaning filmmakers basking like beached lobsters in the sun! The American Pavillion is a great place to get a placement if you want to do Cannes for free, though you will need to work long hours.

(below right) The hotel corridors at Cannes are packed sales booths all adorned with hard sell posters for a dizzying array of low brow B movies.

The only company who showed a real interest was Beyond Films. Being an Australian company they felt more in tune with our way of thinking, and because we knew that they had picked up another low budget UK film, we felt there was more of a connection. At the time, their big success had been *Strictly Ballroom*. A week after Cannes we set up a screening for them in London - we felt everything was riding on this so we hired a screening room in Soho and sat their rep down to watch it in a theater. He liked it. Beyond made an initial offer of something like $12k and then upped it to $35k and finally up to $100k, which was structured over a period of three years. The delivery requirements were quite horrendous and they wanted the film for a term of fifteen years.

We were concerned because of our experience on *The Runner* and the idea of handing the film over to Beyond for fifteen years with a staggered (over years) advance that wouldn't cover our minimal budget didn't sit too well. We had immediate debts that needed to be met so we offered them a $450k buy out for all rights, but they didn't go for it.

Q - In retrospect, would it have been a good idea to take the deal?

Chris - Now that we know what we know, and don't forget they were leaving the UK to us, it would have been a good idea - just to get rid of the film. The thing to remember is that we were acting in the best interests of the investors and the company, we felt at the time that we couldn't accept what we considered a low offer when the film had only just been completed. The other thing is that we did believe in the film, we were confident we had a very high quality low-budget film. It is a hard decision to make and I guess one gets more experienced - what do you do if you believe your product is worth much more than your initial offers? How long can you wait before you have to take one? There are no hard and fast answers, only twenty twenty hindsight. I don't think you can ever get it totally right, but you can let go and move on to your next film.

Q - When you were faced with delivery requirements, was there anything that you didn't know about?

Chris - We knew about basic delivery requirements because we had done *The Runner*, so we knew about the immediate things like the Music and Effects mix or color slides and that kind of thing. What we weren't prepared for from Beyond was the 25 page fax of the most unbelievable requirements, even down to things like alternative out takes on original master negative. Half of these we just didn't have and couldn't get - I'm sure they thought it was necessary but for a low-budget picture, some of the requirements were totally out of the question. Most companies had this kind of list, some differing slightly - but when it comes down to it, if they wanted the film, they would compromise as long as the main elements are in place, and that's no mean feat!

Gen - The one thing that we didn't know about at the time which came as a big shock was the Errors and Omissions Policy (E&O) - an insurance policy which insures the producer and distributor against all sorts of weird legal actions, such as a person saying that the film is based on their brother - the only thing was that this would cost around $10k!

Q - So have a good idea of what you need to deliver and say there it is, take it or leave it?

Chris - If you can't afford to make full delivery, then yes, but you do have to be sure of what the sales agent really does need to sell the film. There are a lot of things that don't actually cost a lot that are on the delivery list, like having the proper contracts with every one involved, waiver forms, release forms, chain of title, legal documents proving the country of origin. All of these are cheap to get together, but they do take time. A delivery list will usually say 75 high quality B&W photographs and 75 high quality color photographs. With the best will in the world you're not going to have that many good quality pictures on a low-budget film, it's just not going to happen.

Q - Apart from Beyond, was there any other interest?

Gen - At Cannes we went to an attorney's party and started chatting to two brothers, Simon and Andrew Johnson who had made a film called *Tale Of A Vampire.* They told us how they had sold the film themselves to a US company, turned a healthy profit and managed to hold onto the UK rights. We felt they were on our wavelength. It appeared they had gone through the same process we were going through and had frustratedly decided to do it all themselves, and they had come out on top. They were very interested in teaming up with us, because we all shared the same goals.

Chris - At the point of us turning down Beyond, Simon and Andrew (of Pilgrim Ent.) told us that they could guarantee deals with America and Japan through their contacts. They only wanted a three month window and ten percent so we decided to let them have a crack. After all they had been successful with their film. Sure enough, within months we did have several deals on the table including a deal memo from Trimark who wanted the US rights plus Canada for US$120k advance plus extras which would top it up to roughly $250k.

Q - How did the American deal come about?

Chris - Michael Cole from Trimark acquisitions had seen the film at the Montreal Film Festival in September where we had four totally packed screenings. He sat in on our last screening with an amazing audience, and negotiations began. Because of their prior relationship with Trimark, we allowed Pilgrim to take over negotiations and they came up with the deal memo. Because of the Montreal screenings we started to get a lot of offers, Germany came in as we stepped off the plane from our return. We had to decide what to do, whether to extend our agreement with Pilgrim as sales agents or to carry on the negotiations ourselves. We decided to extend the agreement and to leave all the negotiating to Pilgrim. The German deal happened and we actually got some money.

Q - How much was Germany?

Gen - Roughly $85k which was paid in three lump sums. Pilgrim took a slice off the top, about half was used to pay off debts and running costs, and the remainder was used to finance our UK theatrical release. Korea also came in at this point with an offer of $35k which we took. So at that point, we had nearly $350k signed, sealed but not delivered.

Chris - Firstly it would take weeks and weeks to negotiate a deal. The one thing that was really infuriating was that somebody would make an offer, and then you wouldn't be able to contact them until they came back from their three week holiday or whatever - time just goes by. And because you can't sit across a table from these people, you had to call and get through their secretaries who weren't speaking the same language - certainly, in Korea, that became a nightmare. Whatever we did, we just couldn't get an answer.

Q - Were you ready to deliver once a deal was signed?

Chris - Aside from making up the clone master tape, and patching up a few problems with the M&E, yes. The problem we had with the US is that Pilgrim negotiated what they called minimum delivery i.e all you need to sell and exploit the film. Trimark agreed and signed in a deal memo, and then changed the goal posts in the long form agreement. They asked for additional items that we didn't have, so we then had to go back to them saying we don't have these, and we've already agreed that you don't need these. Because we only had a one page deal memo that was not specific, they simply stood firm and stated that the detailed delivery list must be completed if they are going to take delivery. One major problem was that in the delivery list they mentioned the master 35mm negative - of course, we had shot on S16mm. While this obviously made no difference to Trimark in terms of quality, they could use it to stall the deal.

Q - Did Trimark have a copy of the film?

Gen - They had a copy for about five months - it's a tricky situation because they said that everyone in the company needed to see it for them to finalize. They could have used that time to show the film to their prospective buyers and field their responses - basically get a commercial assessment of that product. Ultimately we couldn't agree on the delivery items and they refused to take the film.

Q - What happened with your Korean deal?

Chris - After paying the $10k deposit, the company who acquired the rights just disappeared off the face of the earth for six months. After the American Film Market they got back to us and explained that the film had been banned as it had *'immoral social values'* - they faxed through the certificate of *'banning'* (which for all we know could have been an insurance form) and asked for their deposit back. We told them that we had spent it and it was their problem if the film had been banned. Now, not only had we gone stale on the US deal but we had also lost the very considerable balance of the Korean deal.

Q - If you made another film, what could you do differently, how would you overcome this problem?

Chris - You can't. The only thing you can do is make a film that will make the buyers go mad i.e. make a good film, give it to the sales agents and let them go for it. Hopefully you can trust the sales agent, but at the end of the day you can never really be sure - if a sales agent screws up, there's very little you can do as you have assigned the rights to them. I've never heard of any filmmaker being really happy with their sales agent on their first film.

Is this the Korean equivalent of the BBFC's certificate banning White Angel *from public viewing, or is it an insurance form, or even the back of a Korean cornflakes box? We sure didn't know.*

White Angel *premiered at the Montreal Film Festival where it was very well received. The festival paid for the shipping of the print, one flight and accommodation for four in a five star hotel.*

Gen - I suppose try and get a reputable sales agent and build up a relationship to make them want your next film.

Q - So you make a loss on your first film in order to make your second film and get it right then?

Gen - I think our problem was that because we didn't get any money back from *The Runner*, we just didn't trust any other sales agent with *White Angel* - that was the main reason that we went with Pilgrim. In retrospect, it was a mistake.

Chris - The basic problem is that selling a low budget indie film is very difficult. When you're making deals to territories for a few thousand dollars, those few thousand dollars are instantly eaten up on expenses. What could end up happening is that the basic sales merely cover the cost of attending markets in the first place - it's a vicious circle. There really is very little you can do except make as good a film as possible and maybe speak to an agent before setting out - find out what they think they will be able to do with the project before it is committed to film.

Q - How do you get a film into a festival?

Chris - First of all you need to find out which are the best festivals, and where they are, when they are and apply at least 3 months in advance.

Gen - For Cannes, it is hard to get into the festival but you can screen the movie by hiring a theater when you get there - many low-budget films do this to generate a buzz about the movie. For a festival like Sundance you have to make sure that they have seen the film by the end of July and obviously the earlier the better. So really you're looking at nine months. The film only ever has one world premiere so it's important to use that on the best festival you can get - pass it around and field the offers - a good sales agent will advise you which are the best festivals to go for. In some respects we blew the premiere of *White Angel* at the Montreal Film Festival. If we knew more about it, we would have premiered at the Toronto Festival (which followed on from Montreal) as it has a reputation for being a buyers festival whereas Montreal is a bit more arty.

Q - Do they pay for you to attend the Festival, how does it operate?

Chris - Send a VHS tape with the application form to the festival co-ordinator, they will then come back to you with *'no we don't want it thank you very much'*, or *'yes, we would like to invite you to attend the Festival'.* They will then invite the film and probably one member of the filmmaking body which is usually the director, and may possibly invite an actor or the producer as well. Normally the Festival will cover the hotel bills of anybody who can get to the screenings (who is directly related to the film). If it's an international festival, your flights can be paid for by the Festival and for festivals in the US, it depends on the festival and how profile your film is (they may even pay for all shipping of the prints). Essentially the filmmaker should try not to spend a single penny to attend a festival but that isn't

White Angel attended several festivals and picked up several awards. Each time Living Spirit would use the award for publicity, even if neither Chris or Gen attended the festival. (right) A picture of Gen taken in her back garden as she accepts a best 'production' award. The picture made it to several magazines.

Fantastic Burgos 1994
WHITE ANGEL
Premio Feliciano Vitores
Mejor Opera Prima

always the case. There are SO many films being made now that it is getting tougher and entry fees are going to get more common and much higher.

Gen - Watch out for small print - sometimes a festival will say that the producer must take care of the return shipment of the print, which can prove to be expensive.

Chris - We got inundated with requests to attend festivals and it became impractical to attend them all. At a festival in Puerto Rico we met a top sales agent who charges $300 on top of ALL expenses. If a festival comes to us now and we don't want to go, they can have the film for $300 plus all expenses. And the money comes directly to the production, not the sales agent.

Gen - I wouldn't recommend adding a fee if it's a festival you want to attend, particularly if they've agreed to pay for your flight, accommodation and a weeks stay in their country. But if they are asking to screen your film, and they're not going to accommodate you, or you don't really feel as though their festival is going to do much for the film - it's a small festival in the middle of nowhere - then, if the festival wants your film, they will have to pay for it.

Q - Did you find Film Festivals to be useful in the process of selling films?

Gen - Yes, it's a FREE showcase for your product and it can create a profile for your film. If you enter a film and win Best Film or Best Actor, it creates a bit of a buzz about the movie, you get publicity and it becomes an 'award winning film'.

Q - Which Film Festivals did White Angel attended and has it won any awards?

Gen - *White Angel* attended 13 film festivals around the world - Montreal, London, Ankara, Sao Paulo, Puerto Rico, two in Rome, Mannaheim, Emden, Valenciennes, Burgos... and we won two awards - Best First Film at Burgos Fantastic Film and Best Actor for Peter, at Valenciennes. I remember I got a phone call about a terrific film Festival that I should attend, give some lecture, go on TV and generally be a high profile British filmmaker. I said fine, where is it - *'Oh, it's the Gaza Strip Film Festival.'* There was a very long pause. Eventually I was persuaded to go. I was even going to be sneaked across borders with guards being bribed! The whole trip got called off a few days before because some tourists were murdered and the Gaza Strip was closed down. That was pretty weird.

Q - Do the festivals expect you to promote the film?

Chris - Yes, usually local press and radio, sometimes TV. The worst TV interview I had to do was in Turkey where I had been lined up for an interview at the local station (this is during the film festival AND their heated leadership elections). When I got there I was more than a little concerned as it was surrounded by razor wire and I had to pass through metal detectors and sniffer dogs to get in - I realised they were looking for bombs and weapons! Suddenly, it dawned on me, I was going on state TV - exactly the kind that was hated by the extremist terrorists of that country. I was then informed that

UK 1993
Scr: Chris Jones, Genevieve Jolliffe
Leading players: Peter Firth, Harriet Robinson, Don
Henderson, Anne Catherine Arton
R.t: 92 mins
UK Dist: Living Spirit Pictures

15 MON 16.00 & 21.00 ODEON WEST END 1
White Angel
Dir: Chris Jones

White Angel heralds the arrival of two young, talented filmmakers: producer Genevieve Jolliffe and director Chris Jones. More a film about serial killing than about a serial killer, *White Angel* offers a novel and very British view, whilst dealing with the complex (subtle?) differences between manslaughter and murder. Leslie Steckler (Peter Firth) is a soft-spoken dentist who rents a room in Ellen Carter's (Harriet Robinson) house. She is a successful writer on criminal psychology who is being hounded by the police in connection with her husband's

disappearance. Meanwhile, London is in the grips of a serial killer, 'the White Angel', and the dentist and the writer become entangled in a dangerous game of blackmail. The plot is full of surprises, twists and turns (all best left untold) that keep you on the edge of your seat, relying on powerful psychological devices and avoiding unnecessary gore. In many ways it's a first in its chilling (fictional) portrait of a very British way of serial killing. Mesmerizingly good, and a triumph of British independent production. *Rosa Bosch*

my interview was going to be live, and it was out to 47 million homes at prime time 7pm! The interview was nerve racking as it descended from chit chat about movies to hard hitting political rhetoric - I kept saying, *'I'm sorry but I don't know anything about the political situation in your country'* - which was then translated into a three minute speech! The last thing I wanted to be was a Westerner telling the natives what to do in their own seemingly fractured, fundamentalist religious country. After it was over, both Gen and myself were thanked, passed back out, through the metal detectors, past the sniffer dogs and razor wire before being dumped on a dark and cold Turkish roadside.

Gen - The movie *Midnight Express* comes to mind.

Q - How did the London Film Festival come about?

Gen - The London Film Festival is one of the major UK festivals and White Angel was selected to play as the centerpiece film. It was screened in Leicester Square and it was great.

Q - Was this good for the film?

Chris - Yes. At the time it seemed to crystallize what we thought - firstly, we've got a great film, and secondly, it was very commercial. This small film was suddenly put right up there, next to *Remains of the Day* in Leicester Square. We got a lot of press and a very high profile. Suddenly we felt that it was all going to happen right here and right now. We felt very confident that the film was going to be a hit.

Gen - And remember, at this time we were negotiating with America, Korea, and Germany - signed deals were on the table, it's just the money still hadn't come through.

Q - What about the UK theatrical release?

Gen - The theater manager of the Odeon Cinema at Leicester Square told us that he liked White Angel - *'it had an amazing effect on the audience'* - and that he would like the film to be screened at his theater. He told us that if Rank Film Distributors picked it up then he would get it - he had a few colleagues at Rank

(top) Great reviews at the London Film Festival, helping create a false sense of security.

that he would put us in touch with and put a good word in for the picture. We decided to get in contact with Rank Film Distribution who requested a private screening there at their offices. They laid on sandwiches and wine, all the razzma-tazz, and had four or five of their people viewing the film. They told us they loved it, thought it could work very well and they wanted it.

Chris - They made an offer of something like $35k advance against a UK theatrical plus half of the UK video. After several discussions and haggling we got that up to $90k. In reality we believed that if we took that deal we would never see more than the $90k offered, and I still believe that, although it was still a very good deal. Rank guaranteed to do a P&A spend of around $100k, which again sounds a lot, but it's not huge. It would have ended up going out in five theaters with a lot of advertising. We did the math and felt we could make more if we did the release ourselves, so we turned down the deal, which I think was a shock for them. In hindsight we should have taken the deal, we still wouldn't have broken even but we would have been a hell of a lot closer. Out of everything we ever did, I feel that turning down that deal was the only real and stupid mistake we made.

Gen - That said, the money Rank were offering would mean that we still would be unable to pay the cast and crew. As the German, Korean and US deal which totalled $350k were about to come in, we thought that we could afford to take a risk to make more by self distributing. Pilgrim did their own release with *Tale of A Vampire* and did extremely well, certainly better than Rank's advance. We watched *Tale of A Vampire* and in comparison, we felt *White Angel* was a superior film and would therefore do better. It doesn't actually work like that as we later found out. It's more to do with marketing, the type of film and timing - but at the time, we didn't know that.

Q - So you decided to release your film theatrically, so what is involved in doing that?

Gen - Firstly we had to decide how wide we were going to release, on how many screens and work a budget out accordingly. Because of Pilgrims experience with *Tale Of A Vampire* we took a lot of their thoughts on board and they wanted to open quite wide. Initially we were going to open in three theaters only, but they had a screening with the exhibitors who offered them more screens - everybody liked it which meant that it would be picked up by the multiplexes. So our three screens then developed into fifteen scattered around the country in the major cities, which increased our advertising budget. The other thing we had to do, was to get hold of a theatrical booker to actually get the film in the theaters, someone who knew how the system worked.

Q - Who is the booker?

Chris - The booker is the person who engineers and schedules the booking of screens and the moving of the prints. For instance, they will tell you the dates that your film will be screened, and the dates that the film will be moved from one theater to another. With 15 prints we would move from 15 theaters to another 15 theaters, moving around the country until, hopefully, we had covered every major town.

Q - What happened about publicity?

Film Festivals are a great place to win awards. This gets distributers, broadcasters and sales agents interested, and as a bonus you get to collect strange figurines mounted on marble blocks.

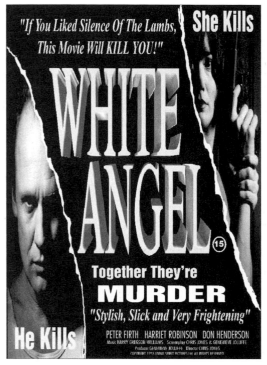

"If You Liked Silence Of The Lambs, This Movie Will KILL YOU!"

She Kills

WHITE ANGEL (15)

Together They're MURDER

"Stylish, Slick and Very Frightening"

He Kills

PETER FIRTH   HARRIET ROBINSON   DON HENDERSON
Music HARRY GREGSON WILLIAMS   Screenplay CHRIS JONES & GENEVIEVE JOLLIFFE
Producer GENEVIEVE JOLLIFFE   Director CHRIS JONES
COPYRIGHT 1993 LIVING SPIRIT PICTURES Ltd. ALL RIGHTS RESERVED

Chris - We had to hire a publicist, but a lot of the publicity we did ourselves, and eventually we became quite good at getting newspaper interviews, radio and TV. We discovered that telling the occasional white lie or even complete outright lie would always be good for publicity - always managing to get a good column in a newspaper. That was a good way of generating interest around the film.

Q- Do you think the London Film Festival's good press had an effect?

Chris - It's fair to say that having the London Film Festival putting us on a plinth and using the phrase *"mesmerisingly good and a triumph of British Independent Production"* perhaps nurtured a false sense of quality in our film that actually may not have been there. It certainly raised the expectations of the critics as what they actually got was a standard, commercial, ultra low-budget thriller. One interesting thing is that almost ALL the magazines gave us fair to good reviews while the *'daily newspapers'* unanimously slaughtered us.

Q - In retrospect, would it have been a good idea to take some of these people out to dinner and tell them how you made the film, win them over so to speak, instead of hyping the film out of proportion?

Gen - Yes, because the journalists who we did sit down with and have long chats with were the people who gave us favorable reviews, and all of them were loyal enough not to mention the budget (as we had asked them not to). The problem here was that we were in essence sitting between two goal posts and we were stretched to the limits. We didn't have the financial resources to schmooze people, nor did we have the contacts in the first place. We didn't have the power to demand a favorable or non committal review, (or we'll pull $15k worth of advertising from your mag for instance), and you read a lot of non committal reviews! Quite simply, we didn't have the resources to do the job properly within the set time frame. That's the job of a distributor.

HAYMARKET
(Piccadilly Circus Tube) **071- 839 1527**

ADVANCE BOOKING
081-970 6016 (Bkg fee)

WHITE ANGEL (15)
In Dolby Stereo
Sep Progs 2.15, 5.15, 8.15

RESERVOIR DOGS (18)
In Dolby Stereo
Sep Progs 1.20, 3.45, 6.10, 8.40

KALIFORNIA (18)
In Dolby Stereo
Sep Progs 1.50, 4.10, 6.30, 8.50

Chris - I think the problem with the *White Angel* release was partly the film itself. We aspired to a big budget style film with very little money. When you see a thriller up there on the screen, people expect Bruce Willis, blue light and a lot of gloss. We didn't have all that. What we had, was a TV style film that was a competent thriller and we were actively marketing it as an 'A' movie super duper thriller.

Chris - To some degree, a film appears to be valued at it's perceived cost. If you go down to a used car salesman and say *'how much is this car?'* and he says *'$1,000'.* Then you ask *'how*

(above) There was so little money for the release that the film's poster had to be put together on a PC by Chris, using Photoshop and Quark Xpress. (left) White Angel may have opened at some top London cinema venues, but due to a number of factors, it didn't last long so the whole exercise became a very expensive PR campaign for Living Spirit.

(right) EPK - The electronic press kit contains shots taken during filming, very roughly edited interviews with key cast and crew plus several clips from the completed movie. It should be delivered on Beta SP and is vital if any TV coverage is to be expected. (lower right) The old 'director pointing' press shot - it was actually taken a week before the London Film Festival in a front garden.

much is this other one?' and he says *$10* - they may both look the same but you'll think there is something wrong with the $10 one. And it's the same with films. Why go and see a film if it only cost $50k to make when you can go and watch Bruce Willis in a film that cost $70m, or another film that has been critically acclaimed? Why bother going to see this small independent thriller? So on the one side of the coin you want to get on top of the building and shout *'you won't believe what we made this film for'* but at the same time you know when you do that you devalue the film, which is exactly what top UK TV critic, Barry Norman, did on his TV film show. He criticised the film, which is fair enough, he's a critic and it's his job. But one particular comment absolutely destroyed us. And that comment was *'...this is no more than a 90 minute student film.'* Why bother going to see a 90 minute student film, when you can go and see a 90 minute *'real'* film. If he had panned the film it would have been one thing, however he put a value on the film and consigned it to the bargain basement.

Q - So you claimed not to be low-budget, but fairly low, you claimed to have made the film for just under a million?

Chris - The phrase we used, was that the film cost less than a million, which is true!

Q - In retrospect, do you think you should have been straight?

Chris - I don't know. I think a lot of critics may have thought where did all the money go, but then again, we never said it cost a million, just under a million. It is impossible to gauge how much of an effect the bad reviews had, they sure didn't help, but I'm not so sure they damaged us terribly. Most people seem to ignore critics. There were probably other factors other than the reviews that helped the film fail at the box office.

Gen - There were other things, like when we booked our opening weekend, we didn't have six months leeway to book in reviews with the big glossy magazines, so we lost a lot of publicity there. The youth magazines could fit us in as they had a quicker turnaround, and luckily we got in there with some great reviews. And we just couldn't afford TV advertising.

Q - Would it have been a good idea at the time of production to have got more journalists involved?

Gen - We did attempt to do that. UK film magazine *Empire* were interested, they came on set for a day and spent another day taking photos - it seemed to go well. But nothing came of it. They never used it in the magazine. Unless you have a star, or really great angle, most journalists aren't interested.

Q - In terms of the prints and advertising, how important do you think the poster is?

"White Angel is stylish, slick and often very frightening - everything you don't expect from British movies"
SELECT MAGAZINE

'Unpretentiously gripping and solidly commercial, White Angel deserves more than a little glorification"
Mark Wyman - FILM REVIEW

"A chillingly impressive film. White Angel is so scarily sinister, it makes Psycho look like an old Ealing comedy."
Sam Steele - NME

"A cracking thriller with plenty of edge-of-the-seat tension. and more twists and turns than a Dune sandworm"
VIDEO WORLD

Chris - I believe they are absolutely vital. It's the only point of sale where you can make your movie look like all the other Hollywood major movies - we made the name as big as we could on the poster so that people would remember it. Two small ads were placed in the London Evening Standard, probably two inches by three inches over the weekend of the release, which cost us around $8k (and the Evening Standard isn't even national). 5000 A1 full color posters cost us $3k. You can see how cost effective posters are.

Q - You had a fairly wide UK release with the film but it didn't go very well, what happened?

Gen - The big thing that went wrong, was that we released on a dreadful weekend, one of the worst weekends in the year. We had no control with the theatrical booker and were naive about the distribution side of the industry. We only found out afterwards by actually visiting the theaters, usually to help promote the film, and talking to the managers. They all said, *'why did you pick this weekend? This is one of the worse weekends in the year'*. Oops.

Q - What weekend was it?

Gen - It was the weekend immediately after the Easter Break. Everybody had gone to the cinema the week before and there were box office records, but the following weekend, our weekend, they were all going back to school, back to college, back to work after their Easter break. Unfortunately nobody wants to open on that weekend, but because we didn't know, there we were in that slot.

Chris - If we had gone with a reputable distributor, or taken the Rank deal, they would have said, we're not having that weekend, forget it. So again we learnt. But in retrospect we now know all these things, which we wouldn't have found out if we had gone the other way.

Q - It occurs to me that films have a short shelf life?

Chris - The film only gets one premiere, people can only hear about it for the first time once - that's the point to hit. If the American deal had been made through a reputable sales agent, the sales agent would, firstly, have a relationship or, secondly, the clout to say *'put up or shut up'*. If that deal hadn't happened, something else would have come into place. But because it hung about on the shelf, nothing happened and *White Angel* was old news.

Q - So the belief you had in the film from the London Film Festival was one of the downfalls?

Gen - It inflated our perception of the value of the film. In our own minds we believed it was worth much more.

Q - Do you feel that sales agents, international buyers etc, are out there to rip you off?

Chris - It's not that they're out to rip you off, but again, it's the inherent problem of having a low-budget film. It's not worth very much, and it's not worth anybody's trouble to sell it. And even if they do sell it, they'll never make enough money to make any real profits, and probably just cover their own expenses. The advice I would extend to a new filmmaker is to get to the best sales agent you can, get to the best distributor you can, get as much money up-front as you can, and write the rest off. Do not assume you'll ever get anything else back. Try and get an advance that covers your debts because your investors may never get paid anything else. The rest is really up to the performance of the film and whether the sales agent is honest. If you cling on to it, you're dead in the water anyway. Psychologically, write it completely off the moment you have completed the film, don't hang around, get going on your next picture or your first film will become a millstone around your neck. That's what happened with *White Angel*.

"this occasionally laughable and often inept British thriller from young hopefuls. hard to take seriously"
Wally Hammond
TIME OUT

Q - What other problems did you encounter?

Gen - We had unexpected events that occurred after our theatrical release which delayed our entire process.

"It's crass and amateurish, and looks as if it was shot for about threepence-ha'penny."
DAILY MAIL

Chris - Basically the film was released and the press were saying how amazingly well we were doing and that we were making loads of money. In real terms we were doing terribly badly. At that point we also lost the US deal and the Korean deal. Suddenly, from having around $350k coming in to us we found ourselves high and dry owing $40k from the losses on the UK theatrical release, which was pretty much paid for by the German deal. Not only had we lost all our deals but we had also lost all the money that we had made.

"I had a bad feeling about this one even before the opening credits had rolled because its young director, Chris Jones, gave a grovelling speech at the premiere begging us to like his movie"
Julian Brouwer
HARINGAY INDEPENDENT

At this very point... (long pause) ...we had a bit of bad luck. We had just got back from the Cannes Film Festival and at seven o'clock in the morning the doorbell rang. Three of us were living in this house. Myself, Gen and another friend. I went downstairs and eight policemen barged in, and arrested all of us, searched the entire house, drawers, shelves, floorboards - you name it, they searched it - and impounded all our Living Spirit files, floppy disks and equipment.

"aaaaargh!"
Alexander Walker
THE TIMES

Gen - This also included sifting through my underwear, reading my diaries, looking through photo albums... They discovered the fake gun that we used for the film and there was a flurry of excitement... *"weapons possession sir - we got em!"* I entered our office to see three policemen holding the gun on the end of a pencil, examining it in every detail. I pointed out that it was a replica used for the film - pause - *"oh yes, of course, we knew that"*...

Chris - Basically, they believed we had been making lots of money without declaring it. At that point we had applied for benefit from the government as we had absolutely no money to live on, especially with everything falling through. They had read all the press and seen the publicity and believed that we were not entitled to that benefit, firstly because the

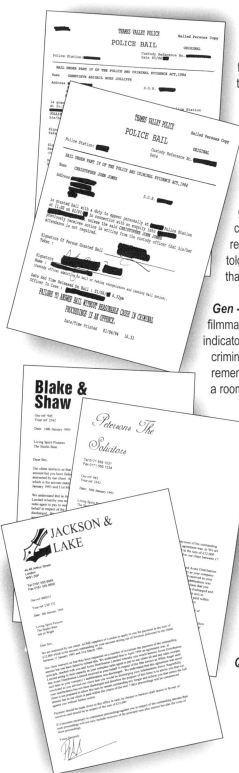

newspapers said we were doing well, and secondly, they couldn't believe that a film company could make and release a film *AND* be broke. Obviously if they read this book they may see things differently. Anyhow, we were taken down to the police station, shoved in a cell, belts and shoelaces taken off to make sure that we couldn't hang ourselves, read our rights - the works.

Gen - That was if you were wearing a belt and shoelaces, and not still in your nightshirt like myself!

Chris - They closed the cell door and it felt like they were throwing the key away. That was it! We asked them to call a lawyer which they finally did, and a few hours later, which felt like days, the lawyer turned up. He asked what was going on as he was used to representing murderers and rapists - and we certainly didn't look like the murderers or rapists he usually dealt with. It was really bloody horrible at the time. We didn't know what the hell was going on. He told us he would sort it out and we would be out immediately. It didn't quite work that way.

Gen - Eventually we were given our interrogation where all our positive attributes as filmmakers, bullshit, bending the truth, running through the wet paint etc, became indicators of criminal intent. They were quite sure that we had committed serious criminal fraud and continued what we felt were ludicrous lines of questioning. And remember, at this time we are surrounded by a bunch of pretty hefty police officers in a room with a tape recorder and pretty much being shouted at. When you hear about it, you always think I would do this or that, but until you have been put in a cell and had your entire life and home opened up in minute detail, you just can't appreciate what it's like.

Anyhow, we were released on bail to appear in one month for an interrogation, sorry, interview! We couldn't leave the country, so it was a damn good thing we had no festivals to attend and in fact, as everything to do with the film or Living Spirit was in the police station, we couldn't actually do very much apart from watch our future go down the tubes. Our bank managers and investors got letters from the Police, asking for information relating to Living Spirit, ourselves and fraud. Our poor friend who lived with us, and who has nothing to do with making films, was considered to be an accomplice in our big operation. They went and interrogated our landlord, not surprisingly we ended up being thrown out of our home a few weeks later. We were all in this together according to the police. It was astounding.

Q - So how did this all happen?

(top) The arrest warrant for Chris and Genevieve. (bottom) And so the floodgates opened as solicitors, undersheriffs and bailiffs made Living Spirit their business...

Chris - Quite simply, they had seen some of our press, wondered what on earth a big film company's directors were doing claiming benefit, put two and two together, got three million and decided to jump on us. They even had press clippings we didn't have, so they must have done a lot of research! They confused off shore bank accounts belonging to my brother, who at that time lived in Germany, with me - they also confused Gen's father's credit card with me - they thought I had about six different identities! Slowly, it became apparent that what they thought was a big fraud operation was actually a couple of people who were completely broke trying very hard to make the best of a very bad situation - and they had just made it infinitely worse.

Q - How long did it take them to solve this case?

Chris - About four months to assess everything and to say *'No, we're not going to press any charges'.* Two months after that we got all our information back. So all in all, six months, after which we got heavily 'fined' by the tax office for not having completed our returns on time - we couldn't as we did not have our own paperwork!

Gen - And that was the end of it - but it had created a ripple effect that, combined with the failure of the film at the Box Office and the falling through of all the international sales, crippled us for twelve months or so. During that twelve months, Pilgrim Entertainment did zero business - we couldn't chase them because our plate was more than full just picking up the pieces. One month after we were in the clear, Rank (labs not distribution) to whom we still owed $40k, sent us a letter saying pay us within 48 hours or we will force you into liquidation. We then had to start negotiating how we were going to get out of this hole. At that point, we decided the best thing to do was to terminate the agreement with Pilgrim Entertainment and take the film ourselves to find new UK distributor and international sales agent. Within days we had The Feature Film company on board to handle the UK video, satellite and TV through Polygram. We had some interest from some international sales agents but couldn't nail anything down. But the UK video was a new source of real cash that could come in for us. We had been made homeless and had no money at all. We were entitled to benefit but just didn't want to take it as the last time we did, we ended up in a police cell. We ended up living with my parents for nearly a year.

Q - When was your video release?

Chris - We had to do yet another re edit of the film to put more sex and violence in which would make the film a lot more commercial and had even thought of retitling the film for the international sales market as *Interview with a Serial Killer.* With a new edit and a new title, we could in some respects reinvent the film for international sales. But with regard to the UK video, it didn't perform particularly well, I don't think that's a reflection on anything apart from the fact that the market was particularly depressed. We did business, I think we sold somewhere between 2,500 to 3,000 units but at the end of the day we only got around $10k which doesn't do much more than put a dent in Living Spirit's debts. We were hoping that we could continue with making more international sales. When Rank sent us the attorney's letter giving us 48 hours we decided to fight, to work as hard as we could to make good the debts. Pilgrim also owed Rank from the UK release but they decided to simply go bankrupt.

Q - In all of this you could have opted for bankruptcy, why didn't you do that?

Gen - We felt a moral responsibility to everybody involved, particularly the investors. When this whole thing happened with Rank, our first reaction was fair enough, we'll go from minus $40k to zero overnight by going under. What a really good way to clear your debt? But it was also a big slap in the face, a big failure and failure doesn't make you sleep well at nights. Not that we've had a great deal of success either, but we didn't want to accept failure and lie down and die, they would have to kill us off with extreme prejudice. We were legally advised to fight it and let them force us into liquidation, but the real reason was that we didn't want to write that letter to our investors and have to say *'Dear investor,* *thanks for your money, by the way, we've given up on it, and we've gone into liquidation'.* That would have been too difficult a letter to write. That may not be good business sense - maybe a good businessman would say, *'Oh well, it's a bad deal, get rid of it and move on'.*

Q - In either of your past lives do you think you did something that meant that White Angel *went through what you could say is the most unlucky curve of all - not only were you practically made bankrupt, your release went totally wrong, you spent time in prison - but then a real life situation was discovered within 20 miles of where you made the film?*

Chris - Yes! Would you believe it! We were on a plane coming back from the Ankara Film Festival, just a few weeks before the film's theatrical release and we heard rumors of a serial killer in Gloucester (where we lived) and my first thought was *'the film must be really getting out there, people are even talking about it on the plane!'* - I didn't realize that it was a REAL serial killer they were talking about. When we found out that it was reality, it was a huge shock. Initially, Fred West was only accused of two murders, but then the body count started growing and we began to worry that the press would jump on us. The story broke on Easter day '94 - *Serial Killer Film made yards from Fred West House - chilling parallels - possible collusion between filmmakers and mass murderer!* Many of the big newspapers carried a small column about it and we tried to play it down. It was a very bizarre occurrence. I think what is most bizarre, when you refer back to when we talk about the screenplay and what we say about why people find serial killers fascinating, that *it's the man next door...?* Well for us, it ended up that way! We used to park our car outside his front door when we went into town! That was very chilling and brought everything into sharp focus - as we were making a piece of fiction, just down the road it was happening in reality!

What was frustrating is that we were being accused of being sick *'cash in'* filmmakers by the people who were printing the story saying *'Sick Fred West Film Made In Front Garden'.* Actually, the only people making any money out of this story were the people selling the newspapers! We pointed out that the film had been completed and premiered at the London Film Festival before Fred West was known to anyone outside family, friends and his unfortunate victims. We had to defend the film and say *'well it's not that sick and nasty',* which diluted the impact for the theatrical release of the film. I couldn't say, *'it's a real shocking, real blood and gutsy thriller',* because the press would say, *'isn't it a bit sick releasing the film the same time as all these revelations about Fred West?'.* What could we do? We couldn't afford to put off the release, we were four weeks away and it was all moving - we were in a no win situation.

Q - Why did you decide to write this book?

Gen - We wanted this kind of book when we started up, a book that gave other people's experiences - showing where they got it right, and where they didn't. There's nothing better than your own experience, but hearing somebody else's really helps and I'm sure we've had a few bad experiences that can be avoided by other filmmakers.

MOVIE OF HORROR

PAT CODD
Showbiz Editor

SERIAL killer West visited a film set - to watch scenes from a movie about a mass murderer.

And there are bizarre coincidences between White Angel and the real-life mass murderer whose wife Rose is now facing 10 murder charges.

Scenes were filmed just yards from West's front door in Cromwell Street, Gloucester, six months before his arrest.

Director Chris Jones said: "It's chilling, particularly as the coincidences were stunning - bodies buried in the wall of the house and garden, 12 young female victims and family members being murdered."

And in the film the killer writes his biography.

West penned his own - eerily entitled I only Ever Loved An Angel - before his suicide in jail in December.

Chris - The other reason why we wrote the book is that it's about the only way we could make money out of our experiences now. That's the tragic reality of the whole situation. It has also been a catharsis too!

Q - What basic advice would you give to somebody about the attitude it takes to make low-budget films?

Chris - There are two kinds of new filmmakers who will go out and attempt to make a film. One is somebody who thinks they want to do it but will lose their nerve, the other is the kind of person who actually believes, quite literally, that they are a genius and that they have no possible way of failing. Quite honestly when we started out we believed ourselves to be mini geniuses, it was absolutely impossible to fail! That is intrinsic to a low-budget filmmakers psyche, it's the only thing that will get you to do these ridiculous things that will destroy your life and financial standing.

Gen - Most new filmmakers, ourselves included, are never prepared for the chaos that will happen after having made the film - making the film is actually the easy thing, dealing with it afterwards is the difficult thing. My basic advice would be, if you can pay yourself, pay yourself and don't put your own money in. Not because you don't believe in the project, but because if it all goes wrong you won't be left so high and dry that you cannot function for several years.

Chris - The other thing is to get out as quickly as possible and start on the next project - don't be too concerned about quality, turnover is much more important. Quality will come later, with experience and serious budgets.

Gen - For a first film, you should make the kind of film you want to make as later you may not have that luxury - many other fingers will be in your pie, each with an opinion.

Q - So to make a film you need to be an optimist, but also a realist?

Gen - You need a vast quantity of optimism, dedication, self will, self motivation, and I believe, honesty and integrity. Those are the things that allow you to get it done properly. The moment you finish the film, take off your director/producer cap, and put on your sales agent cap, or *'now I have to go and make this business work'* cap, then you need to replace your optimism with pessimism and realism - put on your accountancy cap, look at the figures and take as much money as you can, as and when you can, and as quickly as you can. Treat it as a hundred yard sprint. After a hundred yards, kick it into touch and move on, because after a hundred yards you're not going to get any more.

Q - What would you advise the balance between the budget for the actual film production and film sales be?

Chris - It's inevitable that new filmmakers are focused on getting to day one of principal photography and aren't too concerned about things like screenplays or casting - it's just *get the movie shot!* It's an insane desire to shoot and then deal with the chaos that you have created for yourself. With the best will in the world, I don't think that a new filmmaker is going to say, *'well I've got my $100k to make the film, but I'm not going to make it now, because I need another $100k to sell the film afterwards'.* All I can suggest is be aware of it, know that you are going to have problems and say *'I know that I can make the film for $100k, but the real budget is going to be $200k after I have fixed all the problems, paid my rent, been to a few festivals*

CROMWELL St.

It could be the man next door - in Living Spirit's case, it literally was, in the form of serial killer Fred West.

and made delivery to a sales agent'. If at the end of the day the film doesn't sell you'll never make any money, you'll never pay your investors back and you'll have this millstone around your neck for several years. At which point either everyone will get bored and go away or they'll sue you and you'll be made bankrupt.

Gen - Get your screenplay to a sales agent and say *'I have this screenplay, this is the cast I'm thinking about, this is the budget I'm thinking about, what are your ideas?'* And they'll give you a fair appraisal of the films commercial value.

Q - Test your idea out first and be aware that if you are going to make any money you've got to sell it afterwards?

Gen - When we talk about making money out of it, it's nothing to do with profit. Sure, we would all love to have our own yacht in the Caribbean, but what we're talking about is making enough money to pay people back what they have put in and to pay for your rent and food. Any film is going to take at least 12 to 18 months of your life. Who is going to pay for those 18 months?

Chris - Nobody would buy a house for $200k if they didn't know they could pay the mortgage - making a film for $200k is like buying a house and you've got to know that you can pay that mortgage, or you'll lose that money and get repossessed. It's a hard reality. It's naive to assume you're going to make a lot of money. However, if you are prepared to enter the arena and say, *well I'm going to lose it all, and if I do, I don't care*, then great, go for it. *And if I lose it all, I can still survive and start again.* Low-budget filmmaking is designed to launch careers, it isn't about getting rich quick.

Gen - However, I think we've been spectacularly unlucky.

Q - Maybe you are just talentless?

Chris - I think we had better end the interview here!

End of interviews 1996

Chris and Gen completed White Angel *and after being arrested, spent two years as freelance journalists while they worked themselves out of debt. It was during this time that Living Spirit worked on the screenplay for their third feature,* Urban Ghost Story *and wrote the first edition of this book (UK edition). It's worth noting that in the few years between* White Angel *and* Urban Ghost Story, *digital technology had moved on so far that non-linear editing was the best way to edit, and digital features are being made on considerably smaller budgets than the $15k it cost to shoot* White Angel.

White Angel is available on DVD in the USA, under the title, Interview With A Serial Killer. *If you want to buy a copy, buy it from us at www.livingspirit.com so that we can make some money from the sale. If you buy from somewhere like Amazon, we will get zip!*

Q - How did the idea of **Urban Ghost Story (UGS)** *come about?*

Chris - I had seen a documentary on TV about a real poltergeist case and it was really scary. We had always wanted to do a ghost story but the genre felt overpopulated, so we decided to make this ultra real version of a paranormal tale. We originally said it would be like *The Exorcist* if Brit social realist director Ken Loach had made it. We wanted to capture that spooky feeling of late night ghost stories, where not too much happens, but because it's real, it's that much scarier.

Gen - I had some experiences with the paranormal as a kid, my grand-mother was a medium, and I loved horror, so it seemed like an obvious choice. Right from day one we wanted 'real' poltergeist stories and experiences to be the focus of the drama in the movie.

Chris - Yeah, we even spent time hanging out with spiritualists and ghost hunters. It was heaps of fun.

Q - You swapped roles - why?

Gen - Chris directed *The Runner* and *White Angel,* and I directed *UGS.* When we left film school we agreed that we would split everything down the middle, directing and producing. We'd both wanted to direct and it's just the way that the chips fell that Chris directed *The Runner* and *White Angel.* So after producing twice I felt ready to direct.

Chris - In some ways it was a real problem for us. We had two movies behind us, and the first edition of this book (in the UK) which was doing well, but when people read the script for UGS and liked it, we then had to say oh, *'and Gen is directing...'* This was usually a problem as Gen had no real directorial experience, she was young and female, which all seemed to go against us.

Gen - This was all compounded by the fact that a lot of people didn't 'get' what the story was about. We had one company who was interested but wanted to change the end so the tower block was built on a gateway to hell - we just had to say, *'guys, you just don't get what we want to do...'*

Chris - One of the problems we just haven't managed to get over is that of development. We have searched high and low for scripts written by new writers and they are either very poor, or already snatched up by a bigger production company. That means we have to write ourselves, and that means we have to fund that too. And I don't care what anyone says, writing a great 120 page script takes months, maybe years if you can't work on it full time.

Gen - We were disillusioned about what we had made too. *White Angel* and *The Runner* were both genre films, and while *White Angel* was quite good, it still pretty much failed commercially. So we decided to just make a movie that we wanted to make, throw caution to the wind and just do it.

The original image put together by Chris with Photoshop conveyed Urban Ghost Story *as a horror movie. Printed on 1000 postcards for $100 it gave the film a glossy but cost effective presence in Cannes prior to shooting.*

Chris - In some ways it has failed commercially again, but this time it's been a critical success which has meant some very exciting things are now happening.

Q - How much work did you do on the script?

Chris - We spent about 18 months writing but at the same time, we both had to do other work to keep afloat. It was a hard film to write because so much of it was just feel and not plot, it never was a film about a ghost being exorcised. The problem was always audience expectation of a ghost story. We knew the film wouldn't deliver the shocks that a mainstream audience would expect and that it was too paranormal for your average art film fanatic. So we just said, to hell with it, we fall between two posts, but it's a story we want to tell.

Gen - It was so frustrating to have sales agents tell us that there just weren't enough *'blue light'* scenes, or effects. That said, all the actors loved it because it had rich characters for a film that still had a commercial slant.

Chris - We were also taking a risk making the lead a 13 year old. What if she couldn't act?

Q - Why in a tower block?

Chris - We wanted an oppressive and interesting backdrop and a tower block just seemed like the obvious choice. It's cold, dark and scary.

Gen - Glasgow seemed like a good location as the accents are so much more lyrical than say Southern English. I also liked the landscape, it felt dramatic, fresh and new. Setting the movie in southern England/BBC land would have been disastrous, it needed an edge.

Q - Where did the money come from?

Gen - We had produced a budget for $1.2m, set a date, and said whatever we had on that date, we would shoot with. We tried all the usual places but got nowhere - the usual answers were; *'we don't get what it's about...', 'It's too paranormal for us...', 'It's not paranormal enough for us...', 'Who's directing? She can't do it, she has no experience...', 'What about Chris directing instead, then we'd finance it...'*

Chris - It was really hard standing by your agreement when someone is offering you the money if I just cut Gen out of the loop and direct myself. It got Gen down a lot because she felt so devalued. So we stood by our guns, and no industry money came our way.

Gen - Just when we were about to crumble we got this call out of the blue from one of the investors in *White Angel*. His name is Dave and he said that he felt we had been in training

Concept paintings by Alex Fort helped convince all parties at the table that the production was being helmed by a creative team with vision.

on the other two films and now it was time to do it properly. He got a few of his friends together and collectively they put in $350k. This was great, we worked out that we could shoot the movie for that, quite easily actually, but continued to try and get more industry money. Dave then became our Executive Producer.

Chris - The money also meant that we could take an office at Ealing Film Studios in West London, which then meant we were taken seriously by the business... *'yeah, it's Chris here from Living Spirit, we're at Ealing Film Studios and blah blah blah'* - it just made us sound so much better. The room we hired was about the best value we have ever got out of anything - although we are situated next to the boiler room and when they switch on, the office makes a sound like the Millenium Falcon starting up and shudders continuously! It's just a great way to look bigger and more serious than we might be.

(right) Just photocopying a 120 page screenplay on a low budget feature is costly, time consuming, not to mention back breaking. DP Jon Walker helps out just weeks prior to the shoot. (left) The tower block was conceived as a character in the movie, with a life of its own, organic and mechanical. It wasn't in Glasgow, but a short drive from the studios where Living Spirit were based in London.

Q - Did you take the project to Cannes before shooting?

Gen - Yes, Chris did some artwork on the PC and we did some postcards and printed up a pile of scripts. We hawked it around but again, no-one seemed to understand what we were making and why. The best thing that happened was that we met David Thewlis and Amanda Plumber at a party, who were, weirdly enough, the two actors we wanted for the two adult roles. They both turned the film down eventually, but we did get the script to them and they did read it.

Chris - Cannes was great for getting in the mood, but for actually getting the film made, it didn't really help.

Q - What happened when you took the office at the studios?

Chris - We had a friend called Carmen who had worked as a production coordinator on *White Angel* and she was between jobs. We convinced her to come and help out in the office for next to nothing and that made a real difference. Living Spirit suddenly had a consistent voice on the phone and it sounded like we had a secretary. Carmen acted as a filter, making sure we didn't get distracted by unimportant calls, and she also arranged heaps of production things too.

Gen - Because we had set a date, we had some cash and a script we believed in, we absolutely knew the film was going to happen. The only questions left were exactly how much money we would have when we got to photography, and just how good the movie would end up being. The freight train started to move down hill and we both knew it wouldn't be long before it would be impossible to stop it.

Chris - It was a great time.

Q - How did you get the cast involved?

Months of casting and sending out screenplays led to the very best cast we could have imagined. Left to right, Nicola Stapleton, James Cosmo, Heather Ann Foster, Jason Connery, Billy Boyd, Stephanie Buttle, Andreas Wisniewski and Elizabeth Berrington.

Gen - I spent months interviewing actors. Cathy Arton, who had worked on both *The Runner* and *White Angel* stepped in as our casting director. She dealt with agents brilliantly which meant I only needed to see if the actor was the right person for the job. She made a big difference as she would always make interesting suggestions and find a way to get to the actors.

Chris - What was most interesting was that Gen seemed to make really good short lists, but because she was so close to it all, when she came to make the final decision on who would be the best person for the part, we all had to go by our gut instinct. I wasn't as involved in the casting, so when it came to decision time and there was a lot of *umming* and *ahhing* going on, I usually had a gut feeling based on fresh new impressions. Although Gen made a brilliant choice with Heather, the young girl from Glasgow playing the lead.

Gen - I went to Glasgow in Scotland and met about 100 young actresses whom Cathy, our casting director, had found. Heather was the 7th girl I saw and she just shone out immediately. Her dad was a cameraman too, so there was no need to explain how the business worked, they understood.

Chris - We had discovered that all sorts of laws exist for working with kids, all of which were a pain in the butt, so we moved the shoot forward so that we could shoot in the summer holidays and set a shoot date, August 18th. Then we discovered that Scottish kids go back to school weeks before English kids - on August 18th, so we were just as screwed! So we had to adhere to all the laws and get a professional minder and all the rest of the stuff, which was very expensive.

Q - Did you have any problems with unions?

Chris - Astonishingly yes. BECTU, the technicians union blacklisted us. Even after blacklisting, they couldn't tell us why we had been blacklisted, even though we were named for months in their magazine. I asked them to substantiate their position, but they didn't, and never have. It didn't really cause much of a problem for us, just made us look like crooks.

Q - How much did you pay the crew?

Chris - About $150 a week, plus food. It's not much I know but everyone did it because they wanted to be there, everyone was getting a break - art directors got to do production design, gaffers got to operate camera etc. And because

Dave Hardwick, Executive Producer for Urban Ghost Story, *was the only person who believed in both Chris and Gen and the movie itself.*

everyone was on the same money, there were no squabbles, no-one felt less or more important than anyone else - DP, production designer, runner, editor - everyone got the same deal and there was a real team spirit.

Q - But those aren't union rates?

Chris - Who said it was a union film? And what right does a union have to blacklist a company without backing up any claims? Then the thing with the agents happened. We were about a week from shooting when an agent called me and said to me - quote, *'you've just fucked yourself! I'm pulling my actors and you'll never work in the industry again - goodbye!'* I couldn't believe what I was hearing. How arrogant to think that they had the power to tell anyone whether they could work in 'their' industry or not. Then it happened with another agent and another. In the space of an hour, we lost most of our cast, except for Jason Connery's agent who stood by us.

Q - What was wrong with them?

Chris - The Personal Managers Association (PMA), is a group of agents in London who meet regularly behind closed doors. What transpired is that they had got hold of a letter written (for prospective investment) by our investor, Dave, in which he said Low Budget Films don't pay their deferred fees. It's a fact, deferred fee movies don't work. That's why we decided not to make UGS with deferments, but that just didn't matter. I couldn't even get hold of the PMA, they seemed to be more like a secret society than a group of agents who want to encourage nw filmmakers. Anyway, the agents just didn't believe that we were not crooks and insisted that we make the film using the unionised *'PACT Equity registered low budget scheme'*. I just want to say clearly and categorically that because we were forced to use the *'PACT Equity registered low budget scheme'*, we ended up paying the cast 35% less than what we had anticipated. Even so, I was humiliated by the butt licking that I had to go through in order to get our cast back - but I did it.

To crown it all, a top agent who represented a major actor whom we had agreed would play a part in UGS then said, *'yes I know it's registered low budget, but... don't tell Equity and hire my actor as a producer then you can give them an extra $60k deferred fee as well'*. I had already been in hot water with Equity and as this proposed practice was strictly forbidden under union rules, I was damned if I was going to jeopardize it all again, so I just let it slide. Weeks later, this guy wrote to me with all sorts of wild accusations, again telling me that I would never work in the industry in the future. Where do they get these people?

Q - Did you get your cast back?

Chris - Yes, and you can imagine their faces when we told them that Equity, Agents and the PMA had collectively forced us to effectively negotiate their fees down by 35%!

Q - How did you find working with actors?

Gen - Because the production ran so smoothly, nights were early and days relatively short, tempers never frayed. Initially I was daunted by directing and thought that it would be obvious that I had never done it before, but no-one noticed so it was fine! I spent a lot of time talking to them about their characters and they seemed to get the idea that there was a cohesive idea behind what I wanted to get. And because everything had been storyboarded in great detail, I didn't need to spend so much time working on the camera.

Q - Did storyboards help?

Chris - We had never storyboarded before but this was a great experience. Weeks before shooting we could argue out the best ways to cover a scene. Gen would normally say *'I want to do this'*, I would say *'no we can't afford it, why not do this?'*, then she would say *'how about that way then?'* and before you knew it, we had the most creative and cost effective way of shooting a scene on paper. This didn't happen on *The Runner* or *White Angel* and it shows.

Gen - Alex Fort drew many of the story boards, but we ran out of time and stick figure sketches with camera placement diagrams took their place. It's amazing when you look at the boards then at the shots, just how closely they match. There were times when I turned up on location without any idea of what the location would look like. So I'd have to make it up there and then and looking back, these scenes didn't work as well as the ones that were storyboarded, they just weren't planned out.

Q - Did you shoot on location?

Gen - We couldn't afford to shoot in Glasgow, so we shot all the tower block scenes just down the road in West London. We used our tried and tested rule of finding all the locations as close as possible to the main unit as practical. Then we shot all the interiors on a set at the studios. Because we were shooting in London, the local council wanted $thousands for us just to stand out on the pavement with a camera. So we just lied, told them we weren't going to do any shooting, then just did it. No-one ever had a problem and there was not a single complaint.

Q - How did you find working on a set?

Gen - First of all it was Stage 4 at Ealing Film Studios, which wasn't a sound stage, more like a big shed. And some days we were on the flight path with Heathrow airport so that every 90 seconds we'd stop shooting and wait for a plane to fly over, then when it rained we couldn't record sound because it had a metal roof. Other than that it was great. We cut a great deal with the studio which got us the stage, green room, production office, changing rooms etc., and there were on site bathrooms and a canteen so catering wasn't an issue. From a production point of view it was a dream come true. The actors liked it too because there was parking, they could go somewhere quiet to relax, and there were virtually no night shoots. Very civilized.

Q - What happened about catering?

Chris - Because we were shooting at the studios we were able to give everyone $10 per day and they could feed themselves at the canteen. On the very odd occasion when we were on location, one of the production team would go to the local supermarket and buy sandwiches and buffet type food and everyone was happy. Aside from tea and coffee, we always had cold water on tap because the stage wasn't air conditioned and it was the height of summer. With all the lights turned on what was supposed to be a freezing cold Glaswegian flat was more like a furnace and dehydration became an issue. In retrospect it's amazing how much we spent on water, nearly $2k!

Q - Who built the sets?

Chris - When Gen was casting, I was crewing. I met this wild guy called Simon Pickup who seemed to me to be bonkers. But he had extraordinary passion

(left) The beginning of the compromise. An unhappy Genevieve argues for her shots, against Chris who constantly says 'no, it's a half page scene, we don't need to do it in eleven shots!'

URBAN GHOST STORY STORYBOARDS

Sketched by Alex Fort

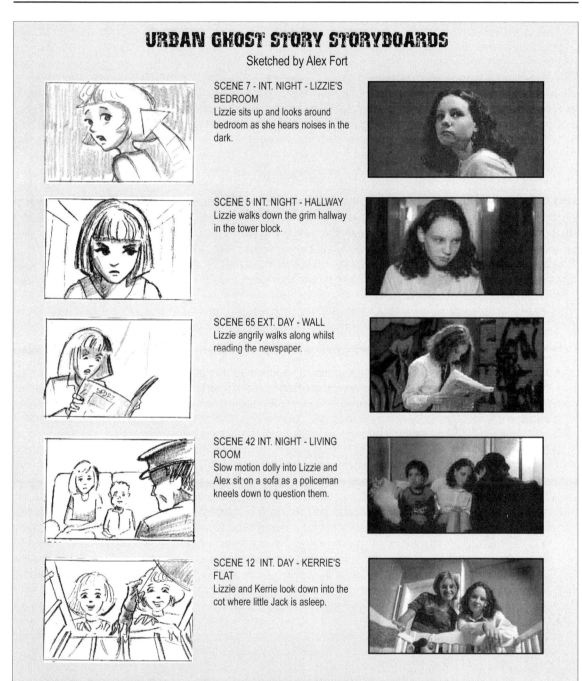

SCENE 7 - INT. NIGHT - LIZZIE'S BEDROOM
Lizzie sits up and looks around bedroom as she hears noises in the dark.

SCENE 5 INT. NIGHT - HALLWAY
Lizzie walks down the grim hallway in the tower block.

SCENE 65 EXT. DAY - WALL
Lizzie angrily walks along whilst reading the newspaper.

SCENE 42 INT. NIGHT - LIVING ROOM
Slow motion dolly into Lizzie and Alex sit on a sofa as a policeman kneels down to question them.

SCENE 12 INT. DAY - KERRIE'S FLAT
Lizzie and Kerrie look down into the cot where little Jack is asleep.

Artist Alex Fort worked with Gen and Chris to storyboard Urban Ghost Story. The storyboards allowed Gen to communicate to every member of the cast and crew, just what was needed throughout each day. It also ensured that what was shot would actually 'cut' once in the edit suite. Overhead camera diagrams were also used to illustrate where actors and the camera would move during a shot. Management of anywhere between 500 and 1000 storyboard images is an issue not to be underrated.

CASE STUDIES

(Left) Stage 4 at Ealing Film Studios, West London. An effects stage with no real sound proofing. Ideal for Urban Ghost Story as it was based at a studio facility, came with green rooms, production offices, storage, bathrooms, canteen, parking etc. It was cheap, BIG and all other locations needed were a short drive away. (Below) It may look convincing on film but it is just plasterboard, plywood, paint and wallpaper.

and a vision. I wasn't too sure about his vision, if it was doable, but I felt that if we were going to build sets, they should be as unique as possible. Simon designed a fantastic set for the film, and gave every ounce of energy in his body to make the film as good as possible. Mark Sutherland, from *White Angel,* came on board as the construction manager, and together they made it happen. A BBC designer came on set one day and proceeded to tell us that what we were doing wasn't the way to do it, it couldn't be done for the money we had, and it was impossible. Well Simon and Mark proved him wrong.

Gen - The level of detail in the sets meant that we could shoot anything, and in close up detail. Walls could be moved, and there was a floating ceiling so lights could be suspended from above. The big problem was that it took longer to build than we expected, so they were still hammering weeks into the shoot. Just as they completed the build we had to rip it all down. One problem we found was that you need lots of space around your set so that you can get lights or a skyline backdrop far enough away to be acceptable. We built the set right up to the wall at times and that was a mistake. The more I think about it, I can't think of a single drawback to shooting on a set. I guess if there isn't time to paint and dress it properly, it might look a bit crap and then it's self defeating. Because you make the sets, everything is bigger, which means there is more space to work in and the actors aren't so restricted. If you look at UGS, it has to be the biggest council flat in the history of Glasgow!

Shooting on a set meant an incredible degree of control over lighting, additional space, flying walls and ceiling for better access. In the pictures, the walls look laughably thin and you wouldn't ever believe that in the movie they look convincingly like two foot thick concrete. We also had a little help from the neighboring, bigger budget dumpsters that were on the studio lot. Many of the sets in UGS were built from junk pulled from BBC drama dumpsters. Many of the sets in UGS were built from junk pulled from BBC drama skips.

One big problem, literally, was Andreas, who played Dr Quinn, was just too, well, big! And his head would often pop off the top of the set. We had a cunning solution which was to put him in a wheelchair, but that was a little too mad scientist, so we just got him to sit down whenever we could.

Chris - We also built a few tiny sets, just corners of rooms or walls. Again, this meant that we kept the equipment, cast and crew all in one place.

Q - How did you approach the style of the film?

Gen - With *The Runner* we'd gone for a glossy look, with *White Angel* we'd gone for a social realist look that ended up looking a lot like TV. For *UGS* we knew we would still have a limited lighting budget but more than we'd had before. Myself, Chris and DP Jon Walker, who had shot both *The Runner* and *White Angel,* all got together and decided on the 'look'.

Combined with shooting in a studio with complete control over the sets allowed us to create a style with which we were all happy. It's hard to quantify the look but we wanted it to look a lot like Luc Besson's *The Professional.* We wanted it to look cinematic and not televisual, so we used a lot of slow motion, long lens shots, fast cutting and ultimately, although this wasn't planned, put it through a bleach bypass at the labs.

The costume and sets were another area that we wanted to control in order to create this look. Simon Pickup and Mark Sutherland, with their crew of die hard set dressers, had created this beautifully detailed set that just meant we could shoot in every direction. Early in the shoot a costume for our lead man was a problem. I hadn't had time to collaborate with costume designer Linda Haysman on everything as there just wasn't time or money. Actors often ended up wearing their own clothes which isn't always the best idea as you don't have much control and personal preferences start to come into play.

Chris - On the first day of shooting with Jason Connery it all went well except I was unhappy with his costume. I thought he looked too dressed up and less like the bit of 'rough' I expected. This 'look' had been a compromise between what Jason was comfortable wearing, budget restrictions and what he had brought with him in his bag. As I was not literally at the coal face directing I was able to stand back and note that the costume was just not quite right. Gen had gone through the whole day and noticed the costume but because it was early on in the shoot and there were other seemingly bigger issues, it just didn't seem like an immediate problem.

This is where a creative producer is useful because the costume issue didn't seem too dramatic at the time but in retrospect it would have changed the dynamics and tone of the film and was actually very important. Linda adapted the costume that night after persuading DP Jon Walker to relinquish his trousers, giving the dressed down 'look' everybody agreed was right.

Gen - Ironically we ended up using these first scenes in the final cut of the movie to create a new story thread where Jason Connery's character comes back at the end of the film, sometime after the main story has finished. The obvious costume difference implied a change in character and a passing of time. Quite funny considering it was a screw up!

Q - You mention bleach bypass - what is this?

Chris - Bleach bypass is a process in the labs where the film isn't put through the bleach bath. It makes the blacks and dark areas of the film almost impenetrable and it adds a kind of rich feel to the image. It's very subjective and is only used in the theatrical version of the film, but it didn't half make it look great. *Se7en* used it in the cinema for instance.

Q - What did you shoot it on - S16mm or 35mm?

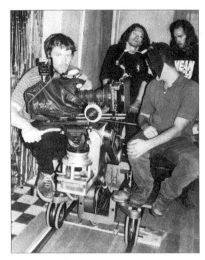

(above) A large main unit and small 2nd unit ensured maximum coverage.

Gen - Even though we had $350k and could have afforded 35mm we chose S16mm. This was because we had a 13 year old girl in the lead and we didn't know if she would be a one take wonder or a take twenty six disaster. In fact she was fantastic. It was also because we had learned from our other films that coverage is paramount. It's a lot like the way Hollywood shoots films, we just wanted to burn stock like there was no tomorrow and we knew that if we shot on 35mm we wouldn't be able to do that.

Chris - We reasoned that audiences were not interested in whether a film was shot on S16mm, 35mm Kodak or Fuji, they were just interested in whether the story and characters were engaging. So we let go of 35mm and embraced S16mm and truly did burn stock! It was the right decision and I know that the film wouldn't have been as good if we had shot on 35mm. We would have crisper shots, but fewer shots and diminished coverage.

Q - Did you use a second unit?

Gen - Yes. One of the things that was different with *UGS* from our other movies were that there were an enormous amount of characters. That combined with the fact that our young actress was legally only allowed to work for a few hours a day meant that often we had to have two cameras running on set. The second camera was usually free and roaming and would grab snippets of anything interesting when it could. A lot of the time, Chris would be directing the second unit while I was on set doing the main unit, which freed me up to forget about doing close ups of newspapers or hands putting a cup down and concentrate on the drama and the actors.

Chris - The other advantage was that I was able to use a stand in for Heather (Niki Ball) and shoot large portions of scenes with her, then Gen would come in with the lead actress, shoot her close ups, then move on. Because we were cutting as we shot I was able to isolate sequences that needed a cutaway to bridge two shots that weren't cutting comfortably and then go and shoot them, or shoot a cutaway to help cut the middle out of a dialogue scene that wasn't quite working - basically invent tiny segments of drama to help with the overall pacing of the movie. Even though we shot for only four weeks, because we pretty much had two units going almost all of the time, it enabled us to nearly double the amount of shots that we were able to achieve had there only been a single main unit.

Q - When did you edit?

Gen - Because we had a budget we were able to hire an Avid which we installed in a room 50 yards from Stage 4 where we were shooting. Our editor, Eddie Hamilton, was fresh out of the corporate video world but loved movies. He appeared to have limitless energy and showed us a short film he'd cut called *Hallraiser,* about a mad axe murderer in a hall of residence at a university. We recognized a kindred spirit who was born from a love of *Star Wars*, so we gave him the job even though he'd never cut drama before. It was a brilliant decision because Eddie's technical expertise, creative knowledge, combined with his almost super-hero like energy levels meant that by lunch time each day he'd already cut the previous days dailies. This meant we could watch the scenes over lunch and plan how we would plug any holes or problems, or just feel damn fine about how good we thought it was looking. We also let the actors look at some scenes which boosted their confidence.

Chris - You have to be careful with this because one of the actors often became unconfident after seeing themselves. I don't know why because they were fantastic. The upshot of having this Avid and Eddie cutting away, aside from plugging holes in scenes, was that by the end of the shoot, Eddie had pretty much cut the whole movie. So within a couple of days of wrapping we actually sat down and watched the movie.

(top) A typical 2nd unit pickup. On the day, we were running late, the baby in the scene was tired and crying and it was unbearably hot. We ended up with no reverse shot of the store keeper, so the following day, the actor was brought back, a tiny set was mocked up and the 2nd unit picked up the shot.

(middle) Working with kids could present a nightmare scenerio. Fortunately, Heather Ann Foster was probably the most profesional cast member!

(bottom) Actress Heather Ann Foster aged 13 (left), with actress double Niki Ball aged 23 (right). We couldn't get a picture of them stood together wearing the same clothes as we only had one set!

Q - How did it look?

Gen - Terrible. It was the most depressing experience of my life. It was a mess, all over the place, full of holes and it just didn't flow. My directorial debut was a disaster!

Chris - I believe all movies are like that and the editing process is designed to smooth everything out and fine tune the story. Editing is an interesting stage because when you think about it, if there's a problem with the script, the editor has to fix it. If there's a problem with the acting, then the editor has to fix it. Problems with the camera, then the editor has to fix it. And so much of post production is just making something that doesn't work into something that does work. And after a few drinks, the cut didn't seem as bad as we thought, but we knew we had a lot of work to do. We discovered there were a lot of holes we hadn't seen and we almost immediately planned a quick re-shoot weekend where we shot an extra 50 or so shots without any actors. These were things like exteriors of buildings etc.

Q - So you held test screenings?

Gen - Yes. The first one was with a few friends and whole sequences were still missing, like the car crash at the end of the movie, so it lacked punch, but we were just trying to find out if people understood the story mechanics that were going on underneath the hood of the film. We isolated a lot of problems and did another re-cut, then we had to plan the stunt sequence which Terry Forrestal co-ordinated for us. Once we had this footage and cut it in the whole movie came to life. To be quite honest, none of us expected the crash to be as spectacular as it was.

Chris - So we had another test screening, this time for a large group of 30 or so people who we didn't know. It was quite an eye opener as we discovered that all our friends had been, on the whole, fairly generous with their criticism. We weren't really interested in finding out whether people liked it or didn't like it. There's nothing you can do about personal taste, we just wanted to know whether the story was working and we discovered all sorts of problems.

Gen - I hated the screening because everything that I knew was wrong with it seemed to glow like a beacon. It was demoralizing listening to

(right) Eddie Hamilton got the job to edit UGS because he had so much energy and loved movies with passion. His technical expertise also meant that we could sleep safely in the knowledge that EDL nightmares, optical effects and sound track laying would all be taken care of.

(left) Micro Set - To plug the hole that had appeared because of the opera subplot, we needed to shoot three new scenes with Lizzie listening to her walkman in the bathroom. The sets had long gone so Chris Burridge built a micro set, simply two sheets of plywood with tiles, a pipe and toilet seat that was screwed into a wooden box. The frame was kept tight and the illusion, helped by dripping water sound effects, was sealed.

what people were saying after Chris had stood up after the film and said to the audience *so 'tell me what's wrong with it?'* - after the invitation to tear it apart, they didn't lose much time. In retrospect this was brilliant because all the problems became apparent, and every problem had a solution, so we were able to go back and fix them all. So while the process might have been demoralizing, in the long run it was the best thing to do.

Chris - We discovered all sorts of strange things. When you write a script and make a film, you create a kind of road map for the story, the idea is that the audience never knows what's round the next corner - the problem is that sometimes you think they're driving along one road when actually they're off on a completely different road because of the way they've interpreted what they've seen. This happened in UGS with two characters - George was a character who was cut because everybody thought he was the father of the money grabbing loanshark. To everyone involved in the film it was an astonishing revelation that anyone could even consider this, yet there we were with thirty people all saying it to us. So we made some brutal cuts and George hit the cutting room floor. It was an important lesson to learn that no matter how confident you are in your own story, you need to show it to people to test out whether it's working on a purely mechanical level. Do they understand who is who and what relations they have and do they understand where they are being led by you the filmmaker. If they don't, invariably they get confused and bored and will fall asleep. And we've all seen films where we don't really understand what's going on, or something in the fabric of the story seems very odd, this is probably because you're thinking one thing when the director thinks you're thinking something else.

Gen - We began fine cutting the movie. Even though Eddie was like Buzz Lightyear with inexhaustible batteries, the whole process began to wear his enthusiasm down. Chris and I argued vehemently in the cutting room, often over frames, or the slightly different delivery of lines, and it was very hard work - not just exhausting but it was a spiritual and emotional marathon.

Chris - Because of the fact that three re-cuts of *White Angel* had happened in the past, each time vastly improving the film, I was adamant that there wouldn't be a single frame in the movie that wasn't absolutely essential. This of course flew in the face of what Gen wanted because she was so in love with the nuances and detail that would inevitably require a few extra frames here and there. Eventually we agreed on a cut and after a test screening we felt sure that it was the right one. It felt lean and mean and everyone was happy. I was sure that the horror of re-cuts as we'd had on *White Angel* would never happen.

George the handyman, a prominent character played by Richard Syms. During a test screening we discovered that the audience believed he was the father of a loan shark character who turned up later. This wasn't the case and we ended up having to cut the character to avoid this confusion.

We had a test screening for some industry people at Polygram. They came out and said it was good but it was too slow. I just couldn't believe it! I'd argued so aggressively to cut, cut, cut! I was sure there was nothing in there that could be taken out. But I knew from experience that even if you're sure, you could be wrong. I went to see Gen, who was recuperating with her family... *'they're all wrong!'* she exclaimed, *'but what if they're not?'* I argued. For eight hours we fought until Gen dug her heels in explaining that it's her art, her film, and nobody was going to *'fuck with it!'* Some time later, I'd secretly arranged for Eddie to drop by to argue the case for a recut of the first 25 minutes, the part of the story with pacing problems. Gen was still opposed, but intrigued to see what would happen if we did cut 15 minutes. An hour later and we'd done it. Having been away from the movie for a few weeks it was incredible to see how baggy it was. The three of us sat in the cutting room with our jaws on the floor saying *'why on earth did we leave all that junk in? - I can't believe we didn't cut it out before - It's so much better - Oh my God... !'* That's the cut that we released, short at 86 mins., but we felt it's better to have a well paced shorter film than a long baggy affair.

Q - UGS uses a famous bit of opera, why and how did that come about?

Gen - We knew we had to get the key sequence at the end of the film right. The car crash formed the pivotal question in the audience's mind, *'what happened?'* - it was also the moment that Lizzie remembered just what did happen, as she faced death falling from a window thirteen floors up in her towerblock.

Chris - We broke this out and did it eight weeks after the main shoot. We knew this one would be hard and fast and wanted to have as much energy as possible, plus half of it was a night shoot. It was shot over two days with seven cameras, some running in extreme slow mo. When we got the footage back and Eddie cut the sequence together it was jaw dropping. It was at that moment that I said, *'I don't know how or why, but we should put opera over this sequence, how can we do it?'* I found an old opera CD and I listened to all the famous tracks, until I heard one that seemed perfect. We put it on the Avid and watched it with the pictures. There was stunned silence as everyone in the room knew that we absolutely must use this opera music.

Gen - The challenge was to work out a way where we could plausibly use this music without it being self indulgent. Perversely this worked in our favor as part of the screenplay's problem had always been what reason was there for Lizzie to conveniently remember *what happened in the crash?* at the end of the movie. We used the opera as a kind of acoustic memory that Lizzie has, and when she finally hears it in all it's glory, it triggers a series a mental flashbacks. We then shot three new scenes to explain it's presence.

Chris - Again this shows that with low budget films as you don't have enough money to write the script and go through as many drafts as is needed, you end up being forced to shoot before you're actually ready. The secret to making this work is to treat the editing as yet another screenplay revision and not be afraid to go back and re-shoot or invent entirely new characters, subplots, scenes etc.

Q - How did you do the joy riding car crash sequence?

Gen - Terry Forrestal, the stunt coordinator on *The Runner,* came back to do *UGS.* He now had even bigger movies under his belt and he really did it as a personal favor. There were two sequences - the car crash and the high fall out of the towerblock. From a stunt point, the car crash was very dangerous but essentially a fairly run of the mill stunt, a car hits a pile of sand, flips over, skids to a halt and explodes. You could probably see this kind of stunt in a TV drama. The reason this sequence worked so well in *UGS* and why it looked much more impressive was because of the quantity and the diversity of coverage. We had seven cameras, all running as fast as they could so that they would slow down time on screen (slow motion). The main camera was on a very long lens about quarter of a mile away and this was running at nearly 300 fps, which meant that when the car flew through the air it slowed down so much that visually it looked stunning and smacked of

(left) Even though there were seven cameras on set, it was camera four, running at 250 fps, with a 500mm lens operated by Jay Polyzoides that was the one that produced the shot that gets the gasps in the cinema.

John Woo! It was a very exciting night and even though the crash seemed to happen over just one or two seconds, it felt like an eternity before Terry was pulled from the wreck.

Chris - Then came the explosion with special effects man Dave Beavis. He had a limp which was vaguely worrying considering he was blowing something up for us, but we knew his credentials and felt confident. We set up all the cameras as he rigged the car to explode. Just before we started the cameras I asked him *how far away do we need to be safe?* - he coolly took three paces back and said *here's safe.* So we called action, the cameras started and Dave pressed the button - BABOOM!!! - I was hit by a blast of heat and then my hair stood on end as I watched a wall of flame come at me with terrifying speed. I glanced over to Dave who was casually scratching his chin as though nothing had happened. I looked over my shoulder at the crew but they weren't there, they were twenty yards away, and running! There were a lot of expletives. None of us had any idea how big the explosion was going to be, but whatever we had imagined it was at least three times bigger. It was a splendid experience! As Jason Connery put it, *'how unlucky for Lizzie to steal a car only to find that there are 40lbs of semtex in the trunk!'*

Gen - The next day we had to do the high fall out of the building. What was supposed to happen here was Lizzie was to be holding on to some pigeon wire attached to the side of the building thirteen stories up, the wire would give way and then she would drop - again coverage and slow motion made this scene work as well as it finally did. In fact this wasn't as dangerous in terms of stunts because the stunt girl, Danielle, was on a very thin cable and was dropped several floors as the pigeon mesh came away from the building. Still the moment that she came away and dropped was absolutely riveting. Even though you know it's a stunt and she's on a wire, and that there's a crash mat at the bottom, it still looks like somebody jumping out of a twenty story window! Two people screamed involuntarily which helped seal the tension on set. There was a guy walking his dog some forty feet away who hadn't seen the film crew and looked round when he heard the commotion only to see what he thought was a young girl falling out of a thirteenth floor window and screaming! We had to stop him ringing the emergency services and calm him down with a cup of tea!

Chris - In Cannes a couple of people came up to me and said *'how did you do that stunt... with the crash and falling out the window that must have cost at least half a million dollars?'* I wryly smiled and said yes, it was a small portion of our budget that was well spent. In fact this entire sequence, with Union rates, including paramedic and the emergency services, the fire service, six extra cameras, pyrotechnic effects, location fees, cars to crash, special wire rigging etc. all came in under $30k. Sure it's a lot of money but for what we got it was the best money we've ever spent.

(upper left) Stunt Co-ordinator Terry Forrestal takes charge . (lower left)To flip the car before hitting the stationary car a pipe ramp was bolted to the floor and greased up. Terry checks the trajectory meticulously as he will be in the car when it hits at 60mph.

Q - What did you learn directing UGS?

Gen - It's so exhausting! You have to keep your mind on everything all the time, constantly thinking on your feet. The other thing that surprised me was the physical rigors of directing. Unlike producing, you never have a chance to stop, there is always a line of people queuing up to ask you questions and the only time that your brain can actually stop is when you switch off the lights to go to sleep, even then your mind is buzzing over the days rushes and thoughts on the day to come. The most disappointing thing about directing is the constant compromise that you have to suffer, camera movements are never quite as good as you visualize, actors deliver performances differently from the way you imagined and there's just not enough time, money or daylight to get what you want.

Chris - There was a funny moment on the first day when I was driving Gen home, She was very depressed and I said *'what's wrong?'* and she said, *'the actors, why couldn't they just act... better?'* First days are always dreadful, and actors tend to do things differently from the way you imagined, but that isn't necessarily bad work.

Gen - In a strange sort of way these compromises become your allies because it allows the other creative people around you, as long as you have chosen carefully, to flourish and bring something new to the movie. We tried to work with the most talented creative people we could find and then let them loose within rigid parameters so that they could produce their best work but at all times it stays true to the spirit, vision, story and style of the movie. There are times when the compromise is difficult to swallow but you have to ask yourself if I go for another take or another shot is it really going to improve what I want? It's easy to go for take after take in vain, hoping that the camera move will somehow get better or the actor will somehow do it differently. There's no hard rule here but I learnt to trust my instinct and not to waste time on something if it isn't working. I knew that I had a second line of defense in the form of Eddie in the cutting room, and he could work wonders with those scenes that I didn't think were working, as long as I had enough coverage.

Chris - Gen always says to me that there is one scene in the middle of the movie that she hates and regrets the day we shot it because I forced her to shoot it quickly the way that she did, because we were so behind schedule. Again with no rules and just opinion, there is no answer aside from the fact that Gen tends to forget about the other times where compromises were made and the compromises didn't show. You have to accept that some scenes will be disappointing and you'll end up hating them.

Q - Did directing ever get the better of you?

Gen - Yes, two thirds of the way through the shoot there was a day that I got so overloaded, stressed, hungry and frazzled that I became sick and I had to stop for a few hours and go and lie down. Fortunately because Chris is also a director and close to the project it was just a matter of him stepping on set and continuing to direct one full scene so we didn't fall behind. Interestingly, although we're not going to tell you what scene it is, you can clearly detect a different directorial style and strangely when I saw it I thought *'My God! That scene's great, I wouldn't have directed it that well!'*

(above) Danielle Da Costa, stunt double for Heather Ann Foster, wearing oversized costumes and wig, prepares to make her leap from the 13th floor whilst attached to a fan descender.

Chris - Then again when I saw some of the scenes that Gen did I said *'My God I wouldn't have done it that way and it works so well!'* Interesting how other peoples interpretation is surprising and that surprise makes it better.

Q - Chris, how did you approach producing?

Chris - My approach to producing was very different from that of Gen's during *White Angel* and *The Runner*. Gen had taken the weight of production on to her shoulders and had taken every single problem as a personal challenge. I on the other hand, being lazy, decided that I would delegate everything, and I mean everything. I had a really good team of production people around me and I told them that the only time that I wanted to hear from them was if we were about to be shut down, somebody was going to die or there is some impending disaster, otherwise, they would fix it. I also developed a peculiar condition called producers cramp which manifested itself in the inability to sign checks! Because I didn't pay anything until after the shoot, I didn't have to keep track of money, and because I didn't have to deal with the thousands of production problems that occurred, my brain stayed clear. Consequently I was able to keep tabs creatively and I became for want of a better description, the cast and crew therapist. Crew members would regularly come to me and bemoan some compromise or condition that they had had inflicted upon them and I would say *'there there, I understand and I care'*. They'd get it off their chest and we'd get on with it. I didn't realize how important this role was in terms of team building but it meant that everybody's gripe was heard and if something could be done about it, it was. Consequently from a production point of view, I wasn't stressed, I could deal with *real* problems in a level headed way and everything ran pretty much smoothly.

Q - Were there any major problems?

Chris - I don't know, the production team dealt with it.

Q - How did you get the music for UGS?

Gen - Harry Gregson-Williams had done the music for *White Angel* and then went to Hollywood to do movies like *Armageddon* and *Antz*. As *White Angel* had been Harry's first feature film and because of personal contacts we really wanted Harry to do *UGS* and Harry wanted to do it too. Unfortunately, the meager music budget we had was severely outweighed by Jerry Bruckheimer and *Enemy of The State*, so Harry had to graciously bow out, but did suggest his brother might do a good job.

Chris - We decided to have a look at a bunch of other composers but bizarrely enough Rupert, Harry's brother, was indeed the best choice. He tapped in to the style of music that we wanted, something contemporary and upbeat. It was important not to give it a Hollywood thriller sounding score and equally we couldn't just pack it with Brit pack band songs. I think the music is one of the strongest elements in the film because it is so left field from what you would imagine from a movie called *Urban Ghost Story*, set in Glasgow, and yet it seems to work so incredibly well.

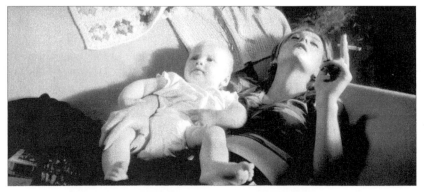

The mix of spooky story, urban setting and social realist with a slash of Hollywood treatment made Urban Ghost Story *an odd movie. A hit with the critics, film festivals and Hollywood executives, all of whom respond to it's unique qualities, but a failure with international sales as buyers just don't know what label to put on it, Ghost Story or Social Drama?*

(right) Directing is a physically rigorous job. Lack of sleep, mental exhaustion, severe backache, poor diet and a crisis of faith are common. (below right) Nightmare compromise.The pharmacist heist scene - it's the first day of shooting, it's the hottest day of the year, the location is a tiny pharmacy with customers coming in and out, there's no air conditioning and the lights make it like an oven, you are behind schedule, the baby is going mad... and it's a really complicated scene. It was eventually shot hand held and the sheer spontaneity of the way in which it was filmed actually helped the scene. Second unit picked up a missing shot the following day and the scene was saved.

Gen - We were also very specific with Rupert about where and how much music we were going to use and in comparison with our earlier films there isn't that much music in the whole movie, probably around 25 minutes. The music was composed of samples, electronic instruments and wherever possible, real performers. We recorded it over Christmas and all of us all got very severe food poisoning from a dodgy curry. The last thing you want to do when you're up against a deadline is to spend a day chucking your guts up, it's not what you call creatively inspiring.

Q - So you completed all your post production. When did you start to talk to sales agents and distributors?

Chris - After we'd recut the movie, we set up a screening in London, with high hopes because we knew that *UGS* was the best film that we'd made. One thing that had surprised me during earlier screenings is that at the end of the movie, people were in tears because they had found the resolution emotionally moving. We never expected people to cry at the end, but the combination of Heather's performance, the lighting, the music and the story worked so well that everybody started sniffling. We were starting to get a sense that the movie we had made actually looked like one thing, ie a ghost story, but was actually another thing, i.e. a story about guilt and redemption. This dichotomy was at the heart of the problems we were going to have as we tried to sell the movie. *'Is it a ghost story? Is it a social realist drama?'* We always said that it was a ghost story in a social realist world and that was it's unique position.

Gen - So the distributors watched it, all smiled and passed on it because they didn't know what box to put it in. In the absence of any good reviews or press they also didn't know whether people would take to it or not. Only one company was interested, Stranger Than Fiction, who were already acting as our sales agents for *White Angel*. We were very excited because they were about to sign a deal where they were going to have an influx of cash, which meant that they would have a high profile at Cannes and our movie would be their number one product.

Chris - We had run out of cash and the laboratory processing bill meant that we owed the lab about twenty grand. We were eager to get sales so we signed with Stranger Than Fiction and they began putting together all the bits. A design agency put together a poster, which was not what either of us had imagined, yet it seemed really fresh and original and we liked it a lot. So we went with it. It was bold red and very eye catching, which meant that when we flyposted in Cannes, it really stood out. The poster definitely worked for the movie and it also conveyed a sense that there was perhaps more to this than just a simple spooky tale.

Gen - We'd already cut a trailer for *UGS* which we liked, but Stranger Than Fiction asked for another one, and this time they said *'make it look like Die Hard with ghosts'*. So Eddie, who is already energetic to start off with, was caffeined up and locked in a cutting room for a day only to emerge eight hours later, eyes bloodshot and hair crazy, explaining *'it's done'*. We watched it and somehow Eddie *had* made it look like *'Die Hard with ghosts!'* It wasn't exactly a fair representation of the film but it was big and ballsy.

Q - What happened when you took UGS to Cannes?

Chris - We wanted a big push at Cannes so decided to take a few friends down with us, all of whom had worked on the film. All in, there were six of us and we were determined to make sure that everybody in Cannes had heard of *UGS*. Every morning we would go up and down La Croisette and fly post anything that didn't move - cars, telephone boxes, railings, Hollywood movie posters. Within a few hours they'd all have been taken down because it's illegal, so in the afternoon we went and flyposted again. The posters were just the red colored image that we had decided on for the film and its simplicity and boldness really worked in our favor. After a couple of days everyone we bumped into would say, *'Oh yeah I've heard of that film Urban Ghost Story'*. It was very labor intensive and damned hot but worth it.

Gen - We had three screenings which we tried to pack - the first was hard, but the second and third were full and the buzz on the street was that UGS was a cool movie. We approached every company and gave them an invite to come to the screening. It's really hard work knocking on so many doors, sensing rejection, but it has to be done.

Q - Did you pitch new projects when you were there?

Chris - One of the fun things we decided to do was to see how far we could get by talking the talk. Myself and fellow filmmaker Simon Cox decided to give it a try. We went to the Noga Hilton Hotel, targeted the companies who make and sell American style B movies, swaggered in, pitched, told them that we had half of the $2m budget already in place. Of course we didn't but it was really an exercise to see how far you could get with bullshit. Within an hour, we had an Anglo-Canadian co-production for a science fiction thriller that we hadn't even written, budgeted at $2.2m, to be shot in Wales and post produced in Canada. Clearly we couldn't pursue this because we didn't have the $1m that we claimed we had, neither the screenplay or even the desire to make it! But it did show how quickly you can put something together if you have something that you want to do and a bit of cash. We also dropped in on Troma, who had their new movie, *Killer Condom.* Over dinner

that night we came up with a concept for a new movie for them and the following day went and pitched it. It was called *The Breath of Death the Killer Fart.* We'd already constructed a story that held water. The guys at Troma got excited and again we talked the talk, but really didn't want to make an end of the world movie about an evil doctor and his Killer Fart potion!

Gen - One major distinction from our previous Cannes visits is that because we had a film that was screening, we were perceived as credible filmmakers. We were invited to parties and dinner and got to hob nob with fairly important people on a more level playing field than we'd ever experienced before. One of the reasons we also got a lot of coverage was because Jason Connery also came down to Cannes and worked very hard with us to get as much good press and exposure as possible. It's really important to have positive and

The poster for Urban Ghost Story *wasn't at all what we expected, but it was different, suggested there was more to the film than just a spooky tale, and it was bold. The red hue made it stand out when fly-posting and everyone seemed to remember the name of the movie.*

(left) It looks great in the photos and on TV, but Cannes is often exhausting, hot, sweaty, and downright expensive.

(below) Chris, with fellow film maker Simon Cox, try to sell a concept to Troma, agents for Killer Condom. Their movie, The Breath Of Death - The Killer Fart.

(bottom) Jason Connery was 100% behind the movie and spent much of his time in Cannes promoting Urban Ghost Story. On this occasion he is doing a live link for Euro channel Sky News. Getting your cast behind your film is extremely valuable because journalists are always up for an interview with an actor, they're just prettier than us film makers!

constructive support from your cast as they represent the glitz that Cannes is really all about.

Q - Did you sell the film?

Chris - Yes, one far eastern company from a small territory came to look at the trailer that Eddie had cut, the one that makes it look like *Die Hard.* They got very excited and bought the film on the spot. A couple of months later we discovered that they were going to do a 15 print theatrical release and we were opening against *Armageddon!* It was *Urban Ghost Story* vs *Armageddon!* I started to wonder whether the guy had actually seen the film. A week later I discovered that he hadn't and when he finally watched it he had a bit of a panic attack because it wasn't the horror movie he thought it was, and that even worse, *'it wasn't even in English but in Scottish!'* The next contact I had was when he asked me if I wanted to buy back 15 prints as he was unable to open the film.

Q - Did you premiere the film at a film festival?

Gen - We chose Edinburgh as our World Premiere because UGS is a Scottish movie, the people at the festival liked the movie, Jason lived quite close and the timing was right. We wanted to make a big impact and from the outset wanted to promote ourselves as filmmakers as well as the movie. We wanted the whole world to hear about *Living Spirit Pictures, Urban Ghost Story, Chris Jones* and *Genevieve Jolliffe.* We hired a publicist who cost us a couple of grand but in terms of what we got it was well worth spending as we had full pages in daily newspapers, excellent write ups in magazines and plenty of TV. Because of the work load in the office, Chris decided to stay behind in London for the first couple of days while I went ahead to do the press. As soon as I stepped off the plane it was interview after interview and before either of us knew it, the story ceased to be about *'Chris, Gen, Living Spirit* and *Urban Ghost Story'* and became *'hot new attractive female young film director makes startling debut film.'*

Chris - Suddenly Gen was everywhere in the press and I was mentioned in the fine print, if at all. It was the first time that either of us realized just how the world views the filmmakers, the producer is ignored and the director is given all the credit. Everybody thinks that the director is the only person who made the film. Whether they've heard of the auteur theory or not, they believe it. Sure the actors acted in it, but the producer, writer, editor, cameraman etc - were all

pawns in the director's grand view. It's sad because there is so much creative talent involved and yet only one person is recognized.

Q - How did the screenings go?

Chris - We had a great response and Q&A session afterward. But then something else happened which neither of us were prepared for. As we were being whisked away from the theater my cell phone rang. It was an agent who had seen the film and wanted to meet up with Gen. Then the phone rang again and it was another agent again wanting to meet with Gen. On the one hand it was exciting because this was a fantastic opportunity and at last we were being taken seriously by the business, but on the other hand, it was a real downer as clearly they were only interested in the *'hot new attractive female young film director who made a startling debut film'*. The positive press had really worked for Gen, but not for me. Whenever an agent would even consider me in the equation, they'd take a look at *The Runner* and *White Angel,* then say *'well they're not as good as UGS, clearly Gen is the one with the talent'*. Of course they aren't as good, we didn't know then what we do know now and the next film we make will be better than UGS! It's common sense. But they and the industry in general, just kept on coming back saying well we don't care what you tell us about collaboration, Genevieve is *'the hot new young attractive female film director who made a startling debut film'*.

Gen - It was difficult because we are both filmmakers and had hoped that one day we would get agents and a chance to move into the bigger playground. Here was this opportunity for me, but it was quite clearly for me alone. It caused a lot of friction between us.

Q - So did you sign with an agent?

Chris - After meeting several agents, Gen met up with one back in London and they got on like a house on fire. She really understood what Gen wanted to do with her career and seemed like she could open doors in Hollywood. Within days, and out of the blue, a FedEx landed on Gen's desk. It was a big studio werewolf movie budgeted at $15m, and they were looking for a hot shot new director. They'd seen *UGS* in Hollywood as we had a print out there. We can only surmise why they liked it, but it's probably because it felt like a unique slant on a ghost story. So Gen read the script and got back to them and before anyone knew it she was on a plane to LA being given the red carpet treatment.

Gen - We put together some concept sketches and asked Phil Mathews, an old effects buddy from *White Angel,* to mock up a werewolf model. Armed with this I marched into the office of the studio head and did the talk. The moment I landed and had my first meeting in LA, I started to get calls from all the other studios wanting to meet me. Hollywood seems to be constantly in search of new talent. The project still hasn't been made, with either myself or another director, and may never happen. I think this is part of the way of Hollywood movies, so many films seem to so nearly happen but falter before the final hurdle. This has happened several times with other projects too. It's really frustrating because I put all my personal projects on pause while I threw everything at these movies and at the end of the day you just have no control over your own destiny. It was also difficult because the opportunities were clearly for me and whenever I tried to bring Chris in, it just seemed to weaken my position.

Chris - When Gen got back from LA we had to have a heart to heart and accept that she was going to go first and that wherever possible I would be standing right behind her on her coat tails. I had to accept that that was the way the business works and because Gen and myself had gone through so much over the last few movies I knew that come hell or high water I could trust her. If you're in a film partnership with another person, I can't stress how important it is that you have a very frank and open minded discussion about what will happen if one of you suddenly gets an unbelievable opportunity, but that opportunity excludes the other. Gen and I had many unpleasant arguments which really boiled down to my frustration at the fact that other people were marginalizing me as a filmmaker. It was out of Gen's hands and I just had to come to terms with the fact that we're a partnership and that if she's going to get an amazing opportunity then hopefully I will be there for the next amazing opportunity. No matter how we looked at it we just couldn't turn away from Hollywood over the question of who gets the glory and who gets to go first.

Gen - A few months later we went to LA to present ourselves as more of a team and pitch our personal projects.

Chris - This was amazing because we'd spent so long complaining that we were ignored by the film industry, and there we were sitting in Dreamworks pitching. It became clear that the only thing stopping us from making a movie was the fact that we didn't have a fabulous screenplay that was ready to go.

Q - Did you meet Steven Spielberg when you were at Dreamworks?

Chris - Yes. We had a wonderful chat.

Gen - You said *Hi* and he said *Hi* back!

Q - So is it that easy to get to meet people in LA?

Gen - Yes and no. If you've made an interesting first film you can take advantage of their perception that you might be the next Tarantino or *Blair Witch*. Ideally this is the point at which they will say *'so what have you got next?'* And you'll put that 120 page script on their desk. They'll have seen the film because they have their own 35mm screening rooms and they'll say *'we can see from your film that you have talent but this film is too small for us, what have you got next?'*

Q - So you are starting to meet more important people who could help your career in LA?

Chris - Yes, since we've started to schmooze with more important filmmakers we've found ourselves in a strange new world. Once we were taken out for dinner to the poshest restaurant that I'd ever been in. I needed to go to the bathroom so

(above) Concept paintings by Alex Fort for the Werewolf movie.

(over page) a six inch maquette sculpted by Phil Mathews all helped illustrate what Gen wanted to achieve with the werewolf movie.

(right) Another Hollywood project that appeared was The Crow Part 4. *Chris and Gen met with Ed Pressman for* The Crow *franchise and pitched a concept about a blind samurai nun. They liked it a lot, suggested some changes, but like so many projects, they passed as they didn't see a female Crow as viable.*

I excused myself and went to the gents - as I walked in I was hit by opulence, the bathroom was polished marble. While peeing I looked at the urinal and said to myself, *'this has got to be the nicest urinal that I've ever peed in, there's all this water sprinkling down, it's made of marble and oh look there's even coins in the bottom'*. I look over my shoulder to see a row of normal urinals and realized with horror that I was pissing in an ornate fountain!

Q - How about people in the UK film industry?

Gen - Before I knew it, I was sitting at a table next to Nik Powell at the First Annual British Independent Film Awards for which I'm nominated as Best Director and Chris is nominated as Best Producer. We're up against films like *Elizabeth, Nil by Mouth,* and *My Name Is Joe.* We had no expectations and we didn't win, but it was another indicator as to how slowly and surely we were working our way into the British Film Industry. The deep irony here is that just as we're breaking into the British film industry both of us can't help thinking about Hollywood.

Q - Did you take UGS around the festival circuit?

Gen - Because *UGS* is an original film it started to get invited to heaps of festivals. Being a hard up filmmaker, when you get offered an all expenses trip to somewhere like Korea or Australia it's hard to turn it down, especially if you love travelling. I spent a good part of eighteen months in airport lounges, sat at dinner tables with important dignitaries, many of whom I don't even know how to pronounce their names. This all sounds great but the problem is that I haven't spent the time I should have spent on writing my next screenplay and whenever anybody says *I've just seen Urban Ghost Story, what's next?* I had to fall back on *'I'm writing and I'll let you have a copy when it's completed'.* I would have been in such a good position if I could just drop that screenplay on their desk, there and then.

Chris - It became a running joke. Whenever Gen went to a festival she'd spend the week before pontificating about how much great work she'd do on her screenplay while abroad in those foreign exotic lands, writing on her laptop and generally living the lifestyle of an ex pat creative.

Gen - Of course when you're on the plane you're asleep and when you're in an exotic place you want to go out and sample exotic food and drinks, see the world and meet the people. The last thing you want to do with your five days is work hard on that screenplay.

Q - Do distributors see the film at festivals?

Gen - Yes and there's no reason why, if you're so motivated, you couldn't cut some kind of deal. If you want to do this though, you really need to think about contacting all the distributors before the festival, sending them flyers and press packs, even a DVD trailer, then when you get to the festival you'll need to do fly posting, a lot of press and make sure that you have both NTSC and PAL tapes and DVD's for distributors who missed the screening. Don't leave this to your sales agent or it might not get done. You'll also meet other filmmakers and possible future work partners.

Q - Is it hard to keep going?

Chris - Fitting everything in is a real problem because amongst developing your new projects, dealing with sales and distribution, going to film festivals etc., you have to do things like answer the phone, do accounts and empty the waste paper basket, never mind have a life! Making a film generates an enormous amount of stuff to deal with and you shouldn't underestimate how much hassle that is. If you can find someone you can trust, delegate as much as you can, because the window of opportunity after you've finished your film can be short and you mustn't be tied down by the hum drum day to day of running a business. You need to be out there pitching and selling yourself as aggressively as possible.

Gen - This problem is exacerbated by the fact that you'll probably be broke and not able to pay an accountant to do your books, and then you have to do stuff like meet with the bank manager because you need a loan. All of this crap is labor intensive, stressful and generally counter-creative.

Every film will have it's premiere. Make the most of it as it will probably be one of the best nights of your life.

Q - How has UGS done?

Chris - It took us a while to secure a UK theatrical deal. At UGS's first Cannes market, Germany bought the film and a few other much smaller territories were snapped up too. Unfortunately our sales agent Stranger Than Fiction was not supplying us with the financial information that we needed so we were finding it very difficult to keep tabs on how well or how badly the film was doing. We had calculated that they owed us over $40k and it was becoming very frustrating because STF were not making contact with us - no return of phone calls and no response to faxes.

The sales agent/distributor dynamic with new filmmakers always seems to be fraught with discontent. Every low budget or new filmmaker we have met has complained about their sales agent and distributor. I think it's fair to say that selling a low budget film is very difficult and that unless you make something fiercely original or blisteringly good it's unlikely that your project will financially succeed. Even if you have made such a good, film there is still a very good chance that it will fail.

Eighteen months after the first sales, we finally got a meeting with Grace Carley who had by then left STF. I think she felt bad about what had happened, and I know there was some serious mismanagement that was out of Grace's hands. No one seemed to know what had happened with our film. No one would produce accounts or contracts and we eventually just had to sever ties. STF did legally give us the film back and we received a few thousand pounds from them. The problem is if you don't know which countries they sell your film to, what are you going to do? There was no one left to take legal action against and so we cut our losses.

Gen - We then made a deal with Lise Romanoff of Vision Films in California to handle all our world sales. She actually sends us checks. Admittedly not big ones as STF seemed to have done so much damage previously. She also sends us a report via FedEx ever 12 weeks detailing deals, the balance and a check if there is one due! So we now seem to have a reputable sales agent representing the film.

Chris - One thing new filmmakers tend to get very upset about is making sure that they have everything contractually tied up. It's just worth stressing that even if you have a strong contract, if somebody wants to breach that contract, or is forced to breach that contract by their own circumstances, they can and may well do so. A simple example of this is with our sales agents STF who, even though they were contractually obliged to supply us with information, simply didn't.

Gen - Again, it's a common story that the filmmaker ends up in some kind of dispute with the sales agent or distributor. It's very sad when you consider that every other person in the filmmaking process, from the camera rental companies to the actors, the caterers to the dubbing mixers, have all bent over backwards with their generosity to help you make your film only for it to end up not getting the exposure it deserves because there are so few sales agents and distributors to go to in order to sell your film. It really does beg the question why not sell the film yourself?

Q - What have you learned from UGS?

CASE STUDIES

Gen - When opportunity knocks you've got to be ready, you mustn't be distracted. If you're in a filmmaking team be prepared to face an imbalance of reward and remember the producer doesn't get the attention. If Hollywood is interested, have your next project ready. Don't have too much fun traveling the world with festivals. Get on to your next screenplay and your next movie. We've both learned that you need certain things, talent not being at the top of the list, but energy and enthusiasm being of paramount importance, original ideas and the ability to tell familiar stories in a different way, but probably the most important factor is your ability to get on with people and nurture your contacts. One strange thing is that you've probably spent years being ignored by the industry, then suddenly you're considered for twenty fully funded films where you'll earn more in ten weeks than you have in the last ten years. It's a quandary. Do

Chris and Gen in the Hollywood Hills prior to their meeting at Dreamworks.

you accept the first one that comes along or wait for the right one? It's difficult when you've been struggling for so long. Also you can't wait too long as people will lose interest in you.

Chris - One important thing is that UGS was a film that we wanted to make, not for a market, but for selfish personal reasons. Thereby it's unique and interesting, and that's what seems to get people excited. They don't want this movie, but they do want you to make one for them. We were also very lucky as we found Dave, our Executive Producer, who was the only person with the vision and belief and the ability to equip us so that we could make the movie. Without Dave we might still be on the phone and sending scripts out.

Gen - It's been echoed by other filmmakers that we've interviewed in this book, but if there's one thing you should do, it's MAKE THE MOVIE YOU WANT TO MAKE! Sometimes I wonder if making films is actually a curse. The strange thing and this is something that some people just don't understand, is that we just have to make movies. I've often thought of what it would be like to have a more normal job with a regular paycheck, especially when I had those days of running out of coins for my electricity meter and water leaking through my living room ceiling into my cold downtrodden London flat. But whenever I lost the faith, I'd go to the movies and the magic that happens on the silver screen is like a drug, I'm elated and addicted all over again.

Chris - Filmmaking isn't taught, it's caught! If filmmaking was a sport, it wouldn't be football, swimming or the hundred meter dash, it would be a marathon. More than anything, I've learned that going the distance is the most important thing. Some of your friends and peers will be able to run the marathon as though it's a hundred meter dash, the very lucky ones get helicoptered to the finishing line, many of your friends will fall by the wayside exhausted and disillusioned, but if you've got the stamina you'll make it to the finish and anyone who makes it to the finish, is a winner.

Q - How did the film finally do with UK sales?

Chris - You would think that we should have had our quota of bad luck wouldn't you. We made a deal with a company called Visual Entertainment, for a UK theatric and Video/DVD release. They gave us the whole spiel, how they were going to do amazing things blah, blah, blah! We went to their offices, large and plush, and they had some other good titles and we felt confident they were the ones for us. A date was set for the theatrical release and a plan made. We would release on two prints only and move them around the country. We would target specifically the theaters we wanted and work hard at getting great, localized PR. We had an excellent publicist who got us tons of coverage and reviews, most of which were glowing. I don't think we even got a single bad review. We opened extremely well in central London, and had a packed weekend. We also did well in Glasgow too. We were held over for a second week in both cities. One thing that worried me though was that I was doing everything for the release and the guys at Visual were doing very little. Every time I made a request they gave me an excuse. I was concerned that the poster was not strong enough, but they refused to do a new one for instance. And they asked me to handle all press too.

A week into the release, they told me they were so happy, they wanted to rush the DVD out. That seemed odd but I let it go. We made a great DVD with tons of extras and really cool documentaries, and we put a lot of effort into it. But all the time, Visual were screaming to move the release date forward! I was starting to smell a rat. The DVD was released and five days later I found out that they had gone bust, taking our money with them.

Gen - There we were again, having done everything right, only to find the distributor just going under and leaving us with nothing.

Chris - What was most upsetting was the fact that one person at this company had really seduced us, been our friend, and when the shit hit the fan, didn't even bother to call to tell us. In time I have dug around and discovered that there is an elusive character behind this company and many other failed video distribution companies. I can't name names for legal reasons, but he is as elusive as Keyser Soze!

Gen - A new company came to our rescue, ILC. Time will tell how we get on with them. We got the TV rights back and immediately cut a deal with David Wilkinson at Guerilla Films, who then made a great deal with the Universal Channel here in the UK. Then, believe it or not, before we got fully paid, the Universal Channel went under! Universal!

Chris - David, being the excellent distributor that he is, managed to control the damage though, and cut a new deal with the Sci-Fi Channel and ultimately we got back pretty much all our losses.

Gen - No matter what we seem to do, the awful truth is that whatever we got upfront is all we ever seemed to get. Due to this, you do ask yourself, why not self distribute? At least then, you're the one in charge. There's a lot to learn when you self release a film, and that can be a benefit of doing it, IF you have the time to devote to it and the incentive.

Chris - I guess that we all want to make films and not necessarily distribute. It's much more fun working with actors and cameras, dreaming up ideas and sitting in a cutting room etc., than it is shipping DVDs or arranging for trailers to screen in a theater three weeks before the film opens, or keeping inventory of your VHS stock. We want other people to do those jobs. The problem, it seems to me, is that bar a few honest small distributors such as David Wilkinson at Guerilla Films, you just can't trust anyone.

Q - Did UGS see a release in the US?

Gen - The film was picked up by a New York distributor, Panorama Entertainment, who wanted to start with a small theatrical release and then hopefully move to more screens around the country. Panorama wanted to focus on getting the film out to US film festivals, so we could drum up the publicity and then through that we'd get interest from the theaters. Not being in the US at the time and the fact that it would be very difficult to handle the campaign from London, we decided to follow their strategy.

In our contract with Panorama, we had a clause that the film would be released in three of the top one hundred markets. We thought that this would be fine and we all hoped that this would certainly be beginning with either New York or LA - both, however extremely tough markets to open in.

The film was released in Monterey (supposedly a very independent market), Savannah (we had played in the film festival there) and somewhere in Louisville, Kentucky. With the first release in Monterey, I was told that there was a publicist on the case, but when I flew out to California a week before the release, I discovered that no publicity had been done for the film and in fact it was opening that Friday and nobody had been contacted. I immediately flew up to Monterey and started trying to get interviews all over the place, trying to persuade the press to put it in the next day's paper - anything to try and publicize the film so people might know something about this movie rather than just seeing the title up in lights. But, it was too late. The limited press that there is in Monterey did do several articles, but they came out several days after the release, and of course the figures on the first night and the consequent two nights are vital to whether a film is pulled or not. We were pulled. With Savannah, we received more press as reviewers had seen the movie at the Savannah Film Festival. We had positive reviews, but we had very little in the way of paid print or radio advertising and the film was pulled. In Louisville, I found out that the film had screened before I could get there, so it was gone before I had a chance to do anything. Although out of this screening we did get an incredibly good review that read... 'what's the greatest horror film of the 90's? So far there seems to be a three-way tie between the low-budget British film 'Urban Ghost Story', Francois Ozon's ghoulish featurette 'See the Sea', and M. Night Shyamalan's new film, 'The Sixth Sense'"...!

There was a possibility of getting a theater in San Francisco to screen the movie, if we could get good press in the local SF papers. Luckily I had a good friend who worked for The Chronicle up there and who was eager to get a story out. However, although this was what we were told was needed to secure a theatrical release in that theater, nothing happened. The theatrical release was very disappointing.

Chris - Panorama told us that they were having difficulty with the film because as it was Scottish, it was deemed to be a 'foreign film' and therefore exhibitors were not interested. Both Gen and I were burnt out with dealing with the US release and combined with what we were still experiencing in the UK, we could not handle the thought of fighting for a better or longer American release. A mistake maybe, but very difficult to deal with constantly when you're in a country miles away.

Gen - I was also in the process of moving to the US and that in itself was eating up much of my time. There soon came a 'shouting match' between Panorama, ourselves and our investors as we tried to do the best for the film. People wouldn't talk to each other, it was kind of ridiculous as though we were back in nursery school. We realized that we were in a very awkward situation. Panorama had already spent money on the film's small theatrical release, and they told us they wanted to make sure that they got the right deal for the DVD/Home Video release and they were prepared to wait. We, however, were used to being 'screwed' by distributors and therefore were extremely concerned that this deal would never come. So was our investor who of course hadn't seen any returns at this point. We were approached with another offer from a different company and so we put them in contact with Panorama, however, neither wanted to do business with the other. We were being asked to pull out of our deal with Panorama and hand everything over to the new company. However, with legal threats back and forth, this wasn't an avenue we wanted to go down. Fortunately and somewhat surprisingly, while this was going on, Panorama told us that the 'right' deal had come along. One that offered the same type of benefits as the other company. We thought it sensible for the movie and for our investors to continue on the path we had started out on. The deal took several months to get into place and finally we nailed it down. April 27th 2004 Urban Ghost Story sees it's US DVD release. Finally it's out there!

Chris - In the next revision of this book we will publish the royalties and expenses for the US release to show the readers how much was spent, how much others took and how much we got. It will be very interesting I think.

Q - So what is next?

Gen - I've been out in LA for a while now and I'm loving it. I got a US agent and hoped to get work. After a year and only a few meetings, I was starting to get frustrated. I was a small fish in a big pond and the larger clients took precedence over me. However, my agent came up with a good solution. She introduced me to a manager who had fewer clients but a fair amount of clout. He handles my day-to-day meetings and pretty soon he got a production company to pick up one of my pitches. Now, the agent comes into play more because she can get my pitch to big stars within my agency which gives me a better chance of getting my stuff made.

My advice to any aspiring filmmaker and take this from my own struggles, once you have written and completed that passion project of yours, go back to your list of ideas and choose another one to start writing immediately. Start coming up with more ideas to keep your list long. You need to keep constantly pushing product out into the marketplace and not get tied up trying to set up one particular project. You never know which one is gonna hit and it could be the one that you thought no one was going to like!

Q - How different is the LA world from the UK?

Gen - There are two main differences. First, in the UK, if you make one type of genre movie, that doesn't necessarily pigeon hole you into making that kind of movie. In LA, they like you to stay within a certain genre because they know what they're getting for their money. The only way you can move from genre to genre is to either have a lot of power or make one of your films be a combination of genres and move to the other one in the script after that. I found this out when I tried to get a romantic comedy script going but I kept hearing 'aren't you a horror director?' So, I started coming up with more horror ideas, which I'm a great fan of anyhow, and all of a sudden more doors started to open. I suppose there is one other way to get out of a certain genre and that would be to make a movie on your own dime but then again, they'd probably pigeon hole you into that genre!

The second major difference is that in the UK I struggled hard against a 'can't do' attitude, whereas over here, everyone wants to make a movie and everyone says 'I love it!' Even if it is a bunch of bullshit, it's at least easier to get out of bed every day when talking to people with a positive attitude.

Chris - What I have learned is that now, after learning on three features, it just isn't worth going through the hell of making another film unless the screenplay is great. That's not true for everyone. I think a new filmmaker with little experience should throw caution to the wind and just go do it, in a smart a way as possible of course, but make the movie now. How else can you learn?

CASE STUDIES

Catherine Hardwicke

Q - Tell me about your background?

Catherine - I am from a tiny town in South Texas on the Mexican border, and we barely had a movie theater. I only remember seeing a few Clint Eastwood westerns and Cheech and Chong films. I went to architecture school and at the University of Texas and it unleashed all this creativity: I was sculpting my architecture models out of clay. I would dress up like my building designs and do a strip tease show that went along with the building presentation, just shocking them! One of the teachers finally said '*I don't know if you should really go into architecture, maybe you should try something else - something that encourages creativity -architecture tends to stifle it.*' I didn't really know anything about film, but I applied to UCLA's graduate film school in animation. In UCLA, you write, direct, produce and finance your own projects, so you're doing everything, which was great. People started saying, '*you're an architect, why don't you design my films?*' and so I started designing sets and doing other weird film jobs. On my first film, for Roger Corman, I was the set director and stunt person who rode the motorcycles, a 2nd AD, and a dialogue coach. I was also suddenly put in charge of all the weapons and a real uzi was stolen during the lunch hour by a PA I had assigned to guard the guns. It turned out that he had just left a mental hospital a month before.

Q - What was the first big job you did?

Catherine - I had Production Designed some $3m and $4m movies and somehow I got to design a $15m studio movie. It was a wacky film based on a TV show. In the early days when I went to interviews, people were like '*whoa, tone it down!*', so I started to make a conservative version of my portfolio, otherwise people would think I was '*out of control.*'

Q - Didn't they appreciate the vitality and energy you brought?

Catherine - Some people didn't, they were scared. Art departments are notorious because it is one element of the budget you can't control much. But, I know how long it takes to build things and how many carpenters I need, how to save money by taking so and so out. I love production design and I was fortunate enough to have had jobs with great directors. I really had a front row seat .

Q - Did you start writing screenplays at UCLA?

Catherine - Yes. I wrote two screenplays, one of which was commissioned by a studio. It was set to be made, but they changed head of the studio and it was shelved.

Q - Did you still know you wanted to do your own films?

Catherine - Yes. In between Production Design jobs, I wrote screenplays and took acting classes. Four years ago, I wrote one I really wanted to make that's a true story set in the Civil War, and I tried to get that going based on, '*look at me, I'm a production designer, I've got all this experience and some 2nd unit directing*'. People said, '*you're never going to get a period film made as your first movie*'.

Q - How long did it take you to write the screenplay for Thirteen and how did it come about?

Catherine - At the time, I was close to the thirteen-year-old daughter of my ex-boyfriend and I was kind of a stepmother to her, and we got along great. I started noticing Nikki was changing and was angry with herself, at her Mom and Dad and she was very negative. She was obsessed with waking at 5.30am and spending two hours getting ready for school, getting her look together, and I was like, '*wow, that's so radical for seventh grade!*' I had never spent more than five minutes getting dressed, but then I started to see that this is the culture. We're obsessed with the beauty myth. We preach it in every magazine. I thought I had to try and help her by broadening her perspectives, so I started taking her to museums and looking at photography and paintings and going to plays. She said she was interested in acting, but I thought that would make her more vain. Then I thought, good actors write their own material, they develop their own projects. Let's start reading literature. Then I got her with an acting coach and paid for her lessons and started filming tiny scenes and cutting them together. She seemed to like that, but she's so lively and brilliant that she needed more to keep her occupied, so I said, '*let's write a screenplay together*'. We had one week over Christmas holidays before she went back to school and I wasn't on a job. She came over here and she would be dancing around, listening to music, making phone calls and I would be like, '*Nikki, concentrate, help me here!*' But then I realized that was what the script was about, these interruptions. This kind of rap music energy of jumping around was good and I had to embrace it, and so the screenplay was made even more chaotic and crazy. So every time I wrote a scene, I'd go, '*come over here and act it out with me*'. So we'd read it all out loud and change the words and improve it, so that was the writing process with her. I was at the computer, but she would fly in with input and the voice of her character.

Q - How long was that for?

Catherine - Six days. At the end, I read it and thought, this had some power in it and I showed it to a couple of people who agreed it was radical and intense. I was so fired up about it when I went to a party a week later and I met this therapist who worked with girls that had done similar things. She said, '*let me tell my producer husband about it!*' I happened to have a copy in my car and so I gave it to him (Michael London), he read it the next morning, called me up by 10am and said, '*I really want to help you make this movie, let's figure out a way to do it*'. So Nikki and I met and he was like, '*okay, lets go*'. I continued diligently to tighten the script and take people's comments, but the essence of what we shot was there in those first six days.

Q - How long was the screenplay after six days?

Catherine - 105 pages and the shooting script was 95 pages. I kept cutting it down because I knew we didn't have enough money to waste one cent on anything extraneous.

Q - What happened after the meeting with the producer?

Catherine - I'm an impatient person and used to doing things right now. I had in my mind that I wanted to shoot it that summer because I wanted Nikki to be in the movie and I wanted her to be the right age. So I said, '*We're doing it this summer*' and I made a backwards calendar from there. I had another producer, Jeff Levy-Hinte, who liked it who I had sent a script to before that party. He met with Michael London and they got along and had different things to offer. Jeff was more hands on. He had produced High Art and Michael used to be a VIP at Fox, so he knew agents and talent people. I think Jeff was about to go to Cannes and at that point, we had about $1m committed, but we knew we needed more, because I wanted to shoot it in LA.

Q - Where did the $1m come from?

Catherine - Jeff has several companies in NY and has produced a couple of other films, so he has some investors. When he saw how obsessed I was to do this, he said, '*I'm going to pull something together for you'*. Through Michael, we got it to Holly Hunter's management company. One person there liked it and sent it to Holly and she liked it. We wanted to get an answer from her quickly so we could announce it at Cannes and try and raise more money. I got a call saying *'Holly will meet you tomorrow at 3pm in New York'*. I was in LA.

Q - Did they expect you to be in New York for that?

Catherine - They said, *'She won't say yes until she meets the director and talks over some issues.'* So I grabbed my video camera and ran over to Nikki's house and said, *'I've got to film you, your Mom and the house'* to show Holly how real and specific it is. Nikki was having a slumber party at my house a week later and she had hand made invitations. I said, *'Write one to Holly'*. So she wrote one and we went through the house, filming her in her bedroom, etc. I got to New York and met Holly. I was in awe of her. I showed her the tape and I gave her the invite to the slumber party. She said, *'This is a real person?'* I said, *'Yeah, I wrote this with this thirteen-year-old girl, and this is her mom'*. Holly is a great actress and very specific. Not that she copied Nikki's mom at all, but she loves real details, so the specificity was exciting to Holly. She was electrified about the idea, and was bummed out that she wasn't thirteen, because she really wanted to play the thirteen year old! She said, *'I'm not going to agree to this project right now because I think there are some things that are missing in the script for my character'*. It's not that she wanted her character to have a bigger part, because she knew it was a thirteen year old's story, but she wanted some shadings. I was listening to her and I started getting ideas too. I got on the plane and wrote on the way back, and she had new pages by Monday morning. She liked them and signed on. She had enjoyed the meeting, saw that I was listening to her and taking her seriously, which was reflected in the scenes.

Q - What about the other girl, Evan Rachel Wood?

Catherine - Any girls that had a growing reputation as actresses were scared of this part. Their agents and managers thought it could ruin their careers, but when Holly Hunter signed on, suddenly they were like, *'Oh, we'll be playing Holly's daughter, maybe we should take this more seriously'*. I think if I had directed before, they would have understood what I was trying to do, but I was unknown. Evan came in to the meeting and we got along great. She's a fantastic actress. One thing I noticed was that during auditions, some kids would get their hands on it and say, *'this thing seems like real life instead of some goofy little girl'*. There were a lot of stories people told me in the auditions about how they could relate to it. Even before Holly signed on, you could see it had really moved a lot of people. Others would be in the waiting room crying. They had been talking to their mothers for the first time about this stuff and I could see that good things would come from this.

Q - Did you have problems getting Nikki cast in the film since she had no experience?

Catherine - I wanted her to play herself but the producers were not so enthusiastic. She had an instinct for what she should do, and she was a natural talent. But, she had crossed over and was not innocent enough to play the lead. The first scene was the most intense scene she has in the whole movie, where she has to walk into Holly Hunter's bedroom and say that she's been molested. That was her first scene with Holly Hunter, Academy Award winning actress, and she pulled it off. One thing that helped was that I insisted the house was a real house and it would be already to go one week before we started shooting. Then I would have six hours a day with Nikki, Evan and Holly, where we would just rehearse and nobody would be allowed to bother us. The stuff is emotionally intense, and if we hadn't hashed it out on our own, we could never have made the shooting schedule. We could only have the kids for 9 hours a day, and then you had to take out the time for the meal and getting them ready, which left 8 hour days, and it was very strict.

Q - Do they have to have regular breaks after every hour?

Catherine - Luckily in filming, you have mini breaks anyway, but they have to feed them and they have strict rules. In the summer, they did not have school, so that was good. But the welfare worker would give no extensions, and you could not buy a meal penalty with a kid and you cannot pay them more to stay longer.

Q - How long was your shooting schedule?

Catherine - It was four, six-day weeks, eight and a half hour days. So really seventeen days, because normally you would shoot twelve hour days. I think part of the energy of the film was having that tight schedule. People were not sitting around, they were hustling every minute. It was go, go, go! With that schedule, we could never put a camera on a tripod, so it was almost all hand held.

Q - What were the reasons for shooting on Super16mm?

Catherine - We wanted to save money. The cameras are smaller and lighter, and we had a lot of bathroom scenes, like the OD scene and nudity scenes, so a lot of times we needed the space. A lot of times we did stuff on the fly, running around Hollywood Boulevard, Melrose. We somewhat had permits, but on Hollywood Boulevard we might have a permit for this thing and this place, but when we went from this location to another one, we just left the camera on and let the actors walk along and when police came along, Elliot would just put the camera down. We didn't have a permit for the scene on the bus. I just went up to Evan and gave her $1.50 in change. She said, '*What's this for?*' I said, '*You're going to pay the bus driver.*' She had only been on a studio movie and a TV show and had never done a guerrilla movie, so she was in shock. I said, '*Come on, it's going to be fine, it's guerrilla filmmaking, you're going to love it*'. So we got her to the back of the bus and the AD blocked the bus drivers view. He stood in the rear view mirror and with the little camera we would shoot. I asked people to move seats.

Q - No-one questioned you?

Catherine - If a cop came up, we would lower the camera. Since our camera was small, I think they just thought we were tourists.

Q - How did you plan your shots?

Catherine - I had my laptop and every day as I travelled to location, I drew little maps to show where we would put the camera and how to do the blocking. I would make a shot list and a timed schedule, saying, '*At 9am we have to be here, and at 9.30 we have to be on this shot*'. I was very detailed about what shots I would drop if I wasn't there by that time. Then I would make copies and give them to everybody. I would write on there how long characters would have for wardrobe changes. There are scenes where we choreographed three minutes of action, where we didn't cut because you feel a certain energy because the camera doesn't stop. The actors loved that as they got to stay within the energy. So then we would only have to do it two or three times. I would sometimes run to the trailer and say, '*Guys, we've got to go now*'. Even if they were in the middle of hair and make up, they would just run out. It took a lot of guts for Holly to go along with that.

Q - Did you do any pick up shoots?

Catherine - No. We didn't have any money to do pick ups.

Q - Did you have to do more takes because of using young actors?

Catherine - We didn't have time for more takes. Fortunately, Evan is a fantastic actress. She nails it. Nikki was really good and Holly would get it first time. The other thing is Nikki and Evan had worked with a coach and myself before we even did the rehearsal thing. On the first day of rehearsal, Evan, Holly and Nikki knew every line in that script and they knew internally where it came from.

Q - Was the video monitor useful?

Catherine - Yes, because sometimes there would be a scene where we would start here and go into five different rooms of the house, or we would do a 360* shot, and it's hard to follow the cameraperson. So for moments like that, you really needed to watch the monitor. Also, since it's all hand held, you don't know the framing. You can't just say, '*There's the shot, I know what I'm getting*'.

Q - How did you structure the viewing of your edit?

Catherine - We would get the dailies tapes and I would try and see them at lunch or in between lighting set ups. But I also had a plan in my mind to focus on the next day and not get too distracted. As a production designer, I've never missed dailies. It was weird. I was very fortunate to have this very experienced editor, Nancy Richardson, who has been a friend of mine for a long time and she would call me if there was anything she freaked out about.

Q - How long did the first assembly take after shooting wrapped?

Catherine - We had the editing suite for eight weeks. Nancy did a cut in the first week and we had a screening five weeks later. We got a lot of UCLA students to come and then we had a few more screenings over the next weeks to get notes. It was going to be rated 'R' so only a few kids that were fifteen came in and saw it.

Q - Did you make changes after the test screenings?

Catherine - Yeah. I made a three-page questionnaire and said I wanted everybody to fill out everything they thought. So people were honest on paper, and if there was something that a lot of people repeated, I took it into account. I also like things to be very tight, like my script. I got it down to about 93 minutes. So if people suggested a scene to cut, even though I was freaked out, I would usually go ahead and try it.

Q - How did you approach the music for the film?

Catherine - That was scary. There's a lot of music in the film as they are teenagers and are always listening to a song. A lot of Nikki's influence in the movie was raunchy, nasty outrageous lyric hip-hop and that's what informs her life, so I definitely wanted a lot of hip hop stuff. But, we couldn't afford the most famous ones. You go through this process of trying to find people that are good and not signed yet and that was ambitious. Some of my friends wrote stuff for the movie.

Q - What was the stage from getting the final cut to Sundance?

Catherine - Since we shot so late, Sundance gave us an extension of a month after the deadline. They saw a tape and then a couple of weeks later they told us we were going. It was a race to Sundance and we worked over Christmas. We didn't show it to any distributors before Sundance. We wanted all the distributors to see it for the first time at the first Sundance screening

Q - Did Fox Searchlight come on board immediately?

Catherine - We sent the script to Fox when we were trying to get money for it, and Peter Rice was like, 'We wouldn't make this movie, but maybe I'll see it at Sundance and buy it'. During the first screening, Peter called Michael and said he wanted it. But there were two or three other companies that wanted to buy it, too. There were days of haggling, but it sold.

Q - What was the audience reaction like?

Catherine - It was in a 1500 seat theatre, and you could hear the audience through the movie laughing and gasping. Then you could hear a lot of crying at the end. Then we got up for the Q&A and it was a positive response. People would stand up and say pretty emotional things about it. At one of the screenings, I left and went to a party and didn't want to go back for the Q&A, but decided I should, as there was a big turn out for a midnight screening. It was the best Q&A ever. One guy stood up and said, '*I hated your film.*' Somebody else said, '*I think every parent should see it*'. Then a fifteen-year-old girl stood up and said, '*I was a heroin addict*' and people got so into it. Holly had a great time. She said she saw two different men, who were fifty something, and they were outside crying. She said they were not the kind of people that looked like they would even go to the movie.

Q - What was it like working with a big actress like Holly Hunter?

Catherine - She is intense. She didn't come with an assistant, and no one drove her. She's very down to earth, but she is very serious about her work and wants the right space and the right things. As a director you have to be really on top of your game every second. She does not like to be directed in any way that is technical. It all has to come from inside the character and internally motivated. It has to be real and specific. If she was making breakfast, we had real food for her to make it. That made it real and for me too. The reason I could survive with Holly is because I knew it really well and I'd seen this first hand, I'd felt it and I'd acted out every scene with Nikki ten times. I never would have made it if I hadn't done that.

Q - How have people responded to the film?

Catherine - People are shocked, but it's not that shocking if you really look at it. There's no violence or sex in the movie. A journalist said, '*I have a thirteen year old daughter and I hope mine doesn't turn into a junkie / prostitute like these girls*', and I said, '*What are you talking about, there's no prostitution?*' She goes, '*weren't they prostitutes by the end with all that money?*' Some people get so scared by it that they imagine it's ten times worse than it is! One reason is because the style is hand held and immediate. There's also a reality where they might have heard their daughter say something similar to them the day before.

Q - Has Thirteen opened doors for you?

Catherine - Yeah. The day that LA Times article came out was the day my life changed. People suddenly took me seriously and other agents jumped onto my team. You get a little overwhelmed by it all. People have said, '*you'd better capitalize on this while you're hot*', and I agree. I have a lot of energy and haven't had a day off in a year and a half, since I started writing this.

Q - What common mistakes have you come across?

Catherine - I could have cut my script even more and I wish I had. There were one or two scenes people told me to cut out, which I didn't, and I wish I hadn't wasted time editing them. As I watched the filmmakers I work with, I noticed some things I thought were good and some things that were bad. One thing was about temperament. Some filmmakers I've worked with have a very even temper and some go off and get mad and create very negative feelings on set. Sometimes filmmakers are not open to listening to other people's ideas. And, sometimes people don't fight for what they truly believe. I almost fell into that trap with the sprinkler scene. Everybody was against that scene because we didn't have the money for it. I said, '*We need the scene for this reason and I will go on Sunday and get the sprinklers and pay for them personally!*'

Q - What single piece of advice would give a new filmmaker?

Catherine - The biggest thing for me is that the whole film came from something not concocted or a plotted out, but it came from the heart. That gave me energy. If it is something you don't believe in, you won't have the passion and physical energy to get your shit together and convince a million other people to believe it. You've got to feel it.

CASE STUDIES

Renè Gil-Besson and James Portolese

BOXES

Q - How did you guys meet, and what are your backgrounds?

James - I studied TV, Film and Radio at Indiana University, then moved out to LA in '94. I started as an assistant, coordinator, 2nd AD, production manager etc. I was doing cool things, but I was still working for someone else. Rene and I met in '98 and discovered that we had this similar film ' background and that we liked the same things. And we knew that we both wanted to make a movie about being trapped in a box. Rene sent me an e-mail saying what do you do in the day, between 8am one day and 8am the next. I wrote down a ton of things and a week later we saw *Fight Club*, which knocked us on our asses. I wrote the script in four days and that is what we shot. We didn't change anything at all. We didn't try to sell it. We did it to make a statement. Before hand we had made a feature length video called *Decade* about a college experience I went though. We learned what to do and what not to do on that, and it cost $4k.

Rene - I studied film in Miami and I realized that things were going the digital way. So, I wanted to learn more about it because my background was more on the artistic side. There was a lot of liberation in understanding the technology.

Q - When you were doing your film for $4k, where you working?

James - Yes. We'd work during the day and meet up at night and shoot at weekends, from Friday to Monday. We really learned how to do it, so when we got to *Boxes*, we had it down to an art. We shot the movie in eleven days.

Q - Was Decade a short?

James - It was a feature about fraternity hazing. It was a really tough subject. A lot of people couldn't relate to it. Something like *Boxes* everyone knows what a cubicle is. Everyone knows what it's like to eat lunch out of a stryrofoam container.

Rene -That was literally the questions we asked during casting. Tell us what it was like before you broke out of your box. Everybody is from somewhere else. Every single one of them knew what that meant. If they didn't then they didn't get a call back.

Q - Why did you choose to do Boxes?

James - We had a couple of other ideas. One guy wanted us to help him make his movie - Rene would direct and I would produce. This guy thought his script was perfect because his friends were telling him so. It was garbage, so we walked away, and then we had an epiphany to make *Boxes*.

Rene - An eruption. Everything came out. E-mails going back and forth. It was a script created by e-mails. We even used the junk e-mails that you get - the mass e-mails you get that tell some ridiculous story or joke? We tried to incorporate those. There was one that was *Top 10 Stupid Things Your Boss Can Say'*. We took those made the boss say those things.

James - Like how the boss mangles clichès. and how all the women are referred to in nicknames. The cute eager office girl, the no job-crunch girl and every time a name is said, the sound drops out. It is a very corporate way of looking at things.

Q - The budget was $300?

James - Yes. We didn't want to spend a lot of money and we knew we could pull it off.

Rene - People would ask us what our budget was for certain things and it would literally be whatever we had in our pockets at that time.

Q - What was the rest of the money spent on?

Rene - We spent $79.87 on tape stock. Hair and make up, $140. That was that one thing. Catering, $32 next door at Bird's restaurant. Craft service, $33.25, which was for peanut butter and jelly and cookies.

Q - How many characters were in it?

Rene - Three main characters, and around fifteen lesser characters.

Q - Did you do open casting for these parts? And, did they know that it was for no money?

Rene - Yes. We put an ad in *Backstage West*. We got a garage full of headshots. It took us a month to go through them all. I was floating around Sony at the time, so I got a conference room there to do casting. We called everybody in and lined them all up outside. Everybody knew they were coming in on a free movie. We cast for two or three days.

James - We put the ad out in December, weeded through the photos and the second week in January we started casting. We shot a month later.

Rene - We would shoot two nights during the week and then Saturday and Sunday. There was a seven page bar scene at the end, and we shot at The Continental in LA.

Q - Did you pay for that location?

Rene - No. Just a thank you in the end credits.

James - And they let us have the party there when it premiered on IFC.

Q - Was there are lot of shooting on the street?

Rene - Yeah. We were shooting a lot of weekend at Sony where I was working. We had shot two weekends and one night there during the week, and we had structured the script so it was mostly phone conversations between people. So we would do the lead actor's coverage and then turn around and find another office space in the building and shoot the other caller. My boss had given me permission to be there and shoot something over the weekend, but on the second weekend when we were wrapping up, her boss came in and we got busted. Two days later I got let go.

James - So we had to shoot the office scenes where I worked.

Rene - We went in the backdoor and shot all the coverage. Midway through the process, we tried an experiment. We had one actor reading his lines off camera to the other camera, and then we said let's try it where you walk in and interact with his environment while you are on the phone with him. It kind of worked and it was early enough where we were able to place that dynamic into the film. So in car scenes, one guy would be in his office on the headset, but he is in the car sitting in the passenger seat with his headset on having lunch while having a conversation with whom he is talking to.

Q - So it was a matter of making it work with what you have?

Rene - You have to be open with your story. A lot of times the first things you come up with is what you have to let go.

Q - How did you meet Chris Gore (from Film Threat)?

James - We met Chris at a party in NYC. We had previously sent him three copies of the movie, but it never got reviewed. So we went to go talk to him, and we became friends. Over Labor Day weekend he called us and said, '*I just watched your movie. I love it. What can I do to help?*' He did a review and a long interview with us and spread the word.

Q - What did you shoot the movie on?

Rene - We shot it on a single chip Sony camera, the PRV-8. It was the cheapest camera out there at the time. It's not a great looking movie as far as resolution, but at the end of the day if the story connects with the person who is watching it, it doesn't matter what you shot it on.

Q - Did you have any lights?

Rene - Most of it is practical. We used a China ball once, which is a Chinese lantern with a regular bulb in it.

James - We also used one clip light that's still in my apartment. It cost about five dollars.

Q - What did you use for sound?

Rene - It was a combination of a little wireless mics and the camera microphone. I had a friend that had another camera and he came in and shot a lot of the B roll. So, when I had sound on that one, I switched to that one. I mixed it up in Final Cut to make it sound it good.

Q - Was there anything else about production that what crazy?

Rene - One day before we premiered, I realized that I had missed one insert shot of when he drives into a Taco Bell and orders something in the drive through. So the night before I drove to KFC and ordered something, filmed the speaker box and edited it in the movie. If you look closely at the movie, any time you see and insert of a finger it is either James or myself.

James - There were times when Rene would give me the camera and I would film myself walking out a door. Or I would be in an elevator and just rolling on people coming in and out.

Q - How long did it take to shoot the whole film?

James - Four weeks. We cast it in February, shot it in March, cut it in April and premiered on May 1st at Sony.

Q - Did you have to get release forms?

Rene - We just cut people's faces out. Or if we were at Ikea we would blur the sign.

Q - So you edited this in Final Cut Pro, were you doing it as you were going along?

Rene - A little bit. It was good to know what kind of coverage we had, so whatever we shot on a Tuesday and Thursday, we could pick up over the weekend. It is always good to cut while you are shooting. In case someone cuts their hair or something.

Q - How much footage did you end up with?

Rene - About 20 hours. There was an economy in the way we were shooting. One thing I recommend is to learn editing as it is going to save your ass when you are making a movie. Every project that I have ever been worked on has been the same, *'how can I get what I need out of this?'* And it all has to do with editing.

Q - Some people say that DV equals amateur?

Rene - You still need a style. We are not fans shaky-cam, nor are we totally into slicked out kind of stuff. We want to make something that works. I have a Steadicam, Jr. and I actually shot everything from my camera with it, so we do have tracking and dolly shots. And, the whole movie was shot with a wide-angle lens. It was never messy.

James - There is only one tripod shot in the whole movie. It happens right at the fifty minute mark. The opening sequence is a six-minute shot, one take. He gets out bed, showers, shaves, dresses, watches a little TV and is out the door. In a big film like *Goodfellas*, that would take three weeks to light. The first shot of our movie is all backlit.

Q - Did you have any ideas for style when you started the film, or was it just to tell a great story?

Rene - For myself, a lot of the way that I operate is on instinct. I try to storyboard, but it is hard because things change. I wish I could be more prepared, but at this level, you just don't know. You could spend four months preparing for something and then at the last minute, the rug is pulled out from under you. So, prepare for that. Prepare for being sensible about how you are going to deal with that and then incorporate your style.

Q - What was the time scale for post?

Rene - Because I had done some precutting while we were shooting, it only took me two weeks. A composer also did some music for the film. I had done some music videos for him in the past and we have a good working relationship. So I approached him with the script and he read it and said, *'What do you want me to do?'* When I had a completed scene, I would send it off to him and say that we were looking for a *Fight Club* kind of vibe. He would then create something new. Then I would send him the next scene after that and he would build upon that. So it is almost wall to wall.

Q - So he was doing it while you were cutting it as opposed to watching the whole movie and planning it out?

Rene - Right. He came up with good stuff while I was trying to fuse certain areas together. A few minor edits here and there and we got everything to work. The next couple weeks were about special effects and color correction.

Q - Did you use any other effects packages other than Final Cut Pro?

Rene - After Effects. I have a partner that I came out here with who has won two Emmys for the graphics work he does, and he did our end titles and some graphics throughout the movie.

Q - What kind of sound effects did you do?

Rene - This may sound misogynistic, so forgive us. If a woman was talking, we would put in baby crying. Or, a dog yelping.

James - Or lots of inappropriate or radical sound effects like if someone would drop a paper document on a desk, we would put in a window shattering. So it was what the actors hear in their head. We really enjoyed playing with sound and images.

Q - Did you use any film look effects?

Rene - On the first film we did, we used Cinelook, but we found that it was heavy in the magenta. It was very grainy and added a lot of noise. What I would do is have the image on one layer, copy it on the top layer and reduce that layer by 50%. And, then on the lower one I would deinterlace the even fields and on the lower one I would deinterlace the odd fields. You create a blend, and you get back the resolution you use. Now, Flicker Filter on Final Cut Pro does this. It took six nights to render the whole movie.

Q - When you were happy with the cut, did you screen it for a bunch of friends?

James - No, the night before we premiered, Rene called me over and I walked across the street and we sat there and watched it. There was nothing else we could do. It's like putting a child out into the world.

Q - What did you screen it on?

Rene - We premiered at the Backstage Theater on the Sony Pictures lot and just plugged it into their Betacam system, out of the same camera we shot it on, and pressed play.

Q - What was the next stage?

James - Once we finished it, we started making copies with videotapes from the 99 cent store, and mailed them blindly to people. A month later we got the call from IFC. They said they liked the movie and started negotiating on the phone.

Rene - There is a shot in the movie where the lead character in the movie is looking down from the 7th floor down at all the 'ants' milling about in the lobby. Right before I received the call from IFC, I was depositing my last check from being let go in the Sony lobby where we shot it. I sat down on a couch and looked up and said, '*I am one of the ants. Where do we go now?*' As a filmmaker, when you finish something you wonder what you are going to do next. Then my cell phone rings. IFC wants to buy the film!

James - Mark Stolaroff at Next Wave was a huge supporter of the film as well.

Rene - Chris Gore got us into No Dance, but they would not put us into competition because we had a distributor. They did say they wanted to showcase us, have a screening of it and have us talk about it.

James - It was such an awesome community and exciting to be a part of it, and to meet other filmmakers. They had a party every night and you would meet the filmmakers and learn about their stories. Everybody wanted to know how you did it. It was the first time Rene had ever seen snow! It was great week.

Q - What has happened since the film came out? Did you get agents?

James - Yes. Chris Gore, our guardian angel, sent the film to his manager. He got it on a Thursday afternoon and on Thursday night I got a call from him saying that he wanted to meet us.
A lot of people wanted to know what we were going to do next. Our manager has been really good, but the most attention that you get is generated on your own. Managers and agents just legitimize you in the eyes of Hollywood executives.

Rene - Mangers and agents will never find you work. They will get you meetings, but you get you work. They will do the legal part of it. But, at the end of the day, you pound the pavement trying to get a job or create that opportunity.

Q - How did the Guiness Book of World Records happen?

Rene - Chris Gore. He read somewhere that some Canadian filmmakers had made a film for $500 with the same name, then called us to let us know a mistake had been made. We e-mailed Guiness and set them straight. We just sent in the materials and then we heard back saying that we were in. We put it in our publicity.

Q - What advice would you give other filmmakers?

James - Just go out and do it. Have your next project ready to roll.

Rene - If you get offered a gig after your film, do it even if you think it is crap. It is a good way to practice your craft and you meet other people, which will lead to other things.

Sean McKittrick   Richard Kelly

DONNIE DARKO

Q - Did you both go to film school?

Sean - Richard went to USC and I went to UCLA. Although I was a physiological science major, I had been interning at film companies like Columbia Pictures all through college. I met Richard at the end of our senior year. We were introduced by a mutual friend who needed a producer for his graduate short and we hit it off creatively. We had the same insane taste in material.

Richard - I got a fine arts scholarship to USC, but two days in I was secretly wishing I had gone to film school. I found a loophole where I could drop the art major but keep the scholarship money and so I wheedled my way into any film class I could, applied to the film program and got in. USC is the hardest film school to get into with the highest profile in terms of its close proximity and ties to the industry, and it has the most money. It's an incredible resource. I fought like a madman to show people I could direct and thankfully, my work wasn't rejected by my peers.

Q - Where are you from?

Richard - Richmond, Virginia. I was under the assumption that in order to get into film school you had to have already made a lot of films. I was very intimidated, I'd never even been to the state of California before. I just showed up with a couple of suitcases, and then I heard through the grapevine that they want raw artists. They don't want some smart ass who's already made twenty student films. That is a strike against you.

Q - So you met in your final year?

Richard - I was prepping an absurdly ambitious grad film. An actress had worked with Sean and he was suggested. The film was really a self financed test for me as a director, and Sean as a producer. It's 35mm, with elaborate digital effects.

Sean - There were over 70 effects shots. The story made barely sense but we knew the acting wouldn't, so we played up to the visual style and let the actors satirise themselves unintentionally. The technique and craft behind it made us proud. We made if for $60k. It is 40 min long, on 35mm and has all these visual effects. It looks like it cost three or four times that.

Richard - That gave us the confidence to say we could do *Donnie Darko,* making it visually and technically far beyond the scope of what the budget allowed.

Q - How long did it take to do the grad film?

Richard - We finished shooting it in August '97. I went off to work at a post production house to try and find someone who wanted to be an editor as I had all this elaborate sci-fi footage but no money. I made friends with Sam Bower while doing the midnight shift as assistant runners. He's like, *'I'd love to take a look at it. I'm an editor. I don't have anything to edit'*. He had been training on the Avid and we would come in late at night and look at the footage for months. I said, *'If you do this for me and I get a feature, you can edit my feature'*. So come September of '98, a year later, the film was finally finished.

Q - How long was it after you graduated that you got Donnie Darko off the ground?

Richard - I graduated in May '97. Sean went and worked in development at New Line Cinema and in the summer of '98, I showed Sean my first draft for *Donnie Darko*. We went through the script, got the length down and in the November '98 (a year and a half after graduation) we sent it to three assistants at agencies in town. We said, *'Please read this and if you like it, show it to your boss'*. We struck gold at CAA and within two weeks, everyone had read it.

Sean - They brought him in and signed him in the room.

Richard - I was writing *Donnie Darko* while in the midst of the anxiety of having borrowed $60k from my family and thinking the grad film would never get finished. If you have a short to show people, it's pretty much worthless unless you also have a feature script. If people like your short, they'll say, *'That's great, what else have you got?'*

Q - Did CAA sign you off the script as the writer?

Richard - Yeah, and I said I wanted to direct. I had this crazy grad film, but it shows I can move a camera. Then they sent the script out in Jan '99, all over Hollywood.

Sean - They wanted to team us with a big brother producer, so we had a meeting with Ben Stiller's company which had a big deal with New Line at the time. It turned out to be a really long, horrible drawn out process as everywhere it went, the only people who love it deemed it unproducable. They said we should turn it into a teen horror movie.

Q - Was it unproducable because they didn't get it?

Richard - You can't have a rabbit talking to people.

Sean - They said there's no real enemy or hero. They didn't realize Donnie was the hero in the story. We were 24 at the time, so we'd walk into a room and we'd sense their chuckle. They want young people because they are cheap and work fast. But as a director, no-one wants to roll the dice on a first timer.

Richard - Especially when they saw the over the top mystery science theater short and they thought it was serious. They said, *'Is this how the acting is going to be in Donnie Darko?'* and *'We know you can't direct actors, because we saw the short'.*

Sean - They said this sometimes to our face and sometimes to the agents. Some people said they would buy the script as long as Richard didn't direct it. They wanted an experienced director.

Richard - They planned to just buy me off and give me some sort of bullshit credit.

Sean - Over the year, I got many calls from people asking if he still wanted to direct it. They were waiting like vultures for us to give up and let them turn it into whatever they wanted. Obviously Richard was never going to abandon his story as it's his thing. We waited it out. We were unaware that Jason Schwartzman loved our script.

Richard - Jason wanted to play the lead. We met with him and he immediately came on board. The development execs loved to declare something as dead, especially if it's not theirs and all of a sudden it had been resurrected by Jason Schwartzman and people were calling. Our line producer warned us that there was no way we could make it for less than $4m unless we chopped thirty pages out of it which would have meant the whole story would have fallen apart.

Sean - We started to get serious financial interest from companies saying, *'We will give you $2.5m'*.

Q - Were these companies or private investors?

Richard - Pandora, based out of Paris. Ernst Goldscmidt used to run Orion. He was the first legitimate financier to come in and say, *'I get it'* and he ended up making the film.

Sean - Then Sharon Sheinwold at UTA sent the script to Nancy Juvonen. She read it and accosted one of our agents and said, *'Can we be a part of this?'* Our agents called and said, *'Drew Barrymore is really into your script'*.

Richard - Two days later, this is early March, we were on the set of *Charlie's Angels* sitting with Drew and Nancy and they said they loved the script and Drew said she wanted to play the part of the teacher.

Q - Did they say they wanted to bring anyone in for it?

Richard - Drew said *'Don't change a word. I'll play the teacher, let my company be involved in producing with you guys and let's go'*. The budget went from $2.5m to $4.5m. Pandora was willing to up their financial commitment to $4.5m based on her market value.

Q - Did you surround yourself with an experienced crew early on?

Sean - Richard is very specific. He probably has more knowledge than some DPs about cameras, so we needed to find someone that was experienced enough to appease the fear of the financiers, but wouldn't come in and take over.

Richard - One resume I saw had second unit for *Blade Runner* and *Close Encounters* on it. We were like, *'We can get someone who shot a Ridley Scott film!?'* It turned out Steven Poster hadn't shot a feature for two years and was taking some time off and just doing commercials. He loved the script and we hit the jackpot. We got a legendary DP to do this minuscule budget film.

Sean - He came in and said, *'Disregard our age difference'* and *'I don't want to be a director, so don't worry about me wanting to direct your movie'*. He's one of the greatest people we've met.

Q - Did he get what you wanted to do?

Sean - Yes. Not to mention from a pure financial standpoint, all talent and creativity aside. He is such a well connected, well respected cinematographer that he got us ridiculous discounts. We shot on anamorphic lenses with negligible cost. He literally was the primary reason why the film ended up looking so good for so little money.

Q - What was your relationship with the producers like?

Sean - They were all good people. They knew I was Richard's partner on this and beyond, so I acted like a filter for Richard and kept all the bullshit away from him so he could do what he needed to do, which was direct the movie. I learned a lot from Tom which was great, because I wasn't a *'numbers'* producer before, but now I understand all the ins and outs of it.

Richard - It's vital for a new filmmaker to have a producing partner of the same status in their career. There are a lot of producers who will turn their back on the director and sell out to the studio. It's better to enter a situation as entrepreneurs. A new director needs a producing partner who can schmooze the actors and the studio, but also get their hands dirty and find out how much things cost.

Sean - A good producer knows the tension between the gaffer and the DP and knows their names. For the first three days, I'm sure a lot of the crew didn't know who either of us were. We were like two PA's running around.

Q - Did Flower Films give you freedom to choose your crew?

Sean - They were our partners. They were not a studio and they were there as a buffer to make a call to an actor's agent, to help us get what we wanted.

Richard - From the first meeting, they said, *'We don't want to come in and tell you how to do things'*. I think for them it was a learning process to do a movie this small. They had done two studio pictures, *Never Been Kissed* and *Charlie's Angels*.

Q - How did your relationship work with them?

Sean - We knew better than to show them the short film. People misunderstood it so badly. As far as them working with us, they were great. They were so busy with *Charlie's Angels* that they weren't too involved until a few weeks before shooting, and in the end, they were with us most of the time.

Richard - Casting a movie is like a pool party. People show up but nobody wants to be the first to dive in, they're all dipping their toe in and wavering. Drew Barrymore dives right into the deep end before anyone else and then everyone wants to go swimming with her.

Q - Did Jake Gyllenhaal come on board through Drew?

Sean - Jason had to drop out because of a scheduling commitment. Then we had to recast and Jake was perfect. Richard and I brought in every actor in that age group. You could see it on Richard's face the moment Jake walked in. It was obvious halfway through the meeting it was done.

Q - How did the shoot start?

Richard - From the moment Drew came on board it was 23 hour days. The most expensive shoots with the most extras and the biggest sets came first, like the school, the Steadicam and the hallway - we dove straight in. The Steadicam took 6 hours to get one shot.

Sean - To be honest, it was fine. We knew what we were doing, we had a great crew and we meticulously planned each shot and storyboarded everything. I think people underestimate just how important it is to get along with your crew. We became friends and still are to this day.

Richard - Dealing with the cast was easy. They are all big stars, but the nicest people. They all loved the script. We had to fire the caterer and a second make-up artist.

Sean - We had originally cast this actress for 'Grandma Death' and done all these make-up tests on her, to age her thirty years. Three days from her scheduled start date, we couldn't find her. She was having a face lift. When you're doing ageing make-up, you have to stretch the skin out to apply the make-up and we couldn't touch her face. The make-up artist said the actress couldn't smile, couldn't move her face and still had some blood lines on her jaw. We had a mad rush to find someone new with her agent still arguing that she could do it, missing the point that she was supposed to be 100 years old, not 20 years younger. Nancy and I just set up one day and brought in thirty people. We sat, read a bunch of resumes, picked our top three and Richard chose the best. She was awesome. We were glad it happened in the end.

Q - Who did the effects in the film?

Sean - Amalgamated Pixels. A bunch of guys from various huge visual effects companies had just formed a new company, so they needed a calling card. They cut their price down to do the film which was great for us. Richard was very specific about what he wanted, we didn't have to invent anything. It was all already in Richard's head exactly how he wanted to shoot it.

Richard - We had some additional scenes, like all the stuff in the bathroom, our opening title design and a couple of other things were done by a friend of ours, Kelly Carlton. Never underestimate the power of friends working in the business who want to work. If the script is good and you're articulate about what you want, you can take advantage of those resources, because people who are desperate to work don't have the opportunity as they don't have access to good material.

Sean - Everyone knows it all comes back around at some point. If you help people out, they will return the favor.

Richard - We owe a lot of favors.

Q - It must have been great to have the editor who is your friend on board as well?

Richard - With Sam, at first they said, *'absolutely not'* but we didn't budge. He had edited an independent feature that had been released straight to video. They had to concede in the end and let him come on board.

Q - Did you have a lot of extra coverage?

Richard - I knew exactly what I wanted so I didn't shoot a lot of extra coverage. When the first week's dailies came back, I was a little concerned that we hadn't shot enough, but there was a positive reaction to it.

Q - Did you have to do any pick-up shoots after you had wrapped?

Richard - They didn't think of giving us the money to do them, but we didn't need to. We did one extra shot three months after we'd finished principle photography, to clarify one more story point and Newmarket paid for that. Thankfully, no additional shoots were necessary.

Q - How many cameras did you shoot with?

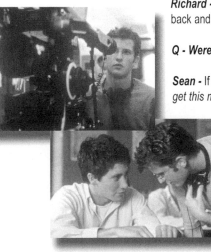

Richard - Three. The second unit would often be working simultaneously so I would go back and forth.

Q - Were there times where you couldn't set up complex storyboarded shots?

Sean - If Steven started to smell disaster, he'd say, *'Richard, I'm not going to be able to get this much'*. We really planned out our elaborate shots. Our key grip, gaffer and in fact the entire crew were amazing and able to put together everything we needed.

Q - Did you storyboard before your DP came on board?

Richard - Steven and I spent a few afternoons going through the entire script, doing a shot list and the visual design behind the film. I then communicated our more elaborate set ups to a storyboard artist. To save money, we went to every location to take photographs to replicate the camera angle we were going for. We just matted out the photographs as pseudo-storyboards.

Sean - It helped out our production designer as the ideas were so specific. Less is more when being specific on shots. It ripples out throughout each department.

Richard - We were very specific with certain color schemes. The film had a kind of comic book stylized vitality to it. I wanted to represent an idealized, stylized version of the East coast.

Q - What kind of inspirations did you have?

Sean - The photography of *When Peggy Sue Got Married* was our biggest reference point and Jordan Cronenweth style of lighting for night exteriors. We looked at Kubrik's movies for a lot of references. *Lolita* was a big influence.

Q - What was your pre-production and production schedule?

Sean - We shot the film in 28 days. We had a little over 2 months to prep. 3 to 4 of those prep weeks were Richard, me and Steve and an office assistant, as we needed those weeks to get crew. We wanted it ready for Sundance, so we had so little time to edit. I forget how many weeks, but it was ridiculous.

Richard - This is where it helped having two editors as we had them in two rooms next door to each other, and Richard would just go back and forth. In the future, I'd prefer to work with one editor, but in this case, their styles complimented each other well.

Sean - Given that we had a lot of footage and the film was running very long, it was great to have two people in there trimming. It was a major challenge to get this film under two hours.

Q - What was your first rough cut like?

Richard - Two and a half hours. I started freaking out about how to cut a half hour out and have it still make sense.

Q - Did you have test screenings?

Sean - No. They didn't want to have to pay. All we cared about was making Sundance.

Richard - We thought it would be a disaster. You have to have made about thirty movies before you can do something challenging and new. If you do that too early, you get criticized for not having made a name for yourself first.

Q - Did Newmarket come on board after it was done?

Richard - We did one additional shot for Newmarket when they came on board. They didn't officially purchase the film until four months after Sundance, which was hell because we thought, *'The movie could go straight to cable.'*

Sean - Our financiers got hold of some arbitrary number of minutes that needed to be cut out from some buyer, and took it as gospel. As each week went by, the film still hadn't sold, people started getting scared, wanting to cash in and were thinking, *'Fuck it, let's cut our losses and take the $1m for the pay cable premiere'.* When we finally closed the deal, all the editing duties were passed onto Newmarket. Luckily, their exec said, *'It's a little too long, here are some of the things we want to remove',* and we just went into the editing room and did the majority of it. The first time we ever saw the things that didn't click was at Sundance, so after the festival we sat down with Newmarket and cut.

Q - Was that an amazing experience watching it in a theater?

Richard - It was crazy. There were ten hours of press a day. We had been working straight for nine months. A lot of people hated our movie being at Sundance as it's a festival for really small movies with no stars. We presented a $4.5m film with stars and special effects, which represented a studio film invading Sundance's turf.

Sean - We didn't realize we resembled the big end by using visual effects and movie stars. We looked like we'd already arrived and who were we to show up at this festival? We made the mistake of going to the awards. The only reason it was fun is because we were sitting next to the *Dog Town and Z-Boys* guys. Literally, everyone was cheering for every movie that was shown and then when our movie came on, there was a polite applause.

Q - What did the audience think of it?

Richard - The audience loved it.

Sean - The elitist critical community and the film snobs dismissed it as an '*impressive failure*'. We had our 2nd screening for a real audience. At Sundance, like most theaters, they lock their prints with all the reels together. We were just over halfway through the film when reel 4 or 5 came on back to front. We had a visual effects glitch in one of the shots, so we had a new reel sent up from LA. They cut it in backwards by accident. It took an hour to unwind the whole thing, taking that one reel from the plate, flipping it over; re-rolling it in the opposite direction and putting it back in, so we had to shut down for over an hour in the middle of the movie!

Richard - It was a 9pm screening. I had a Q&A for ninety minutes while we were waiting, so I ended up talking about my childhood.

Sean - The audience ran out of questions, so I got up and then they ran out of questions for me. One of our cast members came up and started doing this comedy act. No one left and seventy five people stayed after the film played, for more Q&A.

Q - Newmarket saw it at Sundance. Was it then that they approached you?

Richard - They didn't want to show interest because they couldn't compete with the others.

Sean - There was a lot of gossip going round the distributors. They didn't want to buy it, but they didn't want anyone else to buy it, because if it turned out to be a success they would have made a big mistake. The film got tainted by that. No one wanted to buy *Memento* either, and Newmarket distributed that and look what happened.

Q - Did they stay interested?

Sean - They kept quiet and then they waited until everyone had backed away from it and could get a good deal.

Richard - There was still fear because Starz pay cable was offering a lot more than they bought the movie for. We called Nancy and we said we needed Drew to convince the powers that be at Newmarket that this needs a theatrical release.

Q - Was it in your contract that you had to have a theatrical release?

Sean - There were no guarantees. We had Drew ready to come in to the meeting like a godmother and save the movie. She was trying to cut to the chase, '*Are you playing this in theaters or not?*' The guy said, '*Of course we are*'.

Q - Could they go back on that?

Richard - The decision was theirs to make. They intended to put it in theaters, it was more of a negotiation based on this clause that they didn't have to. That was what scared us.

Q - Were you unhappy with the way it did at theaters?

Sean - I was fine with the marketing, up until it came out in theaters. They booked too many. Sometimes, timing just doesn't work out in your favor, though it did find an audience.

Q - Did you find a lot of people were coming up to you asking about your next film at Sundance?

Richard - A lot of people who were like, *'Their stuff is not commercial and it doesn't work'* and also the film didn't perform at the box office. They were like, *'your stuff's really interesting, but it will never make money'*. We are doing bigger budget stuff now, we need studio support. I don't think we'll ever make another movie for as little as we made *Donnie Darko*.

We certainly need to prove that our material is financially possible and it can make a return on the investment. Thankfully, in overseas and home video release *Donnie Darko* has proved to be financially viable.

Sean - The power in filmmaking is with all the actors and there was such an overwhelming response from the acting community for *Donnie Darko*. This really helps because when we send a script to an actor, you know they're going to take it seriously.

Q - Once you finished Donnie Darko, did you have other scripts ready?

Richard - Yeah. I've already written my next five scripts that I want to direct.

Q - Had you done those before Donnie Darko?

Richard - I'd written two or three of them before we even started shooting *Donnie Darko* and then I wrote a couple more while waiting for someone to distribute it. Anxiety about my future makes me a prolific writer. Rejection makes me more confident.

Q - Is there anything you would have done differently?

Richard - I wish I wouldn't have let the stress and anxiety of post production and distribution get to me, it kept me up at night when it's just a process. I was convinced that at any given day, they're going to dump the movie.

Sean - One thing I did want to change was that you don't need to have a *'fuck you'* mentality. We felt like we had to because everybody was looking at us like we were these young nobodies who don't know shit.

Q - What advice would you give new filmmakers?

Sean - You can't roll over because the moment you do, everything will be steamrollered.

Richard - Write something that you can make really cheaply. Stand your ground. I wouldn't be sitting here right now if I hadn't stood my ground and been a pain in the ass. Get people to work for you for cheap. Inspire people. Inspire your crew, actors and they will do anything for you.

Sean - Don't subscribe to the *'I'm a struggling filmmaker ...oh my script's great but no one gets it'*. I believe if it's good, it'll find its way. We worked our way into the system with a great piece of material which is how it got through. So don't go crying that your stuff is great but no one gets it. If it's great, it will find its way.

FROM JAWS 2 to THE SINGING DETECTIVE

Keith Gordon
filmmaker

Q - Have you always wanted to act?

Keith - Yes, although I was interested in filmmaking before acting. As a teenager I ran around with a Super8 camera making really bad unfinished films. I worked as an intern at the Museum of Modern Art in NYC and occasionally they would run obscure movies for me. I grew up in Manhattan. I had no concept of making a career out of filmmaking and acting, it was just something I enjoyed. My parents both worked in the theater, so I did know something about the acting world. Somebody saw me in a school play and said, *'why don't you come and read for our professional play'* and I got the job. Somebody else saw me in that play and said *'we're doing a movie, why don't you come and read for it?'* so I got *Jaws 2*. This acting career not only paid the rent, but gave me the chance to have this sort of paid apprenticeship. I worked with a lot of wonderful directors, particularly Brian de Palma, John Carpenter and Michael Bennet. They took me under their wing and answered hours of nauseating directing questions.

Q - How did Static come about?

Keith - Mark Romanek was a 2nd assistant director on a film I did with Brian de Palma, called *Home Movies*. Brian taught a filmmaking course at Sarah Lawrence by making a film. He, George Lucas and Francis Coppola put some money in and the students did everything else, with Brian directing. They hired professional actors, myself included. So it was half film, half classroom. It was perfect for me, because I got to be treated like one of Brian's students and listen to him explain why he was doing what he was doing and how it worked. Mark was on the crew, and I really liked his short films. He came to me and said, *'I have some connections to money, maybe we could work on something together?'* He had a character he thought I'd be good at and he knew I wanted to get into production, so we wrote a script together and I was also one of the producers. Mark directed it. It was called *Static*. It was a success in the UK, but our independent film movement here had barely started. This was before *Sex, Lies and Videotape*, so no one knew what to make of it, and we never got any real distribution. It did well with the critics and audiences, but people who worked in Hollywood thought it was weird. The major studio people barely made it through the opening credits. Jonathan Crane, who was this young entrepreneur who managed John Travolta among others, wanted to get into production. He really liked our film and said, *'what do you want to do?'* I said, *'I want to direct'* and I had a project I thought could be made inexpensively, which was this book *The Chocolate War*. My pitch was based on the fact that the book had sold hundreds of thousands of copies and I that I thought we could make the movie for $500k. He bought that pitch.

Q - When was this?

Keith - It was 1987. He told me to write the script, and he gave me $500k to make the film and tremendous artistic freedom. I didn't have people staring over my shoulder. I was completely spoiled by the experience. It was a good film to do on that kind of budget. Almost the entire piece took place in and around a boy's Catholic school, the perfect location being an abandoned one in Seattle. We paid the Catholic Church a few thousand dollars for unlimited use of it over a period of months. I was also lucky with the author because the book had been owned by various studios. They were sick of the fact that the book had been a huge literary success for years and yet the people who had owned it had never gotten it made and had_ tried to make it had taken all the darkness out. I said, *'I don't have any money. I can't pay you a fraction of what you deserve, but I intend to make this, not put it in development* hell. And I intend to honor the book you wrote and not make some terrible, watered down version of it'. That was music to their ears. We paid $2.5k for a year option, and when the film got made they were due something like $60k, but I think they were just pleased to see it get made. They also had all sorts of back end deals so if the film made a lot of money, they were protected, and so it wasn't like we were saying, 'give us your book for free'.

Q - Did you have distribution?

Keith - Jonathan Crane' company, MCEG, which financed it, also distributed it. I got to help decide which theaters to put it in and I was carrying a print around, showing it to people. If we couldn't get the right theater in Dallas, we would come back to Dallas later. We did one city at a time, treating each city as its own thing. It probably wasn't the most economically lucrative method, but I loved it as a filmmaker and MCEG didn't mind, since they were trying to establish themselves as a distributor and, it was their first time too, and they wanted to do it in the classiest way. So it was a good experience.

Q - How long was the process from the beginning of the theatrical run to the end?

Keith - Probably close to six months as we did it such a slow way. We played seven weeks in LA, maybe more. It was my first education in the power of reviews with independent films because we'd go city to city. You'd go to Houston and if a couple of big papers there didn't like it, you were gone in a week. You'd go to Dallas and if the papers there did like it, you'd be there forever. It made money because we made it for so little and did nicely theatrically, although it didn't make a profit in the theaters. It probably broke even theatrically ñ the grosses covered the ads, basically. But we did very well with video. This was a time for video when the profit margin per unit sold was very high. It sold about 75,000 copies on video, which returned a profit of something like $30 a shot. With that and the cable sales, I think it returned a reasonable profit for MCEG In terms of cost to return, it was the most successful film I've made. I have long since given up on the thought of ever seeing back end, profit participation money for myself on movies and I don't worry about it. Hollywood's accounting practices make it very unlikely one will see any money that way, even if the film does quite well unless you are powerful enough to get 'gross' points, and not the after-ever-expense-we-can-think-of-to-throw-in 'net' points. My agents and lawyers all sweat about the definition of net profit on each deal and I'm like, 'why are we arguing about this? We're never going to see it!?'

Q - What happened after that film?

Keith - I was called about a project called *A Midnight Clear*. I think Tom Cruise had been involved at one point. It wasn't surprising that studios hadn't jumped on it as it was a dark, anti-war film without much action, but it was a great piece of material. I said I wanted to make it with a reasonable amount of money. I wrote a screenplay from the book and we started to find finance for it, which took four years. It was a nightmare. It wasn't a commercial film. We'd think we'd got the money and then lose it, or companies would be interested but want to change the script too much and other people would say, 'get us these big stars for all the roles'. Several times we were actively casting when the money fell through. Finally a foreign distribution company, cable and a new American distribution company put together $4.5m. Some of the money people freaked out on seeing the dailies, because they saw the characters sitting around talking about existentialism and not having gun battles. If they had read the script carefully, they would have known. It was a bad experience in terms of artistic interference. There were changes made in the edit, over my objections, but I'm still happy with the final film. There were no changes that were so appalling that I wanted to take my name off it. A lot of egos came into play. One person would call at 2am and say, 'I hate this actor. Change his performance' and five minutes later, someone else would call up to say, 'that's not true. Don't listen to them, listen to me'. So that was a lesson in politics.

Since then, I've gotten better at making the money people feel involved rather than seeing them as the enemy. It's their money and they have a right to be concerned. I make really positive contact with financiers as early as possible to make them feel welcome. The more you leave the door open, the less people feel obligated to try and push their way through. I think it was Truffaut who said, 'the way to be a great director is to know exactly what you want at every moment, but to have no ego at all about giving it up the second there's a better idea'. I think that's true, and too many young filmmakers don't realize that.

Q - Was there a long period of time between each film?

Keith - A ridiculously long period. *Chocolate War* was 1987, so we're talking about sixteen years. I wrote my first draft of *Waking the Dead* in 1991, it was released in 2000. *Mother Night* took five years before we shot it. My present projects range from 1 to 7 years of work so far, which is normal and you must factor that into your life. Expecting a miracle, like shooting six months after you've written your script, is like thinking *'I'll win the lottery, that is how I'll pay the rent'*, so you're likely to be disappointed. I try to be very clear eyed about the fact that this is a very slow, painful, inch by inch process and you go down lots of blind alleys and meet lots of insane people.

Q - Especially as a lot of new filmmakers assume that if they get into Sundance, they've made it.

Keith - Absolutely and it's not true. It gets no easier to make your next film. It gets easier to get a job. If your film goes to Sundance, people like it and your goal is to get a job directing an episode of a television show or directingsomeone else's movie then yes, it does make a difference. If you're going to be an independent filmmaker and tell your own stories, it doesn't get any easier. I've spoken to independent movie makers who grossed $40m on their film, they've said, *'yeah, they all want to make my next film, as long as it's commercial'*. If your next film is a difficult subject, it doesn't make that much difference. So people should not operate under the illusion that they will *'make it'*. You don't. It's too difficult and economically challenging a world. I've managed to use television to make money to live on. That made it easier. The cycles in business make it harder. Videos were worth a lot, now they're not. German financing was hot, now it's fallen apart.

Q - What is your present project?

Keith - It's a project with Ethan Hawke and Jennifer Connelly. We only need $5m, which you'd think would be easy, but because it's a dark and difficult subject, none of the usual suspects will commit to financing up front, instead they say *'we're interested in looking at distribution it when it's done'*. We're now investigating other ways of financing.

Q - You'd have thought having those names would guarantee you some sort of pre-sales deal or financing?

Keith - If I wanted to make a violent, love on the run movie about two young, hot bank robbers, we'd be in production tomorrow. But this is from a disturbingly sad and dark novel about a deeply wounded family, and an incestuous relationship between a brother and a sister. Ironically, I think those very things make it a more commercial film in the independent world, because it deals with incest and things that are sexually taboo. Indie films that challenge taboos are often the films that attract the most interest, like *Boys Don't Cry* or *Kids* or *The Crying Game* or *Monster's Ball*. They all did very well theatrically, but people are still nervous to commit up front to make films like that. Particularly in a politically conservative time.. They'll have the meeting, they'll tell you how much they like it, but it doesn't mean they will write you a check. But, on any film, going from nothing to 'almost there' is easy.

Everybody will say all sorts of encouraging things. That's not that hard part. The hard part is getting to *'here's a real, cashable check for $1m'*. I had finished contracts for one film, but it didn't mean a thing as the company never really had any money, which we'd only discovered after months of trying to work through the deal points. They were hoping while we were making the deal that they would finally get their money together, but they didn't.

Q - It's so hard to get pictures out of a company that have gone bankrupt?

Keith - Yes, there's 8 million lawyers arguing over who owns what asset. It's a very common thing. Even moderately large companies are constantly being bought out by other companies or going under. I had that happen on *Midnight Clear*, which was a perfect movie for Europe and never got released there. The company that owned the foreign theatrical rights went belly up and it was tied up in litigation. By the time we got it out, it had already been released on video in most foreign countries. Grammercy Films made

Waking The Dead. By the time we released the film, they had been bought by Universal and half their executives had been fired. New people came in who had no allegiance to the project.

Q - Have you dealt with co-productions at all?

Keith - Not much at all. I wish I was more knowledgeable about it. Everything I've done so far has been financed by one source, other than *Midnight Clear.* That was a mess, but I didn't put that deal together. After that, I produced my own films because I didn't want so little control again. I've made a couple of films in Canada, but they weren't co-productions. We took advantage of the tax breaks and exchange rates. Sale/leaseback is something I'm exploring for future projects. However you do it, the challenge with co-productions is; Everybody wants to put in a third of the money and get ownership of half the movie. They'll say *'we'll finance US, but we get all cable and video rights'.* That means you'll never get a theatrical distributor, because no distributor wants an independent movie without cable or video because that's where they make their money.

Q - What have the budgets been of your films?

Keith - *Chocolate War* was $500k, *Static* was $1.1m, *Midnight Clear* was $4.5m, *Mother Night* was $5.5m, *Waking the Dead* was $8m and *The Singing Detective*'s was $8m. These are not super small. Anything between $2 - $10m is tough right now. They either want to spend $40m or more for an obviously commercial, mainstream film, where you can make an offer to Tom Cruise, or people want to do a $500k video film because there's so little downside. The films in the middle are hard. There's enough money so people feel they can get hurt, but not enough that they feel they can't lose.

Q - How did The Singing Detective come about?

Keith - I thought the original BBC series was amazing. Not long before his death, Potter wrote a script adapting it as a feature film, and I read it and loved it. He condensed it all, change the setting to America, and really re-thought it, both in terms of content and style. The years went by and nobody made it. The script ended up with Mel Gibson who realized that it needed to be done for under $10m, to go back to the core of what it is; essentially an experimental film, instead of trying to blow it up into a big, studio type movie. Potter talked about his frustration with *Pennies From Heaven* because it got too big. He said in interviews he felt it lost its 'home-made' quality. So Mel brought Robert Downey in and they started looking for people to do it on a smaller budget. They came to me about twelve weeks before they wanted to start shooting. I had a meeting with ICON months earlier, but never heard anything for months, so I was shocked when they called. Downey felt comfortable with me doing it and he liked my take on it. So they called me at the last minute. Preparation time is everything on a small budget movie and we didn't have time for that. The clever things you do to help the budget we couldn't do, as Robert had to stay in LA. So it was scary and challenging, but ultimately satisfying.

Q - Did you go to Sundance?

Keith - Yes. We sold it there. *Static* was at Sundance in '85 and *Waking the Dead* was there in 2000. Sundance is such a rush of activity, press and trying to sell your movie you don't get to do much else, whereas, I love going to the festival, just watching movies as a civilian. I'm grateful for Sundance as we did sell the movie, but it was hard work. Four companies were interested, but Paramount Classics had a passion for it so we were happy selling it there. It's experimental, the audiences aren't going to know what to make of it and some of the critics are going to compare it to the original and grumble; it's going to need that careful, loving, passionate approach to it, because if it's thrown out there, it's going to have a hard time.

Q - You also have good cast which should help?

Keith - Sure, but in the end it's still experimental and surreal and you're going to have to seduce people. If an audience is unprepared, they won't know what to make of it. At the Sundance screening, the audience were real film fans, not critics and industry executives, and that had by far the most applause and laughter. They all stayed for the Q&A at the end.

Q - When is the release date?

Keith - It'll be in the fall. You never have the money for huge ad campaigns you want, so I'm sure they'll try to find a moment that's a little less crowded, when Robert and Mel's schedules allow some press time. They are pushing these two guys for Academy Award nominations. Robert making his comeback role and Mel is unlike any Mel you have seen before in this movie. Mel had had fun looking like a weird, nerdy, silly little old man.

Q - As an actor, did you get frustrated with other directors, thinking you could do the scene another way?

Keith - Not as much as you'd think. Back then, as an actor I was just learning. I was anxious to direct but it wasn't painful in that sense. I frankly thought it was going to take me until I was forty to make my first film anyway and I never dreamed I'd get the chance to make the pieces I love on my own terms. I've been so lucky. I've done things like directing television to pay the bills, which has been a lifesaver. I've tried to pick projects where I could ask to have my own vision. It's one thing to put together a $5m movie and say, *'I want you to give me a lot of freedom'*, it's another thing to say, *'I want to make a big, expensive $80 million science fiction movie and now leave me alone'*. I see each job as *'I have to live on this for four years'*, not, *'I have to live on this for six months'*. When you sell your script, don't go out and buy the Porsche because you don't know how long it's going to be until you sell the next one. I saw how much my parent's income (in the theater) would go up and down and I thought, *'okay, live comfortably, but don't get yourself in debt or live above your means'*, so if I have a year where I make zero, I'm alright. Of course, my agents are always trying to get me to do a studio movie.

Q - Is that an LA thing with the agents pushing their clients into doing studio movies?

Keith - The industry exists on short term profit and loss. People's viability to make a lot of money doesn't last long and in turn, agents and studio executives go up and down the ladder of success very quickly. They are often not interested in a long term career investment. They don't care about your little pet project that's going to take ten years. It's a purely economically driven business here, whereas I think New York and other cities regard film as a hybrid art business, in LA, it's business 90%, art 10%. Films in the US open in 5,000 theaters and even if they're successful, their entire life span is six to seven weeks. It's a very short term, instant gratification approach.

Q - How do they distribute independent films?

Keith - Independent films still work the old way. The problem is that even if you make your film for $1m, it's still going to cost $3m to put it in movie theaters and get it exposed enough for people to know it exists. There is no government help and no one cares if you're an independent film. Even a half page ad in the New York Times is $75k at a discount price. It drives companies like Miramax to find 'independent' films that sell like studio films. Independent films become increasingly about finding big hits. The worst thing that happened to the American independent movement was *Pulp Fiction* making $100m. People started saying, *'you can do that with independent films'*. The mentality is shifting so that you may as well be talking to the studio people.

Q - Are the studios saying, 'this could be an independent studio film?'

Keith - They are looking for studio films where they don't have to spend the money on the stars. That's why things are stuck right now. Will people find a way to use the internet to advertise or distribute their films in a less expensive way? If your film comes out and goes straight to DVD, it's seen as a failure. But why? DVD is a great medium. TV is getting better and better. Maybe that could become a real way to have, as Steven Soderburgh said, an *'off Broadway for film'*.

Q - Would you advise new filmmakers to make a short film or a feature as a first project?

Keith - The problem with making a short film is there is so little you can do with it once it's finished. It's a great calling card. But at the end of the day when you've spent your savings or your parents' money, you'll find you'll never make their money back. If it doesn't lead to you getting a job right away, you have an asset you can't do much with. If you can make a feature, the chance of it actually having a life is better. But a feature is more expensive, it takes longer to do, so it's not black and white. It depends on the story. I have seen people take short film ideas and puffed them up to feature length because they want to make a feature. What they end up with is a boring piece that feels wrong. So you need to look at your story and what best serves it. If you have a great ten minute story, then make a ten minute film. If you make a short, you can make something that won't cost $75k. Last year this kid from USC did one and it looked like a Steven Spielberg movie. It was science fiction and the digital effects were amazing. It must have been ridiculously expensive. It was very slick. The story was not important, but that fit his particular ambitions. This is a kid who wants to make *Bad Boys III*.

Q - Should your first film be something from the heart?

Keith - If I'm going to spend eight years raising the money and making the movie, I'd better feel passionate about it. Making movies is hard enough when you love it. You go down so many blind alleys trying to find the money; get the money; lose the money; then you'll have the money if you get a certain actor, and then you get that actor and they change their mind; then you make it and somebody wants to distribute it but wants it re-edited. There are people that make Hollywood movies and are comfortable. You'll ask them about their film, and they'll smile and say, *'piece of crap, I just did it for the money'*. I admire that in a perverse way because I don't think I could do that. How do you get yourself up at 5 in the morning and work for 18 hours a day 7 days a week that hard if you don't care?

Q - Do you think that new filmmakers don't have a grasp of the business side?

Keith - I'm grateful that I produced my own film before I directed, as it made me a realist as a director. Most good independent filmmakers are producers anyway, whether they take the credit or not. I've always come in on or under budget because I see it as a moral commitment: if I'm going to ask you to take a risk on me, and to support my artistic vision, you have a right to ask me to live up to the budget and schedule we agreed to. I think too many filmmakers treat it like it's their money and don't care what things cost, which causes an adversarial situation. I'm also a big believer in rehearsals. I think directors get talked out of rehearsal time by money people. Economically, it's one of the cheapest kinds of insurance you can have. Even on *Chocolate War*, which was a $500K movie, we rehearsed for over a week on location with all the cast, because the costs were minimal: basically a few extra days in the hotel. And, once we were shooting, we were able to move so much faster because of it. It may cost $10k that you think you don't have, but it's crucial, and it can make filming a much more pleasant and efficient experience. Rehearsal gives your actor's time to come to trust you, and gives you a chance to learn how to give them what they need to do their best work without a crew of 40 people standing around while you figure things out. We had three weeks of rehearsals on *Waking the Dead* and it made a huge difference in creating a complicated love story with a rich relationship. That was a film that jumped around in time, and we were able to spend some of the rehearsal time improvising the scenes that weren't in the film at all, but the actors needed to know how the characters got from point a to point b in the scenes that we did see.

Q - Have you worked with directors who haven't understood acting?

Keith - Some, but even if they don't focus on the actors, good directors have a good instinct of how not to screw up actors. Brian De Palma is not going to sit around and talk about your motivation with you for hours, but he's very smart and he wants you to bring your ideas to the table. He would always say, *'we've got a print, which was fine, let's try something different'*. So as an actor, you felt there was some freedom to try things. I've worked with other directors who just say *'stand there, do this, say it this way'* and it's awful. You start wondering why you are there; they could have just used a model. Actors are creative; they may be neurotic, but they are also smart. Why not make them your ally instead of your enemy?

Q - Would you say it's important to know actors' terminology as a director?

Keith - There are no rules for dealing with actors. Some love to improvise, some hate it. Some love to talk intellectually at great length about the characters; others get completely tied up in a knot. Professional actors don't need you to be their teacher. Your job is to give them what they need to do their best work. The most important thing for that is to listen and ask questions.

Q - Do new directors fixate on the technical side?

Keith - Yes. The camera is a *'thing'*, whereas actors are these weird, crazy, slightly neurotic, and complicated *'people'*. The neuroticism of actors comes from the fact that they're very vulnerable. They have to get up on the screen, open their hearts to the world. I've been there and it's terrifying. If you can understand that, you can see the complexity of actors behavior with compassion and empathy. Then, suddenly, even the seeming craziness isn't so bad, and you can use your understanding to become their ally, and to encourage them to become your ally.

I think it is important that people take more time in casting. Most casting directors bring in a million actors, one every five minutes. The problem is that actors can be very slick in an audition, but that is all you will ever get from them; you saw the finished performance. Somebody else might come in and be very rough edged, but if you took a little more time to work with them, you might find that they're rough edged because they are creative and they are going to be a great partner. I take 45 minutes to an hour with most actors for a large role. I think directors need to give themselves that time in casting to get a sense of an actor as a person. Talk to the directors that have worked with them. Were they good to work with? Creative? Difficult? And talk to more than one source. Any two people can have some specific personality conflict.

Q - Are the problems always the same on big budget and low budget movies?

Keith - Sure, it's just scale. The nice thing about independent movies is that although there are more problems because there's less money, problems are solved with intelligence, wit and cleverness, as opposed to big movies, where the answer is to just throw more money at them. It is not creative. I like the high pressured low budget movies as they are more fun. *Jaws 2* was a mess and that was a perfect case of *'when in doubt, build another shark'*. Everybody was scared to come up with creative solutions as they didn't want to rock the boat. We ended up shooting for something like 190 days., The shark would sink and we would all sit around for a week while they dragged it up from the bottom of the ocean.

You get a different kind of person doing independent films. The prop woman on *The Singing Detective* was so great. She was always creating and building things. I have found that the crews on bigger projects just do their job and look at their watches. They are competent, but the gap between competent and enthusiastic makes all the difference in the world to me.

Q - Working on a low budget independent, you're not doing it for the money anyway?

Keith - My AD on *The Singing Detective* had just done *Spiderman* and probably made five times the money. He loved our script and he loved Dennis Potter and he wanted to be part of it, people wanted to be there. It's an energy difference. But as far as the day to day problems go, it's pretty much the same.

Q - Do you find there is a lot of money wastage on big budget films?

Keith - Most of the numbers aren't that different when you look at the budgets for a $4m movie and a $60m movie. The differences are really the big stars, the studio overhead and the special effects, not the film stock and processing. You'll spend $20m up front on the main actors, but the day to day cost of shooting is very similar.

Q - Is TV very different to working on film?

Keith - Yes. The most fun I've had on TV has been doing anthology shows where they want you to come in and create your own little film. That is a blast. The series *Homicide* was very challenging. They had a template of how they did things, a style that they were very serious about. At the end of one show, a character was sitting on the steps of this church, depressed and he wasn't moving. I said, *'get me a tripod'* and there was shock. I said, *'I want to put the camera down'*. They said, *'you can't put the camera down. We never do that.'* I said, *'the whole point of the story is that he's stopped and the investigation has stopped and nothings moving anymore, so let's stop moving the camera for just this one scene'*. So the next day I got a call from the network saying, *'what did you do? You cannot do that. We never put the camera down'*. I said, *'I was making a story point'*. They said *'you don't make points, now go back and reshoot'.* That was a big education for me.

The producers on *Gideon's Crossing* weren't so strict. I'd try something and they'd say, *'that's cool. We'll do that more in the future'*. But that was partly because that was a new show. They hadn't locked themselves in to a way of doing things yet. Television directing is a little like being an actor. You have to take their style, their way of telling a story and make it your own. It's less about the 'art' more about the 'craft'. But, I enjoyed that and it's lucrative too. The DGA minimum is $30k for an hour's show - I can live on that for a while. It's 8 days of prep, 7 days of shooting, 2 says of editing. You basically throw it together the best you can in the two days in the editing room, and then twenty five people are going to re-edit it anyway. With series TV, when you're finished, you put it down and walk away because what you'll see on the air is often not what you intended. The nature of the beast is, they're going to re-edit it, putting things in that you don't like, taking out things you love.

Q - Do you do any teaching for the IFP?

Keith - I have yet to be able to teach a class regularly as my schedule has been too crazy. I was teaching at USC, but three weeks into the semester I got *The Singing Detective* so had to leave. I did a series at the AFI where I screened my films and talked about how I made each one. I've guest lectured and taught individual classes at USC and UCLA and IFP and I go up to Sundance to mentor each summer at their filmmakers' lab. I've mentored 'outsider' aspiring film-makers (poor, minority, older women, gay, etc) for the IFP's *Project Involve*. I've written magazine articles and I hosted a radio show about film.

Q - What is the most common mistake you have come across with new filmmakers or yourself?

Keith - Probably it was being too didactic. Not taking advantage and collaborating with people around me and treating money people as an enemy. It was basically that *'filmmaker as dictator'* behavior as opposed to *'filmmaker as really benevolent open minded dictator'*.

Q - What single piece of advice would you give new filmmakers?

Keith - Don't take any of it too seriously and keep the rest of your life alive. Fall in love, get married, have hobbies and do other things. It's a cruel and strange business and will go up and down. Even if you're as lucky as I am, and you're able to make a living out of it, you're going to have very difficult times if you have pegged your whole sense of self and worth on your career. Consider: One critic told me *'most of us are reviewing 150 films a year and seeing a lot more than that, so we have no time to think about your movie, ponder it or decide whether we like it. We have no time to go back and see it again.'* Essentially, within five minutes, they've decided whether they like it or not. Many, perhaps the majority of the films now considered the best ever made that were not warmly received on their release. Conversely, a lot of the films that were considered the best films in their time have now vanished. It's all just opinions. If you do things that are going to be pushing the envelope, either emotionally or stylistically, you are going to piss off some people. You need to be prepared for that. I am always bemused when I meet filmmakers who have made experimental films and they get really upset when someone goes, *'that's weird and dark'*. If your goal is to show people something new and different, a lot of people won't like that, it comes with the territory of what you're trying to do.

Scott McGehee   David Siegel

SUTURE and THE DEEP END

Q - How did you get into film?

Scott - Neither of us went to film school. We know each other because David and my sister went to art school together, Kelly McGehee. She ended up as the production designer on *The Deep End.* We met up in San Francisco and made a couple of short films to figure out how filmmaking was done. Neither of us had any background in it at all, although David had a done a little filmmaking in his course and I had taken one class at the Film Arts Foundation, and knew the mechanics of what all the pieces were. We were just big film fans. We thought that if other people could do it, why couldn't we?

David - Having not gone to film school and being ignorant about the way movies are made, we just thought, '*Let's try and make some films together*'. So the delineation of credit or responsibility was never defined for us. That was the beginning philosophically, but the reason it kept going that way was that we developed a particular writing process together that formed the foundation of what we wanted to do and it always seemed organic that way.

Q - What did you shoot your short films on?

Scott - Both were 16mm, but a good half to two thirds of the first one was actually shot on VHS video and we transferred it to film. Because we were doing it on video and they were mostly interviews, we could walk in the door with our little camera and people didn't feel like we were making a film.

Q - Did you enter the shorts in any festivals?

David - Both short films played at a few festivals, but nothing that got us anywhere. That's when we started writing the script for *Suture.* We put together a limited partnership, and raised enough money to shoot *Suture* and do a rough edit. We knew we didn't have enough money to finish the movie, but during post, we ended up being introduced to Steven Soderberg. It was with Steven's help that we were able to finally raise the money to finish it after five months.

Scott - We were showing a 'close to final edit' of the film to investors. We invited everyone we could think of to the screenings. Steven was inviting people, showing up at every screening and wore a *Suture* t-shirt. It took forever. The guy didn't give up. He was so good to us. Week after week coming back and inviting new people, trying to talk people into helping us finish our movie.

Q - What stage had he seen 'Suture' at?

David - The rough cut. A friend introduced us and Steven agreed to come and see the film.

Scott - It was the worst screening ever. It was a little screening room and everything that could possibly go wrong, went wrong. They put the wrong gate in the projector, missed reel changes, had reels out of order. But he came to talk to us the next day, and at that point he was talking about re-mortgaging his house to help us finish the movie!

Q - How long was the writing stage on Suture?

David - We spent six months writing that script. We shot super 35mm so we could do a wide screen blow up.

Q - When you approached potential investors, did they want to look at your shorts?

David - It was really finding people who were willing to part with money. It wasn't really industry people. It was a lark for them, just to mess around with it. We started shooting with $600k. In the end it cost $1m, and we spent about a year raising the money to get us into production. We shot *Suture* in thirty days in Phoenix, Arizona, all on location. We brought in most of the crew from LA.

Scott - Arizona is a 'right-to-work' state. It was a small enough for the union to leave us alone. We headed out as short filmmakers, thinking we were going to be producing a longer 'short' film, not knowing what the scope of the production needed to be. We would scout in Arizona, find locations and started getting a feel for what the film should look like. There was a slow dawning that once we'd hired a line producer and an AD that we were getting bigger than we thought. I remember walking through a parking lot, beside the hotel, and seeing all the trailers and trucks that were there on our behalf and being in awe that we'd caused all that.

Q - How did you write the script? Half each? And directing?

David - We outline thoroughly before we get started, so we have a map of the whole piece, and then we write our first pass in chunks. We get the whole thing pieced together in the first pass before we begin rewriting. We each write our first take on a piece and then we revise each others work and it gets broken into chunks until we don't remember who started what or who's last revision changed who's previous revision. It becomes the thing that really is both our work. For us, a lot of directing is planning. We tend to plan the movie, and then the days, very carefully, so that when we're on set, there are two people who really understand what the vision of the movie is and what we're doing. I wind up taking a little more of a forward position, in terms of calling, 'action', 'cut' and driving things a little more directly. But we're both there talking to the actors and dealing with the camera.

Scott - When things are in their smaller formats, such as storyboarding or rehearsing, you can have a much more open and collaborative conversation. By the time we arrive on set, we try to have things pretty well worked out, at least between us, so that we're leading in one direction.

Q - How long was the post before the rough cut of Suture?

David - We wrapped the movie in the middle of November and it premiered at the Telluride Film Festival next September. So it wasn't that long. Steven probably saw *Suture* about two months after we shot. It wasn't fine cut by then, so that was going as we were raising funds. We only had screenings for people that Steven or we knew. That went on until April and we were starting to get a little worried that we wouldn't raise the money. We started the sound and the mix work slightly prematurely, fibbing about the amount of money we had.

Scott - Steven was in Cannes and got some French distributors who ended up coming in with the completion money as our partners. They bought the European rights too. Although the idea was they would sell them and distribute elsewhere. They didn't actually sell it as many places as we would have liked. It played in England, Belgium and Spain, I think.

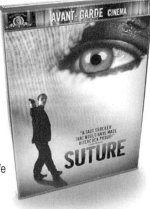

We had been invited to the Toronto festival as well, which was immediately after Telluride. It was there that things started happening. Telluride is such a particular festival. It's a wonderful place to see movies, but not a lot of business gets done there because of the way they work. They don't reveal what movies are going to be there, and a lot of the movies people have seen in Cannes. We sold it out of Toronto and got invited to Sundance.

Q - When you sold the film, was it for a lot?

Scott - No, it was a tiny amount of money. That movie never returned a profit.

Q - They gave you a distribution deal?

David - Yeah and it was getting a lot of attention critically. We got invited to Cannes and it played at London the following year.

Scott - At Sundance, the buzz films are the ones that are for sale. Our film had been around and a lot of people had seen it. It wasn't a bad experience but there was something about the atmosphere which we didn't like. It felt like it was about selling films rather than about filmmaking. We, as filmmakers were all somehow in competition with each other. We've since made our peace. We later took *The Deep End* to Sundance and we love the festival now!

Q - How long did it take to get the next movie off the ground and did you have agents knocking on your door?

David - We had a lot of interest from agents and we signed with Steven's agent. The time between *Suture* and *The Deep End* wasn't happy professionally speaking. We had three separate movies take a lot of time to not happen. We started out with a small studio film that we had written that wound up turning into an ownership fight after a year. Then we were trying to do a difficult film that had become a passion project for us that basically couldn't get going because of difficulties with financing and casting. It was out of that frustration that we hooked up with Robert Nathan and formed Hi5. The idea was to find a way to raise money, not just for a film of ours, but for three or four movies. After we finished the script, Claudia Lewis, who is the senior vice president at Fox Searchlight and a good friend was interested after we showed it to her. But we couldn't come to terms on casting and they would not have made it with the cast we ultimately decided on. For a small film, if the movie's good and people are interested in it, it doesn't matter if there are stars in it. *The Deep End* did great with no real stars in it. But if the movie isn't good, the studio wants to be able to push the publicity angle on the stars and pre-sell territories based on star value.

Q - How did The Deep End come about and how long did it take to write?

David - *The Deep End* is one of the fastest scripts we've written. We spent maybe three and a half months writing. We had already formed I-5 and the intention was to make it through I-5. The little detour that we took through Searchlight was accidental. We weren't expecting them to finance the film.

Q - When you were writing, did you have Tilda Swinton in mind?

David - No, that came later. If you think about fortyish year old women who have to be able to be strong and emotional, there aren't that many women who can do it. We also knew we needed an actress who goes through the experience in a very solitary way. So we were looking for a face. Someone that you feel is thinking when you put the camera on them. As soon as we started looking at stuff, she seemed as good at silent filmmaking as anybody. She's remarkable.

Scott - We sent her the script, and got lucky as she happened to be traveling through LA when we wanted to meet with her. As soon as we started talking to her, it was apparent how in synch we were about what the character needed, what our interest in her was and what her interest in acting was. We were a perfect match for her at that moment.

Q - Water is a big reference point in your movies. Was it difficult setting it in Lake Tahoe with the location?

David - The idea of Tahoe came about very early and we actually went and wrote some of it there at the lake. There wasn't difficulty in terms of dealing with Tahoe. We just had so little money for what we were trying to do that everything was stretched so thin. So when we did the work on the water, we didn't have quite good enough pontoon boats to make it easy. At every stage our ambitions just exceeded our resources, so it was a hard film to make. But we had a great crew and it was never difficult to the point of being frustrating or overwhelming. Once, when looking for the house location, we got caught in a blizzard on the lake in a little boat. We would spot houses and our locations guy would go to the office and ask about them in a blizzard! The guy who was taking us round was an experienced boatsman. We were just too far out and the storms in Lake Tahoe can come on really fast. So we were driving back and could only go so fast because we were all huddled inside. I don't think I've ever been so cold in my life. It's a very unsettling feeling because you don't really feel like you're going to die, but you can imagine a horrible death!

Q - Did you have to convince the owners?

Scott - They were really nice, but the man was a businessman, and it was an expensive location. But it was perfect. They were going to remodel the house that summer, so we had the run of the estate.

Q - How did you find the lead actor, Goran Visnjic?

David - We had seen him in *Welcome To Sarajevo*. Neither one of us watch television, so when we were first talking about him, we didn't know that he was on *ER*. He was one of the two or three people we originally thought of for the role and he's so handsome and manly. In the book, the character was originally an Irishman, and we liked him being outside the culture, so it implies history without having to declare a history. He agreed to do it from the get-go.

Scott - We never thought of him from a marketing point of view. Tilda has a constituency of people who are interested in her, and follow her, and they're very cinematic. It ended up being helpful having someone with a completely different background. Goran was known as an American television star. So totally different people in terms of press wanted to talk to them. The cinephiles wanted to talk to Tilda and weren't interested in Goran, and the more general media people were interested in Goran.

Q - What was the budget of The Deep End?

Scott - About $3m. We wrote a movie that could succeed at a modest budget. It's a movie about a woman who lives in a house, and its got a limited scope in terms of the world we need to show. We thought that was a movie that didn't need more money to be better. So the $3m number was what we could afford to spend and what the film needed.

Q - Do you storyboard everything?

David - We do a combination shot list and storyboard for everything. Occasionally improvisational things happen on set, and we try and allow for that, but we try and go in pretty carefully planned.

Q - Did you find financing The Deep End to be a problem after the seven-year break since Suture?

Scott - It's never easy to raise money. Our pitch was different, and I think that helped. It wasn't investing in a film, it was investing in a company. And it wasn't really a company, it was a group of films, and the idea was by investing in several films, you're not betting everything on a single success, because sometimes the best films don't succeed for reasons you can't control. It wasn't the same pitch you always hear, so maybe that helped us.

Q - Was The Deep End union?

Scott - No. We actually went in trying to shoot a non-union film. We were on a remote location so we thought we'd be safe. We were paying pretty close to union rates and overtime. The

fringes were what really hurt us. Everyone knew the deal going in. People on our set called the union, not because they were mistreated, but because they were from San Francisco and wanted to get into the LA union. So they screwed us a little bit. Our film became a victim of their desire to get into a closed system. There was a rumor that they had heard that Fox Searchlight was financing us, because we had been friendly with them and our friend Claudia actually came to our set to visit us socially.

David - It was disheartening emotionally. Financially, it probably wasn't so different than if we had gone in as a union film in the first place, but seeing all these people you've been working with for weeks cross the street from your set and not come to work, felt like a betrayal. It took us a while to get the feeling on the set back. I believe if you are independently financed and not attached to an industry financing source or a studio, you should be able to make a movie without being a union film. The union doesn't believe that. The IA believes that that's part of the cost of business, regardless of what kind of a movie it is. At this point We'd been shooting for two or three weeks.

Q - Did you know something had happened or did people just stop showing up?

Scott - They have to be pressured by the union to do that, so the union showed up and called a meeting. We lost about of a day. The people who were members of the union, who are on our crew, are required to do what the union tells them. It's the other people who aren't members who were swayed.

David - The word was sent around that there was a meeting at lunch on a particular day and then they didn't come back.

Q - Did money just go up?

Scott - Yeah, it cost us a lot of money. It became a big accounting problem and we only had a few people to deal with it. We worked it out and were able to absorb the cost eventually. It's a labyrinth of rules and rhe low budget agreements aren't that helpful. It depends on the kind of low budget you are. The union budgets force you into a cable film structure where you have limited shooting days, and if you're trying to do something more ambitious, it's difficult.

Q - Do you think it would have been better to go with a union from the start?

David - It varies from moment to moment, the mood of the union, and I think you need to talk to people who have negotiated with the unions recently or hear about how much organizing they have been doing. We should have spoken to them in advance. We did let them know. We didn't try and hide it from them. We just didn't try to negotiate.

Q - What was your cutting period on The Deep End?

David - We cut for 14 weeks and kept the film completely under wraps until Sundance.

Q - Was The Deep End a success at Sundance?

Scott - Yes. No one had seen the movie and we had a big screening fairly late in the festival. Tilda was flying in from Scotland and had been delayed by a day and a half. An attempt to show her the film before the screening had failed and she was actually driving up to the screening changing her clothes in the mini van. We sat down in the theater and had no idea whether people would like it or hate it.

David - I didn't sit down in the theatre. I was drinking beers. It was really something. At the end of the screening, we had a sense that people liked it enough that it wasn't going to be a disaster. We started getting buyers interested.

Scott - Then you go through it all again during the release, too, because we had no idea whether people were going to like it. The release was stronger than the festival release.

Q - Who picked it up?

Scott - We had a situation where we had sold it to Searchlight, and then the next day, Harvey Weinstein really wanted to buy it for a lot more money than Searchlight had offered.

David - We could have just been really creepy and bailed on our deal with Searchlight and made a lot more money with Harvey, but we decided to be honorable.

Q - How much did they buy it for?

David - For just under $4m excluding France and Italy. It ended up being a very profitable film for our company.

Q - What advice would you give new directors and writers?

Scott - It's such a difficult thing to give advice because everyone's experience is so different. No two films have the same story and as soon as you say, '*It's better to do this or that...*' you'll meet someone else who has had the opposite experience. There's a funny story Robert Rodriguez used to tell about when he made *El Mariachi*. He made a list of everything at his disposal, and then wrote a movie about that stuff. We've never worked that way, but it's very clever.

David - There are such a lot of films being made now either on digital video or film. I remember reading something that said, '*by hook or by crook, get your film made.*' But that's such a strange piece of advice because you've got to dig down and ask yourself the question, '*am I going to be good at this?*' and '*do I really want to put the time and resources into making a movie?*' The bar is being lowered as it is so easy to pick up a camera and make a movie. That doesn't really prove the quality of the filmmaker, it's not much of a meritocracy. A lot of lousy movies get bought and they go to film festivals, and you see good movies that don't get bought, and so it comes down to if you really love doing it. I love the process of making movies. Be sure you're making a movie that being small suits. I find it frustrating when watching a movie that feels it didn't have the resources it needed. The successful small movies are the ones that make a virtue of their limitations. Write something within the perimeters of how you think its going to get made.

Q - Do you think it's best to rush into a movie for the experience or for money, or to wait for the right script to come along, or to get your own personal project off the ground that you are passionate about?

David - It's a question you never stop asking yourself. It is a game of persistence.

Scott - As fun as it is, the process is hard. I don't think it's fun enough for us that making real crap would be worth it.

David - As bad as you think the studio system is... it is! Be wary of it.

Scott - But it's still a place to make movies.

Anne Chaisson   Dylan Kidd

ROGER DODGER

Q - What is your background?

Dylan - I loved movies at high school and I was aware that there were directors, but I never thought it was something I could do. I went to college to study philosophy, but then I saw an ad for film school. I knew I wanted to get out of where I was, so I said, *'Let me try this'.* I went with very low expectations as I didn't know how much hard work it would take to major in film. I met a lot of people that I've continued to work with since I graduated in 1991. I then spent my entire twenties sacrificed to filmmaking. It was a unique situation in New York the year that I graduated, in that it was the worst year for film production ever! There was a Writer's Guild strike and a recession. I worked in a pool hall, waited tables, was even a doorman for a while. I thought I wanted to be a cinematographer, so I became an assistant cameraman for a while. It was three or four years after school that I finally decided to do a short film and that's how I met Anne who ended up producing it.

Anne - I studied marketing and economics, after which, I worked for an investment banking firm and then market research and sponsorship. I then met an independent filmmaker who had written a script and wanted to adapt it. He asked me to write his financial proposal, and by actually talking to people about finance within the city, I started raising a lot of the money! It was completely unexpected. We shot on Super 16mm with a two-week shoot in Boston and two weeks in NY six months later. We sold a little bit internationally, but it was a realization that there wasn't much going on in the city to help people like myself. So while I was consultant I started a Film School called The Reel School, and managed to produce another feature that was completely avante garde for $40k, which took us four years to do! Finally I quit my job and decided to become a film producer. I found as many people as I could to produce their short films and started line producing to make my way around the industry.

Q - What was the short film that you made as a partnership?

Dylan - It was a 25 minute psychological horror. I was passionate about it but its primary function was as a reel piece. I would recommend you make movies if you want to be a filmmaker. Even if you end up with 10% of what you intended, the learning curve is so steep, you'll benefit. It was shot on 16mm for $20k, all my own money. It did the festival circuit for about a year, and did fairly well winning some awards. It didn't go internationally, but the internet was starting to explode at the time and I managed to get some work doing internet serials, spec commercials, all while I began writing *Roger Dodger.*

Q - Was Roger Dodger your first feature screenplay?

Dylan - I did write a few others but none that I would let anyone see.

Q - How did the project come together?

Anne - Two years after we did the short, Dylan gave me a draft of *Roger Dodger*, I read and flipped out. I couldn't believe it. We had a reading and worked on the script together after that, working out the problems. It had a different ending than it has now because we went back to it after the screenplay reading. We really collaborated although he collaborated a hell of a lot more with his DP. They pretty much share a brain because they went to film school together. They knew where the locations were going to be and talk about why they are going to do this and that. A lot of people skip that process and sit down with the DP two weeks before the shoot and do a shot list. That's not how you make a well thought out movie. If you're trying to make an independent movie that stands out, you've got to have a plan for your vision. It's not magic, but it takes immense preparation.

Q - The film is centered predominantly around two characters. Is that a writing choice?

Anne - Dylan had a friend in college who was very much like Roger and he thought *'What would happen if he came to town and asked my friend so and so for a night out on the town to understand women.'* Dylan thought it was an interesting dynamic and wrote the script from that. He kept it small as he knew how to make independent film. We had three good cameos that we could get actresses to do for five days each. A name person is willing to work for you for a week at scale. People were excited to work on it. We had a lot of theater people in it, too.

Q - How did you raise the money?

Anne - We had raised about half the money when we were trying to get to this other actor, but they wanted to know that we had all the money. We couldn't tell if the person had actually read the script, and they were giving us the run-around. We met Campbell who loved the project and he's not a gregarious person that would fawn over it. He just said, *'How are you guys doing with the money?'* and we said how much we had and he said, *'I might know some people to put you in touch with'*. So he introduced us to another financier who ultimately financed the entire movie, so we told the other investor, *'No'*.

Q - How did you manage to get Campbell Scott?

Dylan - Anne and I had a typical experience, which is *'No money without a star, and no star without money'*. One piece of advice is actors want to do good roles, so if you don't have a track record like we didn't, your best leverage is to write something that an actor will gravitate towards. If an actor is dying to do a part that you've written, you need to make it known that you are going to be directing too. Most actors will want to do it. The challenge is getting to the actors. People said they would pass the script on and didn't. So I got in this head space where every morning I had to do something to get this movie made. So I started carrying the script with me. I was in a coffee shop with a friend of mine and Campbell Scott walked in. I called Anne and the two of us talked for five minutes. Neither of us had considered Campbell before for the role, but he had one big track record of supporting first time directors and he's a great actor, but he was right there. I approached him cold and tried to be as polite as I could. I said, *'I have a script here and I think you would be fantastic for the lead role, will you read it?'* He said, *'Sure'*. This is not a tried and tested method for getting scripts to actors!

Anne - Campbell went the extra mile by saying that he would read it, AND call us back and tell us what he thinks of it.

Dylan - He's not afraid of first time filmmakers. Good things happen to those people that are a little bit more open to making the initial contact. He said it would take him a couple of weeks to get back to us as he was leaving town. He called back two weeks later and said, *'Hey, this is Campbell. I like it. Let's talk'*. I think he invited Anne and I to a reading he was doing and that was the first time that he sat down with us. Actors know how much money we have. He knew what I needed was a letter of intent saying he wanted to play the role and help get us other actors.

Anne - He said, *'You can have the letter of intent, but good luck getting money with my name'*.

Q - When you did the initial budget, how much were you hoping to get?

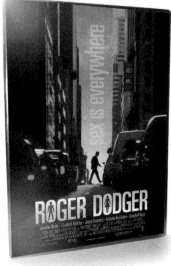

Anne - We had several budgets, based on what kind of money we thought we could get. We had a $500k version and the $2.5m version. So Campbell pretty much executive produced the movie. He put us in touch with the final investor. We raised $500k through private investment. It was someone who didn't know the filmmaking process at all. They said, '*Great. We would love to be involved*'. Campbell was not a tier one actor, but we needed someone who would knock this character right out of the park and we knew that was a key thing. We had Jessie, but we knew Jessie wouldn't be able to carry the project, maybe to the point that he would steal the movie, but that didn't happen as Campbell completely pulled the character on his own. Their chemistry was outrageous. When we did the screenplay reading Jessie sat down with Campbell and they didn't say a word to each other, and they started the reading. I was saying '*This is absolutely amazing*'. The room was electric. At the end Campbell got out of his chair and picked Jessie up, got him against the wall and said, '*Where did you come from? Who are you?*' It was so great!

Q - A lot of filmmakers ask how to get finance?

Anne - It's hard. The first movie I did, it took me going to lots of people asking for $20k each. It wasn't, '*Hey, we're going to finance a large chunk of this movie*'. The God's just conspired and Campbell was the domino for us.

Q - But up to that point, you had $500k?

Anne - It was from a friend. He liked the script and said he'd do half. A lot of people are willing to do half, but there are stipulations. It depends if they've done it before, on getting an actor etc. Put your script out there to people you know in the script world who can give you financing. There are film companies all over that have access to money. Get to the right person, not just the receptionist. If you get to the right person and they are not into it, ask them who you should talk to as they know what other companies are looking for. If they like the script, but say they can't do it right now, it's negative feedback. If you constantly get negative feedback, there is something wrong with your script. So if you only think you can get the money from private investors, maybe you're not developing your script well enough. As soon as you get distribution, doors start to fly open, especially the bridge between the independent world and Hollywood. That doesn't mean as a director you will get everything in the world from Hollywood, but if you've gotten notoriety and a distributor, it happens. It's a shame because there's a lot of quirky independent films out there who don't get a distributor, and they wallow until they get a video deal. The statistics are still what they were in the beginning. Out of all the films that get made, maybe 1 - 2% go to Sundance, and of that, 5-7 of those get bought. So what happens to everything else? I was part of that for some time and it was devastating.

Q - What did you shoot on?

Dylan - We shot 35mm. We made a lot of effort to make the format look more portable than it was because they were heavy cameras. We set out to do something that could be done in 13 days, but it ended up being a 20 day shoot.

Q - Did you come across any problems running around with a 35mm camera in New York?

Dylan - We were lucky in that the exteriors are limited. We have one major sequence where we had to hide the cameras and do a candid camera thing. Extras are a huge expense, so we tried to do things with our production department.

Anne - Our exteriors were all at night so it was easy to move around NY. We shot right after 9/11 as well, so there wasn't a lot going on. The Mayor's office was accommodating to us.

Dylan - But that being said, we did employ a guerrilla techniques, in that there was one scene, which needed the full sense of being in the city. Because of our budget level, we couldn't do the thing where you block off three city blocks.

Anne - We worked out with the restaurants to hide in their basement area and get the shot. Half the day we were doing that, and as luck would have it on any independent film, there was a scaffolding accident a block down, so we got shut down and had to go back and redo it.

Q - Were there any common mistakes that you could warn first time filmmakers about?

Dylan - Because this one went so well, it's easier to talk about what went right. My whole thing is, we fought for rehearsal time. I assumed that rehearsal time would automatically be included in prep, but it wasn't. I insisted on it. A lot of directors are scared of rehearsals as they don't know what to do or say, but that's time to get to know the actors and their needs.

Q - Was it a six day a week?

Dylan - It was Campbell's decision to shoot a 5 day weeks as he has a 4 year old son. I was all for that as I'd been a technician and I know that a 6 day week is hard work. That's the reason we were able to get our crew on reduced rates, because it wasn't a 6 day week, and it was local. They were like, '*Okay, we'll have a weekend*'. We were editing as we shot, which was a huge advantage for us because the movie began to speak to us. We were shooting on Monday and by Thursday I could see the scene cut together and understand if it was working or not. You hear the story about Travolta talking to his director and saying, '*You're not going to see it on set, but you'll see it on dailies*'. That is so true.

Q - Did you storyboard the movie?

Dylan - I don't like to storyboard because I feel like the scenes that I storyboarded and got exactly as I wanted were flat. I think you've got to leave room. So we shot listed, meaning we had the beats that we wanted to get, or certain cutaways. It depends on what you're doing. The Coen brothers made *Blood Simple* and planned out every shot. If you have the time it's probably a good idea, but any independent film is going to have that moment where you walk on set and suddenly it's completely different to when you boarded it. So when you write your storyboards, just remember that the best skill of a director is being able to make quick adjustments and that's where your preparation comes in.

Q - Did you do a lot of improvisation?

Dylan - We did in rehearsal. It loosened people up in rehearsal. We had four afternoons rehearsal time. It was a hard decision as there were days where I was needed to scout locations, but I insisted on being there for the actors.

Q - How did you find Jessie Eisenberg, the kid?

Dylan - We had a casting director for the movie, and I had seen Jessie briefly on TV and jotted down his name and suggested him to the casting director. He turned eighteen ten days before we started shooting, which meant he was an adult and we didn't have to cut him loose at certain times.

Q - How long was the post process?

Dylan - That was more relaxed, but our mix was insane. One lesson I learned was that it's easy to steal money from post in the moment. It's the role of the producer to say, '*I know you want a few extras, but you can only have twenty five and I know you think its ruining the scene, but what will*

ruin it more is not being able to mix it properly'. We ended up having a mix that we didn't have time to do properly, so we convinced them to let us go back and re-mix.

Q - Did you have to do pick ups?

Dylan - There was one shot I should have gotten, but we were lucky. What's great about working at this budget level is it forces you to be careful about what you spend your money on. Having a small budget forces you to go in and say, *'We can only afford to dress one half of this room. Which half is periphery to the scene?'* My DP said, *'If we had $10m to make this movie, we would screw it up',* and he was right! We found a budget level that was perfect for the film, that was tight enough so that we had to be resourceful and smart and prepared, but not so tiny that we were throwing the baby out the window.

Q - Were there any problems getting permits in New York?

Anne - Permits are free in New York, so that wasn't an issue. With any outdoor scene you should have the police involved, but that's free as well. Guerrilla tactics for us were finding a way to shoot the movie without having to shut three blocks down. We hid the camera, ran and got it done. But we had to completely control the number of extras we had. The crew got paid normally. It wasn't a union shoot per say, but we followed union rules. So that makes everybody happy. I still say you can shoot a movie for $500k, but it depends on what your crew are willing to do. It's not because of their obstinacy because they do this all the time. Why would they invest two months on something they get mistreated on? To them, mistreated is having no food, no sleep. You have to take care of those people or you're not going to get your movie made.

Q - Did you get into Sundance?

Anne- - We didn't finish editing until March and we knew we were going to miss the Sundance deadline. So we said, *'Oh, forget it'.* Even if we gave them a rough cut, the film still wouldn't have been ready for the festival in January so we moved on to the next submission date - Cannes and Tribeca. The Tribeca Film Festival was happening that year to honor September 11th and getting people back into the neighborhood. We made a decision to premiere there. We knew it would get tons of press, and it was right there in our neighborhood. So we did it and won. George and I went together with the print to Cannes because everybody went to Cannes the day after we won. So the decision makers weren't in New York anymore, so we had to carry the baby to France. Everybody set up private screenings on their own and we sold it there. We had an offer, but we wanted to hear other people's offers. We were with two companies for a while, but ended up with Artisan. It's a whole unique experience and I feel guilty pleasure because I know how devastating it is when the elements don't come together. But I also know that now, when you have a project that these kinds of things happen to, the right things start to come. We know it will never happen this way again.

Q - How much did Artisan pick it up for?

Anne - Let's just say our investors made their money back. We also sold foreign to Alliance Atlantis. So between those two deals, we paid the investors back and made a tiny bit.

Q - How were the reviews?

Anne - Excellent almost across the board. We also garnered a National Board of Review, NY Film Critics, Chicago Film Critics nods for Campbell Scott and Dylan Kidd.

Q - Where did you meet your agent?

Anne - The agent at CAA that we went with saw our movie at Tribeca. He's a real go-getter. Usually agents rep the writer / director, but due to our strong partnership, we wanted to sign together. There were tons of offers from Hollywood, but Dylan was still writing at that point. Plus we were on a festival schedule, and the movie was getting released. CAA started sending scripts right away, but because of the promotion of the movie, Dylan was on a tour basically, so we were lost in all that. We have lined up a few things we are interested in, so when we came out here we're pretty much setting up his two next years. There are a lot of independent filmmakers who say, '*I'm staying independent*' and then it takes them a year and a half to get their script out. They shun getting an agent. I know four people like that who have never got past film one, and this is four years later. I wish I could tell writers/directors they are not selling out by getting an agent - you're opening up your opportunities. You don't have to take anything they give you. But you never know. They may give you an article that you can write and make it for $2m. The point is you drive your career.

Q - What advice would you give a new filmmaker?

Anne - Work on the material and make sure it's at the best it could possibly be without actors on it. A lot of writers don't take the time to finish the script. They get feedback, but don't listen to the feedback. It's clear if you are hearing the same thing over and over you need to change it. Remember this is a collaborative art. Keep the crew happy because if there's dissension in the ranks, you're not going to get out of them what you're going to need to make the right movie.

Dylan - Have the courage to quit a job that is taking up your time from making your movie. Everything in film is the alliances you form, so you have to donate a ton of your time to it. Every time you work with someone, even if you are a PA, keep in touch. Competent, nice people will gravitate towards each other. Also you'd better love the process and be willing to take the bull by the horns. I would do all the struggling again in a second.

CASE STUDIES

Alex Smith   Andrew Smith

THE SLAUGHTER RULE

Q - What's your background? Whereabouts are you from?

Alex - We grew up in Western Montana, in a small town of about 40,000 people, on a ranch about 20 miles from any urban area.

Andrew - Our mother had been a film producer for a while, on documentaries and she made one feature film called *Heartland*. That was an early indie made in 1979, and I can remember going on set when I was eleven years old and being influenced by the excitement of that. We were both English majors, but we studied film as a sideline. I was accepted into a film studies program at the University of Iowa and studied critical film theory and history.

Alex - I took a lot of film classes and then as I worked on film sets, I sort of got the bug to learn more about film.

Q - What films did you work on?

Alex - We worked on *Little Man Tate* that Jody Foster directed, *A River Runs Through It* and a bunch of bad films.

Q - How easy was it to work on those films without experience?

Alex - No too hard. We started out on very low budget movies. On one, I worked in the art department, which started a domino effect. Someone would get another job and recommend you. It was freelance, so sometimes I would get two films at once and then not get anything for months. When we weren't working, we were writing. On *Little Man Tate* I was an intern and became a clapper loader, but it gave me a lot of time to be around the director and the DP.

Andrew - I had the world's most boring job. I was the video assist.

Alex - On later films, I was a boom guy then I did art department on stuff and I started doing camera work, and that interested me because you were in there with the director, the actors and the DP and you could soak up a lot more..

Q - How did The Slaughter Rule start?'

Andrew - We spent a few years writing before we took the script through the writing and directing lab at Sundance.

Alex - We had spent some time with a filmmaker in Texas who wanted to direct it, and we were going to be the screenwriters. But, it didn't work so we decided to make it ourselves. We sent it to various producers at the same time as submitting it to the Sundance lab. We got rejected from Sundance twice, but each time we made it to further levels.

Andrew - Between the second and third time we had acquired producers, Good Machine, who provided an sort of validation that we were going forward regardless of the Lab.

Alex - Sundance now take more projects that have a chance of getting made. For a long time they were developing projects that were so out there that it just didn't happen. So once we had more momentum, they took a closer look.

Q - How do the Sundance labs work?

Alex - You have the writing lab for a week and they have a bunch of advisors who are top-notch screenwriters in the industry, both indie and studio. They look at your script and everyone takes a whack at it. It's all the most praise and criticism you're going to get in your lifetime, all in a week. You get advisors who weep at the same time another one cuts forty pages. You get incredible reactions.

Andrew - We had Michael Weller, who wrote *Hair*. Peter Hedges, who wrote *What's Eating Gilbert Grape*. Paul Attanasio, who wrote, *Quiz Show* and *Donnie Brasco*.

Q - How many people go on the lab?

Andrew - For the writing lab, it's eight projects a year and that's purely screenwriters. If you do the writing lab, you're not guaranteed to go to the directing lab and some writers aren't directors anyway. The directing Lab is a month long film camp, including actors. You cast three actors out of LA and NY with Sundance's help for your film, pick four scenes from your film and then they give you a DP and editor and you shoot the scenes. They have all these advisors, professional directors, DP's and editors and actors who come on set, and give you advice.

Alex - We had amazing directors as advisors - Alison Anders, Jocelyn Moorhouse, Michael Lehman who did *Heathers*. Sometimes they have big name directors as well as lesser known indie directors like Michael Ritchie. We also had John Toll who shot *Braveheart* and *The Thin Red Line*. They rotate and get divided up onto different projects. The directors lab has about eight projects, and then after you shoot your four scenes and edit it you get feedback. Robert Redford sat in the editing room from time to time.

Q - So you spend two weeks getting your scenes together?

Andrew - It actually takes three weeks. Two for shooting, and one week of feedback. They also do a composers component, which happens at the end of it.

Q - When you did the screenwriters lab, had the script changed significantly?

Andrew - For us it was a ricochet effect where somebody would suggest something that we hadn't thought of and then somebody else would say something that would click with what the other person said. It's an interesting process, because when you put creative people on your script, particularly other writers, there is a tendency for them to take over and run with their own ideas. You end up with six versions of the script.

Alex - It's all really good stuff. Every single one of those suggestions is a choice you could make.

Q - Can you take me through a typical day at the screenwriters lab?

Alex - It's very nice. You're up at a ski resort. It's winter, it's beautiful and you get up and have breakfast with everyone, or at least the lab fellows. Then you have separate meetings. You have breakfast meetings, lunch meetings, then dinner screenings and you'd end up in the bar with the screenwriters telling stories.

Andrew - Some of the best advice you ever get is from your fellow lab participants and some of the most lasting relationships we've had in our film careers is with friends we made at the lab.

Q - At the end of the lab, did you walk away with a new perspective or just a lot of work in front of you?

Andrew - A lot of work. You also get lots of confirmation.

Q - How many people were then on the directors lab?

Andrew - I think it's eight projects again. They can't take more than a certain number as they have limited crews, studio space, equipment and resources..

Alex - You get a skeleton crew of four or five, plus an art department, and then they rotate. You rehearse for a day, then you shoot for a day, you edit for a day, then you have a day off. Even if you're not done cutting your scene, they erase the media from the Avid and you're done! You will of course want to present your scene finished and the editors make sure you don't spend too much time on the first three minutes of your scene and don't get the rest cut. Our editor in the lab, Brent White, eventually cut our film too.

Q - How different were the four scenes you did in the lab to the final ones in the movie?

Andrew - We had very good actors in the lab, but they weren't the right actors for the movie. If you don't have the right guy, you can direct your ass off, or they can work their ass off, but you're still not going to get what you're looking for. We had looked at it as writers for so long, that directing was a new experience.

Q - How did you make the shoot work? Did you split things up?

Alex - We never split things up. We just did our homework each night and prepared what we wanted to do. We'd lived with it for so long, that we knew what we wanted, which is all I think people want from a director. Because of my camera experience, I'm probably a little more lens savvy. We'd still agree on the set up before we pursue the shot. Sometimes, if one of us has a strong note to give an actor, we confirm with each other before giving feedback. We try very hard not to ever give conflicting notes, because then the actors start playing Mom against Dad. We have an emotionally different approach to things, but I think our aesthetics neighbor each other. We also have an agreement if one of us wants to go again, and we didn't get something we wanted, the other one's gotta let him go for it.

Andrew - I'm a more conscious about getting the day done, while Alex is focused on getting what he wants out of the scene. So there were times when I was like, *'are we wasting our time here? Have we got what we needed?'* He'd be like, *'Don't bother me, I'm working'.*

Q - It sounds like perfect harmony as you get the best of both worlds? Producers would love it?

Andrew - Yes, although we're inflexible when there are two of us, and it's hard to persuade both of us.

Q - Did the lab scenes change much from the lab to the final cut of the film?

Andrew - Yes, we condensed and strengthened them.

Q - How did Ted Hope get involved?

Alex - Good Machine optioned *The Slaughter Rule* for 18 months, which basically means they rented it and tried to raise money to get it made. During that time, James Schamus, who wrote *The Ice Storm* and co-wrote *Crouching Tiger, Hidden Dragon*, gave us a lot of notes. Our film used to have one hundred and eighty scenes in it, and James said, *'it's got to have one hundred or less'*. It was a good lesson that we have carried on. We had lots of little quarter page shots with a guy driving a truck, and it was all great stuff, but as James pointed out, it's stuff like that which takes three hours to shoot.

Andrew - Ted came in with his pragmatic notes about production. At the same time, they were taking the script round to the mini majors. They wanted to shoot a $6m film, and it was tricky because one of the cast members was a seventeen year old and the other was a middle aged guy. At that point, we had David Morse, who they loved, but they said, *'we can't finance this film with David Morse'*. So they were suggesting other actors like Nick Nolte, Ed Harris and Harvey Keitel. It was frustrating for us because we loved David and thought he was the right guy. David, being a great guy said, *'this film needs to get made, and if I'm in the way of that happening, I'll step aside.'* But they were unsuccessful getting the Fox Search Light's, the Fine Line's, New Line's and Miramax's to step up. They told us it was basically execution dependent, which means these companies will buy it if we made a good job of making it.

Q - So those companies said, 'go ahead and do it then we'll have a look'?

Andrew - Exactly. Because there was no hook as far as subject matter or casting that would make them want to bank on. Goode Machine said they could get the money together if we shot it digitally, but for our movie we said we couldn't do it digitally, and they said that was cool. They wanted to renew the option for free because they didn't have a lot of money. Instead, we decided we'd try to go out on our own.

Q - How much was the option?

Alex - Very little. $5k. After the lab there was a lot of interest in the script, but we said we wouldn't let anyone option it again. So we decided to do it on a contingency basis, basically let people produce it if they could raise the money. There were a couple of producers interested before we settled on our team. Most of them were from New York and we eventually went with Gavin and Greg O'Connor and Michael Robinson. I met Michael first because he had produced a film called *Trams,* which I liked a lot. We were also close friends with Bob Hawk, who is a consultant for a lot of independent films. He is just an amazing champion of projects that he feels close to. He was behind our film for ten years. He became a producer on the film and helped us at every stage.

Q - What budget were they proposing?

Alex - Greg had a budget that was much lower then what we actually shot and DV came up again. We hired a line producer to budget it on a 16mm shoot, a 35mm shoot and a DV shoot. We were trying to figure out a way to shoot widescreen that was affordable as Super35mm was way too expensive. There was this company in Australia called Multi Vision who modified cameras to shoot two perf as opposed to four perf, which cut your film costs and your processing costs in half and would give you the widescreen look. The other benefit for our movie was that it gave us nineteen minute magazines, so it went through the stock twice as slow, and so there were fewer interuptions to change magazines, which is a real advantage in subzero temperatures.

Andrew - The film is built around three big scenes, which are one-on-one. With those two actors, you wind them up and let them go and it was nice to have the luxury of not having to cut every few minutes.

Q - So you hired your cameras from Australia?

Andrew - Yeah, the guy who owns the cameras came out and was going to be a second shooter on the film. The cameras were falling apart and he had little bits of duct tape and staples holding them together.

Alex - He had a silent, non-synch camera, which a lot of the great shots came from. But it was risky. One camera went down in the first week. We had been shooting with two cameras for a lot of the movie and we had to ship one to LA to get it fixed twice. Eric Edwards, our DP, had many technical questions. Then Brent White, our editor also got in on it because he figured out how to turn two perf back into four perf, which hadn't been done in the US for 20 years.

Andrew - I'm glad we did it because of the look we got, but it wasn't easy. And now I'm addicted to a 1:2.35 ratio.

Q - Do you find industry people are familiar with the technique you used?

Alex - No one has heard of it. Crest who is our film lab looked at it and said, *'Ah, I remember this'*, because those guys are all really knowledgeable. One of them handed me a Xerox list of all the Technoscope films. Our system is not technically Technoscope, because it's not done by Kodak, but it's the same idea. All the spaghetti westerns were shot on Technoscope, *American Graffiti, THX1138.*

Q - What is Technoscope?

Alex - A low budget way to get a widescreen look, even in the seventies. It got outdated because it doesn't take the anamorphic lenses on the camera. We knew it would cost money on the back end, but we figured we would put the money into the production and get the best looking film that we could get. The plan was to make a film for a certain amount of money and use the footage to raise money for post. We were all terrified by the decision, though our biggest problem turned out to be sound. We didn't know that until the cameras showed up. They weren't nearly as quiet as they needed to be. So we had everyone's down filled coats wrapped around the cameras. So that's where we got hammered in post-production. We spent hours in the sound mix taking the camera noise out of it. For this film it was the right decision because it allowed to us to shoot so much film. We had a set up with Eric so that whenever there was something cool going on, a sunset or something, we would just shoot it. I think it allowed us to shoot enough film that we created an impressionistic movie, which is what we were after. Where it really hurt us, is that after we finished our picture lock, put the Avid away, spent a couple of months finishing our post production and doing our sound mix, we started thinking about cutting the film again. But looking at the logistics of what it would take to go back and cut the two perf and blow it up again, it just seemed like we would never get the film re-cut for Sundance.

Andrew - It was a huge risk and I wouldn't want to go through it again.

Q - What were your experiences with sound other than the camera noise?

Andrew - Sound is so crucial. One of the biggest problems with the film now is that people don't get certain lines because they're fuzzy. David Morse had such a powerful, resonant voice, but if it's not clear it people don't understand. So people were looking at a film but they weren't experiencing it.

Alex - You think, *'Ah, I can fix it in the mix'*, which you can if you have a lot of money, but we didn't. We had a great sound lab, Juniper Post, who we paid next to nothing, and they worked their butts off. They gave us a lot of free hours just because they loved our project. But still, there are certain things you can't fix. Such as camera noise.

Andrew - And, because of our stubbornness or fool-hardiness, we were like, *'ADR is the devil'*. It takes you out of the movie. But now if I had the chance, I'd go back and put more ADR in, because I see the ones we put in play and no-ones ever commented on it. With good actors and a good recording session, you can hear the lines so much more clearly.

Alex - What's interesting is seasoned actors like ADR because they can correct things they on set, whereas younger actors resist ADR because they feel it ruins the integrity of the scene. I think not being able to hear a scene is much worse than not being able to see a scene. If there was one person I could have added to the budget, it would have been a sound designer.

Q - How much money did you have to shoot?

Alex - $725k for production. We went a day and a half over, but on our tech day we ended up shooting a lot of stuff that was in the movie, so we snuck a day in, too. We had forty locations in twenty-five days. It was ridiculous.

Andrew - That's again when those cameras paid off, because to cover a football game like that in a day, we needed the extra film. And the small Arri's were helpful, as opposed to big Moviecams for that stuff, because Eric could put in on his shoulder and would be running around with the players, so we were shooting documentary style.

Alex - I ended up shooting quite a bit of film and our gaffer shot some! There were several operators beyond the usual. That was where my former life as a camera assistant paid off.

Q - Were your locations in roughly the same place?

Alex - Roughly in the sense of Montana close! We would drive sixty to one hundred miles to locations. Park View, where we shot some of the Native American stuff was one hundred and fifty miles away, but that was second unit.

Q - How did you operate? Was it a six day week?

Alex - Six day, seventeen hours a day. It was excruciating.

Andrew - It was a weird thing for both of us having worked as crew and knowing what it's like to feel abused by low budget schedules. But we did warn everyone ahead of time.

Q - Did you get the money through private investors?

Alex - Yes, equity financing. We created a limited partnership and you could buy $40k stakes in the film. We raised about $100k that way and then through Sundance, we got a free Avid package and a free titles and opticals package through Pacific Title, who were a great company. Avid donates a Media Composer to Sundance for the year and Sundance loans it to various filmmakers for two months. But we had it for five months. The total budget was $1.2m.

Q - Was Sundance your first festival?

Alex - Yes. We screened a print that had just come out of the lab the day before and we hadn't seen it ourselves! There was a lot of buzz on the project and the first screening went down well. We had great press afterwards. But there was a sense that we weren't getting the offers that we were hoping for.

Andrew - It was weird because our producers, Greg and Gavin, had made *Tumbleweeds* and sold it at Sundance for a lot. It was one of those films that could be said to actually hurt other indie film sales because it was sold for so much and didn't make much money. So, distributors aren't likely to buy films like that again.

Alex - *The Slaughter Rule* doesn't have a kind of commercial saleability. The truth is that our of 20 or more dramatic films at Sundance each year, only four films get awards and only about six get bought.

Andrew - We were just happy to be at Sundance and that was reward enough. You work so hard to get there, and only fifteen films get selected, and then there is this unpleasant expectation that you can't just go there, you've got to sell there. You've got to win some awards and then you have a successful film. Certain films that get bought at Sundance get a lot of heat and then they are released and disappear within a week.

Q - How has your film done internationally?

Andrew - They loved it down under. We went to Sydney, Melbourne and New Zealand. We went to Athens and are going to Stockholm tomorrow. It has been hugely rewarding to see the film play on a screen in front of 1200 eager film goers in New Zealand.

Alex - Cowboy Pictures made an offer at Sundance for theatrical. Unfortunately, they couldn't make an offer that had an advance. With the amount of money that was spent on the film, the producers needed to see an advance. We were optimistic. Lion's Gate saw it two times after the festival. Every distributor watched it. You never know what's going on with sales agents and we have one of the best out there, but he wasn't a producer on our film.

Q - How did your sales agent, Jon Sloss, get involved?

Alex - Our lawyer used to work with him and Michael Robinson had connections with John as well. We had him for a month prior to Sundance.

Q - Did he know the film was going to Sundance at that point?

Alex - Yes. We'd already had some interest from other a sales agents. Some were big, some were more passionate, some made more promises. It was tricky. There were certain things that we learned. HBO wanted to come in two weeks before we started shooting and make it an HBO movie, and they would have doubled the budget. But we would have had to change the format. I think our producers wish we had done it though. Sometimes we also wish we'd done it. I don't think if we'd made it that way, it would have ever played at Sundance though.

Q - Will it be an LA / New York theatrical release?

Andrew - Cowboy has released it in cities like Portland, Minneapolis, Austin. It's going to play in LA, New York, San Francisco, Oakland and after that it will go to Boston and Chicago.

Q - Who is your video release with?

Alex - The Sundance Channel. It's a great deal. The reason we went with them is because of how good the video output deal is. We got an advance from Sundance. It wasn't what we hoped for but they have been extremely good at promoting it on their channel and selling it to video and DVD retailers.

Q - What was the structure of the deal with Cowboy?

Alex - Cowboy has the theatrical for several years*. Sundance has the video rights for twelve years and the cable rights for two years. So in two years, Cowboy will have a second cable. So they can make some money back by selling it to whoever will buy it.

*Editorial note - Cowboy declared bankruptcy in Nov 2003 which, as usual, means the filmmakers will probably never see their fair shares.

Q - What advice would you offer a new film maker?

Andrew - Don't skimp on rehearsal time. It will save your ass on the set if you've been able to amply rehearse your actors before the cameras are going and your money is disappearing second by second. Don't neglect to get the best sound mixer you can get, and pay attention to the sound department's problems on set. You don't want to have to 'fix it in the mix' because it costs too damn much. Don't make enemies with the dolly grip. Don't be afraid to fire someone who is not working out as it won't get better as the shoot goes along. You will learn more about filmmaking AFTER you have shot the film than you will on the set, because the set is all about reflexes, instant decisions, dealing with immediate problems, going with your instinct, letting the magic happen etc. But your film will live and die by the decisions you make near the end of the editing process. Remember, until you reach picture-lock, you are still making your film. After that, it's all about fixing your film, which is something else entirely, and you have many fewer tools at your disposal by that point.

Alex - Do your homework- The most common problems on a filmset stem from not being properly prepared. So many folks are too eager to shoot, and haven't done the work they need to, in order to get the most out of your shoot. We had 8 years prep for 24 days of shooting. That might be too much prep! Hire people you trust, and then trust them to do the job you hire them for. Don't micromanage every department / facet of the shoot. Hire excellent folks, and tell them what you want, but don't tell them how to get it. Accept your actors' ideas about their characters early on - don't fight them about who they are playing from the get-go. If they realize you're open to their ideas, they will work extra hard, because their ideas have suddenly become taken seriously, have suddenly become a reality. Don't freak out. It's only a movie. And you can sleep after you wrap.

28e FESTIVAL DU CINEMA AM
...UVILLE

Miguel Arteta   Matthew Greenfield

Photo by Tony Barson - © WireImage.com

STAR MAPS, CHUCK & BUCK & THE GOOD GIRL

Q - How did you get together and make films?

Miguel - I'm from Puerto Rico, and have liked movies all my life. When I was sixteen I moved to Boston and started watching foreign movies, and that got me inspired to pick up a video camera. I fell in love with the all American movies and I dropped out of Harvard so I could watch movies everyday - that was my real education. I had a friend who I made movies with, and he went to Wesleyan University in Connecticut where he was taught by Jeanine Basinger. She says *'Every great director defines film in his or her own way'*. And when you watch great movies you realize that is the case, like a directors personality and point of view is what effuses, even in old Hollywood. By the time you're done with the program, you realize, *'I don't have to come to Hollywood and imitate Quentin Tarantino or anybody! My most powerful weapon is my own point of view'*. The more particular the ideas I have of the world, the stronger the piece is going to be, so I don't have to worry about trying to compete with other people. I told her I wanted to make a musical, and so I made it, and Mathew produced it, which is how we met.

Q - What's your background?

Matthew - I grew up in LA and I started making shorts in high school on Super8mm. I knew I wanted to work in film in some way and I went to Wesleyan, where they have a great film program and that's where I hooked up with Miguel, and we worked on each other's films there. And after college I went to Seattle where I worked in theater. Miguel went to the American Film Institute, and I came back down to LA and worked on his film. We decided to make *Star Maps* on our own.

Miguel - When I graduated from Wesleyan, I went to NY and I worked as a location scout for Sydney Lumet on a couple of his movies. Then I gave my car mechanic a copy of that musical, and he loved it and he set up a meeting with Jonathan Demme.

Q - Your car mechanic?

Miguel - Yes. He called Jonathan to watch my musical, and Jonathan hired me on the spot to be a PA on the documentary he was working on. Watching Lumet and Demme work was kind of a revelation to me. Demme was a real inspiration. He really encouraged young people to go and do it themselves.

Q - What do you think about film school?

Matthew - The competition can be counter productive. They justify it because they say the real world is dog eat dog and you have to learn. But the whole point of being in school is that you learn in a safe atmosphere so when you get to the cut throat world, you can deal with it from a better place.

Q - When you guys finished at the AFI, was it then that you decided to do 'Star Maps'?

Matthew - We both had day jobs, and we would get together at night and plot out a story and the characters. That took a long time as we were only able to work in the evenings a couple of times a week. From there we got a basic story and wrote a screenplay. It was four years from the day we discussed *Star Maps* for the first time to when we were at Sundance.

Q - How did you raise the money?

Matthew - The script was underdeveloped and way too long, but it was the best that we had at the time. We had to get the movie done and we said, *'We've made short films before. It can't be that different. Let's see what we need, and figure out how to get it.'* We did a whole series of budgets, from what we thought was the minimum we could do it for, which was $65k, up to a couple of million dollars, which we would never get. We made a list of everybody that we thought might put money into the film - friends, family or people who liked our short films - people who might have a reason other than just business sense for wanting to be involved. We started talking to people about it and started showing them the script. We had a reading which was a disaster, it was too long and we left the stage directions in, but somehow a good number of people ended up putting money in the movie anyway.

Q - How many people did you have in the audience at the reading?

Matthew - Twenty. Somebody who had been at the reading said, *'I really liked your script. It's really interesting. I think maybe it should be darker, but I'm interested in supporting it.'* And we were like, *'This is great.'* We thought, *'this is a dark movie. It's a movie about a father prostituting his son, about a kid prostituting himself to be successful'*. So we thought, *'This is a man after our own hearts'* and he committed to putting in a certain amount of money. We kept looking for more money and it took us a year before we found another penny. We found somebody else who we had been talking to for a long time who said, *'Ok, I'll match what you already have.'* Then we found some more people that put in some more little bits and pieces. It took about two years or so to raise the money, full time trying. We put it in the can for $230k, and finished it for $475k. Post was tough because we had no money, and also because there were story problems in the script that we tried to fix but couldn't. We edited for eleven months and then we re-shot parts of the movie for six days. Then we edited it for three more months and screened it at Sundance.

Q - Who was the guy who initially came on board?

Miguel - A friend of a friend who was interested in supporting independent movies. It's always a fluke. You meet someone who is reasonable, and it's the first time they have decided to put some money into independent movies, because they don't do it a second time! He just wanted to support independent film. He liked the short film Miguel made as his second year project at the AFI, which gave us the opening to show him the script and then he came on board. We did all the casting at his house, we shot in his house, we used his cars. He even appears in the movie! He was a part of the whole production from beginning to end and he had invaluable notes on the script and on editing.

Q - Was he supportive or interfering?

Matthew - Very supportive. He did an incredible thing. He said, *'I'm going to invest this much money into your movie and I hope that I'll make money, but you guys make the movie. I'll tell you what I think here and there, and you can tell me when you want my advice. I'm not going to get in the way.'* He was true to his word. We were very fortunate.

Q - How long was the writing process?

Miguel - It took us about eight months to come up with a very detailed thirty-five page outline that Matt and I did together, working nights. Then it took me almost a year to extend that into a script that originally was 189 pages, and that was whittled down to 139 pages. But we didn't know how to write and that became a problem when we edited. Only when I went to the Sundance

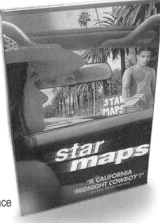

writing lab on another project and showed a bit of the film to a lot of the writing advisors and students did I get anywhere. We wrote it and then we went out and reshot 1/3 of the whole thing. We went back into production for six days and changed shots in some of the movie, and then it was in good shape.

Q - Was the Sundance writing lab beneficial?

Miguel - Yes. The teachers are amazing, and the way Michelle Satter runs the program is supportive and takes the push and the competition out of it. It's like an artists colony that's been applied to independent filmmaking and writing.

Q - Did you do any other test screenings before Sundance?

Matthew - We had screenings for friends and friends of friends. We tried to get small groups of people, some that we knew well and others that we didn't at all. We just screened it on video at people's houses. That's part of how we knew it wasn't working, but also it helped find the solutions. The editing process was eleven months, then we reshot, and then three more months editing.

Q - How did Sundance come about? Did you just submit it?

Matthew - Yeah. We gave them a tape of the cut as it was on the date of the deadline. We crossed our fingers and waited until Thanksgiving to find out.

Miguel - It definitely was a weird transformation. I had sixteen credit cards maxed out from staying alive during the four years. I was very depressed. It was a dark period and to have all that validation in one night was very strange.

Matthew - We didn't have any money, but we rented a condo and said *'Anybody who wants to come can stay is welcome'*. We had seventeen of the cast and crew that just crashed on the floor. It was very exciting and we had no idea what to expect. We were working day and night over the holidays, trying to get the movie ready and still raising money in January of '97. We got the print of the film the day before we left. The first screening we had was on the first full day of the festival, and it was half full. We screened it in a conference room that had been switched over and they put in a temporary projection booth. We had terrible technical problems where the movie started without sound, and we got them to stop it and it start a second time and they didn't want to rewind it or stop it - we thought our lives had been ruined at that point, but we were able to get a projectionist in there to fix the problem.

Miguel - Indie Wire was really helpful. It was their second year, but they spread the word about that screening. A woman at Searchlight was there and after she said *'I really like your movie. I'm going convince more people from Searchlight to come to the next one.'* The second screening was a big surprise because there were lines around the block and we were wondering what the lines were for, and then we realized the lines were for our movie! The movie played incredibly well, but I was really nervous because I kept seeing the Searchlight people getting up and leaving. I was convinced it wasn't going to work and no one would buy the movie. Later on I found out they had been going to the bathroom to call their lawyers and our lawyers and try to do it before other people got involved! Also when the lights came on, I realized that Matthew was gone.

Matthew - There's a Q&A at Sundance after each film. I left and Miguel stayed to do the Q&A!

Miguel - After the Q&A, I made my way back. Matthew and our lawyer were sitting there looking stunned. Fox Searchlight had made an offer - Matthew said casually, *'They've put an offer on the table for $2.5m'*. I drank the rest of my beer. It's a weird experience. There's a one-page document where you write the name of your movie, your name, the amount of money and you sign on the bottom. Then the next day you're in the news. Our lives changed radically, but we still had a lot of work with the movie.

Matthew - When we got back, we were back in the thick of it, working really hard until the release of the movie. The movie came out in July, but then with international stuff and publicity, it took the rest of the year without being able to get to other stuff.

Miguel - We had the premiere at Mann's Chinese Theater and our relatives all came, and went down the red carpet. After four years of hard, nerve wracking work it was really great. I got offered some TV work out of that premiere.

Matthew - Then we started the process of trying to make *Chuck & Buck.* We had had it for a little while because Mike White, who is actually in *Star Maps,* had shown us the script.

Q - How did they pay you your advance? Was it staggered?

Matthew - There was a small amount that came right away to keep us and the movie going. It was divided up, something like 70% with basic delivery and the rest came with full delivery.

Miguel - We tried to look into studio projects, things like *The Mod Squad,* but we couldn't finish the scripts! We couldn't get enough interesting material for a studio picture and Mike's script kept haunting us. We had put it aside and said, *'Maybe we should do a bigger movie',* but the characters in the script were irresistible to us, so we kept going back to that.

Matthew - No one wanted to put any money into *Chuck & Buck.* We were doing it very small. Everybody said, *'Why do you want to make something so dark? You should make something lighter.'* A lot of people appreciated the script, but said, *'Maybe you should wait and do a more successful movie first and then come back and do this.'* But we didn't have any other projects that we liked. We were very optimistic, set up offices in my house and started pre-production while we looked for the money. But we couldn't find the money, so we shut down. I got really depressed.

Q - A lot of new filmmakers think if you have a successful film, you're there, but you've got to keep going?

Matthew - It took us two and a half years to make another movie and that was a low budget $300k movie!

Miguel - *Chuck & Buck* was just as hard. There are no rules. The most important thing you can learn from hearing people's stories is that there are no set, right or wrong ways. You have to really commit to trusting your gut instincts and doing things the way you do them. We could have tried to make *The Mod Squad* and the guy who wrote it went on to write *8 Mile* . He's probably one of the most successful writers in Hollywood right now and that's fine. But we couldn't do that. So we had no choice but to find a project that we could really fall in love with and something that everybody else called *'career suicide'.*

Q - Did Miguel have an agent before or after Star Maps?

Matthew - Yes. He said to me *'I really like your short film, but I'm not going to be able to get you any work.'* It was a very accurate statement. He wasn't saying it to be mean, it was just true.

Miguel - Unless you can write a script that's going to generate interest, or you can align yourself with a script that has a lot of interest, an agent won't be able to do much. If you can write a script yourself, it will represent your own personality and point of view the best. The more unique it is, the more particular it is to who you are, the more it's going to drive people.

Q - How did the finance come about for Chuck & Buck?

Matthew - Blow Up are independent financiers in NY and we had shown them *Star Maps,* but at the time, they didn't want to put money into it, but they were fans of it after it was done. We then showed them *Chuck & Buck* and they said they really loved it, but didn't have access to any cash.

Miguel - We saw *'The Celebration'* in '98, and we were like, *'You know what? The quality of video is different than video, it's different than film. It's a neat thing that works.'* If you're telling a subjective story, using mostly close-ups like a video diary, this is perfect. It's really intimate. Ironically, that same week, Jason and John called us and said, *'We're starting this new digital division and we want to announce Chuck & Buck as our first film if you're willing to do it.'*

Q - What was the budget for that?

Matthew - About half a million. We shot on MiniDV PAL.

Q - What were the major differences you noticed between 35mm and Mini DV?

Miguel - It was very good for the actors because actors get less intimidated when you have a 5lb plastic object that everybody ignores. The actors become more fearless and they take more chances. With a 35mm camera, even if you have a tiny crew, people are really paying attention to the huge monster.

Matthew - And the 35mm camera costs dollars and dollars. So you're really aware of every frame you're shooting. On video, you don't have the same concerns. You still have time limits and things like that, but you have the freedom to shoot more takes when you need to. We were able to work with a smaller crew and work more quickly and efficiently with very little equipment.

Miguel - Also there was a feeling creatively among people from Hollywood and independent film community that if you are shooting video, you can have more of a crazy film. There's more artistic leeway given to a digital project. So in some ways it was great and it bust the door open for doing more interesting work. Before this, it cost more money and everybody was paranoid. They were like, *'There's only X amount of movies to be made and I shouldn't be talking to this director/producer because we're all competing for this money'.* Now we have to talk to each other because we have to help each other with information. That's the first time in many years and that's been a really positive result of doing this. We went to Sundance in 2000 with *Chuck & Buck* and the year before *The Blair Witch Project* sold, but our year was the first time there were digital movies in competition. When we sold the movie, the fact that it was shot on digital didn't come up. They didn't care.

Q - Did you shoot too much footage?

Miguel - Yes! Our editor was miserable with over ninety hours of footage.

Matthew - We had about 2½ times the amount of footage as *Star Maps,* so it was more work. It wasn't that there were more takes being shot, it was more because we were shooting with two cameras and also Miguel would go talk to the actors without turning off the cameras. It takes a while to reset everything, so they wouldn't turn off the cameras, and as soon as they were ready, they could just launch into it. So it gave fluidity to the shooting. You can shoot really long takes without worrying about it too.

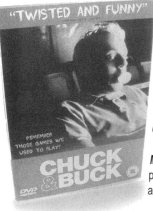

Matthew - We shot both *Star Maps* and *Chuck & Buck* without a generator, just lights that we could plug into house power. We had an incredible DP, Chuy Chavez!

Q - How many shooting days were there on Star Maps and Chuck & Buck?

Miguel - 29 days in the main production and 6 days in re-shoots for *Star Maps.* 24 days for *Chuck & Buck* and 3 days of re-shoots.

Q - Were there any union issues on Chuck and Buck?

Matthew - No, it was too small. We didn't have any trucks, a generator or any equipment. At one point, some of the unions came by while we were shooting *Chuck & Buck* and they didn't even come and find me to ask about it. They just looked at us and said, *'Call us when you have a bigger movie.'*

Q - Do you think the unions thought, 'Oh, it's domestic digital cameras... fine, just go ahead!'

Matthew - I hope they understand that some movies are made low budget because people need to learn, and that's how people get the skills to make bigger budget movies, and that it's good for everybody. I think there's enough work out there that people aren't too concerned with being taken advantage of. I think that unions want to make fair and safe work places and I think if you're conscious of being fair and safe to people then it isn't too much of an issue. When we got to a bigger budget on *The Good Girl*. We did all the unions.

Q - Did you deal with SAG for your cast?

Matthew - We did one of the low budget agreements, and so it was SAG on *Chuck & Buck*. What I found is that on the $500k and below, they're all willing to make it work. Once you start going up to $1m then you have to start working out other things.

Q - Did you have to get permits?

Matthew - We did everything legally. We had permits and insurance. We're a big believer in following the rules for that kind of stuff.

Q - Was acting in it something Mike (actor and the writer of Chuck and Buck) wanted to do?

Matthew - He said, *'I'd like to audition. I'd like to play a part, but its not a requirement.'*

Miguel - When we made a decision on not using name actors, I told Matthew, *'Let's not worry about non-actors, whether someone has an interest in acting or not, let's just think about who is right.'* And Matthew suggested, *'Well maybe Chris Weitz could play Chuck?'* and I realized that that would be great.

Matthew - They had not acted professionally. They were writers and they had just directed *American Pie,* but it hadn't come out yet. They are friends of ours but, we really believed that Mike White, and Chris and Paul are all smart, creative people. We had a feeling that they had chosen to express themselves in one direction of writing and directing but we believed that they could do it through acting too.

Q - Was the post-production process smoother?

Matthew - Yes. We had a better sense of what we were doing, and we had a little bit of a budget. We knew we'd have to do some reshoots, but we kept them minimal. We didn't have a proper amount of money for the music or the mixing or the other things that were costly. So it was still difficult, and we had to work to get it all done. We were fortunate enough to get into Sundance again. Again, we showed them a rough cut.

Miguel - This one was much closer to being complete. Like everybody else, we sent them a tape and crossed our fingers. They called up and said, *'You got it into the competition.'* We were stunned.

Q - How did The Good Girl come about?

Miguel - *The Good Girl* had been written at the same time as *Chuck & Buck*. I wanted to do it from the beginning, but Mike was trying to direct it himself, and finally when we got into Sundance with *Chuck & Buck*, he got too busy, so he let us have the script.

Matthew - *Chuck & Buck* sold well, and this time, we were like, ' *If we can sell the movie we'll go right away and try and find the money for The Good Girl.*' The day after we sold *Chuck & Buck* we showed *The Good Girl* to all the companies that could have come in and bought it. Everybody had the same response, '*We like it but we're not really interested in financing it*'.

Miguel - They were saying, '*That was fantastic, we love it and we were wondering if you could convince Mike White to write something for us*'. Everybody passed on it several times.

Matthew - Kirk D'Amico got involved on *The Good Girl* at the time Mike was going to direct it. He was doing foreign sales and trying to raise money, which was difficult with a first time director and no star. When we started looking for the money he became involved again and over the next summer, he raised money from a German company who basically bought it as part of his company. He said, '*Go for it*' and we said '*We need a final cut which we have had on our first movies*' and he said, '*Sure, go for it!*'

Q - What was the budget on that?

Matthew - It was just under $6m. We were thinking it would be smaller, but once we got Jennifer and knew we were going to shoot on location in LA, the budget started going up. We had to go union.

Q - What were differences are there between a $500k and a $6m movie?

Miguel - We had experienced actors, which was different because the non-actors in *Chuck & Buck* made it fascinating to work with, but it was different working with more experienced cast, too. Different, not better or worse.

Matthew - We had a little more control and on *The Good Girl* we took an empty warehouse and turn it into this store set.

Miguel - When you have several $million and a union crew and you want to improvise, '*Let's shoot over here*', it becomes cumbersome. You be more prepared and willing to give up spontaneity. Until you get to a $60m budget where everyone's like, '*Well, so what if we wasted $1m?*' You don't get that feeling of being spontaneous again.

Q - Why did you choose Jennifer Anniston?

Miguel - We had thought about actresses who had done a lot of dark, independent movies, but Mike suggested that we cast against type, '*How about casting America's Sweetheart, Jennifer Anniston?*' We had a gut instinct that she would be tremendous, and also it would be nice for the film because she's so relateable to her stardom. She doesn't feel out of reach. She's beautiful, but it's not the kind of beauty that alienates you. So we felt it would make these weird characters making strange choices more understandable because they are played by somebody you feel close to.

Matthew - And having somebody with comedic talent would help as well and Miguel had an idea that the best way we could structure this was to have someone who's very funny playing Justine, a role that allows them to do almost no comedy. Then surround them by other funny people.

Q - Was it difficult working with a huge star?

Miguel - I think Jennifer had a better understanding than we did that she was putting her whole reputation on the line. We were thinking that this would be a nice little excursion for her from *Friends*. When the movie came out, I really realized that this was a high-pressured situation for her.

Matthew - She was a dream. We were fortunate. We didn't know her beforehand, but she was such a pleasure, both personally and professionally. She set an incredible tone for the rest of the cast and the crew and for us, for everybody putting their hearts into it and working hard.

Miguel - I would recommend someone making their first bigger project movie to use a star who's excited to do it. Jennifer wanted to do something different, and this represented a whole new opportunity for her. She was very excited and there wasn't a feeling that anyone was doing anyone a favor.

Q - So stars are reachable?

Matthew - I think now actors from all levels understand the value of independent film as a creative experience. Many are open for figuring out creative ways financially to work it and get involved with the movie.

Miguel - It all comes from the script and they are accessible if you have a script that has some integrity.

Q - If they had a choice of making a low budget feature or a short, which would you recommend?

Matthew - You just have to figure out what's right for you. Shorts are helpful, both creatively and for learning the craft. They can help raise money for other projects. I don't think we'd have been able to raise the money on any of these movies without having had shorts to show that we could tell a story.

Miguel - Also it takes away the intimidation about the technology. A lot of young filmmakers are nervous about where they are going to put the camera, what lens to use etc. You make a couple of short movies and you realize that nobody knows what they're doing and it doesn't really matter all that much.

Q - What are the common mistakes you have experienced?

Miguel - When editing I remember something that Jonathan Demme said, '*It's better for the audience to be two minutes behind you than thirty seconds ahead of you*'.

Matthew - Also, edit until you're done. There's tremendous pressure to be like, '*That is good enough and the time is up...*' but a small amount of time more can improve the movie dramatically.

Miguel - Don't let go of the movie just because people say '*You ran out of money, you have to finish*'. If you have a feeling that '*I haven't captured the thing that excited me about this idea,*' then re-shoot the whole thing if you have to, but don't let go of the movie until you feel you have captured the initial excitement of the project idea.

Q - What advice would you give new filmmakers?

Miguel - Write a story and characters the way you see them and don't try and prove anything to anyone.

Matthew - Understand that there are no rules, and you have to do it your own way. You have to, both creatively and practically, find what's right for you and it's really important and helpful to look at how other people have done, it so you can see what the options are. But then you have to say, '*Is this right for me, for my film and the way I'm going about it?*' Also, make your first film first on as little money as you can because there is tremendous pressure in making a feature. The less money you have, the less pressure there is, and there's going to be too much pressure no matter what the budget! And also the less money you spend, the more likely it is that you can have control over your vision and I think that's what leads to success.

Jeff Balis
Producer

BEING A PRODUCER

Q - What is your job?

Jeff - I'm a film producer, specializing in lower budget features that straddle the independent and studio worlds.

Q - What's your background?

Jeff - I first started working on a movie as the director's assistant, which is an ideal job for learning about filmmaking. You make sure the director is happy and has Diet Cokes and has the information he or she needs, and in return, you get a first hand look at how the movie is made. One thing about my first job was I had the chance to work on a film from pre-production all the way through post. That is a fantastic learning opportunity. In pre-production, you see the director and producers making story changes in order to fix plot and character problems. Then you're in production and you can see how those things are implemented. In the editing room, you can see the results of those decisions, and if they worked or not. Other people are making the decisions, but in your own head, you think, '*You idiots, you should have been doing this!*', or '*that's a good idea, this guy's smarter than I am*'. It's only by being involved for a long time that you can get a good perspective on what's happening.

Q - Would you recommend film school?

Jeff - Film school never really called to me. Some people like the structure of a school geared toward what they want to do, and for them it makes sense. But you can definitely get to where you want to go in the film business without it. As far as undergraduate education, I think a good liberal arts education will get you just as far. Reading great books, studying history, and in general soaking up as many stories as you can will give you the perspective to make good movies. That, to me, is more important than technical knowledge about filmmaking. I do think it is crucial to make some short films and shoot actual film or video footage at some point, but you can do that on you own.

Q - How did you meet Chris Moore?

Jeff - He was speaking at my university while shooting *Good Will Hunting*. I had made a Kung Fu action comedy, and after his speech we talked and he said, '*Send me your film*'. So I did. He sent it back to me and said, '*Give me a call when you get out of school*'. So I called him and he hired me as an intern on the Fox 2000 movie called *Best Laid Plans*. I eventually moved up to become the director's assistant. Chris responding to my film is an example of how he is very much a proponent of follow-through. If somebody calls you, you call them back. Another great lesson I learned from Chris is not to '*Step over dollars to pick up pennies*'. When you negotiate with some people, they vigorously grab for everything that they can and try to screw you so hard in the first meeting without realizing that there are fifteen other negotiations you're going to be making over the life of the movie. You have to maintain focus on the bigger picture. You are working with the same people and the same companies, so you need to concentrate on the important things, and that's not always carving out the best deal for yourself.

Q - Did you continue to work for Chris after Best Laid Plans was over?

Jeff - Not immediately. I went with Mike Barker, my boss and the director of BLP, to England for post production. I became friends with the editor and we'd have dinner at Indian restaurants, and talk about the movie. That's where I first started learning about the power of the editorial side of film making.

Q - And when the film was completed, what happened next?

Jeff - After *Good Will Hunting*, Chris got a deal with Miramax and I started working for him, first as his office assistant during *American Pie,* and after that came out and did well, as a development exec. From the beginning, Chris was always very much producer-orientated; if we needed a new copier for the office, it was *'Produce the copier'*. Then *'Produce the wrap party'*, *'produce the holiday cards.'* He didn't want all the information, he wanted me to get the information and synthesize my own solution. I had to be prepared to defend it, which is ultimately what producing is. It's about using information, getting the bottom line, and making sure you're making the right decisions. And being accountable.

Q - When did Project Greenlight come about?

Jeff - The idea for *Project Greenlight* came in to LivePlanet (the company Chris Moore formed with Matt Damon, Ben Affleck and Sean Bailey) by way of Miramax Television. We worked to hammer out the mechanism of the show and the contest, and the question of who would produce the movie came up. Chris was producing *American Pie 2* and had a kid on the way, so I was put onto it to run it day to day. I had done a lot of the producing *'bits'* before, but this was the first time I did it from beginning to end.

Q - Was 'Project Greenlight' set up for the cameras?

Jeff - No. Because of condensing and editing, the show isn't an exact replica of real life, but it does depict what things were like on set and what it's like to make a movie. The conflicts are real and the characters are not too far off their human counterparts. The stories were simplified and some of the successes were cut to emphasis the hardships, but everything you saw really happened. For example, we shot in the rain one day in Chicago, and the crew, which was used to terrible weather, said it was one of the worst days they've ever had. Truthfully, it was a mess. To this day, those guys believe we shot in the rain because it made good television. But, that was just the reality of the situation. Because of out very limited budget and schedule, we were either shooting in the rain or not at all.

Q - That's the rule of low budget filmmaking. You just have to go for it?

Jeff - Now as I'm more experienced, I would say we could have been more prepared. But weather is weather and you're at its mercy. If you have many exterior locations, a twenty five day schedule, and rain is on the forecast, you are going to feel pain. You'd better be prepared, and your director better be ready to compromise. On small movies, you can't throw money at problems, so you have to be creative in coming up with alternate plans. That's the fun of it.

Q - Did you get used to the cameras being there all the time?

Jeff - Kind of. Yes, well, sort of. Maybe. No, not at all.

Q - You became a kind of a hero. Didn't Chris say 'go away' from the shoot and then call you back?

Jeff - In *Greenlight I*, there was a power struggle between the line producer and me that lead to my fight with Chris. Things eventually worked out, but it was rocky for awhile during production. I certainly feel lucky with the way I was ultimately depicted on the show, and it was nice to have people rooting for *'my character'*. Chris and I are about to do *Greenlight II*, and I'm very curious to see how it goes. As strained as our relationship was on the first one, I feel pretty good that we will be able to work together effectively next time around.

Q - What kind of benefits did you get out of the whole thing?

Jeff - From a business standpoint, it seems to have had a positive impact. It's been helpful for getting my calls returned. More than anything, it's been a lot of fun. I got to dip my little toe in fame and see what it's like. It's been pretty interesting but I'm happy to stay behind the cameras .

Q - What was the next step for you after season one of Project Greenlight?

Jeff - I made a $1 million film this summer called *Speakeasy,* which was the *Project Greenlight 1* runner up. Brendan Murphy wrote and directed, and Chris, Matt, Ben and I produced. We're taking it around to film festivals. I also started my own company called Wisenheimer Films. The first Wisenheimer film is called *Waiting,* which is an under $5m comedy about waiters that I'm producing in early 2004. Rob McKittrick is the writer/director and Ryan Reynolds is staring. I've been working on it for a number of years now, and this is my baby.

Q - How do you become a producer?

Jeff - You can blaze your own path, or try and go through the system. If you blaze your own path, it's all about finding access to talent. That talent can be actors, writers, or directors. The most direct way, though certainly not easy, is to find screenplays, even if you have to write them yourself. Align yourself with great writers, and use your literature background to help turn good scripts into great scripts. Pair up-and-coming writers with ideas of your owns. You can also align yourself with directors and actors, but you need to bring something to the table because you yourself don't have any value yet (unless you can bring money). When you look for material, you need to find projects that will get people's attention. People walk out of movies all the time and say '*I can write something much better than that piece of crap*' That isn't good enough. Until you have established yourself in the system and have earned the right to churn out crap, you need to find gems. The studios have plenty of mediocre romantic comedies in their vaults, so you need to bring in something that's original. So when people read it they say '*Holy shit, how do I get into business with you?*' If you want to get into the mainstream industry, it helps if you can afford to work for free for awhile. Then you can be in a position to chose better opportunities, rather than seize the first thing. The goal at first is to get as close as possible to the people that you respect and who are doing what you want to do. Working for people who have the power to get things done is important too. Then just impress the hell out of them, and hopefully they will help you move forward. You can get abused, so ideally you want to work for someone who cares about what you want to do. That's not easy to find, and you have to have a built-in meter for knowing when enough is enough. Thick skin certainly helps.

Q - What sort of negotiating skills do you need to be a producer?

Jeff - If you're starting out, you're going to get pushed around. My personal belief is to allow yourself to get screwed on the first one. Nobody wants to get screwed, but let yourself to give up the money if it's going to get the movie made. That's all you should care about. Then on the next one you'll have more negotiating power.

Q - What is your advice for independent filmmakers on keeping themselves financially afloat?

Jeff - It takes much longer than you think to get a movie made, so you need to have many things going on at once. Hopefully one of your projects will go into production before you run out of money, and if you're lucky, that film will keep you afloat long enough to get another going. Be careful, though, because just when you think your film is a sure thing, it falls apart for some obscure, irrelevant reason, and if you don't have anything else lined up, it can be a cold winter. The objective it to get movies made and do everything you can to turn them into hits. Then you're a guy that can make people money, and that is a good thing.

Q - Fighting for control of the movie must be an issue as well?

Jeff - Always. Everyone thinks they are the smartest person in the room and that they should be making all the decisions. People will usually seize as much control as they can. In general, it helps to have a balanced opinion and recognize that there are two sides to things. Choose your battles, and that applies to everything in life. It's moderation. You can be a tyrannical monster, a real asshole, but you better be a genius. You are probably a miserable person, but you can be really successful. Just make sure you are in fact a genius, and that other people agree with that assessment. You want to work with directors who are decisive and can make strong decisions, but have at least some degree of flexibility. When that director has a few $100 million dollar grosses behind them, they can afford to develop obsessive control issues and God complexes. But hopefully not on the tiny, budget-less indie film you are struggling to pull together. If a writer/director is making the story of their childhood, it can be quite difficult to convince them to relax creative control. '*Compromise*' is not a word they want to hear.

Q - What are the elements you look for in a crew?

Jeff - The most important component of a producer's job is hiring people. If you hire the right people, create good chemistry and treat them well, then you don't have to do very much. Check references. Find people that have experience doing a movie comparable to what you're doing, and who are still hungry and want the opportunity. On low budget film, there's a trade off between experience and hunger. If you've got a 2nd AD who you hire as a 1st AD, that person is going to be hungry and will do it for little or no money, as their real reward is the experience, credit and the step up the ladder. If you find yourself begging a 1st AD who has done $80m movies to do your film for no money, you are opening yourself up to trouble. They're going to be great at the job, but that may come at the cost of a lack of tolerance for other things that your small production cannot provide. Occasionally, you can find both experience and enthusiasm and that is the greatest thing in the world.

On a low budget production, if you're not paying a lot of money, you need at the very least to provide good working conditions. One thing that you can always give to your crew that doesn't cost anything is *respect*. Remember that you are hiring artisans, so they should be treated as such. If you hire the right people, respect can go a long way toward mitigating the long days and low pay. Build a reputation as someone who crew and actors want to work with. You can't substitute for having a happy crew because ultimately, as much as the director is directing the movie, it's the grips, electricians, drivers, etc who are crafting your movie. Naturally, it is important to avoid personality problems. If you have two geniuses that can't work together, you're going to have trouble.

Q - If you're in that situation where you've hired your team and you have an awkward crew member, do you just have to get rid of that person?

Jeff - Firing people is always hard, so it shouldn't be the first option. If someone just isn't working out and all attempts at solutions fail and the film is suffering, then it is an unfortunate necessity. It is particularly hard to fire people in the middle of production, or even once prep has begun in earnest, because you don't know all the groundwork they've done. If it's a location manager, they have contacts with all of your locations. They will also have allegiances with other crew members. If you fire the DP, all the camera, grip and electric crew might leave. That will be painful, but it may be necessary. Make sure you do your homework before you fire someone. Better yet, hire the right crew from the beginning. Time is so expensive that if you see things not working out, you have to do something about it immediately.

Q - Is it always a bad thing having a 'yeller' as an AD?

Jeff - It can be good or bad. You just don't want them to alienate people or generally exacerbate other issues.

Q - What are the main problems when shooting on set?

Jeff - Working with kids, weather, animals, water or special effects are all tricky. The best way to avoid problems, no matter what they are, is to stay close to the project. Try to develop relationships with everyone on the crew so you know what's going on. Watch rushes, and make sure you have a good editor. It should be someone you trust, so you can say, *'How's the footage? Good? Are you getting everything you need? What are we not getting?'* They're the ones who can look at it objectively. When you start to see trouble forming, head it off as soon as you can. Have frank conversations early on. This is a good way of letting people know what's important to you. Anticipation is crucial, but you also need to take the next step and make sure your foresight is relayed to other people so they don't get blindsided. You have to take the information flow very seriously because you potentially waste people's time and resources and they don't like that. If people are busting their ass to do things and then you say, *'Oh but we didn't tell you that we're not gong to be shooting that tomorrow.'* They say, *'We stayed all weekend because we thought you were going to do that.'* The next time you say, *'We're going to do this'* they'll work half as hard. So make sure that you set up effective systems of communication.

Q - Do you have much to do with distribution?

Jeff - Distribution is usually tightly woven into getting the film made. It is often easier to get your movie financed than it is to get it distributed. Finding the pipes to get your product to consumers is expensive and tightly controlled; that goes for films as well as toys and kids cereal. Marketing your film costs a lot of money because it's very difficult to get the general public to learn about your film and decide they want to go and see it. P&A is expensive; even though the 'P' part will decrease as they get to digital distribution, it will always cost money to advertise. Then, there are a limited number of theatres. Depending on your appetite for risk, it's usually a good idea to try and lock up a distributor as soon as possible if you can. That's where getting stars is important. So yes, you can get your dad's friend to give you $1m to make your movie, but how do you get people to see it? Film festivals can only get you so far, but it comes down to how marketable is your movie? Is it a marketable script and is it a genre film? Does it have a good cast? What is it that's going to drive people into the theaters? After you've spent years making your film, you don't want to be that crazy guy trying to sell it out of your trunk.

Q - How important are contacts?

Jeff - Unless you are unquestionably and ridiculously talented, whereby the first person remotely involved with the film business who reads your script will see it as their golden ticket and fight to show it to everyone they know, you should probably have an eye towards cultivating relationships. It is difficult to get things done in the film business without relationships or at the least, relationships to people with relationships (i.e. a producer who can make the calls you can't). If you're an assistant, meet other assistants. In three years, that assistant is now a junior agent and another friend of yours that was an intern at a studio is now working for a production company that has financing. And, off you go. You as a twenty-two year old are not going to become friends with the President of Production at a major studio. But if you begin associating with talented and aggressive people looking to move up in the film business, even if they are just starting out, you can build a network of relationships in less time than you think. Not that you should pick your friends based on where they work, but from a business perspective, it's a good idea to start networking and consider the directions people are going to move.

Q - How do you go about finding money?

Jeff - There are a limited number of institutions that will give you money to make movies - studios, funded production companies, foreign investors and distributors, and rich uncles. Different methods go in and out of vogue, depending on markets and attrition. Financing films by pre-selling foreign is pretty much dead now, though soft money in the US and Europe is becoming more available. You've got to explore all your options. Often, smaller indie films get made by attracting cast before the money is in place, but this is a delicate dance that takes a lot of time. Agents aren't incentivized to put their clients in low-paying movies that don't have financing yet, so you need someone with experience and relationships to get agents and talent to take your project seriously.

Q - Is it easy for a new producer to walk into a studio with a great script with no agent and get noticed?

Jeff - It's hard for a complete unknown to get into a busy person's office because they don't have any reason to take you seriously, yet. But that's where having relationships with people in the business helps. You don't have to know big people. Any assistant at any company is dying to come in with a great piece of material to show her boss. That's how she gets promoted. As much as you want to get your script in her hands, she wants that script in her hands, too. It is important to be selective, though, so don't cry wolf (i.e. don't cry 'brilliant script'). You don't want to pass along every mediocre script you find because you will soon be known as the guy with crappy scripts.

Q - What advice would you give a new filmmaker?

Jeff - Be balanced. You're not the smartest person in the world, and even if you are, that doesn't mean that no one else's opinion has relevance. You need to listen to other smart people and balance their thoughts with your own opinion. I think that generally helps you make better decisions. You want to let people do their jobs and not ride on top of them, but you also want to make sure that they deliver. Whatever position you are in, always remember the bigger picture. Hopefully the ultimate quality of the film you are working on fits prominently into that picture. It's a good idea to try to make films that actually make money, because if you want to continue making films, the people that give you money want to get their money back. It's a risky business, but generally if they let you do it once, they let you do it again, as long as you make them money. Ultimately, the way to be a film producer is to produce movies. Just talking about it or calling yourself a film producer is not being a film producer. It is actually through the process of making a film that you get experience, the relationships, and the knowledge.

Nicole Holofcener

WALKING & TALKING to LOVELY & AMAZING

Q - How did you get into filmmaking?

Nicole - I hid the fact for the longest time that my step-father was Woody Allen's producer, because God forbid anybody would think nepotism got me where I am today. But because of him, I had access to film sets and PA jobs. I PA'd on Midsummer Nights Sex Comedy and decided then to go to film school. I knew I wanted to do something with movies - write, direct or edit, but I wasn't sure what I'd be good at. I graduated from NYU with a short film that was pretty horrific. I wasn't at all ready to be spending lots of money on my own material, that was obvious. I tried to write some scripts, had some boring jobs and eventually worked as an apprentice editor on Hannah and Her Sisters. That was a pretty great job - I learned a lot. I sunk dailies, mostly, alone in a room - the first person to see the material. I felt so privileged. At that point my parents were willing to spring for Graduate school so I went to Columbia. I had started writing screenplays and working in the editing room, while working in a video store and had figured out what I was going to do.

Q - Are you from New York?

Nicole - Yeah. I grew up in New York until I was twelve, then my family moved to LA. I moved back for *Mid Summer Night's Sex Comedy*, and pretty much stayed until I graduated Columbia. I made a short film there as my thesis, and had written a script I wanted to direct. That's when I moved back to LA. I'd gotten an agent already, and was feeling pretty optimistic.

Q - Is it normal at your film school to have agents waiting to sign people up?

Nicole - I guess there were a few people coming out of there every year getting an agent. The school started to have these annual screenings of about 10 shorts. Mine did well. It got into some festivals.

Q - And the screenplay was..?

Nicole - It was called *Inside That Pretty Head* and it never got made. It was similar in tone to my short and I thought that would be helpful because then people could see 'Oh well she did this, so she could do that'.

Q - You were in a good position when you left. People don't normally graduate with anything to show an agent.

Nicole - I was really lucky that I had that. A lot of people didn't like the script, but at least I had something to hand out. I went to a lot of meetings here because of it, none of which amounted to anything, but I felt like I was doing something productive.

Q - Who was your agent?

Nicole - His name was Geoff Sanford. He unceremoniously dumped me after about a year, and I haven't heard from him or spoken to him since. It broke my heart. We couldn't get the movie made, but he always said, 'I'm in it for the long haul'. My subsequent agent, Ronny Gomez, did hang in. She was really supportive and I was with her for about eight years. During this time, I supported myself by writing for a kid's TV show, and I wrote a pilot based on my short that I made at Columbia. I was thrilled to be making a living as a writer, even if it was a tiny living.

Q - Was this all through your agent?

Nicole - The TV show came about through a film school friend, and the pilot was actually through my step father who had a deal at Lorimar at the time. Soon after, I wrote the script for *Walking and Talking*. I showed it to Ted Hope who was a struggling producer, and he said, 'I really like it, it needs a lot of work, but I'm forming this company called Goode Machine with James Schamus and maybe we can raise the money together'. It took six years from that meeting to production. I wanted to give up so many times.

Q - How did you survive in the meantime?

Nicole - I lived on very little. I had the pilot and the kids TV series that I worked on for a couple of years and I was a temp secretary. HBO had optioned another spec script I had written called Everything Matters, and they paid me to write another draft. (it never got made). What else - Good Machine allowed me to make another short - they produced it. They had some short ends from a Hal Hartley movie and a crew that was available for the week-end. It was really fun, and that short played at Sundance, and on cable tv for a long time.

Q - Did Goode Machine say 'we will do it one day?'

Nicole - I thought it would never happen. We would be waiting to hear back from somebody who was forming a company, or the financing had fallen through, or they we needed better casting, or they we had to wait four months for an A list actress to respond. Before I knew it, six years had gone by. My husband and I moved to New York to live in a sub-let apartment, having got rid of our house in LA when we had the financing and the cast. Then the financing fell through. It was like, 'What am I doing here?' I remember saying to Ted 'I can't take it anymore, I'm giving up'. I think three months after that, the financing came through another source and we made the movie with another cast on a lower budget.

Q - So perseverance pays off?

Nicole - It did, especially Ted's. I might have given it up if he'd said, 'I think we should give it up too, write another script.' But he never said that.

Q - Did you write any other scripts during that time?

Nicole - I wrote one called *The Deep End* and one called *My Romantic Getaway*, which I thought I was going to make as my next film, but I was sick of it by then. The material felt ancient.

Q - When they finally got the financing for Walking and Talking, what was the budget?

Nicole - It was $1m at the beginning and a little more when it fell through. It was $1.2m when I made it.

Q - Had you got any cast attached at that stage?

Nicole - The cast and the financing had to come together simultaneously because they were contingent upon one another. Anne Heche's character was pretty hard for me to cast. At one point Julianne Moore was going to play her - that was when we lost the financing the first time, which was disappointing. But six months later Anne was available (Julianne was not) and had some buzz, so I went with her. I really liked what I'd seen of her and she seemed right for the part. Catherine Keener had been my first choice for the part for a long time. I'd seen her in Tom Dicillo's movies and it was love at first sight. She embodied everything I wanted in that character. Humor, vulnerability, realness.

Q - How were the other parts cast?

Nicole - Avy Kaufman was the casting director. She brought in Kevin Corrigan, whom I instantly wanted. I had seen Todd Field in *Ruby in Paradise* and met with him. Liev Shreiber came through Greg Mottola, who had just directed him in *Day Trippers*. Everybody had to be somewhat known, or about to be known, for the financiers to approve.

Q - What did you shoot on?

Nicole - 35mm.

Q - How long was your shooting schedule?

Nicole - 25 days. We had very long days and too many locations for such a short shoot. It was hard, but a lot of fun.

Q - Were you all non-union?

Nicole - Yeah. The DP, Mike Spiller, had a lot more experience than me as he had shot several of Hal Hartley's movies. He helped me so much, in terms of handling my first feature.

Q - Did you have a relationship with the DP before you started shooting?

Nicole - Mike had shot the short of mine that Good Machine produced. It was a good way for us to see if we liked working together, which we did. It helped to know and trust him. That eliminated a certain amount of anxiety going in.

Q - Who was your producer?

Nicole - Ted. He was spread pretty thin during production because he was working on so many movies simultaneously, but he did a great job.

Q - Were you comfortable directing your first feature?

Nicole - I wouldn't exactly say comfortable. I felt nervous and green, not sure what I knew and didn't know. But I was fairly decisive and confidant at the same time. I felt like I was doing what I do best, and that was a great feeling. I didn't pretend to know things when I didn't, and ironically, I think that helped the crew trust me. I certainly had my strong points, and my weak spots. I overshot things, because of inexperience. I ended up covering things in a more traditional way because I wanted options. A lot of master shots ended up on the cutting room floor. Now, I don't shoot so many. I also was pretty clumsy with the transitions, and I'm still working on that. Getting from one scene to another in a graceful yet unobtrusive way, can still be a mystery to me.

Q - How long did post take?

Nicole - It was a couple of months. The deadline was Sundance. No financiers want you to turn in a shitty cut. If it's a mess, they'll probably give you more time. Because it didn't have a distributor, it had to be good enough to get one.

Q - Did you have a test screening before submitting to Sundance? Did you do re-cuts?

Nicole - Yes. The first fifteen minutes were hard to cut and we jumbled it all around. The response at the test screening was bad which was devastating. I thought I'd made a flop. We put it closer to the script and had more screenings which were more successful.

Q - Was the test screening a small, intimate affair?

Nicole - It was everybody's friends who turned up to be honest, but gentle. In case people were shy, Ted handed out a stack of questionnaires.

Q - What was the reaction at Sundance?

Nicole - We were two hours late for our screening, which was really horrible. We were flying the print in, the plane broke so we had to rent a private plane. The audience thought they were going to be seeing *I Shot Andy Warhol*. However, Miramax met with the producers the night after that screening and bought it, so that was great.

Q - What was their offer?

Nicole - $1m. It was great. I got a bonus.

Q - What happened after they started the distribution and you started doing the publicity?

Nicole - We got to go to many festivals all over the country by word of mouth, before its release date. There was no premiere or fanfare.

Q - Where did it come out first? New York? LA?

Nicole - Both, then it went wider and did pretty poorly despite great reviews in New York and LA. Of course I think it could have done better. Ask any filmmaker and they'll say, 'Well if only they...' and 'if they just...' But it enabled me to make another movie and have a career. I didn't make any money.

Q - Do you know how it did at the box office?

Nicole - It made $1.2m. Not good, because Miramax had spent more on prints and advertising. It did pretty well in Europe though.

Q - What happened immediately after that?

Nicole - I had a lots of meetings with people saying, 'We want to make your next film, what is it?' but I had lost interest in *My Romantic Getaway*. It was another 'Girl finding her way'. So I thought I was going to take time and write a new script. Instead I directed *Sex And The City* and I started re-writing for studios, my first one paid me so much money I couldn't believe it. I got caught in that niche, which was great, and I did more studio re-writes when I was pregnant.

Q - What are your views on women working in the industry?

Nicole - I feel there's a general discrimination. It's always white men who are nominated for Oscars or Golden Globes. Occasionally there's an aberration. I'm lucky as I've made movies and made a living. For me, it's very difficult juggling motherhood and a career. When I had my kids, it limited everything. They were young enough to travel when I directed *Sex and The City*. Now that they're in school, I can't go anywhere, and I get offered jobs out of LA. I think it's different for some fathers, generally they feel pretty good about leaving the kids with the wife, going and having a brilliant career, coming back when they can. My kids are much more important to me than my career, so I don't go anywhere. I can do pilots or episodes, but I can't direct a movie. There's no way

I'm going to miss this time in their lives for a paycheck from a movie I don't like that much.

Q - What was the difference between directing your first feature and shooting TV shows?

Nicole - Going from my own work to somebody else's and having producers staring at a monitor watching what I am doing is hideously nerve wracking, no matter how incredibly supportive they were. Incidentally, Mike Spiller was shooting the series, (Sex and The City) so I had a DP I was used to and comfortable with, and I didn't have to prove myself, at least to him. I directed a pilot for NBC. I had support, a great crew, and a wonderful cast. However there were two other monitors for two levels of executives hidden away. This meant I couldn't say 'Print that, lets check the gate and move on' until several people came up to me and okayed it, which sometimes I disagreed with completely, but had to do anyway. These are not bad problems to have. *Six Feet Under* has a very specific look, which as a director, I had to be conscious of. It's very unsentimental, almost unemotional. I did not come near making a statement or putting my imprint on it. I just didn't want to fuck it up. I just hoped it looked like an episode of *Six Feet Under*. If it was a good episode of that show, then I did my job well.

Q - When did you write 'Lovely and Amazing'?

Nicole - I wrote *Lovely and Amazing* when my kids were a year or two old. I was really optimistic because I really thought the script was good, certainly better than *Walking and Talking*. It had Catherine Keener in it from the start, I was determined to get it made, but I couldn't. People read it and said, 'This is a good script', and 'This is amazing' but 'we have no idea how to market it!' That was really depressing, but then we gave it to Blow-up Pictures in New York who were looking to finance $1m movies, shot on digital

video. It took me a day to think, 'Video, shit!' but by the next day, I was like, 'okay. I'll shoot on anything'. I didn't want it to look like a Dogma movie, I wanted it to look like a movie, but that was the deal. They let me put who I wanted in it.

Q - What was the budget?

Nicole - $1m, with 20 days to shoot it, but it was a tighter script than *Walking and Talking*, there was no big re-writing on set or panic. It was a much smoother shoot than *Walking and Talking*. I had a considerable amount of practice in between, which was good thing, because I would have been a wreck if it had been six years since I talked to an actor.

Q - You shot digital. What camera did you use?

Nicole - The Line Producer managed to get a great deal on a Sony PD-3, which was the best hi-def camera we could get. To me it's not as beautiful as film, it's just not as rich and lovely to look at. The camera was so huge I forgot it was digital. The DP treated it as though it was a film. We had a huge crew with tons of lighting.

Q - Were there any effects added in post?

Nicole - If we'd had more money, we could have benefited from the fact that it was digital video. There's a scene in the pool that was shot hand-held from the water looking out onto the girls. It was really shaky and I hated it in the editing room. We were able to stabilize that, so I ended up giving it a really strange texture that jumps out at you, but I chose the texture over the shaky.

Q - How long did post production take?

Nicole - Twelve weeks of cutting in a cheap room in a dungeon of an editing place with an old Avid. At least we didn't have a deadline. The mix also turned out to be somewhat unfortunate as we went with a large and fancy dubbing studio because they loved the movie, but ended up having to change rooms every day. We had only a five day mix which was just awful for a low budget movie. I felt the budget a lot more in post production and prep - where I had to choose my locations based on price - than in production.

Q - Did you change anything after you completed and screened it at Telluride?

Nicole - I didn't change it once it had been screen at Telluride. Prior to locking the picture, I did a couple of pick ups later on that helped the transitions.

Q - What were the events after Telluride?

Nicole - Fox Searchlight was going to buy it for a ton of money and we were all excited, but it didn't happen. The screenings went well and people responded favourably, but I was nervous. Lions Gate saw it at a screening and became interested. I flew to the Toronto Film Festival, unfortunately on Sep 11th. It was a very strange time but that is where Lionsgate bought it.

Q - How much did Lions Gate offer?

Nicole - $350k. But a they were great company who really seemed to love it.

Q - What advice would you offer a new filmmaker?

Nicole - Stick with what you know. It's so hard to get off the ground in the beginning, at least the material itself shouldn't be too foreign to you. Stick with personal stories and don't try and be too clever. And don't let the production value overshadow the content of the movie -- sometimes that is so out of balance, and all that money or production value actually can diminish the impact of the movie if it's a simple, small story.

CASE STUDIES

FILM LINGO

Above the Line - the cast, producers, writer and director of a film. Separated from the rest of the crew by an imaginary line of "importance" in a studio's eyes.

Alligator Grip - This is a spring-loaded lighting grip used to attach a light to pipes, molding or even doors. The most common place to see these used is in a sound stage or studio.

Barn Doors - Flaps attached to lights that when opened and closed can manipulate the direction of light. Barn doors are also the place you clip gels, diffusion, blackwrap and flags to the light.

Below the line - the people involved in the physical production of a film, which included post production. Seen as below an imaginary importance line that separates the creative executives and the physical production.

Black Bag - changing bag that functions as a portable darkroom, used to load a film magazine. This bag is basically two bags, one inside the other and is used from everything from loading film to fixing camera jams.

Brothers - term for electricians, refers to the International Brotherhood of Electrical Workers.

Bullets - clothespins used to attach gels to lights. So called because electricians and gaffers hang them off a string like a bandolier.

The Cheat - technique used to make things fit that wouldn't normally, such as moving furniture forward so a person or camera can fit in the space, or an actor not quite looking in the right direction of another in order to compensate for space restrictions.

 "Check the Gate" - to take lens off camera and look into the camera's gate for hairs, emulsion buildup etc. If there is something found, you need to clean the gate and perhaps reshoot any affected scenes.

Chicken Coop - An overhead, box-like light with a cluster of six, usually 100-watt globes, for top lighting of sets.

Cinching - the practice of pulling the end of a roll to remove slack.

Cookie - a cutout pattern, cut out from a material and placed in front of a light to cast a patterned shadow, such as the outline of a window frame or Venetian blinds.

Crossing the line - crossing the invisible line of action.

Dolly - camera term referring to when a camera moves in or out of a shot. A dolly is usually done on wheels or tracks in order to produce a smooth movement.

Dot - Shadow-forming device in the figure of a small round scrim.

Eye Light - a low-powered light to produce a lively reflection in the subject's eye. The light is usually there to substitute the sun's reflection you get when you're outside.

Finger - a thin rectangular shadow-casting device.

Fishpole - a long lightweight telescoping rod, which a microphone is attached to for recording dialogue.

Flying Moon - a lighting apparatus, which is used to create artificial moonlight. It is in the shape of a cube composed of aluminum pipes and covered with bleached muslin. It houses four 25,000-watt HMIs and is lifted by an industrial crane to 80 to 120 feet.

Flags - metal or foamcore boards used to protect the camera from stray light, creating a gradual transition from light to dark and to avoid or control light spillage in your scene. Can sometimes be called gobos or siders.

Gaffers Tape - wide black tape that is better then duct tape for it leaves no sticky residue on your film equipment. It is also good because it can be ripped quite easily into smaller strips. You can fix anything with gaffers tape.

"Hitting the mark" - when an actor stops at the correct spot in a scene for framing and focusing. The mark is usually a piece of white camera tape set on floor.

Honeycomb - A grid used on soft lights to control the lighting design and direction.

Inky-dink - the tiniest focusable studio lamp with a Fresnel lens and a bulb up to 250 watts.

"In the can" - term that means the film has been shot and is ready to go to the lab. In more generally terms, it means that everything is finished.

Kicker - a form of backlight that shines on your subject off to one side. This serves not to illuminate but to define the edges of it's subject.

Magic Hour/Golden Hour - the time just before sunrise or the time just after sunset when there is enough light to get an exposure on buildings and on various landscapes but car headlights and building lights can still be seen as on. The color temperature of the daylight is pleasant gold color, which makes objects seem magical.

Mark Slate - snapping the arm of the clapperboard against the main panel to provide a mark for the lab to synchronize the picture and the sound.

The Martini - the last shot of the day.

Meat Axe - An informal term for a small flag.

Mike Stew - unwanted background noise that is picked up by the microphone.

Peanut Bulb - A tiny light used for hiding in confined areas.

Practicals - household light fixtures that are placed to be visible in a shot (i.e. that would be there naturally like a desklamp).

Room Tone - This is the distinct sound every film location or set makes. It is used to bridge gaps in the sound track of a film, providing a consistent background.

Snoot - A funnel-shaped light-controlling device used on lamps in place of barndoors for a more precise light-beam pattern.

"Take A 42!" - A 42-minute lunch break which is specified by the union contract.

Tough Spun - A highly heat resistant diffusing material made of synthetic fibers.

Script Doctor - a writer brought in to fix a script just prior to, or during production.

Second Unit - a crew that shoots scenes that require stunt scenes, crowd scenes, battle scenes and battle scenes. Basically they shoot any scenes that do not require sound. These scenes have a different director and camera crew then the first unit.

Sun Guns - Camera-mounted lights that are portable and provide constant and shadowless illumination. Generally used in documentary or news production.

Stinger - an extension power cord for running electricity

"wrap" - the end of the day/shoot.

Wrecking crew - slang term for make up and hair because of the amount of product they have to put on an actor to look good on film.

TOP NORTH AMERICAN FILM FESTIVALS

AFI FEST: AMERICAN FILM INSTITUTE
(November)
American Film Institute
2021 N. Western Avenue
Los Angeles, CA 90027
Tel: (323) 856-7707
Fax: (323) 462-4049
E-mail: afifest@afionline.org
Website: www.afifest.com
Categories: doc, flf, shorts
Fee: early - $40 (flf)/$30 (shorts)
Fee: late - $50 (flf)/$40 (shorts)

IFP/WEST-LOS ANGELES FILM FEST.
8750 Wilshire Blvd., 2nd Floor
Beverly Hills, CA 90211
Tel: (323) 951-7090
Fax: (310) 432-1203
Email: lafilmfest@ifpwest.org

NEW YORK INT. INDIE FILM & VIDEO FEST.
(3 events, Spring, Fall, Winter)
873 Broadway, Suite 303
New York, NY 10003
Tel: (212)777-7100
Fax (212) 387-0873
Email: filmvoice@hotmail.com

SANTA BARBARA
(February & March)
2064 Alameda Padre Sierra, Suite 120
Santa Barbara, CA 93103
Tel: (805) 963-0023
Fax: (805) 962-2524
E-mail: info@sbfilmfestival.org
Website: www.sbfilmfestival.org
Fee: $40 (US)/$45 (foreign) + $10 for late entries

SLAMDANCE
(January)
Held in Park City, Utah
5634 Melrose Avenue
Los Angeles, CA 90038
Tel: (323) 466-1786
Fax: (323) 466-1784
e-mail: mail@slamdance.com
Website: www.slamdance.com
Early fee: $30 (films under 40 min.)/$45 (films over 40 min.)
Late fee: $35 (films under 40 min.)/$55 (films over 40 min.)/$100 (screenplays)

SOUTH BY SOUTHWEST
(March)
P.O. Box 4999
Austin, TX 78765
Tel: (512) 467-7979
Fax: (512) 451-0754
E-mail: SXSW@SXSW.com
Website: www.SXSW.com
Fee: early - $25 (shorts)/$35 (features), late - $30 (shorts)/$40 (features); $5 discount for entering online

SUNDANCE
(January)
Sundance Institute
225 Santa Monica Blvd., 8th Floor
Santa Monica, CA 90401
Tel: (310) 394-4662
Fax: (310) 394-8353
la@sundance.org
www.sundance.org

TELLURIDE
(August & September)
National Film Preserve, Ltd.
379 State Street
Portsmouth, NH 03801
Tel: (603) 433-9202
Fax: (603)433-9206
E-mail: tellufilm@aol.com
Website: www.telluridefilmfestival.com
Fee: $35-$75

TORONTO
(September)
2 Carlton Street, Suite 1600
Toronto, Ontario M5B 1J3
Canada
Tel: (416) 967-7371
Fax: (416) 967-9477
E-mail: tiffg@torfilmfest.ca
Website: www.bell.ca/filmfest
No fee

TRIBECA
(May)
375 Greenwich Street
New York, NY 10013
Tel: (866) 941-3378
Fax: (212) 941-3939
E-mail: festival@tribecafilm.com
Website: www.tribecafilmfestival.org
Fee: $35 (flf)/$30 (shorts)

PRODUCTION BUDGET

This is the production budget for the low budget horror film, CREEP. An industry budget is broken up into two sections. The first is called the Top Sheet and is a summary of how much money is allotted for each major section of making the film such as camera, grip and lighting and visual effects. These are then subtotaled into pre-production, production and post-production lines and finally a 10% contingency (for anything that comes up that you forgot) is calculated and a final negative cost is listed. The second part is a detailed line item account of everything you will need to make the film, the rate, the length of time needed for each item and the cost. Where it gets tricky is when you need to calculate for union requirements like Worker's Comp. or meal penalties. Programs like Movie Magic Budgeting can do this automatically for you and can also provide you with a myriad of budget formats that fit the various studio's tastes. But, if you don't want to spend the cash, you can do what we did, and use an Excel spreadsheet - takes a bit of time to set up the formulas, but worth it in the end. Alternatively there is Budget from Movie Tools which we developed for low budget films (www.movietools.com).

ACCT #	ACCOUNT NAME	UNITS	TYPE	RATE	TOTAL
1000	STORY - RIGHTS AND EXPENSES				$0
	TOTAL 1000				$0
1200	PRODUCERS UNIT				
1	PRODUCERS	negotiated			$50,000
2	EXECUTIVE PRODUCERS				$0
3	ASSOCIATE PRODUCERS	negotiated			$30,000
4	CO-PRODUCERS	negotiated			$20,000
5	PRODUCER'S ASSISTANT	39	weeks		$19,500
	TOTAL 1200				$119,500
1300	DIRECTORS				
1	DIRECTOR	negotiated			$60,000
2	CASTING DIRECTOR	6	weeks	1250	$7,500
	TOTAL 1300				$67,500
1400	CAST				
1	MARCO	6	weeks	1620	$9,720
2	KELLY	6	weeks	1620	$9,720
3	MR. WEIR	6	weeks	1620	$9,720
4	CATHY	6	weeks	1620	$9,720
5	MEGAN	6	weeks	1620	$9,720
6	OMAR	6	weeks	1620	$9,720
7	KAREENA	1	day	466	$466
8	ANDY	2	day	466	$932
9	BILL (EXTRA)	1	day	110	$110
10	STEVE	1	day	466	$466
11	EXTRA MENTAL PATIENTS (5)	5	day	110	$550
12	PAUL	1	day	446	$446
13	INDIAN WOMAN	1	day	446	$446
14	UNCLE ALI	1	day	446	$446
15	PARTY EXTRAS (20)	20	days	110	$2,200
16	PARTY CHILDREN EXTRAS	5	days	110	$550
17	BLACK MAN IN OVERALLS	1	day	446	$446
18	DR. WIGGINS	2	days	446	$892
19	BRIAN	1	day	446	$446
20	MR. FORDHAM	1	day	446	$446
21	BOBBY	1	day	446	$446
22	BOBBY'S MOM	1	day	110	$110
23	BOBBY'S DAD	1	day	110	$110
24	POLICEMAN #1	1	week	1620	$1,620
25	POLICEMAN #2	1	week	1620	$1,620
26	SLAVE JINN	1	week	1620	$1,620
27	EXTRAS FOR HISTORY MONTAG	3	days	110	$330
28	EXTRAS IN KELLY'S RESTAURAN	5	days	110	$550
29	LITTLE BLACK BOY	1	day	446	$446
30	MUNKAR	1	week	1620	$1,620
31	ALEX	1	day	446	$446
32	LITTLE GIRL JINN	1	day	446	$446
33	LITTLE BOY JINN	1	day	446	$446
33	JINN EXTRAS (12)	12	day	110	$1,320
	SUBTOTAL				$78,292
34	CAST FRINGE (13.8%)				$10,804
	TOTAL 1400				$89,096

	TOTAL ABOVE THE LINE				$276,096

2000	DIRECTOR'S UNIT				
1	UNIT PRODUCTION MANAGE	12	weeks	2000	$24,000
2	FIRST ASSISTANT DIRECTOR	8	weeks	1570.2	$12,562
3	SECOND ASSISTANT DIREC	6	weeks	1462.8	$8,777
4	SCRIPT SUPERVISORS	7	weeks	1000	$7,000
5	SUBTOTAL				$52,339
6	DGA FRINGE (20%)				$10,468
	TOTAL 2000				**$62,806**
2100	STUNTS				
1	STUNT COORDINATOR	1	week	3750	$3,750
2	STUNT PEOPLE (2)	2	weeks	1738	$3,476
	SUBTOTAL				$7,226
3	SAG FRINGE (13.8%)				$997
	TOTAL 2100				**$8,223**
2200	ART DEPARTMENT				
1	PRODUCTION DESIGNER	11	weeks	1875	$20,625
2	SET DECORATOR	7	weeks	1000	$7,000
3	PROP MASTER	6	weeks	1150	$6,900
4	ASST. TO ART DEPARTMENT	7	weeks	500	$3,500
5	SET DRESSER (2)	12	weeks	800	$9,600
6	PROPS RENTAL				$7,500
7	IATSE FRINGE (20%)				$9,525
	SALARY SUBTOTAL				$57,150
	TOTAL 2200				**$64,650**
2300	SOUND STAGE				
1	STAGE RENTAL	6	weeks	4000	$24,000
2	PAINTERS (3)	15	weeks	1120	$16,800
3	CONSTRUCTION MANAGER	6	weeks	1750	$10,500
4	CARPENTERS (4)	20	weeks	1300	$26,000
5	PLUMBER	2	weeks	1750	$3,500
6	ASSISTANT PLUMBER	2	weeks	1200	$2,400
7	ELECTRICITY	30	days	60	$1,800
8	AIR CONDITIONING	30	days	300	$9,000
9	CONSTRUCTION MATERIALS				$10,000
10	TRASH	4	bins	45	$180
11	DRESSING ROOMS	30	days	75	$2,250
12	SECURITY	30	days	50	$1,500
13	STUDIO MANAGER	6	weeks	400	$2,400
14	TELEPHONE & FAX	30	days	50	$1,500
15	PARKING (5 Spaces)	150	space	7.5	$1,125
16	REPAIRS & DAMAGES				$1,000
18	IATSE FRINGE (20%)				$11,840
	SALARY SUBTOTAL				$87,100
	TOTAL 2200				**$125,795**
2350	MAKEUP & HAIRDRESSING				
1	MAKEUP SUPERVISOR	7	weeks	1320	$9,240
2	ASST. MAKEUP ARTIST	6	weeks	1121	$6,726
3	ADDITIONAL LABOR	2	weeks	1120	$2,240
4	HAIRDRESSING SUPERVISO	7	weeks	1150	$8,050
5	ASST. HAIRSTYLIST	6	weeks	1025	$6,150
6	ADDITIONAL LABOR	2	weeks	1025	$2,050
7	COSTUME DESIGNER	10	weeks	1400	$14,000
8	KEY COSTUMER	6	weeks	1150	$6,900
9	COSTUMER	6	weeks	935	$5,610
10	BODY MAKEUP				$1,000
11	PURCHASES				$500
12	BOX RENTALS - MAKEUP				$600
13	BOX RENTALS - HAIR STYLISTS				$600
14	IATSE FRINGE (20%)				$12,193
	SALARY SUBTOTAL				$73,159
	TOTAL 2350				**$75,859**
2400	GRIP/LIGHTING				
1	LIGHTING RENTAL				$10,000
2	GAFFER	7	weeks	1150	$8,050
3	BEST BOY	6	weeks	1040	$6,240
4	KEY GRIP	7	weeks	1000	$7,000
5	ELECTRICIANS (2)	12	weeks	990	$11,880
6	GENERATOR RENTAL				$3,000
7	GLOBES AND EXPENDABLES				$750
8	REPAIRS				$2,000
9	FUEL (GENERATORS)				$500
10	PURCHASES				$1,000
11	GRIP BOX RENTALS				$450
12	GRIP TRUCK	30	days	250	$7,500
13	IATSE FRINGE (20%)				$8,634
	SALARY SUBTOTAL				$41,804
	TOTAL 2400				**$67,004**

2500	CAMERA				
1	DIRECTOR OF PHOTOGRAPH	12	weeks	2800	$33,600
2	CAMERA OPERATOR	7	weeks	1650	$11,550
3	1ST ASSISTANT CAMERAMAN	6	weeks	1430	$8,580
4	2ND ASSISTANT CAMERAMAN	6	weeks	1100	$6,600
5	FILM LOADER	6	weeks	940	$5,640
6	STILLMAN	6	weeks	1655	$9,930
7	35mm CAMERA PACKAGE RE	30	days	2000	$60,000
8	CAMERA CRANE				$1,000
9	CAMERA DOLLIES & TRACK	7	days	150	$1,050
10	DGA FRINGE (20%)				$13,194
	SALARY SUBTOTAL				$89,094
	TOTAL 2500				**$151,144**

2600	SOUND				
1	SOUND MIXER	7	weeks	1850	$12,950
2	BOOM MAN	6	weeks	1250	$7,500
3	CABLEMAN	6	weeks	1195	$7,170
4	AUDIO STOCK	20	tapes	10	$200
5	BOX RENTALS				$3,000
6	WALKIE TALKIES				$1,500
7	EQUIPMENT REPAIRS				$500
8	MOBILE PHONES				$1,500
9	IATSE FRINGE (20%)				$5,524
	SALARY SUBTOTAL				$33,144
	TOTAL 2600				**$39,844**

2700	TRANSPORTATION				
1	TRANSPORTATION COORDIN	7	weeks	2500	$17,500
2	DRIVER CAPTAIN	6	weeks	1700	$10,200
3	DRIVERS (3)	18	weeks	1365	$24,570
4	VEHICLE RENTAL				$10,000
5	DRESSING ROOM RENTALS	3	weeks	500	$1,500
6	REPAIRS AND MAINTENANCE				$2,000
7	FUEL				$9,500
8	MILEAGE ALLOWANCE				$3,000
9	TEAMSTER FRINGE (20%)				$10,454
	SALARY SUBTOTAL				$62,724
	TOTAL 2700				**$88,724**

2800	LOCATION EXPENSES				
1	LOCATION FEES				$5,000
2	TRANSPORTATION FARES				$500
3	HOTELS, MOTELS, ETC.				$60,000
4	SITE RENTALS				$2,000
5	OFFICE EQUIPMENT RENTALS				$2,000
6	TELEPHONE				$1,000
7	SHIPPING STATIONARY POSTAGE				$1,000
8	LOCATION LOSS & DAMAGE				$5,000
9	LOCATION SCOUTING				$3,000
10	LOCATION CONTACT				$500
11	TEACHERS WELFARE WORK	6	weeks	1625.6	$9,754
12	POLICEMEN, WATCHMEN, FI	10	days	450	$4,500
	SALARY SUBTOTAL				$14,254
	TOTAL 2800				**$94,254**

2850	TRAVEL AND LIVING EXPENSES				
1	AIR FARES				$10,000
2	PARKING				$1,000
3	PRODUCTION VEHICLE				$1,000
	TOTAL 2850				**$12,000**

2900	TAPE/TRANSFER				
1	35MM FILM STOCK	40	rolls	300	$12,000
2	35MM FILM STOCK PROCESS	40,000	feet	0.49	$19,600
3	VIDEO TAPE STOCK VHS				$50
4	FORCED DEVELOPING				$1,000
5	TIMED DAILIES	24	hours	175	$4,200
6	SPECIAL LABORATORY WORK				$1,000
7	STILLS FILM STOCK	50	rolls	10	$500
8	STILLS PROCESSING	50	rolls	15	$750
	TOTAL 2900				**$39,100**

	TOTAL PRODUCTION				**$829,403**

3000	EDITORIAL				
1	PICTURE EDITOR	6	weeks	1950	$11,700
2	ASSISTANT EDITOR	6	weeks	1140	$6,840
3	ADR EDITOR				$3,500
4	SOUND EFFECTS/MUSIC EDI	6	weeks	1725	$10,350
5	ASST SOUND EDITORS (2)	12	weeks	1195	$14,340
6	FILM MESSENGER				$750
7	VIDEO TRANSFERS				$4,000
8	OFF-LINE EDITING SYSTEM				$15,000
9	COLOR CORRECTION				$1,000
10	IATSE FRINGE (20%)				$9,346
	SALARY SUBTOTAL				$56,076
	TOTAL 3000				**$76,826**

3100	MUSIC				
1	MUSIC SUPERVISOR				$10,000
2	COMPOSER/CONDUCTOR (flat fee all in)				$20,000
3	SYNCHRONIZATION LICENSE (FROM PUBLISHER)				$5,000
4	RECORDING RIGHTS				$5,000
	SALARY SUBTOTAL				$30,000
	TOTAL 3100				**$70,000**

3200	**TITLES & GRAPHICS**				
1	TITLES & GRAPHICS (flat fee)				$3,000
	TOTAL 3300				**$3,000**

3300	**VISUAL EFFECTS**				$40,000
	VISUAL EFFECTS (flat fee all in)				
	TOTAL 3500				**$40,000**

3400	**CATERING & CRAFT SERVICES**				
1	FOOD & LABOR				$47,250
2	TABLE & CHAIR RENTALS				$750
	TOTLA 3400				$48,000

3500	INSURANCE				
1	NEGATIVE INSURANCE				$2,000
2	ERRORS AND OMISSIONS				$8,000
3	LIABILITY				$1,000
4	WORKMEN'S COMPENSATION				$1,000
5	COMPREHENSIVE LIABILITY				$1,000
6	PROPERTY DAMAGE LIABILITY				$1,400
	TOTAL 3500				**$14,400**

3600	GENERAL & ADMINISTRATIVE				
1	MISCELLANEOUS				$5,000
2	TELEPHONE AND TELEGRAPH				$1,000
3	PRINTING AND XEROXING				$2,000
4	OFFICE SUPPLIES				$7,500
5	PAYROLL ORGANIZATION				$170,550
6	ACCOUNTING FEE				$20,000
7	LEGAL FEE				$20,000
8	OFFICE SPACE RENTAL				$3,000
9	SECRETARIES (2)	12	weeks	500	$6,000
	TOTAL 3600				**$235,050**

3700	FESTIVALS & SCREENINGS				
1	FESTIVAL FEES/PASSES				$1,000
2	TRAVEL/LODGING				$7,000
3	PROMOTIONAL MATERIALS				$1,500
4	TRANSFER/DUBS				$1,000
	TOTAL 3700				**$10,500**

3800	DELIVERY CHARGES				
1	COPYRIGHT				$500
2	TRANSCRIPTION CO.				$3,000
3	COPYRIGHT REPORT				$500
4	NTSC MASTER				$500
5	PAL MASTER				$500
6	INTERPOSITIVE				$40,000
7	STEREO PRINT MASTER				$300
8	DA 88				$500
9	MUSIC & EFFECTS				$500
10	DM &E				$500
11	OPTICALS				$500
12	TEXTLESS BACKGROUND				$500
13	EPK				$1,600
	TOTAL 3800				**$49,400**

	TOTAL POST-PRODUCTION				**$547,176**

	TOTAL ABOVE/BELOW THE LINE				**$1,652,675**

STATE TO STATE INCENTIVES

Unlike most of the world, the United States does not offer any national tax incentives or relief for feature filmmaking investment. However, there are options at the state level. Consult each state's website or film office to find out what each one offers. Here's a hint: New Mexico, Hawaii and Louisiana are the most liberal.

Alabama
Phone: 334-242-4195 or 800-633-5898
www.alabamafilm.org

Alaska
Phone: 907-269-8112
E-mail: alaskafilm@dced.state.ak.us
www.dced.state.ak.us.com

Arizona
Phone: 602-280-1380 or 800-523-6695
www.commerce.state.az.us/Film

Arkansas
Phone: 501-582-7676
www.aedc.state.ar.us/Film

California
Phone: 323-860-2960 or 800-858-4749
www.film.ca.gov
www.filmcafirst.com
www.cinemascout.org

Colorado
Phone: 303-620-4500
www.coloradofilm.org

Connecticut
Phone: 860-571-7130 or 800-392-2122
E-mail: info@ctfilm.com
www.ctfilm.com

Delaware
Phone: 800-441-8846
E-mail: cpheiks@state.de.us
www.state.de.us/dedo/new_web_site/frames/film.html

Florida
Phone: 850-410-4765 or 877-FLA-FILM
LA Office Phone: 818-508-7772
www.filminflorida.com

Georgia
Phone: 404-656-3591
www.filmgeorgia.org

Hawaii
Phone: 808-586-2570
www.state.hi.us/tax/hi-tech.html

Idaho
Phone: 208-334-2470 or 800-942-8338
www.filmidaho.org

Illinois
Phone: 217-782-7500
http://www.commerce.state.il.us/film/

Indiana
Phone: 317-232-8829
E-mail: filminfo@commerce.state.in.us
www. http://www.in.gov/film/

Iowa
Phone: 515.242.4726
E-mail: filmiowa@ided.state.ia.us
www.state.ia.us/film

Kansas
Phone: (785) 296-4927
www.kdoch.state.ks.us/kdfilm

Kentucky
Phone: 800-345-6591
www.kyfilmoffice.com

Louisiana
Phone: (888) 655-0447
E-mail: msmith@led.state.la.us.
www.lafilm.org

Maine
Phone: 207-624-7631
www.filminmaine.com

Maryland
Phone: 410-767-6340 or 800-333-6632
www.marylandfilm.org

Massachussets
Film office closed due to lack of funding.

Michigan
Phone: 517-373-0638 or 800-477-3456
www.michigan.gov/hal

Minnesota
Phone: 612-332-6493
E-mail: info@mnfilm.org
www.mnfilm.org

Mississippi
Phone: 601-359-3297
www.visitmississippi.org/film

Missouri
Phone: 573-751-9050
E-mail: mofilm@ded.state.mo.us
www.ded.state.mo.us/business/filmcommission

Montana
Phone: 406-841-2876 or 800-553-4563
E-mail: montanafilm@visitmt.com
www.montanafilm.com

Nebraska
Phone: 402-471-3680 or 800-228-4307
E-mail: info@filmnebraska.org
www.filmnebraska.org

Nevada
Phone: 702-486-2711 or 877-NEV-FILM
(877-638-3456)
www.nevadafilm.com

New Hampshire
Phone: 603-271-2665 or 800-262-6660
www.filmnh.org

New Jersey
Phone: 973-648-6279
Email: njfilm@njfilm.org
www.njfilm.org

New Mexico
Phone: 505-827-9810 or 800-545-9871
www.edd.state.nm.us/FILM/index.html

North Carolina
Phone: 919-733-9900 or 800-232-9227
Website: www.ncfilm.com

North Dakota
Phone: 701-328-2525 or 800-328-2871
E-mail: mzimmerman@state.nd.us
www.ndtourism.com

New York
Phone: 212-489-6710
www.ci.nyc.ny.us/html/filmcom/home.html

Ohio
www.ohiofilm.com
www.clevelandfilm.com
www.filmcinncinnati.com

Oklahoma
Phone: 405-522-6760 or 800-766-3456
www.oklahomafilm.org/

Oregon
Phone: 503-229-5832
Email shoot@oregonfilm.org
www.oregonfilm.org

Pennsylvania
Phone: 717-783-3456
www.filminpa.com

Rhode Island
Phone: 401-222-2601
Email: RSmith@riedc.com
www.filmri.com

South Carolina
Phone: 803-737-0490
www.scfilmoffice.com

South Dakota
Phone: 605-773-3301
www.filmsd.com

Tennessee
Phone: 615-741-FILM or 1-877-818-3456
www.state.tn.us/film/main.htm

Texas
Phone: (512) 463-9200
Email: film@governor.state.tx.us
www.governor.state.tx.us/divisions/film

Utah
Phone: 801-741-4540
www.film.utah.gov

Vermont
Phone: 802-828-3618
Email: vermontfilm@state.vt.us
www.filmvermont.com

Virginia
Phone: 804-371-8204 or 800-854-6233
Email: vafilm@virginia.org
www.film.virginia.org

Washington
Phone: 206-256-6151
E-mail: wafilm@cted.wa.gov
www.oted.wa.gov/ed/filmoffice/

Washington, DC
Phone: 202-727-6608
www.film.dc.gov/film

West Virginia
Phone: 304-558-2234 or 800-982-3386
www.wvdo.org/index.cfm?main=/filmoffice/index

Wisconsin
Phone: 800-345-6947
www.filmwisconsin.org

Wyoming
Phone: 307-777-3400 or 800-458-6657
E-mail: info@wyomingfilm.org
www.wyomingfilm.org

MAJOR US STUDIOS

The Walt Disney Company
500 South Buena Vista Street
Burbank, CA 91521
818-560-1000

MGM
2500 Broadway Street
Santa Monica, CA 90404
310-449-3000

Universal Studios
100 Universal City Plaza
Universal City, CA 91608
818-777-1000

20th Century Fox
10201 West Pico Boulevard
Los Angeles, CA 90035
310-360-1000

Paramount
5555 Melrose Avenue
Los Angeles, CA 90038
323-956-5000

Warner Brothers
4000 Warner Boulevard
Burbank, CA 91522
818-954-6000

Dreamworks SKG
100 Universal City Plaza
Bldg. 10
Universal City, CA 91608
818-733-7000

New Line Cinema
116 North Robertson Boulevard
Suite #200
Los Angeles, CA 90048
310-854-5811

Miramax Films (LA)
7966 Beverly Boulevard
Los Angeles, CA 90048
323-951-4200

Miramax Films (NY)
Tribeca Film Center
375 Greenwich Street
New York, NY 10013
212-941-3800

Revolution Studios
2900 Olympic Bouelvard
Santa Monica, CA 90404
310-255-7000

GLOSSARY OF CONTRACT TERMINOLOGY

ACCRUALS - The accumulation of payments due.

ADJUSTED GROSS - This will be defined in your agreement but generally is the gross receipts minus certain deductions such as prints,advertising, taxes.

ADVANCE - This is money received from your distributor/sales agent when they sign the distribution contract and prior to selling the film. This could also be in the form of the distributor paying for delivery items directly themselves, rather than the Producer.

ANCILLARY RIGHTS - Other subsidiary rights i.e. the right to make a sequel, soundtrack, computer game etc., merchandising, video, novelization.

ARBITRATION - An informal method for resolving disputes (by finding the middle ground) which is usually quicker and less expensive than litigation. Usually an arbitrator is agreed in advance by the parties or it's agreed to use the AFM Arbitration process.

BREACH OF CONTRACT - Failure of one party to fulfill the agreement.

BREAKEVEN - The point when sales equal costs, where a film is neither in profit nor loss.

BUY OUT - This term is used in relation to the engagement of artists where no repeat, residual or other fees are required to be paid to the artist in relation to any form of exploitation of the film or program. Also referred to purchasing the movie for all rights and no repeat, residual or other fees will be paid to the producers if that country makes further deals with the film.

BEST ENDEAVORS - Means you have to do all you can including incurring expense in order to carry out your relevant obligation under the agreement. 'Reasonable endeavors' is less onerous than 'best'.

CAP – A ceiling, upper limit. Try to cap expenses in distributors/sales agents agreements.

CEASE AND DESIST - To stop and not continue in that course of action. This is generally a letter from a lawyer requesting that the other party stops a particular activity that it's persuing or an order issued by a court.

COLLATERAL – Assets pledged to a lender until the loan is repaid i.e. with a bank loan, a house can be put up for collateral. In film business, the assets would generally be the underlying literary property, the physical elements that are created during production and the exploitation rights.

CONTINGENCY - Money set aside for unanticipated costs.

CHAIN OF TITLE - Contracts and documents that hand down the copyright to the present owner.

CROSS COLLATERIZE - This is where a party, usually a distributor, will offset losses in one area against gains in other areas. If you are a producer, you will want to resist this.

DEAL MEMO - A short version of the contract, giving the principal terms of the agreement which can be legally binding – check carefully if this is the intention.

DEFERRAL - Delay of payment of a fixed sum which is all or part of payments for cast and crew and other services, usually paid out of receipts from the film after the distributor or financier has taken their commission/fee/expenses or been repaid their initial investment (plus a %).

DISTRIBUTION EXPENSES - There is no set definition for this term but things to watch for are that the expenses are reasonable and relate directly to the film. It should not include the Distributor's overheads and any expenses payable by the distributor to third parties should be negotiated on the best commercial terms available.

DISTRIBUTION FEE - This is usually between 25-50% of income received. You should try and negotiate a sliding scale for the fee which reduces as the income from the film increases.

EQUITY - The interest or value an owner has in a property but where they have no legal ownership in the property.

ERRORS AND OMMISSIONS - Insurance protection covering against lawsuits alleging unauthorized use of ideas, characters, plots, plagiarism, titles and alleged slander, libel, defamation of character etc.

ESCROW - Monies or property held by a third party for future delivery or payment to a party on the occurrence of a particular event or services rendered.

FAVORED NATIONS - Meaning that the contracting party will be given treatment on an equal footing with others that the other party deals with i.e. could refer to placement of billing requirements, or profit participation.

FIFTY/FIFTY FIRST DOLLAR SPLIT - A film distribution deal where the income is split 50/50 between the distributor and the producer from the first dollar of the Distributor's gross receipts.

FINDERS FEE - A fee or commission that's paid to an individual or company for 'finding' what is desired. I.e. either a project, a buyer, financier.

FORCE MAJEURE - This term is usually defined in the agreement. Generally it means any event which is outside the control of the parties to the agreement i.e. God, fire, strike, accident, war, illness of key persons involved in the production, effect of elements, earthquake etc.

GROSS DEAL - A profit participation for the producer or others in the distributor's gross receipts (unusual).

GROSS RECEIPTS - This term is usually defined in an agreement to meet all income received from the exploitation of the film by the distributor before any deduction of the distributor's fees and expenses but sometimes it's expressed to include the deduction of such fees and expenses.

INDEMNIFY - A promise to make good any loss or damage another has incurred or suffered or may incur. It may not always be appropriate to give an indemnity.

INDUCEMENT LETTER - This is required where a party, usually an artist, director or individual producer, contract through their company (for tax reasons) rather than as individuals. A Producer and/or financier will require the individual to provide personal warranties and undertakings in relation to the ability and authority of their company to state the artist/director/producer will render their services. The letter will also confirm that they have granted the relevant rights to the company which the company then grants to the producer under the principal agreement of engagement.

INSOLVENT - Where one has liabilities that exceed their assets.

LETTER OF INTENT - A written communication expressing the intent of a person or company to perform whatever services they provide. This may not be legally binding.

LIBEL - A false and malicious publication that's purpose is to defame a living person.

LICENSOR/LICENSEE - One who grants a license (generally the producer)/ One who's received a license (generally the distributor/ exhibitor).

LIEN - A creditor's claim on a property acting as a security for a debt.

LIMITED LIABILITY - Reduced risk to an investor or partner in/of a company because the onus of responsibility is placed on a company rather than the individuals.

LIMITED RECOURSE LOAN - A loan which may only be repaid through specified sources of income i.e. income derived from the exploitation of a film.

MORAL RIGHTS - This is a general term used to describe a bunch of rights which belong to the author of a copyright work. These would include libel, unfair competition, copyright and the right to privacy. These so called 'moral rights' give the artist the right to protect their work even though it's the property of another. It should be noted that movies are not covered under the U.S. Copyright Act, however there have been cases where artists have won based on the evidence presented. A distributor would not find it acceptable for an artist to be able to prevent the distribution of a film on the basis that their moral rights had been infringed and would therefore request a waiver of moral rights.

NEGATIVE COSTS - Total of various costs incurred in the acquisition and production of a film in all aspects prior to release. Includes pre production, production, post production costs.

NEGATIVE PICKUP - Prior to the completion of the film, the distributor picks up the rights to a feature film in the way of a contractual commitment and will pay for the film once the film is completed and delivered to the distributor.

NET DEAL - A distribution deal where the distributor recoups all of it's costs and collects all it's fees before giving the producer the remainder of the film's revenue.

NET PROFIT - There is no set definition of this term as in every case there will be much debate about what may or may not be deducted from the gross receipts to arrive at the net profit. The definition of net profit in any agreement should be looked at very carefully to ensure that expenses and commissions are not being deducted twice i.e. once by the distributor and again by the sub distributor.

NINETY/TEN DEAL - A distributor/exhibitor split of box office receipts. After recoupment of House Nut, the distributor receives 90% of remaining box office receipts and the exhibitor receives 10% in the first week of the film's exhibition. Each week after this, the distributor's percentage is reduced by 10% until the minimum distributor percentage is achieved.

OUTPUT DEAL - A contract though which one party delivers it's entire output ot another party. I.e. a distribution agreement between a production company and a distribution company in which the distributor commits to distribute the films that have been or will be produced by the producer.

PARRI PASSU - Means on a like footing i.e. everyone is to be treated in an equal fashion. For instance, on distribution of net profits everyone gets an equal amount irrespective of their contribution.

PRO RATA - Means that, for example, if an artist is entitled to payment on a pro rata basis then if they receive a weekly fee for 6 days work and the artist subsequently works only 3 days, the artist would receive half the weekly fee i.e. the weekly fee would be pro rated according to the amount of time the artist's services were engaged.

PRODUCERS SHARE - Means the net sum remaining to the Producer after deductions of distribution fees, expenses (or other deductions that are agreed) and after other profit participants have received their share. The producers share of net profits may be shared with other third parties.

PROFIT PARTICIPATION - Percentage participations on net profits.

RECOUPMENT - When the costs and expenses of a film production are recovered from the film's revenue i.e. when production costs have been recouped.

RESIDUALS - Payments for each re run after initial showing. In the case of guild or union agreements minimum residual payments have been agreed.

ROYALTIES - Payments to a party for use of the property calculated as a percentage of a defined amount (i.e. net income from video sales).

THEATRICAL RELEASE - Exploitation of the film in the movie theater as opposed to on television or dvd etc.

TURNAROUND - e.g. a screenplay development situation where the purchaser or licensee of the property has decided not to go forward with the production or if the production is not screened or does not begin principal photography within a specified time the owner or licensor can serve notice on the owner/licensee so that the screenplay can be reacquired by the owner/licensor.

WAIVER - A relinquishment or surrender of particular rights.

WARRANTY - A promise by one party that the other party will rely upon i.e. in a distribution agreement, a producer may warrant that the filming is of a particular quality and standard.

WINDOW - A limited time during which an opportunity such as delivering a film to a distributor must be acted upon otherwise it will be lost.

International Film Festivals

JANUARY
Int. Film Festival of India
http://mib.nic.in/dff
dffiffi@bol.net.in

Int. Film Festival of Rotterdam
Holland
www.filmfestivalrotterdam.com
tiger@filmfestivalrotterdam.com

Göteborg Film Festival
Sweden
www.goteborg.filmfestival.org
goteborg@filmfestival.org

Max Ophuls Preis Film Fest.
Germany
www.saarbruecke.de/
filmhaus.htm
filmfestSB@aol.com

FEBRUARY
Mardi Gras Film Festival
Australia
www.queerscreen.com.au
info@queerscreen.com.au

MARCH
Valenciennes Action & Adventure
Film Fest.
France
www.festival-valenciennes.com
fifav@wanadoo.fr

Cartagena Film Festival
Colombia
www.telecartagena.com
festicine@telecartagena.com

Bradford Film Festival
UK
www.bradfordfilmfestival.org.uk
filmfest@nmsi.ac.uk

Creteil Women's Int. Film Fest.
France
www.filmsdefemmes.com
filmsfemmes@wanadoo.fr

Brussels Int. Fest. of Fantasy
Films
Belgium
www.bifff.org
peymey@bifff.org

Festival du Film De Paris
France
www.festival-du-film-paris.com
festival@wanadoo.fr

APRIL
Hong Kong Int. Film Festival
Hong Kong
www.hkiff.org.hk
hkiff@hkiff.org.hk

Dublin Film Festival
Ireland
www.dubliniff.com
info@dubliniff.com

Jamaica Film Festival
Kingston, Jamaica
bjankee@cwjamaica.com

Int. Istanbul Film Festival
Turkey
www.istfest-tr.org
film.fest@istfest-tr.org

Cape Town Int. Film Festival
South Africa
filmfest@hiddingh.uct.ac.za

London Lesbian and Gay Film
Fest.
UK
www.llgff.org.uk
carol.coombes@bfi.org.uk

Singapore Int. Film Festival
Singapore
www.filmfest.org.sg
filmfest@pacific.net.sg

MAY
Cannes Film Festival
France
www.festival-cannes.fr
Accreditation@festival-cannes.fr
Unifrance Film International:
www.unifrance.org/

Toronto Jewish Film Festival
Canada
www.tjff.com
tjff@tjff.ca

Rose d'Or Festival
Switzerland
www.rosedor.ch
info@rosedor.com

Oberhausen Int. Short Film Fest.
Germany
www.kurzfilmtage.de
info@kurzfilmtage.de

World Wide Short Film Festival
Canada
www.worldwideshortfilmfest.com
shortfilmfest@cdnfilmcentre.com

JUNE
Filmfest Emden
Germany
www.filmfestemden.de
filmfest@vhs-emden.de

FantaFest
Italy
www.fantafestival.org
info@fantafestival.org

Midnight Sun Film Festival
Finland
www.msfilmfestival.fi
office@msfilmfestival.fi

Shanghai Film Festival
China
www.siff.com
kane@siff.com

Sydney Film Festival
Australia
www.sydneyfilmfestival.org
info@sydneyfilmfestival.org

JULY
Karlovy Vary Int. Film Festival
Prague, Czech Republic
www.iffkv.cz
festival@kviff.com

Auckland Int. Film Festival
New Zealand
entries@enzedff.co.nz
www.enzedff.co.nz

Giffoni Film Festival
Italy
www.giffoniff.it

Melbourne Int. Film Festival
Australia
www.melbournefilmfestival.com.au
miff@melbournefilmfestival.com.au

Brisbane Int. Film Festival
Australia
www.biff.com.au
biff@biff.com.au

AUGUST
The Montreal World Film Festival
Canada
www.ffm-montreal.org
info@ffm-montreal.org

The Norwegian Film Festival
Norway
www.filmfestivalen.no
info@filmfestivalen.no

Odense Int. Film Festival
Denmark
www.filmfestival.dk
off.ksf@odense.dk

Edinburgh Int. Film Festival
UK
www.edfilmfest.org.uk
info@edfilmfest.org.uk

Locarno Int. Film Festival
Switzerland
www.pardo.ch
info@pardo.ch

Espoo Cine Int. Film Festival
Finland
www.espoo.fi/cine
espoocine@cultnet.fi

Venice Film Festival
Italy
www.labiennale.org
das@labiennale.com

SEPTEMBER
Cinefest: The Sudbury Film Fest.
Canada
www.cinefest.com
cinefest@vianet.on.ca

Atlantic Int. Film Festival
Canada
www.atlanticfilm.com
festival@atlanticfilm.com

Athens Int. Film Festival
Greece
www.aiff.gr
festival@pegasus.gr

Rio De Janeiro Film Festival
Brazil
www.festivaldoriobr.com.br
info@festivaldoriobr.com.br

San Sebastian Int. Film Festival
Spain
www.sansebastianfestival.com
ssiff@sansebastianfestival.com

LUCAS Int. Children's Film
Festival
Frankfurt, Germany
www.lucasfilmfestival.de
lucas@deutsches-
filmmuseum.ce

Toronto Int. Film Festival
Canada
www.e.bell.ca/filmfest
tiffg@torfilmfest.ca

Vancouver Int. Film Festival
Canada
www.viff.org
viff@viff.org

Filmfest Hamburg
Germany
www.filmfesthamburg.de
filmfest-hamburg@t-online.de

OCTOBER
Sao Paulo Int. Film Festival
Brazil
www.mostra.org
info@mostra.org

Int. Film Festival "Molodist"
Ukraine
www.molodist.com
molodist@oldbank.com

Pusan Int. Film Festival
Korea
www.piff.org
program@piff.org

Raindance Independent Film
Festival
London UK
www.raindance.co.uk
info@raindance.co.uk

Flanders Int. Film Festival
Belgium
www.filmfestival.be
info@filmfestival.be

British Independent Film Awards
London UK
www.bifa.org.uk
info@bifa.org.uk

The London Screenings
London UK
www.londonscreenings.com
registrar@londonscreenings.com

Murphy's Cork Int. Film Festival
Ireland
www.corkfilmfest.org
info@ccorkfilmfest.org

Warsaw Film Festival
Poland
www.wff.org.pl
festiv@wff.org.pl

MIFED
Milan, Italy
www.fmd.it/mifed
mifed@fmd.it

Tokyo Int. Film Festival
Japan
www.tokyo-filmfest.or.jp
pr@tokyo-filmfest.or.jp

Leeds Int. Film Festival
United Kingdom
filmfestival@leeds.gov.uk
www.leedsfilm.com

Vienna Film Festival
Austria
www.viennale.at
office@viennale.at

NOVEMBER
Ankara Int. Film Festival
Turkey
www.filmfestankara.org.tr
festival@filmfestankara.org.tr

Mannhiem-Hiedelberg Int. Film
Festival
Germany
www.mannheim-filmfestival.com
ifmh@mannheim-filmfestival.com

London Int. Film Festival
London UK
www.lff.org.uk

Thessaloniki Film Festival
Greece
www.filmfestival.gr
info@filmfestival.gr

Int. Film Festival de Amiens
France
www.filmfestamiens.org
contact@filmfestamiens.org

Stockholm Int. Film Fest.
Sweden
www.filmfestivalen.se
info@cinema.se

Graz Mountain & Adventure Film
Fest.
Austria
www.mountainfilm.com
mountainfilm@mountainfilm.com

Festival of Jewish Cinema
Australia
www.acmi.net.au

Independent Film Fest. of
Barcelona
Spain
www.alternativa.cccb.org
alternativa@cccb.org

Cardiff Screen Fest.
Wales UK
www.iffw.co.uk
sarah@sgrin.co.uk

Cairo Int. Film Fest.
Egypt
www.cairofilmfest.com
info@cairofilmfest.com

Oslo Int. Film Fest.
Norway
www.wit.no/filmfestival
filmfestival@eunet.no

The Southern Africa Film and TV
Market (Sithengi)
Cape Town, South Africa
www.sithengi.co.za

DECEMBER
Cinemagic – The Northern
Ireland Int. Film Fest. for Young
People.
UK
www.cinemagic.org.uk
info@cinemagic.org.uk

Canadian Film Commissions

BC Film Commission
www.bcfilmcommission.com
Ph: 604 660 2732

British Colombia Tax Credits
For more information contact British Columbia Film.
Ph: 604 736-7997
email: bcf@bcfilm.bc.ca

Canadian Federal Tax Credit
For more info. contact (CAVCO) Canadian Audio-Visual Certification Office
Ph: 888 433-2200 or 613 946-7600
www.pch.gc.ca/cavco

National Film Board of Canada
Ottawa, Ontario: Ph: 613 992-3615
Quebec Ph:514 283-9000 Toll free: 1-800 267-7710

Telefilm Canada:
www.telefilm.gc.ca
Head Office: Montreal: Ph: 514 283-6363

Toll free: 1-800-567-0890
European Office: France Ph: (33-1) 44.18.35.30
Toronto:Ph: 416 973-6436 Toll free:1-800-463-4607
Vancouver: Ph: 604 666-1566

Alberta
Alberta Film Commission
Calgary, AB. Ph: 403 297-6241
Email: tina.alford@gov.ab.ca

Alberta Film Network
Calgary, AB. Ph: 403 221-7868
Email: info@albertafilmcommission.com

Alberta Motion Picture Industries Association
Edmonton, AB. Ph: 403 944-0707

Calgary Film Commission
Calgary, AB. Ph: 403 221-7868
Email: beth@calgaryeconomicdevelopment.com

Edmonton Film Office
Edmonton, AB. Ph: 403 917-7623

Edmonton Motion Picture & TV Bureau
Edmonton, AB
Ph: 403 424-7870   Toll free: 1-800-661-6965

British Columbia
Alberni Clayoquot Economic Development Office
Port Alberni, BC. Ph: 250 723-2188
Email: wmellwyn@cedar.alberni.net

Alberni Clayoquot Regional Film Commission
Port Alberni, BC. Ph: 250 720-0027
Email: alfilm@telus.net

Arrowsmith Film Commission
Parksville, BC. Ph: 250 954-0828
Email: lsolecki@shaw.ca

British Columbia Film Commission
Vancouver, BC   Ph: 604 660-2732
www.bcfilmcommission.com

Burnaby Film Office
BC. Ph: 604 294-7231

Comox Valley Film Commission
Courtenay, BC. Ph: 250 334-2427
E-mail: info@filmlocations.ca

Cowichan Motion Picture Association
Ph: 250 748-6117
Paul Douville, City of Duncan, Administrator
Duncan, BC.   Ph: 250 746-6126
Email: duncan@cow-net.com

Greater Victoria Film Commission
Victoria, B.C. Ph: 250 386-3976
Toll Free: 1-888-537-3456
Email: islandfilm@shaw.ca

Island North Film Commission
Represents the Vancouver Island communities
Campbell River, BC
Ph: 250-287-2772
Email: joan.miller@infilm.ca

Town of Ladysmith
Ladysmith, BC. Ph: 250 245-6405
Email: info@town.ladysmith.bc.ca

Nanaimo and Mid-Island Film and Video Commission
Email: jkemp@city.nanaimo.bc.ca
Film Nanaimo
Nanaimo, BC. Ph: 250 754-9614
Email: filmnanaimo@telus.net

Okanagan-Similkameen Film Commission
Kelowna, BC Ph: 250 717-0087
Email: inquiries@okfilm.bc.ca

Powell River Regional Film Commission
Powell River, BC. Ph: 604 485-3899
Email: gerry@prfilm.ca

Sooke Film Commission
Mel Dobres, Film Liaison
Ph: 250 642-6142   Email: mel@film.bc.ca
Linda Gordon, Film Liaison
Sooke, BC. Ph: 250 642-6745
email: admin@film.bc.ca

Manitoba
Winnipeg, Manitoba. Ph: 204 947-2040

New Brunswick
Fredericton, New Brunswick. Ph: 506 453-2553

Newfoundland
St. John's, Newfoundland. Ph: 709 729-5632, Toll free: 1-800-563-2299

Northwest Territories
Yellowknife Economic Development Authority
Yellowknife, Northwest Territories. Ph: 403 873-5772

Nova Scotia
Nova Scotia Film Development Corporation
Halifax, Nova Scotia. Ph: 902 424-7177
Email: nsfdc@fox.nstn.ca

South West Shore Film Commission
Yarmouth, Nova Scotia. Ph: 902-742-0244
Email: SWSDAY@auracom.com

Ontario
Ontario Media Development Corporation
Toronto, Ontario. Ph: 416 642-6634
Homeowners' Hotline: 416 642-6660

Toronto Film and Television Office
Toronto, Ontario. Ph: 416 392-7570

Prince Edward Island
Prince Edward Island Film Office
Charlottetown, Prince Edward Island.
Ph: 902 368-6329

Quebec
Province of Québec Film & TV Office
Montréal, Québec. Ph: 514 841-2232

Montreal Film & Television Commission
Montreal, Quebec. Ph: 514 872-2883

Quebec City Film Bureau
Quebec City, Quebec
Ph: 418 692-5338

Saskatchewan
SaskFILM / Locations Saskatchewan
Regina, Saskatchewan.
Ph: 306 347-3456

City of Regina
Regina, Saskatchewan.
Ph: 306 777-7486

Yukon Territory
Yukon Film Commission
Whitehorse, Yukon Territories.
Ph: 867 667-5400
Email: info@reelyukon.com

SHOOTING OVERSEAS / CO-PRODUCTION

AUSTRALIA

2 programs are aimed at aiding investors: 10BA (which encourages private investment in Australian content by providing accelerated tax deduction of 100% in year investment made) and 10B (that accepts alternative formats allowing tax benefit to be carried over to two years. For more info contact:
Film and New Media, Department of Communications: *Ph: 02 6271 1066, email: film.info@dcita.gov.au, website: http:// www.dcita.gov.au*
The Film Finance Corporation Australia (FFC): *www.ffc.gov.au*
Australia co-production program guidelines and other tax incentive details at the government level are available at www.afc.gov.au

Important web sites:
www.afc.gov.ac Australian Film Commission
www.ffc.gov.au - Fllm Finance Corporation Australia
www.pftc.com (Pacific Film & TV Commission)
www.film.vic.gov.au - Melbourne Film Office
www.safilm.com.au - South Australian Film Corp
www.fto.nsw.gov.au - New South Wales Film and TV Office
www.screenwest.com.au - Screen West
www.fti.asn.au - Film & Television Institute WA.

BELGIUM

The Flemish AudioVisual Fund (VAF): 78% of the funding VAF receives from the government goes toward film production and international co-productions with a Flemish partner. www.vaf.be

CANADA

Please see Shooting in Canada sidebar and Canadian Film Commissions.

DENMARK

The Danish Film Fund provides funding schemes to Danish producers such as the 60/40 scheme. The fund supports co-productions where the Danish producer is the minority partner up to approx $450k. Subsidies under this scheme may be granted to films that are judged to have a reasonable chance of attracting a large audience. www.dfi.dk

EUROPE

Eurimages is the Council of Europe fund for the co-production, distribution and exhibition of European cinematographic works. Additional co-producers from non-member States cannot exceed 30% co-production (i.e. involving at least three Eurimages member States) and 20% for bilateral co-productions (i.e. involving at least two Eurimages member States). The director must be European. For more information:
www.coe.int/T/E/Cultural_Co-production/ Eurimages

FRANCE

1. Tax Breaks: *Offered through film financing companies that operate under Societes de Financement du Cinema at de l'audiovisuel (SOFICA). Individuals can invest up to 25% of their income with a 100% tax write off and companies who invest can write off up to 50% of tax on their investment. Any tax relief given must be paid off by the individual or company within a maximum of five years after their acquisition.*
2. Co-Productions: *Co-producers may access the CNC fund (Centre National de la Cinematographie) as long as the majority of the filming takes place in France with a French or European crew. In addition to the national funds, co-productions might also be eligible for film funding from other regions in France, if the film is shot in their region. Contact CNC: Ph: +33 1 44 34 34 40 or www.cnc.fr.*
3. Taxation: *A 50% tax credit is added to taxable income and deductible from the tax due. For non-resident partners the 50% tax credit is added to a withholding tax at a rate of 25%, which can also be reduced depending on the co-production treaty between France and the foreign producer's home country. Check out: www.Peacefulfish.com*

GERMANY

A levy on exhibitors of 2.5% helps support Germany's main funding program through the German Federal Film Board. Co-productions can access the national funding available and it's not necessary that the production takes place in Germany. There are certain requirements dependent on the nationality of the co-production partners and the existence of any production treaties between Germany and the countries involved. www.ffa.de.

Some regional Film Boards also offer support for co-production. A certain percentage of the funding, which exceeds usually the granted sum (i.e. 150%) has be to be re-invested in the region to pay labs, studios, cast, production facilities, hotels etc. Check out these examples of certain regional Film Boards:
FilmForderung Hamburg: *www.ffhh.de.*
Filmstiftung Nordrhein-Westfalen:
www.filmstiftung.de
Filmboard Berlin Brandenburg: *Ph: (49) 331 721 28 59*
For more information on German Film Funding visit www.film-law.de.

IRELAND

1: Tax Exemption for Individuals: *Individuals who become residents can be entitled to tax-free income derived from publication, production or sale of books, screenplays, plays and musical compositions deemed original and creative, with cultural or artistic merit.*
2: 10% Tax Rate: *This applies to production, film finance and film distribution and licensing companies. There's no withholding tax on dividends paid by Irish companies, which has made Ireland very attractive to foreign investors.*
3: Double Taxation Treaties (includes US): *Foreign owners can receive the after tax profits without any further tax payable by them in their home country and can defer further taxation. Also provides that any dividends, interest or royalties paid to an Irish company suffer minimal, if any, withholding tax.*
4: Section 481: *A tax break for both corporate and private investors which presently operates until the end of 2004. After this date, check with the Irish Film Board that it's still in existence. For guidelines contactwww.gov.ie/arts-sport-tourism/*
5. Co-production Treaties: *Canada and Australia have co-production treaties with Ireland. In order to obtain co-production status, the production must involve at least three co-producers who are members of the ECC. Non-members may also participate, however their total contribution cannot exceed 30% of the total cost of the production. For more info contact the Institute of Ireland: http://www.fii.ie.*

Other Irish contacts:
Irish Business and Employers Confederation: http://www.ibec.ie
Irish Film Board: http://www.filmboard.ie

Irish Revenue Office: www.revenue.ie/services/
film.htm and www.revenue.ie/service/sect35.htm
Minister for Arts, Culture and the Gaeltacht:
www.ealga.ie
Tax relief for investment: www.boylandodd.com

ITALY

There are several Italian subsidy funds where
up to 70% of the total budget can be loaned
through these funds. There is also The Veltroni
Law which requires public service broadcasters
to invest Euro 50m per year in feature film and
TV fiction. Contact the Italian Film Commission:
http://www.filminitaly.com/

MEXICO

Please see Shooting in Mexico sidebar.

NETHERLANDS

1. The Dutch Film Fund: supports filmmakers in
developing, realizing and distributing films of all
formats and lengths. The Fund only provides
financial contributions for a film project to
producers based in The Netherlands and, with
the exception of Research and Development,
funds are not given to individuals. For more info
visithttp://www.filmfund.nl
2. The CoBo Fund: This allows German and
Belgian companies to be involved in co-
productions if the film is shown theatrically in
the Netherlands before broadcast to TV (the
foreign company must be public).

NEW ZEALAND

Tax benefits for private investors if the
production has been certified as a NZ film. The
Film Commission certifies films or television
programs as a NZ Film provided it contains
significant NZ content with respect to the
creative talent or the locations involved in the
film. For more info contact http://
www.nzfilm.co.nz.

NORWAY

The Norwegian Film Fund: www.filmfondet.no

SPAIN

Subsidies are offered by ICAA (Instituto de las
Cinematografia y de las Artes Audiovisuales) to
films that earn more than US$330,000 at the
box office. All Spanish films have the right to
aid, up to 15% of gross takings during first 2
years screening in Spanish cinemas. Grants are
occasionally given for script development,
distribution and exhibition expense, and are
considered on a project-by-project basis. The

2001 Cinema Law also requires broadcasters to
invest 3% of their annual income in Spanish
films. There are 3 major tax credits for
investors:
1. Up to 25% of film production investments are
deductible from corporate income tax.
2. P&A expenses are 20% tax deductible when
occurred through entering new markets or
developing new products.
3. Up to 5% (or up to 20% for non-Spanish
holding companies) of the amount invested in
fixed assets can be deducted from corporate
income tax, up to 25% of the total tax charge.
For more info contact ICAA (34) 1 532 74 39 or
http://www.mcu.es/cine/index.html.

UNITED KINGDOM

The U.K offers four types of tax relief:
1. Production Expenditure: - Development and
Production. Any amount spent on development
of a British qualifying film qualifies for 100% tax
relief in the year incurred, even if the film is not
subsequently made. (Expenditure must not
exceed 20% of the budget.) Any amount spent
on production of a British qualifying film qualifies
for 100% tax write off in equal installments over
a period of 3 fiscal years commencing in the
year in which the film is completed. For British
qualifying films that cost less than $15m, the
relief is extended to a full 100% tax write off in
the fiscal year that the film is completed.
However costs such as financing, completion
bond and publicity costs do not qualify for 100%
relief in one year but follow the normal tax relief
rules.
2. Acquisition: - Provided the film meets the
criteria above for production expenditure, the
same relief is available as above for the cost of
acquiring a film. Here the financing, completion
bond and publicity costs again do not qualify for
100% relief in one year, however, they do obtain
relief over 3 years. Such costs are therefore
excluded from the acquisition price and tax
relief is claimed directly by the producer.
3. Enterprise Investment Scheme (EIS): The
relief available here is 20% income tax relief on
investments up to GBP150k, per individual tax
year. 40% Capital Gains Tax deferral, with no
maximum investment. Disposal of the EIS
shares is outside the scope of Capital Gains Tax
if they have been held for at least 3 years.
4. Sale and Leaseback (S&L): The UK offers a
100% tax relief to investors, which has
benefited filmmakers in the form of the **S&L**
agreement. Primarily for films that have been
completed, however, if they're guaranteed that

the required conditions will be met, many S&L
organizations do advance the funding of
between 5-10% to producers before production
starts enabling producers to use S&L as gap
finance. Also deferments can be included as
part of the production expenditure for S&L. Due
to the complex nature of S&L, carry it out
through a lawyer or an accountant.

How the S&L works: -

1. The producer sells the film to a purchaser.
The purchaser is usually a group of individuals
who are found either through an accounting or
lawyer's firm with taxable profits sufficient to
benefit from tax relief.
2. The purchaser leases the film back to the
producer for a period of between 7-15 years.
Most of the sale price (which is the cost of the
film) is placed on deposit securing the lease
repayment installments by the producer to the
purchaser. The deposit is placed in a bank
account specifically set up for this arrangement
and where lease repayments have been set up.
3. The remainder of the sale price is given to
the producer who receives between 5-10% of
the cost of the film.
4. Purchaser returns to the producer, copyright
and the freedom to exploit the film over the
period of the lease.
5. At the end of the lease period, the rights may
by agreement revert to the lessee.

To Qualify: a film must be made by a company
that is registered and managed in the U.K. At
least 70% of the total expenditure incurred in
the production of the film must be spent on film
production activity carried out in the UK. A film
may still qualify as 'British' if it can satisfy the
terms of one of the UK's official co-production
treaties. Therefore co-producers from Australia,
Canada, France, Germany, Italy, New Zealand
and Norway can be included. Check
qualification requirements at the Dept. for
Culture Media and Sport website:
www.culture.gov.uk.

Other U.K contacts:

www.britfilmcom.co.uk
www.scottishscreen.com
www.mediadesk.co.uk
www.britisharts.co.uk/artsfunding.htm
www.bfi.org.uk/
www.filmcouncil.org.uk/
www.britfilms.com
www.shootingpeople.org/
www.britfilmusa.com

INDEX